D1030510

SOCIAL ETHICS

SOCIAL ETHICS

NATURAL LAW IN THE WESTERN WORLD

By Johannes Messner

Dr.iur.utr., Dr.oec.publ., Dr.theol.h.c. (Vienna)
Dr.rer.pol.h.c. (Freiburg i. Br.), Dr.sc.pol. et soc. (Louvain)
Professor in the University of Vienna

TRANSLATED BY J. J. DOHERTY

Revised Edition

B. Herder Book Co., St. Louis & London

This is a translation of
DAS NATURRECHT: *Handbuch der Gesellschaftsethik, Staatsethik und Wirtschaftsethik,*
third revised and enlarged edition, by Johannes Messner,
published by Verlagsanstalt Tyrolia G.m.b.H.,
Innsbruck, 1958.

IMPRIMATUR ✠ Joseph Cardinal Ritter
Archbishop of St. Louis, November 3, 1964

314 North Jefferson, St. Louis, Mo. 63103
London: 2/3 Doughty Mews, W.C. 1
Library of Congress Catalog Card No. 65-23383
Manufactured in the United States of America
Designed by Klaus Gemming

WITH THANKS
TO THE FATHERS OF
CARDINAL NEWMAN'S ORATORY
AT BIRMINGHAM, ENGLAND
WHERE THIS BOOK
WAS WRITTEN

SUMMARY

CONTENTS

Book I / *The Foundation*

PART II. The Nature of Society: Social Philosophy

PART III. The Order of Society: Legal Philosophy

PART IV. State Dynamics

Book IV / *The Ethics of Social Economy*

PART I. The Economic Process

BOOK I

THE FOUNDATION

PART ONE

The Nature of Man
Moral Philosophy

1. Man

When we inquire into the laws on which the order of human society is founded and by which it develops, must we take as our point of departure man or society? The answer seems evident, since society is the specific object of study. To begin such an inquiry with a discussion of society itself seems the more necessary because society is certainly an entity in itself. For it acts independently of the individual; not only is the individual wholly dependent upon it in the process of development but is largely subject to its will. Furthermore, society outlives man: states survive many generations of men, and nations endure for hundreds of years. Finally, the good of the community takes such precedence over the good of the individual that the latter is required, when necessary, to sacrifice wealth and life itself for the community.

Social philosophy may, indeed, begin with an inquiry into society as a whole, striving to analyze its nature and to discover the laws that govern its existence, its life, and its action. But the further such an investigation proceeds toward discovering the raison d'être of society, the more pressing will become the question: In what does social actuality consist and upon what is it based? The sociologist will then find that man is the indispensable constituent of all social existence. And in the quest for those forces which animate and energize society he will again discover that all activity and function in society is ultimately traceable to men. Again, when he inquires into the purpose of society, a number of ends will require scrutiny, and lastly the question concerning the meaning of human life—What is man?—must be answered. To this fundamental question social philosophy and social ethics must find a clear and unambiguous answer if they are to comprehend the nature, purpose, and order of social life. Hence, it is justifiable, if not imperative, to treat the question of man first.

In fact, both procedures are justified provided that they are handled in such a manner that they can deal adequately with the whole reality

Man and the community are the two poles in this reality. If the method employed is not able to deal with the whole of experience in the field of either of these poles, it is inadequate. The outcome will then be an ideological dogmatism instead of scientific realism.

The social theory of individualism began with the individual as an entity complete in himself and possessing an absolute value, but it never really reached the conception of the community as an entity with a supraindividual existence, purpose, and value. The social theory of all collectivist systems, on the other hand, begins with the social entity as the absolute primary value, but never reaches the full reality of the human person with its suprasocial ends and its value ranking above that of society. Neither the individualist nor the collectivist pattern of values, nor the liberalist or socialist ideologies founded upon them, have ever in practice been or can ever be fully actualized. Human nature does not allow it. Therefore, more or less far-reaching modifications in theory and in practice have resulted from this fact. The purpose of this study in social ethics is not to attempt a criticism of all these in detail; such an attempt has been essayed in another work.* The programs and tactics of the groups and parties which champion such schemes of values change. Social ethics is not concerned with the details of such programs, but with the social theories and value systems underlying them.

It must be borne in mind at the outset, however, that any necessary criticism does not imply an indiscriminate rejection of all the endeavours and achievements of the individualist-liberalist and collectivist-socialistic social movements and social systems of modern times. The liberalist movement with its demands for liberty in all spheres of human activity had as one of its effects a genuine and justified reaction against obsolete systems and institutions in social, economic, and political life. On the European continent it was a vehicle for the uprising against absolutism, against the police state, and against the mercantilist regimentation of economic and social life. The socialist movement, again, with its shifting of the center of gravity of social order to the opposite side, must be understood, partly at least, as a reaction against the failure of society to carry out vital social functions—a failure due to individualist forces. Indeed, these movements in all countries can claim to their credit real and lasting achievements in the field of social reform which are recognized by the champions of all social creeds.

We have said that the question concerning the being and order of society always results in another question: What is man? Therefore, we shall be occupied in the following chapters with the question of the nature of man.

* *Die Soziale Frage, im Blickfeld der Irrwege von gestern, die Sozialkämpfe von heute, der Weltentscheidungen von morgen,* 7th revised ed., 1956.

2. The Nature of Man

We shall begin with a survey of present-day theories of philosophical anthropology. It is a fact established in modern epistemology and the methodology of the sciences that scientific thinking is governed by opinions which are held both consciously and unconsciously. Hence, it is the duty of every scientific author, especially in the sphere of the social sciences, *to examine critically his own fundamental views and then to give a clear account of them.* This will be the subject of the present chapter together with a comparison of the most important views held today on the nature of man. It may, however, be emphasized that we are not going to derive our doctrine of man and the resulting ethical principles from the ideas we are about to explore, but from an analysis of reality and of experience itself. Such an analysis will be our concern in the following chapters. It will provide a number of occasions for dealing in some detail with the method of ethics. The various systems of anthropology are represented today as systems of *humanism,* and it seems best therefore to adhere to this mode of expression.

I *Christian Humanism*

Christian humanism is the humanism of the traditional natural law doctrine since *Augustine,* and it is based upon the following facts and ideas.

1. *Empirical anthropology,* which critically collates and systematizes the data of experience in the human sphere, provides a traditional natural law theory with two findings: first, that man is *physically* very close to the animal world, but constitutes a single "species" in the zoological sense; for all "races" of mankind can interbreed freely. The second finding is that man is a being endowed with *reason.* Because of his generalizing faculty of grasping the relation between cause and effect, he is *homo faber,* the only toolmaking animal. Again, he is the only creature endowed with the power of self-determination in his conduct. His faculties of reasoning and self-determination distinguish him essentially from the animal world as *animal rationale, homo sapiens.*

2. *Metaphysical anthropology,* which, proceeding from experience, inquires into the essence of man, yields two further findings for traditional natural law theory: first, that man possesses a spiritual soul; secondly, that because of his spiritual-physical nature man is a social being, that is, one that attains its full stature only in social fellowship. In the view of traditional natural law theory, metaphysics is founded upon experience and is guided by the conviction that it is adequate to its

task only if it can bring its conclusions into relation with the whole range of empirical reality bearing upon its object. True, there is no metaphysics that could claim to solve all its problems with indisputable certainty. But it is equally true that any metaphysics which refuses to take parts of experience into account or tries to explain away facts of reality lapses into dogmatism of one kind or another, consisting of hypotheses or assertions based on inadequate or nonexistent empirical or philosophical grounds. Metaphysical anthropology of the natural law school holds that, in contradistinction to the animal soul, the human soul is a *spiritual*, self-contained, immortal substance, the seat of the mind. Hence, from this follows the essential dualism of body and spirit: the body is material in substance, the soul spiritual; neither can be derived from the other. Together they constitute human nature as an essential unity, the spiritual soul being the principle of specifically human acts. Because he is compounded of body and spirit man is of a *social* nature. Because individual natures are complementary to one another both in need and in capacity the full development of man's nature is wholly dependent upon the social nexus.

3. From *Christian anthropology* traditional natural law obtains final certainty with regard to the above-mentioned findings of empirical and metaphysical anthropology concerning the spiritually conditioned nature of man. Linked with these are two facts concerning human existence which are of the greatest significance for social philosophy. The first is the fact of original sin, which explains man's proneness to error and his perversity of will with the resulting defects in social systems (the "social question"). The second fact is that God entered the world. By assuming human nature he set the seal on the image of God, which is inscribed in man's nature, thus bearing witness that the value of the person, whose destiny is linked with the spiritual soul, is raised above every earthly value, so that neither society nor state nor nation nor race nor the whole world can outweigh the dignity of the human person.

II *Naturalistic Humanism*

The naturalistic idea of man in its several varieties forms a contrast with that just developed. The varieties of the naturalistic idea have in common: (1) a belief in the "natural" man, the purpose of whose existence is wholly bound by his life span; (2) a belief in the exclusive existence of reality accessible to experience; (3) the rejection of revealed religion.

The following varieties of naturalistic humanism can be distinguished on the basis of the underlying suppositions and meaning of its interpretation of the nature of man (anthropology).

1. *Rationalistic humanism* and its anthropology are mentioned chiefly for their significance in the historical development of naturalistic thought. They are

founded on three assumptions. The first consists in the belief in the all-powerfulness of human reason to comprehend and to mold the world, a belief which, since the days of *Comte* (1798–1857), has grown more and more into a belief in the omnipotence of science. Secondly, there is the belief that man, because of his rational nature, is unreservedly good if only he can find "natural" conditions for its development; hence, the call "back to nature" (*Rousseau*, 1712–78). Thirdly, allied with this is the belief in the "law of progress" without end in all realms of human and cultural values, proclaimed first by *Saint-Simon* (1760–1825) and *Fourier* (1772–1837). The ideal of this humanism is that of the personality reaching fulfillment in the harmony of pleasure, and is not far removed from the idea of the "greatest happiness of the greatest number" which *Bentham* (1748–1832) was then developing in England. The experiences of two World Wars have revealed that rationalistic anthropology is unrealistic. But the belief in science has remained and with it a constantly renewed hope consequent upon the great strides made by the sciences. This is especially true of the following two varieties of naturalistic anthropology.

2. *Scientistic humanism* seeks, in the study of man and of society, to follow exclusively the natural sciences and the sciences of man which work with methods of natural science, viz. biology, psychology, sociology, and ethnology, which rely exclusively on empirical knowledge. In Anglo-Saxon countries some even speak of a "scientific humanism" in the hope that the social scientist and the social technician may at some time become capable of achieving the same results in the organization of social and political life as do the natural scientist and technician in the control of external nature. The immediate forerunners of scientism as a philosophy of life are to be found among the exponents of a "scientific philosophy of life" (*Weltanschauung*) in Germany toward the end of the last century. Scientism largely dominates the thinking of the Anglo-Saxon world and is making great advances on the continent of Europe and in intellectual noncommunist circles beyond. Nevertheless, today it is generally overshadowed by the fear that a misuse of scientific knowledge in a future war may imperil the continuance of the human race, or at any rate of civilization.

Western scientistic humanism combines (with varying emphasis) details from "scientific" theories on the nature of man. These are principally the theories of biological evolution, of analytical psychology, of utilitarian pragmatism, of logical positivism, and of economic social determinism. Eastern scientistic humanism on the other hand assigns to the last an altogether dominant position. A common metaphysics underlies all these scientistic tendencies, since they adhere to premises which cannot be supported by any methods of natural science. The cognitive methods of natural science are restricted to the world of sense experience; therefore, they make possible no scientifically (in this sense) based statements with regard to the nonexistence of a reality lying beyond the world of sense, although all scientism claims to be able to prove "scientifically" that the assumption of such a reality (of a suprasocial moral authority, of a spiritual soul, of a supramundane Creator) is self-deception on man's part. Each of the above-mentioned "scientific" theories has developed its own special variety of naturalistic humanism. Hence, they require separate discussion.

3. *The humanism of dialectical materialism* may be treated by following *Lenin's* exposition, since he justly claims to be the most logical interpreter of

dialectical materialism. The Marx-Engels Institute in Moscow is entrusted with the task of safeguarding and extending the orthodox tradition of the Leninist interpretation of *Marx.* Its principles may be summarized briefly from the writings of *Lenin:* "The psychical, consciousness . . . is the highest product of highly developed matter [and] is a function of that complicated bit of matter which is called the human brain." "The materialist elimination of 'the dualism of mind and body' (materialistic monism) consists in this, that the existence of the mind is shown to be dependent upon that of the body, in that mind is declared to be secondary, a function of the brain, or a reflexion of the outer world." Man's nature thus consists in being highly developed "organic matter." "Matter is of primary nature. Sensation, thought, consciousness are the highest products of matter organized in a certain way. This is the doctrine of materialism, in general, and of *Marx* and *Engels* in particular." Organic matter is "a result of a long evolution" of "eternally moving and eternally changing matter"; "development is a 'struggle' of opposites." Only "the struggle of the mutually exclusive opposites is absolute, as movement and evolution are," [1] and this is the reason why materialism must be dialectical and decline the "recognition of immutable elements, 'of the immutable substance of things.' " [2] Any metaphysic which deviates from dialectical materialism Lenin branded "fideism," "a doctrine which puts faith in place of knowledge." [3] The "fideism" in dialectical materialism itself is certainly obvious enough, since, as we shall see, it rests in its most fundamental features on scientifically unfounded assumptions, i.e. on dogmatisms.

4. *Psychoanalytical humanism.* According to *Freud's* anthropology the human "mental mechanism" is divisible into the Superego, the Ego and the Id. The last embraces what is physically instinctive: the Libido with the sexual element as its chief motive force. The Superego consists in the inhibition automatism in harmony with acquired rules of conduct. Like the Id the Superego belongs wholly to the "unconscious." This Superego with its associated belief in the suprahuman authority of the moral law consists in the introjected authority of parents, who have to deny the child in earliest infancy, before the attainment of self-consciousness, the unregulated satisfaction of impulses, especially with regard to elimination, and instil in it socially valid rules of con-

[1] Lenin, *Materialism and Empirio-Criticism,* 1908. Collected Works, A. Trachtenberg, editor; authorized by the Lenin Institute, Moscow. Vol. XIII, trans. by D. Kvitko, 1927, pp. 26, 34, 52, 65 f., 191, 228, 323 f.

[2] *Ibid.,* p. 220. Another version of this fundamental conception of "dialectics" runs as follows: "In the theory of knowledge, as in other branches of science, we must think dialectically, that is, we must not regard our knowledge as ready made and unchangeable, but must determine how from ignorance knowledge is gradually built up, and how incomplete, inexact knowledge becomes more complete and more exact" (*ibid.,* p. 77). In all this Lenin closely follows Engels. "Nature works dialectically," says Engels; the world, particularly history, is "a process of evolution," i.e., in continual motion, change, transformation, development; this process of evolution cannot find its intellectual conclusion in the discovery of any so-called absolute truth (F. Engels, *Socialism, Utopian and Scientific,* trans. by E. Aveling, 1892, pp. 28–40; noteworthy is the passage on materialist dialectics and its debt to Hegel). Concerning Engels' significance for the interpretation of Marx, Lenin says: "It is impossible to understand Marxism and to propound it fully without taking into account all the works of Engels" (Lenin, *The Teachings of Karl Marx,* 1931, p. 48).

[3] *Ibid.,* p. 311. On fideisms in the anthropology of dialectial materialism, cf. Messner, *Ethics and Facts,* pp. 262–71.

duct, including moral rules. The Ego is the conscious constituent of human nature and is that constituent of the "mental mechanism" which is formed from conscious reaction to the social environment; compared with the other two it is a relatively small part of the constitution of the personality, but its development decides the integration of the personality. This summary of the leading ideas of psychoanalysis [4] will suffice for our present purpose. Freudian psychoanalysis knows nothing of a self-contained spiritual soul forming the essential determining part of human nature; therefore, it belongs as a metaphysical doctrine to the philosophical schools of materialistic anthropology. Our criticism does not imply the rejection of psychoanalysis as a method of psychology and psychotherapy, since, indeed, in the words of *R. Dalbiez:* "Freud's work is the most profound analysis that history has ever known of the less human elements in human nature." [5]

5. *Behaviorist humanism.* This school of anthropology holds, as the American psychologist *E. L. Thorndike* expresses it, that "as a result of nearly forty years of experimental study of animal intellect and the contemporaneous advances in knowledge of human thinking and reasoning it now appears that no clear, general, qualitative distinction between the intellectual possibilities of the genes of man and those of the genes of the lower animals can be made." [6] The anthropology of behaviorism is materialistic: man is regarded as a higher animal without a spiritual soul. With regard to the ability to reason, it "is now known," says *Thorndike,* that man forms mental connexions just as the animals do, but in enormously greater number, and that his power of abstract generalization and reasoning is developed "so to speak" as a byproduct. Chimpanzees using sticks, and rats making use of topographical sense "have at last convinced" *Köhler, Norman Maier, McDougal,* and others that these animals do "something of this sort," namely, the "so-called reasoning." "In general," if the facts interest animals, and if their behavior in relation to the facts is rich and varied, then the animals "seem and are . . . somewhat" like man.

We need not discuss the fact that such a process of generalization and the equation of "seem" and "are" on the basis of "somewhat" is inconsistent with any scientific method. What *Thorndike* says conveys his own personal opinion, but has nothing to do with science. The anthropology of behaviorism rests altogether on preconceived dogmatisms and fideisms.

6. *Biological-evolutionist humanism* may be best illustrated by the book "Evolution" by Professor *Julian Huxley*. He considers that "a phase of synthesis" has now been reached for the theory of evolution.[7] He also comes to the conclusion that evolution "is just as much a product of blind forces as is the falling of a stone to earth or the ebb and flow of the tides. It is we who have to read purpose into evolution, as earlier men projected will and emotion into inorganic phenomena like storm and earthquake. If we wish to work toward a purpose

[4] Cf. Sigmund Freud, *Gesammelte Werke,* Vols. I–XVII, London, 1940. For the philosophical and ethical side of Freud's psychoanalysis cf. *Ethics and Facts,* pp. 57–70, 290–94; *Kulturethik,* pp. 36 ff., 73 ff. Cf. also K. Stern, *The Third Revolution* (U.S.A.), 1951.

[5] R. Dalbiez, *Psychoanalytical Method and Doctrine of Freud,* 1941, Vol. II, p. 327.

[6] E. L. Thorndike, *Human Nature and the Social Order,* 1940, pp. 288 ff.

[7] J. Huxley, *Evolution: The Modern Synthesis,* 1942, p. 13. Cf. for a critique of Huxley's book *The Nineteenth Century, March, 1943.*

for the future of man, we must formulate that purpose ourselves. Purposes in life are made, not found." All values are subject to evolution; the assumption of absolute values and their personification in God was an error, and the recognition of it enables man to make progress in science; on the other hand, evolutionary humanism may be the nucleus of a new religion understood as man's destiny and duty to make fruitful his still unrevealed powers.[8] In the view of this materialist anthropology man is only a highly developed species of vertebrates, "living matter," and as such exclusively a product of the evolution of world-stuff in one particular direction among countless others.

Another neo-Darwinist, Professor *D. M. S. Watson,* admits bluntly that the materialist anthropology of neo-Darwinism is founded on a fideism: "Evolution itself is accepted by zoologists not because it has been observed to occur or is supported by logically coherent arguments, but because it does fit all the facts of taxonomy, of palaeontology, and of geographical distribution, and because no alternative explanation is credible." Why not? *Watson* gives the reason: The theory of evolution is "generally accepted, not because it can be proved by logically coherent evidence to be true, but because the only alternative, special creation, is clearly incredible." [9]

7. *Neo-positivist humanism.* According to the anthropology of *logical positivism,* which has to a large extent dominated philosophical thought in England and in America since before the Second World War, the human soul, if thought of as immaterial, is nothing but "the ghost in the machine" as Professor *Gilbert Ryle,* one of the leading exponents of logical positivism in England, puts it. According to the logical positivists true knowledge is concerned only with that reality which is perceptible to the senses, that is with facts verifiable by sense perception; hence, propositions concerning metaphysical reality and also concerning values cannot be considered true or false—they are meaningless.[10] But it is admitted that it is practically impossible to live without any kind of values. The fideism in the premises of logical positivism has often been pointed out. According to these premises the principle of verification is itself not susceptible of empirical verification and is therefore, by the tenets of logical positivism, a metaphysical proposition and hence meaningless. One of the leading logical positivists, *A. J. Ayer,* has indeed admitted that this constitutes a hitherto unsolved difficulty for logical positivism. There is another fideism in that the logical positivist links mental states and, still more, mental processes with what sense perception presents to him as other men; these states and processes, however, are not verifiable as such by sense perception. Thus, it is only by denying his own tenets that the logical positivist can endeavor to reach understanding with others about such states and processes.

The logical positivists have not even attempted a theory of social order; in

[8] Cf. J. Huxley, *op. cit.,* p. 576; *Evolutionary Ethics,* 1943, pp. 41 f., 84. Cf. also *Evolution in Action,* 1953, pp. 149 f.

[9] British Association for the Advancement of Science, Report on 97th Meeting, 1929, pp. 88, 95, mentioned in the *Nineteenth Century, loc. cit.*

[10] Cf. G. Ryle, A. J. Ayer and others, *The Revolution in Philosophy,* 1956; also: R. Carnap, *Philosophy and Logical Syntax,* 1935; A. J. Ayer, *Language, Truth, and Logic,* 2nd ed., 1948; C. L. Stevenson, *Ethics and Language,* 1944; G. Ryle, *The Concept of Mind,* 1949, 2nd ed., 1950. For criticism, cf. C. E. M. Joad, *A Critique of Logical Positivism,* 1950; F. Copleston, *Contemporary Philosophy: Studies in Logical Positivism and Existentialism,* 1956; Messner, *Ethics and Facts,* pp. 296–312.

their view all social institutions, for example, the family community, can only be a resultant of the individual's value judgments in a society, without foundation in human nature as such.

8. *Existentialist humanism,* although much divided within itself, is distinct from all other trends of naturalistic anthropology by reason of its characteristic doctrine that we cannot know anything about man's essence, but only about his existence; we can know only about the "how" of the human being, not about the "what." As distinct from mere "being there" (*dasein*), man's "true" existence implies the realization of his self in the historical world and hence in the given situation. This self-realization is bound up with man's freely taken decision and thus is possible only through "self-design" (*selbstentwurf*). Consequently, there can be no universally valid standards of value; the law by which man must decide can be revealed to him only in the process of existing itself. Thus, existentialism denies that there is an order of existence constituting a universal moral order to be inferred from the nature of man.

The contrast between existentialist anthropology and any anthropology based on natural law is obvious. The fundamental idea of the latter in all its forms is the assumption that it is possible to know the nature of man, to know his essence and the fundamental order of individual and social existence implied therein. Notwithstanding the ethical significance of the existential philosophy, because of its antideterminist concept of freedom and its emphasis on decision in personal existence, it remains almost exclusively preoccupied with the individual and has hardly approached the realm of man's social existence and the questions of social order because of its one-sided interpretation of human existence in terms of individual freedom[11] (on more recent attempts cf. Chap. 39).

9. *Idealistic humanism.* Whereas monism (the doctrine of the essential homogeneousness of matter and spirit) of a materialistic character makes the human mind an evolved form of matter, idealistic monism conceives of man and of all reality as forms of evolution of spirit, which is the fundamental substance of the universe (this philosophy is also known today as psychism). The philosophy of idealistic monism in the form given to it by *Hegel* is, therefore, of the greatest significance for social philosophy because it makes the state a "higher" form in the self-realization of spirit, being (the state) objective spirit, while the individual has objectivity, truth, and morality only as a member of the state. Thus, a straight line leads from idealistic monism to the totalitarian principle of the "identification of state and individual," as formulated by *Gentile* for Italian fascism.[12] *Gentile* was influenced by *Hegel,* although *Hegel* himself

[11] For existential philosophy cf. the well-known works of Heidegger, Sartre, and also in part Jaspers; and for criticism cf. the more recent literature: F. J. Rintelen, *Philosophie der Endlichkeit,* 1951; Hans Meyer, *Die Weltanschauung der Gegenwart,* 1949, pp. 430–76; Hans Pfeil, *Existentialistische Philosophie,* 1952; O. F. Bollnow, *Existenzphilosophie,* 4th ed., 1955; Emanuel Mounier, *Einführung in die Existenzphilosophie,* trans. by W. Richter, 1949, esp. his penetrating criticism of Sartre; Joseph de Tonquédec, S.J., *Une philosophie existentielle. L'existence d'après Karl Jaspers,* 1945; J. M. Hollenbach, S.J., *Sein und Gewissen. Eine Begegnung zwischen Martin Heidegger und Thomistischer Philosophie,* 1954; Auguste Etcheverry, S.J., *Le conflit actuel des Humanismes,* 1955, which deals also with rationalistic and Marxist humanism.

[12] G. Gentile, *Origini e dottrine del Fascismo,* 1934.

would certainly have rejected every form of modern state totalitarianism, since in his view world history is ultimately the evolution of the idea of freedom. And yet it might well be argued that *Gentile's* actualistic idealism,[13] according to which the spirit exists only by acting and not as a being in itself, would find complete support in *Hegel,* since in *Hegel's* view "spirit is the existing truth of matter," "spirit has objective reality only by dividing itself within itself" and "only is what it does." [14] The most influential contemporary German restatement of Hegelian philosophy in the social field, the universalism of *Spann* with its related concept of "the dividing spirit" (*Gezweiung des Geistes*), arrives by means of a similar metaphysics at the conclusion that "it is the fundamental fact of all social reality and the fundamental truth of all social science . . . that not the individuals are the truly real, but the social whole, and that the individuals have reality and existence only insofar as they are members of the whole." [15]

3. Natural Law

I *The Problem*

We recognize the nature of things from their functioning. The various sciences study inanimate nature and natural laws by observing the forces operating in them, and animate nature by observing modes of behavior, especially in relation to environment. The approach to an understanding of human nature and the laws of conduct proper to it obviously must be the same. Therefore, we must investigate the energies, drives, and impulses which we find at work in man. At first glance we observe in him the instincts of self-preservation, of feeding; the impulse to secure a livelihood, to make provision for the future; the sexual instinct, the parental instinct; the impulses toward family life and social fellowship, the impulses to enlarge experience and knowledge; the instinct for beauty; the desire for the respect of others; the impulse to maintain a well-ordered relationship toward the Supreme Being; and the instinct for happiness, which involves all other instinctive ends.

Some of these impulses or instincts are possessed by man in common with animals; but a distinction can be seen at once: man is capable of becoming aware of his impulses and of grasping the connection between them and their inherent ends. Unlike the animal, man is aware that the feeding instinct serves to maintain the life and health of the individual. He is aware, too, that it depends upon himself, upon his self-determination, whether and how far he fulfills such ends in satisfying his impulses; for example, whether in satisfying his feeding instinct he preserves due

[13] Cf. G. Gentile, *The Theory of Mind as Pure Act,* trans. by H. W. Carr, 1922, pp. 20, 27.

[14] Hegel, *Grundlinien der Philosophie des Rechts,* 1821, pars. 187, 343; *Enzyklopädie der philosophischen Wissenschaften,* 1830, par. 389.

[15] O. Spann, *Gesellschaftslehre,* 3rd ed., 1930, p. 562; *Der wahre Staat,* 3rd ed., 1931, pp. 33 ff.

measure in order not to frustrate the end of the instinct by too much or too little. He knows also with equal certainty, however, that he is not fully at liberty to act as he chooses in this regard; rather, he acts in accordance with his rational nature only if he keeps due measure, whereas by an excess of eating and drinking which prevents him from fulfilling his tasks or from using his reason he acts in a way inconsistent with human dignity, in a "subhuman" way, and inconsistent with the responsibility laid upon him with his rational nature. He is aware also of an inner urge, the command of duty, to act in accord with this responsibility. Finally, he immediately recognizes his fellowman as endowed with the same rational nature, and thus recognizes that certain modes of conduct are due to his fellowman, with converse being just as true.

Thus, we observe spiritual and physical instinctive dispositions in human nature, and we have no reason for not regarding their operation as the operation of a natural law in man as long as we apply the same principles by which we apprehend the natural laws of the external world. Certainly the mode of operation of the natural law in man is not the same as in irrational nature. Nature has its specific modes of functioning in inanimate, vegetable, and animal beings. The same must be true of man; in him also nature has a specific mode of functioning. Indeed, as far back as we can trace man's thinking about himself (e.g., in the Homeric poems, which carry on a tradition reaching far into prehistory) there has been general agreement that the key to the understanding of man's nature is his *reason;* [1] that the hallmark of his human nature is in those modes of conduct which depend on his reason. The *specifically human conduct* which is thus implied by rational nature accordingly signifies man's natural law: man's authentic mode of conduct which depends upon his self-determination and responsibility as a rational being.

This preliminary sketch of our problem, the detailed discussion of which will form the subject matter of the following chapters, shows that the problem comprises the questions that arise from man's experience in the realm of moral consciousness and moral order. Indeed, all systems of ethics agree that the knowledge of good and evil, the sense of duty and responsibility, conscience, are the data of moral experience. In the explanation of the origin, essence, and basis for moral obligation, however, the various systems differ widely.

In the following discussion of the fundamental problems of ethics we adopt principally the line of thought which goes back to *Plato* and *Aristotle,* was continued by *St. Augustine* and *St. Thomas Aquinas,* came to a second climax with the great Spaniards of the sixteenth and seventeenth centuries (notably *Vitoria* and *Suárez*), and has since been continued in an uninterrupted tradition: *traditional natural law ethics.*

We shall certainly have to examine the criticism of this tradition by

[1] Cf. O. Dittrich, *Geschichte der Ethik,* Vol. I, 1926, pp. 24 ff.

modern ethics, and also to make some critical reservations; we shall also, where it appears necessary, attempt to reinforce the foundations and structure of its arguments; furthermore, we hope to bring out a number of fresh aspects regarding the conclusions which it offers for modern society. To rally around this tradition offers at first sight the immense advantage that it is based on an uninterrupted endeavor in human thought over a period of more than two thousand years, and on a system of ethics uniquely self-critical. This advantage seems especially significant in a period of "*crisis in ethics*" when the greater part of present-day philosophy has no positive answer, and often even professes to be unable to give any answer, to the fundamental questions of human existence as expressed in the well-known words of *Kant:* "What can we know, what ought we to do, what may we hope?" and to the question implied by these: "What is man?" Besides all this, the newly awakened interest in the natural law idea and the fresh criticism of it on the part of modern jural thought suggest a re-examination of the fundamental positions in the natural law doctrine as developed in its main tradition. A review of these positions in the light of the unexpected development of the modern social sciences and in the light of the vast enlargement of experience which they involve seems well worth while.

In the following section it will be possible to discuss all the questions of ethics (moral philosophy) only insofar as is necessary for the purposes of natural law ethics and hence of social ethics. For a fuller exposition the reader is referred to my *Kulturethik,* Book I: "*Prinzipienethik.*"

II *The Moral Consciousness*

The basic fact of experience for any discussion of ethics is man's *knowledge of good and evil.* A man of sound mind knows that the murder of a brother in order to obtain his possessions is evil, and that he must therefore refrain from it. Linked with this we perceive the universal injunction: "Do good, avoid evil," which makes not a conditional, but an absolute, claim upon man. It does not say: "Do good if you wish to be respected by others or to gain some advantage." It commands: "Do not kill, even though you have to renounce your brother's possessions which are a temptation to you and even though no suspicion would fall on you." Through conscience everyone is aware of the moral imperative; and the systems of moral principles in force among all peoples, from taboos to advanced societies, admit of no doubt with regard to the universality of the sense of this imperative which underlies the detailed precepts and rules of these systems.

As with the fundamental experience of the universal awareness of good and evil, there is agreement among all schools of ethics regarding the closely related fundamental principles of specifically human conduct. Among these principles are the following: preserve moderation;

act in a way befitting human dignity; do not do to others what you do not wish them to do to you (the golden rule); render to each his own (justice); do not repay good with evil (gratitude); keep your pledged word (fidelity); obey lawful authority. These are the *directly evident moral principles,* that is, truths about obligatory modes of conduct; *directly evident,* that is, recognized as intrinsically certain and therefore universally valid as soon as the meaning of their underlying concepts is grasped by experience; *obligatory,* that is, signifying a claim on man's self-determination absolutely and without exception. All these sides of his moral reason are brought most immediately to man's awareness by the voice of his *conscience* which approves, disapproves, advises, warns, urges, impedes, praises, blames, and summons up powerful emotions when it makes a previous or a retrospective judgment on a decision regarding conduct in the sphere of good and evil.

III *The Root of Morality*

Natural science investigates the empirical data in its sphere with the object of ascertaining inherent and causal relationships. In the same way ethics must inquire into the relationships among the empirical data which it discovers in its sphere and to which we have already referred. There are, then, three main questions which occupy all systems of ethics: the questions concerning the source, the nature, and the criterion of morality. The first two cannot be neglected by any ethical system without failing to meet the essential requirement of every science, namely, to discover the causal connection underlying the empirical data in its sphere. Ethics as a practical science is also concerned with a third question, regarding the principles of order of individual and social life; to answer this question ethics offers a criterion of morality as a guide.

The natural approach to these questions seems to be that of *St. Thomas.*[2] Moral good, he says, can only be a species of the good in general. The question then is: When do we call things good and when bad? It seems noteworthy that the "common-sense philosophers," exponents of one of the most recent trends in philosophy, the "analytical" school, which is founded on common speech usage, go back to the same basic question. Good can signify the fitness of a thing for a special purpose, for example when we speak of a good horse, meaning one fit for pulling loads or one willing and not recalcitrant. But first and foremost a horse is good if its organism functions well in all respects (including of course the normal intelligence of a horse). This is obviously the case if its nature fulfills the ends inherent in its essential functions, for instance, those of the digestive apparatus, of sight, of hearing, of the nervous

[2] Cf. St. Thomas, *Summa theol.,* Ia IIae, q. 18, a. 1. Cf. also his definition of the good in general, Ia IIae, q. 71, a. 1: "In hoc enim consistit uniuscuiusque rei bonitas, quod convenienter se habet secundum modum suae naturae."

system; otherwise it is defective in one way or another and is a bad horse. Thus, we call things good or bad according to their fitness for carrying out the functions which constitute their nature. Good in general is, therefore, the perfection proper to a thing. Thus, the specifically human good must be sought, as *Aristotle* says, in the sphere of the "excellence" proper to man or as *St. Thomas,* following *Aristotle,* expresses it, in the sphere of "perfection" [3] proper to man. Since the expression "perfection" is very commonly used today in its moral sense, whereas it is to be understood here in an *ontological* sense, it will be preferable to employ expressions such as the *full reality of human being* or *full humanity.* Thus, the good is a mode of being and so a quality of a particular kind.[4]

Since human nature as distinct from animal nature is characterized by reason we must seek in reason the ground for the excellence, perfection, and full reality of human existence. If this were not true, a cripple would have to be regarded as bad intrinsically, an idea which calls forth an emphatic protest. Indeed, we know that in a cripple's personality essential humanity can be much more fully realized than in a man who is wholly sound in body. It is, then, in and through the mind that man is man in accordance with the requirements of the full reality of his nature. Nevertheless, he is not inescapably compelled to act in accordance with these demands. Man can, for example, go against his instinct of self-preservation and deliberately commit suicide; the animal, on the other hand, cannot—its instincts compel it to act as its nature requires. Therefore, the animal is always what it is destined to be by its nature. The case of man is not the same. Specifically human conduct is not deter-

[3] Aristotle, *Ethics I;* St. Thomas, *Contra Gent.,* I, 40; *Com. in lib. I Ethicorum,* lect. 1.

[4] The question raised by G. E. Moore in his famous *Principia Ethica* (1903) has, outside natural law ethics, still not been adequately answered. Good, according to Moore, is one of those objects of thought which are ultimate concepts, themselves indefinable, but necessary to the definition of everything definable. What good is, he says, is immediately evident, requires no further explanation, and is not indeed susceptible of any. Rather different is the question of absolute, universally valid principles; these cannot be defined by ethics, since all duties are governed by the situation; what is possible is general truths obtained by generalizations from experience regarding duties in given situations. (Noteworthy is the parallelism between these ideas of Moore and the fundamental views of Scheler: thus, first, that the values good and evil are a category of objects *sui generis,* the apprehension of which rests upon intuition; secondly, that they are not reducible to other realities; thirdly, that principles relating to duties are only generalizations of value experiences in concrete situations. On Scheler cf. n. VII of this chapter.) Like Moore (and Scheler), St. Thomas (*Summa theol.,* Ia IIae, q. 91, a. 3) is also of the opinion that the general moral principles concerning good are the object of immediate apprehension and neither require nor are susceptible of proof; these principles of practical reason are indemonstrable, *naturaliter cognita.* Nevertheless, the fact that they are indemonstrable does not mean that we cannot further investigate their connection with human nature and human existence, whose distinctive feature is the claim to authority of these principles. Only this investigation makes it possible to say what sort of justification this claim possesses and what it demands in the concrete situation. For good and evil, moral value and its opposite are not only, as Moore and Scheler suppose, objects of a speculative nature, but also of a practical nature, i.e., they are wholly related to existence.

mined by blind forces, with the inevitability which is inherent in animal instinct. Man's conduct, whether in accordance with or contrary to the demands of the full actuality of his being as man, depends upon the operation of his reason, upon his self-determination. Hence, this capacity of human nature for self-determination is the reason for responsibility in human conduct and for the phenomenon of morality in man.

IV *The Essence of Morality*

Our analysis of human nature has led us to the conclusion that its fullness of being is not attained as a result of the automatic working of instincts, as in the animal organism, but of the operation of reason, which must come into action whenever specifically human conduct and the specific human good are involved. The functioning of the glands in the human body does not depend upon the direct activity of the mind; but the manner of expression of instincts and impulses—such as those of self-preservation, eating, mating, knowledge, the beautiful—does depend on the mind.[5] Therefore, the question presents itself: Is the human mind also capable of apprehending the proper mode of functioning of the impulses underlying man's self-determination, and hence also of rightly understanding his nature? Man can, as already stated, reach an understanding of his nature only in the way in which he understands the nature of other living things, except that he also has at his disposal inward as well as outward experience. As with other living things he must comprehend the instinctive impulses of his nature and the ends inherent in them. Such understanding calls for no more than the simplest experience and reflection. To understand the organism of a horse and its specific instinctive disposition no detailed knowledge of chemico-biological processes in its brain, heart, digestion, sight, and hearing is necessary, but only such knowledge as that its feeding instinct involves an essential function of its organism. (The word "essential" is used because its end is the preservation of life.)

In the same way, by means of outward and inward experience, man learns to know his own physical and psychical dispositions and impulses and learns what ends are inherent in his impulses. When we speak of

[5] It is through reason, as Plato expresses it, that man is master of his irrational propensities and so "master of himself" (*Republic,* IV, 430[e]). The purpose of reason is "to give the man within man the complete mastery over the entire human creature" (*op. cit.,* IX, 589). On this W. Jaeger (*Paideia: The Ideals of Greek Culture,* Vol. II, 1944, p. 353) comments: "The true man, the 'man in man,' as Plato beautifully expresses the new Idea, is the intellectual part of the soul. It is unnecessary to explain the significance of this image in the history of humanism. . . . It is clear once more that the whole complex structure of the *Republic* was meant only to serve as a background against which to work out this picture of the human soul. . . . The function of education is to train our nobler irrational impulses to harmonize with the intellect so that the weak human element in us may be supported by them, and keep the subhuman part in check."

impulses or instincts, psychical as well as physical are meant.[6] The term "instinct" is chosen not least out of regard for its use by modern psychology and sociology, which employ it to denote both physical and psychical dispositions. It may be necessary to state expressly that this use of the term "instinct" has nothing to do with the narrower notion in which instinct and instinctive disposition are confined to the part of human nature which is unresponsive or hostile to reason. We must also distinguish from instinct proper the instinctive stirrings and inclinations, which may be in harmony or in conflict with the ends inherent in instincts.

To sum up: The specifically human conduct is the conduct of rational nature; the conduct demanded of man by the full actuality of his nature is indicated by the ends designed in the physical and psychical instincts of his nature; because it is dependent on his reason and will (self-determination) the conduct required of man by the full actuality of his nature takes on for him the nature of morality. Accordingly, we may give the following definition of morality: Morality consists in the correspondence of human conduct with the ends designed in man's nature, in his physical and psychical instincts, or, briefly, in "instinct-conformity." Thus, to use the well-known expression of *Aristotle,* the good consists in "right desire," [7] or, as traditional natural law ethics has also expressed it,

[6] At this crucial point in our discussion of the law of human nature we can again find support in an idea of St. Thomas Aquinas (*Summa theol.,* Ia IIae, q. 94, a. 2): "Secundum igitur ordinem inclinationum naturalium est ordo praeceptorum legis naturalis"; *inclinationes* are instincts rather than inclinations. He speaks also of man's instinctive constitution and distinguishes therein three groups of instincts: (1) the instinct which he shares with all creatures—self-preservation in accordance with the particular nature of each ("conservationem sui esse secundum suam naturam"); (2) the bodily instincts which are common to man and other living creatures, e.g., sexual union, rearing the young; (3) the mental instincts proper to man's specific nature, among which he includes the social instinct. With regard to all instincts he proceeds on the principle: "Omnia illa ad quae homo habet naturalem inclinationem, ratio naturaliter apprehendit ut bona, et per consequens ut opere prosequenda, et contraria eorum ut mala et vitanda."

[7] Here again at a crucial point we may turn to St. Thomas Aquinas. When Thomas enters upon the ontological-metaphysical analysis he does so in the precise direction in which we are striving to develop traditional natural law theory, so necessary today: Emphasizing strongly the psychological (apprehension of principles) and the theological (eternal law) sides in natural law, he begins his analysis with ends, and at once conformity with ends becomes his criterion of morality. Thus, he asks in II *Sent.,* dist. 38, q. 1, a. 1: "Utrum sit tantum unus finis rectarum voluntatum" ("Whether the right direction of the will is towards one end only") and comments: "Eodem ordine res referuntur in finem quo procedunt a principio, eo quod agens unusquisque ordinat effectum suum in finem aliquem; et ideo secundum ordinem agentium est ordo finium; inveniuntur diversi fines proprii, secundum diversitatem entium; res referuntur in finem ultimum communem mediante fine proprio; (although the final end is one only, namely God), nihilominus tamen sunt alii fines proximi, et, si secundum illos fines servetur debita relatio voluntatis in finem ultimum, erit recta voluntas." With his characteristic precision he goes on: "Actus morales non specificantur a fine ultimo, sed a finibus proximis: hi autem plures diversorum sunt, sicut et fines naturales sunt plures." The interpretation and development of the natural law doctrine of Thomas would appear to demand: (1) a thorough ontological-metaphysical analysis of human

in "right reason," since it is reason that directs the specifically human instincts toward the ends designed in them and thus man's conduct toward congruence with the true reality of human nature.[8] Since man's whole nature in its physical and spiritual aspects is in question, morality accordingly consists in *being true to nature* (hence, in the social sphere, in being true to what is demanded by the intrinsic "nature of the things"; cf. Chap. 4, par. IV). And since the ends indicated in human nature with its physical and spiritual instincts, which are to be realized by man by his own self-determination (freedom) in the existing circumstances, determine the special character of human existence, we may term them *"the existential ends"* of man. The existential ends will form *the fundamental concept of our ethics.* Owing to the position of end in the traditional natural law ethics, one essential feature of this ethics is teleological (as also it has a eudaemonistic [cf. Chap. 4] and an intuitionistic feature [cf. Chap. 6]).

A survey of the existential human ends makes it clear, I think, that our definition of morality is in harmony with *universal and established human experience.* We may sum up these ends as follows: self-preservation, including bodily integrity and social respect (personal honour); self-perfection physically and spiritually, including the development of one's faculties for the improvement of the conditions of one's life and provision for one's economic welfare by securing the necessary property or income; the enlargement of experience and knowledge; marriage and the rearing of children; interest in the spiritual and material welfare of one's fellowmen as human persons equal in value; social fellowship, to promote common utility, which consists in the maintenance of peace and order and in opportunity for all members of society to attain full human existence by sharing proportionately in the welfare of society; the knowledge and worship of God and the ultimate fulfillment of man's destiny through union with him.

---

nature; (2) a presentation of the special ends inherent in human nature, "fines proprii"; (3) an interpretation of natural law not only as the bidding of reason but also as a force by means of which human nature is impelled to realize in social life the natural order proper to it. It is principally in three directions that we are here attempting a development of traditional natural law theory. Therefore, it would appear to be a misunderstanding when Erich Fechner (*Rechtsphilosophie,* 1956, p. 127) mentions our *Social Ethics* as portraying "the traditional dualism of instinct and reason."

[8] Aristotle, *Nicomachean Ethics,* VI, 2 (trans. by F. H. Peters). This book of the *Nicomachean Ethics* makes it very doubtful whether the classical idea of man can be shaken by the objection that it gives only a negative note to the connection between reason and instinct, as R. Niebuhr (*The Nature and Destiny of Man,* 1941, Vol. I, pp. 32 f.) seems to assume. It is not only a "pattern of human reason" (*ibid.,* p. 30) that is signified by the criterion "right reason." The mere fact that Aristotle bases his ethics on an extensive *ontological* analysis of the human instinct for happiness precludes such a judgment. It was not the classical ethics that derived the moral order from self-contained reason, but the *rationalistic* ethics of the Stoa and modern enlightenment. Herein lay the principal ground of the reaction of the ethics of romanticism, especially that of Nietzsche with its emphasis on the values of vitality.

There is, I think, no doubt that this account of the existential human ends, except the last mentioned, meets with general agreement. This shows that the fully developed individual moral conscience, when it concerns itself with the meaning of life, finds it must refer to the existential ends which it sees are designed in the nature of man. In this can be seen weighty evidence that our principle of morality corresponds to reality. Evidence of no less importance is afforded by the fact that such a scheme of the existential ends, in virtue of the developed moral sense of mankind, is in quite general use for judging of the rightness or wrongness of the functioning of social institutions and social systems, although the points of emphasis may vary in particulars.

[A digression: Since the question under review is human nature as an instinctive constitution and the relationship between instinct and end, no biological or psychological investigation can assist ethics in the *fundamental* questions regarding the nature of man and, dependent upon this, the nature of morality. The case is different with *particular* questions of moral conduct. Fresh knowledge concerning the functioning of human nature and its dependence on environment may lead to new understanding; an example is the findings of biology regarding the sterile period.]

The conception of existential ends

This conception has given rise to many questions. Thus, Professor *Veit* writes:

> Though the schools of present-day philosophy which in one way or another appropriate the idea of existence are drawing ever further apart, it seems hardly permissible to assign Messner to one of these schools. Have we now gone so far that in order to gain attention in Europe it is necessary to make a terminological concession to existentialism? Or is it Messner's purpose to show that the appropriation of a good old idea like existence need not worry us, and that one can use it without incurring a burden of debt to Kierkegaard, Heidegger and other names which Messner hardly mentions? If the latter interpretation is correct then this is a substantial gain. Often stereotyped models of thought have to be penetrated by the elementary force of intuition in order to get to the substance of problems. This is made difficult today by the fact that preliminary questions on the way to the core of a problem claim too much space and that in the process energies are dissipated in discussing model-inspired methods of approach.[9]

The following is the truth of the matter: My object was to avoid needless involvement in largely unfruitful argument about concepts both within and without the confines of traditional natural law theory and in merely theoretical speculations in order to move on as quickly as possible to the root problems of jural, social, political, and economic order in present-day society. Our concept of "existential ends" is not affected by the fashions of philosophical thought. Traditional natural law teaching

[9] O. Veit in his discussion of my *Social Ethics*, in *Ordo*, Vol. VII, 1955, p. 276.

was always familiar with the existential idea in substance, since, although it saw in man's essence, or nature, the basis of the fundamental demands of true humanity, yet it saw the realization of these demands in his personal and especially social mode of existence as dependent on his self-determination (freedom) and the actual situation. The idea impressed itself upon me in England at the beginning of the Second World War soon after I had begun to work upon a natural law ethics adequate to the circumstances of the modern world. At that time existential philosophy as such had aroused no special interest even on the Continent, and in England during the war hardly the name was known.

Among the reasons which decided me to employ the concept "existential ends" I would stress the following:

1. One of the great surprises which await those who come to grips with Anglo-Saxon thought and writing is to find that the accustomed form of metaphysical basis for ethics and legal philosophy is alien to Anglo-Saxon thought, which relies much more directly on *experience;* hence, a foundation as close as possible to experience had to be sought if access to this realm of thought was not to be barred from the outset. Equally surprising is it to become acquainted with an extensive literature which, relying on the remarkable advances made in the empirical sciences of man (biology, psychology, sociology, ethnology), sets forth a purely empirical, indeed scientific, humanism and rejects any metaphysical reality, quite apart from the purely empirical and scientific humanism of dialectical materialism. Thus, the question concerning the nature of man and the natural order of society was given a fresh turn. In view of the new questions posed by the empirical sciences it seemed imperative for the natural law doctrine to allow experience itself to speak as far as possible in the interpretation of the nature of man and thus to conceive it in terms of its functioning, as we are accustomed to do when seeking a scientific understanding of the nature of things. It seemed quite beyond doubt that it must be possible to interpret the order natural to human conduct directly in terms of human nature without digressing into discussion of "last end" and "eternal law," with all the metaphysical questions which they involve. The now apparently simple solution of deriving "existential ends" from the instinctive constitution and instinctive structure of human nature came to me only as the result of long deliberation. At the same time it was clear also that this new conception not only did not mean an abandonment of the natural law tradition but that in fact it would bring out the fruitful character of this tradition for modern empirical thinking. Indeed, the *philosophia perennis,* to which traditional natural law ethics belongs, has always laid great stress on experience as its starting point.

2. The ends thus derived from the instinctive constitution and structure of human nature are the *essential* ends in life, which are bound up with the constant basic substance of human nature. In the light of

the previously mentioned tasks which confront a modern natural law ethics, however, the notion of "essential" ends (although it seems justified in my *Kulturethik*) seemed inadequate. It allowed too much prominence to the conception of man as an abstract rational being, *animal rationale,* which has too long dominated the development of natural law theory, and to the corresponding narrowing down of natural law to a rational a priori of moral law. In fact, man has to actualize the essential order of nature in individual and social life not only as an abstract rational being but always, too, as a concrete historical being, that is, in the historical conditions, or situation, governing his existence. This dependence on circumstances was always brought out by natural law ethics, but its implications were not always fully taken into account. For a realistic modern natural law ethic it seemed necessary at the outset to emphasize that the actual natural law order was dependent upon circumstances; hence, the notion of "existential ends."

3. To equate natural law too closely with the general principles of the moral a priori could have given the impression that they were only of a "formal" character,[10] that is, lacking material content. Our concept of "existential ends" as related to integral nature and to the ontological order recognizable in it emphasizes the *concrete* nature of the natural law order along with the rational a priori. Furthermore, as we shall see, it indicates that even the elementary jural truths are determinate in content in accordance with man's actual mode of existence.

4. Besides the strong emphasis on the ontological order which is involved in the concept of "existential ends" and on their dependence on situation for realization, the special character of the tasks of natural law ethics today is underlined: natural law ethics can work out the natural fundamental order of the various spheres of social life only if it keeps in full and continuous contact with the established findings of the various sciences of man, especially the *social sciences,* and collaborates closely with them. Otherwise there will be continual recourse to generalities, whether about principles or about method.

5. Perhaps nothing can serve better to make evident the status of our fundamental idea of "existential ends," its connection with tradition, and the development of tradition which is contained in it, than the following quotations. *Theodor Steinbüchel* writes: "One idea above all permeates the whole Thomistic philosophy and theology: the idea of end. End is the general category under which the entire universe as well as the life of the individual is considered."[11] *Robert Linhardt* is equally positive: "The fundamental significance of teleology in the

[10] What significance is to be attached to the reproach of "formality" may be gathered from the long exposition of H. Thielecke, *Theologische Ethik,* Vol. I, 1951, pp. 676–92, on the imprecision of the fundamental principle of natural law, *suum cuique.* Cf. Chap. 48.

[11] T. Steinbüchel, *Der Zweckgedanke in der Philosophie des hl. Thomas v. Aq.,* 1912, p. 1.

Aristotelian-Thomistic system cannot be stressed firmly enough," specifically with regard to the "immanent teleology of things, of man, of communities."[12] In contrast with pre-Thomistic scholasticism, which follows the ethics of *Augustine* and in which earthly life was seen primarily as a preparation for eternal life, "temporal ends," says *Steinbüchel,* acquire with *Thomas* "a more important status; they are fully recognized in their own relative values," and scholasticism with Thomas accordingly turns "to dignifying the immanent ends of life and to make their attainment a moral duty." Nevertheless, the idea of the moral personality, which is fundamental to modern natural law theory, occurs in Thomas only in embryo, states *Steinbüchel: personalitas* is understood by him in a purely metaphysical sense.[13] *A. Utz* reaches the conclusion, surprising to many, that with *Thomas* the individuality principle does not yet represent a prepolitical jural principle in natural law. Thus, moreover, the principle of individual rights is not found with him, nor is even the underlying idea of human dignity, "since it would never have occurred to Thomas to uphold an individual right to freedom on the basis of human dignity"; "the age of St. Thomas was not yet ready to visualize in the concrete situation the principle of individuality and of human dignity founded on like human nature, and on this closer to life basis to declare them as natural law . . . This required the social revolution brought about by industrialization and liberalism. All the necessary elements of thought are, however, present in Thomas."[14]

With the notion of "existential ends" *the idea of end remains at the center of natural law theory;* yet man is also understood by his nature as an individual as well as a social, and hence a historical, being; from this notion can be gained the indispensable *criterion of natural individual and social rights* as dependent on the changing state of society.

It may be gathered from the foregoing, however, that to make the notion of "existential ends" the starting point of natural law ethics in fact represented an attempt to penetrate to the substance of problems, as *O. Veit* says, that is, to the demands of the *natural jural order* in the various spheres of social life in present-day circumstances without becoming too involved in the much tilled field of purely speculative or historical inquiry.

We can now describe in a few words the relationship between our conception of existence and that of the existentialists. There is naturally a point of contact, and this lies in the fact that true, authentic, fully real human existence depends on man's self-determination, that is, freedom,

[12] R. Linhardt, *Die Sozialprinzipien des hl. Thomas v. Aq.*, 1932, pp. 32, 55.

[13] Cf. T. Steinbüchel, *op. cit.*, pp. 1, 84, 87, 90 f., 105.

[14] A. Utz, *Recht und Gerechtigkeit* (*Deutsche Thomasausgabe*), 1953, pp. 494, 496, 499 f. In view of the central position given to the idea of end by Thomas, as pointed out by Steinbüchel and Linhardt, it is surprising that in modern presentations of the natural law doctrine of St. Thomas the idea of end is hardly mentioned, much less is its fundamental significance discussed.

and on the situation, as the best exponents of traditional natural law theory have always maintained. Our notion of existence, however, as we shall see, includes also the notion of the *order* of individual and social existence, which man finds indicated in general outline in his nature and which he has to actualize in detail in the situation as it arises, guided by reason and will (the latter being the instrument of his freedom). All trends of existential philosophy outside the philosophy of Christian humanism understand man solely in terms of a freedom linked with no such existential order. According to existential philosophy, therefore, there is no moral order universally and uniformly binding, no "general ethics," but only "situation ethics." That it possesses no direct approach to man's social existence, to his wholly social nature, is, as already pointed out (cf. Chap. 2, n. II), a further objection to its doctrine of man, its anthropology.

v *The Criterion of Morality*

The criterion of morality forms the subject of the third basic question of ethics (cf. above, n. III). The criterion of morality is also termed the "moral principle." It must achieve three things: 1) It must make it possible to discern what kinds of conduct are intrinsically (and therefore always) evil, and must make the reason evident, thus enabling the question to be answered: Why are lying, adultery, and suicide intrinsically (and therefore always) morally wrong. 2) In regard to modes of conduct which are not in themselves evil, the moral principle must make it possible to determine the moral quality of acts in particular situations and of means in the service of ends, and hence of what in a particular situation is commanded, allowed, or forbidden. 3) The moral principle must, in the case of prima facie conflicts of duties or conscience, make it possible to reach a decision about the right line of conduct.

The criterion must follow logically from the definition of morality. The definition of morality has been shown to be conduct in conformity with the existential ends, the ends which man finds designed in the instincts essential to his nature. In order to fulfill its function as described above, the criterion of morality must be objective and concrete. As objective, it must be independent of the purely subjective feeling and thinking of the individual, since it is to serve for the appraisal of true and false in his judgment. As concrete, it must not contain a merely abstract, formal generalization unable to express anything about the individual case. The criterion is *objective* because it is related to being, that is to human nature and its own essential impulses; it is *concrete* because it is related to facts, that is to the individual ends designated in these impulses.

Derived objectively from the full reality of integrated human nature, our criterion of morality allots to the individual existential ends their place in the order of ends ontologically outlined in the order of being in human nature itself. Thus, we come to the *logic of the order of ends.* Notwithstanding many contrary statements (cf. Chap. 47), this order is in no way deduced from the perspective of the Christian world of values; *Aristotle* was already aware of it and saw it as corresponding with the gradation of impulses in human nature. For example: outward material things are not ends in themselves, but means serving the ends of other grades of being, particularly life and health; other ends are linked with these in great number, especially the maintenance of family and home. The family again finds its superior end in the common weal which makes possible for it a life of peace and fully human existence, the "good life" (*Aristotle*); all the ends mentioned flow into the final end of the possession of the supreme good. Therefore, the scale of ends ascends from those lying in external, *material* goods, whose status is that of means toward ends in the *biological* sphere, through those of the *social* and *intellectual* spheres, to the all-embracing *moral* and *religious* sphere.

The gradation in the order of being and in the order of ends is, ethically speaking, of a twofold fundamental significance. In the first place it reveals the uniqueness of human nature by showing that human nature is to be known by the spiritual character of the soul and hence by its freedom and responsibility—its moral character. Secondly, it points the way to the realization of full human being, in that the ends of lower ontological grades are directed toward those of higher grades; in other words, values of a lower order toward values of individual personality and social culture.[15] Primarily, however, the ontological matters involved are in themselves morally indifferent and acquire a moral value quality only when ends establish demands, as existential ends, on the conduct of man or of society.

From the logic of the order of ends we must distinguish the realization of this order; from the *ontological* aspect of the order of ends must be distinguished the truly *ethical* aspect. With regard to the ethical aspect, the ends which are in themselves superior do not impose unconditional obligations, nor do all the ends demand their realization. The reason for this is that the order of realization depends on the "existential" character of ends at any time: its relationship with the conduct demanded by the situation, required by the full actuality of human being in the situation, individually or socially. A feature of human existence is of fundamental significance in this respect: the realization of full human being does not come about in a single act (in contrast with what theology has to say about the one and final volition of the angels), but in *a process continuing throughout life and therefore dependent on circumstances.* The determination of what is at any time morally demanded in this

[15] Thus, what Scheler eloquently termed the "transparency" of the lower values pointing toward the higher is grounded in the order of being and the order of ends; the same idea, that "the *fines proprii* of the several stages of being are perhaps the goal for what is below them, but they themselves in their turn point beyond to what is above them," is found by Linhardt (*Die Sozialprinzipien . . .* , p. 60) in Thomas Aquinas, *Summa contra Gent.*, 3, 2: "Omnia intermedia inter primum agens et ultimum finem sunt fines respectu priorum et principia activa respectu sequentium."

process is made possible by the concrete and definite nature of our criterion, since it indicates on the one hand the special demands of the existential ends in themselves and on the other hand the immediate demands occasioned by their interdependence in the course of realization. In other words: our criterion makes it possible to determine not only whether and when an immediate priority is to be assigned to an end in the lower rank in the process of realization of the order of ends as a whole, but also when and to what extent the ultimate realization of existential ends is not to be prejudiced. For example: it would be wrong for a father of a family to devote himself to the things of the mind, which in themselves occupy a superior ontological rank among ends, while leaving his family without means of support; for him, in his situation, providing for his family is a paramount existential end in the process of realizing the order of ends as a unity determining his full humanity.

On the other hand, a minimum of intellectual development is indispensable for the attainment of full human being by the *individual* in fulfilling the responsibility rooted in the existential ends; therefore, a minimum of intellectual development is an existential end of the highest rank; and a minimum of opportunity for intellectual development for *all* is an existential end of social fellowship and therefore obligatory for social systems. Apart from this twofold obligation, however, the individual person as such need not pursue any special aims in the intellectual sphere; in other words, he need not cultivate his impulse toward intellectual ends and values. For the same reasons, individual ends in particular circumstances may become unimportant to the full realization of human being; or rather may acquire a purely indirect significance (i.e. that of a voluntary or involuntary renunciation, which may then be of direct significance in the service of other existential ends). Thus, the exercise of a profession or trade in society may be pointless for a recluse; similarly, marriage may be inexpedient for someone who wishes to be free for higher ends and to aspire to a form, determined by such ends, of integrated, viz. in the special sense, perfect, humanity. On the other hand, a social system which makes marriage economically impossible for many, or possible only after long delay, is incompatible with the order of ends and hence with the natural moral order.

Our conception of the nature and criterion of morality is by no means discredited, as has been thought, because morality can mean disharmony between man's conduct and some ends of his nature. What is meant is voluntary or involuntary, total or partial forbearance in the exercise of instincts. According to our conception, in the exercise of individual instincts morality consists in the conformity with the ends ordained in them.[16] This does not mean that every single instinct is to be exercised

[16] The reader is referred again to the passage quoted before (cf. note 23 above) in which St. Thomas (*II Sent.*, q. 38, a. 1 ad 3) says quite generally that the morality of an act depends upon its conformity with ends.

generally or by everyone to the same extent. Rather, our criterion enables us, as already shown, to *distinguish* between what is *mandatory,* what is *permissible,* and what is more *perfect;* in other words, to distinguish in the scale between fundamental values and higher ideals, between the claims of mere duty and those of magnanimity, between the demands of law and of what is beyond law, distinctions which are inaccessible to other ethical systems or which are accessible only by reference to extraphilosophical modes of interpretation.

At this point it is necessary to show the application of our criterion of morality to the three problems to which it must indicate the answer. The answer to the first question: Why is lying *intrinsically (and therefore always) evil?* is that it is incompatible with the existential ends designed in man's social nature, since their attainment depends on mutual understanding and trust. Acts which are intrinsically evil, such as lying, are evil under all circumstances, since they are always contrary to the existential ends. Suicide is intrinsically evil because man has to realize his moral existence in a process never completed in itself, and therefore may not arbitrarily put an end to the process; euthanasia is likewise morally wrong: even though gravely and incurably ill a person may achieve an act of fulfillment of the moral personality such as he has never before achieved.

Our criterion proves itself also in the second problem mentioned above, namely, the judging of *what, here and now, is permitted, forbidden or commanded;* that is, moral acts as dependent upon circumstances. Intoxication robs man temporarily of that control of his mental faculties which enables him to act in accord with his existential ends. Therefore, to induce intoxication merely for the sake of pleasure is contrary to the moral order. If, however, it is necessary in order to secure an existential end such as the preservation of life or health, for example, the use of an anaesthetic in an operation, it is justified. Another example: obedience to lawful authority is a virtue; but if a government demands from parents action which offends against their duty to educate their children, thereby preventing the fulfillment of an existential end, obedience becomes morally wrong.

With this we reach the question of *conflict of duties,* the third of the above-mentioned problems which are connected with the criterion of morality. We have the clue to its solution at hand: in the process of realizing the order of ends, existential ends preserve the claim to authority due to them in this order insofar as they are necessary to the attainment of fully real humanity, provided that the ultimate realization of the order of ends is not frustrated. This means that an end, one which establishes duties in a definite situation, of lower rank prevails against those of higher rank provided that the fulfillment of duties established by the latter and linked with another situation is not impaired thereby. Gambling or playing cards may be morally preferable to work when recreation is necessary and these are the only available forms of it. A mother must nurse her sick child in preference to attending divine service if the child's health is in serious danger, although in itself devotion to the child ranks lower than devotion to the Creator; the mother's devotion to the child takes precedence as an end, since the end of preservation of the child's life is imperiled, whereas that of devotion to the Creator can still be attained. Nevertheless, devotion to the Creator preserves its status as the ultimate end if man's relation to the Creator is directly involved and man's final end is in jeopardy: in a time of persecution one must not deny one's religious faith even if one's life and consequently the future of a dependent is at stake (the objection that one's right relation to the Creator can be restored later implies the admission that something integral to full humanity is being sacrificed). The government of a peace-loving nation, if it sees the material, cultural, and moral welfare involved in the essential ends of the state threatened by an aggressor, may be in duty bound to undertake a defensive war involving grave losses, although the assessment of the precedence of existential ends in this connection is a very formidable task. The aim of self-preservation, of securing its very existence, the existential end which underlies all others, can then govern the decision to be made in a conflict of duties; it is otherwise if political, but not moral, religious, or cultural self-determination (freedom) is at stake.

The reason for the *conflict of duties* consists in the fact that they depend on circumstances (on the situation: the conditions *and* consequences of modes of conduct): owing to inadequate perception of the nature and significance of the circumstances, reasons seem to arise for contradictory claims of moral principles. Our criterion of morality makes it possible to ascertain which is the true claim to authority in such a conflict of duties, because by basing moral conduct, namely, duties, on existential ends it relates the claim of individual ends to the order of ends as well as to the process of realizing it. There can never be more than one duty at one time, because in the ontological order ends cannot be in conflict, nor, therefore, can they conflict in the ontological pattern of the situation, since, in its reality too, only the natural order with its unitary order of ends can make claims valid. Therefore, *objectively*, that is, in reality fully understood, no conflict exists between duties (and rights), although *subjectively* such a conflict can often weigh heavily on the individual conscience. The same is true with regard to questions of social order. Conflicts in questions of a political or social nature between groups or states are by no means only devised by interests, but may involve genuine moral conflicts having their cause in conflicting, more or less convincingly based judgments on rights and duties. Just because there are always rights and duties at issue in the sphere of social order and therefore always questions of common good and hence of moral conscience, however, objectivity, or the endeavor to attain objective analysis, becomes the supreme moral obligation in deciding such conflicts. A criterion of morality and right such as ours—allegiance to ends indicated in the natural order itself—makes it possible to proceed to an objectively based judgment concerning the concrete demands of such ends in the given situation and hence also to a definite judgment of conscience on seemingly conflicting jural principles and claims in questions of social order. (In dealing with legal philosophy it will be necessary further to consider the question of the conflict of rights.)

VI *The Concept of Natural Law* (Lex naturalis)

In defining moral good we began with the general idea of good (cf. n. III above), and we interpreted its nature as perfection of being. We considered the apprehension of the general moral principles, but we saw the nature of morality not only as lying in what is *in accordance with right reason*, understood in terms of these principles, but as lying in what is in *accordance with nature,* a wider concept—namely, the conduct designed by man's moral reason and the existential ends. Since the idea of moral "good" conforms with general linguistic usage, one may suppose that the idea of moral natural law (*lex naturalis*) should conform with *general scientific usage*. Otherwise the impression will be aroused that natural law (*lex*) in the human sphere means something altogether different. It then appears questionable whether this notion in scientific ethics can be chiefly or exclusively restricted to moral *reason* or simply to the judgment of conscience. Little is gained if, in view of the inadequate nature of such a definition of natural law, reference is made to the other side, to *being*, but only in such general terms as, for example, moral good is what is in accordance with human nature, and natural moral law is the law of human conduct as recognizable in the essential reality of man and the world. The opponents of traditional natural law ethics who maintain that the moral principles of reason are only of a "formal" character would not be prepared to regard such an ontologically generalizing concept as more than formal as long as the "what" of this being and the "how" of understanding it are not explained. In natural science, general usage understands by natural law the mode of functioning or behavior inherent in the nature of things and conforming with it. The most general idea of natural law in the human sphere need not differ from this: it is the mode of functioning inherent in man's rational nature which brings about conduct in conformity with this nature.

This is a general concept. We must now deal with its details in order to reach a more articulate definition. In accordance with his rational nature, natural law operates in man through his reason and will. *Reason* acquires a twofold function in this regard: on the one hand, that of insight into the self-evident moral principles; on the other hand, insight into the mental and physical impulses of human nature tending toward a fully human being, as demanded by the ends indicated in them. Similarly, two functions belong to the *will:* on the one hand, performing the duties thus recognized as moral commands; on the other hand, allowing itself to be guided by the impulses inherent in man's nature to strive for integral humanity, operating in his impulse toward happiness, a fundamental instinct, especially urging upon him the way to fulfillment through community life. Accordingly, the functions of the intellect and the will are intimately linked, although they have to be separately discussed in order to bring out the special character of the human natural law. This brings into view (and this is fundamental to the concept of natural law as here understood) the *psychological* aspect of the concept, which concerns moral apprehension, in its direct and indissoluble connection with the *ontological* aspect; in this way the impression is not aroused, as often happens, that what comes first is an a priori insight into the elementary truths, to be followed by knowledge of being.[17] Owing to its mode of operation in the psycho-physical nature of man, the ontological order itself becomes a stimulus toward apprehension of the moral principles. But it would be wrong not to see the "deontological order" at work in the natural law just as certainly as the "ontological order," the former understood as insight into the immediately manifest moral principles with their obligating commands. This apprehension, which constitutes the *psychological-subjective* aspect, is as essential to the idea of natural law as the *ontological-objective* aspect.

The natural law of nonrational living creatures operates solely and entirely through their instinctive knowledge. We are familiar with the amazing instinctive certainty of animals in matters of feeding and propagation, in their reaction to environment, etc. If animals possess such a highly developed instinctive knowledge regarding what is demanded by their nature—their full development and self-preservation—it may be supposed that man too possesses, in a manner appropriate to his nature, the necessary immediate knowledge of what is required by his nature and its development.[18] His is the rational nature, and therefore it must be the mind which imparts this knowledge to him. He possesses it in the form of rational insight into the moral conduct demanded of him (judgment and command of conscience bound up with moral in-

[17] It is known to child psychologists today that not even the general categories of empirical knowledge, such as space, time, and causality, belong to a prereflective consciousness, but are acquired in a process of trying out. Cf. among others, Jean Piaget, *La causalité physique chez l'enfant*, Paris, 1927; Engl. trans.: *The Child's Conception of Physical Causality*, 1952; *Le développement de la notion de temps chez l'enfant*, Paris, 1946.

[18] Cf. St. Thomas, *Summa theol.*, Ia IIae, q. 91, a. 4: "Secundum proportionem capacitatis humanae naturae." Cf. the relevant remarks quoted in Messner, *Kulturethik*, p. 32, from the pragmatist C. H. Peirce and the agnostic B. Russell: the former asks why, if a chicken knows at once what to peck and what not, man should not also know what his nature demands; to which B. Russell replies that he knows no answer to this question.

sight as a permanent disposition: *habitus* or *synderesis* as a part of *lumen naturale;* otherwise expressed: aprioristic-moral insight, aprioristic-intuitive apprehension of values). It would be vain to belittle this psychological-subjective side of natural law for the simple reason that man requires the immediate guidance of reason in situations calling for an immediate decision with regard to conduct. This is effected by the natural conscience. (Concerning our definition, developed above, we shall have more to say when dealing with natural law, *jus naturale,* the cognition of it and the proof of it, in Chap. 47.)

The objective and subjective aspects of the functioning of natural human law work, as has been said above, in intimate connection. What is the reason for this mode of operation of natural law? It is the special character of man's social nature. There *has been and is still a much too strong tendency to think of man* philosophically, as an *individual being complete in himself,* or to see him as a *political being,* namely, *in his relationship to the state,* as did the ancient world (and, under its influence, also to some extent the Middle Ages). Much more is *man primordially a family being.* In the family his beliefs about truth and value are formed, as indeed his spirit down to its deepest roots; and in the family group he learns what is his good as a social being and as an individual in the endeavor to fulfill his desire for happiness, that is, in aiming at values. It is this experience urged upon him by his very nature that brings him to pursue modes of conduct in accordance with his nature. Human nature leaves man, on the whole, no other possibility than life in conformity with the order of existence thus set before him. Consequently, the concrete content as well as the general validity of those self-evident principles is grasped from the outset.

In the light of the foregoing, we can see in the operation of natural law the experience of conscience and the experience of being, the insight into principles and the insight into reality indissolubly linked at the very root, and the natural law operative as originally in its ontological-objective aspect as in its psychological-subjective aspect. Thus, we have reached, it seems to me, a *highly important stage in the question of the formulation of natural law* (both *lex naturalis* and *ius naturale*). From the outset the moral principles are not conceived as abstract and formal principles, but in concrete, objective practicability. Knowledge of the ontological order is from the outset intimately and inseparably linked with the rational order. From the outset reason learns to see the elementary moral principles in their relationship to being, conscience learns to understand them as involved in the "nature of things" (*natur der sache*) and hence can apply them further. All the simple moral (and jural) principles such as those of moderation, of peaceableness (the "golden rule"), of justice ("to each his own"), of obedience, of keeping one's word, of being faithful to contracts ("*pacta sunt servanda*"), of probity, are first experienced in their particular application in family life and then grasped in their general significance; at the same time their inherently certain truth is understood and hence their general validity. In connection with this insight the most general supreme principle (good is to be done, evil is to be avoided), the supreme moral value and its obligating nature are seen to be both concrete in content and self-evident and generally binding.

To sum up these reflections a precise notion of natural law must be stated: It is the mode of functioning of man's nature, conferring an obligation upon his will, tending to bring about the conduct demanded by the full reality of his being, by means of the disposition belonging to his mind to apprehend intuitively the postulates of such conduct and to see them in relation to the spiritual and physical instincts and impulses directing and impelling him toward such conduct.

In order to obviate misunderstandings it may be observed that to emphasize the dependence of moral insight upon experience does not mean that general moral principles are founded upon experience; rather it means that experience is a prerequisite for the apprehension of their evident truth as well as of their general validity. That the apprehension of the simple moral truths and of the supreme principle "good is to be done, evil is to be avoided," is dependent upon experience may be seen from the fact that the child attains to this knowledge generally by means of reward and punishment. That is to say, the principle *omnis cognitio incipit a sensibus*—all cognition depends upon experience—is as true in the realm of practical reason as in the realm of theoretical reason. All man's mental capacities belong to his nature only as dispositions; they must unfold and develop, and this they can do to the full extent only in social fellowship, namely, in the primordial community of the family. In the family, these cognitions are first conveyed to the child from without, with the awakening of reason, and hence they do not yet appear as the direct functioning of natural law. They are, however, functions of an indirect character, and their instrument is the family group. It is well to recall again how clearly *Plato* saw this fact; he pointed out that first the moral reason of parents and of educators operates in the child, but as the child attains to the full use of his own reason, his moral reason takes the place of that of the parents and now begins to function independently and from its own insight into what is good and right, what is evil and wrong.[19]

This insight is not primarily the outcome of penetrating reflection; rather, the mind comes to it by means of the impulses operating in human nature. Man's fundamental instinct is his instinct for happiness. In the operation of this instinct, that is, the desire for satisfaction of the various individual instincts and their inclinations, man learns that not every satis-

[19] Cf. Plato, *Laws*, 653c. He says with Freud that, before the attainment of the full use of reason, the principles of the moral law become operative through the unconscious, but, against Freud, that, with the attainment of the full use of reason, these principles are recognized as intrinsically certain and bearing their own authority in themselves.

faction of instinct conforms with the true well-being demanded by his nature. With this experience in the satisfaction of the instinct of happiness, *the first intimations of the ontological order in human nature* in general emerge for the developing mind of the young. He learns this in connection with his experiences in the family group. These experiences are concerned first and foremost with mutual love and with the many experiences closely linked to this primal human instinct, such as that of mutual respect, of obedience, of trusting in one's word, of assured tenure of one's own belongings, of peace if one member does to another what he himself does not want to suffer, and thus of order in the conduct of all those living in fellowship together, which makes their community a happy one. Modes of conduct are thus experienced as asserting a claim to validity, and their significance is gradually understood. As the developing mind becomes conscious of its dependence on the common good of the family, it gains an awareness of the generally valid demands connected with this good which are made upon it, first of all in regard to the existence, order, and well-being of the family as such and the good of all its members; then it gains the awareness of demands relating to conduct toward other men outside the family by reason of their humanity.

Thus, man learns to live the elementary moral and jural principles with their concrete demands, then he learns to apprehend their general nature and their universal authority, and finally he learns to comprehend their inherently evident and absolute claim to obedience.[20] He learns *to live them and understand them as concrete rules:* this is the one decisive factor in our argument. The other fact of decisive significance is that these experiences and the associated intuitions of the awakening and developing mind are *imposed by the ontological order,* that is by the quest for happiness and for value realization originating in the instincts and impulses of human nature as they operate in the family community.

With these are linked *other experiences and insights of equal importance,* all of them being bound up with family life, which is so fundamental to human existence. The most important of them is man's experience of dependence on reality, that is, the complete dependence on the family community. (The experience of "anxiety," or "dread," which certain trends of existentialist philosophy have made the focal point in their interpretation of man, is first and foremost the fear of deprivation the being has of finding shelter in the family.) This experience of ontological dependence opens up a first approach to awareness of ontological de-

[20] Because they are linked with experience, the elementary moral principles may be called synthetic judgments a priori. Cf. Chap. 6; that Thomas Aquinas was no stranger to a mode of observation emphasizing the role of experience in the sense discussed is shown by his words in *I. Eth.,* lect. 11: "In artibus operativis accipiuntur principia per experientiam quandam." Here he is indeed thinking of scientific ethics, but would certainly not exclude the common sense of mankind. Cf. also in *I. Eth.,* lect. 4: "In moralibus oportet incipere ab his quae sunt magis nota quoad nos, i.e., a quibusdam effectibus consideratis circa actus humanos."

pendence on God, the Creator, and so also of responsibility toward him. The experience in the family community is bound up with the insight into the indispensability and working of authority, through whose commandments order is established in community life. From these insights ensues the first approach to the insight into the obligatory character of natural law as originating in the will of God. Thus, even in this respect experience in social life is essential for man's insight into the substance of natural law. This is true, however, not only with regard to insight into moral principles valid in the social sphere, but also with regard to the personal sphere; indeed, it is only as a social being that man becomes a personality, with the attitudes and insights which this involves. Thus, we are given *a new aspect of a fundamental idea of traditional natural law ethics,* namely, that every law, including the natural law, is related to the common good; a new aspect, because in our exposition the ontological side of this relationship emerges more clearly beside the obligatory than is usually the case.

What has been said about cognitions of the ontological order formed by the developing reason is not meant to refer to philosophical knowledge. Nevertheless, it is a widespread error to think that metaphysical and ontological knowledge is reserved exclusively to scientific philosophy. This is entirely wrong. Such understanding may be possible in a higher degree to a simple mind open to reality than to a mind narrowed from the outset by preconceived opinions. Indeed, insight associated with natural law belongs to that "natural metaphysics of the human mind" of which *Bergson* spoke.[21] Throughout the history of philosophical thought, that insight has aroused the deepest controversy; from century to century by ever varying methods it has supposedly been shown to be erroneous, yet because men have found themselves impelled to seek fresh ways, it has never convincingly been shown to be false. Human nature rules this out. This is an additional conclusion from our ontological interpretation of natural law (cf. Chaps. 4 and 5 on natural law as nature and as law).

If today there are controversies in progress, even among the exponents of traditional natural law doctrine, which reveal uncertainties in the fundamental questions of natural law, I think that the cause of this is to be sought in the inadequate understanding of the substance and concept of natural law, since it is too narrowly identified with natural conscience in one form or another, whether as moral insight or simply as moral judgment. The resulting differences of opinion may be traced back to *Thomas Aquinas,*[22] even indeed to *Augustine.* As our exposition shows, natural

[21] H. Bergson, *Évolution créatrice,* 1908, p. 352.

[22] A note in the Turin edition of the *Summa theologica* of Thomas Aquinas (Editio II, Taurinensis, 1888) on Ia IIae, q. 94, a. 1, where Thomas is discussing the nature of *lex naturalis,* says: "On this question the views of theologians are at variance; some say that natural law is rational nature itself and in itself, insofar as particular acts are in conformity or not in conformity with it with regard to its essence; others would see

law is not only a *rational* order (insight into principles and values), working through the natural conscience, but also an *operative* order, functioning through the natural human appetites (pursuit of values, impulse toward happiness) toward a pattern of full human being in fellowship as well as toward the apprehension of the moral principles involved, which, however, after this working of experience, are understood to be independent of experience and thus to be absolutely valid. If the relationship of natural law to the Creator has been restricted simply to the mind's sharing in the knowledge of good and evil, of right and wrong, and has in this sense been regarded as participation in the "eternal law," in our conception of natural law the relationship to the Creator emerges no less clearly: it is a mode of functioning of human nature through the operation of the "eternal law"; that is to say, the wisdom and the will of the Creator, through the ontological order as well as through the deontological order.

Thus, the natural law is understood from the outset not only psychologically but also ontologically; the apprehension of reality and the bidding of reason are seen from the outset in their intimate relationship. This is of the greatest significance for natural law. The way in which I hope, with this conception of natural moral law (*lex*), to clarify certain important questions of natural jural law (*ius*) will be shown when this is dealt with (cf. especially Chap. 47).

Nothing will better illustrate the significance of our shifting of the accent in the conception of moral natural law than the following words of *Michael Wittmann,* whose thorough, luminous, and critical exposition of the ethics of *St. Thomas Aquinas* must surely be considered to be hitherto unsurpassed. Without himself undertaking any extension of the theory of moral and jural natural law as worked out by the scholastics, he foreshadows, in his remarks on natural law at the conclusion of his critique of *Thomas Aquinas* (concerning more details on this, cf. Chap. 47), the conclusion to which we were impelled in our development of

---

in it a permanent disposition (*habitus*); others again hold it to be actual dictate (*dictamen actuale*) of natural reason; it seems nearer to the truth, according to Thomas, that natural law is nothing other than natural intellect (*lumen naturale*) acted upon and informed through the eternal law or the eternal reason." Regarding the *lex aeterna,* just mentioned, it is noted on Ia IIae, q. 91, a. 1 (where Thomas deals with *lex aeterna* and explains it in terms of world government by providence, which he had proved) that the eternal law is the first and primordial mind ruling things (*ratio gubernationis rerum*) and that Thomas himself emphasizes in *De verit.,* art. 1 ad 6 that in God the eternal law does not consist in providence, but is as it were the foundation (*quasi principium*) of providence, so that the acts of providence would correctly be ascribed to the eternal law. For comparison the definition given by Augustine in *Contra Faust.* 27 may be appended: "Lex vero aeterna est ratio divina vel voluntas Dei ordinem naturalem conservari iubens, perturbari vetans." This lays stress on *voluntas Dei* in the sense of the position of the will in Augustinian thought; furthermore, this definition covers *ordo naturalis,* which evidently refers to the ontological order. (Concerning the significance of the natural law in Augustine and Thomas cf. Chap. 47.)

the concept of natural law to meet present-day requirements. *Wittmann* writes:

If natural law is thought of not as the bidding of reason but as the order of being inherent in the nature of things, a different relationship of natural law emerges both with regard to the eternal law and to human reason. Thus understood, natural law would not be restricted to most general and fundamental precepts, but would constitute a *complete and comprehensive order of life* [my italics, J.M.]; the natural law would not in content fall short of the eternal law or the divine will, as on the other hand it would indeed coincide with the law of human reason, since the precepts of the latter extend not merely to the general, but also to the concrete and particular. In substance, eternal law, natural law, and the bidding of reason would denote one and the same pattern, but in different stages: eternal law is the pattern as conceived in the mind of God; natural law as it achieves expression in the life of finite things; the bidding of reason as, through the nature of things, it becomes known to the mind of man. The law would, so understood, represent in part a different movement and different stages of movement compared with the scholastic idea.[23]

VII *Value-ethics and Natural Law Ethics*

Some have thought that it has now become impossible to base ethics on the idea of end in the light of modern value-ethics. In the opinion of *Scheler*, the rejection of end by *Kant* represents one of his significant contributions to ethics,[24] and there is no longer room for the idea of end in the foundation of ethics. He understands by teleological ethics a system of ethics based upon the postulate of a Final End and hence reducing "the values good and evil to mere technical values serving this end." *Nicolai Hartmann* also, who follows *Scheler* in his criticism of teleological ethics, thinks: "In teleological ethics lies a fundamental depreciation of moral values, that is, in the fallacious equation of the latter with the value of the concrete thing pursued."[25] In the light of what has been said here, the position of end as a principle in moral philosophy is wholly different from what *Scheler* and *Hartmann* reject. For what is in question is the "*existential* ends," not the "*intentional* ends" which Scheler and Hartmann are thinking about. In other words, the existential ends are not the subjective ends of volition, but the objective ends of nature.

I agree with *Scheler* that "ethics must be opposed to the idea of good and bad ends. For ends as such are never good or bad." In fact, ends and the spheres of value connected with them are in themselves indifferent (cf. n. V above). Scheler's view is not so far removed from ours as it appears. Value can be nothing else but that which corresponds to an instinctive inclination; accordingly, Scheler speaks also of the connection be-

[23] M. Wittmann, *Die Ethik des hl. Thomas v. Aq.*, 1933, pp. 359 f.

[24] M. Scheler, *Der Formalismus in der Ethik und die materiale Wertethik*, pp. 2 ff., 10 ff.

[25] Nicolai Hartmann, *Ethik*, 1926, p. 234.

tween values and inclination, preference, and love. But if knowledge of value and pursuit of value are inevitably related to instinct, then for philosophical-ethical understanding the essential values are to be explained in terms of the ends inherent in the physical and spiritual instincts. Indeed, as will presently be shown, *Scheler's* philosophical analysis of value follows the gradation of instincts, and hence of ends, first set down by *Aristotle*. On the other hand, in our opinion expressed above, there is (prephilosophical) intuitive knowledge of fundamental moral principles (values); but in view of the only too obvious possibilities of error, knowledge of this kind requires a criterion of truth. The discovery of this criterion is the first objective of scientific ethics.

I agree also with *Hartmann's* view that moral value is at bottom a value of the act itself and hence of the person, since, as we have found, moral good is the good will as the factor determining the conformity of man's conduct with the demands of his essential being. In fact, the basic idea of natural law ethics could hardly be more aptly expressed than in *Hartmann's* own words: "Nature is bound by its laws; he (man) alone bears within himself a higher law by which he works in the world, or, more correctly, which works through him, through him leads up from not-being to being, which it delineates in its ideal form." [26] In our mode of expression, natural law leads man from potential to actual full reality of his being as a person, a full reality which is delineated in his essential nature (concerning the concept of "self-realization" cf. Chap. 13). And *Hartmann* himself cannot escape the verdict that his value-ethics follows the line of thought of the great tradition of ethics of the ancient world and of the Middle Ages—the line of thought which is followed in this study—and that the possibility of this was opened up by the work of *Scheler*.[27]

The fact, however, that value-ethics does not base insight into human nature as a whole but only insight into moral principles on the moral a priori is its fatal flaw. *H. Welzel* sums up (probably correctly) the result of the discussions on value-ethics, especially with regard to the significance of the latter for the question of the ordering of society in accordance with moral law, in this way: "In the value-ethics of Scheler and Hartmann is fulfilled the destiny of every idealistic theory of value, which in Plato and in Leibnitz became manifest. From general a priori value entities it is not possible to infer the right decision about the real situation here and now by means of any laws of preference." [28] The hope which still existed in the first years after the Second World War of developing, under the aspect of social ethics, the philosophy and ethics of value initiated by the monumental work of *Scheler* and *Hartmann* has not been fulfilled.

[26] *Ibid.*, p. 153.
[27] *Ibid.*, pp. 108, 124.
[28] H. Welzel, *Naturrecht und materiale Gerechtigkeit*, 1951, 2nd ed., 1955, p. 181.

No extensive treatment of fundamental and special questions of social, political, and economic order on principles of value-ethics has been given. Indeed, no thorough attempt has been made even to show that such an undertaking is a possibility using the methods of value-ethics. This would require a *criterion of the truth of values,* since this alone makes it possible to work out scientifically the concrete demands in individual cases of the social order, and particularly of the legal order. The inner connection between the idea of value and the order of value, on the one hand, and the nature of man and hence the "nature of the case" on the other, must be clarified in order to throw a bridge between the "essential" and the "existential" reality of value, which forms the subject matter of social ethics. The simple appeal to personality values, which frequently occurs today in writings on questions of legal and social order, after the example of *Scheler* and *Hartmann,* leaves the question open concerning what exactly these values are and what are the grounds for them, and hence the question what they can signify in detail with regard to the understanding of the "nature of the case."

These observations should not be taken to indicate that I wish to dispute the place of the value idea in ethics, especially in natural law ethics. The contrary is true (cf. *Kulturethik,* Chaps. 14, 40, 61–66, 73–76). In fact, if one does not cling to the letter of the expression, the wide field of common ground between value-ethics and natural law ethics, which we are seeking to develop with the category of existential ends, is obvious enough. For the value-ethics of the two great pioneers, in spite of their rejection of any relationship between values and ends, reflects clearly the doctrine of the gradation of instinct-dispositions and hence of ends, as maintained since *Aristotle* by natural law philosophy. *Scheler,* for example, distinguishes four spheres of fundamental value modalities in the ascending order: 1) The agreeable and disagreeable as "self-values." These possess, according to *Scheler,* their own character independently of all other values, whereas "consecutive values" have an inherent relationship to other values, without which they would cease to be "values"; the "consecutive" values in the domain of the "agreeable" are chiefly the utility values, as represented by the technical and other outward aspects of civilization. 2) The noble and ignoble, i.e. the "vitality values," whose consecutive values lie in the sphere of health and of prosperity. 3) The sphere of spiritual values, that is, the aesthetic values and the values of true knowledge; the corresponding consecutive values in this sphere are the "cultural values," including those of science. 4) The holy and the unholy, that is, the modality of value around which the religious values are grouped. These four modalities of value, according to *Scheler,* correspond with the "four well marked stages of feeling which correspond with the structure of our whole human existence: (1) sensory feelings or 'perception feelings'; (2) bodily feelings (condition) and vitality feelings (functions); (3) purely spiritual feelings (pure ego-feelings); (4) mental feelings (personality feelings)."

Indeed, the Aristotelian classification of the instinctive dispositions corresponding with the ranks of being in the ontological order of human nature could not be more perfectly mirrored than it is in the foundation of this philosophy of value.[29] We derive from the instinctive constitution and the instinctive structure indicated by the existential ends the *specific classification* and also the *ontological basis* of the individual fundamental values. There is a further common ground between natural law ethics and value-ethics in that the former, with its assumption of immediate insight into moral principles, actually thinks of what the values represent for value-ethics as the object of intuition. The former, nevertheless, identifies this insight not merely with purposive feeling but also with intellectual reasoning. When we come to deal with jural philosophy it will be necessary to consider the attempts to base it on a philosophy of value.

VIII *Fundamental Questions of the Method of Ethics*

We have already had abundant opportunity to deal with the problems of method. In the treatment of this question a scientific system of ethics must practice an *indispensable self-criticism,* by precising its own procedure and comparing it with others. In the light of what has been said hitherto about particular questions of methodology, there remain still some fundamental questions to discuss. The three definitive methodological touchstones of every scientific system are the *exhaustive analysis* of the facts of experience, *logical stringency* of arguments, and the *consistency* of the system.

Ethics, like every other science, must avail itself principally of two modes of procedure, the inductive and the deductive. Various combinations of these are possible. Each, however, requires methodological justification. It must be shown that the particular procedures are correctly applied and that they are linked in such a way as to permit an exhaustive investigation and elucidation of the whole reality of experience. Our natural law ethics is governed in its methodology by the idea of "nature" as its fundamental concept; therefore, it must secure its foundations by means of the most thorough and comprehensive analysis possible of the data of experience. In our investigation of the essence of morality we did not begin with metaphysical or theological concepts, but adopted from the beginning an *inductive* procedure. This has revealed that inward and outward experience points to something beyond itself. Human nature is not to be explained in terms of number, weight, and measure, in the way the natural sciences deal with their material. To attempt, like the be-

[29] M. Scheler, *Der Formalismus in der Ethik und die materiale Wertethik,* pp. 104 ff., 344.

haviorists, to investigate and to explain the nature of man and of morals from statistics is as fruitless an undertaking as it would be to attempt to understand and to elucidate *Beethoven's Ninth Symphony* by statistical methods. The inadequacy of mere measurement and enumeration is counterbalanced by the fact that, in the question of the nature of man and of morals, inward as well as outward experience is available, namely, man's knowledge of good and evil and the immediately evident principles which this communicates, with their claim to absolute authority. They represent primarily a prescientific direct knowledge possessed by man about his nature and its claims; their investigation and explanation is the prime *theoretical* task of ethics, to be discharged by the metaphysical analysis of human nature. In the course of this inquiry we have found the principle of morality in the existential ends. Our procedure has been that of "inductive metaphysics," which seems to be especially called for by natural law ethics, since, as the very words indicate, it is related to man's nature.

After thus establishing its foundations, our natural law ethics continues with the procedure common to all sciences which are occupied with human action (and are therefore called practical sciences). Ethics is a *practical* science because it has for its object human conduct: it is the science of the moral order of man's individual and social life. Therefore, its method can only be that of applying its general principle, the principle of morality (cf. n. V above) to the conditions in which truly human, that is, moral patterns of life are to be realized. The application of the principle, therefore, depends upon the analysis of circumstances and accordingly involves the logical procedure of inference. This is a *deductive* procedure, one used by every science in the application of its general laws for practical ends. An engineer cannot design an internal combustion engine without applying general scientific laws to particular circumstances. The fact that in the sphere of ethics the *inferential procedure* plays a much more extensive role is due to the fact that the one principle of morality is applicable to the many spheres of human conduct: personal, social, political, economic, cultural, international, in fact, to man's whole relationship to the world. On the other hand, the laws of the physical world, because of the manifold forms and forces of this world, have a largely specialized character; hence, the individual laws find their application in a more limited sphere.

It follows from what has been said on the relationship in our ethics between inductive and deductive method that this ethical system involves an essential connection between *ought* and *being*. They do not coincide, but are distinct, as the activity of the practical reason is distinct from that of the theoretical reason. For the practical reason, the moral truth contains also the awareness of the moral imperative, an awareness which relates not merely to "is" but to "ought." Accordingly, practical and theoretical judgment do not coincide. Because, however, the former expresses a demand of full humanity, the judgment, "One ought to be loyal," can also be expressed as a general ontological proposition: Loyalty "is" conduct in accordance with human nature (human dignity). In all schools of ethics which neglect or dispute this connection between "ought" and "is," moral truth can find its ultimate justification only in an element of "faith,"[30] which, although in different ways, is the characteristic of Kantian and related ethics as well as of the earlier emotive ethics of *Hume* and the more recent emotive ethics deriving from him.

Against the separation of practical from theoretical reason by *Kant* and the schools following him, the well-known argument still holds good which was first applied by the acute *F. H. Jacobi* in his reply to *Kant's Critique of Practical Reason:* that in a philosophical analysis one cannot convince by an appeal to belief alone; that is, in the case of Kant, one cannot set up postulates of practical reason as necessary assumptions, one cannot, therefore, demand belief because we "must" believe. Natural law ethics is not confronted with this difficulty because it refers practical reason to knowledge of human nature, which is a matter of theoretical reason. In a different way from Kantian rational ethics, the emotive ethics deriving from *Hume* trace morals back to beliefs. Its representatives are to be found today among the logical positivists who are developing the Humean tradition. In their view, true and false can only be judgments of fact, so that all moral judgments of approbation and of disapprobation rest upon "beliefs." In fact, however, their own criterion of truth, by this very criterion, rests upon a pure belief (cf. Chap. 2), quite apart from the fact that the denial of knowledge of fundamental moral truths is at variance with the sure conviction of the whole of mankind regarding the truth of moral principles (for example, that lying, cheating, and murder are evil) and regarding the fact that in general there is the distinction between good and evil.[31]

[30] A different matter from basing moral reasoning altogether on a postulate of faith is to assign to an element of faith its definite place in the concrete situation of an individual decision regarding moral conduct or a moral act. In the given situation in which the individual has to fulfill his duty "here and now" it is often impossible for him to recognize with full certainty what mode of conduct conforms with the moral order in view of the conditions and consequences. To act in spite of such uncertainty would mean consent to something possibly evil; such consent would be itself evil according to the supreme moral principle "avoid evil," which conveys an absolute dictate. To reach any decision of conscience on such an occasion, without which we cannot act morally, we must take the only way that is open to us, namely, to do what we believe with sufficient reason—"to the best of our knowledge and responsibility"—to be the right thing. This gives the often misunderstood problem of *probabilism* its great significance, especially if the moral order is understood not merely as an aggregation of norms, but as a true order of existence, linked with the manifold shortcomings of human insight into the conditions and consequences of free and therefore responsible action.

[31] On cognition and certitude in the moral sphere cf. Messner, *Kulturethik,* pp. 237–63.

4. Natural Law as Nature

It is a common idea that the moral law is a kind of divine dictate promulgated by God amid lightning and thunder, a yoke clamped by him around man's neck. The more man feels a part of his nature rebelling against the moral law, the more readily does he feel inclined toward this belief. The belief is strengthened by moral philosophers and educators who give the moral law a pre-eminently or exclusively theological foundation, thereby conveying the impression that God, after creating man, imposed the moral law upon him by his arbitrary will as absolute Lawgiver. Such an assumption is, however, contrary to the teaching of revelation on creation and on the manner and form in which the Creator, as *causa prima,* imposes his will on nature, from the atom to the highest animal organism. He exerts his will by means of the energies and impulses which he has placed in them; that is, by means of the *causae secundae* (the created causes). There is no justification for supposing that the Creator has acted otherwise with man than with the rest of nature. Indeed, in deriving natural law from the nature of man we have proceeded on the same fundamental principles of method in the examination of reality and experience as the rest of the sciences in deriving their laws. What we have found is that the natural law of man is the functioning of his nature in accordance with its own full reality—therefore, that which must mean for him the fulfillment of his life and, hence, happiness.

Everyone in his life is often faced with the question: Why should this or that action be morally bad, although it would bring happiness? Thus, contraception often might make possible a fuller life for the members of a family. The problem underlying these questions is obviously this: What is *man's real good?* From the point of view of natural law this question becomes: Why is moral good for man not *a* good but *the* good? To answer this question we shall take up the line of thought where we left it in the last chapter. In fact, there still remains a wide field of reality and experience to be investigated in the sphere of moral law.

I *The Fundamental Impulse in Human Nature*

On several occasions we have referred to the instincts which belong to the essence of human nature. Can they be brought to a common denominator? *Aristotle,* as is well known, sums them up at the beginning of his ethics as the instinct of happiness. But all desire for happiness is moved through forms of love. Man's seeking for happiness is directed by love of a person, of money, of power, beauty, fame, amusement, etc. In all the various forms of love man seeks fulfillment of his instinct for happiness; that is to say, he seeks that in which he perceives something good, a good for himself. *Love,* therefore, forms the fundamental instinct of human nature. (For these reasons it is no contradiction here to call love, under n. III of this Chapter, the desire for happiness, the fundamental impulse.) Love which can recognize the relationship of goods for the satisfaction of individual instincts and also generally the relationship of goods for the satisfaction of the instinct of happiness, as a whole is possible only to man. Love in the true sense is thus restricted to rational beings and can be attributed to animals only in an analogous sense, insofar as these are guided by their instinctive cognition. The seat of man's fundamental instinct is the will, the power to which the operation of all man's essential instincts is subordinated. Since this power in its turn depends on knowledge, man loves what he loves only on account of the good (*ratione boni*) which he perceives in it for himself, whether his perception is true or delusive. Consequently, the right operation of the fundamental instinct of "right love," depends upon right knowledge in the choice of goods, on "right reason," conformity with instinct, as we have called it.[1]

Since the fundamental impulse toward the good has its seat in the will, the "good will," which is habitually directed toward the true good, is, to use the words of *St. Augustine,* "among all goods of the spirit the most excellent."[2] And since this good will is virtue, virtue consists, again in the words of Augustine, fundamentally in "the order of love."[3] This order is objectively the order of ends. Subjectively, the ends as adopted by the

[1] No one has written on the metaphysics of love more lucidly and profoundly than the great teachers of the natural law doctrine, especially St. Augustine and St. Thomas. St. Augustine likes to compare love to the specific gravity of material bodies: oil thrown into the air strives downwards because of its weight, but upwards if it is put under water (*Epist.* 55, n. 18): "Ita enim corpus pondere, sicut animus amore fertur, quocunque fertur" (*De civ. Dei,* XI, 28; cf. also *Confessions,* XIII, 10; *Epist.* 157, n. 9). Similarly *St. Thomas* describes the fundamental instincts of human nature in *Summa theol.,* Ia, q. 20, a. 1: "Primus enim motus voluntatis et cuiuslibet appetitivae virtutis est amor"; cf. also *Summa theol.,* Ia IIae, qq. 26–28; *Summa contra Gent.,* I, 91. In addition, the following lines of thought concerning the metaphysics of love of traditional natural law ethics may be mentioned. Since love is a motion of desire toward a good in which, as its end, an instinct finds satisfaction and in which it gains rest, the good influences the being of the lover: love brings about the assimilation (*connaturalitatem*) of the lover to the good striven for. Because of this assimilation, love opens up in the lover a new and more perfect understanding of the loved being (*cognitio affectiva*). Love of person for person, therefore, becomes a striving for union and also a striving for the love of the loved being, which will guarantee union. For the same reasons, true love means loving a being for its own sake; otherwise love does not go beyond self-love, which makes the loved being in whole or in part merely an instrument. Concerning knowledge through love Augustine says (*Quaest. oct. trib.* q. 35): "Nullumque bonum perfecte noscitur quod non perfecte amatur." Concerning the metaphysics of love, cf. M. C. D'Arcy, S.J., *The Mind and Heart of Love,* 1946; M. Nédoncelle, *Vers une philosophie de l'amour,* 1946; W. Heinen, *Fehlformen des Liebesstrebens in moralphilosophischer Deutung,* 1954.

[2] Augustine, *De civ. Dei,* XIX, c. 3. Cf. St. Thomas, *Summa contra Gent.,* III, 116: "Homo autem dicitur bonus ex eo quod habet voluntatem bonam."

[3] Augustine, *De civ. Dei,* XV, c. 22; *Epist. 168,* n. 15: "Virtus est caritas qua id quod diligendum est diligitur"; also *Epist. 155,* n. 13.

will determine the "intention" in human conduct. Since, then, the "good will" or the right moral intention consists in the congruence of the subjective with the objective ends, both are, in their mutual relationship, equally constitutive of the morality of human conduct. Hence, objectively good ends can be made evil by subjectively evil purposes, that is, by bad intention (for example, charitable works done from vanity), whereas the best intention cannot convert something intrinsically evil into good. From this correlation of subjective and objective ends in human conduct it follows that the end can never justify the means.[4]

We may now summarize the foregoing argument as follows: The fundamental impulse of human nature is love. Natural law tends to direct man's conduct toward the right "order of love," that is, toward the correspondence of the subjective ends with the objective "existential" ends in the realization of which human nature attains its full reality. Hence, natural law is nature for man.

11 *The Fundamental Fact of Deontology*

The moral natural law, as was just pointed out, directs man toward the full reality of his nature and hence toward his real being, his true self. Because it is linked with no inescapable necessity but with his self-determination, the conduct thus indicated becomes a duty for man. Nevertheless, there is also a necessity in duty, namely, the necessity bound up with the full reality of man's being to act in accordance with the demands of this reality. Man is accustomed to experience this necessity as an impulse of his conscience: he knows that he can act against his conscience, but he knows equally that the moral duty is an absolute one and therefore involves the necessity of a definite mode of conduct; in other

[4] This essential correlation of the subjective and the objective ends excludes both mere intentionism in ethics (*Gesinnungsethik*) and mere pragmatic ethics (*Erfolgsethik*). Intentionism, as expounded by Kant, identifies morality wholly with right intention, regarded as the will to do good for duty's sake alone, excluding, for instance, the desire to promote the good of one's neighbor when performing an act of charity. For both Kant (cf. *Grundlegung zur Metaphysik der Sitten,* Vol. IV, p. 393) and natural law ethics (cf. footnote 2) the good will is the highest good of man, and for both the "good will" consists in conformity with right reason. But in the interpretation of right reason they differ radically. Kant conceives of it as reason in agreement with itself in virtue of its own autonomous maxim, which can become a general law; thus, the absolutely good will is "indeterminate with regard to all objects, and contains only the form of volition in general" (Kant, *ibid.,* p. 444). St. Augustine and St. Thomas, on the other hand, consider right reason as reason in conformity with the objectively good, which is indicated to man by his nature through moral apprehension and the ontological order. Thus, they make the substance of right reason precisely what Kant wishes to exclude. On the other hand, pragmatic ethics bases the nature of morality exclusively on the outward consequences of conduct for the promotion of human-social interests, as these consequences are represented in the judgment of society. It therefore neutralizes the individual moral intention, as guided by moral insight, since it considers the moral character of actions to be determined only by outward conformity with the rules approved by society.

words, that it exists independently of his own "for and against." Thus, as *Kant* expresses it, "the consciousness of a voluntary submission of the will to law" is bound up with "an inescapable compulsion."[5] Duty is at once an absolute and a hypothetical necessity: hypothetical because it depends upon self-determination; absolute (or categorical) because the full reality of human nature admits nothing else but conduct in conformity with the natural law. If man acts against this, for example, if he becomes drunk, he falls from this full reality, he acts "subhumanly."

An example of absolute and hypothetical necessity will make this clear. Hypothetical necessity is exemplified if five dollars is charged for admission to a charity performance. But if invitations are addressed only to persons who are bound by their social position to attend, then the stipulation that five dollars must be paid becomes for them an absolute, categorical necessity. It is an absolute necessity, although dependent throughout on self-determination, that is, on "free will." Similarly, because of his status as a rational being, man is bound to conform his conduct to what the law of his nature requires, whereby alone he can be man in the full reality of his nature. Because on the one hand duty imposes on man an absolute demand, whereas compliance with this demand depends upon his self-determination, the necessity inherent in duty, the impulsion by conscience, is that of "ought."

This is, then, the fundamental fact of deontology: human nature itself binds man to the natural moral law.[6] The moral law is for him *the command of nature*. Consequently, man is in a true sense morally autonomous: natural law is nature and, because of that, law. Thus, we find the element of truth in the ethical doctrines of the moral autonomy of reason, not indeed in the sense intended by *Kant*, that reason gives itself the moral law,[7] but in the sense that the mind recognizes it as a dictate, as a law of rational nature. In exploiting this primary deontological fact,

[5] Kant, *Kritik der praktischen Vernunft*, Coll. Works, Vol. V, pp. 32, 80; accurately though Kant analyzes moral compulsion, he sees the ground of "compulsion to act in accordance with the bidding of duty, and in spite of contrary inclinations, only in man's own reason," in line with his notion of the absolute autonomy of practical reason.

[6] In a review of the first edition of this book a moral theologian maintained that man's nature is not a foundation of obligation of the moral law, but only the will of God. In a public discussion on "Church and Socialism," in which he joined a Catholic layman in opposition to two socialists, an elderly gentleman from the audience asked him in what the basis of obligation of the moral law did consist. He received the answer: "In the fact that it is the law of God." The questioner replied that he was an atheist, yet nevertheless felt himself bound by the moral law, simply by reason of his humanity; he asked whether this was not also true morality, and added that he thought that not a few in the same situation felt themselves bound by the moral law at least as much as many who according to their religious faith should see the command of God in the moral law.

[7] For Kant, because of his view of moral autonomy and his idea of duty (cf. Chap. 7), the situation is exactly the reverse: "The concept of good and evil does not precede the moral law but follows it and is based on it" (*Kritik der praktischen Vernunft*, Coll. Works, Vol. V, p. 62).

natural law ethics was enabled to open up a highly important line of development in ethics with the *differentiation between the good and duty.* Whereas the Greek philosophers concerned themselves in their ethics principally with the good and with virtue, natural law doctrine has made duty and responsibility, to at least an equal degree, the object of ethical inquiry. This line of thought is especially important for natural law ethics because the natural individual and social rights are rooted in the moral responsibilities founded in nature. The distinction between good and duty is important also because, although it is always the good —even though in the form of avoiding evil—that forms the object of duty, yet every good does not represent a duty for man. He is obliged by the good which is indispensable in order that he may remain in harmony with his essential nature, the existential ends. From the connection between good and duty it becomes further evident that the large proportion of our duties which are clothed in the negative form of prohibition are only ostensibly negative. Fundamentally, all are positive. "Thou shalt not steal," accordingly signifies: "Thou shalt preserve the order demanded by thy nature in thy conduct toward the property of others."

III *The Fundamental Fact of Eudaemonology* (theory of happiness; Greek *eudaimonia* = happiness)

Man's basic instinct of love is always directed toward a good, toward something in which man perceives something good for himself, a value: he strives necessarily for satisfaction of his instinct of happiness.[8] Generally, and for all beings determined by instinct, the attainment of happiness means the fulfillment of instinct. The good which is in accordance with man's nature cannot be otherwise defined: it consists in the essential fulfillment of instinct. The attainment of the functioning of instincts in accordance with their inherent ends is, as we have shown, a matter of the self-determination proper to his rational disposition, and constitutes the essence of morality. Hence, the attainment of man's essential happiness is bound up with morality.

Along with the satisfaction of instinct are associated feelings of well-being, which are designated also feelings of pleasure or simply pleasure. If we look more closely we find, as did *Aristotle,* that two kinds of pleasure can be distinguished. The one is connected with the act of satisfying an instinct, as, for instance, the pleasures of the palate with the act of eating; the other is connected with the attainment of the end inherent in the instinct, for example, vitality as the object of eating. Everyone

[8] Cf. St. Augustine, *De disciplina Christiana,* n. 6: "(Homo) unde se fieri putat beatum, hoc amat." This is only ostensibly inconsistent with the definition of love given by Augustine in *Quaest. oct. trib.,* q. 35: "Nihil enim aliud est amare quam propter seipsam rem aliquam appetere" (cf. note 1), as emerges from the ontology of love expounded in the text above, with the relationship which the true nature of love bears to the good in itself and in its tendency toward the *summum bonum.*

places bodily health, the essential end of the feeding instinct, before a gluttonous pleasure in eating, that is to say, if a man does not forget himself, that is, if he does not act in a way contrary to his essential nature and his true interest. Thus, it is evident that happiness is not just synonymous with pleasure. Besides, everyone knows that the satisfaction of individual instincts is always transitory. "All pleasure wills Eternity, wills deep, deep Eternity." With these words *Nietzsche* in his *Zarathustra* (*Das andere Tanzlied*) expresses a most indubitable human experience. Not even an eternity of a limited happiness would satisfy man. It would not raise him above a more or less agreeable eternity of tedium. Everyone is familiar with the experience that things which have seemed necessary to one's happiness lose at least some of their initial effect after one has enjoyed their possession for some time, furthermore, that man's capacity for receiving mere pleasure values exhausts itself is a fact already noted by *Aristotle*.

An eternity of limited happiness, we observed, would not satisfy man: man's instinct of happiness seeks the everlasting and boundless reality of the good. Why? The universal idea of the good, of that which answers to his desire for happiness, enables him to recognize how limited individual goods are with regard to both the duration and the extent of the happiness which they can yield; and it enables him at the same time to grasp the idea of *summum bonum*, the supreme good, infinite in being and duration. And since man comprehends this idea, he knows also that the supreme good alone can fully satisfy his instinct of happiness; and he knows further that his instinct of happiness strives toward the supreme good. Certainly, most men have no very distinct awareness of this truth. The existential unrest of which *Augustine* speaks in a celebrated passage of his *Confessions* leaves him in no doubt, however, that all finite goods arouse in him intimations of the boundless and everlasting supreme good, in the possession of which, and there alone, he will find ultimate satisfaction of the longings stirred by his instinct of happiness. This impulse toward the infinitely perfect good, however, does not afford a cogent proof of the existence of God any more than does man's sense of duty, taken by itself; such proof requires further steps in reasoning. But when man recognizes God as the Supreme Good he will then surely, if he rightly understands himself and his instinct of happiness, turn toward him in personal love.[9]

[9] Against the familiar line of thought (developed, for example, with great care and force by M. Cronin, *The Science of Ethics*, 4th ed., 1939, Vol. I, pp. 46–89), which starts from the *summum bonum* as man's necessary last end and represents moral duty as the necessary application of definite means to this end, it is objected by ethicists of a purely deontological orientation that such an explanation of duty does not correspond to our immediate experience, that is to say, our elementary knowledge of duty. This objection is justified only insofar as the connection between moral conduct and the *summum bonum* is not in itself part of our elementary awareness of duty. This does not mean, however, that it does not form part, and indeed an essential part, of a well-developed moral sense. The fact of death alone makes man reflect on the meaning of

From our analysis, the following answers emerge to the two questions (one concerning the essential values of happiness; the other concerning the significance of pleasure values) which are bound up with man's instinct of happiness. The first is the fact that the pleasure values, the feeling of pleasure linked in time with the act of satisfaction of instincts, as *Aristotle* argues,[10] is something subordinate and accessory in comparison with the permanent values of happiness associated with the satisfaction of instinct in the realization of the ends inherent in instinct. The second conclusion is that for all creatures happiness is the realization of the full well-being of their nature ensuing from the fulfillment of their instincts; for man this means the full reality of his nature brought about by instinct-fulfillment in accordance with the immanent ends. In the conformity of man's conduct with his existential ends we found the essence of morality. Hence, the law of his perfect good, that is, of his happiness, is the moral law.[11] This, therefore, prescribes for man what is demanded by his nature itself. *The natural moral law is the law of his nature striving, in its fundamental happiness instinct, toward essential self-fulfillment.*

It is the rendering of these facts of eudaemonology into small change for the use of a narrow view of human existence which insures an element of truth even in utilitarianism with its assertion that the ultimate motive for moral action is utility and interest. In fact, however, the concept of utility which underlies the fundamental fact of eudaemonology does not refer to the subjective pleasure values as understood by utilitarian ethics, but to the objective values of happiness as demands for the perfect good of human nature. The fact that traditional natural law ethics, however, since *Augustine* and *Thomas,* has always assigned the eudaemonological element its proper place in ethics and has sought the end and function of the natural law substantially in man's "utility," is shown by its thorough exposition of the fact that happiness is a real, although secondary, aim of morality, and that *bonum morale* is the very *bonum hominis.*

Therefore, natural law ethics is *eudaemonological* ethics. It draws the practical conclusion from this by not denying an act moral character because its immediate motive is concern for ultimate happiness and not simply submission to duty or love of God, as long as these last two motives are present, at least unconsciously, in the anxiety for ultimate

---

life, which signifies nothing else but reflection on his last end. Nothing more relentlessly brings before the human mind the question with regard to the meaning of his life than does its physical end. As soon as the awareness of his last end has in this way formed in man, it increasingly takes possession of him and becomes a source of powerful motives of moral endeavor and at the same time promotes an intense deepening and vitalizing of the idea of duty.

[10] Cf. Aristotle, *Nicomachean Ethics,* I, 6 and X. Cf. also Zeller, *Aristotle,* trans. by Costelloe and Muirhead, Vol. II, pp. 136–52.

[11] Cf. Augustine, *Epist. 130,* 3: "Inde necesse est, ut fiat homo beatus, unde fit bonus."

happiness. Natural law ethics has always understood that the final satisfaction of the desire for happiness forms the decisive motive of moral conduct for the great majority of men; that is, they are unwilling to risk the loss of happiness if they must one day render an account of their actions before the Supreme Lawgiver. They may indeed strive for the ends of their choice (interests) in seeking values of happiness as long as these ends remain in harmony with the order of ends. For, although the "order of love" is then only indirectly effective in their conduct, the attainment of their existential ends and hence the fulfillment of their being in the ultimate happiness values of the *summum bonum* is assured.

Now we have the answer to the question: Why is moral good not *a* good, among others, for man, but *the* good? From our examination of the fundamental impulse in man's instinctive constitution, of the absolute character of the claim of duty and of the boundless quest for happiness, we were led to the conclusion that for man natural law means nature, since it is through moral good that he achieves the full reality and the perfect good of his nature. It is, therefore, *the* good for him. To turn to the example mentioned above: birth control can contribute to a kind of enhanced self-fulfillment on the part of the members of a small family. But as soon as it is established that external, material *pleasure values* do not constitute the ultimate meaning of life and that parents and children possess vital conditions for the development of their individual selves in the *personal values* nourished by the family community (love, consideration, self-sacrifice, etc.) and that the existence of society with all that society means for the coming generations is placed in jeopardy if birth control becomes a principle governing the national life, it then follows that birth control cannot be *the* good for man, either individually or socially.

From our analysis of the fundamental human impulse and the basic facts of deontology and eudaemonology we can also discover the reason why *the human natural law is fundamentally a unity,* whereas in the rest of nature we find a multitude of natural laws. These natural laws are the modes of functioning of things determined by their inherent propensities.[12] In contrast, the propensity inherent in human nature, in all its instincts with the "existential ends" indicated therein, is *the* good of man, so that his natural law is but *one:* it directs man's self-determination in his conduct to the single end of the complete reality of his rational nature.

IV *Reality and Morality*

We have found morality to be that which is in conformity with man's nature, in accordance with the existential ends immanent in his nature. Because it is conformity with nature, morality is (as we expressed it)

[12] St. Thomas Aquinas, *De divinis nominibus,* 10, I: "Ipsae naturales inclinationes rerum in proprios fines, quas dicimus naturales leges."

that which is demanded by the full reality of man's nature as an individual and as a social being.[13] Because man's good is the full reality of his rational nature, his moral self and his true self, being and goodness, goodness and truth are fundamentally one.[14] Consequently, scientific (speculative) truth and moral (practical) truth reflect the same reality in human nature (*veritas est adequatio intellectus et rei*): scientific truth reflects reality in its aspect of *being;* moral truth reflects reality from the point of view of the order of ends immanent in it.[15] Accordingly, in practice, in the various domains of social and cultural life, that which lies in "the nature of the case," is morally right: the "objectively" right which is indicated in the essential reality. Therefore, objective truth is in this sense the criterion for the establishment of social institutions.

Hence, a very true sense can be found in the following proposition, which at first sight may seem paradoxical: What is economically right is morally good; whereas the moralists are accustomed to say: What is morally wrong cannot be economically right. And in the sphere of politics the proposition: "What is politically right is morally good," is as true as the principle that nothing that is morally wrong can be politically good. In the former of each pair of propositions the condition is implied that economics and politics are understood in terms of the demands of the essential reality of human being and not in terms of preconceived ideological or party political dogmas. Thus, a social system, social institutions, forms of private property, credit, technology, government, and educational institutions conform with the moral order insofar as they can measure up to the demands of full human reality, that is, ultimately, of the existential ends, including especially the ends of the common good, on whose realization all others depend.

It also follows, however, from this intrinsic correlation between reality and morality, that *genuine ethics does not seek to force moral principles*

[13] This idea is shared by Plato and Aristotle in spite of the difference in their fundamental views and Aristotle's criticism of Plato. Plato starts from the knowledge of good (ideas) which belongs to human nature; Aristotle seeks the fulfillment of being demanded by human nature with its instinct of happiness. But Plato also declares: "Justice corresponds with the natural order," and explains: "Then virtue is the health, beauty and well-being of the soul, and vice is the disease and weakness and deformity of the same"; "the best is the most natural"; "and if there be a pleasure in being filled with that which is according to nature, that which is more really filled with more real being will more really and truly enjoy true pleasure" (Plato, *Republic,* 4, 444; 9, 585–87; 10, 612 ff., trans. by B. Jowett; cf. also *Gorgias,* 470). Aristotle begins by seeking the goal of all human endeavor; it consists, he says, in happiness, and this consists in virtue. The notion of virtue has with him a wider significance than we are accustomed to give it; for Aristotle it means excellence in the modes of being and conduct proper to man as man (*Nic. Eth.,* I, 6 and 13). Hence, for him also what is moral is the same as what is truly natural.

[14] Cf. St. Thomas Aquinas, *Summa theol.,* Ia, q. 5, a. 3; Ia IIae, q. 18, a. 1: "Ens et bonum convertuntur"; Ia, q. 79, a. 11: "Verum et bonum se invicem includunt."

[15] *Ibid.,* Ia IIae, q. 49, a. 2: "Bonum et malum dicitur per respectum ad finem"; *Summa contra Gent.,* III, c. 9: "Bonum et malum dicuntur secundum ordinem ad finem, vel privationem ordinis."

upon reality, but works out the essential order of being with its claims in the concrete situation at any given time. To investigate this reality is the concern of the sciences. Accordingly, we arrive at the conclusion that there is a *very wide area of contact between ethics and science,* in particular biology, psychology, the social sciences, including especially jurisprudence, politics, and economics (cf. Chap. 10). Therefore, it follows that *social ethics especially cannot by any means do justice to its function unless it follows closely the established findings of the social sciences.* Yet, it is only to a very limited extent that the warning uttered by that far-seeing and realistic moralist *F. X. Linsenmann* of Tübingen, has been heeded: "Only if legal is willing to learn from moral theology, philosophy, politics, economics, etc., where these alone are competent, can it also claim that those sciences should accept instruction from moral theology where it has the final word." [16]

But a *still deeper mutual relationship* exists between morality and reality: only good, and not evil, can become final reality. For evil is a deficiency of being, of the full reality demanded by nature. These are lines of thought along which *Augustine* and *Thomas Aquinas* like to dwell.[17] They were aptly summed up by *Franz von Baader* (died at Munich, 1841), whose profundity in metaphysical speculation renders him not unworthy to be mentioned in such close connection with the two named above: "Only that ought not to be (ought to be forbidden) which cannot truly be." [18] For evil cannot become a permanent reality, although it often appears much more powerful than good. It may often simulate a force possessing being, whereas it is really a lack of that perfection of being demanded by nature. This lack must entail for man, when he is no longer able to yield to illusion concerning the ultimate fulfillment of being demanded by his nature, the unquenchable pain of seeing himself remote from the boundless and eternal reality of the good—a pain which is to be measured only by the boundlessness and eternity of this reality from which he is finally excluded.

v *The Experimental Test of Natural Law*

It is often held against the doctrine of natural moral law that in it the term "law" denotes something different from what it denotes in the laws of the physical world. In the latter, it is argued, we are speaking of something that can be verified by experiment in the laboratory: no such test can be applied to moral law. We reply: Certainly it can; it is continually being done. What is tested in the laboratory is the working of a physical or chemical law. Similarly the eudaemonological effect of conduct in ac-

[16] F. X. Linsenmann, *Lehrbuch der Moraltheologie,* 1878, Foreword, p. vi.

[17] Cf. Augustine, *Confessions,* VII, n. 18: "De libero arbitrio," III, p. 38; *De trinitate,* VIII, 5: the will directed toward good "corresponds with nature" ("voluntas congruit naturae"); regarding Thomas cf. Chap. 3, n. III.

[18] F. V. Baader, Coll. Works, Vol. VIII, p. 110; Vol. X, p. 77.

cordance with or contrary to natural moral law is tested by experiment.

In the *life of the individual* this experiment is constantly being performed before our eyes. Of course, the ethicist does not make the experiment; everyone does it for himself. Countless people seek happiness in the sphere of mere pleasure values while neglecting the values of personality founded in the existential ends. The result is an inward impoverishment; they find no real meaning in their lives (often enough through no fault of their own). They may indeed at times attain a lively feeling of happiness, but this is the happiness of escapism. A great many features of our civilization represent, so the critics tell us, the reverse side of modern man's ennui, which arises from his inner emptiness, and results from his attempt to make life bearable by fleeing to illusory values. On the other hand, it is a well-known fact that innumerable men and women who have not been blessed with material or intellectual goods succeed in attaining an existence richly endowed with enduring, and therefore truly human, values: a profoundly contented existence, although full of sacrifices, a life full of inner happiness, although a hard life.[19] All this shows that the natural moral law stands the test of experience. Indeed, quite in harmony with the natural law idea is the universal experience of mankind that man cannot attain completion without self-renunciation in growing out of his lower self. In this we are expressing only the conviction to which so many poets and thinkers have given utterance: that any human love in which man's existential longing is at work is inseparable from sacrifice.

In the *social sphere,* too, the experiment is made in the full view of all. The laboratory is the world. The lesson that undoubtedly emerges from the two catastrophic world wars and from the subsequent international situation with all its unrest and anxiety is that the moral principles prevailing in society during the last few generations up to the present day (those of individualism and collectivism) are false. Indeed, there is no doubt about the empirical fact of this enormous aberration; what is doubtful is whether men are ready to learn from experience. Actually, the principal difference between moral and physical natural law is that in the moral sphere greater latitude is left to the self-assertion of the human will. Here experience and experiment do not produce results quickly enough to bring ridicule upon human pride when it insists on its own arbitrary law, as they would if anyone were to attempt to build a house upside down in defiance of physical laws. In the long run, however, moral law asserts itself in the life of society and in history as inexorably as physical law. Moral natural law is the intrinsic law of life of nations and of civilizations.

The destiny of a society does not, admittedly, depend upon the moral natural law in the sense that a community directly guarantees its own prosperity by observing it. Its well-being is determined also by factors

[19] Concerning this cf. the fuller analysis in Messner, *Ethics and Facts,* pp. 75–135.

lying outside the control of the individual man or of the individual society. Nevertheless, the destiny of society depends upon the natural law inasmuch as in the long run (this proviso must be stressed) no community can thrive while disregarding it. A departure from the moral law may temporarily increase the wealth or power of a community. But when the historian tells us[20] that power and wealth, thought by peoples to be the culmination of their history, are generally the opening chapters in their decline, we must, I think, look for a principal cause in an unbalanced development of energies at the expense of essentially human ends (values), and hence at the expense of elementary life forces. The natural law of social life can be examined only in the process of history, but in this it manifests itself with such certain effect that *world history is indeed also world judgment.* It is not the ultimate world judgment, as it is represented to be in *Hegel's* philosophy of history, and it is no judgment at all insofar as the destiny of a society depends upon causes outside man's influence. But, insofar as history is the work of man it will sooner or later bear testimony against him if he presumptuously rises against the law of his nature.

Like every law of life, natural law shows itself to be *a force by which social life regulates itself.* In every society it expresses itself in energies which work toward an order of life and of society in harmony with the essential demands of human nature, just as the agencies of self-regulation in the living organism work toward its proper functioning and counteract disorders. In times when the "social question" goes to the vital points of the social organism these agencies of self-regulation cause a return to natural order in more or less violent evolutionary or revolutionary developments. Thus, from the point of view of natural law philosophy there is a very true meaning in *Horace's* words: *Naturam expellas furca, tamen usque recurret:* You may expel nature with a pitchfork, but she will still return. When, however, a society loses this power of self-regulation, its final decline is inevitable. Beyond any doubt history itself shows that the regenerative force in the existence of peoples is at bottom moral in nature: it is the force of natural law, of the innermost law of life of peoples.

VI *Ethics, Epistemology, Metaphysics (On the Method of Ethics)*

Again, as in the preceding chapter, we have arrived at fundamental questions regarding the method of ethics. If morality is what is natural, then good and evil are ontological as well as ethical notions, *"ought"* is inseparable from *"is"*: hence, there exists an inherent connection between metaphysics and ethics, between logos and ethos; ethical and speculative judgments cannot be severed from one another. Accordingly, *episte-*

[20] Cf. A. J. Toynbee, *A Study of History,* Vol. V, pp. 15 ff.

mology and logic must possess a decisive significance for ethics. Only if man is in a position to apprehend reality is he capable of apprehending the moral order throughout the whole range of individual and social life. It is, therefore, not least because of the question of moral cognition that traditional natural law philosophy has unyieldingly opposed scepticism and agnosticism and maintained that man's intellect is capable of knowing reality and hence also his own nature and its claims upon his conduct.

On the other hand, ethics, like every other science, rests necessarily on cognitive principles of a metaphysical character. Consequently, ethics, from its beginnings, is indissolubly bound up with *metaphysics.* Just as for every other science, the analysis of experience is bound up with metaphysical principles (e.g. the principle of contradiction, the principle of causality), that is to say, principles which are not based on mere experience or not proved by experience alone.[21] Yet, these metaphysical axioms can provide an approach to reality only if they themselves, in conflict with inwardly or outwardly experienced reality, are not based on arbitrary dogmatism. In this case, when a system of ethics is built upon arbitrary premises it must remain, in part at least, cut off from empirical reality, and must accordingly fall prey to fallacies. Upon such fallacies naturalism in modern ethics rests, with its metaphysical theories of the "natural man" (cf. Chap. 2) founded upon rationalistic and materialistic postulates or upon the equation of part of man's instincts with his whole nature. These naturalistic theories commit the same error, at least from the philosophical standpoint, as do those systems which seek to base ethics, which is a philosophical science, exclusively on theological premises.

Therefore, every ethical system is confronted with *three fundamental metaphysical problems:* 1) It must insure that the metaphysical principles on which it bases its analysis of experience are employed only as the logical principles necessary for the examination of reality and experience, and not as the premises from which the essence and the fundamental principles of morality are inferred. 2) Every system of ethics must offer a guarantee that it submits to scientific examination and explains the whole range of moral experience. Systems which are compelled to leave essential data of experience unexplained, or even to deny them (e.g. the experience that there is a consciousness of duty independent of considerations of interest), certainly do not fulfill this function of self-criticism. 3) Lastly, beginning with the analysis of experience, a system of ethics must succeed in finding a sure way of ascent to metaphysical realities, if it does not wish to leave unanswered the most vital questions. Indeed,

[21] Consequently, metaphysics cannot, as A. E. Taylor supposes (*The Problem of Conduct, a Study in the Phenomenology of Ethics,* 1901, p. 49), simply be placed at the end of the investigation of morals; on the contrary, "The necessity to ethics of a metaphysical foundation" is unquestionable (H. W. B. Joseph, *Some Problems of Ethics,* 1913, p. 15).

a touchstone of the truth of every ethical system consists in whether, in its construction, it succeeds in securely spanning the arches from its initial metaphysical axioms through the whole range of reality and experience to the final metaphysical solutions.

5. Natural Law as Law

I *Natural Law as Command*

The word "law" has a twofold meaning. It denotes tendencies in things, as when in genetics we speak of the Mendelian laws of heredity; and it denotes the command of a lawgiver, as when we speak of the law of the state. Natural moral law is law in both these senses: it is a natural mode of functioning and also a decreed rule. In the previous chapters we have shown that the moral law is the bidding of nature. As such it is also the bidding of the Creator and of his will which is revealed in nature. Therefore, for man the natural moral law is the bidding of nature and, in addition, the command of a lawgiver. We say "in addition," because in its obligating force the natural moral law as divine decree has a warranty quite different from that of the bidding of nature. Nevertheless, it is indispensable for ethics to show that the natural moral law is the intrinsic mode of functioning of human nature itself, and that moral duty is also a demand of human nature as such.

Certainly, the philosophical procedure to which nontheological ethics is committed cannot attain the same power of conviction as a mathematical proof. In point of fact, up to now our argument does not take us beyond what self-respect demands from man in his personal and social life. But even if there were no other reason for striving to obtain truth supported by intellect alone regarding the nature of man and its claims, the fact that today men find themselves constituted in a viable social order, bound to accept a common basis of generally accepted moral principles independent of religious beliefs suggests an examination of these principles by reason alone, quite apart from the justification of such a method because of the character of ethics as a philosophical discipline.[1] It is certainly a weakness of not a few expositions of traditional natural law theory that *theological* beliefs, that is, beliefs derived from faith, are too lightly adopted as a foundation, are taken over into the conception of human nature and then again surreptitiously deduced therefrom. Natural law theory and natural law ethics must work with *philosophical* methods; hence, they must (1) epistemologically and logically account for the

[1] Cf. E. Gilson, "Theologism and Philosophy," *The Unity of Philosophical Experience,* 1938, pp. 37–60, with his observation that St. Thomas was well aware that some pious people "would have branded him as a pagan for his stubbornness in dealing with philosophical problems in a purely philosophical way" (p. 49). Cf. also E. Gilson, *Études de philosophie médiévale,* 1921, pp. 1–29; *Le sens du rationalisme chrétien.*

philosophical nature and grounds of their fundamental concepts, (2) work out the idea of nature by philosophical means, namely, methods proper to reason, and hence (3) delimit precisely what can be gained from reason in natural law theory concerning the notion of the nature of man, namely, *everything essential*, and what is to be gained from faith, namely, *heightened certitude* in the understanding of its essential features. (With regard to the notion of "Christian natural law" cf. Chap. 54.)

On the other hand, it is evident that no ethics can provide an absolute sanction for moral law without tracing it back to the dictate of the divine Lawgiver, whose will prescribes the natural moral order and whose power it vindicates if infringed.

II *The Theonomy of the Moral Order*

Our conscience speaks very clearly about the question just mentioned. In our experience of the moral imperative we find more than just the consciousness of the bidding of nature, the demand of our true self. We know that we are not only responsible to ourselves, but we are aware of the suprahuman authority of the law of conscience. We are aware that there is a Lawgiver who has power over us, and that our ultimate fate depends upon our relationship toward him. We do not assert that everyone has a clear notion on this subject, and the data of individual experience would in themselves by no means afford a cogent proof of the existence of God. However, in conjunction with our natural knowledge of God from other sources, natural law clearly proves to be the bidding of him who created human nature and gave it his law: natural law is divine law, and the divine will is the ultimate source of moral obligation. *M. Scheler* expressed it as follows: "If there is a God, then an absolute autonomy of the practical reason is unthinkable and therefore impossible, and theonomy is inevitable: this proposition seems to us evident." [2]

III *The Promulgation of the Natural Law*

The theonomy of the moral law does not take the form of an explicit decree delivered by God to man; natural law does not rest on a "supernatural" revelation such as is the source of theology. Natural law is promulgated by "natural" revelation: the nature of man reveals to him the will of the Creator and informs him about the things the Creator demands from him. The promulgation which is necessary for the validity of any law (if one is to have an obligation under a law one must know what the law is) is effected for natural law through man's nature itself. Man learns about it through his natural conscience and through the insight into his nature as man, which is linked with this.

Natural law, then, is a natural revelation of the eternal Wisdom which

[2] M. Scheler, *Vom Ewigen im Menschen*, 1933, p. 630.

gives being and order to creation. This eternal Wisdom, which is identical with God's own "law" of being and acting, is called by *St. Augustine* the *lex aeterna*. In the rational creature this works through natural moral law: insight and the bidding of conscience.[3] Hence, *Augustine* says that natural law is the impress of the eternal law on the human mind,[4] while *Thomas Aquinas* says that it is the rational creature's participation in the eternal law.[5] An important conclusion from this can be stated in the following way: Since it is through conscience that it operates in man's power of moral discrimination and decision and is applied to his conduct, man is bound in the individual question of the good or evil of a particular course of moral action to follow the unambiguous decision of his conscience.

IV *The Sanction of Natural Law*

Besides promulgation, every law requires sanction. By sanction of a law is understood the reward or punishment which makes the law effective, thus guaranteeing the order intended by the lawgiver. This order is realized either by obedience toward the lawgiver or by its restoration whenever it is infringed. Two sanctions are linked with natural law. The first is provisional: the satisfaction or the reproach of conscience. This first sanction consists in the sense of guilt occasioned by a definite transgression against the responsibility for his conduct which is imposed upon man by his nature itself, and also in the sense of guilt as consciousness that one is guilty before the Lawgiver of the moral law. Both aspects of this sense of guilt are also found in the second, ultimate sanction of the natural law: if man opposes the law of his nature with his entire and final resolve, his fate must be the irreparable loss of the happiness which alone can satisfy his nature. This means that he will live eternally removed from the ultimate end of his nature, a torment whose measure lies in what man then recognizes to be lost forever. This

[3] With regard to the rational creature St. Augustine (*Contra Faust.*, XXII, 27) defines the eternal law thus: "Ratio divina vel voluntas Dei ordinem naturalem conservari iubens, perturbari vetans"; *De divers.*, q. 79, 1: "Est enim lex universitatis divina sapientia"; *In Ps. 36*, serm. 3: "Voluntas Dei est lex Dei." If we speak of the relationship between "eternal law" and "natural law" the connecting idea is that of the *Creator*, whose wisdom and will give being and order to his creation. He does not give it first being and afterwards a law of order, but with being immediately gives it the law of its order, put into the being as operative force; it must, therefore, not be forgotten that conscience, revealing in natural law the legislative will of God, is also God's creation, and as St. Augustine (*En. in ps. 145, 5*) and J. H. Newman (*A Grammar of Assent*, 3rd ed., 1879, pp. 104 ff., 384 ff.) declare, it is for individual man the primary and most convincing source of the knowledge of God: of his command, but also his power to make this command ultimately effective.

[4] Cf. Augustine, *De lib. arb.*, Lib. I, c. 6, 15: "Aeternae legis notio, quae impressa nobis est."

[5] Cf. St. Thomas Aquinas, *Summa theol.*, Ia Iae, q. 91, a. 2: "Participatio legis aeternae in rationali creatura." Cf. Gilson, *L'Esprit de la philosophie médiévale* (Gifford Lecture), 1932, Vol. II, Chap. 6: "Loi et moralité chrétienne."

torment then remains the one thing by which man is still aware of the Lawgiver, and through which he still can, and therefore must, render satisfaction to the order willed by God and to his glory. Hence, again deontology and eudaemonology are intimately linked: duty shows man the way to achieve that state of being which alone can satisfy his nature, namely, participation in the boundless and everlasting reality of the good. Thus, we arrive at the conclusion that *the moral natural law involves a necessity on which man's destiny depends more inevitably than any event in the material world depends on its physical laws.* Irrational creation is not intrinsically destined to become eternal reality, whereas the moral world must become eternal reality. This is evident as soon as, besides the existence of God, the immortality of the spiritual soul is established.

Man receives certainty about the *immortality of the soul* through the word of God in revelation. The idea of the immortality of the soul as found in *Plato* proves that its conception is not beyond the scope of the unaided intellect. Modern empirical psychology hastily denied the possibility of an afterlife. But, as *Bergson* rightly says, "Psychology dates from yesterday, and psychical research is almost of today." Psychologists still have a vast field of inquiry before them. Some facts which Bergson regards as established by the analysis of consciousness are: "the independence of almost all conscious thought from the body"; and, the fact that we "are bound to regard the mental life as much more vast than the cerebral life." Thus, he comes to the conclusion that survival after death is so probable that "the burden of proof comes to lie on him who denies it rather than on him who affirms it." [6] Another branch of modern psychology, psychotherapy, comes to the conclusion, in the words of *C. G. Jung,* that "it is hygienic . . . to discover in death a goal toward which one can strive; and that shrinking away from it is something unhealthy and abnormal, which robs the second half of life of its purpose. I therefore consider the religious teaching of a life hereafter consonant with the viewpoint of psychic hygiene. . . . It happens sometimes that I must say to an older patient: Your picture of God or your idea of immortality is atrophied; consequently your metabolism is out of gear." [7] Naturally, a real proof of the immortality of the soul cannot be provided by empirical psychology, but only by metaphysics.

v *Divine Law and Natural Law*

Natural law is divine law promulgated by the divine Lawgiver through the human nature which he has created. When, however, we speak of the law of God in contradistinction to natural law, we are thinking of the

[6] H. Bergson, *Mind-Energy,* 1921, p. 79 (trans. of *L'Energie spirituelle* by H. W. Carr); *The Two Sources of Morality and Religion,* trans. 1935, p. 27.
[7] C. G. Jung, *Modern Man in Search of a Soul,* 7th ed., 1944, pp. 129 ff.

Decalogue, the divine law promulgated through the spoken word of God. This could not contradict natural law, for natural law represents nature to man, and as such reveals to him the will of the Creator; therefore, God would contradict himself if he willed to impose upon man a command which was inconsistent with man's nature as it is and with its inherent law. God cannot do that any more than he can alter his own nature and its eternal law, whose impression on man's mind natural law is. In fact, the divine law promulgated in the Decalogue only directs man toward what human nature itself demands from him: it strengthens him in the understanding of his true nature, of his true self, and of his essential good; it supports, as *St. Augustine* and *St. Thomas* say, the working of the natural law in man.[8]

6. The Functioning of Natural Law

We have defined natural law as the way in which human nature functions in order to bring about conduct in conformity with human nature. This mode of functioning pertains to the insight and impulse of the natural conscience. From both points of view we must now look more closely at the functioning of natural law.

I *Natural Law as Intellectual Insight*

The content of immediate moral apprehension, or natural conscience, is made up of the *elementary* moral principles. The chief of these principles declares: Good is to be done, evil is to be avoided (or, preserve right order, in the sense of *St. Thomas' rectitudinem servare,*[1] behave in accordance with human dignity in the words of *Suárez, honestum est faciendum*[2]). As soon as experience and the development of reason enable the individual to grasp the notions they convey, the following principles governing his relation to himself, to others, and to God, are likewise immediately evident: preserve moderation; render to each his own; do not do to others what you do not wish them to do to you; act so that social coexistence is possible;[3] parents must be respected; lawful authority must be obeyed; contracts must be honored; due honor is to be accorded to God. There are also other immediately evident principles

[8] Cf. Augustine, *En. in ps. 57, 1:* "Data est etiam conscripta lex: non quia in cordibus scripta non erat; sed quia tu fugitivus eras cordis tui . . . et ad teipsum intro revocaris"; St. Thomas Aquinas, *Summa contra Gent.,* III, c. 117: "Lex divina profertur homini in auxilium legis naturalis."

[1] Cf. St. Thomas Aquinas, *III Sent.,* d. 37, q. 1, a. 4.

[2] Cf. Suarez, *Leg.,* c. 7, n. 5.

[3] This principle, not often mentioned in expositions of natural law theory, is expressly mentioned by St. Thomas Aquinas, *Summa contra Gent.,* III, c. 129: "Ea sine quibus societas humana conservari non potest"; cf. also *Summa theol.,* Ia IIae, q. 94, a. 2.

which presuppose rather fuller consideration of the nature of man and of the ordering of social life, consideration which is imposed on the young person as experience widens. These are the moral truths that stealing and lying, adultery and unchastity are intrinsically evil. To this realm of universally known principles belong the Decalogue, as *Thomas Aquinas* and *Suárez* state, with the exception of the Third Commandment, which is positive divine law.

Unlike the elementary principles, the *applied* principles are not immediately evident to the majority of mankind; instead, knowledge of them depends on the inferential application of the former principles to particular circumstances and to the modes of moral conduct demanded thereby. In simple conditions it is easy enough to estimate the just wage. But to judge what wages an employer should pay to different categories of workers and staff in the division of labor, in order to satisfy the demands of justice, is impossible without thorough insight into the socio-economic process: comprehensive knowledge and penetrating reflection become indispensable.

The elementary moral principles mentioned above are the *principles of practical reason,* which enable us to practice right conduct (described by traditional natural law theory as synderesis). They have their parallel in the principles of speculative reason, which enable us to practice right thinking; an example is the principle of contradiction, which declares that two mutually contradictory propositions cannot at the same time be true; this is immediately evident to anyone as soon as the underlying notions are grasped. Because the most general principles of right conduct are immediately evident to the practical reason as soon as their sense is understood they are also termed the *moral a priori.* This expression means that the principles are not demonstrated by experience, but are self-evident, although experience may be the cause of an individual person being aware of them. In view of this position which natural law ethics accords to the moral a priori, or to the intuitive apprehension of elementary moral principles as immediately evident truths, natural law ethics may be described as *intuitionist*; and in the light of what has been said before it is also teleological and eudaemonological.

The self-evident principles, as already stated, do not spring from experience, although to grasp them (cf. Chap. 3, n. VI) depends upon experience. This is so if only for the reason that their meaning is not grasped until the sense of the concepts linked in them is understood, which can be conveyed only by experience. We must know the meaning of the words "parents" and "disrespect" in order to recognize the truth that disrespect toward parents is morally bad; thus, the comprehension of the meaning of words and of the moral judgment in question is dependent on experience. The dependence upon experience for the comprehension of the elementary moral principles, however, as we have shown, goes much further. These principles are first lived and experienced, with their special, concrete mode of validity, for example, in the family community. Their general import is grasped and their general validity understood by the developing mind; this is true by reason of the insight into reality on which full human being in the family community depends. In connection with this insight, the most general supreme principle (good is to be done, evil is to be avoided, the supreme moral value and its binding nature) is understood to be both concrete and self-evident and generally binding. Because they are dependent upon experience and determined in content, the elementary moral principles possess the character of *synthetic judgments a priori.* The fact that they are self-evident and hence intrinsically necessary and generally valid propositions does not rest upon the understanding of conceptual relationships alone, but also upon the understanding of the underlying reality.[4]

Experience, however, is not the source of these moral principles either with regard to their self-evident content or with regard to their absolute claim to authority; rather, experience is the means by which they can be grasped by the intellect as principles in this twofold respect. If they are fully understood then they are of an aprioristic character: intrinsically certain and immediately evident. Thus, in the example mentioned, the respect due to parents is not by any means understood as simply a decree of society, but is taken as "a matter of course." These psychological and epistemological facts are not taken into account by all interpretations of morality which base morals on self-interest. The difference between "morality" in a dog and morality in man is clearly that the dog is guided only by experience of its own self-interest, whereas the man who is of sound mind comprehends the intrinsically certain truth of the general principles of moral law.

We have been discussing the insight into the elementary moral principles which is common to the human mind in general. The fact is, however, that to some extent we find aberrations in moral understanding which are in no sense due to bad will but rather to a *defective functioning of the natural law,* namely, to a fallibility of the natural conscience regarding the elementary principles themselves. Natural law ethics has always devoted special attention to this defect. Accordingly, it has pointed out that just because these principles are self-evident does not mean they are innate in man; if this were true, any obscurity or doubt about them would be out of the question. What is innate is *only the faculty* of apprehending them. Like all man's faculties, this one requires appropriate training and also a social environment suited to its development. In unfavorable circumstances, for example, when someone has grown up without sufficient mental training or lives in an injurious social environment, the judgment of the practical reason may be defective. This is true of individuals and also of communities, especially those in early

[4] Concerning the character of the principles of the moral a priori as synthetic judgments a priori, cf. Messner, *Kulturethik,* pp. 237–63, where there is a detailed discussion of their *epistemological* nature and also of the underlying mode of cognition.

stages of development ("primitives"). That is why their moral codes not infrequently have included grave errors; one need only recall the killing of strangers, of old people, and of infants of the same community, or the plundering of neighboring communities as a sport. Ethnologists have astonishing facts to report concerning the deficiency of natural law, one instance of which will be mentioned presently.

To explain defects of this kind, the great natural law teachers have often adduced the fact that outside the human sphere, too, nature is subject to deficiencies in its operation; [5] furthermore, although they see moral understanding as natural to man, they also consider its sometimes faulty development under adverse conditions to be "natural," just as the faulty development of the plant which lacks light and air. Hence, they laid stress on the fact that reason is endowed only with the elementary principles and not with a comprehensive moral code: error is already a possibility with the first steps in their *application,*[6] for it presupposes the appraisal of facts and of situations in which errors are possible. Therefore, natural law ethics has always held that human nature with its practical reason does indeed "in the majority of cases" [7] come fully into effect, but in some cases only incompletely. The investigation of defects in the moral sense of peoples in history and primitives of recent times opens up a wide field of work to *comparative ethics* and *comparative jurisprudence.* For the reasons stated, natural law ethics itself provides the justification and necessity for such inquiry. It need not be concerned about the results, for while maintaining that human nature is equipped with insight into the elementary moral principles, it maintains also, since it views human nature quite *realistically,* that moral reasoning can go wrong.

Among the cases of defective moral sense in communities let us consider one which seems to offer special difficulty to natural law theory: the Eskimos. Père *Buliard,* a Catholic missionary who spent fifteen years with the fewer than 40,000 Eskimos in northern Canada, reports the following facts: as late as 1913 two missionaries were cruelly murdered and dismembered in order to provide food; during his stay with them some Eskimos shot in sport a fellow tribesman whom they saw bathing in open water; immediately after their birth girls were often killed and thrown to the dogs; when the colony periodically moved, the sick and aged were left in an igloo with some food and a light which would soon go out, abandoned to certain death; men were murdered because others wanted to take their wives. In such cases, Père *Buliard* says, "the Eskimo never feels regret for the bad deed." Indeed, "this is even encouraged by the law of the Eskimo community," for "the penal law of

[5] St. Thomas Aquinas, *Summa theol.,* Ia IIae, q. 94, a. 4: "Naturae generabiles et corruptibiles deficiunt ut in paucioribus propter impedimenta."

[6] "In particulari operabili" (*Summa theol.,* Ia IIae, q. 94, a. 6) as Thomas often expresses it.

[7] "Ut in pluribus" is the phrase often used by Thomas Aquinas; cf. *Summa theol.,* Ia IIae, q. 94, aa. 4–5.

the Eskimo people is concerned with one thing only, the preservation of the general weal, and it never concerns itself with individual crimes like murder. The sole crime is an act which weakens the social body itself. Naturally, this tolerant attitude encourages murder as a means for settling disputes. Murder is expedient, simple, and natural for a hunting people used to killing; in passing judgment on Eskimo murder, therefore, one should not arbitrarily apply the moral standard of Western Europe."[8] This explanation of *Buliard* for the facts mentioned is exactly that which *Thomas* would have given. The difficulty, unimaginable for the West European, of the conditions of life and the environment in the Arctic region makes it clear why the Eskimos describe themselves, as Buliard explains, as Inuk, "the man"—indeed, "the man par excellence among men," because they are able to live in this environment.[9] The fact that no one doubts the full humanity of the Eskimos and of their common human moral and jural mental equipment is shown by the endeavors which it seemed natural to make to convey to them all the fundamental principles of moral law of the civilized nations of the West, quite apart from the general admiration which is felt for the Eskimos as an amiable people combatting nature's harshest difficulties.

11 *Natural Law as Effectual Impulse*

Natural law, as we have shown, is an operative impulse which works through conscience and through the desire for happiness.[10] As a moral stimulus it brings about conduct in conformity with the understanding of the individual conscience and brings about social institutions in conformity with the social conscience (especially by way of the moral and jural consciousness of society). As a conative stimulus natural law brings about that order of social life which is called for by the good ("utility") of all. Accordingly, natural law is of an essentially dynamic nature. It is static only insofar as the immediately evident truths are immutable, that is, insofar as the general elementary moral principles are in question. As an efficient force it is a stimulus to the progressive realization of the natural order in personal and social life.

The fact that the operation of natural law in this sense is imperfect,

[8] Père Roger P. Buliard, *Inuk,* 1953, pp. 16, 60 ff., 65 f., 90 f., 93 f.; almost exactly similar facts are reported by a missionary from another Eskimo community from the far north of Canada, R. de Coccola (helped by P. King), *Ayorama,* 1955, pp. 4, 18, 34 f., 49 f., 52, 67, 78, 86, 98, 112 f., 121, 137, 178 f., 205, 219 f., 273 f., 285.

[9] Buliard, *op. cit.,* pp. 1 ff.

[10] Cf. the references on this subject in St. Thomas Aquinas, *Summa theol.,* Ia IIae, q. 94, a. 3: "Naturalis inclinatio inest cuilibet homini ad hoc quod agat secundum rationem; et hoc est agere secundum virtutem"; in *IV Sent.,* d. 33: in the cognitive power natural law is *naturalis conceptio,* in appetitive power it is *naturalis inclinatio.* That natural law is also an impulse is but seldom emphasized; it is, however, by O. Schilling, *Lehrbuch der Moraltheologie,* 1928, Vol. I, p. 96; R. Linhardt, *Sozialprinzipien,* p. 101.

just as moral reason is imperfect, is a fact confirmed bitterly enough both from the individual and from the social aspect by the experience of every man and by history; hence, we need not dwell on it. This constitutes the basic tragedy of human existence, and its source is to be found in the impairment of human nature (cf. Chap. 11). In what follows it will be referred to only by way of example.

In *personal* life natural law is a driving force impelling man to develop his moral personality. This driving force is of such a kind that man can neglect it or resist it, and its effectiveness can be impaired by emotion, indolence, or adverse environment. Every man possesses, however, the experience of a moral force which drives him in the direction of his "better self," just as he is aware of the contrary force of the "other law" in his nature (Rom. 7:23), the law of his lower self. Consequently, maturity of personality is not something in which man comes to share just because his emotions have been stilled; rather, it is the result of a dynamic process in which he strives gradually to transform the motive forces in his instincts so that they come to serve his true self. In this process he sees himself impelled step by step to comprehend the essential reality of his nature in itself and in its relationship to the outer world, and to follow his better understanding in conduct and attitudes. As soon as a man has perceived that he owes charity to his neighbor he will at first grasp the cruder occasions calling for such love; only gradually does he perceive the finer occasions in which love of neighbor is called for; only gradually does he see that it must become "second nature" before he can promptly and fully answer the call of every situation. Meanwhile, even at this stage, more than at any earlier stage, because he has now become more clearsighted about the claims summed up in the phrase "man, become your essential self" (*Angelus Silesius*), man will have intimations of the realization of his highest self, the full ripeness of his moral personality, rather than see it as a reality closely approached. Natural law is an impetus toward such a purpose, although man can struggle against it or, owing to a specially unfavorable environment, may never come near it.

The dynamic character of the moral law is equally evident in the *social* sphere. The evolution of the human mind in its history from the age of the wooden spade to that of the tractor has its parallel in the evolution from taboo ethics to the principles of the Atlantic Charter. Just as men unite their forces in order to explore and to exploit external nature for their common purposes, so also they find themselves urged to set up social institutions in order to bring about progressively the conditions necessary for authentic human life. This process depends on the constant interplay between the development of moral consciousness and the development of social reality, and hence in a true sense on a *dialectical evolution*. Because of the increasing complexity of social relationships and the associated development of reality this inquiry is constantly charged with new and more difficult tasks. No sooner do a greater number of members of society understand the claims of justice under new conditions than they are immediately driven by conscience to aim for the appropriate institutions in their social system. The road to this end is, however, generally a long one, particularly as new goals continually come into sight. Beginning with primitive moral ideas about human relationships, mankind took thousands of years to reach the idea of the universal brotherhood of men as represented by Christian ethics; it was almost another two thousand years before the demands of this moral idea asserted themselves in the efforts for a social order based on equal civil and social rights. And it is unnecessary to emphasize how far we are from completing the task of making this idea current in advanced societies, or indeed how far we are from the full realization of human rights in the whole international sphere, which would of course assure world peace. The dynamic character of the natural law rests, however, by no means only on the development of moral insight, but at least equally on its other side, the impulse toward happiness: social classes strive and fight for conditions of life in due proportion to those of the privileged groups in the political community, and "underdeveloped" nations insist on their share in what the international community can afford in due proportion so as to ensure all its members fair conditions of life.

Nothing else better demonstrates the dynamic power of natural law than the endeavor, which today deeply stirs the whole world, to recast the order of economic, social, and international life. Moral postulates form an essential part of the motive force of this endeavor. Certainly, these forces are not always in complete harmony with the natural law; they may in part be rank growth, such as the organic forces of nature often develop. Yet, none of the reformers and planners, not even the adherents of Marxism or of other revolutionary dogmas, want to exploit the present-day economic and technical opportunities merely to satisfy a passion for adventure; instead, they desire to serve ideals like justice, social equality, and the brotherhood of man. These are ideals of a moral character, and the struggle to achieve them today is an obvious testimony to the restless dynamic force of natural law.

Four essential features of natural law, in which its substance becomes especially manifest, must be discussed more fully in the following chapters: (1) its universality; (2) its unity; (3) its invariability; (4) its immutability.

7. The Universal and Individual Character of Natural Law

A touchstone of any system of ethics is the solution it offers to the problems posed by the relation between individual and universal in the moral law. From our previous considerations we derive the following answer: individual and universal moral law are related in the same way as individual and universal human nature. The essential nature of all men with its existential ends, no matter what race they belong to or what stage of development they have reached, is the same; therefore, moral law is the same for all. The universal moral law can result in special obligations and special virtues: for the individual man, in accordance with his qualities and circumstances; for individual communities, in accordance with their particular character and cultural development. The result is the individual moral personality of the individual man and the specialized social morality of communities—the unique qualities of their *forms of ethos* and *moral codes;* the former consist in the modes of moral feeling, thought, valuation, and conduct which are guaranteed by tradition.

Our question is of special *significance for natural law theory.* The question of the existence or nonexistence of a universal moral order also decides the question of the existence or nonexistence of a fundamental order conferring rights and obligations on all men and peoples equally. Without a universal moral order there is no foundation either for the human rights which belong equally to all men or for an international law equally binding upon all states. Probably there is no one today who would not assign the same human nature and the same human dignity to all men of all nations. Yet, it is maintained by influential philosophers and ethicists that among different communities, especially primitive ones, different fundamental moral beliefs occur ("conscience speaks differently to different peoples"). Such assertions rest on the defective observation of facts. Those who make them should learn from the ethnologist and anthropologist (cf. Chap. 47) that the uniformity of the moral consciousness of mankind is well established; it is a principle firmly held among anthropologists today that only after one has lived a long time with primitive people can one become acquainted with the fundamental beliefs hidden beneath their customs (ethos forms). Indeed, the exponents of these views are inconsistent in that they all believe, with great conviction, that a fundamental order of social life legally binding on all men alike and a fundamental order of international life binding alike on all nations are possible and desirable. This would, however, be illogical if one did not hold that all men are alike in nature, that the same moral reason is owned by all, and therefore that the same fundamental moral order can be known by all who possess a developed intellect.

The proposition regarding the universal nature of natural law means, therefore, that natural law belongs to the rational nature of all men, so that *no man is morally blind.* Thus, it is impossible for a person of fully developed mind to possess invincible ignorance of the elementary principles of the natural moral order. Partial moral blindness is not ruled out since, as we saw in the preceding chapter, human nature works defectively under unfavorable conditions, just as the rest of nature does. Human nature can become fully active only in a suitable environment, just as the nature of every living organism can attain full development only under suitable conditions. A plant deprived of light, air, and space can remain under stones, stunted in growth and perhaps even unrecognizable. Unfavorable circumstances which impede the full development of the moral reason of the individual even among civilized peoples are the following: bringing children up in broken families; faulty education; constant bad example; the decline of public morals; gravely defective social systems. Then the moral sense may be unsure and the power of moral judgment may be defective, especially in the sphere of applied principles, for example, in matters of sexual morality, divorce, birth control, usury, covetousness, and duelling.

The foregoing considerations indicate the importance of moral education in home and school for the development of man's moral nature. Its neglect is an evil not only for the young but also for society. The natural root of social order is stunted if the natural moral disposition of youth is not developed and trained. And since nature requires suitable conditions for the right development of conscience, this can be substantially promoted or retarded by the state of *public morality*. By public morality we mean the moral state of a society measured by what is publicly demanded or tolerated as morally admissible. This will include primarily the press, theatre, the cinema, radio, television, organized entertainment, and advertising. Both of the conclusions with regard to education and public morality are in accordance with the oldest experience of mankind. We find them advocated with great insistence by *Plato* and *Aristotle*. The former would ban from public life all enervating kinds of poetry, music, and the other arts; [1] the latter sees the chief object of politics in "a good moral training." [2]

The *individual* nature of morality not merely finds a place in natural law ethics but forms a primary element in its conception of morality. In this conception morality consists in the perfection of man through the ordered development of the fundamental human instinct of love in accordance with the abilities and energies, circumstances and situations which determine his individuality and his individual destiny. These circumstances and situations include health, heredity, defects of education, and unfavorable environment: in short, everything that gives the moral task of the individual its distinctive character. Because the universal moral order must always be actualized by individuals under individual conditions *there is no standardized ideal of moral personality*. We can best demonstrate the essential features of "individual morality" by trying to bring out its positive and negative aspects. Nega-

[1] Cf. Plato, *Republic*, III, pp. 395–401.
[2] Aristotle, *Ethics*, I, 4.

tively, there is no doubt that the extent of what is morally dangerous and harmful varies from individual to individual. It is a fundamental principle of education, confirmed by the whole experience of mankind, that individuals whose moral judgment and moral character are not firm enough should be shielded from situations which would make excessive demands on them morally. The child must not know or see much that can be safely known and seen by adults. Further instances of how individuality claims its rights in the moral sphere come readily to hand.

Equally obvious is the positive feature in "individual morality." The example of the development of benevolence in the individual alongside the ripening of his personal self makes this quite evident. For the more mature moral personality, finer forms of benevolence become a duty, while for the more primitive moral personality they do not enter the sphere of moral consciousness. For many who possess spiritually robust natures it signifies great heroism to desist from violence in a quarrel, whereas for others it is an effortless duty to see that quarrels never arise. In the sense thus indicated, therefore, it is wholly justifiable to speak of an "individual morality."

We must test our doctrine of the universal validity of the moral order in the light of the relevant doctrine of other schools of ethics.

1. *Kant* undertook, with the whole force of his noble philosophical ethos, to demonstrate the universal validity of the moral order in opposition to the ethical utilitarians who degrade human reason more or less to the status of a bookkeeper of pleasure and unpleasure values in the various modes of conduct, and who make enlightened self-interest the ultimate root of morality, thus according it fundamentally only an individual nature. Nevertheless, *Kant* himself did not rise above a *moral formalism.* Like all principles of cognition the moral principle could only be a wholly general one, because it was only "formal," that is, possessing no definite context. This principle, according to Kant, is: "So act that the maxim of your will can always serve at the same time as a principle of general legislation." [3] Thus, the moral order is founded on a general law of reason, which, consequently preserves its autonomy (cf. Chap. 4, nn. I and II). However, the human intellect does not create the moral principles and values; it discovers them as evident truths and values.

In connection with his formal moral principle, *Kant* reaches only a formal definition of the morality of the individual act: it possesses moral character only insofar as it is performed solely for the sake of duty as such. In fact, man knows with certainty of duties with definite content. And the moral principles of which he is thus aware he recognizes as equally binding on all men because of their common human nature. They rest, as we saw, on the responsibilities immanent in human nature, grounded in the existential ends.[4] By basing the universality of

[3] Kant, *Kritik der praktischen Vernunft* (ed. Preuss. Akad. d. Wiss.), Vol. V., p. 30.

[4] The reaction against Kant's abstract formalism was inevitable as soon as thinkers began to open their eyes again to the reality of human existence. Henri Bergson supplied the first powerful stimulus to this movement. With his concept of "life" and his analysis of consciousness he declared war both on the rationalistic and on the mechanistic view of man. Admittedly, his notion of life with the metaphysical and cosmological conclusions resting upon it, especially in his earlier writings, is open to grave objections. In his later years, however, his view of "life" and the resulting conclusions

the moral order on abstract reason *Kant* bars the approach to individual morality.

Schleiermacher was the first to draw attention to this defect in Kantian ethics and to develop the idea of individual morality. *Kant's* notion of duty, according to which the maxim of conduct must be capable of becoming universal law, leaves no room, says Schleiermacher, for the special and the individual. Besides, he points out, morality is not only the mastering of nature but also the fulfillment of nature, the harmony of reason and nature. Human nature, continues *Schleiermacher,* always appears as something individual; moral duty, therefore, always presents itself to the individual as special and individual.[5] To this emphasis on the individual character of the moral function is due *Schleiermacher's* distinctive position in the development of modern ethics, although in the criticism of his own work it is unanimously held that in spite of his endeavors he has not succeeded in really establishing an intrinsic correlation between the individual and the universal sides of morality.

2. At the opposite pole from *Kant's* formalism stands *Scheler* with his *value ethics.* He rejects the Kantian "duty-ethics" which recognizes as moral only what is done from duty and for the sake of duty, and conceives duty as something opposed to inclination. The fundamental impulse in man, in which he realizes himself as a person, is love, and this is something essentially linked with inclination. A moral imperative is incompatible with the act of love; so also is a moral law claiming universal validity, according to *Scheler,* since love is by nature personal and individual. Morality itself is not comprehended by the intellect by means of a "formal" principle, as *Kant* holds; rather, the moral values are to be found intuitively with concrete precision in emotive acts and preferences, love and hate.[6] This intuition of value involves no obligation;

---

regarding human existence remain not too far removed from our concept of "nature." The exponent of natural law doctrine will be able to find an approximation to truth in Bergson's argument that "all morality . . . is biological in essence," if, that is to say, "one gives to the word biology the very wide sense which it should have" (*The Two Sources of Morality and Religion,* trans. by R. A. Andra and C. Brereton, 1935, p. 82). In fact, it is also our conclusion that morality is "nature" (cf. Chap. 4). The acute criticism which L. Laberthonnière (*Esquisse d'une philosophie personaliste,* Oeuvres, L. Canet, editor, 1942, pp. 288–346) applies to Bergson and which culminates in the assertion that Bergsonism possesses no basis for an ethics was written, as the editor himself points out (p. 334), before the publication of the above mentioned work of Bergson.

[5] Cf. F. Schleiermacher, *Grundlinien einer Kritik der bisherigen Sittenlehre,* 1803; *Entwurf eines Systems der Sittenlehre,* posthumously published, now in: Coll. Works, Vols. I–IV (Leipzig), 1910–13. The ideas quoted in the text and our discussion of them reveal a distinct parallelism between some of his lines of thought and those of natural law ethics.

[6] Max Scheler, *Der Formalismus in der Ethik und die materiale Wertethik,* 3rd ed., pp. 10 ff., 194 ff., 215 ff., 397 ff.; *Vom Ewigen im Menschen,* 1923, 3rd ed. 1933, pp. 484 ff., 698 ff.; *Die Stellung des Menschen im Kosmos,* 1930, p. 111; *Wesen und Formen der Sympathiegefühle,* 2nd ed., 1923, pp. 189 ff. The unequalled wealth of thought in Scheler's work will influence the development of ethics for a long time to come. Scheler's criticism of the errors of rationalistic, formalistic, utilitarian and pragmatic ethics opened up many new and surprising perspectives. In addition, he has broken much new ground in the science and philosophy of value. Had he only shown what the phenomenological method of Husserl can achieve in ethics, his place in the history of ethics would be assured. All this admitted, our interest in Scheler's work remains fundamentally critical. Under the light of criticism, however, this work proves stimulating to an extraordinary degree.

obligation is added in the light of the existing situation as a prerequisite of a definite action; general principles, *Scheler* concludes, can be traced back only to generalizations of such value experiences. As we have seen (Chap. 4), natural law ethics also assumes that the fundamental impulse of human nature is love: natural law ethics is *personalistic* in that since *Augustine* it has maintained that man realizes his true self as a person in moral good; it assigns its due place to the intuitive apprehension of values, the immediate perception of inherently certain general moral principles, of concrete values.

Natural law ethics, however, not only sees value and being in an intimate connection (cf. below n. 3), but also seeks a *criterion* of truth for value, because the fact is very obvious that the fundamental impulse of love as cognitive disposition, like all man's cognition, is prone to error in its acts of choice. Besides, the intellect undoubtedly has its role in the judgment of moral value, as reflection on the worth and worthlessness of conduct in complicated situations demonstrates, whereas only the fundamental values, contained in the general moral principles, are grasped intuitively. The discernment of the particular in the moral realm requires reflective and logical activity like every cognition of the particular in the various spheres of practical human knowing and doing. Hence, in *Scheler's* view axiological intuitionism (value intuitionism, Greek *axios* = worthy) does not stand the test of reality with regard to some of his basic philosophical-ethical views (cf. Chap. 3, n. VII).

3. Only an individual morality is recognized by *deontological intuitionism* (Greek stem *deont* from *dei* = ought), the first form of *situation ethics.* It reduces the moral order altogether to an individual "law." Moral cognition is confined to the intuitive understanding of what is duty at a particular time: man recognizes in particular situations particular modes of conduct as his duty by virtue of direct intuition. Generalized principles of conduct which are derived from such experiences can, according to this ethics, be a great help (e.g. in moments of passion), but they remain principles for the individual and are not universally valid; indeed, even the individual is bound by them only insofar as circumstances themselves establish such an obligation.

The second form of situation ethics which recognizes a purely individual morality is that founded on *existentialist philosophy:* "authentic" existence for man means being in freedom; therefore, it is bound up with self-design in the given situation, which excludes a universally binding moral order; the most that is admitted is the possibility of generalizations of the modes of decision in parallel situations. Natural law ethics also assumes that it is the individual who, in the particular situation, recognizes his duty to act in a certain way. Nevertheless, with regard to all decisions about duties which have to be made in such situations, the question "why" can be put; reason is made especially conscious of it in the case of decisions of conscience which go against one's own inclinations. This question goes back to ultimate moral principles which are gained not only from situation experiences, that is, from generalizations, but, as we have shown, are self-evident truths.

A third form of situational ethics is that of *scientistic* and *neo-positivistic humanism.* From the concept "natural law" itself, objections are raised to the universal validity of the fundamental principles of moral law on the ground that even in the sphere of the natural sciences the certain knowledge of the universal validity of the laws of nature (owing to the impossibility of complete induction) is denied us. Since this humanism admits only outward experience as a source of knowledge it may be argued that our immediate everyday experience itself proves their basic "scientific" attitude to be mistaken. For, the whole of our cultural life, and especially its technical aspect, would be impossible unless we were definitely aware of the general validity of natural laws. Social life would be equally impossible without our definite knowledge of the universal belief in the universally binding validity and intrinsic necessity of elementary truths concerning good and evil, right and wrong, and also of the fact that this validity and this necessity are founded in the likeness of the essential nature of all men, involving for all absolute basic demands on their conduct and equal basic rights as claims on the conduct of others.

8. Unity and Diversity in Natural Law

The natural moral law is one single law for both the individual and the social spheres, for personality and culture, for family and society, for the state and the community of nations. The foundation of this *unity and oneness of the moral order* lies in the fact that human nature is only one, and that on natural law depends the full reality and full development of humanity, and thus all true individual and social culture. Hence, the natural moral law is the basic law of all spheres of cultural life: intellectual, political, economic, social, international. On the contrary, the maxim of "*double morality,*" which is a fundamental element in individualistic as well as collectivistic thought, declares that public and private life are subject to different moral principles. Moral considerations which may be valid in personal and civil life can only have a restrictive influence in political, economic, and cultural life: "You cannot build railways with biblical quotations," was a statement made in a European parliament in the heyday of liberalism. On these foundations arose such principles as Machiavellianism in politics, Manchester liberalism in economics, "free love" in sexual relations, art for art's sake in aesthetics. With the principle of "double morality," the ends and values of the various spheres of human activity are given an absolute authority, and political, economic, and intellectual life have been accorded *absolute autonomy,* claiming not to be subject to universal moral law. This autonomy meant a vital danger to culture, because culture is nothing else but the full development of humanity, and this itself, as we have seen, is bound up with the natural moral law. Cultural endeavor misses its goal when it departs from natural law, for then it is at the expense of the ends essential to the fulfillment of human nature and so must lead to the "crisis of culture."

Natural law ethics, too, admits a kind of autonomy, but only a *relative* one: human activity in political, economic, and cultural life has to abide by the concrete laws imposed by the particular ends of these spheres. Indeed, the Decalogue does not tell us how to establish and to organize a shoe factory or a combine. These concrete laws involve a multiformity of moral principles for the patterns of social life of the various realms of culture. They are, however, the principles of one undivided moral order, divided in its demands according to the multiformity of the "nature of the case" in the individual spheres of life seen from the point of view of the existential ends and the natural order associated with them, and from the point of view of the concrete laws which indicate the means to be used in the service of these ends. The same moral principle, therefore, can call for a variety of modes of conduct. Patient forbearance in the face of unseemly behavior on the part of others can be a noble virtue, yet the teacher may be called upon to react differently if such behavior is met with in those entrusted to his care. Tolerance which may be a virtue in the private citizen, conferring a variety of obligations on him, may be mere irresponsible weakness on the part of the statesman who is obliged to serve the common good of the state with energy and determination. Interest on money loans was contrary to justice as long as money did not possess the quality of capital and capital was not indispensable to the fulfillment of the social end of the economy.

Although modern naturalism insisted on absolute autonomy in the spheres of politics, economy, and culture, some representatives of a misconceived *supernaturalism* have sought to turn all cultural spheres, particularly politics and economics, into departments of an ethics founded on supernatural revelation and religion. The truth is that all these departments of knowledge and activity need only bear in mind the subordination of their own particular ends to the natural law pattern of ends, and after that they have the right and even the duty to search out the best ways and means for attaining their purposes. Although *naturalism* would make the *causae secundae* (created forces) independent of the *causa prima* (the Creator), supernaturalism is inclined to overlook the "relative autonomy" grounded in the *causae secundae*. Hence, recognition is given only to a theological ethics based on the revealed word of God. A supernaturalism of a special kind is advocated by one group or another on the Catholic side in the form of "integralism," with the claim that in the political and social spheres everything is to be placed under the "direct" authority of the Church. Were the Church or its ministers to make any such claim to a direct authority in these fields, the reproach of "clericalism" would be justified.[1]

In connection with the unity and diversity in natural law two domains

[1] For the Catholic doctrine the reader is referred to the definite remarks of Pope Pius XI in the encyclical *Quadragesimo Anno* (*The Social order*), 1931, concerning the authority of the Church in the social and economic spheres. The Church, he says, has no authority in matters of technique or of mere instrumentality in economic life, since for these it can claim neither any special equipment nor a mission; the authority of the Church covers matters of moral law.

of the one moral order, which stand out from each other as a maximum and minimum of morality, must be mentioned. In the social sphere a *moral minimum* is demanded, that is, that minimum of morality which must be observed by all members of society in order that social life may thrive or indeed be at all possible. Most obligations of external daily life belong to this category. This "social morality" is the strongest unifying bond in a society and at the same time the most important part of its common good; it is an indispensable element of its existence as a communal structure as well as of its spiritual and physical continuity.[2] The great majority of individuals find an essential, if not the principal, support for their personal morality in the environment provided by social morality; this may be seen from the familiar experience that people often suffer in their moral outlook with a change in their environment. In contrast to the social sphere, the goal in the personal sphere is a *moral maximum,* because man is destined for the full realization of his moral personality. Personal morality means development for as long as man is alive. With each fresh step toward moral ripeness of personality, man's insight into the implications of the good grows along with his power to comply with them. Only relatively few develop all these capacities to the utmost and strive with all their might after perfection in the realm of moral personality: these are the geniuses in the realm of "personal morality"—the saints. They seek not only their own fully moral existence, but also have the power to enkindle in others moral ideals which they themselves know and live. As such ideals permeate society, social morality as a whole rises to a higher level.[3]

The relationship between personal and social morality which we have just touched upon has received close attention from *Hegel* and *Bergson.* The understanding of the distinct significance of "social morality" by *Hegel* is a cultural-anthropological insight of the first rank. It must be carefully observed that what he means by this is precisely the opposite of the view widely held today that morality is something wholly and entirely evolved from society; for *Hegel,* social morality is that which governs society. He distinguishes the morality belonging to personal, individual life (*moralität*) from the pattern of social conduct guaranteed principally by law (*sittlichkeit*).[4] Nevertheless, *Hegel* considers the individual possessing spiritual being totally embedded in social morality, i.e. in the "objective spirit" (cf. Chap. 2). According to *Bergson,* a state of tension exists between personal and social morality which forms "the two extremes of the single morality." On the ground of its significance for the existence and preservation of society, to which we have alluded above, *Bergson* calls social morality "closed morality," and the society which is informed by it a "closed society": between the two spheres of morality "lies the whole dimension between acquiescence and movement"; in the latter it is chiefly the

[2] On ethos and ethos forms cf. Messner, *Kulturethik,* Chap. 70.

[3] Cf. the fine work by A. D. Lindsay, *The Two Moralities: Our Duty to God and Society,* 1940.

[4] Hegel, *Grundlinien der Philosophie des Rechts,* 1821, pars. 141 ff.

"pioneers of morality" who are at work; "life holds for them unsuspected tones of feeling like those of some new symphony, and they draw us after them into this music that we may express it in action." In his discussion of the connection between the two moralities he concurs almost completely with the natural law idea, and he refers explicitly to nature as the common root of social and personal morality.[5]

9. The Invariability and Variability of the Natural Law

Natural moral law is one and the same for all men. If the principle of equality, which is proclaimed as one of the milestones on the road of human progress, has any significance at all, it means primarily that all men possess equal moral dignity as persons and hence equal original rights. He who proclaims social equality with fundamentally equal demands for all, presupposes equality in fundamental moral responsibilities for all men, that is, that the natural law has equal validity for all. On the other hand, the internal delimitation of the idea of equality is also grounded in the natural law. The diversity of individual talents and hence of social function and status is part of the natural order, with which, as with the moral task of forming the individual personality, are linked far-reaching diversities (concerning the idea of equality cf. Chap. 52).

For nations also there is but one natural law—the same for all—with which, however, the diversity of their individual ethos forms (cf. Chap. 7) can harmonize well. Because of their distinctive gifts and the state of their cultural development, individual nations display a variety of special moral faculties and special moral values, for example, courage, purity, loyalty, sobriety, industry, thrift. Just as some nations are extolled for their outstanding achievements in various fields of cultural life, such as statecraft, philosophy, poetry, and music, so also the moral order common to all mankind shines forth in a colorful spectrum of moral traits distinctive of the various nations. Again, however, it is clear that in the very diversity in the functioning of natural law there is evident testimony of its invariability with regard to its fundamental principles and of the sameness of the elementary moral consciousness of mankind. For, such diversity of moral characteristics can be ascribed to individual peoples

[5] H. Bergson, *Les deux sources de la morale et de la religion,* 1933, pp. 35 f., 47, 56 f.: "La vie a pour eux des résonances de sentiment insoupçonnées, comme en pourrait donner une symphonie nouvelle; ils nous font entrer avec eux dans cette musique, pour que nous la traduisons en mouvement . . . Nous trouvons aux deux extrémités de cette morale unique la pression et l'aspiration; celle-là d'autant plus parfaite qu'elle est plus impersonelle, plus proche de ces forces naturelles qu'on apelle habitude et même instinct, celle-ci d'autant plus puissante qu'elle est plus visiblement soulevée en nous par des personnes, et qu'elle semble mieux triompher de la nature. Il est vrai que si l'on descendait jusqu'à la racine de la nature elle-même, on s'apercevrait peut-être que c'est la même force qui se manifeste directement, en tournant sur elle-même, dans l'espèce humaine une fois constituée, et qui agit ensuite indirectement, par l'intermédiare d'individualités privilegiées, pour pousser l'humanité en avant."

only if the oneness of mankind's moral consciousness, or equality of natural conscience, is established. The contrary assumption would result in difficulty with the logical axiom that the particular as such can be apprehended only by means of the recognized general.

Both individualist and collectivistic thought view morality as varying according to class and race. *Racial ethics* maintains that morality alters with racial endowments; the *dialectical-materialist theory* holds that all precommunist morality is class morality and will, therefore, change with class domination. These collectivistic theories of class and race morality are already adumbrated in individualist-liberalist theory and practice. Was not moral autonomy reserved to the class of "enlightened" people, while a moral code was considered indispensable for the "masses"? And was it not a widely held idea that morality meant different things for colonial powers and colonial peoples, and conferred different rights upon "superior" and "inferior" peoples? These errors gave the "advanced" classes and peoples excuses for an easy conscience when they made the internal and the external proletariat (as *Toynbee* describes the colonial peoples) the object of exploitation.

10. The Immutability and Mutability of Natural Law

In natural law ethics the immutability of natural moral law means that as soon as homo sapiens had appeared, man endowed with reason, there could no longer be any change in what is fundamentally good or evil and is comprehended as such. Human nature with the dignity of the person does not change, nor can self-evident truth change. Hence, there is a *constant* in human nature and existence which remains throughout all historical and cultural change.

On the other hand, we are aware of the fact that there has been a long evolution in moral consciousness from the days of primeval man up to the present day. This evolution is marked in the history of different peoples by the lack of many moral rules which we regard as fundamental to culture and to civilization (e.g., respect for human dignity, freedom of conscience, freedom of religious beliefs). Traditional natural law ethics, at least in its most important exponents, has considered such an evolution to be "natural," owing to the manner in which human reason in all departments of knowledge proceeds from the imperfect to the more perfect (cf. Chap. 40). They saw experience at work in regard to the natural order implied in the general "utility." Here for the third time we have to assign to the idea of utility its place in ethics (cf. above Chaps. 3 and 4). Hence, a pragmatic element undoubtedly enters into ethics (although not in the sense of ethical pragmatism), according to which the moral principles themselves originate exclusively in such experience. Certainly, however, in the moral sphere as in every other, men learn by experience: from the effects of the principles which they have applied, and not least from the effects of mistaken principles, namely, by trial and error.

Since the idea of evolution is inseparable from the nature and the natural law of man there exists, notwithstanding the immutability spoken of at the beginning, a further range of *mutability*. We have referred to the "constant" in human nature and existence: it concerns the fundamentals of the order of truly human existence and the apprehension of the fundamental moral principles of this order. But the fact that the nature of man, of society, and of civilization is subject to far-reaching changes, and involves a very extensive *variable,* can be seen from a glance at the course of development from Neanderthal man to the present day in the region where he once moved. He was unaware of a considerable proportion of the more advanced moral principles which are today the common property of civilized nations. As civilization develops, new demands of natural law arise, so that natural law is itself changeable in its operation. From this *first* kind of mutability of natural law arising from the development of civilization there is to be distinguished a *second* kind, owing to the fact that as circumstances change the application of the same principles leads to different conclusions. Thus, criminal law is a different thing today from the cruel code of the Middle Ages when confessions were extorted by the rack and punishment was meted out by mutilation. As a result of other means of protecting society against lawbreakers and of a new understanding of the psychological aspect of crime and punishment, changes have taken place.

Thus, we come back to the idea of evolution, and at the same time to a *third* kind of mutability in the natural law: the moral consciousness of individual peoples and of mankind as a whole underlies evolution. Even though individual moral "geniuses" may provide stimuli in this direction (cf. Chap. 8), such stimuli have also proceeded from the experience linked with the desire for happiness as driving force in society, from the inquiring mind and philosophical ethics, from the moral sciences and social movements. In this process, truth and falsehood, justice and injustice have generally been mixed. But, as in all domains of the human spirit, in the realm of moral law mankind progresses through the struggle of truth and of error. And it is not the least proof of the potency of natural law that in this struggle it always asserts itself, not continuously and not without reverses, to be sure, yet in the traceable history of mankind it operates in the formation of social systems more in accordance with the demands of true humanity.[1]

[1] We treat the defects in the mode of operation of the natural law, of which we have already spoken (cf. Chap. 6), not as mutability in the natural law. In ascertaining such faults, as in the case of the departure from monogamy in Old Testament Israel, regarding which it has even been suggested that in such cases God "dispensed" men from the natural law, we are not by any means faced with a change in natural law itself; A. Utz (*Recht und Gerechtigkeit, Thomaskommentar,* 1953, p. 440) rightly disputes any act of dispensation by divine authority, pointing out that "it would be fundamentally wrong to seek to divest natural law principles of their absolute normative force," whereas "divine authority . . . alone can deal with concrete, morally permissible, difficult circumstances, while not charging for the ob-

Three evolutionary movements must accordingly be borne in mind if one is seeking to form a judgment about mutabilities in the natural law: (1) the unprecedented development of the social world in the last two centuries, politically, economically, socially. This has been accompanied by (2) a not less far-reaching development of jural and social consciousness; this development is undoubtedly due to the dynamic forces of natural moral law, although it has certainly gained momentum under the impulse of the Christian cultural tradition. The driving forces of the two evolutionary processes mentioned were due in no small measure to (3) the development of the sciences, natural sciences and social sciences including the sciences of man, anthropology, biology, psychology. What does this mean for ethics? The question concerns the relationship between ethics and empirical science, which we have already several times touched upon.

I *Ethics and Empirical Science*

The function of ethics consists in working out the natural order in existing reality. The investigation of actual reality forms the object of the empirical sciences. Ethics, therefore, must rely on these in seeking the natural order in the existing conditions. The social ethicist in particular must be familiar with the whole range of the empirical sciences which are concerned with the actual reality of society, at least with their principal findings, if he does not wish to confine himself to platitudes. In the economic and social fields, which today are so much a part of current thought and political discussion, political economy offers the natural law ethicist the tools which are indispensable for his allotted task of ascertaining the implications of the common good. The fact that Christian ethics for too long concerned itself, as distinct from the natural law ethics of the great scholastics, with generalities was certainly a main factor in its considerable loss of influence on the development of economic and social life since the advance of individualist liberalism at the end of the eighteenth century. The scholastic ethicists up to the sixteenth century were the leading economists of their time; indeed world-famous economists (in contrast with earlier judgments) speak with admiration of their economic ideas.[2]

---

jective defection. The scholastics should have distinguished more clearly between legal rules and moral responsibility toward these rules." For an investigation in, and explanation of, the difficulties in question on the basis of the recent development of the natural law theory, cf. J. Messner, "Contradictions to Natural Ethics in the Old Testament," in *Jahrbuch des Instituts für christliche Sozialwissenschaften* (Münster, Symposium for G. Gundlach), 1962.

[2] J. Schumpeter, *History of Economic Analysis,* E. B. Schumpeter editor, 1954, pp. 91–104; cf. also Schumpeter, "Die Entwicklung der Sozialökonomik zur Wissenschaft," in *Grundriß der Sozialökonomik,* 1924, p. 24, where he writes of the work of the scholastics: "If their predominant aim is moral casuistry this should not prevent us from seeing that the 'cases' and religious rules which are discussed are only the outer form of concrete inquiries which at times make an impression all the more

Although the Fathers of the Church were highly thought of at that time, there was no inclination, when the capitalistic development of economy was setting in, to solve the problem of interest, as has been attempted in the present century, by quotations from the Fathers. The principles have not changed, the reality has. With the development of the uses of capital in the socio-economic process, other conclusions are drawn from the same principles, just as the physical laws of nature have not changed in the transition from earlier extensive to later intensive agriculture, although their application takes another form.

Ethical judgments can of course be based only on definitive and established findings of scientific research, not on mere opinions or hypotheses. The function of ethics is to investigate moral principles by methods appropriate to it and to apply them to the actual reality presented by the society of a given period. What this reality is ethics must learn from the sciences. Should biologists, for instance, be able to show that marriage between persons having certain hereditary traits inevitably involves grave consequences to the community as a whole, a legal eugenic matrimonial impediment would be justified and even imperative; thus, the Catholic Church has laid down a canonical impediment to marriage between first cousins.

11 *Ethical Evolutionism*

There are no absolute moral truths and values independent of time and society; rather all are the outcome of a long evolution—this is the doctrine of ethical evolutionism and relativism. In this evolution it is held that experience regarding the preservation and development of society has been the sole determining factor. Hence, today in the era of the empirical sciences we are to be informed primarily by these as to what is useful and good for individual, for society, and for mankind. Two forms of ethical relativism need to be discussed more particularly.

Concerning *dialectical-materialist* evolutionism *Lenin* says: "Only one thing is, from *Engels'* viewpoint, immutable—the reflection by the human mind (when the human mind exists) of a world existing and developing independently of the mind. No other 'immutability,' no other 'essence' or 'absolute substance' in the sense in which the idle official philosophy portrayed these, existed for *Marx* and *Engels*." But such a proposition is refuted by clear facts: twice two is four—this is certainly independent of the evolution of the material world, it is intrinsically necessary and immutable. The fact that the three angles of a triangle are equal in sum to two right angles remains unaltered even if the whole world of matter were to disappear. The mathematical and geometrical laws are of absolute and unquestionable validity independently of the evolution of matter. From the proposition quoted, *Lenin,* appealing again to *Engels,* goes on to develop his ethical pragmatism. "For a materialist, the 'suc-

favorable the longer one studies them." How highly W. Sombart and J. M. Keynes thought of the economic understanding of the scholastics will be dealt with later (Chap. 170).

cess' of human practice proves the correspondence of our conceptions to the objective nature of the things we perceive."[3] This is supposed to apply to truth in general, and to ethical truth in particular. His conclusion is: "The highest task of humanity is to comprehend the objective logic of the economic evolution (the evolution of social existence), to comprehend the most general and fundamental features with the purposes of adapting its social consciousness and the consciousness of the advanced classes of all capitalistic countries to it in clear, exact, and critical fashion." *Lenin* does not assume that the mind is a "lesser" reality in evolution, since of course its function is to understand the necessities inherent in evolution and to adapt human practice to these necessities. For this process of adaptation of consciousness the natural and social sciences form the sole and exclusive foundation: "If that which our practice confirms is the sole, ultimate, and objective truth, then it follows that the sole path to this truth is the road of science which stands by the materialist creed."[4]

No other form of pragmatist ethics makes it so immediately clear that judgment about success or failure already presupposes value-assumptions on which are based judgments concerning what is success or failure. Thus, when the Soviet government assigned priority to heavy industry in economic planning they were necessarily relying on value-assumptions regarding the aims to be pursued in the socio-economic process. We shall also see, however, when dealing with the Marxist-Leninist view of society, that Marxist-Leninist dialectical materialism is guided by genuinely aprioristic value-principles (cf. Chap. 16).

The immutability of natural law with regard to its absolute principles and values is challenged from another angle by *biological evolutionism. Herbert Spencer* first applied this theory to ethics. Modern evolutionism has a prominent exponent in Professor *Julian Huxley*. Borrowing from Freudian psychoanalytic theory (cf. Chap. 2), *Huxley* assures us that the child's "'intuitions' as to what constitutes right and wrong are derived from its environment, largely mediated through its mother"; "the absoluteness of moral obligations turns out on analysis to be no true absolute, but a result of the nature of our infantile mental machinery, combined with later rationalization and wish-fulfillment." "The appearance of universalist ethics" is taken as the outcome of a long evolution. "By universalist ethics I mean, of course, the conception that ethical principles apply to all humanity, irrespective of race, language, creed or station." The appearance of universalist ethics is explained as follows: "When we look at nature as a whole, we find, among the many directions taken by evolution, one which is characterized by introducing the evolving world-stuff to progressively higher levels of organization and hence to new possibilities of being,

[3] Lenin makes a sharp distinction between the pragmatism of dialectical materialism, which closely follows the objective nature of things, and the American pragmatism of his time, according to which the criterion of truth consists in the "value of its results" seen in the light of the progressive general satisfaction of mankind's desire for happiness. In reality, this pragmatism does not go much beyond Bentham's idea of the greatest happiness of the greatest number, but it imbues the idea with the optimism of faith in unlimited possibilities, which is not surprising in view of the current American philosophy of life.

[4] Lenin, *Materialism and Empirio-Criticism* (cf. above Chap. 2, note 2), pp. 111, 114, 222, 280.

action, and experience. This has culminated in the attainment of a stage in which the world-stuff (now molded into human shape) finds that it experiences some of the new possibilities as having value in or for themselves; and further that among these it assigns higher and lower degrees of value, the higher values being those which are more intrinsically or more permanently satisfying, or involve a greater degree of perfection." *Huxley* further assures us that "we can say that this is the most desirable direction of evolution, and accordingly that our ethical standards must fit into its dynamic framework. In other words, it is ethically right to aim at whatever will promote the increasingly full realization of increasingly higher values." [5] We are here not so much interested in *Huxley's* theory of biological evolution as such as in the interpretation it affords of the "natural."

Criticism does not have a difficult task in dealing with this proof of ethical relativism. The explanation of the authority of conscience and of convictions about moral values which is borrowed from Freudian psychoanalysis is a hypothesis for which the necessary factual evidence does not seem possible, since we have no insight into the development of the unconscious in the first months of life. With his theory of the evolution of the sense of value, *Huxley* openly contradicts himself. "Value," "perfection," "the most desirable direction of evolution," are concepts which can only be correlated to purposes; he has informed us elsewhere, however, that "it is we who have to read purpose into evolution." That this represents a *petitio principii,* namely, a procedure in which a premise consists in a postulate, is unconsciously admitted by *Huxley* himself, since he ends with the surprised question whether his excursion into the field of ethics has not "merely brought us back to the blend of Christian and humanistic universalism characteristic of the ethics of Western civilization." [6]

11. The Impairment of Human Nature

Natural law ethics is realistic. In the course of our discussion we have repeatedly had to emphasize the limitations under which the law of nature works and to refer to the defects of man's understanding and will as well as to the power of the "less human elements" in human nature. Christian anthropology is prevented from idealizing human nature by the doctrine of original sin. Human nature is impaired: man still possesses a rational nature, but he cannot presume himself to be in possession of unerring knowledge of good and of a willing propensity toward it. Natural law, in the sense of the law of man's rational nature, continues to operate through the natural conscience with its perceptions of good and evil, of right and wrong, and as an impulse to act in accordance with them; furthermore, man has retained the power to comprehend reality insofar as this is indispensable to the understanding of the fundamental demands of natural law concerning individual and social life. Man has

[5] J. Huxley, *Evolutionary Ethics,* 1943, pp. 14 ff., 27, 41 f.
[6] *Ibid.,* p. 53.

to struggle toward such understanding, however, with darkened sight and contrary inclinations. Thus, natural law ethics with its realistic anthropology firmly maintains the operation of natural law while being aware of its impairment and taking account of this when inquiring into the nature and order of society.

Traditional natural law theory finds the confirmation of this view of human nature and the functioning of natural law in the teaching of *St. Paul* (Rom. 2:14 ff.), where it is stated that the Gentiles, though they have no revealed (Mosaic) law, are guided by their conscience with its natural insight and its natural impulse: "When the Gentiles who have no law do by nature what the Law prescribes, these having no law are a law unto themselves. They show the work of the Law written in their hearts. Their conscience bears witness to them, and so do their thoughts which accuse and excuse one another: laid open on the day when, according to my gospel, God will judge the hidden secrets of man through Jesus Christ." [1]

Its realistic attitude, founded on its doctrine of original sin, prevents natural law ethics from falling victim to any social utopianism. Thus, the

[1] From the Protestant viewpoint, the interpretation as suggested by the context of Rom. 2:14 f., regarding natural law, is disputed on the ground that "certain pagans, thanks to the renewal of heart which has occurred in them, do the will of God without Law" and hence "they are mentioned as just for their active obedience" (Felix Flückiger, *Geschichte des Naturrechts,* 1954, pp. 295 f.). In his thorough discussion of Flückiger's book, Hans Reiner, *Archiv für Rechts- und Sozialphilosophie,* Vol. XLI, n. 4, 1955, pp. 528–61, objects that Flückiger has not really attempted a proof for his interpretation of the passage, for such a proof would have to be drawn from the whole early Christian tradition concerning the view taken of this passage. Flückiger himself admits (*op. cit.,* p. 295) that the passage "is constantly interpreted in the sense of the stoic idea of natural law and serves for a biblical justification of the natural law theory," but argues (*op. cit.,* p. 387) that Augustine in later years rejected the natural law interpretation of the passage which he had accepted in his earlier days. What Flückiger has not done with regard to early Christian tradition Reiner undertakes to a great extent, with the conclusion: "The supposed testimony of the later Augustine, thus extolled by Flückiger, against natural law theory, utterly collapses. On the whole the thorough inquiry into the interpretation of Rom. 2:14 f. by the Fathers, which Flückiger omits, yields *a comprehensive picture of a biblically based assumption of a natural moral insight.* In this way the passage is clearly enough explained by Justin and Irenaeus; it is then found unanimously interpreted expressly in this sense by Tertullian and Origen, later by Hilary, Ambrose, and Chrysostom, and finally by Augustine and Theodoretus" (*op. cit.,* p. 553). On the doctrine of the Apostle Paul cf. Rudolf Schnackenburg, *Die sittliche Botschaft des neuen Testaments,* 1954, pp. 202–208. From Protestant literature, we may mention C. H. Dodd, *The Epistle of Paul to the Romans* (in: The Moffat New Testament Commentary), 1932, pp. 36 f.: "For Paul the Mosaic Law is the most complete revelation of the will of God there is, in terms of precepts and prohibitions; but the 'law of nature' is not a different law, but only a less precise and complete revelation of the same eternal law of right and wrong. . . . Nor is this a merely formal admission in passing: he makes use of it in his argument that a good pagan is better than a bad Jew (2:25). . . . We note this as against the doctrines of 'total depravity' and the complete impotence of the will, which have been attributed to Paul." Similarly the Norwegian Protestant Bishop E. Berggrav, *Der Staat und der Mensch,* 1946, p. 48, says that the sentence from Paul "meant the welding together of natural law and the law of God."

reality of human nature condemns every belief in flawlessly perfect social and economic systems: *every social system possesses its social question.* Because of this realism, natural law ethics (in contrast with the liberalist belief in the harmony of interests) emphasizes the unceasing duty of social reform falling upon every society. In the light of the fact of original sin, then, the maxim that politics is "the art of the possible" acquires a deeper sense. On the other hand, political realism, regarded as such, is the very opposite of political opportunism with its principle of following the line of least resistance; for natural law ethics makes it a duty of the community to put forth the utmost effort to achieve "the possible" in practice, and hence establishes an inspiring and potent "social idealism." A second unmistakable conclusion for natural law ethics is to be derived from the doctrine of original sin: all social reform, that is, the effort to achieve a more perfect order of political, economic, and social life, is inevitably dependent upon the moral reform of man himself. Hence, natural law ethics opposes the idea (which underlies especially the communistic and socialistic faith in the future) that the betterment of men is to be expected from the reform of the social system as an automatic result. The *realism* of natural law ethics is accordingly as far removed from a one-sided *pessimism* as from a one-sided *optimism* in the interpretation of human nature.

An Exclusively Theological Anthropology?

In contrast with the view just set forth, according to *Luther* human nature has been wholly under the influence of sin since the Fall: man is incapable by himself of realizing the moral order and is wholly dependent upon guidance by faith and the healing powers of grace. According to *earlier Protestantism,* the morality which belongs to the realm of faith is only that of individual life, not that of social order. It rests entirely with the social authority to establish order in those external spheres, and the individual is bound to comply with it since social authority is thus charged with the execution of divine Providence. *R. Niebuhr,* the American Protestant theologian, does not hesitate to speak of *Luther's* "curiously perverse" social ethics and his "defeatism in the realm of social morality," in which he sees a cause of the cult of the authoritarian state and of the progress of the "tyranny" of nationalism in Germany.[2] The older Protestantism saw in the surrender of economic and cultural life to the secular powers, which was implicit in its Protestant ethic, a release of energies in the service of progress, and hence a constructive influence on culture ("cultural Protestantism"). The paradox was that Protestant pessimism and rationalistic optimism, in regard to the conception of human nature, coincided in their belief in the progress of civilization. The optimism of the enlightenment attributed to reason an unlimited ability to attain the true and the good by its own powers. Hence arose the belief in unlimited progress in the intellectual and material spheres which distinguishes nineteenth-century humanism. Undoubtedly,

[2] R. Niebuhr, *The Nature and Destiny of Man,* 1941, Vol. II, pp. 201 ff.

considerable energies were set in motion in all spheres of civilization by the rigid secularization of the social sphere in accordance with Protestant ethics. The resultant split between civilization and morality, between religion and life, because it was in conflict with the law of civilization decreed in the natural law, was inevitably revealed as an error producing the crisis of civilization, which soon manifested itself.

If the doctrine of original sin thus gave rise to a cleavage between older Protestantism and Catholicism in regard to social ethics, a similar cleavage in the opposite direction has emerged with the change of attitude in *more recent Protestantism.*[3] According to modern Protestantism the rules for social ethics are to be derived only from the word of God which is found in Holy Scripture, because as a result of the Fall man's intellect has become incapable of instituting order in the various spheres of social life. Starting from theological principles this ethic reaches a conception of human nature which excludes the possibility for the mind of discovering an order intrinsically designed, and therefore rules out any philosophical ethics (such as natural law ethics tries to be), admitting only theological ethics (cf. below, Chap. 12). Obviously the dispute with this theological anthropology must take place on a theological level,[4] which I do not consider to be the task of the present study in natural law ethics. A few references to clarify the basis of our ethics seem, however, to be necessary.

In connection with the discussion of the doctrine that man is made in God's image, the *imago-Dei* doctrine, *Helmut Thielicke* says concerning the idea of human nature: "I can speak of 'natural' law and, in the developed sense, of 'nature,' only if in reference to sin I assume a merely limited disturbance, and in no case a complete perversion or a loss of this likeness"; the fundamental requirement is lacking for a natural law owing to the "impossibility of recognizing an order of being." Hence, *Thielicke* reaches the conclusion, in discussing the "axiom of the primal *ordo*" *suum cuique:* "Certainly there is due to each person a *suum,*" but "the *suum* is known only to God, and, as a corollary, this *suum* cannot be found by men in an ontological order." The function of theological ethics, therefore, can be only a negative one: "As far as a theological ethics or the Church authorities are concerned it must accordingly be simply a question of setting certain anthropological limits to economic or political or other objectified purposes (*sachlichkeit*), but admitting at the same time a

[3] R. Niebuhr, "A Protestant Looks at Catholics," in *Catholicism in America,* G. N. Schuster, editor (New York), 1954, pp. 30 ff., says, concerning American conditons, that the tension between Protestantism and Catholicism is due not least to their respective attitudes in applying natural law principles to social life, the main issues being principles of marriage and family life, viz. questions of divorce and birth control. Strict natural law ideas represent an introjection of stoic or Aristotelian rationalism into the highly dynamic ethics of biblical religion; the foundation of this ethics is the twofold law of charity. On birth control Niebuhr says that nothing is more obviously true than the assertion that in sexual relations nature aims at reproduction; he considers, however, that the freedom of the human person should take precedence somehow over the primary ends of nature; naturally, the abuse of the new freedom is possible; this attitude to natural law theory does not mean that we surrender to a moral relativism or even nihilism. But what does "somehow" mean?

[4] For the Catholic viewpoint cf. Josef Fuchs, S.J., *Lex Naturae: Zur Theologie des Naturrechts,* 1955; also: Albert Auer, O.S.B., *Der Mensch hat recht: Naturrecht auf dem Hintergrund von heute,* 1956, pp. 194–210.

definite range of possible solutions." Does not this raise the question how theological ethics and the Church can set "anthropological" limits to objectified purposes in the sphere of social and cultural order, if there exists for the mind the "impossibility of recognizing an order of being," which must be that of purposes borne out by essential reality. And with regard to the "anthropological limits" in the revealed word of God, only fundamental values are spoken of, but nothing is said about the details of their implications in view of social and historical institutions (note in the following chapter what *Wendland* thinks about this): faith and charity do not inform directly concerning what is commanded, what is good and right, what is permissible—that is to say, with regard to the conditions and consequences of a given action. But with the help of reason we must seek to attain clarity concerning the way in which to conform with faith and charity in our moral conduct. And is not man bidden by God's own word (cf. Gen. 1:28; 3:23) to use his reason in order to carry out the tasks set before him in the light of his social, historical, and cultural milieu?

It seems to be an inherent error in the basic attitude of Protestant ethics that it is able to regard man only as a being concerned with salvation; thus, exclusively as an individual and not also in his social and historical reality. If one starts with the idea that man's existence as a civilized being is possible only in society, then hardly any question of the knowability of the ontological order can arise: truly human existence would never have been possible in the half a million years of pre-Christian history had not human nature of itself striven toward an order of existence, and that because of the capacity belonging to human nature to apprehend genuine human existence and because of the impulse to bring about the social prerequisites of such existence. In other words, the *suum cuique* basically obtains content in detail in the simple relationships of the family community, by means of the desire for happiness proper to man's nature and of the consequent impulsion toward an order providing for the good of all (cf. Chap. 3, n. VI). What reason enables man to accomplish in uncomplicated society, scientific reason enables him to accomplish in complicated society, namely, the analysis of the general good and the ascertainment of its implications concerning the *suum* of the various social groups. When, therefore, *Thielicke* says, "Thus, here we stand before a crisis of the idea of reality in general; to tackle the problems involved is one of the most pressing tasks of evangelical ethics," he seems to be raising a fundamental question of evangelical ethics which has hitherto scarcely been perceived or dealt with.[5]

In fact, there remain *two epistemological questions for Protestant ethics* to answer. The first is the quite concrete question: If knowledge of the ontological order, as *Thielicke* holds, is simply impossible, what is it that anthropology and especially the social sciences are learning about when they investigate the biological and psychological sides of human nature and its modes of functioning in the various social institutions, such as family, state, social economy, international community; what relationship does the idea of the reality of evangelical-

[5] H. Thielicke, *Theologische Ethik,* Vol. I, 1951, pp. 62, 613, 682 ff., 712. One awaits an answer to Thielicke's question on the conception of reality in his paper, "Was ist Wahrheit?" (read at the inauguration of the theological faculty of Hamburg University in 1954). He deals, however, only with the status of theological knowledge as such.

theological ethics bear to these sciences of human reality? The second question is: How is theological knowledge possible if reason is wholly inadequate and incapable as Protestant ethics assumes? For it is only through reason that man can receive the word of God.

The fact that evangelical ethics has not freed itself from the natural law idea may be seen from *Thielicke's* own words: "Notwithstanding the impossibility of getting to know an order of being and notwithstanding the resulting crisis of natural law, it is fundamental that the question of that order remain a living one and that, as it were, an impulse toward natural law be preserved." [6] What meaning can be given to the question regarding this order if the impossibility of discovering it is accepted? [7] (Cf. also Chap. 12.)

12. Christian Moral Law

Christian moral law differs from natural moral law in that the latter is given to man through natural revelation, while the former comes about through supernatural revelation. In the one the will of the Creator is made known through man's nature, in the other by the direct word of God. In substance, however, even in its social ethical bearing, Christian moral law goes only a little way beyond natural moral law. In the Decalogue, confirmed and expounded by the teaching of Christ and the apostles, no more is laid down (apart from the Third Commandment) than is contained in natural law itself. Insofar as the ethics of Christ point to higher standards of moral and religious life (e.g., in the evangelical counsels), a special vocation is demanded. The law given by the express word of God has a twofold significance for moral understanding: first, man receives a positive clarity and certitude regarding the insights of his natural conscience; secondly, supernatural revelation provides man with a full and clear understanding of his true nature, the importance of which is obvious in view of the fact that he is greatly inclined to regard as "natural" wrong features in his nature, which are really due to the impairment of his nature by original sin. For, supernatural revelation

[6] *Ibid.*, p. 687.

[7] That natural law doctrine had its well-established place in early Protestant tradition was shown by the historian Clemens Bauer, "Die Naturrechtslehre Melanchthons," in *Hochland* 1951–52, pp. 313–23. This early tradition is all the more significant because "Melanchthon's theological life work, after the Lutheran Reformation had become a church, for long represented the theology of Lutheranism." Bauer comes to the conclusion: "Thus Melanchthon's natural law doctrine bears all the essential features of a Christian natural law. It rests upon the broad foundation of a natural theology and has as its central thought the objective divine order of creation. Natural moral law, a primal canon of all human law, and fundamental institutions of human coexistence lie side by side in this natural law." If German Protestantism would turn back to natural law, concludes Bauer, this would accordingly represent only a "revival." Emil Brunner, *Gerechtigkeit*, 1943, pp. 104 ff., also stresses the early Protestant tradition in natural law: "The reformers, who in a new understanding of 'God's justice' made a break with the tradition of a thousand years without hesitation, yet unanimously applied the concept of natural law, as presented by the Fathers and the scholastics, as an integral constituent of their social ethics."

informs man unmistakably of the spiritual character of his soul and its immortality, of God as his Creator, Judge, and last End.[1]

An Exclusively Theological Ethics?

Until quite recent times ethics had been conceived of as a "philosophic" science, namely, one based on rational arguments, as "moral philosophy." Today, in the Protestant view, only the possibility of a "theological' ethics is recognized (for reasons which were mentioned in the preceding chapter; cf. what was said there about *Thielicke's* view); consequently, an altogether new orientation of the Protestant attitude to social order has sprung up. The *older* Protestantism placed the centre of gravity of morality wholly in personal life, and hence thought in terms of individual ethics; since the end of the First World War, criticism has set in against this viewpoint from the Protestants themselves. "In old Protestantism," says *G. Wehrung* in his comprehensive discussion of the fundamentals of a Protestant ethics, "it was presupposed that the Christians led their tranquil lives under the protection of a patriarchal authority and had hardly occasion or opportunity for world-shaking decision; it sufficed if they adhered to the accustomed elementary moral precepts." [2] In line with the already well-advanced reorientation, *Ernst Wolf* says: "Contrary to the frequently expressed view that Luther's ethics is 'individual ethics in the real sense' . . . according to which the individual man realizes his relation to God in his own personality and inwardness, it is essentially social ethics," since

[1] N. Monzel, *Was ist christliche Gesellschaftslehre?* (Munich, inaugural lecture), 1956, pp. 7, 20, disputes the account given by me in the first edition of this book and elsewhere, which is the same as that given above, of the relationship between natural and Christian moral law. In his opinion, "the supernatural-Christian Revelation contains a surplus of socially significant value-determinations and purposes over and above natural or natural-law social ethics" (*ibid.*, p. 8). In my view I believe I am at one with the whole tradition of Christian social teaching since Augustine and Thomas Aquinas (on this cf. Chap. 5, note 8) and also with modern thinkers such as Cardinal J. H. Newman (cf. Messner, *Kulturethik*, pp. 386 f.) and Wilhelm Schwer, whom Monzel with emphasis names as his teacher. Indeed, Schwer, *Katholische Gesellschaftslehre,* 1928, p. 142, writes: "Even in the sphere of redemption and its operation of grace natural law remains the foundation of human social order. It is neither rendered superfluous by it, nor devalued nor replaced by it. *From faith, grace, and from conscience enlightened by grace there emerge no new insights into the fundamental laws of social life, but only new forces in order to attain perfectly the ends set out in its nature-rooted institutions*" (my italics, J. M.). Not only is my view in harmony with that of Schwer, regarding the relationship between natural and Christian moral law, but also regarding the *distinction between insights and forces,* which are imparted by the supernatural Christian reality of Revelation. Monzel, for example, speaks of tender care for the biologically and culturally inferior (*op. cit.*, p. 15) as a specific theme of Christian social doctrine; that, however, the claims of charity in question are accessible to natural reason is shown by the statements of an atheistic biologist like J. B. S. Haldane, already quoted in the first as in this edition of this book (cf. Chap. 147). Charity is, in fact, as I maintain, "the supreme natural social principle" (cf. Chap. 53; cf. also J. Fuchs, S.J., *Lex naturalis: Zur Theologie des Naturrechts,* 1955, pp. 163 f.), and as such also an object of natural knowledge. The "new forces" (Schwer) in the spheres of social life and knowledge which arise from supernatural faith have been emphasized by all exponents of Christian social theory at all times, and also by the present writer, as Chapters 57 ad 67 (taken over materially unchanged from the first edition) show.

[2] G. Wehrung, *Welt und Reich: Grundlegung und Aufbau der Ethik,* 1952, p. 323.

morality is a testimony to God's redemptive act, and "Christian freedom" with *Luther* "means the rights due to each and the duties imposed upon each in his station in relationship to others." [3]

"The first bold approach to an evangelical political ethics for centuries" is the way *Wehrung* justly describes the works of *Georg Wünsch* on political and economic ethics. *Wünsch* expresses his fundamental idea in this way: "The Kingdom of God as an ever present obligation exists for the believer in his earthly existence only as an order of creation; for he knows that it is the same God who commands through the order of creation and who has prepared his Kingdom of hope as the goal of history. . . . But along with [this knowledge is the fact that] the Christian ethics of political life is an affair of the order of creation, not of the Kingdom of God; rather, service in the Kingdom of God, which is not to be regulated by man, is accomplished in obedience toward the immanently self-promulgating order of creation, under God's leadership, through the medium of concrete needs." [4] Concerning *Wünsch's* work, *Wehrung*, however, thinks it necessary to say that, according to *Wünsch*, everything would bind us to creation and to its orders, and all that we have to recognize as God's leadership would be the historical destiny imposed upon us; it would be impossible to draw positive rules for our conduct from what lies beyond human existence and creation; "hence, the growth of the order of creation and growth into the other world is supposed to lie on different levels and proceed on their courses without any approximation of one to the other." In *Wehrung's* view this provides no real answer to the question: What does belief in the Kingdom of God mean for ethics? Leadership through historical necessity actually exists, says *Wehrung*, "but it still calls for a different historical leadership, we call it Revelation, and it discloses to the believer under what destiny all our lives stand." *Wehrung* also seeks to assign its place to the order of creation as such: God does not come to meet us directly in an explicitly declared will, "but first in the ordinances, in virtue of which he lets man share in his work and in which he combines and shapes their common life." Therefore, Wehrung concludes: "If God by his order of creation keeps hold of man quite generally in his conscience, then *natural morality,* at least a *knowledge of God's will gained by natural reason,* with which Luther deals sometimes, is manifest"; [5] *Wehrung* thereby seeks for Protestant social ethics a way which links reason and faith.

On the other hand, *Walter Bienert* in his book, which testifies to a strong Christian ethos, lays the emphasis wholly on divine guidance; the Christian ethos operating through responsibility to Christ and by virtue of the Holy Spirit in the faithful must penetrate and, according to need, reshape existing social institutions: "The quest for the 'Christian' economic or social order has gone so far astray because these dimensions do not exist; instead the Holy Spirit constantly impels man toward new social orders founded on Scripture. But then the Christians also have to concern themselves about a continuous permeation of economic and social life by the Christian ethos and to pray for the constant coming of the creative Spirit." However, "the work-ethos of the Bible is an ethos of believers for believers. It is, therefore, not to be conveyed

[3] Ernst Wolf, "Sozialethik bei Luther," in *Evangelisches Soziallexikon,* 1954, pp. 684 f.; cf. Franz Xavier Arnold, *Zur Frage des Naturrechts bei Martin Luther,* 1937.

[4] G. Wünsch, *Evangelische Ethik des Politischen,* 1936, pp. 90 f.

[5] G. Wehrung, *op. cit.,* pp. 44 ff., 82 ff.

with rational perspicuity like a philosophical ethics; for, this ethos is prefaced by the claim to be grounded in suprarational Revelation. It is an ethos of those who place themselves under this Revelation. That is why it cannot be realized in a secularized world, for instance with the intention of thereby achieving a remedy for social and moral ills. It can be practiced only by a community of believers. This community is then all the more obliged to live and to practice this ethos." [6] In spite of the emphasis which, as mentioned above, he lays on "natural morality," *Wehrung* also reaches similar conclusions: it is a serious temptation for theological ethics to refer the Christian conscience to the general, audibly speaking moral law; in Christ a new and higher power is made manifest: "Hence, the Christian is no longer ruled by law but by the Spirit, the Spirit of Christ, the Holy Spirit of God, who is not to be confused with reason and who also redeems reason"; and, "so also the conscience of the Christian is no longer directed toward a comprehensive law (to be discovered by reason) under the guidance of which it must learn to know what is prescribed for it. The life movement which bears it along gives it the direction of action, it contains all necessary indications"; "He who lives in constant converse with and before God can confidently hope that along with the magnitude of the difficulty he will also be shown its solution." [7]

In view of the doctrines of *Bienert* and *Wehrung* the question arises whether or not with them social ethics is again becoming simply individual ethics, for it does not go beyond the attitude of the individual in social life, whereas social ethics is above all concerned with social order as such, i.e. with the institutional side. Furthermore, the sphere of social ethics is not touched upon by concentrating attention on "charity as an obligatory motive of work," which "draws one's neighbor into a community of love," in order, as St. Paul says, "to take care of the weak" and "to give to those in need." *Bienert* also envisages "relationships immanent in reality," which are the "expression of conduct related to the community (church)," since the work-ethos in question is narrowed down expressly to that of believers in the community of believers. When Bienert finally attributes the efficacy of the Christian ethos to the fact that the Christian submits to the *hodegesis* and *kybernesis* of the Holy Spirit, and says that the Holy Spirit "constantly urges on a new social order founded on Scripture," one wonders where precise indications for such a social order are to be found in Scripture, especially since the quest for the "Christian" economic or social order is so decisively rejected as mistaken. Even though *Wehrung* expects everything from the "life-movement," which keeps hold upon the Christian conscience, and from the signpost given directly by God to the conscience, nevertheless, everything is left to intention (*gesinnung*), concerning which *Georg Wünsch* emphatically declares: "With intention, in general, no moral conflicts are solved, nor is the problem of economic systems for the Christian economic ethics—they are only blurred." [8]

The question of social ethics as an ethics of social order seems to be of special urgency to Protestant thinkers in connection with *"the Church's claim*

[6] W. Bienert, *Die Arbeit nach der Lehre der Bibel: Eine Grundlegung evangelischer Sozialethik,* 1954, pp. 389, 400 ff.

[7] Wehrung, *op. cit.,* pp. 321 ff., 331.

[8] G. Wünsch, *Evangelische Wirtschaftsethik,* 1927, pp. 512, 517; *Sozialismus aus christlichem Gewissen,* 1949.

to publicity," which has begun to gain momentum in German Protestantism since the end of the Establishment. This claim, according to *Ernst Wolf*, consists in the church's claim to competence in public life, "in virtue of its responsibility for the world," which means "the processes and arrangements, functions and needs of public life." He refers to the Stockholm Conference (1925) and the endeavor in progress since then to "tackle the questions of public weal and social needs." [9] At the World Conference at Oxford in 1937 the object was, as *Wilhelm Menn* explains, "to work out fundamental imperatives which could be expounded as Christian demands in face of the existing situation. It was clearly seen that particular rules could be arrived at only if one were fully conversant with the technical side of things, but also that one could not keep to generalities such as that of the 'Golden Rule.' The task would be to find imperatives which lie midway between general propositions of an abstract kind and special demands for the individual case." Concerning the World Conference in Evanston (1954) *Menn* says that tensions similar to those of Stockholm in 1925 were revealed, "in the meeting between Anglo-Saxon activism and the Continental European viewpoint," in which connection, "in face of the eschatological orientation of the European theologians, in America and elsewhere a serious anxiety was aroused lest the church should succumb as before to that false conservatism which withdraws from true responsibility toward those very social questions and tasks." [10]

With the above quoted reference to the Oxford Conference, namely, that it is a question of "midway between general fundamental propositions of an abstract kind and special demands for the individual case" and, in this regard, of complete familiarity with the technical side of things, it seems that the due place of social ethics is accorded to the natural order (the order of creation), which is inferred from reason, and to the order of the Kingdom of God, which is inferred from faith. One would hardly be wrong in supposing that such considerations were of some influence in the ideas which *Wehrung* attributes especially to *E. Brunner*, in that "use is made more or less explicitly of natural law thinking." And *Wehrung* adds in a conciliatory vein: "Evangelical theologians may be glad to make a conciliatory gesture to Catholic theology, which believes that it possesses in the natural law foundation of its world-wide ethos a portion of the *philosophia perennis*, a bulwark which, tested through centuries of trial, has resisted all storms and disintegrating tendencies." [11]

The Oxford Protestant theologian, *Nathaniel Micklem*, well-known for his books, *The Theology of Politics* and *The Theology of Law*, writes in the former book about the connection he considers to exist between the natural order and the Kingdom of God, between faith and reason; the Christian faith is revelation superadded upon common sense (common sense meaning moral reason). *Micklem* continues by saying that, in these chapters, he is relatively little concerned with Revelation but much more with common sense; for what is conceived there as the Christian doctrine of society or the idea of Christendom is but an exalted or quickened expression of that *philosophia perennis* or unchanging

[9] E. Wolf, "Öffentlichkeitsansprüche der Kirche," in *Evangelisches Soziallexikon*, 1954, pp. 586 f.

[10] W. Menn, *Soziale Frage in der Ökumene*, pp. 781 ff.

[11] G. Wehrung, *op. cit.*, p. 201; Wehrung refers especially to E. Brunner's essay, "Das Menschenbild und die Menschenrechte," in *Universitas*, 1947.

philosophy of which Plato, Aristotle and Cicero, as well as St. Thomas Aquinas, are the representatives. Of course he stresses also that reason is not enough, that with the discovery of the coincidence of the law of nature and the Decalogue, natural morality was recognized as the dictate of an omnipotent, transcendent will, and that fallen nature needs the powers of redemption in order to attain to social patterns worthy of man and of Christian man.[12] Among German Protestants the controversy continues. *Walter Künneth*, because of the power of the demoniac forces in this world which prevent reason from attaining knowledge of the primal order of creation, considers only an eschatological mode of thinking, concentrating entirely on the New Man in Christ, to be justified.[13]

On the other hand, *Heinz-Dietrich Wendland* regards it as the first duty of theological ethics "to learn to understand the revolutionary dynamic of the social process," a duty "to which the traditional social-ethical concepts do not measure up." The social-ethical directions of the New Testament are transitory insofar as they refer to a definite historical and social situation: "It is in fact not the meaning of the New Testament message that we should always merely repeat the first beginnings of primitive Christian 'social doctrine.'" Although to the theological mind the "world" is indeed the realm of Satan, it is also the creation of God, to whose order is due "its intrinsic mode of being, because of its institution by God"; hence, "the ontological question about being must arise." Furthermore, "being in Christ must become historical existence in time and place, in social institutions, in historical inheritance." In regard to the social demands put forward at the World Conference at Evanston, *Wendland* asks whether they "are not entirely demands of social reason and humanity, which are universally perceptible and require no special Christian basis"; because they are demands for the sake of "the humanity of man," they are also under the eschatological law of love and are protected from demonization; "In this sense it is true that eschatological and natural law thinking are not in contradiction"; "*We must get away from the paralyzing opposition between eschatology and natural law.*" *Wendland* sees it as an important practical conclusion that *for Christians and non-Christians there exist a wide field of collaboration in realizing the demands of social humanism.*[14]

13. The Human Person

As a being capable of responsibility by virtue of his freedom, his capacity for self-determination, man possesses the dignity of a person. Hence, freedom is the distinguishing mark of his nature. With the responsibility for truly human existence which is accordingly his, moral good becomes the good of the human person as such. Natural law ethics, therefore, is in a special sense "personalistic" ethics. The development of the human

[12] N. Micklem, *The Theology of Politics*, 1941, pp. 54, 62, 158 ff.; *The Theology of Law*, 1949.

[13] W. Künneth, *Politik zwischen Dämon und Gott*, 1954.

[14] H.-D. Wendland, *Die Kirche in der modernen Gesellschaft: Entscheidungsfragen für das kirchliche Handeln im Zeitalter der Massenwelt*, 1956, pp. 19, 34, 58, 85–103, 144 ff.

"person" is, in the light of this ethics, man's *self-realization* in accordance with the order indicated in his "nature." And as natural law directs man toward the world of absolute values in the process of this self-realization, *self-transcendence* belongs to the innermost impulsion of his nature. Indeed, with the return of an increasing portion of modern philosophy to a metaphysical anthropology, a number of philosophers, including *Scheler* notably, have sought the uniqueness and distinction of man in his capacity for self-transcendence.

If the expression of the idea is new, the idea itself has in substance always been part and parcel of natural law philosophy. *St. Thomas Aquinas,* for example, speaks of two ways in which man can transcend himself by virtue of his spirit: first, by means of his intellect, which enables him to range over the entire world and to ascend to God; secondly, by means of his will, which enables him to strive after the good as such and to rise by love, the fundamental impulse of his nature, to the Supreme Good. Nothing bears clearer testimony to the moral dignity of man than the fact that his self-transcendence is at the same time a self-realization. But this also involves man's existential risk: man alone is capable of transcending himself, and he alone is capable of *self-degradation.* Man alone can abase and thus abuse himself. The animal cannot do this; it must follow its instincts and always be what its nature determines it to be. Man can, however, employ his instincts for purposes at variance with the ends designed in them by nature and with the general end of his person.[1]

Man's integration in the "good will" (cf. Chap. 5), that is, in the morally good person, is the creative human act par excellence. Created in the *image of God,* since man's natural law is a participation in the eternal law, man must perfect himself by developing that image of God in himself. It is in the fact of being the image of God that the human person finds the measure of what he is ultimately meant to be. What he thus finds as potentiality in his nature must become reality in his person. In this, however, his nobility is not yet exhausted. Although all men are called to

[1] In this possibility of self-debasement in man's nature lies the root of his sense of shame. Vladimir Solovyof, the great Russian thinker, sees in the sense of shame which distinguishes man from the whole animal world one of the essential characteristics of man's nature. "In being ashamed of his own natural inclinations and organic functions," he says, "man proves that he is not merely a material being, but is something other and higher" (*The Justification of the Good: An Essay on Moral Philosophy,* trans. by N. A. Duddington, 1918, p. 29). In face of the nineteenth-century belief in the autonomy of man Solovyof stood out among philosophers with his defense of the conviction that human nature has an inherent vocation to self-transcendence. He finds a second feature in human nature which testifies to this vocation, namely, man's instinct of pity, which links him with the whole living world (*ibid.,* pp. 28 ff., 59–77). With this he has made a contribution to the analysis of human nature which, one may say, could only come from the Russian temper of mind. Self-transcendence he finds also indicated by a third characteristic in human nature, the feeling of reverence for something which man knows to be higher, a feeling connected with the impulse toward "inward voluntary submission to the superhuman principle" (*ibid.,* pp. 34 ff.).

this assimilation with God, when realized, the divine image will not be the same in individuals. Every man is a particular idea of God, translated into reality by the special act by which the soul is created, with his own special dispositions and conditions for development, including mental and bodily qualities, hereditary and acquired aptitudes and disabilities, the functioning of the biochemical processes of his organism with their psychological reactions, and, not least, environment. All of this forms the "material" out of which the individual has to form his moral personality and with which he has to actualize the thought of God in himself. And God also desires to be loved in a particular way by each man, as by an individual person bearing his image in himself. Thus, God desires from every man an intimate love which is the expression of the whole personality; to this he responds with an intimate personal love which human speech can only symbolize in terms of the love of the betrothed, as we see in the Canticles and in the writings of the mystics.

Man, therefore, although he is a means for the glorification of God, the supreme end of creation, is also an *end in himself;* so true is this that, after endowing man with freedom, God himself cannot make man a mere instrument except by man's own will. Only when he finally makes himself an instrument of created ends does man become, by undergoing the punishment of final separation from God in order to restore the violated order, exclusively a means for the glorification of God, the final end of creation. But, *St. Augustine* says, so great in God's eyes is the dignity of the human person that, for the sake of man's freedom without which man's spirit could not be spirit and could not possess God in love, he has permitted *man's existential risk* of falling prey to evil and to eternal self-loss.[2]

The problem of the *freedom of the will* which confronts us here is a touchstone for every system of ethics. It must not stand as an extraneous body in the entire system, with no internal relation to the general account of morality which the system affords. Although an exhaustive treatment of the problem is out of the question here, we must indicate the direction in which we seek the solution. In the nineteenth century the freedom of the will was passionately disputed on the ground that it was scientifically impossible. Since then, however, the natural sciences have become more cautious. After a review of modern physics Sir *James Jeans* came to the conclusion that after three hundred years of research in physics no reason exists for departing from *Descartes*' view that free will is nothing else but "unconscious determinism." Nevertheless he admits: "The classical physics seemed to bolt and to bar the door leading to any sort of freedom of the will. The new physics hardly does this; it almost seems to suggest that the door may be unlocked—if only we could find the handle." [3] *Lenin* thought that modern physics afforded cogent reason

[2] Augustine, *De civ. Dei,* XXII, 1; *De libero arbitrio,* II, 3.
[3] Sir James Jeans, *Physics and Philosophy,* 1942, p. 216.

for an exactly opposite view, namely, that freedom of the will is conscious determinism: [4] acting in accordance with the necessities recognized in nature. The fact that such contrasting opinions can be expressed in the name of science is possible only because natural science is in no way competent to deliver any final pronouncement on free will. The door leading to the explanation of free will does not lie in the realm of physics; it is not, therefore, the physicist who will find the handle. Free will is not a phenomenon of physical causality, but one of life, of the life of the spirit, indeed of the rational will, and it must be explained as volitional causality and not as physical causality.

How does man's self-determination in the act of free will take place? Everybody would agree that the intellect of man is capable of comparing the goods which he desires, and hence of "valuing" them. The animal is able to do something similar, for example, when a dog chooses between different foods. But what man alone can do is to reflect on his choice. He can make the value-judgment underlying his choice itself the object of *reflection;* he can ask himself "why." Therefore, *St. Thomas* is certainly right in attributing decisive importance in the explanation of free will to the power of the intellect to *judge its own judgments, de suo iudicio iudicare.*[5] On the other hand, the will does not seem to be really free if it is able to act solely according to the judgment of the intellect and if it must automatically strive after an object which the value-judgment of the intellect presents as desirable.[6] This would give the intellect a function like that of a signal box, selecting and determining the track which the will with its motive power must then automatically follow. But the will is itself a spiritual faculty. As the psychologist knows, the will influences the judgments of the intellect. It can do this by moving instincts, emotions, passions, and habits to exert influence on the intellect in forming its judgment. The will can exclude or give special effect to whole groups of motives. Above all, man can do evil knowingly because it lies in his own power to use or not to use his knowledge of the good. *St. Thomas* himself points this out, referring with approval to the passage in the *Nicomachean Ethics* where *Aristotle* rejects *Socrates'* assumption

[4] Cf. Lenin, *Materialism and Empirio-Criticism,* p. 154. Following Engels, he says: "Freedom, therefore, consists in a mastery over ourselves and external nature founded upon the knowledge of the necessities of nature" (*ibid.,* p. 156). Note that Lenin's idea of acting in accordance with the recognized laws of nature constitutes an obvious *circulus vitiosus:* such acting presupposes the self-determination of the will.

[5] Cf. St. Thomas, *De veritate,* q. 24, a. 2.

[6] For a criticism of the scholastic theory of free will cf. Thomas Molina, *Das Leiden im Weltplan,* 1929; Johannes Auer, *Die menschliche Willensfreiheit im Lehrsystem des Thomas v. Aquin und Johannes Duns Scotus,* 1938; Auer points out that Scotus, unlike Thomas, thinks that "the will is spontaneously active like nature in general, but also free as nothing else is"; for "the will is self-moving, is free in respect to its purpose as in respect to its means"; he sums up significantly: "If we finally consider the result of the work we must say: The freedom of the will is a secret for the human mind, which wants not only to accept, but also to grasp, to penetrate, to understand" (*op. cit.,* pp. 286, 288, 300).

that knowledge is virtue and that evil is done from ignorance.[7] The will can make the knowledge of good ineffective.

The will, then, has influence on what is aptly called the *"primary decision."* As an example of this, the child who spontaneously decides not to reflect how nice the forbidden apples look or how good they would be has already gained the victory over the temptation to steal. The importance of the "primary decision" in the act of free will for education and for the conduct of life cannot be estimated highly enough. It may be objected that even in this primary decision the judging intellect is the determining factor, basing its discrimination on previous experience and on its realization that certain classes of motives are opposed to certain values. It is equally certain, however, that the training of the will by education is not only a training of the intellect to judge and to value rightly, but a real training of the strength of the will and its inclination toward good. The purpose of training the will is to enable it to turn toward moral good even when the intellect is not clearly and intensely aware of the motives for such conduct (e.g., during moments of strong passion). Furthermore the movement of the will toward the good is love, which is man's fundamental impulse; and we have learned from *St. Augustine* that through love itself man fully knows a good.[8] Hence, we come to the conclusion that intellect and will mutually influence each other and are both in operation together, as spiritual faculties, in the free act of the will: freedom of the will is not only the concern of the intellect but truly of the will itself.[9]

The self-determination of the will is a problem of the life of the spirit and therefore cannot be solved by the categories of cause and effect, which are more at home in the realm of natural science. Organic life has proved impatient of any explanation by the methods of physics; even more is this true of the life of the spirit. Life is the inherent power of self-movement in a being toward the intrinsic ends of its nature; freedom is the conscious power of self-movement of a spiritually endowed being in realizing the ends indicated in the impulses of its nature.[10] Man's free will is, therefore, the power to make the law of his nature the determining law of his conduct.

[7] Aristotle, *Nicomachean Ethics,* VII, 2, 3.

[8] Cf. Chap. 4, n. I and Chap 4, note 1, concerning affective knowledge.

[9] Our ideas on the problem of free will have nothing to do with voluntarism. Against the narrow emphasis on the role of intellect, however, we would say that this does not distinguish sharply enough between condition and causality. Certainly, awareness of a good or of several goods is the necessary condition if the will is to move in one direction or another, but as a spiritual faculty it possesses its own motive force. Informative on the problem from a scholastic point of view is R. Z. Lauer, "Bellarmine on Liberum Arbitrium," in *The Modern Schoolman* (St. Louis University), Jan., 1956, pp. 61–98. In the light of our analysis of the problem above, it seems very doubtful whether one can agree with the author in ascribing voluntarism to Robert Bellarmine because of the way in which he claims to find in free will, besides the role of the intellect, a genuine self-determination of the will.

[10] Freedom and morality, therefore, are not identical, as Kant, Fichte, and Hegel

Since the law of man's nature is bound up with his self-determination —his freedom—moral responsibility is of the essence of his nature; therefore, he is a person. Man's responsibility concerns the demands of the existential ends designed in his nature, and hence in his natural law. Here a whole new range of questions opens up: Do these ends and responsibilities belong to the individual alone? They would if man were capable of attaining full integration by his own resources. Is he so capable? With this question we pass from the discussion of the nature of man to the treatment of the *nature of society*.

---

suppose. The good does not spring from freedom in the sense of a creative self-determination of the autonomous reason, but freedom is the condition for the development of the good will; it is this that realizes the good. Our argument makes visible, however, the element of truth in the idealistic identification of freedom and morality: Freedom is indeed the potential, but not yet the actual good will. Against the rationalistic shifting of the perspective and the "scientific" narrowing of the problem of free will, Henri Bergson, with his conception of life, reached forward in two directions to the truth: 1) He saw the problem of freedom as that of "life," which belongs to a wholly different sphere from that of physical causality, in which scientific determinism sought the solution. 2) He showed at the same time where the root of the creative essence of freedom is to be sought: in the life of the spirit with the will as the faculty of the spirit coordinated with reason. Cf. H. Bergson, *Essai sur les données immédiates de la conscience,* 1889; *Evolution créatrice,* 1907.

PART TWO

The Nature of Society: Social Philosophy

---

14. Man's Social Nature

By nature man is as much a social being as he is an individual being. The nature of man as an individual person has been the object of our discussion hitherto. The proof that man is a social being is shown by facts which are beyond doubt to a mind open to reality. The first is his physical nature. With regard to his physical constitution he is incomparably more dependent on the family than is the brute, which, because of its natural equipment of instinct, protective covering, and means of defense, is much more fully capable of maintaining and developing itself from babyhood. Besides requiring completion because of the constitution of his bodily nature, man requires it by reason of his spiritual nature. The awakening and educating of his spiritual powers and faculties depend entirely upon his association with others, especially with the communities of family, tribe, nation, and state. In every respect the development of the spirit is dependent upon society. Society is needed in general for the development of the individual mind, particularly in the realms of religion and morals, but it is also needed in the realm of the sciences, literature, and of the arts. The individual development of the mind, therefore, is inseparably connected with the social.

It is surely one of *Hegel's* merits that he made it clear how the spiritual development of the individual is generally dependent on his being spiritually rooted in society, an observation opposed to the rationalism of the Enlightenment, which saw man as dependent only on himself and on his own reason, although *Hegel* claimed too self-subsistent a being for "objective mind." Neo-Hegelian trends in philosophy have more fully presented the development of the individual spirit and of social culture as a process of spiritual interaction—and hence a socially determined process—although they too betray the Hegelian one-sidedness. Recently, ethnology and cultural anthropology have done much to show how very farreaching an influence on man's spiritual formation is exercised by social tradition, the world of experience and knowledge handed down, modes of thought and imagination, beliefs regarding values and rights, customs and attitudes, which in their totality are operative in a society as a form of life.[1] By the gift of speech, the instrument of mental communication, which at first glance raises man above the animal as nothing else does, and which enables him fully to develop his faculties, nature, as *Aristotle* observes, has unmistakably shown that man is a social being.

Thus, man achieves full integration only in society; only through social completion can he fully develop his being as his nature demands.[2] Man's nature is predisposed for integration and hence for sociality. Indeed the instinct for social fellowship is one of the strongest impulses, if not the strongest fundamental impulse in human nature, for none of his other instincts can achieve satisfaction without fulfillment of the demands of this one. The need for completion underlies the whole range of man's nature. By means of this instinct, reason urges man on toward an order of social existence which will fulfill the purpose of his integration.[3] This purpose consists in making possible a completely human existence for all in accordance with the requirements of man's existential ends. Thus, man's nature is a social nature as well as an individual nature, so that *the social end is one of the fundamental existential ends.* Both sides of human nature are thus inseparably bound up: man's individual nature could not develop without social fellowship, and this could not bring him to a state of culture were he not an individual being with a psycho-physical nature and the needs of such nature, that is, its desire for fulfillment through values.

15. The Ontological Root of Society

What is the root of society? To answer this question we must obviously seek the reason in human nature why individual men require integration through mutual assistance and why they are made capable of this. It is agreed that men are alike in their essential nature, with the existential ends indicated therein linked to man's moral responsibility; it is also established that they are unlike in their individual nature by reason of their diverse qualities and faculties. The equality in men rests upon the equality of their spiritual-moral nature; in order to explain their

[1] Cf. J. Messner, *Kulturethik,* 1954, Chaps. 69–72, on civilization as a form of life, and the bibliography given there.

[2] Cf. St. Thomas Aquinas, *Summa contra Gent.,* III a, q. 117, a. 3: (*homo*) "Indiget ab aliis hominibus adjuvari ad consequendum finem"; or, in *Eth.,* lib. I, lect. 1: "Quia homo naturaliter est animal sociale utpote qui indiget ad suam vitam multis, quae sibi ipse solus praeparare non potest, consequens est, quod homo naturaliter sit pars alicuius multitudinis, per quam praestatur sibi auxilium ad bene vivendum."

[3] Hugo Grotius, the great heir of the traditional natural law doctrine, thus expresses its continuous teaching on this essential character of human nature (*De iure belli ac pacis,* Prolegomena 6): "Inter haec autem, quae homini sunt propria, est appetitus societatis, id est communitatis non qualiscumque sed tranquillae, et pro sui intellectus modo ordinatae."

inequality it seems necessary to lay stress on the bodily and sensory side of human nature. The human nature of the individual consists of body and spirit in undivided unity. The human spirit is provided with faculties reaching far beyond the realm of matter, namely, the faculties of comprehending the worlds of truth and value, of ascertaining principles of law in the external world, and of utilizing these in the effort to attain and to realize the values in which civilization consists—to rise in will and understanding into the world of the absolute and its cause, the divine nature, so that self-transcendence is a fundamental feature and a fundamental impulse of man (cf. Chap. 13). Man attains to integral human existence by the striving after values and culture engendered by his spiritual nature and encompassing the sensory, the moral, and the external worlds. Because of its union with the body, the human spirit can become active only by means of the body, whose capacity for action, however, is a limited one in comparison with the faculties and aspirations of the spirit. The spirit, bound up with matter in human nature, is subject to the limitations of matter; hence, the necessity for completion. But precisely because of its physical existence, individual human nature is also predisposed to completion. Consisting of a unity of body and spirit, human nature is individuated by particular qualities and faculties which make completion possible. By virtue of this individual inequality in powers and the identity of the ends proper to their essential nature, men are predisposed to combine their qualities and powers and to cooperate in order to attain to the integral human existence implied in these ends.[1] Thus, man's social nature is rooted in the special character of his human nature as a unity of body and spirit.

Since *Aristotle,* it has been the view of natural law philosophers that society is a reality specifically human, and that the suprahuman and subhuman spheres exclude society in this sense. Animals organize themselves by instinct into various forms of herd life; some, like ants and bees, are directed by their instincts into more or less complex forms of "social" cooperation. But the individual member of animal society is ready made by nature to fit into the whole almost as a part into a machine: its allotted function is part of its compelling instinct. Accordingly, even the highest forms of "social" life in the animal world can be called social only in an analogous sense, although such forms may "function" more perfectly in their own way precisely because their modes of functioning are more automatic in character. Like the nonspiritual being, the pure spirit, such

[1] The theory of individuation of the *philosophia perennis* as applied to human nature need not be discussed here in detail since it would not take us much further in our understanding of the issue in question. On the problem of individuation from a phenomenological point of view, which makes a significant step in the direction of further inquiry, according to which "matter-bound spiritual nature" is "spiritual nature in a state of becoming" (although the social limitation of this becoming is not investigated) cf. J. M. Hollenbach, S.J., *Sein und Gewissen: Eine Begegnung zwischen Martin Heidegger und Thomistischer Philosophie,* 1954, pp. 71 f., 82 f., 151, 338.

as the angel, is incapable of social life in the human sense; since it is fully equipped in itself for the attainment of its proper ends, it is self-sufficient and not predisposed toward completion through others. Thus, *Aristotle* comes very close to the truth with his conclusion: "He who is unable to live in society, or who has no need because he is sufficient for himself, must be either a beast or a god."[2] Only when a human person has absorbed all that social contact can give toward the fulfillment of his ultimate existential ends, and hence is fully capable of continued self-integration from his own resources (cf. Chap. 13), and has thereby outgrown the necessity of completion by society, may solitude provide for further development and even the necessary condition for the highest perfection.[3]

16. The Nature of Society

In the light of the foregoing, society is the association of men for mutual help in the attainment of the full humanity implied in the existential ends. They are associated in a cooperation based upon the need and capacity of the individual for completion. Mutual complementation brings to their combined endeavors a substantially greater effectiveness than the sum of their individual efforts could achieve. Protection against gangsterism, for instance, is beyond the powers of individuals, but becomes possible for them when they combine their forces in a political community. In economic life the fruits of labor are many times greater when the members of society work together in the form of the division of labor than they would be if each individual or family tried to produce its own requirements. Social cooperation, therefore, brings into being something *new*, in which all the members of society participate in the fulfillment of their purposes in life. Thus, society is more than a mere plurality of men, more than merely the peaceful coexistence of individuals; it is a supra-individual unity. It rests upon the active and passive sharing of individuals in the process and in the success of their mutual complementation. This success consists basically in fully human existence for all, to which each could not attain by himself: something essentially new which can only be achieved in social cooperation.

Upon the degree in which a particular society is essential for the integral human existence of the individual depends its ontological rank. Hence, the family is a society in a more substantial sense (viz., possessing fuller being) than the bridge club; the nationality (*volk*) in a more substantial sense than the joint stock company. For, societies like the family and the nationality are more directly demanded by natural im-

[2] Aristotle, *Politics,* I, 2, par. 14.

[3] Cf. St. Thomas Aquinas, *Summa theol.,* IIa IIae, q. 188, a. 8: "Vita socialis necessaria est ad exercitium perfectionis; solitudo autem competit jam perfectis."

pulses and are more indispensable for fully human existence than others; they are rooted, therefore, in more vital existential ends. Such impulses also express themselves in stronger bonds of sentiment and hence in social entities which are in a true sense called communities. We are accustomed to call the family and the nationality communities, but we would not so designate the bridge club or the joint stock company. Natural law philosophy has always drawn a distinction between natural, "necessary" societies which form communities in a narrower sense, and "voluntary" societies which are devoted to freely chosen purposes.

The metaphysical implications of this distinction have not always been fully traced. If, for example, too much stress is laid on conscious and deliberate purpose as an essential element of society (a viewpoint found in some textbooks of natural law theory), under such a concept it becomes impossible to subsume the nationality in the biological-cultural sense as a community. In fact, the nationality, although the awareness of a common purpose hardly exists, is a community in the radical sense of the word, and the formative factors which make it a community have a much stronger influence on the whole personality of its members than, for example, the state (cf. Chaps. 92–95). Besides, the very general conception of society as a permanent, conscious, and willed association of men for the attainment of common purposes covers the state and the family as well as the joint stock company and the bridge club. Only an eye blinded by the individualist social theory can fail to see the radical difference between these forms of society and can regard them as ontologically equivalent.[1] Of course, to a man with a mistaken idea of his true ends, the bridge club may be much more important subjectively than anything else, or a man may be prepared to sacrifice important interests of the state for the sake of the profits of his commercial company. A definition such as ours does not exclude less essential forms of society like the joint stock company or the bridge club, which are related to purposes not directly designed in nature but to purposes derived from these, and hence of an indirect character. It is no real criticism of our definition to say that even "societies" with perverse purposes, such as criminal gangs, must be comprised within a general definition. Such groups can be called societies only in an analogous sense, and social metaphysics in its interpretation of reality can treat them only as symptoms of degeneracy. Similarly, ethics need not give a definition of good or of virtue which includes evil or vice.

[1] Provided that the emphasis on electoral freedom in the formation of patterns of social life does not involve severing the links with the existential ends, a "liberal" conception of the state need not come into conflict with truth. Thus, Ernest Barker (*Reflections on Government,* 1942, p. 290) comments on the liberal English conception as opposed to the German: "We tend to make the state itself into a sort of club, and to extend the methods of the club into the management of the state. In Germany, it may be said, there is a tendency to make a club into a sort of state, and to extend the methods of the state into the management of clubs."

Particularly today metaphysics must undertake the task of clarifying the nature of social reality, because individualism and collectivism have created a mentality inclined toward grave misunderstanding of this reality. *Individualist* social theory conceives of society ultimately as an organization for self-chosen purposes, especially for the securing of such a sphere of freedom for the individual as is compatible with freedom of all. Freedom, not mutual completion through cooperation, is the root idea of individualist thinking. Hence, it tends to reduce the nature of society to a "*social contract*" and to emphasize the arbitrary element in all social forms, that is, to see them without relation to existential ends and to the fundamentally human values originating in them.

According to the *collectivistic* social theory, on the contrary, the nature of society is intrinsically determined by formative forces of biological and economic evolution, so that the social process as a whole and its organization are subject to a "*social determinism.*" For this process, it is not man and his existential ends that are of decisive importance; rather, man is wholly at the service of this process and can claim as a sphere of self-determination (freedom) only what each organization permits. Consequently, even its system of values is imposed on society deterministically, with social values enjoying a primary place. In the following chapters we shall be dealing in more detail with the various aspects of the individualist and collectivistic social theories. Here we shall consider merely the starting point in the two theories.

It was in order to combat the wrong emphasis of individualism that *Toennies* produced his well-known work,[2] but he himself remains a prey to this wrong emphasis. His distinction between "community" and "society" coincides only partly with the distinction made by natural law philosophy between natural and other societies. "Community" he believes to rest on natural dispositions and impulses (the "essential will"), "society" on self-chosen purposes and interests (the "arbitrary will"). Enlightening though *Toennies'* study is in many respects, the antithesis in his conception does not do justice to reality. The pair of categories in the form invented by him can hardly be maintained from the point of view of social philosophy or even of empirical sociology (cf. Chap. 17). Purposes also have an essential determining influence on "communities"—that is, the existential ends—especially the latter on the free selective will of their members. On the other hand, the employers and employees of a firm may go beyond the mere fulfillment of their individual functions and form a community in the true sense, if their cooperation is instinct with mutual trust and if all common concerns are settled in concert, that is, if the principles of justice and charity govern their cooperation. In fact, all functional associations are at least indirectly connected with existential ends, and hence each "society" is subject to demands which do not permit it to constitute itself and to act solely in accordance with arbitrary will. This does not mean of course that, for instance, the workers, managers, directors, and shareholders in a company need cultivate affection for one another, but it certainly implies that their relations must be inspired by mutual respect, justice, and benevolence, and thus be guided by a spirit of partnership. There are also objections of a general nature to the narrowing of the concepts of "community" and "society." In everyday language as well as in scientific discourse the concept society in the wider sense comprises all social forms, both true communities and functional asso-

[2] F. Toennies, *Gemeinschaft und Gesellschaft,* 1887, 8th ed., 1935.

ciations. Furthermore, the concept of society in the narrower sense has long been in use for the distinction, equally important for social philosophy, social ethics and sociology, between "society" and "state," [3] namely, between the respective responsibilities and competencies of individuals, communities, and associations, and the competence of the state: "society" in this sense signifies all competencies which do not belong to the state and therefore set limits to the extension of its competence (cf. Chaps. 68, 136). The confusion of ideas is the more unfortunate at a time when the state, in pursuit of collectivist tendencies, is seeking to expand its competence, especially when the prevailing mechanistic view of the state holds the state to be itself only a functional association whose purposes and forms of organization, in accordance with the theory of the absolute sovereignty of the people and the theory of democracy derived therefrom, are left entirely to the discretion of the popular will.

The collectivistic interpretation of the nature of society, which has had far-reaching international consequences, today is that of *dialectical materialism.* The famous passage in which *Marx* expounds the fundamental idea of this philosophy runs as follows: "In the social production of the means of life, human beings enter into definite and necessary relations which are independent of their will—production relations, which correspond to a definite stage in the development of their productive forces. The totality of these production relations constitutes the economic structure of society, the real basis upon which a legal and political superstructure arises and to which definite forms of social consciousness correspond. The mode of production of the material means of livelihood determines, in general, the social, political, and intellectual processes of life. It is not the consciousness of men that determines their existence, but, on the contrary, it is their social existence that determines their consciousness. At a certain stage of their development the material productive forces of society come into conflict with the existing production relations, or, what is but a legal expression of the same thing, with the property relations within which they have hitherto moved. From forms of development of the productive forces these relations become their fetters. A period of social revolution then begins. With the change in the economic foundation the whole gigantic superstructure is more or less rapidly transformed. In considering such transformations we must always distinguish between the material transformation in the economic conditions of production, transformations which can be determined with the precision of natural science, and the legal, political, religious, aesthetic, or philosophical, in short, ideological forms in which men become conscious of this conflict and fight it out to an issue. Just as little as we judge an individual by what he thinks of himself, just so little can we judge such a revolutionary period in accordance with its own consciousness of itself; on the contrary, this consciousness must be explained from the contradictions of material life, from

[3] This distinction is not merely a common one in the context of traditional natural law theory: it is also a fundamental principle of English social and political theory. Thus, in his criticism of the neo-Hegelian political doctrine of F. H. Bradley, Ernest Barker (*Political Thought in England, 1848–1914,* 1942, p. 66) points out that with Hegel "society" merges into state: "Failure to distinguish between state and society may lead to unlimited state regulation of life. It is safer to distinguish, as we in England have always distinguished, between society (with its social atmosphere, its social morality, and its social institutions) and the state (with its political institutions, its laws, and its officials)."

the conflict existing between social productive forces and production relations. . . . In broad outline we can designate the Asiatic, the ancient, the feudal, and the modern bourgeois forms of production as so many periods in the progress of the economic formation of society." [4]

Writing on historical materialism *Engels* says: "The final causes of all social changes and political revolutions are to be sought, not in men's brains, not in man's better insight into eternal truth and justice, but in changes of the modes of production and exchange. They are to be sought, not in the *philosophy,* but in the *economics* of each particular epoch." [5] His ideas are more concretely expressed by the following excerpt: "The new facts made imperative a new examination of all past history. Then it was seen that *all* past history, with the exception of its primitive stages, was the history of class struggles; that these warring classes of society are always the products of the modes of production and exchange—in a word, of the *economic* conditions of their time." [6]

The arguments against the social theory of dialectical materialism and of social determinism put forward by the various social sciences can be summarized as follows. The facts of history contradict the postulate that the decisive social changes have come about through revolutionary transformations. The historical researches of *Dopsch* show that the transition from the ancient Greco-Roman economic and social structure to that of the Middle Ages (from the "ancient" to the "feudal" forms, as *Marx* would say) was not revolutionary, but gradual and continuous; [7] *Strieder* proved the same with regard to the transition from the economic and social structure of the Middle Ages to that of modern capitalism (from "feudal" to "modern bourgeois"). [8] Again, the forecast by *Engels* of an inevitable social revolution in England, based on *Marx's* materialist theory of history, has proved quite false. So confident did Engels feel that he wrote: "Prophecy is nowhere so easy as in England, where all the component elements of society are clearly defined and sharply separated. The revolution must come." [9] *Halévy,* however, reaches the heart of the matter when he writes: "If the materialistic interpretation of history is to be trusted, if economic facts explain the course taken by the human race in its progress, the England of the nineteenth century was surely, above all other countries, destined to revolution, both political and religious. But it was not to be so. In no other country of Europe have social changes been accomplished with such a marked and gradual continuity." [10] Facts prove also that intellectual and religious forces have much more strongly influenced the order and development of society than have those of the form of production. This has been thoroughly demonstrated by the well-known researches of *W. Sombart* and *M. Weber.* They reach a conclusion just the opposite of historical materialism: it was not

[4] Marx, *A Contribution to the Critique of Political Economy,* 1859, Preface.

[5] Engels, *Socialism, Utopian and Scientific,* trans. by E. Avelyn, 1892, p. 45.

[6] Engels, *ibid.,* p. 41.

[7] Cf. A. Dopsch, *Die wirtschaftlichen und sozialen Grundlagen der europäischen Kulturentwicklung,* 1923; trans.: *The Economic and Social Foundations of European Civilization,* 1937; on the continuity of development cf. also Robert Latouche, *Les origines de l'économie occidentale* (Paris), 1956.

[8] Cf. J. Strieder, *Zur Genesis des modernen Kapitalismus,* 1904; *Studien zur Geschichte kapitalistischer Organisationsformen,* 2nd ed., 1925.

[9] F. Engels, *Die Lage der arbeitenden Klassen in England,* 1845.

[10] E. Halévy, *History of England in the Nineteenth Century,* Vol. I, pp. 334 f.

changes in the modes of production and exchange which created the capitalistic mentality; on the contrary, it was the capitalistic mentality which created the capitalistic forms of production and exchange.[11] The development of juridical and social thought in capitalistic society, and the development of this society itself, has proceeded in a direction wholly contrary to Marxian assumptions: industrial society in the most intensively capitalistic countries has not developed toward the inevitable misery followed by the dictatorship of the proletariat; instead, the working people by their own initiative have organized in order to assert their rights through the trade union movement, and on the initiative of other groups a comprehensive social policy has been created, resulting both in the raising of the living standard of the workers and in a weakening of class hostility, so that the Marxian class war idea was completely dropped by Western socialists. In the hundred years since *Marx* developed his theory of history and of society, the face of industrial society has completely changed: today more than ever before man is aware that social and economic organization depend on his will and his actions. In fact, *Engels* himself in the English edition of his previously mentioned work, quoting the words of *Goethe*, "In the beginning was the act," admits that "before there was argumentation there was action"; [12] it was the creative act in both directions which decisively convicted the Marxian theory of error.

To be sure, one must not underestimate the influence of the molding forces of technical economic development on the process of social relationships. Furthermore, the criticism and rejection by the social sciences and social philosophy of the social theory of dialectical materialism and its evolutionist theory does not mean that they can deny the influence which *Marx's* doctrine has exercised in the field of social science, especially on empirical sociology and social history, with regard to the effect of economic factors on forms of social organization and cultural life. But it is as a method of empirical social inquiry and not as a philosophy that *Marx's* achievement is of lasting value to science, and indeed all the scholars mentioned above as critics of the Marxian theory would hasten to acknowledge their debt to *Marx* in this respect.

17. Society as Reality

What kind of reality is society? Is it a substance or only an accident? Has it only a notional being; does it exist only in our imagination or has it a real being; has it an objective essence? All these statements have been made about society. According to our analysis, we are to regard it as a supraindividual, lasting entity. Against the supposition that the forms of society have only a notional being and exist only in the world of our imagination is the undeniable fact that these forms represent very real

[11] Cf. W. Sombart, *Der moderne Kapitalismus,* 2 vols., 6th ed., 1924. Cf. also Max Weber, "Die protestantische Ethik und der Geist des Kapitalismus; die Sekten und der Geist des Kapitalismus," in *Gesammelte Aufsätze zur Religionssoziologie,* Vol. I, 1920; *Wirtschaftsgeschichte,* 1923. Cf. also R. H. Tawney, *Religion and the Rise of Capitalism,* 1927; A. Fanfani, *Cattolicesimo e Protestantesimo nella Formazione del Capitalismo,* 1934; O. v. Zwiedineck-Südenhorst, *Weltanschauung und Wirtschaft,* 1942.

[12] F. Engels, *Socialism, Utopian and Scientific, op. cit.,* Introd., p. xv.

functioning units. From the ways in which things function, and from them alone, we can recognize the nature of things and the kind of reality which they possess. Let us consider only the most elementary social units, such as nationality (*volk*), family, and state, with their being outlasting the individual. The family continues to exist when a child dies or voluntarily leaves the family circle, and even when the main support of the family goes. Even the nationality, that primal community based on common ancestry, common speech, and common culture—who would seriously maintain that it, with its enduring character, regenerating itself even after severe blows of fate, and with its all-round formative influence on its members, is to be conceived only in terms of the attitudes of its members? To say that the nationality as a social form is to be understood from "unconscious" attitudes and beliefs is no objection. For, precisely here we can perceive a reality which is not attributable to the individual person but to effective forces of a supraindividual nature. Consider the state with its operative forces which largely govern the fate of the individual and whose existence often outlasts by centuries the generations of its members; we shall easily see that the notion that the state consists merely in an idea in the minds of men is quite unrealistic. In fact, culturally complete individuals do not establish the state; rather, through their participation in the communal, actual life of the state the individuals become civilized beings, and are enabled to attain to a fully human existence.

The question of the kind of reality which appertains to social forms raises itself in a variety of ways. In any case, however, it cannot be answered by simply going back to "relations" between men, unless we are to overlook significant and obvious facts of experience. The facts of experience already mentioned about the state may be recalled. The work of social philosophy is to explain how the state exists as an abiding and supraindividual reality. Undoubtedly this reality appears first and foremost as one of modes of conduct in relations between men, yet equally certainly it is also the cause of such conduct. Hence, the question concerning the nature of these causes and the reality revealed therein arises. This question cannot be answered with a mere statement of empirical facts, just as human nature cannot be explained by referring only to empirical facts. Indeed, the question is an ontological and metaphysical one. We have already prepared the way for an answer in the previous chapters by tracing the nature of society to the social nature of man conceived ontologically and metaphysically. But this does not answer our present question, the question of the kind of being which society possesses. We have already ascertained that society has a being of its own and therefore is not a mere abstraction or a baseless idea. What is this distinctive being, this distinctive reality? Is it a self-existent being (a substance) or a dependent one (an accident)? This is *a question of the widest implications.* If society does possess an independent being, then nature itself totally subordinates the individual to society. But if society had a purely dependent being, then it could spring only from the will of the individuals. The result would be the originally unrestricted freedom of the individual. Both alternatives have been held: that society and the individual each possesses only a dependent being; that each is an accident. According to *Hegel* the individual person is an accident: "The state as the reality of the substantial will, which it is in the special self-consciousness raised to its universality, is the absolutely rational. This substantial unity is an absolute unmoved end in itself"; "Since it (the state) is the objective spirit, the individual himself has objectivity, truth, and ethicality in being a member of it"; this objective spirit, or the reality of morality, is "the will, being in and for itself, the objective being and sphere of necessity, whose '*momenta*' (*momente*) are ethical powers which rule the lives of individuals and in them, as their accidents [sic!], have their representation, apparent form, and reality." It is their "highest duty to be members of the state"; thus, "in reality the state is the first entity within which the family forms itself into the civil society."[1] According to *Hegel's* doctrine, then, society as the objective spirit has independent, substantial being; the individual has only dependent being and is an accident. According to natural law philosophy, society does possess a being of its own but not an independent one; only man possesses substantial being. Society in its abiding mode of existence requires individuals to support it. It has being only in virtue of the being of men; it has existence only through the existence of men as its members. The individual, on the other hand, exists independently of society and has full humanity when he has attained it through life in society, independently of society.

In the first edition of this work the matter was dealt with in the following way: Society is an accident, requiring a substance, namely, man, to support it, but an ontological accident, since man is by his nature a social being. From the ontological or metaphysical accident we must distinguish carefully the logical, which denotes something incidental, having no

[1] Hegel, *Grundlinien der Philosophie des Rechts,* 1821, pp. 145, 256, 258. The element of truth is unmistakable in Hegel's statement, erroneous though it is, that the individual, from the point of view of the ontological reality of society, appears as an accident. His notion is false because he assigns to society a primary reality, and to this reality as the "objective spirit" a substantive mode of being, so that the expression accident as a definition of the ontological nature of the human person acquires an untenable meaning. But insofar as the supraindividual and lasting reality of society exists independently of the individual not only in its being, but also continues in existence, the individual is, in a true sense, of accidental significance; that is, he is seen as an "individual," or as a part of the social whole (cf. Chaps. 19–20), whereas man as a person, as we have shown, is ontologically and metaphysically of a suprasocial nature. It is clear from his repeated references to the matter, that St. Thomas also thinks so and that he assigns to the individual also a reality ontologically dependent on society and to society as a totality a supraindividual reality; thus, he says in the *Summa theol.,* Ia IIae, q. 96, a. 4: "Cum enim unus homo sit pars multitudinis, quilibet homo hoc ipsum quod est, et quod habet, est multitudinis, sicut et quaelibet pars id quod est, est totius."

intrinsic relation to the nature of a thing (e.g. the color of the skin has no intrinsic relation to the essential human nature). The use of reason is an ontological accident, because a man who does not have the use of reason still remains man, and is distinct from reason itself, which determines the nature of man, namely, makes him what he is. Today we would say that ontologically and metaphysically, if the expressions substance and accident are given the meaning just set down, society can only be described as an accident. It seems, however, to be another question whether the special supraindividual reality of society can be fully explained in terms of these disjunctive concepts of substance and of accident, so conceived. Certainly society is not a substance in the sense of subsisting in and for itself, independently of individuals. Yet, although society is not a substance in this sense, we cannot conclude that its being in the ontological and metaphysical sense is merely secondary in relation to the individual as such. For, to return to our example, man retains his nature as man without the use of his reason, but without his social nature man cannot achieve his integral humanity. Consequently, the social nature of man is equally original with the individual. We have seen that by nature man requires completion in order to attain his full being, that is, in order to be a being with cultural life, for which he is destined by nature. From this natural requirement of, and capacity for, completion through social cooperation, the new reality in which the individual must share in order to be able to reach full human integration comes about. It is wrong to ascribe primary being to society and only secondary being to the individual; but it is equally wrong to ascribe primary being only to the individual, and only secondary being to society. For then it would not be possible to explain the fact that the individual achieves fully human being only through participation in the life of society, that is, in what is enduring in it.

A principal cause of the misunderstanding of the particular being and reality of society has its origin in *nominalism,* which became widespread after the Middle Ages. It has had effects in the social sphere which are almost more catastrophic than those connected with the recognition of other metaphysical realities. According to the theory of nominalism, universals or general concepts are merely names for which there is no corresponding being or reality. Being is assigned only to individual things; they alone are cognizable, and then only insofar as sense experience is capable of perceiving them. No being is allowed to exist outside of sense experience, namely, no metaphysical reality.[2] Thus, being is abandoned as the ultimate source for the interpretation of things, and with this, the order of being which comprises all individual being. In the social sphere this would mean that fundamentally reality is attributed only to the

[2] Cf. the promising and original resumption of the problem of universals by Ottokar Blaha, *Logische Wirklichkeitsstruktur und personaler Seinsgrund: Zur Ontologie der Universalien, Sachverhalte und Seinsschichten,* 1955.

individuals; in society only an organizational unity dependent wholly on the will of individuals is seen. Therefore, society is denied the order demanded by the order of being itself. In this way the philosophical foundations for later individualism were laid down. Social thought and social will lost the all-embracing, unifying idea of order. Those who look beyond pure sense experience in their thinking and who do not reject suprasensory metaphysical reality (i.e., nonpositivist thinkers) take it as an established fact that the decay of social order, ranging from the family to the community of nations, has its roots in the breakdown, progressing for centuries, of beliefs regarding truth and value, which in the view of former ages are inseparably bound up with the comprehensive idea of order founded in the being of things and ultimately in the divine Being. The order of being, the order of values, the social order, all have been torn asunder by the nominalist thinking and volition of the modern age: the order of society was surrendered to the will of the individuals in accordance with tables of value, which could be chosen by the individuals in virtually unrestricted freedom. The *social philosophy of individualism* is a philosophy which preaches the wholly primary and original being of the individuals. The individuals, therefore, alone are responsible and give themselves their social order in self-determination. The individualist-liberalist doctrine that "each man is his own law" (*Leo XIII, On Human Liberty,* 1888) is not wholly or even primarily traceable to the falling away from Christianity, but to the philosophical error of nominalism. The latest effects of nominalism can be seen today in the world conflict, which is reaching such a tragic pitch and which is a result of the opposed ideologies of East and West.

We have said that society and the individual possess, ontologically and metaphysically, equally original being. Neither can be derived from the other or reduced to the other as the primary being, as the individualist and collectivistic theories suppose. In the view of the *individualist* social philosophy, as just stated, only the individual has real being; society possesses no reality of its own distinct from the relationships of the individuals composing it. To the extent that the ontological question of the existence of society is considered at all, it is answered by the *"fiction" theory* (cf. also Chap. 21). This theory holds that for practical reasons it is necessary to assume the separate existence of society, but that our conception and idea of society as such are only fictions to which no real being corresponds. Ontologically, says the theory, it does not exist independently of the individuals and their interrelations, and there is no supraindividual reality of society. The association of individuals in society indeed consists in interrelations, but not in interrelations of integrated individuals, as all individualist theory assumes; rather, it consists in interrelations through which the individuals achieve full humanity and through which, therefore, a new reality is established.

Collectivistic social theory ascribes primary reality to society, on which the members of society depend for their whole existence. Dialectical materialism explicitly places the realities in this order of rank: "It is not men's consciousness which determines their being, but their social being which determines their consciousness."[3] (We have seen that *Hegel* in the passage quoted says that the moral forces have their representation in individuals as their "accidents"; and so social being as objective spirit constitutes the reality determining the consciousness of men.) The *"universalism"* of *Spann* is a continuation of *Hegel's* philosophy: "Not individuals but the whole of society forms the true reality; the individuals possess reality and existence only inasmuch as they are members of the whole."[4] *Spann* is referring to *Aristotle's* maxim that the whole is anterior to the part. This principle, as we have shown, can be applied to society with good reason. In the scientific examination of an object one may proceed from the whole to the parts, and it is then correct to say that the whole precedes the parts; but this in no way means an ontological antecedence. If we consider a house as such, the house of course comes first from this point of view; but the stones out of which it is built exist first. The house possesses a genuine reality, as do the materials of which it is made. *Aristotle* himself is far too much of an empiricist not to see this point. In the *Politics* he says: "Thus, the state is by nature clearly prior to the family and to the individual, since the whole is of necessity prior to the part." But in the *Ethics* he states as a matter of course: "The love of husband and wife seems to be a natural law, since man is naturally more inclined to contract a marriage than to constitute a state, inasmuch as a house is prior to a state, and more necessary than a state, and the procreation of children is the more universal function of animals."[5] Thus, family (the house) is prior from one point of view, state from another; the same can be applied to the individual.

Social Philosophy and Sociology

Social reality is so varied in its forms and in its strata that an investigation of it demands the cooperation of a considerable number of social sciences. Among these are politics, economics, social ethics, social philosophy, and sociology. Each of these in turn comprises a number of special sciences. The two last-named have in common the endeavor to make an all-round inquiry into the principal phenomena of social reality. Thus, the question arises with regard to the relationship between the two. To answer the question we must first define the objects of inquiry and the methods of the two sciences.

In accordance with traditional natural law ethics the object of social philosophy is the nature of society, the foundation of society's being and the order of being observable in it. The nature of society must be studied in order to discover the laws of order under which its being is fulfilled. Hence, social philosophy is not an ethical science, but an ontological science, with the object of clarifying the question of the fundamental ontological and metaphysical reality of society posed by the reality of social experience. As distinct from social philosophy, however, sociology remains in the field of experience itself and is not supposed to seek to be more than an empirical science. It is divided into special and general sociology: special sociology is concerned with the investigation, analysis, and description of connections, causations, factual situations,

[3] Marx, *Zur Kritik der politischen Ökonomie*, 1859, Preface.
[4] O. Spann, *Gesellschaftslehre*, 1930, p. 562; *Der Wahre Staat*, 1931, pp. 33 ff.
[5] Aristotle, *Politics*, I, 2, 13; *Nic. Eth.*, VIII, 14.

changes, and developments in individual social spheres or in particular social processes. Today these tasks are undertaken by the sociology of culture, of law, of knowledge, of literature, of art, of the family, of industry, of the village, and of religious, ecclesiastical, and pastoral conditions; by the sociology of public opinion, of political parties, and of the changes in thought and in will of social classes, for example, of the working class in the course of generations.[6]

General sociology aims at universally valid findings regarding forms, connections, causes, and processes of development in social life. Here, therefore, we are primarily interested in the relationship between "general" sociology and social philosophy, since both pursue the object of all-round knowledge in regard to social reality. Opinions concerning the ways and methods of inquiry in general sociology are greatly divergent, so that difficulties in determining its relationship to social philosophy arise. On the basis of the "scientific methods" applied, *F. Bülow* in the recent *Wörterbuch der Soziologie* is able to list seventeen main schools of sociology, with many overlappings. In fact, in the discussion of the "socio-biological" trend, names like *Aristotle, St. Thomas Aquinas, Machiavelli, Hegel, Comte, Darwin,* and *Malthus* occur side by side; *Thomas* is also named as the supreme authority on the main trends of the universalist doctrine, and *Spann* as chief exponent of a philosophical "universalism," although there is no doubt of the philosophical difference, even opposition, between the two.[7] In the older *Handwörterbuch der Soziologie,* edited by *A. Vierkandt, Theodor Geiger* enumerates four main directions, but the subdivisions reveal the same multiplicity of tendencies.[8] In spite of this multiplicity of tendencies the relationship between general sociology and social philosophy can be precisely defined, if the former is understood as an empirical science,

[6] On the European Continent the development of this special sociology only began in recent times, especially in the form of "sociography," "field study," "social inquiry" (the investigation and description of facts). In the Anglo-Saxon countries this kind of sociology is still predominant today in the form of case studies, field work, social research—which too often means a mere compilation of data with the aid of questionnaires and statistics. That the development toward general sociology is under way in those countries is evidenced by the volume edited by G. Gurvitch and W. E. Moore, *Twentieth Century Sociology* (New York), 1945. Of the numerous contributions dealing with sociology in America and other countries we recommend that of T. Parsons, Principal of the Harvard Institute for Social Relations, who holds, no doubt rightly, that the stage of development of a science must be judged by the system formation of its theory, and that for sociology also as a single empirical inquiry and description a system of general categories is indispensable. On the other hand, among European sociologists today, compared with former times, there is a justified scepticism regarding a premature general systematization or theory. Thus, A. Gehlen and H. Schelsky say, in a symposium edited by them: *Soziologie, ein Lehr-und Handbuch zur modernen Gesellschaftskunde,* 1955, p. 9: "An overall theory cannot at present be offered. If such were attempted seriously it would constantly reveal its own dubiety"; as a reason for this, they mention the gaps in our anthropological ideas, the everywhere noticeable lack of firsthand findings, and the frequency of tendentious elements in most previous attempts; the compilation mentioned offers a good survey of problems and methods of today's "special" sociology (omitting, however, "departments which are not or only sparsely covered in recent German work," as the sociology of art, of knowledge, of law, and of religion; there is no mention of the sociology of culture). There is an ample international bibliography on the particular fields discussed.

[7] Cf. W. Bernsdorf and F. Bülow, *Wörterbuch der Soziologie,* 1955, pp. 498 ff.

[8] Cf. A. Vierkandt, *Handwörterbuch der Soziologie,* 1931, pp. 569 ff.

as is customary today.[9] Anticipating the outcome of the closer examination of this relationship, which follows, we may say that, if social philosophers and sociologists rightly understand their object, the purpose of their inquiry, and their methods, not only can there be no antagonism between the two departments, but in fact they are complementary.[10]

1. *Social philosophy,* if it is to be equal to its task, must make use of the established findings of sociology in two ways. The philosophy underlying natural law theory has always emphasized experience as the starting point of all knowledge: *Omnis cognitio incipit a sensibus.* Sociology has brought about a great widening of our experience in regard to social life. Because of this increase in knowledge, social philosophy may not have to undertake a revision of its metaphysical findings relating to the individual and social nature of men, although it will have to examine how large a proportion of its "standing" conceptions, which have been passed down from generation to generation, rest on empirical foundations and are thus partly time-bound (cf. Chap. 48). The other respect in which general sociology is of significance for social philosophy is this: with the opening up of new and constantly developing empirical reality, social philosophy will receive powerful stimuli for the understanding of its tasks with regard to the articulation of its methodological tools. On the other hand, it can hardly be denied that among the greatest exponents of traditional natural law theory—*Plato, Aristotle, Augustine, Thomas, Bernardino of Siena, Suárez, Vitoria, Molina*—there is an abundance of sociological knowledge of a general character relating to all spheres of social life. We shall often be referring to their sociological findings in the course of this work, although we shall not be listing them as such.

We have spoken of the importance of "general" sociology to social phi-

[9] The definitions of "Sozialphilosophie" and "Soziologie" given by the Bernsdorf-Bülow Dictionary are hardly distinguishable from those which we have given above. *Social philosophy* is defined as "that study of society which concerns itself with the meaning and nature of social forms of life and their changes in regard to the whole of the phenomena up to metaphysics. It is primarily ontology of social being and becoming and seeks to do justice to ultimate problems which arise in sociology on the border of the findings which it has empirically made and which it passes on to philosophy." *Sociology* is defined as "the study of the forms and varied manifestations of coexistence of men, animals, and plants. It is the science of the social phenomenon, be it as a general, fundamental social science or as a special science, and embraces as a system social structures and social processes. . . . If one surveys its whole development from the beginnings, the main trend is characterized by the fact that it has evolved more and more from a philosophical and metaphysical or an encyclopaedic-historical-philosophical discipline to a specialized empirical science, its object of knowledge being secularized" (*ibid.,* pp. 483 ff., 498 ff.). In any case, the still recurring use of the word "sociology" as a collective name for all social sciences or even as a designation of a comprehensive social theory with a more or less emphasized basis of social philosophy or social ethics seems no longer justified according to scientific usage.

[10] We are here thinking of natural law social philosophy. If, like F. Bülow (*Wörterbuch der Soziologie,* p. 485), one also includes under social philosophy "ideologies" such as those of nationalism, socialism, communism, collectivism, and anarchism, then one can but agree: "There can be no doubt that in the often pungent intolerance with which they assert their intellectual position they have often gone too far and have brought it about that social reality in the variety of its manifestations could not always be objectively recognized." What he adds is generally accurate: "Here sociology as an empirical science has important tasks of elucidation to fulfill, without any need for a split between sociology and philosophy."

losophy. We must not omit to mention the farreaching significance of "special" sociology for natural law ethics: in order to assess situations calling for the application of its principles, natural law ethics will have to take account of the results of sociological investigation in all fields; concerning this we need say no more than has already been said on the method of natural law ethics.

2. *Sociology* can as little dispense with social philosophy as the latter can with the former. Sociology, after initially overlooking the value problem, found itself faced with the fact that value beliefs belong to the most important formative and evolutionary forces in society and that it cannot speak about these forces, their nature, and their significance, either by the method of "understanding" (*verstehen*) or by the method of causal analysis, unless it uses interrelated ideas of value as a reference system. Furthermore, as pointed out by the school of sociology of knowledge initiated by *Max Scheler,* the quest for knowledge and the communication in the domain of the social sciences are governed in part by modes of thinking dependent on social and historical factors.[11] The once vigorously raised demand for a science free from presuppositions and for value-free sociology, has for long been proved untenable by sociology itself. Therefore, it is not surprising that *Helmut Schoeck,* a professor of sociology working in the United States, in his history of the problems of sociology refers to the "growing emphasis with which present-day sociology, particularly in the United States, is taking interest in the problem of value. In the writings and conferences of American social scientists it has been in the foreground not much less than ten years. In Germany, too, *Max Weber's* demand for freedom from values is no longer a principal maxim of social science. . . . We must naturally distinguish between the value problem in the method and the value problem as a sphere of empirical investigation, that is, as a causal factor. In fact, the two are contiguous. One cannot expect to make a successful investigation of prevailing value systems within the social sphere unless one possesses a definite value system and can methodically make out its pattern. From a position of agnosticism or nihilism in regard to values one can hardly give due consideration to the symbolic language and the intensity of value systems alien to one's own." [12] *F. Bülow* comes to the conclusion that sociologists can give up any connection with philosophy only by neglecting "the fact that there are ultimate questions of principle regarding the coexistence of men which require to be dealt with by social philosophy or by a metaphysic of society." [13]

[11] Cf. M. Scheler, *Versuche zu einer Soziologie des Wissens,* 1924; *Die Wissensformen und die Gesellschaft,* 1926; Hans-Joachim Lieber, *Wissen und Gesellschaft: Die Probleme der Wissenssoziologie,* 1952; J. Schaaf, *Grundprinzipien der Wissenssoziologie,* 1956; of the older literature, cf. especially K. Mannheim, "Das Problem einer Soziologie des Wissens," in *Archiv. f. Sozialwiss. und Sozialpol.,* Vol. LIII, 1925; *Ideologie und Utopie,* 1929.

[12] H. Schoeck, *Soziologie: Geschichte ihrer Probleme,* 1952, pp. 348 f.; cf. on the same question Leo Strauss, *Natural Rights and History,* 1953, and the views quoted from there in Chap. 40, note 8.

[13] Bernsdorf-Bülow, *Wörterbuch der Soziologie,* p. 500. That contrary views still exist, namely, the rejection of social philosophy and resistance to the new attitude toward value problems, may be seen from the article "Sozialphilosophie" by Jügen v. Kempski in the *Handwörterbuch der Sozialwissenschaften,* now in progress, part 10, 1955, p. 531, where it is stated: "The very diversified picture which thus emerges seems for the present to forbid any ontologizing of a definite structure such as is character-

3. To elucidate *questions of detail* in the relationship between social philosophy and sociology it seems expedient to cite some of the best-known sociologists who regard their sociology as wholly and entirely an empirical science, and who have exercised a decisive influence on the development of sociology and will long continue to do so. Among these we may perhaps assign first place to *Max Weber*. He defines sociology as "a science which seeks to understand social conduct interpretatively and so explain it in terms of causality in its course and its effects"; in his view, social conduct is understood as conduct (acts, forbearances, omissions) "which in accordance with the sense intended for it by the doer or doers has reference to the behavior of others and in its process is orientated thereto." Social structures, too, such as the state, trade unions, corporations, are "for the interpretative understanding of conduct by sociology, simply processes and connections of specific conduct of individual people." With regard to social structures, says *Weber,* in contrast to biological organisms, we are capable of going beyond the mere observation of functional connections and of achieving something "eternally inaccessible to all natural science: the '*understanding*' of the conduct of the *individuals* involved." Referring to this fundamental emphasis on the individual, Weber rightly criticizes "the enormous misunderstanding that an 'individualist' method signifies (in any possible sense) an individualist valuation." [14]

The same misunderstanding is pointed out by *Leopold von Wiese,* for whom sociology means wholly and entirely an empirical science, in fact, as a "study of relationships (*beziehungslehre*)," whose object is social conduct, that is, conduct related to the behavior of others, wherein "only what is subjectively meant, not the objective sense, is scientifically comprehensible." In this he declares agreement with *Max Weber,* yet the study of relationships aims at bringing the ways of social conduct into a system.[15] The demand for strictness of method is of crucial importance: "It is a matter of observing the actually existing connections between people and their relationships (not the ideologies, wishes, postulates, and objectivizations of them fostered by men), and to analyze them, to systematize them, and as far as possible to 'understand' them." The aims of sociology are stretched further when *von Wiese* thereupon says that "a scientific work on human society belongs to sociology to the extent to which it is fitted to elucidate the nature of society"; its "general theory of relationships is nothing other than general anthropology," which has the task of "laying the historical and social foundations of an empirical ethics," by means of "a

---

istic of the older social philosophy, apart also from all philosophical misgivings based on such a procedure. . . . Negatively it can first be stated that the peremptory principles with which social philosophy (social ethics and legal philosophy) has hitherto worked—and this is true especially for the phenomenological-axiological—are not of such a character that their implications can be discussed within the framework of modern theories of social science." In explanation it seems to be thought that "the answer of a philosopher to the 'essential question' always depends upon what he considers—and for whatever reasons—essential." Such an opinion seems to indicate unawareness of the social philosophy of traditional natural law theory (it is not mentioned in the article) and of the fact that the present world conflict which is deciding the destiny of man is caused by two opposed conceptions of the nature of man and of the corresponding fundamental order of society. Cf. Messner, *Ethics and Facts,* 1952, pp. 136 ff., 214 f.; *Die Soziale Frage,* 1956, pp. 22 f., 204–19, 666 ff.

[14] Max Weber, *Wirtschaft und Gesellschaft,* 1922, pp. 1, 6, 7, 9.

[15] Cf. L. v. Wiese, *Soziologie: Geschichte und Hauptproblem,* 1950.

demonstration guided by experience and psychic analysis of what man has hitherto been for man and what he can be to him."[16] But all this seems to go far beyond the boundary of purely empirical sociology and to attribute to it a task which can no longer be accomplished by empirical methods but only by philosophical ones, namely, the task of explaining the essence of society and of establishing an ethics. The misunderstanding which leads to this encroachment is a widespread one: the view that the difference between sociology and social philosophy is that, as *von Wiese* expresses it, the former is a science of observation, based on what is demonstrable, whereas social philosophy is "an interpretative exercise in wisdom seeking the ultimate connections of being." In reality social philosophy is a social science, which (1) proceeds from external and internal experience; (2) does not interpret by guesswork, but keeps to what can be proved; and (3) aims at ontological cognition in contradistinction to the dicta of the sage.[17] *Von Wiese,* however, goes still further in overstepping the bounds of empirical sociology: "It is impossible to deny that all social forms exist only in the world of our imaginations, that they are ideas." It cannot be more clearly indicated that a sociology of this kind professes nominalism in the sense described above and thereby becomes social philosophy. This is shown by emphatically expressed further views on the idea of man, which underlie this sociology. It is based on what is generally human, where "general" is only given the meaning of the type which makes possible the "fiction" of the "universal figure" of homo sapiens: "It is of course only by generalization of individual phenomena that we reach the fiction of the universal figure." The nominalist basic feature of this anthropology is again unambiguously expressed: "The universal does not move in bodily form over the earth."[18] Certainly it does move over the earth in the human nature which is common to all men; any doubt about this can only be due to philosophical preconceptions, as is shown by the conviction prevailing today in the social sciences as elsewhere of the universal equality of human nature, human dignity, and human rights. Thus, the critic who has suggested that *von Wiese* would not be in agreement with my description, in the first edition of this work, of his theory of relationships as a social philosophy, is no doubt right. On the other hand *von Wiese* rightly says: "There is not a vestige of individualism to be found in the theory of relationships." He is right if individualism is understood in the socio-political sense, with its presupposition of freedom intrinsically unrestricted but limiting itself only in accordance with enlightened self-interest; this demand is based on a socio-philosophical view of man with which the theory of relationships has nothing in common. This

[16] L. von Wiese, *System der allgemeinen Soziologie als Lehre von den sozialen Prozessen und den sozialen Gebilden der Menschen* (Beziehungslehre), 2nd ed., 1933, pp. 4, 88 f., 613 (page numbers are identical with the 3rd ed., 1956).

[17] L. von Wiese is perhaps right in saying that Catholic social philosophy was opposed, critically, to sociology as long as sociologists were not clear about the limits of their province; but the general attitude of Catholic social philosophers today is probably, as he puts it, that they welcome the fact that sociologists "do not contest the claims of theology to dominate the duty-sphere of life and regard it as a matter outside the competence of their inquiry to state views on ethical and metaphysical questions" (*ibid.*, p. 87).

[18] L. von Wiese, *Ethik in der Schauweise der Wissenschaften vom Menschen und von der Gesellschaft,* 1947, pp. 184 f., 188.

form of the individualist view is held now by very few social scientists (e.g. *L. v. Mises, F. Hayek*). And yet that *von Wiese's* theory of relationships means something more than an individualist "method" (cf. above on *Max Weber*) can be seen, apart from what has been said, from the fact that it is unable to see a supraindividual entity in society. Instead, it tries to conceive of society exclusively in terms of the sole reality of the individuals, and hence sociality as just "the inter-human processes generally." Thus, according to *von Wiese,* the family is an institution for regulating sexual relationships, and hence is "first and foremost the true organizational form of reproduction." More particularly he says: "In the service of the goal of bringing about an ordered sexual life, which in itself is not a natural 'goal,' 'society' transfers special tasks to the family," which, over and above the biological function, then fall to the family, namely, the protection of helpless children, the control of the exercise of the sexual instinct, the reduction or control of antagonism between the sexes and the generations, and especially the protection of the aged. Is an ordered sexual life not a "natural" goal? And are the tasks enumerated conferred on the family by society? Today we learn differently from the early history of mankind and also from biology (cf. Chap. 47, n. II); the anthropology and sociology of culture, quite apart from the philosophy of culture, have established that the family is in exactly the same degree a transmitter of culture, in the sense of a way of life, as it is at the service of the preservation of the species; and that its cultural function is not less than its biological function. It is not surprising that *von Wiese* also states expressly that by "society" he does not mean a "totality," assuming, it seems, that social totality can only be understood as "substance." [19] Social morphology can be nothing but the study of social processes: "If social processes occur in a definite rhythm of countless similar quasi-repetitions it becomes necessary to represent these formations as imagined for thousands of years by learned and unlearned: as quasi-unities." Furthermore, "such simplifications" are called "fictions." But in consequence of his philosophical nominalism, the reality of social structures, of the social entity, and of the "institution" is overlooked [20] (cf. Chaps. 39 and 42). In the following chapters

[19] Cf. L. von Wiese, *System der allgemeinen Soziologie* etc., *op. cit.*, pp. 89, 128, 158, 639.

[20] To show the quite different view held by anthropologists and sociologists of culture, who see social structures as realities and not as fictions, we pick out two voices: Alfred Weber, *Prinzipien der Geschichts- und Kultursoziologie,* 1951, p. 110, says of the individualist sociological method of Max Weber, who sees in a social structure "merely the courses and connections of the specifically human action of individual men": This method "is not to be used by us here because we wish to illuminate complex wholes in their complexity, consciously leaving them as a unity, since our whole purpose is the tolerable understanding of inexplicable, fundamentally irrational historical collectivities in their unity, great compounded total phenomena permeated by countless individual causal connections of the most heterogeneous kind which do not concern us." Werner Ziegenfuß in the *Handbuch der Soziologie,* 1955, p. 242, says of the cultural sciences: "Truly one can speak of a culture and its special 'social' forms sociologically only if an essential and 'eternal' meaning is recognized and if a permanent objective composite picture freed from contingencies and from the continuous decay of communal life is firmly established, which makes it possible to understand society as 'pregnant with culture' and 'social in entity.' " Only under this condition have the sciences of culture their own objects of inquiry, so that in consequence a sociology of culture can investigate and study civilized society in relation to its findings. Although it is not to be expected that the sciences of culture will ever attain to a definitive and conclusive knowl-

we hope to show that although society is a totality, it is not therefore also a substance, and that social forms possess a real being of their own and hence are not "fictions." Our observations on *von Wiese* are directed against encroachments which are contrary to his own principle of strict method in empirical sociology, not against the rich yield of his investigations and labors in this same field.

We must also refer briefly to a third outstanding sociologist, *Franz Oppenheimer,* in order to show how dangerous are the encroachments of sociology into the sphere of social philosophy. Thirty years ago Oppenheimer anticipated ideas which today are beginning to come to the fore over a wide range of sociology: that sociology can and should be an instrument for social engineering guided by a technical view of society. According to him, sociology is a science of what "is," "a purely theoretical, a purely rationalistic science," whereas social philosophy is only a science of what "ought" to be. He thinks of sociology as a "universal science" comprising all specialized social sciences. It embraces the other social sciences by "first the fusion of theoretical economics with historical science in the widest sense, i.e., not merely with political history, but with ethnological history and the history of all so-called ideologies: law and language, religion, art and custom"; for he understands the intellectual aspect of the social process as ideologies these and only these governed by economic life. He continues: "Sociology must be strictly 'deterministic'—or it is impossible as a science. . . . To us it is an a priori axiom that a given set of circumstances calls forth a definite motive in every man according to his disposition, and this motive calls forth a definite action. This axiom does not as yet state whether the action so determined is also calculable by us. It depends on this question, to be answered only a posteriori, whether sociology is or can be a science in the strict sense." In fact a principal law of all sociology says: "To a definite situation of the group there corresponds a definite motivation, and to this motivation a definite activity of the members." But here the sphere of social philosophy has long been invaded: What is being advocated is a deterministic social anthropology and social philosophy. With this principle, according to the author, individual psychological motivation loses any independent significance, and instead "the group has so determined its members psychologically that they spontaneously will this activity because it seems to them dictated by reason and morals." Today, many who side with *Oppenheimer* see it as the task of sociology to prepare the means for realizing the vision of the social technician and social engineer in the hope that it will be possible to guide "the social process" like a machine. *Oppenheimer* even speaks of social pedagogy and the art of social organization as "practical" sociology based on general sociology, a technology of the socio-psychological determination of the members of society: "It is of course, if not the only at least the most important function of the theory to provide a foundation for such a technology; all sociologists of any standing have from this thought alone derived the courage to devote themselves to this formidable task. Civilization can really begin only when mankind has learned to control the powerful elemental force

---

edge of their objects, and even though they themselves form part of the living progress of cultural work, their dominant purpose must continue to be the "comprehension of permanent, stable, and normative relationships, although these, on the other hand, must not be made absolute."

which is operative in the social process, of all elemental forces by far the most powerful and dangerous."[21] Certainly the social process is the most powerful and dangerous. Precisely because in visions such as *Oppenheimer's* the realm of empirical and therefore realistic sociology is left behind, everything depends upon the hope that reality itself will prove stronger, that is, the essential nature of man, which is so completely misrepresented philosophically in such visions.

In the following chapters it will be necessary to examine the reality of society ontologically and metaphysically.

18. Society as a Unity

In order to elucidate the kind of unity possessed by society, it is customary to use the convenient method of distinguishing it from the unity of a herd and from the unity of an army. The unity of society is neither a mere aggregation of self-sufficient individuals nor a "formation" organized for an external purpose. It is a unity of order, that is, a unity in virtue of an immanent end coordinating the conduct of its members by means of their self-determination. Order signifies unity due to an inner principle of form. This principle may be an efficient cause, like the principle of gravitation in the solar system, or it may be a final cause, like the purposes which govern the activity of the directors of a company. All social units depend on a connection between efficient causes and final causes. Man's social nature impels him toward social life and in doing so becomes an efficient cause. His conduct and activities, however, are governed by the will; through the will the unifying end of society operates, thus becoming a final cause. This is, therefore, the inner principle which determines the character of the social unit and the conduct which it demands of its members. "Inner principle" means, then, that the unity of society rests not on external compulsion but on the self-determination of its members. The unity of society is not like that of a herd, which is held together by unconscious instincts compelling definite behavior; nor is it like that of a military formation, which is organized from without for an external purpose. The unity of society is order, having as its *inner formative principle* the end proper to itself and functioning through the self-determination of its members. The recognition of ends and self-determination in realizing them are faculties of mind-endowed nature. Hence, society's most essential bonds of union are spiritual.

This does not mean that spiritual bonds form the whole essence of society. External ties, institutions, are indispensable for its unity: the inner formative principle of society must be supported in its operation by

[21] F. Oppenheimer, *System der Soziologie,* Vol. I, 1922–23, Preface, pp. xx, 69 f., 133, 199 f., 600 ff.

externally uniting bonds. The state, for example, requires a legal system with executive machinery; the family too requires a number of external institutions for the fulfillment of its communal ends. For several reasons, the effectiveness of the intrinsic formative principle of social unity depends on institutions. The deeper reason for this lies in the two-sidedness of human nature as a unity of body and spirit; hence, the two-sidedness of society as a unity based on spiritual and external forces. Furthermore, institutions have the effect of directing the activities of the individuals surely to the common end because they bring and keep this end before their intellects and self-determining wills, and also because they dispose of physical compulsion in the event of antisocial conduct. Continuity in the functioning of society in the service of the common end (e.g., in the state), throughout changes of government and throughout succeeding generations, depends upon institutions. Thus, since unifying institutions and bonds are indispensable for the very existence of social entities, society involves, as an essential feature, *organization,* the coordination by external institutions of all activities in accordance with the implications of the end underlying its unity.

The mechanistic and even technical view of society, which is so widespread today, apprehends society principally as an organization serving man's self-imposed ends, be they understood in a more individualist or a more collectivistic sense. Hence, today more than ever before it is necessary to emphasize the essence of society, that is, the order indicated in its very nature. Because it is so bound up with the natural order, the organization of society is only partly a matter of human volition. Arbitrary planning and organization contrary to the natural order must substantially limit the degree of attainment of the end of society and hence of the self-fulfillment of the members of society—humanly, economically, and socially. Attempts at ordering social life are primarily a matter of seeking after the requirements of the natural order in the light of existing conditions. Within the framework of the natural order much is certainly left to human planning in accordance with what is found to be expedient with the aid of science and technology. But any planning and organization at variance with this fundamental order can erect only towers of Babel doomed to become testimonies of man's self-deception.

19. Society as a Whole

The import of the concept of the social whole may be seen from the fact that we are accustomed to call certain social systems totalitarian, when they embody the view that individuals are primarily only parts of the social whole and therefore totally subordinated to its purposes. The collectivistic theories underlying such social systems seek to justify themselves by pointing to the disintegration of the individualist society.

According to the individualist theory, individuals are not interconnected in society as parts of a supraindividual whole, but interact only externally like atoms, remaining unaffected in themselves and each being a world to itself; hence, this social theory is called "atomistic." In fact, the unity of society has the character of a whole; the individuals form the parts of the whole, and as such are dependent upon the being and activity of the whole. They can be fully men only as members of the social whole, as members of the family, of the neighborhood community, the nation, the state. Hence, we have the principle that the whole precedes the part.

Immediately the question arises concerning how much man is a part of society and how much he is not. His immediate consciousness tells him of a domain of personal being, of personal responsibility, and of personal will in the shaping of his life; metaphysically, suprasocial ends are rooted in the nature of man—ends which, therefore, point beyond the social totality. Yet, the fulfillment of these ends, as well as all other existential ends, is also dependent on society, since man requires society in order to develop fully all of his capacities. Insofar as he can attain fully human existence only by means of society, he is wholly a member of society, and society is prior to the individual. Thus, the statement, "The social whole precedes the individual" is true in view of the dependence on society of man's full integration. On the other hand, the statement, "The individual precedes the social whole," signifies that man possesses an independent being of his own which has suprasocial ends. Therefore, it is obvious that in both the former and the latter order of precedence, the being and end of society are ultimately rooted in the being and ends of its members. The status of being prior to and superior to any social whole belongs to man as a person.

Since the social whole is a unity of order with its own end as a formative principle, the character of social wholes varies according to the character of their ends. Hence, the teleological aspect is inseparable from the totality aspect in social theory. If one views it only ontologically as a whole (*ganzheitsbetrachtung, O. Spann*) one comprehends only half the reality of society. One runs the risk of overstressing the totality aspect of society and thus of furthering its "totalitarian" character. Nevertheless, the teleological view should not rule out the view of society as a whole; otherwise there is a danger of failing to grasp fully the supraindividual reality of society and hence of the social entity as such.

20. Society as an Organism

In everyday language as well as in the language of social philosophy we speak of society in terms that are properly used only of an organism: as a unity, society is spoken of as a "body"; we speak of social groups as "corporate" units; the parts of society are referred to as "members"; and the various functions of society are exercised by "organs." The term "organism" is taken from biology and denotes a bodily entity with an inner principle of life and activity by means of which all its parts are directed in their functioning toward the end inherent in the whole. Society is not a bodily unity; it possesses no principle of life and unity operating with the necessity of forces belonging to the body, and hence it is not an organism in the biological sense.

In reference to society, therefore, the term organism can be used only in an *analogous* sense. Yet, to call it an organism is no mere metaphor based on an external resemblance. There does exist an intrinsic, essential similarity: there operates in society an inner vital principle, the final cause, whereby the manifold activities of its members and organs are linked together into a unitary, vital process. It is the formative principle of the common end which guides this vital process of the "social body," viz., the activity of the "members" in their self-determination and the activity of the "organs" following from the ordering functions assigned to them for the purpose of insuring the continued fulfillment of the end of the community. Rational beings are the agents of this final causality; therefore, society is primarily a spiritual organism as distinct from a bodily organism which is an organism in the biological sense. Because they are rational beings, the individuals are "members" of the social whole, yet they harmonize their conduct with the end of the whole by self-determination. This fundamentally "spiritual" nature of the social organism is meant when we describe it as a "moral" organism; here, the word "moral" is used in a wider sense for what is essentially different from the "physical" world.

Society in the comprehensive sense, however, is not a single organism but an *organism of organisms*. For, the various particular ends underlying the cooperation of men in realizing their full human existence originate a variety of social organisms. These particular organisms in their turn, however, have ends in common, in which the total organism of society finds its principle of life. The following example will illustrate the point: The employers and workers who cooperate in factory and vocational groups do so to secure a livelihood, which of course corresponds to a primal end of life; but in doing so they help to provide society as a whole with the goods and services which it requires. The occupational groups are thus social units in the sense of member organisms of the all-embracing organism of the universal society. Thus, for the first time in our inquiry the ontological foundation of *social pluralism* comes into view: the fact that society is not an uncoordinated mass of individuals, but is coordinated as a plurality of communities and groups each with its own end, responsibility, and competence. The comprehensive society (the state) is a coordinated unity with lesser social units as intermediate members between it and the individual.

In opposition to the "organic" social theory,[1] the "mechanistic" theories speak of the "body" of society and its "members" and "organs" in a purely figurative sense. They see in society only correlations of individuals acting on one another mechanically, by attraction and repulsion, like physical things; or all of them organized mechanically into a unity like parts of a machine. In individualist social theory the unity of society is ultimately the effect of individual special interests, which by their interplay achieve a certain "equilibrium." As a result, the fundamental ideas of individualist social theory are "mechanistic." The same is true of the collectivistic theory. The distinctive idea of collectivistic thinking is in the category of coordination, in the sense that the governing authorities have the task of directing all activities within society toward the ends set by themselves. Society is treated as a mechanically understood unity, the state in particular being regarded as a machine for the actualization of its plans and schemes; this is true especially in Marxist theory.

On the other hand, the idea of the social organism is overdeveloped in social theories which see society as an organism in a higher sense, subsisting in itself. This error, to a greater or lesser degree, is found in all systems influenced by *Hegel.* They substantialize the social organism or at least make it an entity in which individuals are merely parts. This conception of society is termed "organicistic," as distinct from the organic conception. *Plato* sees the best state as the one which "most nearly approaches to the condition of the individual." [2] Neo-Hegelian organicistic theory, in the form of *Spann's* universalism, sees in the social "partial whole" a mere "ramification" of the social "totality." Also influenced by *Hegel,* the Italian school of actualistic idealism arrived at a similar overvaluation of the social totality. The danger of all such exaggerations is that the self and the rights of the individual man are sacrificed to the supposedly "primary" reality of the state, so that in fact, although not in intention, totalitarian trends are encouraged.

21. Society as a Person

Throughout the centuries since the Roman era, communities and associations have been regarded in practice as legal persons capable of

[1] To dispute the organic social theory, a standing object with individualist-mechanistic social theorists, has by now been rendered virtually impossible since A. N. Whitehead (*Science and the Modern World,* 1925; *Process and Reality,* 1929; *Nature and Life,* 1934) extended the category of organism to the atom as the ultimate unit in the organism of organisms, which for him represents the world as a whole. In fact, every system of energies with an inherent principle of functioning makes possible an analogy with the organism. Yet, the analogy itself does not explain anything. It is the task of science to determine and explain the variety of principles operating in the different kinds of "organisms." The principle is physical in the atom, biological in the plant and animal, spiritual in man, spiritual but not substantial in society. Thus, the reality of these organisms is essentially diversified. It would be no explanation of reality to bring all units from the atom to the universe to the same analogical common denominator. And such a method could by no means explain the difference between animate and inanimate or between rational and irrational beings, or between the biological and the moral organism. Cf. the criticism of Whitehead in R. G. Collingwood, *The Idea of Nature,* 1945, pp. 173 f.

[2] Plato, *Republic,* trans. by B. Jowett, V, 462c; cf. also IV, 443.

acting in a valid legal manner and with legal responsibility. But the fully elaborated conception of juridical personality is of modern date. When individualist social and legal philosophy began to inquire into the nature of this aspect of the community, at first it could find no reality behind it, because it was blinded to the essential reality of society by the prevailing nominalist thinking. It saw only the individuals and their will, guided by self-interest, but regarded the corporate personality as pure "fiction" (cf. Chap. 17).[1] The development of society itself, however, with its manifold economic and social associations, forced upon nineteenth-century social theorists a gradual reorientation of social theory and finally the recognition of the really juridical personality of social bodies. We shall have to deal with this development in detail later. Here we are concerned only with the nature of society as a person.

In view of what has been said in the preceding chapters concerning the nature of society, we need not emphasize that society is not a person in the same sense as the individual man. In the well-known definition of *Boethius,* person in the strict sense means *rationalis naturae individua substantia;* society, however, has no substantial being of its own. But society is not a person merely in a metaphorical sense; rather, it is a person in a well-grounded analogous sense. What are the features common to natural and social, or, in other words, to physical and "moral" persons? Like the natural person, the social person has a real but not substantial being of its own, which outlives even generations of its members. Like the natural person, society as a unity possesses self-determination in the pursuit of its essential ends, and hence it has the capacity to will and act. Just as the natural person is responsible for his existential ends, so also the social person; hence, like the natural person, the social person possesses rights. It acts also with juridical consequences: a state concludes legally binding treaties with other states; similarly, trade unions and employers' associations conclude legally binding agreements with one an-

[1] One of the most distinguished pioneers in the elucidating of the personality aspect of society is Otto von Gierke, although he is inclined to overemphasize the selfhood of social bodies and their personal character. Thus, he finds fault with Pope Innocent IV (1243–54) for coming very close to the "fiction theory," because he says of the social group: *Fingatur una persona.* But the pope clearly speaks of it as *res incorporalis,* thus putting it beyond doubt that in his view it is more than a mere "fiction" without any reality of its own; by the expression quoted he intends to bring out the essential difference between the juridical person and the natural person (cf. Gierke, *Das deutsche Genossenschaftsrecht,* Vol. III, 1881, pp. 271–82). Innocent's view is exactly that of natural law ethics in his day, as expressed by St. Thomas Aquinas. St. Thomas does not concern himself explicitly with the question, but makes it clear that for him the corporate person is a reality differing as much from a mere fiction as from the natural peson: it possesses an intrinsically analogical nature, but nothing more (note the *quasi* and the *similitudinarie* in the following quotations); in the *Summa theol.,* Ia IIae, q. 81, a. 1, St. Thomas says: "Omnes homines qui nascuntur ex Adam possunt considerari unus homo, in quantum conveniunt in natura, quam a primo parente accipiunt; secundum quod in civilibus omnes homines qui sunt unius communitatis, reputantur quasi unum corpus, et tota communitas quasi unus homo; sicut etiam Porphyrius dicit, quod 'participatione speciei plures homines sunt unus homo' "; in IIIa, q. 8, a. 4, he says: "Unum autem corpus similitudinarie dicitur una multitudo ordinata in unum secundum distinctos actus sive officia."

other. The social person has another characteristic in common wi
as an individual person: it can in its turn be a member of a
society, just as man himself is a member of a social whole. Thus, the
family and municipal and vocational bodies are members of the state, and the state itself is a member of the community of nations. Furthermore, like the human person, the communal person—or the group person with its own being, its own end, its own responsibility—is never merely part of a larger whole, but always remains a distinct self with its own rights. Hence, again we come to the conclusion that the natural constitution of the great society involves a *social pluralism,* with the consequence that all the lesser communities and associations, directly or indirectly rooted in existential human ends, are instinct with elements of the dignity and freedom of the human person.

Another consequence of the fact that the community has the character of a person is the collective responsibility of the members for the acts of the corporate body. How far, for instance, can the citizens be made responsible for the acts of their government in case of war? (We shall be dealing with particular questions later in connection with international law.) From our argument on the nature of society, the following distinction emerges: first, there can be no doubt about collective responsibility insofar as the acts of the community as such have sprung directly or indirectly from the will, consent, toleration, or nonresistance (where resistance would have been possible) of the members of society. Secondly, however, it is just as certain that in questions of responsibility on the part of communities a careful distinction must be made between the responsibility of the community, of its organs, and of its individual members. For, the community cannot act except through its organs (e.g., the state through the government). Hence, the citizens of a state should be held responsible as individuals or collectively for the conduct or acts of their government only insofar as they have shared directly or indirectly (through culpable inaction) in the formation of the political will and in the decisions of the government. If, for example, a nation is physically terrorized by a government and intellectually blinded by monopolistic propaganda, its members cannot really be held responsible for the deeds of the government. Different from collective responsibility is the responsibility of individuals and groups, who participate in the carrying out of governmental orders which are obviously at variance with law and morals; it is on this account that individual persons can be charged with responsibility (e.g., war criminals).

22. The End and Function of Society: The Common Good

Society, as we have seen, finds the reason for and the order of its being in the nature of man: the reason for its being is human nature with its need and capacity for completion in the attainment of full humanity; the order of its being is found in the conditions prescribed by man's individual, social, and personal nature for the attainment of this full humanity. Consequently, the end of society is the *help* which all require for the fulfillment, on their own responsibility, of the vital tasks rooted in the existential ends. Because this help is made possible, but also necessitated, by the cooperation of all members of the social unit, it is called the common good or common utility or the social good.

The nature of society as presented in our analysis yields immediately a further determination of the common good or the help which society must make available to the individual. Ontologically and metaphysically the nature of man has shown itself to be in need of completion, yet at the same time it is destined to realize its existential ends entirely on its own responsibility: in order to achieve full humanity man requires society, but his full humanity depends essentially on his *personal responsibility* and self-reliant activity in carrying out the demands of his being. This may be illustrated by the example given previously: the animal can be provided with all that it requires without impairment to the full reality of its being. Man, however, cannot be simply allotted everything that is necessary, because full humanity is essentially bound up with personal responsibility and personal activity; in other words, full humanity is a person. Hence, it follows, in regard to the ontological and metaphysical nature of the common good, that although founded on the need and capacity of individuals for completion, the common good does not consist primarily in a piecemeal collection of goods and services made by individuals and put in a common pile, nor in the simple allocation of goods from common stores to which the members of society have contributed. Rather, the common good means that social cooperation makes it possible for the members of society to fulfill by their own responsibility and effort the vital tasks set for them by their existential ends. Accordingly, although a domestic animal is not harmed in its essential nature by being provided for, the "provider state" does impair man's natural status because it takes away from him a sphere of self-determination and personal responsibility. Thus, since it harms man in goods of the highest rank it is contrary to the common good, notwithstanding great achievements, for example, in the interest of social security.

The second conclusion arising from the nature of society is the following: The notion of the common good signifies a reality determinate in being and not subject to arbitrary will. In its basic features this reality is metaphysically and ontologically determined by human nature whose need and capacity for completion is in the fulfillment of the demands of the integral existence of all members of society. Only within the framework of this *natural order* and the corresponding order of ends, therefore, is the design and planning of the common good a matter for the will and discretion of society. Within this orbit, the planning and shaping of the common good is indeed a matter of the common will with its own sets of values, for it has to serve their interests and wishes. In particular, the means of realizing the common utility, their character and their application, are a matter of this will. Indeed, in this regard there is no limit to the discretion of the community except the necessity of insuring that the means are not incompatible with the existential ends.

A third immediate consequence of the natural order of society concerns the two *basic functions* of the common good. The first is taking steps to preclude antisocial impulses in human nature from interfering with the social order, the necessary condition for fully human existence. First and foremost, the members of society must be protected against interference by others in the pursuit of their essential tasks in life; only through social cooperation can such encroachments be averted. This defense is one aspect of the help which the common good represents for the members of society: the establishment of *peace*. This function is largely fulfilled by the law, which has the power of coercion behind it. The second basic function of the common good is making possible an integral human existence for the members of society: the establishment of public *welfare*. In this respect man's need and capacity for completion are highly versatile, so that, as our metaphysical and ontological analysis of society has shown, man is dependent in many respects upon social units in the pursuit of his full humanity: hence, the variety of existential social ends to which the spiritual, intellectual, moral, religious, cultural, economic, and social development toward the individual's full self is linked. Therefore, the idea of the common good and the help which forms its essence does not relate only to the state and to the political community; it also relates to the family and the nation, to local and vocational communities, to religious bodies and the community of nations.

The conception underlying the *individualist* interpretation of the end of society is that of the *"harmony of interests,"* a condition which is to exist when the legal system insures the freedom for individuals to pursue their interests. Behind this idea lies the concept of a pre-established harmony: men's aptitudes and energies are directed by the Creator toward bringing about the greatest general good of men, and would therefore, if left to develop freely, lead to the best for all. This is the idea of the *ordre naturelle,* from which the French physiocrats of the eighteenth century, led by *François Quesnay,* derive their name, and by which the ethics and the economic theory of *Adam Smith* are clearly inspired.

Gradually the theistic element was dropped from the concept of the harmony of interests. The concept was then given the interpretation that "enlightened" self-interest requires everyone to take account of the endeavors others make to attain their interest, in order that his own may be best realized. The most familiar expression of the social idea of individualist ethics, the idea of the common good, is "the greatest happiness of the greatest number," upon which *Bentham* founded modern utilitarian ethics.[1] In it Bentham seeks to sum up both the essence and the criterion of morality. However attractive this principle

[1] Cf. Jeremy Bentham, *Introduction to the Principle of Morals and Legislation,* 1789; *Deontology or Science of Morality,* J. Bowring, editor, 1834.

may seem at first glance, and whatever significance the general happiness may possess as a practical, secondary criterion of the moral rightness of individual conduct and of social institutions, it offers no explanation of what the terms moral and social mean. *Bentham's* criterion of morality is happiness, an abundance of pleasure, which comes as a result of certain conduct. But this offers only a formal principle of morality, a principle with no determinate content ("formal" like that of *Kant,* although contrary to it). Although *Bentham* undertakes a thoroughgoing classification of pleasure feelings, he does not say which feelings determine the nature of morality. Instead, the content of the "greatest happiness" is left to be determined by the "greatest number," that is, by the popular will. Logically, he places the moral sanction for the observance of what is demanded by the "greatest happiness," the common good, in the rewards and punishments laid down by the lawgiver, with the pleasant or unpleasant feelings associated with them. This means that his failure to relate the sanction of morality to God hands it over to the state. *Bentham* also leaves unanswered the question concerning where the motive for moral action is to be sought if there are no state penalties for opposite conduct or if actions against the social good can circumvent the penal law. Today, this utilitarianism has been abandoned theoretically, but in practice it forms the intellectual basis of "liberal democracy," with the predominant position which liberal democracy gives to the popular will and to the majority will, even in questions concerning the moral natural law. There is no denying, however, that the Benthamite principle proved a stimulus to social legislation to counteract the effects of unfettered individualist capitalism in nineteenth-century England.

In *collectivistic* theory the original utilitarian principle received a new presentation because of its obvious failure to determine the social good. Professor *Harold Laski,* for instance, aimed at developing the Benthamite theory on the lines of socialistic theory, with its emphasis on society as the dominating entity. He defines the social good as the search for things of value for themselves by the individuals, thereby enriching society as a whole.[2] Even in this collectivistic interpretation of *Bentham's* principle, the ultimate criteria for the substance of the social good continue to be the subjective pleasure of the individuals and the popular vote. For, the citizen considers the state to be an institution which exists to make his happiness possible, and he judges it by its capacity to fulfill his expectations; but that in which he wants to find happiness is private to himself.[3] Yet, *Laski* admits that universal franchise has disappointed expectations concerning the judgment of subjective reason in this regard; indeed, he even thinks that the mass of men are not clear about their real wants.[4] The collectivistic answer to this failure is the *planning of society* by the "experts" in accordance with the development of the technical forces of economic production. Thus, the end of society, according to collectivistic views of social philosophy as expressed by *Engels,* is seen in "the possibility of securing for every member of society, by means of socialized production, an existence not only fully sufficient materially, and becoming day by day more full, but an existence guaranteeing

[2] Cf. H. Laski, *A Grammar of Politics,* 1941, pp. 24 ff. (Laski speaks of evangelistic assumptions in Bentham's formula but does not say what they are.)

[3] Cf. H. Laski, *Liberty in the Modern State,* 1930, pp. 78 ff.

[4] Cf. H. Laski, *A Grammar of Politics,* p. 16.

to all the free development and exercise of their physical and mental faculties."[5] This is the collectivist postulate. What remains to be proved, however, is that man would not be delivered up to the "experts," i.e., to the managers, in this provider state with its inevitable planned economy.

23. The Common Good: An Actuality

Man's individual good, as we have seen, is wholly dependent on social cooperation and on spiritual, intellectual, moral, economic, and social participation in the common good. The individual good, therefore, which we have also called fully human existence, exists ontologically and metaphysically as part of the social whole as such. Thus, the common good is not a reality formed by the summation of the personally achieved individual good of the members of society; on the contrary, that is what makes possible their individual good. Compared with what the individuals could achieve for themselves, it constitutes *a new reality*. Like society itself (cf. Chap. 17), the common good possesses a supraindividual and enduring being of its own. Certainly, the sole basis for the existence of the common good is the individual members of society: without the individuals, there can be no common good. On the other hand, as with everything else, we must infer its nature from its functions. If we think of the persistence of family tradition and ethos, of ethico-cultural traditions largely rooted in and effective through the unconscious, of the organized system of peace and public well-being which continues in the state for generations and which is so necessary for all cultural activity, then we can see a reality of goods and values which belongs to the social whole as such. This reality is independent of the individual; in fact only by sharing in it can man attain the full reality of a cultural being. Hence, there is no doubt about the supraindividual and distinct character of the common good. We must conclude therefore: The common good is ontologically and metaphysically a distinctive reality in the social whole as such, making possible an integral human existence for the members of society.

We have deliberately spoken of goods and of values which are included in the common good. From these we must distinguish means and devices in the service of the common good. They too are component parts of the common good, but they belong to a subordinate realm of values, to the domain of instrumental values. Since, as we have seen, the individual good of the members of society forms part of the common good, it is not the instruments of social cooperation, namely, the various organizational and technical institutions and devices, which ultimately represent the common good, but their effects in the integral human existence of the members of society. A society may be equipped with the most perfect

[5] Engels, *Socialism, Utopian and Scientific,* trans. by E. Avelyn, 1892, pp. 80 f.

economic apparatus (e.g., a communistic totalitarian state), and yet the essential common good may be only partially realized in it. The institutions mentioned are, of course, goods of society, but they possess only the nature of means in the service of peace and of the general well-being of society in its members as a totality. A long list of such goods serving the common utility could be made. They would include chiefly the legal system, the public educational system, the public health service with its hospitals and research institutes, social welfare institutions, the defense forces and the police, and public utility services for transport, water, and light. All these institutions are means in the service of the common good, which ultimately consists in goods and values: in law and order in society, the guaranteed freedom of its members, the opportunity for all to pursue their essential tasks in life on their own responsibility and by their own efforts, a sound state of health in society as a whole, the insuring of the foundations of economic life for the immediate future and for the coming generations. The significance of the organizational and institutional side of the common good should certainly not be underestimated. We are concerned here, however, with the ontological nature of society and of the common good. It cannot be too strongly stated that the common good consists ultimately only in goods and values actualized in the members of society. This must be stressed particularly at a time when the progress of society is viewed too much in terms of institutions, organization, and technique.

The *institutional side of the common good* is, however, an indispensable and essential component of its reality. This is true for a number of reasons: 1) Much of the mutual complementation which is achieved through social cooperation is made possible by the provision of means for the use of all in the pursuit of their own interests. 2) The institutions are a means of storing up intellectual and economic values, labor and experience for the good of all. 3) The institutional side of the common good especially renders possible the progress of society, since in this way succeeding generations can utilize the experience and successes of earlier ones for the enrichment of the common good, and hence of the individual good of the members of society. Thus, we come again to the central point of the question: Only the attainment of a fuller and richer personality by the members of society constitutes real social progress, not the perfection of the institutional apparatus as such.

As an actuality, therefore, the common good is not merely a state of equilibrium in the interplay of interests, as the individualists and liberalists think. The fundamental error of their doctrine of the free play of forces is not taking into account the inequality of individuals, of their external circumstances, and of their mental and physical faculties. Furthermore, the common good is not, as the collectivistic theory holds, the actualization of a mechanical principle of equality. In the *Communist Manifesto, Marx* expressed it in this way: "Each according to his capacities, to each according to his needs." Individualist theory does not see that individual inequality in the mechanism of the unfettered free play of forces must place the less favored members of the community at a disadvantage; collectivistic theory misunderstands the reality of human nature by leaving out of account the significance of the fullest possible mobilization of all capacities for the complete actualization of the common good by means of the impulsion of individual interest, quite apart from the neglect of the significance of the personal responsibility of the individual which can only result in impairment of the development of the individual and hence of the common good itself.

24. The Common Good: An Order

Since the common good consists in help for all the members of society in fulfilling the tasks allotted to them by the existential ends, its reality is bound up with the order of ends laid down in man's nature; the same is true with regard to the order of proportional participation in the goods and values of the social whole which result from social cooperation. It should be noted that our present inquiry is concerned with the *metaphysical nature* and the *ontological reality* of the common good, namely, with the inquiry into the order of being, from which the conclusions regarding the moral-legal order will be drawn later. We have just spoken of the reality of the common good as a reality of order from two points of view.

In the first place, we have spoken of the order of ends rooted in human nature with the existential ends. It is especially important to refer to this today because the common good is all too generally understood as an order of distribution of goods in economic and social life, while at the same time the essence of the order of justice is placed principally in this sphere. Certainly, this aspect of the common good should not be underestimated. But man's chief good, fundamental to all others which are linked to existential ends, is his freedom, which is particularly fundamental to his full humanity as a person. The order of the common good, therefore, is essentially an *order of freedom* related to the spheres of responsibility of the individuals and of the member societies, this responsibility being based on the existential ends and the order of ends. Furthermore, the values of the common good which belong to the spiritual, intellectual, and moral spheres are incomparably more essential than the material ones. The fact that this is not just metaphysical speculation is understood today by the exponents of empirical cultural anthropology and of cultural sociology: the vital roots of culture lie in the spiritual-intellectual-moral sphere. The *culture of a society*, understood in its essential import, is nothing but the reality of the common good extending into all spheres of value, participation in which enables the individual man to become the cultural being which he is destined to be by his nature, and to possess what we call fully human existence, the necessary condition for which is afforded by society and the common good.

The spiritual-intellectual-moral values of this fundamental reality of the common good are transmitted to the individual by social tradition, which functions primarily through family and ethnic tradition. A conclusion of great significance follows from this: A society deviates farther and farther away from the full reality of the common good the more *family values* lose acceptance and the family pattern of life fails as the vehicle of those basic values in the common good. This shows how false is the view of a large proportion of present-day empirical sociologists who teach that the family is to be regarded only as the institution for the preservation of the species (cf. Chaps. 17, 47). The traditional natural law theory, if it described the child as the first purpose of marriage, always saw this end as naturally involved in the whole range of common good values in question; today it will have to stress emphatically this much wider range of values if it is to avoid the imputation that it is thinking of the child only in regard to the preservation of the species. In discussing this aspect of the order of being of society and of the common good, we have drawn attention to one of the most essential features in the supraindividual and lasting nature of the common good: in it are gathered together the thought and endeavor, the labors, experiences, and successes of countless generations, and in it they become a spiritually, intellectually, and morally creative factor. All this includes the fundamental convictions regarding essential human values, truly human attitudes, and the basic patterns of social life: in brief, everything which makes civilization the way of life of a society, with its proper ethos as the nucleus. The manner in which the common good is communicated and shared in the course of its realization in this sphere is unknown in part to the members of society. Thus, the common good is the reality which bears within itself the harvest of past generations as well as the source of life for future generations, as acres thrive from the sweat of fathers and of forefathers, thus promising fruit to children and to their offspring.*

We have spoken, secondly, of an order of *proportionality*. As distinct from the spiritual-intellectual aspect of the order of being of the common good, the aspect now to be discussed belongs more (but not exclusively) to the external sphere with its material values. In contrast with the values of the spiritual-intellectual sphere, a greater number of participants means smaller shares for the individual. There is a fur-

* I am not unaware that in certain forms of social life and ethos, for example among primitives, tradition can also involve erroneous beliefs and attitudes, which impede spiritual and intellectual progress, and may be influenced by the interest of ruling classes: the long life of such forms of society and culture proves, however, that in them the fundamental human values, even if in questionable external forms, are effective in determining the common good reality. They can be recognized by the ethnologist only if he is able to live a considerable time as a full member of such communities. In fact, such inquiries have shown that, in regard to these basic values of community life, especially those connected with the family, but also a number of other basic moral values concerning the behavior of members of society to one another, the "primitive" societies compare very well on the whole with "civilized" societies.

ther difference: the development and functioning of the spiritual-intellectual common good is not to any great extent present to the consciousness of the members of society; but the economic-social process is in the foreground of consciousness, since it means daily work and daily effort for the individual. The members of society experience social cooperation consciously, because it is linked with a *twofold individual interest,* namely, that of lightening the burden of one's work while also increasing earnings from it. The reality of the common good consists, even with regard to this aspect, in the help which all receive from their social cooperation in the performance of their essential tasks in life, tasks which are the same for all and based on the existential ends. Hence, the order of the common good involves an order of proportionality. The fruitfulness of social cooperation depends upon the application of greater and lesser individual capacities as well as upon the individual effort of the members of society. Thus, the order of the common good involves, on the one hand, unequal participation in the fruits of social cooperation, otherwise the services necessary for the realization of the common good will not all be available. On the other hand, by its nature, the purpose of social cooperation is to enable all to achieve a fully integrated human existence such as is demanded by their existential ends. Since these ends are essentially the same for all, the order of the common good consists in a proportionate equality of conditions for all in the attainment of their existential ends, in the light of what the total output of social cooperation makes possible for all groups and of what actually accrues to individual groups therefrom in virtue of existing privileged positions in regard to distribution.

When we describe the order of the common good as an order of proportionality, the aspect of *equality* and the aspect of *variety* are thereby comprised in their intrinsic relationship: the equality of the human nature of all members of society, which implies that all should have the opportunity to pursue their radically equal tasks, and the variety in men's contributions to social cooperation and its output, which involves corresponding differences in their participation in these fruits. The intrinsic relationship of the two aspects consists in the fact that the social cooperation of all with their different contributions, which makes possible for all the fulfillment of the tasks in life arising out of their uniform existential ends, is ordained by nature. These reasons, which are drawn from the order of ends, make it evident metaphysically and ontologically that the common good is an *order of distribution* of the material and cultural goods in a society.

As an order of proportionality, the order of the common good is *constantly developing.* The essential feature which distinguishes man from all other living creatures is his sense of value and his striving toward the realization of value. His mind urges him on toward the increasing of the goods and values serving his welfare and the satisfaction of his impulse toward happiness, and also toward the extension of his interests and purposes in life, and toward the improvement of the means of attaining them: *man is the creative animal.* The bird builds its nest without thinking about new possibilities in architecture, and the cow grazes without attempting to improve the pasture. In contrast, man is impelled by his instinct and desire for value enrichment to improve the conditions of his material and intellectual life. Hence, the progress made from the primitive cart and boat to the airplane and ocean liner, from flint and tinder to the atomic pile, from the cave dwelling to the modern house, from the primitive forest existence to the international civilization of today. The medium of creative development is social cooperation. The forces and the fruits of social cooperation change, so that the common good is actualized only by the continuous renewal of proportionality in the sharing of the product of social cooperation in accordance with the changing contributions of individual groups and the productivity of social cooperation as a whole. As an order of proportionality, the common good, therefore, is essentially an order of *dynamic evolution.* Both aspects of this order will be more fully discussed in the following chapters.

Both individualist and collectivistic philosophy fail to recognize the fact that by its nature the common good is related to an intrinsic order of society. *Sismondi,* one of the first important precursors of modern socialism, pointed to the basic cause of the abuses of individualist capitalism when, in his critique of its fundamental economic theory based on the principle of unrestricted freedom, he said that this was a theory of accumulation of wealth, whereas the function of political economy is to find ways to promote the general welfare. *Marx* begins his critique of political economy with the same ideas. The collectivistic theory goes to the opposite extreme because it sees the realization of the common good in an organization of society in which a share of welfare is provided for all individuals on the principle of abstract equality, to be guaranteed by regimentation and control of all activities: the human person becomes a mere statistical unit in schemes of planned production and consumption.

25. The Common Good: Its Causes

In order to bring about the good of its members, the community has no hands and no intelligence but theirs. Thus, the *efficient cause* of the common good is the endeavors of individual men engendered by their needs, wishes, and interests. The common good, therefore, can be realized and perfected only if the individuals can apply their faculties with as little hindrance as possible to the satisfaction of their needs and interests in social cooperation. It is to be noted that in social cooperation the individuals keep primarily in mind their own good, their own ends, and their own interests. Certainly, their interests and endeavors must be harmonized and coordinated with the common interest; this is the task of the social authority, which constitutes the *formal cause* of the common good. It operates by watching over, directing, stimulating, and facilitating the free activity of the individuals and of their associations. But since the efficient cause of the common good is ultimately the hands and brains of the individuals, the common good will be best promoted if the social authority can so influence their activities that, on the one hand, the efforts of the members of society to pursue their own interests are able to develop with as little hindrance as possible, and at the same time these efforts come to serve the general interest. This is probably the most important principle of good government.

The creation of effective institutions is the principal medium at the disposal of the social authority for serving the twofold aim mentioned. These institutions consist in laws, regulations, and administrative machinery (cf. Chap. 23). Since they serve the common good they belong to the class of *intermediate causes.* Their ontological status as social goods is not free from ambiguity. Some, like legal institutions, also share in the value-substance of the common good itself; others, like traffic regulations, are purely technical in character. Since both individual and social activities belong to the sphere of man's self-determination in their relationship, the common good becomes the *final cause* (cf. Chap. 18). The final cause operates in two ways. In the action of the organs of society the causality of the end must be direct; in their acts and forbearances they must be guided consciously and deliberately by the common good ends underlying their functions. It is otherwise with the actions of the members of society in pursuing their own interests and endeavors: it is not their affair directly to serve the common good; indeed, generally the common good is best served when they can look after their own interests in self-determination and use their own resources without harming the interests of other members of society. As an end in their actions, therefore, the common good need only be effective indirectly: it need not be the directly determining motive of action. We said "generally," because in particular cases, when the member of society takes on the character of an organ, the common good becomes the direct and primarily determining purpose, for example, in the exercise of one's right to vote in the election of the legislative body, or again in defending one's country against unlawful aggression either from inside or from outside.

All of this shows from a new vantage point the difference between the idea of the common good in natural law ethics and in individualist and collectivistic social theory. In individualist theory the general interest is basically the harmony of individual interests, considered as an automatic balance in the assertion of their interests by the individuals in the free play of forces; laissez faire, therefore, is its fundamental principle in economic and social policy. In collectivistic theory the main cause of the social good, in the words of *Engels,* is the systematic planning and organization of economic production, "whereby the struggle for individual existence disappears." * Although individualist theory does not see the necessity of harmonizing individual and group interests through social authority as a formal cause of the common good, collectivistic theory disregards the function of self-interest and the self-responsibility of the members of society in the service of the common good as an efficient cause.

26. The Common Good: Its Effects

In its effects the common good means proportionate participation by all members of society in the fruits of social cooperation. Why not *equal* participation so that all could have similar conditions of life? The reasons are both personal and social. Such equality is not implied in the integral human existence, which, as individual good, is ontologically part of the common good. Integral human existence consists in the shaping of the personality in an individual manner in the fulfillment of the tasks imposed by the existential ends, and not in a schematic equality of individual existences; it means the full maturity of the greatest possible number of personalities participating in the common good, not a universally equal humanity. Socially, too, the common good can become a complete reality only if the talents and capacities of the greatest possible number of persons are fully developed and at the same time their powers are fully effective, with the varied quality and quantity of their contributions on which the common good depends (cf. previous chapter). Because human nature cannot be switched on and off like a machine, and its activities depend on self-determination, this self-determination must, in the interest of the common good, be made effective through proportionate sharing in the fruits of social cooperation in relation to individual contributions. Even if one regards this proportionality as simply due to the need for higher endeavor, its explanation would by no means be merely psychological, as is often thought. What is at issue is the functioning of human nature in general. For this reason, the ontological aspect has been brought into the foreground in our argument. *Aristotle* devoted close attention to both sides, although he treated the entire matter almost exclusively as a question of the political common good in democracy; in a number of places he returns to this crucial question of the order of being to which the common good belongs, and he answers it with the principle of proportionality: proportionate equality as distinct from "numerical," quantitative equality.†

By means of two arguments, one of a personal and one of a social character, we have shown that the common good cannot mean equal participation by all members of society in the fruits of social coopera-

* Engels, *Socialism, Utopian and Scientific,* trans. by E. Avelyn, 1892, pp. 74–82.
† Aristotle, *Politics,* V, 1 and 7, 9.

tion. Nevertheless, the *proportionate* nature of this participation belongs to the essence of the common good. There are also two reasons for this, one personal and one social. The social reason is that the cooperation of all is equally necessary to attain the full reality of the common good; the work of a common laborer is as indispensable as that of the company director, the one depending upon the other. The other reason is the common essential nature possessed by all members of society—their personal nature—which means that their contribution toward the fruits of social cooperation is to be measured not only by external standards, like the work of machines, but by the standard of the functions which are laid upon all men alike by the existential ends. To facilitate the performance of these functions is an existential end designed in man's social nature. Thus, it is the social as well as the personal side in the full realization of the common good, the nature of society as well as the nature of the human person, that set a limit to the inequality in material and cultural existence of the groups in society and entail the proportionate participation of all members of society in the fruits of social cooperation.

The ontological factor which we have discussed makes evident from another point of view the essential feature of the common good: the common good is a reality only in a process of constantly renewed realization. The sum of the values implied in it can increase generally and lastingly only if all social groups share in such increase. This is a *fundamental law of all cultural progress.* Cultures stagnate when privileged classes are able to secure for themselves substantially increased shares at the expense of the rest of society. For long periods of time an elite can acquire socio-cultural functions of vital importance and along with them a privileged status. The future of their status, their function, and the extension of the class culture linked with these, materially and intellectually, is dependent on the continuing enhancement of the cultural state of the other classes. The reason is that for everyone a reciprocal relationship exists between readiness to contribute effort and to share in its fruits. If the common good is to expand, new creative intellectual and technical forces must be brought to bear, and through changes in the political and social status as well as in the economic and cultural standard of life of such new groups, new impulses must be awakened in the development of the common good. The transformation of ancient society and especially the emancipation of slaves were largely due to the fact that a greater part of the essential work and functions of society (e.g., in crafts, education, soldiering) passed into their hands, with the result that they developed into a new social status. The "political" upheaval brought about by the French Revolution and the present-day social movement toward full participation by the working class in the economic and cultural welfare of the community rest on similar grounds. The abovementioned law, therefore, signifies also that the growth of the common good is necessarily linked with changes in the character and structure of social cooperation. The desire for value attainment, which belongs to man's nature, keeps in motion the economic structure of society, and also the social structure, which again, if it leads to new effort, becomes the cause of an increasing value enrichment for all groups. Thus, we find ourselves turning again from the question of effects to that of efficient causes (cf. preceding chapter). For, it is self-evident that the principle of proportionality concerns the common good not only with regard to effects, but also with regard to the efficient causes. The two aspects are inseparable in the static as well as in the dynamic reality of the common good. All claims by groups to shares in the common good, which are not matched by a proportionate readiness for service, therefore, in the end go against the interest of these groups themselves for the reasons stated.

The conception of the common good outlined here and in the preceding chapter, stressing constant development in its actualization, is the *dynamic* conception. In this conception the constantly renewed realization of the common utility is conceived as a driving force in social progress; it underlies, as we shall see, the notion of social justice. In earlier chapters we developed the *static* conception of the common good, focussed on the unchanging end of society as derived from man's unchanging nature. The static conception affords a means for the understanding of the various social forms (family, local community, vocational community, state, international community) and their functions as based upon their essential ends. The dynamic conception, on the other hand, makes possible the understanding of the implications of social progress and the related tasks of social reform.

27. The Common Good: Its Structural Proportionment

Since the common good is realized only if the members of society share proportionately in the fruits of their social cooperation, the question arises with regard to what the proportional structures of the common good are to be: Is it possible to determine the shares of the groups in society, and if so how? Obviously, an exact mathematical calculation is out of the question, for the contributions of the individual groups to social cooperation, and still more those of the individual members of society, resist exact calculation. Not only is the quantitative effectiveness of the individual efforts dependent on others, because of the reciprocal relationship among all efforts, so that the importance of each individual contribution cannot be precisely assessed, but changes in the general pattern of contributions are constantly occurring also with the changes and progress in knowledge, in technical aids, in labor capacity, and even in interests, which prevent exact assessment of the outcome of individual effort.

Notwithstanding the impossibility of exact mathematical proportionment of the common good, the personal and social criteria (cf. preceding chapter), nevertheless, offer adequate standards. Social cooperation takes place in the form of the structure of services, which is again determined by the pattern of needs in society. In both directions social cooperation is determined by data regarding the ontological reality of man's nature and hence of the nature of society itself. Ontologically, the *pattern of needs* is founded on the bodily and spiritual needs of man. However complex this pattern may be in society as culture develops, the basic structure cannot change because of its dependence on nature; in fact it can be recognized, distinctive and unvaried, in all societies known to history. There is an ontological foundation also for the *division of services* and hence for the variety of occupations in social cooperation. This follows the diversity of needs; in addition, there is the ontological fact that the forms of service corresponding to these demand special ability, which is gradually learnt and handed on by tradition through the generations and at the same time operates as a builder of tradition and hence of community life. *Vocation and occupational groups are thus basic categories of social ontology.* It is the pattern of vocational groups, so based, that indicates the proportionment of shares in the common good by the application of personal and social criteria. First consideration is not due to the individuals because differences in their individual good, as we shall presently see, are not evidence against the full reality of the common good. Differences between the occupational groups in their respective shares in the common good, however, indicate a corresponding deficiency in the actual common good; the occupational groups carry out the services demanded by the common good in the division of labor. This organization of services makes it possible, in the first place, to assess the importance of the service performed by the individual occupational group, and secondly, to assess the comparative shares of occupational groups in the fruits of their cooperation. Thus, by means of an essential feature of social cooperation, the personal and social criteria make it possible to determine the structural proportions. A further criterion is afforded by the structure of social cooperation itself, since the quantity and quality of the services demanded by the common good (including the numerical strength of the occupational group) depend on the interrelation of effort and yield, thus showing whether the distribution of shares is in accordance with or contrary to the common good.

Hence, integral human existence, as dependent on the common good, proves to be a *relative entity:* it signifies the material and spiritual minimum of existence, dependent upon the state of the common good, but signifies also the material and spiritual higher level of existence, depending upon its extension through increased efforts by the various groups. As a relative quantity, therefore, the full reality of the common good depends ontologically not only upon the occupational groups' being allotted an appropriate share in the product of social cooperation, but also upon the facilitation of an ampler contribution of service with a view to the attainment of a higher productivity. Thus, the full reality of the common good involves the possibility of greater endeavor as the prerequisite of a greater share in the correspondingly developing material and spiritual culture. It is only by way of simplification, therefore, that one could sum up the structural proportionment of the common good with the statement that it is revealed most clearly in the relative living standard of the individual groups and classes. Such a formula leaves out of consideration important conditions for the full actualization of the common good. These include the opportunity to improve the standard of living of groups and the opportunity for social betterment for their members by means of improved efforts in both quality and quantity. The common good is all the more fully a reality, the more it avails itself of new efforts. If for large sections of a society there exists no possibility of performing social functions through social cooperation, for example, because of chronic unemployment, or no possibility of making such functions more productive, or for example, as a result of monopolistic restrictions on production by individual groups, obviously the common good, and with it the system of social cooperation in a society, is gravely prejudiced. The formula mentioned also does not make it sufficiently clear that with relatively equalized living standards of the social groups, some groups can enjoy a share of the goods of economic and intellectual culture without rendering adequate service, particularly because of positions of power, whether these are based on property, on organization, or on electoral majorities in mass democracy.

The actual distribution of the product of social cooperation on the principle of proportionality, and the order of the common good which this brings about, do not exclude *contrasts of wealth and poverty* which have their origin in differences of individual circumstances (e.g. personal abilities or disadvantages), and which cut across the various social groups. Such inequality, then, is not the effect of deficiences in the social system; the remedying of them is a matter for charity and for welfare institutions. Even the existence of privileged groups need not run counter to a true common good order if the political and cultural development of a society necessitates the existence of classes carrying out certain special cultural, political, military or economic functions; for this reason, such classes are endowed with special benefits according to the particular services they render to the community.

We have spoken often of the full reality of the common good. The metaphysical and ontological inquiry is concerned with the *essential reality* and hence with the essentially fully real being of the common good; it is the way to ascertain the order of being of society and of the common good, and hence is the only way to discover the moral order of society and to acquire standards for judging the *actual reality* of the common good. In this connection there is a universally existing fact of the greatest ontological significance: that, measured by the essential being of the common good, the common good is always more or less imperfectly realized. The reason is at the same time metaphysical and ontological, universal and necessary: the impairment of human nature (cf. Chap. 11). The order of being of human nature is disturbed, and hence the order of society, and in consequence also the order of the common good.

This double aspect of the conception of nature contained in the traditional natural law theory, according to whether attention is directed to the essential or to the actual reality, is objected to in the often and variously repeated criticism of traditional natural law: that on the one hand the order of being is derived from the nature of man, of society and of the common good; on the other hand, man, society, and the common good will attain to the full reality of their nature only in accordance with the demands of this order of being. This criticism is exactly parallel to an assertion that although medicine as a science works with an idea of the human organism and its proper functions, nevertheless, it regards bringing this organism to its proper functioning as its first task. As a matter of fact, all social sciences and social endeavors which make use of the concept of human dignity work with the same mode of procedure as natural law theory. They link the idea of human dignity with the nature of man, but regard it as a task, in the domestic and the international fields, to actualize the full humanity demanded by human dignity. The opponents of natural law theory should be particularly cautious with this criticism at a time when the thinking of social scientists, like natural science for a long time past, is coming more and more under the influence of evolutionary ideas.

From the point of view of traditional natural law theory, as we have shown, the idea of *evolution* proves to be inherent in the primal essence of the common good, since it is linked ontologically, metaphysically, and ethically with the law of man's nature. The cultural and social history of mankind provides the empirical evidence for evolution as it is seen by traditional natural law theory, with its progressive and reactionary forces, witness the manifold patterns of social dependence in the five thousand years of known human history, and today's ideal of internationally guaranteed equal human rights for all, the many stages of progress having seen steps taken forward and backward, yet with the final clear emergence of the ideal and the endeavors to realize it. The evidence contained in these facts for the evolutionary idea of natural law theory is incontestable.

This notion of evolution contains the key to one of the most perplexing phenomena of human history: throughout such a long period of human history large parts of society lived in conditions remote from the natural order of the common good. We may give in example slavery, or the intellectual and economic "minimum of existence" of large groups even in culturally advanced societies up to the most recent times. Empirical sociology has much to say about this and about the causes, which show themselves with great regularity: the warlike subjection of some peoples by others, the domination of some groups by others in society owing to the striving for power, the formation of classes to protect economic interests, the dependence of the development of the higher cultures on the existence of elites and socially dependent classes, and the restrictive effects of social tradition and custom. Natural law social philosophy with its social metaphysics and social ontology can bring to light the deeper reasons for the obstacles to development involved in the impairment of human nature in the faculties of reason and will; but it can also reveal the impulses to development in the human natural law, which have remained effective, though blunted, and on which is founded the state of the common good in advanced societies today; it can show also that this degree of progress is itself only a stage on the way from the imperfect to the more perfect.

28. The Common Good: Its Functional Proportionment

The common good is the good of society with respect to the totality of its members and the totality of its ends. It is a reality only if it carries out its functions adequately. We say adequately because, as shown in the preceding chapter, the common good can never be more than imperfectly, approximately realized. Two concrete questions regarding the degree of adequacy require answer. First: How far does the supraindividual nature of the common good make its realization independent of the existence of the *individuals in their totality* as members of society? Because the members without exception are not only individuals, and as such parts of the social whole, but also persons with suprasocial ends, the social whole is not only a unity existing per se, but also a *collectivity*, namely, a totality of individual persons existing per se and directed toward their particular good. The important conclusion which follows is that the common good is not something which exists independently of the collectivity of the members of society. The common good cannot be a reality except in the good of the members of society, just as the social whole has no being outside of its members. Although it is supraindividual, the common good cannot be gained by the sacrifice of a great part of the community, just as the well-being of the human organism is not to be increased by destroying a vital part of it. A fundamental error of totalitarian political theories is to consider that the good of the whole is something transcending the community as such and existing independently of the collectivity of its members, whether in the form of political power or national greatness (national-socialism), or of a social system (communism). Such conceptions have led to the sacrifice of great numbers of people for supposed ends of the state or the nation, as in aggressive wars. The principle in question, on the other hand, often makes decisions extraordinarily difficult, for example, in cases when war is forced upon a nation for the sake of its highest goods, its freedom, and its honor, and when defense would mean the destruction of its best forces and even then seems hopeless. Nations which have fought "to the last man" have often covered themselves with glory in the eyes of posterity. But, in fact, as long as a nation is not threatened with annihilation by the enemy, the common good may require it to take the opportunity of self-preservation and to renounce the glory of heroic self-defense.

The second question arises with regard to the *totality of the ends* involved in the common good. How far may the realization of essential ends and the fulfillment of essential functions of a society fail before its common good ceases to be a reality and the community forfeits the basis of its existence? A realistic social theory, like that of the traditional natural law school, will avoid confusing idea and reality and will not shut its eyes to the failure of community life, which has proved to be one of the most potent causes of suffering in human history and a cause of the gravest dangers to the essential individual good as based on the existential ends. The fact that communities can sacrifice their raison d'être is true of the family and of the state particularly. The institutional bonds may remain, but this does not mean that a community itself as such really continues to exist. A *family* may continue to reside in the common home and the legal ties may remain in force, but instead of serving the good of its members their common life may be a source of irreparable harm to all (this, of course, does not touch the question of divorce). Many *states* have been known to history, in which the extent of the common good represents a very doubtful minimum. A state of this type is the dictatorial state, the state of tyrannical rule, in its ancient and modern forms, in which vital goods of the commonweal, such as the rule of law, human rights and social rights, are gravely prejudiced. If such a state is denied its raison d'être, the question with regard to its replacement arises. In this respect natural law theory is realistic almost to the point of appearing self-contradictory. Thus, on the one hand it may regard as possible serious injury to the common good which would justify attempts at revolution, yet it warns against such attempts because they may still more gravely jeopardize the common good (cf. Chap. 132 on the question of active resistance). It is obviously considered as possible that the lesser evil may itself be regarded as a form of the common good.

In fact, like full human existence, the common good also can *be only a relative quantity* (cf. Chap. 27). It never becomes a reality except in the interplay of social forces, both the social forces which are intent on the general interest and those which aim at special group interests. If "never" seems too strong, it must be remembered that without exception the realization of the common good is defective owing to the impairment of human nature by original sin: to original sin are due the forces of evil in human nature and also man's merely gradual advancement in the knowledge of his nature along with the demands of the common good essential for the development of culture. The successes achieved in man's quest for culture, we are told by the sociology of culture, for long periods were possible only through the "division of labor" between elite and dependent classes, with a disproportionately low minimum of existence for the latter. One will have to be cautious, however, in making comparisons regarding particular societies in history. It has often been said that in the ancient civilizations, which possessed a higher sense of responsibility on the part of the governing class, the dependent class, including even the slaves, held a more secure footing in the order of the common good legally (because of protective measures), economically, and intellectually than did the working classes during the relentless progress of industrialization in Europe in the mid-nineteenth century; even *Marx* was of this opinion. But if one is to compare the common good of societies it should be noted that the price being paid today for industrialization in sacrifices of the common good in communist countries is certainly not less than that paid in the nineteenth century for industrialization in capitalistic Europe. There too, however, as in the Western World—perhaps in it only after generations—the dynamic nature of the common good will prove itself to be the relentless motive power toward an ever more complete realization of the ends of the common good, especially human rights and social rights.

Human nature decides what debasements of their common good nations and their underprivileged classes are willing and able to bear. Good evidence of how much they can bear is provided by the century of European industrialization. What those in Asia and Africa are willing to bear will decide the fate of the Western World insofar as the West will have first to convince those nations that what it has to offer them is an essentially more complete reality of the common good than what is promised by the other side. This will be the more difficult for the West because African and Asian peoples have little experience of the goods of an advanced common good reality, on which are based the freedom and standard of life of the West. Complete human existence and the common good are, as we have indicated in this and the preceding chapters, relative entities; but, precisely for that reason also, they are entities in a proportionality which, from the point of view both of society and of world politics, decisively influences the course of history. The fact that the reality of the common good possesses a relative and therefore dynamic nature, that is, carries within itself forces making for progressive development, is a law which I hope to have shown, metaphysically and ontologically, to be one of the fundamental laws of history.

29. The Ancillary Character of the Common Good

Our analysis of the common good has shown it to be something complementary and subsidiary: it is the help men receive from their social cooperation for the fulfillment of the tasks arising from their existential ends; it is *not an end in itself*. The conclusions to be drawn from this are of great moment in face of the individualist and collectivistic social theories, which are not as perverse on any other point. The individualist social theory narrows the auxiliary character of the common good to the securing of the free play of interests. In collectivistic thought the common good has not merely an ancillary position, but it is indeed the paramount end of human existence. In fact, the common good has only an ancillary character, but one that concerns the whole of human existence, since for the pursuit of all his existential ends man is in need of the aid of social cooperation. From this it follows that the common good cannot be a reality as long as a society seeks to develop it at the expense of the development of the human person, which is implied in these ends.

Linked as it is with the existential ends, the common good can be realized only within the framework of the order of ends. This means primarily that the *human person* can never become a mere means toward the common good without the common good itself forfeiting the essential ground of its existence. Even in the realm of ends of a lower category any interference is only in accordance with the common good itself, if it is the only way in which the ancillary function of the common good can be maintained in the service of goods of a higher order. Consequently, the promotion of the material prosperity of the whole body politic may demand from individuals sacrifices of material possessions, for example, in the form of heavy taxes or capital levies. A restriction of personal freedom in the form of general conscription or compulsory direction of labor has no justification in the common weal as long as the freedom of the community itself is not at stake. But an imminent or actual threat to the freedom of a community may require limitations on individual freedom. Even the sacrifice of man's bodily "existence" may be an indispensable means for the preservation of the existence of the community, and hence is, for the individual, a demand of the essential ends of his social nature. No trespassing on man's personal responsibility, where it is linked with his moral and religious conscience (e.g., regarding religious worship, the fundamental education of one's children), can take place without putting an alleged common good at a higher teleological level than the human person, and valuating the human person as a mere means in the service of such a common good.

The ancillary status of the common good is hardly doubted in the free society as far as the *intellectual life* is concerned. From the ontological point of view, our analysis has shown that great harm is done to the reality of the common good if society arrogates to itself in the fields of science, of art, and of literature, the function of regulating or directing creative activity instead of confining itself to its auxiliary function. Anyone who is not dazzled by collectivistic ideology will admit this. In regard to *economic life,* on the other hand, today there is a widespread inclination to look to state planning, organization, direction and control for everything essential. Little reflection, however, is needed to see that even in economic life the common good cannot be fully realized if its function is expected to be more than subsidiary. We must simply bear in mind the variety of men's needs and capabilities, in virtue of which the individual himself wishes to determine how he shall apply his powers and his income. The common good becomes real by opening up the widest opportunities to the desire for fulfillment in values, arising from these two sides of his nature. We do not deny that good planning, organization, and guidance of the economy by a socialist state may perhaps bring about increased production in certain directions. What is denied, however, is that such increase is synonymous with the realization of the common good. Just as the accumulation of wealth does not mean welfare, as *Marx* rightly points out in his critique of individualist capitalism, in the same way the wealth attained by a managerial economy under state socialism is not the common good. The economic order is identical with a true order of the common good only insofar as it ministers to the development of the creative personality of the greatest number of the members of society. In the state-socialist managerial economy the individual person is largely a subject of calculation as a unit in production and consumption. Even a higher standard of living attainable in this way, reckoned according to the values of the material sphere, may be far removed from the full reality of the common good just because economic riches are not identical with human culture. The common good cannot be purchased at the expense of the development of the human personality.

30. The Difference between Common Good and Individual Good

Our ontological analysis has shown that the good of the community and the good of its members are in a close reciprocal relationship, but are for that very reason disparate in kind. The common good consists in the factors resulting from social cooperation which make possible for the members of society the fulfillment of their tasks rooted in the existential ends; the individual good is the individual's capacity for attaining these purposes in self-determination. In other words, the common good consists in the opportunity provided by society for a life of fully integrated existence for its members; the individual good is the life of fully integrated existence lived by the members of society by their own power and responsibility.

Thus, the specific difference between social and individual good is a difference between perfections of being—that of society and that of the individual. Therefore, at bottom the difference is between society and the person as individual. To be more specific, the following differences have emerged: the good of the social whole is a supraindividual reality; the good of the human person is a suprasocial reality. The common good is the good of the social whole comprehending the good of its individual members as parts; the individual good is the good of the human person in the full humanity and is made possible by social cooperation. We have called the common good and the individual good perfections of being. Because they are perfections of being which make possible the attainment of fully real humanity they belong to the world of goods and hence of values: the common good and the individual good are actualizations of a different kind of value. The common good is the social reality of values which forms the ground for the complete human existence of the members of society; the individual good is the actualized values, lived in complete human existence, and bound up with the personality values. Thus, the common good is a social reality with a supraindividual rank in being and value by virtue of the plurality of members whose complete being depends on it; the individual good is a reality with a suprasocial ontological and axiological rank proper to the human person. If we describe as social culture the actualization of values and goods springing from social cooperation and making for man's complete existence, we may conclude: the sphere of the common good is *culture,* that of the individual good is the *person;* the two spheres are essentially different but essentially interdependent.

There is no essential difference between social good and individual good, the individualists and collectivists say, although for opposite reasons and with opposite conclusions. In the individualist view the social good is at bottom nothing more than the sum of the individual good of the members of society, and hence does not differ from that. In the collectivist view, an individual good consists only in participation in the social good of the collective whole, and hence it is one with it. As we have shown, the individual good is a participation in the social good insofar as it cannot be realized except with the help arising from social cooperation. The social good consists in the conditions necessary for the members of society in the pursuit of their individual good by their own effort and on their own responsibility.

31. The Pluralistic Character of the Common Good

Since the various existential ends, for the realization of which man requires social completion, involve various forms of social union, and hence various forms of social ends, the common good is by nature pluralistic. These particular ends of the social units are the basis of their particular responsibility and competence in the pursuit of their own common good. Because of the nature of the common good, the pluralism characteristic of it is seen to mean *autonomies of communities* in the service of existential ends. The greater and lesser communities with nature-ordained ends are, among others, the family, the local community, the vocational community, the state, the greater national and international regional communities, and the community of nations, each with its special common good. In addition there are associations based on ends freely chosen, such as those devoted to various cultural, economic and social purposes; these include, among others, charitable organizations, trade unions, employers' associations, and animal welfare societies.

This multiformity of the common good does not mean a mere sum or coexistence of different communities or associations, but a unity of order in conformity with the order of ends. The ordered unity of individual and social ends is indicated in the oneness of human nature, and with that the ordered unity of responsibilities and competences of the greater and lesser communities, the latter each having its own independence and being subordinated to the former insofar as they are parts of them. Thus, the pluralistic nature of the common good involves *a hierarchy of communities,* the greater or lesser extent of whose competences is determined by their ends. Each is autonomous within the sphere of its own ends, yet subordinated to the greater society insofar as the wider end of the latter is concerned. Hence, the autonomy of individual communities is described as relative. This may be illustrated by examples. A number of ends and functions fall within the sphere of care for the needs of daily life which pertain exclusively to the family. But families in the same neighborhood are in need of cooperation, which results in the local authority, which provides common requirements such as roads, bridges, water, lighting. Provision for the common needs of the local communities in a region forms the basis of the competence of the regional unit in the sphere of functions connected with this end. All the smaller communities need the "great community," the state, to secure law and order internally, peace externally, and to provide certain services for all and for the general welfare in such fields as transportation, money, health, and education. The social hierarchy in the pluralism of the common good is thus essentially correlative with the autonomy of the smaller social units, with their own responsibility and competence.

The pluralistic order of being of the common good is, as we shall see more fully later (Chap. 44), at the root of the order of subsidiary function with the autonomy and hierarchy of functions springing from social ends. Hence, like all other natural law social principles, the *principle of subsidiary function* is *primarily an ontological principle,* and hence also a principle of order.

Individualist and collectivistic social theories are equally *antagonistic to the idea of a social pluralism* founded on a plurality of social ends. In the individualist view the fundamental function of society is merely a negative one, namely, the exclusion of the interference of individuals in the spheres of other individuals. This view leaves no room for lesser communities intermediate between the individual and the state with their own ends and relative autonomy. Following out this principle, liberalism, in the course of the nineteenth century, initiated a shifting process in society. Previously society had lived in a framework of traditional community bonds (many of which were undoubtedly obsolete). This society was now set in motion from inside by the individualist interest mechanism, having as its moving principle the freedom of the individual in the pursuit of his interests. Vital binding forces of the community organism were severed, individuals in growing numbers were "set free" within, and exposed to the social interest mechanism. The accompanying transformation of society into the mass society constitutes the *liberalist revolution of the nineteenth century*. Because of its gradualness it is rarely ever thought of as a revolution, although in its effects it represents perhaps the most complete and far-reaching revolution in world history. In its effects it is the precursor of totalitarian collectivism in its various forms. Collectivism is unthinkable without the mass society which emerged from the liberalist revolution. The predominant position of the collectivistic ends of the all-embracing society entails for the collectivistic social theory the principle of "total coordination" (*gleichschaltung*), the exact opposite of individualist laissez faire, i.e., the coordination of the activities of the members of society throughout the range of public life into the pattern of collective ends set up by the holders of political power. Accordingly, this coordination leaves no room for a plurality of independent social ends as a basis for smaller communities with their own common good and relative autonomy. All the particular questions connected with the principle discussed will engage our attention in the following Books.

32. The Structure of Society

The structural order of society is founded on the pluralistic nature of the common good: the universal society, the state, is built upon, or divided into, relatively autonomous large and small social units. When we speak of the *integration* principle of social order we are looking first at the smaller units, and we pass by way of the greater to the comprehensive society; when we speak of the principle of subdivision we pass from the larger to the smaller. These two principles are often spoken of as the federal and corporative. The term *federal* connotes the alliance or federation of smaller social units, and hence their uniting into a greater whole while retaining their relative autonomy. The term *corporative* points to the branching or articulated division of the social organism into lesser social bodies as member communities with self-determination. Thus, these two principles illuminate different sides of the social organism as a whole consisting of parts. All these expressions, "organic," "corporative," "federal," as well as the two principles in question themselves, emphasize the same fact: that the comprehensive society is a unity composed of smaller communities with relative independence or autonomy, and that these all have their own social ends, their own common good, and hence their own functions (and hence again, as we shall see presently, their own competences and rights).

Of these member communities the family is the most vital, the life-cell of society. From the family, the social fabric extends outward in two main directions, political and economic. Politically, it is made up of local and regional units and, beyond those, of wider territorial communities such as the states of the United States of America, the national groups of the United Kingdom, and the Bundesländer in Germany and Austria; economically, the social organism (in essence, if today only to a rudimentary extent in places) is made up of vocational groupings with their local, regional, and national associations of employers and employees in the various branches of industry.

Another important conclusion can be drawn from the natural order of society as here described: It is not the individuals who directly form the members of the comprehensive society; rather, they are members of it through the intermediacy of the family and of the territorial and vocational groups, great and small. In a naturally ordered society there is relatively little direct contact of the individual with the state. Surprising as this statement may seem to minds accustomed to the individualist-collectivistic image of society, it is confirmed by the experience of citizens in every state community in which natural social pluralism has not been wholly ousted by state centralism. In normal times the citizen is hardly at all aware of the state in the sense discussed. He is in direct contact with the state mainly through military service and taxation, and even in the latter case only when he is paying direct taxes. In modern democracy, admittedly, universal direct suffrage in the election of parliaments represents a highly important form of contact between the citizen and the state; yet, the crisis of mass democracy shows at least that here there is a one-sided development which undoubtedly calls for redress, or, better, counterpoise through the strengthening of the regional and vocational communities. In the well-ordered society it is not the state that stands in the foreground of consciousness of the majority of citizens; rather, apart from the family, the local and vocational bodies are foremost, and, last but not least, voluntary associations of all kinds. As long as a society preserves its essential structural pattern, social life moves preponderantly in these smaller social units. Even where direct relations between individual and state do exist, as in the sphere of the functions fundamental to society, for example, the maintenance of peace and order internally and externally, they do not involve any pronounced "political consciousness" as long as national and international order are not affected by profound disturbances.

Everything is changed, however, when social pluralism is increasingly strangled by state centralism as a result of the dynamism of an individualist-collectivistic society. This can be summed up as one single dynamism since forces are at work which, although intellectually and politically different because they come from opposed origins, yet result alike in the elimination of the social units which are intermediate between the individual and the state. The result is a predominance of direct connections between the individual and the state, so that either the individuals collectively (as pressure groups in the liberal-democratic society) make the state the instrument for realizing their sectional interests, or the state (totalitarian socialistic) makes use of the organized groups politically and economically in order to subject society to its short-term and long-term purposes.

33. Society as a Value in Itself

Because in origin the common good is aid, society holds an essentially subservient position. This does not mean, however, that society lacks any value of its own. Indeed, it does possess intrinsic value of a very high order, not in the sense that it can lay claim to an ultimate value based on an independent end, but by reason of its auxiliary function. For, insofar as society fulfills this end, it becomes, as we have shown, itself an actuality with its own rank of being and of value. The individual good of its members as parts of the social whole then becomes itself a part of the common good, since it comes into existence with the aid of society and by causation through society. Hence, *St. Thomas* could say that the common good stands higher in its intrinsic value and is the more "divine" in proportion as it embraces a greater number of goods in its effects, thus drawing nearer to God, the final Cause of all good.[1]

Indeed, in bringing about its common good, society, like every other actualized order, becomes part of the order of the universe as intended and planned by God in his creation, to be completed by man in the cocreation to which he is called in order to share in the carrying out of God's law and plan for the world. With the realization of its common good order, therefore, society, as *Augustine* points out, becomes part of the beauty of the universe, since the idea of beauty is inseparable from that of order.[2]

Social reality even outlasts temporal existence, since men's association in the pursuit of their ends is reflected in the final attainment of these ends in the life to come. And love, the fundamental constituent of all human community life, insofar as it has been an impulse toward man's self-perfection through union with others, will form an integral part of

[1] St. Thomas, in *Eth.*, lib. I, 2g.

[2] St. Augustine, *De vera religione*, n. 76: "Ordinantur omnes (all beings) officiis (functions) et finibus suis in pulchritudinem universitatis; n. 77: Nihil enim est ordinatum, quod non sit pulchrum; n. 80: Quaedam gradatio . . . ordinata convenientia pulchra judicetur."

the life to come, and hence will be a lasting reality, entering into the union of all with the *communi et immutabili bono* (*St. Augustine*). Thus, the life to come essentially will be community life. How, says *St. Augustine,* could we speak of the City of God were not the life to come social life—*si non esset socialis vita sanctorum.*[3]

[3] St. Augustine, *De civ. Dei,* XIX, c. 5.

PART THREE

The Order of Society: Legal Philosophy

---

34. The Basic Question

If at this point we seem to be approaching the real object of Book One, legal philosophy, for the first time, this is not an altogether correct impression. Hitherto we have been concerned principally with the nature of man and with the "existential ends" indicated therein. Indeed, without exception, all important legal philosophies and social theories start from the idea of ends: the object of their endeavors is the order of purposeful conduct, which is indispensable in man's communal life.

The question of ends may be posed with greater or less emphasis in this or that school of legal philosophy, but it is common to them all, whether we think of the metaphysical and theological conception of law, which seeks the order of ends in the divine will; or of the positivist, which sees the existing order of ends as rooted in the will of the ruler or the ruling group; or of the utilitarian conception, which finds the order of ends in the people's will as ascertained by democratic methods. In day-to-day political and professional life it is the same. When right and wrong are discussed, the question at issue is always the order, or relative importance, of ends, that is, of interests in the purposive behavior of individuals or of groups or of society as a whole or of states toward one another. We have this order of ends in view whenever we speak of human rights in general, whether of fundamental rights constitutionally guaranteed or to be guaranteed, or when we speak of the question of superior or inferior claims on the total economic output of society to be enjoyed by vocational groups, or of the advantages and disadvantages of the capitalistic economic and social system, socialism, communism, or world peace. The question of law or rights always involves the question of the ordering of man's purposive conduct. Always underlying this question is that of the inner *rationale* of the ends governing this conduct and of the order sought. In this, all answers are based on an implicit or explicit interpretation of human nature.

It has been suggested that to *base legal philosophy on social ontology,* as we have done, is a roundabout procedure, and that the reverse is the better, namely, to base social metaphysics on law: the ontological basis of the being of society, it is said, lies in the dependence of each person's rights on the equal human rights of every other person. At once, however indisputably the question arises what these human rights are and, more importantly, why equal human rights; indeed, the greater part of the history of civilization reveals no such equality in practice. The idea behind this view is similar to *Kant's*. *Kant* described freedom as the sole original right of man, and from that he came to his principle of the freedom of every person consistent with that of every other in accordance with a general law (cf. Chap. 36). Yet, this principle, because it is purely formal, that is, of no definite content, satisfies equally well the individualist conception of law, as represented by *Kant,* and the collectivistic conception as represented by *Marx,* whereby "the free development of each is the necessary condition of the free development of all" (cf. Chap. 41). If, as the view in question implies, one were to seek the ontological basis of society in law, one would then have to inquire into the ontological foundation of law, unless one were to explain law in terms of itself. To say that it is responsibility is unsatisfactory for the simple reason that responsibility is not "is" but "ought." To trace this ought-ness to its foundation is one of the principal tasks of ethics in general and of legal ethics in particular. To make the equality of personal value the foundation of legal and social order is by itself no explanation, because it is then necessary to answer the obvious question, what man's personal value is and in what it is rooted. In fact, both *Kant* and *Marx* endeavor to ascertain the ontological basis of law. The former begins from the nature of the individual, the latter from the nature of society, and, linked together in this, they both also begin from the idea of equality: to *Kant,* the equal right to freedom has its origin in the equality of rational nature; to *Marx,* the equality of all is the goal, which is dependent on the evolution and implicit in society, toward a social order of equality. Thus, in their inquiry into law these doctrines take their departure each from its own form of humanism, its own conception of the nature of man, just as, in fact, *every answer to the question of the nature of law (and of the state) is founded on a definite conception of the nature of man, an anthropology, a special kind of humanism.* For this reason we have had to lay the foundation of our natural law ethics by making an analysis of man's personal and social nature.

St. Thomas Aquinas also makes use of an idea of equality in his answer to the question on the nature of law, in order, however, to show that the answer cannot come from the mere idea of equality, but only from the determination of what equality is in the concrete. In treating of virtues he comes to speak of the virtue of justice and says that it has to do with a kind of equality (*aequalitatem quamdam*) and hence, obviously, its characteristic implies relationships between people (as distinct from other virtues). He points out that in popular speech mutual settlements are spoken of as *iustari* or "getting even." What is to be settled, or balanced, can be determined from the "nature of the case" (*ex ipsa natura rei*), which is called "natural law"; or it can be determined by private or public agreement or by decree of the lawgiver, which is "positive law." Accordingly, the object of the virtue of justice is the "equalizing" of what is given to what is due, *suum cuique:* "Ideo proprius actus iustitiae nihil aliud est quam reddere unicuique quod suum est." * With his idea of equality *St.*

* St. Thomas, *Summa theol.,* IIa IIae, q. 57, aa. 1–2; IIa IIae, q. 58, a. 11.

Thomas wishes to establish two essential features which belong to the virtue of justice as distinct from other virtues: (1) that it concerns external relations between men; (2) that there is a measure in accordance with which must be performed what justice commands (e.g., something agreed by contract as distinct from an obligation of a charitable nature), namely, the *suum* in the sense of a claim based on a definite legal basis to a particular behavior or a definite payment on the part of others. The equality idea has, therefore, in *Thomas'* arguments, a wholly different function from the function it has in *Kant* and *Marx* and in any legal philosophy working with only a formal idea of law.

35. The Origin of Law

Law, as we have just seen, is the order of purposeful conduct in the realm of relations between people; this is accepted both by jurists and by other thinkers. The ends by which men's actions are determined are of different kinds. One group of ends is distinguished by the fact that to aim at them involves moral responsibility. As we saw when discussing the ontological basis of morality, ends may be designed in human nature; these are the existential ends, which constitute responsibilities. They are ends which man has a moral duty to fulfill. Responsibility in some matter, because of its moral nature, implies a claim to be respected by anyone who is capable himself of responsibility by reason of his nature. Thus, for everyone for whom existential ends establish responsibilities, these ends imply titles to comply with them, and this first and foremost by the exclusion of any interference by others; in other words: rights to act in self-determination.[1] Rights, and therefore law, thus have their *origin in man's existential ends.* The subjects of rights are individual persons and joint persons; for, the common good, since it is an existential human end, is a source of responsibilities for the community as such, assigning to it a sphere of its own authority in virtue of this end. In a true sense,

[1] Fundamentally the same idea of the basis of law seems to be expressed by Gustav Radbruch in *Einführung in die Rechtswissenschaft,* K. Zweigert, editor, 9th ed, 1952, pp. 38 f.: "The doctrine of the essence of duty—however its content may be determined—involves *absolute demands on law.* Law cannot of course set itself the task of ministering directly to the fulfillment of ethical duty. The performance of ethical duty is necessarily an act of freedom and therefore not to be carried out by legal compulsion. Law cannot enforce the fulfillment of ethical duty but only make it possible. Law is the pre-condition of conduct in accordance with moral duty or, in other words, that measure of external freedom without which the inner freedom of ethical decision cannot exist. It is the core and essence of *human rights* to guarantee that external freedom. Thus, it follows that these rights are absolute in nature, not indeed in the sense that they have assumed this or that form of positive law, but in the sense that they are necessary in order to make possible the fulfillment of moral duty." With this, clearly Radbruch is already on the threshold of natural law, if not already within. Concerning the development and change in Radbruch's thought on legal philosophy cf. the Introduction by Erik Wolf to his new (5th) edition of Radbruch's *Rechtsphilosophie,* 1956, and especially Radbruch's supplementary essay "Gesetzliches Unrecht und übergesetzliches Recht."

therefore, to quote the well-known phrase of *Ihering:* "End is the author of law." By assigning this place to end in the foundation of law (cf. Chap. 3, n. IV), traditional natural law ethics acquires a *teleological* character.

The attainment of man's existential ends depends upon his social connections: this truth was the outcome of our inquiry in the preceding chapters into the interdependence of men in their attaining to integral humanity. We found social cooperation to be designed in human nature itself, and one of the most important aims of this cooperation we discovered to be the securing of the spheres of responsibility of the individual and of society, and of their self-mastery in accordance with their existential ends, against encroachments from without. Against attempts at violent encroachment upon such spheres of self-competence, such security is feasible only by force. Thus, already in the origin of law we find enforcement bound up with it. To sum up: The ends which are designed in human nature constitute responsibilities for individuals and communities, and hence titles to carry out these responsibilities unimpeded [2] and the right to protect these titles, if necessary, by force.

Since the Creator assigns these responsibilities to individuals and to communities through the ends designed in human nature, rights and law have their ultimate source in God. From this point of view we appropriately speak of "natural and divine law" as one and the same thing. Such a statement does not go beyond the bounds of legal philosophy as long as law is not directly inferred from the will of God. Indeed, an exhaustive investigation of the phenomenon of law must go back to the ultimate source of the order of being and of ends. Thus, *Constantin Frantz,* that distinguished German Protestant political thinker, is only drawing a logical inference from clear premises when he says that the idea of law implies the idea of a personal God.[3] Only if a personal God is recognized as creator and lawgiver can the idea of the "might of right" possess its quite definite authority; otherwise, there is no compelling reason why the principle "might is right" should not in one way or another prevail. The sanctity of law, which we are wont to speak of, has no real meaning apart from the existence of a personal God.

The various *theories of legal and political philosophy* ultimately attribute the origin of law to: (1) the social contract (the individualist school: Chap. 37); (2) the social "institution" (the French school: Chap. 42); (3) the autonomy of the individual (the rationalists and the Kantian school: Chaps. 36, 38); (4) the popular will (the liberalist theory: Chaps. 37, 38); (5) the popu-

[2] Since animals have no awareness of existential ends and therefore no moral responsibility for the accomplishment of such ends, they have no rights in the true sense of the word. But to inflict unnecessary suffering on them is against man's own existential ends since it hardens him in his feelings toward human beings. To inflict suffering on animals may, however, be necessary for man's own existential ends, and thus for his good, e.g., in experiments to further scientific knowledge.

[3] Cf. C. Frantz, *Die Naturlehre des Staates,* 1870, p. 194.

lar mind (the historical school: Chap. 40); (6) social experience (the purely empirical and evolutionist theories: Chaps. 40, 54); (7) individual utility (the individualist-utilitarian school: Chap. 39); (8) effective authority (the positivist and analytical school: Chaps. 38, 41, 49, 54); (9) coercive power (the physical force theory: Chaps. 38, 54); (10) the "mode of production in material life" (the dialectical materialist theory: Chaps. 39, 41, 54); (11) social utility (the socialistic-utilitarian school: Chap. 39); (12) social functions (the collectivistic schools: Chaps. 36, 37, 39); (13) the utility of the people (the national-socialist theory: Chaps. 36, 39); (14) the objective spirit (the idealist, Hegelian and neo-Hegelian schools: Chaps. 36, 38, 39, 49); (15) the initial legal hypothesis (the pure theory of law: Chaps. 42, 50, 54); (16) law identical with its actual effects (the sociological school: Chap. 54); (17) the sense of justice (the psychological-subjectivistic school: Chaps. 41, 50); (18) the consciousness of duty (the recognition theory: Chap. 38); (19) personality values (the value-ethics school: Chap. 39); (20) man's existential ends (the legal philosophy developed in this work on the basis of traditional natural law theory).

36. The Nature of Law

Now we can educe a very general concept of the nature of law: Law is the order of rights to act in self-determination. Law consists in guaranteed titles in the sense that one is empowered, under guarantee of noninterference by others, to do, to have, or to demand something, namely, to act in self-determination. In essence, a right is a title or power to act. Thus, our definition remains in harmony with the common sense of mankind, for whom law primarily means authorization. Since law is one of the fundamental facts of human existence, this link with common sense must remain evident in the scientific development of the notion of law. (Here it must be stated again that this does not mean titles conferred upon individuals only, but also those of communities and particularly of the state.) As a title or authorization, each right is a kind of power of control. The second essential feature of law, order, equally belongs to it in conformity with the common sense of mankind. Law consists in titles or powers with the property of precluding interference by others. It is a pattern of the mutual delimitation of competences, together with a guarantee of the behavior implied by these competences on the part of others toward those entitled. This behavior is social behavior; from this derives the third feature of law: it is of a social nature.

The titles conferred by law are conferred along with the responsibilities bound up with man's existential ends, and hence they are *definite in content.* In this question too common sense is not uncertain, e.g., regarding man's title to his life, to the inviolability of his person, to his good name, to bring up his children, to the disposal of his rightfully acquired property. Scientific-philosophical analysis has shown us that the existential ends are the basis of the rights which constitute the essence of law.

Thus, we arrive at the closer definition of law, which is also our supreme *principle and criterion* of law: Law is the order of social relationships in harmony with the existential human ends.

In many definitions, law is seen only as the pattern of external limitations of competences, of the pursuit of interests, and of freedoms. In a conception of law founded on the nature of man, such as that presented here, these competences, freedoms, titles, that is, the original individual and social rights, are seen to be by their nature *intrinsically limited.* In the first place, the power in which a right consists does not go beyond the end in which it is rooted. Man's right to freedom of worship does not entitle him to coerce others to adhere to his religious profession against their convictions. Secondly, rights are limited because of the respect for the rights of others which are rooted in their equal existential ends. The right to self-preservation does not entitle one to kill another directly even in a case of extreme danger, for example, when one is sharing an inadequate supply of food with a fellow mariner after having been shipwrecked. Hence, we may conclude: *No unqualified right* belongs either to an individual or to a society.

Because their roots are in moral responsibilities, natural rights are *inviolable and inalienable.* The exercise of rights may be impeded, but this does not cancel the rights themselves, for rights are inviolable. It is evident to anyone whose property is stolen that his ownership continues and that he has a title to recover his property. Man cannot divest himself of his elementary rights, since he cannot divest himself of the moral duties on which they are based. Parents cannot renounce their right to bring up their children. They may wholly or in part delegate this function to others, but their responsibility, the right itself, is inalienable. The duty in question falls back on the parents themselves if the education provided by those to whom the function is delegated does not conform with the end from which the right springs.

The inviolability and inalienability of rights indicate their twofold relationship to duty. Rights are primarily bound up with duties which are rooted in the ends underlying these rights; secondly, the rights of one person impose on everyone else the duty of respecting them. Law, therefore, comprises juridical powers, that is, claims based upon rights, and juridical duties, that is, duties relative to jurdical claims; these are obligations of justice with the special property that their fulfillment can be enforced. Consequently, the basic feature of the order of society is one of juridical relations.

As a power of control, every right implies a legal subject, which is in possession of the title to control, and a legal object over which the subject is empowered by the right to exercise control. Legal subjects can be physical or corporate persons. Legal objects can be things or services rendered by persons. A *thing* in the legal sense is a legal object over which unrestricted control may be exercised; hence, only by a departure from the natural juridical order in a given legal system can man become a "thing," like the slave in ancient law. "Things" in the sense of legal objects can be material things like machines; or forces bound up with material things, like electricity; or immaterial things, such as a musical work or an invention.

With regard to the *human person,* in a society with fully developed juridical consciousness rights can only establish a title to services and then only insofar as such services are not in conflict with existential ends. Hence, there is no right involving immoral acts on the part of a person (e.g., acts contrary to a person's own religious convictions); no contract and no court can turn such "legal" claims into true rights. Every labor contract, for the reason given, includes an implied condition that the person of the worker and his responsibilities rooted in existential ends will be respected; it is, therefore, a distortion of the natural order of law if an economic system, either individualistic or communistic, imposes working conditions which prevent the worker from fulfilling his duties toward his family, whether by overworking or underpaying him. His own person is, of course, the legal object of man's rights to his body, to his freedom of movement, to his working capacity, etc.

The essence of law as an order of competence to act in self-determination seems twisted when it is conceived of as a system of compulsion and rules, the essence of which is a *heteronomy* imposed on the members of society. Such a system of rules is what law means for *Kelsen* and his school. *Hans Nawiasky* defines the legal order as "the definite and concrete system of prescriptions, maintained by a social community (delimited in space and time) or by its governing class, for the outward behavior of the members of society, noncompliance with which entails coercion or punishment"; with the attribution of legal order to the will of the state "the character of law as heteronomy is obvious." In fact, in face of the state systems of rules and compulsion there always arises the question of their justification; and indeed to the common sense of humanity there is no doubt that the state does possess a right to establish rules and employ coercion to ensure compliance, but not an absolute right, because man as man also possesses rights. The general opinion of mankind is able to distinguish between the rights of the state and the assumed right of leading classes of society who know how to use the state system of compulsion for their own interests. *Nawiasky* thinks that if natural law exponents start from original titles, such "prelegal" titles can exist only in the moral sense; immediately before that, however, he expressly admits the possibility that "subjective rights reached consciousness earlier," and that the natural law "demands respect from the lawgiver in the exercise of his functions"; nevertheless, he declares, "it does not ultimately belong at all to law as a system of compulsion." [1] This is true if it is correct to say that law is only a system of compulsion. But this concept is again questioned largely because of recent experience with systems of state rules which were imposed by leading groups with the totalitarian heteronomy

[1] H. Nawiasky, *Allgemeine Rechtslehre: System der rechtlichen Grundbegriffe,* 2nd ed., 1948, pp. 18, 23 f., 29, 170 f.

of man, in contrast with the essence of human rights, which imply titles to self-determination. This is not to deny, however, that there is an element of truth in *Nawiasky's* view, as in legal positivism generally, and to this we shall return.

Both essential features, as shown above, belong to law: "competences" to act in self-determination and the "ordering" of social relationships bound up with these. *G. del Vecchio's* definition is based exclusively on the idea of order: "Law is the objective co-ordination of the acts possible among a plurality of subjects according to an ethical principle which determines their development and precludes interference." [2] This conception of law, however, leaves open the question concerning the nature of justice and injustice. Not only is man aware of definite rights, whose infringement means injustice; he is also aware that the responsibilities designed in his nature and in its order of being and ends, and hence ontologically based, yield a concrete order of concrete rights. The definition of *del Vecchio* says only that an ethical principle "determines" the development of subjects but leaves indeterminate in content what this claim to development involves; the "ethical principle" is confined, as with *Kant*, by whom *del Vecchio* is influenced, to a merely formal conception of order; furthermore, the "subjects" are obviously thought of only as individuals and not also as communities enjoying equally elementary rights.

The fact that *Kant*, in his supreme legal principle, is committed to individualist thinking, is placed beyond doubt by sociology of knowledge: "There is only one innate right. Freedom (independence of the compelling will of another), as far as it can coexist with the freedom of everyone else according to a general law, is this one, original right, due to every man in virtue of his humanity." *Kant's* general jural principle declares, therefore, that "law is the totality of conditions under which the will of one can coexist with the will of the other according to a general rule of freedom." [3] In his formula, *Kant* expresses the principle of the equality (cf. Chap. 34) of the elementary rights to freedom of all individuals. But the formula does not offer any definition of what freedom itself consists in and to what in particular it entitles one. Indeed, he himself leaves no doubt that according to his philosophy the general jural principle, like the moral one, can be only a formal one. In his critique, *Hegel* dealt accurately with the weakness of *Kant's* principle, often pointed out later in various forms. *Kant's* definition, says *Hegel*, "on the one hand contains only a negative determination, that of limitation; on the other hand its positive element, the general or so-called law of reason, the agreement of the will of one with the will of another, amounts to nothing else but the well-known formal identity and the principle of contradiction." [4] In spite of its purely formal character, however, *Kant's* jural principle possesses the value of *a secondary criterion of law* (e.g. for judging the justice or injustice of a social system in regard to the state of freedom and equality as bound up with its distribution of property or power). Following the neo-Kantian philosophy and ethics, *Stammler* also maintains that the supreme legal principle can only be a formal one, although

[2] G. del Vecchio, *Lehrbuch der Rechtsphilosophie,* trans. by F. Darmstaedter, 2nd ed., 1951, p. 371.

[3] Kant, *Einleitung in die Rechtslehre* (Supplement, Ges. Werke, Pr. Akad. d. W.), Vol. VI, pp. 230, 237.

[4] Hegel, *Grundlinien der Philosophie des Rechts,* 1821, par. 29.

he seeks to remove what is unsatisfactory in the Kantian principle by bringing in the "social ideal": "The community of free willing men"; law is a coercive norm, and the substance of a norm of conduct is correct if it accords with the social ideal in the existing special situation. *Stammler's* legal philosophy, with its emphasis on the moral basis of all law, was one of the principal forces opposing the then prevailing legal positivism; his principle, however, remains subject to all the criticisms levelled at *Kant's* formal principle of law.[5]

To *Hegel,* law is the realm of actualized freedom (par. 4),[6] freedom as such, as idea (par. 29), since it is the identity of the universal and the particular will (par. 155). As idea, freedom is "ethicality," the concept of freedom which has become an existing world (par. 142). "Ethicality" is distinct from individual "morality." It is socially objectivized morality since "the ethical has a definite content, which is necessary in itself and is an existence raised above subjective opinion and arbitrariness"; it is "the self-subsisting laws and institutions" (par. 144). The "ethical" in the form of custom appears as a "second nature" (par. 151), in that the universal proves to be "the ground and necessary form of the particular" (pars. 184, 186). In ordinary language one might interpret *Hegel's* thoughts in the following way: Law is "ethicality" in the sense of a socially secured and therefore universally binding morality (*Austin's* "positive morality," morality as socially established, comes nearest to the idea in English legal philosophy), whereby the freedom of the individual, integrated into the social morale, is guaranteed (freedom as actualized idea). In his view, therefore, law is the "spirit objective" in its actualization in the state; hence, the state is the actualization of the ethical idea (par. 257). *Hegel* tries to overcome the formalism of *Kant's* jural principle by seeking the essence of law in the actuality of socially established morality. But an explanation of law would be provided only if we were given a criterion by which that morality ultimately is to be judged. In fact *Hegel's* idea of law amounts to an identification of the essence of law with positive law (par. 211). Yet, it cannot be denied that his idea of law deserves much consideration as a practical secondary jural principle. Natural law doctrine also sees theoretically in positive law that minimum of actualized morality which is necessary for the existence and functioning of society, and, principally, has always held that the citizen can assume that he is satisfying justice when he acts in accordance with the laws of his community, as long as he has no reason to think that they are unjust. The oversimplified identification of law and state, based on the omnipotence of the state, the law being the instrument of its arbitrary will, as in all shades of collectivistic theory, is certainly contrary to *Hegel's* real idea.

This appreciation of Hegel's philosophy must not, however, prevent us from recalling that in practice his doctrine resulted in a strengthening of legal positivism and state omnipotence, although he himself would have rejected the principles of totalitarian collectivism. *K. Larenz,* a neo-Hegelian, lays prime emphasis on the ethnic legal consciousness, by conceiving the following as the supreme legal principle: "Law derives its force from the fact that it is the spirit

[5] Cf. R. Stammler, *Die Lehre vom richtigen Rechte,* 1902, pp. 197 f.; cf. also E. Kaufmann, *Kritik der neukantischen Rechtsphilosophie,* 1921; the appreciation by H. Coing in *Grundzüge der Rechtsphilosophie,* 1950, pp. 288 ff.; Burkhard Mathis, *Rechtspositivismus und Naturrecht, eine Kritik der neukantianischen Rechtslehre,* 1933.

[6] Cf. Hegel, *op. cit.* The paragraph numbers are given in parentheses.

objective of the ethnic community (*volk*), with which the individual is linked by his nature; it binds, because and insofar as by its very idea it is the unity of the universal and particular will." According to this "objective idealism," as *Larenz* calls his legal philosophy, the particular state of legal consciousness of "a race, a *volk,* a concrete community" at a certain moment is the valid form of concretion of the ethnic spirit.[7] In spite of the obvious objections to *Larenz's* theory, he does not fail to observe the natural law reality immanent in the juridical consciousness of society, as is shown by his acknowledgment of the debt of (secularized) modern German natural law thinking, in its development and in its fundamental ideas, to traditional natural law ethics.[8]

In various forms all *collectivistic legal theories* look for the essence of law in the universal will totally informing the individual, and thus actualizing freedom as participation in the universal will. The aim of this will is understood as the well-being of society—racial, national, political, or social. The socially expedient and therefore necessary functions serving this aim form the practical criterion for the shaping of the legal order with its duties and rights. Thus, in collectivistic theory, law has a merely "functional" character. Although the self-fulfillment of the individual is treated in all collectivistic theories as an end of society, they do not credit man as a person with rights of his own, which are inviolable by society; the determination of socially expedient and therefore necessary "functions," and hence rights, is in one way or another left to the discretion of those entrusted with it by the "universal will." They are divided only on the aim of this collective will. One form regards it more as racial and political welfare, explicitly giving economic welfare a second place; another conceives it as economic and social welfare, assigning (theoretically at least) a secondary role to political and national values; we have met the term "functional" in dealing with *H. J. Laski* and his theory of law (cf. Chap. 39). *H. Kelsen* comes to the conclusion that (Soviet) communist legal theory law has only a functional character, although he does not use the expression.[9]

37. The Moral Character of Law

Because law is rooted in the existential ends of man, it has a moral nature. What we have found in philosophical analysis to be the supreme jural principle, the ordering of social relations in accordance with the existential ends, has proved that law is bound up with man's moral

[7] Cf. K. Larenz, *Rechts- und Staatsphilosophie der Gegenwart,* 1931, 2nd ed., 1935, pp. 114, 155, 163; *Sittlichkeit und Recht, Untersuchungen zur Geschichte des deutschen Rechtsdenkens und zur Sittenlehre,* 1943.

[8] K. Larenz, "Zur Beurteilung des Naturrechts," in *Forschungen und Fortschritte,* 1947, parts 4–6.

[9] H. Kelsen, *The Communist Theory of Law* (New York), 1955; Kelsen is not concerned with Soviet law itself, but with the legal theory (ideologically influenced) of the jurists of Soviet Russia, who adhere to the principles of communism. Their adherence to the principle that jurisprudence must be aligned with politics represents, Kelsen thinks, a shameful degradation of legal science, which is to be taken very seriously at a time when everywhere the power of the state is constantly on the increase. Kelsen contrasts his interpretation of law as a system of delegated rules with the "ideological," but he leaves open the question on what the delegating authority is ultimately founded.

responsibility. Man's immediate moral-legal consciousness, the natural law, informs him of the fundamental requirements of the order of social relationships. The natural conscience is aware not only of moral duties and moral values, but is in the truest sense also jural conscience. Principles such as the following belong to the *jural a priori* of the moral natural law (cf. Chap. 3): render to each his own (*suum cuique tribuere*); do not act toward others as you would not wish them to act toward you; lawful authority must be obeyed; social evildoers must be punished; contracts must be fulfilled (*pacta sunt servanda*). These are the legal principles on which are based equal fundamental rights for all human persons; the power of command belonging to the legislative authority; the right to enforce the legal order; and the validity of rights springing from contracts as a condition of social cooperation in the political community (not least in the economic field) and the international community (the law of nations). We have said (Chap. 35) that there is an essential teleological element in traditional natural law theory; it follows that its *intuitionist* feature, according to which directly evident general principles of law are apprehended by virtue of intuitive reason, is equally marked.

The jural a priori as part of the natural law implies two elements of law. First, it is immediately evident to anyone who has attained the full use of reason that it is morally bad to violate definite rights of others; secondly, it is immediately evident to anyone that if he possesses certain rights he has a claim to a certain kind of behavior on the part of others which does not depend on their good will. The payment of a debt may be enforced, but not a contribution to a charitable fund.

The jural a priori makes it quite clear that in this sense rights mean entitlements. It is likewise certain that the jural a priori, exactly like the moral, contains only *general principles* and not a detailed system of legal rules, still less a legal system valid for all time. But it makes it possible to apprehend particular juridical obligations under simple conditions and thus the fundamental relationships of social order (concerning the content and nature of the social a priori in detail cf. Chap. 47).

The supreme jural principles, therefore, are that part of natural law which relates to social order. In Latin this part is termed *ius naturale* (*naturrecht, droit naturel, diritto naturale,* as distinct from *lex naturalis, naturgesetz, loi naturelle, legge naturale;* the difficulty in English is that the one expression, "natural law," is made to cover both meanings, although the term jural, or juristic, can be added to keep them distinct. The Japanese translators of this work have intimated that they experience the same difficulty in their language, which has the single expression *shizen-ho*). Law, then, is the *minimum of morality necessary for the existence of society.*[1]

[1] Agreed with by St. Thomas Aquinas, Ia IIae, q. 96, a. 2, where he says that it is a matter for the enacted law to prevent breaches of order, "sine quorum prohibitione

The following consequences arise from the moral character of law:

1. Since it is founded on natural law as a *source,* and on the duties bound up with it, law has the essential characteristic of involving obligation. Philosophically, moral responsibility has proved to be the concept linking morality and law (the merely natural fact of immanent ends would not by itself be a legal rule, nor could it constitute one). The existential ends derived from man's nature are the object of moral obligation and, therefore, involve a claim to noninterference in their fulfillment and hence to an order of social relationships that guarantees this.

2. Therefore, real law cannot exist in conflict with natural moral law. If an enacted law is incompatible with man's existential ends, it conflicts with the moral nature of law. Natural law theory, therefore, has always held, for example, that the *legislative power,* insofar as it is in conflict with those ends, is a usurper, having no real juristic foundation and conferring no moral duty of obedience; hence, resistance is morally justifiable.

3. Different from such intrinsically void pretensions to rights is the *abuse* of intrinsically genuine rights. This abuse consists in the exercise of a right for some purpose incompatible with its intrinsic end or incompatible with natural law. Such abuse does not abrogate the right, but its exercise may be restricted insofar as it infringes on the rights of others. Misuse of private property, for instance, even when this violates the moral law, does not invalidate the right of ownership itself, within the limits mentioned; nobody, therefore, acquires a title to appropriate misused property. The mistreatment of one's body in dangerous sporting activities does not deprive one of one's right over one's own body. The reason why misuse of a right does not cancel it is that the essential function of a right is to guarantee the possibility of exercising moral responsibility and hence the corresponding spheres of freedom. What use each person makes of this freedom is a matter of his own personal responsibility. Were rights to be abrogated by misuse, the opportunity for personal responsibility would be removed, whereas it is precisely the

---

societas humana conservari non posset"; a full exposé of the relevant teaching of St. Thomas is offered by Linhardt, *Sozialprinzipien,* pp. 122 f. G. del Vecchio (*Lehrbuch der Rechtsphilosophie,* p. 384), referring to the passage in St. Thomas which has been mentioned, points out that the idea of law as the "ethical minimum," which since the expression was coined by Georg Jellinek, "many regard as entirely modern, was not unknown to the old masters of legal philosophy." The criticisms levelled by G. Radbruch (*Einführung in die Rechtswissenschaft,* 9th ed., 1952, p. 21) against Jellinek's desciption of this function of law are not convincing, since (according to Radbruch's standpoint of 1929) they are based upon the complete disparateness of moral and legal points of view—indeed upon the general rejection of a universally valid moral order. The idea of an ethical minimum "sacrifices the multiformity, indeed contrariety, of the individual moral conscience," which suggests, according to Radbruch, "a denial of the possibility of tragic conflicts between personal morality and the general juridical system." In fact, this conflict is radically understood only when the moral foundation of legal order is recognized, for only then is it wholly and exclusively seen as a conflict of conscience.

function of law to insure this possibility for man—the possibility of continuing to aim at the fulfillment of duty and responsibility in spite of failure, thus attaining the fulfillment of his essential self. Of course every exercise of rights which infringes on the rights of others or on the community is liable to compulsory restriction. Our statement regarding the continuance of misused rights cannot be interpreted to mean that man has a "right" to perform acts contrary to the moral law. He has only a right to protection against interference by others in spheres which affect his moral responsibility. Much the greater part of moral life is truly of a private nature. Immoral conduct in the private sphere falls outside the legal sphere, which, as we have seen (cf. also following chapter), is confined to the ordering of social relations.

4. Rights in the true sense are, therefore, also something different from the "rights of God," if this expression is applied to the relationship of the Creator to the creatures. *St. Thomas Aquinas* leaves no doubt about his view [2] when he restricts law expressly to the human sphere, referring to *Cicero's De Officiis* (1, 7): *Justitia ea ratio est, qua societas hominum inter ipsos et vitae communitas continetur.*

If absolute freedom and autonomy are the basic feature of man's nature, as held by individualist thinking, law cannot have its foundation in the moral order, but only in this autonomy itself. This thinking, therefore, looks for the solution in the *social contract theories. Hobbes* (*De Cive,* 1642; *Leviathan,* 1651) bases his version of the social contract on the assumption that nature itself has given everybody the right to everything, and the consequence of this "state of nature" is the struggle of all against all. Out of fear, and guided by the instinct of self-preservation, men agreed upon the social contract in order to guarantee an equal, although restricted, freedom for all, thus securing peace in society. Law, then, in this theory, springs exclusively from the decree which vests power in the human legislator by agreement, and is identical with this decree. Yet, the question remains why "asocial elements" in the national and international communities are not in the right when they find that the original absolute freedom is in their interest and adopt the "state of nature" in which, according to *Hobbes,* "nothing can be unjust": "for the notions of right and wrong, justice and injustice, have no place there." [3]

In contrast to *Hobbes, Rousseau* does not regard the "state of nature" as a state of anarchy, but rather as a state of well-ordered community life, which makes possible man's full development through the realization of his freedom, to which he is born. Society and its law, therefore, must be conceived in terms of a social contract founded on the general will, so that each person is obeying himself when he obeys political authority.[4] Oversimplifying *Rousseau's* thought, by wholly leaving out of consideration the problem, which he did at least see, of the distinction between *volunté générale* and *volunté de tous,* liberalist, so-

[2] Cf. St. Thomas, *Summa theol.,* IIa IIae, q. 58, a. 2.

[3] Hobbes, *De cive,* Chap. 12, par. 1, says: "Regulas boni et mali, iusti et iniusti, honesti et inhonesti, esse leges civiles, ideoque quod legislator praeceperit, id pro bono; quod vetuerit, id pro malo habendum esse."

[4] Cf. Rousseau, *Contrat social,* I, 6: "Chacun, s'unissant à tous, n'obéisse pourtant qu'à lui-même, et reste aussi libre qu'auparavant."

cialistic and collectivistic schools of legal philosophy have sought to place the whole basis and nature of law in the "popular will" or majority will. The rights of man were understood increasingly to mean, says *Laski,* defining his own view of law,[5] that only the popular will was the effective source of power. According to the consensus theory upheld by traditional natural law ethics (cf. Chaps. 118, 130), the legislative power and law are linked with the popular will, and the popular will assuredly affords a *secondary criterion* for determining law. The fact that this is also the view of natural law theory can be seen from unambiguous remarks made by *St. Thomas Aquinas,* one of which agrees almost word for word with the passage from *Rousseau* quoted above; in another, he deals with the basing of statutory law on common utility, which is ultimately related to the popular will.[6] He makes it clear, however, that the popular will is not the ultimate source of law and that there are rights which, being rooted in man's moral nature, are not to be infringed by the popular will or by any other will.

38. The Specific Character of Law

The distinction between morals, morality, and law was unknown to Greek philosophy. The Greeks comprehended the whole range of responsible human action under the wide conception of *dikē:* that which is "just." The ancient idea of law proceeds from the notion that, generally speaking, something is right if it is in accordance with a rule, a prescription, an order. The Middle Ages, too, regarded law principally as a part of the moral order, the moral natural law. With *St. Thomas Aquinas,* the specific difference between the law and morality remains almost wholly in the background.[1] That *St. Thomas* was nonetheless able to present the social function of law in so clear a manner, and perhaps still unexcelled, is due to the paramount position held by teleology in scholastic thought and in the metaphysical assurance with which the scholastics traced the substance and function of law to the ends inherent in the nature of man and society. Those who know of the status of law in Thomistic legal philosophy were not surprised when *Ihering,* a Protestant scholar, in a footnote to the second edition of his work *Der Zweck im Recht,* observed that he would perhaps not have written his book if his attention had been drawn in advance to the position given to end in the legal philosophy of *St. Thomas.*[2]

[5] Cf. H. J. Laski, *The Rights of Man,* 1940, p. 9.

[6] Cf. St. Thomas, *Summa theol.,* Ia IIae, q. 90, a. 3: "Ordinare autem ad bonum commune est vel totius multitudinis [people], vel alicuius gerentis vicem totius multitudinis." He follows this by saying: "Et hoc modo unusquisque sibi est lex, in quantum participat ordinem alicuius regularis."

[1] Cf. Linhardt, *Sozialprinzipien,* p. 101; cf. also Chap. 47 of this work.

[2] Ihering, *Der Zweck im Recht,* 8th ed., 1923, Vol. II, p. 126 (2nd ed., 1886, p. 161), says of the legal doctrine of St. Thomas: "I ask myself in amazement how it was possible that such truths, once they had been uttered, could have fallen so completely into oblivion in our Protestant learning. What errors it could have avoided if it had borne them in mind! For my part, I might not have written my book at all if I had known them, for the fundamental ideas with which I had to deal are already set forth by that powerful thinker in perfect clarity and most pregnant formulation."

The specific character of law lies in this, that it constitutes a rule of external conduct and accords the power to insure the required conduct by force. Hence, law differs from morality in four respects: (1) it has regard only for external relations between men, and (2) for definite concrete obligations; (3) it empowers the community to enforce compliance, and (4) to establish legal security.

Law concerns, first, *external conduct* only, not the inner disposition, which is essential for moral conduct. Social order, which is the purpose of law, is guaranteed when the external conduct of the members of society is in harmony with the legal rules. Social order does not depend upon whether the motive of this conduct is consideration for others or fear of punishment. Certainly the perfection of public order also depends upon an interior disposition causing men willingly to perform duties which spring from the legal order. And the common good is certainly more perfectly realized when society is ruled more by love of justice than by fear of the police; when, therefore, the order of law is strengthened by the moral will and attitude of the members of society.

Secondly, rights mean *concrete claims* by individual and corporate persons; therefore, they constitute concrete obligations on the part of all other persons to respect these claims. They are determinate in quality and in quantity (cf. Chap. 50) as a *suum* (what belongs to, or is due to, each person). The legal claim of each person to bodily integrity imposes on the motorist quite definite legal duties, distinct from the moral obligation to give a lift to someone in distress. The *suum* can have a juridical basis in natural law (e.g., a demand of human rights), in contractual law (an agreement about services given and received) or in positive law (a constitutional, common, or statutory law).

Thirdly, the external conduct demanded by law must be assured if there is to be social order. Hence, law involves essentially the power to guarantee this conduct by means of physical force as a function of social cooperation: *St. Thomas Aquinas* and *Hegel* agree in maintaining that *coercive power* is an essential component of law (also in stating that this is not the only element in it). Both of them give the same reason: Coercive power is necessary because of the lawless conduct of members of society.[3] For this reason, however, argues *Hegel,* compulsion is not the fundamental element in law. Compulsion is bound up with law, he says, because force must be met with force when it violates a right; to make force the essence of law is to conceive of it in terms of a consequence which comes into existence only as a result of injustice.[4] This argument seems irrefutable. It lays bare the logical root in the errors of the individualist and collectivistic coercion theories of jurisprudence, which identify law wholly with the coercive power. These theories are also

[3] Cf. St. Thomas, *Summa theol.,* Ia IIae, q. 95, a. 1; Ia IIae, q. 96, a. 5: "Lex de sui ratione duo habet: primo quidem quod est regula humanorum actuum; secundo quod habet vim coactivam."

[4] Cf. Hegel, *Grundlinien der Philosophie des Rechts,* 1821, par. 94.

obviously inconsistent with the universal sense of mankind. Two things are evident to the jural consciousness. First, it is quite certain that a right is a right, even when there is no possibility of enforcing it; no one doubts that his right to freedom still exists even if he is unjustly deprived of his freedom. Secondly, the jural consciousness is well aware that every right implies a title to compel a given mode of conduct. Both principles belong to the a priori of man's jural sense. The third a priori insight is that in the organized community the exercise of coercive power, exceptions apart, is not a matter for the individual, but for the public authority. The very function of law, namely the establishment and preservation of social order, precludes the use of force by the members of society in order to secure their rights.

The conditions necessary for a proper use of force, namely, an unprejudiced inquiry into the facts in order to ascertain the extent of the violation of rights and of the interventions necessary, are secured only when the use of force is exclusively in the hands of the authority responsible for public order. Only when there is no possibility of appeal to authority does law sanction a direct use of force, and then only insofar as the higher rights of others are not infringed. Thus, in the case of a murderous attack, the right of forcible self-defense comes into play immediately. Coaction, therefore, is essential for law, but not the exercise of coaction. In a similar way, reason belongs to the nature of man, but he remains man even when, through derangement or some other cause, the use of reason fails. The essence and dignity of law lie in the fact that it consists in a moral title to unhindered action in self-determination, and to the guaranteeing of it by the exercise of force. For these reasons it is an error to deny natural law the essence of law on the ground that its principles have no actual coercive power behind them. When totalitarian states deny their citizens fundamental human rights, is not everyone convinced that they can be deprived of only the exercise of rights, and not of the rights themselves? If so, then natural rights are rights in the fullest sense of the word, although they are rights which are not always guaranteed by the power of external compulsion, but "only" by the power of conscience. The legal positivist who thus uses the word "only" should be convinced by recent experiences that the power of conscience affords a stronger sanction than the most powerful systems of coercion.

The fourth essential feature of law is promulgation and due process of administration of justice, which we would sum up as legal certainty or the rule of law. Thus, the legal order (customary law or statutory law) has to provide for a sure knowledge of legal claims and duties. For the members of society this means that, with regard to modes of conduct, they can be certain of being in accordance with the will of the lawgiver and will not be left to the arbitrary will of the judge; to the administrators of justice and authorities responsible for public order it means fixed principles governing their official functions. Like actual coaction, legal certainty is not the only essential feature of law. Thus, even when justice in the totalitarian state is at the service of the monopolistic party and disregards positive law or natural rights in its treatment of citizens, natural rights remain rights; those affected know it and so does the rest of the world insofar as it is not deluded by ideologies.

Legal philosophy and jurisprudence are of course entitled, or rather, by reason of their method, compelled to distinguish between *moral rights and legal rights,* the latter comprising rights actually guaranteed by physical force and the former those not so guaranteed. As long as moral rights are not denied the nature of law, and as long as the moral character of law, the soul of all law, is not disputed, jurisprudence may concentrate on "legal" law with its coercive character, just as the medical sciences concentrate on the human body without inquiring into the nature of the spiritual soul. But a conception of law which identifies it exclusively with a compulsion imposed by the state, is not only at variance with inner experience, which has complete certitude regarding rights prior to the state, but is also proved false by external experience, i.e. by the fact that by far the greater part of the community obeys the law in response to a moral impulse and not through fear of compulsion and punishment, a fact which was admitted even by *Austin* and which can be regarded as undisputed among jurists today.

In individualist and collectivistic jurisprudence, the *compulsion theory of law* attained predominance. It was not an accident that it developed in England first. *Hobbes,* in his *Leviathan,* had placed the essence of law in the command issued to one having a duty of obedience toward the person commanding. In his celebrated and much discussed theory of law, *John Austin* attributed law exclusively to the command of a sovereign made effective by penalties. Law, in his theory, is essentially command, a rule given to regulate the conduct of a rational being by another rational being having authority over the former. A relationship of superior and inferior, and the power of compulsion are considered to be immediately bound up with the demand for obedience.[5] Against *Austin's* theory, it has often been said that law, in various forms, i.e., customary law, has been and is in force, which is due neither to the command of a sovereign nor is guaranteed by compulsion; and furthermore, that English constitutional law does not rest upon the command of a sovereign, but upon traditional rules; and even less the American constitution, which rests upon explicit consent. *Austin* found himself compelled to admit the fact mentioned, namely, that by far the greater proportion of the juridical community obeys the law not from the fear of punishment but by reason of the bidding of conscience.

In Germany, the compulsion theory of law found its classical expression in the definitions of *Ihering,* although he (cf. Chaps. 36, 47) is not among the wholly one-sided exponents of legal positivism. In his view, law is the "system of social ends guaranteed by force"; "the state is the sole source of law"; "law is the sum of the conditions of life in society, guaranteed by the power of the state

[5] Cf. J. Austin, *The Province of Jurisprudence Determined,* 1832. Cf. the appreciation of Austin by C. A. W. Manning, *Austin Today;* or, "The Province of Jurisprudence Re-examined," in *Modern Theories of Law,* W. Ivor Jennings, editor, 1933.

through external compulsion in the widest sense of the word." [6] *Otto von Gierke* rightly says of the compulsion theory of law that "while it reverts to the older conception of positive law, but wipes out its natural law complement, it strikes at the very root of the idea of law. In this new mode of thought, the idea of law, in the end, replaces its meaning by the idea of utility, and its own efficacy by the idea of might." Law is, however, says *Gierke*, anterior and superior to the state. In a clear and convincing exposition *Gierke* develops his arguments for disproving the materialist theory, which equates law with coercion and regards the state as the sole author of law: "Law, being the system of external rules for free wills, cannot in its own existence be will itself; where will governs will, it leads always, by logical necessity, to the notion of power. If there is a binding rule not just for this or that will but for the will itself, it must be rooted in a mental faculty independent of the will. This faculty is reason. Hence, law is not the collective will that something shall be done, but the collective conviction that something is." [7] The identification of law and force received no small support from Kantian legal philosophy. "Strict law" is, according to *Kant*, "that in which nothing ethical is mixed, that which requires no other volitional causes than the external ones"; "law and the power to compel, thus may mean one and the same thing." [8] *Hegel* (cf. Chap. 36) disputes *Kant's* formal conception of law; he is opposed both to the severance of law from ethics and to its identification with force: "The general foundation of law," he says, "lies in the spiritual sphere, and its particular place and foundation is the will which is free, so that freedom constitutes its substance and determination; the system of rights is the realm of actualized freedom, the world of the spirit produced by the spirit, as a second nature." [9] In fact, however, by equating state law and law he gave an impetus to the compulsion theory of law.

Law is conceived as law of actualized freedom also by the *recognition theory* of law. Among the outstanding exponents of this theory in the last generation is Sir *F. Pollock*, and probably the most notable today is Professor *A. L. Goodhart* of Oxford. According to this theory, the sanction of enforcement does not belong to the essence of law. Its force depends upon its recognition as a binding rule. *Goodhart* recalls *Pollock's* definition: "A rule of law must at least be a rule conceived as binding," and *Pollock's* statement: "Law is enforced by the state because it is law; it is not law merely because the state enforces it." [10] *Goodhart* himself defines law, in his fine work on morality and law in England, as any rule of human conduct which is recognized as being obligatory; an essential distinction must be made between obedience to a rule and recognition of its binding character. *Goodhart* develops *Pollock's* recognition theory with the idea that enforcement has its basis also in the recognition of the obligatory character of the legal rule, since this involves, as indispensable, the application of sanctions in case of transgression of the law. The delimitation of the jural species of law found in religion, in morals, and in law is seen by *Goodhart* in the variety

[6] R. von Ihering, *Der Zweck im Recht*, 8th ed., 1923, Vol. I, pp. 247, 250 f., 511. For an appreciation of Ihering and for an understanding of his thought in the light of the intellectual situation of his time cf. Erik Wolf, *Große Rechtsdenker*, 3rd ed., 1951, pp. 616 ff.; Ernst von Hippel, *Rechtsgesetz und Naturgesetz*, 2nd ed., 1949, pp. 76 f.

[7] O. v. Gierke, *Johannes Althusius*, 1880, 4th ed., 1929, pp. 317–19.

[8] Kant, *Einleitung in die Rechtslehre*, Ges. Werke. Pr. Akad. d. W., Vol. VI, p. 232.

[9] Hegel, *Grundlinien der Philosophie des Rechts*, 1821, par. 4.

[10] F. Pollock, *A First Book of Jurisprudence*, 1896, 5th ed., 1923, pp. 26, 29.

of their mode of obligation and in the basis of obligation; in jural law the obligation subsists toward that society which is organized to establish peace, namely, the state. In reply to the question why we recognize a law as valid in the sense of binding with an obligation, *Goodhart* gives as the first reason the vague feeling of duty arising from the habits of the people; [11] another reason he gives is the feeling of respect in England toward the monarch; a third, the awareness that otherwise anarchy cannot be avoided; but finally, he says that only the moral law can be regarded as the decisive reason. This theory of law doubtless appears totally unacceptable to the legal positivist. Its important content of truth is indicated by the generally recognized fact, already mentioned, that laws are for the most part obeyed from a sense of duty, that is, because of the sanction of conscience, and not because of a fear of the sanction of coercion. On the other hand, the recognition theory seems to underestimate the ordering power which, along with the establishment of peace and legal certainty, is rooted in the common-good end of society as an essential function. Certainly, however, the ordinary power need not take the form of a "sovereign" in *Austin's* sense; in legal systems, which are characterized by customary law, it is present in the form of the social authorities in charge of the administration of justice.

39. The End of Law

If individual and social ends are the origin of law and if these ends are the individual good of all and are the social good, then the general end of law is utility, the common utility. This seems a simple inference from what we have said in the preceding chapters about law and the nature of society. Indeed, natural law theory has never sought the end of law, or, what is the same thing, the function of law, in anything else but *utility*. It is true that utility as the end of law was not as clearly emphasized in the natural law doctrine as it developed after its climax in the great Spanish thinkers of the sixteenth century, and with *Grotius* in the seventeenth century. Forced to take up a defensive position against the nineteenth-century utilitarian conception of law, the traditional natural law theory had to champion the idea of justice, thus neglecting the idea of utility. But the great champions of the natural law doctrine, such as *St. Thomas Aquinas*, make it quite plain that they regard the end of law and justice as utility.[1]

[11] A. L. Goodhart, *English Law and Moral Law,* 1955, pp. 18 ff.

[1] The excerpts which follow are from the *Summa theol.*, Ia IIae, q. 95, a. 3: "Finis autem humanae legis est utilitas hominum"; *ibid.*, q. 96, a. 1: "Finis autem legis est bonum commune"; *ibid.*, q. 97, a. 1: "Rectitudo legis dictur in ordine ad utilitatem communem" (the common utility is the criterion of true law); *ibid.*, q. 96, a. 4: "Dicuntur autem leges justae et ex fine, quando scilicet ordinanatur ad bonum commune . . . et ex forma, quando scilicet secundum aequalitatem proportionis imponuntur subditis onera in ordine ad bonum commune"; (utility also governs the alteration of the law), *ibid.*, q. 97, a. 2: "Lex humana intantum recte mutatur, inquantum per eius mutationem communi utilitati providetur"; (regard for common utility inhibits even the suppression of some forms of conduct which offend against public morality), IIa IIae, q. 78, a. 13: "Leges humanae dimittunt aliqua peccata impunita propter conditiones hominum imperfectorum, in quibus multae utilitates impedirentur, si omnia peccata districte prohiberentur poenis adhibitis."

Is not our view of law also utilitarian? It would be if we had not *objectively* defined the ends and the goods implied in the ends, from which our conception of utility is inferred. But this leaves scope enough for the *subjective* value-motives, purposes, and interests within the framework of the ends which we have termed existential. These subjective purposes and interests concern both the personal and the social spheres. Within that framework natural law leaves it to each man to shape his own life and leaves it to nations to mold their communal life as they please. Indeed, the natural law demands that no one should hinder them in this. If rights are founded on the existential ends, as we have shown (cf. Chap. 36), this implies an internal limitation of rights and hence of freedoms, but it also implies that outside the limits thus drawn, freedom remains unhampered as the condition of the creative development of man and of his culture (cf. Chaps. 24–26).

The framework within which these subjective purposes can take effect is fixed, therefore, by the objective order of ends. Providing the opportunity of complying with the responsibilities founded upon the existential ends through social cooperation constitutes objective utility, which it is the function of the law to serve; in this lies the essence of the *common good.* Since these ends are designed in human nature itself and therefore are independent of subjective choice, utility as the end of law is fundamentally objective in character, although, as already mentioned, a wide scope may remain for utility values of a subjective character, that is, for freely chosen motives and purposes.

Thus, we arrive at the conclusion that utility as the function of law involves *three groups of ends:* (1) the *individual* ends bound up with the dignity of the human person, at which the basic function of the common good aims, principally by the guaranteeing of human rights and the realm of freedom, which makes possible purposes within the framework just described; (2) the *social* ends of the common utility, namely, those linked with the establishment of peace and order and the creation of the prerequisites for general welfare; (3) the *cultural* ends, in the sense of a universal and social humanism which is the goal of cultural progress. Doubts about cultural progress as the end of law can only arise if the notion of culture is confined to intellectual culture and if the creative "realization of cultural values as such," or the "task of inspiration" is attributed to the state lawgiver. *Scheler,* therefore, certainly is right in saying that "no kind of positive task" falls to law in the hands of the state. But *Scheler* also sees a task for the state and for law "as far as the values of law, of welfare, and of power are reflected in cultural forms"; he stresses the dependence of the "realization of these political values" on the total cultural formation of the people, with respect to which the state acquires its function.[2]

[2] Cf. M. Scheler, *Der Formalismus in der Ethik und die materiale Weretethik,* 3rd edition, 1927, pp. 575–79.

If one thinks of culture in what I think is the only true sense, the wide sense in which it is understood today in the philosophy and anthropology of culture, that is, as developing and still further to be developed humanity, there can hardly be any doubt that the dynamic function of culture belongs to the essence of law. Progressing humanity means progressing jural consciousness and progressing jural culture. It cannot be denied that the essential tasks of legal evolution include the progressing assurance of human rights, the creation of an international law to guarantee world peace. These are the tasks which are bound up with the aims of *universal and social "humanism,"* as I have propounded in *Kulturethik.*[3] *Roscoe Pound,* the celebrated American jurist, referred in the first edition of his work on the philosophy of law (1921) to the evolution of the idea of end in law. Until the sixteenth century the end of law had been seen in the maintenance of the status quo in society; then, the idea of the Spanish scholastics on the natural equality of man introduced endeavors, which culminated in the nineteenth century, to guarantee the natural rights of man. This implied a new conception of the end of law, still further in the civilized society of the twentieth century the end of law is thought to be the satisfaction of social needs without disproportionate sacrifices in regard to other claims.[4] They are functions of law in the service of cultural progress. If today the understanding of the historical character of legal systems is thought to be a task for us, it would undoubtedly be inconsistent to view the historical character of law only in the light of the past and not to see also the dynamic evolutionary function in the present and in the future.

Like the common utility and the establishment of order, peace and freedom are the fundamental aim and fundamental purpose of law: *All law is of a social nature.* The nature of man links his development into complete humanity as a person with social cooperation and hence with the common good and with law. The ontological basis of the latter, therefore, can be found only in the nature of society, and not exclusively in the nature of personality and the personal values of the individual, since the individual good which is bound up with these can become a reality only as part of the common good, much as the common good order itself is determined by personality values. For these reasons we have had to deal at length with the ontology and metaphysics of society. The conclusion (cf. Chaps. 16–33) was that being, value, responsibility, and original rights are possessed not only by the individual person but also by the collective person in its many forms of communities. We also discovered that the individual personality cannot be a complete reality without the collective person; rather, the realization of the values of the

[3] On the notion of culture and the position of law in culture, and also on universal and social humanism as objectives of present-day culture cf. Messner, *Kulturethik*, pp. 336 ff., 368 ff., 463 ff.

[4] Cf. R. Pound, *An Introduction to the Philosophy of Law*, 2nd improved ed., 1954, pp. 38 f., 46 f.

personality is dependent on the realization of the values of the common good. Hence, *law* itself, with its ordering function, also proves to be at bottom *a common good value:* it is of a social nature.

Value Ethics in Legal Philosophy

This school takes its origin from the value and the values of the personality; the categories of the community reality and common good values essential for law and juridical order, if they are mentioned at all, are receding. The reason for this lies in the present state of value-philosophy, which is focussed primarily on the individual person; therefore, it has no real access to the social entity as an independent reality and the social good as an independent value. Thus, when *Erich Fechner,* in his thorough appreciation of *H. Coing's* natural law theory, which is founded on value-philosophy, speaks of a "narrowly individualistic conception" which leaves largely out of account "the values of the supra-individual and social," his rebuke aptly characterizes present-day value-philosophy, whose range of vision does not take in the supraindividual, social reality in its own being and value.

Against *Coing's* attempt to base timeless legal principles on the value-ethics of *Scheler* and *Hartmann, Eduard Spranger* has also pointed out that this value-ethics is fundamentally only a "map of the modern Western sense of value strongly influenced by Christianity." [5] We shall deal here only with the first objection; we shall deal with the second objection in Chapter 47.

I should like to pursue (cf. Chap. 3) my criticism of *Scheler,* while recalling how much this work and others of mine, notably *Kulturethik,* owe to him. It is part of the fundamental attitude of his value-philosophy, according to which values are comprehended as immediately evident in acts of feeling and of choice, that personal values form its object almost exclusively, and that the approach to the social realm of values is hard to discover. In his view, personal values are immediately evident fundamental data, particularly in the form of value-qualities in the realm of conduct and of attitude (virtues). Surely a majority of them concern relationships between people—for instance, truthfulness, loyalty, obedience, justice and especially charity. But this concerns not the reality and value of society proper. Indeed, *Scheler,* in his endeavor to comprehend society, comes back logically to an attitude of the person, that of "solidarity." He speaks of this not without express reference to "the wholly new element in the ancient Christian community idea," according to which "no longer is the community all-responsible," the individual only "sharing in the responsibility for it," but "coresponsibility between the individual and the collective person, the state, is reciprocal, without at the same time excluding the individual responsibility of either." So positively is solidarity seen as the fundamental attitude that even "the contractual principle has its root in the solidarity principle." "The solidarity principle in this sense is to us, then, an eternal constituent and at the same time a basic article of a cosmos of finite moral persons." *Scheler* then asks: "On what essential foundations, however, does this great and elevated principle

[5] E. Fechner, "H. Coings Grundzüge der Rechtsphilosophie," in *Archiv für Rechts- und Sozialphilosophie,* Vol. XXXIX, n. 3, 1951, p. 410. Cf. E. Spranger, "Zur Frage der Erneuerung des Naturrechts," in *Universitas,* Vol. IV, 1948, p. 408.

rest?" He answers: "In the last analysis on two propositions": first, that "the community of persons belongs to the evident essentiality of a possible person"; and secondly, "that even the possible union in thought and in values of such a society possess an a priori structure" independently of its actualization. Here already one wonders whether *Scheler* is not overstraining his aprioristic method and elevating assertions, which need to be proven, to the status of "a priori propositions." In any case, "the great principle of solidarity" is seen only in terms of the attitudes of individual persons; it tells us nothing about the special reality of the common good and nothing about the special value of the common good and of its order, with law as a fundamental constituent.

This is made especially clear by *Scheler's* arguments on the "values of the social person." Here he proceeds again from the idea that "every finite complete person has an intimate sphere and a social sphere," the former being strictly separated "from the empirical content of all forms of self-experience which occur in explicit, or somehow implied, reference to being a member in a fellowship, i.e., of the social person." The *social person*, according to *Scheler*, is what must be carefully noted, not the social body, but the individual person "as far as it experiences itself and knows itself to be experienced as the subject of any social acts having reference to other persons" (individual or joint persons). A "social person" then, it seems, can be either an individual or a joint person; in fact, however, he deals chiefly with the social sphere of the individual person. The joint person itself, in the light of his fundamental idea, is logically only a center of experience, "insofar as the relevant centers fully correspond with the definition of person given earlier." Concerning the person, he says that "it actualizes its existence only by living its possible experiences"; its essence consists wholly and entirely in the performance and in the process of its acts, so that it "requires no permanent being maintaining itself throughout this succession in order to establish 'the identity of the individual' "; that has (he says) nothing to do with the actualistic conception of the person, "yet, insofar as the actuality theory of the person only denies that the person is a 'thing' or a 'substance,' which performs acts in the form of a substantial causality, it is probably wholly in the right." One wonders what, according to these arguments about the individual person, the reality of the "joint persons" as centers of experience can be. Concerning the individual person itself, *Scheler* argues that as a social person it is the vehicle of a special group of values: "These values are called—in accordance with the special membership of the individual in a social unit—for example, good or bad reputation, fame, prestige, honor, dignity, renown, sanctity, etc." [6]

We have quoted *Scheler* liberally in order to show, first, how he tries to find an approach to the value of the social entity and, secondly, to show that this endeavor is a vain one. Of course, he has a great deal to say concerning social relationships and social units, and concerning the joint person and the community, that is of great significance. But the ontological reality of society, the structure of society as such (what French social philosophers call *l'institution;* cf. Chap. 42), he is unable to bring into the range of vision of his value-philosophy. Above all, his value-philosophy presupposes the person with his full capacity for understanding value; neither does it inquire how the person as such reaches full reality, although *Scheler* in the passage quoted above speaks

[6] Scheler, *op. cit.*, pp. 399 ff., 523, 542, 553, 555 ff., 585, 590 f.

of the "complete person" as a necessary condition for its experiencing the intimate and social spheres, nor does he ask how the understanding of value is possible. Man attains to the full humanness of the person, however, only by reason of his social fellowship, in which the juridical order is the fundamental condition for the development of the person and the personality. Thus, the question of the ontological reality and of the value of society, namely, of the community and the common good, proves to be a basic question for value-philosophy, which, however, does not seem to offer any approach to the real answer. But apart from *Scheler's* failure to establish a satisfactory interpretation of the human person, there arises the question of the apprehension of value in the realm of the social. The apprehension of values, which according to value-philosophy takes the form of the apprehension of "a priori qualities" through acts of feeling and choice, is doubtless conceivable in the realm of personality values. The reason for this is that the immediate inner "experience" (*Scheler* places value on this expression) plays the decisive role, but not in the social sphere, that is, the special reality of social forms and social values as distinct from relationships between individual men. For, in this sphere (apart from the values of the family community as such), values are apprehended only by means of the existing social orders in their particular historical settings. These criticisms extend to *Hartmann* also, who, although he emphasizes "order" as an essential feature and characteristic value of the community, he does not explain more clearly how the knowledge of this value is attained.[7]

On the other hand, the categories of *ethos* and of *ethos-forms,* which *Scheler* treats thoroughly in his value-philosophy and which are of the greatest significance for natural law theory, have not been applied in the endeavors of value-philosophers to provide a groundwork for legal philosophy. They are especially significant because they relate to realities which are constitutive of the state and of law. The special goods proper to the state, says *Scheler,* can be traced to the spheres of law, of power, and of welfare, of which only the jural values are purely spiritual, the rest possessing a vital nature. The state is "naturally a spiritual subject of will which has value in itself. The ethos, however, in accordance with which it performs those basic functions does not originate from it, but from the spiritual joint personality within it and, in a certain sense, above it; directly from the cultural personality of the nation or the wider cultural sphere to which it belongs, and indirectly from the joint personality of the church's religious community." By ethos-form he understands more particularly the structure of value experience and of the rules of preference immanent in various peoples, namely, as a social and historical reality. With this he links the two ideas: "Rightly understood absolute ethics peremptorily demands" on the one hand the variety and on the other hand the openness in principle of the formative stage of any particular ethos; wherefore, the full experience of the cosmos of values is dependent on the historically evolving forms of ethos.[8] We may note also one of his insights which is of great importance to natural law theory, namely, the one concerning "the inner history of ethos itself, this most central history in all history." Nevertheless, these significant categories are founded not on value-philosophy analyses but on sociological findings. *Scheler* sees in this the dependence on social and historical

[7] Cf. N. Hartmann, *Ethik,* 1935, p. 293.
[8] Cf. Scheler, *op. cit.,* pp. 312 f., 314 ff., 569.

factors of what we call the moral-legal consciousness of individual societies (peoples). Of course, the findings bound up with the two categories themselves are not as new as some of his immediate or later followers would have us think, for they do not go very far beyond what *Hegel*, with his notion of social ethicality as distinct from individual morality, made the basis of his legal philosophy (*Scheler* distinguishes "ethos" and "morality," as can be seen from the passages quoted, expressly in the same sense), or what *Savigny* called the "jural consciousness living in the people" and the "people's spirit" (*volksgeist*), or what *J. Austin* termed "positive morality."

But if in spite of the many unsolved problems, the personality and its value are made the foundation of legal philosophy, then the difficulty arises that the legal order was a reality long before this value, and indeed before the idea of personality, rose to consciousness. In the historical portion of his exposé of the "law founded on the personality," *Heinrich Hubmann*, who is close to the value-philosophy trend of natural law ethics, states: "One might think at first that the value of the personality is immediately and directly self-evident, so that it could be recognized by anyone without difficulty. But this value is in itself exceedingly complicated; it contains a number of antitheses which conceal from reason the higher connection, the deeper meaning, the true value"; in fact, "not all cultures have so clearly worked out the idea of personality as Western culture has, not even the Chinese and Indian, although they can look back on almost as long an evolution." [9] *H. Coing* points to another difficulty in the legal philosophy founded on the personality and its value: an agreement among men, especially of different cultures, would not be thinkable at all, he says, if a generally equal sphere of being were not opened to men in the moral sphere as well as in that of sensory perceptions, while "there remains the disturbing phenomenon that in history at different times and in different cultures we find different values proclaimed as supreme value." [10] This implies a major difficulty for a legal philosophy based on the value of the personality because, according to the philosophy of value, as *Scheler* expresses it, "community has its ultimate foundation in the idea of the person, and the highest values are not the values of the community but those of the person"; [11] or, as *Hartmann* expresses it: "The values of the individual surpass the macrocosmic values of the universal in axiological rank. Consequently, it is clear that, as a bearer of value, the individual himself has higher value than the universal, and that individual ethics has a deeply rooted claim as against a one-sided community ethics." [12] I concur entirely, of course, in these latter views of the two great exponents of value ethics. It is another question whether the value of the person can be made the basis of legal philosophy in a manner philosophically justifiable—if, on the one hand, the knowledge of this status of the personality is such a late product of the evolution of the human mind, and, on the other hand, the community values have for so long and so positively and among such a wide sector of humanity been regarded as the higher. This came about undoubtedly because the reality of experience induced in men the awareness

[9] H. Hubmann, *Das Persönlichkeitsrecht*, 1953, pp. 6 f.; cf. also his article "Naturrecht und Rechtsgefühl" in *Archiv für die civilistische Praxis*, Vol. CLIII, 1954, pp. 297–331.

[10] H. Coing, *Rechtsphilosophie*, p. 108.

[11] Scheler, *op. cit.*, p. 546.

[12] N. Hartmann, *op. cit.*, p. 295.

that the realm of social values, that of "common utility," is the prerequisite of fully human being and existence, the prerequisite in fact of that in which we apprehend the value of the human person today in the more advanced world of historical evolution of the human mind and of moral consciousness.

Seen from a purely historical point of view, it seems undeniable that the immediate findings in the moral sphere, as in the juridical sphere, are not connected with the knowledge of the value of personality as such; rather, the moral and legal a priori belongs simply to the fully developed human mind, whereas the full development of the mind itself is bound up with the world of values of the common good lived in the reality of the community. *Ontologically,* therefore, personal and social values are interdependent; although this does not prejudice the priority of the former, it is of decisive importance to legal philosophy: *The value of law as a fundamental social value must be derived from society as well as from the personality, from man's social as well as from his individual nature.* Without doubt, law is basically and above all an order of society, in order that the social structure as such can exist and fulfill its function in the service of man as a person. In other words, the question of the essence of law is not only that which stands in the forefront of value ethics, namely, how is coexistence of free personalities possible, but equally, how is personality itself possible. Only if the fact is fully seen that personality is possible only through the reality of the community and the values of the community, can law too be fully apprehended in substance and value as the fundamental value of society, on the reality of which depends any actualization of personal and cultural values.

The Existentialist School in Legal Philosophy

Attempts in this direction are still in their infancy. Although *Georg Cohn* places the word existentialism in the title of his book, it cannot be reckoned among the works of that philosophy in the light of the views expressed by its authoritative exponents. The book merits notice, however, because its author is a member of the Permanent International Court at The Hague, and because presumably it reflects a variety of prevailing views. What he takes over from existentialism is only an incongruously simplified conception of situation, applied to the individual legal case. According to *Cohn,* only the individual legal case possesses a juristic reality, although it also possesses its own norm. The decision of an individual case required by this cannot, he maintains, be taken by the single judge alone, but only in association with experts and lay judges as a "characteristic cross section of society." In the adjudication of a particular case there is an important role for common sense as well as for expertise. The author is directing his fire chiefly against "conceptual jurisprudence," but is sceptical in general about logical thinking because it is based on a static view of the world, whereas the world is in fact in a process of dynamic evolution in every respect (man's intellect too, he holds, is a product only of evolution).[13] *Cohn's* doctrine is an unlimited legal historicism.

A notable attempt to provide an existentialist foundation for legal philosophy as a step toward an ontology of law has been made by *Werner Maihofer.* Fol-

[13] Cf. G. Cohn, *Existentialismus und Rechtswissenschaft,* 1955, pp. 22 ff., 35, 143 f., 154.

lowing *Heidegger, Jaspers,* and *Sartre,* his analysis of existence leads "to a twofold 'natural law' basis of law: the existential natural law of the exception (of self-being) and the institutional natural law of the rule (of qua-being), through whose polarity of 'subjective' and 'objective' natural law, perhaps the level of thought for the ontological inquiry into natural law 'as such' is attained." In accord with existential philosophy, he understands existence as "self-being," although his analyses "lead to a second category of existence, which equally originally determines the structure of being of all humanity—qua-being." In the autonomous sphere of the self is rooted the "existential natural law springing from the uniqueness of the self," namely, "in the free area of such absolute autonomy," in which, as *Maihofer* says with *Jaspers,* there is nothing universally valid, but only "that 'absolute ought' of the autonomous freedom of existence, which hears and obeys itself," namely, what "the individual hears 'as right' through the ear of his conscience" and what, "according to the interpretation of conscience by the existential philosophy," results in his self-being. Yet, existence is being in the world. It "acquires at the same time a social character 'determined' by the social standpoint of others and comparable with others. In this social form it enters the world of order and that of law." "With the development of his humanity," man grows into the world of nature (e.g., the mother into the relationship to the child), which is "ordained by nature," and into the world of culture, through which he enters into "the world of others." "Human existence in the world is not only being in the sense of that incomparably unique self but also equally originally being in the connections designed by the world—that being which is comparable with others and similar to others, the qua-being." All individual development becomes reality only "by entry into a definite social form, whose being and significance are not determined and invented by existence arbitrarily, but are discovered in the world, by whose all-comprehensive connections it is determined." The law of qua-being is the "institutional natural law"; "everything legal is concerned fundamentally with nothing less than the authenticity of the qua-being," the person as social person; for example, "being as man and wife, as parents and children, as owners and possessors, as buyers and renters, as citizens and neighbors, as members of a definite profession, of a nationality, of a religious denomination, comparable with and distinguishable from others." Furthermore, through the "heteronomous imperative of the common world," "there is designed for every social type the authenticity of its being as a definite someone: as (= qua) tenant or purchaser, doctor or judge, father or neighbor." The points of contact between *Maihofer's* and our own social and jural ontology are obvious (including expressions like: "designed" in the nature of man, social nature and individual nature being "equally original"). For both *Maihofer* and for us, natural law is an "order of existence." As *Maihofer's* illustrations show, however, he sees (like *Scheler,* cf. above) the "social person primarily only as an individual person in its qua-being—that is, in its social relationship—not the social structure itself in its specific being." The qua-being is illustrated by examples which are explained phenomenologically rather than ontologically. Thus, from the *prolegomena* to an ontology of law set forth here it is not yet evident in what the criterion for the authenticity of the qua-being is to be sought, although *Maihofer,* doubtless with reason, regards his "ontological finding" as significant to the questions of the "order" and the "rightness" of law. It will also have to be shown how "absolute" autonomy of self-being can be reconciled with the heteronomy of qua-being, unless the order of personal and social existence is understood as the order of moral uniformity "designed" in man's nature with responsibilities of the individual (self-being) and the community (social being with its own reality). Concerning the rights of the community as such, rooted in its own responsibilities, *Maihofer* does not speak, nor does he indicate where they may be thought to be located.[14] Finally, the question arises whether the concept of qua-being is to be grasped without giving existential philosophy an interpretation of its notion of freedom hitherto foreign to it. Now that its problematical nature is becoming more and more evident, however, there is nothing to prevent the further development of the logical and ontological categories of existentialism in order to bring out fully their relationship with reality, with an eye to the unity of man's individual and social nature.

Theories on the End and Function of Law

Theories concerning the end and the function of law are divided according to the various views taken on the nature of man and on his relation to society. When *Rudolf Sohm* assumes that the function of law is the development of the individual personality in contrast to the complete herd life of primeval times,[15] the question presents itself in this way: In what are the ends and values of human personality to be found? Turning to *Ihering's* proposition that the function of law is to serve "social purposes" which arise from practical human needs and interests,[16] we must ask which interests are to be protected by law and which are to be restricted. And when *C. A. Emge* declares that the end and criterion of law are to be found in "value-carrying evolution as a whole," the question inevitably follows: What decides what is of value? No answer is possible, however, if, like *Emge,* one is sceptical of the question concerning the apprehension of values. Again, when we find that *Kohler* thought the function of law to be the advancement of culture through a coercive order of things,[17] we are compelled to ask what the determining values and ideals of culture are: Should the coercive decree of law be aimed at the "Hegelian Aristocracy," as *Kohler's* own ideal has been termed, or at the further development of the Western Christian civilization, or at a kind of "Americanism" or "Sovietism"? Or, is it the function of the law to be of use to the people ("Law is what benefits the people"), as the *National-Socialist* principle of law maintained, rather than the contrary—that only true law can really and ultimately benefit the people? Or again, is the function of law, as *Marxist and communistic* legal philosophy maintains, altogether dependent on the process of economic evolu-

[14] Cf. W. Maihofer, *Recht und Sein: Prolegomena zu einer Rechtsontologie,* 1954, Vorwort, pp. 83, 98, 101, 108, 113 f., 117, 120, 125; *Vom Sinn menschlicher Ordnung,* 1956.

[15] Cf. R. Sohm, *Institutionen, Geschichte und System des römischen Privatrechts,* 16th ed., 1919, pp. 25 ff.

[16] Cf. R. Ihering, *Der Zweck im Recht,* 2nd ed., 1886, 8th ed., 1923.

[17] Cf. C. A. Emge, *Einführung in die Rechtsphilosophie,* 1955, p. 348. (Emge very clearly shows how concrete law is governed by situation, but he makes it finally merge completely into the situation.) Cf. J. Kohler, *Lehrbuch der Rechtsphilosophie,* 3rd ed., 1922.

tion? In feudal and capitalistic society, according to this philosophy, law is the organization of property interests, and hence simply the expression of exploitation relationships based on class structure; in the period of transition to the new socialistic society, law is the means of securing the class interests of the proletariat; in the classless society, law will have a purely functional character —it will be an instrument for organizing the production of the material basis of life, while realizing general social equality. The views of all these schools have points of contact with our viewpoint of the threefold function of law, which is that law is in the service of individual, social, and cultural ends. By relating them all to man's existential ends, our natural law theory is able to define the claim to validity and to show the extent of the validity of individual and social rights. The definitions which have been quoted concerning the function of law, undoubtedly merit the status and the value of *secondary criteria* for judging how far law fulfills its end. None of them constitutes an ultimate criterion, since none is related to all aspects of the reality of human nature which has its personal, social, and cultural spheres of value. In fact, *the question* concerning the end of law is, as *Roscoe Pound* remarks, *fundamentally one of the criteria of values.*[18] I suggest that we have discovered these criteria in the existential ends and the order of values determined by them.

Utilitarian Theory of Law

Bentham's individualist utilitarian theory of law sees the function of law in utility based on a purely subjective judgment. He has, as we have noted (cf. Chap. 22), no other ultimate criterion of utility than popular opinion. Nevertheless, his formula, "the greatest happiness of the greatest number" will not be denied the value of a *secondary criterion* by the champion of natural law theory, since he must assume that man's essential nature asserts itself to a large extent in the moral-legal consciousness of society and in popular opinion. As a practical principle, undoubtedly it proved its value in the legal and social development of England in the nineteenth century; and even though it was inadequate because of its individualist presuppositions there remains a certain logical consistency in the original Benthamite principle. This is changed with the adaptation of the principle by collectivistic and *socialistic* legal utilitarianism. Thus, *Laski* finds the test of rights in utility; but, to whom are the rights to be useful? Since the demands of each citizen for the fulfillment of his best self must be taken as of equal worth, the utility of a right, therefore, is its value to all the members of the state; hence, rights are related to functions because the citizen has rights in order to make his contribution to the social end. But then *Laski* goes on to explain that the mass of men and women are scarcely articulate about their needs; and even when they are articulate, they are not able to judge how their wants are to be accomplished. Thus, there can be no system of government in modern society without a body of experts whose work in the interest of all will be judged by the result.[19] We miss logical consistency in the two statements because in the one the utility concept is based on the good of the individual citizen and is assigned to the subjective judgment; the other

[18] Cf. R. Pound, *op. cit.*, p. 45.
[19] Cf. H. J. Laski, *A Grammar of Politics*, 1941, pp. 16 f., 40, 92, 94 f.

is based on the social good, which is to be assessed, not by the citizens themselves, but by experts who decide on needs and their satisfaction. Furthermore, if according to this "functional" theory of law, rights are based on contributions toward the social good, the question remains: On what ground can one speak of the equal human rights of the individuals? In fact, this is the socialistic theory of law, which seeks to justify the planning of the economy and of society, for which the "experts," that is, the managers, are competent, whether they function in industrial concerns or in government departments.

40. The Historical Factor in Law

One of the greatest difficulties for juristic thinking lies in the doctrine of the traditional natural law school that there is a core of natural law which is invariable, valid for all times, and universally binding for all peoples. In fact, law exists always in historical, and therefore varied, forms. Legal history has accumulated an immeasurable quantity of material on this. Regarding this material, probably no one today would dispute *Maine's* contention that evolution rules in the realm of law as elsewhere.[1] Textbook versions of the traditional natural law doctrine have not always paid full attention to this aspect of law,[2] but it is inherent in its character.

The best representatives of natural law theory from *St. Augustine* onwards were intent, nevertheless, on making it clear what they take to be the unchanging substance of natural law: according to them, it is confined to the most general principles of the moral-jural a priori (cf. Chap. 37); the realization of these principles, however, is governed by historical factors, according to the best natural law tradition. Concerning this, *Augustine* explicitly says: Even the just law is altered justly as times change and varies with different peoples. Hence, he sees the existing legal systems with all their farreaching differences among different nations as justified, "provided that they are not in conflict with the commands of God," namely, with the *principles* of justice which are those of the moral-jural a priori. The legal *forms* (institutions and codes) themselves he traces back to the union of wills of the legal community at any given time, which he understands as a community of values.[3] *St. Thomas Aquinas* follows *Augustine;* he does not speak directly of the

[1] Cf. Sir H. Maine, *Ancient Law,* 1861.

[2] On the same idea cf. G. Stadtmüller, *Das Naturrecht im Lichte der geschichtlichen Erfahrung,* 1948.

[3] Cf. Augustine, *De civ. Dei,* XIX, c. 17 (union of wills: *humanarum quaedam compositio voluntatum*); c. 24 (community of values: *coetus multitudinis rationalis, rerum quas diligit concordi communione sociatus*); on the scope attributed to *communis utilitas* cf. *De lib. arb.*, I, c. 6, quoted in Chap. 47. In the same place he speaks of the dependence of law on historical developments: "Appellemus ergo istam legem, si placet, temporalem quae quamquam justa sit, commutari tamen per tempora juste potest."

"evolution of law," but his theory on variations in law shows a clear perception of the evolutionary character of law and the historical features of legal systems.

In this, *Thomas* follows two lines of thought.[4] The first is concerned with the progress of reason. "Human reason is mutable and imperfect," he says, and it seems "natural" that in juridical thought also it should advance from the imperfect to the perfect. He illustrates his thought by reference to the sciences, whose theories are at first imperfect and then become more perfect. In the practical life of society, he says, we note the same development. Those who first set out to discover something useful for the community were not able to observe everything at one time, and consequently established institutions which were defective in many respects. These institutions were later altered and improved, but may still be defective from the point of view of the common utility. In his commentary on the *Ethics* of *Aristotle,* he even states that "the barbarians do not use rational laws"; and in his commentary on the *Politics* he says that people of primitive times were ignorant and base and their laws were very primitive and strange.[5] The second argument of *St. Thomas* refers to the change in "man's conditions." Under different conditions different laws are expedient; the criterion of the right content of laws is the common utility. Accordingly, as *St. Thomas* declares, the limit of the evolutionary idea in legal philosophy lies only in the immutability of the general principles of natural law. He sees a *twofold evolution.* First, human codes and *systems of law* change with the development of the human mind and with the application of these principles to the changing conditions of social life. Secondly, the emphasis with which he describes the merely gradual progress of the human mind from the imperfect to the perfect as something "natural," leaves a wide scope for the development of man's *juristic consciousness* itself.

We need not consider the barbarian peoples; the *legal history* of the Western civilized peoples provides an extensive enough evolution. Its stages are marked by the general acceptance of slavery, the denial of rights to women and children in ancient society, the lack of any conception of the personal rights of the individual,[6] the suppression of freedom

[4] Cf. St. Thomas, *Summa theol.,* Ia IIae, q. 97, aa. 1–2; cf. S. Deploige, *Le conflit de la morale et de la sociologie,* trans. by C. C. Miltner, *The Conflict between Ethics and Sociology,* 1938.

[5] Cf. Thomas Aquinas, *in 7 Eth. 1; in 2 Pol. 12:* "Primi homines fuerint imprudentes et ignavi, [their laws are] valde simplices et barbaricae, i.e. irrationales et extraneae."

[6] Nevertheless, one may say with G. Stadtmüller, *Das abendländische Rechtsbewußtsein,* 1951, p. 11, if one is thinking only of the "historical basis": "The historical basis of the Western sense of the worth of the individual personality as against the state is Roman law"; on the other hand, it would be difficult to refute Hegel's statement, *Grundlinien der Philosophie des Rechts,* 1821, par. 2, that "for Roman Law no definition of *man* is possible, for the slave cannot be subsumed under man, rather the concept is infringed in his status," so that in the general concept "what is contradictory, here what is unjust, is visible in its nakedness." In St. Thomas Aquinas himself the dependence of jurisprudence on development is evident from the fact that "it would

of conscience, the progressive recognition of the freedom of the human person, the establishment of the equality of all before the law as a fundamental rule of the legal system, and finally the growth of international law. This entire evolution could be summed up as the recognition of the "rights of man," although this expression was unknown before the eighteenth century and was later linked with erroneous views. In this evolution, the most powerful driving forces were those of early and medieval Christianity,[7] even though they did not assume the clamorous tone of some later freedom movements. Indeed, the rationalistic and individualist trend in modern development is still inspired by these forces to a large extent.

The process of the evolution of the jural sense and of legal orders may well be described, with *Hegel,* as the evolution of the spirit "objective," provided that the social consciousness is not reified, but is sought in the moral, jural, and cultural principles and values which shape

---

never have occurred to Thomas to uphold a right of freedom for the individual on the ground of human dignity," as A. F. Utz states (*Recht und Gerechtigkeit,* Vol. XVIII, St. Thomas-Ausgabe, 1953, p. 494). On the other hand, R. Linhardt, *Die Sozialprinzipien des hl. Thomas,* 1932, pp. 134 f., speaks precisely of a "proclamation of human rights" by Thomas, referring to the *Summa theol.,* IIa IIae, q. 64, a. 2 ad 3, where Thomas speaks of the jural status of man by reason of "human dignity": "Dignitas humana, prout scilicet homo est naturaliter liber et propter seipsum existens"; Linhardt sees in this an essential step in the evolution of legal thought, since it shows "how far beyond any Greek or Roman conception of law Thomas goes in his personalism." Linhardt also points to a series of "inborn rights of human nature" which Thomas refers to, not forgetting to mention *Comm. in Lib. 4. Sent.,* d. 36, q. 1, a. 3, where Thomas says that some of the inborn rights cannot be prejudiced even by slavery ("Servitus, qui est de iure positivo, non potest praeiudicare his, quae sunt de lege naturali [as eating, sleeping, marriage]"). Nevertheless, Thomas' attitude to slavery as such shows again how his legal thought is conditioned by the historical period in the development of law. There is a balanced discussion of the lines of development just mentioned by Professor A. Egger in his important book, *Über die Rechtsethik des schweizerischen Zivilgesetzbuches,* 2nd ed., 1950, pp. 92 f., 95 f.: "The ancient masters of law in fact develop—it cannot be otherwise—a radical doctrine of freedom. The Roman spirit, of strong virility, created its proudest work in its law. This is altogether imbued with the idea of freedom—that is why it was able to become a law for all humanity. Ancient Rome was an abode of free citizens. . . . But in Roman law, beside the idea of freedom there appears the idea of power. Only the Roman citizen and head of household shared in the freedom. To the Roman legal order belong the bondage of the household staff, slavery, and the outlawry of the non-citizen. The modern notion of freedom is a different one, much wider, more unconditional, universal—the outcome of immense struggles in an unbroken chain of emancipations: of domestic servants, of classes, of foreigners. The history of marriage and the change in the position of women, children, and wards, menservants and maidservants, the history of the third class, especially its uprising in the French Revolution and that of the Fourth Republic in the nineteenth century; the development of the law relating to foreigners; the legal recognition of religious tolerance; and, finally, the liberation of Jews, bear witness to these struggles, which were fought on a thousand battlefields with one single purpose. Ultimately they are all concerned with one sole idea: humanity, its inalienable dignity and sanctity, prefigured in the Old Testament and in ancient philosophy and comprehended by Christianity in all the depth of its significance as the condition of the children of God."

[7] Cf. A. J. Carlyle, *Political Liberty, a History of the Conception in the Middle Ages and Modern Times,* 1941.

the mental outlook and the practical attitude of a particular society. One of *Hegel's* real achievements consists in the emphasis which he lays on the existence of what we today designate the ethos-form, including jural ethos, that is, socially guaranteed "morality" (as distinct from individual morality), which assumes a life of its own and shapes the mind of the individual, the spirit "subjective," to a substantial degree. We need not concern ourselves here with the question how far *Hegel's* system involves panlogism or even pantheism, but only with what the mental sciences gain from his work.

Legal Historicism

Traditional natural law thinkers regard law as subject to historical evolution throughout the historical existence of man and of civilization. The historicists, on the other hand, conceive all law as an exclusive product of evolution and deny that rational nature is equipped with a primal jural conscience or that there exist principles of law and value independently of historical development; all these, they hold, are merely the outcome of long experienc in man's historical evolution of endeavoring to establish patterns of coexistence. This historicism not only represents a hypothesis without scientific foundation (its exponents should recall the words of *Newton: Hypotheses non fingo*), but it is also in conflict with today's established findings of research in the fields of history and social science, with which we shall (Chap. 47) be dealing later at some length. Man's sense of law has not evolved from nothing, as the exponents of legal historicism believe. In the beginning there was the knowledge belonging to the natural conscience that wrong is not right, that is, knowledge of universal jural truths which belong to human rational nature and which are invariable.[8]

[8] Leo Strauss, in *Natural Right and History,* 1953, points to the politicization of philosophy as the starting point for legal historicism in the eighteenth century: the political philosophy of that time was fundamentally a natural law theory which with its denial of the suprahistorical being of the "eternal order," until then the principal object of philosophy, led to historicism (*ibid.,* pp. 31–34). Strauss is especially at variance with Max Weber, who described himself as one of the followers of the historical school, and with Weber's principle of the freedom of sociology from values. Weber, he says, proceeds from the baselessness of so-called invariable principles of value and from the impossibility of deciding about conflicting values by rational means; sociology must therefore be concerned solely with facts, it must be free of values. Strauss points out, among other things, that Weber never explains what he means by values; besides, Weber himself constantly uses value-judgments in his sociology, he has not seen that sociology is simply not possible without value-judgments; how, for instance, can it speak of morality, religion, and culture as sociological phenomena without value-assumptions and value-judgments. In fact, Strauss sums up, Weber's own value-judgments underlying his sociology are those of continental Europe since the time of the French Revolution (*ibid.,* pp. 36–78). Only sketchily does Strauss mention the foundations of his own conception of natural law, while stressing that a fundamental factor in the understanding of the natural law idea is common sense insight into the nature of the world, which in fact was the starting point of classical philosophy in its thinking about the world and man. What it has ascertained is adequate, especially in conjunction with the basic knowledge conveyed by the Bible, for the comprehension of the essentials of the natural world and hence also the origin of the natural law idea (*ibid.,* pp. 79 f.). We have also referred to the "natural metaphysic of the human spirit" (Bergson) as a starting point for natural law theory,

The mode of thinking of the school of legal historicism is exemplified in the work of *William Seagle*. According to *Seagle*, any law is only a transitional stage in man's evolution; mankind has lived much longer according to usage and custom than according to law and legal codes; law takes its origin in the pathology of social relationships; the purpose of law has always been a rearrangement of relationships of power and of domination; every change in law simply means the victory of a different social class; in the age of science we may achieve liberation from the tyranny of law, so that, in spite of our present faith in law as an eternal idea, a future society will know nothing of "justice according to law." *Seagle* is unmistakably thinking of a future classless society along the lines of *Marx*. *Seagle* does not stand by his own correct sociological finding that it is a mistake for a present-day jurist to see the social institutions of primitive people with the unprejudiced eyes of his own culture. *Seagle* allows himself to be guided by a preconceived sociological conception of law, according to which law is a mode of regulating human conduct with the aid of sanctions imposed by the existing political organization of society. Thus, he is led to declare that the customs and usages of the primitives cannot be regarded as law, since these people do not possess any political organs: and some do not possess even a word for "chieftain"; others may manage well without any judicial organ. He is of the unfounded opinion that the prevailing anthropological school of today is the school of the critical anthropologists, who scarcely admit the existence of any universally recognized rules. This is pure "belief," however, and is not by any means an established scientific finding. *Seagle* himself declares, for example, that *Malinowski's* book, which appeared in 1926 (*Crime and Custom in Savage Society*), is a kind of classic, but feels compelled to engage in polemics against *Malinowski*, whose main thesis is that "savages" are not slaves of custom, but that a concatenation of obligations forms the foundation of their civil law, that is to say, of a law in the full sense of the word. In spite of his wide outlook and excellent individual observations, *Seagle* inevitably falls into error in his quest for law, since, as he himself says, primitive law cannot be stretched out on the "procrustean bed" of modern legal concepts (cf. also Chap. 47 on the evolution theory of law).[9]

The Historical School of Law

The historical school of law in Germany, as understood by *Savigny*, is not to be classed with historicism. Its antinatural law attitude is due less to the traditional natural law doctrine which held sway up to the beginning of the seventeenth century than to the rationalistic natural law theory of the eighteenth century. To appreciate correctly the significance of the rationalistic theory, one must bear in mind that in the eighteenth century the *Leibniz-Wolff* school of legal philosophy not only was dominant in Germany but also exercised a great influence on French legal development; the French Code of 1804 clearly bears the stamp of this philosophy which claimed unalterable authority for its

---

whose chief function, however, lies in the epistemological, ontological, and metaphysical examination and explanation of natural law. For the history of natural law, the critical presentation of natural law theory by Hobbes and Locke, Rousseau and Burke is of significance in Strauss's book.

[9] Cf. W. Seagle, *The Quest for Law* (New York), 1941, pp. 7, 27 f., 31 f., 35, 374.

law of reason.[10] *Christian Wolff* (1679–1754) set out to systematize the philosophical world of *Leibniz* and to simplify the wealth of his thought, but he overemphasized his rationalistic, mathematical method. Thus, he attempted to develop an aprioristic natural law system whose detailed legal rules he regarded as a permanently and universally valid foundation for any positive law code. It was the almost exclusive dominance of this rationalistic theory of natural law, with its "arrogance and shallow abstractions," which *von Savigny* (1779–1861) wished to overcome, as he himself clearly indicated,[11] by means of his historical method. He desired to use the historical method in order to open the way for a jurisprudence and a codification of law in accordance with modern needs. At the same time, he thought that with the historical method he could overcome the formalism of *Kant*, which was then beginning to supersede the school of *Wolff*, and replace *Wolff's* rationalism by a new rationalism, that of basing a formal jural principle on abstract reason.

Abstract reason, says *Savigny*, is not the ultimate source of law, but "the sense of law dwelling in the people," the *volksgeist* (folk spirit), operating chiefly in usage and in custom. Close investigation of the roots of existing law and the freeing of its original spirit from the more technical framework, which is a device for producing a closed system, would enable jurisprudence to fulfill its ever-changing functions. With this should be linked a familiarity with Roman Law, which has never ceased to influence law on the Continent; its practical feature encourages jurisprudence to exert the necessary sense of reality. Thus, says *Savigny*, theory and practice, legal philosophy and historical actuality, are inseparably correlated.[12] A legal philosophy based on historical data would take on an objective and scientific character and would inevitably replace the natural law theory with its subjective and abstract speculations. He was, however, far from denying what the traditional natural law school up to *Grotius* had considered to be its fundamentals; he himself asserts as an established fact that everywhere on earth as soon as questions of juridical relations arise, general jural principles already exist for solving them; furthermore, every

[10] Cf. F. Gény, *Méthodes d'interpretation et sources en droit privé positif*, 1899. The abstract natural law doctrine of Wolff held the field for a considerable time against the legal philosophy of S. Pufendorf (1632–94), who was concerned with a continuation of the natural law doctrine of Grotius, although he was unable to keep clear of rationalistic influences, while on the other hand he sought to base the binding force of natural law directly on the will of God. C. Thomasius (1655–1728) had likewise been thrust into the background; he followed Pufendorf in the main, but rejected Pufendorf's theological foundation for natural law, and sought to liberate legal philosophy from theology. On the development of natural law theory associated with these names, cf. the wide-ranging book of Erik Wolf, previously mentioned: *Große Rechtsdenker der deutschen Geistesgeschichte*, 3rd ed., 1951; also cf. G. Stadtmüller, *Das Naturrecht im Lichte der geschichtlichem Erfahrung*, 1948.

[11] Cf. Fr. K. von Savigny, *System des heutigen römischen Rechts*, Vols. I–VIII, 1840–49. Savigny was not the first in Germany to rely on the historical method: Gustav von Hugo (1764–1844) was already in the field with many works, of which we shall mention here only his *Naturrecht als Philosophie des positiven Rechts*, 1798, 4th ed., 1819.

[12] Cf. Fr. K. von Savigny, *Vom Beruf unserer Zeit für Gesetzgebung und Rechtswissenschaft*, 1814; cf. the new appreciation of Savigny and his significance for modern legal science by Carl Schmitt, *Die Lage der europäischen Rechtswissenschaft*, 1950; also cf. Schmitt's critic Fr. A. v. d. Heydte, "Carl Schmitt und die Lage der europäischen Rechtswissenschaft," in *Hochland*, Feb. 1951, pp. 288 ff.

national law contains two elements, an individual element proper to each people and a universal element belonging to common human nature.[13]

In its further development, the historical school closed its eyes to this fact which *Savigny* regarded as historically established, broke with the spirit of the great juridical thinker, put itself at the service of legal positivism, and with its positivist narrowing of view drove the rising science of legal history largely into wrong directions, from which it is only now beginning to be set free by the latest research. Sir *Frederick Pollock* described as an inquiry into the "natural history of law" the undertaking of *H. S. Maine* (1822–88), the founder of the historical law school in England.[14] According to the Preface to his *Ancient Law, Maine's* object was "to indicate some of the earliest ideas of mankind, as they are reflected in ancient law, and to point out the relation of those ideas to modern thought." If such historical research is sufficiently comprehensive and penetrating, it may lead to fresh corroboration of the thesis of *Giambattista Vico* (the first exponent of the historical method in jurisprudence), which he set down in his famous *Scienza Nuova:* the evolution of law throughout history is a progressive approximation to natural law and to a fuller realization of it.[15] (To refer to *Vico* here is appropriate, since *Savigny's* theory was influenced considerably by him.)

41. The Social Factor in Law

Every legal system is dependent on social factors: it is always a compromise between principles of justice and interest forces. The jurist has a keen eye for this compromise character of law; for this reason he is intent on the distinction between the reality of law and the idea of law, and is inclined to see in natural law an ideal rather than real law. Traditional natural law theory, as propounded by its chief exponents, by no means overlooks the dependence on social factors of every historical legal system; it sees the character of compromise and their merely approximate value in the light of what is demanded by natural law. One may recall the references to *Augustine* and *Thomas* in the previous chapter concerning the diversity of legal codes among different peoples and on how they are conditioned by social factors rooted in ethnic and cultural traditions. Furthermore, the doctrine of original sin could not fail to keep traditional natural law thinkers alive to the possibility of social forces contrary to justice, and hence to the inevitable imperfection of every historical legal order. Regarding the *problem of power* itself, the opposition between right and might, today it seems much easier than ever before to see *Augustine's* distinction (cf. Chap. 124) between the

[13] Cf. Fr. K. von Savigny, *System des heutigen römischen Rechts,* Vol. I, pp. 7, 15.

[14] Cf. H. S. Maine, *Ancient Law,* Frederick Pollock, editor, 1930, Introduction: note the latter's remarks on the neglect of the scholastic tradition in England through two centuries (pp. 77, 120 ff.) and the clear statement of its principles, as understood in England up to the sixteenth century, by Richard Hooker (1554–1600) in his *Ecclesiastical Polity.*

[15] Cf. G. B. Vico, *De uno universi iuris principio et fine uno,* 1720; cf. Chap. 159.

kingdom of this world and the Kingdom of God in the perspective of the dependence of legal systems on social factors arising from power relationships. The same may be said of the discussions, remarkably penetrating for their time, by *Thomas Aquinas* and especially by *Suárez,* on the right of resistance and the right of self-defense against the unlawful holder of authority, and also of their teaching on the sovereignty of the people and the obligation of the ruler to conform with law (cf. Chaps. 130–32). When people too hastily reproach natural law theory for its vindication of slavery and other legal institutions, as being fitted "merely" for the justification of the existing social order, they are forgetting that *its extensive occupation with "relative" natural law represents a struggle with the question of the dependence of law on the actual social circumstances.*[1] Many will be surprised at the extent of the varieties in law which were regarded as possible within the order of justice: they range from liberal democracy to dictatorship (cf. Chap. 45).

Indeed, the dependence of every historical legal order on actual social factors forms a principal feature of the "social question" which besets every social order. Its ideological and institutional causes, which largely condition every actual legal system, will occupy us at some length (Chaps. 57–59). These causes form a principal object of the general *sociology of law.*[2] It might be claimed as a fact established by history and sociology that, in the life of nations, in most cases the positive law enacted after the period of customary law, was effected by politically dominant groups to a greater or lesser extent in their own interest by forcible means of an ideological or physical kind. Means are of a physical kind when the origin of laws is bound up with repression. Means of an ideological kind are religious and traditional forces, which express themselves in the forms of jural ethos underlying legal orders. To these latter forces we may attribute the fact that throughout long periods of known history the division of society into ruling and dependent groups was accepted without objection. Ideological formative forces also proceed from more permanent conditions of domination and from the conscious endeavors of ruling classes. The institutional side of legal order, concerning the regulation of outward relationships, likewise results in in-

[1] Certainly, however, we must agree with Gerhard Ritter in his *Vom sittlichen Problem der Macht,* 1948, pp. 17–22, when he says that insight "into the essentially warlike character of political power" appears (with Machiavelli) only in the sixteenth century and was never so clearly obtained and formulated either in clasical antiquity or in the Middle Ages. Although for the latter "the true objective of real statesmanship is to establish rational, just peace," it is, in fact, says Ritter, impossible to construct a legal community or to establish ordered peace without an assured possession of material power; but no power can be asserted without constant struggle, so that there exist "inescapable necessities of struggle."

[2] Cf. Eugen Ehrlich, *Grundlegung der Soziologie des Rechts,* 1913, reprinted 1929; Max Weber, *Wirtschaft und Gesellschaft,* 1922, Chap. VIII, "Rechtssoziologie"; *Staatssoziologie* (prepared by Weber as *Soziologie der Herrschaft*), J. Winckelmann, editor, 1956; *Rechtssoziologie,* J. Winckelmann, editor, 1960; Franz W. Jerusalem, *Soziologie des Rechts,* 1925; *Kritik der Rechtswissenschaft,* 1947.

equitable developments in legal systems. For, institutions are always meant for existing conditions. But these conditions change. Today, institutions provide persons and bodies with rights and powers. Influential groups in the community strive to fortify and to insure the continuance of the legal system which secures their advantages and their "vested interests," and to obstruct innovations which would work to their disadvantage.

Since rights of this kind relate to the sphere of *property* in no small measure, and since property gives power, the property-owning groups are able, to a considerable extent, to influence the legal system in their own interest. Furthermore, economic cooperation in a society is largely dependent upon the technical resources at any given time, which again influence the legal system as a whole because of the particular forms of private property and of private interests linked with these. Thus, the gap increases between legal reality and the ideal of law. The actual legal order (this is our conclusion) is never merely the outcome of the efforts of legal reasoning, but of a legal will which is the expression of *class relationships* and which rests upon power.

A further social factor which is part of the compromise character of every legal system was found by *Maine* in his researches into legal history. Although he may have exaggerated its significance as an element in the consolidation of legal systems, it is assuredly one of the strongest factors: it consists, as he says, in the resistance of human nature to changes.[3] The result of these forces of inertia in human nature is that, generally, a measure of disagreeable, often bitter, experience is necessary before underprivileged social groups generate motive forces for a reshaping of the social and legal order and become capable of carrying it through. Men are basically conservative, they are under the power of habit. Thus, a large proportion of the community is always more inclined toward stability than change. But just because there are groups which, from pure self-interest, wish to stabilize the legal system with its faults, other groups arise which, also from self-interest, seek to bring about changes in the legal system and in so doing exceed justifiable bounds. Thus, the legal order becomes the *resultant of opposed social forces.* For the reasons mentioned, legal systems inevitably represent *compromises* between contrary interests. In spite of "conservative" and "progressive" social groups wishing to assert their own sectional interests, the art of the lawgiver is to bring about the common good to the greatest extent possible in face of the unavoidable compromise in every realization of a law of the natural jural order.

Because of its compromise nature, every existing legal order is encumbered with *legalized injustice.* If a state of peace is engendered and preserved by law, then the most essential thing for a community in the sphere of the common good is achieved. Herein lies the answer to the question

[3] Cf. Sir H. S. Maine, *Ancient Law,* 1861.

why even a defective legal system possesses the binding force of law. Nevertheless, the demands of the natural law order remain undiminished in authority, as do demands for its progressive realization. We have described this impulsion toward the realization of the maximum common good as the dynamic force of natural moral law, and we shall further show that it is the dynamic force of natural jural law. The dynamic side belongs to natural law in both senses just as much as the static. Social systems are thus "legitimized" by natural law, in spite of their defects, if they are efficient, that is, if they realize that minimum of the common good which is necessary for the existence of society. To exclude any error, however, we must add that this "legitimization" does not mean justification. Slavery and individualist capitalism cannot be justified in themselves, but must be examined in the light of the relevant historical conditions in which the common utility (*utilitas communis* of the scholastics) is being realized. In this process a more profound idea of the common good, seen in its dynamic nature, will preclude any doubt that, notwithstanding the social limitations of a legal system, justice demands the progressive actualization of the legal goods bound up with the value of individual personality (the scholastic *bonum hominis*).[4]

Marx's Sociological Theory of Law

Our argument about the social-economic-technical factors in law existing at any time follows a course obviously parallel in part with the ideas of *Marx*. In fact, *Marx* was the first who undertook to show on the sociological plane the dependence of every legal and social system on economic and technical factors, as well as on ideological and political factors. Traditional natural law theory does not dispute this dependence; it admits wide scope for sociological method in jurisprudence and legal philosophy. It rejects, however, the basic idea of Marxian dialectical materialism that law is a by-product, indeed a mere subordinate of class-relationships, exclusively determined by technical and by economic factors. Certainly, the legal forms which are required for the organization of economic cooperation change as forms of production change; but it is the sense of justice, as *Marx* unconsciously admits, and it is the fundamental thought of natural law ethics, that promotes the defense of human dignity against any domination by technical-economic forces and promotes the endeavor to improve the legal order. We said that *Marx* unconsciously admits this. Indeed, he himself appeals to principles of law, a fact which can only be understood as an absolute a priori with regard to any technical conditions of economic cooperation. For example, he states the principle: "Each according to his capacities, to each according to his needs"; he considers the ideal of a community to be "the free development of each is the

[4] Cf. Augustine, *De civ. Dei,* XIX, cc. 14, 16, on respect for the personal nature of slaves. He points out that the *ordo naturalis* so clearly prescribes this respect that it has given rise to the expression *pater familias,* meaning one whose family obligations extend not only to wife and children but also to the *servi familiares,* so that a man bears this name even when there are no children.

condition for the free development of all." [5] What interests us here is not the content of these principles, but the fact that *Marx* himself assumes principles of justice independent of society and time, that is, he considers principles as intrinsically necessary and generally valid, in accordance with which efforts toward social order must be guided. The Marxian philosophy of law with its hypothesis that the critical evolution of law always proceeds by means of social revolutions, in a dialectical process, receives no confirmation, as we have shown (cf. Chap. 16), from social and legal history.[6]

42. The Juridical Order: Plurality of Rights, Unity of Law

Law, as we have found, is essentially an *order*. But what kind of an order is it? Is it only the consistency of the precepts of a legal system? This is the view of the analytical school. It narrows jurisprudence, in the words of *Ihering*, to a mere "conceptual jurisprudence" incapable of seeing the reality behind the conceptions. *Ihering* himself thought he had found the reality behind these conceptions in the manifold purposes of human endeavor, which had to be brought into a harmony, into an order,

[5] Marx, *Kritik des Gothaer Programms; The Communist Manifesto.*

[6] Positive law, as this chapter has indicated, is always a reflection of social relationships; but it is at the same time a mirror of the jural sense of society which precedes positive law, and this sense is a mirror of the natural jural conscience with its awareness of right and wrong (cf. Chaps. 37, 40, 47). "The Mirror Character of the Legal Order," says W. R. Beyer in his essay under that title (1951), concerns only social being: "It is self-evident"—he refers to Lenin—"that a copy cannot exist without the thing copied" and "there is no other being but material being"; the essence of law as a reflected image is "an 'essence' dialectically coinciding with the essence of the society which institutes the law"; in this sense he designates his dialectical legal philosophy "existential." The dream-picture of a natural law is no mirror-image, for this would presuppose the reality of the thing reflected, which does not exist (*ibid.*, pp. 7, 9, 11, 14 f., 30). In his *Rechtsphilosophische Besinnung: Eine Warnung vor der ewigen Wiederkehr des Naturrechts* (1947) Beyer says that all consideration of law must proceed from the concept of law: "Law can only be what functions as law." This concept of law is aprioristic. With this preconceived idea in mind, again aprioristically, he declares: "From the limitation of law to the field which alone is proper to it, it follows a priori that natural law must be denied the essence of law and that a concept of law must be sought which stands close examination." Yet, in spite of the subtitle of his essay, Beyer does not dispute the justification for a natural law doctrine: "The idea of natural law cannot be constructed a priori. Only the contemplation of natural law in its multiform, continuous change will make possible the attempt to deduce the concept of natural law and at the same time to demonstrate, outside legal dogmatism and legal philosophy, the only possible significance of natural law for legal policy" (*ibid.*, p. 15). The question is, who "constructs a priori": he who attributes reality only to material being, or he who is also ready to see immaterial reality in the nature of man? Because Beyer constructs his concept of law with a narrow view of reality and also restricts it to "functioning" law, we have called him aprioristic. Indeed, Beyer forgets that he himself says: "Every theory is more or less conditioned by general outlook and anchored in a philosophical system, also every legal theory" (*ibid.*, p. 14). In the light of these statements of Beyer there can be no doubt that his theory of law is founded on a very distinct world outlook and a metaphysics. Cf. Chap. 54 on a similar attempt by Laski to reach a new natural law.

by the will of the legislator. But an order of interests thus founded can, as we saw in the preceding chapter, place law at the service of the political and economic interests of power groups. On the other hand, if law has to serve human purposes with a view to the full human reality, namely the personal dignity of man as distinguished by responsibility and self-determination, the will of the lawgiver cannot prevail as the exclusive basis of legal order. Today, legal philosophy and jurisprudence are prepared, to a large extent, to consider what *Eugen Ehrlich*, one of the outstanding jurists and legal sociologists of the previous generation, said about the essence of law: "Thus, from the conception of law as a system of state coercion, which customary jurisprudence has always held tenaciously in substance, although not always in form, three elements at any rate are to be eliminated. It is not essential to the conception of law that law originate from the state, or that it form the basis for decisions of the courts or other authorities, or that it form the basis for the subsequent legal coercion. A fourth element remains, however, in the conception of law, and from this, I think, one has to start: Law is an order." [1]

What, then, is the basis of unity in legal order? *Ehrlich* thinks it possible to understand law sociologically in terms of the will of "society" as distinct from the state, and thus to understand legal order solely as a resultant of the juridical ideas and aims operative in society. This theory may be influenced by an idealizing view of modern democracy, yet it surrenders law to the stronger groups (and hence ultimately to arbitrary force) and ends by equating might with right. Therefore, the question remains: What is the basis of unity in order which forms the essence of law? There can be no doubt about the answer if one regards as the end of law man with his individual and social ends and values, which are presented to his individual responsibility acting in self-determination. Thus, we shall have to seek the basis of the unity of legal order in the nature of man, and the basis of legal order in the order outlined in man's existential ends. The order of law, whose fundamental end, as we have seen, consists in the good of man attained through actualization of the common good, is that of the order of ends, which are to be found in the *objective* individual and social existential ends (personal and communal values) and which are binding for the state lawgiver in his choice of *subjective* ends and of interests of individuals, groups, classes, and of interest groups, which are to be made legal by the legal system.

The following principles emerge as conclusions:

1. Enacted law is true law insofar as it conforms with the pattern of

[1] E. Ehrlich, *Grundlegung der Soziologie des Rechts*, 1929, p. 17; Ehrlich shows (*Freie Rechtsfindung und freie Rechtswissenschaft*, 1903, p. 7) by scientific sociological arguments why it is that in present-day legal thinking law is equated with the law of the state: "We are all children of the civil service state which has already been dominating all social life for centuries, and hardly one of us will be able without great effort to free himself from the ideas and lines of thought which the civil service state creates and nourishes. Indeed, from the true civil servant standpoint, law is nothing else but a command from the state to its officials."

ends indicated in the essential reality of human nature and with the responsibilities based on this pattern. Accordingly, "true" expresses conformity with objective reality.

2. The "objectivity" of law[2] thus refers to the fact that there is a sphere of law and rights precluded from the subjective will of the lawgiver or of the people, since it is founded in man's personal and social nature. In general usage itself, "objective" means "conforming with the nature of things"; if, therefore, the "objectivity" of law is seen only in a system of rules guaranteed by the power of the state, this is an arbitrary misuse of the word.

3. The legal order is fundamentally a matter of objective judgment and not of merely subjective feeling; hence, it demands an understanding of the nature of things. No one regards it as merely a matter of personal feeling if he is robbed of his freedom by unjust laws; rather, he knows that the jural order existing prior to and independently of personal feeling and of the political order is violated.

4. The objective fundamental order of law, which is indicated in human nature itself, does not mean that wide responsibilities do not devolve upon the state lawgiver; indeed, they are allotted to him by this order itself (cf. the following chapter).

5. Because its substance is determined by man's personal and social nature with its existential ends, the order of law is by no means a mere formal one, resting on an unreal or hypothetical principle; rather, it is of a concrete, and indeed "positive" essence, viz., an essence determined in its basic content and in its obligatory character.

Formal and Hypothetical Theories of Law

In modern legal philosophy and jurisprudence we find two outstanding attempts to base law on a formal concept of order. The first is that of *Stammler*, already mentioned (cf. Chap. 36); the other is that of *Kelsen* (cf. also Chap. 50). With his "pure theory of law" *Kelsen* does not seek a principle for judging "true law"; he admits that "true law" cannot exist since there are intrinsically only interests and conflicts of interests, which are solved by the order established by the legal system. The authority of the several rules of a legal system, therefore, cannot reside in the sphere of interests, but only in another rule; furthermore, since law belongs to the category of "ought" as distinct from that of "is," its unity in order must be derived from its concept as of a rule and

[2] The German "Recht" as distinct from the plural "Rechte" ("rights") is not a merely abstract expression or collective noun, but denotes the *order* of rights or law ("subjective" rights also belong to "objective" law in this sense of an order). The notion of order is also clearly implied in the words *ius, droit, diritto;* "objective law (recht)," therefore, does not only mean "abstract" law, as T. E. Holland, the English jurist, suggests in his widely read book *Elements of Jurisprudence* (13th ed., 1924, p. 84). There would be no problem if the English word "right" corresponded with the German "Recht" (meaning "order of rights"). As it is, recent translations of Hegel's *Philosophie des Rechts* have got over the difficulty by using "right" instead of "law"; this usage, commoner in America than in England, is confined to specialized literature.

not from a source outside law. The individual legal rules, therefore, can possess binding force only by reference to a higher rule within the legal system, namely, by "delegation." By a logical regress in the sequence of delegations, *Kelsen* is led back to the constitutional law, i.e. to the "fundamental law" or "law of origin," as the basis of the concrete legal system. This cannot be derived further, but is the "hypothetical foundation" of the whole legal system. *Kelsen's* theory, as he himself emphasizes, is a continuation of the nineteenth-century positivist theory of law.[3] Three essential features of legal order emerge more clearly in *Kelsen's* "pure theory" than in any other theory of legal philosophy: it exists as a unity; its binding force rests in detail on "delegation"; this delegation must have an ultimate source (cf. Chap. 49). Since, according to *Kelsen,* this source consists in a hypothetical concept, the first link of the sequence of delegations hangs in the air. *Nawiasky* points out that *Kelsen* arrives at a contradiction of his positivist fundamental assumption, since "to derive the validity of a constitution from a hypothetical law, which in fact means from a hypothesis, is to deny the historical existence of the constitution and to replace it by a mental operation, thus robbing the constitution of its positive quality." [4] This ultimate source, if law is to be law in accordance with man's juridical consciousness and not just the enforced command of a ruler, can only be the will of the Creator of the moral world order.

Law is an order embracing *a plurality of categories of equally original rights,* none of which can be simply derived from another. A legal monism is inherent in every totalitarian collectivistic philosophy of law: the denial of the original character of the rights of the individual and of their derivation exclusively from the supposedly primary and only original law of the state community. This is the inverse of individualist legal monism, which maintains with equal firmness that there are ultimately no original rights other than those of the individual. Rights have their origin in the existential ends prescribed in man's nature. These ends are both individual and social in kind; there exist, therefore, original rights of individuals and of communities. The rights of the individual are freedom of conscience, of religious worship, of association, of contract, and many others (cf. Chap. 51). The rights of every community involve its special authority in the sphere of its particular end, with relative independence of other social authorities; in other words, the community enjoys autonomy.

This *juridical pluralism* is a much more complex phenomenon than it appears at first sight. A great variety of social entities exist which have rights of their own. The modern industrial society can enjoy peace and order without the social function which is fulfilled by the sports clubs organized by many firms, but not without the occupational organizations which are necessary for bringing about collective labor agreements. Both club and trade union are associations with their own responsibilities and rights. In character and extent, however, these rights differ widely. For,

[3] Cf. H. Kelsen, *Reine Rechtslehre,* 1934, pp. 15, 25, 65 ff., 129.
[4] H. Nawiasky, *Allgemeine Rechtslehre,* 1948, p. 35.

the rules of the club are binding only upon its members, whose membership is wholly voluntary, whereas the rules of the collective labor agreement are binding not only upon the members of the trade union and the employers' association who freely enter into it, but in countries with an advanced system of collective agreements are also binding upon the whole branch of industry concerned in a particular area (just as state rule binds everyone, even those who have taken no share by their consent in its formation). Thus, the club performs a social function in the private sphere, the trade union in the public sphere. Within their own association, of course, their rules with regard to, for instance, subscriptions and members' claims are binding only upon the members; in this respect, the trade union does not differ from the club. Another trend in economic development points in the same direction. The public utility corporation (e.g., the gas company) may present the same legal structure as a private commercial undertaking. Yet, in reality they differ essentially because of their different functions. The latter exercises a social function in the sphere of private commerce and in its price formation is governed by competition; the former, on the other hand, exercises a function in the public sphere and determines prices by decree, independently of competition. The private monopoly also fixes prices, but under other conditions and with other results than is the case with price-fixing by public utility corporations.

In fact, there are as many autonomous social groupings as there are necessary and voluntary social functions serving needs inherent in human existence. The lesser communities in the private sphere extend over the whole field of human activity—cultural, economic, social, charitable, and sporting—and take such varied forms as the tennis club, the limited liability company, the reading circle, and the charitable trust. The lesser communities which have socially necessary functions are the family, local and regional communities, and occupational groupings. The autonomous rights of all these lesser communities have their limits only in the order of ends founded in man's personal and social nature. Since it is the function of the authority of the "great society" to give effect to that order and to coordinate the functions of the lesser communities within that framework, the lesser communities are subject to the ordering power of this authority within its proper competence.

The *distinction between private and public law* originates from the pluralism in the juridical order. Private law comprises rights whose end is the individual good, public law those which have the common good as their end. The distinction has often been disputed with the argument that all law is either of an exclusively private or of an exclusively public nature.[5] The

[5] That our definition of the distinction between public and private law does not lack confirmation from an established tradition in jurisprudence may be seen from the words of Sohm: "Public law is the law of power relations concerned with common utility; private law is the law of power relations concerned with individual utility" (*Institutionen, Geschichte und System des römischen Privatrechtes,* 16th ed., 1919, p. 25).

difficulties jurists have experienced in past centuries and even up to modern times in interpreting and applying this distinction, which was already found in Roman Law (*ius publicum quoad rem publicam spectat, ius privatum quoad singulorum utilitatem spectat*), are due to two reasons. The first is practical: in the course of history new legal institutions have sprung up which have not been exactly covered by either definition, especially during their period of development; thus, in the Middle Ages the guilds were communities with their own social rights and functions. In modern times collective agreement committees are set up by trade unions and employers' associations, that is, by groups on a private footing, but beginning to exercise public functions. The second reason is more essential and refers to the already-mentioned legal monism: individualist thought had forgotten that society consists not only of individuals but of social groups, so that the juridical order is characterized by a multiplicity of original rights of social groups and indeed always has been. It is not surprising, therefore, that *O. von Gierke* [6] and *F. W. Maitland,*[7] in their study of legal history in Germany and England found a plurality of groupings with social functions in the public sphere and endowed with corporate rights and a measure of autonomy.

In nineteenth-century France, the question of the nature of the juridical order was taken up with special emphasis by the school of legal philosophy and jurisprudence which expounded the "*institutional theory*." Their ideas were greatly stimulated by the developing forms of groupings and institutions in economic and social life. Much of the discussion has centred on the notions of social and legal personality and the nature of the rights associated with the autonomy of corporate units. The ultimate source of these rights has been sought in various directions: *Gierke* sought it in the unity of the group will; [8] *Duguit* in the principle of solidarity; [9]

[6] Otto v. Gierke, *Das deutsche Genossenschaftsrecht,* Vols. I–IV, 1868–1913, esp. Vol. II, pp. 25–42 (translation of parts by E. Barker, *Natural Law and the Theory of Society,* 1934); *Das Wesen der menschlichen Verbände,* 1902, p. 25.

[7] F. W. Maitland, *Introduction to Gierke's Political Theories of the Middle Ages,* 1900; *History of English Law* (with Sir F. Pollock), 1911; *The Collected Papers,* 1911.

[8] Gierke wishes to replace the distinction between public and private law by that of social and private, thus conceiving the all-embracing community, i.e., the state, solely as a federal union of the lesser communities and nothing more. He mistakes the substance of sovereignty, which is rooted in the end of the state, namely, the maintenance of the order of law in the all-embracing society. A second objection to Gierke's theory is that he bases his "social law" on a conception of the community which makes it simply a *genossenschaft,* or fellowship, i.e., an association by the will of the members, in which he comes close to the social contract theory. These reservations, however, cannot prejudice Gierke's merits as a champion of the understanding of juridical reality against individualism and positivism in legal philosophy.

[9] Cf. M. Duguit, *L'état, le droit objectif et la loi positive,* 1901; *Manuel du droit constitutionnel,* 1907; *Le droit social, le droit individuel et la transformation de l'état,* 1908. In Duguit's thinking, social law is *droit objectif*. He sees it as based on the solidarity of the group and this on objective realities. One of these is the common attitude of a group toward encroachments from outside; another is the common awareness that this attitude must be given an organized form and must become a recognized rule of action, involving coercion. This "objective law," therefore, does not ultimately derive its validity from state legislation or the state judicature.

Hauriou in the idea common to a group; [10] *Gurvitch* in the *faits normatifs*.[11] The latter traced back to *Proudhon* the whole tradition in French legal thinking represented by these names. We need not discuss all of these attempts in detail, since they can be reduced to a common denominator without difficulty: The end which underlies the "unity of will," the sense of "solidarity," the "common idea" of the group, the unifying "factual situation." It would be easy to show that the ends thus understood are essentially related to the ends which, according to our legal philosophy, constitute rights. *Gierke, Duguit, Gurvitch,* and others term this kind of community rights "social rights" (*droit social*), but without giving the term exactly the same meaning. A common factor in these jurists is that they conceive of the social unit as a group with an order governed by an inherent end, with a being of its own, with a duration and capacity for action independent of its individual members, and with autonomous corporate rights. The "institution," the social unit as such, is, according to *Hauriou,* more than merely a group equipped with legal capacity and is completely different from a union founded only on a contract: the contract can only create a "legal" situation, whereas in the "institution" a general will operates without a contractual basis; the individual can belong to a number of such institutions, of which the state is a special kind. *Hauriou,* the founder of the institutional theory, does not deny the influence of traditional social and legal philosophy upon it. *Duguit* and *Gurvitch* seek to think in purely empirical-sociological terms and hence to concern themselves only with factual data, although both postulate an intuitive sense of justice as an essential datum alongside the objective facts. The outstanding contribution of these theories toward the pluralistic conception of law is to have brought to light again the institution, the social unit as such. Their positivist critics find a fundamental element of natural law theory only in the idea of an intuitive

[10] Cf. Maurice Hauriou, *Principes du droit public,* 1910; "La théorie de l'institution et de la fondation," in *Cahier de la nouvelle journée,* 1925; cf. also *Précis de droit administratif.* Hauriou is the initiator of the "institutional theory." Another outstanding exponent is Georges Renard, *La théorie de l'institution,* 1930; *La philosophie de l'institution,* 1939. Renard made the institutional theory fruitful for traditional natural law theory.

[11] Cf. Gurvitch, *Le temps présent et l'idée du droit social,* 1931, esp. pp. 113–53. Gurvitch conceives of "social law" as *droit positif intuitif* in contradistinction to *droit positif formel;* he seeks its origin in the *faits normatifs,* which he interprets in a way similar to Duguit's and in which he sees original sources of rights. René Toulemont, *Sociologie et pluralisme dialectique* (Louvain), 1955, shows in this book, which is mainly occupied with Gurvitch, that Gurvitch regards his sociology as a positive or empirical science, which as such has nothing to do with abstract notions and ideal natural law. His notion of *faits normatifs,* on the other hand, according to Toulemont, makes it impossible to derive moral values and fundamental jural rules of conduct exclusively from man's will and social customs, so that in the idea of *faits normatifs* there is to be seen an affirmation of the essential elements of natural law; the more so as he sharply repudiates the centralist, atomistic state with its elimination of the lesser units, a development which is inconsistent with the order implied in the *faits normatifs.*

sense of justice; the endeavor made by these theories to ascertain the ontological grounds of the rights of communities seems, however, to afford a much deeper parallel to natural law doctrine.

In the light of the foregoing there exists a *plurality of rights of like origin, although they are not all of equal kind.* The right of the state is sovereignty, which includes the right to command the smaller social entities; for, the function of state sovereignty is to establish the legal order of society as a whole, including all individual and communal members.[12] In reality the autonomous rights of the different social units cannot always be sharply defined. Continuous evolution and complex relationships prevent this. The development of new legal forms which are required has hardly been begun; thus, the rules which arise from the collective labor agreement and which concern whole branches of industry still have, according to the letter of the law in many countries, as in England, only the character of civil law contracts; where the collective agreement law and the social assurance law present new elements of social law these remain often unrelated to a general concept of social and legal order.

Meanwhile, political, economic, and social life urgently call for a reorientation. If this does not take place, two serious dangers threaten. The first is the pluralistic society in which, instead of a pluralism of autonomous communities which conform to the order of law there is a pluralism of interest groups acting on the principle of power; the other is the centralist state which, because of the lack of autonomy on the part of member communities, constantly gathers to itself wider powers in all fields of administration. Since the turn of the century, this evolution has had one of its roots also in a legal monism of an individualist and of a collectivist stamp. Positivist jurisprudence was blind to the wealth of elementary rights with which nature endows the many *intermediate social entities* which have their place between individual and state; particularly alien to it is the idea of an organization of society according to vocational groups (cf. Chaps. 85, 181, n. V). Only the division of powers in accordance with competences for selfgovernment, founded in the pluralism in the legal order, forms an effective protection against state centralism and all forms of open and concealed state omnipotence and omnicompetence.

The pluralism in the legal order, as discussed above, excludes jural monism, or the derivation of all rights from a single kind of original rights, but it does not exclude the *inner unity of the legal order,* in the

[12] The state and lesser communities cannot be placed on the same level. Surprisingly enough, such opposed social philosophies as that of Laski (*A Grammar of Politics,* 1941, pp. x ff., although he here modifies an earlier, much more levelling opinion) and that of Spann (*Der Wahre Staat,* 1931, p. 184) reach the same view in conceiving the state as only one community among others, all of which are held to be fundamentally equal in their sovereignty. For all such attempts, the remark of Morris R. Cohen (*Reason and Nature,* 1931, p. 398) holds good: "The evils of an absolute state are not cured by the multiplication of absolutes."

sense that there can be no contradiction between the manifold original rights of individuals and of social entities. This unity of law is intrinsically rooted in the unity of the order of ends, in which the various individual and social rights have their origin. The order of ends itself is an intrinsic unity as a result of the unity of man's individual and social nature. Thus, we conclude: The unity of the legal order does not spring essentially from the mutual coordination of unlimited rights; rather, individual rights, private and public, are themselves inherently limited (cf. Chap. 36), since the competences which accompany them are restricted to the jural end underlying them. The supreme end of society confers on the authority which is based upon it the right and duty to uphold the unity of law in its system of rules; not least in importance, this unity results in legal certainty which, as already mentioned (cf. Chap. 38), belongs to the nature of law itself.

In fact, however, the unity of the legal order is always only approximately, and never wholly, realized. Every legal system is instinct with *unavoidable frictions* which arise from historical and sociological factors, each being a compromise resulting from the endeavors of the groups in society to mold the social order in their own interest. But even if all groups in society were intent only on justice, the legal order would present no absolute unity, since on the one hand human reason cannot become conversant with all the individual claims of justice in every detail and with complete certainty, especially in a complex society (cf. Chap. 48), and on the other hand the lawgiver is able to define the legally relevant facts only in a more or less general way, not in such a way that every possible individual case is covered. Furthermore, the conditions underlying the legal system vary in societies stirred by evolutionary forces, whereas in the interest of legal security the existence of fixed legal rules is unavoidable. Hence, the traditional natural law theory thinks realistically in the present question, too, and sees the inevitability of frictions in every existing legal order and the necessity of insuring, by external means and in the interest of legal security, consistency within the legal order. Such means may be described as technical, whether they occur in the drafting of laws by the lawgiver or in the powers conferred by him upon the judicature. Natural law ethics, nevertheless, will emphasize that the lawgiver has to provide for possibilities in order to comply with justice in cases in which a defective statutory law would run counter to clear principles of justice or of equity (on conflicts between law and justice and on loopholes in the law cf. Chaps. 48, 49).

The unity of the legal order is also called in question by a second phenomenon: the *conflict of rights* and the conflict of duties. This means that there may be legal claims apparently equally well-established, but not capable of being fulfilled at the same time. No conflict, however, can exist between real rights, but only between judgments on the jural situation which result from faulty appreciation of the relevant factual situation. This includes the facts of human nature itself as well as those of the external circumstances in question. And since, finally, the facts of human nature are decisive, any real conflict of rights is precluded. Nevertheless, the traditional natural law theory oversimplifies the matter when, as happens in some expositions, it leaves the question with such abstractions and admits only a contradiction between right and apparent right.

In reality, it would often require an all-knowing mind to penetrate the facts from both aspects mentioned and to elucidate the jural situation. Furthermore, there are the unavoidable frictions in the legal order, which have just been mentioned. These can result in cases of conflict between rights and can be solved only by compromise, as sometimes happens in courts of law (e.g., in cases of mutually incompatible property rights which have been acquired bona fide). Regarding the factual situation, even in the sphere of moral natural law sometimes not merely external circumstances must be taken into consideration, but also psychological factors, which are partly concealed from the judgment of others. If a girl is faced with the choice between her natural right to marriage and her parents' natural right to her help, it is evident that subjective factors must be taken into account on both sides and the decision must then be left to the individual conscience, because the nature of the actual data eludes an exhaustive examination.

Again, in political life we may consider the case of the natural right to resistance, the exercise of which depends on weighing the consequences for the common good; but often in the actual political situation no judgment is possible which can claim more than probability, so that in the face of a given situation a decision for or against the exercise of the right of resistance can hardly ever be given in the name of natural law ethics; instead, the decision must be left to the individual conscience, and natural law ethics can only develop the applicable principles. Recent experience has reminded us how heavily such conflicts of rights can burden the individual conscience, when, for example, not only the right to resist and considerations of the common good are at stake, but the individual conscience also has to take into account obligations toward his family, his following, his parish community. Another familiar example is the conflict between rights of natural and contractual justice in interstate relations. Viewed in the abstract, all these cases can be solved smoothly enough, but in actual life they very often involve the gravest *human tragedies,* whose cause lies in the inadequacy of man's understanding.[13]

A touchstone for every philosophy of law, and hence for natural law ethics, is how far they can offer *principles and criteria* for a solution of the conflict between rights and between jural obligations (on collision of duties cf. Chap. 3, n. V). We can derive these from our supreme principle and criterion of law, which consists in the existential ends:

[13] Cf. Messner, *Ethics and Facts,* pp. 136–41. On the problem of genuinely tragic situations cf. Messner, *Kulturethik:* in general, pp. 587 ff.; in the sphere of law, pp. 603 ff.; in the religious-moral sphere, pp. 609 ff.

1. Rights founded on *existential ends* of a more comprehensive and more immediate significance for complete human existence, that is to say, rights which safeguard goods of a higher rank in this sense, have priority over rights founded on ends of less comprehensive and immediate significance. If a nation is engaged in a life or death struggle, the right of a union to strike must be kept in abeyance if a strike would impair the war effort; the duty of the workers toward the community is prior to their duty toward the union which calls them out on strike. On the other hand, the supreme right, that of the moral conscience, whereby man is entitled to act in accordance with the clear voice of his conscience, must give place to the right of the community to peace and to order, since goods of a like nature, but more comprehensive, and therefore higher, are endangered. Thus, when someone feels himself bound in conscience to perform a violent deed for political motives, priority must be given to the right of the community to use appropriate means for its protection. Using the same principles, the position of conscience is different under the conditions for violent resistance (cf. Chap. 132).

2. The first-mentioned principle suffers a restriction by reason of the fact that the securing of the goods protected by rights depends upon *time factors.* For, the attainment of goods indispensable for existential ends may depend on a good of lesser significance. In such cases the rights which protect lesser goods and duties have priority. If, in a struggle for life or death, a government makes inroads into the fundamental liberties of the human person without justification on grounds of national emergency, and if there is no prospect of these liberties being later restored, then a general strike would be justified by reason of the time factor, although intrinsically the common good of the community and the rights rooted in it have priority when in conflict with the individual good and the rights rooted in it. For, if the individual good of the members of society were permanently and substantially impaired in its principal existential ends, the common good of the community would itself be illusory.

3. A third principle is the priority of duties founded on *inalienable rights* over those founded on alienable rights. The latter usually rest on contracts. Thus, a state may have bound itself by treaty to come to the help of another in case of war; but if war would mean inevitable defeat and disaster, then the inalienable right of self-preservation for such a state would assume priority over the treaty rights of allies. In general, all contractual rights as such give way to original rights with which they are in conflict, since the original rights always serve directly to safeguard the fulfillment of existential ends. If, for example, an actress has entered into a film contract which is prejudicial to the upbringing of one of her children, the rights of the child take precedence; if, however, the harm is not irremediable and the work is indispensable for their livelihood, the second principle, that of temporary urgency, may come into play.

4. Natural rights and duties which are *established by law* have priority over rights and duties which have only a natural law basis; for, it is the state's function by natural law to circumscribe natural rights and to codify them in its laws. Thus, the right of free assembly is subject to the conditions laid down by the state legislation. The situation alters, however, when the law of the state comes into conflict with natural law. If the state tries to eliminate any possibility of free assembly, then the original right of free assembly assumes priority over the law of the state, even though it can be exercised only in the form of "underground movements."

43. Juridical Order and the Ordering Power

The state's power of legislation and of coercion is as fundamental a part of the natural jural order as the rights of its members. This fact is overlooked by jurists when they argue that the natural law principles are too indefinite to fulfill any real ordering function in society. Although the natural law in itself offers only general principles, these are definite enough, in conjunction with knowledge of the factual situation, to guide the ordering power in its function of establishing the basic juridical order. The natural law doctrine does not hold that the natural law principles alone, without legal definition and enforcement, could establish and maintain order, peace, and the common good; it holds, rather, that the legal power of the social authority as *power to command* is grounded in the natural laws principles. The task of this authority is to define the fundamental requirements of the natural law order in rules of conduct binding upon the members of the community, and to guarantee their observance. Although most people are aware of the natural law principles and are able to apply them in simple situations, in less simple circumstances they lack the clear understanding of the facts which is necessary for the appreciation of the juridical duties bound up with those principles; furthermore, many lack the reliable will necessary for the assured fulfillment of such juridical duties and hence for the assured maintenance of peace and order in society.

The fact that these principles, along with knowledge of the facts, are clear enough to enable the lawgiver to establish the natural juridical order with its rights and duties can be seen from the undeviating uniformity with which the elementary rights and duties recur in the codes of law of the whole civilized world. For this reason, we find uniformly prevailing in these codes of law such fundamental rights as freedom of conscience, freedom of religious worship, the right to life, the right to reputation, the rights to one's property, the right of parents to educate their children, the right of free expression of opinion, the right of free association, etc. The principles which are thus to be realized by the social authority are those of justice, which assign "to each his own," namely, the rights which the natural law order guarantees to man, because he is man, with his existential ends, and with his spheres of self-responsibility and of self-determination. If some of these rights, the essential ones, have only gradually come to be more clearly apprehended in the course of the development of man's jural consciousness, or if, once realized, they have been suppressed, the human conscience has striven after their recognition with obvious success. The guaranteeing of these fundamental rights and hence of the peace of society is the one principal end of the common good to be realized by the state legal system; the second consists in welfare, in making it possible for the groups in society to share proportionately in the fruits of their social cooperation (another task in line with the principle "to each his own").

Social ordering power in large measure is also *power of decision*. The choice of the ends, interests, goods, and values in which a juridical community seeks the particular features of its common good is a matter for its own will; besides this, however, the question concerning the best means of serving the demands of the common good often admits of no unequivocal solution. Therefore, a large part in the shaping of the common good and hence of the legal system is left to sound common sense, to practical judgment, to group influence, and to the popular will. A large pragmatic element, therefore, exists in legal systems: to a great extent, legislation is a question of expediency, materially governed by the preference of a society for certain values and formally governed by the necessity for inner unity in the juridical order. Since in every society there is inevitably a great variety of purposes and values, blameless in themselves, and a great variety of opinions on the merits of different aims and on ways for best realizing the common good, in order that the common utility may indeed become a reality legislative authority also implies power of decision with regard to which ends and means are to obtain the sanction of the common good principle and hence come within the binding force of law. Thus, we again find an aspect of positive law which indicates an element of truth in legal positivism. Indeed, since this power of decision is founded on the end of the common good itself and hence forms part of the state administrative authority, obedience is a natural juridical duty for the individual and for the group members of society, when in such questions of pure expediency the lawgiver has taken a decision, and even if they feel certain that his decision on the expediency of a measure is bound to prove mistaken. For example, the measures taken by the legislature to curb or to stimulate economic development impose a duty of obedience on individuals and on groups, even though they believe them inexpedient, just as the lawgiver possesses the moral right to compel obedience to such decrees.

The functions of the state authority, however, are not exhausted with the rights and duties just mentioned. A very important function which belongs to it is *legal certainty.* This forms, as we have seen (cf. Chap. 38), an essential constituent of law. In the first place, legal certainty signifies the possibility of clear and certain knowledge by all members of society with regard to what actions are lawful. Legal certainty is also of immediate interest for the application of law, because the judge, the lawyer, and the jurist are concerned with the law's application. The lawgiver performs his task by framing the system of rules which lays down what is lawful in the civil, social, political, and economic relations peculiar to the particular legal community. In this task of the lawgiver, founded in the natural juridical order itself, we can again perceive an aspect of positive law which points to a strong element of truth in legal positivism. The establishment of legal certainty by the state authority involves as a second task the guaranteeing by legal compulsion of the maintenance of the juridical order by the members of the community.

Natural law theory has accordingly always upheld as *functions of the lawgiver:* (1) the definition of the general principles of natural law in order to exclude ignorance and uncertainty about them (*per modum declarationis*); (2) the application of the general principles to special conditions in the light of the historical development of society (*per modum conclusionis*); (3) the decision in regard to suitable institutions for realizing the common utility (*per modum determinationis*); (4) the exercise of coercion to insure the observance of the juridical order (*per modum executionis*).

It has often been stated by jurists that jurisprudence would take much more readily to the idea of natural law if it were represented not as a detailed and finished juridical order independent of time and society but rather as a basis and outline of such an order.* What has been said previously in this regard should show that acceptance of the doctrine of natural law need offer no difficulties to the jurist. Although this doctrine maintains that true and genuine rights are rooted in natural law, it certainly does not hold that the pattern of society in every detail is laid down by natural law in particular national, political, economic, social, and cultural circumstances, or that codes of law and legal systems valid for any society independently of time can be deduced from it. On the contrary, natural law theory expressly states that, in this respect almost everything has to be done by the human lawgiver; legal codes and systems are the affair of the lawgiver and not of natural law ethics.

In the above, the ruling authority of the state has been placed in the foreground, because this power is fundamental to and has the most far-reaching influence on the peace and order of society as a whole. Never-

* In isolated instances, however (cf. Chap. 47), the contrary objection is raised that natural law is unable to develop a complete system of rules which the lawgiver could simply put into force, but assigns him a very wide range of tasks in the establishing of rules. But this overlooks the character of the natural law principles and the fact that their application depends upon the situation, and also that positive law is dependent upon historical and sociological factors.

theless, it is only one of the forms of social ordering power, for just as the common good of the state as an end is the basis for the rights of the ruling power of the state, each species of common good originates a special kind of ruling power. Hence, there is a *plurality of social authorities,* which form part of the juridical pluralism (cf. Chap. 42, n. II). Every form of social authority, since it has its root in a special existential end and in the moral responsibilities implied therein, represents a right, and indeed a right of control, which is the nature of every right. Social authority represents a right of a special kind in that it consists in control over men and over part of their conduct: In its innermost nature it is the power to command, with the powers necessary to secure the common good. Social authority exists, therefore, wherever an objective social end, a common good, is to be realized (e.g., in the family, in local and regional communities, in the state). One's relationship toward such an authority is not subject to arbitrary notice, like membership in a free association, a club, a trade union, or in a charitable society; in these cases, adherence rests upon voluntary agreement. In the case of the natural communities it is founded on the objective order of the common good of society, namely, on the objective end appropriate to the particular social entity (the "institution," as the French school expresses it; cf. Chap. 42). Although authority differs in kind in the various natural communities with their special objective ends, it remains essentially one and the same as the power of command. The basis of the state's administrative authority is also the objective social end, and not the agreement of individuals, not a social contract or the will of the people, as assumed by the legal and political theories of individualist and collectivistic schools. Indeed, authority is an essential element in the natural "constitution" of the state, which is true of every original community.

From the nature of the ordering power in society which we have just been discussing, the following *essential characteristics* may be derived: 1) The ordering power in society is part of the natural juridical order, since it springs from man's existential ends as involved in the common good. 2) Obedience to lawful authority, therefore, is a moral duty, and indeed a duty in justice. 3) Obedience to social authority, accordingly, is liable to enforcement. 4) Because it is founded in human nature all authority has its ultimate origin in God: "There is no power but from God; and those that are, are ordained of God" (Rom. 13:1). 5) The authority of every community is inherently one and undivided by its nature; the "division of powers" (legislative, judicial, executive) is not a division of social authority itself but the assignment of its exercise to different organs. 6) The authorities of the communities which are rooted directly in man's social nature are part of the juridical order as a whole; the compass of each authority is limited by the end it has to serve, so that every social power of command is limited by its nature. 7) Only the power of command as such is founded on the end of society, not the investment of this power in a particular person, which requires a special legal title. This title may originate in natural facts, such as parenthood in the family, or an agreed constitution, as in a democracy, or the right of succession, as in a hereditary monarchy. 8) Because it belongs to the natural moral and juridical order, in all its measures social authority is bound by the principles of this order. 9) Only as the ordering power in society in the sense discussed is the power of social control legitimate juridical power in contradistinction to despotism founded on external power relationships (concerning the problems thus posed for legal and political ethics cf. Chaps. 40, 41, 48, 49, 131, 132).

The principles laid down here must be more fully considered in the two following chapters from the point of view of the justification and limitation of the social ordering power.

44. Juridical Order and the Principle of the Common Good

Fundamentally, the juridical order is the order of the common good: an order of society implied by the help which is required by all the members of society, and which must be made available through their social cooperation in the tasks set before them by their existential ends which are to be carried out under their own responsibility. To provide such *help* is the essence of the common good. Making this help possible by means of social cooperation, therefore, is itself an existential end, the end which determines the whole order of society and primarily determines all law as the foundation of social order. All this has been dealt with at length in our discussion of social ontology (cf. Chaps. 22–31). Now we must draw conclusions with regard to the nature of the common good principle, the special range of its authority, and the mode of obligation which it imposes. Although the principle of the common good is often quoted in present-day literature and in traditional natural law literature as the fundamental principle of all social and juridical order, little is said about what the common good is by its nature. The first task of natural law theory is to analyze nature from every point of view, that is, the personal and social nature of man as a unity, but especially the nature of society and of the common good. For this reason, it has seemed necessary to deal fully with social ontology and social metaphysics.

1. The first conclusion concerning the common good principle is that it is a *concrete* principle, insofar as it is founded in concrete reality and is characterized by concrete contents. For the integral humanity of the members of society is dependent upon the realization of the common good order. Therefore, by no means, as is often maintained, is it a merely formal principle without definite content or a too general one to have any significance for the functions of social, economic, and state policy.

In fact, most demands in these fields are made with appeals to the common good, even when in present-day democracy they are put forward by groups employing the methods of power politics. When claim and counterclaim come into conflict, however, and the path of negotiation must be followed, then real common good interests are discussed. Discussions take place with reference to "the nature of the case," as seen by the different sides, that is to say, by the negotiating parties themselves and by the public organs. The fact that they are seen differently by different sides is not to be wondered at, for with the complexity of all social, political, and economic relationships it is no simple matter to discover "the nature of things." Furthermore, the fact that discussions are possible in the consideration of arguments and counterarguments shows sufficiently that the common good principle itself is not a formal but a concrete principle, although the results of such discussion in most cases may outwardly bear the stamp of compromise. A reason for this is that, along with the concrete considerations and arguments, those of power politics always arise. What concerns us here is the fact that arguments in such cases are governed by the idea that above the sectional interests of groups, the common interest of all groups, the general interest of society, is to be kept in mind, and that the possibility exists of discussing it in concrete terms. Statements that the common good principle is only a formal principle, one that is too general, too impractical, and too unusable, issue from groups associated with party ideologies or from social theorists whose outlook regarding the reality of life is "scientifically" impaired. Both sides exhibit a promising field of sociological investigation.

2. We have already touched upon a second essential feature of the common good principle: the *jural* principle. As a principle of justice, the common good principle is concerned with the *suum cuique,* that is, the *suum* of society as a whole and that of its members as parts of the whole. In content, the *suum* comprises the original rights of the members of society, the safeguarding of which forms part of the fundamental end of society: it comprises the right of society as a whole to secure what is necessary for its own existence and for the performance of its due functions; and it comprises the rightful claim to the corresponding efforts by the members of society, the claim by the members to their share in the general welfare made possible by the cooperation of all, and finally the claim that this cooperation with regard to efforts and to fruits is ruled by the principle of proportionality (cf. Chaps. 26, 27). In addition, this principle does not mean vagueness, when once the measuring rod is sufficiently determined. It is sufficiently determined when a judgment on the amounts concerned is possible, for example, the necessary yield of a tax and the capacity of the taxpayers, or the levels of productivity and wages in the economy as a whole and in particular branches of industry. Who would deny today that due proportion in these matters can be ascertained with sufficient accuracy? Although, of course, this does not mean that it is accepted as a rule of action by the parties concerned.

3. The mode of *obligation* imposed by the common good principle primarily has the character of a natural law. This means that the obligation imposed by the common good does not depend solely on the will of the lawgiver, which is merely one of the forms of its mode of obligation (one which basically has the character of a natural law); but it concerns also obedience toward the will of the lawgiver, which settles what demands the common good makes on conduct. Besides this, a wide field of natural law duties exists which is founded on the common good principle. First among these duties are those of the state legislator himself, who must carry out the measures required by the common good. Since the whole social sphere does not fall under the control of the lawgiver, however, it is subject to the common good obligation of natural law, even if the lawgiver is not primarily responsible for the common good order of a certain sphere or as in the case of the community of nations, even if there is no lawgiver capable of regulating the obligations originating in the common good. The lawgiver is not primarily responsible in the "social" sphere in which natural communities or free interest groups have to comply with their common good obligations on their own responsibility. Such obligations exist for the first of the natural communities, the family, concerning which *St. Augustine,* who bases his thought so firmly on the family (cf. Chap. 47), states that it represents a beginning and a part of the state as "the ordered union of citizens, practiced in commanding and obeying," and "like every beginning tends toward the ultimate goal and like every part toward the perfection of the whole." To stress the common good obligation of the family in natural law seems necessary for natural law theory at a period when, owing to the failure of the family as the biological cell of society, society is threatened at its vital root. The common good obligation is stressed also in order to counteract the impression that the family has only claims to make on the state, founded on the common good principle, without obligations to fulfill which are based on the same principle. Among common good obligations of natural law in the "social" sphere we have to note those of political parties with respect to the subordination of their party interests to the general interest, and the obligations of occupational groups with regard to the apportionment of the social product through the price and wage structure. No lawgiver's will has yet been able to prescribe to the members of the community of nations the demands of their common good; nevertheless, for them too juridical duties exist that are based on the common good principle—and not derived merely from treaties—duties which vary according to the importance of their position in the community of nations. We shall have to deal later in detail in various connections with the obligations and rights of legal, political, social, and international justice, rooted in the common good principle, which we have here touched upon.

4. With regard to the *range* of authority of the common good principle, it must be pointed out first that it not only can establish obligations, but also can provide independently existing obligations with further binding

force. Every mode of conduct demanded by the moral law (i.e., virtue) can also fall within the requirements of the common good and hence assume the character of a fulfillment of an obligation of justice; as such it can be enforced. Moderation in eating and drinking is enjoined by the moral law, but in wartime it can be demanded by the law of the common good and enforced by the legislature through food rationing. Since in certain circumstances every mode of conduct can come under the binding force of the common good principle, this principle has been described by the traditional natural law school as that of "general justice" (cf. Chap. 50). From the range of authority of the common good principle there follows, secondly, the *priority principle:* the common good takes precedence over the individual good. The individual existential ends cannot be attained independently of the common good; hence, the latter represents the "universal" good, in comparison with the individual good, and, therefore, is the higher jural good.

Because the natural jural law order is intrinsically related to the order of ends (or order of values), the common good principle as a principle of priority has a *twofold limitation,* a qualitative and a quantitative one.

Qualitatively it remains valid only within the same rank in the scale of goods (values). Since the common good, as we showed (Chaps. 23 ff.), is a reality only insofar as it results in the good of the individual, goods which are essential for existential ends (human values) of higher rank must not be subordinated to community goods (values) of lower rank. Personal services, therefore, must not be demanded from the members of the community when material contributions will suffice. No community has the right to demand a sacrifice of conscience, for man's entire moral personality is rooted in conscience (cf. Chap. 51, n. 1).

The *quantitative* limitation of the common good principle as a priority principle: The priority of the common good continues only if there is a well-founded prospect that the fundamental ends of society as a collective unity will continue to be realized. The ontological aspect of the present question was dealt with fully when we considered the functional proportionment of the common good (cf. Chap. 28). If the physical and cultural self-preservation of a nation is so threatened by a superior enemy that a defensive war would leave only a small portion of the nation, and even for them physical and cultural survival would be in jeopardy, then the common good principle loses its binding force and becomes void of purpose. But situations in which not the whole existence of a state is radically threatened can lay upon the statesman the grave decision whether he is entitled to sacrifice a relatively large part of the community in order to save the state as a whole. With regard to the smaller community of the family, the priority law of the common good also can forfeit its validity: if a family becomes so disrupted by parental discord that it cannot fulfill its principal ends as a community, then the individual good of the children and of the parents themselves may receive preference over the common good of the family community, which is no longer fulfilling its main purposes, and may justify the breaking up of its unity.

Our task here has been to discuss only the essential features of the common good principle; its requirements in detail will occupy us in the following books (II–IV), which deal with the ethics of social, political, and economic life.

45. Juridical Order and the Principle of Subsidiary Function

As we said in the preceding chapter, the juridical order is fundamentally the order of the common good; and the common good principle demands that the help required by all the members of society in accomplishing the tasks set down for them by the existential ends, to be accomplished through their own responsibility, must be made possible as a result of their social cooperation. Since the fulfillment of the tasks imposed upon individual responsibility is in question, the common good, although by its nature it is help, is help *only* in the service of such tasks: it possesses a subsidiary nature. The principle of subsidiary function, therefore, means that the common good does not establish for society any right or authority over what the individual person or the member society can do by his own power. We say that "the common good" establishes no right for society beyond this limit, in order to emphasize the fact that every right to social activity is founded on the common good, the end of society, and that hence the subsidiary principle is inherent in the nature of the common good.

Basically, therefore, the common good principle and the subsidiary function principle are one. Both declare that the common good empowers them to perform all functions necessary for its actual realization. Thus, the common good confers powers and at the same time limits them: it empowers them to do everything necessary for its actual realization, but *only* that. The common good principle and the principle of subsidiary function are concerned with two sides of one and the same thing. Thus it was that *Pius XI*, when he coined the term "subsidiary function," called it [1] the "fundamental principle of social philosophy" (*Quadragesimo*

[1] In the encyclical *Quadragesimo Anno* (1931, on the 40th anniversary of *Rerum Novarum,* par. 79) it is said: "Just as it is wrong to withdraw from the individual and commit to a group what private enterprise and industry can accomplish, so too it is an injustice, a grave evil, and a disturbance of right order, for a larger and higher association to arrogate to itself functions which can be performed efficiently by smaller and lower societies. This is a fundamental principle of social philosophy, unshaken and unchangeable. Of its very nature the true aim of all social activity should be to help members of the social body, but never to destroy or absorb them." Recently, opinions were voiced to the effect that the Latin of *Quadragesimo Anno* does not speak of a "fundamental" principle. Our socio-philosophical analysis (Chaps. 24–32) has shown

Anno), while *Leo XIII* described the common good principle as "after God, the first and last law in society" (*Au milieu,* Breve to the French clergy, February 16, 1892). In the sections which follow we shall treat of the subsidiary function principle, as we did with the common good principle in the preceding chapter, with reference to its nature, its specific character, the range of its authority, and its mode of obligation.

1. The principle of subsidiary function is a *concrete* principle, not less so than the common good principle itself; it is founded in concrete reality and its content is concrete. For, the common good cannot be a reality if it is treated as something more than an aid to the fulfillment of the tasks, rooted in existential ends, of the individual and of the member societies. This is the conclusion from our searching ontological analysis of the common good (cf. Chaps. 22–29). The reasons may be briefly summarized: the full reality of the common good consists in the actualized integral human being of the members of society. For man, however, fully integral being is being which is realized in self-determination and responsibility in the fulfillment of the tasks imposed by the existential ends. As such, fully integral being belongs to the person and is characterized by moral responsibility; it belongs also to lesser social units insofar as they have moral responsibility for their own ends. The reality of the common good, therefore, is impaired insofar as it is pursued by means of a diminution of the spheres of responsibility and of competence belonging to the members of society. Since the full actuality of the common good is by its nature an auxiliary agent in the fulfillment of the tasks derived from the existential ends, the principle of subsidiary function, as a principle delimiting social competencies, is an ontological principle and, because it belongs to the ontological order of the common good itself, it is not less an ontological principle than is the common good principle: like the common good principle, it has its origin in the unity of man's personal and social nature, and its substance is determined by the order of ends indicated thereby.

The concrete nature of the common good principle is questioned if it is seen as merely a formal principle. (This was pointed out in the preceding chapter.) The principle of subsidiary function is also held to be a formal principle by some representatives of the traditional natural law doctrine: "The principle only gives information about the norms which are to be applied to a division of competencies and makes the narrower entity take precedence over the wider insofar as the narrower is capable of fulfilling the task. Whether, however, this is actually the case, the principle of subsidiary function itself says nothing." [2] In fact,

that the subsidiary function principle and the common good principle are two different aspects of the same reality, and hence they are equally fundamental. With regard to these opinions cf. J. David, S.J. and W. Bertrams, S.J., in *Orientierung,* 1957, nn. 2, 7.

[2] G. Küchenhoff, "Staatsverfassung und Subsidiarität," in A. F. Utz, editor, *Das Subsidiaritätsprinzip,* 1953, p. 80; cf. Utz, *Formen und Grenzen des Subsidiaritätsprinzips,* 1956; E. Link, *Das Subsidiaritätsprinzip,* 1955 (comprehensive but completed

the principle of subsidiary function, because it is rooted in the order of being and of ends, assigns quite definite and concrete responsibilities, competencies, and rights to definite narrower social units, for example, the family, the narrower and wider neighborhood community, and the narrower and wider occupational community. Hence, it is a concrete principle of justice.

If the principle of subsidiary function were only a formal principle, then all natural law principles would have only a formal nature, and the opponents of natural law, who see in it nothing but formal principles (cf. Chap. 47), would be right. Traditional natural law ethics recognizes, however, only one single formal principle—the principle of equivalence —which has no definite concrete substance, drawing its substance rather from the facts which in particular cases establish a right. For instance, when a customer buys a pound of sugar in a shop he establishes a contract whereby he pays the agreed price and the shopkeeper gives him the desired quantity of sugar of a certain quality; hence, service and return service are agreed upon, and indeed they are agreed upon by the principle of equivalence. The equal value is ascertained from the right-establishing fact of a contract of sale and purchase. The principle of equivalence demands that the contract be kept to the full measure of the equal value; the purchaser who pays too little and the vendor who sells tainted sugar violate the obligation to render service in accordance with equal value; but this value is determined materially by the contract of sale, not by the principle of equivalence as such. Hence, this is a formal principle.

The principle of subsidiary function declares a quite definite distribution of competencies based on the order of being and of ends. Certainly, the mode of obligation and the extent of authority are, as we shall show, dependent upon circumstances. Consequently, *Küchenhoff* is right when, in the passage quoted, he continues by saying that the principle of subsidiary function, "with respect to the division of competencies, leads to different results at different times or under different conditions." This is true, however, of all natural law principles, although this does not mean that therefore they become merely formal principles. The application of all natural law principles depends on circumstances; nevertheless, they are not devoid of content (empty principles, as the natural law principles have been called, because of their supposed formal character) but are determinate in content. The reason why their mode of application depends on circumstances is that the natural law principles possess a general character, which is a wholly different thing from principles possessing a purely formal character (concerning the logical and ontological nature of natural law principles cf. Chap. 47).

The concrete nature of the principle of subsidiary function is misun-

---

in 1948, more recent literature not dealt with); O. v. Nell-Breuning, S.J., *Wirtschaft und Gesellschaft,* Vol. I, 1956, pp. 67 ff.

derstood in an almost diametrically opposite way when it is conceived not as a principle of division of competencies, in the sense of limitation of competencies, but as a principle binding society to give help; (the word "help" is understood to be the meaning of the Latin *subsidium*). Yet, it belongs to the essence of the common good to provide help by creating the necessary conditions in which the members of society can carry out their essential tasks on their own responsibility; the state's obligations to help, therefore, belong to the sphere of the common good principle and the order of justice which this postulates. Contrariwise, the principle of subsidiary function is a limiting law in regard to all social activity: this must be "help" *only* insofar as the powers of the members of society are inadequate for the fulfillment of their tasks.[3] The Latin word *subsidiarius,* although it derives from *subsidium,* does not connote help pure and simple in its fundamental military sense, but rather in the sense of "reserve," a word used of those forces which were to provide help when the frontline troops failed.[4]

2. Accordingly, the principle of subsidiary function regulates competencies which are rooted in spheres of responsibility. It is thus a *jural* principle. Competencies based on responsibility are rights; the juridical order is an order of competencies; the ordering power in society is one of the kinds of competencies, namely, that founded in one social end; the order of subsidiarity is the order of competencies or rights founded in the various social ends; hence, the principle of subsidiary function is a fundamental natural law principle of juridical order. Social competency belongs to a social authority, and our principle, therefore, is that of the subsidiarity of all authority. Like every other right, the right of social authority is a kind of domination; but it is characteristic of this authority, unlike all other rights, that it is domination over men, and hence is the power of command. The limits of this domination are set by the order of subsidiary function. These limits protect natural rights which are proper to the member societies and to the individual; as natural particular rights, they protect autonomies. For this reason, we have said that our principle is the principle of the subsidiary character of all authority.

Rights, authorities, and autonomies signify spheres of domination or power; hence, the principle of subsidiary function is the natural law *principle of the division of power in society.* It refers to all power rela-

[3] Since the passage in which the encyclical *Quadragesimo Anno* enunciates the principle of subsidiary function declares so emphatically that what private individuals can accomplish by their own industry and initiative must not be "withdrawn" from them and handed over to a group, for this would involve injustice, it seems certain that the principle of subsidiary function is considered to be a principle limiting the competence of the state and not one establishing its obligations to help. A confirmation of this view may be seen in the fact that the issue of the encyclical obviously gave expression to an already widespread anxiety regarding the rapidly expanding claims of the state.

[4] A particular use of the word is in the expression *subsidiarii cohortes,* or "reserve cohorts," formations which could be brought into action when the main forces could not fulfill their task unaided.

tionships; hence, it refers not only to the relationship of the state to other social entities and to the individual, but also to the relationship of the organizations in modern pluralist society to their members: political parties, industrial associations, trade unions, cooperative societies, social insurance institutions. The principle of subsidiary function stands *opposed to the omnipotence of organizations just as it is opposed to the omnipotence of the state.* Because the subsidiary function principle protects the particular rights of the natural and the free associations against the state's claim to omnicompetence, it is a *fundamental principle of the pluralistic society:* the subsidiary principle stands against the totalitarian claim of the state to competence; the subsidiary principle is the natural *fundamental law of the free society,* guaranteeing the particular rights of "society" as distinct from the state.

3. The mode of *obligation* of the subsidiary function principle is that of a natural law principle; it concerns the order of competencies in society in its entirety. Competencies are grounded in responsibility. Hence, the subsidiary function principle is by no means merely a principle binding the state (as is much too easily assumed in the literature on the subject), although, of course, today it is of special significance in this respect because of the constant extension of the state's sphere of competence and of power. Yet, the principle of subsidiary function also confers an obligation (and this seems of special significance in the light of the evolutionary tendency just mentioned) *on the member societies and individuals,* since it protects their own competencies and rights. Nothing is gained by merely appealing to the subsidiary function principle in reply to the state's tendency to expand. The competencies and rights protected by the subsidiary function principle must be used with vigor; the responsibilities underlying them as far as possible must be fulfilled through one's own power and initiative. In fact, if the subsidiary function principle can be defined in these terms: "As much freedom as possible, as much state as necessary," then the order of subsidiary function can become a reality only insofar as the principle, "Freedom imposes obligations," is effective in the form of the principle: "As much *individual responsibility* as possible, as much demand for state intervention as necessary." Any other attitude in a society is bound to work out in a manner contrary to the order of subsidiarity, with the state predominant and all-powerful.

Closely linked with responsibility is the *self-help principle.* The principle of subsidiary function also means: As much self-help as possible, as much state help as necessary; self-help being meant in the sense of cooperative alliance. The obligations linked with freedom are first of all those of the individual, for the actualization of the order of subsidiarity in the sphere of the member societies, for example, at the local and the regional levels, depends on the attitude of the individuals. The subsidiarity principle, nevertheless, lays obligations on "society" as a whole. As an order of competencies, the subsidiarity order depends on *institutions:*

it depends on an organization of society which will give the necessary external safeguards and reinforcements to the order of competencies. It is the task of "society" to establish this organization, and the task is all the more urgent the more vigorously the "state" strives to centralize all powers. Here, then, is the fundamental task of social reform today: to reform society with a view to the organization of strong autonomous bodies, both regional and occupational. We have shown (cf. Chap. 32) that the ontology of the common good points to the "federative" and to the "corporative" principles of order. They are sectional principles of the subsidiarity principle and they show, once again, that this is an ontological principle.

According to what has just been said, the subsidiarity principle means the *decentralizing* of competence and of authority. Thus, we return to the mode of obligation of the subsidiarity principle as it concerns the state: it obliges the state authority to take heed of the common good, preferably by means of subordinate authorities, namely, those of member societies in an organization of the state community based on the federative and corporative principles. The principle of subsidiary function, however, certainly does not signify a weak state standing without authority face to face with a pluralistic society. On the contrary, the more strongly the character of society develops in its federative and corporative branches, both regional and occupational, in conjunction with a plurality of free associations based on economic group interests, the more clearly does the common good principle call for a state with strong authority which will enable it, in a *pluralistic* society with diversified competencies and interests, to carry out its essential functions: namely, to care for the common good and the general interest.

4. As with other natural law principles, the application of the principle of subsidiary function is also dependent on the situation. Hence, the *range* of its authority widens or contracts according to the energy and will of the individual members of society to undertake responsibility in looking after their rights, the protection of which is guaranteed by the jural principle of subsidiarity. Because limits are set by the subsidiarity principle to the authority of the state, it is often understood too much in a merely negative sense as a defense against the claims of the state. In fact, its jural purpose is entirely a positive one, namely, the safeguarding of spheres of responsibility and competence; therefore, in reality, it possesses a thoroughly positive nature. Thus, it can also be expressed positively as a *principle of priority for responsibilities, rights and freedoms.* The following is a first important conclusion from this: The burden of proof that any extension of powers in society is justified lies, according to the principle of subsidiarity, with the social authority claiming such extension, which today, in view of the tendency mentioned above, generally means the state. It has to be shown that those primarily responsi-

ble and competent are either not capable or not willing to carry out their responsibility. A second important conclusion: Any such proven right to extend the area of state intervention and subvention does not mean anything final; rather, the subsidiary principle requires that state intervention and subvention maintain the subsidiary nature of its activity in order to make them superfluous as quickly as possible. It does this when it provides the members of society (groups) with the prerequisites which will enable them independently to fulfill the tasks falling within their responsibility. Where the will to moral responsibility in a society shrinks, the range of validity of the subsidiarity principle contracts and the common good function expands to the extent that the moral will to responsibility in society fails. In such cases, even dictatorship may be compatible with the principle of subsidiarity, as *St. Augustine* indicates in a famous passage: "If a people is self-disciplined and is itself the zealous champion of the common utility, so that every man places the public interest before his private interest, is it not then just that such a people be empowered by law to select the magistrates who are to administer its own business—for that is what the state is? . . . If, however, a people becomes degenerate, and men place their private interests before the public interest, selling their votes and taking bribes from ambitious men, allowing unscrupulous men to rule over them, is it not equally right that some capable and respected man should then take away from such a people the power to confer offices and should place the supreme power in the hands of a few good men or even of a single man?" [5]

Our purpose here has been to consider only the essential features of the principle of subsidiary function. Detailed considerations belong to the later books of this work.

In *actual life* the order of subsidiarity, like the order of justice generally, will never take shape in perfect form. The reason is not only the impairment of human nature, which means that the order of justice can never come to full realization, but also the motive forces belonging to human nature, which are expressed in the cultural will of every society. Our principle concerns not least the much discussed relationship between *individual and community, freedom and authority,* a problem which arises anew in every historical epoch. The spheres of value and endeavors toward their actualization which center round the two poles of individual and community are, in their interdependence and in their restless self-assertion, the cause of a large part of those energies which instill vigor and richness into social and cultural life. Therefore, the correlation between the individual and the community can be regarded, in actual life, as a condition of *tension.* The reasons are, besides those already mentioned: First, society is a living whole composed of member communities and individuals. Both the whole and its parts pursue their own ends and

[5] St. Augustine, *De libero arbitrio,* Bk. I, Chap. 6, 14.

interests in self-determination and by their own activity. Their nature urges them to the greatest possible fulfillment of life. Hence, antagonisms and tensions inevitably arise.

Since, furthermore, a great part of the social order is determined by considerations of expediency within the framework of the common good, there remains wide *scope for freely chosen ideals.* Hence, one social order may place greater emphasis on personality values as objectives, and another on social values. Thus, the choice between a more democratic or a more authoritarian form of state lies with the citizens as long as existing rights are not affected. A nation whose citizens exercise strong self-discipline may regard as desirable a wide measure of "liberal" institutions; another may prefer, in the interest of national or social objectives, a close-knit and more centralized form of polity, notwithstanding the inevitable sacrifice of some inessential individual freedoms. In all this lie the origins of the rich diversity in the life of nations and in their political and social systems of which history tells us.

From the principle of subsidiary function we can derive *three criteria* for judging the value of a social system: 1) A social system is the more perfect insofar as the individuals are able to pursue their own interests unhindered, while at the same time being compelled by appropriate institutions to serve the common good. A touchstone of the true art of government is whether it succeeds, with the least possible curbing of the activity of the members of society in the pursuit of their interests, in finding suitable institutions to make this activity serve the achievement of the common good to the greatest possible extent. Thus, the greatest effort will be mobilized for the common good; and every furtherance of the common good is due ultimately to the activity of individuals. 2) A further criterion of the value-quality of a social system, originating in the subsidiary function principle, lies in the extent to which the central authority works through subordinate authorities; in other words, it lies in the extent of decentralization and of actual self-government enjoyed by the lesser social units. Then, the supreme authority confines itself to its essential function of facilitating, stimulating, promoting and supervising the activity of the member societies. Indeed, from their experience in their own particular spheres, these communities must know best what they expect from the common utility and by what particular methods this may best be achieved. 3) Finally, a criterion rooted in the subsidiarity principle is the paucity of direct state interference. The ideal of social order lies in the maximum measure of freedom for the individual within the framework of a community permeated by moral forces or, in the words of *Franz Xavier Linsenmann,* one of the greatest and most farseeing moral theologians of the nineteenth century, in the state "in which the greatest freedom exists within the bounds of a moral order of life." [6] Thus, the fewer the legal precepts with which a community can succeed

[6] F. X. Linsenmann, *Lehrbuch der Moraltheologie,* 1878, p. 416.

in attaining public order and the common utility, the closer it comes to this ideal. In fact, one of the oldest experiences of mankind shows that the nations with the most laws are not the happiest. The present trend of evolution is quite contrary to this experience: the maximum of economic and social progress is expected from a maximum of state interference. The underlying principle of state socialism and collectivism, "As much state as possible," was first countered by *Nietzsche*'s opposing principle: "As little state as possible." *Nietzsche* certainly has the facts of experience on his side.[7]

46. Natural Law

The whole of our previous discussion of the nature of law, and the preceding discussion of the nature of man and of society, has been concerned with natural law. The present chapter and those following, which deal particularly with the questions posed by legal science and practice for natural law theory, will have to probe further into its foundations. From what has been said on the moral and specific character of law, we can derive the following *definition:* Natural law is the pattern of the individual and social competencies rooted in human nature by virtue of the responsibilities designed in it. "Competency" means the authority to act in self-determination within the limits of men's social relationship, so that the relevance of all law to social life is implied. "Responsibilities," as indicated in the personal and social nature of man, are moral. They are responsibilities either of a "social" or of an "individual" character, each linked with its own competence, including those of the state. "Pattern" (or, order) has reference to the uniform nature of all law, notwithstanding the multiplicity of competencies rooted in man's personal and social nature; at the same time, however, since the complete development of the human nature of all members of society is bound up with this pattern, it points to the common good relationship, the social nature of all law. "Rooted" in our definition indicates two things: the particular competencies are assigned, first, by the responsibilities proper to human nature, and secondly, they are guaranteed by the rational moral law which belongs to human nature. In this context "nature," which seems necessary for the concept of natural law, has its fundamental significance in two respects: first, as ontological order with the spheres of competence grounded in its intrinsic ends; secondly, as deontological order with the immediately evident legal principles which belong to it. Taking both aspects together, natural law is the natural order or what is proper to human nature in social relationships, whether direct or mediated by means of things (technical or institutional).

Thus, with equal force our definition emphasizes the *two aspects of*

[7] Cf. Nietzsche, *Menschliches, Allzumenschliches,* par. 473; *Morgenröte,* par. 179.

the order of nature: on the one hand, natural law is that which is demanded by nature as an order of being, that is, by the "nature of things"; on the other hand, natural law is that which is demanded by nature as an order of reason, that is to say, by the natural moral conscience as an integral part of it. The natural order, which can be referred to as the *"nature of things"* (*Thomas—natura rei, natur der Sache,* meaning a legal object in all its relations, i.e., with regard to essential humanity as well as to the actual situation), reveals itself in two ways: first by the (ontological) investigation of the nature of man in general; secondly, by the investigation in detail of the historically and sociologically determined conditions relating to the nature of man and of society thus understood. The *rule of reason* also, the jural conscience, has a twofold function: on the one hand, it guides man in his immediate decisions regarding conduct affecting the particular competencies of others; on the other hand, it offers a moral sanction for law in general, namely, a guarantee of the competencies and entitlements provided in natural rights.

The aspect of natural law which is bound up with the nature of the case can be designated its *objective side;* that which is bound up with the moral jural conscience can be called its *subjective side.* It must not be overlooked, however, that the jural conscience itself is in a general sense part of objective nature. Juristic thinking sees rules in law primarily; hence, in natural law itself it sees the jural principles belonging to man's reason. It is the jurist too who says that these jural principles are not sufficient for the establishment of the order of law itself, but that other factors are indispensable. He knows also that these factors are not arbitrary, since such an idea would be diametrically opposed to that of law; rather, they must possess an objective nature and exist in the "nature of things." The connection between the two aspects of natural law, namely, the legal rules which belong to reason itself and insight into the nature of the case as regards the actual situation, will engage our close attention in the next chapter. Here we must consider two further conceptions of the nature of law peculiar to juristic thought, which affect also the views of jurists on natural law.

Juristic thought sees two features as especially bound up with the nature of law: the source of law and the guaranteeing of law. This means that law naturally involves a relationship to a lawgiving will and a guarantee of the maintenance of the legal rules by the lawgiver. Both essential features of law belong also to natural law. For natural law, the moral-jural conscience constitutes the *fundamental law,* namely, the natural moral law with its injunctions; the guaranteeing power is the compulsion of conscience. From either aspect the essential legal character of natural law seems indisputable. It is true that the legal rules, the principles of justice, given in the law of nature (*lex naturalis,* the law of conscience), are of a very general kind. But the laws of the state legal system, of which the jurist is accustomed to speak, are also of a general kind. "The legal system," says *Nawiasky*, "apart from exceptional cases, can only lay down generally abstract rules for foreseeable groups of facts. But the groups of possible facts are themselves too multiform; hence it is impossible for the appropriate rules to be laid down for all in advance. Instead, a further simplification must be established by the formation of general concepts, themselves again embracing a wealth of facts or fact characteristics." The legal system, says *Nawiasky*, cannot directly offer a concrete rule for every individual case, "for the circumstances of the individual case are not ascertainable in advance; these emerge first from the actual happening, which always arises new and in a new form." [1] That which is stated here concerning statutory law is accurate also with regard to natural law and to the general character of its legal principles contained in it, except that their general character is stretched wider, whereas the general character of the concepts of the positive law of the state, being formed in the light of concrete historical and social conditions, is drawn tighter. Logically, however, there is only a difference of degree between the general character of the rules of positive law and those of natural law, and no essential difference.

Besides the fundamental law, the jurist also considers the *guaranteeing power* an essential factor in law. The guaranteeing power in natural law has at least as much effective force as that in statutory law, even though the nature of the coercive power is different. The observance of the norms of the latter is assured by external compulsion; the norms of the former are assured by inner compulsion, by conscience. One may recall that *Kant* spoke of "compulsion" in connection with his idea of duty.[2] It may also be pointed out that the empirical and the scientific findings regarding the valuation of this inner compulsion have completely changed since the beginning of the century, along with the attitude to the questions of moral conscience then current. Thus, *Hobbes'* erroneous idea that positive law is obeyed only through fear of penalties is opposed by *John Austin*, who declared, although he maintained a positivist outlook in regard to law: "The man who fulfills his duty because he fears the sanction, is an unjust man, although his conduct be just." The prevailing view today among exponents of the legal and social sciences is that obedience to the law on the part of the great majority of the community does not rest upon fear of compulsion but upon grounds of conscience.[3] It can hardly be doubted that the legal system could not go on existing and functioning if this were not so. We may also recall what psychology has to say about the fact of the compulsion of con-

[1] H. Nawiasky, *Allgemeine Rechtslehre*, 2nd ed., 1948, p. 54.

[2] Cf. Kant, *Kritik der praktischen Vernunft* (Coll. Works, Pr. Akad.), Vol. V, pp. 32, 80 f.

[3] Cf. J. Austin, *The Province of Jurisprudence Determined*, 1832, p. 449; on the position of the conscience cf. R. M. McIver, *The Web of Government*, 1947, p. 76.

science.[4] Particularly recent history, with its records of the struggle against the totalitarian obstruction of man's rights in Germany and elsewhere, yields sufficient evidence of the fact that the guaranteeing power of the conscience is at least equal to that of state compulsion.[5] These testimonies to the power of the law of conscience as the source and guarantor of natural law, with its authority and compulsion, made no small contribution to the change in positivist legal thinking. What should have emerged from all this is the fact that natural law, and not only positive law, is safeguarded by a guaranteeing power.

I *Special Points of View in Present-Day Natural Law Discussions*

In our discussion of natural law, in this and the preceding chapters, we have tried to give due place in determining its nature to the different points of view arising in the present-day discussion of natural law, namely, the ethical, psychological, ontological, historical, sociological, and theological. It seems that the *large area of common ground* which exists in fact is lost sight of more because of a narrowing of one's viewpoint to a particular line of thinking than to any irreconcilable differences.[6]

Present-day jurisprudence which is occupying itself with natural law, is interested chiefly in the ethical side of law; moral principles, including those linked with religious beliefs, are not, so it is said, to be separated from law, yet natural law and its principles of justice belong only to the realm of morality (the *ethicizing* of natural law) and not to the domain of law itself. We have tried to show the inseparable connection between

[4] Freud's doctrine of the "Superego" and the claim of the law of conscience to absolute authority signifies recognition of the fact of the claim and of the compulsive power of conscience, even though his interpretation of it as "introjected police" (Max Scheler) is untenable.

[5] Cf. *Die Vollmacht des Gewissens, Gespräche und Gutachten aus dem Kreis der Deutschen Widerstandsbewegung* (Europäische Publikation E. V., Munich), 1956. Cf. also Mary A. Gallin, *Ethical and Religious Factors in the German Ressistance to Hitler* (U.S.A.), 1956, p. 164, where the author, like the previous book, makes clear the power of conscience in resistance to the seemingly incomparably greater power of the totalitarian state.

[6] Cf. Thomas Würtenberger's thorough and critical review of German literature on natural law in *Archiv für Rechts- und Sozialphilosophie,* XXXVIII, 1949: *Wege zum Naturrecht in Deutschland,* 1946–48, XL, 1953: *Neue Stimmen zum Naturrecht in Deutschland,* 1948–51, XLI, 1954; *Zur Geschichte der Rechtsphilosophie und des Naturrechts.* Cf. also Erik Wolf's *Das Problem des Naturrechts: Versuch einer Orientierung,* 1955, 2nd enlarged ed., 1959, the leading idea of which (from the Introduction) is "that in the apparent confusion of contradictory doctrines on natural law there operates a secret pattern which becomes visible when one follows the process of their dialectic"; M.-E. Schmitt's *Recht und Vernunft, ein Beitrag zur Diskussion über die Rationalität des Naturrechts,* 1955, was intended as a kind of bulletin on the literature on the questions dealt with. Dealing mainly with works in the German language, this book also mentions the principal works in other languages and the most significant legal theories of the past in its critical discussions. As a starting point it uses the natural law theory of St. Thomas Aquinas. Cf. Albert Auer, O.S.B., *Der Mensch hat Recht, Naturrecht auf dem Hintergrund von heute,* 1956.

the ethical aspect of natural law and the ontological aspect (which is linked with the reality of man's essential nature), while strongly emphasizing the law of nature understood as moral-jural reason. Nevertheless, in the understanding of natural law, the ontological aspect has seemed of equal rank with the ethical aspect; hence we have devoted our special attention to the ontological aspect. Thus, we have not restricted the law of nature (*lex*) to the natural conscience, but have understood it as the mode and order of operation as designed in nature; furthermore, from the beginning we have tried to grasp natural law (*ius*) as an order determined by being, by objective facts. On the other hand, it seems one-sided to attempt to derive from the order of being a kind of system of legal rules (the *ontologizing* of natural law), rather in the way that the rationalistic natural law theory sought to derive a system of legal rules from pure reason. No doubt the jurist is right when he thinks of natural law first and foremost in terms of general principles of law, and when he asks about their nature and origin (source), as well as about the manner and form of their authority in the formation of law (the lawgiver) and in the administration of law (the judge); indeed, he is then largely in line with the questions posed by the principal exponents of traditional natural law theory, who proceeded from moral and juridical insight to moral-legal principles of a general character (norms).

If thinkers today, in reconsidering the natural law idea, look for points of support rather remotely in the philosophy of value, and if directly evident values, principles of value, and ideals of value are referred to, in which standards are to be sought for judging the existing patterns of law, and goals to be obtained for the future development of law, we too have noted important common elements in value-philosophy and natural law theory: the concrete, evident, intuitively grasped moral and legal principles of which traditional natural law theory speaks are the concrete, evident, intuitively grasped values of which value-philosophy and value-ethics speak. Because, however, the comprehension of values and of the order of values is ascribed to feeling, and consequently their essential relationship to being and to the order of being is disregarded (the *psychologizing* of natural law), the question of the inner connection between value and being remains open; consequently, the question of the objective criterion for determining the content of law, which is true to values in the existing historical and social reality, also remains open.

It seems understandable that the scientific juristic thinking of today is focussed especially on legal realities; and in the light of our present-day historical knowledge of the varieties of legal systems and legal beliefs, it views with reserve the notion of invariable, suprahistorical legal rules with distinctive content. On the other hand, contrary to the idea that all law represents merely a product of evolution (the *historicizing* of natural law), we find a realm of legal beliefs and legal forms whenever history tells us about social life. The same may be said of attempts to understand natural law as merely the expression of social forces and as a motive factor in the evolution of legal and social systems (the *sociologizing* of natural law). The purely sociological interpretation of natural law leads to two contrary propositions: first, natural law is an invention of ruling groups to support the existing order; secondly, natural law is an invention of oppressed groups in the process of their efforts to secure a better social order.

The complete sociologizing of all law could not but result in the endeavor to explain law exclusively in terms of man's desire for power or of his will orientated by expediency (the *secularizing* of natural law). In fact, sociological interpretations of natural law, although they will not admit this, think of the force of a moral-legal conscience when they refer to the idea of justice as motive force of social change; it is this basic fact of the moral-legal sense, operating through the natural conscience, in which natural law theory sees its foundation. The theory itself, however, will have to exercise caution with regard to what it will recognize as moral-legal sense, and it will have to confine itself to the general jural principles which, at the height of the traditional theory, as we have indicated, were thought to be the jural a priori. The jurist who shares the Christian outlook will unreservedly recognize religion generally and revealed religion in particular as the final source and sanctioning power of natural law. On the other hand, the approach to natural law is made more difficult for those who are remote from Christian belief if natural law is interpreted in terms of theological beliefs (the *theologizing* of natural law) instead of reason. This is especially true because the jurist is accustomed to seeing reason at work in so exemplary a fashion in that great legal system—the Roman—which has undeniably helped to form our legal systems and legal thinking up to the present day. There is certainly no real objection to a "theology of natural law" embracing a rich fund of problems of a material, epistemological, and methodological character (cf. Chaps. 11–12). Of course, the theological discussion of the question of natural law will appeal most to those who hold a theological belief.

Nevertheless, the philosophical investigation and foundation of natural law as the central task of natural law theory should be questioned today less than ever. It was certainly not by chance that *Thomas Aquinas* and the best minds of the Middle Ages, in spite of their prevailing uniform Christian outlook and their own prevailing theological interests, treated natural law theory *philosophically*. In this connection, recall *Étienne Gilson,* one of the best authorities on medieval Christian philosophy, who said, and his remarks were applied to the natural law doctrine of the Middle Ages, that all the original contributions made by the Middle Ages to the common treasure of philosophical knowledge have been made by theologians; furthermore, the deepest expression of their philosophical thought is found in their theological works.[7]

With regard to *traditional natural law theory itself,* it seems necessary today that it should avoid giving the impression that the form of philosophical natural law doctrine reached by medieval scholasticism is something absolutely definitive. Today, much more persistently than even recently, the traditional natural law school is emphasizing the variableness of legal forms derived from natural law as distinct from legal principles belonging to natural law. Due allowance, however, is not always made for the partial dependence on historical factors, well-established sociologically, of the natural law thinking of the Golden Age and of later scholasticism. And although in this work we are certainly following the path laid down by the traditional natural law school and particularly by *St. Thomas Aquinas,* it is equally certain that his natural law doctrine is not *the end of the scientific development of natural law theory.* Hence, if concrete reasons are lacking, we do not consider that because new ideas diverge from those of *Thomas* this in itself forms any conclusive argument against them. First of all, as *Thomas* himself points out, scientific knowledge is always on the move in all fields; secondly, since his time the social sciences in particular have made quite remarkable advances; thirdly, as anyone would admit who knows *Thomas's* scientific manner of working and his position in the intellectual history of the West, *Thomas* would have been the first to make use of the findings of the modern social sciences.

11 *A Concise Conspectus*

By summarizing the results of our inquiry in this chapter, in the foregoing chapter, and in the chapters following, we may now answer the question: *What is natural law?*

1. Natural law is a *body of legal realities,* and this in a twofold way:

a) a body of *jural rules* (of the natural conscience with its knowledge of the principles of right and wrong, i.e., of justice);

b) a body of *original rights* (of the individual and the various communities).

2. Natural law is a *science,* that is, the philosophy and the ethics of law, with two main tasks:

a) the investigation of *the foundation and the criterion* of natural rights and justice. (The problems mentioned up to now in this conspectus are treated in *Book I* of this work.)

b) the *application of the general principles of justice* in the fields of *social, political,* and *economic life.* (This will be the subject of *Books II, III,* and *IV* of this work.)

[7] Cf. E. Gilson, *History of Christian Philosophy in the Middle Ages,* 1955, p. 543.

47. Natural Law as a Reality

A number of objections are raised to the notion of natural law as a reality: it consists only of formal, meaningless propositions; in any case, it does not consist of legal rules in the proper sense, and still less rules of permanent validity; in general, it is not possible to speak of a juridical sense common to all mankind. Thus, there are four questions that demand an answer: What is natural law as an actuality? How is the knowledge of it acquired? Can its actuality be proved? And, if so, is it anything more than merely a phenomenon of evolution in origin? It will be seen that, like all ontological and epistemological problems, the first two questions are inextricably intertwined and must therefore be treated as one question. Similarly, the last two questions concerning origin and proof can hardly be answered separately.

I *Is Natural Law an Actuality? How Is It Apprehended?*

(The problems of ontology and epistemology in natural law theory.)

Let us consider first, in the striking versions put forward by *J. Sauter* and *K. Bergbohm,* objections to the reality of natural law repeated in similar form again and again up to the present day. *Sauter* says that the "greatest error" of natural law theory is the "self-evidence of natural law": "In complete contrast to this widely prevalent doctrine we most definitely declare that natural law is not self-evident. . . . The supreme principles, which are said to include *Bonum est faciendum, malum vitandum,* or *Quod tibi non vis fieri* etc., or *Suum cuique tribuere,* or *Honeste vivere,* are no doubt self-evident, since they represent nothing but purely formal propositions *about* natural law; but 'what' *bonum, honestum* etc., are 'in themselves' or 'for us' we do not know at all by means of such propositions. To achieve this we must first follow the laborious path of the ontological order in which we have been placed, and which was already clearly known to Aristotelian-scholastic idealism." [1] *Bergbohm* goes a step further. He sought to show that there cannot be a natural law, for it claims to be "eternal, universal, absolute, or a law in itself," in contrast to the actual "relativity of law." "Law is willing and able to control only the external form of man's relationships: but it is the content of these relationships which determines what law and what legal forms are possible." The relationships differ, however, according to epoch, nation, and civilization; whence it follows "that there cannot be an eternal, universal, absolute law." [2]

We do not deny that *Sauter*'s arguments contain some truth. The su-

[1] J. Sauter, *Die philosophischen Grundlagen des Naturrechts,* 1932, pp. 222 f.
[2] K. Bergbohm, *Jurisprudenz und Rechtsphilosophie,* 1892, pp. 410, 416, 419.

preme principles of the moral reason (the natural conscience) are indeed principles "about" the obligating nature of natural law; furthermore, the substance of the demands of natural law can be known only through an understanding of the order of being. He errs, however, in supposing that those supreme principles, namely, the basic juridical truths which form the nucleus of natural law, possess only a formal character. All objections, such as those of *Sauter,* are founded on the presupposition already touched upon (cf. Chap. 3), that there exists first a knowledge of general principles, after which must follow knowledge of being and then the growth of the apprehension of objective juridical claims. A conception of this kind leaves two questions open: (1) The psychological-epistemological question which asks how man comes to the apprehension of principles; (2) The ontological-epistemological question—how we come to reach the assumption of a correspondence between the matter conveyed in such an "innate" cognition of principles and the correspondence inherent in being itself. Today, probably no one would be prepared to accept a prestabilized harmony, involving divers further questions, in order to explain such a correspondence. The trend of thought in question is generally based on the idea that the self-evident principles of logic in the various realms of cognition, including the moral and legal, are "innate" to the mind and are not to be acquired like any knowledge. In fact, the supreme logical principles in the moral and juridical, as in all intellectual spheres, are *by no means an inborn possession of the mind.* What is inborn consists not in ready-made knowledge of even the simplest moral and legal truths, but only in the capacity to apprehend them. In addition, all such objections overlook the fundamental fact that there are impulses inherent in human nature tending to bring about that knowledge in the process of development of the full use of the reason.

How does man come to the *apprehension of the most essential jural rules?* The Middle Ages were content to describe it as participation in the "eternal law." Present-day thinking, with its fervid interest in modern epistemology, logic, psychology, anthropology, ethnology, and sociology, would not be satisfied with this, apart from the fact that today, for many who deny any metaphysical reality, the "eternal law" also signifies no reality. If one is faithful to experience itself it becomes evident that underlying the theories of *Sauter* and *Bergbohm* there is *a false question which leads immediately to a false answer.* For, as a matter of fact, reason and factual knowledge are inseparably linked from the outset as soon as knowledge of the elementary jural principles arises, as we saw in discussing the basis of natural law (cf. Chap. 3, n. VI). In its operation, natural law shows itself to be a unity: there is an indivisible interaction between intellectual and instinctive endowment, between rational nature and physical nature, and between rational order and ontological order. The impulse toward an integral human existence, attainable only in community life (the impulse toward happiness, which makes for the attainment of individual good and common interest), does *not leave it to man's arbitrary will whether or not he shall perceive what is objectively right or wrong.* Man's nature as a family being is fundamental to this effect of natural law in that man is wholly and entirely dependent upon the family community for his full development.

Human nature itself impels the human being toward an order of social life in the family community; this alone makes possible a human existence for all its members. It is not theoretical knowledge of human nature that leads the members of the family to this conclusion, but their experience of what they need in order to feel satisfied in their vital bodily and spiritual requirements. All living things strive for well-being through the satisfaction of their fundamental instincts and needs. That human nature does not work otherwise is a fundamental idea of the great exponents of the traditional natural law theory, although this idea was not carried through logically enough and was too much neglected by later scholastics. This seems to be *the crucial idea leading beyond the purely abstract mode of thought:* it is in accord with the epistemological principle, *Omnis cognitio incipit a sensibus,* its full validity in the realm of practical reason, and *establishes the direct connection between apprehension of the self-evident moral and jural principles (values) and apprehension of the order of being,* or, in other words, between apprehension of the validity of principles and apprehension of the nature of things (in the wider sense of this term as pointed out in Chap. 46). The elementary moral and jural principles are experienced and learned with definite content at the first movement of the will toward social order, which is urged upon man by his very nature. These first steps are completed in the primal society (understood ontologically as well as historically), viz., in the family and tribal group. In this the natural impulses of love, of mutual respect, and of mutual good will (and hence of the will for the good of all and of the community as a whole—the common good), prove to be in full operation as a function of the law of nature in its twofold meaning of cognition and conation.

There is, accordingly, an important significance in the efficiency of the natural instincts mentioned, because love and respect come to have a determining influence on the conduct of the members of the family community toward one another and toward the whole: the moral-legal truths, principles, and values on which the order of the family community is founded are experienced and lived in this community and as such are recognized as binding truths. The simple truths about right and wrong, which rise into consciousness at the same time, are those which are bound up with *man's "fundamental social situation," the social situation of the family community:* the principles concerning its peace and its common good. Thus, we reach the conclusion: The notion of a merely "formal" character of the supreme natural law principles is a theoretical misconstruction, resting on an unreal idea of man. In fact, at man's first steps into the social existence proper to his nature these principles already possess their definite content.

Accordingly, the outcome of our inquiry into the reality of natural law is this: Natural law is an order of existence, the fundamental *order of man's existence as man,* in the truest and fullest sense of "existence"; the order whose demands, in regard to their definite content, become known to him in this process of existence in accordance with the fact that all knowledge, including knowledge of the principles of jural reason as part of the practical reason, depends upon experience. Primarily apprehended in this way, these demands are then perceived by the fully-developed mind in their general, intrinsically certain truth and in their universal binding force.[3]

In our analysis of the reality of natural law, *two fundamental ideas of all ethical thinking seem to be intimately connected,* the severance of which has been greatly to the disadvantage of progress in ethics: the *eudaemonistic* and the *intuitionistic;* in other words, the school which places the starting point of ethical thinking in value-conation and the school which places it in value-cognition. The former, the "impulse towards happiness," man's primal impulse, gave *Aristotle* his starting point; *English utilitarian ethics* is narrowly based on the happiness instinct. Medieval natural law ethics incorporated the value-conation in its framework, yet, as we shall see, not with all its consequences; rather, it placed the emphasis on direct perception of the supreme moral and jural principles. *Continental rationalistic ethics* has also taken up a very narrow position, making the exclusive assumption of innate principles, intuitively and aprioristically given to the mind, the foundation of ethics. In our own line of argument the two great currents of scientific ethical thought are brought together. In our attempt to combine the two lines of thought we owe much to the profounder researches of English ethics into human value-conation (into lasting happiness, as distinct from pleasure), and to the new perspectives of German value-ethics which concern the

[3] We are speaking of the simplest juridical truths or the elementary juridical principles. The fact that there are a variety of forms of law and ethos in which certain of these principles do not receive the expression we expect with our present axiological and juridical consciousness does not refute our exposition of the reality and apprehension of natural law. One may think of legal systems which admit slavery and marriage law codes which degrade women. Forms of ethos and law are the products of long evolution, in which a variety of causes (cf. Chaps. 6, 11) may bring it about that the natural law is impaired in its operation. In fact, however, the validity of the elementary natural law principles is still recognizable even in such legal forms, as Augustine observes regarding slavery (cf. Chap. 41, note 4). With regard to polygamy, it can hardly be doubted that even in such a family community the experience and the apprehension of the elementary natural law principles is present in the manner we have outlined, otherwise it would not be practicable as a form of human coexistence. It must not be overlooked that polygamy never became the rule in human history, but remained on the whole the exception, if only for the reason that the possession of several wives was linked with special economic conditions which imposed limits on its extension.

intuitive-aprioristic perception of value, and which we owe particularly to *Scheler.*

Against English ethics, we hold to aprioristic-objective value-cognition critically in conjunction with subjective value-conation, which seeks happiness; against German value-ethics the connection between value-cognition and value-conation in the process of understanding and realizing values. At the connecting point of the two currents of thought there stand, as will have become apparent, ontological insights of a third school of thought, namely, those of *existential philosophy,* which are bound up with the following concepts: existence, being, true existence, and essential being (nature). Critically, in regard to this trend, we hold as unrealistic the disregard of natural value-conation and natural value-cognition and of their significance for man's "fundamental situation." We can therefore infer: *The insight into the fundamental moral and legal truths is neither founded exclusively on man's experience of his desire for happiness (value-conation), as is assumed by the exclusively eudaemonistic ethics, nor on a purely aprioristic apprehension of principles (value-cognition), as is held by the exponents of exclusively intuitionistic ethics; rather, experience is a condition for insight into them. But when man has become aware of them through experience, these truths reveal themselves as being of an immediately evident and hence intuitive character, and hence of apriori validity: thus, they constitute synthetic propositions a priori.*[4]

To avoid misunderstandings, it may be advisable to add a few qualifications regarding the epistemological aspect of the cognition of the elementary natural law principles. When we resort to the whole nature of man with its cognitive and conative faculties, this is *as far removed from irrationalism with its assumption of merely emotional factors as it*

[4] Cf. for further epistemological analysis: Messner, *Kulturethik,* 1954, p. 237, where I have first undertaken to show that the fundamental moral, legal principles are synthetic judgments a priori. Karl Rahner comes to the same conclusion: *Bemerkungen über das Naturgesetz und seine Erkennbarkeit; Orientierung,* Nov. 30, 1955. In the present chapter, as already in Chap. 3, we have to refer continually to the indissoluble bond between the experience of truths (principles, value) and the insight into them, a bond which has been neglected because the foundations of cognition have been thought exclusively to reside in a priori judgments or in empirical data. Nickolai Hartmann, *Kleine Schriften,* Vol. I, *Abhandlungen zur systematischen Philosophie,* 1955, expressly emphasized this bond, especially for ontology, to which he attributes the nature of a fundamental science for the whole of philosophy: "A uniform base for philosophy can be seriously sought only in the direction of an ontological foundation" (*ibid.,* p. 62). Since philosophy itself consists in knowledge, its basis, he says, cannot in turn be sought in knowledge. Of the *bond between experience and knowledge,* to which we attribute such decisive importance for moral-legal cognition, he says (*ibid.,* p. 230): "Between experience and knowledge there is no assignable content frontier. Even in the forms of experience there is already latent an element of cognition; on the other hand, knowledge is also a form of experience—an emotionally faded experience but expanded in content." Knowledge itself, he emphasizes, is for the sake of life: "It is the great instrument for the orientation of the human being in its environment, primarily, therefore, in external nature. This orientation is an objective one, not one which refers everything to the self, as with the animals, but vice versa, an orientation of the self to the world."

is from rationalism with its empty rational a priori. On the contrary, the all-decisive position of reason becomes quite realistically evident in the unity of nature as a whole by virtue of which man is impelled to understand the natural law order as the order of his existence in his endeavor to attain the integral human existence postulated by his being, or, in the ancient and medieval manner of expression, in his endeavor to fulfill his impulse toward happiness, in which endeavor the two aspects of the functioning of the law of his nature, the rational and the ontological, determine and aid each other reciprocally. Furthermore, our course of argument does not leave the apprehension of natural law principles psychologically to an evolutionary process; rather, the functioning of natural law is shown ontologically as the functioning of human rational nature in its psychophysical unity, which, as soon as homo sapiens exists, urges him to institute the natural law order as the social order of existence in conformity with this unity. Finally, our argument does not mean that the fundamental moral and legal principles are derived in a form of "inductive ethics" from the experience of man, with the desire for value-realization proper to his instinctive nature; rather, it shows that although experience stands at the beginning of the apprehension of the self-evident natural law principles, as with all cognition, experience itself urges man toward the ontological-metaphysical insight into the elementary ethico-legal truths as well as into the duty involved in the order bound up with them (cf. Chaps. 4–5).

If the argument whereby the experiencing and knowing of natural law principles is traced to the family community, which has its origin in human nature, is correct, then *two facts fundamental to natural law theory* are established. The first fact is that the elementary natural law principles or fundamental human values are not read into nature on the basis of either an interpretation of man's nature preconceived in ideological terms (cf. *Welzel* below, n. II) or of a system of values governed by historical cultural factors (cf. *Spranger,* Chap. 39). They are, on the contrary, "established" by human nature itself as the principles postulated by the order of man's social existence and enforced by nature itself. The second fact which emerges as fundamental to natural law theory is this: What man learns right from the start in the family group because of the functioning of natural law, namely, to live the simple jural truths in their concrete determinateness and to apprehend them together with apprehension of the nature of things, *continues as the mode of functioning of natural law in the development of legal sense and of legal will.* This is true for the *individual legal conscience,* since this, as each one's experience tells him, can form a clear idea of right and wrong in all simple situations, and for the good reason that from the beginning it is trained to see into the real nature of the case and hence can apply the general principle. This is true also, however, especially for *historical evolution.* Legal and social history yields clear proof of this, since in it the natural impulse to attain a measure of well-being (the impulse toward value realization, happiness) has played at least the same role as the natural knowledge of the general principles of justice (insight into value-principles).

We do not maintain that the operation of natural law in bringing about the natural law order is perfect. Nevertheless, even in the light of faulty manfestations (e.g., the low minimum of existence in high civilizations among slaves and others socially dependent, including the proletariat in the last hundred years) our concept of natural law reveals its further significance: the impulse toward well-being becomes, for groups at that minimum stage, a force leading to assimilation in the more fulfilled forms of human existence enjoyed by other groups, and hence becomes a strong *motive force for social development and at the same time for the development of the moral and legal consciousness* as well as of legal and social order. Both are at work in the one natural law in inseparable alliance: the experience-guided impulse toward the good which conforms with human nature and the mind's constantly increasing apprehension of the demands of the natural law order as demands of justice. The development of legal consciousness and of legal endeavor takes place chiefly in *the development of the association, established originally by human nature itself, between the apprehension of principles (order of reason) and the apprehension of facts (order of being)* and the development of the faculty to apply the elementary moral and legal principles thus apprehended, which, with concrete content man lives, learns, and understands as a family being.

These principles contain the basic insight into duties and claims with regard to the preservation of life and of the bodily integrity of the individual, with regard to keeping one's pledged word, to respecting the good name of others, to respecting the lawfully acquired property of others, to honesty in complying with agreements, to the authority required for the maintenance of peace and order in society and the duty of obedience which it implies, to the necessity of using compulsion to safeguard and insure the claims and obligations already mentioned, including the punishability of offenses committed, to fitness of punishment to crime as regards its nature and extent, and finally also to the insight into the general jural principle *suum cuique* as one of entitlement and obligation.

Has not *Bergbohm,* however, shown that there "cannot" be such a natural law reality as we have tried to establish? Few would be unwilling today to admit that *Bergbohm* proved too much, and so, in accordance with the well-known rule of logic *qui nimium probat, nihil probat,* proved nothing. That this was also the impression of his contemporaries, in spite of the prevailing legal positivism, is revealed by the review of his book in the *Archiv für öffentliches Recht,* which soon followed its publication. It indicates, with an emphasis quite unusual for that period, that questions of the "epistemology, methodology, and logic of jurisprudence" are involved; *Bergbohm* subscribes, according to this account, to a formal philosophy of law which refers law to the formal source of the legal command, whereas without a concrete philosophy of law one cannot do justice to the reality of law as we recognize it. The separation of the two disciplines is especially unrealistic when one seeks to answer the question what law is "in its inmost essence and final end" (*Bergbohm*); furthermore, it is unrealistic also if law is regarded simply as "an internal technical concern of the jurists" (*Bergbohm*) and if one is unwilling to see the element which is common in part to jurisprudence and to other sciences, especially ethics.[5]

It may be advisable to pursue this line of internal criticism further by pointing to some inconsistencies in *Bergbohm's* argument; especially: Bergbohm is not sure of the concept of law; a "well-rounded definition forms a difficult problem in my eyes"; as the requirements "of which one might say that they contain the least that *all jurists* demand of law," he proposes:

> Law must in all circumstances mean rules which in some way relate to men's practical activity toward one another etc., and are of a special obligating force. By emphasizing this function at least, this much is said, that law does not consist merely of feelings and thoughts, cannot mean something subjectively psychical or purely rational; rather, it is an obligatory rule with the tendency to assert itself in the external world through people and with people. In this "validity"—and such a "validity" all regard as "law," notwithstanding what they otherwise mean by it, taken along with an energy belonging only to law, which obtains even against the contrary view of the individual—the idea is conveyed that law is an objectively existing fact, an entity, which *is* only insofar as it functions.

Apart from the last few words, *Bergbohm*'s statement is nothing more than the concept of law according to traditional natural law theory. *Bergbohm*'s definition, however, is inconsistent in two respects: first, his concept contains nothing of the "competent law-forming power" which is the "formal source of law" and, according to his analysis of the nature of law, confers on a rule the quality of law; [6] secondly, his much-quoted statement that law "*is* only insofar as it functions" is not only quite unrelated to the previous long definition but also inconsistent with the focussing of his analysis on the law-forming power, since law "functions" in many forms and not just because of the "will of a law-forming power," as he claims. He himself says concerning the fundamental question regarding the sources of law thus posed, that it is "a difficult concept"; but he makes bold to declare that, as distinct from positive law, "natural law exists of itself as soon as one makes up one's mind to think it"; that it rests on the assumption of "innate ideas," is an error into which he

[5] Cf. A. Merkel, *Archiv für öffentliches Recht,* 1893, pp. 608–12; the passages quoted by Merkel, one of the most significant jurists of his time, from Bergbohm, pp. 103, 359, 526, 529 f.

[6] Cf. Bergbohm, *op. cit.,* pp. 360 f., 549.

may have been led by the rationalistic idea of natural law (cf. Chap. 40), and perhaps also by oversimplified presentations of medieval natural law theory. Our principal endeavor in this chapter has been to show that the elementary principles of law are of an entirely different nature. Because of his preconceived notion of law and of natural law, *Bergbohm* sees natural law as a kind of "ideal" law and even as a legal system, in contrast with "positive" law; in the traditional law theory, however, natural law is by no means a code of law (this also we have shown in detail).

If *Bergbohm* had read the few relevant pages of *Thomas Aquinas* he would not only have seen that *Thomas* by no means assumes that natural law involves an elaborate legal system, but he would also have seen that *Thomas* thoroughly discusses the "relativity" of positive law, its fluidity owing to social, historical, and cultural conditions, of which *Bergbohm* makes so much. On the subject of variability in human nature, *Thomas* indeed goes so far that it was possible to speak of "the immense breadth and changeableness which *Thomas* ascribes to the norms of natural law," whereas only "natural law, insofar as it builds upon common human nature, that is, upon the specific essentiality of man, is invariable." [7] Nevertheless, in the light of his demonstration of the "logical inconceivability of any nonpositive law" *Bergbohm* states: "Anyone who, in spite of all that, wishes to achieve still another 'universal' legal maxim, may well take care that he translates it into every language so that all nations understand him—and so that all equally understand him." [8] Precisely this is being aimed at by the United Nations with its Declaration on Human Rights.

A digression must be made at this point which concerns not only *Sauter* and *Bergbohm.* Many misunderstandings in the discussion about natural law are due to *imprecise use of the concepts "general" and "formal."* They are often taken to be identical in meaning, although "general" has a threefold meaning. The fact that elementary natural law principles are of a general character means, first, that they concern not just particular cases of modes of conduct, but an objectively definite kind of modes of conduct; hence, they concern all particular cases of this kind, as long as the perception of the concrete nature of the particular case makes it possible to recognize it as coming under the general kind and the general rule. Our whole daily life rests on rules of this kind of logical nature. This is true not only regarding modes of conduct between man and man but also regarding modes of conduct dependent on the general natural laws of the external world. We apply the *"general"* law of gravity a hundred times a day both in our movements and in our handling of material objects. An ordered daily life would not be possible, as far as modes of conduct between people are concerned, were not particular

[7] A. F. Utz, *Recht und Gerechtigkeit, Thomasausgabe,* Vol. XVIII, pp. 401, 440.

[8] Bergbohm, *op. cit.,* pp. xv, 132, 410, 424, 478 f.; cf. for a criticism of Bergbohm, H. Coing, *Grundzüge der Rechtsphilosophie,* 1950, pp. 155 ff.

cases subsumed under general rules, whether they concern road traffic or the *suum cuique* in business.

A further logical prerequisite of the regularity of our daily life consists in our certain knowledge that the general rules of conduct are recognized by all as such and are as binding on all, and that the particular cases are recognized as coming under the general rules, which are held as obligating in all such cases. Here we have a second meaning of "general," that of *universally valid.* The first meaning, logically, is the meaning of the "universal concept"; the second is that of an obligation binding on "all" and "in all cases." The first meaning makes it possible to subsume the special case under the general concept; the second meaning declares that an obligation holds good in every individual case which comes under the general principle. The question of the general validity of the principle concerns its obligating force, so that, as a natural law question, it points beyond the purely logical nature to the question of the ontological and metaphysical foundation of the natural law principles. The two meanings of "general" discussed here in connection with the natural law principles are very closely linked together; yet, in a large number of apparent problems clarification would be easily reached if the two sides of the question were kept separate.

The third meaning of "general" is *"common to all mankind":* belonging to the "universal" moral consciousness, and hence known to every man throughout mankind. In this sense logical and ontological meaning are linked together again in a new way: it is the "general" rational nature, that is, as common to all men, which causes the same knowledge in all men of the elementary moral and legal principles. For this last meaning of "general," *Augustine* and *Thomas* use the expression *communia principia,* which excludes any conceptual uncertainty from the outset.

"Formal" propositions, as distinct from all three meanings of "general" propositions, are those which predicate generalities without any positive concrete content (concerning particular cases or a category of them), for example, *Kant's* principle of morality (cf. Chap. 3). They are empty propositions; *Sauter* understands "formal" in this way. The same holds true with regard to the term *"abstract";* the natural law principles are in no other sense, only in degree, abstract and thus are of as general a character as the state laws (cf. Chap. 46). In the language of logic they are concrete though general; they are concrete with regard to their cognition and to their mode of functioning, and are, as such acquired neither by generalizing nor by isolating abstraction.

The fact that natural law in the sense discussed is an order of existence provides the most illuminating arguments in support of our concept of *"existential ends"* (cf. Chap. 3). For, they are involved in the well-being demanded by the nature of man and they codetermine both the value-conation (impulse toward happiness) proper to man's nature and the elementary juridical insight proper to everyone's nature. Our first concern in this chapter was with this elementary insight. It is necessary to distinguish between this elementary knowledge and the scientific knowledge of natural law. The function of the latter consists in elucidating the implications of natural law in the conditions prevailing. To this end, scientific natural law ethics requires a criterion for judging the detailed implications of natural law. The question of the *criterion of morality and law* is one of the fundamental questions of scientific ethics and of legal philosophy (which is intrinsically bound up with ethics). Indeed, the discussions on natural law which have been taken up again since the Second World War are concerned to a large extent, if not expressly, with this question of the criterion of natural rights. Through our empirically grounded metaphysical analysis of human nature we have found the criterion of law in the "existential ends." The fact that natural law has proved itself to be the social order guaranteeing to man a truly human existence, in which the cognitive and instinctive endowments of man's nature are inseparably correlated, shows the significance of our concept of "existential ends," both from the viewpoint of "elementary" natural law insight and from the viewpoint of the "scientific" tasks of natural law ethics.

Our account of the reality and apprehension of natural law follows a route which is new and probably surprising to many. It seems opportune, therefore, on the one hand (1) to indicate what distinguishes these views from those found within the traditional natural law doctrine, and on the other hand (2) to see how far points of contact exist with the most recent work on natural law outside the traditional natural law school.

On the development of natural law theory within the scholastic tradition

Throughout the whole course of our argument we have frequently referred to the great exponents of traditional natural law doctrine, while emphasizing, also, the fact that with *Augustine, Thomas,* and the scholastics up to the present day, *essential questions have remained open. Augustine, Sauter* explains, is aware that what he designates the supreme moral-legal principle, *suum cuique tribuere,* in itself contains no information with regard to what *suum* is, so that the principle requires further definition. *Augustine* follows two paths, according to *Sauter,*[9] in order to overcome this difficulty. One way consists in his relying additionally on the principle, *Ne aliquid faciat quisque alteri, quod pati ipse non vult.*[10] But this principle also says nothing about what the natural rights originating in man's nature are in detail. The second way consists in his bringing the moral order into relationship with the ontological order. If I am to formulate a concept of the natural law which is impressed upon us, says *Augustine,* that which is just (*iustum*) has to comply with the purpose *ut omnia sint ordinatissima.*[11] Here he is thinking of the gradation of perfections of being, with the *summum bonum* as supreme and with the observation that God

[9] Cf. J. Sauter, *Die philosophischen Grundlagen des Naturrechts,* pp. 61 ff.

[10] Augustine, *Epist.* 157, 3, 15; elsewhere, *De ord.,* 2, 8, 25, he calls this principle "hoc vulgare proverbium."

[11] Augustine, *De lib. arb.,* Bk. I, Chap. 6, 15.

gradibus ordinavit creaturam a terra usque ad coelum, a visibilibus ad invisibilia, a mortalibus ad immortalia.[12] Then, however, he returns again to the eternal law and to the eternal truths, and principles in our souls.[13]

This is, however, *not the whole Augustine.* We find in him *important suggestions toward an interpretation of natural law such as we are attempting.* We see a beginning of this kind especially in the position which he accords to common utility in the process of apprehending the supreme principles of law, and particularly in connection with the immediate experience of man in social life. Quoting *Cicero* (*De inv. rhetorica,* II, 53) word for word, *Augustine* describes justice as "an attitude of mind governed by common utility, which concedes to each his dignity," and adds that although this attitude is grounded in human nature itself, the first steps in the shaping of human community life are taken by "customs forming for the sake of utility." [14] Furthermore, where *Augustine* goes beyond Cicero and expresses his own ideas on natural law and common good, the *family* obviously holds the central position in his thought. Men, he says, in seeking their good (complying with their impulse toward happiness) strive first and foremost for peace in their community life; peace is the most fundamental aim in the impulse toward happiness, man's primal instinct (*sicut nemo est qui gaudere nolit, ita nemo est qui pacem habere nolit*); peace consists in "ordered concord" (*ordinata concordia*), toward which man is impelled by virtue of the "laws of his nature" (*naturae suae legibus*); the source and type of all peace is the natural order (*naturalis ordo*) of the family. Here *Augustine* gives emphasis chiefly to "the father's care for his own"—which is bound up with natural love—as the "source" of concord and peace in the family, in commanding and obeying; fathers command "in loving care" and "thereby serve those whom they seem to command." [15] *Augustine* does not concern himself any further with the mode of operation of natural moral law (*lex*) and the mode of apprehension of natural jural law (*ius*). From the beginning, however, he recognizes the family as the "fundamental situation" governing experiences and perceptions relating to social order, and also the desire, which belong to man's nature and is conditional upon the family, to attain the well-being of the family with mutual love and respect as the fundamental impulse.

With regard to *Thomas Aquinas,* we may well rely on *Wittmann's* penetrating exposé of his ethics, already referred to (cf. Chap. 3., n. VI). Although *Thomas* is ever aware of the order of being, nevertheless, for him natural law is basically the reason's endowment with the general principles of moral order. *Wittmann* says plainly: "The notion of natural law developed by *Thomas*

[12] Augustine, *En. in ps. 144: 13.*

[13] Similarly, J. Mausbach, *Die Ethik des hl. Augustin,* 2nd ed., 1929, Vol. I, pp. 88–104.

[14] Augustine, *De div.,* quaest. 31: "Justitia est habitus animi, communi utilitate conservata, suam cuique tribuens dignitatem. Eius initium est ab natura profectum: deinde quaedam in consuetudinem ex utilitatis ratione vertunt: postea res et ab natura profectas et ab consuetudine probatas, legum metus et religio sanxit." This passage, with which we shall be concerned again later, has undergone a shift of meaning as compared with Cicero, insofar as Augustine's idea of nature differs from Cicero's stoic idea and to Augustine God and nature are not one, as the Stoics held, nor is human reason a part of the divine cosmic mind.

[15] Augustine, *De civ. Dei,* Lib. XIX, cc. 12, 17.

is not of a metaphysical or ontological but of a psychological and epistemological character; just as in the purely speculative, so also in the practical reason there is a natural knowledge, and this is the natural law."[16] Hence, says *Wittmann,* "in order to elucidate the notion of natural law *Thomas* proceeds not so much from human nature as from the eternal law." The sciences, on the other hand, *Wittmann* says, understand by natural law, a law, an order, "which is prescribed for things and creatures by their own nature"—"an order of being residing in the nature of things." According to *Thomas,* law generally points to reason; hence, "natural law, by its very conception, points directly to reason. The principle that law *aliquid rationis est* is strictly followed out. A distinction may be found only insofar as intellectualism is still more stubbornly upheld in regard to natural law than in the view of the eternal law."[17] *Wittmann* lays stress on the fact that at times *Thomas* emphasizes the metaphysical side of natural law, seeing its basis chiefly in the nature of things and seeking knowledge of it through the ends inherent in things. Nevertheless, "Even then for *Thomas* the natural law is still chiefly dependent upon reason; the manifold human inclinations and impulses, he says, are subject to natural law insofar as they are regulated by reason (*Summa theol.,* Ia IIae, q. 94, a. 2 ad 2). Thus, law as such appears first in the mind, and the train of thought returns from the objective order of being and nature to the mind." In general, "from this point of view, order does not form the object of a special inquiry. *Thomas* treats of the eternal law, of the natural law in the sense of a law of reason, but not also of natural law in the objective sense; he even incidentally observes that the natural law is primarily contained in the eternal law and only secondarily in human reason (*Summa theol.,* Ia IIae., q. 71, a. 6 ad 4); the connection with nature he seems to pass over" (*ibid.,* pp. 343 f.) The natural law, as rational insight, as *Thomas* sees it, "in no case penetrates beyond completely abstract and fundamental norms"; human law must join natural law, and only "when the two are taken together do they yield a complete order of living," whereby "the practical reason by appropriate reflection gains from the prescriptions of natural law prescriptions of a more positive kind, namely, those which are described as human laws (*Summa theol.,* Ia IIae, q. 91, a. 3)." Reason is now again the source, namely, the reason "of a superior"; human law also is "in this sense a command of reason. Thus, Thomas adheres even at the last stage to the intellectualistic conception of law": "Law always ranks as a work of reason."[18]

[16] A. Mitterer, *Die Entwicklungslehre Augustins im Vergleich mit dem Weltbild des hl. Thomas und der Gegenwart,* 1956, pp. 314 ff., shows how, following out Augustine's (limited) idea of evolution, it is possible to form an idea of evolution which comprehends the whole created world, in which the law of nature and the law of civilization, understood as the law of being, becoming, and ought, are seen in intrinsic connection with the eternal law.

[17] Wittmann, *Die Ethik des hl. Thomas v. Aq.,* 1933, pp. 328, 335, 338 (cf. Chap. 3).

[18] *Ibid.,* p. 353; he refers to a passage in the *Summa theol.,* Ia IIae, q. 92, a. 1: "Lex nihil aliud est quam dictamen rationis in praesidente quo subditi gubernantur." However, says Wittmann, this "intellectualism" of Thomas seems to have become fully developed only in his later works, whereas in his commentary "he refers political order not to reason but to the will of the ruler" (*Sent. IV,* d. 49, I, 2. Thus, I, 4: "Dicimus . . . rectum ordinem civitatis, qui est ex voluntate gubernatoris civitatis"). On the primacy of will or intellect as the foundation of law and rights in medieval thought cf. T. E. Davitt, S.J., *The Nature of Law,* 1951; the author adduces six authorities (from Heinrich of Ghent to Suárez) in support of the primacy of will, and six others (from Albert the Great to Bellarmine) in support of the primacy of intellect.

As above in regard to *Augustine,* we should like to say now that *this is not the whole Thomas. Thomas* not only says natural law represents a "natural knowledge" in the cognitive faculty and a "natural impulsion" in the conative faculty (cf. Chap. 6); [19] we have also pointed out that he links the obligatory order of natural law to the instinctive order (cf. *Summa theol.,* Ia IIae, q. 94, a. 2: *Secundum ordinem inclinationum naturalium est ordo praeceptorum legis naturae*); also a basic idea with *Thomas* is that the impulse toward happiness is a natural instinctive disposition for man, not a matter for his arbitrary will.[20] Finally, we must recall the role which *Thomas* allots to *communis utilitas* as the purpose of law (cf. Chap. 39). To *Thomas,* unlike *Augustine,* however, the order of being operating through its impulse toward happiness plays a secondary role. Furthermore, *Thomas* does not keep the family at the centre of his thoughts; rather, with *Aristotle,* he holds that the state "is by nature prior" to the individual, and the family itself is by nature directed toward the political commonweal as the fundamental requirement for complete human existence,[21] whereas with *Augustine* the nature of the state is conceived as an order of peace with reference to the peace of the family community.[22]

We have said that even to the *present day* there remains an uncertainty in scholastic natural law teaching with regard to the relationship between the jural a priori of human reason and the ontological pattern of human reality. One may recall the celebrated dispute between *V. Cathrein* and *J. Mausbach* regarding the definition of the morally good, which is also fundamental to the conception of natural law in its general and in its jural sense. *Cathrein* sees the starting point in "rational human nature 'as such,'" whereas *Mausbach* seeks it in the "final end." [23] *Cathrein* is closer to reality, yet he never reaches an objectively adequate definition of what this nature is; he understands the natural order basically as only the rational order which reveals itself in the natural conscience, and hence natural jural law (*ius*) as "the body of natural moral laws which concern men's social life and instruct them to render to all others their own." [24] How is "their own" to be determined? *Cathrein* does indeed hint at the order of being, but he is actually thinking (as *Wittmann* declares of *Thomas*) only of the rational order: "By rational human nature we must understand the whole moral nature of man with body and soul, with spiritual and intellectual faculties—in short, with all its parts, but insofar as they are parts of a rational nature. Reason must, so to say, spiritualize all man's activity, must raise it to the rational sphere." [25] Apart from the fact that the functioning of human nature, which points to the natural law order, remains out of consideration, the "so to say" leaves the main question unanswered: In what, for scientific natural law ethics, does the criterion of "rational" in determining good and right consist?

[19] Thomas Aquinas, *Sent IV,* d. 33, I, 1: "Oportet quod in vi cognoscitiva sit naturalis conceptio et in vi appetitiva naturalis inclinatio."

[20] Cf. Thomas Aquinas, Ia, q. 19, a. 10: "Non ad liberum arbitrium pertinet quod volumus esse felices, sed ad naturalem instinctum."

[21] Cf. Thomas Aquinas, *in I Pol.,* lect. 6; of course, Thomas does not overlook the rights of the family and the state's duty to respect and protect them. Cf. also on this question O. Schilling, *Die Staats-und Soziallehre des hl. Thomas v. Aq.,* 2nd ed., 1930, pp. 71 f., 327 f.

[22] Cf. Augustine, *De civ. Dei,* Lib. XIX, c. 12.

[23] Cf. *Philosophisches Jahrbuch der Görres-Gesellschaft,* Vol. XII (1899) and XIII (1900).

[24] V. Cathrein, *Recht, Naturrecht und positives Recht,* 2nd ed., 1909, p. 222.

[25] V. Cathrein, *Moralphilosophie,* 5th ed., 1911, Vol. I, p. 196.

A standpoint almost opposite to that of *Cathrein,* and also opposed to *Wittmann's* interpretation of *Thomas,* is adopted by *A. F. Utz;* he places the centre of gravity of *Thomas's* natural law doctrine in the "objective state of nature": "Everything must count as natural law that is objectively rational, viz., that can be objectively analysed." "The main fundamental thought of Thomas's conception of natural law," he says, is that "all natural moral claims, i.e., all commands of the moral law, insofar as they follow from *natura humana,* possess not only a moral but also a juridical character." *Natura humana* is for *Thomas* the basic notion of natural law ethics and the norm of natural law: "Thomas proceeds from *natura humana,* which as an absolute norm is the measure for all human action, including that of society." [26] *Utz* is no more concerned than *Thomas* (cf. *Wittmann* above) or *Cathrein* with the functioning of human nature as a pointer to the natural law order, nor does he embark on an analysis of the order of being and the order of ends revealed in human nature. The understanding of the natural law order of individual and social life is regarded by *Utz* as that of a process of "juridical logic," because of his view that "man in himself, just because he possesses *natura humana,* has enough reasoning power to be able to recognize the norms, and, by reference to the concrete facts, to draw the conclusion in accordance with the facts, namely, what must rightly be realized by society here and now. The result of this logical process is natural law." In explanation he adds: "In the teaching of *St. Thomas,* the practical reason, insofar as it correctly analyses the objective facts, namely, insofar as it is true, possesses law-creating force." [27]

This raises, however, the crucial question: When does practical reason "correctly" analyse the objective facts, and when is it "true"? *M. E. Schmitt* touches on the core of the question in her critical survey of the literature concerning natural law questions: "Thus, we are concerned with the crucial question, how one recognizes the human person and any principles at all taken from life as jural rules, and acknowledges them as binding on society," especially since it is at present clear, in the light of a legal philosophy rooted in a positivist anthropology, that "one cannot without qualification designate nature as a legal category if one does not wish to succumb to an evil naturalism." [28] If this is so, it seems that for natural law theory everything depends on showing how it reaches the following concepts: nature; nature of man; *natura humana;* natural law; nature of the case; order of being; and hence the criterion of "true" and "correct" in the logical process of inference bound up with fact. This is possible only if the concepts mentioned are thoroughly examined from the empirical-phenomenological and ontological-metaphysical points of view, especially the concepts of human nature and natural law, whence we have thought it necessary to devote so much attention to them.

[26] Utz, *op. cit.,* pp. 433, 482, 566. In the light of the interpretation of Thomas by Wittmann, which we have quoted in the text above, it seems questionable how far the elaborated conception of the natural order as an objective order, as set forth by Utz, can be found in Thomas' writings (the expression *natura humana* itself is not a common one with Thomas); the purpose of this present work, however, is not an interpretation of Thomas, and so we confine ourselves to recording the theories insofar as they are of significance to our argument.

[27] Utz, *op. cit.,* pp. 443 f.

[28] M.-E. Schmitt, *Recht und Vernunft: Ein Beitrag zur Diskussion der Rationalität des Naturrechts: Sammlung Politeia,* A. F. Utz, O.P., editor, 1955, p. 7.

It is not our concern here to discuss the attempts at interpreting *St. Thomas* or to discuss contradictions therein. Only the natural law problems underlying such contradictions concern us. They involve not least *the relationship between natural moral law in general and jural natural law.* The related uncertainties in present-day scholasticism are due, we think, to the fact that it one-sidedly locates the functioning of human nature and its law in reason, while disregarding the impulse toward value-realization (happiness), which operates through the order of being. In his book, *J. Fuchs* states that he would not maintain the distinction between moral natural law in general (*lex naturalis*) and jural natural law (*ius naturale*), because medieval scholasticism does not observe the distinction either.[29] Contrariwise, *A. F. Utz* declares with great emphasis in his commentary on *St. Thomas:* "Law (*ius*) is always a concrete entity. . . . Law (*lex*) can manifest itself in general principles"; "The time has come, therefore, for natural law thinkers who follow *St. Thomas* to take this distinction between natural law in general and jural natural law seriously." [30] *Albert Auer* adopts a widely different position. He builds on the *lex aeterna,* and only briefly at the end of his book as a "supplement" does he refer to the connection between *lex aeterna* and *lex naturalis.* He begins with "the fact that the supreme and ultimate elements of law are contained in the *lex aeterna* and that it is at the same time a really valid law"; "the content of natural law is the content of *lex aeterna*": "if we speak, therefore, of natural law, we do not mean simply a law arising somehow from the meaning of nature or having something to do with a law of nature. Natural law cannot be seen primarily from nature": "The principles of all law are metaphysically necessary principles and as such are contained in synderesis, as *lex aeterna.*" *Lex aeterna* "is law insofar as it means the anchoring of human nature in God; but man's own nature insofar as its content is meant." [31]

R. Linhardt, on the other hand, says: "*Thomas* has given generous attention to the materials of the legal mode of life, especially private law. But in distinguishing between the specific idea of law and the specific idea of morality he has not advanced beyond clarity to distinctness, and especially he has not reached the logical application and elaboration of a distinct notion of law. We are left with suggestions which must be extracted from various treatises in order to construct his idea of law." [32] *Wittmann* reaches a similar conclusion: "The Middle Ages does not always and strictly distinguish law and morality; the two notions of natural law, *lex* and *ius,* regularly coincide." [33] Today there can be no doubt that natural law ethics has to work with a clearly conceived specific idea of law (*ius*); this is why we have devoted so much attention to it (cf. Chaps. 36 ff.). There seems, however, to be equally little doubt that natural law (*lex*) and natural law (*ius*) must be seen in connection with one another as follows from our dissertation on natural law (*lex*). This was necessary because of the intimate and indissoluble relationship between the two categories: *the doctrine of natural moral law* (lex) *is not to be regarded merely as introductory and preparatory to the doctrine of natural jural law* (ius), *but forms an essential*

[29] Cf. J. Fuchs, S.J., *Lex naturae,* 1955, Preface.

[30] Utz, *op. cit.,* p. 433.

[31] Albert Auer, O.S.B., *Der Mensch hat Recht. Naturrecht auf dem Hintergrund von Heute,* 1956, pp. 59, 124 f., 162, 196, 373.

[32] R. Linhardt, *Die Sozialprinzipien des hl. Thomas v. Aq., op. cit.,* p. 86.

[33] Wittmann, *op. cit.,* p. 356.

part in it. Natural jural law (*ius*) can be shown to be a pattern of obligations only in conjunction with general natural moral law; furthermore, it is only by means of general natural law, as the proper functioning of human nature, that it can be shown to be the order of existence to which man sees himself impelled in his quest for integral humanity, and will ever in the future see himself impelled as civilizations change.

Present-day natural law theory outside the scholastic tradition

Since we always endeavor to find what is common between our line of thought and the notions of others it seems important to show that our conception of the reality of natural law and its apprehension reveals *a number of points of contact with the latest work outside the traditional natural law school.* A discussion of these also will make it possible to define more precisely our own views. *Helmut Coing* ascribes key significance for the elucidation of natural law to the "fundamental social situations" of man, pointing to the family as the "basic type" of community; natural law "is to be understood as a body of supreme legal principles which form the foundation of positive cultural law." The moral conscience, he says, shows us the way in detail, in the concrete situation, and one must not disregard the fact that human life "is bound up with certain typical situations." The historicists overlook the fact that there is not only evolution, but also "basic phenomena which always return." From this *Coing* draws the conclusion: "It is possible to describe the content of moral values with respect to such typical situations and also—without, of course, exhausting it—to give a picture of its essence, transcending the individual situation. In this way I can somehow define the notion of justice, at any rate the core of it." [34] Clearly, *Coing* seeks to link together empirical (in contrast to *Kant*) and a priori matter. Thus, we go along with *Coing* in great part. The question seems to arise, however: What is the reason that, under the influence of the moral conscience in the "typical situations," modes of conduct arise on the basis of which we are then able to describe the content of moral values? If it is assumed in advance that conscience already possesses principles of value which point out the way to man in the concrete situation, is this not assuming what has to be explained? It seems to us that if one seeks to base the moral content of law and of justice on the value-cognition, then one must inevitably go back to the value-conation natural to man, in other words, to the impulses striving for satisfaction and happiness. This is the starting point chosen by *Aristotle* with the incontrovertible statement that the impulse toward happiness is man's primal instinct. Aiming at happiness is nothing else than value-conation. *Coing* himself declares that "the idea of 'the nature of the case' embraces the nature of man, his natural capacities, instincts, conations etc."; it "comprises, furthermore, the modes of instrumentality proper to the various spheres of man's activity and to his communities." [35] This is our view also; yet, our analysis of human nature has shown perhaps that in human nature itself the order of being (pattern of impulses, value-conation) and juridical insight (moral sense, sense of value) are bound up together still more originally and directly, intimately and indissolubly, that is, they are experienced and recognized in the "fundamental social situation" of the family community. Without this close

[34] H. Coing, *Grundzüge der Rechtsphilosophie,* 1950, pp. 106 f., 110 f., 165, 179 f.
[35] *Ibid.,* p. 119.

connection between the order of being and the order of value, the perception of value can be based only on "feeling" (as *Coing* sees [36]), and justice then remains without an objective criterion or a material standard.

For *Mitteis,* too, the *juridical conscience* with its rudimentary perception of the demands of justice is central; he strongly emphasizes the reality of natural law: "Natural law is the authentically valid law; positive law by comparison has a derived conditional validity, prima facie resting on a presumption. Positive law is a rule for a judgment which is itself subject to judgment, a measure which itself requires measurement. Positive law cannot avail anything against natural law; it is only the transformer in which natural law is made practicable for real conditions. Positive law must give way if it no longer corresponds to the claims of justice, that is to say, of natural law. Natural law transgresses positive law—in this way our whole argument may be summed up." *Mitteis* also thinks it necessary to emphasize the fact (which seems to us so crucial) that, in community life man attains to comprehension of his own nature and the realization of values which this postulates; hence, when he describes natural law as "that law which corresponds with the idea of human community and which, therefore, as community-ruling has reached its most proper, authentic nature, its own self." He also speaks of natural law as "an existential prerequisite of human community"; thus, "the personality in society" proves itself to be a supreme value, and mutual loyalty, resulting in joint responsibility for common destiny, a basic duty of conduct: the personality bears the standards within itself.[37] We agree with all of this, but believe it to be necessary to establish the idea of personality and of community ontologically; it was in order to find this basis that we proceeded from the interaction of man's natural intellectual capacities and natural striving toward values.

Again, we find a common element in *Wilhelm Sauer.* He himself makes the following remarks concerning our *Naturrecht:* It "treats of natural law as something rooted in the nature of man and of society, with the result that it is very close to the view of this book [cited below]: as an order of ends." Like the present writer—and no doubt it is of this that he is thinking—he ascribes a vital role to the *striving for values and to the common good* in the establishment and apprehension of law. Legal and social philosophy, he holds, are right in treating law as a constituent part of society: "Every true community is a value-community," in which, accordingly, "every member of the community remains at the same time an independent personality"; the deposit of the general will, which forms in the community, is universal usage with the social order rooted in it; formal, state law "is thus explained in its organic evolution as living law from social life by way of the general will and custom, and is sociologically established." Justice "is the handling of men's striving for values (of volition and action) in accordance with their value for the community," according as they tend to enhance or to diminish the common good; "the true good of the community," "the law-establishing common good," is not identical with the subjective "common will," but calls for a "critically refined, socio-ethical orientation on the idea of culture"; this idea is founded on the value idea, and this in turn, and "value-metaphysics" on life and experience. "Out of life

[36] Cf. *ibid.*, pp. 106 f.

[37] Cf. H. Mitteis, *Über das Naturrecht,* 1948, pp. 7 f., 18, 33 ff., 38.

arise the vital values (cultural values) which alone make life worth living."[38] He refuses an ontological explanation of values on the ground that the "distinction between *is* and *ought* (the value-judgment) is lost on the ontological level." In fact, the values, if they are understood in terms of life and of striving for values, are already seen in part ontologically, i.e., as founded in human nature. On the other hand, the experience of that which alone makes life worth living varies so much for the individual that it becomes impossible to base super-subjective, absolute values, which *Sauer* also recognizes, on mere experience. Hence, our endeavor to establish an ontological basis for them in terms of the order of being and of the order of ends found in human nature. *Sauer's* idea of value leads him to an idea of culture which includes the possibility of a "law-establishing pantheism" and a conception of the divinity "as the body of supreme values thinkable for man, the absolute values."[39] On the other hand, says *Sauer,* employing his notion of end and his ideas of the common will, of the common good, and of the justice determined by it, "one reaches, on a strict methodical line, to a supralegal standard, the idea of law. With this, positivism is overcome or (what is the same) the idea of law acquires positiveness."[40] If the idea of end is understood not merely subjectively, then such a conception comes very close to the traditional natural law idea, especially when accompanied by the notion that the idea of law so founded, itself acquires positiveness (cf. below, Chap. 49). With his concrete conception of law based on the idea of end, *Sauer* opposes the formal conception which comprehends law exclusively in terms of legal rules and the legal decree.

Hans Ryffel also thinks of establishing a concrete conception of law. Following the theory of conduct of *Carlo Sganzini* he starts from "conduct-projecting" in human social life. Because this is always a response to an actual reality, and hence wholly and entirely dependent on the situation, he thinks, like many before him, that the following conclusion is inevitable: "There cannot be any universal validity of the supreme natural law idea"; "The real conduct-projecting and universal validity are incompatible"; hence, "actual reality and absolute standard must be radically distinguished," with the consequence that natural law must not itself be understood as actuality but only as idea of natural law; the natural law idea, therefore, can signify only "unavoidable reference to the absolute standard and to the likewise unavoidable falling short thereof."[41] The idea of social conduct-projecting brings out features in natural law which we have stressed a good deal, namely, that knowledge of natural law depends on experiencing reality and that the realization of natural law depends on the situation. Similarly, we emphasize the fact that any legal system, which is measured by the absolute standard of the natural law order, is always imperfect, and hence misses the ideal, even though it stands in "unavoidable reference" to the ideal as a binding command. However, the impossibility of generally valid

[38] W. Sauer, *Einführung in die Rechtsphilosophie,* 1954, pp. 1, 5, 18, 30, 32, 44 f., 99 ff. Cf. also W. Sauer, *System der Rechts- und Sozialphilosophie,* 2nd ed., 1949; *Metaphysik auf sozialwissenschaftlicher Grundlage,* 1951.

[39] *Ibid.,* pp. 18, 101.

[40] *Ibid.,* pp. 13 f.

[41] H. Ryffel, *Das Naturrecht,* 1944, pp. 57 f., 114 f., 118, 120 f., 128 f.; "Emil Brunners Buch über die Gerechtigkeit," in *Archiv für Rechts- und Sozialphilosophie,* Vol. XXXVIII, 2, 1949, pp. 267 f.

natural law principles we do not find proved by their depending in the actual mode of validity upon situation, since of course there are situations common to men in general and constant in character; furthermore, as we showed with reference to *Nawiasky*, positive law itself can never completely anticipate the existing reality, but can only lay down "general abstract rules" by means of "general concepts." [42] For *Ryffel* the question how man comes to knowledge of the absolute standard as the foundation of the natural law idea remains open. The question also arises, how anything can be a standard if it is not concrete and generally valid, since both properties seem necessary to the concept of a standard. Indeed, the fundamental question for all theories of natural law is this: *What* is the standard for judging of true law? "Nature" itself, in my opinion, gives the answer in that by means of experience of the "social conduct-projecting" in reality it urges upon us the apprehension of the principles which contain the "absolute standard" for the legal order. They contain it because of their definite content and their general validity, both of which are communicated to the intellect by the rational nature common to all as it works in bringing into effect the order of existence in its basic features, which are demanded by nature itself. To this order belongs love, in which *Ryffel* seems to see the absolute "directive," but of which he also says that, "in world affairs it can never assume the concrete form of absolute rightness."

We find a common element particularly in a legal philosophy which stresses the idea of love. *Günther Küchenhoff* in his interpretation of natural law, which follows the traditional doctrine but gives it a decidedly Christian meaning, assigns to the *love* of man for man, in which the fundamental natural social command consists and which Christianity has made the most important "personal motive," so vital a place in the world of law and justice that he speaks of a "law grounded in love," although he sees it working, not in real legal claims, but in mental attitudes in legal usage in private and public life.[43] Lastly, *Walter Schönfeld* bases law and also a "theology of law" entirely on the *Christian precept of charity*.[44] We ourselves, while giving an ontological foundation to law and to the knowledge of law wholly within the framework of philosophy, since we regard as decisive the nature of man as a family being, assign an essential place to love, and to love of one's neighbor in general a place no less essential than that of "supreme social principle" (cf. Chap. 53), but consider it imperative for "natural law theory" to remain wholly within the philosophical framework and for legal philosophy in general to distinguish sharply between the specific essence of law and rules of conduct otherwise determined.

Finally, our discussion of the reality and of the apprehension of natural law will, I think, have shown that we share specially in the endeavors to establish a *criterion of law*, and that we are at one also with the criticism levelled against over-simplified treatments of this question in presentations of natural law. Nevertheless, there is no substance in the charge against *Thomas Aquinas*, which *H. Welzel* renews, that he arrives at the "typical natural law petitio principii. What has been previously perceived to be good is represented as 'natural' and is then used as a criterion of good. Thus, even *Thomas* sets out

[42] H. Nawiasky, *Allgemeine Rechtslehre: System der rechtlichen Grundbegriffe*, 2nd ed., 1948, p. 54.

[43] Cf. G. Küchenhoff, *Naturrecht und Christentum*, 1948.

[44] Cf. W. Schönfeld, *Grundlegung der Rechtswissenschaft*, 1951.

the already established Christian world of values as natural and then apparently proceeds to derive the Christian world of values from this concept of 'nature' " (*Welzel* claims to find the same error in *E. Brunner's* natural law idea, viz., "the old natural law vicious circle": "All . . . value beliefs which the author has previously inserted into the concept of natural he subsequently derives from it again.") Certainly, however, neo-Thomistic natural law theory will find itself increasingly opposed by the keen weapons of the positivist school of linguistic analysis with regard to its concept of "nature." Thus, *F. C. Copleston,* S.J. issues a warning: "Thomists may find themselves urged to reconsider the foundations of their metaphysics in the light of modern empiricist criticism and of linguistic analysis and their status in relation to pure tautologies on the one hand and to empirical hypotheses on the other." [45] Present-day Thomism is in a quite different situation from *Thomas* himself, who in his own day with its prevailing common conception of human nature was able to dispense with any thoroughgoing scientific discussion of it.

Indeed, in view of the opposing conceptions of man which are current today it seems necessary to provide an inductive-ontological-metaphysical foundation for natural law theory. *Thomas* does not fail to trace back what is according to nature to the order of being and ends (cf. Chap. 38); and *Welzel* himself, who first thinks "that from the principle of what 'is in accordance with nature' no world order can be developed," has to admit finally: "The enduring results of natural law theory lie not in the central axiological sphere but—generally unnoticed—in the peripheral region of ontology." The foundation of being (ontological) of concrete law, he says, is to be sought in the "objective-logical structures"—in the object; therefore, it is of vital importance to ascertain the criterion of "*correct*" objective-logical structural analysis. For, *Welzel* thinks, as we do, "that the practical problem of correct social conduct in ethics and in law is the same in principle"; and hence also, the "concrete endeavor of natural law continues unaltered to discover the practical principles of correct social action." What, then, is "correct" social action? *Welzel* seeks an answer by going back to *Kant's* maxim that man must always be an end in social action, never a mere means. *Welzel* thinks: "If one could define an inviolable good of action more closely, the desire of natural law would not have been in vain. *One* practical ethical principle of lasting validity could then be pronounced, to which a multitude of other relatively ascertainable propositions could be annexed on the principle of consonance." That principle would be: "That man, that is, the autonomous (self-responsible) person, must never be regarded purely as a means, but always also as an end in itself." [46]

Obviously, the important question which follows is: How far is man a means and how far is he an end? *Welzel* thinks this can be more closely determined with the aid of the principle, "to use the person in his empirical existence as a means only as far as his doing and suffering is to complete or destroy the moral person himself." This is undoubtedly a demand corresponding to very high

[45] F. C. Copleston, S.J., *Aquinas,* 1956, p. 251.

[46] Kant, *Grundlegung zur Metaphysik der Sitten,* Coll. Works, Vol. IV, p. 429, expresses himself thus: "Act so that you always use mankind, in your own person and in that of everyone else, at all times as an end, never merely as a means"; this undoubtedly defines a criterion of morality of great practical significance, yet one of only secondary character, since it is not given a more precise ontological foundation and it therefore remains formal in nature.

moral and humane ideals (cf. Chaps. 39, 42). It leaves out of consideration, however, the social entity as such (cf. Chap. 39). Moreover, the fact that it provides no real criterion of the "inviolable good" or value and hence of morality and law, is seen by *Welzel* himself, for, with an eye on the encroachment of the totalitarian state, he adds: "But the precise definition of this idea, especially with regard to what practical-ethical bounds it sets to political power, has remained open until today. Yet, only when this task is completed can we hope to give firm contours and a legally applicable structure to the great idea of 'human rights.'" Precisely to this task we have turned with our concept of the "existential ends," including those proper to society and to the state. From the "existential ends" understood in terms of the personal and social nature of man, we can derive not only firm contours but also a very definite pattern of "human rights." We have shown, moreover, in detailed analysis, how man in fact through "empirical existence" itself, to use *Welzel's* expression, that is, in the human "fundamental situation" of the family community, reaches the perception of the supreme practical principles of law.[47]

The objection of *A. I. Meldon* of the University of Washington to this is no objection at all. He says that cases can always be imagined in which it would not be practicable to actualize what, in an article of the (U.N.) Declaration of Human Rights, is established as man's human rights. This declaration is concerned about concrete, definite principles, yet their application remains dependent on circumstances. It is particularly surprising that exponents of the linguistic analysis school of philosophy, to which he belongs, cannot advance to the recognition of this fact. *Meldon* himself does indeed say, with natural law ethics, that the validity of all general moral principles is to be understood in the connection in which they are applied; but from this he draws the conclusion that moral principles "are linguistic, not natural signs." Along with the logical positivists, he says that the manner of their application is altogether different from that of utterances in which we describe matters of fact: the moral principles consist in general admonitions to realize that we live in a world in which a conversation about moral questions is possible. The linguistic analysis school spends much intellectual energy in opposing the often repeated and self-evident fact that a statement regarding values is something different from a statement of facts. Similarly, it is self-evident that no mere sociological, anthropological, or psychological data will enable us to deduce that a man has any rights; it is self-evident because they can be explained only on an ontological and metaphysical basis. Yet, the data of experience in the realm of morals and of law urge the mind that is responsive to reality to inquire into their ontological and metaphysical foundations; one of these empirical facts is the individual and general conviction regarding the existence of original rights of man. In fact, *Meldon* himself not only does not wish to dispute this "common sense persuasion," but regards its defense as an object of his study, although he acknowledges these rights to be only invitations to men not to relapse into vengefulness and cruelty, but to act as moral beings.[48] The cause of human rights is, however, hardly likely to be served if they are thus thrust, by a kind of nominalism, into the realm

[47] Cf. H. Welzel, *Naturrecht und materiale Gerechtigkeit*, 2nd ed., 1955, pp. 61, 165, 168, 171, 182, 196 f.

[48] Cf. A. I. Meldon, in *Science, Language and Human Rights* (Philadelphia: University of Pennsylvania Press), 1952, pp. 167 ff., 187.

of "signs." Fortunately, by far the greater part of mankind are at least as certain of the *metaphysical reality* in question, namely, that of conscience with its witness to law and to justice, as they are of sense-reality. Otherwise there could never have been any United Nations Declaration on Human Rights or any hope to ensure general recognition of the principles laid down in it. The fact that the epistemological theory of the linguistic analysis school is not in a very healthy state even with regard to the truth of facts (not to speak of values) is suggested by the remark of *Max Black* in the same volume of essays to the effect that the sense-datum language exposes those who use it to the danger of perpetuating the confusions with which the minds of its inventors were beset.[49]

We can also appreciate what is of merit in the *criticism of traditional natural law theory,* as may be seen from our discussions all throughout this work, although indeed this provides occasion for rebutting often repeated unfounded criticisms. Thus, Professor *Adolf Merkl* points to numerous inconsistencies in the "Christian natural law doctrine," such as the rejection of absolute freedom of conscience and of freedom of opinion by *Pope Gregory XVI,* compared with the recognition at about the same time of religious freedom and of religious equality in Germany by *Bishop von Ketteler* "in the existing circumstances." Inconsistencies regarding the legal valuation of the personality and the protection of its dignity are said to be revealed in *Augustine's* opinion that the emancipation of slaves belongs to the realm of Utopia, by the justification of slavery still maintained by *Thomas Aquinas,* whereas people of strong religious affiliation cooperated in the achievement of emancipation; and again in the American Civil War there were members of the great Christian confessions on both sides. Another inconsistency is that the social natural law of the papal encyclicals *Rerum Novarum* and *Quadragesimo Anno* put all the social teaching contained in papal pronouncements of the eighteenth century in the shade. In addition, *Mausbach* says in *Naturrecht und Völkerrecht* that natural law calls for the punishment of crime, but that the assessment of the penalty is a matter of positive definition by the lawgiver; thus, observes *Merkl,* a distribution of roles between natural law and positive law comes about which assigns to the state the determination of the crime as well as the assessment of the penalty, so that the question arises whether, for example, the criminal acts defined by a communistic penal code are always without exception binding on the conscience (e.g., listening in to a papal declaration from the Vatican radio). It betokens the "bankruptcy of natural law if it refuses to give an independent judgment with regard to what modes of conduct are deserving of punishment and in what way, but instead delegates the state lawgiver, in his autonomous prescriptions, with the task of giving substance to the natural law principle, 'crimes are to be punished.'"

Opposing views, says *Merkl,* are also to be noted in questions of education. Organizations which base the rights of parents on natural law demanded "the confessional school" in one country in 1952, in another "the Christian community school." In the question concerning the form of the state, theological writers, statesmen, and laymen have, he declares, pronounced certain forms of political power or certain historical situations hallowed as specially pleasing to God or

[49] Cf. M. Black in *Science, Language and Human Rights,* p. 40 (see note 48); for a criticism of the philosophy and ethics of linguistic analysis cf. Messner, *Ethics and Facts,* pp. 294–312.

in conformity with Christian natural law, whereas *Leo XIII* (1881) held that the question of the form of state is a neutral one for present-day Catholicism and left it to the peoples' own choice, with the proviso that justice be safeguarded. Thus, the decision with regard to the admissibility of a form of state is made dependent on the question, "What is truth?"; this question greatly has occupied the mind of man without any wholly satisfactory answer being found. Finally, with regard to the purpose of the state, "the Catholic Church, substantially in agreement with the other Christian denominations, has developed a fundamental natural law line which has recently been designated in natural law literature as the principle of subsidiary function," and which signifies a "distribution of roles between the liberal constitutional state and the totalitarian state." Now, "the collectivist and socialist frequently will see the conditions laid down by Christian natural law for state intervention fulfilled, whereas the individualist and liberal, or in general the exponents of a restricted purpose for the state, will infer from this same natural law principle the prior right of the individual or of the free associations. Thus, even this very substantial natural law rule is ambiguous."

To Professor *Merkl's* surprise and perhaps to the surprise of many of our readers, let it be stated first that it has always been taken as a matter of course in natural law theory that the natural law principles are "ambiguous" with regard to the situations governing their application; also, that in the interpretation of one and the same situation in complicated circumstances opposite opinions can exist in the sphere of traditional natural law theory. In such cases the question is: What are the concrete reasons for and against the one or the other interpretation and application of natural law principles? In exactly the same way, as we shall see, opposing opinions can arise even among experts in the realm of the natural sciences as soon as theory is left behind and the applications of the laws of nature are discussed, when the concrete reasons decide the issue. Since it is a matter of the "nature of the case," one cannot see how it is possible to speak of a "specific natural law" (*Merkl*), congenial to the value-judgments of party ideologies; and ideological natural law would undoubtedly be a contradiction in terms, like wooden iron. In regard to the "rejection of absolute freedom of conscience" and the simultaneous acceptance of religious tolerance, of which *Merkl* makes a point, two principles are involved which at the same time, are both rooted in and delimited in human nature. By virtue of his rational moral nature (cf. Chap. 5) the individual is bound by the clear voice of his conscience; therefore, he possesses the primal right of freedom of conscience with the consequent obligation to respect this right in his dealings with men, which is the principle of tolerance. Man's social nature itself (apart from moral law and its theonomy; cf. *loc. cit.*) admits neither an absolute freedom of conscience, nor an absolute freedom of opinion, nor an absolute principle of tolerance, since there are no absolute rights at all which could be used without regard to others; this is true especially of the public exercise of the rights in question. As a matter of fact, even the liberal legal systems impose limits upon freedom of conscience and of expression (e.g., they prevent assassination of political opponents even if a command of conscience is appealed to, the misuse of freedom of expression for the purpose of overthrowing the state, the distribution of publications harmful to the young) with the full concurrence of the general juridical consciousness. Because application of the principles of freedom and of tolerance, like all natural law principles, depends on the situation, the regulation of the position in public law of the religious denominations together with the school question cannot but be dependent on circumstances; therefore, it can take different forms from country to country, according as the great majority of a population belongs to one denomination or another.

With regard to the passage cited by *Mausbach* from *Merkl*, even a fleeting glance at the most cursory presentations of traditional natural law will show that they give as little free scope to the state in penal law as elsewhere; rather (as generally in the question of the relationship between natural law and positive law), the principle—"provided that justice is safeguarded"—obtains, which *Merkl* quotes from *Leo XIII*, concerning the choice of a form of state. Because the natural principles of justice—natural law—make possible a judgment about the right and wrong of political measures, the Vatican radio station has been able often and unmistakably to express views on the suppression of natural rights by the totalitarian state. *Merkl* observes only incidentally that in natural law theory a changeable natural law also is spoken of. We admit that this aspect of natural law for a long time has had too little attention in traditional natural law writings. (Soon after the end of World War II, I submitted an article on request to the illustrious editor of a well-known Catholic review, in the course of which I mentioned "variable" natural law. The horrified editor returned it with the remark: "Where should we get to if we did not hold firmly to the absolute validity of natural law?") It is unnecessary to repeat what has been said in previous chapters about natural law as dependent on temporal and social conditions, that is, "relative" as distinct from "absolute" natural law, involving dependence on development, both of legal consciousness and of legal order. In this connection, considerable significance is attached to the question of certainty, with which we shall deal later.

In any case, the question of the truth of natural law is not to be simply disposed of with *Pilate's* question, "What is truth?"; for man knows with certitude *that* there is both right and wrong, and the simple conscience also knows very well *what* is right or wrong. In complicated questions, the *objective reasons* decide for or against—for instance, whether a measure conforms with the subsidiary function principle or not. A quite different matter exists in a democracy generally, in that only compromise solutions are to be attained because of the ideological attitudes of parties and of groups who think in liberalist or socialistic terms: this has obviously nothing to do with the question of truth as such. This general question is equally little affected by the fact that in particular cases it is not always possible to reach an ultimate degree of certainty, or by the fact that legal history can point to errors of jural consciousness and of legal administration. To deny the existence of objective truth and of true knowledge for such a reason would be tantamount to inferring that no objective truth can exist or be known with regard to the nature and motions of the sun, moon, and stars because of the many false beliefs which have existed and still exist in regard to them. Or, if someone disputed the possibility of a scientific natural law theory on the ground that contradictory opinions and even ridiculous statements concerning specific postulates had been put forward by scientific exponents of natural law theory, the possibility of a medical science would also have to be placed in doubt, on the ground that "medicine men" have uttered ridiculous statements and illustrious exponents of medical science have aired contradictory or false medical opinions.

We have spoken of *objective* reasons, which are of as much consequence in natural law questions as in the realm of natural science. Objective appraisal of conditions and of suitability to purpose of legal measures is, of course, more difficult as conditions become increasingly complicated. This is true in the application of *the laws of nature in the technical sphere:* although the laws of steam pressure may be clear, if they are to be applied in the construction of a heavy mountain locomotive, a number of questions of suitability to purpose arise which cannot be solved with ultimate certainty but only with *sufficient certainty,* since otherwise it would be impossible to build efficient locomotives of this kind. The same is true in the natural law sphere. History shows that mankind knows of the claims of justice with sufficient certainty, although it is undoubtedly always in conflict with untruth and injustice, to find its way along the difficult path of cultural progress. In the service of this certainty there are two powerful forces: *experience and interest.* Experience keeps in constant motion the discussion concerning the rightness or wrongness of legal measures and regulations. Experience and discussion promote scientific knowledge in all spheres, and, in the social sphere, promote insight into the concrete demands of justice, which depends on the comprehension of truth. It also happens in the social sphere that the interests of groups and the insight of the natural conscience collaborate in keeping the development of the legal system in motion, with the purpose of a progressive realization of the common good, the *common utility* (cf. Chap. 39), mentally and economically, namely, of the supreme natural law principle of the legal and social order. This is the principle which is fundamentally involved when, for example, in Anglo-Saxon countries it is said that the accepted criterion for social measures, which of course in a democracy are always legislative measures, consists in their long-term effect on human happiness.

Merkl himself finds the answer to his objections incidentally when he writes that *Joseph Mausbach* (*Naturrecht und Völkerrecht,* p. 37) says with deep wisdom: "One must not imagine it to be an easy thing to formulate the law of nature, apart from the simplest principles; as I have said before, it calls for the same comprehensive, sober, and loving absorption as any other inquiry into profound truths; it calls for . . . not only the work of the study, but also knowledge of human life, the exploration of popular wisdom, probing into the spirit of tradition and history. Otherwise, even highly intelligent men, in formulating natural law imperatives without regard to subjective and historical conditions, make disastrous errors. A Clement of Alexandria declared the wearing of earrings and the cutting of the beard by men as an 'offense against natural morality.' The even stricter Tertullian holds the dyeing of woollen clothing impermissible 'because God did not color the sheep red or blue by nature.'" For scientific self-critical natural law theory the absurdities of important philosophers and theologians mentioned by *Mausbach* form as little reason for questioning the objective foundations of natural law and the scientific character of natural law theory as do the errors of great medical men prove anything against the scientific character of medicine. *Merkl* concludes his criticism with a mention of present-day developments, not without a powerful declaration for natural law:

"At the moral low-water mark to which positive law sinks all the easier, the greater is the power of the state; the effectiveness of natural law postulates of no matter what ideology is the sole hope of checking the abuse of state power and of human impotence." [50] Unquestionably, salvation will not come from natural law postulates that spring from ideologies, but only from endeavors aimed at objective truth and justice. That the existence of these cannot be denied *Merkl* admits by implication, in spite of his contrary statements. On what grounds and by what other standard could he speak of the "moral low-water mark" to which positive law is liable to sink?

An original line of thought regarding the *epistemology of law* is pursued by *Rudolf Stanka,* the much too early deceased professor of the philosophy and history of law at Vienna. He tackles both the question of the nature of law and the possibility of legal science at the same time.[51] He considers it wrong to base the apprehension of law on pure reason, like *Kant,* because at the apex of legal thinking stands the imperative, the "ought." *Stanka* refers to the concept of "transcendental self-consciousness" which *Kant* uses in various senses: "I call self-consciousness transcendental insofar as it finds itself independent of the laws of nature in the phenomenal world, but practically transcendental insofar as it represents freedom and independence in the will." As such it is orientated toward the future. "The primal experience of the self . . . is the self-determination of the human personality, which establishes itself in the self and must necessarily oppose the exterior world, the non-self, to the self, although this exterior world at the same time and above all provides the material for exercising the will." Thus, man establishes himself, i.e., his self, as the cause which intends to realize ends and purposes. The opposition of self and not-self is eliminated at one point, which is of great significance to all mental sciences, namely, in the "We"-experience, in which subject and object coincide, so that the dualism of subject and object is overcome: "The subject 'I' is indeed not opposed to the object 'We,' but 'We' is felt as directly thinking and willing and demanding." This "*social experience*" represents a new form of attitude not observed by *Kant*. "The nature of social experience involves the practical and also the epistemological inseparability of the transcendental 'I' from such a 'We.'" *Stanka* describes this experience as "the experience of the membership of the 'I'"; with this "we are at the threshold of legal consciousness": The position of the self as a vehicle of values in the totality of values, as *Ihering* understood it, must be linked with a deepened conception of the nature of rules as directed to objects; this is in complete opposition to *Kant,* who conceived law as an end in itself. The conclusion is that both the transcendental I-consciousness and the transcendental We-consciousness require the law in order to safeguard their "identity in the future." Although our point of departure and our line of thought differ from *Stanka's,* there exist a number of common elements in his and our answers to the epistemological question in legal philosophy, especially: the apprehension of the fundamental juridical principles is bound up with the "social sphere" and it is not a matter of pure reason but rather of practical reason, since "the proper object of reflection of the practical reason is the social sphere,

[50] A. Merkl, "Einheit oder Vielheit des Naturrechts?" in *Österreichische Zeitschrift für öffentliches Recht,* Vol. V, 3, 1953, pp. 260, 266 ff., 270 f., 273 ff., 280, 309 ff.

[51] Cf. R. Stanka, "Der Ursprung der rechtlichen Erkenntnis," in *Archiv für Rechts- und Sozialphilosophie,* Vol. XLI, 1, 1954, pp. 19–31.

to which man is bound by virtue of this very practical reason." We seek the *ontological* basis of law still more directly in the community sphere; *epistemologically* we hope to have shown with our analysis of the community experience that the natural law principles are synthetic judgments a priori, and *metaphysically* to have expounded the intrinsic relation of the rule to the object by our investigation into the law-establishing objective "existential ends."

11 *Can Natural Law be Proved? Is It Merely a Phenomenon of Evolution?* (The problems of evidence and evolution in natural law theory.)

In this chapter we are concerned with "natural law as a reality." Thus, we have dealt with the questions concerning the character of its reality and of the apprehension of it. But what if its reality is called into question completely? Is it possible to prove the existence of a natural law proper to man and hence independent of time, or is the origin of all law to be explained as a phenomenon of mankind's evolution from animal ancestry? To *prove* natural law *three possibilities* exist: the metaphysical-theological; the empirical-historical; the inductive-ontological. The first, which goes back to the "eternal law," is the one used almost exclusively for a very long time by traditional natural law theory. The second method of proof, which purports to show that the same moral and jural consciousness is to be found, in its essential features, among all mankind known to us, has been attempted first in recent times; a sketch of such a proof will be undertaken in the following pages. Obviously, its probative force can extend only to that portion of mankind known to us, that is, to a period of ten thousand years at the most.

We know today, however, that the age of mankind on earth covers some half a million years. Since, on the other hand, we know of extraordinarily low developments of jural consciousness and jural forms among primitives, the evolutionists and historicists will seek to find arguments for the view that the whole realm of intellect, of morals, of law, and of values is to be explained simply as a product of evolution in the transition from animal to human existence. Therefore, we have tried to work out a third line of argument, the inductive-ontological, which makes it possible to refer back to the earliest period of man's emergence, to his conduct and the jural principles underlying it, with the one *presupposition* that he is recognizable as homo sapiens and hence as a being capable of culture. The clue for recognizing the beginnings of a culture distinguishing the human status from animal status is the use of tools, and especially fire. This proves the knowledge of the principle of causality, and hence the presence of man, who strives in the community urged on him by his nature to extend his sphere of life in order to satisfy the needs peculiar to himself as a rational creature. *Our presupposition* is justified because no representative of evolutionism would assume that jural consciousness developed before the knowledge and application of causal connections had appeared and had made possible the manufacture of tools.

An inductive-ontological proof

The last-named line of argument, which we have mentioned, proves natural law to be the order of human existence; it argues on inductive ontological grounds from the nature of man as a family being. Our procedure requires support principally in two respects. To begin with, however, we must recall what has been said in this chapter about natural jural law (*ius*) and earlier (Chap. 3) about natural moral law in general (*lex*). The basic idea is the *interdependence* of man's *experience* in the life of the primal social order of the family, urged upon him by his physical and spiritual nature, and his developing *insight* into the basic jural principles. The separate steps of our procedure are as follows. Man is by nature a *family being,* his nature and its law operate in the family community in order to bring about mutual love and respect among its members and an order of existence which guarantees an integrated human existence. Thus, the development of his rational nature and its faculty to grasp simple juridical principles proceeds in the *interaction of cognitive and instinctive dispositions.* These principles are lived first of all, and therefore are, from the outset, *determinate in content;* then, their *general* truth and *absolute* validity is apprehended, and their specific character which relates to *rights* and *duties* understood. This includes the experiencing and understanding of the principles that are valid for conduct between individuals and also for the good of the community as such.

Because cognitive and instinctive apparatus interact inseparably, the principles of jural order are apprehended from the beginning in their relationship to the order of being, that is, they are related to man's being as it is bound to the community, and to the fact that all its members strive after the specific well-being of human nature (the desire for happiness). Hence, from the beginning, the simple *insight into being* is bound up with the simple *insight into principles;* and from the beginning there grows the capacity to see the legal world in its inner relationship with the order of being. Thus, natural law is evidenced ontologically by the nature of man with its striving after integrated human existence, which is to be achieved through life in the community. From the interaction of this basic factor of reason and the gradually widening experience in circumstances which change under the influence of cultural motive forces in society, new insight into jural duties and claims emerges, with which the *evolution of legal consciousness and legal order* is linked. In brief: The nature of man, with its instinctive and cognitive apparatus, tends, by means of the family community, toward a life lived according to the natural law order and according to the appropriate juridical insight, on account of the natural love and respect of the members for one another and of their common bond of care for the good of the community as such.

If our basic idea regarding moral natural law and jural natural law (cf. Chap. 3 and this chapter) is correct, it leads to a conclusion of great significance: The *fundamental principles and values* belonging to natural law (only these, not, for example, the value of personality, the democratic rights; cf. Chaps. 39, 51) are, because they are bound up with the nature of man as a family being and hence native to the most elementary community order, *universal to mankind and independent of history.* Their origin is neither to be ascribed to evolution from a pre-human status nor is the present-day pattern of values read into human nature. Those basic principles of law and value are rooted invariably and everywhere in man's mode of existence as a family being and hence in his nature and in man's natural law.

As already stated, *our proof of natural law actuality requires foundation on two sides.* It must be shown, (1) that the perceptions of the principles governing the order of the family community, which are conveyed to man through this order, relate to principles of a *legal* and not merely of a *moral* nature; and (2) that the family community forms the situation fundamental for integrated human existence in the sense we have adopted.

1. The question is one of perceptions relating to *legal* obligations, claims, and competencies of a personal as well as of a social character. *All elements of the nature of law are to be found in the family's order of existence.* Especially do we find the regulated and secured order in the service of the good of the community as a whole and of the good of its members individually. Indeed, an order regulating and securing the *suum cuique,* which lies in the essence of law, is the order of the family community. It not only checks selfish antisocial impulses (the specific purpose of law), but also it allots the duties which are indispensable for the maintenance and prosperity of the whole (the common weal as the purpose of law). This order of *suum cuique* is not least an order of Mine and Thine (in the sense of a right to property in objects of personal use) induced by the instinct of ownership proper to human nature, which makes itself known in earliest childhood. Such property rights can be demonstrated in the primitive family in which common property is prevalent; this emerges from the work of *Fritz Kern,* not only in respect to "consumer goods" such as articles of clothing, adults' ornaments and children's toys, but also in respect to "producer goods," such as hunting gear, although these may serve to provide food for the community. The order of *suum cuique* and of legal obligations is also recognized in the mutual relations of the members of the family community. Thus, wrong (what is unjust, not only what is morally bad) is recognized in the defamation of character, in calumny, in dishonesty with regard to one's given word, in theft, and in fraud. We need only recollect how early a child recognizes right and wrong as such if it is unjustly punished, and recognizes the twofold wrong if the punishment is the result of libel by a brother or sister; he knows with full certainty that a wrong is done to him, and not just that an

offense is committed against moral precepts [52] (As to *Fritz Kern,* cf. below.)

The apprehension of an order that is indispensable to society is accompanied by the apprehension of the indispensability of the ordering power and of its right to command in the service of peace and of the good of the community, to guarantee the preservation of the established order by threatening punishment, and, when order is violated, to exercise the penal power. Finally, the ultimate basis of obligation of the order of the community and hence of law is recognized also; it is revealed by the moral law of conscience, since the conscience nowhere else speaks as clearly as in the family community, which is a "source of metaphysical revelation," as *Spranger* calls it.[53] We do not maintain of course that the apprehension of the elementary principles of law, which is gained through life in the family community, provides a methodologically ascertained conception of law (which not even jurisprudence itself possesses), but we do say that jural rights and duties are recognized as such as distinct from purely moral duties.

2. Secondly, our inductive-ontological proof of natural law requires empirical-scientific support insofar as it must be shown that man is *wholly and entirely a family being, and this first and foremost and in an altogether more elementary sense than the sense in which he is an individual being or a political being.* In this, one's gaze turns not from the family to "society" ("the family as the cell of society"), but in the opposite direction, from the family to the "individual" and to the dependence of an integral human existence on the family. Man was regarded too exclusively as a *political* animal (*zoon politikon*) by the ancient schools of social philosophy and is still regarded quite exclusively as such by the naturalistic collectivistic schools of today. On the other hand, anthropologists of the rationalistic individualist school and, following in their footsteps, the last generation of sociologists have regarded man solely as an *individual.* We need only recall what is said or rather left unsaid about the family by such celebrated authors as *Max Weber, L. von Wiese, F. Oppenheimer, K. Mannheim, H. Freyer* (cf. Chap. 17). In fact, above all man is a family being; through the family he receives the mental and physical equipment for an integral human existence. This is, I think, confirmed by recent findings of *empirical anthropology,* and particularly in the fields of biology, psychology, cultural anthropology, and cultural history. What they say about man as a family being appears so obvious, if one sees it in context, that our efforts may appear superfluous. It is indeed quite remarkable that so primal a fact of human existence and its bearing on social science could have remained to such a large extent concealed from the attention of sociologists of such caliber. Because for natural law theory everything depends on the concept of the nature of man, we must speak of his nature as a family being at least to the extent of referring to the main facts and findings which today belong to the stock-in-trade of the empirical sciences.

What has *biology* to say about man as a family being? Differences between

[52] The following is, I think, a convincing example of insight into right and wrong in the young child: A child notices a red star in the sky among all the others and asks its mother what it is; Mars, is the reply. The child asks how we can know its name when it is so far away. She replies that it is we who have given it that name. On the other hand, the child will not ask how we can know that right is called right and wrong wrong, but knows that each is determined in itself as such.

[53] Cf. E. Spranger, "Zur Frage der Erneuerung des Naturrechts," in *Universitas,* IV, 1948, p. 419.

human and animal family life have often enough been pointed out since ancient times, particularly the fact that man, at a much later age than animals, reaches maturity in his physical and mental disposition, which enables him to maintain self-preservation in his environment and to procure the necessities of life. But modern biology has substantially more to say. Let us consider the work of Professor *Adolf Portmann,* the well-known Swiss zoologist. We are not so much concerned with his establishment of the fact that the essential processes in the development of man's physical nature (attitude and movement) occur in the period after his birth, whereas in the most highly developed animal (the anthropoid ape) no essentially new features appear. Of much greater importance for our present purpose are his conclusions as a biologist regarding the psychical and cultural aspects of human nature as distinct from those of the animals. He shows that the child's first attempts at speech are something essentially different from animal sounds. The animal sound is only an expression of inner conditions, whereas in the first stirrings of the power of speech in the child one can recognize an understanding of the relationships of meaning in external processes; with regard to this, the child's recognition of analogous situations in his solving of problems and his progression from subjective to objective is especially important.[54] *Portmann* further points out that man is distinguished from the animal by his dependence on tradition. Each individual animal, he says, even the most highly developed, finds itself at the same starting point for its development. With man it is quite different: "Man appears in a series of generations which hand on from one to another the result of their work and for which, accordingly, with each generation there arises an entirely new situation as starting point; and yet this situation is not influenced by any hereditary change in man and does not itself have any such hereditary change as a consequence." [55]

Today, the family is also seen by empirical *sociology* as the vehicle and imparter of tradition. This is emphasized by *Portmann.* Characteristically, the empirical American sociology, since it is closer to reality, succeeded in establishing this fact before European sociology, which is largely theoretical and systematic in method. Typical of American thinking is the handbook of sociology by *Ogburn* and *Nimkoff* (these two authors represent a naturalistic evolutionist point of view). According to these authors, the family is the point of transmission of culture as a form of social life and folk-custom, with their proper modes of conduct and value-beliefs; in many fields of research, they say, findings converge on the family as the principal social influence in the life of the individual. As distinct from other forms of social organization (e.g., the United Nations), the institution of the family rests neither originally nor in its more developed organizational forms on deliberate planning, but rather on the fact that there are certain basic human needs, like that of food, procreation, and the training of the young.[56] According to both authors, the roots of law are to be

[54] Cf. A. Portmann, *Biologische Elemente zu einer Lehre vom Menschen* (Basel), 1944, pp. 33 ff., 45 f., 50, 75 ff. The opposite theory of the origin of language is in Arnold Gehlen, Ernst Cassirer, Julian Huxley; cf. G. Kraft, *Der Urmensch als Schöpfer: Die geistige Welt des Eiszeitmenschen,* 2nd ed., 1948, pp. 216–29; cf. also Messner, *Kulturethik,* pp. 353 ff.

[55] Portmann, *op. cit.,* pp. 16 ff., 60–64; cf. also Portmann, *Natur und Kultur im Sozialleben,* 1946.

[56] Cf. W. F. Ogburn and M. F. Nimkoff, *A Handbook of Sociology* (London), 1947, pp. 7 f., 26, 34, 120, 364 f., 368 f.

sought in the family and in the family group, that is, in usages that are governed by perception of what is required for the peace and good of society, whereas later the state is organized to guarantee customs. Such statements could not be regarded as self-evident at the turn of the century; the authors show this by their frequent reference to *William G. Sumner* and his book *Folkways,* which appeared in 1906. In contrast with this, the sociologists mentioned in the beginning of this section see in marriage an institution for the regulation of sexual relationships and for the organzation of propagation, namely the biological aspect, while surprisingly neglecting the spiritual and cultural aspect as revealed in tradition and folk-custom, the last aspect being hardly mentioned. *R. M. MacIver,* the well-known American sociologist, places the family right in the center of his political sociology. According to him, the regulation of sexual relationships is not the origin of the family, as was commonly believed, it is "the nature of the family" which necessitates the regulation of the sexual relationship. Indeed, he says, the child "makes" the first coherent society; modern social psychology and psycho-analysis show how deep in the family community the whole later personality is formed. In the family community the child learns what is right or wrong; and, he declares, it is easy to show that the family is a microcosm of political life for the child.[57]

Today, *cultural anthropology,* one of the youngest experimental sciences, is completely at variance with rationalistic individualist thought in stressing the entire social nature of culture. Culture is basically a form of life and a "style of life" (*Erich Rothacker*) through which man receives experiences and knowledge in the mastery of his environment and in the shaping of life; especially, however, he acquires beliefs about truth and value, i.e. traditional ones, which he never fully outgrows.[58] As *T. S. Eliot* points out in his study on the idea of culture (in opposition to *Mannheim*), the family community hands this tradition on with the value-beliefs and modes of conduct which it involves.[59] Lastly, the analytical psychology of the individual and collective unconscious unwillingly, perhaps, or even "unconsciously," notwithstanding its otherwise hypothetical character, brings into great prominence the fact that man's spiritual nature is formed fundamentally by the family: thus, *Freud's* psychology of the "individual" unconscious with its theory of the persistence of parental value-beliefs from earliest childhood throughout life (the "superego"), and equally *Jung's* psychology of the "collective" unconscious with its theory of the archetypes, primordial images handed on by the family community from generation to generation in earliest childhood, namely sets of mental attitudes in the ways of thinking and behaving as an elementary part of tradition.

Legal history informs us no less clearly about developments which have their origin in the legal consciousness formed in the family community and the greater family group. It reveals the fact, which *H. S. Maine* upheld in his famous controversy with *J. Austin* and with his positivist conception of law, and to which the latter had no real answer, that before sovereignty and without it legal order existed in the form of customary law,[60] which arises from the

[57] Cf. R. M. MacIver, *The Web of Government* (U.S.A.), 1948, pp. 28 ff.

[58] Cf. E. Rothacker, *Probleme der Kulturanthropologie,* 1948, pp. 191 ff. On culture as a form of life cf. Messner, *Kulturethik,* pp. 345–95.

[59] Cf. T. S. Eliot, *Notes toward the Definition of Culture,* 1948, pp. 43 f.

[60] Cf. H. S. Maine, *Early History of Institutions,* 1875, lects. 12, 13.

family and the greater family group; this bears out clearly our conception of the position of the family as the original soil of the natural law order of man's social existence. The fact that customary law is the prelude to all legal development and was in antiquity and in the Middle Ages the actually predominant law has been very convincingly demonstrated by *Eugen Ehrlich*. It would be difficult to dispute his contention that the famed works of law of early times, such as those of *Hammurabi, Zarathustra, Lycurgus,* and the Twelve Tables, contained only customary law.[61] Similarly, even *William Seagle,* in spite of his evolutionist theory of law, feels impelled to say that, although the difficulties which customary law offers to jurists are great, primitive law is "customary law" par excellence, and that when a community recognizes that from certain acts of its members spring definite claims, legal obligations exist, although no organized coercive power is available to enforce them.[62]

Another empirical science, the science of the *early history of mankind,* has quite essential things to say about man as a family being. It confirms all that we have quoted from the other empirical sciences. In his thorough exposition, *Fritz Kern* states: "The small family is the most solid association provided by nature. If we meet it in the first Hunting Period still without competition we are justified in seeing in it a primal condition and in assigning this to the protoliticum"; "The family is the naturally firmest core of all group formation"; "The children are the chiefest joy of adults, their upbringing is the unbroken chief instinct of all family cares"; "The right of the child to love and to care," as the center of gravity of marriage, lies not in the relationship of the spouses but in the family. In the training of the young personality "close family life and harsh living conditions work favorably together." "The importance of one's good name soon becomes evident; among life-long acquaintances one feels the steady accompaniment of one's good name to be a precious possession." "The *property* (*Kern's* italics) of the group on the soil is the first established law of the hunting culture"; "the protection of public property, i.e., the values of the hunting area against unauthorized persons, is the principal object of primal international law"; "from the most intimate and strongest group, the family, the warmth of mutual responsibility in the community radiates to all others." In his concluding chapter ("Lived Natural Law") *Kern* points to a circumstance of great importance for the growth of the early natural law order and for the corresponding recognition of "human rights as demanded by freedom": the tribe which grows out of the family lacks the requisite conditions for the emergence of despotism, for the claims of the individual are slight. As a member of the tribe, each is born with the right to use earth, air, water, and fire; each has enough property and opportunity to work. Landed property is not private; private property is only for the minimum needs of each person and therefore is not accumulated. *Kern* does not hesitate to describe this earliest culture, wholly bound up by the family, as "by far the most stable of all cultures." Professor *Hermann Trimborn,* who wrote a preface to *Kern's* book after the latter's death, sees in the myth of the golden age, "by contrast with an age which believes in progress and ascribes everything repellent and offensive to a 'primitive period,'" "the higher degree in which a natural law flowing from man's 'human'

[61] Cf. E. Ehrlich, *Freie Rechtsfindung und freie Rechtswissenschaft,* 1903, p. 15.
[62] Cf. W. Seagle, *The Quest for Law,* 1941, pp. 11 f.

nature has been realized in a primitive period still within the reach of history."[63]

The empirical sciences of man in their most recent development, as we have shown, admit of no doubt with regard to the soundness of our inductive-ontological foundation for natural law: that man is first and foremost a family being; that within the family community men are impelled by their natural impulses to love, respect, and care for one another as well as by their natural impulses to strive for their own good and the good of the whole to establish an order of the family community in which they experience natural law as the order of existence, acquire the knowledge of the relative juridical principles, and finally recognize their immediately and intrinsically evident claim to validity.

The empirical-historical proof of natural law

The empirical-historical method shows natural law to be a universal reality, concluding from this that it is a reality proper to man's nature. The argument points out that all peoples and races known to us possess insight into the elementary natural law principles. This argument was first put forward comprehensively by *Cathrein* at the beginning of the century in his large three-volume work on the uniformity of man's moral consciousness. He makes use of the method of *comparative ethics* on the basis of facts then known to ethnology. At the same time, *L. T. Hobhouse,* the outstanding scholar in the sphere of comparative ethics, without aiming to prove any specific theory, similarly established the fact of the uniformity of moral consciousness.[64] Yet, in 1910, *L. Lévy-Brühl* still wanted to dispute the fact of man's universal similar rational equipment, to ascribe to primitives only a "prelogical" mode of thinking, and to deny them the prerequisites of logical thought (knowledge of the principle of contradiction, the principle of causality).[65] The uniformity of man's natural mental equipment was also denied by ethnologists from the legal and moral aspects, on the ground of the variety of moralities among primitive peoples. Today, this line of thought is taken by the school of *legal historicism* (cf. Chap. 40 and the end of this chapter), which seeks to explain all culture, and hence all law, as the outcome of a process of evolution from precultural beginnings. Thus, human nature is divested of essential constancy and of the fundamental moral-

[63] F. Kern, *Der Beginn der Weltgeschichte,* with Introduction by H. Trimborn, 1953, pp. 61, 73, 157 ff., 186, 196. On the whole question, cf. Fritz Valjavec, editor, *Historia Mundi,* Vol. I, *Frühe Geschichte der Menschheit,* 1952.

[64] Cf. V. Cathrein, *Die Einheit des sittlichen Bewußtseins der Menschheit,* 3 vols., 1910; L. T. Hobhouse, *Morals in Evolution,* 1st ed., 1906, 4th ed., 1951, with Introduction by Morris Ginsberg, where the latter says (p. 28) that the comparative study of ethics in its earlier stages left the student with a bewildering sense of the diversity of moral judgments, but now gives him a picture of a fundamental and far-reaching uniformity; throughout history and all over the world a recurrence of the common features of ordinary morality is an established fact. Ginsberg, *Essays in Sociology and Social Philosophy,* Vol. I, *On the Diversity of Morals,* 1956 (Vol. II, *Reason and Unreason in Society,* 1956), Introduction, p. vii, points out that, according to his knowledge of the relevant facts, the moral cannot be elicited or constructed from the nonmoral, and that sociology or psychology can never take the place of ethics. We are bound to assume primary valuations which are not further reducible. On the other hand, sociologist Ginsberg, quite rightly, is very decided regarding the significance for ethics of sociological and psychological facts, saying that an adequate treatment of morality involves taking into account moral principles as well as the relevant psychological and sociological facts.

[65] Cf. Lucien Lévy-Brühl, *Les fonctions mentales dans les sociétés inférieures,* 1910.

legal principles of suprahistorical, universal, and absolute validity. *Lévy-Brühl* himself later withdrew the views mentioned; [66] among ethnologists of today, one can observe a return to the assumption of the uniformity of the most general basic logical and moral-legal insight among men known to us historically.[67] Indeed, *Fritz Kern* says about primitives known to us: "Today, only ignorance or insincerity can refuse to acknowledge the humanity of law in the nomad culture"; "The (human) natural law actually corresponds to the positive law of primitive times." [68]

Metaphysical-theological proof of natural law

This line of argument makes use of *natural theology.* It attributes the apprehension of the general moral-legal principles (values) to the *lex aeterna,* to the mind and will of God. Of course the simple appeal to *lex aeterna* is no evidence, as is sometimes assumed, of the reality of natural law. To obtain a real proof, a wide field of epistemological, metaphysical, and theological questions must be covered.

One may note, for example, how thoroughly *Suárez,* building upon the work of his predecessors from *Augustine* onwards, devotes four long chapters to *lex aeterna,* dealing particularly with the question how man attains to the knowledge of the eternal law and its content. It might surprise many to know that *Suárez,* along with the whole preceding tradition, teaches that "the eternal law is known to men not in itself but only in other laws and through them," that is, only from its effects (since everything that man comes to know naturally from God he can learn only in this way). Hence, he names as the principal means of getting to know the eternal law, "participation in it (through the medium of the law of nature), and in consequence thereof, just laws, temporal laws, and positive law, since, as created causes point to the First Cause and created things to the Creator, temporal laws, as participation in the eternal law, indicate the Source from which they flow." He continues: "Yet, not all men attain this knowledge, because not all are capable of inferring the cause from the effect"; hence, they lack the conceptual awareness of the eternal law, even though they all, by virtue of their rational nature, necessarily participate directly in the eternal law, *quia nemo utens ratione est, qui non iudicet aliquo modo, honestum esse sequendum et turpe vitandum;* one should note the *aliquo modo,* which indicates how cautiously classical scholasticism proceeded in this whole question. Immediately following this, in order to be precise he defines again: Not all men reach the conscious conceptual insight into the eternal law, but only an unconscious participation by means of natural law; yet some (*aliqui*) reach conceptual knowledge of it by means of natural reasoning or, in a perfect manner, through revelation: "Therefore, I said that to some the knowledge of the eternal law comes only in inferior laws, and among them to some again not only in them but also through them"; one should note the gradations of knowledge of fact and content by means of "in" and "through," and likewise the distinction between natural reason and supernatural revelation.[69]

[66] Cf. Maurice Leenhardt, editor, *Carnets de Lévy-Brühl,* 1949, p. 182.

[67] Cf. Wilhelm Koppers, *Der Urmensch und sein Weltbild,* 1949, and the literature mentioned therein; cf. also Clyde Kluckhohn, *Mirror for Man,* 1950, pp. 28, 249.

[68] F. Kern, *Der Beginn der Weltgeschichte,* 1953, p. 249; *Geschichte und Entwicklung,* 1952.

[69] Cf. Suárez, *De legibus,* lib. II, cc. I–IV, esp. c. IV, 9.

It is of great interest to scientific ethics that *Augustine,* from whom medieval natural law theory took over the idea of the eternal law, seeks in different ways to prove its existence by the methods of natural reasoning (as distinct from revelation), and also that he endeavors to base his proof much more directly upon experience than has been the more recent practice. Thus, *Augustine* avoids the very involved metaphysical problems which are bound up with natural theology (which *Suárez* too only partially discusses). *Augustine's* methods, which will certainly surprise many, are as follows. According to human law, he says, outwardly similar acts are quite differently judged, so that killing is at one time a crime, at another time permitted as punishment for crime, or again commanded as a duty for soldiers. We find also that quite opposed forms of conduct can be equally right and just, so that a nation conscious of responsibility is entitled to self-government or a nation lacking in responsibility is deprived of self-government by conscientious men. From such variation in "temporal" law, which is just in either case, says *Augustine,* one must conclude that an invariable eternal law exists which is the supreme guiding principle, which in any case must be followed, and in harmony with which temporal law is justly decreed and also justly altered.[70] The likeness of the method chosen by *Augustine* to demonstrate the eternal law with the proof of the existence of God from the contingency of created beings is unmistakable.

Augustine also offers a proof by analogy. We find in the realm of law, he says, that the judge has not to judge the "temporal" law when once it has been laid down by the lawgiver, but only to judge in accordance with it. The good and wise lawgiver himself, however, takes counsel with a law which man has only to recognize, and not to judge (*fas est cognoscere, judicare nefas est*), the "eternal law." *Augustine* deals with this question in discussing the manner in which the mind ascends from the realm of appearances to the realm of suprasensory realities and thus to the existence of God. He discusses first the idea that the mind judges beauty in nature and in the work of man, and thereby distinguishes beautiful and less beautiful, but can only do this because "above man's thought stands the law which we designate as truth," namely, "the immutable truth" which can only be the eternal wisdom of God. Likewise, the human mind finds a standard in the sphere of law: the immutable eternal law which can be only the law of the divine wisdom and of the divine will.[71]

Still another kind of proof by analogy, starting from universal immediate experience, is taken up by *Augustine* with his reference to our knowledge of the "absolutely certain and unchangeable law" of the world of numbers; in the same way man knows also of the idea of "wisdom," in which the moral world and its law are revealed and whose rules are as true and immutable and common to all as the rules of numbers; through wisdom we apprehend "truth itself," "that truth in which the supreme good is seen and grasped." [72] *Augustine* finally undertakes the proof from the universal inner experience of mankind concerning the knowledge of one definite principle of natural law: "In the mind of every man who is endowed with freedom there is a law, written by nature in the heart;

[70] Cf. St. Augustine, *De lib. arb.*, I, cc. V, VI, par. 11–15.

[71] Cf. St. Augustine, *De vera religione,* cc. 29–31.

[72] St. Augustine, *De lib. arb.*, II, cc. VIII–XIV, pars. 20, 37.

[73] St. Augustine, *Epist. 157,* 15. Concerning Augustine's inquiries on the possibility of philosophical knowledge of the eternal law, Alois Schubert, *Augustins*

it warns him not to do to another what he is unwilling to suffer himself" [73] (cf. note 10).

In any case, from *Augustine's* and *Suárez'* discussions of the eternal law it can be seen that the proof of natural law from the eternal law, particularly in view of present-day mentality, poses a number of epistemological, metaphysical, and theological questions. From the *epistemological* point of view, the question must be answered, how we reach the knowledge of the eternal law, its existence, and its content. From the *metaphysical* point of view, today we must deal with the question of the existence and nature of God, since in contrast with the Middle Ages neither is the existence of God universally believed in nor is the idea of God uniform. *Theologically,* from the point of view of both natural theology and revelation, it is necessary to elucidate the manner and form of our knowledge of the eternal law and its operation in man, because appeal is made to the biblical doctrine of man (concerning Protestant theology, cf. Chaps. 11–12) to call into question the law of nature in general and hence the possibility of the eternal law operating by means of human nature as such. This strict procedure, which is so thoroughly consolidated on all sides, has not been undertaken in the more recent literature of traditional natural law ethics. Often there is only the appeal to the "eternal law," with references to the teaching of *Augustine* and medieval scholasticism. I do not think it the function of this book to follow out the line of argument which would put the reasoning from *lex aeterna* on a philosophically sound foundation, but I hope that the comprehensive treatment devoted to the problems associated with natural law in its general and jural aspects, from the beginning of this book until now, may have advanced one or two suggestions for such a metaphysical-theological argument.

The problem of evolution in natural law theory

The period of human history known to us, and on which we must rely for evidence in support of the uniformity of the moral-legal consciousness of mankind, does not comprise much more than the last five thousand years. On the other hand, we know today, as mentioned previously, that the prehistorical development of mankind, about which there is no documentary information, comprises some half a million years. *Evolutionist anthropology* and *generalizing historicism* see in this fact new opportunities for establishing their hypothesis that man, his nature, his intellect, his moral and jural mental apparatus, and his legal customs and legal systems are exclusively the results of a progressive evolution of man from a prehuman animal condition. But the student whose thinking conforms with *strict scientific requirements* will find himself disillusioned when looking for evidence in the ethical and juristic sphere. What has been preserved for us from prehistoric times conveys nothing with regard to moral and legal views and forms of conduct. Yet, we can learn a sufficient amount to show the fully human nature of early men from the caves which they left behind serving religious purposes, decorated with drawings, and from their graves which point to beliefs of a religious kind and relate to survival after death,

Lex Aeterna—Lehre nach Inhalt und Quellen, 1924, an instructive work on the history of ideas, mentions nothing, but concerns himself solely with Augustine's doctrine on the communication of the eternal law to human reason by God (impression, illumination, irradiation).

namely, beliefs [74] which much more readily suggest the assumption of moral and juridical ideas than the opposite (concerning legal historicism, cf. Chap. 40).

Because *legal historicism* seeks support for its hypothesis in evolutionist anthropology, this must be discussed. Outstanding among such theories is *Arnold Gehlen's biological theory of man.* Owing to the lack of an environment naturally adapted to man, he is constructed in order to transform and to subdue nature, and hence also in order to be capable of an articulate experience of the world: "In order to be capable of existence," man must, constantly urged by his "surplus force of drives," by his constraint towards self-leadership, and by his concern for the future, make effective his nature by means of self-activity. This comes about according to the "relief principle," the proof of which *Gehlen* describes as the chief object of his theory: "Man must, by his own means and by his own activity, relieve himself, that is to say, convert the defective conditions of his existence into opportunities of securing his existence"; the human consciousness is to be understood as a "phase of the action" itself, so that "from there one has a direct approach to the answering of the questions: Why speech; why imagination; why inner life; why memory?" Speech expressions are primarily movements like any other, arising from immediate motor or sonomotor contact with things. "Self-intentional" images are products of speech, and reflective thought is also primarily the "intention" induced by the sound of speech toward something.[75] *Gehlen*'s theory undoubtedly contains very important observations concerning the biological equipment of human nature regarding its destiny as rational being. Yet, it is unable to solve the question of conscious experience (the epistemological problem) by its methods, and still less that of self-conscious (reflective) thought with the possibility of generalizing (a further epistemological basic problem); rather, the theory reads into the observed facts what has already been established with regard to man's capacity by reason of his special mental apparatus. Besides, *Gehlen*'s theory has to answer the question how nature brings about a defective being of the special kind assumed by him (which conflicts with basic assumptions of the theory of evolution), and also, how the hypothesis that this defective being is "built" for a definite activity is justified. The inference from man's faulty biological nature, the "defective conditions of his existence," seems to us to be principally this: he is "built" (*Gehlen*) for social completion and, as we showed, he is wholly and entirely "built" for the family community, "in order to be capable of existence," in the sense of the fully integrated human as distinct from all animal being. The fact that this fundamental significance of the family community and, for that matter, of the social factor is altogether missed in *Gehlen*'s theory of human existence seems one of the strongest objections against his anthropology.

The idea of the *theory of evolution* itself is much more vigorous. We follow *Julian Huxley,* one of its foremost interpreters. The evolutionists regard man's consciousness as a product of evolution, the progress man makes in gaining control over his environment. Genuine cultural development has taken place

[74] On connections of the latter kind Alfred Weber has something to say in *Kulturgeschichte als Kultursoziologie,* 1951, p. 30; for an appreciation of the findings in question cf. Johannes Maringer, *Vorgeschichtliche Religion: Religionen im Steinzeitlichen Europa,* 1956.

[75] Cf. A. Gehlen, *Der Mensch, seine Natur und seine Stellung in der Welt,* 4th ed., 1950, pp. 38 f., 91 f., 140, 208, 284 ff., 333 f. Cf. the more detailed discussion of Gehlen's theory in Messner, *Kulturethik,* pp. 353 f., 581 f.

only after four-fifths of the time has elapsed since the emergence of homo sapiens. This development took place through the process of "divergent" adaptations to environmental conditions (climate, etc.) and resulted in the formation of various races. At the same time, this development also took place through a process of "converging" mutual biological and psychological adaptation of races, and of the understanding and interchange of their cultures. This theory (and *Gehlen*'s) has not been able to explain the following facts: all the various human groups in the most varied environments have developed fundamentally the same needs as cultural driving forces; all have come to the same basic forms of common life; all have developed "symbols" for the appropriate description of reality and convictions regarding truth and value of no biological (!) value; all can communicate on these matters with the aid of speech. It is indeed, *Huxley* admits, a great disappointment for the evolutionists that, in spite of all our understanding of the process of evolution and the work that has been done on developing the animal intelligence, it has not been possible to teach them to speak in the true sense.[76] *Portmann,* a zoologist, draws attention to one feature in the nature of man which is of great significance in the present connection: the handing on of tradition is not influenced by any inherited change in man and does not result in any such change.[77] In other words, *the mode of functioning of human nature is not a product of evolution;* it remains constant in its basic features, which justifies us to conclude scientifically that it has *always been impelled toward life in the order of existence appropriate to human nature.* Hence, at the same time, it has been impelled toward the apprehension of the moral and jural principles which determine this order; this has been true from the beginning, through all generations of human development, and primarily by means of the *family community.*

We must refer finally to an exclusively historical interpretation of natural law according to which natural law is a European phenomenon, like Roman Law. Legal history and comparative law, *Paul Koschaker* says, may find what is common to private law systems, namely, "typical forms and juristic thinking," "which today dominate the whole civilized world and all more or less have experienced the influence of Roman Law or have had to come to terms with it." He has to defend his position against a Romanist colleague who thinks that inquiries of this kind must lead to natural law. This objection, says *Koschaker,* has in mind an absolute natural law. He continues: "There is no question, however, of an absolute natural law. There is a relative natural law, however, and it is such a relative, that is, European natural law, that we are dealing with here. This natural law is not derived speculatively from the mind but, on strict historical grounds, from the comparison of those private law systems which have contributed to the European legal structure and hence to that of the whole civilized world. Roman Law is at the head of those systems and forms the link between them; it is a natural law which gathers up the legal experiences of all the civilized peoples who have helped to build Europe." As so often happens, *Koschaker* equates two things which should be sharply distinguished: the

[76] Cf. J. Huxley, *Evolution in Action,* 1953, pp. 87, 100, 104, 109, 137. Cf. also the more detailed criticism of Huxley's theory in Messner, *Kulturethik,* pp. 98 f., 447 f., 583 f.

[77] Cf. A. Portmann, *Biologische Fragmente zu einer Lehre vom Menschen* (Basel), 1944, pp. 16 ff.; also A. Portmann, "Die werdende Menschheit," in *Frühe Menschheit, Historia Mundi, Vol. I* (cf. note 54).

reality of natural law and the *theory of natural law*. Even if this error could not be gathered from his whole presentation, it would be obvious from the fact that, for him, natural law, like the German pandects, is "professors' law": In fact, natural law theory is a science, and the reality of natural law is by no means synonymous with it. From various points of view, this reality can be the object of scientific investigation. The fact that ancient and medieval natural law theory bears a largely European stamp has been stressed in previous chapters. It is no less a fact, however, that this theory has been able to reach the foundation of natural law reality proper to man's nature scientifically, by virtue of the scientific spirit of European man. *Koschaker* himself comes close to reality with his statement that natural law "has raised a claim to be effective in every positive law independently of state decree. Thus, natural law, while creating the basis for a critical valuation of existing law, was certainly the driving force for progress and reforms in the legal sphere." To accomplish this, a large role was played by the "professors' law." The decisive factor, however, was natural law reality, which the theory traced out in the jural conscience and in the legal consciousness of peoples which depends upon it. Again *Koschaker* writes: "If natural law was to be effective against any positive law one could expect to find it not merely in Roman and German law. Thus, attention was called to other laws, and natural law became the mother of comparative law." The reality of natural law is thus found through a comparative law science open to reality, especially general natural law with its timeless legal principles. General natural law, as we have shown, expresses itself in the legal consciousness and legal system of particular peoples in various ways, because of historical and social conditions. Therefore, perhaps one can speak with *Koschaker* of "a natural law bound up with territory and nationality"; but if one wishes, like *Koschaker,* to describe this as relative natural law it becomes evident that logically the ascertainment of something "relative" is possible only with the aid of established standards. Only because natural law theory was able to ascertain such standards scientifically in universal human nature could "natural law become the mother of comparative law science." And only this (very seldom recognized!) achievement of natural law theory authorizes the hope nourished by *Koschaker* that the history of law and the comparative study of law "can contribute toward forming elements of a supranational dogmatic body of law, as earlier the dogmatic Romanist embodiment of law did." [78] This would involve a task of the greatest importance for jurisprudence, which would be linked with the others (cf. Chap. 48) set for it by natural law reality. In comparison with all the other forms of legal historicism, the one discussed above leaves the traditional natural law school with the least impression of an unbridgeable gulf. In fact it carries the conviction that the historical legal sense and the historical legal systems of nations will give the unprejudiced eye testimony to the basic idea of natural law theory, namely, that the same human nature with the same fundamental sense of values and the same fundamental impulse toward happiness by value-realization urges toward the order of social existence which makes a fully human life possible: the order which is in conformity with the principles of natural law.

[78] P. Koschaker, *Europa und das Römische Recht,* 2nd ed., 1953, pp. 249, 253 f., 268, 345 f.

48. The Mode of Operation of Natural Law

Man's natural law expresses itself in many forms in the establishment and development of the order of law and justice in social life. The questions involved concern absolute natural law, applied natural law (conscience, custom, positive law, development of law, developing natural law, jurisprudence, natural law ethics), original sin in natural law, *ius gentium,* cognition, and certainty in the realm of natural law.

I *Absolute Natural Law*

Absolute natural law is concerned with the general juridical principles of the moral conscience. They are general in content, having reference to kinds of conduct; and knowledge of them is general, being common to all men. These principles are described as "*absolute*" natural law in order to indicate that, in their validity, they are independent of time and of human will and that the "ought" implied in them constitutes a categorical imperative. Because the knowledge of them is a function of man's moral reason, the natural conscience, they can also be called "original" [1] natural law; and because this knowledge comprises only the general, simple juridical principles which, nevertheless, are fundamental to all further juridical insight, they can also be called "*primary*" or "*elementary*" natural law. The most general principle is *suum cuique,* which is synonymous with the concept, "Avoid injustice"; this is the fundamental principle of the natural moral-jural conscience, which cannot mistake it when the reason is fully developed. Similarly, the principle, "Do not do to others what you do not wish them to do to you," which unmistakably suggests experience, is of a most general nature; known as the "Golden Rule," it has been found among a great number of peoples [2] and is also mentioned in the Gospels.[3] The simple insight into human relationships (apprehension of the "nature of the case") proper to the fully-developed reason is sufficient for recognizing the *suum* in the fundamental interhuman relationships (cf. Chap. 47).

These general principles concern especially the following legal claims

[1] In the early Christian centuries primary (general, absolute) natural law was seen as "original." Cf. the historical study by O. Schilling, *Naturrecht und Staat nach der Lehre der alten Kirche,* 1914, and *Die Staats- und Soziallehre des hl. Thomas v. Aquin,* 2nd ed., 1930, pp. 8 ff., 330 ff.

[2] Cf. the informative work by Hans Reiner, *Die goldene Regel: Die Bedeutung einer sittlichen Grundformel der Menschheit,* in *Zeitschrift für philosophische Forschung,* Vol. III, 1948; cf. also the work by Reiner mentioned in Chap. 11, note 1.

[3] Cf. Matt. 7: 12; Luke 6:31; both give the golden rule in positive form: "As you will that men do unto you, do you also unto them." Matthew also adds "for this is the Law and the prophets."

and duties: respect and obedience toward father and mother; nonviolation of the life (arbitrary killing of an innocent person, or murder, is wrongful) and bodily integrity of fellowmen; nonviolation of the conjugal partnership; nonviolation of the honor and good name of other members of the community; nonviolation of rightfully acquired property; faithfulness to one's pledged word and to concluded agreements; obedience toward the lawful authority in society; the suitability of the punishment to the wrong committed. All of these refer only to the general principles of the natural conscience, and not to legal forms in a developed society.

Among individual peoples the expression of the principles linked with these rights and duties can vary. Western thinking is familiar with the expression given in the Decalogue (Fourth to Tenth Commandments). The knowledge of the general principles in question is always first inculcated along with the rules of conduct which a child is required to observe in the family community. In early society this knowledge is further confirmed and developed by means of the ethos that is operative through custom, juridical consciousness, and legal usage. In the society with statutory law, the lawgiver, as traditional natural law teaching has always emphasized, has the task of rendering the jural principles of the natural conscience clearly understood by making their demands positive law. It is necessary to note, however, that the lawgiver only creates conditions for the apprehension of principles whose substance, once grasped, is immediately evident to the developed reason with regard both to truth and to obligation.

All the principles mentioned above form, according to the traditional doctrine, the *primary* natural law principles or, what is the same, principles of natural justice. They are self-evident, but not without a kind of inferential insight, which will presently be dealt with, depending on simple empirical knowledge of social relationships; when understood, however, these principles are directly evident.

In consequence of what has been said, the clear and certain knowledge of these principles, it must be repeated, is not innate in the mind; only the *faculty* for it is innate. This faculty, like all other bodily and mental faculties, requires training. If training is lacking, the knowledge of some of the principles mentioned may be defective or even wholly wanting in one respect or the other. Thus, the individual, and the lawgiver too, is liable to error. For this reason, traditional natural law teaching at the height of its development was intent on stressing the "*general*" character of the immediately evident principles of law. This character is emphasized from two points of view: insight into universal validity may be defective, for example, because foreigners may be regarded as not protected by the principle "Thou shalt not kill"; and insight into the general validity may be defective insofar as individuals or social groups do not grasp the import of one or the other of these principles. If individuals grow up outside law and order, or if social classes, perhaps in the name of "justice," are to a considerable extent robbed of part of the fruits of social cooperation, they may be misled in their judgment concerning private ownership of the means of production. Even zeal and enthusiasm for truth and goodness can deceive individuals and societies and lead them to stray over the boundaries set by elementary natural law principles; examples of this are the attempts to convert peoples to Christianity by the sword and the refusal of freedom of conscience and freedom of religious practice in the persecution of heretics in all parts of Christendom.

11 *Applied Natural Law*

Applied natural law means the claims of justice issuing from the general principles under existing circumstances.[4] The circumstances can involve, notwithstanding the absolute, the unvarying validity of the general principles, varying legal demands. Since it is dependent on circumstances, this natural law is also described as "*relative,*" and in this way is distinguished from the previously discussed "absolute" natural law. The mode of application of general natural law principles can take only the logical form of inferential judgments. Hence, the question is, to what logical species such a judgment belongs. It consists in a conclusion, the major premise being a general natural law principle, the minor premise a judgment on the nature of the actual circumstances, whereas the conclusion conveys the substance of legal claims and duties implied in the premises. Natural law derived in this fashion is also called "*secondary*" to distinguish it from the directly evident "primary."[5] The

[4] Objections have been raised to the expression "applied natural law," although no convincing reasons have been given. The understanding of the import of natural law under particular circumstances involves an intellectual process in which perception of the general principles and of the special nature of the case work together. This is the procedure of every practical science and it is often described as the "application" of principles to the special facts and requirements of the case. In particular, the expression "applied natural law" can hardly be opposed with the appeal to St. Thomas; for Thomas (*Summa theol.*, IIa IIae, q. 47, aa. 3–4) described the procedure in question as *applicatio rectae rationis ad opus*, which implies knowledge of both principles and facts: "Id quod applicandum est, et id cui applicandum est." The procedure is that of a syllogism with major and minor premises, namely, judgment with regard to principles and judgment with regard to facts. In the choice of this simple expression I have been guided in part by the fact that it is used by such a Thomistic scholar as Gallus A. Manser, *Angewandtes Naturrecht*, 1947, but especially because it brings out the logical nature of the procedure. If one prefers to speak of legal logic or factual logic in the process, of course, there is no objection to either; but it seems necessary to declare what judgments enter into this logical process and what is their logical nature, for a logical process can be completed only in a sequence of judgments.

[5] With this interpretation of "secondary" natural law, which is current in traditional natural law theory, one should not confuse the Protestant conception, which understands by "secondary" natural law that of the "fallen world," and by "primary" natural law only that of the "primordial state." Cf. H. Thielicke, *Theologische Ethik*, Vol. I, 1951, pp. 654 ff.

logical nature of a judicial judgment (the "subsumption" of a particular case under the general rule) is the same. The logical procedure in the natural law judgment must be clearly grasped because the truth and certainty in the apprehension of concrete natural law form a basic epistemological question for scientific inquiry; to this question we shall devote careful attention.

1. In its operation, undoubtedly natural law first comes into direct effect through the *moral conscience.* This makes it possible for man to recognize right and wrong in simple situations (e.g., the injustice of appropriating what belongs to another, if it is so recognized). In other words, as we have tried to show, with the development of the use of reason in early life man acquires not only the perception of the general natural law principles but also the faculty of judging the "nature of the case" in the social relationships of daily life. One of the modes of this way of functioning of the natural legal conscience requires special mention. In most cases man needs no very profound reflection on the right and wrong of conduct that depends on the circumstances in his everyday life. This does not mean that the logical character of the judgment of conscience is any different from that already described, but only that man's judgment becomes practiced through a familiarity resulting from the repetition of similar cases, and he sees "*at once*" what his legal duties are. Because they are based on habit and therefore do not appear to be logical processes, they are thought to be a matter of "feeling" and are often so described. There is no objection to this as long as the insight into right and wrong is not altogether ascribed to feeling, to a "legal sense" or to a "feeling for justice," instead of to reason. "Immediate judgment" does not confine itself to the application of natural law principles; the same is true with regard to the application of the physical laws of nature in daily life, which is fundamental to our behavior (e.g. of the law of gravity in walking or riding a bicycle); such application is accomplished by habit.[6]

2. The next form of applied natural law is the original *customary law.* Habit plays an entirely different role in this from the role it plays in the form previously discussed. For, in the customary law not the individual conscience is in question, but a social phenomenon, namely, the legal usage which prevails in a community. We call this "original" customary law in order to bring out the difference between it and the rules or rights of present-day customary law, which are based on long actual usage. The legal custom we are dealing with here rests directly on the legal consciousness of a community. Following *Augustine* (cf.

[6] St. Thomas, *Summa theol.,* Ia IIae, q. 53, a. 1 (and in many passages) describes this capacity to apply general principles, even in the realm of the sciences, as *habitus conclusionum,* as distinct from *habitus principiorum;* by the latter he understands the apprehension by rational nature of the general ontological, logical, moral, and jural principles.

Chap. 47) we have pointed out the unique significance of customary law as an expression of the legal consciousness and hence as a form of applied natural law. We have followed *Augustine* also in declaring that, in its origin and development, positive law is to be understood primarily as confirmation of the legal order established and sanctioned by the natural juridical conscience and legal custom.

The principles reached through the individual conscience and through social usage form the *secondary* natural law principles or principles of natural justice in terms of traditional natural law doctrine. Error is possible to a much larger extent in this category than in the first.

3. The position of *positive law* as a question of applied natural law has already been discussed (cf. Chap. 43) and will require still further consideration from different aspects (cf. Chap. 10).

4. Applied natural law is further effective as the potent motive force of *legal evolution*. We have devoted close attention to the evolution of law, and also laid stress on the fact that the exercise of authority, which is inseparably bound up with legal order, is always subject to misuse in the interest of sectional groups, the "ruling classes." The injustice which in this way characterizes the actual legal systems has proved to be a powerful impulse toward the development of the legal consciousness; this in turn has become a powerful impulse in legal reform. Therefore, legal development consists of a process of the interaction of these two factors. On both sides, as we have shown, this process is again largely influenced by the cultural development of society in general, including not least the development of its technical, economic, and political culture. Indeed, the necessary conditions for new law-formation can clearly emerge and be recognized only in the course of evolution itself.

Thus, it pertains to the essence of applied natural law that, to a large extent, it be *developing natural law*. There are several reasons for this: first, the implications of natural law demands presuppose perception of the nature of the facts, which, when in full development, can elude judgment of their natural law significance. Secondly, even if these facts were clearly understood, successful new legal enactments presuppose an indispensable development of the legal consciousness (cf. Chap. 49). Thirdly, since vested interests are involved in legal order, there are always conflicting social groups at work in the process of legal evolution, which to a large extent allow the natural law order to come to realization only in a process of development. Fourthly, if in the course of legal evolution the legal order of a society is developed in accordance with the claims of natural law, the result, measured by natural law, is always imperfect and faulty, so that the legal conscience immediately finds itself confronted with further tasks. For all of these reasons the realization of the natural law order is subject to a process of evolution, and the applied natural law integrated into the existing legal system to a considerable extent is the product of evolving natural law and the origin of new evolving natural law.[7]

The forces of evolving natural law largely operate in *social movements* which therefore must be mentioned in this connection. In the name of law and of justice they seek to bring about changes in the existing social and legal order, regarding themselves as champions of new demands of justice and at the same time striving to arouse consciences in order to give real force to these demands. An example of this is the preparing of the way for the social legislation of the 1880's in Germany and Austria as a demand of justice, that is, of the social conscience, by scientific, ecclesiastical, employer and labor circles. Social movements serving the development of law do not need, therefore, to be merely mass movements of the legally "underprivileged," although these can be of great significance at many stages. Examples of social movements acting as forerunners of an advanced jural will and of evolving natural law are the movements to have human rights guaranteed by positive law in all the member states of the United Nations and to establish a legal order in the community of nations which will actually guarantee world peace.

5. Applied natural law also becomes operative by means of legal science, especially by means of *jurisprudence in teaching, in literature, and in research,* and also through the professional *ethics of judges, of lawyers and of administrators.* Naturally, jurisprudence must see its principal object in the system of norms of positive law, although until far into the modern era it found the ultimate principles of its thought in the natural law bound up with the Christian interpretation of human nature. This is true of the great tradition of jurisprudence in the Latin countries and also in England.[8] Throughout Europe far into the nineteenth century,

[7] Among the rare examples in literature in which mention is made of the "developing natural law" deeply rooted in the nature of law, the following may be noted: Gustav Ermecke (Jos. Mausbach), *Katholische Moraltheologie,* Vol. III, 1953, pp. 140 f.; cf. Erich Fechner, "Naturrecht und Existenzphilosophie," in *Archiv für Rechts- und Sozialphilosophie,* Vol XLI, 3, 1955. In contrast with positivism, which is at present again gaining ground in Germany, Fechner sees in the natural law problem "the central problem of legal philosophy." He lays the emphasis on "a natural law with growing content," rejecting a ready-made natural law; by the latter he understands rather a fully formed codification of natural law than what the traditional natural law school understands by absolute natural law (cf. above). In contrast with the existential philosophy, which holds that no order of existence can be known, Fechner himself maintains: "Man *is* under ordering forces over wide areas and is not delivered up to nothing" (*op. cit.,* p. 324); but the precise meaning of this being "under ordering forces" remains an open question with Fechner, even in his *Rechtsphilosophie,* 1956, where the proposition is again stated (p. 263).

[8] Cf. Sir F. Pollock and F. W. Maitland, *History of English Law,* 1911, Vol. I, pp. 132 f.: "But in the twelfth, and even in the thirteenth century . . . English law was administered by the ablest, the best educated men in the realm; not only that, it was administered by the selfsame men who were 'the judges ordinary' of the church's courts. . . . It is by 'popish clergymen' that our English common law is converted from a rude mass of customs into an articulate system; and when the 'popish clergymen,' yielding at length to the pope's commands, no longer sit as the principal justices of the king's court, the creative age of our medieval law is over."

jurisprudence, legislation, and legal practice, as *Hans Thieme* has shown, was strongly influenced by natural law doctrine. The opposition of legal positivism to supreme legal maxims linked with the moral order is a late development, while the modern works of legislation on the Continent, in Austria, Prussia, France and Switzerland, were, as *Thieme* proves, influenced in part by natural law thought produced by Western Christian civilization, a thought carried on in England in the form of case-law: "Thus, in fact, natural law belongs to the remaining general cultural heritage of Europe." It was the legal positivism of the second half of the nineteenth century which first sought to ban the natural law idea from legal science and legal practice.[9] Legal science itself, however, was soon profoundly affected by the consequences of its equating law with the positive law of the state, so that *Walther Schönfeld* writes: "[Modern] positivism, we hope, will return from its secularism and bow to the judgment which has come upon it."[10]

The effects of this positivism, however, are by no means at an end. Nearly all countries are moving in the direction of the legislative omnipotence of the state. In view of the accompanying crisis of "positive-statutory legality," *Carl Schmitt* conjures up the highly menacing image of the development "which set in with the splitting up of law into legality and legitimacy and ended with the complete conversion of historical into revolutionary legitimacy" and has led us into the present "age of motorized law and motorized decrees," into a period "in which legality has become a poisoned weapon with which one party stabs another in the back." At such a time, *Schmitt* continues, "*jurisprudence becomes the last refuge of legal consciousness.*" The fact that respect for the natural law foundations of positive law is in question here, may be seen from the description of the task which according to *Schmitt* devolves on jurisprudence: "In the changing situation we preserve the foundation of a rational humanity, which cannot dispense with the principles of law. These principles also include a recognition of the person, which persists even in battle and rests upon mutual respect; a sense of logic in ideas and institutions; a sense of reciprocity and for a minimum of ordered procedure, a due process of law, without which there is no law"; with the preservation "of *this indestructible nucleus of all law,*" "we fulfill *a task which cannot be taken over by any other form or method of human activity*" (my italics, J.M.).

This task of course does not belong exclusively to jurisprudence; but

[9] Cf. H. Thieme, *Das Naturrecht und die europäische Privatrechtsgeschichte,* 1947, pp. 19–42, 43, 45 ff.; noteworthy is Thieme's reference to Vitoria ("Natürliches Privatrecht und Spätscholastik," in *Zeitschrift der Savigny-Stiftung für Rechtsgeschichte,* 1953, pp. 235, 237, 241), where he points out that Vitoria emphasizes the divine origin of *naturalis ratio,* which forms the basic idea of scholastic natural law theory, reaching the conclusion: "Quare non multo incertior erit definitio, si ex naturalibus procedat, quam si ex sacris literis argumentaremur." Thieme observes: "This is certainly a bold proposition, important in the history of ideas."

[10] W. Schönfeld, *Grundlegung der Rechtswissenschaft,* 1951, 2nd ed. of *Die Geschichte der Rechtswissenschaft im Spiegel der Metaphysik,* 1943, p. 538.

the fact that it is called to assume a primary place in the successful preservation and defense of legal consciousness is not likely to be questioned by anyone duly informed about the influence of jurisprudence in historical and modern times. In comparison, the actual influence of legal philosophy and legal ethics takes second place, if only because their influence operates in turn by means of influence on jurisprudence and on the legal thought shaped by it, of lawgivers, of judges, and of lawyers. If, however, jurisprudence must see in the preservation and defense of the legal consciousness one of its principal functions, this must doubtless include its moral-legal root soil. For, in its historical development, the legal consciousness of society draws its powers of growth from the moral conscience, that is, from natural law itself. It is not by chance that *Schmitt* emphatically recalls *Savigny* and his belief that "the statute is only one of a number of manifestations of law." [11]

Indeed, it seems that in today's conflict between legality and legitimacy, *legal science, in order to protect its own existence and its own right as a science,* will find it necessary to reflect again on the supralegal principles of justice. For, without these the principle of legitimacy is deprived of its strongest supports against the threatening domination of the principle of legality, which seeks to make all law the business of the will of the state legislature, and hence today a matter of the will of those groups which control the legislative machinery. *Schmitt* speaks of jurisprudence's own right, which it has won for itself in the course of intellectual progress against its former inclusion in the philosophical, ethical, and religious spheres of science. How much this right is imperiled by the development indicated by *Schmitt* is shown by *H. Kelsen* in reference to the state of jurisprudence in Soviet Russia, which is governed by the ideologically based principle of legality, and also with the warning that in the West the power of the state is steadily growing (cf. Chap. 36).

6. We come now to the tasks of *natural law ethics* in the sphere of applied natural law. These form the principal part of social ethics as a science of the moral and juridical order of society in all its spheres, under the existing historical-cultural conditions. Its chief task will be to work out *juridical principles* which are yielded by the primary and secondary principles in the light of the "nature of the facts" proper to these spheres. This is the wide range of principles which traditional natural law theory has always been wont to call *principia remota* (derived or remoter principles).[12] From these *legal principles* we must distinguish *legal rules* as well

[11] Carl Schmitt, *Die Lage der Europäischen Rechtswissenschaft,* 1950, pp. 24, 30, 32. Cf. the criticism by Fr. A. Frh. v. d. Heydte in *Hochland,* 1951, pp. 288 ff.; cf. also, Chap. 40, the criticism of Savigny.

[12] R. Linhardt, *Die Sozialprinzipien des hl. Thomas v. Aq.*, p. 105, designates these principles as "tertiary conclusions," as understood by Thomas. St. Thomas, *Summa theol.,* Ia IIae, q. 100, a. 3, says that, although the primary and secondary principles are comprehended immediately or after only slight reflection, the reasonableness of the "derived" principles is a matter for the experts; Thomas is thinking mainly of the lawgiver and the representatives of the relevant sciences ("per diligentem inquisitionem sapientum inveniuntur rationi convenire").

as definite legal claims and obligations, which arise as demands of one of the three kinds of juridical principles in the light of the clearly recognizable nature of the facts ("situation").[13]

The distinction between legal principles and legal rules may be illustrated by the question of human rights. In a great number of states today the definition and guaranteeing of human rights in the form of *legal rules* forms an essential element in the constitution. The way in which they are defined and guaranteed, and therefore realized, cannot but vary from state to state in conformity with the cultural, political, and social development of the individual states. If, on the other hand, human rights in general are in question, natural law ethics will have the task of developing in full the *legal principles* underlying the individual human rights and giving guidance for their application. A "codification" by natural law ethics could only take the form of a casuistical description of kinds of situation and their relevance; this, however, would never do justice to the great variety of conditions in individual societies.

Thus, when *Jacques Maritain* declares equal franchise for all to be a natural right, summarily identifies the rights of the citizens with those of the people and then includes among the natural rights "government of the people, for the people, and by the people," [14] without reference to the dependence of the statutory form of all these rights on the development of a people's juridical consciousness, on its political education for demo-

[13] This division has been accepted by natural law ethics since St. Thomas Aquinas. If one thinks how thoroughly the exponents of natural law ethics have occupied themselves during the last century, as we shall see, with the application of natural law and with its demands in regard to the order of society in all spheres, it seems questionable whether the development can be rightly described in the following way: "It is gratifying that in modern times there is a movement away from the limitation of natural law to the most general principles" (Josef Fuchs, S.J., *Lex Naturae, zur Theologie des Naturrechts,* 1955, p. 110; Fuchs quotes also A. F. Utz, O.P., Vol. XVIII of the German edition of St. Thomas, 1953, pp. 432 f., and J. Funk, S.V.D., *Primat des Naturrechts: Die Transzendenz des Naturrechts gegenüber dem positiven Recht,* 1952, pp. 133–38). What Fuchs himself refers to as "natural law" very largely means the three catagories of principles we have mentioned above: "In general we can consider as natural law the most general principles . . . or the first conclusions . . . or the application to more concrete facts, or finally the application to concrete individual situations." Fuchs mentions among the primary conclusions: "One must not deliberately kill, steal, lie," and he thinks also of the *principia secundaria* appearing in the Decalogue. With regard to the application to "more concrete facts" it is said that "they of course largely presuppose a definite soteriological situation; for instance, the question of the interruption of pregnancy in especially difficult circumstances"; this is obviously the realm of the *principia remota.*

[14] J. Maritain, *The Rights of Man,* 1944, pp. 40 ff.; *Man and the State,* 1954, p. 102; that Maritain himself at bottom means legal principles and not statutes claiming universal validity can be seen from his essay "On the Philosophy of Human Rights," contributed to *Human Rights, a Symposium,* Unesco editor, (London), 2nd ed., 1950, p. 74, where he maintains that no declaration of human rights can be complete and definitive, but must always be historically dependent upon the state of moral consciousness and the development of civilization arrived at, although he is again thinking of mankind as a whole and it is not stated that the legal enactments of human rights by individual nations vary according to existing conditions. The social and historical limitations of the statutory definition of human rights are impressively described by Erich Fechner, *Die soziologische Grenze der Grundrechte,* 1954.

cratic life, and on its general standard of education (here one thinks of the illiteracy of great peoples, who today are entering the dynamics of world history), it is quite obvious that such a general summing up cannot set forth human rights in the sense of definite legal rules, but only legal principles which it is the task of the individual state to concretize into positive laws after careful examination of the existing relevant conditions.

The three categories of juridical principles convey only fundamental relationships of the juridical order of society. These principles, therefore, by their nature represent only *fundamental principles of justice*. From some quarters today an objection is raised (cf. note 13 above) to the restriction of natural law to fundamental principles and relationships.[15] We have already pointed out that in particular cases quite concrete demands

[15] It is hard to understand how, commenting on the natural principles of justice as discussed in the first edition of this work, Arthur Kaufmann, *Naturrecht und Geschichtlichkeit,* 1957, p. 24, can interpret our view of natural law, which confined it to an "outline of juridical relations" (cf. Chap. 87), as meaning that "only the grossest excrescences of injustice in statutory law would be eliminated from the realm of the legally binding." In the passage referred to, I say that the fundamental principles and relationships contained in natural law clearly comprise the jural principles directly evident to the natural conscience, as well as those which become evident with the evolution of the jural consciousness. The latter include in modern Western democracy (the passage quoted by Kaufmann is dealing with democracy and parties) human rights, understood not in an ideological party sense, but precisely in a natural law sense (derived ontologically from the nature of man and society). In this passage, I pointed out that, in natural law, there is to be found only an outline of jural relationships, and "the details are left to the will of the members of society." St. Thomas, *Summa theol.,* IIa IIae, q. 57, a. 2, may be noted: "Voluntas humana ex communi condicto potest aliquid facere iustum in his, quae secundum se non habent aliquem repugnantiam ad naturalem iustitiam." But because in the first edition I discussed in detail the application of the natural law principles to society, to the state, and to the economy, in complete contrast to Kaufmann's observation, Fr. A. Frh. v. d. Heydte, in *Archiv für Rechts- und Sozialphilosophie,* Vol. XLIII, 1957, pp. 223 f., declares that in a "thousand pages" I have attempted "somehow to codify natural law and to compare and contrast this codification of natural law with the codification of positive law in the constitution and legislation." In fact, in the first edition of this book, as in the text above, I firmly and repeatedly rejected the idea that natural law offers a code of law or that such can be derived from it. When, on the other hand, v. d. Heydte observes that our natural law ethics consists "in raising ethical postulates with regard to the positive norm, postulates which are doubtless all justified, but not all law," he is obviously guided by the idea that only positive law is real law and therefore that the jurist logician analyzes the positive legal rule "without finding the natural law soul in it." What I attempted, however, was by no means merely to define "natural law" *ethically* in relation to positive law, but with an eye to the existing order of society, of the state, and of the economy, which is fundamentally that of positive law, I tried to ascertain what is demanded by the natural *juridical* order of society in its various spheres. Indeed, from the Middle Ages until modern times (cf. text above) all important exponents of traditional natural law theory have regarded as their main task: to examine existing legal systems and legal institutions in the light of natural law principles and to set out the demands of the latter with regard to historical systems always encumbered with greater or lesser deficiencies in law and justice, laying stress on the idea that justice and law in the true senses are the issue, even if they are deprived of their authority in positive law. Not only is positive law real law, and not only does natural law exist in the realm of conscience, as v. d. Heydte seems to assume; indeed, the relationship between the two could be understood as "dialectical tension," as v. d. Heydte suggests, if real law existed only on the one pole.

of natural law may exist in clearly defined situations (e.g., do not damage "this" property of another). A natural law ethics which goes beyond this and thinks of a natural law capable of being completely codified in concrete terms would seem, however, to be yielding to a misunderstanding of the nature of the third category of natural law principles, the "derived" ones, of which applied natural law chiefly consists, and seems to regard to some extent as concrete legal rules or concrete entitlements and obligations what are in fact principles. Because of this, new life is again given to the apparently ineradicable error that, for traditional natural law theory, the historical legal systems, with their immense variety of legal rules (among the primitive peoples of today as well as in the highly developed civilizations of history), and the suprahistorical essence of all law which it upholds, represent an insoluble antinomy.[16]

The fact that the limitation of natural law to fundamental principles and fundamental social relationships in no way signifies a misunderstanding of the functions of applied natural law is quite evident if one thinks of the exponents of traditional natural law idea in continental Europe in the last hundred years, who today are credited with a too narrow conception of natural law. In harmony with the view of the natural law scholars of the classical Middle Ages that applied natural law yields almost entirely principles and not completed concrete statutes, they saw in *the questions of justice in their own society the main field of natural law ethics.* They were convinced that its task is to develop the principles of justice as they bear upon concrete questions regarding the reform of society, of the state, and of the economy and the appropriate law to be created, but not to produce draft laws and texts of laws with an exclusive claim to authority legitimated by natural law. It is a different matter that some of them, whether officially or unofficially, have taken a share in the drafting of laws. Although concerned with what is entirely concrete, they themselves have given emphatic warning against the disregarding of the limits in question.[17] They engaged less in theoretical discussions of natural

[16] Following Erik Wolf, who thought the core of Catholic natural law study to be the quest for an absolutely supratemporal law, Fr. A. Frh. v. d. Heydte, *Natural Law Tendencies in Contemporary German Jurisprudence,* in *Natural Law Forum,* Vol. I (Notre Dame Law School), 1956, p. 116, also assumes that Catholic natural law theory finds itself faced with the permanent antinomy between supratemporal natural law and the historical nature of positive law. Thomas Aquinas, because he sharply distinguished general absolute natural law and its application, has no difficulty in admitting in full measure the historical nature of positive law, as is shown by his simple, realistic statement (cf. *Summa theol.,* Ia IIae, q. 95, a. 2) that general natural law leads to different applications among different peoples "propter multam varietatem rerum humanarum." Wherefore, as he says in *III Sent.,* d. 37, I, 3, statutory law is different among different peoples. Concerning the whole question cf. Chaps. 40, 43.

[17] So experienced a practitioner in the application of natural law as Joseph Mausbach, a moral theologian who played a considerable part in the shaping of laws in Germany after the First World War, and an exponent of Christian social doctrine of the stature of Wilhelm Schwer find it necessary to utter similar warnings against the obliteration of the boundaries between legal principles on the one hand and legal rules, "concrete natural law," on the other. The passage from J. Mausbach, *Naturrecht*

law than in the discussion of its practical demands in the light of the social crisis of their time, and indeed wholly in accordance with the view of *Thomas Aquinas,* who held that the center of gravity of the endeavors in the natural law sphere lay in applied natural law. We may recall such names as Bishop *W. E. Frh. von Ketteler, K. Frh. von Vogelsang, G. Ratzinger, von Hertling, F. Hitze, T. Meyer, V. Cathrein, J. Mausbach, P. Tischleder.* With a bold sense of responsibility and with brave determination they put their hands to the many difficult questions of justice with which their times were faced—owing to the crisis in society, in the state, in economy, and in international relations, and treated them as questions of applied natural law.

Their aim was not an order of society fixed in codifiable natural law rules, but the working out of natural law principles relevant to the situation, in order to deal with the problems which the "social question" of the day raised for the moral conscience. We thought it best to follow this tradition and the tradition of natural law theory in its classical period, when in the first edition of this book we confined ourselves to the barest fundamentals of *theoretical* natural law in order to cover the wide range of social, political, economic, and international questions as questions of *practical* applied natural law. The present interest in natural law, however, has made it necessary to devote much more space to the theoretical problems in the present edition than was originally intended. It remains our conviction that, as *Thomas Aquinas* held, *the center of gravity of natural law ethics lies in applied natural law.*[18] For, "he declares again and again

---

und Völkerrecht, p. 37, was quoted in the previous chapter. Wilhelm Schwer, *Katholische Gesellschaftslehre,* 1928, p. 142, writes that natural law is only the "scaffolding" (what we should call the "fundamental relationships") of the social structure; "Hence, *there is no question of deriving from it positive rules for the concrete organization of the social system insofar as its most elementary foundations are not at issue.*" Even one versed in the history and development of the traditional natural law theory, a theologian deeply engaged in questions of applied natural law at the present time, Otto Schilling, *Lehrbuch der Moraltheologie,* Vol. I, 1928, p. 106, likewise declares: "Christian natural law knows but few evident and fundamental principles elastic enough to be applied to all conditions, however various, which of course is their function." Similar warnings are being issued again today by eminent Catholic jurists who take their stand entirely on natural law but are opposed to an overstraining of the natural law idea. Thus, Professor Karl Siegfried Bader of Zürich, speaking at Salzburg (cf. *Berichte und Informationen des Österr: Forschungsinstitutes für Wirtschaft und Politik,* 11th year, H. 527, p. 743), and R. Stanka, mentioned in the following chapter. One of our most important teachers of international law at the present day, Alfred Verdroß, *Völkerrecht,* 2nd ed., p. 29, sees in primary natural law only those fundamental principles "which are necessary for the existence of a rational and moral peace. These principles form the common groundwork of the main natural law theorists from Aristotle to the present day."

[18] Only a failure to distinguish adequately between legal principles and legal rules can explain the paradox whereby exponents of traditional natural law theory have commented that I confine natural law to an outline of juridical relationships, whereas the same people again have declared that my book would correctly bear the title *Sozialethik* and not *Naturrecht* (*Natural Law,* the title of the German edition): as if *natural law ethics,* as understood by Thomas Aquinas, were not *essentially and inevitably social ethics, and vice versa.*

that the principal effort of all ethics and social ethics is not the exposition of general principles, but their application to the ever varying concrete situations of life."[19] *St. Thomas* thought the general principles were familiar to the natural conscience.

7. The preceding detailed discussion of applied natural law has been necessary because it seems that *a wholly new task in the sphere of applied natural law has arisen for natural law ethics today, which did not exist for medieval natural law ethics.* This is the task of producing an outline of the order of society, of the state, of social economy, and of the society of nations, which can be understood from natural law principles in the light of the social situation of the world as it is at present. Hence, we insist on "principles" as distinct from "rules" of law. If such rules were present in detail and in their entirety in the "nature of the facts," they would yield ready-made legal, political, and economic systems. But this is prevented by the nature of the facts, not only because the conditions governing the application of natural law principles are subject to constant historical development, but also because natural law principles themselves leave very wide scope to free will in the arrangement of social institutions. Hence, in the traditional natural law school, once sociological thought had been focussed on "social systems," it soon became evident that natural law does not provide a social system in the sense of a detailed pattern of legal, political, and economic organization. Undoubtedly, however, the principles of applied natural law yield the basic order of social, political, economic, and international life.

We have said that the social conditions of today pose a wholly new problem for natural law ethics by comparison with the Middle Ages. One can indeed speak of a new function of natural law. The classical natural law theory of ancient and medieval times rests on the idea that, in substance, the order of society then prevailing was a realization of the natural order. Medieval natural law theory was no exception to the findings of the present-day sociology of knowledge about the historical dependence of the formulation and solution of problems in all branches of knowledge.[20] In part, classical-medieval natural law is the natural law of the Greek-Roman-Christian civilization of the day. *Aristotle, Augustine, Thomas,* and *Grotius* knew nothing of the other high cultures, either the Near Eastern ones beginning from about 3000 B.C., or those of the Far

[19] R. Linhardt, *op. cit.*, pp. 12 f., cf. the passages cited by Linhardt, *op. cit.*, pp. 33, 39 ff., from St. Thomas, especially on the extent to which the natural law ethics of Thomas is related to circumstances and the concrete situation.

[20] The first scientific sociological references to the natural law doctrine of Thomas Aquinas are found in Albert Mitterer, "Naturwissenschaft und Naturrecht," in *Die soziale Frage und der Katholizismus, Festschrift zum 40jährigen Jubiläum der Enzyklika "Rerum Novarum,"* Jakob Strieder and Johannes Messner, editors (publ. by Görresgesellschaft), 1931, pp. 436–52; again in R. Linhardt, *Die Sozialprinzipien des hl. Thomas v. Aq.*, and more recently in A. F. Utz, O.P., *Recht und Gerechtigkeit,* Vol. XVIII of the Latin-German edition of St. Thomas with commentary, 1953.

East, which were contemporary with their own, not to speak of the previous half a million years or so of human existence.

It seems of especial significance for our question concerning the new function of natural law that in the Middle Ages natural law ethics considered the "existing" social order as permanent, and, as we should say today, not merely in its essential features but as a "social system." Just because it was a product of the Christian outlook on life and on the world, and rested on the universally and firmly held interpretation of man's nature, the existing social order was believed to correspond in a special way to the natural law order, even if theoretically the idea of development was emphasized in regard to juridical order and juridical consciousness (cf. Chap. 40). In modern times, however, because of the sharp divergence from this outlook the dispute about the social order itself has arisen: the existing *social order as such is called in question.* The question concerning the "natural order" of society, and hence of social order as such, became the fundamental question of *individualist liberalism,* then of *collectivistic socialism;* and with the ideological war between East and West, today it has become the fateful question for mankind.

Hence, *three great historical epochs in the development of natural law* seem to emerge. The first period: For hundreds of thousands of years natural law was confined to the family community and to the larger family group, with the accompanying development of legal custom, legal usage, and the earliest customary law, a development which among primitive peoples reaches to the present day. The second period: With the growth of the high civilizations and their complicated forms of social life and of common utility, practical natural law took on new forms; yet, as far as we know today, it was only to the philosophical spirit peculiar to the classical-medieval high civilization that natural law itself became a theoretical scientific problem. Thus, the foundation and the basic principles of natural law were worked out in a lasting general pattern, namely, for all humanity of all times. Without this great inheritance the third epoch in world history, which was marked by demands for human rights, for social rights, and for a comprehensive system of international law, would have been unthinkable. *The question of the social order as such* has most deeply stirred the Western world for the last two hundred years and is reaching a climax today in the acute ideological cleavage between opposing world fronts with their contrary interpretations of *the nature of man.* Thus, today social order itself has become a fundamental question of natural law and natural law ethics is charged with the task of *indicating positively and constructively the basic features of the natural order of society in the conditions of today.*

The headlong developments which have taken place in every direction since the beginning of the modern age in the intellectual, economic, political, and social spheres have prevented natural law ethics, at the critical historical moment of the collapse of the medieval guild system and the emergence of the capitalist economy in the fifteenth and sixteenth centuries, from pointing out for the new developments the way to the natural order of economic and social life in conformity with the new situation, although there was no dearth of warning voices. One need only think of the century-long troubles in the Tyrolese mining districts or the misery among the Flemish weavers; it is to *that* period that we should assign the failure of the Christian natural law conscience, and not to the nineteenth century, as is commonly done. It is pertinent also to recall the largely defensive attitude with which the development of modern democracy has been received, and the supposed problems in discussions of "popular sovereignty," which have so greatly occupied traditional natural law thinkers. These problems have by-passed the real questions; and the valuable suggestions found in the natural law doctrine of the scholastics of the sixteenth century, as we shall see (Chap. 130), were pushed aside while the traditional natural law school combated the errors of Rousseau and engaged in internal disputes without any external effect. Since today the question of social order as such has reached such momentum and such threatening force for the future of mankind and its culture, it becomes one of the principal questions, if not *the* principal question, for a natural law theory true to the great tradition; and in consequence, it points to one of the principal tasks, if not *the* principal task, in the sphere of applied natural law. This perspective from the beginning has governed our endeavors to form a natural law ethics appropriate to the modern world.

Two other significant kinds of applied natural law must be discussed in greater detail.

111 *Natural Law after Original Sin*

Human nature is impaired by original sin. This impairment, as was shown earlier (cf. Chap. 11), concerns man's intellect and will. In it is rooted a fundamental situation of human existence, which has consequences of a general character for the natural order of social life. From the viewpoint of intellect, the consequence consists in the necessity of positive law to define legal duties, even though they are recognizable in themselves by the natural conscience; such a definition must be provided by the lawgiver and by his rules in order to obviate any uncertainty and deficiency in knowledge of these duties on the part of the members of society. From the viewpoint of the will, the consequence of the impairment of human nature consists in the necessity for compulsory measures to be taken by the social authority in order to guarantee law and order, by making the unwilling carry out their obligations. The result of all this is a *wide extension of the natural-law competence of the political authority.* This mode of functioning falls under "applied" natural law: the mode of application of natural law as conditioned by the impairment of man's nature. It remains true natural law because it is rooted in man's rational nature, although it has suffered in its intellectual and volitional powers owing to the effects of original sin. Indeed, the development of the greater proportion of non-Christian peoples shows that reason is by no means incapable of understanding the special character of human nature, and the basic requirements of the order of social relationships which it involves, and of realizing them in their legal systems.

From the fact of the impairment of human nature by original sin and hence of the functioning of natural law, there follows an important consequence for all endeavors in the sphere of legal order: *legal realism.* This has a twofold meaning. First, owing to the impairment of human nature, an essentially new function falls to positive law, that of establishing legal certainty, by the definition of rights and of duties in applied natural law and by the guaranteeing of its observance by compulsion. Therefore, after original sin the element of truth in legal positivism has some foundation in the natural law. The legal realism which is rooted in this natural law signifies, secondly, that *every legal system is necessarily imperfect,* not only because of the inadequacy of the lawgiver's understanding, but still more because of the possibilities of misuse (arising from the desire for power of social groups) of the ordering and commanding power of law.

The legal realism suggested by the doctrine of original sin must guard against expecting more from legislation than it can achieve in view of the basic facts of human existence which we have discussed. Exaggerated expectations are as dangerous as they are mistaken. Christians, liberalists, and socialists yield to such expectations when, much as their viewpoints differ in other respects, they hope that legal means can produce a perfect or nearly adequate economic and social order. The legal organization of social life always remains a task burdened with the effects of passions and, therefore, with deficiencies, so that it can never be perfectly or finally discharged. For these reasons, as history sufficiently shows, the paths of progress toward a more perfect order of law and of justice are again and again interrupted by periods of regress. On the other hand, for the *Christian conscience* which is aware of these dangers and their deeper cause, a tireless endeavor to achieve a more perfect order of justice in every sphere of social life becomes a greatly heightened obligation.

IV *Ius gentium*

The peoples of all ages have founded their legal systems upon the same human nature which has the same reason, the same conscience, and the same weaknesses; and in the process, aided by experience, they have discovered what was necessary and expedient for the attainment of the common utility. All consequently reached the same fundamental concrete principles in their legal systems. This part of applied natural law was termed *ius gentium* by the Roman jurists. *Ius gentium* is, accordingly, natural law as actualized through the common experience of peoples in the establishment of their municipal and international institutions. *Ius gentium* is essentially different from what we today call international law; the latter is contractual interstate law. The questions which concern us here are: What is its character as applied natural law and what is its significance today?

Regarding its *municipal law aspect,* the relationship of *ius gentium* to natural law has always been the object of discussion. We need not go into detail here, but a few observations seem necessary. The older natural law theory subsumed *ius gentium* under positive law, because, springing from human reason in conjunction with human experience, it belonged to the basic stock of positive law of all nations. At the same time, however, it emphasized the fact that the natural law principles belonging to reason itself guided the peoples in this, so that at bottom no explicit legislation was required.[21] Its actual origin, although today this is often too little considered, must be sought in the development of custom and of legal usage in the course of operation of the natural conscience in conjunction with experience.[22] The historical school deriving from *Savigny* has contributed much toward the clarification of this process. The reason why the earlier traditional natural law school classed *ius gentium* so decidedly under positive law as distinct from natural law lies in the intention of the school to stress the variability of *ius gentium.* In this, in spite of its essentially static views of society, it kept the door open for the understanding of the dynamic development of mankind's sense of law and for the expression of this development in a progressive common human law.

In its *international law aspect, ius gentium* consists in the legal principles rooted in moral-jural reason and prevails in the intercourse between nations, the recognition and observance of which is due not to express agreement but to custom and to legal usage. The *ius gentium* concerning the relations between peoples is not restricted to international relationships as such (e.g. respect for ambassadors), but embraces also the mercantile, immigration, and residential rights and duties of the members of the individual peoples in their mutual relationships. A sign of the reality of the scientific natural law thinking of the scholastics in the late sixteenth and early seventeenth centuries is their immediate occupation with the question of the natural law principles which should govern the relations between the peoples of the Old and New Worlds. Although the notion of *ius gentium* in its original significance designates predominantly legal principles which were embodied in the internal law of the nations of the Roman Empire, attention now turns to questions of interstate relations.

[21] Thus, St. Thomas, *Summa theol.*, IIa IIae, q. 57, a. 3, includes *ius gentium* in human law, but explains: "Quia ea, quae sunt iuris gentium, naturalis ratio dictat, puta ex propinquo habentia aequitatem, inde est quod non indigent aliqua speciali institutione, sed ipsa naturalis ratio ea instituit." On the question of the view of *ius gentium* held by Thomas cf. R. Linhardt, *op. cit.*, pp. 106 ff., and A. F. Utz, *op. cit.*, pp. 445 ff.

[22] Thus, Suárez, *De leg.*, lect. II, c. 19, n. 6, says: "Praecepta iuris gentium in hoc differunt a praeceptis iuris civilis, quia non scripto, sed moribus, non unius vel alterius civitatis vel provinciae, sed omnium vel fere omnium nationum, constat."

Ius gentium is no longer seen now as merely law which prevails "within" the national sphere, but also as law which holds good "between" the various nations and their members. This new feature is dealt with tentatively at first by *Vitoria,*[23] then with assurance by *Suárez.*[24] The nations have, so to speak, agreed (we would say "tacitly"), says *Suárez,* to recognize the principles of this *ius gentium,* their authority resting more on tradition and on legal custom than on formal prescription.[25] The emergence of this new feature in the idea of *ius gentium* is completely in harmony with its character: it is the *expression of the development of the moral and legal consciousness of mankind* based on its experience in the organization of social life in all its spheres, both internal and international.

Under both aspects *ius gentium* is the repository of *a growing heritage of applied natural law principles.* As the relations between peoples broadened and intensified, this heritage grew and at the same time extended its influence. The traditional natural law theory included under *ius gentium* the fundamental institutions of civic law, first those connected with private property and with contracts of purchase and sale, then the principles of international law guaranteeing the safety of ambassadors and merchants. The generally recognized principles of law today, by contrast with earlier times, include freedom of conscience, of religious practice, of speech, of association, and also include the principles, realized in

[23] It is noteworthy that with Vitoria *inter omnes homines* becomes *inter omnes gentes,* where he cites the *Institutes* of Justinian, I, 2, I (in *De indis et de iure belli relectiones,* rel. I, sect. III at the beginning): "Quod naturalis ratio inter omnes *gentes* constituit vocatur ius gentium." Cf. J. Brown Scott, *Francisco de Vitoria and the Law of Nations,* 1934, pp. 139 f., 163. Concerning the position of Vitoria in the historical development of the idea cf. J. Höffner, *Christentum und Menschenwürde, das Anliegen der spanischen Kolonialethik im goldenen Zeitalter,* 1947, pp. 231 ff., and the bibliography given there; there also cf. the justified criticism of L. Molina, *De iustitia et iure,* Tractatus II, disp. 105, n. I, regarding the too generalizing nature of some principles stated by Vitoria.

[24] Cf. Suárez, *De legibus,* Lib. II, c. 19, n. 8: "Duobus modis (quantum ex Isidoro, et aliis iuribus, et auctoribus colligo) dici aliquid de iure gentium: uno modo quia est ius, quod omnes populi, et gentes variae *inter* se servare debent; alio modo quia est ius, quod singulae civitates, vel regna *intra* se observant; per similitudinem autem, et convenientiam ius gentium appellatur. Prior modus videtur mihi propriissime continere ius gentium re ipsa distinctum a iure civili, prout illud explicuimus. Et ad illud pertinent exempla de legatorum, et commerciorum usu, qua explicuimus." On the variability of *ius gentium* cf. Suárez, *op. cit.,* c. 20, nn. 6–9. On *ius gentium* in Suárez cf. H. Rommen, *Die Staatslehre des Franz Suárez,* 1929, pp. 285 ff., especially on its variability, p. 288; cf. also J. Höffner, *op. cit.,* pp. 234 ff.

[25] Cf. Suárez, *ibid.,* Lib. III, c. 2, n. 6: "Aliqua communia iura quasi communi foedere et consensione [are recognized, but] magis traditione et consuetudine quam constitutione aliqua introducta sunt." He assigns so wide a role to custom in establishing principles of *ius gentium* in the international sphere that present-day thinking cannot follow him in some respects (for example, when he assumes a right to enslave prisoners of war). Suárez seeks to justify his "realism" in subsuming customs, like the enslavement of prisoners after the defeat of an aggressor, under *ius gentium* (*ibid.,* Lib. II, c. 18, n. 9), by pointing to the fact that the internal law of the state has to tolerate evils like prostitution, mild deception in contracts, etc., because this seems necessary owing to the frailty of men and the nature of commercial dealings (*ibid.,* c. 20, n. 3).

social legislation, which guarantee a certain minimum of protection of human labor. Since the content of these principles represents the natural juridical consciousness of peoples at the present stage of their development, it forms *present-day ius gentium.* This reference to a *ius gentium* of today is intended, on the one hand to draw attention to the essentially progressive character of *ius gentium* and, on the other hand, to the evolutionary impulse which it transmits to the legal consciousness. The stage of development reached by individual peoples in their legal consciousness operates as a motive force in the development of the legal consciousness of other peoples. It seems more profitable to devote increased attention to this motive force inherent in *ius gentium* than to enter overmuch into discussions about the conception of *ius gentium* in the course of history.

Indeed, *ius gentium* is by no means a merely historical category. Its history is itself evidence of its evolutionary character, which embraces the present time. A significant testimony of this is afforded by the judgment on *slavery* in early and high scholasticism. Slavery was ranked among the institutions of *ius gentium,* since it was found in the legal systems of most nations, and the available facts of experience made slavery seem to be an integral part of the society and civilization of these nations. The idea that, over and above this justification by circumstances, some men should be considered as destined for domination and some for bondage owing to the variety of individual endowments, and that this should be regarded as a permanent institution, today seems intolerable; the idea was the result of a too narrow basis of anthropological experience. Sociology today offers the material necessary for the explanations of such views; it will find with regard to the institution of slavery that essential feature of variability which the natural law theory so emphasized in *ius gentium,* since, indeed, it was the impulsions of conscience operating in *ius gentium* which provided unyielding opposition to slavery. In order to appraise the outlook of medieval natural law theory in its true perspective sociologically and historically, we should remember that not a few members of the "enlightened" nations of the nineteenth century reconciled the slave trade with their humanitarian ideals. Furthermore, quite apart from the slavery still existing in the Near East, the twentieth century is disfigured by slavery on a gigantic scale in the labor camps of the totalitarian states. This is a new form of slavery which violates the most essential human rights and which so far has elicited from the rest of mankind nothing more than paper protests, accompanied by a continuing readiness to trade in merchandise which undoubtedly includes products of such slave labor.

v *The Regenerating Force of Natural Law*

Natural law in all its modes of operation is a powerful force in the history of nations; indeed, among such forces, except those of external nature, it is the strongest and most persistent. The moral jural conscience and the jural will, which it legitimizes, urge the realization of the order of justice; in doing so continually, they also urge the questioning of legal systems and social forms and their alteration if they do not conform with basic precepts of justice. The revitalizing and progressive force of natural law does not proceed solely from the natural jural conscience; it proceeds at least as much from the jural will of underprivileged groups in society, which is kept in motion by the impulse toward happiness-values and which seeks its justification in these principles. Such groups endeavor, by the adaptation of the legal system, to secure their *suum,* that is to say, their due share in the economic and cultural goods produced with their cooperation as well as their social standing commensurate with their part in cooperation.

If opponents of natural law maintain that this is something essentially inflexible, and hence a hindrance to social and cultural progress, they are generally thinking of the undeniable exploitation of natural law theories by ruling classes, who favor the existing legal system for their vested interests. In fact, all decisive advances in the legal and social order in the West received their strongest impulses from the struggle for natural justice. The natural jural conscience and the jural will which obtained its sanction from it in view of the changing social world brought about the fall of the system of slavery and of the feudal system; and with the developing consciousness of human and social rights imposed radical changes on the individualist-capitalistic system. The driving force of the natural law conscience is obvious enough in the development of international law, as will be shown later in detail.

Ernst Troeltsch ascribed a narrowly conservative character to both Catholic and Protestant natural law theory.[26] Doubtless, as we have indicated, the natural law doctrine of the early and high Middle Ages largely reflected the social order of its time, was broadly static in its thinking, and as a science had to pay the inevitable tribute to the conditions of the period. Although thus, in part, it read the social system of its age into natural law, it never made it a principle that natural law imposes an absolute duty of submission to the existing social system, a principle which *Troeltsch* held was predominant in Lutheranism until the most recent times, and was the doctrine underlying its social ethics. If nothing else, the development of international law emanating from the Catholic natural law doctrine of *Vitoria* and *Suárez* would show that *Troeltsch's* generalizing statement does not correspond with the facts.[27] The opinion of Sir *Frederick Pollock,* the well-known jurist (not a Catholic), that natural

[26] Cf. E. Troeltsch, *The Social Teaching of the Christian Churches,* trans. by O. Wyon, 1931, Vol. I, p. 305, Vol. II, p. 529; cf. also the book by O. Schilling, *Naturrecht und Staat nach der Lehre der alten Kirche,* 1914, intended as a critique of Troeltsch.

[27] Cf. E. Troeltsch, *op. cit.,* Vol. II, p. 543.

law theory up to the seventeenth century was on the whole progressive fits them better.[28]

VI *Truth and Certainty of Knowledge in Natural Law*

The cognition of applied natural law rests, we said, on inferential judgments, whose premises on the one hand are general principles of natural law and on the other hand are facts governed by circumstances. The conclusions express what the former demand in regard to the latter. Therefore, insofar as full certainty in regard to those facts is not attainable, it is also lacking in regard to the demands of the natural law principles in question.[29] Whether and how far we are able to recognize these facts is not primarily an ethical question, but an epistemological one, namely, how far man is enabled by his reason to understand reality and truth. Knowledge of the facts is largely what jurisprudence understands by insight into "the nature of the case." There are two avenues of approach to true knowledge regarding the facts of the case: common sense and the sciences.

Unless one is willing to go against the whole experience of mankind one can hardly deny that the human mind is able to comprehend simpler matters by means of experience and of reflection. One will be equally unwilling to deny that the sciences concerned with man and society can comprehend a wide field of reality and truth. Insofar as these two modes of knowledge communicate truth, natural law ethics also can reach assured conclusions in the field of applied natural law. The knowledge thus gained no longer comes within the sphere of epistemology, but simply of logic, that is, the logic of the syllogism (the process of inference). Insofar as they concern the common sense we made it our business to show (cf. Chap. 47) that man learns to understand being or facts simultaneously with percep-

[28] Cf. Frederick Pollock, in the notes to his edition of H. S. Maine, *Ancient Law,* 1930, p. 120.

[29] Surprisingly, this whole range of questions regarding truth and certainty of knowledge has altogether retreated into the background in recent traditional natural law theory; rather, there is often expressed a belief in a wide realm of established natural law, quite concrete in its provisions, sometimes with emphatic reliance on St. Thomas Aquinas. On this question, as always, Thomas' thinking is very realistic and arrives at very cautiously held conclusions. For the principles of applied natural law he claims to a considerable extent only a *probabilis certitudo* (*Summa theol.,* IIa IIae, q. 70, a. 2); for most cases of individual application of natural law principles, which concern primarily *singularia* and therefore *contingentia,* only *veritatem nisi contingentem* (*in III Sent.,* d. 35, I, 3, solutio 2). R. Linhardt, *op. cit.,* p. 40, who deals with the question thoroughly, sums up: "The sound core of sociologism and economism in the modern conception of history and morality is no new invention of the twentieth century, originating with Marx, Durckheim, Lévy-Brühl etc., but an ancient Aristotelian-Thomistic matter of course." The first and still the most thorough work on the position of Thomas on this question is that of Prof. Simon Deploige, *Le conflit de la morale et de la sociologie,* 3rd ed., 1923; Engl. trans., *The Conflict between Ethics and Sociology* (U.S.A.), 1938, especially Chaps. 7 and 8. Cf. also Werner Schöllgen, *Die soziologischen Grundlagen der katholischen Sittenlehre,* 1953.

tion of the general principles of law. Thus, he learns to judge whether a remark about another is likely or not to harm his good name and prospects; if it is, then he knows that it would damage a *suum* of the other and hence be an injustice. Scientific knowledge of the effects of nuclear weapons on life and body, a *suum* of man, leads to the conclusion that the uncontrolled use of such weapons is wrong.

We do not always, however, possess certainty in our acceptance of such inferential truths. In the two cases mentioned, there is certainty of factual judgment and hence of judgment regarding the natural law duties. The factual situation, however, can be more complex, for instance, when in a particular case the conditions and consequences of a mode of conduct under consideration cannot be clearly made out. The question of defamation can become unclear if the withholding of a harmful statement about someone would harm someone else. The appraisal of the factors, the ascertainment of which forms the *condition* for a proper decision, may in itself and in relation to others concern the professional position of the persons in question, with respect to the prospect of avoiding harm or of making restitution if one keeps silence. The appraisal of the *consequences* can, for example, involve the comparison between the prospective harm on either side respectively: the harm accruing to the families concerned in their particular situations; the injury to others involved in the case in question, one's own liability if one spares the other person. In cases of this kind it is often impossible to attain complete certainty with regard to the details of the facts.

The same is true of the *lawgiver.* His authority is naturally limited by every *suum* included in the common good, whether it be that of the political community as a whole, or that of the occupational groups, or that of the individuals with their human rights. For example: What can the farming community of a state demand as their economic, fiscal, social *suum,* involving for example minimum price guarantees and subsidies from taxation? The social sciences will be able to offer varied help toward a judgment on the facts in question, particularly in regard to general relationships in the total price structure of an economy: the relationship between agrarian prices and industrial wages, the position of this price-wage structure in the export-import process. Insight into the general relationships form, however, only one of the means for judging the facts of the situation in the case we are discussing. For in a case of this kind, not only quantitative relationships are in question but also the position of agriculture in the structure of an economy and its position as an enduring element in the political structure, which again raises considerations of internal and external politics of a quite special kind. Obviously, the questions of justice to be judged in these matters permit of no precise, much less mathematically precise, decision: perfect certainty is impossible.

We have deliberately chosen two examples which are unquestionable in regard to the *bounds of truth and certainty in the sphere of applied natural law.* Natural law ethics need not fear to recognize as a consequence that the conscience of the individual and of the lawgiver, in questions of legal duties and of claims, must often rely on judgments of fact, which can claim only a greater or lesser degree of probability.[30] Consider also the question of what would be quantitatively the exactly just wage for a given category of labor in an industrial undertaking using a complex division of labor, or indeed for the actual work done by the worker in such an undertaking. To answer such questions with full certainty is impossible. The only justifiable conclusion from this is that, *like everything human, any order of law and justice is imperfect,* because man's intellect (quite apart from man's imperfect readiness of will to apprehend the truth and to recognize its claims) is imperfect. This imperfection of the existing legal order is part of the intrinsic tragedy of human existence. But we are by no means justified in concluding that, because justice is imperfect owing to the inadequacy of understanding, it is therefore not justice at all, just as it would be wrong also to deny all morality to man because defective moral insight makes him morally imperfect. (We are here concerned with the question of knowledge; the fact that a political system basing right upon might is in conflict with the order of justice has nothing to do with the question.)

It was said that any existing legal system, measured by the demands of justice rooted in the nature of the facts (the demands of *suum cuique* for social groups and individuals), is imperfect like all things human. Even if human nature and its faculties may be more or less pessimistically judged, however, it is a fact that, in the course of man's historical development, his intellectual faculty has proved increasingly capable of recognizing right and wrong in order to enable him to live in social systems which have permitted civilized life and development. Civilized life is the life natural to man and the legal order is the fundamental condition of its realization.[31] The more strongly the evolutionary side is stressed today, especially when it is pointed out that in order to understand himself man is to a large extent dependent upon history, the more highly must we appreciate the fact, proved by history, that *man has always had the ability to know the elementary requirements of the order of justice with the certainty necessary for his existence and for his development as a cultural being.*

The fact that the development of reality has not always kept pace with true and certain knowledge in the sphere of legal order must not, as has already been mentioned, be confused with the present question. It should be remembered further that true and certain knowledge in the sphere of law is by no means a matter of "pure" reason, but that, in the sphere of

[30] St. Thomas, *Summa theol.,* IIa IIae, q. 70, a. 2, quotes Aristotle: "Certainty cannot be demanded equally in every matter"; hence, especially in the realm of human actions, "eo quod sunt circa contingentia et variabilia. Et ideo sufficit probabilis certitudo, quae ut in pluribus [i.e., generally] veritatem attingat, etsi in paucioribus [in some cases] a veritate deficiat."

[31] Cf. Messner, *Kulturethik,* pp. 335 ff., 368 ff.

law, *knowledge and interest are intimately linked*: the *suum* in any given circumstances is an object of interest for the one for whom it establishes a right. Interest, therefore, provides strong motive forces for and against ways of judging the facts. But just because forces and counterforces are in operation they contribute to the greatest possible understanding of the nature of the facts, whether the juridical order as a whole or a particular right is in question. As we have seen, the development of jural consciousness and of jural order depends on this to no small extent. The question is one of forces intimately connected with the functioning of man's natural law. They help bring about the securing and extension of human existence. To these are added the forces which are operative through the moral jural conscience itself; and by its own imperative, the moral jural conscience must aim at not less than the best possible knowledge of the legal situation governed by the nature of the facts—indeed, it knows this to be a legal duty.

The remaining lack of certainty in applied natural law leads to conclusions of importance for the position of the lawgiver. First: *The lack of certainty establishes the power of decision for the lawgiver.* If legal certainty or the common good require it, he has to decide by legislation what is to be regarded as law, as long as an absolutely clear knowledge of the nature of the facts cannot be obtained. Positive law must answer the knowable demands of the facts, yet must give a valid legal decision on the existing "disputed" sphere. As an example, we may recall what has been mentioned regarding economic legislation in the field of agriculture. This provides further corroboration of the kernel of truth, which undeniably exists in legal positivism. Another conclusion can be brought out: Just as the endeavor after factual knowledge is a jural duty, being a condition of the knowledge of the order of justice, so also there is, in the conditions of modern liberal democracy, *an obligation in justice to be objective in discussion on all questions of legislation.* Only through objective discussion is it possible to reach the best possible approximation to true knowledge in regard to the jural claims rooted in the nature of the facts. Indeed, the basic assumption of the theory of modern democracy is that, by means of objective discussion,[32] the greatest possible measure of objective factual knowledge is brought to bear in it (cf. Chap. 134). The fact that not only objective considerations enter into the discussion, but also interest group and ideological party considerations, reduces the approximation value of the knowledge in question. This has, however, nothing to do with the question of the possibility of knowing the order of justice; rather, it has

[32] It may surprise many to find how realistic even in this respect the thinking of the great exponents of traditional natural law theory is; they do not simply place the center of gravity in an intellectual faculty ascribed to abstract reason in regard to every matter, but know that the understanding of the nature of the facts, the discovery of the truth, and with that the clarification of questions of justice is often only possible *ex collatione multorum*, as Thomas Aquinas expresses it in *II Pol.*, lect. 1. In other words, it can only result from discussion, argument, and debate.

its roots in the defective will for law and justice and indeed is, because of this fact, a matter of conscience as such; and conscience, we must not forget, is willing to be deceived by spurious reasons in order to justify its attitude—indeed, it seeks for such reasons in more or less good faith.

The difficulties in the way of true knowledge and certainty lead to *important conclusions for natural law ethics*:

1. As a science concerned with the essential and factual nature of society, today natural law ethics is faced with incomparably more difficult tasks than ever before in the ascertainment of the natural law order of society. For, its chief task lies not so much in questions of the moral order of individual life, which are questions of application of the moral law of nature, but in questions of the order of society in regard to its law and institutions. But, to penetrate into the nature of the matters concerned represents an immeasurable task in the present-day complexity of social, economic, and political relationships. In this task, natural law ethics will look for substantial help from the social sciences, especially from the legal sciences, the political sciences, the economic sciences, and the cultural sciences, and, in conjunction with the sciences mentioned, from empirical sociology. Natural law ethics, however, will be well advised to accept only the assured findings of these sciences. Everyone knows that a great deal is still under discussion in these sciences, and so is not yet established knowledge of truth and reality. As long as there are such limits to certainty of knowledge, natural law ethics should *not, by way of generalizing, attempt to set up concrete natural law imperatives*; it can discuss only the mode of application of assured natural law principles in the relevant circumstances. For these reasons, natural law ethics can only rarely succeed in establishing quite concrete principles of justice and in the name of natural law demand their recognition as fully authoritative rules for the legal order of the state. Its task is, rather, to reason out the mode of application of natural law principles in relation to the conditions and possibilities of their realization in given circumstances.

2. Although natural law ethics must be cautious with general demands, another conclusion emerges immediately for the representative of natural law ethics: Because of the unavoidable element of uncertainty and the consequential risk attached to his work, he must be aware that *his professional ethos calls for a high degree of courage.* The more he has to deal with particular questions of the natural law order in society, in the state, in the economy and international community, the more he has to work in regions where the objectively based judgment which his scientific code obliges him to form presupposes a considerable measure of familiarity with the contiguous social sciences, although the mastery of these is now no easy task even for the experts themselves. On the other hand, the natural law ethician makes his task too easy when he confines himself to the sphere of general principles and attempts to leave their application to the individual sciences. His task simply remains unfulfilled. He will have

to incur the risk which *Thomas Aquinas* (cf. Chap. 61) saw was linked with diagnosis and therapy regarding the social body: the necessary factual information involves incomparably greater difficulties than those which face medical science in its diagnosis and therapy of the human body. Yet, *all social diagnosis and social therapy is fundamentally a question of the natural law order* in the various spheres of social life.

3. Thus, we reach the conclusion that *the weight of argument* is the deciding factor *in applied natural law,* since the discovery of the operative reasons, and hence of truth, can often be made only by a process of clearing up differences of opinion—the process by which all sciences, and human knowledge generally, progress. It seems important to emphasize this because, as we have already pointed out (cf. Chap. 47), many jurists conclude from the differences of opinion apparent in traditional natural law that it possesses no scientific basis at all, or that it works primarily only with "ambiguous" rules. Were this charge true, methodologically jurisprudence too would be in an awkward state. *Theodor Viehweg* points this out in his work on the foundations of jurisprudence, which goes to the root of countless misunderstandings,[33] since its essence, as he insists, does not consist in a closed system of rigidly distinct conceptual relationships and established findings, but rather in "problem-thinking." Such a method is also largely demanded by applied natural law on another level in the process of learning what is just, that is, in working out the validity of the natural law principles in cases where their application is made complicated by the circumstances.

But do not the difficulties already exist in *establishing truth and certainty regarding even the fundamental principles of natural law*? Indeed, natural law could not be disputed if the same kind of certainty existed about its basic principles as that which exists for the laws of physics. The difference is that, in the realm of fundamental moral and legal principles, *inevitable certainty* does not exist as it does in the fields of mathematics and of natural sciences, but only *discretional certainty* when free will has to play its part. Man could not be endowed with freedom if his acceptance of fundamental moral and legal principles were necessitated like that of mathematical truths. This does not mean, however, that certainty in the ethical sphere must be essentially less assured than that in the other spheres of knowledge.[34] For even in these spheres, truth and certainty of knowledge is possible only with the aid of fundamental axioms which are susceptible of no exact scientific demonstration (e.g., regarding the knowability of the external world, or of the utterances of others as conveying their thoughts). Since the certainty attainable in the knowledge of the

[33] T. Viehweg, *Topik und Jurisprudenz,* 1953, esp. pp. 15 ff., 53 ff.

[34] The proof that this is true has been missing in natural law ethics for a very long time. Because it concerns equally the moral and jural fundamental principles, I have undertaken it within the framework of general ethics. Cf. Messner, *Kulturethik,* pp. 237–63; cf. also, *Ethics and Facts,* pp. 296–315.

fundamental principles of morals and law is a certainty arising from decision, it is much harder to reach agreement; hence, the dispute for and against natural law will certainly not be decided on the purely theoretical plane, in the sense that it could result in a generally accepted scientific conviction with regard to the basic metaphysical and ethical questions of natural law (essence, foundation, content, authority, range). In today's "crisis" of philosophy and ethics, the assumptions are too varied to permit the hope of a uniform conception of natural law.

This is not meant to question the justification, indeed the necessity, of discussions on these fundamental issues. In many quarters, they have led, at least among those guided by a scientific ethos wholly devoted to truth, to increased self-criticism, and thus to an understanding of the views and assumptions of others. Self-criticism and understanding of others have always proved to be most valuable allies in the history of the scientific quest for truth. In fact, of course, *a very significant measure of agreement* exists not only between the exponents of the several present-day and earlier conceptions of natural law, but also between all these and the critics of natural law, with regard to the elementary principles of justice upheld by natural law ethics, surprising though such a statement may appear prima facie. At stake are the *fundamental values of Western civilization,* which underlie man's personal rights to freedom and to the democratic order of society. Opinions differ widely with regard to their conceptual definition and metaphysical explanation, but in the *actual legal conscience* there is not the divergence of view regarding these fundamental values and the legal principles resting upon them as one might suppose from the disagreements in the theoretical sphere. This should suggest, it seems, to the various metaphysical and philosophical schools, the great opportunity common to them: for natural law primarily thinks in terms of the "nature of things." In the purely theoretical field, rigidity and pedanticism easily set in from ideological motives. It is otherwise when the discussion proceeds from the nature of things and of facts in the legal world and with the appropriate concrete argument.

To a part of the *Protestant school of social ethics* the question of certainty forms the occasion for criticism of traditional natural law theory. This is particularly true of *Thielicke.* He begins with the alleged impossibility (cf. Chap. 11) of knowing an "order of being" (*seins-ordo*), "so that there can be no transformation formula" which would permit a concrete and detailed order of justice to be derived from the most general natural law principles. The factors of uncertainty "are rooted in the objective world-structure itself," namely, in "the world *post lapsum,* whose injustices *cannot* be clearly demonstrable since there are no clear zones of justice in it with which those injustices could be contrasted." *Thielicke* then undertakes to show this by reference to the axiom *suum cuique;* for the reason given, this axiom, he says, has a completely variable character, "so that as men we are unable to know this *suum* and are consequently not in a position to declare general rules by means of which the *suum* could be assigned in concrete cases." "The *suum* is known only to God"; it derives "from the function, unknowable to us, which a man possesses in the totality of God's plan of salvation," and cannot appear until the last judgment. *Thielicke* illustrates his opinion with the question: "What is, for example, in this sense the *suum* of Judas Iscariot? And not simply in the sense of what punishment befits his betrayal, but especially in the sense of what function or destiny was allotted or granted to him." [35]

Insofar as *Thielicke* is attempting a soteriological interpretation of the *suum cuique,* he will be opposed by no one who takes his stand on revelation; *Thielicke* is bound to come up against the problem of predestination, as is shown from the last passage cited. He is right in thinking that, with such a purely theological conception of justice, one cannot approach the question of justice as a human task. An inconsistency, however, seems evident here: the judgment that the existing order of this world is at bottom, as he insists, an order of injustice is only possible on the basis of a knowledge of the fundamental requirements of justice; this is as indisputable logically as the fact that judgments about the particular as such are only possible through knowledge of the general. On the whole, however, his far-ranging discussion of the problem of certainty must give the impression that tremendous efforts are being made to prove that there is no such thing as something which mankind always does and has done, namely, to judge with adequate certainty about right and justice in the existing circumstances of practical life with the aid of the natural jural conscience.

Thielicke argues exhaustively that, as the outcome of the *conclusiones* (his expression), only general a priori principles "emerge in the manner of deduction"; to this, he says, there is added the subsumption in the inferential process, which "results from experience and therefore proceeds a posteriori." Admittedly, medieval and modern presentations of traditional natural law doctrine make it appear that the general principles of justice consist of purely a priori propositions; this is, however, by no means true, for they represent rather, as we have shown, "synthetic judgments a priori" which, being already originally linked with insight into reality, are therefore not in any phase of their apprehension purely a priori propositions. They are experienced and known in relationship with life. Hence, in the process of their application *there are not two separate worlds standing face to face, the purely deductive a priori one and the purely empirical a posteriori one, but it is always the one reality, whose general aspect is recognized in the principles, while the particular element of circumstances, determining their actual bearing, is recognized in their application.* According to syllogistic logic, in the *conclusio* from general principles, different conclusions result in accordance with circumstances. Like many others before him, *Thielicke* thinks that this proves

[35] H. Thielicke, *Theologische Ethik,* Vol. I, 1951, pp. 670 f., 675, 682, 683 f.

the dubiety of general principles. He uses in illustration the command, "Thou shalt not kill": "Even this commandment in its concrete application reaches a crisis, which arises because of the empirical components. The state kills the murderer, and in self-defense one may kill one's attacker." The example seems badly chosen just from *Thielicke's* point of view. First of all because the principle repeats God's spoken word; secondly, the natural jural conscience and the clear reason leave no one in doubt that this commandment does not protect the life of the murderer or the aggressor. In fact, God has declared by his spoken word only the mode of application of the commandment as already knowable by the natural conscience (Exod. 21:12–15).

Thielicke is certainly right in saying that "often the situation is distorted to the point of unrecognizability in the question of a just war."[36] In fact, however, conscience and reason do not leave man so completely in the lurch even in this question, difficult though it is, as *Thielicke* suggests. For apparently the question will be whether a war is for the purpose of attack or defense. On this point the judgment of history in individual cases is nearly always clear, from the verdict of *Thucydides* on the Athenian aggression against Melos until the verdict of the world's conscience on *Hitler's* aggressive war. Undoubtedly, for the citizen called to arms, an objective judgment on the situation (on the causes of the war, etc.) is often very difficult, if not impossible; the "transformation formula" for this case is the duty of obedience toward the lawful "authority," subject to the proviso that a command recognized with certainty as wrongful must not be obeyed. It may be recalled that this "transformation formula" is advocated by *Luther* not only for the special case in question, but also quite generally from the point of view of theology, and particularly from that of injustice of this world. The point we are trying to make is that placing the question of certainty on the theological level does not lead toward its solution. On the other hand, traditional natural law ethics is fully in agreement with *Thielicke* with regard to the fact that even the best legal system conceived and created by men is necessarily imperfect; but it maintains that even the imperfect order is still order, and indeed the order which makes possible man's existence as a civilized being.

This basic function of legal order itself seems to provide a last decisive argument against *Thielicke's* exclusively theological legal ethics; an argument which at the same time concerns his fundamental views on the *suum* as the supreme principle of justice. He says: "Certainly for every man a *suum* is due to him," but "what is concretely due to each is unknown to the extent that the relevant differences are unknown, and hence the ultimate presuppositions are lacking for calculating the *suum*." Furthermore, he says, they are unknown because we do not know the order "which alone

[36] H. Thielicke, *ibid.*, pp. 667 f., 682 f., 686.

would inform us of the key to the distribution by means of which it could be determined what is due to each with respect to the whole." This is the widely held opinion that the *suum cuique* principle is conceived as a principle by which, according to a "distribution key," all ideal and material goods are exactly calculable and must be allocated to the individuals. All such arguments, however, *overlook the radically basic situation of human existence,* which consists in its freedom. This also forms the basic situation for the legal order and is of effect on its whole nature. An order of justice with appropriation of a *suum* in all goods, calculated exactly for each person according to a distribution key, must either cancel the freedom of man in the use of the goods so allotted to him or must at every moment reallocate all goods in accordance with new conditions created by the self-determination of individuals. The *actual legal order can be only a defective one because it depends upon the freedom of human nature*: just as the freedom of man in his personal life is essentially and unavoidably bound up with the risk of evil, so also in his social life it is essentially and unavoidably bound up with a measure of injustice.

Because of this risk linked with freedom in social life, the legal order has the basic function of securing and of guaranteeing the sphere of freedom necessary for the life of man as a responsible person. Because it is bound up with the freedom and responsibility of man and is dependent on them, however, it is also the duty concerning which man's moral jural conscience instructs him to strive unremittingly to remove the injustice attached to the historical legal order, thus *proving himself distinguished by freedom and responsibility, and indeed giving ever-renewed proof of this in ever-changing historical and social situations.* The fact that man is capable of this in spite of the uncertainty existing in applied natural law is shown by legal history itself: by its records of the development of legal consciousness and of legal institutions; by the standard of respect for human and social rights already achieved; and by the indubitable awareness of new aims and tasks in the sphere of international law and of the world-wide task of social justice presented by conditions in underdeveloped countries.

49. Natural Law and Positive Law

The arguments for and against legal positivism which occupied jurisprudence and legal philosophy before the Second World War were often so one-sided that, in the end, natural law and positive law simply appeared to be opposites. Thus, a primary fundamental fact of jural reality was largely lost from sight: namely, that natural law, to a quite substantial extent, enters into all historical legal systems.

1 *Natural Law as Part of Positive Law*

That natural law forms part of positive law is a fact which should admit of no doubt to natural law theory. For, if natural law has an inner connection with man's nature and with its specific mode of functioning (viz., as the law of its nature), obviously no positive system of law in society can endure for any length of time unless it realizes natural law to a considerable extent. Therefore, it must be considered indisputable that *positive law is imbued with natural law,* even if it does not fully realize natural justice, since the functioning of the natural law, as traditional natural law theory has always held, is imperfect. Even the dictatorial state which perpetrates a great deal of legal injustice, as is exemplified in both historical and present-day instances, is forced to realize a substantial measure of natural law or its contrariety to nature will terminate its existence.

Natural law's realization, to a large extent, in positive law, was the fundamental belief both of *Augustine,* notwithstanding his criticism of the *civitas terrena,* and of *Thomas Aquinas. Augustine* found the idea in *Cicero* and did not hesitate to understand *Cicero's* conception of natural law in the sense of the Christian view of the world and to include in this interpretation his view of the relationship between natural law and positive law. The relevant passage from *Augustine* [1] has been more fully discussed elsewhere (cf. Chap. 47); to summarize that law has its origin in nature, that it has been first realized by way of experience regarding the general utility in custom and legal usage, and finally that law so engendered reaches guaranteed authority through enacted laws and religion. Citing the same passage in *Cicero, Thomas* also sees natural law realized in positive law, apart from particular exceptions. In addition, following the Aristotelian notion of state and law, *Thomas* places such strong emphasis on the position of the legislative authority that, as *Linhardt* says, *Thomas'* whole general theory of law seems written in the light of positive law, so that a superficial reader of *Thomas* on the subject of positive law might perhaps take him for a legal positivist.[2] *Hegel* too states definitely that "natural law or philosophical law is different from positive"; yet, concerning the specific character of natural law and of positive law he says: "To recognize these as being opposed or conflicting would be a great misunderstanding." It would be a misunderstanding also to bring forward the degeneration of positive law as a reason for such a contrast: "That force and tyranny can be an element of positive law is incidental to it and of no significance to its nature." [3]

It is not to be wondered at that scholars like *Gierke, Maitland,* and

[1] Cf. St. Augustine, *De divers. quaest.,* 31.
[2] Cf. R. Linhardt, *Die Sozialprinzipien des hl. Thomas v. Aq.,* p. 116.
[3] Hegel, *Grundlinien der Philosophie des Rechts,* 1821, par. 3.

Ehrlich, who did not allow themselves to be blinded to the reality of law by the positivist theories of their time, established customary law historically and sociologically as the principal content of positive law,[4] just as *Cicero, Augustine,* and *Thomas* did. At the same time, since original customary law is rooted in the legal sense arising from the natural jural conscience, they were able to see natural law in positive law. Therefore, we would agree with *Rudolf Stanka* that the *"immanence of natural law"* in positive law is established, but that, on the other hand, the theory of a "transcendence of natural law" on the part of legal positivism, just as on the part of natural law ethics, is equally questionable. In fact *Stanka* says that positivist thought, in the face of reality, especially in matters not dealt with by the law, but in which the jurist must find his way, will be compelled to seek after suprapositive principles: "These principles—they are simply the philosophical foundations of law—transcend law, in the view of rigid legal positivism; in fact, however, they are necessarily immanent in law"; "not less untenable is the thesis which represents law as a part of ethics; natural law thinkers hold this thesis especially. . . . They fall into the error censured above, of conceiving natural law norms as transcending positive law, and thus, even though involuntarily, render aid to legal positivism." [5] In a similar manner, *Karl Larenz* sees in natural law "the immanent foundation of every historically realized law." Hence, he considers it erroneous to see the relationship between natural law and positive law as an antimony.[6] On the other hand, *Stanka,* whose own position is traditional natural law theory, rightly says in the same place: "Those who approve of this rebirth (of the idea of natural law), nevertheless, will not believe that the age of legal positivism has been without influence on the natural law idea. The criticism of the natural law idea on the part of the legal positivists was too deep for anyone now to be able to pass over its sound core." In our exposition of natural law we have made a special point of doing justice to the positivist criticism of natural law.

11 *Natural Law and Legal Positivism*

In the preceding chapters we endeavored to do justice to the *element of truth in legal positivism* from various angles; now we can sum up our findings. First, *legal certainty,* whose establishment belongs entirely to positive law by its very essence, presupposes the promulgation and guaranteeing of the law, two basic functions of legal order which can be carried out only by the lawgiver. Positive law with its system of rules is the prerequisite for assured knowledge of what is valid law in the relation-

[4] Cf. regarding Gierke, Chap. 38; on Maitland, Chap. 42; on Ehrlich, Chap. 41.

[5] R. Stanka, "Zur Wiedergeburt des Naturrechts," in *Wissenschaft und Weltbild* (Vienna), May 1960, pp. 208 ff.

[6] Cf. K. Larenz, "Zur Beurteilung des Naturrechts," in *Forschungen und Fortschritt,* 1947, Parts 4–6.

ship and intercourse between citizens mutually and in their relationship to the state. It also forms the prerequisite for that aspect of the guaranteeing of law and order which is associated with *judicature,* that is, for the ordered administration of justice. The significance of positive law for legal certainty under this aspect, gives legal positivism a second support for its content of truth. Apart from exceptional cases, when a positive legal rule obviously collides with a clear natural law principle, the judge is bound by the norms of positive law; we shall presently discuss this more fully.

The element of truth in legal positivism finds its third corroboration in the *defects of knowledge* (this was discussed in the preceding chapter). The legal relationships rooted in the nature of the essential and actual reality, in complex situations are not always ascertainable with absolute certainty; therefore, it belongs to the sphere of the lawgiver's competence to state what is to be regarded as law. Fourthly, the core of truth in legal positivism is borne out by the wide sphere of functions belonging to the *juridically neutral area,* on which natural law does not pronounce but only authorizes the lawgiver to make decisions without setting before him definite legal principles. What is left to the decision of the citizens and of the lawgiver, however, concerns not only questions of expediency concerning the safeguarding and enhancement of the common good, but also questions of value, in the sense that it remains within the province of a people to decide in the neutral area to what values it shall, out of preference, devote itself.

The core of truth in legal positivism is supported, fifthly, by *legal continuity,* an essential feature of legal order. The maintenance of continuity can even mean for the lawgiver, in the light of natural law ethics, that he must forgo changes in statutory law which are demanded by natural law, if the change, owing to deeply rooted legal custom, would involve difficulties, impair the authority of the law, and damage instead of enhancing the common utility. Legal reforms, therefore, must be decided not simply according to natural law postulates but also according to factors of a positive law character.[7] Sixthly, and lastly, we have had to refer to the *impairment of the nature* of fallen man as the deepest reason for the position, essential to juridical order as such, of positive law in the spheres of legis-

[7] Much of what is set forth above has already been illustrated in detail from St. Thomas Aquinas, and some further considerations will follow presently; for the general question, note especially St. Thomas, *Summa theol.,* IIa IIae, q. 60, a. 5 and the distinction he makes there between what possesses force in positive law by reason of natural law and what by reason of legislative power: "Nam legis scriptura ius quidem naturale continet, sed non instituit: non enim habet robur ex lege, sed ex natura: ius autem positivum scripturam legis et continet, et instituit, dans ei auctoritatis robur." On the question of legal continuity, it is said in Ia IIae, q. 97, a. 2, that when laws are altered, even when the alterations in themselves mean an improvement from the point of view of natural law, it must be observed that the effective force of the existing law (*vis constrictiva legis*) rests largely on legal custom; hence, Thomas continues, as the jurist Ulpian states, if legal reforms involve any departure from law long regarded as just, their utility must be beyond doubt. For, as Thomas again declares, quoting Aristotle: "Leges habent maximam virtutem ex consuetudine."

lation and of the administration of law, and thus for the increased competence of positive law.

Accordingly, if there is room in natural law theory for the element of truth in legal positivism, natural law theory can, on the other hand, demonstrate the *unreality of dogmatic legal positivism* by reference to the nature of the facts involved in law. The fundamental assumption of legal positivism in its varying shades is that law can be only positive law and that there are no suprapositive legal imperatives rooted in the moral order and binding upon positive law. Today, only comparatively few still adhere to absolute legal positivism; rather, the belief has widely taken hold that with legal positivism itself the "crisis of the idea of law" has arisen. With the emergence of legal positivism, legal philosophy and jurisprudence were deprived of a universally recognized conception of law. As a milestone in this development *John Austin's* famous *The Province of Jurisprudence Determined* may be mentioned; the discussions set in motion by his positivist theory have still not come to an end. *Austin* held the only source of law to be the command of the sovereign of the independent political society; obedience to his command is assured by the application of physical force. In a century of criticism of *Austin's* definition in England, legal historians and sociologists have drawn attention chiefly to the facts of diversity in binding rules and of varying degrees of dependence of sovereign political communities on foreign powers. Today, *Austin's* definition has been abandoned as untenable. Currently, the most generally held conception of law is that of Sir *Frederick Pollock:* Law is "a rule of conduct binding on members of a commonwealth as such." [8] This concept of law is, in fact, not very far from that of the traditional natural law doctrine. Law, it says, is a rule given for the sake of the common good by him who has charge of the community.[9]

The difficulties in the way of a positivist definition of law have not yet been overcome. A jurist of the rank of *Nawiasky,* whose theory is a "methodical" legal positivism, defines law as "a system of precepts for the external conduct of the members of society, non-compliance with which is met by coercion into obeying or by punishment." In discussing the state's constitutional "fundamental law," as the basis of a definite juridical order, however, he finds it necessary to explain that "it contains no forcibly guaranteed rule for external conduct"; it is permissive and not mandatory. Yet, *Nawiasky* thought he had established the essentially mandatory character of law; this proves inconsistent with his interpretation of "the fundamental law." Furthermore, the statement that the constitutional law (as being permissive) "empowers" to something is logically hardly consistent with the rejection of the natural law idea that law originally "entitles" to something,[10] since the two ideas do not lie so very far apart (cf.

[8] Frederick Pollock, *A First Book of Jurisprudence,* 1929, p. 29.

[9] Cf. St. Thomas, *Summa theol.,* Ia IIae, q. 90, a. 4: "Quaedam rationis ordinatio ad bonum commune, ab eo, qui curam communitatis habet, promulgata."

[10] Cf. H. Nawiasky, *Allgemeine Rechtslehre,* 1948, pp. 2, 24, 31, 35 f., 171.

chap. 36). On the whole, as we shall show with regard to *Nawiasky's* conception of legal positivism, an understanding between the positive law and natural law modes of thinking should be possible if both sciences respect the frontiers of their own methods and if the reality of law as a whole is kept in view.

Besides the question of the concept of law, the legal positivists had to face the question concerning the *authority of the lawgiver* for legislation. To the modern mind, as soon as it was recognized that all men are by nature equal, it was clear that no man, on his own authority, is entitled to bind others by juridical obligations. We have dealt with the various answers to this question, which are opposed to natural law. The prize for logic may well go to *Kelsen*. No legal rule as such, he says, can have binding force through mere reference to a fact (e.g., ruling power), but only by reference to another rule. This means that the legitimation of every legal rule of positive law results from delegation from another rule, so that an unbroken *sequence of delegations* must lead back to an ultimate legitimizing authority. *Kelsen* himself concludes that the originating rule, the fundamental law on which the whole structure of rules rests, possesses only a "hypothetical" character; it is thought of as "presupposed." [11] Thus, the fundamental question of its authority remains open: From where does the legislator derive his authority.[12] The orginating fundamental law is the natural law.

111 *Natural Law and Lawgiver*

The idea of *delegation* has always been a fundamental notion in traditional natural law theory. All human law ultimately derives its binding force from natural law, which in turn rests upon the eternal law (cf. Chaps. 3, 47). Thus, the principal links in the chain of delegation are: *ius positivum; lex naturalis; lex aeterna.* Positive law rests either directly on natural law insofar as it embodies principles of natural law, or indirectly, insofar as its rules are concerned with matters which are left to the arbitrary will of the legal community, but as law acquires binding force through the power of command rooted in natural law.

From this we may conclude, first, that positive law receives its moral *sanction* through natural law: the duty of obedience toward positive law is furnished with the sanction of conscience. Apart from exceptional cases in which the conditions for "equity" are present (cf. below), only the law-

[11] Cf. H. Kelsen, *Allgemeine Staatslehre*, 1925, p. 104.

[12] Those who, like Nawiasky (*op. cit.*), reproach Kelsen on the ground that with his "presupposed" fundamental law and the system of rules understood by him as a chain of delegation has no real foundation, and that this is to be sought in the fact of the establishment of the fundamental law by the social community or leading group in power (cf. Chap. 36) do not do justice to the inner logic of Kelsen's view that laws are to be understood only by means of other laws, not by mere reference to a fact.

giver himself can cancel the duty of obedience (the morally binding force of his law), by the direct or indirect declaration of his will. Thus, purely penal laws, namely, those whose infringement does not, according to the legal sense of the people, involve any moral opprobrium, are not binding on the conscience; the lawgiver, taking account of this fact, attaches wholly disproportionate fines to such breaches, as in some countries to offenses against customs regulations. The binding force of a positive law is cancelled for a greater or lesser portion of the community by custom (a practice contrary to a law with the tacit consent of the lawgiver, which is equivalent to an indirect expression of his will), by privilege (an explicit exemption from a law granted by the lawgiver to certain members of the community), or by dispensation (exemptions granted in particular cases). However, any detailed discussion of the questions involved would be far removed from the object of our natural law ethics.

The second conclusion emerging from the sequence of delegation is that *no moral sanction* for positive law exists where the law is in opposition to the moral and jural order of nature. The duty of obedience toward the latter then comes into force: "We ought to obey God rather than men" (Acts 5:29). Judges and public servants may face severe conflicts of conscience if they are expected to cooperate in the execution of laws which are contrary to natural law (e.g. in applying laws relating to divorce or sterilization; or again parents, if they are compelled to send their children to schools or youth organizations where they will be exposed to religious and moral influences contrary to those of the parents). The associated questions of the right and duty of "resistance" will require special treatment (cf. Chap. 132).

A third conclusion to be drawn from the position of the lawgiver in natural law concerns the validity of natural law in cases when positive law is defective. Natural law comes into play in the form of *equity*. Equity (*epieikia*), says *Aristotle*,[13] with his usual clarity, is a law complementary to statutory law, this being necessarily defective because it can be framed only by the lawgiver in more or less general rules. Therefore, at times it has effects which are contrary to the principles of justice governing the intention of the lawgiver (*rigors in the law*); again, it contains no provision for a case which the judge must decide (*loopholes in the law*). Equity or the law of equity means the direct recourse to principles of natural law. Thus, we are not dealing with a principle which attenuates the principles of justice or even contravenes them, but with a true principle of justice; in fact, we are dealing with the supreme principle of the whole order of justice. For, it means that the suprapositive law prevails where positive law becomes injustice or reveals loopholes.

This complementary force of suprapositive law has consequences for legislation, for jurisdiction, and for the administration of law, as well as for individual conduct. It involves for the lawgiver the jural duty to pro-

[13] Cf. Aristotle, *Nic. Eth.*, V, 14.

vide for the administration of law to have recourse to the law of equity, so that in the cases mentioned the deficiencies of the law can be made up.[14] The position of the judge will require special treatment. As an instance of the applicability of the law of equity, the case is often mentioned of a person in danger of death from hunger, who is then entitled to appropriate what he needs; but this falls under private law. However, equity rights exist no less in the realm of public law; in a state of emergency the government of a democratic community is entitled to measures exceeding the powers provided in the constitution, if this is necessitated for the purpose of securing essential ends of the community. Nevertheless, the government remains bound to give an account of its actions to the lawgiver as soon as possible. Individuals are subject to the superior rule of equity if the enjoyment of rights which are theirs by positive or even natural law would undoubtedly place someone in grave spiritual or physical jeopardy (e.g., if the collection of a debt would bring too great a hardship on the debtor). For his part, the individual may have resort to the equity principle of *epieikia* in a case which the lawgiver for certain would not subsume under his general law; such equity may constitute a high virtue, even if the conduct in question may be punished by the relevant judicature.

[14] Repeated references are made in legal literature to cases of such provisions by the lawgiver, e.g., in the Austrian General Civil Code (ABGB) of 1811, which in par. 7 gives points to be considered by the judge in arriving at a decision and states that in case of any doubt remaining after the application of these points, the case is to be decided "with regard to the carefully assembled and maturely considered circumstances, according to principles of natural law." Reference is likewise made to the general clauses of the German Civil Code (BGB) concerning good faith. In the sphere of international law, Article 38 of the Statute of the International Court of Justice is pointed to as an example of the application of natural law principles in positive law, since, besides contract law and customary law, "the universal principles of law recognized by civilized peoples" are mentioned as a third group of legal rules which the Court is to use in coming to a verdict. In England, natural law principles were for a very long time fundamental in the administration of justice in accordance with common law (which is essentially customary law) and especially for the development of case law: the legal principles of equity. From this is to be carefully distinguished the equity jurisdiction which the Lord Chancellor, as "Keeper of the King's Conscience," was empowered to exercise. Although this equity jurisdiction could not nullify decisions of the common law courts, it was capable of preventing a party to a dispute from taking their case further according to common law; the decisions of equity jurisdiction formed a system of rules in addition to those of common law and statutory law. By the Judicature Act of 1873, the two systems were unified, so that today jurisdiction is carried out uniformly in accordance with statutory law and case law (judgments given in accordance with precedent). Besides, equitable jurisdiction still maintains its place in the courts, especially in the Chancery Division, one of the three divisions of the High Court of Justice (also known as the Supreme Court). On English law and English judicature cf. the much used book by T. E. Holland, *Jurisprudence,* 13th ed., 1924, new impression 1937, pp. 38 f., 72 ff.; the valuable summary by R. Rubinstein, *John Citizen and the Law* (Pelican Books), 3rd ed., 1953, new impression 1955. Of developments on the Continent Heinrich Mitteis, *Vom Lebenswert der Rechtsgeschichte,* 1947, p. 118, pointed out how often it is overlooked that "natural law had a practical side too, and, apart from other reforms, gave rise to great codifications (ABGB). Its influence on practice has hitherto hardly been examined."

A fourth conclusion from the idea of delegation in accordance with natural law concerns the lawgiver's obligation regarding the principle of the *common good* as the guiding principle for all his measures. All law is related to the common good (cf. Chap. 39); hence, the common good is the supreme natural law principle for the lawgiver. But this general principle also is dependent on the situation in its application. Hence, we can say: In his legislation, the lawgiver on the one hand need not and on the other hand must not go beyond what existing conditions make possible in the way of best realizing the common good. Morally reprehensible conduct which does not affect the common good is not a matter for his intervention. And in some circumstances he need not suppress everything which is morally bad even when it results in actual harm to the community. For, a community can be in a situation in which too strict laws cause more harm than good. The injunction of the common utility may then make necessary the tolerance of abuses by the lawgiver. A special reason why it may be in the general interest not to make certain evils punishable by law will often consist in the fact that this would give the authorities a certain opportunity to inform themselves about abuses which it has not the power to abolish. Freedom of conscience must be respected, as long as the manner in which this freedom is used does not prejudice public order. These are the considerations with which the lawgiver must approach questions of prostitution, of usury, of toleration of false religious beliefs, of the sale of contraceptives. The three first-mentioned examples are often discussed in the natural law doctrine of the Middle Ages.[15] Because of these considerations, it was generally upheld that the lawgiver is by no means obliged to incorporate all the demands of natural law in his legislation. This realism in Christian thinking may clash with the utopian belief of the many who think that all ills in political, economic, and social life can be cured by laws. Besides, it is an established fact of experience that the moral forces of a people must first be awakened before legislation can succeed in attaining higher goals.

In connection with the obligation of the lawgiver under natural law we must, fifthly, again deal with the question of the *legalization of injustice* by the existing law. For various reasons already discussed, the legal system always realizes the order of justice in an imperfect way. Insofar as these reasons, for instance historical factors governing the legal system, are outside the scope of the legislator's influence, they do not fall within his

[15] Cf. St. Thomas, *Summa theol.*, IIa IIae, q. 10, a. 11: "In regimine humano illi qui praesunt, recte aliqua mala tolerant, ne aliqua bona impediantur vel etiam ne aliqua mala peiora incurrantur." For this reason it may be necessary to tolerate the rites of infidels; in this connection he refers to Augustine, who adduces similar grounds for the toleration of prostitution by the lawgiver in *De ordine,* II, n. 12: "Aufer meretrices de rebus humanis, turbaveris omnia libidinibus." Augustine is thinking of public morality. It can easily be seen how erroneous is the opinion often put forward, even by serious thinkers, that in Augustine's opinion prostitution is necessary for society or for human nature. What he does hold is that in certain circumstances it may be the lesser evil and then may be tolerated by the lawgiver.

responsibility. It is a different matter when the legalization of injustice is due in part to social forces, that is, when the ruler or social groups exploit in their own interest the means which are in their power for shaping the legal system. This may result in the material-social, spiritual-cultural, or even in the personal-political disadvantage of social groups, as in the case of the deprivation of personal and of political rights in the dictatorial state. *In the democratic state also, social groups contribute to the legalization of injustice* if they use power influence on the legislative machinery to advance their sectional interests, politically or economically. This is the source of the danger threatening free democracy today, namely, that legality will more and more stifle legitimacy in that the groups which assert their interest contrary to the general interest by means of the legislative machinery can appeal to the formal legality of their conduct. In natural law, on the other hand, they are guilty according to the principles of justice, which form the essential basis of legitimacy and constitute the supreme duty for the lawgiver and for all groups having part in the mechanism of legislation.

IV *Natural Law and the Judge*

The position of the judge is indisputably marked by two essential features: *he has an obligation toward justice as well as to the legal community.* On behalf of the community he pronounces sentence in court: he is its representative. Accordingly, in deciding the individual case he is bound by the legal sense and will of the community as expressed in the positive law enacted by the ordering power. In this the principle of legal certainty, which, as we saw, has a natural law character, is of significance. But the judge is also under an obligation of justice, which pertains so much to the essence of his function that when he is appointed by the community it regards it as a matter of course that justice is his decisive obligation. The conception of justice which belongs to the legal community, however, is by no means that of literal justice if a decision according to the letter of the law in a particular case would offend against justice in accordance with the nature of the case. The natural legal conscience is principally at work in this notion of justice and in the will of the juridical community founded thereon. By virtue of this concept of justice and of juridical will, the application of natural law principles for jurisdiction in the cases of deficiency of the positive law, which was just mentioned, is legitimized by the will of the community, apart from the legitimation which exists in moral natural law.

It seems to me, that in this virtually unassailable account of the position of the judge we have perhaps the *main clues for elucidating the relationship between the administration of law and natural law*: first, the judge is above all bound by positive law; secondly, his obligation toward justice may in particular cases call for the application of suprapositive principles; thirdly, these principles do not belong merely to the individual conscience of the judge, but, fourthly, they belong to the "legal conscience," that is, of the juridical sense of the community. Through the juridical consciousness of society the legal conscience of the members of society is on the one hand substantially formed, and vice versa, the legal conscience plays a substantial part in the formation of the juridical consciousness of society, in the course of which the conscience of the judge has a greatly enhanced influence. All this obviously restricts the immediate application of natural law principles in jurisdiction to a very narrow field, indeed almost entirely to cases in which the application of a legal rule would set the community at variance with itself or the judge at variance with his legal conscience. Only in the latter case can one speak of a true conflict of conscience on the part of the judge: when he is obliged by his office to conform with enacted laws while his conscience does not allow him to do so. In the former case there is not a genuine conflict of conscience, because the lawgiver himself does not intend to link the administration of law with a rule which, in a particular case, would result in an injustice undesired by him and contrary to the jural sense of the community. The question with which we are engaged is one which specifically concerns nations with a highly developed legal culture. When treated as a question of natural law, this must be done in the light of possible related concrete situations. Purely abstract views for or against natural law or for or against positive law cannot do justice to the essence of the question.

With regard to the real *conflict of conscience* on the part of the judge, if today the right of freedom of conscience is recognized as an essential human right it can hardly be reasonably disputed that it must also be recognized in the judicial sphere. The conclusion seems to be that the lawgiver must make provision for the case of a genuine conflict of conscience. The most important provision might well be that the independence of the judiciary (with freedom from removal or transfer) should be extended to include the case of a judge obeying the well-founded voice of conscience; at the same time, of course, the way should be open for the parties in such a lawsuit to appeal to a higher court and a special function should be assigned to the supreme court of the community.

In order to settle correctly the question of the judge's conflict of conscience one will have to consider wherein lay the sociologically relevant facts for such a conflict. We have previously referred to the juridical consciousness of the legal community. In fact, positive law in modern democracy is an expression of the juridical consciousness of the community; but in the process, necessary for legislation, of shaping the political will of the community and in the operation of the appropriate mechanism, forces may become influential which are not motivated by the moral sense of a nation but by party ideological considerations. In this way, legal rules can be arrived at (e.g., the laws relating to marriage, education, sterilization) which are at variance with the moral conscience of a substantial proportion of the people and of a substantial proportion of the judiciary. We have seen in the section on "Natural Law and the Lawgiver" to what severe conflicts of conscience judges can be exposed if they are required to give judgments on the basis of laws repugnant to their consciences.[16] Anyone, of course, who assents to freedom of conscience for judges in the manner described must also concede it to judges who happen to be in harmony with the legal rules in question. The party in a lawsuit, whose conscience feels aggrieved by the decisions of such judges, can likewise obtain satisfaction through recourse to courts of appeal. In fact, in the liberal democracies one seldom hears of true conflicts of judicial conscience, since in the appointments of judges to the courts account can be taken of their moral convictions.

Concerning the provisions of constitutions, this is almost entirely confined to a right of examination regarding the compatibility of a legal rule with other rules of positive law. But even when a right of examination is not expressly provided, no genuine conflict of conscience arises for the judge, if, as *Karl Peters* explains, a law can be recognized as non-law, viz., "an intolerable deviation from the higher rule"; and if, therefore, "in spite of the legal form no binding precept exists." Cases of this kind, remarks *Peters,* "in view of the legal certainty and the ordering function of the legal system, can only be very rare. We can speak of the nonvalidity of a law enacted in accordance with the constitution only when there is an

[16] If we confine the true conflict of conscience to a *clear* verdict of conscience this is because the judge is justified in conscience in appealing to the judgment of his conscience only after thorough reflection on the ethical considerations in question. A conflict of conscience is a conflict between two duties, namely, obedience to a rule of law and obedience to a rule of conscience. Karl Peters, "Das Gewissen des Richters und das Gesetz," in *Gegenwartsprobleme des Rechts, Veröff. d. Sekt. f. Rechts- und Staatswissenschaften des Görresgesellschaft, neue Folge,* Vol. I, 1950, pp. 34 f. illustrates the considerations which a judge may have to bear in mind in a particular case before his conscience can reach a decision: "The judge's moral decision as to whether he can take part in the carrying out of a law or not is difficult for the reason that, as a rule the question cannot be settled with a plain Yes or No. . . . The difficulty can be illustrated by the example of the participation of a Catholic jurist in divorce proceedings. Here the following points are to be considered, evaluated, and balanced against one another: Is civil divorce in itself wrong or not? To what, after all, does divorce apply? To civil marriage? Or are civil and sacramental marriage so interwoven that the effects of civil divorce touch both? Does participation in civil divorce proceedings mean an obscuring of the indissolubility of a validly concluded and consummated sacramental marriage? Does it cause well-founded scandal? Does the present age with its intellectual confusion demand a clear stand and attitude? Does the cooperation of judges who are lenient toward divorce stem the flow of divorces? What significance has divorce for children? Are the justified consequences of divorce (in regard to family rights and inheritance rights, e.g., the regulation of care of persons, property arrangements, loss of inheritance rights) made possible only by divorce or also by other legal processes? What significance does it have for the rule of law and the ordering function of law that it is precisely here that the judge opposes the law?" Another consideration also seems to impose itself on natural law principles: how far the judge, because of his own moral convictions, may compel divorce seekers to preserve their married state when they themselves are acting on a conviction of their conscience, although a mistaken one, as is easily possible in the prevailing chaotic state of religious and of moral beliefs.

evident and intolerable violation of general, fundamental human laws (e.g., forced marriage, compulsory divorce, compulsory contraception, compulsory abandonment of religious observance, laws for the destruction of races or nations). . . . The conflict between judge and law is much more prone to arise where the law is valid." But also, in case the jurist recognizes, along with this limitation of the judicial conflict of conscience, the more general one just outlined, natural law ethics will agree with *Peters:* "One should guard against seeking the conflict of conscience too soon." [17]

After the abandonment of narrow legal positivism, probably few jurists would be prepared today to dispute the authority of natural law in the special cases mentioned. Differences of opinion are concerned much more with the *question of degree.* Two natural law principles have to be brought into harmony: legal certainty and legal truth. The latter refers to true law in the individual case in accordance with the relevant natural law principles of justice. Legal certainty is one of the most important, if not the fundamental, value of the legal order within the common good. This is stated by *St. Thomas* with an emphasis which will surprise many. To the question whether and why positive law is necessary, he answers (among other things): Since the judgment of the judge may be influenced in any particular case by sympathy, antipathy or other feelings, it is necessary, as far as possible, to pin down judgment by statute and *"to leave only the minimum to the discretion of the judge."* Therefore, to the question "whether judgment must always be given in accordance with positive law," he answers logically: Because what is just according to natural law and positive law is explained or defined by statutes, "jurisdiction must be carried out in accordance with the statutory law." [18] In support of this, *Thomas* appeals to the passage in *Augustine* which we mentioned in another connection (cf. Chap. 47), where he says that the judge must not judge "about" laws, but according to them.[19] For *Augustine,* as for *Thomas,* the question of justice concerns the lawgiver primarily, whereas the judge's duty is linked primarily with legal certainty, one of the highest values of the common good, which consists in peace. On the other hand, of course, *Thomas* considers it as established that "if positive law contains anything contrary to natural law, it is unjust and possesses no binding force" and that "such statutes are not to be called laws, but rather corruption of law; consequently, law must not be administered according to

[17] K. Peters, *Das Gewissen des Richters und das Gesertz,* 1950, p. 33.

[18] St. Thomas, *Summa theol.,* Ia IIae, q. 95, a. 1; IIa IIae, q. 60, a. 5. In IIa IIae, q. 67, a. 2, Thomas goes so far as to say, in answer to the question whether the judge may pronounce judgment at variance with the truth as known to him: "The activity of the judge is exercised on public authority; hence, he must base his judgment on what he is cognizant of in his official capacity and not on what he knows as a private person"; but he can allow his private knowledge to cause him to deal more severely with the evidence brought before him.

[19] Cf. St. Augustine, *De vera religione,* Chap. 31.

such statutes."[20] The difficulties arising out of this for the judge, however, he discusses no further. Many will also be surprised by the strong realistic emphasis, which emerges from the foregoing references, placed by *Thomas* on the status of the judge as one who functions by virtue of public authority (*publica potestate*),[21] on this, *Thomas* bases the judge's dependence on positive law.

We should be doing less than justice to the question of the relationship of the judge to the natural law if we did not once again devote special attention to the position of the judge in the *evolution of jural consciousness and of the legal system.* We are faced with the question of the relationship between positive law and natural justice from a new point of view. *Roscoe Pound,* the illustrious member of the Harvard law faculty, rightly observes that nearly all questions of jurisprudence fundamentally coincide in this one question. We must devote some space to his ideas, since in the course of his argument he speaks of the *law-creating activity of the judge.* The legal rule, he says, cannot but be general, whereas the individual case is governed by particular circumstances. Therefore, its relationship is one of general to particular. The question arising out of this concerning the position of the judge is not, says *Roscoe Pound,* uniformly answered by jurisprudence. The various theories of the application of law, he tells us, can be summed up as belonging to three main schools: the analytical school, which lays its chief emphasis on the logical interpretation of the text of legal rules; the historical school, which says that the judge's decision is only declaratory, namely, understanding the existing positive law, whether codified law or law of precedence, in terms of a process of historical development and thence interpreting it in the application of law by a purely logical process; the third school, represented especially in Europe, sees in the legal rule more a signpost for the judge to enable him to reach just findings, with wide scope for discretion; here he is obviously thinking of the so-called *Freirechtsschule* (free law school).[22] None of the three theories, says *Pound,* stands up to criticism: each presents an element of truth one-sidedly. He envisages a theory that recognizes the administrative element as a legitimate part of the judicature, because individualizing application of law is as important as its content itself. Such a theory, it appears, must unite the elements of truth in all three theories mentioned: first, the law must always form the fundamental idea; secondly, however, it must be understood not strictly according to the letter, but in accordance

[20] St. Thomas, *Summa theol.,* IIa IIae, q. 60, a. 5.

[21] Cf. St. Thomas, *Summa theol.,* IIa IIae, q. 67, a. 1–2; he refers, for further confirmation, to IIa IIae, q. 60, a. 6, where he says that just as laws cannot be binding unless enacted by public authority, so also no one can be entitled to administer the law unless empowered by public authority.

[22] One of its chief spokesmen was H. U. Kantorowicz, *Der Kampf um die Rechtswissenschaft,* 1906. In referring to the position of the judge in England, the free law school considerably overestimated the scope left him for free decision, for before the end of the century the judge found himself bound by statutory law and case law. Cf. the comments of Pound in the text above and note 14.

with the jural consciousness of the community in its historical character; and, thirdly, it must be interpreted, when legal injustice may be in question, in accordance with the principles of equity indicated by the nature of the case. Let us follow *Roscoe Pound* further. His arguments are by no means restricted to American and British conditions, although he expressly refers to the elimination of equity and of natural law from jurisprudence in these countries. He makes the distinction, familiar in Anglo-Saxon thought, between theory and practice, which might serve to induce thinkers in other countries to reflect whether there the problem is not seen in too narrowly theoretical a way. With regard to England, *Pound* declares that equity law and natural law were indeed banished by the reaction which set in against them in the nineteenth century. This exclusion, however, operates more in theory than in practice and more in appearance than in reality, for justice is administered to a great extent in accordance with legal standards which allow the facts of particular cases to be taken into account; in addition, there is a degree of judicial individualization through the discretionary application of equitable principles, handed down from equity law and natural law.

Thus, *Pound* sees two kinds of principles, equity law and natural law, operative in the judicial process: one originates directly in equity and natural law, and, indirectly, another grows out of legal practice itself; both, however, ultimately come from the same source and work in the service of justice. In short, a form of moral judgment on modes of conduct enters into practice, while no definite ground for such judgment is provided by legislation or precedence. *Pound* thinks of judgments on modes of conduct such as fair, conscientious, rational, wise, careful. By means of this analysis of the administration of law, *Pound* reaches his answer to the question concerning the law-creating activity of the judge: *the judicial function and the legislative function intermingle with one another.* The legislative organ has to make laws, but from the nature of the case it cannot make laws so definite that the judicature will not also obtain a law-making function to some degree; although this function will be subordinate only, namely, one of supplementing and of developing, nevertheless, it will play a necessary part in the judicature's competence.[23] The legal order is something living, constantly involved in an evolutionary process, like society itself. For the sake of legal certainty the administration of law must abide by positive law, but it will constantly keep in touch with historical sources and with the natural jural conscience as the primary source, and will understand itself at the same time to be *a vital organ in the continuous historical evolution of the legal system,* which is a living entity and not a repository of statutes to be understood by adhering to the letter.

Throughout our study of the judge and natural law we have stressed the juridical sense of the community in order to obviate the impression

[23] Cf. Roscoe Pound, *An Introduction to the Philosophy of Law,* 2nd improved edition, 1954, pp. 51, 54 ff., 60 ff.

that the position of the judicial conscience in the giving of judgments implies natural law maxims which the individual judge produces out of the hat and uses in place of positive law. Only in very rare cases and quite exceptionally can there be any question of a judge acting by completely certain principles of his individual jural conscience; fundamentally and in general, it will only be the legal principles living in the conscience of the community itself which can come to be applied. Natural law theory must mistrust the *subjective* conscience by itself, if one considers to what few, general principles the natural conscience is confined, and if one considers also how often in present-day society moral judgments are at variance even in some fundamental questions. The subjective conscience of the judge, as a sound natural law theory must hold, always will have to look first to the juridical consciousness of the community for an *objective* criterion of the applicability of the natural law principles which he adduces. Of course, this juridical consciousness is not an ultimate criterion of true law, but it represents, as we saw in connection with *Augustine,* a primary operative form of the natural law conscience, which, being linked with the community sphere, is also linked with the self-criticism of this conscience.

For all these reasons, the traditional natural law school, even though the natural law possesses binding force in the framework indicated, can understand the voices of the jurists who warn us against an overstraining and indeed a misunderstanding of "what natural law can yield"—"a misunderstanding, guided ultimately by the opinion that there is an intrinsic antinomy between natural law and positive law, that natural law is a kind of superlaw which, thought to be fixed in all details, competes with the closed system of positive law." *Peter Schneider* is right in adding a further warning: "But it is just this opinion that drives thinking into the vicious circle of natural law against positivism and positivism against natural law." [24] *Roscoe Pound* also points to the same dangers. Although in the discussion mentioned above, he lays stress on nonpositive law principles in the administration of law, he asks, "Who would respect the law, if the courts failed to do so?" Nevertheless, again looking more at the practical side of the question and referring to the fact that the parties to a lawsuit need not remain satisfied with the decision of the court of first instance, he concludes his observations with the statement that, "In the rare application of nonpositive law principles the sacrifice of legal certainty is more apparent than real, because when reached by mechanical application of fixed rules to human conduct, it always has proved to be delusive."

Notwithstanding the theoretical skirmishes between positivist and natural law schools, they are not as far apart as one might expect in the *practical question of the interpretation of law.* Even positivist legal thinking cannot manage without "suprapositive" ideas. The natural law doctrine, on

[24] P. Schneider, "Naturrechtliche Strömungen in deutscher Rechtssprechung," in *Archiv für Rechts- und Sozialphilosophie,* 1956, Vol. XLII, 1, p. 109.

the other hand, as we have seen, firmly maintains that the judge is bound by positive law rules, exceptions being confined within narrow limits. With regard to positivist thought, *Hans Nawiasky* rejects suprapositive ideas for legal administration, but considers it necessary to assume a fourth method of interpretation in addition to the verbal, logical, and systematic methods, namely, to call into service "the pre-legal ideas underlying positive law, which form an integral part of it." [25] This seems to make into positive law something which is not expressed in positive law, and hence, according to positivist suppositions, represents a logically different category and could not be made an integral part of it. A further question also arises, namely, how the exact content of these ideas is to be ascertained. *Nawiasky* answers by suggesting that it is to be gained from positive law or from the legal persuasions underlying it. But presumably this must be the legal sense of the community which we have so much emphasized; and, the legal sense of the community, it can hardly be denied, is rooted in the soil of natural law, that is, in the natural moral-jural conscience. *Nawiasky* himself admits that natural law "addresses itself to the lawgiver." [26] Obviously, it enters into his "fundamental law of the state" and forms "an integral part" of positive law in the light of his own conception, just mentioned, although as a "pre-legal idea." Thus, in reality the conceptions are not as far apart as the antagonistic positive and suprapositive law theories suggest.

This is confirmed by the similar conception of the status of pre-legal ideas in the positive legal order as outlined by *Hermann Weinkauf,* then President of the Federal Court of the German Federal Republic, who at the same time speaks of a law "superordinate" to positive law; law of a higher rank is, according to *Weinkauf,* to be found in constitutional law, in the general basic juridical persuasions outside it, and in the "fundamental juridical principles which it is customary to speak of as supralegal justice or natural law"; [27] these principles, *Weinkauf* says, "are binding because of God's disposition. . . . Here human legal order finds its limit." Basically, *Weinkauf* means that, with the interpretation given to human existence by the revealed word of God, there is provided a body of natural law principles, among which he mentions those concerning the dignity of man, his freedom, and property.[28] If we compare the views of such decided exponents of their own opinions as *Pound, Nawiasky,* and *Weinkauf,* it seems to be undeniable that, from the point of view of reality and practice, the difference between their antagonistic views is much slighter than appears at a first glance. The antagonism is more apparent than real, espe-

[25] Hans Nawiasky, "Positives und überpositives Recht," in *Juristenzeitung,* nn. 23–24, 1954, p. 719.

[26] H. Nawiasky, *Allgemeine Rechtslehre,* p. 29.

[27] H. Weinkauf, "Richtertum und Rechtsfindung in Deutschland," in *Berliner Kundgebung 1952 des deutschen Juristentages* (Berlin), 1952, p. 24.

[28] Cf. H. Weinkauf, "Das Naturrecht in evangelistischer Sicht," in *Zeitwende,* 1951, pp. 95 ff.

cially when on the one hand "pre-legal ideas" are recognized as a constituent part of the positive legal order (*Nawiasky*), and on the other hand "supra-legal justice," as *Weinkauf* sees it, is not conceived as definite legal rules or as a system of such rules, but as the elementary principles of the moral-jural conscience, whose true understanding of itself is guaranteed by the spoken word of God and whose correct understanding of these principles is thus provided with the supreme objective criterion.

v *Natural Law Thinking and Juristic Thinking*

This chapter has been concerned with the question of scientific thinking as represented by the legal theory and the natural law theory. A number of epistemological and methodological issues are yet to be discussed. The legal theory, which is concerned mainly with positive law, and the natural law theory, which is concerned with supra-positive law, are sciences having the same sphere of reality of law as their common object. Conflicts between sciences, which are concerned with the same fields of inquiry, are by no means confined to juristic and ethical sciences; they occur also between other sciences whose object and common sphere of reality is man, for example, between medicine and ethics, between sociology and social philosophy, between empirical and metaphysical psychology, between biological and philosophical anthropology. The dividing line between the *two principal groups of sciences* concerned with man and society is to be drawn in accordance with the diversity in their aims and consequently with the diversity in their methods. One group sees its immediate object of inquiry in the human reality which is accessible to *external experience,* such as medicine, experimental psychology, sociology, political science, jurisprudence; accordingly, its methods are the ascertainment of facts, of causes, and of the interactions between modes of conduct, relating to the actual regulation of relationships between men. The other group of sciences sees its object of inquiry in the sphere of human being, which forms the object of man's *metaphysical experience,* that is to say, the object of the "natural metaphysics of the human spirit," to quote *Bergson's* expression again. Concerning this sphere, the unprejudiced human mind is as certain as it is of external reality. To this sphere belongs man's knowledge that his nature is not only characterized by the animal reality (*Augustine* concretely expresses it: "man knows immediately that he is more than the beast" [29]), but also by the facts that conscience belongs to the primal reality of his nature, that he possesses self-determination and freedom, that he participates in a world of absolute values, including especially the values of the moral order, with which is linked an awareness of the Creator, of responsibility toward him and, attested by this, of survival after death.

This "natural metaphysics of the human spirit" embraces prescientific

[29] St. Augustine, *De genesi contra Manich.,* Lib. II, cc. 11, 16.

knowledge and forms the object of scientific inquiry and explanation in the various departments of philosophy, namely, ontology, metaphysics, psychology, epistemology, logic, methodology, natural law theory, social ethics, and the ethics of the state, of political economy, and of cultural life. Whereas the methods of the first-named group of sciences are *empirical* in the wide sense of the word, that is to say, they belong to direct or indirect sense experience, the methods of the other group are *metaphysical* in their specific sphere. Even though they proceed from external or inner experience, they aim, by progressive analysis of the phenomenologically ascertained data existing therein, at knowledge of the nature and of the basis of the suprasensory reality and at knowledge of its significance for man and man's existence. In this, they seek especially the answer to the questions, what man is, what is the origin and meaning of his existence; what in particular, following on the answers to these questions, the moral order of his individual and social life is. Natural law theory in particular is faced with the question, what are the essence, the foundation, and the implications of law as the part of the moral order concerned with society.

We have said that the dividing line between the two great groups of sciences of man rests upon the diversity of the aims of knowledge and of the methods dependent thereon. Because they correspond with the object of knowledge, the *methods* are limited as means of knowledge. If this limitation is not understood in the sphere of departmental sciences, and if it is assumed that the sphere of reality accessible to one method represents the whole of reality, then conflict must arise between these sciences. This was the case when medical science maintained, in the name of science, that the soul does not exist because none is discoverable by the surgeon's knife; or when it was held by ethics that the economic science which investigates the interactions of economic factors as such is irreconcilable with the nature of man as a free, morally responsible, creative being. Experimental and metaphysical psychology came into conflict because the former rejected the possibility of the human soul, whereas the latter, with its doctrine of the soul and relying on its methods, behaved too sceptically toward the new empirical psychology. The jurisprudence and natural law theory were opposed because the former had become "jurisprudence without law" to a large extent (*L. Nelson*), whereas the latter had become accustomed to see all law as merely part of the moral order.

Conflicts between the sciences always go back ultimately to infringements of their methodological limits by one side or the other. Relying on its own method a science will monopolize a whole field of reality of which only part is accessible to it by means of its method. The rapid growth of specialization in the sciences in modern times was accompanied by narrowing the mind's horizon to particular specialist departments; thus, conceptual systems and the knowledge of reality came into conflict. This conflict gradually became a problem. After the First World War a rethinking process was inaugurated; it concerned the basic questions of the epistemology, of the logic, and of the method of most of the sciences, namely, in the spheres of the natural sciences and of the mental sciences. To this movement toward the methodological self-awareness of the several sciences belongs the change in attitude toward the natural law idea in the sphere of the legal sciences since the Second World War; to it also belongs the new outlook of natural law theorists themselves to the boundaries in the field of inquiry accessible to natural law methods.

Mankind has always known of a law by which man-made law must either be legitimized or else be proved unjust. When the totalitarian state undertook to create "its law" on the principles of legal positivism, the knowledge of "law proper," with its claim to recognition of its authority, made itself felt. On the other hand, in traditional natural law theory, today it is accepted as certain that natural law contains no ready-made definite legal system; rather, law is very largely dependent on historical development and social conditions. Certainly, both sides have more work to do. Perhaps for the first time we have undertaken to show, from the standpoint of traditional natural law ethics, the true content of legal positivism. From the legal philosophy of *Hans Nawiasky,* today one of legal positivism's most outstanding exponents, it can be seen that a legal science which methodically confines itself to its own sphere need not be positivist in a sense contrary to natural law. He wrote in the Preface to the second edition of his book, which we have referred to several times:

> It is of the essence of law to be positive, that is, given. It is the absence of this factor that, of course, distinguishes a draft bill from an enacted law. Obviously, by legal positivism is understood a strictly verbalistic and in this sense formalistic legal theory which, of course, merits rejection. To a jurisprudence equal to its task, the wording of the laws only provides the first clues for ascertaining the inner meaning of legal rules. In other words, enacted rules are not laws, but sources of law from which laws are to be derived; law is prior to laws, as the intrinsic nature of an object is prior to its external forms of appearance.

Juristic thinking is bound to see the reality of law principally in "*what it does.*" Natural law theorists will be concerned primarily with "what it ought to do," namely, achieve justice. The jurist will always see in *legal certainty* the first guiding principle of his thinking; the natural law theorist, however, will see in *legal truth* the goal of inquiry governing his thought. On both sides attention will be directed toward the common good as the end of law: the jurists will give more immediate consideration to legal certainty as the foundation and basic value of the common good order; natural law will give more immediate consideration to the ultimate values and implications of the order of the common good, as they are bound up with man's personal and social nature. *The relationship between the two sciences will always be one of tension.* The tension, however, can be fruitful—fruitful for the two sciences and, what is more important, fruitful for the development of the legal consciousness and the legal system in the service of the common good of the legal community, and hence in the service of man as a personality.[30]

50. Justice

I *The Notion of Justice*

The word justice denotes a balance between claim and fulfillment (cf. Chap. 34). Consequently, the word is often used with a twofold meaning. When we say that justice demands something we are thinking of rights which ought to be complied with; but we are also thinking of the obligation to comply with them. In the first case the idea of the *order of justice* is of principal concern, since legal claims exist by virtue of natural law or positive law. In the second case the idea of the *virtue of justice* as a readiness to fulfill legal obligations is in the foreground. The two aspects of the idea are inseparably linked and therefore must remain visible in the virtue concept. We may define justice, then, as a habit of the will to comply with existing legal claims; [1] or, in other words, the will to give to everyone his due. Justice is thus the virtue governed by the supreme directly evident juridical principle of *suum cuique*. The actual *suum* consists of a right grounded in objective law; to comply with objective

[30] The Protestant theologian and ethicist likewise says: "If the biblical-Christian idea of justice has played so influential a part in the forming of the Western principle of justice; if, for example, the idea of human rights has demonstrably arisen and been declared in connection with Christian thinking (reference is made to Gierke's *Johannes Althusius*), it will be impossible to deny the right and duty of the theological thinker to take part in this reconstruction work (in the social field). . . . Conversely, one who lives entirely within the world of biblical ideas cannot fail to observe that on the theme of secular justice, on questions of justice in the political and economic sphere, it is not primarily to the biblical expert and theologian that people will turn for advice and authoritative guidance; rather, the questions involved are such that even the most orthodox and exclusive biblical experts among Christian teachers from time to time consider it obligatory to apprentice themselves to philosophers and jurists. The question of justice in secular matters is thus obviously a question impinging on different faculties and a problem in which Christianity and the ancient world have cooperated, not by chance, to solve. The frontiers, however, are, not only in politics and war, but also in the history of the mind, the places where the most vital decisions occur. A frontier guard must be one who looks across the frontier. It is high time that once again theologians, philosophers, and jurists should combine in order to examine together the meaning of this great idea, the idea of justice, and to make clear what justice means, so that a halt can be called to the devastation and so that social reconstruction in accordance with justice can be undertaken in the devastated areas" (Emil Brunner, *Gerechtigkeit: Eine Lehre von den Grundgesetzen der Gesellschaftsordnung*, 1943, pp. 10 f.).

[1] St. Thomas, in discussing justice, *Summa theol.*, IIa IIae, q. 57, a. 1, within the framework of his theory of virtue, starts from the notion that the speciality of justice is that its object is what is right, and he defines, with reference to the *corpus iuris civilis* (1, 10, Dig.: De iustitia et iure I, 1): Iustitia est habitus secundum quem aliquis constanti et perpetua voluntate ius suum unicuique tribuit.

law in acts and forbearances as a subjective habit, forms the obligation of justice. Hence, it follows: *Justice is based upon rights, not rights upon justice.* Rights are primary; conduct in harmony with the rights of others is the virtue of justice. It seems to be important to stress that the *suum* does not only concern material goods, still less only property rights; and not only does the individual have a claim to a *suum,* but also the political community and the social groups (hence, the various kinds of community justice as pointed out further on). Thus, the *suum* includes, for instance, man's life and bodily integrity; his freedoms, honor, and good name; conjugal fidelity; and from the viewpoint of the political community, all goods of the common weal (cf. Chap. 48, "Absolute Natural Laws," and Chap. 100, "The Equal Rights of States").

Justice, therefore, is not to be founded either on conscience alone or a mere feeling or sense of justice; nor can it be founded on the experience of utility or on the sense of value. All attempts to explain the ordering function of law in such a way go only half way, like the attempt to base morality on moral feeling. We are speaking here of scientific legal philosophy and of legal ethics and of their foundations. It has already been pointed out that we attach the greatest importance in several respects to the jural conscience as an intellectual aptitude and an emotional force; but jural conscience, jural feeling, and sense of value cannot suffice by themselves because of the possibility of subjective error. Rather, objective criteria are necessary for the scientific investigation of truth in law as well as of truth in value. In the reality of law itself, the subjective conscience does not form the basis of its ordering function in social life; rather, the juridical consciousness of society, which is objective in character, does this, because although it arises from the natural conscience, its operation is bound up with the objective demands grounded in man's social nature (cf. Chap. 47). And yet, a jural conscience thus objectivized does not suffice for a determination of the essence of justice, since the legal consciousness of society can err also and has proved itself fallible to a high degree. Moral feeling, juridical sense, sense of justice, and even the individual jural conscience and the juridical consciousness of society taken simply by themselves do not lift law and justice above the subjective sphere. Principles of justice which have objective and universal validity are to be founded only on the "nature of reality." This reality is man's nature and, in relation to his nature, his social and physical environment. To declare that, in the sense of justice, the consciousness of such a validity is also present, does not remove the difficulty that mere subjective consciousness offers no objective criterion as to what is good and right. Such a criterion can be obtained only from the investigation of the intrinsic connection between the subjective juridical conscience of man and the objective reality of human nature. Our examination of this connection has found the "existential ends" indicated in human nature to be the objective criterion of law and justice.

11 Kelsen, Del Vecchio, Schmitt, *on the Concept of Justice*

Hans Kelsen, in answer to the question, *What is justice?* states: "I know not and cannot say what justice is, absolute justice. . . . I must content myself with a relative justice and can say only what justice for me is." By way of explanation he goes on: "Human reason can grasp only relative values. . . . Absolute justice is an irrational ideal. From the standpoint of rational knowledge there are only interests and conflicts of interest. For their solution only two methods are available: either to satisfy one interest at the expense of the other or to effect a compromise between them. It is not possible to prove that the one solution and not the other is just. . . . The moral principle, which undertakes a relativistic theory of values or which can be inferred from it, is the principle of tolerance. . . . It is self-understood that no right to absolute tolerance follows from a relativistic philosophy; rather, tolerance only within the framework of a positive legal order, which guarantees peace among those subject to the law while forbidding them any use of force, but not constraining the peaceful expression of their opinions." But with this principle of tolerance is set up an absolute principle of justice, yet without real foundation, being merely derived from the other absolute principle, also set up without foundation, that the legal order has to guarantee peace among those subject to the law. Thus, *Kelsen* contradicts his own profession of ignorance concerning the meaning of absolute justice; indeed, with *Augustine* (cf. Chap. 47) he knows precisely that the impulse toward peace and order in social life is a fundamental impulse of human nature, so that the nature of justice is to be understood from the nature of man. *Kelsen* contradicts himself again when he links with his profession of ignorance in regard to absolute justice, a declaration that truth is the goal of science, which can only thrive under the protection of relative justice, of "justice for me," in the protection of relative tolerance, that is, tolerance of the peaceful exchange of opinion as an aid to mutual understanding. But he desires, precisely in the name of science, to establish principles of justice (tolerance, peace, freedom) rooted in true knowledge, and yet says at the same time that "the judgment of human reason by which anything is declared to be just can never put itself forward with the claim that it excludes the possibility of an opposite judgment of value." [2] This can mean only that two mutually contradictory propositions can be at one and the same time true (which means abandoning the principle of contradiction, the fundamental principle of scientific thinking). In fact, *Kelsen* can hardly deny that propositions such as, "Willful murder is unjust," or "Totalitarian dictatorship which excludes tolerance is unjust," represent universal and absolutely valid judgments concerning truth and value. To deny that no knowledge of truth is possible in this regard would simply mean the bankruptcy of science. This is the conclusion reached also by *del Vecchio.* Commenting on *Kelsen's* similar statement (in his *Reine Rechtslehre,* 1934) that the substance of justice cannot be ascertained by rational process, *del Vecchio* observes that this latter statement would mean "a complete condemnation of reason." The question, therefore, is what is irrational, the ideal of absolute justice, as *Kelsen* holds, or his science with its conclusion that the content of this ideal "cannot be determined by Pure Jurisprudence." [3]

[2] H. Kelsen, *Was ist Gerechtigkeit?,* 1943, pp. 40 ff.

[3] G. del Vecchio, *Die Gerechtigkeit,* 2nd ed., 1950, pp. 131 f.; Kelsen, *Reine Rechtslehre,* 1934, p. 13.

Giorgio del Vecchio himself comes to the conclusion, with regard to *the substance of justice,* that the core of the formal notion of justice is "an absolute claim" which is expressed by the "transsubjective consciousness," in the sense of a form of consciousness "on the basis of which the subject sees itself confronted objectively with others and comprehends itself as belonging to an order of relationships." The content of this order of relationships consists, "in accordance with pure reason, of a uniform and complete acknowledgment of the property of personality in oneself and in all others, and in respect to all the conceivable mutual relationships between the several subjects"; "from this ideal issue the concrete demands of justice as they arise continuously in our conscience." These demands, however, do not go beyond what is described commonly as the moral-legal rational a priori "what can be termed the sap of life or the core of truth" of the natural law doctrine—so that "conscience which is common to the whole human race . . . offers the most valuable confirmation of the conclusions to which our inquiry has led." Since *del Vecchio* has only a *formal* conception of law (cf. Chap. 36), his conception of justice must remain formal also; this is not altered at all by the introduction of the personality idea, since even the recognition of the same property of personality in all by all does not in itself convey any information concerning the precise content of the *concrete* rights and liberties of the person. Indeed, *del Vecchio,* instead of suggesting a philosophical derivation of concrete rights and liberties, suggests that "the concrete demands of justice . . . arise in our conscience." Thus, he admits that his philosophical conception of justice does not make possible an adequate criterion of the concrete demands of justice. In addition, in *del Vecchio's* conception of justice, the social entity is not comprehended as such—not in its proper essence and right—because he seeks to base the conception of justice on the idea of personality alone, namely, on man's individual nature. Thus, for example, the rights of the state could be understood as only a consequence of this individual nature; in fact, however, it is rooted in man's nature exactly as are the rights of the person, namely, in man's social nature. Only when, as we have suggested, the concrete rights and demands of justice are based on the individual and social sides of the unitary human nature, can the concrete conception of justice be reached, according to which justice represents a mode of conduct related to a concrete *suum.* These critical remarks should not give the impression that we do not appreciate fully the importance of the work of *del Vecchio* with its unusually wide survey of the literature on the subject.[4]

Carl Schmitt says, concerning the fundamental question of all legal philosophy, *What true law is,* and hence what justice is, that the answer is a matter of jurisprudence as the guardian of the sources of law (cf. Chap. 48). Obviously, the governing idea is that the "social" juridical consciousness of the legal community reveals itself in the historical sources of law; in this idea is to be sought the objective criterion of true law. He recalls the fundamental idea of *Hegel's* legal and political philosophy, namely, that (in *Hegel's* words) "law must become usage, custom, the state must have a rational organization . . . only this makes the will of individuals really legal." *Savigny* too, in *Schmitt's* opinion, notwithstanding criticism, correctly recognized that "statute is only one of several manifestations of the concrete patterns of law": "Law as a concrete order cannot be separated from its history. True law is not decreed but arises in an unintended evolution. What true law is, is determined today in the concrete

[4] Cf. G. del Vecchio, *op. cit.,* pp. 85, 118–21, 177.

historical form of jurisprudence, in which growth comes to consciousness." [5] Important as the historical-social legal consciousness of the community is as a form of expression of the natural jural conscience and as a source of law for jurisprudence, an ultimate objective criterion of what is right and what justice requires is not to be found in it. For, a glance at comparative legal history reveals that the legal consciousness of peoples and the legal orders resting on them show differences which have always kept legal philosophy questioning, making it a fundamental task for legal philosophy to work out an objective, ontological, and not solely historically based criterion. The same applies to earlier attempts in the field of legal philosophy to base legal order on "the feeling for law in society," and in this to see the "sovereign," as does the Dutch scholar *H. Krabbe*. It applies no less to the attempt of another Dutchman, *H. Kranenburg*, to obtain an objective foundation for the notion of justice and to overcome subjectivism by an empirical examination of the "sense of justice" and by demonstrating its uniformity in a legal society.[6] All these attempts are confronted by the arguments with which *Kant* refuted the error of basing morality and law on mere experience (cf. Chap. 3).

III *The Measure of What Is Just*

From the fact that the virtue of justice, as stated, relates to definite rights, it follows that it possesses a character different from all other virtues: *any obligation of justice involves a certain measure*. This is conveyed in the definite claim to what is due, whereas all other virtues lack any such standard. The duty of almsgiving prescribes no definite sum, whereas a debt to the grocer can be discharged only by full and exact payment. The standard of such an obligation may be of either of two kinds: (1) *strict equality*, when someone has a strictly determined claim as in the case of a creditor; (2) *proportionate equality*, when it is a question of a claim related to the common good. This is the standard of justice applicable to the claims of social groups to their due share of the economic welfare of the community, in relation to their contribution to social cooperation. The same is true of burdens allotted by the lawgiver for the sake of the common good, the assessment of which must be on the basis of proportionality, that is, the burdens imposed for the common good should be relatively equal for all according to their capacity. Since the standard of justice in both cases is not equally definite, the obligation also differs. Obligations of the first kind, of "strict justice," which demand strict equality in their fulfillment, remain in existence until they are fully satisfied. Hence, the *duty of restitution* binds until the jural obligation is fully met. On the other hand, when the standard is proportionate equality, there is no duty of restitution, since the obligation is not a strictly defined debt, but the proportional

[5] C. Schmitt, *Über die drei Arten des rechtswissenschaftlichen Denkens*, 1934, pp. 45 f.; *Die Lage der europäischen Rechtswissenschaft*, 1950, pp. 23 f.

[6] Cf. H. Krabbe, *The Modern Idea of the State*, 1927, pp. 45 ff.; H. Kranenburg, *Political Theory*, 1939, pp. 143 ff.

participation of all members of society in the common good. This implies a continuous process of adapting manifold factors to one another and to the requirements of the common utility; hence, it denotes a *permanent obligation* of justice to be constantly renewing the pattern of the common good correspondingly.

IV *The Forms of Justice*

Justice imposes duties either toward a community or toward individual men and individual groups to give them what is due to them, their *suum*. From this fact we derive the classification of justice into community justice and individual justice.

1. The object of *community justice* is the common good of the various kinds of communities (cf. Chaps. 31, 42), that is, a *suum* of one of them to be met by its members complying with it. Hence, this form of justice may be subdivided, on the basis of the subdivision of communities, into the following: *legal* justice, whose object is the common good of the great community, or the "state," insofar as that depends on its enacted law; *social* justice, whose object is the common good of "society" (as distinct from the state; cf. Chaps. 68, 136) in its groups and classes cooperating in social economy, insofar as this depends on the distribution of the social product; *international* justice, whose object is the community of nations, insofar as its common good depends on the conduct of nations toward one another. Granted that other forms of communities with their common good also exist, in particular the family and other social groups, further classifications of justice could be made to correspond with these; for example, we could speak of a domestic justice for the family circle; one might also consider the possibility of a concept of *political* justice as a form of state common weal. In the classification of community justice set down here, attention is directed toward the common good in its various relationships and hence to public life in the light of present-day developments of society and of civilization. It offers the necessary tools for the treatment of all the important questions of social life today; we hope to show this in the succeeding Books of this work. The chief aim of a classification in the sphere of ethics is not a theoretical, speculative one; rather, it is practical: to facilitate the discussion from every point of view of questions arising concerning the moral and legal pattern of social life.

2. *Individual justice* is subdivided into distributive justice and commutative justice. The object of *distributive* justice is the individual good as part of the common good, that is, the claim on the community of individual persons and social groups to a fair apportionment of burdens and benefits. The object of *commutative* justice is a definite legal claim, a claim which must be satisfied according to the principle of equivalence. The relevant *suum* consists in the right to one's life, freedom, honor, to the fulfillment of contracts, etc.; since this form of justice concerns, above all,

the claims which arise in the course of economic exchange, it is called commutative justice.

No classification of justice can cover the full reality of social life in all its aspects, especially in the complexity of its present-day ramifications. This qualification applies to the classification set forth here, as well as to that commonly followed by the scholastic textbooks, which will be considered at the end of this chapter. One advantage of our classification may be noted here: it admits of a clear separation of *natural justice,* whose obligations spring directly from natural law, and *legal justice,* whose obligations are rooted directly in positive laws.

Legal justice

Legal justice comprises, in the first place, all the obligations to comply with the demands of the common good. These obligations are determined by positive law and belong to two categories: first, the lawgiver's obligations to make whatever laws are necessary for the establishment of the common good; secondly, the citizens' obligations to keep the laws. In modern states the laws are made by parliaments. In the parliamentary democracy the parties are under an obligation to consult the interests of the common good primarily and only secondarily those of their party. No member of parliament or of congress may justifiably promote unjust measures. It is equally contrary to legal justice to obstruct necessary measures. The "political" obedience of the citizens falls within the second of the two spheres mentioned; for them it is an obligation of legal justice. States themselves as members of the community of nations are bound by legal justice to comply with its laws when they are enacted by an international authority.

Social justice

In origin, the expression "social justice" refers especially to the economic and social welfare of "society," in the sense of the economically cooperating community of the state. Owing to the division of labor, the national economy constitutes a cooperative economic unit, whose members in their various groups and classes are all interdependent in their work, making provision for their sustenance. The national economy, therefore, constitutes a socio-economic community whose common good demands for all groups and for their members a due share in the fruits of their cooperation which is commensurate with their contribution. These shares are distributed in the form of prices, wages, interest, dividends, rents, and social and private insurance benefits. Economic cooperation in society and the consequent distribution of its fruits give rise to obligatious of natural justice as distinct from legal justice (which is concerned with, for example, compliance with the social legislation of the state for economic life). The social groups, primarily, are subject to the obligations of social justice. In the negotiations and agreements of the various groups, these must allow one another their due share in the output of their socio-economic cooperation. Social justice, therefore, imposes obligations on employer and on employee in the course of negotiations of collective labor agreements. It not only demands a just distribution of the social product, but also binds the groups cooperating in society to make the efforts in rendering their services, necessary for the firm establishment and development of the common good in all spheres and for economic and social progress. Very high profits, resulting not from a high standard of services but from the monopolistic power of cartels, and uneconomic wages, which are enforced by the power of trade unions and not justified by productivity, are contrary to social justice. The obligations of social justice also relate to the will and to the cooperation of the social groups in creating the social institutions necessary for the most perfect fulfillment of the demands mentioned, that is, vocational organizations. (The implications of social justice for the ordering of social economy will be found in Book IV of this study.) After the conclusion of a collective labor agreement, the observance of its conditions becomes, for both parties, an obligation of commutative justice involving the duty of restitution. The obligation of social justice, which is outstanding among all other obligations and which binds the economically advanced nations, means giving help to the underdeveloped countries so that they will be able to build up their economies and to reach an average income proportionate to that of the other nations. This is not only an obligation of social justice but equally of international justice, because the common good of the family of nations is in question (cf. Chap. 197, on international social justice).

International justice

International justice directs states toward the common good of the community of nations; its obligations are obligations of natural justice. They concern cooperation in the struggle against common dangers and evils, especially against war, and also against other dangers to the well-being of the family of nations (e.g., crime, slavery, the white slave traffic, the traffic in narcotic drugs, etc.); they also concern cooperation in the service of the general material and cultural welfare, through the exchange of raw materials and finished goods, ideas, and ideals; finally, they concern cooperation in organizing the community of nations and in creating institutions enabling it to carry out its work. As soon as such an organization can establish an international (or, better, supranational) authority, the obligations of the nations, which spring from its laws, fall under legal justice. International treaties between individual states create firm and definite obligations, the honoring of which, therefore, falls within the scope of commutative justice under the rule *pacta sunt servanda,* which is the fundamental principle of natural law in this domain of international law. Modern "international law" belongs principally to the sphere of contractual rights and obligations which are binding on the signatory states.

On the other hand, to cooperate with other nations in the building up of an "international law" for the good of the community of nations is an obligation of international justice for every nation. A special kind of international justice, that is, international social justice, the obligations of which are among the gravest, has just been mentioned under social justice, namely, to help the underdeveloped countries.

Distributive justice

Distributive justice is that form of justice which imposes an obligation to share burdens and benefits in accordance with the proportionate equality demanded by the common good. Whereas legal justice directs the authority in society toward the good of the social whole, distributive justice directs it toward the good of the members of society. The state authority is it that is chiefly bound by distributive justice. This distinguishes distributive justice from social justice, since the latter, which also has for its object a right apportionment in the common weal, does not impose obligations primarily upon the state but upon socio-economic groups. In particular, distributive justice has to guide the action of the sovereign and of the legislative, administrative, and executive organs (a special kind regards penalties and is called vindictive justice). Disproportion in the distribution of fiscal burdens and military service, partially and favoritism in the award of public offices, honors and grants from public funds, are contrary to the dictates of distributive justice. An obligation is the avoidance or abolition of privileges not founded on services, that is, benefits enjoyed by one part of the community to the detriment of another part. One of the most important obligations of distributive justice consists in the building and carrying out of a *social policy* and social institutions to protect social groups which suffer from the malfunctioning of the social system; distributive justice also promotes measures of *economic policy* to enhance all-round economic productivity and the just distribution of income and property.[7]

Commutative justice

Commutative justice obliges the individual and corporate person to render to each his due in accordance with strict equality. The object of commutative justice may be the right to one's own person, to the services of another, to a thing, to a discovery. The right concerned may be someone's right to possess something which has already passed into his ownership (*ius in re;* it is not synonymous with possession, for it exists when the owner has lent a thing to another), or a right to demand the transfer of

[7] There is much misapprehension in economic and political writings regarding social and distributive justice; to the former is often assigned the duty of equalizing incomes, which is considered to be primarily the task of the state (cf. Chap. 142, the reference to J. Maritain); but this obligation of the state is one of distributive justice, whereas equalizing, equivalence in what is given and what is received agreed upon by way of contract, is a matter of commutative justice.

ownership in something to which a claim has been established (*ius in rem*). In the former case, the object of the immediate claim is the thing itself; in the latter it is the transference of the thing into ownership. Again, the right in question may be the right to performance or nonperformance of an action by another, or to the rendering of services. Commutative justice is *"strict justice"*: until satisfaction commensurate with one's entitlement has been rendered, the obligation to restore "strict equality" remains in force. Hence, the duty of *restitution* arises, which lasts as long as a just claim has not been met. Since rights and claims of commutative justice are based mainly on contracts, it is also called contractual justice. It governs man's civil intercourse in particular; thus, it governs the greater proportion of the daily processes of social life—those concerned with the exchange of goods and services by way of payment in money; because of this aspect, the expression "commutative justice" is derived. Since it demands strict equality between what is given and what is received, its governing principle is that of equivalence.

The Concept of Social Justice

The subdivision of justice and the definition and classification of social justice have been the object of repeated discussions within the framework of traditional natural law theory since the thirties.[8] These are theoretical discussions. Regarding the practical demands of social justice, there seems to be no substantial difference of opinion. The traditional scholastic doctrine dealt with three categories of justice: legal, distributive, and commutative. Many of its present-day exponents now treat legal justice and social justice as identical, and likewise

[8] A long list of those who in the thirties took part in this discussion is to be found in Messner, *Die Berufständische Ordnung*, 1936, p. 301; detailed reasons for regarding social justice as a special form of justice were first given in my inquiry, "Zum Begriff der sozialen Gerechtigkeit," in *Die soziale Frage und der Katholizismus, Festschrift der Görresgesellschaft zum vierzigjährigen Jubiläum der Enzyklika Rerum Novarum,* 1931. Departing from contemporary usage in the discussion of social problems and from modern political, economic, and social development, and going back to the distinction between "society" and state which the traditional natural law theory made its own, I placed its sphere of operations in economic-social life, as explained above. The comprehensive study of Joachim Girs, "Zum Begriff der justitia socialis, Ergebnisse der theologischen Diskussion seit dem Erscheinen der Enzyklika Quadragesimo anno," 1931, in *München, Theologische Zeitschrift,* 1956, pp. 61 ff., in which the essential literature since then is mentioned, shows clearly that my definition has been upheld. Cf. also A. F. Utz, *Recht und Gerechtigkeit, Die deutsche Thomasausgabe,* Vol. XVIII, 1953, pp. 564 ff.; a divergent view is represented by Joseph Höffner, *Soziale Gerechtigkeit u. soziale Liebe,* 1935; "Soziale Gerechtigkeit und die überlieferte abendländische Gerechtigkeitslehre," in *Karl Arnold, Festschrift,* 1955, pp. 35 ff.; Höffner himself in his first-named work points out that my definition has been accepted by authors such as Albert Schmitt, S.J. (*Das neue Reich,* 1932, pp. 563 f.), Josef Pieper (*Die Neuordnung der menschlichen Gesellschaft,* 1932, p. 15), Anton Retzbach (*Die Erneuerung der gesellschaftlichen Ordnung nach der Enzyklika Quadragesimo anno,* 1932, p. 9), *Cassianus Hentzen,* O.F.M. (*Commentaar op Quadragesimo Anno,* Vol. I, pp. 304–8, containing full discussion of the various views set out in pp. 18 ff. in Höffner's first-named work). That social justice is a special kind of justice has been maintained more recently by William F. Drummond, S.J., *Social Justice,* 1956.

legal and general justice (cf. Chap. 46). The expression "legal justice," however, suggests positive law and the obligation to enact it and to obey it (most scholastic textbooks following *St. Thomas Aquinas* considered this to be its object). A second difficulty in the way of the identification of legal and social justice arises from the fact that the obligations of the latter are chiefly obligations of natural justice, whereas those of the former have their basis chiefly in positive law; this difference hardly seems compatible with the logical consistency necessary for a classification. A third difficulty is of a similar kind: the concept of legal justice would, according to the textbooks mentioned, include also international justice (as distinct from international law, which is based on treaties and hence belongs to commutative justice); in the absence of supranational legislation, however, the obligations of international justice are obligations of natural justice, not founded on a positive law. Exponents of traditional natural law ethics who view social justice as *a special form of justice* can point to the fact that, in the social movement dating from the middle of the nineteenth century, whenever social justice has been spoken of in the struggle for the reform of the social system, the reference has been, in the sphere of natural law theory, principally to duties of natural law on the part of the social groups, whereas the obligation of the state to carry out a social policy must, as such, obviously belong to distributive justice. Besides, the equating of social with legal justice in an age of all-engrossing state intervention may well contribute to misconceptions concerning the function of the state in the social sphere; for example (cf. Chap. 142), it may lead to the assumption that social justice is primarily a matter for the state, whereas primarily it is a matter for the groups concerned in the economic process (of "society" as distinct from the state). Finally, it may be pointed out that the object of any classification is to facilitate the understanding and application of principles to constantly developing social conditions; but the extent of economic and social evolution since the Middle Ages has been so enormous that this alone seems to demand a development of the theory of justice.

51. Freedom

We speak here of "social freedom" as distinct from the freedom of the will (cf. Chap. 13); it implies religious, civil, political, economic and social liberty. Social liberty consists in man's self-determination in regard to his existential ends, without hindrance from individuals or society. From these ends spring man's original rights to freedom. Hence, freedom is based on rights, not rights on freedom. It is not to be forgotten that within the framework of the common good exists the wide sphere of freedom of the members of society for the pursuit of their various interests, since in the free development of man and his personality consists one of the existential ends (cf. Chap. 3. IV and below 11–13).

At this point, the natural law conception radically differs from the individualist and collectivistic conceptions of social freedom. It differs from the *individualist-liberalist* in the following way: first, freedom is a positive conception and does not signify merely the absence of encroachments by individuals or society; it is positive because it means self-determination based on individual responsibility in the performance of obligations grounded in the existential ends. Secondly, since these ends and their order, including the end of the common good, determine the substance and the limits of rights to freedom, there is no unrestricted freedom. Thirdly, because of his existential ends, man has rights which are anterior to any arbitrary will and therefore are not subject to any social contract or majority principle, any public opinion or poll. Fourthly, if the common good or the rights of others are affected adversely by any abuse of the rights of freedom, the community has the right to prevent such abuse. In the *collectivistic-socialistic* conception of freedom, elements of the individualist conception are reversed: freedom is given its significance by the predominant collective end; this end defines the limits of freedom for individual men; there are no rights of the individual anterior to the state, and the state has the unrestricted right to subordinate the exercise of individual rights to the general interest as understood in the collectivistic sense. Thus, if a collectivistic system guarantees the "fundamental rights of the citizens," as the constitution of the Soviet Union does in a number of articles, these rights have a meaning that is different from the one which similar constitutional provisions have in the Western democracies: the citizen enjoys no political freedom which could safeguard his rights against the state, since the right to nominate candidates for political elections is, by the constitution itself, reserved to official organizations, and primarily to the communist party organization, which controls all other organizations; with the withdrawal of the most essential political liberties, all the other fundamental rights lose their significance in the service of the jural ends underlying them.

A new conception, characteristic of the collectivistic trend of social development which is steadily creeping into discussions of economic and social planning,[1] that of *"lesser liberties,"* needs close attention. In fact, there are only inviolable and inalienable rights, no major or minor ones. The notion of lesser freedoms is an aftermath of individualist-liberalist thinking with its conception of unrestricted liberty, which may be used to impose restrictions on it. Freedoms are confined to the end inherent in them (cf. Chap. 36); since the common good is essentially correlated with the existential ends, the original rights of the individual springing from them are guaranteed notwithstanding the temporary requirements of the common good. What can be restricted, according to these requirements, is the exercise of rights, but only in accordance with the law of the common good and the law of subsidiary function (cf. Chaps. 44–45). To describe some rights (e.g., the right to strike) as "lesser" rights is as dangerous as it is false. For, once the formula of "lesser" freedoms is accepted, what is the

[1] Cf. Lord Beveridge, *Full Employment in a Free Society: A Report*, 1944, par. 17.

criterion for deciding which liberties are "essential" and which are "lesser"? Neither the individualist nor the collectivistic theories of law provide a criterion. The danger is that the "notion" of "lesser" freedoms may contribute to the shifting of society toward a conception of rights dominated by the formal idea of legality (cf. Chap. 48), whereby the substance of rights in liberal democracy is made dependent on the popular will as governed by social forces.

The Rights of Man

The rights upon which the social sphere of freedom is founded, in modern times have been called the rights of man.[2] The expression aptly conveys the fact that the rights in question are rooted in human nature itself. The particular relevant principles belong partly to primary natural law and partly to applied natural law, which results in variations in their application from country to country (cf. the further discussion in Chap. 48). The human rights guaranteed in state constitutions are often termed fundamental rights. The principles of natural law concerned with human rights may be summed up briefly as follows:

1. *Freedom of conscience* is the right to act according to one's own conscience. Man may not rightfully be compelled to do what he considers morally impermissible or be prevented from doing what he considers to be his moral duty. Natural law guarantees the freedom even of the erring conscience, but on the condition that there is no violation of the rights of others or of the community.

2. *Freedom of religion.* This right is closely linked with the right of freedom of conscience. It is an absolute right insofar as private religious observance is concerned. The right of public religious observance is conditional; it depends upon there being no infringement of the clear rights

[2] A history of human rights, which accords the like importance to the deeper-lying impulses in the development of the moral-jural consciousness with regard to the immediate sociological impulses leading to the first "declarations," has not yet been written. The exposition by G. Jellinek, *Die Erklärung der Menschen- und Bürgerrechte,* 4th ed., 1927, is criticized as inadequate especially in England, because the influence of Thomas Paine (English Quaker, 1738–1809)—this "greatest pamphleteer" of the English nation, who was at the same time the mirror and propagandist of the prevailing ideas of his time—on the declaration of human rights in America and France is made too little of. After emigrating to Pennsylvania in 1774, he produced numerous pamphlets, summarizing his ideas in the tract *Common Sense* in 1776, with which he exercised a powerful influence on the American Declaration of Independence. Returning to England in 1787 he defended the ideas of the French Revolution in his book *The Rights of Man* (1791–92), which was against Burke's conservative view of the state. His book *The Age of Reason* (1794–1807), with its attacks on the Bible, derives from the rationalistic-deistic conception of human rights of the French enlightenment and revolution. Cf. on the history of human rights Heinrich Kipp, "Die Menschenrechte in Geschichte und Philosophie," in *Die Menschenrechte in christlicher Sicht,* A. Wimmer, editor, 1953. Many references are to be found in the compilation *Die Grundrechte, Handbuch der Theorie und Praxis der Grundrechte,* H. C. Nipperdey and U. Scheuner, editors: Vol. I, *Die Grundrechte der Welt,* 1956; Vol. II, *Die Freiheitsrechte in Deutschland,* 1954.

of others (as in human sacrifice) or of public order. The right of the free exercise of religion means, on the one hand, that no one may rightfully be compelled to practice a religion that is contrary to his convictions, even if it were the true religion; on the other hand, no one may be compelled rightfully to perform actions which conflict with his religious faith or which are directed against the religious community to which, in accordance with the bidding of his conscience, he belongs.

3. *The right to life* means man's right to his life as the prerequisite for the fulfillment of his essential ends. Only when higher goods of the community are at stake can the risking of human life be rightfully demanded. The right to life includes the right to defend oneself against an unlawful attacker, with the use of such force as is necessary, even involving the risk of death for the attacker. The right to life is violated by genocide (the murder of nations or groups for racial, political, or religious reasons) and by abortion directly intended (the destruction of the life of the child in the womb for medical, social, or eugenic reasons, and hence on the principle that the end justifies the means). Euthanasia, painless killing for humanitarian or eugenic reasons, also violates the right to life. The right to life demands protection in the first case from an international authority and in the last case by the state authority.

4. *The inviolability of the person.* There is nothing man can more truly call his own than his body with its faculties and energies designed to enable him to carry out his existential ends. A grave threat to its integrity justifies the use of means of defense involving even the danger of death to the attacker if no other form of defense is possible. For the same reason, sterilization laws are a violation of justice, since the exercise of one's bodily powers to the detriment of the common good does not cancel one's right to bodily integrity, but only justifies the prevention of such exercise; thus, the community has the right to isolate the insane if it is necessary to prevent their propagation. One of the most important rights safeguarding personal inviolability is the right to one's honor, to one's good name in the community. Honor is the highest among the exterior goods; the loss of one's good name deprives one of that bond with society which is indispensable for the full development of one's personality. The right to defend one's honor, however, does not go so far as to justify the killing of the attacker, for the means of defense must be appropriate to the violated right, and honor, unlike life, can be restored by means of legal proceedings. Hence, duelling is not morally permissible. Violation of honor is an offense against strict justice and involves the obligation of restitution not only of the good name itself but also of any other losses which have been occasioned. The right of the human person to social esteem includes the right to recognition of one's legal personality and the claims to equal status before the law, to equal protection by the law, and, in the event of prosecution, to an impartial trial in accordance with established, impartial law before an impartial tribunal. The person's right to inviolability in-

cludes also the right of free movement; unlawful withholding of this freedom by the state, by institutions, or by private persons is a violation of this right. The following are examples of this violation: prolonged detention in custody under suspicion of crime without the person detained being given an opportunity to defend himself; imprisonment as a political means of suppressing opposition to a government in power; the confinement of mentally defective persons in institutions without real necessity (e.g., as a means of robbing them of property claims or other rights). A further implication of the person's right to inviolability is the home's right to inviolability. A man's home is his extended self; hence, its inviolability is founded in man's self-determination within the sphere of his own responsibilities. Within the home, encroachments by the state are justified only in regard to activities detrimental to the public interest or to the rights of others; only well-grounded suspicion entitles the state authorities to search a house. Another right bound up with the inviolability of the person is the privacy of correspondence.

5. *The right to marriage and family.* The right to marriage consists in the right to seek a partner freely and to enter into marriage in free consent without hindrance from state or society on any grounds other than those dictated by nature itself. The right to found a family, under the conditions of the society with a high degree of division of labor, implies for such a society the juridical obligation in relative natural law to pursue a family policy which will make possible the economic and cultural existence of the family.

6. *The right to educate one's children.* Parents have the exclusive right to determine the religious and moral education of their children and the primary right over their general and vocational training (cf. Chap. 73).

7. *The right to make a livelihood,* that is, to secure the necessaries of life by work. The goods of the earth are destined for all men in conjunction with their responsibility for the accomplishment of the essential tasks indicated in their existential ends. Hence, man has the right to acquire the necessary means by economic activity within the framework of the socio-economic cooperation. This activity may be exercised in independent enterprise or by working for wages. The right to obtain a livelihood implies the duty of the state in justice to pursue an economic policy of full employment in harmony with the juridical principle of subsidiary function (concerning the right to work, cf. Chap. 172).

8. *The right to property.* This means man's right, alone or in conjunction with others, to own material goods, with the exclusive right to use them for purposes of consumption or production and the right to disposal by sale or bequest. Private ownership over other men is out of the question. The right of private property is infringed upon by expropriation, except for sound reasons of the common good, and by failure to compensate when expropriation is carried out for such reasons. For reasons of common utility, the socialization or nationalization of certain kinds of

property or confiscation as a punitive measure may be justified. The social duties bound up with private property entitle the authority responsible for public order to take measures of social policy in order to insure the fulfillment of these duties.

9. *The right to asylum.* This is the right of persons liable to persecution in one state for political reasons to obtain refuge in another state.

10. *The right to choose one's occupation.* Man's talents are as much his own as his life; the possibility of using them for his own good and for the common good is the prerequisite for the development of his personality. The realization of the end of this right depends upon proportionately equal educational facilities and upon a market economy which makes possible the choice of employment. Regimentation of labor in the course of a centralist planned economy and especially any kind of forced labor, except in extreme cases of national emergency such as wartime (cf. Chap. 186), conflicts with this right.

11. *The right to develop one's personality.* Primarily, this signifies the right to a measure of education sufficient to enable man to carry out his essential tasks. It comprises, furthermore, the right to the facilities of higher education, so that one may be capable of enjoying a proportionate share in material and intellectual culture. Finally, this right also implies that, within the framework of the socio-economic process, a man's work should leave him time and strength enough to develop his personality (persistent excessive demands on labor in industry by means of the assembly line or of piece-working systems, whether in the free or the communistic economic system, infringes this right, as does the manager's total absorption in his work to the detriment of his physical or psychical personality).

12. *The right of free expression* by means of the spoken or the written word, especially in the press, in science, literature, and art. The public authority is entitled to impose limitations on this right only because of the real necessity of the common good. The basis for this right is founded both in the individual good and in the common good; in the individual good because man's mind, by its nature, requires for its development free activity in a give-and-take participation in intellectual culture; in the common good because the conduct of public affairs, the enrichment of cultural life and economic progress, all depend on the free interchange of opinion.

13. *The right to free association.* By virtue of this right people may associate together for all religious, cultural, economic, and social ends which are compatible with the rights of others and with the common good. It is rooted in the fact that the full development of man's nature depends on social cooperation. The most outstanding example in social history is the workers' "right of combination" to protect their economic and social interests against the employers; this right has long been disputed by individualist liberalism and, when once attained, denied again by the totalitarian states.

14. *The right to a voice in the administration of the life of the community.* This right is rooted in the dignity of man and in the nature of the common good. The common good has a bearing on the duties of all the members of the community, which are based on the existential ends; since they concern man's responsibility toward these ends, which is linked with his moral dignity, he cannot rightfully be the mere object of control by others for their fulfillment. This juridical principle of applied natural law does not speak concerning the manner and form of its fulfillment (e.g., by means of one type of democratic system; cf. Chap. 133); this depends on historical and social conditions. But it implies that, for peoples who possess cultural maturity, the right of participation in government should be limited only insofar as its actual abuse prevents the realization of the end of society.

52. Equality

As a social principle, equality means that all members of society enjoy a legal status which is not the result of the exercise of social power by individuals or groups. It is not to be wondered at that, after a century of talk about the equality of men, even a professed communist biologist declares [1] that there is no such thing as *individual* equality among men, either physically or intellectually, except in their common human nature. Men are alike in their essential nature; in their individual nature they are unlike. Physical and mental qualities and talents differ greatly from man to man. Because of the inequality of men and of their need for completion they are under an obligation to strive for the attainment of their integrated existence through social cooperation. The fundamental aim of social cooperation is to create, for all members of society, the conditions for such existence. History shows that the idea of *social* equality was lacking for long periods; the state of affairs regarded as "natural" in the class structure and in the distribution of welfare was inequality based on power factors. The idea of equality is a late fruit of the evolution of the moral consciousness. Little more than a century ago the social pattern which granted privileges to particular classes to the economic, social, or political disadvantage of other classes was felt to be "natural."

A general, complete *definition* of social equality has rarely been attempted. It means primarily the equality of all before the law with a guarantee of equal civil and political fundamental rights in accordance with the requirements of the rights of man (cf. the preceding chapter); it means also a proportionate equality in the participation of all groups in the material and spiritual cultural goods resulting from social cooperation. Our conception also comprises the equality of all members of society in their coresponsibility and codetermination in the administration of the

[1] Cf. J. B. S. Haldane, *Heredity and Politics*, 1943, pp. 13 ff.

life of society, which safeguards the ends of the common good. This equality of rights in regard to responsibility and the direction of affairs includes especially the political and social spheres. Hence, social equality is much more than a mere distribution problem to be solved by the state, as it is conceived by socialism, communism, and those social programs which regard the social welfare state as a provider state. On the other hand, social equality is by no means merely equality before the law and equal protection of "freedom of the person and of property"; this should lead automatically, according to individualist-liberalist thinking, to general social welfare. The purely *formal equality* of the latter kind is repudiated by the moral nature of the individual personality; the *mechanistic equality* of the former kind is repudiated by the moral nature of the social common good. Social equality can become a reality only if all participate with equal rights in the direct control of the functioning of the legal system in the service of the economic-social and spiritual-cultural common good. By fulfilling his social functions in the form of shared responsibility and decision, man attains to self-fulfillment as a personality. And through his personal self-fulfillment, he is at the same time enabled the better to fulfill his social functions. The more the individual is able thus to develop his special abilities, the greater will be the flow of mutual help, which results from men's cooperation in society, for all.

Hence, the *criteria* for judging the fitness of a social system for bringing about social equality are: first, how far it results in a cosmos of individualities, of personalities conscious of responsibility and ready to perform their part; secondly, how far it forms a hierarchy of social functions which, without admitting social power, can utilize all the abilities and energies of individuals for the good of all. Indeed, a widely developed hierarchy of social functions is indispensable to any social system as long as skilled and unskilled labor, craftsmen and traders, doctors and technicians, managers and governments are necessary. Hence, social justice cannot mean equality of income, *not "to each the same,"* but *rather, "to each his due,"* because the productive will of the members of society depends on it, and on that in turn the productivity of the economy and size of the shares to be distributed. What must be avoided under the principle "to each his due" is the measuring out of apportionments by social power, whether the power of property or the power of management, instead of by the standards of justice.

The Socialist Idea of Equality

The collectivist-socialistic theory of equality fails in regard to both aspects of social equality, namely, that in the social economy everyone can have a direct share in the responsibility for and the direction of affairs, and that no one by reason of his social function may acquire social power over others. Socialistic theory does not provide for a sharing by all in the direction of the social economy, nor does it prevent the growth of social power. The reason is that in it the purely abstract, formal idea of equality is transferred from the political to the economic-social sphere: just as the citizen, according to the theory of political democracy, by exercising his vote in the selection of a government, takes part in the conduct of government, so also, according to the socialistic equality theory, he takes part in the planning and control of the economy through the government which he has elected. In fact he remains just as dependent and planned as he was under the individualist-capitalistic economic system; indeed, the power of the managers in the socialistic economic combines must threaten even more seriously the rights of social equality, since socialism rests on a union between political and economic power.

The *abstract, formal nature of the collectivistic-socialistic idea of equality* calls for further discussion.

1. Any idea of equality is erroneous which works toward a mass society instead of toward a multitude of personalities with a full measure of responsibility. Mass society is the society based on *abstract equality*. It has been largely the outcome of the individualist social system. Any collectivistic system, including the welfare state as understood in the socialistic sense, and the provider state which covers the "same" risks for all, can only further this process. Nothing makes this clearer than does Marxian socialism. *Marx, Engels,* and *Lenin* emphasize that men are physically and intellectually unlike, but they look for the roots of social inequality in the institution of private ownership. The Marxian critique of laissez-faire capitalism made it a cardinal point that the worker was legally on an equal footing with the capitalist, but that he did not in fact enjoy social equality since he was subject to the power of the capitalist. Capital represents "*social power*" (*Marx*) and enables the owners of capital, as a class, to exploit other classes. Hence, the demand for equality is a demand for the elimination of the class society. To achieve this, private ownership of the means of production must be abolished. Such private ownership is of its nature, and therefore always, "social power," and accordingly it results in social inequality. In this latter idea lies the root error of the socialist theory concerning social equality. It is due to individualist capitalism and not to the nature of private ownership that capital is endowed with social power. Accordingly, the object of social reform is to remove this power from private ownership of the means of production and by suitable institutions to compel private ownership to work equally for the general interest as for its own. *Private ownership is the indispensable condition for the realization of the principle of social equality,* for private ownership is the prerequisite for a market economy, and the market economy is a prerequisite for the consumers as well as the workers to be able to assert their will regarding the fulfillment of the end of social economy: the best possible satisfaction of needs. In the communistic economy the will of the workers and of the consumers is denied any influence; in the socialistic economies of the West, such influence is permitted only insofar as the market economy is maintained. Private ownership and market economy are also, as we shall show (cf. Chap. 181), the necessary condition for the cooperation, with equal rights, of all the members of society in steering the socio-economic process toward the realization of social justice. The abolition of private ownership would add to the abstract equality of individuals, that is, equality at the polls, only another abstract equality, that of the dependent worker with no determining influence on the functioning of the economic system.

2. The centralism bound up with the socialistic idea of equality robs the members of society of their rights, not only in the sphere of production but also in the sphere of *consumption.* The types and qualities of goods to be produced are worked out in the planning centers, so that the consumer loses any say in how he is really to be served. The result is standardized goods for the standardized consumer. The effect of the remaining freedom of demand on supply planning can, if it occurs at all, be only indirect and delayed. The collectivistic concept of equality thus involves a further abstract element since, although the planning authorities are formally commissioned by the consumers, the *consumers retain no direct controlling influence* on the nature of supply. Even very big differences in income in accordance with social function do not alter this.[2] The deciding factor is not the inequality of incomes, but what can be done with them for the fulfillment of the individual life and personality. (Under communism man can, in the intellectual sphere, which is decisive, even with a higher income spend his money only on books, music, art, and entertainment which have received the stamp of government approval, and which are produced under collective ownership of the means of production, and therefore are coordinated with the ideologies and value-patterns admitted by those in control of these means of production.) From this it becomes evident how far the abstract, formal socialistic idea of equality in its consequences must go against freedom.

3. The abstract and formal nature of the collectivistic-socialistic idea of equality emerges not least in the solution of the *problem of distribution.* In principle, this solution would be, each according to his needs. The U.S.S.R. Constitution of 1936 says, however, in Article 12: "In the U.S.S.R. the socialistic principle, 'Each according to his ability, to each according to his work,'" is realized; and in Article 118: "Citizens of the U.S.S.R. have the right to work, that is, the right to guaranteed employment and payment for their work in accordance with its quality and quantity." *Marx* himself declared that this principle governed the first phase of communistic society, the stage of transition from capitalistic to communistic society. Only in its final phase, says *Marx,* would communistic society bring full equality into play by realizing the principle, "Each according to his capacity, to each according to his needs." [3] *Every socialistic theory sees the solution of the problem of equality as* Marx *saw it:* equality conceived of as a problem of distribution and narrowed down to the equality of all as consumers, instead of the joint responsibility of all in the conduct of matters of common concern in the economic field. Social equality will certainly pattern distribution, but services as well as needs must form the criterion. This is also the demand of justice, of common sense, and of general interest. For, the supply of goods available for distribution depends upon the extent of contributory effort, and hence also on an apportionment of the fruits of economic cooperation corresponding with such effort. Underlying the collectivistic socialistic idea of equality there is an *abstract unrealistic idea of man.* As long as men are more ready to signify their needs than to render their services, that is, as long as human nature is what it is, the mechanistic idea of equality in distribution is bound to lead to the same relative impoverishment of all, in

[2] According to reliable sources, eleven to twelve per cent of the Russian population in 1938 received fifty per cent of the national income, whereas for comparison in the U.S.A., ten per cent of the population were receiving only about thirty five per cent of the national income. Cf. J. Burnham, *The Managerial Revolution,* 1942, p. 42.

[3] K. Marx, *Kritik der Gothär Programmes,* 1875.

comparison with what true social equality can bring about with its demand for the maximum of individual effort toward the promotion of the common interest and the enrichment of the well-being of all.

53. Love of Neighbor and Social Charity

I *Love of Neighbor*

The order of justice is only part of the social order indicated to man by his nature. The fundamental principle of this order is charity. The oneness of human nature, the sameness of man's existential ends, the common ultimate goal, God, God's love for every human being, all these make charity man's fundamental duty toward his fellowman.[1] *The supreme natural social principle* is, therefore: Thou shalt love thy neighbor as thyself. Charity is man's habitual readiness to respect his fellowman as himself, and to desire and to work for his good as determined by their common nature and common final end. Love of self is thus the model for love of neighbor; on the other hand, it is a simple conclusion from our argument that the commandment to love one's neighbor is inseparable from the commandment to love God: it is "like to it" (Matt. 22:39). The connection between these two supreme precepts, which are, it should be observed, precepts of natural as well as of Christian moral law, shows that brotherhood, which is only another expression for charity (and one of Christian origin), makes sense and can acquire social relevance only if there is a common Father and if he is acknowledged as such. Owing to their secularistic foundations, therefore, individualist philanthropy, liberalist humanitarianism, socialistic fraternity and communistic comradeship cannot replace the social function of charity; nor can it be done by any education in community sense and community morality, which is based on secularistic principles and designed to produce the "socialistic man" or "communistic man." Lacking the vitalizing belief in the Fatherhood of God, all these movements lack the power to counterbalance the self-interest of individuals and groups.

Being directed toward the human person as such, charity alone can make the order of justice fully effective. Respect for another's right indeed depends ultimately on respect for him as a person with the same moral nature and the same existential ends. Thus, *justice has its deepest*

[1] Charity, like law, possesses its precise ontological foundation; cf. Chap. 4, n. III. Paul Tillich emphasizes this in *Liebe, Macht, Gerechtigkeit*, 1955, pp. 25 f.: Most pitfalls in social ethics, political theory, and pedagogics are due to the fact that the ontological character of charity is not understood. If, however, the ontological nature of charity is understood, the relationship of charity to justice and power is seen in a light which illuminates the basic unity of the three concepts and the limited character of their conflicts. The power of charity is not something added to an otherwise completed process, but life bears charity within itself as one of its constituent elements.

root in charity and receives from charity its inmost life. This dependence of justice upon charity does not mean, however, that it always precedes justice in the conduct of men and society. The following three principles, rather, govern the *relationship between justice and charity*:

1. When demands of justice conflict with demands of charity, other things being equal, the former takes precedence over the latter. The order of justice is the prerequisite for peace and order in society; it represents the minimum of order, which then can be completed and perfected by charity. Hence, duties of justice, based as they are on definite rights, are not to be handed over to charity. The working population, therefore, was justified in demanding its rights and in refusing to be satisfied with philanthropy. Another example is the fact that the duties bound up with property cannot be discharged by almsgiving.

2. Claims upon others, when based upon justice, are never exempt from the bidding of charity, for charity is the first precept governing the relation of man to man. When there is a conflict between the strict application of rights and the bidding of charity, the former must be brought into harmony with the latter. In particular, charity prevents the enforcement of a right if this would be disproportionately oppressive. Equity, then, becomes a command of charity as well as of superior justice (cf. Chap. 49).

3. Rights have by their nature a considerable sundering effect, since it is their function to mark the bounds of exclusive spheres of competence within society. Charity must bridge these divisions. The social order, therefore, is the more perfect the more completely it is permeated with charity. Furthermore, the obligations of justice extend only to outward conduct; charity brings about that inward disposition which contains the strongest motives for the willing observance of the requirements of justice. Charity bridges over the impersonal element which is instinct in law; law, for example, regards only the payment of a debt without regard to the personal circumstances of the debtor, whereas charity takes these circumstances into consideration. Only the binding, unifying force of charity can infuse into society the warmth of real peace and establish fellowship with all that this word means.

11 *Social Charity*

The expression *amor socialis* can be found in *St. Augustine* and *St. Thomas*. They associate with it, however, no other meaning than the love of man toward man by reason of their common nature;[2] from this is derived the supreme social principle on which human society is morally based. On the other hand, "social charity" as a special virtue distinct from individual charity, has always been recognized in particular forms, such as patriotism, public spirit, the fraternal spirit, community sense. The en-

[2] Cf. St. Augustine, *De Genesi ad litt.*, 1, XI, 20; St. Thomas, *De veritate*, q. 20, a. 2.

cyclical *Quadragesimo Anno* (1931) of *Pope Pius XI* added the expression "social charity" finally to the vocabulary of ethics. The pope spoke of it as "the soul" of the social order.

Thus far little attempt has been made to provide the exact *definition* of "social charity." The method of eliminating obviously inappropriate conceptual elements can be of some help in assigning social charity its place in ethics. Thus, it cannot be simply identical with individual love, love of neighbor; otherwise, a new term would not be required. A positive indication of where the essence of social charity is to be sought may be gained from *St. Thomas.* Charity, he says, referring to *St. Augustine,* implies an order of obligations in accordance with the order of precedence of the goods in question, so that on the same level of values the good of the community takes precedence over the good of the individual.[3] We base our definition of social charity on this; thus, social charity is a habit of thinking and of acting out of concern for the community and its good. The object and the immediate foundation of social charity, accordingly, is the good of the community, not the individual good as such (as in individual charity). The obligation of social charity extends to all members of the community, individuals as well as groups; it demands attitudes and modes of conduct serving a fuller realization of the common good, which cannot otherwise be attained. Just as individual charity directs man first and foremost toward the good of those with whom he is in direct contact ("love of neighbor"), so also social charity directs the conduct of individuals and groups in society primarily toward the common good, insofar as this is dependent on their conduct toward other men or groups as members of the community. Social charity, therefore, implies community sense. This we should call the fundamental obligation of social charity.

Among the *chief individual obligations* of social charity in the society of today is that of mutual respect on the part of races, classes, and nations as members, equal in value, of the state or of the community of nations. Such respect implies readiness to promote a proportionate distribution of material and cultural welfare within the political and international community, even at some sacrifice. Caste spirit, class spirit, national passions, and the lack of a spirit of mutual understanding are the milder offenses against social charity; class hatred, relentless class war, chauvinism, vengefulness, hostility toward other races are the graver offenses.

A further obligation of social charity is a readiness to settle by agreement the conflicts of interest between different groups, classes and nations. This aspect of social charity is especially important because it is not always possible to define exactly the extent of, and sometimes even establish the existence of, obligations of justice in questions arising among the individual groups, classes, and nations. Herein lies one source of quarrels and discord in the social and international spheres. For this reason alone,

[3] Cf. St. Thomas, *Summa theol.,* IIa IIae, q. 26, a. 4 ad 3.

much depends on social charity, which requires the parties to such conflicts to have the will to come to an understanding in the interest of the common good and for the maintenance and consolidation of a social and international peace, and requires them to be ready to do all that is in accord with ordered self-love. Other obligations of social charity are these: love of one's country and people; readiness for sacrifice on the part of the citizen as well as the soldier, if necessary, for the life of the community; prayer for the body politic and for those in authority, so that with goodwill, perspicacity, and energy they may act in the best interest of the community; prayer for the religious, moral, material, and cultural good of the nation, and for social and international peace. Social charity shows itself also in careful treatment of public property, in moderate use of public resources (whereas many think that they cannot draw too much upon public resources), and in restraint in applying for benefit from public funds (against the attitude of those who consider their long-continued contributions to justify them in making every possible demand on social insurance benefits). In all these cases, obligations of social charity are in question only as long as no obligations of justice itself are involved (e.g., to avoid false claims on social insurance funds).

Today, social charity also involves *duties regarding the organization of society,* such as the willingness for an order of society based on the principle of fellowship. The modern great state with its mass society allows only a small sphere of influence for social charity; for, the bigger a social unit is, the more the good of the whole becomes merely an abstraction for the individual. For most men the nearness of the object is a psychological prerequisite to prompt charity. Just as individual charity is much more animated in response to facts close to experience, whereas it remains comparatively untouched by more remote occurrences, even those involving fearful human suffering, similarly social charity is more lively and active the more immediately individual men are in contact with a *particular common good.* Social psychology, therefore, places it beyond doubt that social charity, if it is to be a living force, presupposes a ramification of society into *smaller communities,* whose individual members have a direct share in the life, the cares, and the endeavors of their particular community, in short, in self-government. This applies to the vocational as well as to the regional division of society (cf. Chap. 32).

Charity is made difficult in today's society not least by the growing *anonymity* of all relationships between individuals. The society of today is largely impersonal in character. Administrative and technical *apparatus,* from state bureaucratism to mechanization of the division of labor, hampers personal contact in all spheres of society. The individual man becomes an abstract quantity in the organization of the body politic and economic, an appendix of anonymous institutions. The result is the mass society, the reverse of a living community. This means that *social charity is the more difficult today the more urgently it is needed.* Only the reorganization of society in the direction of a whole compounded of lesser communities and based on vocational and regional principles can remedy this vital weakness in modern society and liberate the forces of social charity. Only then may a live community, fed from moral sources, grow, and radiate from its foci in the smaller communities to the whole of society and restore to it the condition of a life-breathing community feeling itself bound together by the strong bond of social charity in its manifold forms.

The Notion of Social Charity

We have had to confine our attention here to the idea of natural social charity; we cannot enter into the theological questions, although perhaps this will be possible in some other connection. A great divergence of opinion exists among theologians themselves. *J. Höffner* has made a first attempt to clarify the conception from every aspect. First, with regard to the virtue aspect of social charity, he sees in it, on the one hand, a *natural* virtue, by reason of which goodwill and esteem are conveyed directly to the social whole (nation, fatherland, state) and to all its members; on the other hand, he sees in it the *supernatural* "theological" virtue of charity. Therefore, he holds, it belongs also to the third of the infused supernatural virtues, whereby the love of God "obliges us to cultivate inner goodwill toward our neighbors and sincere esteem for the children of God." Hence, it would follow that we can fulfill all the obligations laid upon us by the previously described social charity also by means of the *"theological" virtue* of charity. But, *Höffner* goes on, social charity may also be understood as a "supernatural *moral virtue* belonging to the cardinal virtue of justice, as a *'virtus annexa.'*" Since "all the obligations of the moral virtue of social charity can also be fulfilled by the 'theological' virtue of charity," *Höffner* sees no reason for treating the obligations of these two virtues separately. Among these virtues, he cites as the most comprehensive "a true attitude of love toward our country and fellow citizens," whence the act of love proceeds spontaneously. As special expressions of social charity he mentions readiness for self-sacrifice for the common good, especially in times of grave emergency, then care for the vital common good values of religion and morality. He sees another sphere of duties in the relations of professions, groups, and classes, and again in the preparedness of individuals to help others as members of society (not just as men).[4] "The essential feature in social charity is benevolence, the positive esteem for the state community and all the citizens." He adds: "One recognizes at once that we can perform all duties toward the common good of the state, including legal duties, from the motive of social charity." One can, he explains, speak of true justice only when a real legal duty exists; on the other hand, "we can perform works of social charity even when we have no obligation at all to do so." Hence, says *Höffner*, one could agree with *O. v. Nell-Breuning*, S.J., when he writes: "In substance, social charity adds nothing to social justice."[5] In the well-known work edited by *O. v. Nell-Breuning* and *H. Sacher*, social

[4] Cf. J. Höffner, *Soziale Gerechtigkeit und soziale Liebe*, 1935, pp. 93–102.

[5] Cf. *ibid.*, pp. 97–101; O. v. Nell-Breuning, S.J., *Die soziale Enzyklika*, 1932, p. 245.

charity is also conceived as natural moral virtue which can rise to the rank of a theological virtue.[6]

On the other hand, *A. F. Utz,* O.P., declares: "If one proceeds from St. Thomas' teaching on virtue, it is simply impossible to describe the supernatural virtue of social charity as a supernatural *moral* virtue which itself 'rises' to the level of a theological virtue. All relations between man and man and between the individual and the collectivity of men, insofar as they go beyond justice, are regulated in the supernatural order by the theological virtue of charity. . . . Social charity, therefore, is nothing but a special sector of the wide sphere of duties and activities belonging to the theological virtue of charity." In the domain of natural moral life, however, social charity denotes "a moral virtue which aims to realize the ideal social order which strives after the common good where all coordination of the various claims and contributions remains simply inadequate." [7]

Those who are not familiar with the scholastic division and subdivision of the virtues will be struck by *Höffner's* description of social charity as a virtue belonging to (*virtus annexa*) the cardinal virtue of justice. These attempts at subdivision and coordination are listed in detail by *Cathrein.* They reveal almost uniquely the existing difficulties in the definitions. Thus, even love of neighbor is described as a "subsidiary virtue to justice." Similarly, the position of equity is defined as that of a virtue kindred to justice, but then again is described as "natural justice," through which, in the administration of justice, natural law may be asserted as against the rules of positive law. The difficulties in the definitions become still more complicated when it is said in the same connection that, by the cardinal virtue of justice "is to be understood singly and solely the particular justice" to which commutative and distributive justice are ascribed, whereas legal or general justice, owing to the lack of a strictly defined object, "cannot be a cardinal virtue and still less a part of one." In addition, however, it is also stated with regard to distributive justice that it is a justice in a less perfect sense than commutative justice, which alone "is termed strict justice (*iustitia rigorosa*)." [8]

Social charity is seen to be linked with the common good justice by *A. F. Utz:* "The social good which is to be realized by social justice . . . is never realized to the full by a legal community in which the emphasis is purely on the individual. Gaps always remain if society is based on the individuality principle. Making good such gaps in the realization of the common good, which in spite of all continues to be a natural obligation, is the function of another moral force, the so-called social charity." *Utz* illustrates this by the duty of paying taxes in view of the widespread evasion prevalent today. "For the sake of the common good—we think today—the individual is obliged to render his contribution to the common weal in the form of taxes as well as in other ways. But this obligation based on common good justice recedes in proportion as the other members of the state do not fulfill their share. The good citizen, therefore, no longer can be held bound, on the ground of common good justice, to contribute

[6] Cf. *Beiträge zu einem Wörterbuch der Politik,* 3 Heft, O. v. Nell-Breuning, S.J., and H. Sacher, editors, 1949, Sp. 36.

[7] A. F. Utz, *Recht und Gerechtigkeit, Die deutsche Thomas-Ausgabe,* Vol. XVIII, 1953, p. 571.

[8] V. Cathrein, *Moralphilosophie,* 6th ed., 1924, Vol. I, pp. 359–63, 595.

the full share levied upon him. Is he, therefore, to be content to look on at the decline of the common weal? In spite of all, the natural moral duty binding on his conscience remains to him to save what can be saved, for the sake of the people with whom he is associated. He corresponds with this moral responsibility by making his contribution from social charity." [9]

Thus, the concept of social charity is, according to *Utz*, limited to what should be performed from social justice, but owing to existing conditions is not performed. Starting from this, *Utz* objects that I seem to identify social charity "with a generally conceived community sense, which is at bottom nothing but a rightly understood common good justice." [10] I do indeed say that social charity demands "community sense above all," but my account of the individual obligations coincides with that given above from *Höffner*. Hence if we endeavor to give the full significance to the expression "community sense" in face of the modern pluralistic society, it coincides with what *Höffner* designates in the "attitude of charity" as the most universal obligation of social charity. (It is evident from our argument, however, that we should not care to confine the obligations of social charity to the conduct of social groups toward one another, as *Cassianus Hentzen*, O.F.M., suggests in his Dutch commentary on *Quadragesimo Anno.*) [11]

Utz also criticizes our view of charity as the supreme principle of social order; he considers that in our argument "after the thorough discussion of law as a principle of order, charity is suddenly designated the 'fundamental principle' of social order. We should not like to recommend this, but to let law stand as the first principle of order, since society is essentially a unity based on law and not a unity based on love." [12] We do call law a principle of order, but charity, deliberately, a "fundamental principle"; we immediately add in explanation, it is "the supreme natural social principle." For, law as a principle of order, as we have shown and as is, I think, generally held today, points beyond itself to the common human nature and common human dignity. In the behavior of man toward man this can only mean mutual goodwill and mutual esteem; precisely in these natural charity exists. *In the essential reality of society, law and charity are ultimately linked ontologically:* the ontology of law can only be completed in the ontology of charity. Our conception of the position of charity is clearly linked with *Augustine's* conception. For him, it is an established fact that, *in the precept of charity "all social duties are rooted."* What significance he assigns to charity as the supreme principle of social order follows from the adjoining sentence on these social duties; the sentence states that (for common sense) "an error on this subject is hardly possible." To obviate any error about the fact that he is thinking first of the *natural* virtue of charity, he adds, indicating the ontological root of the matter in his remarkably pregnant mode of expression: "What is closer to man than man?" [13]

[9] Utz, *op. cit.*, pp. 567 ff.

[10] A. F. Utz, *Divus Thomas*, Vol. XXIX, 1951, p. 508.

[11] Cf. C. Hentzen, O.F.M., *Commentaar op Quadragesimo Anno*, 1933, Vol. I, p. 297.

[12] A. F. Utz, *op. cit.*, p. 507.

[13] Cf. St. Augustine, *De mor. eccl. cath.*, cc. 26, 49: "Ex hoc praecepto nascuntur officia societatis humanae, in quibus non errare difficile est. Agendum autem in primis est, ut benevoli simus, id est, ut nulla malitia, nullo dolo malo adversus hominem utamur. Quid enim homini homine propinquius?"

That the definition of social charity is not yet clarified may be seen also from the fact that most authors concerned with it asume that their particular views are endorsed by *Quadragesimo Anno*. Just as in the discussion of the diversity of opinions on the concept of social justice (preceding chapter), I think it is true to say that, with regard to the modes of conduct enjoined by social charity, the varieties of opinion which might be supposed from the disagreements in definition do not exist. Our own analysis is not intended to be more than a contribution to the discussion on the subject; the course of discussion up to this point, however, does not seem to have yielded any ideas which could cause us to abandon the view we have been holding.

54. The Three Main Schools of Natural Law Theory

The main schools of natural law theory which have emerged in the course of history have a common element in that they base their theories on what is "in accordance with nature," the conceptions of nature being different.

I *The Three Schools*

1. *The Traditional Natural Law Theory.* We call this the traditional one since it can look back on more than two thousand years of continuous intellectual effort. Its foundations consist of two facts in the reality of human nature: man's awareness of the moral-jural self-evident truths with their claim to binding force; and, linked with that, man's awareness of his nature with its claims on the social order to provide for fully integrated human existence. Both facts are fundamental to traditional natural law theory. In the course of centuries the discussion of natural law has circled principally around two topics: the significance of conscience and the requirements of the nature of reality. These two topics are clearly established at the outset of this discussion by *Plato* and *Aristotle:* by the latter in the often quoted passage of the *Ethics* (V, 10) where he is speaking of law "which everywhere possesses the same authority and is no mere matter of opinion"; by the former in the statement that "justice itself is best for the soul itself according to its nature" (*Republic* X, 612). Countless references in the medieval scholastics bear witness to the debt of traditional natural law theory to the natural law ideas of the stoics, especially in the form given to them by *Cicero,* and again to the Roman jurists such as *Gaius* and *Ulpian* (second and third centuries A.D.), and in general to the work of *Justinian.* Light is thrown on the history and development of natural law theory in the Middle Ages by a great volume of material in the comprehensive work of the brothers *A. J.* and *R. W. Carlyle,* which we shall presently mention. Since our task is the development of traditional natural law theory with an eye to present-day society, the *history* of natural law theory lies outside our scope. Nevertheless, we have had to

keep constantly in view, and must continue to do so, the peaks of this historical evolution as represented by the works of *Augustine, Thomas Aquinas, Vitoria,* and *Suárez.*

2. *The idealistic natural law theory.* We sum up as idealistic those natural law theories which seek to understand legal reality only in terms of the mind and its world of ideas. We use the term idealism in the wide sense customary today in the language which has grown out of the history of philosophy.[1] The expression covers such widely divergent schools as the empirical, psychological, epistemological, transcendental, metaphysical, logical, and volitional schools of idealism. Among present-day natural law theories we include in this group chiefly those based on a philosophy of value, with the two main tendencies of the empirical (e.g., in *W. Sauer, V. Kraft*) and the psychological (e.g., the trend which proceeds from the a priori awareness of fundamental values and derives from *Scheler* and *Hartmann*). Among the idealistic trends we count also the various natural law theories of rationalism; they range from the natural law of the Enlightenment and the attempts to set up a detailed legal code independent of time (*Wolff*) to the systems which work predominantly with formal principles derived from reason (*Kant, Stammler*) and to the interpretation of existing historical legal systems as revelations of absolute reason (*Hegel* and the neo-Hegelians).

3. *The materialistic theory of natural law.* According to this theory, all order in the world is only the order of the material universe; its natural law is also the natural law of man, and it prescribes for him what is "according to his nature" for the order of society. The foundation is the materialistic view of man as the most highly developed matter. We have already dealt with the philosophies underlying the materialistic theory of natural law, which emphasize the physical or biological or psychological side of human nature. These are dialectical materialism (the Marxian social philosophy, also modified, e.g., as social utilitarianism, by *Laski* and others), materialistic evolutionism (*J. Huxley* and the schools of evolutionist sociology), naturalistic psychology (the social theory founded on *Freud's* doctrine of man and the behaviorist social theory).

11 *Plurality of Natural Laws?*

The foregoing division, it should be noted, concerns the main schools of natural law *theories.* The assumption of several *kinds* of natural law, for example, when we speak of a plurality of natural laws, is a different matter. Such a plurality is spoken of in two senses: first, a plurality of natural laws based on ideology; secondly, a plurality of natural laws differing on an ethnic basis.

[1] Cf. the article "Idealismus" by Rudolf Eisler in *Wörterbuch der philosophischen Begriffe,* 4th ed., 1927, Vol. I, p. 672, and Walter Brugger, S.J., *Philosophisches Wörterbuch,* 5th ed., 1953, p. 140.

With reference to conceptions of law associated with political ideologies, individualist and liberalist as well as collectivistic and socialistic conceptions of the nature of man and society (cf. Chap. 47), the first view is represented by *Adolf Merkl. Merkl* concludes that, in view of the plurality of ideologically and politically derived interpretations of natural law, there remains only the alternative either "to content oneself with the skeleton or indeed with merely the first beginnings of a natural law order, or to maintain that the prevailing positive law is delegated by natural law, and thus to understand it in its local and temporal particularity as secondary natural law."[2] This does not seem to deny the reality of jural conscience, which is uniform and common to all men and proper to rational nature as such, with its knowledge of general juridical truths and principles, or therefore the unity of primary natural law. On the other hand, a plurality of natural laws with equal material justification but with only ideological foundations would only be possible if truth also were grounded not in reality but in will, and if in consequence the individualist and communist fundamental conceptions of the nature of man and their implied legal conceptions could equally be true.

Josef L. Kunz, in an examination of the question how European natural law can be valid and effective "as a universal law of nations in a world of very diverse natural laws," speaks of a "plurality of natural laws" in the second sense, namely, different forms of the sense of natural law among different nations. He sums up his argument thus: 1) The international law of today is historically the international law of Christian Europe; it is built on the foundation of Roman law and Christian, especially Catholic, natural law. 2) As the result of a historical process, this international law today has universal authority. 3) In the free West there are two great legal systems of common law and civil law, the natural laws of the Catholic and the Protestant philosophies of life. 4) Today, there is in addition, within the Western culture, Soviet law and the natural law underlying it. 5) Furthermore, we see the awakening of the non-whites, who form the greater part of mankind. Even primitive natural laws of Africa are already asserting their authority. But above all, new states have arisen—and there are further independence movements—which correspond to the three great non-Western legal systems and which rest partly on fundamentally different natural laws. These states appear actively on the international scene and are steadily gaining in significance. They are tired of being regarded by the West as merely sources of raw materials, export markets, strategic bases, or tourist attractions, and of being considered inferior. They are pressing for recognition of their own culture; they demand to be heard with their own ideas in questions of international conflicts and in the shaping of international law. 6) It is recognized that no legal system can be fully understood without a knowledge of the

[2] A. Merkl, "Einheit oder Vielheit des Naturrechts?" in *Österreichische Zeitschrift für öffentliches Recht,* new series, Vol. V, 1953, p. 310.

natural law on which it is based and that the effectiveness of a legal system depends on its being, on the whole, in agreement with the natural law of at least the great majority.[3]

Kunz seems to wish to dispute the uniformity of the moral-jural consciousness of mankind. He does not distinguish between the natural law which belongs to the natural juridical conscience, the *universal human* natural law, and the natural law which is bound up with culture-forms, the *historically specialized* juridical consciousness of a particular people. The uniformity of the moral-jural consciousness of mankind is established just as is the diversity of forms of juridical consciousness molded by cultures and characteristic of particular peoples (cf. Chaps. 40–41). It is an untenable proposition that common law and civil law, the Catholic and the Protestant laws, rest on different conceptions of the fundamental principles and values of law; otherwise, precisely according to the theory put forward by *Kunz,* a uniform effective legal order would not be possible in the European area. Equally little justification seems to exist in making the policy of economic and political exploitation toward underdeveloped countries a constituent part of any form of natural law of the "West." And the idea of a right to self-determination, to which the peoples of Asia and Africa today so emphatically appeal, derives entirely from the development of the Western juridical sense and the associated knowledge that the juridical principle of self-determination is founded on the general natural law, but that, in its concrete demands, depends on conditions of social and cultural development. The fact, which *Kunz* emphasizes, that the natural law of the West has been able to attain universal recognition by reason of a historical process, is sufficient proof that peoples have common insights into fundamental truths of law, just as they recognize the basic colors of red, blue, green, and yellow as such. Hence, *Kunz* cannot forego mentioning that *F. S. C. Northrop,* the outstanding legal philosopher of the Yale Law School, on whose works he particularly relies, "hopes and believes in a common world natural law." [4]

It is not surprising that *Kunz* considers it necessary to come to grips with the theory maintained by *Alfred Verdroß,* the professor of international law at Vienna, of a "universalism of a uniform natural law based on universal human values." *Kunz'* arguments in discussing *Verdroß's* theory are by no means convincing. He begins from a conception of law which confines the binding character of law to positive law, and then reaches the conclusion that the law which binds in conscience represents a system of rules completely different from positive law; a similar logically inadmissible argumentation underlies the assertion that "the natural law people are compelled to assume a right of resistance and even

[3] Cf. J. L. Kunz, "Pluralismus der Naturrechte und Völkerrecht," in *Österreichische Zeitschrift für öffentliches Recht,* new series, Vol. VI, 1955, p. 215.

[4] *Ibid.,* p. 216; he refers to F. S. C. Northrop, *The Taming of the Nations,* 1952, Chap. 16, and to "Contemporary Jurisprudence and International Law," in *Yale Law Journal,* Vol. LXI, 1952, pp. 623–54.

a duty of resistance, but are always in great embarrassment over it. A 'natural law' right of resistance is no legal rule, and a positive law right of resistance to positive law is a *contradictio in adjecto*." [5] The actual natural law conscience of the world knows better. The whole of mankind believes in a right of resistance in natural law as a genuine right of opposition to the unlawful exercise of power by the state; this is clearly demonstrated by the Hungarian people in the October uprising of 1956.

III *The Renaissance of the Natural Law Idea*

The new approach to natural law has proceeded in *two stages*. One of these stages, which commenced after the Second World War, is distinguished by a far-reaching reconsideration of the natural law idea and an extensive literature on natural law questions. Experience of the violation of law and of justice by the totalitarian states brought about the change. We have considered in detail this *latest development* in the renewed approach to natural law and we need not go further into it here.

The first phase in the reawakening of interest in the natural law idea begins before the end of the nineteenth century with isolated statements against legal positivism. In the train of the political, economic and social crisis, which began with the First World War and continued unremittingly thereafter, voices of criticism were increasingly raised against the prevailing positivist legal doctrine. In order to appreciate the intellectual change implied in this, one must realize that in the second half of the nineteenth century, when positivist legal thought reached its apogee, the natural law idea was considered to be finally disposed of. The more radical exponents of the historical and analytical school went so far as to reject any principle which did not arise from positive law and even included Benthamite utilitarianism under the sentence passed on natural law. The existing statutory law was thought to be the beginning and end of law and of justice. It seems necessary today to cast a glance at this *earlier development* in order to make it clear that the recent trend did not come about spontaneously but had been in preparation for a considerable time. This came about in the interest in legal philosophy which set in in all countries after the beginning of this century. Certainly, writers often declined to have anything to do with natural law ideas. Yet, in one way or another the problem of the principles of just law constantly came up, unquestionably because of a critical attitude toward positive law. The

[5] *Ibid.*, pp. 187–91; he quotes Alfred Verdroß, *Völkerrecht,* 2nd ed., 1950, but not Verdroß, *Die Einheit des rechtlichen Weltbildes auf Grundlage der Völkerrechtsverfassung,* 1923. Hans Thieme, *Das Naturrecht und die europäische Privatrechtsgeschichte,* 2nd ed., 1954, pp. 49 f., puts in a nutshell the answer to the question posed by Kunz: "The idea of a 'particular' natural law need not therefore be rejected, for we cannot go back beyond the historical school. Nevertheless, it requires completion by obedience toward the one universal idea of law and justice, embodied in those *principia* which alone guarantee unity in plurality and can prevent the disjunction of national laws."

name "natural law," the outstanding American agnostic philosopher *Morris R. Cohen* says, is not unduly applied to the new doctrines because they are, in essence, a reassertion of the old in a form more in correspondence with modern thought. The scientific possibility of this reassertion is the purpose of his thesis; he seeks to prove it by a critical examination of the four usual arguments against natural law theory, namely, the historical, the psychological, the legal, and the metaphysical.[6] Although we wish to sketch this early phase in the renaissance of the natural law idea in various countries, we shall refer to comparatively few references. In this we must chiefly refer to legal thinking outside the traditional natural law school.

In *England,* where jurisprudence had almost completely abandoned the natural law idea, Sir *Frederick Pollock,* one of the leading jurists, took it up again and pointed out its unbroken tradition in the English legal system ("The History of the Law of Nature," in *Journal of the Society of Comparative Legislation,* 1900; reprinted in *Essays in the Law,* 1922, pp. 31 ff.). The various conceptions of natural law, he says, are based on "an ultimate principle of fitness with regard to the nature of man as a rational and social being, which is, or ought to be, the justification of every form of positive law. . . . Such a principle, under the name of reason, reasonableness, or sometimes natural justice, is fully recognized in our own system, but the difference of terminology has tended to conceal the real similarity from English lawyers during the last century or more. The neglect of medieval learning which followed the Renaissance and the Reformation has also caused us to forget that the law of nature has a perfectly continuous history down to the date of its greatest and most beneficent achievement—one might also say its apotheosis in the foundation of the modern law of nations by Grotius." In a letter to Justice *Holmes,* the leading American jurist of his time, Sir *F. Pollock* gives an excellent interpretation of what is meant by natural law (*The Pollock-Holmes Letters,* 1874–1937, publ. 1942, Vol. I, p. 274): "If you mean to imply that no one can accept natural law (natural justice—reason as understood in the common law) without maintaining it as a body of rules known to be absolutely true, I do not agree with you. (See my studies in *Journal of Comparative Legislation,* 1900.) The Roman lawyers made no such assertions about *ius gentium,* which was simply general custom and for most purposes equivalent to *ius naturale.* In the Middle Ages natural law was regarded as the senior branch of divine law and therefore had to be treated as infallible (but there was no infallible way of knowing what it was). If you deny that any principles of conduct at all are common to and admitted by all men who try to behave reasonably well, I don't see how you can have any ethics or any ethical background of law." This is precisely the view of natural law theory that we have been trying to develop. A comprehensive attempt on the part of English jurists to make up for the neglect of medieval learning, which Pollock complains of, has been made by the brothers *R. W.* and *A. J. Carlyle* in their work, *A History of Medieval Political Theory in the West* (Vols. I–VI, 1903–6). It has been pointed out already (cf. Chap. 48) that English common law is rooted in the traditional natural law idea. Its principles exercised a

[6] Cf. Morris R. Cohen, *Reason and Nature,* 1931, p. 402.

formative influence in turn on the legal systems of the British Dominions and of the United States. The determining influence of traditional natural law thinking in the evolution of common law can be clearly traced from the twelfth to the seventeenth century, and it is associated with such names as *John of Salisbury* (twelfth century), *Henry Bracton* (thirteenth century), Sir *John Fortescue* and Sir *Thomas de Littleton* (fifteenth century), *Christopher St. Germain* and Sir *Thomas More* (sixteenth century), Sir *Edward Coke* and Sir *Henry Finch* (seventeenth century).[7] *J. W. Gough* points out that, although today in England natural law as law may no longer form an element of the legal system, English jurists freely write about "the fundamental legal relationships" and "fundamental legal doctrine," and that no English lawyer thinks of law as wholly divorced from morality. *Gough* closes his historical review by declaring that their interpretation of fundamental law may differ, but when Englishmen appealed to it throughout their history, they were in fact confessing the same faith.[8] The long estrangement observed by Sir *Frederick Pollock* between English jurisprudence and the natural law idea, however, is so potent in its effect that natural law, particularly applied natural law, is far outside the customary range of thought.

In the *United States, Roscoe Pound* shows that natural law ideas were always, in practice if not in theory, of great influence on legal decisions and jurisprudence (cf. Chap. 49; cf. also his work on legal history, 1923, 2nd ed., 1946). The basic ideas of his discussion of "jural postulates" are largely in agreement with my development of the fundamental ideas of natural law: they are not rules of law but ideas, principles, of right and wrong to be made effective by legal institutions and legal precepts (*Interpretations of Legal History*, 1923, p. 148). Further details regarding the revival of the natural law idea are given by *C. A. Haines* in *The Revival of Natural Law Concepts* (1930). The growing interest in natural law in the United States was revealed in the extraordinarily widespread interest in an article on "Human Rights and the Law" by *Edward S. Dore,* a well-known Catholic jurist, in the *Fordham Law Review* (March, 1946), which was reprinted in substance in *Life* magazine, which has a circulation of millions. In America, as in England, natural law thinking, at least with regard to applied natural law, is still not customary among jurists. For this reason, it seemed advisable to give the American-English version of this work the title *Social Ethics,* with *Natural Law in the Western World* as subtitle, thus avoiding the impression of a historical treatise or a purely philosophical discourse. Characteristic of the new development is the book by the professor of

[7] R. O'Sullivan, *Natural Law and Common Law* (London: The Grotius Society), 1946, pp. 119–30, comes to this conclusion: "The law of nature was throughout the creative centuries of the common law a familiar idea and a guiding principle among lawyers and judges; and it may even be said to be the source and spring of the common law as it was conceived and developed by Bracton and Fortescue and Littleton and Thomas More and Christopher St. Germain, and Coke and Holt, and even by Blackstone"; "in fact the principle of an overriding law of nature was for many centuries accepted and followed by Parliament. Until the seventeenth century, one may say that the principle was a commonplace of jurisprudence and familiar to the political and the public mind of England." For a similar statement on the strength of the natural law idea, and in fact against the legislative power of Parliament in England up to the seventeenth century, cf. C. H. McIlwain below, Chap. 130, note 1.

[8] Cf. J. W. Gough, *Fundamental Law in English Constitutional History,* 1955, pp. 211 ff.

philosophy at Harvard University, *John Wild, Plato's Modern Enemies and the Theory of Natural Law* (1953); *Wild,* in order to provide an ontological basis for natural law, starts from the active tendencies inherent in human nature (pp. 194 ff., 203). Also worth mentioning is the journal *Natural Law Forum* (Notre Dame Law School) founded in 1956, which claims to be independent of any single school or conception of natural law; its imposing list of editors and co-editors commands respect.

In *France,* the new approach to natural law is seen chiefly in the school of law which finds in the "institution" the basis of rights claiming validity anterior and superior to the state and its law; we discussed this school (cf. Chap. 42) in connection with *Proudhon* and *Hauriou* and the theory of institutions built upon their work. *Renard* and *Gény* belong to this school although they are to be reckoned as traditional natural law theorists. Concerning the latter, *Roscoe Pound* points out (*Harvard Law Review,* Vol. LI, 1937–38, pp. 464 ff.) that in his development of traditional natural law doctrine two features are especially important: he sees society as the basic fact for the concept of law and he sees natural law as immanent in positive law (concerning the features of natural law that we have stressed, cf. Chaps. 47, 49). A review of progress in France is offered by *J. Charmont* in *La renaissance du droit naturel* (2nd ed., 1927).

In *Germany,* original approaches to the clarification of the fundamental principles of the philosophy of law by way of a revival of natural law ideas were made by followers of the phenomenological school of *Husserl. Adolph Reinach* in "Die apriorischen Grundlagen des bürgerlichen Rechtes," a study on the a priori foundations of civil law (*Jahrbuch für Philosophie und phänomenologische Forschung,* ed. by Edmund Husserl, 1913, pp. 685–847; in book form 1953) reaches these conclusions: "The so-called specifically basic legal conceptions have existence outside the sphere of positive law, just as numbers possess existence independently of the mathematical sciences. Positive law may define and transform them as it will: they are found, not produced by it" (*op. cit.,* p. 690). *Reinach* points to the many legal rules that are not codified and need no codification, because they are self-evident (*op. cit.,* p. 842), for example, the binding force of contracts. He says of natural law: "Its search for a sphere which retains its eternal truth without being influenced by the various forms of positive legal systems was absolutely justified." When he continues: "Thus, one of the fundamental tendencies of the natural law doctrine finds its fulfillment in the aprioristic theory of law" (p. 845), he seems to overestimate the possibilities of pure phenomenology. A vigorous attempt to rediscover the basic reality of jurisprudence, which had become a "jurisprudence without law," is made by *Leonard Nelson* in *Die Rechtswissenschaft ohne Recht* (1917), and *System der philosophischen Rechtslehre und Politik* (1923). On the growing interest in natural law, the following is also instructive: *Alfred Vierkandt, Der geistig-sittliche Gehalt des neueren Naturrechts* (1927). The works of *Rudolf Stammler,* whose doctrine of "right law" has already been referred to, must be mentioned here: *Wirtschaft und Recht nach der materialistischen Geschichtsauffassung* (1896, 5th ed., 1924); *Lehre vom richtigen Recht* (1902, 2nd ed., 1926); *Theorie der Rechtswissenschaft* (1911, 2nd ed., 1923); *Lehrbuch der Rechtsphilosophie* (1923, 3rd ed., 1928).

A long list of authors in other European countries could be given in whose writings on jurisprudence or legal philosophy there is recognizable a tendency toward the natural law idea, even if natural law as such is treated with scepticism or is rejected. For Holland, we should mention *Krabbe* and *Kranenburg* (cf. Chap. 50); for Italy, chiefly *Gustavo del Vecchio* with his works: *I presupposititi filosofici della nozione del diritto* (1905); *Il concetto del diritto* (2nd ed., 1912); *Il concetto della natura ed il principio del diritto* (2nd ed., 1922) (these studies were translated by *Lisle* under the title *The Formal Basis of Law,* 1914); *Lezione di filosofia del diritto,* (1930). *Costamagna, Pannuzio,* and others adopt fundamental ideas from the "institutional" theory of *Hauriou.*

IV *The Three Main Trends of Opposition to Natural Law*

1. The sociological theory of law

This theory found its most consistent scientific formulation in the sociology of *Max Weber. Weber* sees in sociology a "value-free science," and in law an order which is "externally guaranteed by the *chance* of physical or psychical *compulsion,* through action on the part of a staff of men specially engaged in that task, directed toward enforcing observance or punishing violation." The "chance" as a conceptual instrument of sociological method is undoubtedly a discovery of great significance. Its application, however, is by its nature restricted to the sphere of sociology, as a purely empirical science. Indeed, to *Weber* belongs the merit of having shown epistemologically what sociology as a purely empirical science is: the investigation of social phenomena with regard to their factually ascertainable relationships. Nothing but what "is" interests this sociology: behavior, causes, effects. It is the consummation of *Comte's* idea of positivist sociology. Religious and ethical values, rights and law, ideas and ideologies are taken as causal factors on the same footing as technique, economy, organization, enforcements, power seeking. All these factors are likewise constituents of the interaction of causes in which sociological phenomena originate and of consequences which proceed from them.[9] Law, too, is examined as just an actually ascertainable "chance" without regard to the primary fact of the natural jural conscience and the question which it poses concerning the ontological basis of law. On his conception of law quoted above *Weber* remarks: " 'Externally' guaranteed orders can also be 'internally' guaranteed. The relationship between law, convention, and 'ethics' is no problem to sociology." Empirical sociology cannot do otherwise than "decide in accordance with that conception of 'ethical' which is or has been *actually* accepted in the circle under discussion. It may not make general statements on the subject." A method of this kind is certainly justified, within limits, and indeed is indispensable for the exact investigation of causes and effects in the social reality. It is equally certain, however, that the reality of law is not wholly accessible to the methods of a purely positivist sociology. A whole world of most certain experience, man's consciousness of being in possession of original, definite, and inviolable rights (even though not enforced), would be overlooked.

The sociological theory of law of Justice *Holmes,* according to which law is just what the courts do, goes even further than *Weber:* neither statutory law nor any other rules of law have real existence until a court has applied them to cases that are brought before it.[10] This is pure nominalism. Certainly the onto-

[9] Cf. Max Weber, *Wirtschaft und Gesellschaft,* 1922, pp. 17 ff.

[10] Cf. Justice Holmes, *Collected Legal Papers,* 1920; cf. also Jerome Frank, *Law and the Modern Mind,* 1931.

logical questions, how law exists and what kind of being it possesses, are very difficult, just as is the question of the ontological mode of existence of society itself (it leads into the realm of ontology of the social relation and institution; cf. Chap. 17). In the nominalist theory of law, rights are only words without reality; reality begins when legal norms produce an effect which is due to the application of law by the courts. All such sociological theories contradict an evident fact of experience: the legal order of a community is a reality, because most people act in accordance with it without feeling that they live under the eyes of the police or are liable to be summoned before the courts. No legal system could function if it were based only on the executive power of the courts and not on the force of the moral conscience.

2. The formalistic theory of law

This is *Kelsen's* pure theory of law, which bases law on a juristic hypothesis (cf. Chaps. 49–50). Among the declared opponents of natural law today *Kelsen* is probably the most outstanding.[11] He rejects natural law because its claim to validity is not guaranteed by physical compulsion and also because its claim to validity is sought outside man's autonomy (and this is irreconcilable with man's dignity). He sees another reason for its rejection in the possible and actual misuse of natural law for political ends, especially for the support of existing legal institutions. According to *Kelsen*, the fundamental question of legal theory is, in contradistinction to the natural sciences, not why something happens but why legal rules are binding; the question concerns the "validity" of legal rules, which is derived only by delegation from a higher rule, not sought in facts outside the existing law. Hence, he also refuses to pursue the question what "true" law is, thus professing positivism. Nevertheless, *Kelsen's* pure theory of law, as we have previously noted, has the merit of logical consistency. Logically, says Kelsen, there cannot be a multiplicity of delegating powers, and hence no multiplicity of absolute sovereignties.

Indeed, outside natural law theory the postulate of absolute sovereignty has received no more devastating criticism than *Kelsen's*. According to existing legal theories, says *Kelsen*, the legal system of a sovereign state can become valid for any other sovereign state only by being included in its own legal system; this assumption of a plurality of sovereigns with absolute supreme legislative power involves an insuperable self-contradiction. The theories of absolute sovereignty have so far failed to give a satisfactory answer to *Kelsen's* criticism. The answer which he himself gives consists in the hypothesis that the legal systems of the individual states derive their validity ultimately from international law, namely, from the legal system of the most extensive community. The "fundamental norm" of this community is, says Kelsen, not the will of the individual state but the juristic postulate, *pacta sunt servanda*. Thus, as his critics allege, by the inner logic of his theory he arrives at a natural law idea.[12] The possibility of misuse of the natural law idea, which *Kelsen* holds as an objection to it, can no more

[11] Cf. H. Kelsen, *Die philosophischen Grundlagen der Naturrechtslehre und des Rechtspositivismus*, 1928; *Das Problem der Souveränität und die Theorie des Völkerrechts*, 1920; *Reine Rechtslehre*, 1934, pp. 12–16; *Der soziologische und der juristische Staatsbegriff*, 1922, p. 200: The unity of the legal system of the state is only the product of the mind working on the material of legal rules.

[12] Cf. Alfred Verdroß, *Völkerrecht*, 3rd ed., 1955, pp. 18 ff.

be adduced as an argument against natural law than can the possibility of human degradation be held against the dignity of man, whether it comes from within man himself or from society. Furthermore, no harm is done to man's moral autonomy, as *Kelsen* fears, by the assumption of natural law, since rightly understood it is only the law of man's nature itself and hence in fact actualizes man's essential autonomy (cf. Chap. 4).

3. The evolutionist theory of law

According to this theory, all law, like all values, is a product of evolution; hence, it possesses an entirely historical nature without any foundation in a metaphysical reality independent of time. This is pure legal historicism, two schools of which we have already discussed: the more recent historical school, and the school of biological evolutionism (cf. Chaps. 40, 47). A third school is that of dialectical materialism; this also we discussed previously (cf. Chap. 41). Here we must mention the attempt made by *H. J. Laski* to transform the natural law idea in accordance with the dialectical materialist view of human nature and thus to establish a basis for a socialistic theory of law. *Laski* says that a revival of the medieval effort in the study of natural law would be highly desirable. Rights, he says, are the foundation of the state which give to the exercise of its power a moral character; they are natural rights which are essential to the good life. They do not imply a natural order which lies behind the changing appearance of a contemporary society; rather, the natural order is a problem for pragmatic analysis at any given time; its only permanence lies in the certainty that it will change.[13] We must seek to revive the effort of the medieval schoolmen and the great Spanish thinkers of the sixteenth century in order to obtain an adequate theory of the state. This has to be done without their theological outlook, however; instead the present-day facts are to be interpreted in economic terms.[14] Only the Marxian interpretation of law is apt to explain the substance of law.[15]

Thus, accepting the view of human nature associated with Marxian dialectical materialism, *Laski* complains of the individualist prejudice, as he sees it, dominating English law, with its guaranteed rights of freedom, which are not based on the more recent collectivistic and corporate habits, but on the liberal-atomic principles developed from the seventeenth to the mid-nineteenth century.[16] In criticism, only the caustic remark of *J. W. Gough* need be referred to; in effect, he said that we have learned enough since *Laski's* time about the so-called "people's courts" under totalitarian regimes to be thankful for the "bias" of our judges in favor of the ordinary citizen.[17]

v *The Concept of "Christian Natural Law"*

As we have pointed out (cf. Chap. 2), underlying every doctrine of law and state, justice and social order, there is a certain idea of man, a

[13] Cf. H. J. Laski, *Grammar of Politics,* 1941 ed., pp. 40, 89.
[14] Cf. H. J. Laski, "M. Duguit's Conception of the State," in *Modern Theories of Law,* W. I. Jennings, editor, 1933, p. 66.
[15] Cf. H. J. Laski, *Grammar of Politics,* p. VIII.
[16] Cf. H. J. Laski, *Parliamentary Government in England,* 1938, p. 22.
[17] Cf. J. W. Gough, *op. cit.,* p. 210.

definite conception of the nature of man. In Chapter 2, we have also spoken of "Christian humanism," or the Christian idea of the nature of man as the basis of our natural law ethics. Nevertheless, we do not use the expression "Christian natural law." Clearly, natural law theory cannot, without falling victim to the most superficial of all contradictions, a contradiction in terms, take its concept of human nature openly or tacitly from religious faith. It must be drawn from reason. Equally clear, however, is the fact that natural law theory may assure itself, in everything essential to its concept of human nature, of the further certainty rooted in faith (cf. Chaps. 11–12). Only in this sense can one, without falling into self-contradiction, speak of "Christian *natural* law." The expression is, however, used in this sense with full justification, especially to distinguish clearly the great fronts of philosophical thinking concerning man and society, morality and law: "Christian" thinking being on one side and, on the other, "naturalistic" thinking with its denial of the spiritual soul, the basis of man's nature as person. The "naturalistic" doctrines of man to which we have alluded are the scientistic, the dialectical materialist, the logical positivist, the biological evolutionist, the utilitarian pragmatist, and the idealistic monist (cf. Chap. 2). In the realm of scientific natural law theory itself, it is preferable to choose a designation which emphasizes its *philosophical* basis in the understanding of human nature, especially since the philosophical evolution of natural law theory goes back essentially to pre-Christian thought, that is, thought which relied wholly on reason. Hence, in this work we speak of "*traditional natural law theory.*"

PART FOUR

The Failure of the Social Order: Social Question and Social Reform

---

55. The Modern Social Question

In the previous parts dealing with the nature of society and the social order we have been discussing what might be called social physiology, that is, the theory of the structure and the essential functions of the social body. But what if this structure is in disorder and these functions are only inadequately performed? Then disease symptoms in the body of society are inevitable. Therefore, we must turn our attention to social pathology: the study of the diseases of the social body, their symptoms, their causes, and their treatment. This is what is meant by the doctrine of the social question.

The expression "social question" was first coined just before the middle of the nineteenth century. The effects of capitalism were then beginning to take forms pointing to the existence of grave defects in the individualist economic system. The widespread pauperism of the working classes was a first clear sign that it was failing to carry out essential functions. Craftsmen too were impoverished, owing to their weakness in competition with industry, or were totally deprived of the economic basis of their existence. New methods of agricultural production in overseas countries brought about a fall in grain prices and consequently very great difficulties for agriculture throughout Europe. Soon the social question had eaten into the very life-cell of the social body, the family, as mothers in great numbers were drawn from their homes into the factories and a ten-hour or even longer working day threatened masses of children with physical and spiritual ruin. The disruptive class war, the increasing impoverishment of large sections of the middle class, periodical mass unemployment, and finally the threatening fall in the birth rate below reproduction level called in question the existing *social order as a whole.*

56. The Essence of the Social Question

The social question arises from the failure of the social order to realize the essential end of society, the common good, with the result that social groups, to a considerable extent, are unable to share proportionately in the fruits of social cooperation. Although the expression "social question" is of modern origin, frictions in the social order and their perception are as old as human social life itself. But the full comprehension of the nature of the social question required a sufficiently clear idea of the end and the essential functions of the social order. On the other hand, the disorder of social life formed the strongest incentive for investigating the essential foundations of social order.

This process can be clearly recognized in *Plato's Republic*. *Plato's* inquiry into "justice" is obviously occasioned by the condition of the Athenian polity, but it penetrates to the very foundations of social order in general. There is still another feature in Plato's inquiry which is important for the progress of man's mind toward understanding the nature of the social system. Although his inquiry is centered on the question of justice, that is to say, the moral side of the social question, he also views its institutional side, although not in all its implications. Because his analysis of the institutional side remains inadequate, he is led to construct an order which can possess only an imaginary existence and was hardly thought of as anything else. His ideal republic, with its philosopher rulers and its communism of property, women, and children, is the first of the *Utopias* which have expressed much of the dissatisfaction of great minds with the political and social conditions of their times and their reflections on principles of reform. From another famous Utopia, that of Sir *Thomas More* (1516), we derive the general term for such works of social and political thought.

Another method of dealing with the social question is found in the denunciation of social evils by the Hebrew prophets; their condemnations sprang from a sense of justice which was deeply rooted in religion and testified to a remarkably realistic insight into the social situation. Awareness of the facts of the social question also accompanies the whole development of the traditional natural law doctrine in the Middle Ages: its concern with the moral principles of society and their application to the economic and social conditions of their time. In fact, one may say that these phenomena determined the surprisingly penetrating interest of the medieval natural law theorists in the central questions of economic theory, such as prices, wages, and interest, and in the analysis of the legal and mercantile aspects of economy.

Not until the nineteenth century, along with the "social question," were doubts cast upon *the social order itself*. In former times, religious allegiances, social traditions, and political forces prevented the emergence of ideologically based revolutionary social movements resulting from failures in the social system, and prevented the growth even of any consciousness that the order of society as a whole could be submitted to a radical change. Owing to the loosening of the religious, moral, and institutional ties of society, rationalism and the Enlightenment worked toward a gradual withdrawal of the checks to the critical judgment. Thus, they prepared the human mind for a keener perception of the obvious malfunctionings of the capitalistic social system for which they themselves, by fostering a disintegrating individualism, were in a large part responsible. At the same time there gradually developed in the socialistic criticism of individualist-capitalistic society *the concept of the social system* as a unity of principles and institutions expressed in the class structure, on which the achievement or nonachievement of the common good depends.

The idea of the social system differs from that of the social order inasmuch as it stresses the correlation of the functioning of the latter with the historical form of the class structure. "*Social order*" relates more to the nature and the essential functions of the common good as such; "*social system*" relates more to the influence of the class structure on these functions and the actual state of the common good. The two expressions, therefore, relate to two different aspects of the same reality. As long as neither of these aspects demands special attention, they need not be scrupulously differentiated. Of course, a particular "social system" is inseparably linked with every "social order" throughout the history of mankind. But the discovery of its nature and implications depended on the development of legal consciousness, especially in connection with individualist ideas of freedom and human rights and with the idea of social justice, which emerged in the reaction against unjust social conditions in individualist-liberalist society. All the ideas of the social sciences which we have just discussed developed to a great extent concurrently with the progressive socialistic criticism of individualist society.

Consequently, the social question must be defined as the question concerning the *deeper causes* of the failure of the social order to carry out its purpose and concerning the means to remedy this. When the expression "social question" was coined, the disease of the social body was diagnosed principally by one symptom, the "labor question." It can still be used in this sense today, but the situation of the working classes is now generally seen in the wider perspective of the functioning of the social order as such. It is a natural process in the development of the sciences that conceptions with a historical tone widen their meaning in conformity with a wider understanding of reality. For us today, the social question is not just a question of the condition of one class or another, but of the social order as a whole. Today, this means that the social question is to be seen particularly in its world-wide character. In discussing the *theory of the social question* we shall not be occupied in detail with the faulty developments of the present social order, nationally or internationally, but with the social question as a general phenomenon, in the sense that every social order is liable to fail in the execution of its essential function.

Thus, in the chapters which follow we shall have to deal with the causes and effects of the distorted developments of society insofar as they belong to the general feature of social life, and not with their particular historical form today. Hence, we shall be discussing only in general the principles of solving the social question by way of social reform and social policy, and not the particular remedies for the present social evils. The social question of today and the means for overcoming it will be dealt with in the following Books of this work, which cover natural law as applied to present-day society, to the state, and to economic life. In the present section, references to historical examples of social distortions and to individual methods of social reform are made, therefore, by way of illustration.

57. The Principal Cause of the Social Question

Is a perfect social order possible? The individualist and collectivistic social theories contend that it is. Social harmony, says the former, will be achieved when all interests can develop as freely as possible. The society of plenty, says the latter, will be brought about by social planning with the aid of science and technology. Reality, however, as envisaged by the Christian doctrine of man, suggests the conclusion that *no social order can more than approximately attain its end.* This means that no social order is without its social question; *original sin,* with its consequences for man's nature, constitutes the principal cause of the social question.

Man is not just a being destined for unlimited progress and perfection, as is assumed by the social theories we have mentioned. The shortcomings of the human intellect as a result of the impairment of human nature by original sin affect men's understanding of what is required for a useful pattern of social order, the adjustment of their wills in order to coordinate their interests, and hence the organization and functioning of social cooperation. Social order and the common good, therefore, can unavoidably be actualized only to the accompaniment of frictions, great or small. It is also a consequence of original sin that the fruits of the earth will always be scarce and labor toilsome: "Thorns and thistles shall it bring forth to thee. . . . In the sweat of thy face shalt thou eat bread" (Gen. 3:18–19). This entails disputes and strife in the allocation of labor and in the distribution of its fruits. Frictions in the social order are also inevitable for this reason.

Two fundamental features of man's social existence are thus rooted in original sin: first, every society possesses its social question, even though its particular manifestation varies in accordance with the conditions of the existing social system. If the perfect individual, the "saint," is an exception, the perfect society is impossible. Even what the individual can attain is only an *approximation* to the perfection of life according to the moral order. Society can never attain the same degree, for "good and evil" (Matt. 5:48) dwell in it together and, as experience shows, the forces which more readily deviate from the moral order are often more resolute and vigorous.

It would be wrong to conclude from this that Christian ethics leads to a pessimistic view of society. The doctrine of original sin does not state that the social order is corrupted at the roots, just as it does not state that man with his fallen nature has become incapable of achieving the integration of his nature. But it does hold that there is a propensity toward distortion in the social body, and toward frustration in the social order, and that therefore unremitting vigilance and continuous effort are necessary to reduce the shortcomings to a minimum. Thus, the acknowledgment of the fact of original sin leads to a *social realism* that fully takes into account the tendency toward social distemper and makes social reform a constant moral duty of every society. Christian ethics, on the other hand, rejects a *social optimism* which rests on the erroneous conceptions of human nature mentioned at the beginning of this chapter.

The second implication of the fact of original sin for the social problem is this: the approach to a real solution of the social question of society depends upon how far it remains open to the regenerative influences of the *Redemption*. Consequently, since the teachings and the graces of the Redemption are deposited in the hands of the Church, the beneficent influence of the Church on society, as St. *Augustine* points out in a famous and eloquent passage,[1] reaches to the roots of society even in its natural existence.

58. Ideological Causes of the Social Question

Ideologies, in the sociological sense, are views of the nature and purpose of man and of society which influence the form and functioning of the social order. The study of ideology as a sociological phenomenon is of recent origin. It was stimulated by the Marxian theory of dialectical materialism, with its concept of the ideological "superstructure" over the process of technical-economic development. According to this theory, man's social existence, with the conflict between material productive forces and the existing production relationships, determines man's consciousness, and not vice versa. Thus, ultimately the forms of economic production determine and transform "the legal, political, religious, aesthetic or philosophic, in short, ideological forms in which human beings become conscious of this conflict."[2]

The social sciences then began to investigate the question of how far

[1] Cf. Augustine, *De moribus Eccles. Cathol.*, 63; cf. also *Epist. 138*, 15.
[2] K. Marx, *A Contribution to the Critique of Political Economy*, Preface.

these ideological forms were in fact determined by technical-economic reality or themselves represent an original reality, and in what relationships the two realities stand toward each other. The criticism of dialectical materialism (cf. Chap. 16) by different philosophical disciplines and social sciences has shown that Marxian determinism has no basis in reality insofar as it maintains an ultimate dependence of all "ideological forms" on the socio-economic productive forces. Nevertheless, the interdependence of the "ideological forms," which characterize a social system and its economic-technical foundations, is an established fact, but it is also a fact that the former are of primary nature and hence exercise a determinative influence on the pattern of the social system. Marxian dialectical materialism does not deny the potent effect of the "ideological forms" on a society; what it denies is that "ideological forms," that is, ideas and values, exist and possess validity independently of the forms of economic production.

Although fundamentally mistaken, the Marxian theory stimulated a closer inquiry into the correlation between the ideological and economic forms as effective forces in the life and in the development of society, and also a closer investigation of the origin, mode of operation, and influence of ideological forms. The *concept of the "ideological"* still owes much to *Marx,* although it is freed from its materialistic perspective. The first and decisive contributions to these inquiries come from *M. Weber, W. Sombart,* and *E. Troeltsch.* The historical and philosophical works of *W. Dilthey, H. Rickert,* and their schools, including *T. Litt,* tended in the same direction. Among those concerned especially with the theory and criticism of ideology, *Vilfredo Pareto, Max Scheler, Karl Mannheim, Theodor Geiger, Erich Rothacker,* and *Hans Freyer* should be noted.[3] Further contributions came from the numerous studies in the fields of mass psychology, of public opinion, and of modern propaganda, in which the ideological trends in modern society strive for influence and gain currency.

The ideological forces interest us here because of their effect on the

[3] V. Pareto, *Tratato di sociologia generale,* 3 vols., 1916–23; M. Scheler, *Schriften zur Soziologie und Weltanschauungslehre,* 3 vols., 1923–24; *Die Wissensformen und die Gesellschaft,* 1926; K. Mannheim, *Ideologie und Utopie,* 1929; T. Geiger, *Ideologie und Wahrheit,* 1953; H. Freyer, *Theorie des gegenwärtigen Zeitalter,* 1955. In these works sociological, psychological, and epistemological considerations are often too little differentiated; ideology criticism and sociology of knowledge are also often too readily equated; the metaphysical side especially (including the metaphysical experience of man as a primal phenomenon) is almost completely ignored. On the other hand, all the books mentioned, from the point of view of a general outlook on the world, would provide a rich field for critical examination of ideologies in the sense of Erich Rothacker's opinion, *Logik und Systematik der Geisteswissenschaften,* 3rd ed., 1948, p. 32: "All methodological proceedings, every judgment of value, every term in a scientific work is conditioned by a philosophy of life." On the history of the concept of ideology, according to which every ideology seeks to be "an exact science, and yet at the same time a philosophy of life and a political programme," cf. Otto Brunner, "Das Zeitalter der Ideologien, Anfang und Ende," in *Neue Wege der Sozialgeschichte,* 1956, pp. 194–219.

social order. All ideas and values, and hence ends, which exercise a formative influence on the functioning of the social order, we sum up as the ideological factor. The concept is thus marked by *three main features*:

1. The concept is restrictive. Not all lines of development of ideas such as the history of philosophy reveals, are of sociological interest, but only those which influence the pattern and working of the social order. Hence, the ideological element is seen to be *a determining factor in the social system;* other groups of such factors are the institutional (cf. the following chapter), the aversion to changes in the accustomed mode of life (which *H. S. Maine* regards as one of the strongest shaping forces in social life; cf. Chap. 40), political forces with the struggle for domination and power in a community, and the technical forces which influence socio-economic cooperation. The ideological element not only includes the ideas which are in the forefront of the consciousness of a society, but at least equally comprises those which are operative in usage, in custom, and especially in national tradition, and which actually possess enormous power when in conflict with other formative forces. Only by gaining influence on the minds of a portion of a society does the ideological element have an effect on the social order. Modern technique makes the exploiting of the ideological factor by various kinds of propaganda one of the most powerful instruments for the planning and guidance of society. The purposes for which it is thus used are three primarily: first, in all states it serves to support and sustain the political system; secondly, to bring about changes in the social system which sections of the community are interested in; thirdly, to create a groundwork in public opinion for changes already made. In all these cases the ideological element is used in the form of propaganda: in the first two cases, for example, by political parties and social classes in the democracies; in the last case, especially by governments in totalitarian states.

2. Thus, we come to another principal feature of the ideological element: it is *essentially pluralistic.* No social system is informed by one ideology alone. The ideological factor always operates as the resultant of various conflicting ideological trends. In the totalitarian states, which are dominated by a single ideology, this may mean nothing more than that other ideological forces must be taken into account by the group in power. No social system is in reality what it should be according to the predominating ideology. Of the ideological forces operative in "Western" society, those representing the Christian view of life are by far the strongest, although their influence derives in part from tradition alone. On the other hand, from the point of view of empirical sociology, Christianity must be considered one of the ideological forms which contend with one another for influence on the shaping of the social order. Among the other ideological forces may be counted rationalism, liberalism, capitalism, socialism, communism, nationalism, racialism, and behind all these

the materialist-secularistic antagonism to Christianity which they share. The importance of the ideological element is vividly illustrated by the fact that the Second World War has been aptly called a war of ideologies. Undoubtedly, the ideological element in the form of propaganda has proved to be one of the strongest and most decisive weapons of modern warfare. And after the end of the Second World War the "ideological war" continues on a new worldwide front; indeed it has assumed unprecedented scale and forms.

3. Lastly, the third feature: the ideological factor is characterized by *social purposes.* The ideologies exercise influence through the sets of values which they represent, and hence through the ends derived from them. *Homo economicus,* man as seen in the governing ideology of individualist liberalism, functions in a scheme of ends dominated by the profit motive. The individualist idea of nationalist sovereignty determines the scheme of international relations in the period of liberalist supremacy. The position of the collective ends in every totalitarian system needs no detailed description.

If we draw the logical conclusion from what has been said about the effect of the ideological element on the social order we can say the following: Insofar as the ideological forces inspiring a social system deviate from the essential ends of human nature, such a system is bound to fail to realize the common good and so to make possible the "good life" of all members of the community. The ideological factor determines the selection of ends in accordance with which the functions of the social order are directed, and thus it becomes *a primary cause of the social question.*

59. Institutional Causes of the Social Question

The whole body of legal, political, educational, economic, and technical institutions—in short—the social institutions which are intended to serve the end of society, will here be termed the institutional factor. From the very outset these institutions are unable to fulfill their end, the common good, perfectly, because their forms are always, in part, the outcome of the endeavors of antagonistic interests and forces in society. But even if their expediency at the time of their establishment was fully adequate, their efficiency would in course of time be reduced from various causes. From among such causes we select six as the chief ones.

1. The institutions are subject to a natural process of decay, for the intellectual, technical, and economic conditions of social cooperation alter, and with them the conditions to which they were fitted. A tendency toward permanence inherent in the institutional factor tends to counteract change; this is due on the one hand to the force of habit which largely

governs social life, and on the other hand to the influence of those interested in preserving institutions because they are linked with economic or political advantages for them ("vested interests").[1] A social order may excellently meet the needs of general utility at one period in the development of a society, but in the course of further development, with changes in the social functions of large groups or classes, it may produce antisocial effects if it is not changed.

2. A second source of danger lies in the *misuse* to which all institutions are liable. The members of the community who operate these institutions are prone to use them in their own interest, which may lie in the direction of profit, or power, or both. The most familiar example of such a perversion of ends is the banking and credit system in the individualist capitalistic economy, with its parasitic profit policy and its tyranny over the social economy.

3. Institutions, which in themselves are only *means, can exercise domination* over parts of society. Today, technology not only largely determines the rhythm of labor and of life in the community, but with the progress of mechanization and rationalization, it often degrades the worker to the status of a component of the machine which he operates. Thus, "the technical age" (*Saint-Simon*), which promised so much help to man's labor, has become largely an era of technocracy. A similar reversal of the relative roles of means and ends exists on the supply side of the social economy, because of the standardization of goods, which tyrannizes over demand.

4. Institutions may become incapable of fulfilling their ends because of *overcomplication* of their structure and functions. They then become inaccessible to the ordinary member of society who has no professional intermediary. In present-day society, law and legal procedure are such a complicated business that the lawyer has become an indispensable agent. Apart from the considerable expenses which this involves for the citizen, he is frequently dependent upon what the lawyer makes of his case and what interest he takes in it. A similar development can be observed in state administration. The management of the complex administrative machinery of the modern state presupposes such detailed expert knowledge, that the senior officials of the various departments are, to no small extent, able to impose their will on the community, independently of the responsible ministers and of the parliament.

5. Another source of danger lies in the *hypertrophy* of the institutional element. Institutions are liable to expand beyond the scale necessary for their immediate purpose. All institutions of a political, economic, or cultural character offer to those entrusted with their administration not only income but power. Consequently, the institutional factor has an

[1] On the tendency to permanence in the institutional element, in the social apparatus, there are valuable comments in V. Pareto (*op. cit.*). In general, much less attention has been paid hitherto to the general sociology of the institutional factor than to the ideological factor.

inherent tendency to disproportionate growth (e.g., the bureaucracy in the modern state or supercombines in the economic world). This tendency, long known to sociology, has recently been aptly set forth in Parkinson's Law, so-called after *N. C. Parkinson* (Parkinson's Law, 1958).

6. A not insignificant source of perversion of the institutional factor lies in its inherent tendency to *autonomy,* in virtue of which it makes itself independent and imposes organizational forms on society. One example is the working of the profit motive under unrestricted competition which as *Marx* showed, becomes, to a great extent, an unyielding driving force which works even contrary to the will of the capitalists if they wish to survive in this competition. Since then, the transition from competitive to monopoly capitalism with its cartels has revealed a technico-economic autonomy in the opposite direction. The combination, with its complex production organization, its managerial apparatus, technology, finance and pricing systems, and market manipulation, also follows its own laws of functioning. These forms of managerial and technical organization, *Burnham* has shown,[2] largely subject every society, whether its ideological basis be liberal or socialistic, capitalistic or communistic, to their own laws.

All these tendencies which we have described must, to a greater or lesser degree, involve a shifting of purposes in the sphere of functions of social institutions; as a result, the common good is only imperfectly realized. Thus, the institutional element becomes a powerful *cause of the social question.*

60. Manifestations of the Social Question

Every social system necessarily operates through institutions in concrete "historical" forms. Hence, their failures in the realization of the common good will also always assume special forms. Consequently, *each historical social order has its particular social question.* A few examples will illustrate this multiformity.

The social question of the *Athenian City-State,* resulting in the tragic

[2] Cf. J. Burnham, *The Managerial Revolution.* In this much discussed book Burnham intends to offer only "a descriptive theory" of the present-day socio-economic development with the purpose of predicting, at least in general, its outcome (Penguin ed., 1945, p. 11); but he concentrates his analysis on the institutional side of the development, whence he arrives at deterministic conclusions. In a more realistic perspective, necessary for a purely "descriptive" theory, at least equal attention should be devoted to the moral forces which endeavor to influence the speed, the direction, and the future of the development. If indeed the greater forms of managerial and industrial organization function like machines, as this theory seems to suggest, regardless of the moral beliefs of those who operate them, one can find no real point in Burnham's statement that no attempt at a social program or a social morality may be made without resorting to his theory (*ibid.,* p. 11).

decline of Athens after a century of the greatest cultural achievements, culminating in the Periclean Era, was due to the special form of its democratic constitution. This constitution encouraged demagogy by the distribution of offices by lot, ostracism, popular law courts, and the swift rotation of office and responsibility.[1] These weaknesses are the reason "Athenian democracy ran its course from infancy to decrepitude with unexampled speed." [2] In Rome, the special feature of the social question toward the end of the Republic was the depopulation of the land because of military levies, the tax system, and the exploitation of the remaining smallholders by the city financiers; this resulted in the formation of *latifundia,* with a corresponding increase in the urban proletariat as well as a disproportionate increase in the number of slaves and in the importance of their social functions.

Although many who are captivated by the ideological basis of the *medieval guild system* frequently paint it as an ideal social system, it too had its special social question. Certainly the regulation of production, of prices, and of incomes by the guilds was inspired by the principle of "adequate subsistence" for all their members and by the principle of the best possible provision for the towns, and had for its aim the realization of social justice. This aim, however, was achieved for only a few decades and even then only approximately. The economic system could not have functioned even to this extent had there not been, on the Continent of Europe, the possibility of a constant outflow of surplus population from the towns into the eastern colonial regions, where the sons and daughters of the master craftsmen could find the livelihood which was no longer possible at home. In this way, the German economic area was doubled in the period from the eleventh to the thirteenth century. The Italians, and later the English, were able to expand their economic resources many times over by commerce overseas. When, however, the master craftsmen in the towns began to protect themselves against the difficulties arising from competition by closing the guilds and by guild monopoly, it became practically impossible for journeymen to become masters. These and the apprentices, who were mostly prevented from becoming journeymen, and hence in accordance with prevailing regulations could not marry, constituted the *proletariat* of this social system; strikes and occasional armed risings are part of the social history from the thirteenth to fifteenth centuries. A working day of twelve to fourteen hours was usual, and even a sixteen-hour day was not uncommon.[3] On top of all this came the great

[1] Cf. H. A. L. Fisher, *A History of Europe,* 1941 ed., p. 20.

[2] Lord Acton, *History of Freedom,* 1907, p. 11.

[3] Cf. Josef Kulischer, *Allgemeine Wirtschaftsgeschichte,* Vol. I, *Das Mittelalter,* 1928, pp. 210–15. On the intervention of the Landesherren in the fifteenth century against the "disorderly and terroristic agitation of the journeymen among themselves and against the masters," and on measures of social policy in favor of the journeymen and apprentices, cf. G. von Below, *Probleme der Wirtschaftsgeschichte,* 1920, pp. 547 ff.

welfare burdens of economy.[4] History, therefore, does not support the notion of an ideal economic system in the Middle Ages unaccompanied by its social question.

We do not need to go on to point out the special features of the social question in the nineteenth and twentieth centuries, which are well-known: pauperism, child labor, social insecurity, unemployment, the proletariat, the class war, capitalistic-imperialist war, and the failing will to live (declining birth rates) of industrialized nations.

61. Social Criticism

A diagnosis of the causes of the failure of the existing social order is the task of social criticism. From natural law ethics we derive the following principles for social criticism.

1. Social criticism primarily involves a sense of *responsibility.* This is meant in two senses: first, watchfulness over the manner in which the social order functions is a constant duty; secondly, it is also a duty to avoid any harm to society by merely factious, sensational, negative, or destructive criticism. Responsible social criticism, therefore, demands a high degree of competence and community sense on the part of those who see it as their function to throw a critical light on social evils and to diagnose their causes, whether such persons are representatives of class or group interests, politicians, journalists, writers, or ministers of religion. This competence presupposes sufficient acquaintance with the details of the social system and with its legal, political, economic, and technical institutions, with the needs and interests of the different groups in the community, with the manifold requirements of the common good, the available resources of the economy, etc.* Only after long study is a physician considered competent to diagnose the ills of the human

[4] In medieval cities of Central Europe, which today would rank as small towns (not more than 7,000 to 10,000 inhabitants), there was a chronic shortage of labor owing to the heavy losses caused by repeated epidemics, famines, and feuds. On the other hand, the number of those obtaining "assistance" was so great that it at least equalled the highest percentage of unemployed between the two World Wars under capitalistic economy (ten percent of the population); amongst the beneficiaries of the extraordinarily heavy assistance burden (according to K. Bücher, *Die Entstehung der Volkswirtschaft,* Vol. I, 12th and 13th ed., 1919, pp. 398–407) were women, whose incorporation into the social economy was prevented by their social standing and who found shelter in convents and welfare institutions. Many had bodily and mental infirmities. A high proportion of old people was occasioned by the aging of the population, which was a consequence of a high rate of infant mortality.

* For this reason, says St. Thomas Aquinas in *V Eth.,* 15, social criticism and social reform, in accordance with the demands of justice, are much more difficult than the work of the physician: "Hoc autem, scilicet accommodare convenienter negotiis et personis, est magis operosum et difficile, quam scire sanativa, in quo consistit tota ars medicinae. Major enim est diversitas rerum voluntariarum, in quibus consistit justitia, quam complexionum, in quibus consistit sanitas."

body; yet, almost anyone can presume to diagnose the body politic in public without even attempting to produce evidence for his competence in the field. Social sentiment often runs away with judgment here. It is not denied, however, that the awakening of consciences to social evils is sometimes more a matter of social feeling than of economic or sociological expertise.

2. Social criticism must go beyond the observation of mere *symptoms.* A dramatic and sensational exposure of symptoms of social malaise is easy, but is of no real use in itself and is in great danger of becoming mere demagogy. In fact, social criticism is always bound up with two positive tasks at the same time: to indicate ways for the speedy alleviation of existing evils and for the removal of their deeper causes. Facile rhetoric directed against "capitalism" is a much less useful contribution to the attainment of social well-being than careful study of the causes of unjust prices and interest rates forced upon the public by industrial and financial trusts, and the formulation of immediately effective countermeasures. The touchstone of any true social criticism is its endeavor to be positive and constructive. On the other hand, it is of equally little benefit to the social good to judge socialism only from doctrinaire ideological points of view, without seeing the forces pressing for a radical reshaping of the economic and social system (which it is the task of social reforms to put to fruitful employment). Furthermore, if high authorities in a particular country, knowing of their responsibility for the state of public conscience, declare that wages, to conform with social justice, ought on the average to be twice as high, this amounts to a severe self-accusation: for generations there must have been a lack of effective, constructive social criticism by these authorities, working toward social reforms (increase of productivity), which could have made such wages practicable.

3. True social criticism presupposes *self-criticism with regard to one's own ideological persuasion,* for ideological prejudice can see only a caricature of reality. It is always ready to underestimate the historical factors of all social reality. In order to be constructive, social criticism must not lose sight of the fact that each particular social system, with its foundation of ideas and institutions, is the product of a historical process; it cannot be simply exchanged for another social order like an old garment without involving grave harm for the social good. If the essential functions of the social order are to remain effective, it can be perfected only in a process of evolution. A more perfect order cannot be created by an act of switching over to ideologically conceived systems. The ideology-based view of the social question is an impediment to true diagnosis. Any social criticism based on ideological "systems" simplifies reality. This is the reason the capitalistic conception of socialism is as inadequate as the socialistic conception of capitalism. To a large extent, both are bogies serving the ends of class warfare.

62. Social Reform

Social reform consists in the renovation of the spirit and institutions of a society in order to achieve the end of society more perfectly. It aims at the alleviation and elimination of social evils by removing their causes. Our inquiry into the causes of the social question has shown that these causes operate chiefly in two directions: mistaken ideologies and perverted institutions. Thus, this settles the main tack which countermeasures must take if the social question in a society is to be dealt with. Correspondingly, social reform has two equally important aspects: spiritual reform and institutional reform.

Spiritual reform means the renewal of social morality in harmony with the existential ends of man and society, or, in other words, the renewal of social morality in harmony with natural law. It concerns the attitude of a society toward the essential values and the awakening of moral forces. The one cannot be attained without the other. Both issues involve reeducation, which is essential to a real solution of the social question of a society. It is a fundamental error of Marxian socialism to expect the perfect society principally from a reshaping of the social system and of its basic institutions. But the very fact that all totalitarian systems find themselves compelled to make the most vigorous efforts to imbue society with their ideologies provides testimony for the importance of spiritual forces to the social order, an example that is unparalleled in history. In fact, the spirit ultimately gives life to a social system, making it work and inspiring it to accomplish great achievements. Experience has shown that even the best institutions fail when a society lacks the appropriate spirit.

Mental reform, however, must be linked with *institutional reform.* During the nineteenth century, there were strong groups of Christian liberals in several countries, who held that everything depends on the moral attitude or spiritual disposition of those using the existing social institutions: capitalism would measure up to all that is implied in social justice if only men could be brought to pay greater respect to moral principles. Certainly, both competitive capitalism and state capitalism would function wonderfully if all men were saints and full of self-denial; but neither the considerable number of socially minded capitalistic employers nor the success of the "Jesuit state" in Paraguay provides evidence that spiritual reform alone suffices. Greed exercised in the various forms of individual and social profiteering is too great a temptation in the light of the reality of human nature for social institutions not to be necessary to insure the realization of the fundamental requirements of social justice. Obviously, Christian liberals would not deny that appropriate political institutions are necessary for the control of government powers in a state based on other principles than those of a religious community. The fundamental error of individualist and liberalist social theory is not to admit the need for protecting the social good by suitable institutions, but simply to trust in the automatic development of harmony of freely operating interests. Hence, in its heyday liberalism was opposed to the idea of genuine social reform and wanted to restrict it on principle to the facilitating of the free play of forces.

63. The Aim of Social Reform

The aim of social reform needs further definition. Not everything that contributes to an alleviation of social ills or even to the improvement of social conditions can be called social reform. Costly governmental subsidies for threatened industries, family allowances, and social security schemes for large sections of the community may be necessary at certain times, but they do not mean social reform in the sense of serious efforts to cure social evils at the root; rather, they are palliatives. Just as in the realm of medicine, the aim in the social sphere is the *vigorous health of the body* so that it can itself fully perform all its functions. Were there no other reason for this, the cost of prolonged treatment of the social body with mere palliatives would be sufficient reason for real reform. Social reform must aim at a functioning of the social order in such a way that economic and social relief measures are confined to the limits fixed by the subsidiary function principle and that the *members of society themselves are enabled* to discharge their essential tasks on their own responsibility, which is implied in the nature of the existential ends.

What concerns social reform is the failure of the social system to fulfill this function; it must get down to the roots of social evils. This does not prejudice social legislation and social welfare measures, especially since we have pointed out that no social system is free from defects and, therefore, that efforts are always necessary to remedy shortcomings in the social order. The primary aim is *to adapt the system as such to the fulfillment of its essential end:* the fullest possible realization of the common good. The social system is a complex, living organism of functions and of institutions which, in fact (at least to a certain extent), always serve the interests of all members of society, and always function in the interest of the common good, since otherwise a society could not continue to exist. The first task of social reform, therefore, is to discriminate and to alter what is functioning unsatisfactorily, and to preserve and to strengthen what is fulfilling its function. It is a bad physician who always recommends the surgeon's knife. Social reform is equally misguided if it relies solely on surgical methods. The constant pruning of defective functions and institutions does not signify social reform; rather, their restoration to full efficiency signifies it.

Today, one of the *commonest errors* of a "social attitude" is to think that *any curtailment of freedom in economic life is synonymous with a measure of social reform.* Private ownership, it is said, causes social evils; therefore, away with it. Socialization is then the panacea. But it is evident that every private interest and private enterprise based on private ownership form powerful driving forces for economic and social progress if they can be set to work in such a way that they benefit the common good as much as the private good. In cases where socialization seems expedient, three questions remain: (1) whether the common interest would not be better served by the splitting up of big combines and the re-establishment of smaller private holdings; temporary socialization could be a means for achieving such a reorganization of the structure of private ownership; (2) whether the socialized concerns should be run as government concerns (like the railways in some countries) or as independent corporations in which the government holds a controlling share of the capital; (3) how far the general interest demands, as a branch of the economy, the nationalization of dominant industrial concerns or of other concerns also. The socialization of large-scale agricultural property may be inadvisable because of the lack of capital for investment in equipping the small holdings which are planned; the neglect of this problem after the First World War in central and south-eastern Europe turned out to be gravely detrimental to the common interest.

Thus, we come to another essential feature of the purpose of true social reform: the common good is a *continuous process* of assimilation of new forces and of adaptation to new needs (cf. Chaps. 25 ff.). These forces and needs are related to purposes, to interests, to desires, and to the productive and creative impulses which govern the application of man's energies. Hence, the extent to which the common good is actualized depends on the degree of self-determination possessed by the members of society in formulating their needs and in applying their energies. Seen from the point of view of life itself, the social principle of subsidiary function is the following: As much freedom as possible, as much regulation as necessary. It means that the reality of the common good is essentially incompatible with the drawing-board plans of social economy, with state direction, and with solutions which would cure everything at the pulling of a switch. Examples of this are projects for getting rid of all economic evils by the abolition of capital profit or of the gold standard or by means of social credit or a social dividend (profit sharing, in addition to wages, established by law).

What has been said points to another important characteristic of true social reform: There is *no ready-made ideal of a social order* for all times. This is particularly true for Christian ethics. Natural law offers no more than an outline of social, political, economic, and international life. Although it is a commonplace that Christian ethics has no absolute preference for one form of state over another, nevertheless, many cling to the mistaken belief that the same does not apply in the economic field and that the medieval guild system represents a unique ideal. For the same reason, Christian ethics cannot produce a slogan to sum up an ideal Christian social system. This may appear to be a disadvantage, especially in comparison with socialistic programs with their mass psychology and mass propaganda effects. Christian social programs cannot compete in the field of slogan making. Nevertheless, Christian social ethics and Christian social reform have a very powerful ally on their side if they will but learn to make use of it: reality itself. If today's debate about economic planning and socialistic programs is brought into the light of the reality of the immediate and essential demands of the common good, the public may well become convinced that all such schemes of organization, which treat the human person as a statistical unit of production and consumption, are bound to fail in the task of insuring a progressive standard of life and of civilization for all classes of people.* On the other hand, our task in the following parts of this study, when dealing with applied natural law in the spheres of society, of the state, and of the economy, will be to show how definite, even in details, are the implications of natural law principles for social order and social reform in the face of a definite social reality such as we see before us today.

64. Evolution and Revolution in Social Reform

Social reform is essentially a process of evolution: only for exceptional reasons may it follow the path of revolution. The cry for social "revolution" was universal after the Second World War. Even church authorities have joined in the cry demanding social revolution, although certainly in a very different sense from that of the communists. The much-used term "revolution" in a rhetorical sense stresses the circumstance that only radical changes in the social system can remove social evils. In times of social unrest, it may be necessary to use strong words to obtain a hearing at all. The social sciences, however, whose task it is to examine the laws of social life and of social progress, must be cautious in the use of such terms.

The difference between evolution and revolution lies in the extent to which immediate changes in the functions and institutions which are fundamental to the social order and the social system, take place. Since the constitution of the state regulates such changes, one can also say that evolutionary changes in the social order proceed by constitutional methods, revolutionary changes by unconstitutional methods. Evolution thus preserves the functions vital to society, especially those of law, and tries

* A unique example of the persuasive power of reality over preconceived ideological thinking is provided by the need for a complete reorientation of Marxian socialism in Europe in the light of the experience of Marxian socialism in Russia.

to transform the existing institutions gradually so that they will better conform with their end. Revolution, however, attacks the foundations of social order in spite of the risk of a temporary intermission of these functions. Anarchist revolutionaries who commit actions which render law and rights ineffective, even those functions of the state which protect life and liberty, do so with unburdened consciences. "How can you even imagine a bloodless revolution?" the author was asked at a meeting with revolutionaries after the First World War.

There are three main reasons for stating that the path of evolution as a rule is the only expedient method of social reform. First, no society can be in a condition so unnatural that its social system does not contain some elements of order. Certainly the perverse energies in human nature may gain the ascendancy in a considerable part of the community, but opposing forces in the rest of society, which have clear notions about individual and social duties and are anxious to preserve the functioning capacity of the social order in accordance with its essential ends, are never lacking. In fact, society could not exist at all if it did not consist for the most part of responsible citizens and if its social system did not function, partly at least, in the service of its essential ends. The second reason for the evolutionary method of social reform is the complexity of the structure of social institutions. Abrupt, radical changes in the greater proportion of institutions involve the danger of complications which must lead to far-reaching disturbances in the vital functions of the social body, notably in the economic process, and are thus injurious to social well-being. Revolutionaries are all too ready to risk such dangers and to rely on the benefits expected from their new order. The third and most vital reason for the evolutionary road of social reform is the organic character of the community and the common good. To cure an organism it is necessary to build on functions still in regular working order, even though they be enfeebled or partly disordered. In any case, one must not kill the patient in order to cure him. The same is true of the social organism. Hence, a better social order must be sought for in the existing one and developed from it. This is the essence of the evolutionary method.

The situation, however, may make it necessary to incur the risk of revolutionary measures for the sake of reform. Three conditions must be observed if such measures are to be justified. First, the action must be necessitated by a state of emergency in the community; its social good must be gravely threatened and the evolutionary method must be without prospect owing, for example, to an actual misuse of governmental power, which, in consequence, is detrimental to the common good. Secondly, there must be a guarantee that the continuance of the vital functions of social order is assured or that any insecurity will be removed in the shortest possible time. Thirdly, the new conditions aimed at must secure the basis for a quick recovery and for the favorable development of the social good. The initiators must know what they intend and what they can achieve; otherwise they are merely desperadoes. For, revolution is never an end in itself.

Obviously these three conditions can more readily be present to justify a *political* than a *social* revolution. The former aims directly at a change of government or form of government, the latter at a change in class structure and its influence on the functioning of a social order. In the light of what has been said, social revolution would never be justified as long as the government in power is ready and able to carry out necessary social reforms. The details of the problem of revolution, however, belong to political ethics (cf. Chap. 132).

To say that in general social reform is confined to the evolutionary method does not, however, imply that it cannot, if necessary, and ought not to be *radical*. Because of its dynamic character, natural law establishes *three principles* for the evolutionary method of social reform: first, that the social order by all expedient means be made an efficient instrument for bringing about the common good, so that only the time factor remains flexible and even this only within the limits set by the assured preservation of vital functions in the process of a fuller realization of the common good; secondly, that the existing social order be not merely patched up with superficial relief measures, but renewed in its spiritual energies and institutional functions conformably with its purpose; thirdly, that all reforms are carried through deliberately (each reform must prepare the way for others) with all the determination which seems to be demanded by one of the gravest human obligations: the obligation to develop the common good to the best possible standard as a condition of lasting peace in society. Thus, the evolutionary principle of social reform calls not only for vigilance and will, to exploit every possibility of reform with the intention of a constant perfecting of the functioning capacity of the social order, but also for resolution and energy of a kind that can be derived only from moral principles.

65. Competence for Social Reform: The Primary Competence of "Society"

Social reform is first and foremost a matter for the regenerative forces of the social body itself. In this respect, society resembles the human body. No physician can restore a sick body to health and vigor unless the organism's own powers undertake the process of recovery. Thus, the doctor's first endeavor must be to liberate these regulative forces, to strengthen them, and to direct them to the intended goal. The state itself can ultimately do no more than this for the diseased social body: the inherent energies of the social body itself must first be brought into play. These are the personal responsibility and interest of the members of society. They are moral as well as selfish forces, in virtue of which the members of society are concerned to secure an adequate functioning of the political, economic, and social order. Hence, the social body, like the animal body, carries its own *self-regulating forces* in the truest sense, and any remedial process must ultimately work from these.

The moral and selfish forces, as soon as they find expression in the endeavors of social groups and classes, are generally very closely interwoven. The egoistic forces are the more insistent, but *conservative and progressive forces are always in interaction.* This is of crucial significance for society's self-regulating power. On both sides, strong selfish motives are at work, because for some groups and classes there are advantages bound up with the existing social order which they strive to preserve ("vested interests"), but for others there are disadvantages which they strive to eliminate. On both sides, therefore, there are dangers of bias. Important conclusions are to be drawn from this, and Christian social reformers must not shut their eyes to them. Social movements imbued with one-sided "*progressive*" ideas always carry with them real and valuable regenerative forces, although actually, owing to the neglect of the natural principles of social order, they may cause far worse disorder than they wish to cure. On the other hand, narrow "*conservatism*" is not less dangerous and fateful, since it not only seeks to perpetuate the diseases of society but may even call forth revolutionary developments. Genuine "conservative" forces, however, which aim to preserve the existing social order, insofar as it fulfills its essential functions, and to develop a better order out of the existing one, may actually be much more progressive than the "radical" ones because their goals of reform can be more in the interest of a lasting removal of social evils. On the whole, as long as their activities are confined within the bounds of the essential groundwork of social order, the rivalries between the more conservative and the more advanced groups perform an indispensable function in social reform. The interplay of thrusting and of retarding forces keeps in motion the sound development of the social order, preserving it from the danger of revolutionary frictions detrimental to the social good. As a rule, therefore, it is best for society if these forces balance each other and if neither side is able to dominate the other. For then, there exists a reasonable prospect of a creative synthesis of the "progressive" and "conservative" interests and powers in a social system.

Such a synthesis can only take the form of a *compromise.* The question is whether it is to be a positive and constructive pooling of forces which, although differing in their views as to ways and means, make it their aim to achieve at least an understanding of all groups. Thus, a common basis for an all-round discussion of the most expedient means for increasing and enriching the common weal, will be preserved; and the common good, as we have already indicated more than once, sets such complicated problems that discussion from all angles among the interested groups offers the best prospect of their solution. If unimpeded, such discussions do not proceed by way of subdued conversations behind closed doors. Among the opposing forces, class interests are at work with their claim to a share in the control of the social process and in the shaping of the social order. They take the form of social strife and of class warfare. Then, compromises are often based more on the relative strength of the opposing groups than on real arguments. This strength may rest on the power of such groups in the social system, or on the number of their adherents in the community, or, as often happens, on a mixture of these factors. Every such compromise in a free society then becomes an impulse in the development toward a regrouping and a resynthesis of social forces. Nevertheless, it is evident from the foregoing that social reform moves toward a maximum of social good only if all social forces retain the necessary freedom for their activity. Otherwise, "social reform" becomes a usurpation of power by one class or group over others, with a reshaping of the social system to its end.

What can be achieved directly by the regenerative forces of the social body itself (as distinct from state measures) in social reform, by the creation of institutions, is uniquely exemplified by the manifold organizations in capitalistic society for the coordination of group interests, especially the development of organs for concluding collective labor agreements for the purpose of balancing the interests of capital and labor. This has proved to be one of the most important real steps toward a refashioning of the social system. As another example, the cooperative movement and its development since the days of Rochdale may be mentioned. No less significant is the autonomy of joint vocational organizations in all countries and the ordering functions which they perform in the social system.*

66. The Competence of the State in Social Reform

The state is competent to undertake social reform since the establishment and furtherance of the common good are its essential functions. The common good principle and the principle of subsidiary function are equally valid here (cf. Chaps. 44–45). What these principles demand is as far removed from the individualist doctrine of nonintervention by the state as from the collectivistic omnicompetence in the molding of the social system. For, it is a function of the state (contrary to individualist theory) to protect the common good in the interplay of interests, and hence also in the functioning of the social system and its institutions. On the other hand (contrary to the collectivistic theory), the function of the state is basically confined to the service of the regenerative forces of the

* Illustrated by the example of chambers of commerce by Alfred Klose, "Grundlagen und Perspektiven der beruflichen Selbstverwaltung," in *Wirtschaftspolitische Blätter* (Vienna), 1957, n. 5, pp. 46 ff.

social body, that is to say, to the task of arousing and of supporting them and of mutual coordination.

Thus, the state is competent to initiate *social reform* where "social" forces fail, particularly when opposing forces are engaged in destructive conflicts. In case of critical developments and of imminent grave dangers to the common weal—in case of "emergency"—the initiative of the state may even extend to the curtailing of political or economic liberty, that is, of rights which in normal times are assured to individuals and groups by natural law. Such interference can be justified on the following conditions: (1) that the basic functions of society are jeopardized by a social crisis, as in a class struggle which is passing over into civil war; (2) that such measures conform with the principle of subsidiary function vis-à-vis society's own ordering forces, so that no permanent extension of state powers is intended; (3) that as soon as the danger is over the constitutional rights of control over governmental actions are at once restored. In such cases, state authority may be obliged by justice itself to take drastic steps to overcome the state of emergency.

Even apart from such emergency cases, state authority, in face of necessary social reforms, need not shrink from showing vision and energy; success itself generally depends on real statecraft. An outstanding example of such leadership was President *Roosevelt*'s New Deal experiment undertaken in the crisis years after 1932 in the U.S.A., even though some of its measures do not perhaps stand up to criticism. A wise government can create, step by step, the necessary legal conditions for the most far-reaching reforms, if it is capable of simultaneously arousing public opinion and of bringing increasing numbers of the community to see the fulfillment of their own will in progressive social reform.

The *social policy* of the state is distinct from social reform. The two ideas are often taken as synonymous, but for the social sciences and especially for natural law ethics, there is an essential difference between them. Social reform is primarily a function of "society," social policy a function of the "state." Social reform aims primarily at a change in the working of the social system, social policy at the immediate alleviation of particular faults arising out of the social system. Genuine social reform concerns itself primarily with the causes, social policy with the symptoms of social malaise. The state's obligation to pursue a social policy is dictated by legal and distributive justice (cf. Chap. 50), and since no social order can be perfect there will always be a need for some kind of social policy.

Perhaps we should also recall the principle that *the best social policy is that which makes itself superfluous* while preparing the way for real social reform, so that the social body itself becomes healthy and capable of integrally fulfilling its functions. The borderline between social policy and social reform, therefore, in reality often is not precisely determinable. Nevertheless, it is certain that the necessity of real social reform is the more obvious the more a state finds itself compelled to take measures of social policy. It is equally certain that an excess of social policy to the neglect of real social reform is the direct road to state collectivism. We are concerned here only with the definition of concepts and of principles; detailed questions of social policy within the framework of political ethics, will occupy us in Book Three.

67. The Competence of the Church in Social Reform

The cooperation of the Church is indispensable for the attainment of the vital aims of social reform. For, the social order is, as far as man's existential ends are concerned, part of the moral order. By reason of her mission, the Church is called to be the *guardian of the moral law,* and hence guardian of the conscience of society. Therefore, she has the right and the duty to raise her voice in admonition and in warning when society deviates from the natural order, thus failing in the essential functions laid down by man's existential ends. Accordingly, the authority of the Church is not confined to the mere enunciation of the moral law; it extends also to the valuation of the principles governing economic thought and economic policy where they impinge upon the moral law. It is also the Church's task to pass moral judgment on the institutions of a social system when these are not in harmony with natural rights; for example, the educational institutions of totalitarian states. Thus, the competence of the Church extends to *both aspects of social reform,* the *spiritual* and the *institutional,* but only insofar as the moral law is in question; it is not her mission to enter into questions of a purely technical or organizational character in political and economic life.

The Church is, however, not only the divinely appointed teacher and expounder of the moral law. Her vocation to cooperate in the solution of the social question goes further. The failure of moral judgment on the part of men and of society is but one side of the consequences of original sin (in which lies the final cause of the social question). The other side is the tumult of human instincts and passions—egoism, avarice, pride, desire for power—with all their disintegrating effects on the social order. Thus, society depends on the Church not only as the guardian of the moral law but also as a *source of moral regeneration.* The Church holds this position because of the graces and the powers of Redemption, that is, of the supernatural order, entrusted to it.

In face of the acuteness of the social question today both within societies and internationally and the catastrophes accompanying it, which arise out of the secularization of society by individualist and collectivistic forces, no prophetic vision is required to see that, without the reawakening of moral and of religious forces, any hope of constructing a social order worthy of the vocation of the human person will be disappointed.

The re-Christianization of society is indispensable if social reform is to achieve decisive results. The universal fears engendered by the invention of nuclear weapons shows that mankind is always in *danger of having its moral progress overtaken by its scientific progress.* The tremendously increasing forces put at man's disposal by the advance of science can serve destructive as well as constructive ends. They will be used for the good of the human race only if its moral forces grow correspondingly. Thus, social progress depends increasingly on moral progress.

68. Social Ethics and Social Reform: Applied Natural Law

The Divisions of This Work

Social criticism and social reform belong to the proper sphere of social ethics. Ethics is primarily a "practical" rather than a "speculative" branch of philosophy. Its object is not knowledge for its own sake, but knowledge of the principles necessary for the ordering of personal and social life. Hitherto we have discussed natural law in general. The principal task of *social ethics,* however, is the application of its principles to the manifold phenomena of actual social life. Its function, therefore, is to be applied natural law. Thus, on the one hand there arises for social ethics the task of examining the existing social institutions with regard to the extent that they are in harmony with man's existential ends and with regard to the extent that they are fitted to realize them (social criticism), on the other hand, social ethics has the task of ascertaining the natural order of the spheres of social life, as far as this can be known from natural principles applied to existing conditions (social reform). The two sides are inseparably linked. Social criticism and social reform, therefore, fall equally into the domain of social ethics. Obviously, it can do justice to neither of these tasks without detailed knowledge of those conditions; therefore, social ethics is largely dependent upon the findings of the various social sciences.

The road we must take in our further endeavors to perform these particular tasks in the study of applied natural law is broadly indicated by the results of our preceding discussions. We have found that, as a whole, society is built up of smaller communities united into the state. The object of the latter is to enable all the smaller communities, as well as individual men, to live together and to work together, as far as this is necessary for the realization of the vital tasks of all men (the existential ends). Thus, the function of the state is only a subsidiary one; a wide field of autonomous functions and rights is left to smaller communities and extends as far as they can realize their own ends by their own powers, independently of the help of the state. This part of social life is called "society" in the narrower sense, as distinct from the "state." It is not necessary to show again how important this distinction is in principle and practice; we have dealt fully with the subsidiary character of the state's function with regard both to its ontological foundation and to its juridical effects.

In the light of what has been said above we may, for our present purpose, *define* the "*state*" as a community within a certain territory directed toward the attainment of the fundamental social ends; "*society*" consists in communities within and above the state directed toward the realization of their particular ends. Thus, the specific difference between them lies in the diversity of their ends: the end of the state is the general good implied in the fulfillment of the fundamental functions of social life; the end of the greater and lesser communities constituting "society" and of the individuals is their individual good. We may also say that the state is the unified social life of a people based on the fulfillment of vital functions through the cooperation of all; society is the multiformity (pluralism) in the social life of a people based on the various essential functions incumbent on individuals, groups, and communities.

From this distinction between society and state, it follows that, for the *construction of our system of natural law ethics,* the ethics of society and the ethics of the state community must form separate parts. A further subdivision of social ethics as applied natural law is suggested by the following consideration. The groups which make up society exist either within the state or above it. Among those within the state community economic cooperation represents a unity which, although it comprises the whole population, is nevertheless "society" rather than "state" in character, since it concerns the free activity of the individuals and their free associations. Certainly this cooperation requires, as all the other activities of man do, the help of the state, but only its help: the task of the state in economic life is clearly only a subsidiary one. Thus, the treatment of national economy would fall within the province of ethics of society. Because of its wide scope and implications, however, it requires discussion in a separate portion of this work (the ethics of political economy).

This work, then, may be subdivided as follows:

Book One: The *fundamentals* of natural law (herewith concluded).
Book Two: The natural law of "*society,*" comprising the ethics of society within the state and beyond it, the latter being the international community.
Book Three: The natural law of the *state,* comprising political ethics or the ethics of the state.
Book Four: The natural law of *economic life,* comprising the ethics of social economy and of international economy.

The subdivision of Book Two is suggested by the following considerations. The social groupings within the state are: (1) the *family* as the cell of society; (2) the *smaller groupings* with community rights based on reasons of neighborhood, occupation, and free choice; (3) the *nation* as a large grouping of special significance for modern society; (4) among the suprapolitical communities which belong to society as distinct from the state there are two of outstanding importance: *the community of nations and the Church.* Only the former is an object of natural law ethics as such.

BIBLIOGRAPHY

Ambrosetti, G., *Razionalità e storicità del diritto,* Rome, 1953.

Antweiler, A., *Das Problem der Willensfreiheit,* 1955.

Arnold, F. X., *Zur Frage des Naturrechts bei Martin Luther,* 1937.

Aron, R., *La sociologie allemande contemporaine,* 1936; Engl., 1957, German, 1953.

Auer, Albert, O.S.B., *Würde und Freiheit des Menschen,* 1952.

——— *Der Mensch hat Recht: Naturrecht auf dem Hintergrund des Heute,* 1956.

——— *Reformation aus dem Ewigen,* 1955.

Auer, J., *Die menschliche Willensfreiheit im Lehrsystem des Thomas v. Aquin und Johannes Duns Scotus,* 1938.

Austin, J., *The Province of Jurisprudence Determined,* 1832.

Ayer, A. J., *Language, Truth and Logic,* 2nd ed., 1948.

——— *The Problem of Knowledge,* 1954.

Baader, F. v., *Gesammelte Werke,* 16 vols., 1851–60.

——— *Grundzüge der Sozietätsphilosophie,* 1837, reprinted 1917.

Barker, E., *Principles of Social and Political Theory,* 1952.

——— *Political Thought in England 1848–1914,* 1942 ed.

Benedictis, M. de, O.F.M., *The Social Thought of Saint Bonaventura: A Study in Social Philosophy* (Washington), 1946.

Bentham, Jeremy, *Introduction to the Principle of Morals and Legislation,* 1789.

——— *Deontology or Science of Morality,* ed. by J. Bowring, 1834.

Berg, Ludwig, *Der Mensch, Herr seiner Rechte: Die Metaphysik der Gottesebenbildlichkeit im Personsein des Menschen hinsichtlich der Rechtsherrschaft des Menschen,* 1940.

——— "Das Soziale im Lichte der Theologie," in *Jb. f. d. Bistum Mainz,* 1950.

Bergbohm, K., *Jurisprudenz und Rechtsphilosophie,* 1892.

Bergson, H., *Essai sur les donnés immédiates de la conscience,* 1889.

——— *Les deux sources de la morale et de la religion,* 1932.

——— *Evolution créatrice,* 1907.

Bernsdorf, W. and Bülow, F., *Wörtenbuch der Soziologie,* 1955.

Beveridge (Lord), *Full Employment in a Free Society: A Report,* 1944.

Beyer, W. R., *Der Spiegelcharakter der Rechtsordnung,* 1951.

——— *Rechtsphilosophische Besinnung: Eine Warnung vor der ewigen Wiederkehr des Naturrechts,* 1947.

Black, M., "Phenomenalism," in *Science, Language and Human Rights* (U.S.A.), 1952.

Blaha, O., *Logische Wirklichkeitsstruktur und personaler Seinsgrund: Zur Ontologie der Universalien, Sachverhalte und Seinsschichten,* 1955.

Bochenski, J. M., *Der sowjetische dialektische Materialismus,* 2nd ed., 1956.

Bollnow, O. F., *Existenzphilosophie,* 4th enlarged ed., 1955.
—— *Neue Geborgenheit. Das Problem einer Überwindung des Existentialismus,* 1955.
Braceland, F. J. (Editor), *Faith, Reason and Modern Psychiatry.* Sources for a Synthesis (U.S.A.), 1955.
Brugger, W., S.J., *Philosophisches Wörterbuch,* 5th ed., 1953.
Brunner, August, S.J., *Der Stufenbau der Welt,* 1950.
—— *Die Grundfragen der Philosophie: Ein systematischer Aufbau,* 4th ed., 1956.
Brunner, Emil, *Gerechtigkeit: Eine Lehre von den Grundgesetzen der Gesellschaftsordnung,* 1943.
—— *Christianity and Civilization,* 2 vols., 1948–49.
Brunner, Otto, *Das Zeitalter der Ideologien: Anfang und Ende, in ges. Vorträge und Aufsätze; Neue Wege der Sozialgeschichte,* 1956.
Buliard, Père Roger P., *Inuk,* 1953.
Burnham, J., *The Managerial Revolution,* 1942; Penguin ed., 1945.
Carnap, R., *Philosophy and Logical Syntax,* 1935.
Cathrein, V., *Die Einheit des sittlichen Bewußtseins der Menscheit,* 3 vols., 1910.
—— *Recht, Naturrecht und positives Recht,* 2nd ed., 1909.
—— *Moralphilosophie,* 5th ed., 1911, 6th ed., 1924.
Charmont, J., *La Renaissance du droit naturel* (Paris), 2nd ed., 1927.
Coccola, R. de (with P. King), *Ayorama,* 1955.
Cohen, Morris R., *Reason and Nature,* 1931.
Cohn, G., *Existentialismus und Rechtswissenschaft,* 1955.
Coing, H., *Die obersten Grundsätze des Rechts: Ein Versuch zur Neubegründung des Naturrechts,* 1947.
—— *Grundzüge der Rechtsphilosophie,* 1950.
Collingwood, R. G., *The Idea of Nature,* 1945.
Copleston, F. C. S., S.J., *Aquinas,* 1956.
—— *Contemporary Philosophy: Studies in Logical Positivism and Existentialism,* 1956.
Coreth, E., S.J., *Grundfragen des menschlichen Daseins,* 1956.
Cronin, J. F., *Catholic Social Principles,* 1950.
Cronin, M., *The Science of Ethics,* 2 vols., 4th ed., 1939.
Culler, A. D. (ed.), *The Imperial Intellect: A Study of Newman's Educational Ideal,* 1955.
Dalbiez, R., *Psychoanalytical Method and Doctrine of Freud,* 1941.
D'Arcy, M. C., S.J., *The Mind and Heart of Love,* 1946.
—— *Communism and Christianity* (Penguin ed.), 1956.
Davitt, T. E., S.J., *The Nature of Law,* 1951.
Dawson, C., *Religion and the Rise of Western Culture,* 1950; Germ. 1953.
Dempf, A., *Theoretische Anthropologie,* 1950.
—— *Kulturphilosophie,* 1932.
—— *Die Einheit der Wissenschaft,* 1955.
Deploige, S., *Le conflit de la morale et de la sociologie,* 3rd ed., 1923; Engl. (U.S.A.), 1938.
Dietze, G., *Über Formulierung der Menschenrechte,* 1956.
Dittrich, O., *Geschichte der Ethik,* 4 vols., 1926–32.

Doms, Herbert, "Die Stellung des Menschen im Kosmos," in *Vom Unbelebten zum Lebendigen,* ed. by B. Rensch, 1956.
Doms, Julius, *Gedanken zum Recht auf die Heimat,* 1956.
Dopsch, A., *Die wirtschaftlichen und sozialen Grundlagen der europäischen Kulturentwicklung,* 1923.
Driesch, H., *Der Mensch und die Welt,* 1945.
Drummond, W. F., S.J., *Social Justice* (U.S.A.), 1956.
Dubarle, D., *Humanisme scientifique et raison chrétienne* (Paris), 1953.
Duff, Edward, S.J., *The Social Thought of the World Council of Churches,* 1956.
Duguit, M., *L'état, le droit objectif et la loi positive,* 1901.
—— *Manuel du droit constitutionel,* 1907.
—— *Le droit social, le droit individuel et la transformation de l'état,* 1908.
Egenter, R., *Von christlicher Ehrenhaftigkeit,* 1937.
—— *Von der Einfachheit,* 1947.
—— *Das Edle und der Christ,* 2nd ed., 1948.
Ehrlich, E., *Grundlegung zur Soziologie des Rechts,* 1913, reprinted 1929.
—— *Freie Rechtsfindung und freie Rechtswissenschaft,* 1903.
Ehrlich, W., *Ethik,* 1956.
Eickhoff, A., *Christliches Ordnungsbild und soziale Wirklichkeit,* 1949.
Eliot, T. S., *The Idea of a Christian Society,* 1939; Germ. 1948.
—— *Notes toward the Definition of Culture,* 1948.
Emge, C. A., *Einführung in die Rechtsphilosophie: Anleitung zum philosophischen Nachdenken über das Recht und die Juristen,* 1955.
Engels, F., *Socialism, Utopian and Scientific,* trans. by E. Avelyn, 1892.
—— *Die Lage der arbeitenden Klassen in England,* 1845.
Engisch, K., *Die Idee der Konkretisierung in Recht und Rechtswissenschaft unserer Zeit,* 1953.
d'Entrèves, A. P., *Natural Law,* 1951.
—— "The Case for Natural Law Re-examined," in *Natural Law Forum* (U.S.A.), 1956.
Ermecke, Gustav, *Die natürlichen Seinsgrundlagen der christlichen Ethik,* 1941.
—— *Der Familiarismus als Ordnungsidee und Ordnungsideal des sozialen Lebens,* 1947.
—— (J. Mausbach), *Katholische Moraltheologie,* 3 vols., 1953–54.
Esser, J., *Einführung in die Grundbegriffe des Rechts und des Staates,* 1949.
Etcheverry, A., S.J., *Le conflit actuel des Humanismes* (Paris), 1955.
Europäische Publikation E. V. München (ed.), *Die Vollmacht des Gewissens, Gespräche und Gutachten aus dem Kreis der deutschen Widerstandsbewegung,* 1956.
Fagothey, Austin, S.J., *Right and Reason: Ethics in Theory and Practice* (U.S.A.), 1953.
Fanfani, A., *Catholicesimo e Protestantesimo nella Formazione del Capitalismo,* 1934.
—— *Summula sociale,* 3rd ed. (Rome), 1956.
Fechner, Erich, *Rechtsphilosophie,* 1956.
—— *Die soziologische Grenze der Grundrechte,* 1954.
Fellermeier, Jakob, *Abriß der katholischen Gesellschaftslehre,* 1956.
de Finance, J., S.J., *Existence et Liberté* (*Problèmes et Doctrines* 9), Paris, 1955.
Fischl, J., *Geschichte der Philosophie,* Vols. I–IV, 1947–53.

——— *Was ist der Mensch,* 2nd ed., 1949.
Fisher, H. A. L., *A History of Europe,* 1941
Flückiger, Felix, *Geschichte des Naturrechtes;* Vol. I, *Altertum und Frühmittelalter,* 1954.
Frank, Jerome, *Law and the Modern Mind,* 1931.
Freud, S., *Gesammelte Werke,* Vols. I–XVII (London), 1940.
Freyer, H., *Theorie des gegenwärtigen Zeitalters,* 1955.
Frodl, F., *Gesellschaftslehre,* 2nd ed. 1962.
Fuchs, Josef, S.J., *Lex naturae: Zur Theologie des Naturrechts,* 1955.
Funk, J., S.V.D., *Primat des Naturrechts: Die Transzendenz des Naturrechts gegenüber dem positiven Recht,* 1952.
Gallin, Mary A., *Ethical and Religious Factors in the German Resistance to Hitler* (U.S.A.), 1956.
Geck, A., *Zur Sozialreform des Rechts, die soziale Problematik in der Rechtsphilosophie der Neuzeit,* 1957.
Gehlen, A., *Urmensch und Spätkultur: Philosophische Ergebnisse und Aussagen,* 1956.
——— *Der Mensch, seine Natur und seine Stellung in der Welt,* 4th ed., 1950.
Gehlen, A. and Schelsky, H. (editors), *Soziologie, ein Lehr- und Handbuch zur modernen Gesellschaftskunde,* 1955.
Geiger, T., *Ideologie und Wahrheit,* 1953.
Gentile, G., *Origini e Dottrine del Fascismo,* 1934.
——— *The Theory of Mind as Pure Act,* trans. by H. W. Carr, 1922.
Gény, F., *Méthode d'interpretation et sources en droit privé positif,* 1899.
Geppert, T. S.J., *Teleologie der menschlichen Gemeinschaft: Grundlegung einer Sozialphilosophie und Sozialtheologie,* 1955.
Gierke, O. v., *Das Wesen der menschlichen Verbände,* 1902.
——— *Das Deutsche Genossenschaftsrecht,* III, 1881.
——— *Johannes Althusius,* 1880, 4th ed., 1929.
Gilson, E., "Theologism and Philosophy," in *The Unity of Philosophical Experience,* 1938.
——— *Études de philosophie médiévale,* 1921.
——— *Le sens du rationalisme chrétien.*
——— *L'esprit de la philosophie médiévale,* 1932.
——— *History of Christian Philosophy in the Middle Ages,* 1955.
——— *The Christian Philosophy of St. Thomas Aquinas,* 1957.
Ginsberg, Morris, *Essays in Sociology and Social Philosophy,* 2 vols.: I. *On the Diversity of Morals,* 1956; II. *Reason and Unreason in Society,* 1956.
Goodhart, A. L., *English Law and the Moral Law,* 1953, 2nd ed., 1955.
Gough, J. W., *Fundamental Law in English Constitutional History,* 1955.
Guardini, R., *Das Ende der Neuzeit: Ein Versuch zur Orientierung,* 1951.
Gundlach, G., *Zur Soziologie der katholischen Ideenwelt und des Jesuitenordens,* 1927.
——— (editor), *Die sozialen Rundschreiben Leos XIII und Pius XI,* 1931.
Gurvitch, G., *L'école du droit social,* 1932.
——— *Le temps présent et l'idée du droit social,* 1931.
——— *Déterminismes sociaux et liberté humaine* (Paris), 1955.
Gurvitch, G. and Moore, W. E. (editors), *Twentieth Century Sociology* (New York), 1945.
Haecker, T., *Virgil, Vater des Abendlandes,* 1946.

——— *Was ist der Mensch?* 1949.
Häfner, H., *Schulderleben und Gewissen: Beitrag zu einer personalen Tiefenpsychologie,* 1956.
Haines, C. A., *The Revival of Natural Law Concepts,* 1930.
Haldane, J. B. S., *Heredity and Politics,* 1943.
Halévy, E., *Histoire du peuple anglais au XIXme siècle,* 1913.
Hänsel, L., *Unsterblicher Humanismus,* 1956.
Häring, B., *Das Gesetz Christi,* 1954.
——— *Macht und Ohnmacht der Religion: Religionssoziologie als Anruf,* 1956.
Hart, H. L. A., *The Concept of Law,* 1961.
Hartmann, N., *Ethik,* 1935.
——— Kleine Schriften, Vol. I, *Abhandlungen zur systematischen Philosophie,* 1955.
Hauriou, Maurice, *Principes du droit public,* 1910.
——— "La théorie de l'institution et de la fondation," in *Cahier de la nouvelle journée,* 1925.
——— *Précis de droit administratif,* 1910.
Hawkins, D. J. B., *Crucial Problems in Modern Philosophy,* 1957.
——— *Christian Morality,* 1963.
Healy, Edwin F., S.J., *Medical Ethics* (Chicago), 1956.
Heer, F., *Der Aufgang Europas,* 1949.
——— *Europäische Geistesgeschichte,* 1953.
Hegel, *Grundlinien der Philosophie des Rechts,* 1821.
——— *Enzyklopädie der philosophischen Wissenschaften,* 1830.
Heinen, W., *Fehlformen des Liebesstrebens in moralphilosophischer Deutung,* 1954.
Hellpach, Willy, *Sozialpsychologie: Ein Elementarbuch für Studierende und Praktizierende,* 3rd ed., 1951.
Hengstenberg, H. E., *Grundlegungen zu einer Metaphysik der Gesellschaft,* 1949.
——— *Philosophische Anthropologie,* 1957.
Hentzen, C., O.F.M., *Commentar op Quadragesimo anno,* 1933.
Hering, H. M., O.P., *De iustitia legali* (Freiburg, Schweiz), 1944.
Hessen, Johannes, *Religionsphilosophie,* 2 vols., 2nd ed., 1955.
Hildebrand, D. v., *Metaphysik der Gemeinschaft,* 2nd ed., 1955.
——— *Christian Ethics,* 1954.
——— *Wahre Sittlichkeit und Situationsethik,* 1957.
Hippel, Ernst v., *Künder der Humanität,* 1946.
——— *Die Einführung in die Rechtstheorie,* 4th ed., 1955.
——— *Rechtsgesetz und Naturgesetz,* 2nd ed., 1949.
Hippel, Fritz v., *Die Perversion von Rechtsordnungen,* 1955.
Hobbes, T., *De cive,* 1642.
Hobhouse, L. T., *Morals in Evolution,* 1st ed., 1906; 4th ed., 1951.
Höffner, Joseph, *Soziale Gerechtigkeit und soziale Liebe,* 1935.
——— "Die soziale Gerechtigkeit und die überlieferte abendländische Gerechtigkeitslehre," in *Karl Arnold Festschrift,* 1955.
——— *Christentum und Menschenwürde, das Anliegen der spanischen Kolonialethik im Goldenen Zeitalter,* 1947.
Holland, T. E., *Jurisprudence,* 13th ed., 1924, reprinted 1937.

Hollenbach, J. M., S.J., *Sein und Gewissen: Eine Begegnung zwischen Martin Heidegger und Thomistischer Philosophie,* 1954.
—— *Der Mensch als Entwurf: Seinsgemäße Erziehung in technisierter Welt,* 1957.
Holmes, Justice, *Collected Legal Papers,* 1920.
Hommes, J., *Der technische Eros: Das Wesen der materialistischen Geschichtsauffassung,* 1955.
Hooker, Richard, *Ecclesiastical Polity,* 1595.
Hörmann, K., *Wahrheit und Lüge,* 1953.
—— *Leben in Christus, Zusammanhänge zwischen Dogma und Sitte bei den Apostolischen Vätern,* 1952.
—— *Handbuch der christl. Moral,* 1958. Engl.
Hubmann, H., *Das Persönlichkeitsrecht,* 1953.
Hugo, Custav v., *Naturrecht als Philosophie des positiven Rechts,* 1798; 4th ed., 1819.
Hürth, F. X., S.J., "De Ethica situationis," in *Periodica de re morali, canonica, liturgica,* Vol. XLV, n. 2, 1956.
Huxley, J., *Evolution: The Modern Synthesis,* 1942.
—— *Evolutionary Ethics,* 1943.
—— *Evolution in Action,* 1953.
Ihering, R., *Der Zweck im Recht,* 2nd ed., 1886; 8th ed., 1923.
Jaeger, W., *The Ideals of Greek Culture,* 3 vols., 1944–55.
Janssen, A., *Leergang van algemene moraalphilosophie* (Löwen), 3rd ed., 1953.
Jeans, James, *Physics and Philosophy,* 1942.
Jecht, H. and Schraeder, R., *Handwörterbuch der Sozialwissenschaften,* 1952 ff.
Jellinek, G., *Die Erklärung der Menschen- und Bürgerrechte,* 4th ed., 1927.
Jerusalem, Franz W., *Soziologie des Rechts,* 1925.
—— *Kritik der Rechtswissenschaft,* 1947.
Joad, C. E. M., *A Critique of Logical Positivism,* 1950.
Jolowicz, H. F., *Roman Foundations of Modern Law,* 1957.
Joseph, H. W. B., *Some Problems of Ethics,* 1913.
Jostock, P., *Grundzüge der Soziallehre und Sozialreform,* 1946.
Jung, C. G., *Modern Man in Search of a Soul,* 7th ed., 1944.
Kaibach, R., *Das Gemeinwohl und seine ethische Bedeutung,* 1928.
Kant, *Einleitung in die Rechtslehre, Ges. W. Pr. Akad. d. W.,* Vol. VI.
—— *Kritik der praktischen Vernunft, Ges. W.,* Vol. V.
—— *Grundlegung zur Metaphysik der Sitten, Ges. W.,* Vol. IV.
Kantorowicz, H. U., *Der Kampf um die Rechtswissenschaft,* 1906.
Karrenberg, F. (ed. by order of the Dr. Evang. Kirchentages), *Evangelisches Soziallexikon,* 4th. ed., 1963.
Kaufmann, A., *Naturrecht und Geschichtlichkeit,* 1957.
Kaufmann, E., *Kritik der neukantischen Rechtsphilosophie,* 1921.
Kavanagh, J., *Manual of Social Ethics* (Dublin), 1950.
Keller, W., *Psychologie und Philosophie des Wollens,* 1954.
Kelsen, H., *Was ist Gerechtigkeit?,* 1943.
—— *Reine Rechtslehre,* 1934, 2nd ed., 1960.
—— *Allgemeine Staatslehre,* 1925.
—— *Die philosophischen Grundlagen der Naturrechtslehre und des Rechtspositivismus,* 1928.

——— *Das Problem der Souveränität und die Theorie des Völkerrechts,* 1920.
——— *Der soziologische und der juristische Stattsbegriff,* 1922.
——— *The Communist Theory of Law* (New York), 1955.
Kern, F., *Der Beginn der Weltgeschichte,* Preface by H. Trimborn, 1953.
——— *Geschichte und Entwicklung,* 1952.
Kipp, Heinrich, "Die Menschenrechte in Geschichte und Philosophie," in *Die Menschenrechte in christlicher Sicht* (ed. by A. Wimmer), 1953.
——— *Naturrecht und moderner Staat,* 1950.
Klubertanz, G., *The Philosophy of Human Nature,* 1951.
Klüber, Franz, *Christliche Soziallehre:* Part I, *Das Naturrecht,* 2nd ed., 1955; Part II, *Gerechtigkeit;* Part III, *Sozialprinzipien,* 1957.
Kluckhohn, Clyde, *Mirror for Man,* 1950; Germ. 1951.
Knoll, A. M., *Von den drei Wesenstheorien der Gesellschaft,* 1949.
Kohler, J., *Lehrbuch der Rechtsphilosophie,* 1908, 3rd ed., 1922.
König, Franz, "Der Mensch und die Religion," in Vol. I of *Christus und die Religionen der Erde,* 3 vols., ed. by Franz König, 1951.
Koppers, W., *Der Urmensch und sein Weltbild,* 1949.
Koschaker, Paul, *Europa und das römische Recht,* 1953.
Krabbe, H., *The Modern Idea of the State,* 1927.
Kraft, G., *Der Urmensch als Schöpfer: Die geistige Welt des Eiszeitmenschen,* 2nd ed., 1948.
Kraft, Victor, *Die Grundlagen einer wissenschaftlichen Wertlehre,* 2nd ed., 1951.
Kranenburg, R., *Political Theory,* 1939.
Kraus, J., *Situationsethik als pastoral- und moraltheologisches Problem,* 1956.
Küchenhoff, G., "Staatsverfassung und Subsidiarität," in *Das Subsidiaritätsprinzip* (ed. by A. F. Utz), 1953.
Kulischer, Josef, *Allgemeine Wirtschaftsgeschichte,* Vol. I, *Das Mittelalter,* 1928.
Künneth, W., *Politik zwischen Dämon und Gott,* 1954.
Kurz, E., *Der Einzelne und die Gemeinschaft beim hl. Thomas v. Aquin,* 1933.
Laberthonnière, Lucien, *Esquisse d'une philosophie personaliste,* oeuvres ed. by L. Canet, 1942.
Lamont, W. D., *The Value Judgment* (Edinburgh), 1955.
Larenz, K., *Rechts- und Staatsphilosophie der Gegenwart,* 1931, 2nd ed., 1935.
——— *Sittlichkeit und Recht: Untersuchungen zur Geschichte des deutschen Rechtsdenkens und zur Sittenlehre,* 1943.
Laski, H. J., *Grammar of Politics,* 1941.
——— *Liberty in the Modern State,* 1930.
——— "M. Duguit's Conception of the State," in *Modern Theories of Law* (ed. by W. I. Jennings), 1933.
——— *Parliamentary Government in England,* 1938.
——— *The Rights of Man,* 1940.
Laun, Rudolf, *Das Recht auf die Heimat,* 1951.
——— *Recht und Sittlichkeit,* 3rd ed., 1935.
Lazerowitz, M., *The Structure of Metaphysics,* 1955.
Leclercq, J., *Leçons du droit naturel,* Vols. I–IV, 2nd ed., 1946–50.
——— *Les grandes lignes de la philosophie morale,* 1947.
Leenhardt, Maurice (ed.), *Carnets de Lévy-Brühl,* 1949.

Lenin, *Materialism and Empirio-Criticism,* 1908, Collected Works, ed. by A. Trachtenberg, authorized by the Lenin Institute, Moscow, trans. by D. Kvitko, 1927.

Less, Günther, *Von Wesen und Wert des Richterrechts, eine rechtsanalytische und kritische Studie,* 1954.

Lévy-Brühl, Lucien, *Les fonctions mentales dans les sociétés inférieures,* 1910.

Lieber, H.-J., *Wissen und Gesellschaft: Die Probleme der Wissenssoziologie,* 1952.

Lindsay, A. D., *The Two Moralities: Our Duty to God and Society,* 1940; Germ. trans. by H. Scherer, 1947.

Linhardt, R., *Die Sozialprincipien des hl. Thomas v. Aq.,* 1932.

Link, E., *Das Subsidiaritätsprinzip, sein Wesen und seine Bedeutung für die Sozialethik,* 1955.

Linsenmann, F. X., *Lehrbuch der Moraltheologie,* 1878.

Litt, T., *Individuum und Gemeinschaft,* 3rd ed., 1926.

——— *Die Sonderstellung des Menschen im Reiche des Lebendigen,* 1948.

Lottin, Odon, O.S.B., *Morale fondamentale,* 1954.

Lotz, J. B., S.J., *Das christliche Menschenbild im Ringen der Zeit,* 1947.

Maceina, A., *Das Geheimnis der Bosheit: Versuch einer Geschichtstheologie des Widersachers Christi als Deutung der "Erzählung vom Antichrist" Solojews,* 1955.

McFadden, C. J., O.S.A., *Medical Ethics* (Philadelphia), 4th ed., 1956.

Maihofer, W., *Recht und Sein: Prolegomena zu einer Rechtsphilosophie,* 1954.

——— *Vom Sinn menschlicher Ordnung,* 1956.

——— (ed.) *Naturrecht oder Rechtspositivismus?* 1962.

Maine, H., *Ancient Law,* 1861; ed. by F. Pollock, 1930.

——— *Early History of Institutions,* 1875.

Maitland, F. W., *Introduction to Gierke's Political Theories of the Middle Ages,* 1900.

——— (with F. Pollock) *History of English Law,* 1911.

——— *The Collected Papers,* 1911.

Mannheim, K., "Das Problem einer Soziologie des Wissens," in *Sozialwissenschaft und Sozialpolitik,* Vol. LIII, 1925.

——— *Ideologie und Utopie,* 1929.

Manning, C. A. W., "Austin Today, or 'The Province of Jurisprudence' Re-examined," in *Modern Theories of Law,* ed. by W. I. Jennings, 1933.

Manser, Gallus M., O.P., *Das Naturrecht in thomistischer Beleuchtung,* 1944.

——— *Angewandtes Naturrecht,* 1947.

Maringer, Johannes, *Vorgeschichtliche Religion: Religionen im steinzeitlichen Europa,* 1956.

Maritain, J., *The Rights of Man,* 1945.

——— "On the Philosophy of Human Rights," in *Human Rights, A Symposium,* ed. by Unesco (London), 2nd ed., 1950.

——— *Christlicher Humanismus: Politische und geistige Fragen einer neuen Christenheit,* 1950.

——— *The Rights of Man and Natural Law,* 1944.

——— *An Essay on Christian Philosophy,* trans. by E. H. Flannery (New York), 1955.

——— *Moral Philosophy: An Historical and Critical Survey of the Great Systems,* 1964.
Markovics, R., *Grundsätzliche Vorfragen einer methodischen Thomasdeutung,* 1956.
Marrou, H. I., *Histoire de l'education dans l'antiquité* (Paris), 1948; Engl., *A History of Education in Antiquity,* 1956.
Martin, Alfred v., *Ordnung und Freiheit: Materialien und Reflexionen zu Grundfragen des Soziallebens,* 1956.
Marx, Karl, *Kritik des Gothaer Programms,* 1875.
——— *The Communist Manifesto,* 1848.
——— *A Contribution to the Critique of Political Economy,* 1859.
Mathis, P. Burkhard, O.M. Cap., *Rechtspositivismus und Naturrecht, eine Kritik der neukantischen Rechtslehre,* 1933.
Mausbach, J., *Die Ethik des hl. Augustin,* 2 vols., 2nd ed., 1929.
——— *Naturrecht und Völkerrecht,* 1918.
McIver, R. M., *The Web of Government,* 1947.
Meldon, A. I., "The Concept of Universal Human Rights," in *Science, Language, and Human Rights* (U.S.A.), 1952.
Merkl, A., "Einheit oder Vielheit des Naturrechts?" in *Österreichische Zeitschrift für öffentliches Recht,* Vol. V, heft 3, 1953.
Messner, J., *Kulturethik mit Grundlegung durch Prinzipienethik und Persönlichkeitsethik,* 1954.
——— *Die Soziale Frage,* 1933, enlarged 7th ed., 1964.
——— *Ethics and Facts: The Puzzling Pattern of Human Existence,* 1952.
Meyer, Hans, *Die Weltanschauung der Gegenwart,* 1949.
——— *Christliche Philosophie,* 1952.
——— *Weltanschauungsprobleme der Gegenwart,* 1956.
Meyer, T., S.J., *Grundsätze der Sittlichkeit und des Rechts,* 1868.
——— *Institutiones iuris naturalis,* 2 vols., 1885–1900.
Micklem, N., *The Theology of Politics,* 1941.
——— *The Theology of Law,* 1943.
——— *Law and the Laws: Being the Marginal Comments of a Theologian,* 1952.
Mitteis, H., *Vom Lebenswert der Rechtsgeschichte,* 1947.
——— *Über das Naturrecht,* 1948.
Mitterer, A., "Naturwissenschaft und Naturrecht, Zusammenhänge bei Thomas v. Aquin," in *Die soziale Frage und der Katholizismus,* ed. by Jakob Strieder and Johannes Messner, 1931.
——— *Die Entwicklungslehre Augustins, im Vergleich mit dem Weltbild des hl. Thomas und dem der Gegenwart,* 1956.
Molina, Thomas, *Das Leiden im Weltplan,* 1929.
Monzel, N., *Was ist christliche Gesellschaftslehre?* 1956.
Moore, G. E., *Principia Ethica,* 1903.
Mounier, Emanuel, *Einführung in die Existenzphilosophie,* trans. by W. Richter, 1949.
Muckermann, H., *Vom Sein und Sollen des Menschen,* 1954.
Müller-Armack, A., *Diagnose unserer Gegenwart: Zur Bestimmung unseres geistesgeschichtlichen Standorts,* 1949.
Müncker, T., *Die psychologischen Grundlagen der kath. Sittenlehre,* 1953.
Murray, J. C., S.J., *We Hold These Truths,* 1960.

Nawiasky, H., *Allgemeine Rechtslehre: System der rechtlichen Grundbegriffe,* 2nd ed., 1948.

Nédoncelle, M., *Vers une philosophie de l'amour,* 1946.

Nell-Breuning, O. v., S.J., *Reorganization of Social Economy,* transl. by B. Dempsey, S.J., 1936.

—— *Gesellschaftsordnung,* 1956.

—— *Einzelmensch und Gesellschaft,* 1950.

—— *Sozialer Katechismus* (Code sozial, Mechelner Studienvereinigung), 1950.

Nell-Breuning, O. v. and Sacher, H., *Beiträge zu einem Wörterbuch der Politik.* I, *Zur christlichen Gesellschaftslehre,* 1947; III, *Zur sozialen Frage,* 1949; V, *Gesellschaftliche Ordnungssysteme,* 1954.

Nelson, L., *Die Rechtswissenschaft ohne Recht,* 1917.

—— *System der philosophischen Rechtslehre und Politik,* 1923.

Newman, J. H. (Card.), *A Grammar of Assent,* 3rd ed., 1879.

Niebuhr, R., *The Nature and Destiny of Man,* 2 vols., 1941.

—— "A Protestant Looks at Catholics," in *Catholicism in America,* ed. by G. N. Schuster (New York), 1954.

—— *Moral Man and Immoral Society: A Study in Ethics and Politics,* 1952.

Niedermeyer, A., *Philosophische Propädeutik der Medizin: Einführung in die allgemeinen geistigen Grundlagen* (Geschichte, Philosophie, Biologie, Psychologie), 1955.

Nink, Caspar, *Metaphysik des sittlich Guten,* 1955.

Nipperdey, J. C. and Scheuner, U. (eds.), *Die Grundrechte, Handbuch der Theorie und Praxis der Grundrechte.* Vol. I, Die Grundrechte der Welt, 1956; Vol. II, Die Freiheitsrechte in Deutschland, 1954.

Ogburn, W. F. and Nimkoff, M. F., *A Handbook of Sociology,* 1947.

Ohm, T., *Vom Christentum des Abendlandes, des Ostens und der Zukunft,* 1951.

Oppenheimer, F., *System der Soziologie.* Vol. I, 1922–23.

O'Sullivan, R. (Q.C.), *Natural Law and the Common Law,* ed. by the Grotius Society, 1946.

—— *The Inheritance of the Common Law,* 1950.

Ottenwälder, P., *Zur Naturrechtslehre des Hugo Grotius,* Foreword by C. Brinkmann, 1950.

Owens, J., C.SS.R., *St. Thomas and the Future of Metaphysics,* 1957.

Paine, Thomas, *The Rights of Man,* 1791–92.

—— *The Age of Reason,* 1794–1807.

Pareto, V., *Tratato di sociologia generale,* 3 vols., 1916–23.

Parkinson, N. C., *Parkinson's Law,* 1958.

Paton, H. J., *The Modern Predicament,* 1955.

Peirce, Charles, *Philosophical Writings of Peirce,* ed. and Introduction by Justus Buchler (New York), 1955.

Peters, Karl, *Das Gewissen des Richters und das Gesetz,* 1950.

Pfeil, Hans, *Existentialistische Philosophie,* 1952.

—— *Überwindung des Massenmenschen durch echte Philosophie,* 1956.

Pfliegler, M., *Dokumente zur Geschichte der Kirche,* 2nd ed., 1957.

Piaget, Jean, *La causalité physique chez l'infant* (Paris), 1927; Engl., *The Child's Conception of Physical Causality,* 1952.

—— *Le développement de la notion de temps chez l'infant* (Paris), 1946.
Pieper, J., *Die ontische Grundlage des Sittlichen nach Thomas v. Aq.*, 1929.
—— *Die Wirklichkeit und das Gute nach Thomas v. Aq.*, 1931.
—— *Glück und Kontemplation,* 1957.
—— *Über die Gerechtigkeit,* 1953.
—— *Die Neuordnung der menschlichen Gesellschaft,* 1932.
Pollock, F. and Holmes, Justice, *The Pollock-Holmes Letters,* 1874–1937, 1942.
Pollock, F. and Maitland, F. W., *History of English Law,* 1911.
Portmann, A., *Biologische Fragmente zu einer Lehre vom Menschen,* 1944.
—— *Natur und Kultur im Sozialleben,* 1946.
—— "Die werdende Menschheit," in *Frühe Menschheit, Historia Mundi,* Vol. I, 1954.
Pound, Roscoe, *An Introduction to the Philosophy of Law,* 2nd improved ed., 1954.
—— *Interpretation of Legal History,* 1923.
—— *The Spirit of the Common Law,* 1921.
Przywara, E., *Humanitas,* 1951.
Radbruch, Gustav, *Rechtsphilosophie,* ed. by Erik Wolf, 5th ed., 1956.
—— *Einführung in die Rechtswissenschaft,* ed. by Konrad Zweigert, 9th ed., 1952.
Rauch, W., *Abhandlungen aus Ethik und Moraltheologie,* ed. by R. Schlund, 1956.
Reding, M., *Metaphysik der sittlichen Werte,* 1948.
—— *Der Aufbau der christlichen Existenz,* 1952.
Reinach, A., *Zur Phänomenologie des Rechtes: Die apriorischen Grundlagen des bürgerlichen Rechts,* 1953.
Reiner, Hans, *Pflicht und Neigung,* 1951.
—— "Antike und christliche Naturrechtslehre," in *Archiv für Rechts- und Sozialphilosophie,* Vol. XLI, n. 4, 1955.
—— "Die goldene Regel: Die Bedeutung einer sittlichen Grundformel der Menschheit," in *Zeitschrift für philosophische Forschung,* Vol. III, 1948.
Renard, G., *La théorie de l'institution,* 1930.
—— *La philosophie de l'institution,* 1939.
Retzbach, Anton, *Die Erneuerung der gesellschaftlichen Ordnung nach der Enzyklika Quadragesimo Anno,* 1932.
Riezler, E., *Das Rechtsgefühl,* 2nd ed., 1946.
Rintelen, F. J., *Philosophie der Endlichkeit,* 1951.
Ritter, Gerhard, *Vom sittlichen Problem der Macht,* 1948.
Rommen, H., *Die ewige Wiederkehr des Naturrechts,* 1936, 2nd ed., 1947.
—— *Die Staatslehre des Franz Suárez,* 1926.
Rosenmöller, Bernhard, *Metaphysik der Seele,* 1947.
Rothacker, E., *Probleme der Kulturanthropologie,* 1948.
—— *Logik und Systematik der Geisteswissenschaften,* 3rd ed., 1948.
Rousseau, *Contrat Social,* 1762.
Rubinstein, R., *John Citizen and the Law* (Pelican Books), 4th ed., 1958.
Ryffel, H., *Das Naturrecht,* 1944.
Ryle, G., Ayer, A. J., *et al., The Revolution in Philosophy,* 1956.
Sacher, H. (editor), *Staatslexikon der Görresgesellschaft,* 5 vols., 1926–32.

Salmon, E. G., *The Good in Existential Metaphysics* (Aquinas Lecture, 1952), 1953.
Sauer, W., *System der Rechts- und Sozialphilosophie,* 2nd ed., 1949.
——— *Metaphysik auf sozialwissenschaftlicher Grundlage,* 1951.
——— *Einführung in die Rechtsphilosophie für Unterricht und Praxis,* 1954.
Sauter, J., *Die philosophischen Grundlagen des Naturrechts,* 1932.
Savigny, Frh. K. v., *System des heutigen römischen Rechts,* Vols. I–VIII, 1840–49.
——— *Vom Beruf unserer Zeit für Gesetzgebung und Rechtswissenschaft,* 1814.
Schaaf, J., *Grundprinzipien der Wissenssoziologie,* 1956.
Schasching, J., S.J., *Katholische Soziallehre und modernes Apostolat,* 1956.
Scheler, Max, *Vom Ewigen im Menschen,* 1923, 3rd ed., 1933.
——— *Die Stellung des Menschen im Kosmos,* 1930.
——— *Wesen und Formen der Sympathiegefühle,* 2nd ed., 1923.
——— *Der Formalismus in der Ethik und die materiale Wertethik,* 1921, 3rd ed., 1927.
——— *Versuche zu einer Soziologie des Wissens,* 1924.
——— *Die Wissensformen und die Gesellschaft,* 1926.
——— *Schriften zur Soziologie und Weltanschauungslehre,* 3 vols., 1923–24.
Schilling, O., *Lehrbuch der Moraltheologie,* 2 vols., 1928.
——— *Naturrecht und Staat nach der Lehre der alten Kirche,* 1914.
——— *Die Staats- und Soziallehre des hl. Thomas v. Aq.,* 2nd ed., 1930.
——— *Katholische Sozialethik,* 1929.
——— *Christliche Sozial- und Rechtsphilosophie,* 2nd ed., 1950.
——— *Christliche Gesellschaftslehre,* 1949.
Schindler, F., *Die soziale Frage,* 4th ed., 1908.
Schleiermacher, F., *Grundlinien einer Kritik der bisherigen Sittenlehre,* 1803.
——— *Entwurf eines Systems der Sittenlehre,* now in *Ausgew. Werke,* Vols. I–IV.
Schmitt, Carl, *Die Lage der europäischen Rechtswissenschaft,* 1950.
——— *Über die drei Arten des rechtswissenschaftlichen Denkens,* 1934.
Schmitt, M.-E., *Recht und Vernunft: Ein Beitrag zur Diskussion über die Rationalität des Naturrechts,* 1955.
Schmittmann, B., *Wirtschafts- und Sozialordnung als Aufgabe,* 2nd ed., ed. by A. Lotz, 1948.
Schnackerburg, Rudolf, *Die sittliche Botschaft des Neuen Testaments,* 1954.
Schoeck, H., *Soziologie: Geschichte ihrer Probleme,* 1952.
Schöllgen, Werner, *Aktuelle Moralprobleme,* 1955.
———*Die soziologischen Grundlagen der katholischen Sittenlehre,* 1953.
——— *Grenzmoral: Soziale Krisis und neuer Aufbau,* 1946.
Schönfeld, W., *Grundlegung der Rechtswissenschaft* (2nd ed. of *Die Geschichte der Rechtswissenschaft im Spiegel der Metaphysik,* 1943), 1951.
——— *Über die Gerechtigkeit,* 1952.
Schrey, H.-H., "Die Wiedergeburt des Naturrechts," in *Theol. Rundsch,* 19, Jg., 1951, ed. by R. Bultmann and E. Dinkler, heft 1–3.
Schulte, L., *Die schöpferische Freiheit: Versuch einer ontologischen Grundlegung,* 1954.
Schuster, J. B., S.J., *Die Soziallehre nach Leo XIII u. Pius XI,* 1935.

Schwer, W., *Katholische Gesellschaftslehre*, 1928.
Scott, J. Brown, *Francisco de Vitoria and the Law of Nations*, 1934.
Seagle, W., *The Quest for Law*, 1941.
Sellmair, Josef, *Humanitas Christiana: Geschichte des christlichen Humanismus*, 1948.
Siegfried, W., *Der Rechtsgedanke bei Aristotles*, 1947.
Siegmund, Georg, *Die Natur des Menschen: Das Bild vom menschlichen Wesen als Grundlage seiner Heilbehandlung*, 1955.
Simmel, G., *Soziologie*, 2nd ed., 1922.
Smith, T. V., *The Bill of Rights and Our Individual Liberties* (New York), 1954.
Sohm, R., *Institutionen, Geschichte und System des römischen Privatrechts*, 16 ed., 1919.
Solovyof, V., *The Justification of the Good: An Essay on Moral Philosophy*, Engl. trans. by N. A. Duddington, 1918.
Soukup, L., *Grundzüge einer Ethik der Persönlichkeit*, 1951.
Spann, O., *Gesellschaftslehre*, 3rd ed., 1930.
——— *Der wahre Staat*, 3rd ed., 1931.
——— *Das philosophische Gesamtwerk im Auszug*, ed. by H. Riehl, 1950.
Stadtmüller, G., *Das Naturrecht im Lichte der geschichtlichen Erfahrung*, 1948.
——— *Das abendländische Rechtsbewußtsein*, 1951.
Stammler, R., *Wirtschaft und Recht nach der materialistischen Geschichtsauffassung*, 1896, 5th ed., 1954.
——— *Lehre vom richtigen Recht*, 1902, 2nd ed., 1926.
——— *Theorie der Rechtswissenschaft*, 1911, 2nd ed., 1923.
——— *Lehrbuch der Rechtsphilosophie*, 1923, 3rd ed., 1928.
Steffes, J. P., *Das Naturrecht in metaphysischer und religiöser Weltsicht*, 1932.
Steinbüchel, T., *Die philosophische Grundlegung der katholischen Sittenlehre*, 2 vols., 3rd ed., 1947.
——— *Der Zweckgedanke in der Philosophie des hl. Thomas v. Aq.*, 1912.
Stevenson, C. L., *Ethics and Language*, 1944.
Stratenwerth, G., *Die Naturrechtslehre des Duns Scotus*, 1951.
Strauss, Leo, *Natural Right and History*, 1953.
Strieder, J. and Messner, J. (editors), *Die soziale Frage und der Katholizismus, Festschrift zum 40 jährigen Jubiläum der Enzylika "Rerum novarum" im Auftrage der Görresgesellschaft*, 1931.
Szilasi, W., *Macht und Ohnmacht des Geistes: Interpretationen zu Platon und Aristoteles*, 1956.
Taparelli, L., *Saggio teoretico di diritto naturale*, 1839.
Taylor, A. E., *The Problem of Conduct: A Study in the Phenomenology of Ethics*, 1901.
Thielicke, H., *Theologische Ethik*, Vol. I, 1951.
——— *Was ist Wahrheit?* 1954.
——— *Der Nihilismus: Entstehung, Wesen, Überwindung*, 1950.
Thieme, H., *Das Naturrecht und die europäische Privatrechtsgeschichte*, 1947.
——— *Natürliches Privatrecht und Spätscholastik, Zeitschrift der Savigny-Stiftung für Rechtsgeschichte*, 1953, pp. 230 ff.
Thorndike, E. L., *Human Nature and the Social Order*, 1940.
Tillich, P., *Love, Power and Justice*, 1954.
Tillmann, F., *Die Verwirklichung der Nachfolge Christi*. Part I, "Die Pflichten

gegen Gott"; Part II, "Die Pflichten gegen sich selbst und gegen den Nächsten," 1951.
Todd, J. M. (ed.), *The Springs of Morality: A Catholic Symposium,* 1956.
Toennies, F., *Gemeinschaft und Gesellschaft,* 1887, 8th ed., 1935.
Tonquédec, J. de, S.J., *Une philosophie existentielle, L'existence d'après Karl Jaspers,* 1945.
Toulemont, René, *Sociologie et pluralisme dialectique* (Louvain), 1955.
Toynbee, A. J., *A Study of History,* 10 vols., 1936–54.
Trethowen, Dom Illtyd, *An Essay in Christian Philosophy,* 1954.
Troeltsch, E., *Die Soziallehren der christlichen Kirchen und Gruppen,* 1919.
—— *Christian Thought in History and Application,* 1923.
Utz, A .F., O.P., *Recht und Gerechtigkeit.* Vol. XVIII, *Dt. Thomas-Ausgabe,* 1953.
—— *Das Subsidiaritätsprinzip* (Sammlung Politeia), 1953.
—— *Formen und Grenzen des Subsidiaritätsprinzips,* 1956.
—— *Wesen und Sinn des christlichen Ethos,* 1942.
—— *Sozialethik: Mit internationaler Bibliographie.* Part I, "Die Prinzipien der Gesellschaftslehre," 1958. Part II, Rechtsphilosophie, 1963.
Utz, A. F. and Groner, J. F., *Aufbau und Entfaltung des gesellschaftlichen Lebens: Soziale Summe Pius' XII,* 2 vols., 1954.
Valjavec, F. (Fritz Kern, editor), *Historia Mundi.* Vol. I, *Frühe Geschichte der Menschheit,* 1952.
Veatch, H., *Realism and Nominalism Revisited* (Aquinas Lecture, 1954, Milwaukee), 1954.
Vecchio, G. del, *Lezioni di filosofia del diritto,* 1930.
—— *Die Gerechtigkeit,* 2nd ed., 1950.
—— *Essenza del diritto naturale,* 2nd ed. (Rome), 1954.
Veit, O., "Existentielles Naturrecht und existentielle Ethik," in *Ordo,* Vol. VII, 1955.
—— *Soziologie der Freiheit,* 1957.
Verdross, A., *Grundlinien der antiken Rechts- und Staatsphilosophie,* 2nd ed., 1948; 3rd ed., 1955.
—— *Völkerrecht,* 2nd ed., 1950; 3rd ed., 1955.
—— *Die Einheit des rechtlichen Weltbildes auf Grundlage der Völkerrechtsverfassung,* 1923.
—— "Die Erneuerung der materialen Rechtsphilosophie," in *Zeitschr. f. Schweizerisches Recht,* Vol. 76, 1957.
—— *Abendländische Rechtsphilosophie: Ihre Grundlagen und Hauptprobleme in geschichtlicher Schau,* 1958.
Verpaalen, A. P., *Der Begriff des Gemeinwohls bei Thomas v. Aquin,* 1954.
Vico, G. B., *De uno universi iuris principio et fine uno,* 1720.
Vidler, A. R. and Whitehouse, W. A., *Natural Law: A Christian Reconsideration,* 1946.
Viehweg, T., *Topik und Jurisprudenz,* 1953.
Vierkandt, A., *Der geistig-sittliche Gehalt des neueren Naturrechts,* 1927.
—— (Editor), *Handworterbuch der Soziologie,* 1931.
—— *Gesellschaftslehre, Hauptprobleme der philosophischen Soziologie,* 1923.
—— *Familie, Volk and Staat,* 1936.
Weber, Alfred, *Kulturgeschichte als Kultursoziologie,* 1951.

——— *Prinzipien der Geschichts- und Kultursoziologie,* 1951.
Weber, Max, *Wirtschaft und Gesellschaft,* 1922.
——— *Staatssoziologie,* ed. by J. Winckelmann, 1956.
——— "Die protestantische Ethik und der Geist des Kapitalismus, die Sekten und der Geist der Kapitalismus," in *Gesammelte Aufsätze zur Religionssoziologie,* 2 vols., 1920 f.
——— *Wirtschaftsgeschichte,* 1923.
——— *Gesammelte Aufsätze zur Wissenschaftslehre,* 1922.
Wehrung, G., *Welt und Reich, Grundlegung und Aufbau der Ethik,* 1952.
Weinkauff, Hermann, *Über das Widerstandsrecht,* 1956.
Welty, E., O.P., *Gemeinschaft und Einzelmensch* (nach den Grundsätzen des hl. Thomas v. Aquin), 1935.
——— *Die Entscheidung in die Zukunft,* 1946.
——— Herders Sozialkatechismus, Vol. I, *Grundfragen und Grundkräfte des sozialen Lebens,* 2nd ed., 1952; Vol. II, *Aufbau der Gemeinschaftsordnung,* 1953.
Welzel, H., *Naturrecht und materiale Gerechtigkeit, Prolegomena zu einer Rechtsphilosophie,* 1951, 2nd ed., 1955.
Wendland, H.-D., *Die Kirche in der modernen Gesellschaft: Entscheidungsfragen für das kirchliche Handeln im Zeitalter der Massenwelt,* 1956.
Wenzel, A., *Philosophie der Freiheit,* 1947.
Wetter, G. A., S.J., *Der Dialektische Materialismus: Seine Geschichte und sein System in der Sowjetunion,* 3rd ed., 1956.
——— *Ordnung ohne Freiheit: Der dialektische Materialismus,* 1956.
Whitehead, A. N., *Science and the Modern World,* 1925.
——— *Process and Reality,* 1929.
——— *Nature and Life,* 1934.
Wiese, L. v., *Soziologie: Geschichte und Hauptproblem,* 1950.
——— *System der allgemeinen Soziologie als Lehre von den sozialen Prozessen und den sozialen Gebilden der Menschen* (Beziehungslehre), 2nd ed., 1933.
——— *Ethik in der Schauweise der Wissenschaften vom Menschen und von der Gesellschaft,* 1947.
Wild, John, *Plato's Modern Enemies and the Theory of Natural Law,* 1953.
Williams, Melvin J., *Catholic Social Thought: Its Approach to Contemporary Problems,* 1950.
Windolph, F. L., *Leviathan and Natural Law,* 1951.
Winter, E. K., *Christentum und Zivilization,* 1956.
Wittmann, M., *Die Ethik des hl. Thomas v. Aq.,* 1933.
——— *Ethik,* 1923.
——— *Die moderne Wertethik, historisch untersucht und kritisch geprüft,* 1940.
Wolf, Ernst, *Zur Frage des Naturrechts bei Thomas von Aquin und bei Luther,* 1954.
Wolf, Erik, *Griechisches Rechtsdenken,* 3 vols., 1949–54.
——— *Vom Wesen des Rechts in deutscher Dichtung,* 1946.
——— *Das Problem der Naturrechtslehre: Versuch einer Orientierung,* 1955; 2nd ed., 1959; cf. the review by W. Maihofer, "Das Problem des Naturrechts," in *Archiv f. Rechts- u. Sozialphilosophie,* 1960, XLVI, pp. 407 ff.
——— *Große Rechtsdenker der deutschen Geistesgeschichte,* 3rd ed., 1951.
Wünsch, G., *Evangelische Ethik des Politischen,* 1936.

—— *Evangelische Wirtschaftsethik,* 1927.
—— *Sozialismus aus christlichem Gewissen,* 1949.
Würtenberger, T., "Wege zum Naturrecht in Deutschland 1946–48," in *Archiv. f. Rechts- u. Sozialphilosophie,* Vol. XXXVIII, n. 1, 1949.
—— *Neue Stimmen zum Naturrecht in Deutschland 1948–51,* Vol. XL, n. 4, 1953.
—— *Zur Geschichte der Rechtsphilosophie und des Naturrechts, deutschsprachige Beiträge seit 1948,* Vol. XLI, n. 1, 1954.
Wust, P., *Die Krisis des abendländischen Menschentums,* 1927.
—— *Ungewißheit und Wagnis,* 4th ed., 1946.
Ziegenfuß, Werner (editor), *Handbuch der Soziologie,* 2 vols., 1955–56.

BOOK II

THE ETHICS OF SOCIETY

PART ONE

The Family

69. Marriage

Marriage is the lawfully constituted life union and sexual union of man and woman. The chief force impelling human beings to unite in marriage is a *love* which is based on the difference of sex. Since man and woman have a spiritual personality by nature, however, the spiritual and corporeal sides of their love are correlated. This love is creative in a twofold sense, both because the lovers transcend themselves in the child, and because in themselves they transcend what each would have accomplished alone. As long as it lives, love makes the lover see clearly what is deepest and best in the beloved and desire that it be fully realized. And this call is answered by love in the other, with never-ending growth and blossoming and ripening of the personality, in which the lover finds continually renewed satisfaction and at the same time finds his love perpetually rekindled. Thus, to guard this sacred fire of married love and to keep it nourished is a moral obligation for those who marry. It is also their duty, before entering this union, to examine carefully whether it is really this holy fire that is melting their inmost beings into one, or merely a flame of passion, which can never truly unite because in its essence it is egoism.

Thus, existential human ends, which are designed in man's strongest impulses and which touch the innermost personality, are involved in marriage. And so, considered as a union of love between persons, marriage manifestly implies oneness and indissolubility, that is, the lasting union of one man with one woman. Every other form of sexual union is inconsistent with the essence of real love between persons, in which the existential ends in the sexual sphere can only be part of the totality of the existential human ends. Otherwise, the sexual instinct, although meant to strengthen love, must, by its force, lead to egoism.

Needless to say, love between persons must not be confused with its merely emotional side. Emotion is transitory, love by its essence is lasting. Polygamy, in its ancient and modern forms, and dissolubility are incompatible with the love which engrosses and informs the whole existence of the lovers. They prevent the fulfillment of the self in married love and thus are contrary to the *personal end* which the lovers have in view in marriage. This love demands the entire and exclusive personality of the partner and a union without limit of time. Everything that poets have ever sung of true love testifies to the unanimity of human thought and feeling on this point. Hence, we have tried to develop our argument for the unity and indissolubility of marriage from the individual end, the personal end of the partners in marriage, which plays such a prominent role in their first approach to marriage.

The *social end* of marriage is unquestionably shown in the natural fruit of the sexual union. Thus, besides the personal end, the marital union has to fulfill a social end, the rearing of the offspring. Hence, the marriage contract contains conditions that are not left to the will of the contracting parties, but have been decreed by natural law. Hence also, anyone who concludes a marriage contract binds himself *ipso facto* by the conditions intrinsic in the social end of marriage. These conditions are oneness and indissolubility. The latter is the condition chiefly disputed today; but it is demanded by the good of the offspring, a good which is involved in the nature of marriage. Since this is the social end of marriage and since the common good takes precedence over the good of the individual, marriage is indissoluble by its very nature. This is true even when one or both parents are unable to find their personal happiness in it.

But what of a childless marriage? Or what if the parents are obliged to live apart (separation being the dissolution of the marriage association, not of the marriage bond), because otherwise their bodies or souls or the welfare of their offspring would be endangered? Even in such cases nature demands the indissolubility of marriage for the sake of its social end, an end which transcends the individual marriage and concerns society in general. Because of the social end, there can be no exception to indissolubility. If there were any exception, many of those contracting marriage would not seriously endeavor from the very first to make their marriage a success in achieving its personal and social ends. Monogamy and the indissolubility of marriage considered as a positive, divine law, and other detailed questions are beyond the scope of social ethics; social ethics itself, in the endeavor to answer these questions, will always take us back to one or other of the ideas we have deduced from the nature of marriage and of wedded love.

Marriage and the State

As a contract involving legal consequences for the married pair, for their offspring, and for society, marriage comes within the province of state legislation. In all civilized countries, legislation defines the conditions of marriage insofar as these clearly concern the interests of society (e.g., the form of the registration of the contract); it protects the marriage bond by punishing adultery; it determines the rights and duties of husband and wife insofar as these rights have social consequences, especially those which concern the care of the children or the economic position of the members of the family (e.g., as heirs). What right has the state to set up economic, racial, and *eugenic impediments to marriage?* The first of these impediments was, strangely enough, advocated by such a thinker as *John Stuart Mill,* who thought the government justified in preventing marriages among the poor.[1]

Today, the other two impediments are the most discussed. In some colonial countries a racial impediment to marriages exists between people of different races, namely, against marriages between whites and natives. Experience has shown that sexual promiscuity, with all its disastrous consequences to the health of body and soul, was much increased by these prohibitions, as also were the prostitution of colored women and the spread of venereal disease. The enactment of "eugenic impediments," which would forbid the marriage of those afflicted with a hereditary taint, belongs to the same class of state prohibitions of marriage. In a case of this kind the most urgent investigation of all possible future consequences is obviously a stern moral duty for those who contemplate such a marriage. The state may use its influence suitably to procure a really thorough self-examination on the part of candidates for marriage. An obligatory "eugenic certificate," issued after examination by an experienced doctor, may well prove proper to the purpose in view. But it is not within the province of the state to make permission depend on such a certificate; this could be enforced only by violating personal rights and liberties.

The state, then, in a subsidiary capacity, may encourage a sense of eugenic responsibility, although it would be a far different thing were the state to usurp a direct advisory function, for instance, by the establishment of *marriage advisory councils.* In some countries such councils have been set up by the state or with state subsidies for the purpose of dealing indiscriminately with as many applicants as possible. In all questions concerning marriage, however, moral principles are involved, and these principles are inseparable from religious conviction. It follows that such marriage advisory councils can acquit themselves fitly of their task only by employing doctors who have the same religious persuasion as those whom they are advising. "Neutral" state advisory councils for marriage would, therefore, be of use only to those without any religion, while advice about marriage will best be given to Christians through institutions set up within the framework of their Churches.

As a consequence of a purely secular idea of marriage, the state increasingly tried to bring the marriage of Christians entirely under its own jurisdiction. In some countries it did so by refusing to recognize or even to allow a marriage between Christians unless it had previously taken place in the presence of civil authorities (obligatory civil marriage); or the state offered Christians the possibility of concluding a purely civil marriage, thus evading Church jurisdiction (optional civil marriage). In many countries, however, the function of representing the state is dele-

[1] Cf. J. S. Mill, *On Liberty,* 1878, Chap. 5.

gated to ministers of the Churches. Marriage between baptized persons is a sacrament and as such falls within the competence of the Church; the state violates natural and divine law by usurping an exclusive jurisdiction over marriage between Christians. On the other hand, a modern state may not be able entirely to avoid making divorce possible, if consciences have been warped by misleading influences in regard to this question. But the more the state facilitates divorce (in some countries within the sphere of Western civilization as many as ten per cent of marriages end in divorce), the further it weakens its own life-cell, the family, which we are now about to discuss.

Individualism and *collectivism* join hands in ranging marriage among those contracts all of whose conditions depend on the will of the contracting parties. The fallacy involved has produced the ideas of free love, of companionate marriage (i.e., living together without contracting marriage), and of trial marriage —all of which were raised to the status of a programme with the rise of individualist liberalism and liberal socialism. Dialectical materialism regards marriage, like any other social institution, as subject to social evolution: "Monogamy arose from the concentration of considerable wealth in the hands of a single individual—a man—and from the desire to bequeath this wealth to the children of that man and no other. . . . What will quite certainly disappear from monogamy are all the features stamped upon it through its origin in property relations; these are, first, the supremacy of the man, and, secondly, indissolubility." [2]

70. The Family

The family is the community of parents and children. The ties of blood uniting parents and children are the source of inclinations and impulsions within the family which leave no doubt of the fundamental law of its natural constitution and functions. Yet, it is possible to err in this matter. Even such an eminent thinker as *Aristotle* defended the exposure of children; and *Plato* went so far as to contemplate the complete setting aside of family life, as well as permitting promiscuity of men and women, the state bringing up their children. But since the law of nature speaks so clearly, *Aristotle* is compelled to admit that the general feeling may turn against the exposure of children,[1] and he finds many objections to *Plato's* common possession of women and children; [2] *Plato* himself, in his later work, *The Laws,* no longer advocates this idea. Indeed, the hearth, the symbol of family union, was held sacred by the ancients, and was coupled with the domestic altar. *Constantin Frantz* is right when he

[2] F. Engels, *The Origin of the Family, Private Property, and the State* (London), 1940, pp. 81, 89.

[1] Cf. Aristotle, *Politics,* VII, 16, par. 15.

[2] Cf. *ibid.,* II, 1, par. 3.

stigmatizes as misrepresentation and falsification of this fundamental order of things the coupling of throne and altar; whereas, he says, it is really "hearth and altar" that are united by the law of nature.[3] No natural reality impresses more closely upon man his relationship to the Creator than the responsibilities and mysteries in the continuous creative process of begetting and rearing offspring. Christ gave divine sanction to this natural order in the sacred character of the family by his birth of a woman and by his life and work in his family. In his teaching the family is the first and most important social unit.

The end of the family is threefold: to provide its members in body and mind with the necessities for an ordered daily life; to bring up the children; to be the cell of society. Upon these individual and social existential ends rests the primacy of the family among all other social units, including the state. For, the existential ends and the functions based on them determine the position of a social organism within the pluralism of the social and juridical order. Hence, the family is prior to the state and holds natural rights which the state is bound to recognize. To make it possible for the families which form the political community to fulfill their natural functions is the prominent task of the state. Only insofar as the assured exercise of the family functions depends on the establishment of peace, order, and welfare in society can *Aristotle's* declaration that the state is prior to the family claim any justification (cf. Chap. 17).

Nature indicates beyond any doubt that the ordering power, the authority, which is essential to every community (cf. Chap. 45), belongs equally to both parents in the family. From all points of view, the family authority is best exercised by the parents jointly and harmoniously. But when decisions are necessary and the parents cannot agree, the ultimate power of decision rests as a rule with the father. The reason is that in every community a supreme authority is indispensable, and the father, as the one responsible for providing its support, is designed by nature to exercise this authority. Basically, therefore, in the fifth and sixth chapters of Ephesians Paul is expounding the natural law principles when he sets out the duties within the family community, although he aims at teaching the Christians the highest motives for their observance. The state family law regulates the exercise of parental power of decision in all essential questions. How far this power of the state may extend is not defined by natural law for all times, since it is largely dependent on the prevailing social conditions. This in general is strikingly expressed by *Constantin Frantz,* who in this matter also gets to the heart of the principle: "About this the law can decide in different ways. Everything which is compatible with the being and end of marriage is to be considered as permissible, everything which serves to maintain the purity of marriage

[3] Cf. C. Frantz, *Naturlehre des Staates als Grundlage aller Staatswissenschaften,* 1870, pp. 126 f.

or to safeguard its end as commendable, but everything which is at variance with the character of marriage or endangers its end as inadmissible." [4]

Both *individualist* and *collectivistic* society uphold the state's claim to primacy. The first does not conceive the state community as an association of families but of individuals; hence, there is no room left for a primacy of the family. The individualist-capitalistic society condemned itself by its destructive effects on the family, by the "family crisis" (cf. Chaps. 71–80). For dialectical materialism the existing social-legal family system is only part of the superstructure of the economic process and wholly subject to the development of this process. Hence, "the bourgeois family," a notion in which the Communist Manifesto obviously includes the idea of the family as based on absolute values and rights, "will vanish as a matter of course with the vanishing of capital; thus, the family is a subordinate element in the social process."

71. Family Community

Aristotle, and in this he is followed by *St. Thomas,* defined the family as "the association established by nature for the supply of men's everyday wants." [*] He indicates which need he is primarily thinking of when he adds that the members of the family are called by the poets "companions of the cupboard" or "companions of the manger." Today, too, when its members, frequently both parents as well as grown-up children, are kept away from home by their work and the younger children in the daytime by school, it is the common table that most often unites them. However, family life has no less a part to play in satisfying man's other needs. To begin with, we have man's craving for play and recreation. If the family is sound at heart, it will readily find ways and means to this end, for nature itself, it has been justly observed, gives the young parents the loveliest and noblest of toys, which they never tire of, namely, the child. We may add with equal justice that the child sees in its parents and later in brothers and sisters its most beloved playmates. This fits in with one of the highest functions of the family; it is an old pedagogic truth that hardly anything offers so many educational possibilities as play.

Furthermore, the communal life of the family has to allow for the satisfaction of man's natural thirst for the things that lift him above his everyday life and its difficulties—for communication, for beauty, for self-education, for friendship, for hospitality. Fairy tales, myths, and legends—in short, storytelling in the home—plays an important role in this respect. The cultivation of music at home, when the members of a family play one or more instruments, perhaps with the assistance of friends, is an especially fertile source of activity and joy in common. What arts

[4] *Ibid.,* pp. 130 f.
[*] Aristotle, *Politics,* I, 2, par. 5.

and crafts did for the home in former days, is now made possible for the family by the techniques of art reproduction, so that any home desiring it can have a small "art museum" at a slight cost. Phonograph records have brought the mightiest creations of musical genius into the home. Broadcasting and television can perform a similar task. Thus, in many ways the progress of technology could serve to consolidate the family community as much as it has contributed to its destruction in the industrial period, and help to form its communal life during the hours dedicated to entertainment, or to interest it in the different domains of science, aesthetics, and knowledge of the world, as well as in the time spent in social intercourse. All this does not mean an idealization of the family; rather, it provides a natural pattern, which is not made less valid by the fact that present-day family life for the greater part is far removed from it; it shows clearly to what extent cultural life in the family has been lost.

The fostering of a family's life in common in such a way that its members are given all they need for body and soul in their daily life in the spheres we have mentioned may be called *family culture.* Its foundation is the personal and moral attitude of its members to one another and to the values which are rooted in the existential human ends and in which alone they can find their best selves. Family culture expresses itself first of all in the manners of the members within the home, in the unselfishness of their mutual love, in their readiness to help one another in daily life, in the development of the personality, and, generally speaking, in all that is implied in good upbringing, the results of which accompany a man throughout life. Family culture is strongly supported by habits and customs in which part of the family culture of an entire people assumes the form of established tradition. Each generation nourishes its family culture on tradition and on custom, and at the same time, may exercise a powerful, creative influence of its own on that of the next generation. These traditions and customs are often closely bound up with religion (which, indeed, is an essential part of family culture). In fact, religion is an indispensable source for the realization of the family's most vital values.

Through the individualist and liberalist undervaluation of the family and overvaluation of the freely-formed association, the individual members of the family—father, mother, child—were drawn to various organizations (union, party, club, sports associations), and these ties kept them away from the family circle. In addition, there were the consequences of having to work in factories that were far from the home, thus necessitating long daily journeys. Thus, the home often becomes, for the members of the family, merely "a place to sleep in"; in large part, their lives run their course elsewhere. Added to this, we have the modern pursuit of pleasure, the tavern, the dance hall, the motion picture theater, the music hall, and other places of entertainment, which make inroads upon family life. Needless to say, all of these organizations and institutions have also a genuine social function.

The process of dissolution received a further strong incentive from collectivistic trends of social development. The Marxian *socialistic* movement on the European Continent may be recalled, with its powerful propaganda aimed at drawing young people into its political and cultural organizations, and to imbue them with its idea of community life. The immediate consequence was that the rest of the community was increasingly compelled to use similar organizations in the attempt to offset the growing socialistic influence. Even the Churches have been obliged to try to counteract this development and its influence on the young by creating their own clubs, associations, and "parish halls." In so doing, however, they have themselves partly contributed, although under compulsion, to loosening the bonds between the young and their families. The desire to obviate the aforesaid dangers in practice has sometimes led the Churches to lose sight of the fact that they have to find in the family, in the solidity of its union and in its spiritual foundations, one of the most important objects of their pastoral ministry. The inroads made by all totalitarian systems on family life—by forcing the children into state youth organizations—form one of the most far-reaching usurpations of the things that are not Caesar's. For, by such organizations the totalitarian state aims at impressing its creed, its conception of life and of values, on the minds of the young, quite apart from the endeavor to encroach upon the family community by inducing the young to spy on, and to denounce, the other members of the family.

72. Family Economy

The provision by the family for the needs of an ordered life is very largely an economic task, and hardly any of its other tasks is entirely independent of this. In times when the division of labor in industry was relatively restricted, the family was an economic unit in a perfect sense: man, wife, and grown-up children worked in house, fields, garden, and workshop. Every able-bodied child increased the working power and at the same time the output and the proceeds. Conditions are quite different now that a large part of the population is obliged to earn the means for family subsistence away from home and in the form of currency. Today, the income of the wage-dependent father of the family takes a prominent place in the discussion. The answer to the question concerning the family wage demanded by natural law principles, is dependent on historical and social conditions. Chief among these conditions are economic productivity, the standard of living incidental to cultural development, the state of morale, and the will of a people to propagate. In accordance with natural law, therefore, the just *family wage* is a relative quantity, and the deciding principles are governed by relative natural law.

We would be mistaken, however, if we considered the family economy merely a question of income, as is usually done, and not also a question of making ends meet. The development of technical and of economic productivity will never make it possible to disregard the limitations of income; hence, as a rule the family economy will always involve a moral struggle for "economy" in the true sense of the word, that is, the application of limited means to the best possible satisfaction of all vital needs, in proportion to their urgency in the order of ends. When girls marry with no preparation and no interest whatever in housekeeping, one can apply the old proverb that the wife can throw more out through the window than the husband can bring in through the door. Deficiencies in the satisfaction of essential needs, caused by the irresponsible spending of wife or husband (drinking, smoking, amusements), are known today as "secondary poverty."[1]

If, therefore, the economic position of the family is always half a question of household management, nevertheless, certainly it is equally half a question of family income. This must make possible the satisfaction of material and cultural needs, which is the object of family life and therefore is clearly a fundamental question of the order of economy. The discussion of the family wage has its starting point in the natural law principle that the man without means, as long as he is fully capable of work, is entitled, by virtue of his sharing in social cooperation, to an income sufficient for the foundation and support of a family. Man's natural impulse toward the foundation of a family and a share in the fruits of the earth (cf. Chap. 171) speaks so clearly on this point that no room is left for difference of opinion.

Three things must, however, be taken into consideration. First, because the family is an economic community providing for the material livelihood of its members, all who are able should contribute toward the upkeep of the household; this also applies to adolescent children, whether by helping in the house or, when there are younger children to be provided for, by helping financially from their own earnings. Indeed, in agricultural homes the participation of sons and daughters in the work is taken as a matter of course. The second consideration is that the average family wage cannot be intended for the very large family but for a normal family, one with three or four children. For larger families special provision will always have to be made in one of the ways yet to be discussed. Thirdly and lastly, it would be erroneous to suppose that a family wage should simply make possible the "living standard" adequate for a childless couple. Quite apart from the question of economic practicability, in such an assumption, external criteria of the living standard would be brought to the fore, whereas the family values themselves are beyond estimation by such standards. Basically, *family policy* has to aim at providing the conditions for the fullest realization of the essential family values belonging to the realm of personality and community values, which indeed make possible life's richest fulfilment[2] (cf. the following chapter;

[1] Cf. F. Zweig, *Labour, Life, and Poverty*, Preface by Lord Beveridge, Foreword by B. Seebohm Rowntree, 1948, pp. 2, 20 ff., 118.

[2] Therefore, all possible measures must be taken to secure a sufficient income for the family so that, in its community, its everyday needs can be supplied. To replace the function of the household by family assistance is questionable. As already men-

on the economic theory of this question cf. Chap. 163, last par. and note 4).

Having established these principles, we must now leave the domain of theory. In practice there is no doubt that, for some time to come, the full family wage in accordance with present-day minimum standards of living, in most countries will not be reached in many branches of industry. Yet, provision for a sufficient family income is such an obvious demand of natural justice that it brooks no delay. Therefore, measures must be taken to satisfy this demand. What are the principles of natural law on this? Our task here is to discuss only these, and not the particular measures and efforts of family policy in the various countries.

1. Even though children's allowances are indispensable, it is certain that the key to the provision of a family wage, especially in times of the security of employment and of rising incomes, is to be sought in the *fiscal policy* of the state. The state is bound by distributive justice to apportion equally the burden of taxation; therefore, in taxing the family income it is bound to have regard for specific expenditure necessary for the fulfillment of the family's essential tasks. This will be achieved by separate taxation of the family income, on the basis of half for both husband and wife, after deducting the generally applicable tax-free proportion of income on each half of the income and tax-free proportion of income based on the number of children. The provision of tax-free income for bringing up the children may also be achieved by including the children in the divided family income, for the purpose of separate taxation. Details must vary in relation to income and to the system of taxation prevailing. Thus, in the United States (Tax Law of April 2, 1948) the income of the wage earner (meaning the joint income if both husband and wife are earning) is taxable, after deduction of the appropriate tax-free allowance, on the basis of half for the husband and half for the wife ("splitting"); in addition, there is a tax-free allowance of six hundred dollars annually for each child. Other than this fiscal policy of protecting family incomes there are no real measures of family policy (apart from assistance in rent when family incomes are less than five times the customary rent of the district), and the public opinion of the country does not consider them to be necessary. In France, taxation of the family income is based on a division of the total income, including family allowances, according to the number in the family, and, after deducting the appropriate tax-free allowance, each part is taxed separately; in the division, husband and wife each count as one, the children

---

tioned, only the total misapprehension by socialists of the nature of the family makes it possible to think of replacing that basic function of the family by the state; in the words of Engels: "With the transfer of the means of production into common ownership, the single family ceases to be the economic unit of society. Private housekeeping is transformed into a social industry" (Engels, *The Origin of the Family, Private Property, and the State* [London], 1940, p. 81). The failure of the Chinese communist attempts at such "reforms" in recent years may be taken as evidence for the reality of the natural law.

as half; family allowances are payable for each child after the first, increasing when the child is ten years old; in addition, a number of grants are available, maternity allowances, a grant for the birth of a child, housing grants, reduced fares, and allowances for mothers unable to work. Public opinion regards the problem of family assistance in France as solved.

2. Insofar as the minimum family wage (cf. above) is not attained by means of a fiscal policy (whether on account of the system of taxation or because wages are too low), its supplementation by *children's allowances* is a demand of justice. There are today two methods of achieving this: Family Equalization Funds; state subsidies.[3] In the first, the means are raised through contributions from the employer, while the payment of children's allowances is made from Equalization Funds organized by professional self-governing bodies. The French[4] and German forms (*Kindergeldgesetz* of November 13, 1954) belong to this category. From the point of view of natural law the system of Equalization Funds has substantial advantages: the raising of means from the administrative revenue preserves the connection of family allowances with the wage income (as distinct from welfare payments); the payment of the allowances by vocational bodies widens the sphere of self-government of the latter (cf. Chap. 85). In the second system (state family endowments), this is effected by means of taxation. It was first introduced in 1927 in New South Wales, Australia. In England a family allowances scheme was introduced (1946) on the basis of the Beveridge Report (1944), and is paid regardless of the parents' income. The reason given in the report for this radical solution is that "with its present rate of reproduction, the British race cannot continue." In fact, there is only one real reason which justifies the exclusively governmental solution. This reason is that a large proportion of families are in such a critical position, or that the downward movement of population is becoming so catastrophic, that no other solution promises to have any effect. For obvious reasons, children's allowances as a rule should be paid to the mother.

[3] A survey of the form and extent of monthly cash payments in 33 countries is made by A. and R. Scherer and J. Dorneich, editors, in *Ehe und Familie,* n. VII in the series *Wörterbuch der Politik,* 1956, pp. 241 ff.

[4] The first beginnings of the Family Equalization Funds (*Caisses de Compensation pour Allocations Familiales*) in France, before the turn of the century, were made by the industrialist Léon Harmel, who was supported in his efforts by such economists and theorists as P. A. F. LePlay and gained a further incentive from the papal encyclical *Rerum Novarum* (1891). In 1918 the first real Family Equalization Funds were formed by a number of industrialists; in 1920 there were 56 funds aiding half a million workers; there were 230 in 1930 aiding nearly two million workers. It was especially furthered by state contracts being granted to firms on the condition that they join the Funds. The experience of these Equalization Funds in France may well be summed up in the fact that the communist unions, which on doctrinaire grounds were against them at first for fear of a delay in the dialectical revolutionary process, found themselves obliged to declare in 1926 that the majority of the proletariat approved of the system and that it was therefore futile to oppose it.

3. It is generally impossible to compensate by means of a taxation policy and family allowances for the relatively heavier burdens imposed on family incomes by special short-term or long-term expenses. Such expenses should be supplemented in accordance with circumstances by state measures and by a municipal social policy. In various countries the following are found: marriage loans subject to a graduated remission of repayment after the birth of children; maternity grants before and after the birth of a child; free maternity hospitals; provision for help in the home for maternity cases; housing subsidies in accordance with the number of children; grants to mothers who refrain from going out to work; reduced fares for large families; free school meals; children's homes; holiday homes for mothers. In addition, justice clearly demands some further measures which have up to now received too little attention in state social policy: when there are at least three children, an adequate income tax allowance should be made to pay for domestic help; the extra expenditure of families on public services should be partly eased by a reduction in tariffs.

4. Alongside the assurance of the necessary family income there will always remain something that is too often forgotten today, a considerable scope for private family assistance by charitable institutions on a denominational basis, such as the Caritas Organizations, the Conferences of St. Vincent de Paul, the Unions of St. Elizabeth and St. Joseph, the Mother's Unions, etc. On these will rest the provision for the economic needs of the family in the special circumstances which lie outside the orbit of state social policy, particularly when, in addition to economic support, help with regard to health, morals, and religion is also necessary. They also have an important task in preparing and training adolescent girls for their future career as mothers and housewives, and consequently in giving them the indispensable preparation for marriage.

73. Family Education

When the subject of family education is touched upon, our minds turn primarily to the education of the children by their parents. In fact, however, family education goes much further. Every member of the family has both an active and a passive share in it. In the family educational community we note effects in three directions: parents on children; children on parents; and children on one another.

When we speak of the *education of the parents,* a need that is by no means unimportant, we are thinking chiefly of the self-discipline which the family community demands from them in their relations with one another and with the children. Family education promotes the avoidance of quarrels, self-control over moods and whims, mutual respect, thrift, readiness to help and to render service, and especially readiness to sacrifice self for others and for the family as a whole. Last but not least, the family brings an educative influence to bear on the parents by the continual stimulus of having to put forth their best self in order to achieve fully the great and noble aim of the family community. The importance of the educative influence of the family on the parents is all the greater since young married couples have not yet fully integrated their personalities and since marriage gives to them a new status in life and new responsibilities. Responsibilities complied with are one of the most efficacious means of education. Thus, the authority assigned to them by nature is an educative stimulus for themselves. For, only those parents can fully educate their children who have succeeded in educating themselves in the family association, thus being able to give the children that good example without which no education is possible.

The *child* will be formed most effectively by growing up to the image of his parents. He must be able to see in his parents the kind of human being that he is to become. On the other hand, education is not a training in clichés of behavior but an awakening of that which in human nature points toward man's best self. For natural law is, first and above all, nature, and thus education has its function in making it alive, progressive, and fully developed. Accordingly, authority as a means of education is only a guide, but one that is indispensable.

The family is no less an educational community by reason of the education which the *children give one another;* the importance of this fact cannot be overrated. Such education is lacking where there is only one child, and it attains its maximum effectiveness in a large family. It consists in this: from the very beginning the children learn from the experience of their daily lives to control themselves, to be tolerant, to claim no more rights than the others, to respect the others, to be obliging, to help the others and try to cause them pleasure, to be self-sacrificing for the sake of others—in short, being and doing whatever may make their life in common a true fellowship, and giving to all the members the comfort and happiness that nothing but the home with its natural incentives of love can give. The fact that greater sacrifices and greater self-denial are demanded of the children in larger families, is the very reason why these families give their children more inward strength to carry them through life and why they provide society with men and women who often prove to be of outstanding quality. We are, of course, presupposing that care be taken so that the children of a large family lack none of the things essential to their full physical and mental development.

I *The Educational Rights of the Parents*

By education we mean the developing and training of the children's aptitudes of body and of mind, so that they become capable of fulfilling their essential tasks in personal and social life by virtue of their own responsibility. Already in antiquity (*Plato*), then in the literature of early and "scientific" socialism, and still today in the school of analytical psychology (*Freud*) the thought recurs sporadically that the education of children should be transferred from the parents to persons especially qualified philosophically, politically, and scientifically. Reality itself, that is to say, human nature, presents four features which clearly assign the function of education to the parents and which provide scientific ethics with the means to prove the parents' right of education:

1. The natural impulse in man to marry and have children has already been stressed by *Aristotle,*[1] showing that man strives to leave an image of himself in his offspring. Education, which is the only thing that can develop this image in children, is therefore the task and privilege of the parents. Indeed, there is no other reason in natural law which so definitely assigns the function of education to the parents as this. No other argument for the primary educational rights of parents can make so clear what has been so uncompromisingly maintained by traditional natural law theory, namely, that the religious and moral education of children is a matter for the parents. It is well known how emphatically *St. Thomas*[2] answered negatively the question, to which he devoted a special article, whether a child of Jewish parents might be baptized against their will; he said that it would be contrary to natural law. Similarly today, traditional natural law ethics rejects interference in the right of communist parents, while, however, it is equally definite in rejecting the usurpation of the parents' rights in the totalitarian communistic state.

2. Again, nature speaks clearly for the parental function of education through the natural dependence of children on the parents and the resulting responsibility of the parents. The human child needs a much longer time than the animal to develop fully his physical and psychical dispositions and to prepare for fulfilling his life's tasks. During this entire period the child is to such a great extent the subject of parental responsibility that his existence clearly forms part of the human existence of the parents. If further proof is needed of parents' undoubted consciousness of this responsibility, it may be furnished by the whole legal consciousness of mankind: legal institutions do not assign legal responsibility to children, but, in their place, to the parents. This means that the child, in the course of his development toward existence as an individual person fully responsible for his conduct and thus for the fulfillment of his existential ends, remains part of the existence of the parents and of their responsibility for their own existential ends; therefore, the right and the duty to educate rests with the parents.

3. Nature gives clear testimony of the parents' right to educate in the strength of the parents' natural love for their children. Love is an unsurpassable and an essential power in education. A psychology which fails

[1] Cf. Aristotle, *Politics,* I, 2, 2.
[2] Cf. St. Thomas, *Summa theol.,* IIIa, q. 68, a. 10.

to see this has lost sight of the reality of the human soul. From the child's viewpoint, too, no better predisposition for education can be found than his natural love for his parents.

4. Nature itself endows the parents with the necessary authority for education. Long before the growing child realizes himself as an individual and can understand the duty of obedience as a matter of conscience, he sees himself only as part of the family community and therefore wholly subject to the guidance and direction of the parents. Then, with the full development of reason this will be understood as the natural power of command which is based in the family community (cf. Chap. 47).

The parents' educational right embraces:

(1) the exclusive right of the parents to determine the basic education of their children, that is their religious and moral education;

(2) the primary right of the parents to educate in every respect, that is, to instruct as far as they are able and willing, in conformity with the schemes of instruction set up by the state;

(3) the right of the parents to provide their own educational institutions (schools) where the children's education and training is in accordance with their own religious and moral outlook, while at the same time fulfilling the aims of instruction set by the state. Basically the parents have the right to delegate this right to educate, that is, to appoint others to represent them. Even the state works by virtue of delegated rights in its schools for young children, and therefore is acting in behalf of those who possess the primary educational rights, the parents; the same applies to kindergartens maintained by public corporations.

(4) the right of parents who maintain their own schools to a proportionate contribution from the state, namely, an amount equivalent to the expense saved to the state through such private schools. The rights with regard to schools may be summed up as the "right to free schools."

The parental right to educate is *exclusive* and *inalienable*. It is exclusive: Just as a child cannot be reared if it is subjected to the continually changing diets of different nurses at the same time, all with equal authority, so also the basis cannot be laid for the development of a personality capable of knowing and developing its essential self if its education is subject to various authorities, influencing it in different directions. The parents' right in this, therefore, must be exclusive. It is also an inalienable right: Parents cannot rid themselves of the responsibility laid upon them by their natural vocation to bring up their children. They can of course appoint others to represent them: tutors, private schools, state schools. But they themselves remain ultimately responsible for the children's being taught and brought up to fulfill their existential ends, especially the religious and moral ones, in virtue of their own responsibility.

II *The Educational Rights of the State and of the Church*

When we call the parents' right to educate an exclusive right, this does not mean that the state does not also possess educational rights. As we shall show later (Chap. 143), under present-day conditions the state is entitled by natural law on various grounds to prescribe standards of instruction and to maintain schools to secure their attainment. From what we have said it follows that the whole activity of the state in the matter of education is subject to the law of subsidiary function. This means that the state can have no primary right in the sphere of the fundamental education of children, and its activity can be nothing more than that of helping the family. Furthermore, state and local authority in all activities affecting educational ends, therefore not only in schools but also in children's homes, act merely in the name of the parents. Lastly, the state, even when acting in its own right in imposing obligatory standards of instruction, still remains bound by the primary educational rights of the parents.

From our discussion of the position of the existential ends in education it follows that the one community whose mission concerns the absolute existential human ends must be invested with rights in the sphere of education. Hence, the right of the *Church,* her teaching office, and her pastoral office extend to education and school. Christian parents resist this divine right when they refuse the Church the necessary collaboration in education; the state resists it when it arrogates to itself a right to educate children while denying the Church the fulfillment of her mission in its schools.

Liberalism as well as socialism claims a direct right of the state in the education of children, prior to the right of the parents as well as that of the Church. The liberalist state, where it had the power, aimed at an exclusively controlled and compulsory education of a secularized kind (state school monopoly and state compulsory schools). Marxian socialism advocated secularization of education in state schools with the principle: "The care and education of the children becomes a public affair." [3] The Constitution of Soviet Russia (Art. 124) explicitly asserted the separation of school and Church: "In order to ensure the citizens freedom of conscience, the Church in the U.S.S.R. is separated from the state, and the school from the Church."

74. The Family Home

A physically and morally healthy family life presupposes a home corresponding to the needs of the family, that is, a home enabled to fulfill its

[3] F. Engels, *The Origin of the Family, Private Property, and the State* (London), 1940, p. 81.

communal and educational functions. For this reason, some natural law aspects must be discussed. These concern family dwellings and housing policy.

I *The Family Dwelling*

That a dwelling may be really a home for a family, three things are needed. 1) It must be sufficiently roomy for all the purposes of family life. It must allow a separate bedroom for the parents and at least individual rooms for adolescent girls and boys. It should contain a spacious sitting room and another living room so that the family need not all be together.[1] 2) A second requirement of a real home is a certain separation of families from one another. The plan of a family dwelling should make possible the intimacy and privacy proper to the family alone among all existing communities. A garden is an essential part of the family environment; it is necessary, not only for the bodily health of children and parents, but because it gives an opportunity of being together out of doors, and also the feeling, so important from a psychological and sociological point of view, of possessing a little bit of land, however small. For all these reasons a one-family house with a garden should be required in principle as a standard dwelling. The two-family house with a divided garden should be the exception. All these reasons speak against blocks of flats for families, which should be destined as much as possible for unmarried people and childless couples only. 3) Lastly, a prerequisite of true family homes is suitable town planning. In many densely populated industrial towns dating from the last century, where houses are packed close together in street after street, each inconsistent with the dignity and functions of family life, in districts where no tree or even a blade of grass is to be seen, it cannot be expected that a family can make a home in the full sense of the word. Present-day town planning is largely governed by principles which also and not least are determined by the needs of the family.[2]

[1] The housing scandal in the era of individualist capitalism is one of the most grievous facts to its discredit, and the slums are merely the worst exterior symptom of that scandal. With special reference to England, Miss Eleanor Rathbone (*The Case for Family Allowances,* 1940, pp. 17 ff.) describes impressively how the man finds himself uncomfortable in his home with the numerous children roaming about in a confined space, the smell of cooking all over the place, the cheap furniture wearing out, with no quiet corner where he can enjoy his pipe and a book or a talk on politics or football with a friend. Hence, he sees himself driven to the public house. The wife being left alone and becoming more and more absorbed in the difficulties of housework sees her vision of family life vanishing in a dreadful reality.

[2] Progressive town planning, in which England leads the way today, considers the one-family or two-family house to be the basic type of town dwelling. The principle is generally held that there should be dispersion of housing estates, so that separate communities may grow up and form their own townships with a sphere of self-government. Rapid communication with the town center, with work and shopping centers, with theaters and concert halls, should be made possible by well-planned transportation services. The townships should not lack churches of their own both

11 *Housing Policy*

Housing presents one of the chief tasks, if not the foremost, for all those who are responsible for family welfare. Nothing so strongly threatens the roots of a family life in conformity with natural law as the lack of suitable housing. Indeed, natural law principles leave no doubt that in this question, as in all other questions of social order, the accomplishment of this task is only possible through the cooperation of all those responsible. Those responsible are (1) the family itself, (2) then those whose duty it is to care for the general welfare, that is to say the state and the municipality. When we say, primarily the family, we think of meeting the costs of the family home from the family income. The principle in question means that self-help takes the first place in providing family dwellings, whereas the state, among general welfare functions, has the duty to provide housing only in exceptional situations. Such situations exist when there has been a long period of falling housing production and when houses have been destroyed during wars. The state can even resort to measures of housing control, as it did in most European countries after the First and Second World Wars. There is today, among all those who are capable of realizing the connection between social policy and economic policy, the conviction that housing control is not only no suitable method of housing policy, but rather the opposite of this, that the inclusion of housing affairs in the general market economy is the only way to recover from a serious housing shortage and the grievances which it entails.

By this is not meant unrestricted competitive economy; indeed, the extent and type of housing provision is one of the darkest blots on individualist capitalism. The provision of an adequate supply of houses imposes special social tasks on the market economy. The difficulties are of two kinds: procuring capital and procuring building sites. Every social economy with a progressively expanding productivity finds difficulties in *procuring capital,* since capital is a scarce commodity and for this reason its use is determined by considerations of productivity. The unconcealed housing shortage in the Soviet Union shows that this applies as much, if not more, to the planned economy of state capitalism as to the market economy of private capitalism. The difficulty, due to the reasons stated, of obtaining capital for building at market rates of inter-

---

for the joint family observance of Sundays and feast days, and for occasions such as births, weddings, and funerals. Indeed, contact with the local church forms an integral part of family life and a vital condition for the realization of its finest values. On the question of house and town planning cf. especially Richard Neutra, *Survival through Design,* 1954; W. H. Maclean, *Planning the Modern City,* 2nd ed., 1949; sociologically informative is G. Krall, L. Rosenmayr, A. Schimka, H. Strotzka, *Wohnen in Wien.* Results and suggestions drawn from an inquiry into Viennese dwelling conditions in city surroundings can be found in *Der Aufbau,* issued by the Stadtbauamt Vienna, 1956.

est, results in too great a proportion of income being demanded for a rent which will be sufficient to repay the necessary capital expenditure on house building. This applies equally to the payment of interest on capital raised for a single house and to payment of rent in the case of a rented flat. The prerequisite for a rent sufficient to repay cost is an adequate income. This gives special significance to all the previously mentioned means (Chap. 72) for securing a family income. There also must be a readiness to set aside from one's income the necessary amount for satisfying housing needs. Before 1914, the average amount required for housing was one-fifth of income, today, owing to an increased housing shortage following the two wars and a greater scarcity of capital, it has risen to a quarter or more of income. In all countries, however, which were faced with the necessity of a lengthy period of housing control with artificial restriction of rents, the readiness to assign so high a proportion of income to rent is undermined to a great extent.[3] With regard to such countries one has to admit the critical position "that the majority of people assign only an insufficient part of their income to housing needs, the burden of which falls, to a considerable extent, on the community as a whole (partly results in inadequate maintenance of housing property)."[4] Only slowly is the way being prepared for a real change, not least indeed by the general raising of incomes in the course of the continuous economic growth. The chief signs of this are to be found in the various kinds of building savings.

State aid in housing, which is certain to be necessary for a considerable period, should be sought, therefore, chiefly in measures of taxation to encourage building savings and the investment of capital in social building,

[3] This is true to such an extent that even a "right to be housed" (on the continent: flats) is advocated, and not only by the socialists. Following from this, the state is regarded as having the duty to implement this right. No real reason can be given for such a right to be housed; rather, there are many reasons immediately evident which speak against it. That is to say, if by the right to be housed is meant a real legal claim, then there must be somebody with an obligation to comply with this claim. This could only be the state, and under its guiding influence the municipal authority. Such a legal claim could be met only by socialization of housing affairs, and, accompanying this, complete housing control. Thus, the family would be, to no small degree, dependent on the state, which would influence its own rights in the fulfillment of its ends at a crucial point, the home. Moreover it must not be forgotten that the "state" in modern democracy is the party state, and, as the housing policy and housing distribution policy of large municipalities shows, the striving for power in the service of party interests makes itself felt in housing matters. In addition, a national and municipal housing policy based on a supposed right to be housed would affect the natural law order of property at a decisive point, since private ownership of houses is equally important for the establishment and the distribution of property. The relation of public and private responsibility in matters of housing can be briefly expressed in the words of O. v. Nell-Breuning, "Wohnwirtschaft," in *Staatslexikon der Görresgesellschaft*, Vol. V, 1932: "In the sphere of housing the public authority should give guidance to the economy instead of wishing to take possession of it. It must definitely be maintained that the cost of housing should be borne, not by the general community, but by individuals."

[4] O. v. Nell-Breuning, S.J., *Wirtschaft und Gesellschaft*, 1956, p. 67.

by which is chiefly meant the building of workers' dwellings by large industrial and agricultural concerns.[5] A further task of state economic policy is to exert the necessary influence to reduce building costs, a task to which too little attention has been given. In many ways this can have important results. It could prevent the increased costs of building materials resulting from building supply industries forming cartels. Moreover it must work against the excessive cost of building caused by inefficiency in the building industry and building material industry if they have a semi-monopoly as a result of long standing tariff protection. An improvement in building methods, which would make it possible to continue building work in winter, is also to be considered; efforts are already being made in different ways which, if successful, would mean a substantial rationalization of the building industry.

The question of the *provision of land* is largely one of the building land law. The question is chiefly a double one: the provision of urban building land, and at economically justifiable prices. Both involve particular difficulties, for with the rapid growth of towns and of the demand for houses and offices, the natural scarcity of land has been greatly intensified, with the result of a severe rise in price. The questions of economics, social ethics and social policy connected with this have been the subject of discussion for many years. For a long time land speculation was blamed for the high price of land and the housing shortage, and in the unearned value increment tax was seen the chief means for bringing about an offer of land at a price compatible with economic conditions and requirements. This view is no longer held.[6]

[5] Among examples of tax concessions on building investments which followed the Second World War in individual countries, the following may be mentioned: tax free allowances (deductions from taxable income) for contributions to building societies for the purpose of obtaining building loans; for repayments to public funds, from which building loans would be drawn; for amounts that are paid for erecting or acquiring housing property; limited tax free allowances for expenses incurred by industrial undertakings in erecting their own workers' dwellings, and for donations to general beneficial housing and settlement associations for the purpose of building workers' dwellings; temporary exemption from land tax for house building and particularly for building by building, housing, and settlement associations; likewise, exemption from taxes raised by the municipal authority on house building and house ownership.

[6] These errors may be traced to the misunderstanding of the economics of urban land rents, which were seen as the cause of prices for plots of land instead of the result of price-formation for land, whereby special profits are obtained for plots of land in particular situations. It may still be advisable to point this out, since in consequence of the long-standing formation of public opinion very false ideas are still to be met with. One of the first to turn against these errors was Adolf Weber, *Bodenrente und Bodenspekulation,* 1904; *Boden und Wohnung,* 1908. The view generally held at the present time may be expressed in the words of Professor Friedrich Lütge, "Wohnungswirtschaft und Wohnungspolitik," in *Evangelisches Soziallexikon,* F. Karrenberg, editor, 1954, p. 1162: "Speculation (forming of syndicates, purposive reservation of land, etc.) may have contributed to the rising of prices. This development, however, is not the outcome of speculation, as criticism by land reformers at that time maintained; but it is to be understood in the light of the market situation of that time as well as of urban building policy, which, unfortunately, was only lately perceived to be mistaken. . . . Contrary to this policy, the taxing of unearned value

In most countries the local authorities have begun to organize the land supply, making provision for transportation routes and for municipal public services; by this means the development of urban land rents is largely precluded. With this is associated the legal provision for the expropriation of land if it is not sold voluntarily to the municipality and if its inclusion in the town planning scheme is necessary. Natural law ethics agrees with *F. Lütge* that "all deprivation of property by force is an evil," but equally sees its justification in case of necessity, since "land is a good of a special kind, not merchandise in the sense of goods that may be increased at will, but rather the living space of the entire nation." [7] In fact, the natural law basis of such a right of expropriation consists wholly in the exigencies of the common good. It is naturally bound up with the obligation of compensating for the value of the land, in which respect justice demands consideration of the many factors influencing supply and demand. Only in conjunction with those mentioned, as a supplementary third measure for land supply, the taxation of unearned land value may be considered. It is "unearned" in the sense that it originates not from any economic activity but from the extension of urban housing areas. In this the fiscal purpose should not take first place; rather, the social policy purpose connected with housing policy should take precedence. In accordance with this end, unearned land value tax must be elastic.

In the foregoing only one part of a housing policy serving the needs of the family has been discussed. The other part concerns urban and rural settlements. From the point of view of natural law this system is significant for many reasons. If one thinks of the family community and its importance for the nation and for society, then land settlement provides conditions obviously closer to nature than any other solution of the housing question, "nature" being understood as the whole milieu suitable for the development of the family community. Undoubtedly, the consciousness of possessing a plot of ground of one's own is inestimable, a consciousness which includes a wealth of values not to be assessed in money.

---

increments had barely a significance in land policy, while their financial efficacy suffered from the dilemma that it had to be greater, the higher the price of land rose. The financial effect is thus in direct contrast to the social and political aims." Also, O. v. Nell-Breuning, *Wirtschaft und Gesellschaft,* 1956, pp. 354 f., says of the unearned value increment tax and its significance in influencing land demand: "Meanwhile, we have also learned that here even the taxing of unearned increment cannot help—contrary to the opinion propagated publicly by the land reformers, an opinion which I also held until experience taught me better. The tax on unearned value increment does not help here but acts in the opposite direction. It puts a premium on the man who is strong in capital, who himself utilizes his land through business, housing, and industrial building, and is detrimental to the man not capable of that, who, therefore, must sell his land for the purpose of building or other use." Cf. also O. v. Nell-Breuning, "Wertzuwachssteuer," in *Handbuch der Finanzwissenschaft,* 2nd ed., W. Gerloff and F. Neumark, editors, Vol. II, 1956, pp. 557 ff.; E. Lubahn, *Die städtische Grundrente,* 1952; F. Lütge, *Wohnungswirtschaft,* 2nd ed., 1949.

[7] F. Lütge, *Evangelisches Soziallexikon,* pp. 1158 f.

They are the values associated with the joy, deeply rooted in human nature, of possessing something affording protection from vicissitudes; the values bound up with a sense of union with the elemental creative forces; the values, similarly rooted in human nature, of the possibility implied in this, of a creative development of personality through working to gain the fruits of the earth; the values of the will to save and to establish further property; the values of the knowledge of safety and security; the values of the many deeply rooted feelings for one's native land; the values of being in union with external nature and with the natural healthy environment of life; and, in addition, the values which greatly enhance all these and are fundamental to them, namely, the values of what the primal community and the home imply. With these are associated the values connected with the social and economic order issuing from the formation and distribution of property.

What has been said applies equally to urban and rural settlement. By town settlement I mean the one-family house with cultivable ground ("small settlement"), which affords the settling family an additional income from their own vegetable growing and from keeping livestock. The undoubted inference from the foregoing is that, to the extent that help for municipal house building comes from public sources, it should be primarily directed toward family settlement, insofar as the settlers seem likely to realize these values.[8] The problems of rural settlement press from year to year in Europe with greater urgency, on account of the importance of the farming community for the social and economic order, the undiminished and continuing flight from the land, the losses of agricultural land through road building to meet the demand of increasing motor traffic, and not least the decreasing resistance of the farming community to the influx from urban areas, an influx which is destroying their way of life and their spiritual substance. In the question under discussion, the natural law points of view are therefore not in doubt. The questions of land provision and capital endowment take particular forms, so that wider aspects of economic, social, and national policy as well as of family, population, and cultural policy [9] come into play.

[8] Nikolaus Ehlen, "Familiensiedlung," in *Ehe und Familie,* A. and R. Scherer and J. Dorneich, editors, 1956, p. 276, estimates by reason of many years' experience, that "today not much more than ten per cent of the population is willing and capable of such settlement," an economically feasible settlement for one family being estimated at 2,000 square meters.

[9] In contrast to the period between the World Wars there is little new individual literature on rural settlement. Cf. especially the *Zeitschrift für das gesamte Siedlungswesen* (*Forts. v. Archiv für innere Kolonisation und von Siedlung und Wirtschaft*), I. Jg. u. folg., 1952 ff.; W. F. Boyens, *Siedlung und Bodenreform als Aufgabe des Bundes* (Deutsche Bundesrepublik), 1950; L. D. Stamp, *The Land of Britain, Its Use and Misuse,* 1948; Hans-Jürgen Seraphim with Jürgen B. Heuer, "I. Ländliche Siedlung, II. Städtische Siedlung," in *Handwörterbuch der Sozialwissenschaften,* Vol. IX, 1956, pp. 238 ff., 248 ff. Cf. also J. Messner, *Die Soziale Frage,* pp. 423 f., 468 f., 565 f.; still valuable from the historical, economic, national, state, and social policy points of view is the article by A. Hermes, O. v. Nell-Breuning, F. Degenfeld-Schonburg, "Siedlung" im Staatslexikon der Görresgesellschaft, Vol. IV, 1931.

75. The Family: The Cell of Society

The family is the cell of society. If there are not sufficiently numerous and fruitful marriages, society cannot last, increase, and renew itself. Therefore, the family is the cell of society in the *biological* sense. The fact that the natural law is really the law of life for nations is made evident because the biological development of nations is dependent on the observance of the rules which natural law imposes on marriage and the family.

But it would be quite erroneous to see in the family nothing but the biological cell of society. The family is the cell of society at least as much from a *moral* as from a biological standpoint. We have shown that the development of a human being's mental and moral powers depends on education within the family. The two most important social virtues, charity and justice, are basically taught in family life. Next to these come the two social virtues of due obedience and just rule. Due obedience presupposes respect for authority as a moral and ultimately God-given power of command; just government presupposes the awareness that authority is given only for the benefit of those governed. In family life man has to learn that obedience can never be a self-debasing subservience, but rather it must be a submission to the order designed in his social being, without which his individual self remains stunted. Until he has learned both how to obey and how to command in the family, a man is not in a position to give authority in society a form compatible with the dignity and rights of a human being. And only those who have learned in their families that government must not be tyranny, but a provident service of the community and of its members, will truly serve the community and its good when they wield social authority.* The family is, therefore, from the point of view of education for social life, irreplaceable. Man also learns in the family all the other social virtues, namely, all those involving respect for others because they are persons with the same human nature and equal human rights—readiness to help, kindness, patience, consideration, fairness, sincerity. The family is morally as well as biologically the cell of social life.

From a *cultural* point of view also, the family is the cell of society. It may be called a law of sociology that in nations with a diminishing birth rate, if the birth rate falls below the rate of reproduction, civilization also is on the decline. The deeper reason for this is that the most important stimulus to maintain the finest values of civilization, that is to say, moral and spiritual values as the formative forces of life, tends to decay with the collapse of the family. Married people who shirk the responsibility of children out of sheer selfishness have no contribution to make to

* Cf. St. Augustine, *De civ. Dei,* Lib. XIX, c. 14.

the culture of a nation. Such a nation may indeed have a better position economically for a time, but it will lack the spiritual forces essential to rising civilizations.

Because the family is the life-cell of society, one can explain sociologically, from long experience, that the condition of a society, its inner power of life and regeneration, can be deduced from the state of its families. Whoever desires a correct *diagnosis* of a society's condition, must look at its families, as a doctor first feels a patient's pulse. If the family is despised in society, neglected by the state, its bonds relaxed, the economic foundations of its existence insufficient, or its reproduction not assured, and if divorce is on the increase, these are all infallible symptoms of a crisis in the social body. History provides sufficient evidence that the decay of family life is the deepest cause of the decline of nations. The consequence of the position of the family as the cell in society is that all true social reform must begin with the family. All so-called social reform which overlooks this law or acts against it is ultimately doomed to failure. Individualism, liberalism, Marxist and liberalist socialism, all condemn themselves by seeking the center of gravity of social reform elsewhere than in the family with its functions as the biological, moral, and cultural cell of society.

76. The Normal Family

What is the natural size of the family? Many sociologists and experts on questions of population decline to answer this question. If they are liberalist or socialistic in thought, they hold fast in principle to the neo-Malthusian axiom that the planning of the size of a family is purely the concern of the married couple themselves. Indeed, the concept of the normal family can have little meaning if the family is regarded individualistically as existing for itself alone or if family planning is regarded from a collectivist point of view only as part of the general planning schemes. If, however, we take into consideration the biological and moral function of the family in the life of society, then we find an unequivocal concept of the natural, or, equivalently, the normal size of the family.

Actually the *biological* function of the family leaves no doubt about its natural size. A nation would replace itself in the next generation if in the present generation there were an equal number of boys and girls, who, later married, would in their turn have two children. But all do not live to marriageable age; others are prevented by illness from marrying; others have a vocation which presupposes freedom from the responsibilities of a family; others cannot find the partner whom they would choose; and of the marriages which are contracted not a few remain childless involuntarily or intentionally. From all these facts we see that a nation cannot remain in existence unless the average number of children in a family is three or four, and that the number must be higher if the population is to increase.

The *moral* function of the family as the cell of society proves the same thing. Where families are generally limited to one or two children, the family cannot fulfill its tasks of education for social life. An only child misses the training in the most important social virtues that common life with brothers and sisters would have provided. Moreover, it is a matter of daily experience that an only child is spoiled by its parents, thus strengthening its egocentric dispositions, instead of developing its sense of duty to society. The two-children system has similar results: between two there cannot be a fellowship calling for such a high standard of social virtues as there would be among three, four, or more children. When the children are more numerous they remain children longer. They learn to amuse themselves and to make toys for themselves; they have a world of their own in their games; they learn to live the social life directly from experience. On the other hand, a single child, or two children, begin much earlier to share the thoughts and lives of their elders and mature too fast, a precociousness that is undesirable both physically and mentally. Everything seems to point to the fact that the family needs to be of normal size (that is, it should consist of three or four children), in order really to fulfill its moral function as the cell of society.

77. The Wider Family

Aristotle includes even the slaves in the family which provides for the needs of daily life.* Natural law ethics has followed him in always regarding domestic servants as members of the family group. It was all the more bound to accept this point of view since Christian thinking recognized the full dignity of the person in every human being, including members of the domestic staff. For this reason Christianity founded the family group more on internal moral union, whereas the pre-Christian family was based more on the external, legally recognized jurisdiction of the father. This Christian ideal of a household is still valid, although during the last century the social relationship between the domestic servants and the family has changed into a mere labor contract. It is true that service in a family does depend on a free contract, but from its very nature a contract of this kind includes much more than exactly calculated work and payment. The relationship between the family and its domestic servants is, on both sides, one of loyalty.

The family, in the performance of various tasks, needs help whose value cannot be precisely measured in terms of money, as can the labor of a worker in a factory, but depends upon a sympathetic interest on the part of the domestic servants in the welfare of the family. In the interest of

* Cf. Aristotle, *Politics,* I, 2.

the domestic staff the contract of service, by its nature, includes more than mere payment of money for service rendered; the family is responsible for the welfare of its domestics in body and mind. For when these give their services for a long time and link their lives with the burdens and joys of a growing family, they are indeed part of the family community. Since they devote their lives to it, the family must provide for their essential needs, especially for their need of respect, of affection, of recreation, of security in sickness and in old age, and of suitable lodging, time off, holidays and whatever else concerns their external good.

As in all relations involving output and return, money becomes, in the liberalist society, the almost exclusive factor in the relationship of domestic servants with the family. The masters come to expect certain definite services, the domestics are paid for these services with a fixed sum of money. For them, particularly the women servants, and especially the finer type among them, this often implied an unimaginably heavy burden of degradation, loneliness, physical and moral frustration, and exploitation (usually endured in silence); this is one of the social sins of the liberalist society. In such conditions the extension of the provisions of social legislation to domestic service, subjecting it to legally established rules of a labor contract, marked an important advance. The state had to protect their basic rights. At the same time, both self-help and charitable organizations (servants' clubs) tried to make up for the servants' lack of community life in families. The result of this development is that today, in industrial countries, girls prefer to go into factories rather than into domestic service, where they get more time off and better social security. But the disadvantages include: the loss of community links so necessary for the young, and the loss of training for family life, which a girl best obtains in the family and in actual housekeeping. The socialistic systems provide only very exceptionally for domestic help; instead they provide for help outside the family in kindergartens and schools, where the children can be influenced and indoctrinated.

78. The Family Inheritance

The problem we must discuss at this point concerns the succession of the children to the property and to the rights of their parents. Nothing is more certain than the fact that the parents have the strongest desire to help their children even after their own death; wishing to secure the children's prosperity, they hand over their own possessions to them by will. One of the strongest motives a family has for working and saving would to a great extent disappear if the right to dispose of the family property by will ceased. For these reasons, parents possess a natural right to dispose of their property to such an extent that they are able, in case of death, to fulfill their responsibility for the continued welfare of the family. For the same reasons and to the same extent, the right of the family to inherit still exists even if there were no will. For it must be presumed that it is the parents' will to fulfill an obligation inherent in the nature of the family group. Small family properties left to children by their parents, therefore, should be free from inheritance taxes. Very large inheritances, far beyond the needs of the children and of their families, may be subject to an inheritance tax not exceeding the limits set by the principles just developed in their particular bearing upon the equitable claims of descendants with families to keep up their living standard in society. Consequently, the rights of the family forbid confiscatory taxation on private property that is of more than average size by indiscriminate progressive death duties. No principles binding in natural law and founded on the functions of the family can be applied to inheritances coming from other relatives except that the lawgiver must have consideration for families in need. However, the lawgiver is bound to make provision for relationships similar to family ties; for example, when a legatee undertakes parental duties for the testator's children, or when a bequest expresses gratitude to servants for long years of service. The consequences of confiscatory death duties for the social order and for cultural development will be shown when we deal with fiscal policy (Chap. 148).

Among the various forms of the laws of succession in different countries, those come nearest to the demands of natural law which give parents a certain freedom of bequest, so that they are able to leave larger shares to those children most in need of them (e.g., to ailing children), or to those who merit them most. Many states do not limit the freedom of parents in this matter beyond obliging them to leave to all children at least a minimum of what they would have had if there had been equal division among all. The form of inheritance which (as in France) compels an absolutely equal division among all the children does not accord with the idea of the family group, since it treats the children who do not comply with its functions and duties in the same way as the others, and moreover gives no support to parental authority. Again, such forms of inheritance result in the splitting up of land belonging to farming units, which often makes their continuation impossible. Factories often have to be sold to make the obligatory division of property feasible. Experience shows that parents frequently limit their families in order to escape such consequences. A very different form of inheritance, existing in some countries for agricultural property, great or small, is the right of primogeniture, by which the eldest son inherits the whole estate and the other children get little or nothing in accordance with the principle, "The farmer has only one child." This may also result in birth control, when, for instance, parents are afraid that a too rigid application of such laws may prevent them from providing by will for the second and third child, and others. If such rigidity in legislation were avoided, then a preferential treatment of the child who will be obliged to carry on the management of the family property need not be incompatible with the natural rights of the parents and may, indeed, serve the idea of the family group.

79. The Position of Women

"Are dogs segregated according to sex, or do they both share equally in hunting and in keeping watch and in the other duties of dogs? Or do we entrust to the males the entire and exclusive care of the flocks, while we leave the females at home, with the idea that bearing and suckling of their puppies is labor enough for them?" [1] With these words *Plato* begins his argument for the complete equality of men and women in his concept of society, which holds women and children in common. But he does admit that women are weaker than men, saying that this fact must be taken into account in the allotment of duties. With reference to *Plato's* opinion, *Aristotle* remarks: "It is absurd to argue from the analogy of the animals, that men and women should follow the same pursuits; for animals do not have to manage a household." Thus, *Aristotle* gives the decisive reason against putting men and women on the same footing: the family community and maternal duties are as different in the animal world and the human world as man and beast are different.[2]

Modern champions of the absolute equality of men and women retort that woman is, like man, a complete human person, and therefore must possess the same rights. Certainly, considered as a person, woman has all the rights that a human being possesses. But she is also a social being, and as such has special functions which are assigned to her by the aptitudes of her particular nature and their ends. Thus she has to fulfill special social functions and she also has special rights. These functions are the tending and rearing of children, which takes a far longer time and makes far greater demands than does the rearing of the young in the animal world. It implies the established family community in which lasting attention can be given to the children physically and mentally; in a word, it necessitates the institution of the household. Hence, woman is assigned by nature a special position in the social cell. From this follows the principle that whatever is prejudicial to woman's task as mother of a family, whether in the case of a particular woman or of women in general, is contrary to nature and to natural law.

The claim for indiscriminate equality between man and woman is incompatible with the principle that rights and duties depend on the ends and functions designed in nature. The nature of the family as well as the particular nature of woman point clearly to the family as the first and most important scene of her social activity. Thus, it is certainly a fundamental truth that *the mother's place is in the family.* That the father should be assured the necessary family income (cf. Chap. 72), so that the mother is not obliged to gain an income from work outside or from work within

[1] Cf. Plato, *Republic*, 5, 451.
[2] Aristotle, *Politics*, II, 5, 24.

the home, is therefore a fundamental demand of justice. Exceptions can be justified, as when, to give a concrete example, in a large family with a preponderance of girls money must be earned to provide dowries or to save for a family home and the children are properly cared for during the parents' working hours by grandparents or in children's nurseries. The principle of family well-being, that the mother's place is in the family, also provides the key to conflicts of duties (cf. Chap. 42), for example, if there is a labor shortage in a country as a result of an overexpanded economy. In this case is it compatible with the family good to draw mothers into the labor field, as is attempted by extensive propaganda? The good of the family, depending on the mother's care, undoubtedly takes precedence; it is different in the case of war, when the harnessing of all the forces of the community is necessary to defend the country.

This is something quite different from the simple maxim: woman's place is in the home. The extensive changes in social conditions have assured girls and women (we are now thinking chiefly of unmarried women) *their place in economic life*. Much that was formerly produced at home is now, owing to the modern division of labor, produced in factories, and chiefly by women (e.g., in the textile industry). Moreover, for a number of modern careers women are as suited as men, or more suited, especially since their admission to universities. Thus, today we find women engaged in social welfare work, as teachers, nurses, doctors (especially for women and children), typists, factory inspectors, sanitary inspectors, in libraries and museums, in handicrafts, in art, in scientific research, and in many other spheres. Nor must we forget that in many countries, especially after wars, a large number of women are unable to marry and are obliged to find remunerative work, often without ever feeling full satisfaction in it or ever growing resigned to their celibate lot. But definite reservations apply to the functions of women and girls in industrial life. The kind of work allotted to girls and women should correspond to their nature. This difference includes not only woman's weaker physique in comparison with men, but her entire being, for, as modern psychology assures us, the sex characteristics of woman color her whole personality. Hence, her physical and also her psychical constitution need special consideration. Moreover, the dignity of woman's sex requires careful protection, especially where work in common with men is unavoidable, whether in offices, factories, restaurants, places of amusement, and particularly during night shifts.

If the principle of equivalence is not accepted as the unconditional principle of justice for individual labor contracts, the *payment for women's work* is bound to be the subject of contrary opinions. The principle of equivalence means the due return for services rendered and equal payment for equal services. No collective labor contract may circumvent this principle. The repudiation of this principle is unmistakable wage usury, resting on exploitation of women's work. It is a fact that in most countries of the free world (not to mention the Near East and Far East) the wages of women, on an average, are considerably lower than those of men. The reasons for this are to be sought not only in the employers, but also in the workers, who regard the lower payment for women's work as, to some degree, "natural" in spite of equal services. One reason, of course, why statistics show that women's wages are on an average twenty to thirty per cent lower, is the fact that a great number of women perform unskilled work, because when they were young the facilities or incentive for training were lacking. On the other hand, it must be kept in mind that a too rigidly understood principle of equality of women's work, having regard for services and appropriate wages, results in competition for jobs, which must in many ways cause the overrating of women's inherent potentialities, as well as the disregarding of the kind of work and working hours appropriate for them. Furthermore, such competition could result in the displacement of fathers of families from jobs, especially in a time of underemployment and above all when younger people, as often happens nowadays, are given preference.

Once woman had entered industrial and professional life, it was natural for her to claim her share in public and *political life* by means of the vote. Moreover, the developing consciousness of the equality of human rights for all could only result in the equality of men and women at the poll in modern representative democracy. Universal suffrage, which includes all male and female adults, is established in almost every country of the Western world (up to now Switzerland and Portugal are exceptions). Experience of the effect of women's votes has not been uniform, but on the whole, in times of radical change women seem inclined, as electors, to hold back and to make their vote felt in favor of more conservative policies. The eligibility of women for parliament was another consequence of their entering public life and of universal suffrage in modern democracy.

Our principles lay bare the besetting fallacy of all programs and *movements for indiscriminate equality* between the sexes. They always measure woman in terms of man, whereas in reality neither man nor woman can be judged by the standard of the opposite sex, but both have their own aptitudes and functions by which alone their particular value can be judged.[3] Contrariwise, the individualist mechanistic idea of equality, as well as the predominating capitalistic evaluation of man as "labor force," produced the idea of indiscriminate equality between men and women which largely underlay the feminist movement, including the suffragette movement and the movement for the "emancipation" of women in general. Both liberal and Marxist socialism follow the same idea and further emphasize it by their characteristic demand for the liberation of woman from "compulsory childbearing."[4] The Constitution of the Soviet Union (Art. 122) declares: "Women in the U.S.S.R. are accorded equal rights with men in all spheres of economic, state, cultural, social, and political life."

80. Education for Family Life

We cannot leave the family without touching on the problems of social

[3] Particularly clear on this is Albert Mitterer, "Was ist die Frau?" in *Um die Seele der Frau,* Karl Rudolf, editor, 1953.

[4] Cf. August Bebel, *Die Frau und der Sozialismus,* 1879 (since then over 60 editions).

pedagogy connected with it. As is usual in times of crisis among civilized peoples, today educational problems are in the foreground of discussion in the West. The problem of school reform is an urgent topic in political and social programs in many countries. Imprisoned in individualist and collectivistic ideas, modern pedagogy, in most of its trends, is remote from the spirit of the family idea. Discussion of education for family life is, if present at all, only incidental. Furthermore, in the family movement, which has developed rapidly in European countries in the last few years and which cannot be too highly estimated for its encouragement of family thinking and family policy, there seems in some places to be too little attention paid to education for family life and too great an emphasis placed on the economic side of the family question.

How can the rising generation be trained for family life, to love the family and to fulfill the functions and duties of family life? Among all possible means, the first and by far the best is the family itself. Therefore, the healthy family life that still exists must be utilized to the full and be made the fertile soil of education for family life. Secondly, the family in general must be put into a position to carry out its economic and educational functions. The family will not fulfill its functions as the biological, moral, and cultural cell of society until society again fulfills its duty toward the family. Thirdly, it is indispensable that the family be held in renewed esteem in society and in public life. Just as a man condemns himself if he allows his parents to be publicly disparaged, so also any society that allows marriage and family life to be publicly disparaged condemns itself. Only when a young man sees the family universally respected will he acquire a lasting love for it. Fourthly, the mutual respect of young people of opposite sex for one another is an essential part of education for family life. Nothing destroys this respect and spoils this education more than sexual libertinism. We cannot do more here than stress this point and refer the reader to writers on sex ethics and sex education; perhaps we may also mention Chapters 1 and 2 of our study, *Ethics and Facts.* Fifthly, if the school rightly grasps its social function, it must educate for family life by constantly instilling appreciation of family values, by instructing in housekeeping, and by encouraging thrift and domesticity. Besides this, courses in household management can be immensely useful to young wives and to girls who have left school. Sixthly, as a means of training for family life, we must not forget to emphasize its purpose of companionship. Nowadays the family is split up by clubs and associations, but in every society the family should be incontestably the first "club." Young people especially should meet one another as much as possible in their families, find their amusement there together, play games, enjoy music, literature, and art together, and together keep up the family traditions—in a word, preserve in all their doings their connection with the family, both with their own family and with the families of their friends.

PART TWO

The Lesser Groups

81. The Local Community

Next to the family, the local community is the smallest of the lesser groups that have functions of their own, and therefore rights, within the state community (cf. Chaps. 32, 42). We can see that its function in the daily life of its members, however, surpasses in importance the function of all greater communities if we disregard the maintenance of the juridical order by the state. Yet, persons living in towns are hardly ever conscious of this importance. They take for granted the provision of roads, water, lighting, drainage, clinics, schools, cemeteries, public baths, parks, libraries, and many other services for which the local authority is responsible. The village communities perform these functions by combining with others to constitute regional units.

As may be seen from the examples mentioned, the services proper to the local community fall into two main categories. The first concerns needs on whose fair and adequate satisfaction the greater part of the community depend in their daily life and occupations; these services cannot be left to private enterprise. The second class embraces services in the domain of recreation, hygiene, and cultural life, which are of no interest to private enterprise since they offer no adequate return. Such services relate to the needs that are common to a group living in proximity and that can be satisfied only by their social cooperation. The neighborhood, therefore, is the origin of the social function of the local community.

The social function of the local community establishes its *right to self-government* (autonomy) in the conduct of its own affairs. The delimitation of the spheres of the local community and of the state is not always easy in practice; the principle of subsidiary function provides, however, a firm basis in that the burden of proof of rights which it claims lies with the state. For, the local community has a natural right to self-government in all matters, insofar as its own general interests alone are in question and it is capable of managing them with its own resources. No less clearly established are the rights and spheres of competence of the state. They include, first of all, safeguarding the juridical order, protecting the constitutionally guaranteed rights and freedoms of individuals, of the family, and of the other smaller social units (today, safeguards are necessary against the politically inspired encroachments of municipal authorities). In the second place, it includes the influence exercised by the state in coordinating, directing, and controlling the activities of the local communities, by setting up certain obligatory standards in matters such as health, housing, schools, and welfare services. Thirdly, the administration of municipal finance, including the making of loans, calls for supervision by the state, since it would be at the expense of the great society if municipalities became insolvent through financial mismanagement.

When state legislation began systematically to circumscribe the sphere of municipal self-government in various countries in the course of the last century, the development of the modern centralizing state was already making itself felt. On the other hand, the basic principles and implications of natural law make possible a considerable variety in the forms of local self-government, and therefore allow full account to be taken of historical development.[1]

The experience of local government in free societies and the complex problems of cooperation with the central government indicate the necessity of employing a salaried staff for the administrative and routine work, but placed under the direction and control of elected representatives of the local community. In the rural community, with its relatively simple undertakings, the local administration can carry out the administration with the help of one of its members who has received some training.

Municipal self-government has often been spoken of as a school for training the citizens for active participation in the conduct of state affairs, and thus

[1] In *Germany* local self-government received a decisive impetus from the famous Stein-Hardenberg reform of local administration in Prussia at the beginning of the nineteenth century. The principle was that the authority of the municipal government extends to everything which the municipality is capable of doing in the general interest of its citizens, including their material and intellectual progress, by utilizing the resources available to it. The limiting conditions, therefore, are the general interests of the community and the use of the municipality's own resources to satisfy them. This principle, indeed, came very near to the ideal delimitation of the spheres of state and municipality. From this reform a rich development of public municipal activity in all fields of public interest resulted. The towns created their own social welfare organizations, municipal savings banks, fire insurance societies, municipal theaters, opera houses, picture galleries, and athletic stadiums. In *England,* the municipalities can undertake hardly any such works unless they are empowered in each case by a special Act of Parliament, of which they themselves have to bear the cost. The scope of their autonomy is defined by law, and in comparison with that of the German municipality is far more restricted. In *France,* before the Second World War the communes possessed no autonomy whatever except in trifling matters. Nothing could be done by the local council without the sanction of the Minister of the Interior. The mayor was appointed by the prefect of the *département,* and the latter by the Minister. Centralization was almost complete. For a long time local administration in the *United States* enjoyed such independence that a marked degree of arbitrary action was possible on the part of groups, of parties, or even of individuals. With the growth of the towns, the American municipalities largely went over to government by experts under the control of a body of elected representatives. The central authority possesses relatively slight powers of interference in municipal activity. Such a form of self-government undoubtedly comes very close to the principles we have discussed.

has been considered as the bastion of live democracy. Much can be said for this view, since the citizens' own direct interests are at stake in the municipality; it is the scene of their daily lives and they are charged with its government. Yet, this view is not altogether borne out by experience. The citizen tends to be contented if the municipal services function to his satisfaction and if the taxes and rates are not too high. Any further interest in local administration is the exception. Relatively few are aware that the right to autonomy also carries with it obligations for the citizens. But only when it is sustained by the active interest of the citizens does municipal autonomy continue even to exist. To arouse this interest is a function of civic and political education. A necessary condition for a direct interest seems to be that the larger municipalities should themselves be divided into smaller units possessing their own functions, and that rural district authorities should be allowed some functions worthy of interest.

Lack of interest on the part of the citizens is, however, not the only danger for local autonomy. A still greater danger, the centralizing tendency of the modern state, threatens. This tendency is partly bound up with the changed character and the increasing extent of the functions of the local authority. In education, in social welfare, in health services, the local authority has immensely greater claims to satisfy. The funds required for these functions are notably in excess of the resources of many municipalities. The result is that the state with its financial support extends its controlling powers until the local authorities more and more become merely executive organs of the central authorities.

Collectivistic socialist thought seeks to guide evolution deliberately in this direction, since according to it there is no basis for the social and juridical pluralism which is constitutive of the natural order of society. For, as *Laski* maintains, in strict theory no reason exists for the necessary functions of government not being discharged by a single authority with the help of local officials.[2] If Professor *Laski,* nevertheless, finds many convincing reasons for the self-government of local communities and earnestly recommends them, he is unwittingly showing anew that in this as in other points the socialistic theory is at variance with reality. There is but one remedy in free society against the constant tendency of the state to extend its competence: the local communities must learn to defend their own autonomy and responsibility. In this sphere almost more than in any other the familiar truth holds good, that freedom must be vigilantly defended if it is to exist. Only if the citizens are vigorously aware of the special functions of their communities and of the special responsibilities and rights attached to them, will they be able to remain master in their own house in face of the increasing centralizing tendencies in the present-day state. Clearly, then, the principle of subsidiary function, which is in question, not only implies an obligation for the political authority but also for the citizen: everywhere to defend the rights which are endangered by an encroaching state.

82. The Regional Unit

The large modern territorial state is subdivided as a rule into regional units: the United States in America; the Länder in Germany and Austria;

[2] Cf. H. J. Laski, *A Grammar of Politics,* 1941, p. 410.

Scotland, Wales, Northern Ireland, and England in Great Britain; the republics in Soviet Russia. Among the factors responsible for such subdivision of big states, psychological factors are not the least important. The love of home and kin, the familiar landscape and all that leads to regional patriotism are elements which cause great national and territorial states to be parceled out into provinces. Thus, France means something different to the man from Auvergne and to the man from Normandy. Secondly, strong interests of a practical nature are factors in the cooperation of local communities in large neighborhoods. The regional unit can supply essential services to the whole area far beyond the capacity of the local communities individually. Transport facilities of all kinds, electric light and power supply, hospitals, universities and other higher educational establishments have in the past been largely based on the effort of the regional unit.

At the same time the regional unit has a third function: the reconciling of the conflicting interests of town and country. The concentration in the town of most of the services and institutions mentioned above, the centralization of commercial life, the convergence of traffic routes, the possession by the town of educational and cultural centers such as libraries, theaters, musical enterprises, art galleries, amusements, the higher social standards of living and working conditions, all these give the town and its inhabitants attractive advantages. The surrounding country, on the other hand, carries the burden of supplying the town with food, often under unfavorable transport or economic conditions, unfavorable conditions of work, and unfavorable conditions for higher education. In the capital city of the regional unit the provincial offices of the regional and state administration are located. Hence, the country is placed somewhat at a disadvantage in comparison with the cities. To bring about a just balance is one of the most important functions of the regional self-governing body.

Nearly always in the history of territorial states the regional units have formed the strongest defensive bulwark against the efforts of large political organizations to extend their powers. To be sure, history itself offers evidence that slowly, but irresistibly, those forces have prevailed which led to the unified great state with its far-reaching concentration of powers. These forces were power politics, economics, and a fiscal policy, but national consciousness and cultural factors also played their part. Today, the regional units have become one of the last strong bulwarks against a permanent overexpansion of the state's power and competence, which proceed from forces of a collectivistic nature in present-day society. They have this position and the resulting responsibility because they embody in themselves a large proportion of the citizens, and are therefore able to protect their autonomous rights effectively, not merely by making protests. The natural law principle of federalism (cf. Chap. 32) involved here, is one of the decisive principles determining the order of state subsidiarity. The organs of regional autonomy are chiefly the regional representative and legislative bodies, and formed from them the separate administrative services. The objection of double working and double costs is an illusory argument, as the experience of totalitarian states proves. Not only is the centralization of all authority accompanied by a powerful growth of administrative bureaucracy in general and especially in the "provinces," but there are no checks on central protection of provincial bureaucracy and its false decisions.

83. The Ethnico-Cultural Group

We shall discuss here groups whose members are united by blood, language, and cultural and natural bonds within a state community. The term "nationality," as applied to the Scottish or the Welsh groups within the United Kingdom, is often used synonymously with nation. But in the sense just mentioned it denotes a smaller group which is distinct from a political nation and forms part of it. In a similar sense the Westphalians, Bavarians, Prussians, Saxons, and the other ethnico-cultural groups called *Stämme* were always thought to be units in themselves within the political unity of the German nation. *Stamm* denotes a federal element within a larger whole, just as does the idea of nationality in the sense pointed out above.

The binding factors of such ethnico-cultural groups are ties of blood, common dialect or language, common historical experience and natural milieu, common local patriotism and modes of life. The picturesque and live quality of dialect as compared with the standard language reveals how much more the people think in it and are at home in it, and hence feel conscious of a closer unity by comparison with other groups of the wider nation. To a considerable extent it is through the use of dialect that the other factors mentioned exercise their power for building up a community and obtain the position of original values in the life of the ethnico-cultural group.

Ties of family, home, custom, and tradition, which unite the ethnico-cultural group, are primary communal values. They form a substantial element in the immediate human surroundings, which, as social biology and cultural anthropology tell us, are vital for the development of personality and provide the indispensable milieu for the sound development of human nature. Hence, the cultivation of those values is closely related to the existential ends; it constitutes a social function, and therefore a natural right for such ethnico-cultural groups.

The ethnico-cultural unit also has a function of its own toward the political community as a whole. The culture of a nation will preserve its vitality and vigor only as long as its roots remain embedded in the natural soil. The cultural sterility of the big town is due in part to its severance from these sources. Indeed, the ethnico-cultural community lives its fruitful and distinctive life principally on the land. The big town is a product of the uniformity imposed upon life by modern technical and industrial civilization. To a large extent it dictates to the whole people their mode and conduct of life. This again prepares the ground for the development of the mass society, the collectivization of its life, and the centralization of its administration. All of this cuts through vital arteries in the life of the ethnico-cultural groups.

The conceptions of the regional unit and the ethnico-cultural group may be found to overlap when applied to the analysis of a concrete political society. The significance of the ethnico-cultural bonds affords a further argument for the principle of federalism with its implications for the structure of a large society such as the modern territorial state. The right of the ethnico-cultural community to its own life is primarily the right to self-administration. Therefore, the desire to restrict autonomy to the cultural sphere would certainly be unrealistic, since without its own political rights the ethnico-cultural unit has no guarantee that it can withstand the desire of the central authority of the federated state to extend its rights and competence. If this principle regarding the status of the ethnico-cultural unit is recognized, then the question of the way in which it should be constituted as a self-governing body is of secondary importance. The concrete solution largely depends on historical factors and on the vigor of the group's will to self-assertion. The position of Scotland in the United Kingdom and the movement there to extend the sphere of its autonomy, as well as the similar efforts in Wales, show that the advocates of federalism are as yet by no means willing to leave the way clear for centralism. In Germany the national-socialist totalitarian state could not crush the forces bringing about the re-emergence of the *Länder*. After the Second World War the federalist structure at once re-established itself in Germany.

84. Minorities

Owing to the predominance of the national idea in the political thought of the nineteenth century and of the recent past, the minority problem is generally thought of in terms of *national* minorities. Until the nineteenth century, from the time of the Treaties of Augsburg (1555) and Westphalia (1648), the minorities which regularly figure in the provisions of international treaties are "*religious*" minorities. On the other hand, the assumption that freedom of worship should be a fundamental right of all citizens, constitutionally guaranteed, was taken so much for granted in most civilized countries that there seemed to be no pressing need for further discussion about religious minorities in state documents. The question of "*linguistic*" minorities is likewise one that had been settled in the constitutions of most civilized communities. Such minorities (e.g., the

German-speaking or Italian-speaking citizens of the United States) do not form groups in the sense of national minorities; they enjoy all the civil rights which they require for the pursuit of their own distinctive cultural values.

The problem of true national minorities arose with the trend toward nationalism and reached the climax of its development with the principle of national self-determination, which inspired the peace treaties after the First World War. This principle applies individualistic thinking to the collective unity of the national whole. Gradually at first, and indeed only during the course of the Second World War, it was realized how the historical tragedy of Europe and the world was bound up with this principle. The most far-reaching outcome of the *principle of national self-determination* was the breaking up of the political structure of the Austro-Hungarian Empire. Today, no one can doubt that if this political union had continued, National-Socialist Germany could not have convulsed the basis of European order to such an extent, and that the incursion of Russia into the very heart of Europe could not have taken place. The principle of national self-determination was also appealed to by National-Socialist Germany in her efforts to incorporate the German minorities from all the neighboring states. With the end of the Second World War there came the anticlimax to this untenable principle. Not only was there scant consideration for minorities, but whole nations were dealt with without any regard for human rights and for rights of national self-determination, but were left to the "spheres of interest" of the great powers, as if the world had never been inflamed by the idea of national self-determination. Indeed, the problem of minorities was disposed of after the Second World War by the barbarous method of wholesale, indiscriminate deportation. All the great efforts that had been made hitherto to find a solution in accordance with the standards of a civilization inspired by moral principles seemed to be forgotten. One such solution of minority questions, which was not advocated as a principle and method of solving the minority problem even by the barbarian peoples known to us, is *genocide,* that is to say, the extermination of unwanted racial, national, religious, and political groups. The original rights of these minority groups as such and primal human rights, such as the right to life, inviolability of the person, religious and moral convictions, by this means have been sacrificed to political interests.

A national minority may be *defined* as a group united by ethnical cultural bonds, occupying a common territory, and forming part of a political community; because of these bonds it is often akin to the dominant nationality of a neighboring political community. In order to settle the question of who belongs to the minority in national frontier areas, a problem which, as experience shows, can lead to great difficulties in estimating the claim of an area to minority status, there is one sure criterion: the language spoken in the family circle. This criterion was successfully applied by the League of Nations.* To provide minorities with the possibility of direct appeal to the organized community of nations and of obtaining definite action if a representative portion of a minority wishes to raise a complaint about a violation of internationally established rights, seems an indispensable step toward a genuine solution of the minority problem.

A minority is entitled to autonomy insofar as it is necessary for its functions as a community for material and cultural purposes. Common descent, communal life, common speech, tradition, and culture in a large group constitute not only a bond of unity but a vital soil for nurturing the whole personality of its members. They are therefore functions bound up with the existential ends, upon which is based the right of the minority to make fruitful by suitable institutions the values implied in those factors for the life of the group and of its members. This constitutes cultural autonomy, an expression intended to differentiate the autonomy of a minority from the full political autonomy of, for example, a federal state.

The cultural autonomy of a minority comprises the following three main groups of rights: 1) The right to equality with the majority in the enjoyment of all civil rights guaranteed by the constitution, including the rights to protection of life, to personal freedom, to free practice of religion, to free exercise of political rights, such as the right of suffrage, freedom of association and of assembly; the right to possess their own press and publishing houses. 2) The right to free use of the mother tongue in private life, in public worship, at public meetings, in press and literature, in communication with the authorities in the area, in schools and other educational institutions, the right to the homeland, that is, the undisturbed possession of the common territory on which the minority lives, and to the cultivation of all the ethnico-cultural values which have just been referred to. 3) The right to a proportionate share in the funds made available by state and local authority for religious, social, economic, educational and charitable purposes; the right to a proportionate share of official posts in the state administration in the minority regions. As long as the

* The peace treaties after 1918 contained two fundamental clauses affecting national minorities. In the first place, they gave the minorities a political status in the organized community of nations by defining their rights. Secondly, they guaranteed this status by declaring the right of intervention on the part of the organized community of nations. The political status given to the minorities meant that their rights were no longer merely a matter for the good will of the state in which they lived, but were anchored in positive international law. A minority could, in cases where it considered its rights infringed, bring a complaint before the League Council, submitting it at the same time to the government of its own state. However, the Council was not considered to be officially cognizant of the matter until one of its own members laid the complaint before it. Yet, not even then was the Council obliged to take any definite steps; everything, including appeal to the Permanent International Court, was left to its discretion. Only the states affected by the peace treaties after the First World War were bound by the above-mentioned regulations; nothing essentially new was produced after the Second World War.

minority is not represented in administrative posts, a hostile national majority can easily make the constitutional rights of a minority ineffectual.

85. The Occupational Group

The organization of society into occupational groups is much more highly developed in capitalistic society than the class structure of that society would lead one to expect. We must not seek for it, however, with an eye that is accustomed to the guild organizations of the Middle Ages. A great number of modern occupational corporations in all civilized countries, however, such as those of craft guilds, universities, doctors, and lawyers do go back to the tradition of the Middle Ages. Capitalistic society has given birth to new occupational bodies, such as joint industrial committees and councils, in which representatives of large occupational bodies, stratified on a class basis, combine together to settle matters of common interest. These new beginnings, which in themselves are contrary to the capitalistic class dynamism, show that natural forces in society as everywhere assert themselves in spite of all adverse circumstances. The individualist liberals and the Marxian socialists were likewise unable for a long time to reconcile themselves to the idea that, contrary to their respective deterministic theories of the struggle of interests in unrestricted competition and in unrestricted class warfare, the employers and workers should be ready to take the initiative toward mutual understanding. But the resistance of orthodox liberalism and Marxism was unable to stay the development of the collective agreement as an instrument of understanding between the two sides of industry.

With collective bargaining and collective agreement, however, the development toward the occupational organization of society has not reached its term. Indeed, the International Labor Conference (twenty-sixth session in Philadelphia, 1944) set a much wider task for the collaboration of employers and workers, namely, "the cooperation of management and labor in the continuous improvement of productive efficiency, and the collaboration of workers and employers in the preparation and application of social and economic measures." [1] In England, after the Second World War we find the Regional Production Boards, constituted on the joint body principle; in the United States certain features of the New Deal movement; in some other countries (we name only countries of such different political atmospheres as Switzerland, Portugal, Brazil, Austria, Ireland) we find a movement toward, or at least a strong interest in, democratic (as opposed to fascist) corporatism. It is not too much to say that with the development of the measures for joint negotiation, most of the organizational elements for the development of occupational, industrial,

[1] *Official Bulletin, International Labor Office,* Vol. XXVI, 1, June, 1944, p. 3.

and, in general, economic self-government are already in existence.[2]

In order to inquire into the nature and function of the occupational group, it is perhaps best to start from the indisputable *democratic principle* that all who contribute to the economic and cultural welfare of the community should be entitled in equal measure to participate in the forming of decisions on matters directly affecting them. This contribution is not made by individuals as such but by social groups, for the community is supplied with various commodities and services by particular groups in society, for example, the agricultural community, various branches of industry, the teaching profession, publishers, provision merchants—in short, vocational groups including employers *and* employees. Their members are bound together within the framework of social cooperation by their social functions, and thus form a *vocational group* to meet the demands of the members of the greater society.

An occupation or vocation is the economic activity of the individual by which he participates in social cooperation. From both aspects, the social and the personal, occupational work is closely bound up with the existential ends. From one aspect there is social cooperation, from the other the taking part in the exercise of a social function by the members of the community to obtain their livelihood and to secure the material basis for the attainment of their essential tasks founded on the existential ends. Indeed, the significance of his occupational work for the development of man's self may be seen from the mere fact that it occupies a considerable portion of his lifetime. On the other hand, countless persons are compelled to earn their livelihood in work that is uninteresting and often of inferior value. But even the scavenger may be conscious of accomplishing a socially indispensable task. This is what gives nobility to all work. The Christian sees a still further moral and religious nobility in work as vocation. In the natural abilities and environment that prescribe the way the individual can contribute to social cooperation, the Christian sees the will of the Creator.[3] Because it is bound up with so wide a field of social

[2] On all problems dealt with in this section, cf. J. Messner, *Die berufständische Ordnung*, 1936, which may be described as a comprehensive theory of the occupational organization from its legal, political, economic, and social aspects (with extensive bibliography). Cf. also, *Report of the Commission on Vocational Organization* (Dublin), 1943. On ideas and endeavors in the U.S.A. cf. P. S. Land, S.J., and G. P. Klubertanz, S.J., "Practical Reason, Social Fact, and the Vocational Order," in *The Modern Schoolman*, Vol. XXVIII, 1951, pp. 239–66. For further literature cf. P. Berkenkopf, *Aufgaben und Aufbau einer berufsständischen Ordnung*, 1948; M. Simonett, *Die berufsständische Ordnung und die Politik*, 1951; O. v. Nell-Breuning, *Wirtschaft und Gesellschaft*, Vol. I, 1956, pp. 219–305.

[3] Max Weber, *Gesammelte Aufsätze zur Religionssoziologie*, 1920, has made the idea of vocation the central point of his well-known and fruitful investigations into the history of the origin of modern capitalism. His critics have rightly objected, however, that he links the genesis of the idea of vocation too closely with Calvinist ethics, and hence does not do justice to the great power of the idea as an influence molding society, as it was fully developed in the medieval guild system (on pre-Calvinist times cf. W. Schwer, *Stand und Ständeordnung im Weltbild des Mittelalters*, 1934).

and personal existential ends, including the moral and religious ends, vocational work must form a substantial part of personal self-fulfillment. The fact that, for the most part, this is not the case in industrial society is one of the chief reasons for the crises in its development up to the present day. The aim of a vocational order is to make provision for the comprehensive fulfillment of man's social and economic existence by a change in the social system.

Given the social function of the vocational group in modern society (as we have illustrated by examples), *vocation becomes the natural principle of organization in the market community.* The social function of the group establishes communal interests and communal responsibilities on the part of all those concerned in it. The knowledge of this responsibility has often enough proved decisive for the peaceful settlement of disputes between capital and labor in individual branches of industry: for the sake of the general interest both sides in an industry have been prepared to strive to maintain production in spite of all conflicts of interest. Thus, an industry recognizes that it is responsible as a whole for providing the community with the goods which it is its social function to produce. Undoubtedly it would be unrealistic to ignore the fact that interest is the immediate driving force of both organized labor and organized capital. But this itself demands an awareness of responsibility, for the workers find that in the long run they can secure satisfactory and increasing wages only if their branch of industry prospers as a whole and is well able to hold its own within the framework of the national and international economy. Similarly, the employers tell themselves that the prosperity of their undertakings depends substantially on the social contentment of their workers and their active interest in the productivity of their labor.

Thus, we find a double *responsibility on the part of the vocational community* with regard to its place within the framework of social cooperation: first, responsibility for proper effort in the service of the greater society, which means productivity in both quantity and quality; secondly, responsibility for its own members, which means, on the one hand, insuring due participation by the whole occupational group in the fruits of social productivity and, on the other hand, insuring an income from the united efforts of the vocational community proportionate to the respective interests of property and labor. This double responsibility assigns to the vocational community special competencies, its *autonomy,* and its self-government, throughout the whole range of regulations necessary for the fulfillment of the tasks implied in this responsibility. The connection of this double responsibility with man's existential ends is self-evident from what has already been said: man fulfills an essential social task by participating in social cooperation, and fulfills an essential personal task by gaining, through this participation, the means of subsistence. Responsibility for the fulfillment of essential tasks, which originate in individual and social existential ends, establishes, as we have seen (cf. Chap. 35), natural rights, in this case the rights of the vocational communities.

To prevent misunderstanding, let us trace the *limits of this autonomy* more closely. Since the state must see that all activities and efforts of groups are consistent with the general interest, this function devolves upon it with regard to the various vocational communities. The political ordering power (legislative and administrative) must first see that the vocational groups do not simply act as mere interest associations; otherwise, contrary to social justice, the stronger ones would undoubtedly know how to secure their advantage at the expense of the weaker. In order to be capable of fulfilling this function, the state must be set free from its present dependence on the will of interest groups. This dependence, as we shall show (cf. Chap. 116), portends a great danger for democracy; we shall also show (cf. Chap. 134) that only the occupational order offers the key for this apparently essential task in the political sphere. Thus, the autonomy of the vocational community is restricted by the political ordering function. On the other hand, it is restricted by the rights of its subgroups, capital and labor, to preserve their own interests. These groups remain wholly entitled to form associations, trade unions, and employers' federations for the safeguarding of their interests. Further, these subgroups would have the right to combine with similar organizations for the purpose of mutual support, just as trade unions and employers' federations at the present time combine on a national basis. Lastly, the right to strike as a last resort must be assured. The vocational organization of society will, of course, within its sphere of self-government, create organs and institutions that will make possible the peaceful settlement of disputes on the principle of equal rights for employers and workers. Such a machinery of conciliation and arbitration working according to absolutely democratic methods will make trials of strength like strikes and lockouts less promising as means of settling social disputes, since their use might not be endorsed by public opinion in view of the possibility of avoiding them and their serious effects.

In fact, democratic corporatism, or, to use another expression, socially integrated democracy ("integral democracy"), seeks to *raise labor to the full status of a principle of order in society and economic life.* Individualist liberalism had made property, indeed capital property, the decisive ordering principle in economy and society; it considered dependent labor as a commodity and as a means of production in the service of capital and its profit interest. The socialist, on the contrary, thinks chiefly of the social function of labor. He thinks the solution to the social problem is to be found by securing for labor exclusive control over the whole social process; this would be based on collective ownership of the means of production as well as state planning and control of the whole economy. In such a system, however, labor would remain as rigidly planned as in the capitalistic economy; the individual worker in the socialistic economy cannot have any direct share and responsibility in the running of the social process and in determining the fulfillment of its ends. Only such a coresponsibility and control could free labor from being a factor of production, planned, directed, and controlled by others, and could secure for the worker the fulfillment of his own self through his occupation; that is, he would have the knowledge that he fulfills a function in his own interest as well as in the interest of society through his direct participation in the direction and success of the economic process. The vocational order provides the conditions for this. It makes it possible for the worker to engage his personality in the whole sphere of his occupational work. This is the problem which socialism has not grasped and cannot solve with its form of administrative centrally planned economy. The reason is that the socialization of the means of production places all power in the hands of the central planning and controlling administration. Labor remains planned and controlled like the capital appropriated to the state. The direct coresponsibility and voice of the worker in the social process presupposes the equality of labor, with property as a regulative principle in the national economy; hence, it insures parity in self-government for employers and employees within the occupational groups. This would mean the realization of integral democracy.

The foundation of occupational self-government is the *principle of parity between workers and employers* in the arrangement of all matters of common interest: the two parties work together on an equal footing. What is decisive is not the number of heads on either side but an equality of status between the two separate groups—employers and workers—in settling their common affairs. By this principle of parity joint committees for collective bargaining regulate such matters today. The management of the enterprise does not itself come within the sphere of matters of direct common interest; rather, this remains the concern of the employer.

A *matter of common concern* to the vocational groups is *prices* in the various branches of industry and in the national economy as a whole. The general welfare is best secured when competition fulfills its social function and prices move toward minimum cost level; for then the purchasing power of consumers' wages tends to rise. To work unremittingly toward the realization of the social function of competition is therefore one of the most important functions of self-government in the society organized along vocational lines. This task should be performed by committees drawn from all groups directly interested in the competitive situation concerning a particular price with parity of representation between workers and employers. In no sense is this a matter of competition control by price-fixing; on the contrary, it is keeping the prices moving through competition in order to maintain the optimum social productivity. Price-fixing was the method of governmental price control during and after the two World Wars. Today, fixing of prices by interest groups largely governs the economy. Against both forms of price-fixing, only a competition that is fulfilling its social function should determine prices. It fulfills this function insofar as it functions according to the basic general social principle: as much freedom as possible, as much restriction as necessary. The control of competition is necessary in order to provide the optimum social and economic productivity. Every kind of harmful competition by price-cutting, therefore, is incompatible with this. Equally incompatible is the curtailment of competition by price-fixing, which restricts production. To safeguard the social function of competition against both is a basic function of the vocational community in its contribution toward the optimum realization of the social end of economy, namely, the fullest satisfaction of the needs of the community out of its supply of raw materials and labor forces, in accordance with the demands of social justice. This basic function of uniting labor and property in sharing equal responsibility and influence in price formation and wage structure is the decisive advance of the vocational order over the liberalist and socialistic economic and social orders. But it is also this function which, and this is of great significance, coordinates the particular interest of the individual vocational group with the general interest of the community, since it is brought into harmony with the social end of the economy as a whole. All this will be discussed in detail when we deal with the economic order (cf. Chap. 181).

Thus, we should *attain to a social and economic order such as the one described by J. M. Keynes:*

> I believe that in many cases the ideal size for the unit of control and organization lies somewhere between the individual and the modern state. I suggest, therefore, that progress lies in the growth and the recognition of semi-autonomous bodies within the state—bodies whose criterion of action within their own field is solely the public good as they understand it, and from whose deliberations motives of private advantage are excluded, although some place it may still be necessary to leave, until the ambit of men's altruism grows wider, to the separate advantage of particular groups, classes, or faculties—bodies which in the ordinary course of affairs are mainly autonomous within their prescribed limitations, but are subject in the last resort to the sovereignty of the democracy expressed through Parliament. I propose a return, it may be said, towards medieval conceptions of separate autonomies. But, in England at any rate, corporations are a mode of government which has never ceased to be important and is sympathetic to our institutions.[4]

What would be the *spheres of self-government* in a developed vocational organization of society? Again, we try to derive them from elements which in substance can already be found in various existing occupational organizations or functional bodies.

Self-government would be concerned with the following aims:

1. The securing of social peace by *collective agreements* to regulate wages

[4] J. M. Keynes, *The End of Laissez Faire*, 1926, pp. 41 f.

and other conditions of work in each occupation, as well as by conciliation and arbitration in labor disputes.

2. The *advancement of industry* through the setting up of functional bodies for "the cooperation of management and labor in the continuous improvement of productive efficiency," as the above-mentioned Philadelphia Declaration of the International Labor Conference puts it.

3. The carrying out of tasks of *social policy* within the framework of the state's social legislation with respect to the conditions of the particular industry: "The preparation and application of social and economic measures," in the words of the Declaration.

4. In the sphere of *economic policy,* the control of the economy by securing the fulfillment of the social function of competition, which, as already pointed out, would be one of the chief objects of self-government in an economy organized on a vocational basis.

5. The cultivation of a sense of *professional responsibility and honor* among the members of the industry or profession, without which none of the individual and social tasks in the occupational life could be carried out in accordance with the actual demands.

6. The exercise of limited *judicial powers* in matters of professional conduct. Some professional organizations, such as the medical and legal professions. already exercise such powers in many countries, often including the power of striking members off the professional register.

7. *Vocational education,* including not only the necessary training but also further occupational education for adults. Both would equally promote personal ability and interest in the work, in its productivity, in the general interest as well as the ability of the individuals to take their full part in the functions of occupational self-government.

8. The institution of a *charter* by each occupational group as a legal basis for the performance of all these functions of self-government within the framework of the coordinating measures taken by the state.

Simultaneously with the extending *self-government* of occupational organizations there must be a substantial curtailment of the spheres of competence and excessive bureaucracy of the modern *state administration.* To reverse the development toward state omnipotence and omnicompetence, so dangerous to free society and genuine democracy, would be one of the most important fruits of a democratic corporatism. Indeed, to leave the hypertrophied state administration unchanged while opening up self-government to the occupational organizations would be to increase the evil and the complication instead of curing it. Above all, a very great part of what is done today by so-called delegated legislation, which is one of the chief means for the exercise of uncontrolled authority by the government (cf. Chaps. 134–39), must be handed over to the self-governing vocational bodies, because it is they which are very often concerned with the details and application of such ministerial decrees, so prevalent today. For the period of transition, the most natural step seems to be to form advisory committees made up of representatives of the vocational organizations to collaborate with the government departments to which these powers are delegated, and thus to exercise the necessary influence.

A strong deterrent to interest in the vocational organization of society appears in the doctrinaire efforts of some of its advocates who present detailed elaborations of schemes involving hosts of organizations and institutions. In fact, however, this problem has long been solved in practice. In all civilized countries we find a far-reaching parallelism in occupational organizations. Nature itself, as it takes effect in social reality, here too shows the way. The solution is to be found in the various actual social services and functions which mark off the occupational organizations from one another. The pattern of these functions corresponds primarily with the pattern of the developing needs of commodities and services in society and the occupational groups connected with them. Today, there are organizations of trades and crafts: bakers, shoemakers, hairdressers; in the professions, doctors and lawyers; in industry, employers' associations and trade unions, which parallel one another (the associations of the two sides in the coal, iron, and textile industries); of more recent development, the organizations of engineers, accountants, dentists, and journalists. The occupational groups which are organized into separate associations of employers and workers will form functional bodies for the purpose of attending to their common concerns. Here again reality shows the way in the already developed method of collective bargaining.

The development of modern society also offers sufficient indications for the *general pattern of the principal groupings* of vocational communities. One need only observe how the state administration has been divided into departments which are almost exactly parallel in all civilized countries and which correspond to the natural divisions of activity in the life of the community. Even such a novel experiment in organizing society as that made by Soviet Russia has followed the same scheme in substance. The pattern must, then, be founded on reality itself. Its main branches are these: defense, civil service, education, agriculture and forestry, industry, trade, commerce, transport, finance, and health. In this connection, it may be well to note that the occupational organization of society extends no less to the cultural sphere (universities, teachers, press, artists, and so on) than to the economic and, within this, no less to agriculture and the crafts than to manufacturing industry, by which we have chiefly exemplified its pattern and working. Along with all this the provincial economic and cultural differences are to be taken into consideration.

To sum up, we may set out *four principles for the organization* of modern society into vocational branches. In the first place, the division and further subdivision must start from the existing organizations; it must not adhere to a preconceived, artificial scheme. The second formative principle is that any such scheme must be based on the ordering functions which are already exercised by the individual occupational groups, such as those found in the joint committees in industry; similar functional bodies may easily be developed for other branches of economic life. On the whole, organizations of this kind must form, as it were, a framework for such functions of the individual groups rather than force a doctrinaire pattern on society. Thirdly, the focal center of occupational autonomy lies in regional groups, and in large towns in local groups, or even in the big economic unit, but not in central, national boards. The principal spheres of operation of these last-named are: the provision of courts of appeal for the former in conciliation and arbitration cases; the appointment of representative committees to collaborate with the state legislature and administration; the establishment of statistical and other research centers in the interest of the whole national group. Fourthly, the vocational organization of a society as a whole must be elastic and adaptable to the progressively increasing complexity of needs and of production: it must leave room for subdivisions as they are required when new industries or professions are evolved (like the radio industry out of the electrical industry).

The Difference between Modern and Medieval Corporatism . .

The similarity between his recommendations and the medieval guild system, to which *Keynes* refers in the previously quoted passage, relates chiefly to the corporative principle as such and to the principle of self-government associated with it. In considering medieval and modern forms and functions, however, the difference is so great that it must be considered comparable only with the changes from medieval to modern society and economy. The difference is many-sided.

1. An occupational organization of modern society, as a means of realizing socially integrated democracy, would stand in the closest relationship with modern political democracy, which it would thus substantially complement, although it would also have a strong counterpoise in political democracy. Obviously this can be of the greatest advantage to both, if occupational self-government and political authority balance each other. This they can do if vocational self-government is strong and if at the same time political authority is strong enough to subordinate the special interests of the vocational groups to the general interest. The political parliament will then be able to concentrate on the general interest and the interest of the state, since the institutions and representative bodies of the vocational organizations, including a central economic chamber, will promote the satisfaction and the reconciliation of group interests. The immense advantages of such a shifting of functions for the further development of political democracy are evident: it makes it possible to base parties and Parliament on the best minds of the nation instead of on the representatives of particular group interests. Here we approach a problem which *de Tocqueville* has described as a vital problem of modern democracy (cf. Chap. 134), the solution of which cannot be found in formal democracy, but presupposes its evolution to integral democracy in the vocational order. On the other hand, in a vocational order there is the danger that the financially and numerically stronger occupational groups will seek to press their special interests at the expense of weaker groups. Therefore, a state authority is necessary, one strong enough to deal with this danger, against which democratic corporatism is not more secure than any other form of democratic institution.

2. The dualism of capital and labor, caused by the development of production technique, forms another important difference between the medieval and the modern ideas of corporatism. This is certain to result in the separate organization of the two sides of industry in order to safeguard their respective interests. This difference of character will be further accentuated by the principle of complete parity in the working of the machinery for the harmonizing of these interests, a feature hardly developed at all in the medieval guild system. The main concern of the medieval journeyman was to become a master

craftsman, and the major social difficulties of the guild system were due to the fact that the apprentice often did not become a journeyman (and hence could not found a family), and also that on account of the closed guild he had no prospect at all of ever becoming a master. In modern society, it is obviously a task for democratic corporatism to secure for the worker the status of a full member of the body to whose system of social cooperation he contributes, and thus to bring about full social equality in a socially integrated democracy.

3. The third difference lies in the fact that the decisive control of the economic system in the medieval town was in the hands of the masters, who formed the main body of the guilds. Modern democratic corporatism, however, would give labor a footing equal to that of property as a formative principle in social economy, thereby assuring to labor an equal voice in the control of the economic process, as we have indicated above.

4. The medieval guild could close its doors to new masters and thus prevent the exercise of a trade. The surplus population in the towns of the Middle Ages was mostly diverted to colonial territories in the east of Europe (Austria and Prussia) and to overseas trade. The modern economic system, to a far greater degree, must provide room for the increase in the working population by internal economic growth, thereby extending the division of labor. The occupational organization of the present day must, therefore, in principle remain open to new enterprise and employment. This principle necessitates an elasticity of organizational structure in modern corporatism which was utterly foreign to the medieval structure. The latter was static in its nature. Modern corporatism should be dynamic and should create the social conditions needed to enable technical and industrial progress to minister to the greatest good of the community. The monopoly problem is closely connected with this. By "closing the guild" the masters in the Middle Ages could set up a guild monopoly. The motive was basically the same as that which leads to industrial cartels and monopolies today: to secure a certain income by excluding competition. It would be a primary function of a modern vocationally organized society to control the formation of monopolistic bodies and to guarantee freedom of competition. Not that it should be forbidden to form cartels, insofar as they are in the general interest. Competition would be ordered as well as safeguarded by a control exercised according to a parity of representation, as we have indicated above. Ordered economic freedom would thus be the basic feature of such a democratic corporatism.

5. In modern democratic corporatism, as in the medieval, the agreed rules would be automatically binding upon the entire occupational group; and all of its members, both employers and employees, would have to contribute toward the expenses of their respective organizations. Through the joint bodies, the agreed will of the vocational group as a whole would be established. But whether the individuals take a more active part in the business of their union or association depends to a much greater extent than in the Middle Ages on their own individual decision. The right to vote in the election of the leaders and managing officials of the unions and associations would, however, be conditional upon membership in these organizations. Such indirect pressure toward active participation in forming the will of the vocational group is not undesirable in the interest of a vigorous social democracy. Those, however, who exclude

themselves from participation remain bound by the agreements and rules reached by the joint bodies, just as in political democracy every citizen is bound by the laws of the state, even when he is not a member of a party and has not taken part in electing the legislative body.

The Difference between Democratic and Fascist Corporatism

Our discussion of the occupational organization of society must not be concluded without laying stress on the absolute difference between a democratic corporatism as described here and the fascist corporatism of Italy between the two wars. Reduced to a brief formula, the difference may be expressed thus: In fascist corporatism the vocational organizations are organs of the state administration; in democratic corporatism they are self-governing bodies. For fascist corporatism the occupational organization of society is a means of subordinating society to the totalitarian political authority; for democratic corporatism it is a means of realizing integral democracy in a free society. The ideological basis of fascist corporatism consists in the principles of the "immanence of the state in the individual" [5] and the "identification of society with the state." [6]

These principles, with their rejection of the dualism of state and society, do not permit of any individual autonomy of vocational or occupational organizations. This does not prevent their receiving a limited and delegated autonomy as instruments of state government. Against the attempts of some jurists and sociologists in fascist Italy to secure for corporations the theoretical status of a juridical personality and hence an original right to autonomy, the decree (of June 1st, 1926, Art. 43) regulating the execution of the law on the collective settlement of labor questions (of April 3rd, 1926) positively declares: "The corporation has no legal personality, but is an organ of the state administration." This is made more precise in Article 46: "The corporative organ is in every respect dependent upon the Minister of Corporations." The *Carta del Lavoro* (1927) further states: "The corporations form the unitary organization of productive forces and represent the totality of their interests. In virtue of this complete representation and because these interests of production are national interests, the corporations are justly recognized as state organs." *Bottai* explained: "The syndicate multiplies its power in the state, although only yesterday it was arming itself against the state or obligingly offered its cooperation under certain definite conditions. The whole originality of fascist syndicalism lies in this: the state absorbs the syndical function into its sphere of authority without destroying it or allowing itself to be dominated by it." [7] By reason of the totalitarian claim of the state, on the principle of the identity of state and society, the occupational organization of society inevitably became what fascist corporatism meant to make it: an instrument for the domination of society and of economy by the state. On the other hand, the aim of democratic corporatism is to be the support of political democracy by means of socially integrated democracy.

[5] G. Gentile, *Origini e dottrina del Fascismo*, 3rd ed., 1934, p. 51.
[6] G. Bottai, *Grundprinzipien des korporativen Aufbaues in Italien*, 1933, p. 6.
[7] *Ibid.*, p. 21.

86. Class

Is class merely a faulty development in society, as is sometimes assumed by Christian social reformers? Is there only a destructive idea of class, as in Marxian theory, or is there also a constructive idea of class? A glance at history shows that in almost every stage in the development of any society we find class antagonisms. If we turn to the Psalms, we can see that the people of Israel were not without their socially repressed stratum. In the ancient state, which was based on slavery, the antagonisms reach their climax in the slave uprisings. In the medieval town the journeymen rise against the masters in strikes and even in bloody revolts. In the feudal system we find the classes of landlords and serfs. In capitalistic society employers and employees, bourgeoisie and proletariat, are divided by class interests. This fact indicates that class antagonism must be something more than the consequence of a particular economic structure, it must originate in the *nature of man and of society itself*. A sociology which tries to look squarely at reality, therefore, will neither seek the causes of class warfare exclusively in the workings of Marxian class ideology nor regard as possible a social order free from any class differences.

Class antagonism is not only an actual characteristic of every society, but the real *progress of society* itself has resulted to a very large extent from the interaction of classes. The whole history of Western civilization provides evidence that its progress toward the realization of higher social ideals is invariably bound up with the dialectic of class movements. The history of liberty in the Western sphere is, indeed, the history of the antagonisms and of the interaction of classes. In the action and counteraction of classes in ancient, feudal, and capitalistic society, some striving for their social rights, others preventing the swing of the social pendulum to the opposite extreme, the abiding values of social liberty crystallized and obtained their progressive actualization. This dynamic impetus springing from class antagonisms radiates from the social into the political, the legal, and the cultural spheres. It continually brings fresh blood into the veins of the social process and sets powerful regenerating forces at work in the institutional structure of society.

To an undoctrinaire, realistic view of history, *the roots of class antagonisms* present themselves as follows:

1. Conflicts of interests are natural and inevitable as soon as the satisfaction of needs is no longer a function of the individual household but of the social division of labor, since in human behavior selfish motives commonly outweigh altruistic motives. The tendency to rate one's own efforts and needs higher than those of others is psychologically rooted in human nature itself. The natural conflicts of interests will reveal themselves more and more in proportion to the progress of division of labor for the supplying of vital human needs in a society.

2. The "institutional" (cf. Chap. 59) is closely connected with the division of labor as a source of class antagonisms. These are largely influenced by "production relations" and "ownership relations," with which are linked "vested interests," that is to say, interests whose fulfillment is guaranteed by social institutions. Institutionally protected interests are, however, by no means confined to those based on economic power relations, but, to a much greater extent, are based on political power. The fact that some interests are thus bound up with institutions has an ossifying effect on the social system, thus intensifying the clash of interests. In spite of their extent, the social and political power relations are a secondary factor in comparison with the human factor, to which we drew attention earlier. They influence the form of class antagonisms, but are not their ultimate root; the ultimate root lies in human nature itself.[1]

3. Social history points no less conclusively to another universal human factor in class antagonisms: the moral factor—the natural sense of justice of the groups in society that are deprived of their due social status and of the share of economic well-being and cultural values corresponding to their share in social cooperation. They know that justice is on their side if they strive to effect a change in the social system. The Marxist movement itself would never have gained such strength had not the belief in the justice of the workers' cause brought the masses into its ranks. The dynamic force of the natural moral law forms the motive power of class dynamism: through the natural sense of right the socially deprived groups are aware of the legitimacy of striving for a social order better able to realize the common good.

4. An important cause of class divisions is of a biological nature. In the course of time the ruling and wealthy classes degenerate, a fact well-known in history. They then fail to fulfill the social functions imposed by their social status. The ancient social system based upon slavery collapsed not because of developments in the technique of economic production, as suggested by Marxian theory, but because more and more of the essential functions in the economic, cultural, and military spheres passed into the hands of slaves, who were thus able to win for themselves a new status in society. Similarly, the emergence of the third estate in modern times is largely a consequence of the new part played by the middle classes in the performance of legal, administrative, and military functions in the modern state. The French Revolution, it is generally admitted today, was fundamentally a political and not a social revolution. These facts alone would be enough to show the fallaciousness of the Marxian thesis which attributes the class phenomenon to technico-economic factors.

5. In addition to the causes of class antagonisms already mentioned,

[1] The sociological theory of class society underestimates the universal human factors in class formation and reduces them exclusively to social factors; thus, Max Weber, *Wirtschaft und Gesellschaft,* 1921, pp. 177 ff., 631 ff.; K. Mannheim, *Ideologie und Utopie,* 1929, pp. 172 ff.; H. Freyer, *Soziologie als Wirklichkeitswissenschaft,* 1930, pp. 264 ff.

those found in human nature and those found in social institutions, there are the historico-political causes. The chief form they take is in the subjection of a nation through war and its servitude under the conquering nation. Historically, two kinds of relationship between the ruling and the dependent strata must be distinguished: the internal—both sides living in one political community; and the colonial—the conquering nation, without such a community, takes advantage of its political predominance to exploit economically external territories ("external proletariat," *Toynbee*).

Our discussion suggests the following general *definition:* Classes are groups in society whose members are linked by a common desire to initiate or to hinder changes in the social system. In the concept of class, then, parallelism of interests is primary, and community of function in the process of social cooperation is secondary. In the concept of occupational community (cf. preceding chapter), on the other hand, the primary element is common social function, while common interests are secondary. Since defects of greater or lesser degree are unavoidable in any form of social system, class antagonisms of greater or lesser degree belong to the *inevitable* sociological phenomena of the advanced society. Class antagonisms, however, will arise at different times in various forms and with varying intensity. They will sometimes be softened and balanced by evolutionary social reforms without any appreciable strain on society. At other times they will lead to revolutionary changes in the whole structure of society and in its fundamental functions. In all cases the question concerns the actualization of the economic and cultural common good; therefore, social justice is always at issue in conflicts of interest between classes. In every class struggle, the appeal to justice has been made, usually emphatically, by both sides alike. One party thinks predominantly of the pattern of justice realized in the existing social system, the other of principles of natural justice demanding changes in the social system and in its institutions.

As groups working to modify the social system for the purpose of safeguarding their group interests, classes have the *status of lesser social groups with natural rights.* These rights are:

1. The right to *class organization.* Without this right the classes would not be able to strive for the reorganization of the economic and cultural common good and the reshaping of the basic functions of society. The right of classes to have their own organization in advanced society is based not only on the right to free association for all lawful purposes, but also on the real demands of the common good, because by class antitheses, as already said, forces of economic and social progress are released. Chief among such organizations in society today are the trade unions and the employers' associations. All totalitarian systems deny the right in question. These systems are all built on a form of class or party monopoly, or both. The ideologies and the will of such monopolistic groups are the only formative forces admitted in the "classless society" of the totalitarian systems.

All totalitarian systems claim to have overcome the antagonisms of class society; in fact, they only suppress class differences by eliminating the free society.

2. The right to *class struggle.* By class struggle is meant the employment of all means within the limits of justice and charity by one class against another in order to preserve and to promote its interests. Among the more pacific forms of class struggle are election campaigns, parliamentary debates on measures of social and economic reform, and the efforts of employers' and workers' unions to secure stronger positions in collective bargaining, which, as recent social history shows, is as much a means of class struggle as of adjustment of class interests. Strike, lockout, and revolution are the more serious modes of class struggle.

3. The right to *class solidarity.* Within the limits just set down, class solidarity is a genuine moral attitude. It consists in the individual's sense of unity with his group in its efforts to secure its social rights and in his consequent disregard of his private interest for the sake of promoting the cooperative endeavor of the group as a whole. Of course, this disregard must not prejudice his inalienable duties toward others (e.g., the family or the community at large). If the methods employed in class struggle are incompatible with the demands of justice and charity, it may be impossible for the individual to show class solidarity in a particular case. Indeed, a tendency to identify fraternity with class solidarity exists, whereas the obligations of the former, properly understood as identical with charity, concern all the relations of man to man: no wrong can be justified by the appeal to a pretended "higher" moral value of class solidarity. Class mentality, as a mental attitude which considers everything in social and political life exclusively from the point of view of class interest, is inconsistent with the loyalty which individuals and groups owe to the community. Still more is class hatred incompatible with that natural obligation of love which man owes to man.

Class Warfare in Industrial Society

Modern class warfare has not been invented by modern socialism. It was present in individualist capitalistic society under the terrible form of class warfare "from above" before *Marx* conceived his class idea. Its chief instrument was the social power which the ownership of the means of production put into the hands of capitalists. But *Marx* discovered that capital in this form of capitalism became a "social relationship" (*Communist Manifesto*), which endowed the owner of the means of production with "social power." For, upon capital and its profit interest depended not merely whether the workers were employed, but also on what conditions. Thus, the worker was socially dependent and was liable to exploitation. The capitalistic class for a long time was able to utilize the state and law to a large extent for the protection of its class interests, since even in the liberal democracies it exercised a determining influence on politics: directly through the governmental machinery; later indirectly by molding public opinion through powerful press organs and the like. The ruling class also possessed its class theory as an ideological substratum for its class struggle. This was the economic theory of liberalism, according to which, as a remedy against overpopulation (*Malthus*), the "iron law of wages" (on account of the competition of the workers, wages could not rise above the minimum physical existence level), and the misery of the working class belonged to the "natural order" of things. This class theory enabled the capitalistic bourgeoisie to preserve an "easy conscience," since responsibility for the existing conditions of the laboring classes was cast upon Providence.

The "bourgeoisie" in the sociological sense embraces those classes that regard their own interests as bound up with the interests of capital within the social system of individualist capitalistic society and, at least to some extent, share its scheme of values, with property values and economic and technical utility values predominating. This classification includes not only capitalists in the narrower sense, but also those working in the interest of capital as managers of industrial concerns, banks, and trusts, and a considerable part of the wealthier property owning middle class and even of the white-collar workers. This indicates sufficiently the diversity of vested interests existing in the capitalistic class.

The "proletariat" as a class became a historical power through Marxism. What *Marx* effected with his class theory was the growth of the class consciousness of the worker in Europe into a political factor of the first rank. *Marx* further gave the fighting proletariat the consciousness of a historical mission in overturning the capitalistic class society. And with his historical determinism and materialism he tore down, to a large extent, the barriers against unrestricted class warfare, which were effective in the Christian scheme of values relating to social fellowship and in respect for the good of the community at large.

Some have questioned whether one can still talk of class warfare in *present-day* Western industrial society. In European socialistic circles, where the Marxian class theory is still maintained, the answer is decidedly affirmative. But since *Marx's* time capitalism has changed so fundamentally that today social scientists who think more sociologically than ideologically generally prefer to speak of "industrial society" than of "capitalistic society." The changes have come from developments which *Marx* neither foresaw nor was able to cover with his theory of the "laws of development" of capitalism. These include social policy, full employment, market stabilization, economic growth policy, the cooperative movements, and the regulation of labor relations by collective agreements. Yet, those who, like us, do not think in terms of Marxian class ideology and class warfare may, as we have just done, speak of class strata and class warfare in present-day industrial society. With the Marxian theory, however, it is not possible to do justice to the facts. The extent to which one is forced to do violence to them by this theory can be observed from the fact that in the original homeland of industrial development the Marxian class warfare theory has remained something alien; and significantly the Marxian theory has not been able to obtain a firm footing in the highly industrialized society of the United States. In both countries the working class has rejected the expression "proletariat." Since the Second World War it has also become alien to the working classes of European countries, with the exception of the communistic ones.

The Marxian Class Theory

The actual class character of each society and class dynamics as a factor in social history have been appreciated in all their implications only since *Marx's* investigations. In his analysis of the roots of class antagonisms and of their function, *Marx* was misled by his materialistic, dialectical misinterpretation of history, which suggested to him the famous proposition: "The history of all hitherto existing society is the history of class struggles" (*Communist Manifesto*). The class theory is the focal point of Marxian social and historical determinism. The ultimate cause of class divisions is found in the "production relations" and in the "exploitation relations," based on specific "ownership relations" resulting from the "material productive forces of society." Man can only hasten or retard the resultant historically determined process. No moral issue is present in this process, *Marx* holds; on the contrary, all moral and legal ideas and institutions are nothing but a part of the "superstructure" of production relations. Had empirical evidence been necessary to prove the error of the Marxian theory, the recent political experiments based upon it would have amply provided such evidence; for experience shows that the ownership of the means of production by society does not prevent the emergence of a class structure. Instead, it favors an unheard-of concentration of political power in the hands of the ruling class (i.e., the monopolistic party), and does not exclude class differences between the upper political, managerial, and technical groups and the rest of the proletariat. All this points to the fact that what ultimately determines class differentiation is an original element in human nature.

Proceeding from his conception of capital as "social power," *Marx* logically regarded the elimination of private property in the means of production as a condition of the classless society. The fallacy lies in the fact that he makes the "social relationship" which he finds in individualist capitalistic private ownership the universal characteristic of private property within the socio-economic process. He fails to see that private ownership may have a basic social ordering function and that the real problem is how to prevent it from turning into a social power relationship.

Marx found all the separate elements of his class theory in the French socialists, *Saint-Simon, Fourier,* and *Proudhon.* The form he gave to it is determined by three features: 1) He tried to explain the capitalistic class relationship as a stage in social evolution on the basis of his theory of history. He considered a former stage of it to be the relation of lords to serfs in the feudal system. 2) He tried to provide a foundation for his doctrine of class struggle with the value theory and the surplus-value theory (cf. Chaps. 160, 170), whence he came to the conclusion that the unrelenting class struggle is an inner necessity of capitalistic society. 3) Capitalistic society, *Marx* declares, is the climax in the development of class society. The capitalistic epoch "is distinguished by having simplified the class antagonism; the whole of society is splitting more and more into two great hostile camps, into two great classes directly confronting each other: bourgeoisie and proletariat" (*Communist Manifesto*). Out of the final clash of class antagonisms in capitalistic society there would arise the dictatorship of the proletariat and then the classless society.

The last mentioned postulate of *Marx's* theory is directly irreconcilable with the facts. Neither the bourgeoisie nor the proletariat in capitalistic society grew into a single united class. On the side of the proletariat we find the large group of workers which is organized in trade unions and is in part even led, by a clear regard for its own interests against those of other workers, to the monopolistic policy of the closed shop. Unskilled labor forms a large group, for the greater part unorganized, with its own social standing within the proletariat. In addition, there is the separate grouping of the proletariat into the ideologically different socialist, Christian, and communist labor movements.

Furthermore, out of the proletariat a new middle class developed, which was itself divided into a number of groups. These range from clerks, bookkeepers, and white-collar workers, up to the dependent but highly paid engineers, etc., each of these subgroups having a consciousness of its own social standing and class distinction. Thus, we arrive at a conclusion that may be summarized in a statement based on an exhaustive investigation of the social structure of such a highly industrialized country as England and dating back to the 1920's: "The belief in the existence of social classes, or even of one social class, the interests of the members of which are identical, or nearly so, and opposed to the interests of the rest of the community, is the result of studying social theory of doubtful value and of neglecting social facts." [2]

87. The Political Party

Many will be surprised to find political parties classified under "lesser groups," each possessing individual rights. It has indeed been remarked that it is strange to see parties dealt with in this part of *Social Ethics*. Undoubtedly parties must be discussed in connection with the state, and we shall have to deal with them again when discussing the state; but parties are not the state. They are generally defined as voluntary associations of people for the purpose of attaining political power; *G. C. Field* thinks it well to add to such a definition the words "by constitutional means," in order to exclude from this conception those groups which, by party organization, aim at the violent suppression of all other parties. On the other hand, he points out that, strangely enough, in Great Britain, where the modern party system first began, political parties are still unrecognized by the law. No act of Parliament or judicial decision mentions any political party, and parties, as such, have no legal rights and no legal obligations.[1]

Parties are not the state. Recent developments show that there are grounds for drawing strict limits when parties in free democracies actually claim to be the state, that is, when they consider that the form and method of regulating public affairs lies exclusively within their province. In the sphere of economic and social life, differences are settled under the influence of interest groups by means of party understandings and agreements, and the representatives of the people merely vote to legalize their

[2] A. M. Carr-Saunders and D. C. Jones, *The Social Structure of England and Wales*, 1927, p. 72.

[1] Cf. G. C. Field, *Political Theory*, 1956, pp. 165, 168.

decisions. Whenever parties think they can be identified with state and people in questions of mental-cultural life, this is quite contrary to the spirit of the democratic common good. Parties, even governing parties, are not representatives of the actual will of the people in the individual questions of public life, particularly in cultural questions and in those which affect the religious and moral conscience.

Parties are not the people. If parties arrogate to themselves exclusive power of decision in questions concerning education and schools, broadcasting regulations, public morality in regard to films, obscene literature, protection of the young, etc., they then work against the will of the people, who are not prepared in such questions to identify themselves with party ideologies and party interests. The people prefer their own associations and communities, among them parents' associations and church communities and the numerous associations serving cultural interests, to serve these most fundamental convictions. We are now in the sphere of "society" and its rights, which have to be considered as inviolable by the state and still less as belonging to the exclusive competence of parties. How extensively, in general, formal democracy rests on fictions with regard to the position of parties will be the subject of discussion when we deal with political ethics (cf. Chap. 134). No one who is acquainted with the sociology of modern democracy can deny that parties are not the people, and even less are they the state.[2]

Parties are not organs of government, that is, organs for executing the will of the state, but means for the formation of the political will of the governed. Only in totalitarian states are they organs for executing the will of the state and making it effective throughout the nation. To attribute this function, and only this function, to a monopolistic party and to identify that party with the state is obviously in contradiction to the party idea as it has been understood throughout the history of democracy. Indeed, the one-party system of totalitarian states is a contradiction in terms, for the word "party" implies part of the nation and thus presumes the possibility of a division within it. The possibility of such a division and the formation of parties constitute one of the decisive characteristics of *social pluralism.* Nothing shows so clearly as the totalitarian one-party state that

[2] G. C. Field, *ibid.,* pp. 177 ff., points emphatically to the well-known fact that parties are in themselves "oligarchies," that is, organizations in which a very small minority exerts the ruling influence. He refers to the very informative work of Maurice Duverger (Professor in the Institut d'Études Politiques de l'Université de Paris), *Les Parties Politiques* (Paris), 1951, English ed., *Political Parties,* 1954, where he maintains that the enrolled party members form only a fraction of the voters (e.g., the enrolled members of the socialist parties in Europe in the ratio of only twenty per cent); and that, moreover, those taking an active part in the affairs and activities of the party form only a small proportion of the party members; and above all, that even among the elected representatives of a party only a very limited number, the group of leaders, make all the main decisions. Well-known is the similar conclusion reached by Robert Michels, *Zur Soziologie des Parteiwesens,* 1910, 2nd ed., 1924, reprinted, with concluding remarks by Werner Conze, 1957 (extensive bibliography).

the party must be considered among the social groups which have rights of their own.

As a part of the nation, the party seeks to bring the opinions, interests, and will of a group of citizens to bear upon the shaping of the polity and the common good. Its function, therefore, is to make effective the valuations and interests (including also class interests) of a portion of the nation in the policy of the state. Society organizes itself in parties in order to determine the basic functions of the state community by molding the government and deciding the guiding lines of governmental policy. The right to form parties is thus a right of society within the state and even against the state. Party formation along the lines of modern electoral law presupposes a definite mode of will formation on the part of the political community, that is, a particular historically determined form of state, that of free parliamentary democracy. As soon as the historical evolution in nations ripens the will of the people for political self-government and they decide to take parliamentary democracy as the form of state, the conditions arise for the emergence of the *natural right* of party formation and party activity. The root of the right in question lies in the concomitant responsibility of man to shape and to direct his political common good. The citizens can only exercise this responsibility by grouping themselves around the values and interests which, according to their will, are to have determining influence on the government of their polity. The will of the various groups is represented in the parties.

Against our account of the function of the party, it is no argument to say that for Christian ethics the structure of the state is fixed in outline by natural law. Rather, it may be asked once again: What is fixed in this way? The repeated efforts to base absolute monarchy on natural law show that prudence is necessary in answering this question. Actually, natural law affords only an outline of juridical relations, whereas the details are left to the will of the members of society as soon as democracy is established as the lawful form of government.[3] Common utility is the purpose of the state system just as it is the purpose of law. Therefore, the citizens must say where they consider their interests to lie. Besides, common utility is largely a question of the most expedient means of realizing it, so that discussion and interchange of opinion are indispensable. To facilitate this discussion, to keep it in motion, and to guide it toward common utility,

[3] In this connection it may be remembered that Augustine, even with regard to the forms of democracy known to him (cf. the famous passage mentioned in Chap. 45, note 5), explains emphatically, and in direct connection with the discussion of natural law as a body of general principles, that the state is the affair of the nation. To quote the sentence above in the text and omit "as soon as," which stresses the development of juridical consciousness, seems particularly surprising in the course of considerations of "natural law and historicism" (cf. the work of this title, *Naturrecht und Geschichtlichkeit,* by Arthur Kaufmann, Chap. 48, note 15), especially since we are speaking in explanation of general utility and (in the following paragraph) of naturally guaranteed rights of men, of society, and of the state, by which, since the whole chapter treats of present-day democracy, is meant the historical condition of juridical consciousness.

is the function of the party system. Hence, the right to form parties and to engage in party activity is a natural right. It is a right dependent on historical conditions, such as the fact that a society has attained its political majority and is conscious that its government is its own responsibility and its own concern.

The social function of the party not only confers rights upon it but imposes certain *duties* to govern its activity. The first and fundamental obligation is that the parties should know they are bound, in all their actions, by the common good of the community. Therefore, the fundamental natural rights of man, of society, and of the state, guaranteed by natural law, must remain outside party controversy. No party should support the least governmental encroachment on essential rights, such as the right of the parents to educate their children. By so doing it would be undermining the foundations of its own rights, the rights of society as distinct from the state. Party concessions to state usurpation will, in the end, always prove to be a danger to the democratic party system itself and thus to free society. It is equally at variance with the actual rights of parties that they should make their influence and their power ends in themselves. Parties thus placing their interest before the interests of the community are the gravediggers of democracy. The liberalist conception of freedom, self-interest, and the majority principle implied the idea that the common good of the state was to be regarded as simply a result of the power relations of group interests combining in political parties. Thus, the way was paved for the party state. The state became a machine in the hands of the parties for securing group interests. The emergence from this party state ("the state is the party") of the single-party state of the totalitarian systems is the logical development of the same principle to its extreme. There will be further opportunity to discuss the way parties tend to ossify and to become entangled with interest groups when we deal with political ethics (cf. Chap. 134).

According to the theory of democracy, an important task falls within the province of the parties: to arouse and to train in the people the spirit of responsible, active participation in the life of the political community. As a condition for this the parties have to adhere to two principles: they must be actuated first and foremost by a sense of responsibility for the good of the community as a whole and be alert to what is demanded in its interest; and, secondly, the parties, in harmony with this sense of responsibility, will see that their strongest weapon is truth and truthfulness, and that the road to the best solution of their problems is honest discussion. Democratic theory says this, and yet everyone knows that life in the various democracies is more or less far removed from this ideal. The literature from all countries on the sociology of parties gives ample information. Here it only remains to say that parties, insofar as they deviate from these two natural law principles, are moving in the direction of demagogy.

Demagogy is influence exercised on the popular will, contrary to permanent common interests, by parties linking their own interest with pseudo-interests of the polity. Thus, it is always a speculation on the supposed obtuseness of the majority of citizens and, if it succeeds, it involves the frustration of the true common good. Only the nation as a whole can protect itself against party demagogues. Individuals, especially in the mass society, are their easy prey. A nation as a whole can take constitutional precautions against such dangers by means of institutions designed to make impossible the exploitation by partics of their temporary possession of power, thus reserving for the nation the possibility of manifesting anew its actual political will; this is one of the fundamental problems for the future of free democracy (cf. Chap. 134).

88. The Trade Union

Trade unions belong to the class of voluntary *self-help organizations* which serve to protect and to promote the economic interests of individual groups in the market economy. Consumers, workers, and producers provide themselves with protection through self-help organizations such as cooperative societies, workers' unions, employers' associations, and cartels. In the cooperative societies, consumers protect themselves against producers; in the trade unions and employers' associations, workers and employers protect themselves against the "other side" of their industry; in cartels, the producers protect themselves against the effects of competition within their own group. All the groups mentioned pursue a policy of defense against the effects of the market economy. Cooperatives and cartels are self-help organizations in the commodity market, almost exclusively intent on their group interests; they will be treated in our discussion of social economy. In comparison with these the workers' unions and employers' associations exercise *a social ordering function* in the general interest which goes beyond the protection of their group interests. This function is the establishment of social peace in the particular branch of industry by means of collective agreement.

We shall concentrate on the *trade unions,* because what is true for them, is true, *mutatis mutandis,* for the employers' associations. In the trade unions the organized workers of the individual branches of industry present a united front in their negotiations for minimum conditions in their labor contracts and thus protect themselves against the domination of capital in the labor market. The trade unions naturally tend toward organization on occupational lines, since the labor market itself follows the lines of division between industries. This does not, however, exclude organizations of the unskilled or semiskilled workers or of general workers (although they more often change their occupation, a fact which creates difficulties for their organizations). Besides their regulative function in the labor market, a chief purpose of the workers' unions is directed to mutual (cooperative) assistance in the case of illness or unemployment.

The development of modern trade unionism and of its regulative function in the labor market is the cause of the most far-reaching *modification of capitalism and its social system.* It reversed the laissez-faire mechanism of individualist economy in a vital point. As *Marx* graphically expressed it, under this latter system there were always twenty workers chasing one job, and they, competing with one another, had to accept unfavorable working conditions: thus, wages could not rise above the existence minimum. With the advance of the trade union movement the internal mechanism of capitalism was thrown out of gear. No wonder capitalistic society tried with all its might to dispute the right of the workers to free association (freedom to combine) for the protection of their economic and social interests. On the other hand, however, the trade union movement shook the Marxian theory to its foundations in two ways. *Marx* had rightly seen that in laissez-faire capitalism capital represented social power, that is, economic and social power over the worker; by this he meant a monopolistic predominance. In the trade unions the workers themselves became a "*social power,*" and thus broke the economic and social monopolistic predominance of capital power. It was of decisive significance for the course of the social system that now "labor" was placed on an equal footing with capital and for the first time was free to oppose it in the settlement of conditions in labor contracts. Moreover, the trade union movement has proved false *Marx's* assertion that the proletariat would become increasingly impoverished. With the trade union movement the workers took their social destiny into their own hands instead of waiting for their impoverishment and the resulting "dictatorship of the proletariat." Trade unionism thus became the champion of "revisionism." Without having to free themselves from Marxian ideology, the trade unions in the Anglo-Saxon countries became a "social power" by reason of the spirit and disposition of the pluralism inherent in free democracy. In Western industrial society, today the organized working class is equal in social power to the rest of the great social forces: employers, agriculture, industry, trade, and finance capital. The will of organized labor asserts itself with equal effect, along with the will of the rest of the social forces, in the regulating of social economy. Since they are a social regulative force, not only is it possible for trade unions to preserve the rights of labor intact, but a responsibility falls to them extending to the development of the political economy as a whole and beyond that to the development of the social and political order itself. Trade unions are becoming more and more aware of this responsibility. Thus, the *philosophy of trade unionism* is presented with new aspects of status and function of the trade unions, in which appear new suggestions for progress toward a fuller realization of democratic principles in pluralistic society (cf. Chap. 181).

The necessary adaptation of trade unions to the market mechanism of the capitalistic economy in the exercise of their function in the labor market has not been without *reaction* on them. They became, as their critics have not failed to point out, capitalist-minded. Without doing violence to reality, it seems difficult to deny the justification of this criticism. It points out, in the first place, that the trade union is a self-protecting organization in the labor market and is based on the same principle as the cartel in the commodity market; it aims at employing the market mechanism in order to achieve higher wages by controlling the supply of labor. Secondly, the trade unions act according to the profit principle of capitalism; they seek as much advantage as their strength allows though the wage policy of trade unionism varies in different countries. Theoretically, everywhere it is recognized that wage demands should not overstep the limits of the increase of economic productivity; in practice, however, especially since the end of the Second World War, these limits have been exceeded in many countries, as is shown by the progressive inflation to which the trade union wage policy undoubtedly contributes. In England, annual wage claims by the trade unions have become the rule, giving rise to a competition between the trade unions to raise their demands at an opportune time, before public opinion is restive and might cause them to fail. On the other hand, it is generally admitted that the "miracle of German economy" after the Second World War and the stabilization of the West German mark would have been unlikely without the wage restraint of the trade unions. Thirdly, critics of trade unions raise the point that in various countries they apply the cartel principle as extensively as employers. They form monopolies to the detriment of groups of workers. The "closed shop" is their instrument: a trade union compels the demand on the labor market, namely, the employers, to accept labor only from the supply which the union has organized, that is, to employ only its members. It prevents nonmembers from securing employment in such factories, just as the cartels often tried to make economic activity impossible for non-organized "outsiders" in their branches of industry. The closed shop and trade union monopoly will be dealt with presently in detail.

To discuss the rights and duties of the trade unions from a natural law point of view, it is evident one must start from the *basic function* assigned to them by the free market economy. This function in the labor market is that of a self-help organization for protecting the economic and social interests of the workers by the settlement of working conditions, particularly wages, in collective bargaining. The parties to the collective agreement are the trade unions and employers' associations. It provides for minimum standards of labor conditions (wages, breaks, holidays, length of notice), which are then the basis of the individual labor contract between the worker and the employer. (Concerning the natural law and positive law aspect of the collective agreement and concerning the position of trade unionism with regard to labor law cf. Chap. 142.) In close connection with this economic and social function of the trade unions in the labor market is the influence which they exert on labor supply by prescribing certain standards of occupational training for their members and by organizing further training for their members as required by technical developments. Then there is the machinery for studying tendencies in the labor market in connection with general economic trends. This can be undertaken only by the combined unions of each country. The national organizations of trade unions have offices for economic, social, and statistical research, for the publication of papers and periodicals to inform their members and public opinion, for the training of trade union officials and shop stewards, and for the general education of the workers. In their centers of social research, industrial development at home and abroad, the development of the labor market, of capital, of production technique, of rationalization, and of population movement are studied; and in this way the scientific weapons are prepared to help in the struggle for social progress. These endeavors are powerfully assisted by international cooperation between the national trade union movements (concerning the I.L.O. cf. Chap. 111).

Among the natural law principles [1] pertaining to the *rights of trade unions,* the following call for special attention. 1) In the first place there is the fundamental right to existence and to activity: the *right of free combination.* In not a few countries the workers had to make great sacrifices to win this right. Yet, soon after the First World War the question arose in Europe whether the worker should be compelled to belong to a definite trade union under pain of losing his job; this became a question of conscience for many workers. Trade unions connected with parties subscribing to materialistic-atheistic socialism often, in factories where they had a majority, would not tolerate any worker who belonged to a trade union with different religious and moral convictions. No one who does not subscribe to their ideology could deny that by doing this these trade unions overstepped their right. In Austria, as early as 1930, a "Law to protect industrial freedom" was passed. By the actions of such trade unions, however, one thing was made strikingly clear: that the workers' right of free association is not an absolute right, just as no other natural right is an absolute right and cannot originate an absolute right (cf. Chap. 36). 2) The second right of trade unions is similar, the right to use *suitable means in the labor struggle,* that is, in the struggle to press the just claims of the

[1] Since in what follows it may seem to many at first sight that too much stress is laid on certain reservations, may I explain that hardly anyone can go further than I do in the assessment of the decisive importance of trade unions for the reform of an unjust capitalism and for the future of a just social order. Indeed, the organization of the workers in trade unions for the purpose of obtaining their rights has become for me actually the starting point for the study of modern social questions. In my earliest youth the question was forced upon me, why my mother had a considerably higher wage than my father; the reason was that where she worked there was a strong trade union organization, but not where my father worked. In the present connection what is wanted is a comprehensive, conscientious, scientific examination of the natural law principles and sociological facts bearing upon the rights and duties in question.

workers in industry or factory. The strike, as an extreme resort in the hands of the trade unions, raises special questions, and will be, therefore, dealt with separately. 3) A further right of trade unions, which they claim today in an increasing number of countries, is the right to strive for *a social reform* by which labor would be entitled to share equally with property in the direction of the social economy and in controlling the pattern of incomes (cf. Chap. 181). This, in many ways, touches on basic questions of the economic and social order as such, as well as on the order of society and the state in general. To the extent that the natural rights of individual or group members of society might be infringed, there are limits to these endeavors, especially when it is a question of particular purposes which could not be accepted by all the union members. Certainly, however, there are possibilities of a gradual movement of social reform endeavors in the direction of cooperation between trade unions and employers, and also to an effective advancement of the general interests of society and economy. This could lead to a continuous increase in productivity and hence to an increase in output, which would result in an assured progressive rise in the standard of living. (Concerning the question of trade unions being built into the constitution or at least being provided for in it, as well as the other interest groups, cf. Chaps. 116, 134.) 4) The right of trade unions to participate in the sphere of *politics* cannot be doubted, once it is admitted that in industrial society they have incurred a responsibility which transcends that of collective agreements dealing with individual cases. With their present-day strength, they essentially share responsibility for the functioning of the economic order, indeed of the political order; moreover, a far-reaching social reform in the sense mentioned can come about only by political means. The question of the political attitudes of trade unions is no problem if there is unity in the fundamental convictions of a society with regard to its order, and if disagreements among the parties are concerned more with details within the framework of this unity. Then, debate, which is of great importance, is not conducted along party political lines, but rather is governed by the concrete facts. In the political atmosphere of the United States, the right of trade unions to express their political will in unison with the program of one or other party was regarded as a matter of course, if it were exercised by the trade unions with caution; thus, the union, out of respect for the political convictions of members, decides to take a stand on important political issues only after undertaking an investigation of opinion. On natural law principles there is no objection to such a party political attitude in a trade union, as long as complete freedom of membership of a trade union and a large measure of democracy within the union are assured. The position is quite different in European countries where parties disagree in their fundamental convictions with regard to the nature and purpose of man and hence of the political and social order. Trade unions in such countries, which occupy a monopolistic position in the form of a unitary union but allow themselves to be influenced in their outlook and activity by party politics, can obviously cause some of their members severe problems of conscience. This, according to natural law principles, decides against the right of such a trade union organization to work for political aims, insofar as these bear upon the fundamental convictions mentioned.

Among the *duties of trade unions* those of social justice take first place. The fundamental right of trade unions, that is to say, the right of self-help by means of voluntary association, is a right which serves social justice. It enables them to secure working conditions in conformity with the demands of social justice. This, however, not only confers rights, as is often one-sidedly assumed, but also imposes duties upon them. Especially are they bound, when making wage claims, to consider the general economic interest and the state of their branch of industry. If they make a progressively rising income a basic principle of their wage policy, they must also share in the responsibility for a proportionate rise in productivity in the whole economy, in the separate branches of industry, and in the factories. In any case, justice demands that they consider themselves bound by a standard of output corresponding to their wage claims ("go slow" tactics might involve the duty of restitution, which is a duty in strict justice according to the principle of value equality in the "give and take" of exchange). Wage demands which overstep increases in productivity conflict especially with social justice, insofar as the stability of currency (a fundamental demand of social justice) is threatened and a creeping inflation harms groups which have no possibility through collective action of making successful income demands to offset currency depreciation.

Another group of duties of trade unions comprises the duties connected with their right of free association. There are two. One concerns respect for the freedom to belong to a trade union (negative freedom of coalition). This is a natural right of the worker, even though it is restricted in cases of conflicts of rights, in which the natural law principles applying to such conflicts establish unequivocally a contrary right of the trade union. Such a right must be established with certainty, because in a case of doubt the individual right takes precedence. This principle of precedence stands on its own, but also stands the test as a basic principle of free democratic society. For, as soon as this principle is no longer recognized, the sure criterion for the encroachment of collectivistic forces in the sphere of individual freedom is lacking, whether these forces be the state, the cartel (trust), the trade union, the cooperative association, or the employers' organization. The right of free association also imposes upon a trade union the duty of internal democracy: the trade union rests on free association, so that the management of the union, in all essential questions, is dependent upon the will of its members. Certainly a leadership exercised according to democratic principles may try to mold the will of the majority in the trade union, but it must equally be aware of its duty to provide opportunities for the members to express their will, and not to allow the principles of trade union policy to become the affair of an oligarchy within the union or to become a one-man affair. Lastly, the trade union and its leaders have educational duties whose object is getting the members to recognize and to take into account the indissoluble connection between their group interests and the general interest of the economy and of the political community. Indeed, the best of the trade union leaders, with the experience gained from their activities, have learned to understand and carry out these tasks: they know that their success and the success of trade union policy is dependent on the fate and prosperity of the economy as a whole.[2]

The Strike

The strike is the refusal to work on the part of the organized workers in order to attain economic, social, or political ends. The lockout is the refusal of employers to admit the workers to work in order to further their own interests. The one or the other may occur in the course of collective bargaining when one or the other side of industry cannot otherwise secure the conditions it desires. The same natural law principles apply for both. The lockout is comparatively rarely used today. Therefore, it seems desirable to set forth the natural law principles as applied to the strike. First of all, the right to strike is established by these principles; it is based on two natural rights: first, on the freedom of man to work or not to work according as he has agreed or not agreed about relevant conditions; and secondly, in freedom of combination for the purpose of all aims which do not conflict with the common good. The strike can be an indispensable means in the hands of the organized workers for the attainment of justified demands. However, it is always detrimental to one or more business firms or to a whole branch of industry or even to the general public; moreover, because it leads to bitterness it has detrimental effects on social peace and often on political peace. Therefore, there are limits set by natural law principles to the use of the strike weapon. Its justification depends on the nature and rank of the jural goods whose infringement it is to prevent, and the jural goods whose infringement is connected with the strike. In all such circumstances it is a matter of applying the appropriate principles for collisions of rights and duties (cf. Chaps. 8, 43).

Among the *general principles of strike ethics* the foremost is the following one: The strike as a means of struggle, because of its involving more or less extensive harmful effects, is justified only as a last resort when all peaceful means of settling differences have been earnestly tried.[3] With this is linked the general

[2] The questions dealt with in the present chapter are the subject of trade union ethics; the sociological aspect is the subject of the philosophy of trade unionism, developed first in Germany; cf. Goetz Briefs, "Gewerkschaftstheorie," in *Internationales Handwörterbuch des Gewerkschaftswesens,* L. Heyde, editor, 1931, Vol. I, pp. 694–700.

[3] The fact that the strike can be considered only as a last resort in an extreme case is a principle which, as Günter Triesch, *Die Macht der Gewerkschaftsfunktionäre: Macht der Verantwortung der Gewerkschaften,* 1956, p. 284, points out, has become predominant in trade union policy, especially in the light of experience, which shows

principle that methods of settling labor conflicts are to be developed which severely limit the justification of the strike as a weapon; these methods must guarantee, in collective bargaining and in arbitration, impartiality and regard for all the interests of the opposing parties as well as those of the general public; these methods, therefore, must be fit as much to gain the trust of the opposing parties as to enable public opinion to form a reasonable judgment. Furthermore, it must be pointed out as a general principle that, as long as a collective agreement is in force, a strike can only be justified if the agreement is not kept by the other partner. Lastly, a general principle comes into play in a strike by groups such as civil servants; because of their duty of loyalty and obedience, based on an oath, on their security of employment, and on their economic security, as well as on the essential services they perform in the interest of public order, a strike would only be justifiable in the case of grave injustice.[4]

A general strike, because of its severe effects on the well-being and order of the whole society, can be justified only if most important rights are in jeopardy, for example, if the highest goods of the community, the general constitutional order, the basic rights of freedom, or the trade unions' right to free association are directly threatened or already violated by an illegal, or even by a legal government. The general strike is the principal means of nonviolent resistance to the political authority (cf. Chap. 132). In Germany recently a strike of a particular kind was under discussion: the *political strike*. This is a strike to further economic or social aims which cannot be attained by constitutional legislation. In our discussion above of trade union rights we have spoken also of the possibility of setting justified aims of social reform and of political activity; the means to attain them must not violate the existing constitution and the moral and legal order fundamental to democracy itself; in the sense in question, therefore, a political strike is not justified in practice as long as a government does not

that the undue use of the strike weapon is fraught with grave risks for the trade union movement and even more for trade union leadership. On the right to strike itself cf. Goetz Briefs, *Das Gewerkschaftsproblem gestern und heute*, 1955, pp. 60–68.

[4] With regard to the various forms of strike, for the token strike, which is a demonstration of strength, or aims to influence in advance the willingness of the employers to make concessions in a new collective agreement, there is never any justification, because there is no real labor conflict involved. Exceptionally, the lightning strike, in which a sudden stoppage of work takes place, can be justified, in case of a serious injustice which could not be remedied by a postponement of the strike (such as a delivery of materials being in progress which the government of another country could use to suppress a just national uprising). The sympathetic strike, that is, a strike by a trade union in support of another union, can hardly be squared with the principles of justice, except in the case of a strike in undertakings which belong to the same concern. Otherwise, undertakings will suffer which have nothing at all to do with the labor conflict leading to the strike. The unofficial strike (not declared or approved by the trade union) need not in all circumstances lack justification; for example, it can be justified if there is a serious lack of internal democracy in the trade union which obstructs just judgment by the trade union management in a big business labor dispute (reference will be made in what follows to discussion of this kind in England). In general, however, the unofficial strike is inadmissible if only on account of the severe harm to the trade union movement which it involves. There is no justification for the protest strike (which is not occasioned by any real labor conflict but rather by measures necessary to business, such as rationalization and automation, which necessitate a discharge of workers); it is otherwise if such measures are thought of by the business management as measures to undermine the position of the trade unions or of the workshop in a labor dispute.

use unconstitutional measures which justify political resistance. The distinction between a direct and indirect political strike, the latter involving, although not aiming at, anticonstitutional means, could not prevail against the principle that the constitution holds first place.

For some years discussions have taken place in various countries about the possibility of *strike legislation.* From the natural law point of view no objection could be raised to legislation protecting the common good against the misuse of the strike weapon, as long as the right to strike itself with its essential function of making effective the just demands of the workers is not prejudiced. On the contrary, the obligation of preventing strike methods which have a detrimental effect on the common good rests on the lawgiver. The principles governing the actual extent of his obligations, however, are those which prescribe the best possible protection of the interests of the common good in a given situation, in that he is forced in many instances to permit damage to the common good in order to avert greater evils (cf. Chap. 49). No wonder that the above mentioned discussion is chiefly occupied with the almost insurmountable difficulties of strike legislation. Proposals have been suggested which would make the declaration of a strike by a trade union punishable by law, if all the existing methods of negotiation are not first brought into use; or if a strike takes place when a verdict of compulsory arbitration exists; or if the strike is not approved, by means of ballot, by the majority of the workers in the undertakings which are concerned in the strike. Among the questions arising from these proposals the following need special attention: Who is entitled to vote? Only trade union members? Why not also the nonmembers? The trade union members may form only a part of the personnel employed, and of these perhaps a great number do not take part in the ballot. And trade union leaders may refuse the proposal on the grounds that a ballot can compel them to call a strike against their better judgment. In addition, and not least in importance, the question is raised, to what extent, to be free from pressure, a ballot must take place under state supervision, thereby creating the danger of encroachment by the state upon the workers' freedom of association and of action. Compulsory arbitration procedure is almost unanimously rejected by all sides, because by it freedom of action of the trade unions and the right to strike itself seem to be assailed; furthermore, in each individual case responsibility for the decision reached would fall upon the state.

Against this the experience of *voluntary arbitration* (as in the United States) is favorable particularly when the award may be set aside through refusal by one or other side to accept it within an appointed space of time. The objection raised against such legal regulation, that the employers' side could prolong arbitration procedure to save paying increased wages, could be met by a regulation by which the wage increases granted under arbitration were made payable retrospectively to a fixed date after the commencement of such proceedings. In answer to the objection that possibly the strike would be continued by the workers against the will of the trade union leaders, merely a few contemplate measures for implementing the arbitration decision (such as the suspension of social benefits in the event of refusal to work, as envisaged for individual cases in the Beveridge Report), if only for the reason that it would mean a strengthening of the predominant position of trade union officials; rather, one should rely on the fact that when once the decision, along with its reasons, has been made known, it is hardly possible to go against it without very good reason because of the effect on public opinion. In any case where legislation is used, it should make the provision that, if the principle of democracy within the trade union is given due weight, strikes should be possible in exceptional cases without liability to penalty, that is, strikes which have occurred without the arbitration procedure taking place. Therefore, on the one hand, a legal settlement must protect the common good and forbid strikes (and lockouts) which are incompatible with the duties of the state (such as self-defense, health protection, public supply undertakings; in the United States these three types of strikes can be stopped for a period of eighty days: the Taft-Hartley Act, 1947); on the other hand, the freedom of workers and management must be protected by law against measures of force or of intimidation directed against those willing to work (there is no objection to pickets who only seek to persuade by means of explanation) and against strikes intended to prevent mechanization and rationalization measures necessary to an understanding, or to enforce employment of unnecessary workers.

The tendencies in the free society, with its market and competitive economy, seem to be in the direction of a general legal control, to eliminate encroachments, emanating from monopolistic forces, upon the spheres of freedom fundamental to the free society. The fact that the trade union, with its efforts to monopolize supply on the labor market, and the cartel, with its efforts to monopolize supply on the commodity market, form organizations on the same principle has been pointed out above. Certainly there are grounds in the competitive economy for organization on the part of labor: to prevent labor from being put on a par with commodities and from being assigned a weaker position in labor agreements. On the labor market as well as on the commodity market, however, limits are prescribed to self-help in the group interest as much by individual rights to freedom as by the common good of society as a whole. To intervene against infringements by monopolistic forces in both directions is without doubt a task of the lawgiver.

The Closed Shop

The closed shop, or the trade union labor monopoly, means that a trade union excludes from work, in undertakings under its control, workers who are not members of their union. The worker, therefore, is compelled, under penalty of losing his job, to join the trade union. The monopoly can be given effect by threat of strike, in case of opposition from the employer, or with the consent of the employer, who expects to gain from maintaining good relations with the trade union a better atmosphere in the shop, that is to say, a peaceful development in collective bargaining. On the part of the trade union, two reasons in particular are put forward for the closed shop: it is necessary for the attainment of the workers' demands, which are based on social justice; furthermore, all workers should be obliged to make financial contributions since they benefit by the advantages obtained by the trade unions by virtue of collective agreements. In the United States the question of the closed shop has been the subject of animated discussions, compulsion to join a union is repugnant to English thought; in Europe the labor monopoly of trade unions, which is based on ideological grounds, has been the subject of vehement discussions and of legislation.

If one glances at the pros and cons that were brought forward in the debate, especially in the United States, no argument seems to have been raised which would make it necessary to change what we wrote in the first edition of this book on the principles of natural law ethics governing this question. As we said, the right of the trade unions to a closed shop is in conflict with the natural right of individuals to work and to gain a livelihood by work; the closed shop, therefore, can be justified only under very special circumstances, such as defense against a grave injury to the rights of the group concerned; in each individual case, therefore, a decision with regard to the justification of the closed shop must be based on the principles which govern the solution of conflicts of rights and of duties. There certainly is no right to a closed shop policy which is used to serve party ideological convictions or party political aims; this would mean an infringement of the original right of men to freedom of religious and moral conscience. But if there are no such issues at stake, a situation may arise where the recognition of the workers' demands, founded in social justice, can be secured only through their united action. Then the rights of the group may prevail against those of the individual; but whether united action is essential is a question of fact. From these natural law principles, which have been discussed already and which can hardly be disputed, it follows that, firstly, there is no absolute and universal right to the closed shop, and that, secondly, in case of doubt the natural right to work prevails. This means that in each individual case where a trade union claims the right to a closed shop, it must provide evidence that it is essential for the purpose of attaining considerable economic and social claims, which are founded in social justice and which are within the sphere of its activity.

The answer given here to the question of the closed shop is borne out, too, it seems, by further considerations. The natural right of free association exists only for purposes which are not incompatible with the natural order of rights; this means that the activities and methods of free associations must not contradict this order. Within this order is found the natural right to work, which only yields to another right such as the closed shop, if such a right can be clearly proved in the circumstances. In addition, not only the question of the right to work but also the right of free association itself is involved. This is the right of any man to enter into an association with others, but also to do this voluntarily, that is, the right to refrain from entering into an association as long as no greater good of a community or group is in question, as in restrictions on the personal freedom of the individual. A danger threatening a local community or district can make it a duty for individuals to belong to an organization for the purpose of warding off the danger, and also can give the competent authority the right to make membership compulsory, but only insofar and as long as circumstances make it necessary. These same natural law principles apply also to the right of the trade union to claim financial contributions ("solidarity contributions"). The funds from these contributions are no more than a means for attaining the objects aimed at in the exercise of the right of combination. Therefore, again the facts decide whether the demand of a compulsory contribution is essential for attaining the trade union aims, which are founded in social justice. And again, there are conflicting rights to be considered, such as the right of an individual to his private property as well as to the disposal of it, and the right of a trade union to a compulsory levy in return for the exercise of the right to work to earn a livelihood. The principle applies that, if the situation does not establish a clear right of the trade union, the original right to work and to exercise the ownership rights regarding wage earnings takes precedence. This is even more true if there are greater calls on the working wage, such as that of maintaining a large family. No one could seriously maintain it to be an intrinsic principle of justice that trade union contributions should be paid in accordance with the principle of a return for the benefits received by individuals through collective agreement, if only for the reason that today the collective agreement is mostly taken for granted by employers; indeed, it has become a requisite of ordered business management, and pays (for itself) by guaranteeing reliable labor relations which are so important for long-term calculations, particularly in big business. This does not even take into consideration the enormous funds at the disposal of the trade unions, which are not always expended with the knowledge (by making accounts readily available) and will of the members from whose contributions they are built up.

Although this means that membership in a trade union is a duty of justice only in special circumstances, there may be many other kinds of obligations. This presents a no less important side of trade union ethics. The foregoing inquiry, qualified by so many distinctions and provisos, was necessary, because rights, namely, claims and duties in *justice,* are involved. Undoubtedly, however, from the point of view of trade union ethics, membership in the unions, payment of contributions, and cooperation can very well come within the demands of *other virtues* and duties. Among them we mention first the virtue of solidarity (cf. Chap. 86), the exercise of which can mean, again according to circumstances, various attitudes and ways of acting on the part of individual workers with regard to the trade union: mere payment of contributions, membership, ordinary cooperation, more positive cooperation, cooperation in a responsible position, as well as striving to exert a lasting influence on trade union leadership.

It should be noted that while the duties of justice have an inherent standard, determined by the rights which are their object, such a standard does not exist for the other virtues. This is the ultimate reason why the nonexercise of moral virtues, among which is the virtue of solidarity, is not always to be connected with the guilt of a violation of duty (sin), since of course there are degrees of perfection in the practice of virtue. In fact, many differences of opinion in present-day questions would be more readily cleared up if greater attention were paid to the distinction made in more recent developments of moral theology and ethics between the doctrine of virtue, of duty, and of sin. Apart from the possibilities of a duty of justice, there may exist a higher duty of solidarity, which could only yield to more important reasons, as in the case previously mentioned, when, although a real duty of justice is not evident, owing to circumstances trade union activity is made more difficult and its success is not assured. There would be a serious duty of cooperation in the trade unions if their internal development embarked on a course which would be critical for itself or for the common good; one thinks chiefly of groups within the trade unions which seek to use the trade union movement in the service of communist (party) politics. Indeed, when a trade union is under the control of a communistic group, there can be a grave duty to belong to the union, if there is a reasonable prospect of success, in order to employ all the methods of internal trade union democracy to secure a change of management; but if there is no prospect whatever of success, there may be a duty to withdraw from such a trade union and eventually to form a union free from party ideologies, in order to realize the basic values of the democratic common good. We must distinguish, from the cases mentioned, a trade union whose leading official, although a communist, leads the union in a politically neutral manner; in such a case all the previously mentioned rules for the application of the general principles stand, including those for the obligation of trade union membership as a duty of justice or another category of duty. All these questions have been touched upon because in various countries they form the subject of vehement discussions.

Similar decisions are in question in the case of the unitary trade unions' organization, as on the European continent, which, relying on the party ideological attitude of the majority, pursues ideological party aims, which the minority must oppose on grounds of conscience; above all, there should be unremitting effort to bring about a neutral attitude in the trade union by democratic methods within the union and within the unitary trade unions' organization. In the case of an insoluble perplexity of conscience, however, individual or collective withdrawal from the union may become imperative. The responsibility for the possible inception of a weakening of the trade union movement lies then with those who disregard the obligation of the trade union to maintain a policy of ideological neutrality.

In the course of the preceding discussion we have found again and again that although *principles* are at stake, *facts* determine the application of principles, as with all natural law principles. We must now consider such facts. To establish generally the right of the trade unions to a closed shop would mean being certain that the trade union movement of today cannot attain its aims of social justice without a closed shop. For an unprejudiced appreciation of the facts, one must note the decisive part played by trade unions in bringing about the radical change in capitalism compared with its form a hundred years ago, and also the position which is enjoyed by the trade unions in present-day industrial society, namely, that today "labor" no longer lags behind "property" (capital) in "social power" (cf. Chap. 86). Even at a time when the trade unions did not yet hold such a position, *Goetz Briefs* wrote in a "classic" article on the problems of trade unionism: "The free association characteristic of the trade union means that the trade union does *not* comprise *all* the workers. Indeed, the aim of association does not demand the union of all. But not even the 'cartel aim' of representation of interests demands it. It may be pursued and realized with a changing quota of the workers in question for the purposes of the trade union. A minority often satisfies the purpose, so much the more as it proves, in accordance with experience, at critical moments to be the factual or recognized leadership of the greater part or even of all the workers." [5] That this view of the character and potentialities of trade unions is right is shown by the unimaginable

[5] G. Briefs, "Gewerkschaftswesen und Gewerkschaftspolitik," in *Handwörterbuch der Staatswissenschaften* (Jena), 4th ed., Vol. IV, 1927, p. 1118; cf. also *Zwischen Kapitalismus und Syndikalismus*, 1952, where Briefs' most noteworthy sociological contribution on present-day development tendencies in the trade union movement is presented.

rise since then of the trade unions to social power. *Briefs'* statement of the general factual situation may claim complete validity today. With regard also to trade union finances, there can be no doubt that with the funds at the disposal of the unions, their pursuit of the aims of social justice as a rule is not hampered by lack of funds. Such a factual situation, therefore, does not support either the right to a closed shop or an obligation of justice to be a member of a trade union. On the other hand, in today's society there exists a vital reason for exercising great caution in asserting rights of free associations and of obligations of justice vis-à-vis them; this reason lies in the persistent advance of collectivistic forces, which are inclined to concede absolute pre-eminence to group interests over individual rights, and, by accumulating power, hope to decide conflicting interests in their favor. In all this, the "official" of the association, the union, a *"key man" in the pluralistic society,* should not be overlooked; *his law of action is success for his organization.* In addition, it is a fact that in most Western countries today there is a lack of internal democracy in trade unions, which has resulted in an authoritarian position for the trade union leaders; indeed, in some countries an ever-increasing prominence is given to political aims. I refer the reader to my recent book, *Der Funktionär, seine Schlüsselstellung in der heutigen Gesellschaft,* 1961 (i.e., *The Executive in Present-day Society*).

In the foregoing we have tried to show when and to what degree, according to natural law principles, the original rights of individuals take precedence over the rights of groups. To protect these rights is one of the foremost tasks of the *state.* For, the order of the common good, whose establishment and protection is the fundamental function of the state, is radically the order of freedom. The right to work and to gain a livelihood is one of the original and primary rights of man. Since this right pertains to the substance of the order of freedom, the state must protect it insofar as other rights do not take precedence, that is, the rights of a group or of the community as a whole. The principles mentioned, therefore, support the justification of legislation against the closed shop policy which makes membership of the union a prerequisite of the right to work (called in the United States the Right-to-Work Laws), under two conditions: first, that freedom of association, as a fundamental right, is fully protected with all facilities for free activity, among them particularly those which serve the chief object of association, namely, the conclusion of the collective agreement in settling conditions of work; secondly, that provision is made for exceptional cases, in which the trade union may show evidence for the necessity of a closed shop to help the workers in their fight for their rights in accordance with social justice.[6]

89. Free Associations

The groups with special rights, which have been discussed in the foregoing sections, belong in part to the sphere of free associations. This

[6] Such laws were made in the U.S.A. between 1947 and 1954 in eighteen states. Thus, Edward A. Keller, C.S.C., *The Case for Right-to-Work Laws: A Defense of Voluntary Unionism,* 1956, pp. 11 f., 95 f., reproduces as an example the text of the North Carolina Right-to-Work Law; the book conveys a very lively impression of discussions in Catholic circles in the U.S.A. about the closed shop and the trade union labor monopoly in the workshop.

sphere is very wide, since any purpose that may be made the object of arbitrary human desires and activities can also serve as a basis for forming an association. The literary society, the sports club, the industrial corporation, the Society for the Prevention of Cruelty to Animals, illustrate the wide range of possibilities. Such associations are voluntary in a threefold sense: 1) They are not indispensable, that is, as social entities demanded by the nature of man for his full development. 2) They are set up by the free choice of the members, with no compulsion to join them. 3) They are based on the original natural right to freedom to form such associations, that is, on a human right. The family, the local community, and the state are societies required by nature. Their existence and their own especial social function are indispensable for the full integration of the self and for man's cultural being; man's obligation to them is outside the realm of human choice. True, it is not necessary to live in a particular local community or in a particular state. Wherever one lives one must observe the laws of the local authority or of the state. Since communities such as the family and the state are indispensable for the integration of the human self, their basic functions occur in a basically similar form at every stage of the historical development of social life. It is a different matter with "free" associations. Their patterns and functions are much more subject to historical factors, such as the particular form of political, economic, and cultural life of a society.

Free associations in modern society are divided into *two main groups*. One group, including occupational organizations, political parties, and social self-help organizations, among them federations and trade unions, perform social functions within the *public* sphere, since their objects involve the life and order of the community and the actualization of the social good. The great majority of the voluntary groups perform a social function in a different sense. Although they also owe their origin to man's need for social supplementation, their activity is confined to the *private* sphere. The forming of free associations is a natural right, and has its basis in their importance for the development of the individual's self. So important indeed are these associations that very many men feel a club or association to be incomparably more necessary to their lives than the local or the state community. It would be wrong of course to say that such associations play a really larger part in the life of the individual; an individual is generally unaware of the extent to which his whole life depends on the local and the state community. The free associations themselves could not even exist if the state failed to perform its function of preserving law and order.

Thus, these associations do not stand on the same level as family and state, even though the individualists think they do. Still less is the right of association based on an original unrestricted freedom of the individual. Contrary to individualist thought, no right is in itself unlimited, and the right to association does not extend to purposes adverse to the existential social ends. Man's claim to seek the development of his self in association with others is rooted in the many-sidedness of human nature and in the defectiveness of the individual's nature. Hence, freedom of association is ultimately derived from men's existential ends and therefore must remain in harmony with them. The state, on the one hand, being the guardian of the common good, has to recognize and protect the freedom of association, but, on the other hand, it has the right and the duty to make legal provisions for facilitating the supervision of their purposes. Along these lines and with these limitations the modern state expressly recognizes in its constitution the right of free association as one of the fundamental rights of its citizens and seeks, by demanding registration, to create the conditions for protecting the interests of the common good. The right of free association is so much a fundamental basis of the "free" society that its *pluralistic* character is largely determined by it.

The orbit of the right of free association extends to all ends that are compatible with the end of society, the common good. All spheres of value, therefore, are open to it. In each such sphere the individuals, by uniting, may seek opportunities for the development of their interests and their personalities, as in associations of a charitable, political, social, literary, artistic, or religious character. Thus, the special purposes underlying the formation of free associations include the whole field of human cultural life. Therefore, their sphere embraces purely social clubs: dancing clubs, bridge clubs, athletic clubs; business associations, cartels, and cooperatives; associations for promoting and popularizing science, literature, and art; charitable institutions, youth organizations, religious associations whose aim is the education of their members for their station in life. Lastly, we must mention also such purely religious bodies as mothers' and young men's associations, which belong exclusively to the province and to the competence of the Church; their foundation in natural law must, however, be especially noted in view of the denial and violation of their rights by totalitarian states.

The particular right of the free association to autonomy consists in the full right to frame its purpose and statute as long as the public interest or the rights of others are not affected. To define a general criterion for determining when the common interest is affected and when the political power has rights and duties to prohibit or limit the activities of associations is impossible. Many circumstances of the particular situation must be examined. Merely abstract reflections will not serve; only a realistic weighing of what the general utility requires in the circumstances of the case at any given time will yield an objective judgment. A government may be compelled to tolerate associations that are obviously planning a revolution, if interference would only hasten its outbreak. There are circumstances when the maintenance of law and order may justify severe restriction by controlling association activity, as after a revolutionary uprising when a community has to be watchful against the enemies of the fundamental freedoms and must take measures to safeguard them by restricting opportunities for the regrouping of the revolutionary forces.

Individualist and *collectivistic* political theories are both inconsistent in their interpretation of the right of association. Thus, for example, although the workers' freedom to combine was at one time passionately disputed in the name of freedom by the exponents of the individualist and liberalist doctrine today the right of associations to propagate contraception and nudism is proclaimed on the same principles; or while the totalitarian state refuses the right to form religious and cultural associations, the right of association and of public activity of atheists has been positively established. Since, in the individualist view of society, the free associations were, in essence, understood to be rooted in unrestricted individual freedom in the same way as the state itself, individualist "free society" developed into the uprising of society against the state; this happened primarily through a social pluralism caused by the conflicting interests of groups, which gave the groups extensive domination over the state. In reaction to these individualist disintegrating forces, the collectivistic doctrine and policy imposed communal values on "society"; it claimed the absolute validity of communal values and gave the state absolute power over society. The consequence was the elimination of free society and of the right to free association. The activity of any association is "coordinated" with the collective purposes set up by the political power. The result is the absorption of society by the state.

PART THREE

The Nation

90. The Idea of the Nation

The nation is a modern phenomenon. To the Greeks and Romans the city was the whole compass of their communal life. *O. Spengler* rightly warns us not to think of nations in the modern sense when we speak of the Greeks and the Romans, as we have been inclined to do since the time of *Shaftesbury* and *Montesquieu.*[1] In origin the word "nation" indicates a large group united by the common descent of its members. The example of the Swiss nation, however, in which four different groups are united, shows that even common descent and the associated element of common language is not an integral characteristic of the idea of the nation. Indispensable, however, are the elements of a fellowship in socially relevant values and the common will to assert this fellowship within the society of nations. This fellowship is chiefly rooted in common historical experience and presupposes a common territory.

Since historical development is of such significance in the origin of the nation, historical factors must be taken into account, as determining its individual features, more than in any other concept of the social sciences. Whereas the family is an elementary social unit guaranteed by unvarying functions, the nation, its status, and its functions are subject to far-reaching change. Some features are conspicuous at certain times and others recede. The idea of the nation, therefore, is elastic. National consciousness, the will to self-assertion and the political means used to further this purpose can take various forms. The sense of a common destiny can be powerfully effective in moments of threatening danger from without, but in times of security it can give way to internal discord. The fellowship in values may comprise all the fundamental cultural and social values, even religion; it may, however, be confined to a few human and social values of a general character.

This elasticity in the idea of the nation is well expressed in the classical definition of *John Stuart Mill:* "A portion of mankind may be said to constitute a nationality if they are united among themselves by common sympathies which do not exist between them and any others. . . . This feeling of nationality may have been generated by various causes. Sometimes it

[1] Cf. O. Spengler, *The Decline of the West,* 1917, Vol. II, p. 173.

is the effect of the identity of race and of descent. Community of language and community of religion greatly contribute to it. Geographical limits are one of its causes. But the strongest of all is identity of political antecedents; the possession of a national history, and consequent community of recollections; collective pride and humiliation; pleasure and regret, connected with the same incidents in the past." [2]

But when *Mill* goes on to explain that the fellowship he describes implies a tendency "which makes them desire to be under the same government and desire that it should be governed by themselves or a portion of themselves exclusively," there is already present what gave the modern idea of the nation at the climax of its development its individualistic stamp: self-determination. The individualist conception of the nation at once met its ideological antithesis in Marxian internationalism. The nation, says *Marx*, is based on the prolonged historical interdependence of classes, economically, socially, politically; now, however, with the emergence of the world proletariat industrial development is bringing about the unification of mankind, with its climax in the proletarian world revolution. Before this final stage, says the *Communist Manifesto,* in every industrial state the proletariat must become "a national class and constitute itself as a nation." Hence, in Marxian political thinking, the highest importance is attributed to national movements in the various countries, which are seen within the perspective of the dynamics of the proletarian communistic development with the ultimate goal: "Proletarians of all lands, unite!"

91. The Origin of the Modern Nation

Until the end of the eighteenth century, Europe thought in terms of states, and the peoples of the various states saw themselves as unities represented in their princes. Among the causes bringing about the emergence of the national idea as a formative factor, mention must be made first of the French Revolution (1789). Its outcome, the Napoleonic domination of Europe, caused the awakening of resistance in the subjugated peoples and thus of their will to national self-assertion. This will arose in Germany after the subjugation of the small states and of Prussia; at the University of Berlin, *Fichte* delivered his famous *Addresses to the German Nation;* Spain rose, Austria followed; in England the Blockade had stimulated the already lively national consciousness; in Russia the flames of Moscow were a signal for national liberation.

If the new order of Europe, framed at the Congress of Vienna, was as yet a tribute to the sovereignty of the princes, nevertheless it made effective the decisive stimulus to the development of national thought which emerged from the French Revolution: the centering of sovereignty in the

[2] J. Stuart Mill, *Considerations on Representative Government,* 1861, Chap. 16.

princes is replaced by the sovereignty of the people. The political community becomes conscious of itself as a self-acting unity and wishes to take its destiny into its own hands. Then, the next steps in the establishment of the modern nation came about in the risings of 1848 in Germany, Italy, Bohemia, Hungary, Poland, and Ireland, in each case under the banner of nationalism. These achieved no decisive results. But later, results were achieved by the unification of Italy after the war of 1861, by the relative autonomy of Hungary gained in 1867, by the founding of the German Reich in 1871; the national movement in Norway led in 1905 to the separation from Sweden, just as Belgium had split off from Holland in 1830; the Serbs, Bulgarians, and Rumanians also attained to national status. The newly found national consciousness obtained many kinds of nourishment from literature, since now there arose a great interest in folk songs, folk tales, and folk sagas. At the same time, the work of prominent European poets became inflamed with the national idea and powerfully influenced the national movements.

Another factor contributing to the national unification of peoples should not be underestimated: the technical and economic revolution of nineteenth-century Europe. The new means of transport and communication brought the members of each individual nation closer together. Intellectually, the interchange of ideas and opinions was rendered possible to an unprecedented degree, mainly by newspapers, periodicals, and books. In the economic field, industrial developments effected the unification of the home market, thus forming the whole population of a country into a unit and bringing national economies into being. Along with the growth of capitalism came an increase, among all the European nations, in the strength of the prosperous middle class, a class which became the repository of nationalism. Growing economic prosperity made possible great advances in institutions for higher education (e.g., the German universities), which played an increasing part in the national movement. The general introduction of elementary education in state schools became at the same time a means for instilling the national idea into minds from childhood onwards.

The nationalist movements in the Americas and in the East, in India, China, and Japan, are by no means mere imitations of the European movement, although European influences have certainly been at work and parallels with the European development are manifold. The movements in the East, in contradistinction to the European, have one cause and one denominator in common: opposition to domination by the European nations. Apart from that, distinct forces are at work everywhere. Japan's national idea, for instance, like that of no other people except the Jews, rested largely on a religious basis. Undoubtedly, however, the new nationalism of the peoples in Africa which recently gained independence, is strongly influenced by European nationalisms.

92. The Bond of Blood in the Nation

Kinship by blood is, as we have said, not an indispensable factor in the constitution of a nation. Where it is present, however, it possesses great unifying force. For with it is linked community of language and, with this, a rich abundance of common cultural values with a great formative power. Hence, we must look to the enhanced unity of the mental constitution of a nation to find the significance of the bond of common blood.

Modern race feeling is an altogether different phenomenon. *Toynbee* sees one of the predominant causes of modern race feeling in Protestantism. With the disintegration of the European community of Christian spirit, it first emerged, *Toynbee* points out, in the consciousness of the White overseas settlers who adapted the Old Testament idea of the "chosen people" to their own situation and intermingled with it the fear of losing their new possessions through the defensive action of the natives. In his analysis of the factors in the genesis of civilization, *Toynbee* emphasizes the fact that up to the last quarter of the fifteenth century the members of our Western society did not divide the human family into Whites and Colored, as we do today, but into Christians and Heathens. When he emphasizes the English Protestant version of our Western culture as the determining factor in the development of race feeling in our Western society, *Toynbee* declares in a footnote that his view should not be misinterpreted as an expression of anti-Protestant religious prejudice, since he was brought up as a Protestant and has not become a Catholic.[1]

This modern race feeling, again, is altogether different from blood consciousness, which the advocates of blood mysticism and theorists of the racial sociology school of National Socialism postulated as an essential feature in the idea of a people. Certainly, anthropologists and biologists do not deny that the racial correspondence or noncorrespondence of intermingling ethnical strains exerts its influence both on the physical and on the mental constitution. If, however, anthropological and biological theory is not biased by political preconceptions, there is no doubt that, as *M. H. Boehm* (the outstanding representative of the Volk theory) says, a scientific analysis of the social phenomena of people and of nation offers no possibility of "gaining conceptions of anthropological species which would really allow us to conceive of the people as the common bearer of a particular mingling of blood, while recognizing the diversity of its racial traits, and to raise this aspect of its nature to the level of consciousness." [2]

In full accord with our estimation of the factor of common origin in

[1] Cf. A. J. Toynbee, *A Study in History*, 1934, Vol. I, pp. 209–24.
[2] M. H. Boehm, *Das Eigenständige Volk*, 1932, p. 21.

the making of the nation, *W. Draeger,* another of the few theorists of racialist sociology who deserves to be taken seriously, records it as a fact of experience that, for example, "in its spiritual and moral constitution the German national constitution presents a much more unified aspect than could be expected from its physical structure." [3] Our inquiry, therefore, demands a brief treatment of the racial problem.

We describe as races those large groups of men who exhibit common physical characteristics, such as stature, complexion, and shape of head, by reason of common descent. Although pigmentation shows striking differences, yet the customary division into white, yellow, and black races has only a limited scientific justification, for anthropologically these form groups of races. Thus, in spite of their considerable racial diversity, the negro, negroid, and negrito (the short, dark, curly-haired families in southeastern Asia and Melanesia) groups are all assigned to the black race. It is an established conclusion of racial research that the physical variations between individual members of the same racial group are much greater than the average variation between different races; in fact, the variations between races affect only about ten per cent of the features that are common to all men as a species.

According to the unanimous view of serious students, the variations between European nations (between Englishmen, Frenchmen, Germans, Italians) consist only of some secondary features, inherited traits, which stand out from the racial blend common to all; there are no peoples of pure race, and in Europe not even of relatively pure race. The peoples of Western Europe are mixtures of Nordic, Alpine, Mediterranean, and Dinaric (Balkan) racial elements. Therefore, we are bound to conclude that racial consciousness, that is, the consciousness of belonging to a particular race, cannot be a decisive element in the life of a nation. Indeed, history offers no example of racial consciousness playing a pre-eminent part in the progress of a people toward nationhood. The racial idea which was conceived between the two World Wars, first in Germany and then in Italy, as the paramount force in the national movement, has not struck genuine roots even among the peoples of those countries. Instead, these peoples have, in the majority, taken up an attitude of indifference or have rejected with more or less firmness the cruelties perpetrated in the name of this idea. That the idea of the Aryan race, which has been of such significance in National Socialist ideology, lacks any scientific foundation, is a fact accepted by all scholars, not excluding National Socialist theorists like *H. Guenther.*

Biology provides no evidence for the proposition that some races as such and their average members possess higher physical and mental qualities, and are thus superior to others.[4] Such racial superiority has been postulated by racialistic sociology with its biological view of the world.

[3] W. Draeger, *Primat des Volkes?* p. 34.

[4] Cf. Haldane, *Heredity and Politics,* 1943, pp. 143 ff.

According to this view, the whole mental and spiritual nature of the individual as well as the culture of a people are subject to the determinism of the blood; therefore, "the true picture of humanity reveals no equality among all who bear a human countenance, but instead diversity and inequality in kind," which provide the conditions for racial superiority.[5] It is not quite the same when the biologist, not establishing philosophical principles but making only the technical distinctions necessary within the scope of his special science, says, "Technically (!) speaking, there is no such generalized being as 'man'; there are only men and women belonging to particular races or particular racial crossings."[6] Nevertheless, such formulations are not without danger, for in a biological sense there is such a generalized being as man, since all the human races are capable of crossbreeding and thus belong clearly to a single species.

What is the real significance of the racial problem in the lives of nations? Common ancestry provides a people with a common environment in two senses: a common spiritual environment resulting from a community of language, the medium for that common world of ideas and values in which a people lives; and an external environment resulting from living together in a common territory. Through the common environment, the common lineage of peoples and of nations works strongly as a unifying factor. In thus urging the importance of environment, sociology agrees with biology and genetics which, as we shall see later, generally attribute the same, if not a higher, importance to environment in the development of living beings as to hereditary qualities themselves. This problem of the change of environment is chiefly involved in the intermarriage of members of different races; as such, it is a problem which equally concerns eugenics and ethics. Marriages resulting in the transplantation of one or both parties into an entirely different cultural environment may have very unfavorable psychological effects. It is mainly by experience that the effects of such intermarriages must be judged, and the experience up to the present day, especially within the British Commonwealth, does not seem to permit the formulation of a general principle, except that, on the whole, the parties must be aware that it is a matter of grave responsibility to contract a racially "mixed" marriage.

In this connection, the *Jewish question* cannot be ignored. A just and objective judgment in this much-discussed problem can be reached only if a careful distinction is made. From the beginning, however, it must be recognized as *the* certain principle in any such discussion that all men, Jews and non-Jews alike, are endowed with equal rights which are founded in the human person as such. In the question of granting equal civil rights, however, the distinction must be made between Jews who form part of a nation by assimilation and those of recent arrival. The Jewish national consciousness itself varies in character from country to country. A substantial portion regards itself as belonging to the

[5] Cf. E. Krieck, *Völkisch-politische Anthropologie*, Vol. II, p. 47.
[6] E. Fischer, E. Baur, and E. Lenz, *Human Heredity*, 1931, p. 209.

nation with which it has lived for generations past, while others, especially those living in more self-contained communities, develop a national consciousness of their own. The old-established and assimilated Jewish populations of England, France, the United States, Germany, and Austria regard themselves as Englishmen, Frenchmen, Americans, Germans, and Austrians. On the other hand, Hungary after the First World War was justified in protecting herself against the indiscriminate immigration of Galician Jews, just as the United States is justified in protecting herself against immigration from Japan.

There remains, then, the question of the position of the assimilated Jews. This question arises chiefly from the fact that, in various countries, Jews occupy positions of eminence in branches of cultural and commercial life out of proportion to their numbers: as bank directors, directors of industrial companies, members of the stock exchange, in trade, in the legal and medical professions, in the press, in the motion picture business, and in the theater. From two points of view it is a question of justice whether a nation may or should protect itself against such a preponderance of the Jewish part of the population in economic and cultural life. Economically, it is a question of a just distribution of leading positions in the professions, of higher incomes, and of economic power; culturally, it is a question of a disproportionate influence wielded by a small fraction of the population on the intellectual life and public opinion of the nation.

Wide circles of nationally conscious Jews in various states recognize that it is inconsistent with justice that Jews should hold a virtually privileged position. On the other hand, no just solution can be found by way of exceptional legislation that would restrict the civil status of the assimilated Jews, denying to them the full and equal rights of every citizen.

Thus, we arrive at the conclusion that we must regard as unjust such measures as the *numerus clausus.* (In Hungary the *numerus clausus* limited Jewish students to a number corresponding to the proportion of the Jewish population in the nation as a whole). Likewise unjust is the limiting of the rights of the Jewish population to those of a national minority. Even more unjust are measures excluding them from *commercium* (economic and social relations with non-Jews) and *connubium* (marriage with non-Jews), which were put into practice under the racial laws of National Socialist Germany.

The following appear to be the only measures defensible before the forum of justice for limiting a virtually privileged position of the Jews in economic and cultural life: 1) If the advantages enjoyed by the Jews at educational institutions are due to their more favored financial position, a remedy can be found in the creation of equal conditions for all, in granting assistance to those who are financially at a disadvantage, and by selection on the basis of abilities alone. 2) If a disproportionately rapid economic advancement is the result of greater unscrupulousness in competition, measures of general application can be taken to eliminate unfair methods. 3) Even if there were evidence of an influence detrimental to cultural values exercised through the medium of literature, the theater, the motion picture, and the press, in an endeavor to make capital out of a compromise with libertinism, such a problem could be solved only within the framework of general, and not exceptional, measures. For, it is not Jews alone who trade upon licentiousness; and like members of other nations, Jews have rendered outstanding services in almost every field of culture.

93. The Bond of Soil in the Nation

It has been the established and general conviction of sociologists that common territory, the bond of soil, is an indispensable constituent of nationhood. Sociology has in particular attached due importance to the deep influence exercised upon the character of a people by the natural conditions of the country and by the kind of work determined by these conditions. We must consider the effects of the natural environment, notably the climate, on habits of life, from food to house building. And we must not forget the particular world of feeling which a people associates with the landscape, with its horizons, with its atmosphere and its moods, with the changing seasons of the day and the year. Truly, therefore, much that derives from the soil influences a people and is dear to it.

All these conditions belong to that unique treasury of experience which all peoples associate with their native land. One of the deepest human emotions is devoted to it; it provides the most universal theme of folk song and poetry. Indeed, the feeling for home and homeland is a primary element of national consciousness and is concerned with values that are, in the full sense of the word, vital values for man, values for which he is prepared to make the greatest sacrifices. But the soil is merely the condition for these values, nothing more; it has thus an entirely different status from that attributed to it by the mystical soil cult of the racialistic theory. From what has been said of the physical and spiritual significance of the soil, the interest of ethics in this needs no further explanation, for surely the love of the native soil is one of the strongest conservative forces in human life, and closeness to the soil is one of the strongest regenerative forces.

Considerations of population, culture, and world politics likewise compel the Western nations today to realize how much their physical and spiritual constitution depends on their contact with the soil; hence, efforts have been made, by the planning of new residential areas, to enable a larger part of the nation to live close to the soil in contact and familiarity with nature. By shifting large masses of the population from the land to the factory towns, industrial capitalism has, for many people, destroyed much that is contained in the values associated with the native soil. This uprooting and severance from the soil, with all the consequences that such a state of homelessness in the sphere of those values must bring, has become a leading characteristic of the development of the proletariat. Other results of the individualist-capitalistic system were the neglect of agriculture and the consequent flight from the land. In this movement away from the land, socialism, especially Marxian socialism, saw nothing objectionable, regarding these as normal symptoms of the development of capitalism, with the result that the uprooted would seek their home in socialism.

94. The Nation: Common Destiny

The decisive moment in the emergence of a nation occurs when a people becomes conscious of itself and thus finds its soul. "Would-be nations must find their own souls" to be real nations.* This consciousness is stirred especially through the experience of being linked by a common destiny. It is nourished by memories of a common history, of common tribulations, of wars and victories, of heroic figures of the remote and recent past, of warriors, saints, statesmen, who succeeded in rousing the people to the service of common ideals. The consciousness of a common destiny comes to the fore especially in times of resistance to pressure from without, when a people is fighting for its freedom, or for life and existence. Then is the time it awakes most fully to consciousness of itself.

We would be mistaken, however, if we regarded the consciousness of a common destiny in a people as exclusively bound up with more idealistic values. Realistic factors enter into play, and, above all, economic factors. Modern national economies have become economic organisms that are obliged to compete with one another as units for raw materials and markets. Every member of every nation sees himself affected by the outcome of this struggle; his income, his standard of living, and the future of his children depend upon it, whether he stands on the side of the employers or on the side of the workers. After the First World War the consciousness of a common national economic destiny received a fresh incentive from the industrial crisis and unemployment, the solution of which became the primary national task of almost every state. It was then that the slogan "Economy is destiny" was coined and that the primacy of economics in national policies was recognized. But governments pursued a shortsighted policy of economic isolation (restrictions on trade and on currency conversion), which was greatly to the detriment of true national interests. After the Second World War the view has gradually developed that the latter are best served through large-scale supranational market units.

95. The Nation: Unity in Spirit

The nation is first and foremost spiritual in nature. The common ideas, values, forms of life, traditions, usages, and customs with which men grow up from childhood and which play so great a part in their basic upbringing constitute the spiritual world binding the nation together. Only a relatively small part of this is made up of those distinctive works of creative genius in the fields of literature, art, and science which are often thought of when culture is discussed as a unifying force in the nation. The broad

* Cf. A. J. Toynbee, "The New Europe," in *The Nation*, Vol. XVII, 1915, p. 826.

mass of the people often knows comparatively little of such works and scarcely takes a keen enough interest in them to make them grow into a unifying force. Only in the educated classes do such cultural values become directly effective as a power inspiring national consciousness. Moreover, *Bach, Mozart, Beethoven, Wagner, Dante, Shakespeare, Raphael,* and *Michelangelo* no longer belong to individual nations, but have long since passed into the cultural treasury of all mankind. Nevertheless, if no one would deny these masters a special relationship with the German, Italian, and English nations, this is because their works have grown out of the particular character of the spiritual world of these nations, out of their ideas and ideals, out of their conceptions and ways of life, out of their customs and traditions, that is to say, out of their culture in the widest sense.

This common world in which a people lives, half aware and half unaware of it, and from which spring the forces that fashion its culture, is what enables a people to become conscious of itself as a unity. This spiritual world cannot be more accurately designated than by *Hegel's* expression "spirit objective," since it exists independently of the individual, although each individual has his spiritual roots in it. It is also often referred to as the soul or the personality of the nation, and there is no objection to this provided no hypostatizing of such spiritual entities is intended. When this common spiritual world rests on a common mother tongue, it then permeates the individual mind most effectively and, other things being equal, it provides the strongest of all unifying forces.

The fact that a nation's spiritual fellowship does not depend upon language, however, is shown by the existence of multilingual nations. In such cases, that which constitutes the creative, unifying spiritual world is sets of values in the moral, political and social spheres, such as the values of a free democracy. In North America, a land young in tradition, they reveal themselves as the truly spiritual substance of a nation's common world; the same values have bound together four different peoples in a single nation in Switzerland, a country of long tradition, while yet largely preserving their cultural individuality. The same applies to Belgium with its union of Walloons and Flemings. Indeed, these nationalities find that the political values and ideals which unite them offer the best conditions for their own cultural life. Such national groups, with their own way of life, largely merge in the common spiritual world of the nation in which they are united. The French-speaking and German-speaking Swiss do not think of themselves fundamentally as French or Germans, but first and foremost as Swiss.

The sociology of customs, usages, and traditions investigates these social phenomena as part of the spiritual world of common ideas and values which unite a people. In customs, usages, and traditions, it feels itself to be held together, and it lives by them in virtue of institutional bonds, which enable its spiritual world to endure throughout the generations.

These customs and traditions, therefore, have significant social functions. They may be summed up as follows: 1) Because of customs and traditions, families and individuals are ceaselessly drawn into the common spiritual life-stream on important occasions in life and in the course of the year's labors. Examples of this are the customs connected with betrothal, marriage, baptism, burial, and the spring and harvest festivals. 2) They demand the creative cooperation of the individual. To go to a motion picture theater to be transported into a world of illusion is a very different matter from taking an active part in the communal experience of folk song, folk tale, folk dance, folk drama, and folk art. What is true of the motion picture is no less true of the entertainment provided by the radio. An immense range of original and vital creative power in a people is lost when, with the decay of customs and usages, men are educated to a purely passive acceptance of art values and entertainment values; this is one reason why present-day art, having little contact with its deeper roots, has become largely intellectual, esoteric, artificial, and moded. 3) The traditions, usages, and customs give the individual a joint responsibility for upholding the values whose expression they are. They make this responsibility a public one; in upholding it the community asserts its self-respect. Here we see the significance of national costume: it is the outward sign of an inherited closer fellowship. 4) In the times when these customary observances were still most vigorous, they always revealed themselves also as points of closest contact between religion and life. Not only popular religious customs, which made religion live in the home and in the family, but also those customs surrounding trade and agriculture possessed this feature. An example of this is the prominent place held by religion in the customs of the guilds.

For all these reasons it is clear that traditions, usages, customs, and modes of life are of like interest to ethics and to sociology. For, a nation's world of ethical values is largely embodied in them and at the same time finds its social institutional support in them. Thus, obviously a sound sociological reason exists for the moralist's anxiety at their decay. From the point of view of ethics we may have no doubt that the widespread decay of traditional customs among all civilized peoples results in a change in the fundamental values of their spiritual world. It is this change that is associated with the development of individualist, collectivistic mass society. The very causes that led large classes of the people to be estranged from the land in the period of individualistic capitalism, resulted also in a spiritual uprooting, in a breach with the spiritual world of a community living in its customs, usages, and traditions. Fellowship personally experienced in traditional forms of social life is replaced by a collectivity of socially anonymous individual existences; the workman, instead of ranking in society according to his craft, is classed as a "hand." In the world of industry "the people" becomes "the masses"; its common element is not so much a spiritual world as the absence of one. Thus, there is a vacuum into which ideologies can stream from outside; and with their help the masses can be controlled and mobilized. The spiritual homelessness of the industrial worker is thus closely correlative with proletarian internationalism. That *Marx* wholly misunderstood the radical strength of the values present in the experience of home and fatherland is one of his basic errors in dealing with human nature. Because of this, in the *Communist Manifesto* he attempted to find in internationalism an essential characteristic of the proletariat and to meet the reproach that the workers, deprived of social rights, would be dissociated from their own country, with the observation that the worker cannot be deprived of what he does not possess.

96. The Nation: Unity of Will

The concept of nation always includes the relationship with other peoples, and hence a political element. The self-consciousness and the will to self-assertion that spring from the unity of destiny and of culture give a people something corresponding with the ego-consciousness of the individual man. A people becomes an individual in relation to other peoples. It becomes conscious of its own separate existence amid the concourse of nations and, at the same time, of its right to its own special character. This right is realized by the people's will to foster its own character, to prove its value and strength, to assert it in the community of peoples, to strive for status and respect in the community of nations in the consciousness of its specific function in the social and cultural progress of mankind: the people becomes historically conscious.

Only by organization can a people make effective, in a unity of will and of action, all the nation-molding forces which we have discussed; and since the object of this will and action is the relation of the nation to other nations, its form cannot be other than that of a political organization. Thus, the individuality of a nation within the society of nations is actualized when there is among its members, as *A. J. Toynbee* puts it, "a present will to cooperate in a political organization." [1] Certainly this will need not be equally explicit among all the members of a nation. It operates vigorously only in a relatively small portion of the nation. This portion, however, tries to arouse a similarly active will in the largest possible part of the nation. To this end it employs various methods of exerting mental influence, from elementary education to university education, and by forming public opinion. But ultimately, the unity of will, based on common language, culture, tradition, and environment, is indeed, as *Toynbee* urges, the decisive element in the concept of the nation. Nationality is "a will to cooperate," and a nation is "a group of men bound together by the immanence of this impulse in each individual." [2]

[1] A. J. Toynbee, "The New Europe," in *The Nation,* Vol. XVII, 1915, p. 826.
[2] *Ibid.,* p. 315.

Let us dwell a little on the significance of the emergence of the individuality of the nation. A nation's *consciousness of its individuality* is a modern phenomenon. Within the unitary spiritual world of the Middle Ages and within the unity of the Holy Roman Empire the various peoples played their special parts; but, except on rare occasions, as in the crusades, the individual people did not form any distinct consciousness of communal aspirations and purposes based on its own individuality. The active contribution of the peoples to common culture and political development was chiefly confined to individual personalities, such as kings, statesmen, princes of the Church, theologians, artists, and poets. With the modern nation the situation is entirely the opposite. With the rise of modern democracy the peoples begin to feel and act as units: they become conscious of themselves and their particular interests among their fellow-nations; they view the society of nations from the standpoint of their particular interests and, in cooperating with it, they seek to secure for themselves a position that will allow them their due share in the material and intellectual cultural enrichment of mankind. This process of individualization, although the fact is often overlooked, is indispensable for the development of an organized community of nations. Just as in the Renaissance period the individual, self-conscious personality began to emerge from the close social ties of tradition, thus making possible the rise of modern democracy with its ideas of liberty and equality, in the same way peoples must first become individualities in order to become conscious and fully active members of a wider community and eventually to form a free democracy of nations.

97. The Nation: Its Political Status

All political theories agree that the idea of the nation contains essentially a political element, which involves a right of self-determination and hence the right to its own political organization. With regard to the nature and extent of this political autonomy, however, opinions vary widely. Since the middle of the nineteenth century it has been thought to be equivalent to separate state existence or even absolute sovereignty. As a result of the experience of the last two world catastrophes, however, we find at present a more reserved and critical attitude, at least among political theorists, toward the individualist conception of national self-determination as absolute political autonomy. Social theory, like the theory of the traditional natural law doctrine, which never lost sight of the pluralism within the one and universal juridical order, could never admit an absolute political autonomy of the nation, although a degree of political autonomy is clearly rooted in its end and its functions as a community, as we have seen from our analysis in the foregoing sections.

Like every other right, national autonomy has its due place in the cosmos of rights, which assigns their rights and relative autonomy to all social groups with their own ends, such as people, state, Church, and international community. Thus, the right of autonomy is by no means the preserve of the state, but allows full play to the pluralism of major groups, such as nations, to their independence as well as to their coordination. In seeking to define exactly the political autonomy of the nation, we are greatly assisted by the elasticity of our concept of autonomy (cf. Chaps. 32, 42). This concept does not draw its concrete substance from preconceived ideas but from the actual pattern of functions which have their reason in social ends. Thus, it allows room for historical development.

In the case of the nation this is of especial significance, because hardly any other social entity is so much determined by historical factors as the nation. Hence, the definition of the political element in the concept of the nation itself has to be an *elastic* one. This is even more true since another element in this idea is, as we have found, intrinsically correlated to the society of nations. The society of nations is, in its form, however, to a very large extent also subject to evolution. We need only remember the different forms it takes in the Roman Empire, in the Holy Roman Empire, in the nineteenth century, and in the nuclear age. Hence, the orbit of the political autonomy and thus of the political status of the nation necessarily varies because of its very nature and the nature of the society of nations.

To define the substance of the political status of the nation, we must further distinguish two aspects in the nation's political autonomy: an internal aspect and an external one. The *internal* aspect comprises all functions necessary for organizing the nation as a community and vitalizing this unity in the interest of its own individual development and the development of its members. For this purpose the nation requires the autonomy of a quasi-state organization. The real end of the nation does not warrant any more extended political functions. Hence, this right to political autonomy can be satisfied, depending on the particular historical situation, either in federation with other nations or by independent statehood within the framework of the community of nations. For an advanced nation, the minimum requirements of this autonomy may indeed imply full sovereignty within the framework of the international or the federal system to which a nation belongs. Our conclusion is, therefore, that autonomy is in itself only a relative concept, and that in the case of the nation it becomes still more relative inasmuch as it depends on the historical situation. The *external* political autonomy of the nation, on the other hand, demands at least the possibility of direct contact with the organized international community and with its organs and institutions in order to safeguard its rights, when for good reasons it considers these to have been infringed. One of these rights is the right of the nation to self-advancement and to life-enrichment by a growing participation in the functions and fruits of international political, economic, social, or cultural cooperation. Thus, the international system must leave room for the dynamic element in the very essence of the nation which operates in the self-interest and self-assertion of the individuality of a people, but must also make provision for the direction of these forces into channels that are compatible with the interests of the nations as a whole.

All these principles are of the greatest actuality in view of developments in Africa and the Far East. Therefore, let us glance once more at the result of our discussion of this *critical problem.* There is essentially a political element in the idea of the nation; therefore, the nation needs a measure of political autonomy for an existence and a life of its own and the functions connected with them. It follows, however, from our discussion, that this political element need not be, and indeed can never be, absolute state sovereignty, as the *principle of national self-determination* suggests. The underlying fallacy of this principle is the attribution of sovereignty to a social entity to which it does not essentially belong. Sovereignty is an essential characteristic of the state, not of the nation. If, however, sovereignty is not essential to the nation, then equally the essential thing cannot be the element of power, which plays so dominant a role in conceptions of the modern nation. Yet, even such a cautious and fine thinker as *M. H. Boehm,* to whose interpretation of the political element we have frequently referred, defines the nation as "a people which develops in the element of power to a unity of will and as such . . . constitutes itself anew." *

In fact, however, the existential ends of a nation limit the political element in the nature of the nation to the political autonomy necessary for the performance of the functions based on these ends. The identification of this element simply with power instead of with the power of law made effective through an adequate, internationally guaranteed self-government is the fallacy in the individualist idea of the nation. Not only the functional sphere of a nation, proper to its end, but also the fundamental concepts of international order allow a national political autonomy only a limited range. In political theory today there can already be distinguished tendencies leading to a revision of individualist conceptions of the nation's right to self-determination and to a more cautious assessment of its right to political autonomy. On the other hand, there is no lack of historical experience of the forms in which autonomy of the kind we have discussed has developed. As an example, we may point to the status of the member countries in the British Commonwealth of Nations. Along similar lines, federations, more or less free, may arise under the urgent necessity of organizing political security systems or large economic areas. If further evidence had been needed, the nuclear age makes it absolutely clear that it was a mistake to invest the nation with absolute sovereignty. Only with a clear understanding of the nation's right to autonomy and of its possible extent and correct delimitation, can we solve the immense international difficulties involved.

* M. H. Boehm, *Das eigenständige Volk,* 1932.

98. Nation and State

Should nation and state coincide? The nineteenth century answered this question with increasing assurance by the principle of nationality: Every nation should possess its own state, and the state should comprise a national unity. This principle of nationality was largely the reverse side of the nonexistence of an efficient order of international life. For, as long as the status of nations is not guaranteed by an international order, each nation must look to state sovereignty as the guarantor of its own national autonomy. Smaller nationalities living within a state dominated by a big nation must fear denationalization by the latter as long as power politics is the only deciding factor in international life and as long as the big state is only answerable to itself. The dominant nation will tend toward stricter uniformity and will be inclined to consider the endeavors of the smaller nationalities within its boundaries to be a source of weakness. The nation-state principle in its absolute form is thus the last link in a chain of fallacious principles.

On the other hand, the very factors which in the nineteenth century contributed to the establishment of nation-states are today pressing in a new direction. The principle of one nation–one state belongs to a period when technical and economic development, as we explained in Chapter 91, demanded units of a certain magnitude which naturally crystallized in autonomous national states. Since then, however, this same development has exceeded those limits and now demands units of a size incompatible with a multitude of absolutely autonomous member states. These external, indisputable, empirical factors show that it can be of great advantage for two, indeed for numerous nations to unite in a single state or federation.[1]

The dividing line between *state* and *nation* is no different from that between state and society. They are two different forms of community. The state is a community whose function is to organize order and peace; the nation is a community rooted in a common destiny and culture whose function is to make this culture fruitful for its members and for the other nations. The state is by nature a necessary form of social organization without which men cannot live together; the nation is a form of community which depends on historical factors. Since it is directly required

[1] The complete dissolution of the Austro-Hungarian monarchy into national states provides an object lesson. It is now generally recognized as an error even by those nations which pressed hardest for it. All the successor states had to pay for the breakup of this great economic and political organism and for their own political independence at the price of great economic difficulties and a reduced standard of living, quite apart from the political consequences which followed the elimination of a Central European organization, which was so essential for European peace and security. With good reason, it has been maintained that the world would have been spared the Second World War and the consequent continuous cold war had not this former instrument of order in Europe been brought to ruin.

by human nature, the state possesses something of the essential unchangeableness of human nature; the nation is a product of development and can reach a high degree of self-awareness or recede into relative unconsciousness. The community links, the life, and the function of nation and state are different. Equally certain is the fact that, as "society" and "state," they can fulfill a function for the other, if each preserves its own life. This is true even when the two coincide in the national state. The nation can bring rich life to the state. If, however, it seeks its greatness only in the power of the state, this fact is probably a sign that it is deficient in genuine vitality. Therefore, "nationalistic movements are extremely treacherous."[2] The state can give indispensable support to the nation in achieving self-consciousness and self-expression in the unity of will, but it is liable to hinder the nation in finding its true self and developing its true character if it makes itself the nation's schoolmaster and drill sergeant.

The line between *state* and *people* is even more sharply drawn than between state and nation. Between state and people stands the nation, sharing in the political consciousness and purposes of the state, but also needing constantly to nourish itself from the living stream in the ethnic fellowship of the people. In the people there runs that deep current of life which becomes ever richer in the thousandfold daily contacts and in the community of language, common descent, and home, and which infuses the growth of cultural and social values into the national heritage. The people is elementary and organic, turning its gaze inward; the state, on the other hand, is purposeful and organized, turning its gaze outward. It is important to mention in this connection that great minds of various nations have called their homeland (i.e., the land of their people), in which their whole being is rooted, their motherland, as against the state to which they belong, which is their fatherland. The people is wholly society, and the only contribution the state can give toward its real life is to guarantee it the facilities for inner development. But the function of the people is to permeate the state with its own creative forces; to give to the state a character of its own in all spheres of social and cultural life and thus to transmit to it its own vitality. If, however, the state dominates the people and exploits the people for arbitrary collective ends by means of organization, propaganda, and regimentation, then to that extent the people will dissolve into a "mass," losing its springs of vitality and its creative ability. As long as it is true to its nature, "the people is unwilling and unable, even as a nation, to become a state, but is ready to yield and make sacrifices to it on a large scale. If it makes concessions beyond certain limits, then both state and people together suffer detriment."[3]

[2] M. H. Boehm, *Das eigenständige Volk*, 1932, p. 306.
[3] *Ibid.*, p. 290.

The principle of "one nationality, one state" could develop only from individualist and liberalist thinking and its conception of freedom as the complete autonomy of man applied to all spheres of the social order; hence, the attempt made to correlate the principle of national self-determination with that of state sovereignty, as in the individualist theory of democracy. "Free institutions," says *J. S. Mill*, "are next to impossible in a country made up of different nationalities," because "the united public opinion, necessary to the working of representative government, cannot exist"; their mutual antipathies are too great; these necessarily result in an accumulation of power in the hands of the state. "Each may reasonably think that it consults its own advantage most by bidding for the favor of the government against the rest. Above all, the grand and only effectual security in the last resort against the despotism of the government, is in that case wanting: the sympathy of the army with the people." For these reasons, "it is in general a necessary condition of free institutions that the boundaries of governments should coincide in the main with those of nationalities." [4] The logical inadequacy of this argument is shown in that it can apply equally to classes, in the Marxist sense of the word, and to the nation.

Out of the same concern for freedom, Lord *Acton* demonstrates with realistic arguments the opposite thesis, namely, that the national plural state, the state comprising several nations, is a guarantee against dictatorship. "No power," says *Acton*, "can so efficiently resist the tendencies of centralization, of corruption, and of absolutism, as that community which is the vastest that can be included in a state, which imposes on its members a consistent similarity of character, interest, and opinion, and which arrests the action of the sovereign by the influence of a divided patriotism. The presence of different nations under the same sovereignty is similar in its effect to the independence of the Church in the state. It provides against the servility which flourishes under the shadow of a single authority, by balancing interest, multiplying associations, and giving to the subject the restraint and support of a combined opinion. In the same way it promotes independence by forming definite groups of public opinion, and by affording a great source and center of political sentiments, and of notions of duty not derived from the sovereign will. Liberty provokes diversity, and diversity preserves liberty by supplying the means of organization. All those portions of law which govern the relations of men with each other and regulate social life, are the varying result of national custom and the creation of private society. In these matters, therefore, the several nations will differ from each other; for they themselves have produced them, and they do not owe them to the state which rules them all. This diversity in the same state is a firm barrier against the intrusion of the government beyond the political sphere, which is common to all, into the social department, which escapes legislation and is ruled by spontaneous laws. This sort of interference is characteristic of an absolute government, and is sure to provoke a reaction, and finally a remedy. That intolerance of social freedom which is natural to absolutism is sure to find a corrective in the national diversities, which no other force could so efficiently provide. The coexistence of several nations under the same state is a test as well as the best security of its freedom. It is also one of the chief instruments of civilization; and, as

[4] J. S. Mill, *Considerations on Representative Government,* Chap. 16.

such, it is in the natural and providential order, and indicates a state of greater advancement than the national unity which is the ideal of modern liberalism." [5] The natural law arguments in favor of social pluralism at the national level cannot be better expressed.

[5] Lord Acton, *History of Freedom and Other Essays,* pp. 289 f.

PART FOUR

The Community of Nations

99. The Natural Community of Nations as Idea and Reality

The idea of the community of nations in its full significance came late in the *development* of the moral consciousness of mankind. We can distinguish *four periods* in the process. As soon as peoples enter upon cultural life, history is able to point to usages which have been observed in their intercourse. Outward and inward experience are the souces of these rules. In outward experience these rules showed themselves useful in peaceful contact and in warlike conflict; in inward experience they were urged by the untutored conscience with its awareness of the common nature of all men. Such principles of natural law needed no formal agreement, but were enshrined in usage and thus became part of the *ius gentium* (as we have pointed out and shall presently illustrate). Outstanding among them was the usage of respect for treaties and for envoys.

With its doctrine of the origin, nature, and end of man, Christianity illuminated the idea of the oneness of mankind and of peoples as a natural community. We find the idea of the society of nations already in *St. Augustine.* Under his influence, the theologians of the Middle Ages saw the nucleus of that society in the international organism of the Holy Roman Empire. Inspired by that reality, *Dante,* in his book *De monarchia,* even considered the ideal of the society of nations to consist in a kind of world state, governed by an international authority. The theologians, however, for reasons to be discussed later, preserved the idea of the society of nations as a society of political societies. Because they held on to this aspect of the interrelation of nations, they were able to develop the first conceptions of international law. The immediate stimulus for their efforts was their concern for the respect due to all men and peoples which was demanded by Christianity, and now due also to the peoples of the newly discovered regions of the earth. Among those theologians, mention must be made of the Dominicans *Francis de Vitoria* (1486–1546; *De Indis et de jure belli relectiones*), his pupil *Dominic Soto* (1496–1560; *De justitia et jure libri septem*), and the Jesuit *Francis Suárez* (1548–1617; *De legibus*). Significantly, these three men belonged to Spain, the nation of explorers and conquerors.

The next step in this development was the recognition that the cultural, economic, and social progress of all nations depends on their cooperation. The nations were made fully conscious of their mutual dependence by the growth of the means of communication, of economic links, and of intellectual exchanges resulting from the technical developments made since the beginning of the nineteenth century. Civilization and its progress proved to be the concern of all mankind. No nation can keep up with this progress except by cooperation with others, and civilization itself cannot be safeguarded without an international order that wards off the destructive forces within the society of nations. Since nations are interdependent to this extent, they have common interests and ends whose fulfillment is integrally linked with the realization of the existential human ends. Thus, the idea and reality of a concrete common good of the society of nations emerge, and with this the consciousness of the obligation to establish the necessary international institutions to secure it. The period we are speaking of is the period of international law, in which states are trying to provide for order and collaboration in the family of nations by mutual agreements.

The development is not yet ended. The community of nations cannot accomplish its task as long as international cooperation depends, as hitherto, upon the free will and the free agreement of the individual states. It requires an international authority with legislative, judicial, and executive powers, and institutions for promoting the economic and social wellbeing of all its members. Thus, to organize the community of nations and provide it with the necessary institutions will be the task of international cooperation in the present and in the future. Indeed, today more than ever before since the days of its emergence, international law is in a state of transition. Since the coming of the nuclear age mankind is becoming aware that it can be saved only by a big step forward in establishing a stable international organization.

100. The Prerequisite of the International Community: Equality among States

A true community, which is more than merely the organized domination of some by others, exists only when, in spite of their individual inequality, a minimum of equal rights is accorded to all its members. In the same way, a community of states is possible only if all states are accorded a minimum of indispensable rights in spite of their inequalities of territories, population, natural resources, political and economic organization, and social system. Equality is founded on their fundamentally equal ends and functions which assign to the political communities a substantially equal status within the social and juridical pluralism. This status is, as we have pointed out, constitutive of the social order (cf. Chaps. 32,

42). Insofar as such a minimum of equality is denied to states, there can be only a more or less open or concealed domination of some states by others.

What are the *equal rights* which should be common to all states? They are the following:

1. The right of existence. Any state possesses this right if it has shown itself capable of fulfilling in an orderly way the functions of a political community. This right to existence is an original natural right and is not dependent on recognition by the society of nations or by other states. Even if this right should be guaranteed by other states, this is without prejudice to its character as a natural, equal, and inviolable right. Still less is this right of a state weakened when another state causes difficulties in the exercise of its functions; incitement to revolution in a neighboring state in order to cast doubt on a state's title to existence and to justify intervention, has become a policy exemplified by many instances in the period preceding and following the Second World War. To prevent such encroachments will be one of the most important tasks of the organized society of nations, because such encroachments conflict with every state's fundamental right to existence.

2. The right to freedom. This right guarantees the state's self-determination in shaping its political order, that is, the right to its sovereignty to the full extent of the functions assigned to it by the existential ends. Only the rights of others—of individuals, minorities, states, or the community of nations—and definite interests protected by these rights restrict the sovereign freedom of states.

3. The right of self-defense, including the necessary preparation by arming and by the conclusion of defensive alliances, is a natural right of the state. The extent of this right depends on the kind of institutions which the organized society of nations possesses for the securing of peace. If such institutions are in existence and are effective, the right to arm freely can be restricted by the international authority except insofar as is needed for the preservation of internal order. This will be dealt with in detail later.

4. The right of the state community to freedom by no means applies only to political freedom, it includes also the freedom of self-determination in the economic and social field, that is, the right to give to social cooperation in the economic sphere the form which the community itself desires. This implies the natural right to its own economic and social system, insofar as it is not in conflict with the moral and juridical principles of municipal or international order.

5. The right to a proportionate share in the material well-being which the earth affords to peoples when they cooperate. There is nothing "natural" in a proletarian status for some nations with relatively low standards of living or even continuous want. Each nation is entitled to have access to the necessary means for a proportionate assimilation of its standard of living to the average within the society of nations. Although the natural

resources of a country must first serve its own people, no people has the right to exclude others from sharing in the surplus. The monopolizing of selling markets is as inconsistent with equality of rights for all states as is the monopolizing of the sources of raw materials.

6. Finally, the state has a right to extend protection to nationals and to their property abroad. Since this right comes into conflict with the right of other states to sovereignty, it can be exercised only in agreement with them, that is, by the method of international treaty. Since it is a question of a natural right, states are bound to hold themselves ready to make such agreements.

The equal rights of states are *limited* internationally only by the equal rights of every other individual state and by the good of the society of nations. The greater political or economic power of some states does not justify any restriction on the rights of weaker states, but only the inevitable requirements of the common good of the international community. Does this mean that, for example, Norway with a little over three million inhabitants (1952) has the same part to play in the organized society of nations as Russia with her population of two hundred million? Certainly not. Just as in the state community, in spite of their equality before the law and of their all possessing the same fundamental rights, individuals differ in abilities, influence, and wealth, so also we have unavoidable *differences* between states in the international community. In fact, it is even in the interest of the society of nations that there should be scope for the historical dynamism engendered by inequality among states, provided that the minimum of equal rights for all is assured. Obviously, more important tasks fall to the lot of the great powers in the international field than to the lesser powers, especially with regard to the chief task of the society of nations, the preservation of peace; thus, they will also have a weightier voice in the council of the nations. To do justice to this claim in the organization of the society of nations without infringing the rights of the smaller nations is a crucial question, which will occupy us later (Chap. 106).

Along with these general natural law principles are linked a series of particular principles concerning rights and duties of states in the society of nations, such as the right of sovereignty, the right to make treaties, the right to associate, the duty to cooperate in setting up a stable order of international law, to abstain from a policy of isolation. At this point we have to turn our attention to these separate questions.

101. The Consequence of the Natural Community of Nations: No Absolute National Sovereignty

Family life becomes impossible if each member of a family insists on being completely his own master. The same is true of the family of nations. It is this absolute self-dominion which the *modern conception of sovereignty* demands for the individual state. This conception grants the state unlimited autonomy in its actions both inside and outside its own frontiers. The development of the modern conception of sovereignty went hand in hand with the modern conception of law which derives all law from the will of the state, whether this will is that of the prince, of the people, or of the ruling party. For the state, according to this theory, there can be no legal restraints except those willed by the state itself. On this basis, legal theorists even argued that the very idea of an international law was a misconception, since in international life rules can be established only when states bind themselves by treaties; and indeed, the state's will to make treaties, they urged, is in fact determined only by its enlightened self-interest, which in turn depends on the power at its command.

The theory and practice of international politics in the recent past have been largely founded upon this notion of absolute sovereignty. The policy of interest had become the predominant factor in international life. The key to international order was seen in the principle of the *balance of power,* based only on the concentration of actual military strength. Perhaps no way could be found but the method of insuring peace by the equilibrium of power groupings, as long as there were states that measured their rights by the opportunities which military force presented to them. Such a peace could not, however, be anything but precarious, for it was apparently not more than the uncertain outcome of the perpetually oscillating dynamics of power politics. This uncertainty was furthered by the fact that states sought to improve their prospects by an armaments race, and growing nationalism demanded a policy of prestige which expressed itself with a hysterical sensitiveness in the mutual relations of states and with demonstrative exhibitions of force ("saber rattling").

What is the *law of sovereignty?* The full discussion of the nature, origin, and location of sovereignty will form part of our inquiry into political theory and ethics. Here, we are chiefly concerned with the natural law principles of the international society. Sovereignty is the autonomy of the state in realizing and preserving its common good. This autonomy is concerned with the fundamental social functions, particularly with the safeguarding of the peace of the community both internally and externally, and also with providing the other conditions for the attainment of the common good of the great society. This autonomy, therefore, is the most extensive possessed by any community concerned with man's material and cultural welfare. But it is only one of the manifold kinds of autonomy having their origin in the social good of the various forms of communities. It is bound up with the hierarchy of rights and is neither unlimited nor independent. This is a straightforward conclusion from what we have said (cf. Chaps. 31, 42) about the pluralism in the social and juridical order. The limitation of the autonomy of the state does not mean that the state has not full legal supremacy. The state has the power to control its affairs and to obligate all its members as far as the good of the state requires, a power which the state exercises without responsibility to any other power and in the exercise of which, therefore, it is entitled to freedom from interference by other powers, political or ecclesiastical. State sovereignty is, therefore, real autonomy, but it is not unlimited autonomy.

The outcome of this application of the natural law principles to the conception of sovereignty obtains full support from legal history. *Jellinek* was the first who emphasized [1] that unlimited sovereignty in the modern sense has been regarded as an indispensable element in the state only in recent times, whereas in former times the incorporation of a state in a larger unit was considered in no way repugnant to the nature of the state. This holds true for the incorporation of the Greek city states in their confederacy of Delos, and of the incorporation of states into the ancient Roman Empire and later into the Holy Roman Empire. But when *Jellinek* declared that the idea of sovereignty was to be regarded in some sense as a *"historical category,"* he was opposed from all sides. Schooled by the First and Second World Wars and by the failure of the League of Nations, a failure which was caused chiefly by the conception of the absolute sovereignty of the member states, political theory is today much more willing to give *Jellinek* his due and to recognize limitations to sovereignty.[2] An international order safeguarding peace excludes unlimited sovereignty for the individual states; every step toward such an order must bring fresh evidence that sovereignty can be only a relative term. All sincere efforts toward international control of the testing of nuclear weapons necessarily presuppose limitations of the sovereignty of individual states, and also a number of other tasks of peace and welfare in international order. A realistic theory of international law, therefore, must today first and foremost plan the *revision* of the hitherto prevalent concept of sovereignty.[3] External sovereignty is, then, the state's right to autonomy while respecting the equal rights of every other state and the rights of the society of nations.

The actual *extent* of rights to a sovereignty based on natural law is conditioned by circumstances, it depends on the demands of the common good of the international society. Therefore, the question is one of relative natural law. The rights of sovereignty in the nuclear age are more limited than in any other of the previously mentioned periods of development of large international units. The right to sovereignty is by no means something rigid, as it is made to appear by modern schools of municipal and international law. Only an autonomy based on a minimum

[1] Cf. K. Jellinek, *Die Lehre von den Staatsverbindungen,* 1882, p. 37; on the historical development cf. Frh. A. v. d. Heydte, *Die Geburtsstunde des souveränen Staates,* 1952.

[2] Cf. P. E. Corbett, *Postwar Worlds,* 1942, pp. 104–14.

[3] Today, with many others, P. C. Jessup, *A Modern Law of Nations,* 1949, p. 12, sees in absolute state sovereignty the archfiction of international law.

of equal rights for states (cf. previous chapter) is essential for sovereignty. For the rest, wide scope is left for adaptation to historical, political, economic, social, and cultural forces. Indeed, in actual international life, sovereignty does not present so uniform a picture that it would always be easy to say whether a restriction of the autonomy of a state affects its sovereignty, or whether the actual autonomy of a partly dependent state can already be called sovereignty. By the peace treaties of 1919, conditions such as disarmament control and financial control, which signified a restriction of autonomy, were imposed upon a number of states. To take an older example, the Anglo-Russian Entente of 1907 established British and Russian spheres of influence in Persia and Afghanistan under conditions which implied considerable inroads into the autonomy of these countries. But in none of these cases was the sovereignty of these states called in question. On the other hand, the British dominions of Australia and Canada, long ago obtained their full autonomy and consequently were already represented in the League of Nations, although formally they derive their authority from the mother country.

The Right of Intervention

If, as has been shown, according to natural law principles there is no absolute sovereignty, but only a sovereignty in conformity with the order of individual state and of international society, as indicated by those principles, it necessarily follows that there is a right of intervention against a state which seriously offends against this order. Traditional natural law theory has always upheld the right of intervention against such states. Under present-day conditions there is, according to natural law principles, a right to intervention chiefly in these four cases: (1) against a state which is guilty of armed attack against another; (2) against a state which encroaches on the right of freedom of another state (e.g. by supporting a party's preparation for or attempt at revolution); (3) against a state which is guilty of gravely injuring the natural rights of large groups of citizens, such as those belonging to a particular political party or national minorities; (4) against a state which directly or indirectly offends seriously against international regulations in matters such as the drug traffic or the colored or "white" slave trade.

In all four cases not only the state, which is directly affected by the conduct of a state, is entitled to intervention for the sake of the violated rights, but also other states; indeed, it can be a definite duty for all states to cooperate in such intervention, so that neutrality would be a neglect of duty (cf. Chap. 106). The reason is that the violation of fundamental rights of states or of groups of people may affect international peace, and also that, in the developed society of nations, a common responsibility exists to insure respect for these rights. Since no man with a good conscience can say, "Am I my brother's keeper?" so also no community can excuse itself from cooperating in safeguarding that minimum of moral and legal behavior in international life which mankind has reached at such great sacrifice and on which the future depends. The organized community of nations must consider the conditions and methods of intervention as one of the most important matters to be settled by statute, and the use of the right of intervention in the best interest of an order of peace or law which is threatened or impaired as one of its most important tasks.

In modern natural law theory and in international politics in modern times no such right of intervention was recognized up to the twentieth century, but actually it was extensively claimed; for example, spheres of interest were awarded to great powers, giving them a possibility of intervening in one state or more. The first recognition of this was in the statute of the League of Nations, whereby the prevention of wars of aggression was sought by threatening sanctions, by provisions of the United Nations Charter instituting united action against breaches of the peace or acts by states tending to lead to warlike developments. The intervention of the United Nations in Korea and in the Suez crisis is an example of the effectiveness of the principles which are now acknowledged. In a very small way since the Second World War, the principle already accepted in nineteenth-century international law theory, of intervention to safeguard human rights (*intervention d'humanité*) has been brought into use.[4] A whole range of countries in the free world, to say nothing of those under totalitarian communistic domination, have rejected in recent years the United Nations' expressions of sympathy for violated human rights and rights of minorities on the ground that they represent "interference in the internal affairs" of the states concerned. Such states incur the gravest responsibility for the injury they cause to the moral esteem of international law and the consequent loss of its effectiveness.

With regard to the manner in which the right of intervention is to be exercised, this right is dependent on the situation more than almost any other right of natural law, insofar as the possibility of attaining the end of the right must be carefully weighed against the danger of bringing about worse evil. For this reason, justified intervention can take the form of radio transmissions to peoples who are deprived of their human rights, if by other methods of intervention, a war, even a world war, might be brought about. Forms of justified and unjustified intervention exemplified in the past are diplomatic action, enforcement of political conditions in loan and trade agreements, partial or general economic blockades, insistence on the appointment of ministers of state with a particular party alignment, radio transmissions to peoples of other states, economic sanctions, breaches of diplomatic relations, and war.

102. International Law

International law embraces, just as municipal law does, three types of law: natural law, customary law, and positive law. If, and this follows from what has been said, the states form a community bound together by the common existential human ends of their members, natural law principles govern the fundamental relationships of states within this community. Therefore, a *natural international law* exists. Just as in the other spheres of social life, so also in the international sphere, primary natural law does not go beyond general principles. The chief one is *suum cuique*,

[4] Cf. A. Verdroß, *Völkerrecht*, 3rd ed., 1955, pp. 77, 481 ff.

which as a principle of international law signifies above all the respect for the natural fundamental rights of all states (cf. Chap. 100); in addition, there are the principles: "Do not do to others what you would not wish them to do to yourself" (preserve peace); "Behave toward others as you wish them to behave toward you" (preserve the common good); "Contracts must be kept" (the principle of abiding by treaties).

These principles were applied in the *customary international law* of *ius gentium*. Peoples, urged by experience of the benefit for all, formed customs of conduct for their intercourse in correspondence with the demands of their common human existence. This *ius gentium* embodies principles of applied international law. *Vitoria,* the great Dominican friar and the founder of the theory of international law, enumerates the following: visitors and strangers are not to be ill treated if they do no harm; everyone is free to travel and sojourn where he likes, with the same proviso; running waters, rivers, the sea, and harbors are common to all (*Vitoria* here refers to the *Institutes of Justinian,* 2, 1); every nation is entitled to trade with any other, with the same proviso; envoys must be held inviolable; prisoners of war may be made slaves.[1] In the customary substance of *ius gentium* there is, as in *ius gentium* generally, an element of tacit understanding or consent involved. This has a double bearing: it establishes its general validity, but also its variability. First, as *Vitoria* realized, it is binding upon all nations even when not all mankind has explicitly agreed to it, but only the large majority; for, it is the result of the moral legal impulse of conscience common to all mankind. Natural law does not always and in all circumstances operate infallibly, but only in the majority, *ut in pluribus,* to recall again an expression of *St. Thomas Aquinas.* If, therefore, in the great majority of cases of mutual conduct of nations it leads to definite legal principles, these must, reasons *Vitoria,* rank as principles of natural law, and therefore are generally binding. A further conclusion is that they confer the right to act in accordance with them against those who do not abide by the moral consciousness of the majority of mankind. On the other hand, *ius gentium,* with its element of consent, is mutable, because it is guided by a discernment of the changing prerequisites of the general utility. In fact, among its principles specified by *Vitoria* there is one which has not been accepted by modern *ius gentium:* the right to enslave prisoners of war.[2]

[1] Cf. Francis de Vitoria, *De Indis et de jure belli relectiones,* 1532, rel. I, sec. 3. The fact that Grotius has drawn from Vitoria in establishing the fundamental principle of his *Mare liberum* (1608) is shown by his reference to Vitoria; cf. the 1916 Carnegie edition of Hugo Grotius' *Mare liberum* (*The Freedom of the Seas*), p. 7; Grotius states his fundamental principle as follows: "Fundamentum struemus hanc iuris gentium, quod primarium vocant regulam certissimam, cuius perspicua atque immutabilis est ratio; licere cuivis genti quamvis alteram adire, cumque ea negotiari." Cf. the analysis of sec. 3 of Vitoria's discourse in J. Brown Scott, *Francisco de Vitoria and the Law of Nations,* 1934, pp. 140 ff.; on the subject as a whole cf. Josef Höffner, *Christentum und Menschenwürde,* 1947, pp. 299 f.

[2] Vitoria, *loc. cit.,* brings out clearly the first of these two consequences of the character of *ius gentium,* not the second.

The customs of *ius gentium,* with their element of consent, already form the transition to *positive international law.* Its development, and thus the development of international law in the modern sense, began when rules of conduct regarding international relations were set up by express treaties and conventions between nations, based on the generally accepted principle that contracts must be kept. Included in this was the understanding that the rules of established customs in general should be binding. Positive international law thus comes into being by the tacit consent or the express agreement of political communities which possess full legal competence. Only states can be parties to contracts in the realm of positive international law, not nations as ethnico-cultural groups. The morally binding legal force of this positive international law is derived from the general principle of natural law: *Pacta sunt servanda.* It would be a mistake, however, to confine natural international law, as is sometimes done, to this single principle, as can be seen from the principles mentioned above.

That international law is *true law* is contested on two grounds. In the first place, there is no legislator; whereas the laws of the state originate with a lawgiver, whether a ruler or a parliament, international law springs only from implicit or explicit agreement between states. In the second place, it is argued, compliance with the law of the state is enforced by the power of the state; but there is no such authority to enforce international law. The latter objection has been repeatedly raised, particularly since the time of *John Austin.* No wonder this objection was raised, since the jurisprudence of his time sought the essence of law in the power to enforce it and denied to moral-juridical law, natural law, the character of real law.

In the development of modern international law, however, facts emerged which could not be explained without the recognition that the universal consciousness of justice itself performs the function of a *sanction.* In fact, all states are greatly concerned to show, in their dealings with other states, that they have justice on their side. For, no nation can violate established rules of international law without forfeiting its moral standing in the eyes of the world. Furthermore, experience shows that states adhere even to conventions to which they are not themselves bound by treaty; for instance, the two parties in the Spanish-American War, both of whom observed the terms of the Declaration of Paris although neither of them was a signatory to it. Such facts prove that a natural juridical conscience exists, indicating an order of law as something which should govern international conduct and with which governments consider themselves more or less obliged to conform. In addition, present-day efforts to establish an international force to take action in case of any unlawful aggression are testimony that there is not wanting in the moral consciousness the principle of vindicating law by higher authority, even though this consciousness has only gradually emerged, and the principle of vindicating law and order is very difficult to implement.

With regard to the argument stating that there is no *lawgiver* in the sphere of natural law, it comes from the unproved assumption (cf. Chap. 38) that there is no law except those made by the legislator of an individual state, and that it is valid only in the territory of that state. At the other extreme, the legal theory of *Kelsen*[3] urges that ultimately even municipal law can be legally based only on international law. When a universal consciousness of fundamental principles of law and of justice is recognized, as in the natural law doctrine, there is no difficulty in seeing in it a true ultimate lawgiver. Of course these principles have to be applied and interpreted in detail by international customs and treaties.

The Development of Positive International Law

The strongest incentive for positive legislation within the state came from experience and the same was also true for international legislation. The horrors of war provided the most powerful impulsion toward positive international law. The first beginnings can be seen growing out of the armed conflicts and sea-trading disputes of the Italian city states of the Middle Ages: the distinction between combatants and civilians in war, sea-traffic rules for the avoidance of conflicts, rules for humanizing sea warfare, the development of forms of courtesy and of diplomatic communication between states, and the provision of passports for travellers. The experience of the Thirty Years' War with its cruelties and misery led to such thoroughgoing regulation of state sovereignty rights and religious matters that the Peace of Westphalia (1648) is regarded by many as the birth of modern international law.

Nevertheless, the first agreed establishment of real international law was not made until the Declaration of Paris in 1856, to which all European powers, including Turkey, were parties: privateering is abolished; enemy property under a neutral flag and neutral property under an enemy flag, contraband excepted, are not lawful prizes of war; the blockade obligates neutrals only when it is effective. The first Hague Peace Conference (1899), at which twenty-six states were represented, undertook a codification of international law in three conventions; yet, only the first two, concerning the laws of war by land and sea, were ratified by the participating states and thus made legally binding upon them; not so the third, which contained proposals for a peaceful settlement of interstate disputes. At the second Hague Peace Conference (1907) further vain efforts were made to secure obligatory arbitration for the participating states

[3] The flaws in Kelsen's natural law doctrine are particularly noticeable in his book on international law, *Principles of International Law* (U.S.A.), 1952. General international law is customary law binding for all states which belong to the international community (p. 19). He regards the binding force of customary international law as originating in the hypothesis that international custom is a law-creating fact, and he calls this hypothesis the fundamental norm; this norm is not created by acts of will but constitutes a juridical assumption (p. 314), namely that the states ought to behave as they have customarily behaved. The norm *pacta sunt servanda* comes under this customary law (pp. 417 f.). The flaw in Kelsen's theory is, if not otherwise obvious, very obvious (cf. Chap. 50) in that he uses the word norm in three different senses: as a factually valid norm (founded on a fact); as only a juridically theoretic norm (based on a hypothesis), as a pre-positive ethical norm (favoring the origin of custom and consisting in an "ought" ruling this).

and to bring about a reduction in armaments. Further efforts, however, resulted only in the setting up of voluntary arbitration; nevertheless, new conventions on the laws of war were adopted, which governed the opening of hostilities, the status of enemy merchant ships at the outbreak of war, the conversion of merchant ships to warships, the laying of submarine mines, the shelling of undefended localities by naval forces, and prohibiting the use of poison gases and weapons causing unnecessary suffering, such as dumdum bullets. The London Conference of 1907, at which ten sea powers were represented, formulated a convention on some questions of warfare (blockade, contraband, prize law, convoys), stressing anew the principle of the freedom of the seas and of the legal status of ships as virtually portions of their national territory.

The chief advance made by the *Covenant of the League of Nations* (1919) consisted in the obligatory recourse to arbitration in interstate disputes, the provision of sanctions against an aggressor, the institution of the International Labor Organization. The peace treaties based on the covenant marked a further step in the development of international law with provisions for international labor law, minority law, the law of inland water transportation and of transit traffic. In 1920, the Permanent Court of International Justice envisaged in the covenant was set up at The Hague. At the Washington Conference of 1922 the leading naval powers agreed to a ten-year limitation in the construction of capital ships.

The Second World War brought the *Atlantic Charter* (1941), which, although it contains only principles whose application has been disappointing, is a document of paramount significance in the development of the moral consciousness of mankind regarding international relations. The *Charter of the United Nations* (1945) does not so much mark a decisive step forward in fundamental principles, as it shows an attempt to set up a more efficient machinery for preserving peace. The organ for this purpose is the Security Council. This, as well as the two other new institutions, the Economic and Social Council and the International Trusteeship System, will be discussed later. The following matters are considered to be corollaries to international law: international agreements on the treatment of nationality, naturalization, patents, trade marks, authors' copyrights, the extradition of criminals, the position of married and divorced persons before the law when marriage or divorce has taken place abroad.

103. The Foundation of International Law: The Sanctity of Treaties

Since today the greater part of positive international law arises from treaties between states (pacts, conventions, general acts), the theory of international law since the time of *Vitoria* and *Grotius* has concerned itself closely with the binding force of such treaties, the conditions under which they come into existence or expire—in short, it has concerned itself with the sanctity of treaties and the corresponding legality of international conduct. Just as every other contract is an agreement of wills between two or more natural or corporate persons in order to create legally binding obligations, so also an international treaty is an agreement between states that is dependent on similar conditions.

The conditions necessary for the existence of a valid international treaty are, accordingly:

1. The international legal capacity of the contracting states; only states, not nations as such, and only independent states, can conclude international treaties.

2. The moral and legal admissibility of the object of the treaty; without this the treaty is invalidated at the outset. Therefore, an aggression pact cannot have any legal existence, and the same is true of agreements in which a third state is recognized as belonging to the sphere of interest or of influence of one of the contracting powers, if this violates or threatens rights (belonging by nature to every state; cf. Chap. 100) of the third state in question.

3. Freedom of decision of the contracting states. This involves difficult questions for the ethics and the theory of international law. Is the peace treaty valid which is imposed upon a defeated state as the result of an unjust aggression? The oppressed nation will reply with a decided No, and the natural sense of justice will approve the answer. *Hugo Grotius* answers with a decided Yes, and justifies his verdict with the argument that there would be no end to wars if every state which considered itself unjustly treated could unilaterally declare such treaties null and void; their observance is, therefore, "in the interest of the human race." [1] *Grotius* would probably be even more positive in his view in the present age of nuclear weapons. The majority of international jurists agree with his judgment and point out that the state which considers itself injured would be acting as judge in its own case and that thereby the stability of international order would be most gravely imperiled, if in such cases peace treaties could simply be denounced as invalid. But all, including *Grotius*, admit that treaties of this kind do not create any true right, or even treaties which are justified in themselves, if they make unjustified exactions (e.g., a treaty imposed by a state victorious in a defensive war, which goes beyond what the state is really entitled to in indemnification and security requirements). It is further agreed that the victorious aggressor state may not retain what is unjustly gained by such treaties. Other jurists deny the legal validity of treaties dictated in this way, but admit that the state which acquiesces under duress may, nevertheless, be under an obligation to fulfill the treaty if it is in the interest of a community which would otherwise be plunged into a war of annihilation, or in the interest of the international community, in order to save it from armed conflict.[2] In practice, the two views amount to the same; especially since the advocates of both stress the necessity of an international machinery to eliminate injustice of this kind.

The binding force of a treaty expires on the termination of the period agreed upon, or on the fulfillment of the terms, or by mutual consent. Any

[1] Hugo Grotius, *De jure belli ac pacis,* Bk. III, Chap. 19, par. 11.

[2] Cf. *A Code of International Ethics,* prepared by the International Union of Social Studies, 1937, p. 50.

other process of termination is beset with complications. The case appears simple when one party to a bilateral agreement breaks the contract, for it then ceases to be binding upon the other party. Since, however, the fact of the breach of contract is itself partly a question of interpretation as well as of actual circumstances in accordance with the contractual obligation, an objective judgment of the case may often not be easy. Especially difficult is the case of a breach of a joint international treaty. Is the convention forbidding the use of poison gas invalidated if one of the belligerents uses gas? To be sure, not without further qualification; for, the whole purpose of such treaties is to guarantee the upholding of definite moral and legal standards. Only when no other means exists of securing respect for international obligations and of resisting the unjust aggressor is there any justification for replying with the same weapon.

The most difficult case occurs when a state pleads an alteration in its circumstances since the conclusion of a treaty; it no longer feels bound by the terms it accepted in totally different circumstances. Let us suppose that a state has entered into a defensive alliance with another state and then sees that to take part in a war in fulfillment of its obligation would cost its existence. Is a state bound to adhere to the terms of its alliance? Certainly not, if the facts are clear. Far-reaching and unforeseeable changes in circumstances relieve the partners of their obligations. Since the binding force of a contract originates in the will of the partners and the international circumstances are often subject to great and rapid change, every treaty contains the clause: *Rebus sic stantibus.* Relatively slight changes in circumstances, however, of a kind that could have been foreseen, do not relieve partners of their obligations; such changes must always be reckoned with, and since the partners only make treaties because they expect advantages from them, they must also reckon with disadvantages if the principles of loyalty to treaties is not to lose all meaning. Experience shows that the powers interpret the above-mentioned clause with a very elastic conscience, and that they simply set aside treaties which do not prove useful to them. Yet, the interpretation of treaties is not a matter of utility, but of justice. It is, therefore, a breach of law to allege a changed situation merely as an excuse for evasion. Such pacts fall within the sphere of commutative, strict justice. Hence, the obligations of a defensive pact go much further than the obligation to intervene, where the latter springs only from natural international justice, that is, from the obligation to cooperate in securing international peace.

What is the effect on treaty obligations when one partner loses legal capacity? The contractual financial liabilities of a state, such as repayments of loans or payments on justly imposed war debts, indisputably pass over to a state which has incorporated it, whether lawfully or unlawfully, since the annexing state will also acquire its financial resources. A partner to an alliance is not freed from the obligations of a defensive alliance with a state which is annexed by another as long as the annexed state has not given explicit or tacit consent to its incorporation, by abandoning, for example, all efforts at self-defense. A nonaggression pact is not invalidated by the fact that one of the partners is the victim of an attack by a third power; if the other seeks to gain territory by annexation, not only is it a violator of a treaty but it becomes an aggressor. In all these cases the chief difficulty consists in the interpretation of facts: Has the partner to the treaty ceased to exist? What will to independence does it possess? What are the prospects of its regaining independence? The difficulties of interpreting treaty obligations, as well as the facts, show how urgently the society of nations requires an authority with power to watch over the principle of the sanctity of treaties and to call treaty breakers to account.

Individualist, collectivistic *political utilitarianism* in the course of the last century openly professed or tacitly followed the principle of the "sanctity of interests," making the interest of state openly or tacitly the only ultimate imperative in international politics. Whether it assumes cruder or more refined forms or even a moral veneer, political utilitarianism is Machiavellianism. Indeed, what *Machiavelli* described as *frodi onorevoli*, honorable deceits in statesmanship, makes treaty breaking a means of international politics. When one reflects on the multitude of treaties that have not been implemented since the middle of the nineteenth century, one is tempted to find substance in the judgment of those who describe the age of international law as the age of open or concealed treaty breaking. In more modern times, political utilitarianism was practiced under the maxim of *sacro egoismo*, and in recent times under the principle of political realism, when states put aside obligations undertaken in treaties which turned out to their disadvantage. The obvious consequence of the principle of the sanctity of interests is international power politics, the antithesis of international law.

104. The Paramount Purpose of International Law: The Preservation of Peace

Peace and order are the primary issues in any community. This is all the more so in the community of nations, since safeguarding peace means preventing such a fearful evil as war. To safeguard peace the community of nations must aim at three international regulations: 1) Each state must submit to international arbitration before taking steps to make war on its own behalf. 2) The state which, neglecting international arbitration, proceeds to war, *eo ipso* is reckoned an aggressor. 3) The executive power of the organized society of nations must take action at once against a violator of the peace, in order to restore order. The first step to set up such a security system was undertaken by the League of Nations after the First World War. This system fell short of its purpose. Article 16 of the *League Covenant* declared that any state which proceeds to war, neglecting the machinery for settling the dispute by arbitration, is an aggressor; and it provided for the application of economic sanctions. These consisted in breaking off economic relations as a first measure. On the invasion of Manchuria by Japan (1931–33), however, the machinery of the League of Nations showed itself from the beginning too cumbersome and slow to hold up military developments, and the application of sanctions, as is well known, came to grief not least because of capitalistic interests in the Far East and particularly those connected with the armaments industry. In the Abyssinian war, the indecisiveness of the sanctions policy brought about a complete debacle for the League; it was quite impossible to secure the application of the decisive oil sanctions. In 1939 it was clear that "the whole machinery for the preservation of peace has collapsed." * It is evident today that economic sanctions are not sufficient to avert aggression, but that the organized society of nations must dispose an *executive force* strong enough to prevent any war of aggression or to quell it at once.

Opinions on the composition of the force are varied. One school thinks in terms of analogies from the life of the state; it postulates an international police force which would have sufficient military strength to make acts of aggression hopeless from the start or at least to render them harmless at once. Such proposals are unrealistic as long as there is one great power unwilling to permit the necessary international control of armaments and which, therefore, is a potential originator of an annihilating surprise attack. More realistic proposals, which are in part realized, are those for strong and large *regional defensive alliances* of states with common defense interests, the war potential of the allied states being combined under joint control. The most resolute adherents of such a system of safeguarding peace even demand the formation of a joint defense government by the allied states to be elected directly by the electorate of all the states of the defensive league. Thus, this government, deriving its authority from the citizens of the several states, would possess first claim on all the human and material resources of the countries concerned. Therefore, it would be in a position to arrange for a fair contribution of air force, ground forces, and naval contingents to be made by the individual states. The states joining such an alliance would have to give up a part of their sovereignty to the common government. There are very strong reasons for such regional security systems as long as there is the danger of a surprise attack with nuclear weapons, which would deprive half the world within a few hours of all prospects of self-defense and self-preservation.

In these proposals the idea of safeguarding peace is based on the *principle of balance of power*. In fact, regrettable though it is, any future schemes will have to be based primarily upon some form of balance among the great powers. The next step toward infusing ethical and legal principles into the system by which peace is secured in the society of nations

* Letter of the British Government to the General Secretary of the League of Nations, September 7, 1939.

seems to lie in raising up to an ethical plane the balance of power principle itself, thus eliminating it in its old forms in which it has been guided by a policy of the self-interest of individual states. This is possible if the principle of balance is bound up with the common good of the international community in such a way that obligations are undertaken by all the states jointly for the common good.

One of the forms of such a system of balance would be the union of states, small as well as large, in large regional defensive systems, as has been suggested earlier. Such a system, with its integration of obligations, would prevent small states, as in 1939, from seeking to save themselves by neutrality, which now even more surely than then would give a great power the best chance of a successful attack. A second conceivable form of a system of balance would apply exclusively to the great powers. The small states would possess no greater military resources than would be sufficient to maintain order within their borders. The great powers would bind themselves to a system of equilibrium in armament reduction under international control. The disarmament commission, which the organized society of nations must set up, must have power freely to inspect the state of preparations for war in all states, including the potential war industries, and particularly the production and stocks of nuclear weapons. Three apparently insuperable difficulties confront such a system. First, the possession of the secrets of production of nuclear power can be kept hidden; in fact, the suspicion of one side that the other possesses advanced methods is one of the chief obstacles to discontinuing nuclear tests. Secondly, the totalitarian state can hardly permit such a control without endangering the very conditions of its existence, since it would necessitate close contact with the staff and workers of the large industrial undertakings. Thirdly, there is the lack of free expression of public opinion in the totalitarian states. This is essential for the existence of totalitarian states, and makes every armament control unsatisfactory, if a state commands an area which, by reason of its extent and inaccessibility, makes the possibility of reliable control doubtful.

In fact, there is *only one really effective guarantee of international armament control:* the free expression of public opinion nationally and internationally. This is the decisive characteristic of a free and open society (cf. Chap. 136). Only in the free and open society can the amount of information be gained which is needed for an effective international armament control. The freedom of public opinion, if operative in all countries, would constitute the decisive bulwark of international peace. The principles which inform the free and open society are those ordained in the existential ends themselves; therefore, they are the fundamental moral principles of national as well as of international life. In the nuclear age, obviously, peace can ultimately be based only on moral principles; the indivisibility of peace, so often referred to, proves to be ultimately the indivisibility of the moral order.

The *security system of the United Nations* (1945) fails in the fundamental tasks of universal disarmament and universal disarmament-control. Its charter retains the obligation of states to settle disputes by peaceful means, as provided by the League, but in the Security Council it sets up a new organ charged with the "primary responsibility for the maintenance of international peace and security" (Art. 24). This shall, when necessary, call upon the parties to settle their disputes by pacific means (Art. 33). It may investigate any dispute or any situation that might lead to international friction (Art. 34). Any member of the United Nations may bring any such dispute or any such situation to the attention of the Security Council or of the General Assembly (Art. 35). Furthermore, in case of any threat to peace, the Security Council shall decide on measures to be taken; these measures consist in the suspension of trade, communications, or diplomatic relations; only if such measures prove inadequate may it take action by air, sea, or land forces, including demonstrations, blockade, and other operations by the armed forces of the members of the United Nations. All members undertake to make available to the Security Council, "on its call and in accordance with a special agreement or agreements," armed forces, particularly airforce contingents (Arts. 39 ff.). Finally, the Security Council shall be responsible for formulating plans to be submitted to the members of the United Nations for the establishment of a system of armaments regulation. The Security Council consists of eleven members: five permanent (China, France, Great Britain, the United States, and the U.S.S.R.) and six others, who are elected by the General Assembly.

The criticism of this machinery for the preservation of peace must be based on the fact, first, that it does not itself constitute a system of universal disarmament imposed on all states by international authority and made effective by international control. Consequently, the armaments race has continued since the end of the Second World War, disillusioning all hopes for a guaranteed international peace. The second fact on which this criticism is based consists in the right of each of the five permanent members of the Security Council to *veto* action by the Security Council; thus, the primacy of the principle of absolute sovereignty over the principle of law is still maintained.

105. The Substance of International Law: The Laws of War

Remarkable as the achievements of international understanding have been in various spheres of international collaboration, its main achievement is the humanization of war.[1] Indeed, it was from the experience of the horrors of war that endeavors to establish international rules chiefly

[1] "Force and fraud," says Hobbes (*De cive*, Chap. 13) "are in war the two cardinal virtues"; for, "where there is no common power," he argues in this well-known passage, "there is no law: where no law, no injustice." Indeed, war is the suspension of all law; its only law is to cause the enemy as much harm as possible. Such has been the predominant practical morality of war in the history of mankind. Not even the international usages of war which have been accepted by treaty deter belligerents from using any effective methods, especially in a protracted war; the only deterrent is the fear that the adversary may reply with reprisals in kind.

sprang. Even the titles of the famous books forming the first attempts to investigate the law of nations, such as those of *Vitoria* in the sixteenth century and of *Hugo Grotius* in the seventeenth century, show that the laws of war, the causes of war, the just war, the just means of warfare, and the just settlement after war are their chief subjects. We shall deal with the causes of war and the just war later (cf. Chap. 146), when we discuss the defensive function of the state. At present, we have to restrict ourselves to the natural law principles for war itself.

There is no generally accepted *definition of war* in the theory of international law; therefore, the law of war which actually prevails must be examined. This may be done by a reference to a practical question such as whether and when francs-tireurs, guerillas, and "partisans" must be recognized as belligerents and enjoy the rights of belligerents. According to older usage, in a country occupied by an enemy, if armed groups harmed the enemy from ambush or in any other way, they were not protected by international law, but were left to the enemy's mercy. Modern war, owing to the great areas over which it moves, has revealed the possibility of supplying arms to organized groups, so that these are able to offer organized resistance, and obtain a status similar to that of the regular forces. Another question concerns the status of organized forces in civil war. Hitherto, a narrow line has been drawn between civil war and interstate war. The last civil war in Spain with the participation of nationals, even regular troops, of other states, has shown that the idea of war in international law does not admit of too rigid an interpretation. In this instance, the insurgents, as in the former the partisans, have been treated as belligerents according to the international law of war, if only for the reason that they would resort to reprisals if their prisoners and wounded had to go without the benefit of that law. Such authorities on international law as *Hugo Grotius* and *E. de Vattel,* the author of the first systematic study in international law, subsumed armed conflicts between groups other than political communities themselves under their definition of wars.[2]

The demands of natural justice follow from the *fundamental principle*

[2] Cf. Hugo Grotius, *De iure belli ac pacis,* 1625, Bk. I, Chap. 1; E. de Vattel, *Le droit des gens, ou Principes de la loi naturelle, appliqués à la Conduite et aux Affaires des Nations et des Souverains,* 1758, Bk. III, Chap. 1. Apparently they did so in view of the many strifes and wars during the Renaissance and at later times between rival princely houses or parties within the same political unit of state or town. This wide conception of war is the more surprising since it deviates from that which the earlier natural law doctrine had established (cf. Suárez, "De bello," in *De fide, spe et caritate,* Bk. III, disp. 13, beginning): war, in contradistinction to sedition and private strifes, is a dispute between princes or states. In practice, the actual provisions and customs of international law for such critical questions as those mentioned above are decisive. Having regard for the viewpoints discussed, the *definition of war* may be taken as a relationship of states, or large organized groups similar to states, based on their readiness to use force. We speak only of the readiness to use force, since states could find themselves in a state of war without actually proceeding to the use of weapons against each other; moreover, we speak of large organized groups similar to states in order to take into account cases such as that mentioned in the example of the Spanish Civil War.

that no kind of action in warfare is justified except as a means of defense against aggression, since war itself is justified solely as a means of defense. Among the particular principles the following are the most important:

1. The opening of hostilities should be preceded by a declaration of war, whether by the recalling of envoys or by the delivery of an ultimatum, and the time should be stated from which a state of war exists. The reason is not only the serious legal consequences entailed in war, but also because provision must be made for the protection of the unarmed population in the prospective theaters of war.

2. The lives of the noncombatant population remain inviolable. The deliberate killing of the defenseless, of women and children, whether directly or indirectly, is murder in war as in other circumstances, whether it is ordered by the military command or is merely the isolated acts of units or of individuals.

3. The freedom of the citizens in the occupied territory is also protected by natural international law. Compulsory transfer and deportation of workers from enemy territory and their forced employment in war production is unlawful because they are thereby compelled to support the war effort against their own country.

4. The military authorities may, on entering enemy territory, possess themselves of state property, but they have only so much right over the private property of citizens in the occupied territory as the citizens' own state possesses, namely, such as is derived from its defensive function in war, e.g., requisitioning billets or food not otherwise obtainable. The fact that so enlightened a spirit as *Hugo Grotius* defends the right to booty,[3] appealing to Roman legal doctrine and to an Old Testament instance (Deut. 20:14; which, however, applies only in the Old Testament dispensation), shows with what difficulty mankind advances along the road of law and with what jealous care it must strive, never to retreat from any stage in the development of law once reached.

5. Since the principle of defensive war justifies only the military defeat of the enemy, the killing of enemy wounded or prisoners is murder. The treatment envisaged for them by international law corresponds with what is demanded by natural law: enemy wounded must receive the same care as one's own wounded; prisoners must be given the same scale of food rations as one's own soldiers; they may be employed in civilian work for pay, but never in the production of war material or in military operations.

6. Since intrinsically immoral acts are never justified, they are not justified in war. Consequently, promises to abstain from hostilities (hoisting the white flag) merely to deceive the enemy are never permissible stratagems. Falsehood remains falsehood even in war, and nothing can

[3] Cf. Hugo Grotius, *op. cit.*, Bk. III, Chap. 6; cf. also St. Thomas, *Summa theol.*, IIa IIae, q. 66, a. 8.

justify the orgies of lies in which propaganda indulges in modern war.

With this we have already entered upon the question of what *weapons of war* are permissible. It concerns particularly such methods as the hunger blockade, the bombing of towns, the bombardment of open towns with hydrogen bombs, the employment of atomic bombs, poison gases, bacterial warfare, dumdum bullets (soft-nosed bullets designed to cause severe injury). Our principle of restricting the means of warfare to self-defense provides an unambiguous answer. Self-defense never justifies directly any of the methods mentioned, for they cause unnecessary injury to combatants or they injure the defenseless in general. Every state which starts to use such weapons in a war commits a serious injustice against countless individuals as well as against the order of international law as a whole. The state attacked has not even the right to employ such means when the aggressor uses them if other means are adequate to the purpose of self-defense. The use of these means for the purpose of retaliation, therefore, is not permissible even as instruments of reprisal to dissuade the enemy from using them himself, if other and lawful means are available, even though these may involve material sacrifices. By observing these rules, the belligerents also protect themselves, since experience shows that, once law is forsaken in the question of war weapons, the biddings of humanity are increasingly set aside to the detriment of both parties. Only one reason can be adduced to justify the use of one or other of the methods we have mentioned, namely, that the aggressor uses them and that it is certain no other means exist of repelling the aggressor, who thus threatens the fundamental goods of a state. (On the many "ifs" and "buts" connected with this question, cf. also Chaps. 28, 146, 149.)

War with Nuclear Weapons

The same principles that govern a just war (cf. Chap. 146) apply to a just war with nuclear weapons, above all that war does not jeopardize still higher goods than those which are to be defended, and secondly, that the means employed must be unobjectionable. In accordance with the last-mentioned condition, nuclear weapons which are uncontrollable in their effect owing to radioactive fall-out, or for other reasons, are inadmissible, since not only large masses of the noncombatant population of warring states but also, on account of the drifting fall-out, large numbers of nonparticipating states would suffer severe injury. Insofar as this condition is not satisfied, the first can hardly be upheld, since the defending state itself would be exposed to retaliatory measures by weapons that would result in most severe injuries. The reason for the inadmissibility of the use of these weapons is that, on account of the uncontrollable effect, they would necessarily amount to the directly willed killing or severe injury of unarmed masses of the population of the enemy state and of nonparticipating states.[4] From this follows, as the first principle, that the use of such a weapon in a war, even in a defensive war, is inadmissible according to the principles of natural law. The objections mentioned are not applicable when atomic weapons have no, or hardly any, fall-out, and are used for the purpose of rendering unserviceable military objects and formations, centers of war-production, and important communication centers. The indiscriminate bombardment of open towns, however, remains inadmissible, now as always, on the grounds previously mentioned.

What is the position, however, if a power striving for world dominion and being a serious menace to the vital fundamental goods of mankind, threatens a war of aggression, using nuclear bombs of the first kind? The most urgent aim will then be to avert war. This gives the right to the world so threatened to make the utmost efforts to arm with similar and more effective weapons in order to avert such a fearful method of attack by that power. The justification for such arming lies in the indubitable fact that an attacking state prepared to use such devastating bombs will believe the defending state to be capable of the same, and can therefore only be effectively intimidated from the use of such weapons by the same or higher war potential of the other side.[5] The use of inadmissible weapons, such as bacteria and gas, has not occurred up to now because of the fear of retaliation with like weapons. A one-sided renunciation of such weapons in a defensive war against such an aggressor would mean a renunciation of

[4] In dealing with the question of the use of weapons, which of necessity are directed against the unarmed (such as the hydrogen bomb or the hunger blockade), the argument that the effectiveness of present-day weapons is only relatively more far-reaching than that of weapons used in earlier times, is unsound; to assess this fact one would have to compare the entire territory of the enemy state with a fortified town of earlier times. Too little consideration, it is said in this argument, is given to the fact that in the *Christian Middle Ages* natural law ethics made no intrinsic distinction between the various methods used in laying siege to cities with reference to the relative amounts of harm done to combatants and to noncombatants; this is true of the starvation weapon, the blockade, as well as of incendiaries and other projectiles with which cities were attacked. Such an argument is fallacious, inasmuch as the moral consciousness of man has since developed, as is shown by present-day international law. Otherwise, the argument could indeed be set out as follows: Uncivilized peoples have always, almost up to the present time, when they are not prevented by the civilized peoples, conducted their disputes by burning one another's villages and murdering or enslaving their populations; civilized peoples have, therefore, the right to do the same among themselves. According to such ethics of war, no bounds would be set to the use of nuclear weapons generally. It must be admitted from the point of view of the development of moral legal consciousness (cf. Chap. 40), that the ethics of war of medieval natural law was just as time-bound in the question of making war as in the question of the enslavement of prisoners of war (cf. Chap. 146).

[5] The opinion, often held, that immunity could be purchased by complete renunciation of nuclear weapons, rests on a false assessment of an enemy that is ready, on principle, to use them. According to the Soviet Russian Encyclopedia (1951) a communist state, as a socialist state, by its very nature wages only just wars against capitalist states (cf. *Zeitschrift Ost-Probleme,* 1955). In addition, according to the opinion of the Soviet leaders, a war with nuclear weapons would only abolish "capitalism"; it is a fiction of the West that mankind or culture would be destroyed (so said the President of the Soviet Union, Marshal Voroshilov, before the Supreme Soviet on May 26, 1955).

self-defense; in this situation, the threatened state is not justified by natural law principles in such a renunciation, since the highest goods of mankind, freedom of mind and of conscience, including the values of religion, are gravely threatened.

With regard to the present world situation, all the demands for the safeguarding of international peace, which are founded in natural law principles mentioned in the previous chapter, have a greatly increased obligatory force. They imply *for all states* the following grave obligations: The fundamental obligation is that of ready cooperation in establishing a general disarmament system with fully effective international armament control, for the immediate purpose of the complete elimination of any further *production* of nuclear weapons with uncontrollable effects, and for the remoter purpose of preventing the production of nuclear weapons in general. Since this aim is not attainable in the present-day situation, there is the obligation to conclude an international agreement which on principle excludes the *use* in war of nuclear weapons of an inadmissible nature in the light of what has been said above, even though in the prevailing circumstances this would have at first only a moral significance. If more is not attainable, the obligation arises to conclude an international agreement to put a stop to nuclear weapon tests. The agreement reached under the Kennedy administration only admits of underground tests. The ultimate aim remains the ending of the production of nuclear weapons, and the destruction of existing stocks of them, both under international control.

106. The Organized Society of Nations

International law in the form which it has hitherto taken has been unable to guarantee the peace and order of the family of nations. It is sufficient to mention the general fear of a third world war. The disintegrating forces have only become all the stronger. The causes of this failure of international law are now almost unanimously attributed to the lack of an international legislative, and of juridical and executive authority. First, international law in the past has been founded exclusively on the will to agreement of the states, and therefore it has an "individualist character" (as *Verdroß* expresses it). Peace and security would, however, be assured only if there were an international authority for the purpose of establishing international law, which would be binding upon all peoples independently of their individual wills. Secondly, only a compulsory jurisdiction can prevent self-help by force, when states believe that their rights or interests have been violated Thirdly, the lack of effective executive power is given as a reason for the failure of international law. The society of nations must be invested with a control of forces sufficient to guarantee its legal order, and thereby peace and security.

Correct though this diagnosis of existing international law is, one should look for the chief reason of the failure of international law in the *lack of the necessary foundation of generally accepted legal principles.* It must have as result "that the international community is seriously affected if a large nation or group of nations tries to detach itself from the common, legal ground of mankind. . . . It must fall asunder if no common values are any longer recognized." [1] This is the case today, since one of the two ideological world fronts adheres to an interpretation of man and society, of basic human value and social legal principles, which is completely incompatible with that of the free world. In spite of this the hope must not be abandoned that the moral consciousness common to mankind will finally prevail; indeed, "reason and conscience" are in like manner proper to all men, as expressly stated in the first article of the *Declaration of Human Rights* of the United Nations. Therefore, in spite of all setbacks, it is the task of natural law ethics to develop the principles which should govern the organization of the community of nations in accordance with the existential human ends to be realized.

Of what nature would such an organization be? A World State is the answer given, not only by such a writer as *H. G. Wells,* but already by *Dante* and, in the nineteenth century, by such a political theorist as *Bluntschli.*[2] Its authority, as the most advanced advocates of the World State urge, must be in the form of a democratic system of universal equal suffrage for all of the inhabitants of earth.

With a world population of some three thousand millions, representation at the rate of one deputy to one million people would give a World Parliament of three thousand deputies, which, it is claimed, appears by no means excessive for the world as a whole. The division of the world into constituencies of a million voters each would, however, have to cut across national frontiers and commit portions of populations, whose differences would far exceed their common characteristics and interests, to the election of deputies in common. Such theorists overlook further factors of reality which urge the grouping of men in separate political communities; the most important of these factors is the spiritual individuality of the political community. This fact has been noted ever since the historical school of law investigated the basis of the systems of municipal laws, from the legal philosophy of the Middle Ages to *Hegel* and *Bergson. Bergson* finds this fact so important that he even feels justified in characterizing every society as a somewhat closed society.[3] The ethnical, geographical, historical, and spiritual conditions essentially determine the needs and interests of men and give its special character to the common good of

[1] A. Verdroß, *Völkerrecht,* 3rd ed., 1955, pp. 12, 78.

[2] Cf. Bluntschli, *Allgemeines Staatsrecht,* 4th ed., 1868, Vol. I, p. 44: "The World State or the World Empire is the ideal of progressive humanity."

[3] Cf. Bergson, *The Two Sources of Morality and Religion,* 1935.

every political community.[4] Although the development of technology has brought peoples nearer to one another, the conditions individuating the common good of each of them mould them into different corporate personalities within the society of nations. Another strong argument against the idea of a World State in the present-day world, permeated as it is with collectivistic totalitarian forces, is the fact that freedom is much better secured by a *pluralistic international society* than by the formation of one World State, because each nation will then be a guardian of its own liberty, whereas a one-state system more easily affords the conditions for world domination and world dictatorship by a single nation or party which may happen to gain control of the executive apparatus. All the arguments we have quoted from *Lord Acton* (cf. Chap. 98) in support of his proposition that the multiple nation state will be a better guarantor of freedom, apply in a higher degree to the principle that the organized society of nations will serve the existential human freedoms better as a federal union of states than as a single state.

What would be the character of a society of nations organized for the purpose of establishing a collective authority, if it is not to be a World State or merely the resultant of arbitrary treaties between absolutely sovereign states? The organized society of nations is the society of states in which each, although it has its own right to autonomy, at the same time is ordained to form part of a society of all on account of the need of establishing and safeguarding the good of the international community. According to this, the *essential character of the organized society of nations is that of a federation,* that is to say, an association of relatively autonomous corporate bodies for the pursuit of their common interests. Because it is demanded by the common good of the international community, the formation of such an association is, for the nations, a precept of the natural law principles of international justice. Natural law doctrine has never been in doubt concerning the nature of the organized society of nations as a federation since it first formed specifically international law conceptions in the sixteenth century.[5] The international authority, which the

[4] To their surprise the advocates of a World State would find all the decisive arguments against their proposition already in Suárez (*De legibus,* Bk. III, Chap. 2, n. 5; Chap. 4, n. 7). He investigates the question of the World State when he deals with the legislative power. A universal legislative authority to bind all men in the whole world is neither necessary nor expedient: not necessary, because it is not required by the preservation or any other good of human nature; not expedient, because, if Aristotle finds the government of too large a state difficult, the government of a state with the size of the whole world seemed to Suarez obviously impossible. To be sure, however, in applying the natural law principles to the world of nuclear weapons, Suárez would insist on the necessity of an international authority with definite powers for the prevention of war and for armament control; but this would, of course, by no means involve world government proper or a world state.

[5] Cf. Suárez, *De legibus,* Bk. III, Chap. 2, n. 6: "Nam licet universalitas hominum non fuerit congregata in unum corpus politicum, sed in varias communitates divisa fuerit; nihilominus ut illae communitates sese mutuo juvare, et inter se in justitia, et

community of nations has to form for the performance of the functions designed in the international common good, has been adequately designated by *Suárez* as a "quasi-political" unity.[6] The authority of the organized society of nations would not, however, according to natural law, be based on an act of agreement on federation, but on the common good of the international community (just as political authority after the constitution of the political community is not based on the act of constitution, but on the political common good). The individual tasks proper to the international authority will be dealt with in the following chapters.

From the nature and functions of the organized society of nations, just discussed, *two fundamental principles* regarding its organization follow directly: it must be *open to all nations;* and it must be *obligatory for all.* First, it must be universal; this principle excludes every proscriptive policy. No state must be excluded. If not open to all nations, an international organization is easily degraded to an instrument in the political interest of those nations which predominate in such an organization. This helped not a little to bring about the doom of the League of Nations. International justice does not allow the exclusion even of a defeated aggressor nation, if it provides guarantees that it will conform with the principles of the legal order in the society of nations. Besides this, it is a pertinent question whether, from a merely realistic point of view, such a measure could ever be in the interest of peace and the common good of the international community. The second principle excludes the isolationism of individual states. In the present state of international development, all nations are obliged by international justice to cooperate with the organized society of nations, because peace, the future of civilization, and the economic and social welfare of all depend upon such cooperation. Any isolationism, especially on the part of big powers, which seriously hampers the attainment of these ends, is an infringement of grave obligations of international justice.

There are *two further principles* for the organization of the society of nations. The one is concerned with *freedom of treaty making:* all states are free to enter into mutual agreements within the framework of the organized society of nations, just as the individuals enjoy freedom of association within the state. This freedom is the natural right of the individual state within the society of nations. As a corporate person it is entitled to seek its advantage by treaties with any state, as long as no wrong is done to other states or to the international community. Such treaties may be concerned with any matter in the political, economic, social, or cultural sphere that affects the interest of a nation. Needless

pace conservari possent (quod ad bonum universi necessarium erat) oportuit, ut aliqua communia jura quasi communi foedere, et consensione inter se observarent." Although directly Suárez derives only the idea of *iura gentium* from this principle, his view of the association of the nations with its implications under developing circumstances is quite clear.

[6] Cf. *ibid.*, Bk. II, Chap. 19, n. 9.

to say, this freedom of treaty negatively denotes the right of any state to have no such treaty forced upon it against its will and interest. Economic treaties, in fact, often have been used by Great Powers as a means of bringing smaller states under their political influence. One of the paramount functions of the organized society of nations is to prevent such treaties which, in truth, serve to screen aggression and domination.

This brings us to the second principle, *freedom of confederation.* In contradistinction to the principle of federation, which characterizes the organized society of nations, as explained earlier, confederation denotes a regional association of a number of states with a view to closer collaboration for common ends. By confederation the individual federated states give up a considerable part of their sovereignty in order to constitute a common authority to insure their common interests. If the establishment of such an authority is necessary, in the idea of confederation all the member states must give up an equal portion of their sovereignty; for all must be granted equal political rights if there is to be a confederation and not merely domination of some states by another. No less essential to its nature and function is the freedom of the states to enter or remain outside a confederation. Such a confederation is being considered in the efforts to create a United States of Europe.

The Right of Neutrality

According to prevailing international law, neutrality is an attitude tenable exclusively during the progress of a war, and neutrality has no rights or duties prior to the outbreak of war.[7] For this reason we should have spoken of neutrality in the previous chapter in connection with the ethics of war. The first question, however, according to natural law principles is: Does a right to neutrality exist? In fact, after the First World War "the conception began to gain ground, that every state was obliged to make a stand against an aggressor," since "a war of aggression constitutes an offense against the international community, against which all states jointly must intervene." [8] The exposition of natural law principles on neutrality presupposes the exposition of the principles binding the states to participate in creating an international legal order both in the tasks of the organized society of nations and, consequently and above all, in the task of securing peace and defense against an aggressor. Because this participation in present-day conditions is obligatory upon all states, there is no longer any right to neutrality. Only *special circumstances* could still justify such a right of a state. Such a circumstance can be the granting of neutrality to a state by the international community itself, if the state can point to a long tradition based on the interest of a large area. Likewise, an arrangement by the great powers, recognized by the organized society of nations, can establish rights and duties of neutrality for a small state, if this is in the interest of easing international tensions. An example of the first is Switzerland, of the second Austria.

First among the general duties of neutrality is the avoidance of any behavior

[7] Cf. Oppenheim-Lauterpacht, *International Law,* 7th ed., 1952, Vol. II, p. 655.
[8] A. Verdroß, *op. cit.,* p. 423.

which would involve a state in taking sides in a possible war, such as entering into a military alliance or granting military bases (aircraft bases). A further duty consists in the avoidance of any direct or indirect military assistance to a state taking part in a war, or to one side in a civil war of another state. In addition, neutral states have the duty to ward off encroachments by combatant states on their territory, if necessary by armed force. The privilege of neutrality, therefore, is bound up not only with the right but the duty of arming for such cases. The neutral state is also bound to prevent openly offensive disparagement (press, radio, television) of other states, and causing them damage by intentionally misleading reports. The duty of neutrality, however, does not inhibit either membership in the organized society of nations by sharing in its tasks which are not connected with war affairs, or by joining in the cooperation of states in a large area for peaceful purposes (Council of Europe, the European Common Market). According to natural law principles, the duty of military neutrality does not imply the duty of surrendering fundamental human rights, such as freedom of opinion and of the press; it is no duty of military neutrality to suppress the actual taking of sides for or against the fundamental principles of political, economic, and social order advocated by other states (ideological neutrality), and to refrain in home politics from discussions of world policy (political neutrality).

107. The Organized Society of Nations: Its Authority

The end of the common good of the international community establishes, like every public common good, two chief tasks: safeguarding the peace of the community and providing the conditions for its welfare. Any concrete common good originates, as we have shown, a right, an authority, vested with the legislative, judicial, and executive powers necessary for establishing and safeguarding that common good. What, then, would be the difference between the present-day international law and the law proceeding from the authority of the organized society of nations? The new international law (1) would not be the outcome of interstate treaties, but of the legislative will of the community of nations expressed by an international legislative body; (2) it would be binding not only upon the states that have ratified it and thus incorporated it in their own legislation, but upon all states directly and without exception; (3) thus, it would not be subordinated to the sovereignty of the individual states, but rather the sovereignty of the individual states would be subordinated to the constitutional law of the community of states. Treaties between states would continue to play their part in international relations, but the fundamental order and the functions of the organized society of nations would in substance be, as it has been called, supranational law.[1]

[1] As found in P. E. Corbett, *Postwar Worlds*, 1942, published by the International Secretariat, Institute of Pacific Relations, with a Foreword by its Secretary-general, E. C. Carter. Professor Corbett makes the supranational character of the international authority a fundamental idea of his international theory.

Although the change in the attitude to sovereignty in international law is unmistakeable, there is little hope that such an international authority will be brought to actuality in the near future. In no sphere of human life is the road from theory to reality longer than in that of international affairs, especially since man's memory of the sufferings and lessons of catastrophes such as wars is relatively so short. For, the existence and functioning of such an authority would depend upon the readiness of states, and of the Great Powers in particular, to accept a constitution of the organized community of nations involving the sacrifice of their unrestricted sovereignty. Until this readiness exists, the international society with each fresh step toward such an organization, will have to learn chiefly from experience. Experience up to now [2] shows quite clearly that, in the organized international society, the status of the Great Powers must be appropriate to their actual political power, but in such a way that the legal status of the smaller nations, which is equal for all nations, is insured. What is this status of a Great Power? *A. J. Toynbee* defines the great power as a "political force exerting an effect coextensive with the widest range of the society in which it operates." [3] The emphasis on force in *Toynbee's* definition need not surprise us; we are in the sphere of politics, in which might has an essential function. We have already emphasized (cf. Chap. 100) that the equal fundamental rights of states in no way excludes significant differences in the influence of these states on the affairs of the community. It is only necessary to delimit this influence in order to safeguard the minimum rights of smaller nations to equality.

What is the *function of the smaller states* for the good of the community of nations? In the community of nations they are the goalkeepers of humanity and civilization. The smallness of their power preserves them from the idolatry of power politics and induces them rather to seek respect among the nations by their cultural achievements, whether in the field of spiritual or of material culture. The freedom and the rights of individuals meet with more favorable conditions in the smaller states. "The

[2] Unanimous opinion assigns the cause of the failure of the League of Nations to the attitude of the Great Powers. The United States had retired into isolation and took no part in the League; Russia saw herself for a long time virtually excluded by the distrustful attitude of almost all the rest of the world; and Germany was for many years refused admittance. Britain, disagreeing with the French policy of intransigence toward Germany, pursued a policy of reserve, so that the League became, to a large extent, the instrument of the wishes of France and the Little Entente. As a conclusion from all this, it may not be too severe a judgment to lay the principal blame for the failure of the League on the "stupidity and selfishness of the Great Powers" (Corbett, *op cit.*, p. 186). In fairness, however, it must also be said that in the League organization they did not receive the place that was due to them as Great Powers. In the League Assembly and the League Council each member had one vote, Great Power and small nation alike. The only consideration given to the Great Powers was that the Council was composed of five permanent members representing these powers, together with four nonpermanent members chosen by the League Assembly. But owing to the attitude of the Great Powers just mentioned, the ascendancy in the League Council passed from the permanent to the nonpermanent members.

[3] A. J. Toynbee, *The World after the Peace Conference*, 1925, p. 4.

small state exists," says *J. Burckhardt,* "so that there may be a spot on earth where the largest possible proportion of the inhabitants are citizens in the fullest sense of the word, a goal which the Greek City State more nearly attained in its heyday, in spite of the slavery system, than all the republics of today." [4] Thinking more of mankind as a whole than of the individual, *St. Augustine* expressed a similar thought; it is desirable, he says, that the states of the earth, just as the homes of the citizens in a town, should be numerous.[5] *St. Augustine* is thinking of the enrichment and deepening of life that would result from such a multiplicity of commonwealths freely developing in neighborly association. For these reasons, then, the safeguarding of the rights of equality of the small states is one of the paramount functions of the organized community of nations in the interest of the fundamental values of civilization.

The *Charter of the United Nations* (1945) departs substantially from the lines indicated by these principles for the constitution of and the exercise of authority by the society of nations. All authority is invested in the Security Council, whereas the General Assembly is only entitled to discuss, to make recommendations, and to consider general principles (Arts. 10 ff.). At the same time a virtual right of veto is given to the five Great Powers individually, so that any one of them is able to prevent a decision by the Council in any matter, when this is in its interest. Thus, the function of the Assembly and the smaller nations is restricted chiefly to the mobilization of the public opinion of the world, but the principle of the absolute sovereignty of the Great Powers is left in operation. Hence, there remains the very obstacle to the effective working of an international authority for the common good that became fatal to the League of Nations after 1919.

108. The Political Functions of the Organized Community of Nations

The functions for an organized community of nations to be created are as follows:

1. *Legislation.* The object of legislation is the establishment and protection of the international organized community. The international community, like every other community, requires a constitution and a code of laws. It is for the constitution of the organized international community to define the competence of its legislative authority. Under this come provisions for the preservation of peace, the laws of war, minority laws, international labor law, international economic and financial cooperation, control over the administration of colonies and mandated territories, and, in general, "the respect for, and observance of, human rights and fundamental freedoms for all without distinction with regard to race, sex, language, or religion"; in this way the *Charter of the United Nations* (Art.

[4] J. Burckhardt, *Reflections on History,* trans. by M. D. H., 1943, p. 37.
[5] Cf. St. Augustine, *De civ. Dei,* Bk. IV, Chap. 15.

55) formulates the end of international cooperation. This suggests that a statute of rights may well be regarded as an integral part of the constitution of the organized community of nations, which would have to insure the respect of all nations for political and social liberties and at the same time a right of petition for citizens whose government is lacking in respect for the principles enshrined in such a statute.[1]

2. *The codification of existing international law.* This would consist in the systematic compilation of laws created by interstate conventions and international usages. A necessary condition of this is that all states shall be obliged by the constitution of the community of nations to register treaties, whether they are of a political, an economic, or other character, as provided in Articles 102 ff. of the *Charter of the United Nations.* This provision would likewise prevent the conclusion of secret treaties endangering third states.

3. *Frontiers and frontier peoples.* Frontier disputes may fall either within the competence of the international judicature or within that of the community of nations. The *Charter of 1945* (Art. 94) assigns a function of intervention to the Security Council. In the practical execution of frontier settlements, the international organization will always have a direct part to play because of the interlocking interests of the states, national groups, and individuals concerned.[2] In complete contradiction to the clear principles of humanity and of human rights (the right to live in one's homeland), after the Second World War the solution of the problems in question was left to mass deportation (Russia), to mass emigration (Poland, Czechoslovakia), and to mass flight (Arabian refugees).

4. *Migration and colonization.* Today, already the overpopulated countries present problems of the greatest consequence for the peace and welfare of the international community. With the further increase in world population the existing difficulties will rapidly and progressively become more acute. Yet, consideration of the problems presented has hardly begun. The first of these is to make land accessible for the settlement of migrants; indeed, this is an apparently insoluble problem at first sight, but one which cannot be indefinitely postponed. It is necessary, in addition, to lay down binding principles for all interstate agreements relating to movements of population, concerning not least the legal status of im-

[1] For a strong case in behalf of such a bill cf. H. Lauterpacht, *An International Bill of Rights of Man,* 1945.

[2] An example of lasting importance is the success of the Mixed Commission and Arbitration Tribunal set up by the League of Nations Council after the partition of Upper Silesia in 1922. Georges Kaeckenbeek, the Chairman of this Commission, can rightly claim in his detailed report, *The International Experiment of Upper Silesia, 1922–37,* London, 1942, on the Upper Silesian Settlement, that the Convention concluded between Germany and Poland under the auspices of the League of Nations is one of the boldest and most progressive diplomatic documents. As he says, never before has such a thorough attempt been made to safeguard individual rights by international means, and never before has such an abundance of methods of cooperation, supervision, and arbitration been resorted to.

migrants, including their right to preserve and to foster their ethnic values. A further group of functions comprises direct assistance during the process of migration itself, assistance in the initiation and preparation of individual agreements between emigration and immigration states, the organization of collective movements as a result of such agreements, and the securing of capital funds for newly arriving settlers in foreign countries.

5. *The protection of minorities.* The protection of the rights of minorities, which should extend equally to national and religious minorities, must be established by statute. A right of decisive importance would be the right to petition the organized community of nations if the minority considers its rights infringed and if a substantial part of it can be shown to be in favor of such a step. This is obvious in the sphere of legal theory. In the sphere of political reality, however, in the present state of affairs the organized international community will, in the face of the sensitiveness of states and especially of Great Powers, often see itself compelled to try to obtain for the injured minority what can be obtained by the procedure of mediation, in order to avoid legal proceedings. No provisions for safeguarding the interest of minorities have been made in the *Charter of the United Nations.*

109. The Administration of Justice in the Organized Community of Nations

One of the most important functions of any community in the interest of peace and of order is to provide for the administration of justice. If this function is to be performed in the international community, it must be constitutionally established: there must be generally binding laws governing the obligation to submit to the judgment of an international court of justice. The *Charter of the United Nations* (Art. 33) provides for obligatory judicial proceedings: disputes between member-states, if their continuance is likely to endanger the maintenance of international peace and security, are to be submitted to arbitration, mediation, conciliation, judicial settlement, or other peaceful means chosen by such states. "The International Court of Justice," says the *Charter* (Art. 92), "shall be the principal judicial organ of the United Nations. It shall function in accordance with the annexed statute, which is based upon the Statute of the Permanent Court of International Justice and forms an integral part of the present Charter."

What law has the International Court of Justice to apply? The statute just mentioned specifies it as follows: (1) the international conventions to which the disputing parties are committed; (2) international custom, which can be adduced to show that there is in existence a certain general practice recognized as law; (3) the principles of law accepted by civilized nations; (4) the court's own judicial precedents and the opinions of recognized international jurists of different nations, although these opinions can serve only as a means for determining the rules of law, not as binding norms in themselves. As soon, however, as a code of international law is set up by the organized community of nations, this would be the primary law applied by the international court without rendering obsolete the principles of law we have mentioned. But the settlement of international disputes by the passing of a sentence may rarely prove the ideal solution, since questions of prestige and of sovereignty stand in the foreground. Therefore, negotiation between the parties themselves, their voluntary submission to arbitration through a tribunal on whose composition they have agreed, or to conciliation initiated by the good services of a third power, or by the mediation of organs of the international community, is greatly to be preferred to a judicial decision.[1]

The following matters should, in principle, be assigned to the *competence of the international judicature.*

1. *Legal disputes.* As such these were pertinently detailed in the *Covenant of the League of Nations* as follows: (1) the interpretation of a treaty; (2) the interpretation of international law; (3) the investigation of facts that would imply the breach of an international obligation; (4) the nature and extent of the reparations to be rendered for the violation of an obligation under international law.

2. *Legal changes.* Provision must be made by international law for states to have recourse to international machinery in order to obtain alterations in international agreements and rulings if the circumstances previously relating to them have changed. Historical developments may render positive international law obsolete; law arising from treaties can become wrong. In such an event, natural law is stronger than positive law, and justice demands that the existing law be altered. The principal kind of change that may be required is the revision of peace treaties and of the conditions imposed on a defeated enemy, when these have become unjust or unreasonable in the course of time. Otherwise, such treaties provide a cause of bitterness, of rebellion against international order, and of new wars. The reformulation of such treaties is itself, of course, a mat-

[1] From this point of view the much discussed question of the inclusion of representatives of the disputing parties in the body of judges must be considered. The present *International Court of Justice* consists, according to its statute, of fifteen members; the parties to a case brought before it are also represented. Being of the nationality of the parties does not prevent judges from exercising their function. Absurd though the proposal seems, that the parties to a dispute should be allowed to be represented on the judicial bench of a civil court, yet in the international sphere it does not seem to the same degree paradoxical that the powers between whom a dispute is pending should be members of such a court as long as there exists no organized society of nations and an international authority invested with all necessary power for the execution of judicial decisions. The fact that they are represented in the College of Judges may even make it difficult for a Great Power to reject a decision which its representative on the judicial bench has not been able to prevent by the presentation of evidence and legal argument. On the other hand, their participation in the judicial proceedings may lead to conciliation and make a verdict unnecessary.

ter for the states concerned or for the community of nations, and not for the international courts.

3. *Creation of new law.* Provision must also be made for the cooperation of the international judicature in the development of new law. The most urgent demand for such development arises when a population outgrows its territory and must find new land for settlement. It would not be possible to quote a single historical case in which any state, however large its surplus population, has obtained territory for colonization from another state by peaceful means, however much underpopulated the latter has been. Population pressure has been one of the chief causes of armed conflicts. The organized society of nations, if it is to prevent wars, must set up a machinery for the peaceful solution of these problems of international justice. The principal means are emigration from the overpopulated country or the facilitating of participation in international commerce for the development of its economic basis. This, as we have pointed out, is one of the political functions of the organized international community. But the member states must themselves be entitled to seek justice through the international judicature. Its function would not be restricted to the pronouncing of judicial decisions, but would include the giving of documented advisory reports to the organized community of nations and its organs, such as the International Court of Justice is called upon to render by the *Charter of the United Nations* (Art. 96).

4. *Criminal jurisdiction.* In every civilized state the supreme principle governing the administration of justice is that no criminal may be punished without a proper judicial trial and verdict. Undoubtedly, justice demands something similar in international life. An unbiased examination of the charges is a prerequisite for the just judgment of the liability of an aggressor to punishment. If there is no such objective examination and if after a war the assessment of the degree of punishment required is left to the victor, the elementary presupposition of a just procedure is missing. However long the road may seem toward a constitutionally organized International Criminal Court, the organized society of nations must stride on if the progress of civilization is not to be seriously hampered.

5. *The punishment of war criminals.* In this much-discussed question, our principles lead to the following conclusions. A distinction must be made between two kinds of war criminals. One class comprises persons occupying responsible positions in the aggressor nation; they are answerable for an aggressive war. It can hardly be seriously disputed that a criminal proceeding against such persons, as at the international Military Court of Justice at Nuremberg, when positive law is lacking, should be based on natural law.[2] Today in the non-communistic world there is com-

[2] In connection with the Nuremberg trials, jurists pointed to the difficulty that no positive international law existed by which the accused could be tried in accordance with the principles of criminal procedure accepted by civilized nations, the chief being the universally accepted rule of criminal law in civilized society that there should

plete agreement in condemning wars of aggression as a means of politics. But, a trial based on these principles is involved in several difficulties. First, the trial would have to be conducted by a court consisting of members taken from strictly neutral nations and not from nations that were parties to a conflict. Secondly, such a court would have to pass judgment on any aggressive actions of any state within the same period. In a different category is the trial of those who have committed crimes against the existing international or municipal laws by murder, atrocities, violations of property rights, and looting. An international regulation could insure that such war criminals are tried according to the laws of the country in which they were committed, or that of the defendants, by a regular procedure before courts composed of impartial judges. Again, however, justice would require that all crimes of this kind committed on whatever side in a war must then equally be brought before such courts.[3] The conclusion from our discussion of this intricate subject can only be that the organized society of nations must, as soon as possible, make provisions for an international criminal code and for the rules of procedure in such a criminal court in whose competence both kinds of crimes would fall.

110. The Organized Community of Nations: Its Economic Functions

It cannot be denied today that the chief problem facing the organized society of nations is the position of *underdeveloped countries.* It is generally seen from the point of view of the situation brought about by the imperialistic efforts of the communist world powers. This provides only one of the motives for giving the necessary help to underdeveloped countries gradually to raise their standard of living to that of industrialized

be *nulla poena sine lege* (so says Manfred Lachs, *War Crimes: An Attempt to Define the Issue,* 1945). Others tried to invoke the authority of Suárez for the justification of the procedure. But Suárez himself expressly bases the justification of the punishment of a defeated aggressor, such as the enslavement of prisoners, on existing law, namely, on *ius gentium* (Suárez, *De legibus,* Bk. II, Chap. 18, n. 9; Chap. 19, nn. 8–9; Chap. 20, n. 8). However, no modern *ius gentium* could be relied on that would legitimate such punishment of the members of a government that was responsible for an aggressive war.

[3] Thus, the late Professor Gilbert Murray says in a letter to the *Times* of May 2, 1946, with regard to the Nuremberg trials: "Granted that the trials are being conducted with the most scrupulous justice; granted further that since the acceptance by the League of Nations of the rule that 'aggressive war is a crime against the international community,' certain actions not previously regarded as criminal may have become so; granted lastly that the monstrous and demoniac cruelties introduced into warfare by the Nazis must receive some definite world-wide condemnation; nevertheless, how can it be just, or to future generations ever seem just, that after a war the victors, because they are victors, should judge the offenses of the vanquished, and, merely because they are victors, escape all judgment themselves? Do we claim that no war crimes were committed by any member of the British, American, or Russian armies?"

countries. In fact we are faced with one of the most serious demands of *international, social, and commutative justice.* There are obligations of commutative justice for those nations which for generations have been guilty of the exploitation of such peoples. The obligations of international justice come wholly within the province of the organized international community, because they concern the international common good. Individual states have the primary obligations of social justice, but essential tasks of cooperation fall on the international society, such as consultation about the particular needs of necessitous countries, the best methods of providing for them, the setting up of institutions to serve the countries which are obliged to give their help.

The organized community of nations will have to consider the general promotion of *world trade* as one of the most important ways of fulfilling this task, particularly as it is conditioned by the present situation. Its fundamental economic task is to exert its influence to enlarge the volume of world trade, to supervise and prevent checks on international trade by the restrictive policies of states or cartels, to use influence to maintain price stability in raw materials and foodstuffs, and to initiate a concerted antidepression policy among the nations. The lessons of the period between the two World Wars should not be forgotten: all countries sought individually to protect their own internal markets and employment level; the means used were prohibitive customs tariffs, devaluation, import quotas, barter agreements, clearing agreements, and state control of dealings in foreign currency. The outcome was the extensive disintegration of world trade and the rise in unemployment of up to ten per cent of the population in most industrial countries, and, what weighed most heavily in the scales, the chronic character of the unemployment. The shortsighted, selfish nature of this world economic policy was one of the most potent causes leading to the Second World War. But for this, National Socialism could not have established itself in Germany. Next come the individual tasks of the international economic policy of the organized community of nations. One thinks of the provision of loans for the economic reconstruction of economically weakened countries,* support to endangered currencies, assistance in credit operations for the relief of countries suffering from repercussions of international price fluctuations or from pressure of debt service, and similar tasks. The organized community of nations needs for these purposes a range of organizational means, among them efficient financial institutions.

The economic functions of the organized community of nations and the agencies necessary for their performance will be discussed in detail in the part of this study dealing with international economy (Chaps. 191–201).

* The League of Nations has two outstanding successes to its credit in the handling of such tasks: the financial reconstruction of Austria (1922) and of Hungary (1923), preparations for which were made in both cases by the Financial Committee of the League.

The *Charter of the United Nations* (Arts. 55–72) shows a recognition of fundamental principles of the kind discussed. An Economic and Social Council of the United Nations is provided for, consisting of eighteen members elected by the General Assembly. The guiding principles for its activities are described in Chapter IX, Article 55, as follows: "With a view to the creation of conditions of stability and well-being, which are necessary for peaceful and friendly relations among nations, based on respect for the principle of equal rights and self-determination of peoples, the United Nations shall promote: (1) higher standards of living, full employment, and conditions of economic and social progress and development; (2) solutions of international economic, social, health, and related problems; and international cultural and educational cooperation; and (3) universal respect for, and observance of, human rights and fundamental freedoms for all without distinction as to race, sex, sex, language or religion." To be sure, up to now these principles remain almost entirely only on paper, since the Economic and Social Council has not yet developed any substantial activity.

111. The Social Functions of the Organized Community of Nations

The tasks in question are those which were formulated in the introduction to the international agreement instituting the International Labor Organization after the First World War (1919): General peace can be assured only if it is founded on social justice; this demands equitable labor conditions; these include the fixing of a maximum working day and week, the prevention of unemployment, provision for an adequate living wage, protection for the worker against sickness, disease, and injury arising out of his employment, the protection of children, young persons, and women, provision for old age, the protection of the interests of workers from foreign countries, recognition of the principle of freedom of association, and the organization of vocational and technical education.

The *International Labor Office* (I.L.O.), one of the successes of the League of Nations, has three principal functions: 1) It prepares for the annual meeting of the International Labor Conference. 2) It collects and distributes information on all subjects relating to international industrial questions, in particular in accordance with instructions by the International Labor Conference. 3) It maintains continuous contact with governments, and in particular with labor ministries, and also with workers' organizations in the individual states. The *International Labor Conference*, by a two-thirds vote, can pronounce decisions which may take one of the following forms: (1) draft Conventions, which have to be brought before the legislative authority of the member states and become law if ratified by them; (2) recommendations, which lay down general principles and are intended to be put into effect by the member states to the best of their ability.*

* At the head of the I.L.O. is a governing body composed of representatives of governments, of employers, and of workers, which elects the Director of the I.L.O.

With these endeavors the I.L.O. laid injunctions upon the social conscience in every country, set goals before social legislation, and rendered powerful aid to the labor movement in its endeavors. A wealth of information obtained from inquiries, statistics, and research concerning the social and economic conditions of individual countries has been made available, together with the international interdependence of these conditions. Out of this, the I.L.O. has rendered unique pioneering services in the field of international cooperation: Germany after the First World War was represented in the governing body of the I.L.O. before she was a member of the League; the I.L.O. maintained close contacts with the United States and Russia for purposes of information, although neither country belonged to the League. As an experiment in international organization, the I.L.O. has pointed the way for other institutions of the organized international community. Although it was an institution of the League of Nations, it had far-reaching autonomy; its activity was not directed by the League but by its own governing body and by the director appointed by it; its decisions were not subject to the control of the League Assembly; its communications with member states did not pass through the League Secretariat, but were direct; its director was not subordinate to the General Secretary of the League. The limitations in the activity of the I.L.O. have hitherto been those of the existing international law: thus, states were not obliged to accept the Draft Conventions but only to introduce them as bills before their legislatures; and even if they were passed, it depended partly upon the strength of the labor movement in individual countries how far they were implemented.

112. Colonies, Mandates, and Trusteeship

Colonial possessions afford a nation great advantages, chief among which are these three: opportunity for providing work and land for its surplus population; raw materials for home production; military, naval, and air bases. The fact that colonial powers think first and foremost of these advantages is sufficiently borne out by older and more recent colonial history. The much canvassed principle that the colonies are to be administered primarily for the good of the colonial peoples does not alter this fact. No one will maintain that the considerations determining the retention of colonial possessions are humanitarian. The argument advanced until very recent times that colonial rule over the native popula-

---

Each member state sends to the annual International Labor Conference two representatives of the government, one of the employers, and one of the workers; the last-mentioned are also nominated by the government, but in agreement with the principal employers' and workers' organizations. Not only, therefore, are states represented, but also the organized employers and workers. Every delegate is empowered to bring forward motions at the Conference. Many of the Draft Conventions have not been ratified by a considerable number of states.

tion must be continued because the natives are politically immature and a danger to international peace in general, is revealing, since it indicates how little, even in centuries, has been done for the political and educational development of "backward" peoples.

This raises three problems for social ethics: What are the rights of the indigenous population, of the colonial powers, and of other nations? From the general principles which are implied in social and political pluralism, we may draw the following complementary conclusions: 1) The dependent peoples constitute communities with their own common good and with a right to an autonomy rooted in it. 2) To the extent that such peoples are not capable of fulfilling the duties involved in their particular common good, more advanced communities may have a subsidiary function in relation to them. This function may fall to the colonial or mandatory power for historical reasons or to the international community for reasons of natural law. 3) If a colonial power does not fulfill its duties, the greater community, the organized international community, must perform its subsidiary function toward the dependent peoples. The organized international community, therefore, has a right always and in all cases to an effective control of colonial administration.

Among the *rights of the native peoples* the first is the right of autonomy within the limits of their capability of performing the functions of self-government, such as maintaining peace and order, protecting the life and property of foreigners, making provision for the intellectual, hygienic, economic, and social welfare of the community. Modern colonial history is the history of a disregard of this right. Let us refer merely to its latest phase. When the greater part of the African continent was divided up by the European nations between 1878 and 1914, the native communities were never asked to give their consent. In extensive areas of the Congo they were oppressed with a forced labor which could only be described as a form of slavery for the benefit of European capital; and up to recent times labor conditions in certain districts and industries in India at times have been far below the standards demanded by human dignity.* The colonial peoples have a further natural right to be allowed the opportunity to progress toward increasing self-government and eventually complete home-rule, although not necessarily to the extent of full sovereignty. The next right of dependent peoples is the right of petition to the organized international community in case of unjust treatment; an international machinery corresponding to this right must be set up. The right to promote their own welfare by utilizing the resources of their own country gives the colonial peoples the claim to a colonial administration conducted really in their own interest. Not the least right of each people is the right to their own customs and traditions insofar as they do not involve infringements of human rights.

The *colonial and mandatory power* possesses two main rights: the right

* Very informative is H. N. Brailsford's *Rebel India*, 1931, and *Subject India*, 1943.

to sovereignty over the colonial territory and the right to derive economic and military advantages from it within the limits set by the rights of the colonial peoples and of the community of nations. Limitations of sovereignty over the colonial peoples may spring from historical causes; for example, when the colonial peoples are approaching the stage of autonomy. The second right of the colonial power is that of utilizing the colonies for economic and military purposes. Obviously, this claim is limited by the primary right of the native population to the resources of their country for their own material and cultural needs; in addition, it is limited by the right of other nations to have access to raw materials by way of trade, and also their right, if circumstances permit, to purchase of land for emigrants.

The *rights of the organized international community* follow from what has been said. They comprise principally a twofold right of control with respect to the colonial powers, one in favor of the colonial population and one in favor of the common interest of the society of nations. With regard to the first, the following questions arise: 1) Whether the colonial administration is really being conducted in the interest of the colonial people; whether the latter is protected against exploitation; and whether serious efforts are being made to promote its physical, economic, social, and cultural welfare. 2) Whether the claim of the colonial people to a relative autonomy is being met, especially by education for gradually increasing independence, or whether the colonial administration is aimed at the perpetuation of colonial rule. In the exercise of this right the organized society of nations should be constitutionally empowered to provide for on the spot inspection through standing or *ad hoc* commissions and, after receiving a documented report, to take the measures necessary to protect the rights of the native population. Regular routine inspections should take place with an opportunity for the native population to speak its mind freely, in addition to the already-mentioned right of petition.

These are the natural law principles. The *Charter of the United Nations* is disappointing in its "Declaration Regarding Non-Self-Governing Territories" (Chap. XI), that is, colonies and mandates, because it is only a declaration of general principles and does not make any provision for the creation of institutions for their realization, which should be the task of the international community. The fundamental principle is declared to be "that the interests of the inhabitants of these territories are paramount," and thus their political, economic, social, and educational advancement, their just treatment, and their protection against abuses should be insured, and their self-government developed. The colonial powers are "to transmit regularly to the Secretary-General for information purposes, subject to such limitation as security and constitutional considerations may require, statistical and other information of a technical nature relating to economic, social, and educational conditions in the territories for which they are respectively responsible." This last sentence, hedged about with limitations as it is, almost amounts to underscoring the principle of the absolute sovereignty of the colonial powers and of the principle of non-intervention by the international community. In reality, representations of the United Nations against abuses are being regularly rejected by the states concerned, on the pretext that they concern affairs which fall within the sphere of the exclusive rights of their sovereignty.

BIBLIOGRAPHY

Abel, W., *Die Landfamilie,* 1953.

Allen, V. L., *Power in Trade Unions: A Study of Their Organization in Great Britain,* 1954.

Azcárate, P. de, *League of Nations and National Minorities,* trans. by E. E. Brooke (Washington, Carnegie Endowment for International Peace), 1945.

Bebel, August, *Die Frau und der Sozialismus,* 1879 (since then over 60 editions)

Belshaw, H., *Population Growth and Levels of Consumption: With special Reference to Countries in Asia,* 1956.

Bergson, H., *Les deux sources de la morale et de la religion,* 15th ed., 1933.

Berkenkopf, P., *Aufgaben und Aufbau einer berufsständischen Wirtschaftsordnung,* 1948.

Beyerle, K., "Föderalismus," in *Staatslexikon der Görresgesellschaft,* 5th ed., 1926–32.

Bigler, F. W., *Die Praxis der Allgemeinverbindlicherklärung von Gesamtarbeitsverträgen* (in der Schweiz) (Bern), 1956.

Bluntschli, *Allgemeines Staatsrecht,* 4th ed., 1868.

Boehm, M. H., *Das eigenständige Volk,* 1932.

—— *Volkstheorie und Volkstumspolitik der Gegenwart,* 1935.

Bosch, W., *Familienrechtsreform: Eheschließung, Ehescheidung, Gleichberechtigung von Mann u. Frau, Rechte der unehelichen Kinder,* 1952.

Bottai, G., *Grundprinzipien des korporativen Aufbaues in Italien,* 1936.

Boyens, W. F., *Siedlung und Bodenreform als Aufgabe des Bundes* (Deutsche Bundesrepublik), 1950.

Brailsford, H. N., *Rebel India,* 1931.

—— *Subject India,* 1943.

Brauer, T., *Gewerkschaft und Volkswirtschaft,* 2nd ed., 1954.

—— *Die Gewerkschaft als Organ der Volkswirtschaft,* 1921.

Briefs, G., "Gewerkschaftstheorie," in *Handwörterbuch des Gewerkschaftswesens,* L. Heyde, editor, Vol. I, 1931.

—— "Gewerkschaftswesen und Gewerkschaftspolitik," in *Handwörterbuch der Staatswissenschaften,* 4th ed., Vol. IV, 1927.

—— *Zwischen Kapitalismus und Syndikalismus: Die Gewerkschaften am Scheideweg,* 1952.

—— *Das Gewerkschaftsproblem gestern und heute,* 1955.

Buytendijk, F. J. J., *Die Frau: Natur, Erscheinung, Dasein,* 1953.

Carr-Saunders, A. M. and Jones, D. C., *The Social Structure of England and Wales,* 1927.

Chadwick, H. M., *The Nationalities of Europe and the Growth of National Ideology,* 1945.

Clegg, H. A., *General Union: A Study of the National Union of General and Municipal Workers,* 1954.

Clegg, H. A., Fox, Alan and Thompson, A. F., *A History of British Trade Unions Since* 1889. Vol. 1: 1889–1910, 1964.

Code de morale internationale, ed. by the Union Internationale des Études Sociales (founded by Cardinal Mercier) (Mechlin).

Cole, G. D. H., *Studies in Class Structure,* 1955.

Corbett, P. E., *Postwar Worlds,* 1942.

Coudenhove-Kalergi, R., *Die europäische Nation,* 1953.

Croner, F., *Die Angestellten in der modernen Gesellschaft: Eine sozialhistorische und soziologische Studie,* 1954.

Curtis, Lionel, *Faith and Works, or A World Safe for Small Nations,* 1943.

Dahrendorf, R., *Soziale Klassen und Klassenkonflikt in der industriellen Gesellschaft,* 1957.

David, J., *Der Lebensraum der Familie,* 1943.

—— *Die Welt auf dem Wege zur Familienpolitik,* 1954.

Dawson, C., *The Judgment of Nations,* 1943.

Delos, J. T., *La société internationale et les principles du droit publique* (Paris), 1929.

—— *Le problème de la civilisation: La nation: I. Sociologie de la nation; II. Le nationalisme et l'ordre de droit* (Montreal), 1944.

Doms, H., *Vom Sinn und Zweck der Ehe,* 1935.

—— *Vom Sinn des Zölibats,* 1954.

Dräger, W., *Primat des Volkes? Ein Beitrag zur Grundfrage einer völkischen Staatslehre,* 1935.

Duverger, M., *Les parties politiques* (Paris), 1951; Engl., *Political Parties,* 1954.

Egner, E., *Der Haushalt: Eine Darstellung seiner volkswirtschaftlichen Gestalt,* 1952.

Ehlen, N., "Familiensiedlung," in *Ehe und Familie,* A. and R. Scherer, and J. Dorneich, editors, 1956.

—— *Das familiengerechte Heim,* 1950.

Eliot, T. S., *The Idea of a Christian Society,* 1939.

Engels, F., *The Origin of the Family, Private Property and the State* (London), 1940.

Eppstein, J., *The Catholic Tradition of the Law of Nations,* 1935.

Field, G. C., *Political Theory,* 1956.

Fischer, E., Baur, E., Lenz, F., *Menschliche Erblichkeitslehre,* 1927.

Flanders, A., and Clegg, H. A., editors, *The System of Industrial Relations in Great Britain,* 1954.

Frantz, C., *Naturlehre des Staates als Grundlage aller Staatswissenschaften,* 1870.

Freyer, H., *Soziologie als Wirklichkeitswissenschaft, logische Grundlegung des Systems der Soziologie,* 1930.

Fröhner, R., Stackelberg, Maria v., and Eser, W., *Familie und Ehe. Probleme in den deutschen Familien der Gegenwart,* 1956.

Furtwängler, F. J., *Die Gewerkschaften, ihre Geschichte und internationale Auswirkung,* 1956.

Gehlen, A. and Schelsky, H., editors, *Soziologie: Lehr- und Handbuch zur modernen Gesellschaftskunde;* in collaboration with Carl Jantke, René König, Gerhard Mackenroth, Herbert Kötter, Otto Stammer, Karl H. Pfeffer, Elisabeth Pfeil, 1955.

Geiger, T., *Die Klassengesellschaft im Schmelztiegel,* 1949.
Gentile, G., *Origini e dottrina del Fascismo,* 3rd ed., 1934.
Ginsberg, Morris, *Nationalism: A Re-Appraisal* (Lecture at Leeds University in 1960; pub. by Leeds University Press), 1961.
Goldstein, J., *The Government of British Trade Unions: A Study of Apathy and the Democratic Process in the Transport and General Workers' Union,* 1952.
Gonella, Guido, *The Papacy and World Peace,* 1945.
Grote, H., *Der Streik: Taktik und Strategie,* 1952 (extensive bibliography).
Grotius, H., *Mare liberum,* 1608; Carnegie edition, *The Freedom of the Seas,* 1916.
——*De jure belli ac pacis,* 1625.
Gundlach, G., "Stand, Ständewesen," in *Staatslexikon der Görresgesellschaft,* 5th ed., 1926–32.
—— "Klasse, Klassenkampf," in *Staatslexikon.*
Haldane, J. B. S., *Heredity and Politics,* 1943.
Häring, Bernhard, *Soziologie der Familie,* 1954.
Hellpach, Willy, *Einführung in die Völkerpsychologie,* 3rd ed., 1954.
Hermes, A., Nell-Breuning, O. v., Degenfeld-Schonburg, F., "Art: Siedlung," in *Staatslexikon der Görresgesellschaft,* Vol. IV, 1931.
Hobbes, *De cive,* 1642.
Höffner, J., *Christentum und Menschenwürde, das Anliegen d. Spanischen Kolonialethik im Goldenen Zeitalter,* 1947.
Hollenbach, J. M., S.J., *Der Mensch als Entwurf: Seinsgemäße Erziehung in technisierter Welt,* 1957.
Huber, Max, *Heimat und Tradition,* 1947.
Huizinga, J., *Wachstum und Formen des nationalen Bewußtseins in Europa bis zum Ende des 19. Jahrhunderts,* 1942.
Jeismann, K.-E., *Das Problem des Präventivkrieges im europäischen Staatensystem mit bes. Blick auf die Bismarckzeit,* 1957.
Jellinek, G., *Die Lehre von den Staatenverbindungen,* 1882.
Jessup, P., *A Modern Law of Nations,* 1949.
Johnson, A., *This Housing Question,* 1954.
Jolles, H. M., *Wien, Stadt ohne Nachwuchs: Sozialwissenschaftliche Betrachtungen über den Geburtenrückgang in der alten Donaustadt* (Assen, Holland), 1957.
Kaeckenbeek, G., *The International Experiment of Upper Silesia,* 1922–37, 1942.
Kaiser, J. H., *Der politische Streik,* 1955.
Kampmann, T., *Anthropologische Grundfragen ganzheitlicher Frauenbildung unter besonderer Berücksichtigung des religiösen Bereichs,* 2 vols., 1946.
Keenan, A. and Ryan, J., *Marriage: A Medical and Sacramental Study,* 1956.
Keller, E. A., C.S.C., *The Case for Right-to-Work Laws: A Defense of Voluntary Unionism,* 1956.
Kelsen, H., *Principles of International Law* (U.S.A.), 1952.
Keynes, J. M., *The End of Laissez faire,* 1926.
Kissinger, Henry A., *The Necessity for Choice,* 1961.
Kohn, Hans, *Propheten ihrer Völker: Studien zum Nationalismus des 19. Jahrhunderts,* 1948.
—— *The Idea of Nationalism* (New York), 1944.

Koren, H., *Volkskunde der Gegenwart,* 1952.
Kothen, R., *et al., Responsabilités internationales des Chrétiens* (Paris), 1956.
Krieck, E., *Völkisch-politische Anthropologie,* 1936.
Lachs, M., *War Crimes, An Attempt to Define the Issue,* 1945.
Lacroix, Jean, *Force et faiblesse de la famille,* 1949.
Laski, H. J., *A Grammar of Politics,* 1941.
Lauterpacht, H., *An International Bill of Rights of Man,* 1945.
Leclercq, J., *Le mariage chrétien,* 2nd ed., 1949.
——— *La famille, leçons de droit naturel,* 3rd ed., 1950.
Lippmann, W., *U.S. Foreign Policy: Shield of the Republic,* 1943.
Lubahn, *Die städtische Grundrente,* 1952.
Lütge, F., "Wohnungswirtschaft und Wohnungspolitik," in *Evangelisches Soziallexikon,* F. Karrenberg, editor, 1954, p. 1162.
——— *Wohnungswirtschaft,* 2nd ed., 1949.
McCarthy, W. E. J., *The Closed Shop in Britain,* 1964.
Macartney, C. A., *National States and National Minorities,* 1934.
Mair, Erich, *Die Psychologie der nationalen Minderheiten,* 3rd ed., 1947.
Mannheim, K., *Ideologie und Utopie,* 1929.
Marriot, J. A. R., *Federalism and the Problem of the Small State,* 1944.
Martin, C.-N., *Hat die Stunde H geschlagen? Die wissenschaftlichen Tatsachen über die Wirkungen der Wasserstoffbombe,* Preface by Albert Einstein, 1955.
Martini, R. de, O.F.M., *The Right of Nations to Expand by Conquest* (U.S.A.), 1955.
Maturi, Giacomo, *Il problema giuridico della Communità Internazionale: Studio theologico-morale sulla dichiarazione dei diritti e doveri degli Stati elaborata dagli Organi delle Nazioni Unite* (Milan), 1956.
Mausbach, J., *Naturrecht und Völkerrecht,* 1918.
Messineo, A., S.J., *Il Problema delle minoranze nazionale* (Rome), 1946.
Messner, J., *Die berufsständische Ordnung,* 1936.
——— *Der Funktionär, seine Schüsselstellung in der heutigen Gesellschaft,* 1961; Engl. *The Executive. His Key Position in Contemporary Society.*
Michels, R., *Zur Soziologie des Parteiwesens,* 1924, Epilogue by W. Conze, 1957.
Mill, J. S., *Considerations on Representative Government,* 1861.
——— *On Liberty,* 1878.
Miller, J., *Moderne Ehe: Probleme in christlicher Sicht,* 2nd ed., 1955.
Mitterer, A., *Elternschaft und Gattenschaft, nach dem Weltbild des hl. Thomas v. Aquin und dem der Gegenwart,* 1943.
——— "Was ist die Frau?" in *Um die Seele der Frau,* Karl Rudolf, editor, 1953.
——— *Die Zeugung der Organismen, insbesondere des Menschen, nach dem Weltbild des hl. Thomas v. Aquin und dem der Gegenwart,* 1947.
Muckermann, H., *Der Sinn der Ehe, biologisch, ethisch, übernatürlich,* 3rd ed., 1952.
——— *Ewiges Gesetz,* 1947.
——— *Ehekrise,* 1948.
——— *Die Familie im Lichte der Lebensgesetze,* 2nd ed., 1952.
——— *Die Normalfamilie,* 2nd ed., 1923.
——— *Vererbung und Entwicklung,* 2nd ed., 1947.
Murdock, George, *Social Structure,* 1949.

Nell-Breuning, O. v., S.J., "Wohnwirtschaft," in *Staatslexikon der Görresgesellschaft,* Vol. V, 1932.
—— *Wirtschaft und Gesellschaft,* 1956.
—— "Wertzuwachssteuer," in *Handbuch der Finanzwissenschaft,* 2nd ed., W. Gerloff and F. Neumark, editors, Vol. II, 1956.
Neutra, R., *Survival through Design,* 1954.
Oeter, F., *Familienpolitik,* 1954.
Oppenheim-Lauterpacht, *International Law,* 7th ed., 1952.
Pfeifer, H., Pd., *Möglichkeiten und Grenzen der berufsständischen Selbstverwaltung,* 1936.
Politis, N., *La giustizia internazionale* (Rome), 1945.
Rathbone, Eleanor, *The Case for Family Allowances,* 1940.
Raumer, Kurt v., *Ewiger Friede, Friedensrufe und Friedenspläne der Renaissance,* 1953.
Reibstein, E., *Völkerrecht, eine Geschichte seiner Ideen in Lehre und Praxis,* Vol. I, *Von der Antike bis zur Aufklärung,* 1958.
Roberts, B. C., *Trade Union Government and Administration in Great Britain,* 1956.
Rosenmayr, L., "Die Wiener Familie der Gegenwart, Ergebnisse soziologischer Forschung und deren Bedeutung für die psychische Hygiene," in *Wiener Zeitschr. f. Nervenheilkunde und deren Grenzgebiete,* Vol. XIII, 1957.
Rumpf, M., *Religiöse Volkskunde,* 1933.
Schaumann, Wilfred, *Die Gleichheit der Staaten: Ein Beitrag zu den Grundprinzipien des Völkerrechts,* 1957.
Schelsky, H., *Wandlungen der deutschen Familie in der Gegenwart: Darstellung und Deutung einer empirisch-soziologischen Tatbestandsaufnahme,* 3rd ed., 1955.
Scherer, Alice, editor, *Die Frau, Wesen und Aufgaben* (Heft VI der Beiträge zu einem Wörterbuch der Politik), O. v. Nell-Breuning, S.J. and H. Sacher, editors, 1954.
Scherer, A. and R. and Dorneich, J., editors, *Ehe und Familie* (Heft VII der Beitr. zu einem Wörterbuch der Politik), 1956.
Schmitz, Wolfgang, *Der Ausgleich der Familienlasten,* 2nd ed., 1955.
Schneider, F., *Katholische Familienerziehung,* 1951.
Schnürer, Gustav, *Die Anfänge der abendländischen Völkergemeinschaft,* 1932.
Schreiber, Georg, *Großstadt und Volkstum,* 1933.
—— *Deutsche Bauernfrömmigkeit,* 1937.
—— *Die Sakrallandschaft des Abendlandes,* 1937.
—— *Hochschule und Volkstum in der neuen Zeit,* 1945.
Schürholz, Franz, *Die deutschen Gewerkschaften seit 1945: Praktische Arbeit und Reformbedürfnis,* 1955.
Schwer, W., *Stand und Ständeordnung im Weltbild des Mittelalters,* 2nd ed., N. Monzel, editor, 1952.
Scott, J. Brown, *Francisco de Vitoria and the Law of Nations: The Spanish Origin of International Law,* 1934.
—— *The Catholic Conception of International Law* (Georgetown, U.S.A.), 1934.
Seipel, Ignaz, *Nation und Staat,* 2nd ed., 1930.
Seraphim, H.-J., *I.* "Ländliche Siedlung"; *II.* "Städtische Siedlung" (II in coll.

with J. B. Heuer), in *Handwörterbuch der Sozialwissenschaften,* Vol. IX, 1956.

Simonett, M., *Die berufsständische Ordnung und die Politik,* 1951.

Soder, J., *Die Idee der Völkergemeinschaft: Francisco de Vitoria und die philosophischen Grundlagen des Völkerrechts,* 1955.

—— *Die Vereinten Nationen und die Nichtmitglieder,* 1956.

Speck, O., *Kinder erwerbstätiger Mütter,* 1956.

Stadtmüller, G., *Geschichte des Völkerrechts,* Vol. I, 1949.

Stamp, L. D., *The Land of Britain, Its Use and Misuse,* 1948.

Stein, Bernhard, *Der Familienlohn, Probleme einer familiengerechten Einkommensgestaltung,* 1956.

Sturmthal, Adolf, editor, *Contemporary Collective Bargaining in Seven Countries* (New York), 1957.

Tannenbaum, Frank, *A Philosophy of Labor,* 1951.

—— "The Social Function of Trade Unionism," in *Political Science Quarterly* (Columbia University), 1947.

Thibon, G., *Ce que Dieu a uni: Essai sur l'amour,* 1945; Engl. trans. by A. Gordon Smith, *What God Has Joined together: An Essay on Love,* 1952.

Thomas, J. L., S.J., *The American Catholic Family* (New York), 1956.

Torff, Selwyn H., *Collective Bargaining* (U.S.A.), 1953.

Triesch, G., *Die Macht der Gewerkschaftsfunktionäre: Macht und Verantwortung der Gewerkschaften,* 1956.

Verdroß, A., *Völkerrecht,* 3rd ed., 1955.

—— "Die völkerrechtliche Neutralität im Wandel der Geschichte," in *Anz. d. phil. -hist. Kl. der Österreichischen Akademie der Wissenschaften,* 1957.

Vergnaud, P., *L'idée de la nationalité et de la libre disposition des peuples dans ses rapports avec l'idée de l'état, Études des doctrines politiques contemporaines* (1870–1950), Preface by J. J. Chevalier (Paris), 1955.

Vitoria, F. de, *De Indis et de iure belli relectiones,* 1532.

Weber, Adolf, *Der Kampf zwischen Kapital und Arbeit,* 6th ed., 1954.

—— *Bodenrechte und Bodenspekulation in der modernen Stadt,* 1904.

—— *Boden und Wohnung,* 1908.

Wengler, Wilhelm, *Der Begriff des Politischen im internationalen Recht,* 1956.

Willgeroth, Hans, "Familienlastenausgleich und Sozialreform," in *Ordo,* Vol. VIII, 1956.

Wright, D. McCord, editor, *The Impact of the Union: Eight Economic Theorists Evaluate the Labor Union Movement* (U.S.A.), 1956.

Wright, R. F., *Medieval Internationalism: The Contribution of the Medieval Church to International Law and Peace,* 1930.

Wurzbacher, G., *Leitbilder gegenwärtigen Familienlebens, Methoden, Ergebnisse und sozialpädagogische Folgerung einer soziologischen Analyse von 164 Familienmonographien,* 2nd ed., 1954.

Zweig, F., *Labour, Life, and Poverty,* Introduction by Lord Beveridge and Preface by Seebohm Rowntree, 1948.

BOOK III

THE ETHICS OF THE POLITICAL COMMUNITY

PART ONE

The Nature of the State

---

113. The Universal Society

Is the state an institution for the protection of all from one another, as it is represented in many individualist political theories, or is it a universal provider, as various schools of collectivistic thought conceive it? Is the state a product of nature or a man-made device? Is it a contractual unity or an enforced organization? Is it an order of justice or only a resultant of the class structure of society? Is it the reality of the moral idea or the incarnation of the will to power? Does it draw its life from the forces of the human mind or only from the forces of irrational instinct? Does it derive from divine will or from human volition? Is it essentially fellowship or domination?

All the opposing elements in these concepts, which we shall treat in detail in the following chapters, have been tried as cornerstones for political theories. In fact, all these elements are to a certain degree bound up with the nature of the state. Primarily and fundamentally, however, the state is a *community*, rooted in man's social instinct and characterized by his social end. It is in the nature of man to seek to attain his tasks in the material and cultural spheres in social cooperation: only thus does he grow to his full human stature and to cultural maturity. Only in larger groups do there occur, quantitatively through the number of their members and qualitatively through the variety of talents which these represent, all the potentialities for such a full mutual complementation of their members and for such a perfect integration of human nature, so that the attainment of man's purpose in life as indicated by the various existential ends is assured. The society that fulfills these conditions, that possesses and actualizes these potentialities, is the universal society, the state.

Consequently, a sharp differentiation exists between the end of the state and the ends of all other forms of community. This end is the fulfillment in all respects of the fundamental social functions which are required for the integration of human nature, namely, the self-defense of the community, the safeguarding of its legal order, and the promotion of the general economic and cultural welfare. Hence, the state has been described in natural law doctrine as the "*perfect society*," a conception that will be seen to have justification in the light of our previous argument: It is the abiding function of the state, by initiating, fostering, and directing all-round social cooperation, to create the necessary conditions for the full development of human nature. In the concept of self-sufficiency (*autarky*), which for *Aristotle* and the traditional school of natural law formed the essential mark of the perfect society, the economic aspect was very pronounced. This view was held because such self-sufficiency was the necessary basis for the self-defense of the ancient and medieval city-state.

This fact does not, however, affect the essence of the idea of the perfect society. The expression suggests the responsibility of the state, rooted in its end, for the fulfillment of the fundamental social functions, by providing the basis of the "good life" (*Aristotle*) or, as we should say today, the common good. Indeed, in the adequate fulfillment of these functions under modern conditions, the individual political community largely depends on international cooperation, but the responsibility for the performance of the fundamental social functions always falls primarily upon the individual state itself. The reason is that the customs, culture, way of life, the legal system of the political nation, and the particular requirements of its common good, necessarily will always be substantially differentiated. Hence, the merging of the individual state in a world state (cf. Chap. 106) is as Utopian an idea as that of a community of nations based on their absolute sovereignty.

The idea of the perfect society today is, for these reasons, of a more relative validity; nevertheless, it is still capable of conveying the particular nature of the state as distinct from other social structures. According to natural law doctrine, the idea of self-sufficiency is bound up with the notion of international cooperation, and clearly has nothing to do with the modern idea of the economic self-sufficiency of the nation-state. This second kind is directed against international cooperation and is intended principally as a means of realizing absolute sovereignty, if not indeed intended as a means of arming for war.

The end of a community and the functions bound up with it determine, as we have shown in our discussion of social philosophy, the authority of a community. The wide authority of the state, therefore, rests on the fundamental and comprehensive nature of its end. The indisputable exercise of the power of command to establish the legal order and the common good presupposes the definite territorial delimitation of the state community, all individuals and lesser groups in a territory being subject to its competence. Thus, the state is essentially a territorial body, and territory is an essential characteristic in the idea of the state. In spite of the immense difference between the ancient city-state and the modern territorial state, territorial delimitation is equally necessary to both.

Four chief *constituents of the concept of the state* thus present themselves: population, end, power, territory. The state, therefore, may be defined as a community constituted by a people inhabiting a definite area and endowed with supreme authority for the all-round establishment of its common good.

114. The Origin of the State

The *historical* origins of the state, as far as research permits a judgment on the subject, are by no means uniform. On the whole, however, history confirms the conclusion which *Aristotle* reached on the basis of the facts available to him: the state has grown out of the family. The family widens as children and grandchildren live together under the more comprehensive authority of one or more elders (patriarchate or matriarchate). With the formation of tribes, in which a fairly large number of families live together, although not within the same household, the transition to a new form of communal order takes place. This form differs from the family order inasmuch as the authority in the individual family continues to exist as a separate authority and to fulfill functions of its own, whereas the new authority receives functions that concern all families. Chief among these functions is the organizing of food procurement and of defense. Along with this situation another element enters into the historical origin of the state: war. War very often attends the birth of states, and very often attends their end. Tribal communities make it a principal task to defend themselves against raiding tribes; indeed, often they organize such raids themselves. Primitive forms of state expand by incorporating and assimilating subjugated groups. In other cases, groups combine for defense against a more powerful third party, and gradually come to be a political unity. By a contrary process, new independent states can arise by splitting off from large states, for example, the United States of America or the Succession States of the Austro-Hungarian monarchy. Here, too, we find war involved in the origin of states.

Political philosophy is primarily interested, not in the historical origin of the state, that is, the process by which it came into existence in the course of human history, but the *ontological* root of its nature. As in other spheres, so also in the sphere of society, scientific thinking cannot be satisfied with the knowledge of how phenomena originate, but must also ask why. The process of man's origin tells us nothing about "why" he is endowed with moral dignity. The actual origin of the state can, of course, throw light on its deeper foundation; but then the question of what the dignity of its authority is and why it may claim political obedience arises. The question to be answered by political philosophy is, then, not "how" but "why." The question concerns the foundation of the state's being, and so it is the ontological question of the origin of the state in contradistinction to the historical. All philosophies of the state have this question ultimately before their eyes. And all have answered it by reference to the nature of man. *Hobbes,* for instance, maintains that the state is necessary to overcome the "natural state" of man, which is the struggle of all against all; *Rousseau,* on the other hand, says that the state is necessary to lead man back to the "state of nature," which is one of universal freedom. In fact, every theory of the state has its own *corresponding doctrine of man,* as every materialistic or spiritualistic doctrine of man implies its specific political philosophy. For us, too, the root of the state lies in the nature of man. The state has its origin in the social nature of man: man achieves integration only in the community which fulfills the basic social functions, thus enabling him to realize his existential ends (as we have urged in our study of social philosophy). Thus, his nature impels him to organize those fundamental functions by forming a community. The state is part of the nature of man, the order of the state is a postulate of the law of his nature.

Our derivation of the state from human nature does not mean that all the characteristics of the modern state manifest themselves from the outset in fully developed form, still less that the human mind has possessed from the beginning a clear knowledge of the essence and functions of the state. *Von Gierke* rightly points out that in the Middle Ages, not to speak of ancient times, there was, for instance, no clear knowledge of the juridical personality of the state.* Understanding the reality of the state, like that of every other reality, is a matter of the development of human experience and of the human mind. Nevertheless, even primitive men have not failed to see that the social life of the group presupposes a communal system that insures their self-defense as well as internal peace and the possibility of their procuring their sustenance. At first this knowledge may have existed solely in the consciousness of the moral principle that lawful authority must be obeyed, while the conception of tribal authority as something possessing a character distinct from simple family authority was still lacking. As soon as the development of the special communal functions of the primitive state brought this distinction before the human mind, however, the reality of the political community was uncovered, even though analytical knowledge of its inner substance might have been wholly absent. Long before this knowledge ripened, man was urged to perfect the structure of simple states. He was impelled by his own nature to strive for a life of peace and order.

115. The State: A Legal System

Of the two fundamental functions of society, that of establishing and safeguarding the legal order is the prerequisite for all other characteristic activity of the state. Unless this function is fulfilled, not only is men's social coexistence impossible but also their cooperation in fulfilling the tasks indicated in their existential ends is impossible. Law can perform its unifying function only if it is assuredly binding on the community as an intrinsically consistent order derived from one source. State authority

* Cf. O. von Gierke, *Das deutsche Genossenschaftsrecht,* Vols. I–IV, 1868–1913; Vol. III, pp. 556 ff.

has its root, as we have argued in our study of legal philosophy, in the function of creating and safeguarding this order. In this respect, *Kelsen* and his school rightly speak of the identity of law and state: a plurality of absolutely valid legal systems within the state is irreconcilable with the ordering function of law, and therefore is excluded by the nature of the state. From all this it follows that the state is first and foremost an association for the establishment of law or of a legal community (cf. Chap. 44).

The legal systems which can be found in the historical development of states correspond with the essential ordering function of the state only more or less approximately. No state legal system is a full actualization of true law. Every legal system is at the same time a mirror of the instinctive, political, economic, and technical forces peculiar to the society. Thus, in its actual condition, it is inevitably permeated with frictions and is also made to subserve interests that are discrepant with the true end of law; for example, the vested interests of economic classes, political parties, military castes, ruling classes. But, because the political order must be realized, notwithstanding the social dynamic of human passions and powerful group interests, the firmly established legal order represents the *fundamental value of the common good* of the political community, even when it corresponds only inadequately to its essential function. It is the primary condition for fully integrated human existence, so that any degree of true order is of immeasurable value by comparison with the complete lack of the fundamentals of order.

The *constitutional state,* which guarantees in principle and respects in fact legally defined civil and political liberties against arbitrary action of the ruler, is a late product of the evolution of law. The fact that this stage in the evolution of law does not yet belong to the assured possessions of mankind is shown by the recent experience of totalitarian states. On the other hand, the nineteenth-century individualist interpretation of the function of law is too narrow because it restricts the function of law to the protection of the individual, of his freedom, and of his property. Such a state has, it is well known, been characterized by *Ferdinand Lassalle* as the "night-watchman state." Today, the legal consciousness of mankind is firmly convinced that human rights, the guaranteeing of which is a primary legal task of the state, extend far beyond the individual sphere to the social sphere.

A merely *juristic conception of the state,* therefore, is inadequate. In fact, there can be no juristic concept without the power concept, just as there can be no sociological concept (cf. Chap. 116) without the legal concept. When the advocates of the former maintain that power is included in law, they overlook the obvious fact that illegal power, as well as legal power, can exist in the state. The task of subduing power to law shows that there also resides in power an element foreign to law, but an element of potent force in the life of the state. Power, therefore, is not to be comprehended solely in terms of law; hence the exclusively juristic conception of the state is inadequate. To be sure, the juristic conception of the state does not do justice to the welfare function. The consequences of the individualist interpretation of law, with its ban on the social function and social policy of the state, bear out the inadequacy of the mere juristic conception. The fact that the full reality of the state is not to be grasped by the juristic conception alone is shown also by the logical conclusion to which the conception is drawn in *Kelsen's* "pure jurisprudence."[1] The identification of law and state to which it leads leaves no room whatever for any distinct reality of the state: the state is only law. The result is a "theory of the state without a state."[2]

All varieties of *anarchism* maintain common error the idea that the basis of all political authority and coercion is to be sought in the private ownership of the means of production. Collectivistic anarchism arose in the middle of the nineteenth century with the idea of the collectivization of the means of production, the call for direct revolutionary action against the capitalistic system, and the rejection of any participation in parliamentary activity and of the belief in the self-destruction of capitalism. *Michael Bakunin* (1814–76) became the champion of this revolutionary and terrorist anarchism and leader of the opposition to *Marx* in the First International. He described himself as a "collectivistic" anarchist, although in his constructive ideas, as far as he suggests any, he comes rather close to the "communistic" anarchism of *P. A. Kropotkin* (1842–1921). The latter assigns the organization of production and of distribution to the commune in order to avoid the coercive power that would be necessarily bound up with the economic administration in state communism, failing to see that even municipal communism cannot succeed without such power.

All anarchists fail to see that even a propertyless social order is unable to function without coercive power behind its administration. The expression "anarchy" was first coined by *Pierre Joseph Proudhon* (1809–65) in his *Qu'est-ce que la propriété?* (1840). He rejected communism, however, as sharply as capitalism and looked for a solution in his mutualism, a system of exchange on the basis of labor certificates, which was meant to establish the full freedom of the individual by excluding capital profit and thus the social and political power of the property class: "Each individual will at the same time be both producer and consumer, citizen and sovereign, ruler and ruled." His anarchism, therefore, is termed "individualist" anarchism. In England, ideas of individualist anarchism (rejection of state power and state law as irreconcilable with human freedom; demand for a new system of property on the principle of equality and need) are found in *William Godwin*[3] (1756–1836), but they have exercised no noteworthy influence. State power as such is also disputed on religious and moral principles by modern reformers, such as *Leo Tolstoy* and *Mahatma Gandhi,* who wished for a return to simpler modes of economic life, stressing agriculture and craftsmanship and demanding a property system freed from the goad of domination.

[1] Cf. H. Kelsen, *Hauptprobleme der Staatslehre,* 2nd ed., 1923; *Allgemeine Staatslehre,* 1925; *Der soziologische und der juristische Staatsbegriff,* 2nd ed., 1928.

[2] Cf. Hermann Heller, *Staatslehre,* 1934, pp. 95 ff.

[3] His *Enquiry Concerning Political Justice* attracted great attention on its appearance in 1793.

116. The State: A Power Organization

Power belongs to the state in two respects: as an association for the establishment of law vested with the right of physical coercion which law implies, being therefore by its nature an association wielding power; as an association for self-defense to safeguard the peace of the community against external aggressors. With the progress of civilization the function of preserving peace may become one of international cooperation, but it requires adequate force for its fulfillment in any case. On both grounds it follows that power is not only an essential element of the state but a high good for the state, that is, a constituent of its common good. Thus, the significance and position of state power are governed by the end in which the state finds the origin and significance of its being. Since this end is the protection of the peace of the community internally and externally, and since its peace may be in danger from the use of power by internal and external enemies, the chief function of *ordered power* can be described as a means of combating arbitrary, illegal power.

A realistic political philosophy must hasten to admit that "ordered" political power never exists except in a form partly contrary to the common good. The Christian natural law in particular must remember that the power instinct is not exempt from the perversion to which the instincts of man's actual nature are subject. That the instinct for power is one of the strongest primary impulses [1] was realized by mankind long before social theory and social psychology began to analyze the *power impulse*. Political power, instead of serving the general weal, is to some degree always made to serve group interests. In the hands of ruling classes, political power becomes the means of influencing, more or less in their own favor, all essential functions of the social system, including law and order, administration, economic policy, distribution, and educational services. Hence, the actual form of political power in a state is always a resultant of the class structure, or of the balance of power between opposing groups in the community. Or, instead of being a means of self-defense for the state, power becomes a means of aggression, since the temptation to abuse power seems always to be associated with the desire for expansion. Hence, forms of imperialism occur throughout the whole known history of mankind. Or, the consciousness of power prestige, within a balance of power system, may take the form of extreme sensitiveness in matters of prestige, following with suspicion all military and economic events and changes in other states and replying to them with "demonstrations" and increased armaments. All these manifestations of the power element in the state belong to its actual nature, just as the partial perversions of other instincts

[1] Cf. A. Vierkandt, *Gesellschaftslehre,* 1923, p. 290.

belong to the actual nature of man. But just as the latter do not make up the essential reality of man, the former do not make up the essential reality of the state.

The natural law doctrine cannot leave the discussion with the two conclusions we have reached, namely, that state power is subject to the moral order, and that it appears always in a partially perverted form. By its very idea of man's nature, it must show how, in the actual reality of the state, the dynamic of natural law counteracts the dynamic of the irrational elements, and how the latter challenges the human spirit to assert itself against them and overcome them. Thus, the *realistic conception* of human nature preserves the natural law doctrine from the optimistic belief in any final elimination of the problems arising from the existence of irrational elements in the state; this conception equally preserves natural law doctrine from any tendency toward a pessimistic theory of the state, one which speaks only of an ineluctable tragedy in which states and community of nations are ultimately delivered over to the dynamic of power.

The fact that the sheer dynamic of power does not constitute the whole nature of the state may be gathered from the experience of history, which shows that no state can base its existence exclusively on force. None other than *Machiavelli* himself, whose *Principe* is the source of essential elements in the modern theory of the power state, finds himself compelled to admit that princes begin to lose the state at that hour in which they begin to break the laws.[2] The fact that no state can be based solely on power is today a commonplace of political theory. In fact, power always sees itself standing *before the forum of the spirit* and, willy-nilly, is called to account. This forum is the political community's consciousness of its right to the safeguarding of the fundamental values of the common good by the ruling power, and further, the consciousness of its right to meet force with force if these values are withheld from it.

The practical effect of this is that the state, in its *internal policy,* must always face the necessity of justifying itself morally by services rendered to the people. This truth is demonstrated not less by the history of the ancient tyrannies than by the history of modern dictatorships and the various forms of absolutist city aristocracies, that is, the types of state in which power seems to form the decisive element. The services such states have rendered the community to justify themselves have been various. They have consisted in the provision of security from external foes or internal chaos, such as the tyrannies of ancient times provided, or in brilliant economic and cultural development, such as was promoted by the Italian city aristocracies. It is of great interest to see the way in which so extreme an advocate of the power state theory as *Treitschke* has to pay tribute to these facts in his treatment of the state forms in question, thus

[2] Cf. Machiavelli, *Discorsi sopra la prima deca di Tito Livio,* III, 5: "Sappiano adunque i principi come a quell'ora e'cominciano a perdere lo stato, ch'ei cominciano a rompere le leggi, e quelli modi e quelle consuetudini che sono antiche, e sotto le quali gli uomini lungo tempo sono vivuti."

admitting that the pure power state theory ultimately receives no confirmation from history.[3] Power is always driven to seek justification before the mind. In this, the natural law of man is at work. It tends toward the *moralizing of power.* Admittedly the process is a slow one and one subject to severe setbacks, but it is unmistakably one of evolution toward an increasing realization of the ideals of individual freedom and social equality based upon the moral dignity of man, that is, toward *control of political power* and of the power groups behind it by subjecting them to law. Hence, the endeavor to subdue the power element inseparable from the state is no less a part of the reality of the state than the power element itself.

In the *external relations* of the state, the same irrational elements in power operate with immensely enhanced effect. Were the enhancing factor nothing but the state's need for security, in view of the historical fact that even a relative weakness by comparison with neighbors may be fatal, it would suffice to call forth from this danger pressure toward the utmost extension of power. In fact, the law of action within the sphere of international power dynamics is partly independent of the will of the individual state; rather, the entire life of the state is substantially governed by the exigencies of foreign policy. This interstate dynamics implies the further law of its own intensification, since each increase of power by one state is followed by similar increases on the part of others, a phenomenon known as the armament race, open or secret. A strong additional impulse is given to this process by a lust for power that is coupled with pride, neither of which can obtain in any other sphere as much satisfaction as they obtain from mastery over other nations.

Against all these irrational power factors in international relations, however, reason tried to assert itself: the desire for peace, order, civilization, and social progress. The constant threat of danger compels reason to organize power for the purpose of securing peace (and hence to *moralize power*). Reason offers men, besides the establishment of an international police force for opposing the dynamics of power politics, yet another way, namely, the direct enlistment of moral forces. The nuclear bomb has finally made it clear that the international organization for peace cannot rely solely upon physical force, but must insure that moral energies have a chance to operate. There is, in fact, only one way to preclude the use of the nuclear bomb for offensive purposes: *complete freedom of public opinion in all countries.* States that prevent freedom of public opinion and access to information by the outer world must be regarded today as potential aggressors. The enlistment of moral factors to overcome the dynamics of power in international life thus assumes the form of preserving certain minimum standards in the internal political life of every state. These are the standards demanded by man's dignity and freedom.

Thus, we arrive at the conclusion that the human spirit does not find

[3] Cf. Heinrich von Treitschke, *Politik,* II, 1895, pp. 189–249.

itself impotent in face of the irrational forces of power politics. On the contrary, the development of power politics and its methods impels mankind to oppose these forces, more and more resolutely, with the power of the mind, and the law of man's nature leaves him in no doubt about the way to be chosen, particularly in face of the latest complication of the situation, the possible use of nuclear weapons.

The purely *sociological idea of the state* is as inadequate as the purely juristic for explaining the nature of the state. One of the most consistent exponents of the sociological idea, *Max Weber,* defines the state in this way: "We mean by state an organization of a political institution when and so far as its administrative body successfully secures the monopoly of legitimate physical coercion for establishing the order of a community imposed by its superior." [4] The definition itself shows, however, that the sociological conception cannot really exclude law; the legitimacy of physical coercion can refer only to law. A great number of other forces and impulses operate in the state: the striving after security, freedom, prosperity, happiness, as well as group interests and national ambitions. To examine the actual influences of all these forces and impulses upon the structure and life of the political community is, in fact, the task of sociology as an empirical science.

And the department of sociology which examines these influences, not only in particular historical instances in this or that state but in their general effect, may very well be designated *"political science,"* a science that can be of great importance for the practical art of government.[5] Thus, besides political philosophy and political ethics we have the general and special sociology of the state. These are all departments of the mind's endeavor to comprehend the state, and they can no more be completely disjoined in realistic political theory than can the elements forming the state be separated from one another. But there can be no objection on the part of social ethics to a methodological separation of the scientific disciplines of the state as long as no one discipline maintains that it alone is an authentic science and that the others have no right to existence. Should it do this and declare that, by a philosophical, an ethical, a juristic,

[4] M. Weber, *Wirtschaft und Gesellschaft,* 1922, pp. 17 f., 29. Two further definitions of Weber's may be added in explanation: "Organization signifies a continuous activity of a definite kind directed toward a purpose"; "Institution signifies a corporation whose appointed order within a specifiable orbit of operation is (relatively) successfully imposed upon every action specifiable according to definite characteristics" (*ibid.,* p. 28).

[5] The justification and limitation of political science are probably correctly described by R. M. MacIver, *The Web of Government,* 1948, pp. 7 f.; he declines to take sides with the purists who would not speak of "science" except when eternal laws are presented or quantitative terms are used, but equally rejects the claim that political science could tell the statesman how to govern as medicine and engineering do in their fields. The traditional natural law school could readily agree with the statement of George E. G. Catlin, who, although a consistent champion of politics as an empirical science, firmly observes that behaviorism as a philosophy may be untenable, but as a scientific method it may be useful. Values have indubitably immense influence on social life, but must, for the purposes of political science, be judged by this influence (*A Study of the Principles of Politics,* 1930, p. 41). Cf. also G. E. G. Catlin, *The Science and Method of Politics,* 1927; Eric Voegelin, *The New Science of Politics* (U.S.A.), 1952. Among the few German works cf. especially, Adolf Grabowsky, *Politik im Grundriß,* 1952.

or a sociological view of the state, it has comprehended the whole nature of the state, it becomes the instrument of fallacious and dogmatic thinking.

Natural law ethics has no need to dispute the right of other political sciences since it can be in no doubt that all sciences which treat of the reality of the state from whatever point of view and do not dogmatically narrow their field of vision, are certain ultimately to discover the moral and legal reality also (which cannot be unrecognized in the state as a fellowship of human persons). For, if the fundamental idea of the natural law doctrine is correct, then there must indeed be a *Physiology of the State,* as *Constantin Frantz,* the distinguished Protestant political thinker and one of the best political writers of the nineteenth century, has named one of his books.[6] But a physiology of this kind, it may be gathered from his book, will inevitably discover the moral nature of the state, if it does not close its eyes to a part of the reality which it has to investigate.

The Political Theory of Dialectical Materialism

Among the political theories which see in the pre-communistic state only the resultant of power relations, the leading position today belongs to dialectical materialism. The state, says *Karl Marx,* is rooted, not in human nature as such, but in class antagonisms. The owners of the means of production (in the course of history: slave owners, feudal lords, capitalists), that is, the exploiting classes, create for themselves in the state the power organization for dominating the exploited classes, and hence for maintaining the social system that serves their interests. With the cessation of class conflict after the elimination of private ownership of the means of production, the state would lose its function of serving an exploiter class; it would "wither away"; it would then belong to the museum of antiquities like the spinning wheel and the bronze axe.[7]

The Marxist theory of the state is open to critical objections on many grounds.

1. It stands or falls with dialectical materialism, its philosophical basis, and is liable to the same criticisms as the anthropology, the theory of history, and the jurisprudence of dialectical materialism.

2. It contradicts the experience of mankind. The political impulse, namely, the impulse toward an ordered communal life, which will enable man to live in peace and to fulfill his existence, is one of man's original impulses. This experience of mankind is justified in those conceptions of the state which, with *Aristotle,* firmly maintain that man is a political animal seeking peace and order as necessary conditions for the good life, so that, as *Aristotle* says, "he who first founded the state" must be called "the greatest of benefactors." [8]

3. It is no less a fact of universal experience that the power impulse itself is an original human impulse which, independently of economically determined class relations, expresses itself socially in the creation and utilization of the power organization of the state. *Nietzsche* even thinks that "the will to power

[6] Cf. Constantin Frantz, *Die Naturlehre des Staates,* 1870.

[7] Cf. *The Communist Manifesto;* Engels, *The Origin of the Family, Private Property, and the State,* 1940; Lenin, *State and Revolution,* 1942.

[8] Aristotle, *Politics,* I, 2, pars. 9, 15.

is the primitive form of impulse; all other impulses are only derived from it." [9] Even though *Nietzsche* errs in one direction by overestimating the power impulse, *Marx* errs in the other by underestimating its original character proper to human nature.

4. *Marx* likewise overlooks the predatory impulse in human nature, which is neither brought about by the class structure of society nor makes exclusive use of the class structure for its satisfaction. History affords countless examples of nations that have made other nations tributary to them; and often only as a result of this process, with the aid of state organization and state power, conditions of class structure have been created. Thus, the order of cause and effect is often the reverse of what Marx suggests.

5. The Marxian theory of the state is further contradicted by experience, because the state throughout its history has exercised a greater number of functions bearing no relation whatever to the class structure of society; for example, the functions of internal order and external defence. It is sheer dogmatism to suppose that after the suppression of private property these functions would disappear, so that there would be no antisocial behavior in national and international society to be combated. As long as human nature cannot be altered, the state will be needed to insure law and order.

The Power State Theory

The view that the state is fundamentally power and therefore that in its conduct it must be guided by the desire for power is the foundation of almost all modern international politics. To be sure, if the modern state pursues a power policy it generally clothes it in the garb of justice. The power state theory gained support from the rationalistic as well as the irrationalistic philosophies of the state. From *Hegel*, the most influential representative of the former, it even gained an apparent moral justification, since he identified the state with the reality of the ethical idea. *Hegel's* philosophy of the state is a variation of the ideas "that the mind, free and rational as it is, is in itself ethical, and the true idea is the real rationality, and this is what exists as the state"; that the state is "the self-knowing, ethical reality"; that the state receives "its absolute right" in world history at "that moment in the idea of the world spirit which is its present stage"; lastly, that against this absolute right "the spirits of the other nations have no rights." [10] (In various connections we have already touched upon the element of truth in *Hegel's* philosophy).

Other thinkers, such as *Treitschke,* have altogether abandoned the notion of incorporating power in a general idea of morality. Instead, they simply make power the essence of the state and conclude that it is "the highest duty of the state to be solicitous for its power." Although he rejects *Machiavelli,* whose conclusions he considered "horrible," and makes power not an end in itself but a means "for protecting and furthering the higher goods of men," he makes all moral standards relative: "The chief thing is that one should know his own self and develop it to the highest attainable perfection." [11]

[9] Nietzsche, *Der Wille zur Macht,* pars. 688, 786; Engl. trans., *The Will to Power,* 1913–14.

[10] Hegel, *Grundlinien der Philosophie des Rechts,* 1821, pars. 270, 345, 347.

[11] Treitschke, *op. cit.,* I, pp. 90 ff., 100 ff.

Machiavelli is more logical. The fundamental categories of *Machiavelli's* political theory are *virtù, fortuna, necessità. Virtù* consists in performing with energy and prudence whatever is bidden by the ends of the state in the given situation. This virtue, therefore, is not connected with any moral norm.[12] To form a fair judgment of *Machiavelli,* we should not forget that he had before his eyes the policy and political methods of Popes *Sixtus IV* and *Alexander VI* as well as of *Cesare Borgia,* the son of the latter, and that he expressly undertook to form a theory of statesmanship from what he found done in practice. Today, he is often designated as the first conscious exponent of political science (cf. above in connection with *Max Weber* and also footnote 5). His power state theory, Machiavellianism, is characterized by the complete separation of politics and morality: religion and law are lumped together by him with armed forces as political instruments.[13]

Nietzsche considers the state an inevitable tool for the purpose of forming society into a soil in which culture can grow; if the state exceeds this purely instrumental function, it becomes an obstacle to culture and to the breeding of the "Superman." In its hypertrophy the state is the foe of culture; it is "organized unmorality," "the coldest of all cold monsters." *Nietzsche's* solution is, therefore, "as little state as possible." In this he takes issue with every form of socialism on the ground that each seeks the goal "as much state as possible." Power politics drew strong support from *Nietzsche.* The "transvaluation" of values proclaimed by him, with the will to power and the idea of the Superman as the determining elements of his new "tables of values," could be readily turned to use for the power state idea. "What is good?" says Nietzsche: "Everything that increases the sense of power, the will to power, and power itself in men. What is evil? Everything that springs from weakness." That one must be cautious, however, in classing *Nietzsche* among the exponents of the power state idea and even of a materialistic interpretation of power, is indicated by his warning: "There is no harder misfortune in all human destiny than when the powerful ones of the earth are not also the first men. Then everything becomes false and crooked and monstrous." [14]

117. The State: An Elemental Force

The state, as we have seen, is rooted in man's impulse toward life in an organized community that will make possible the satisfaction of his existential needs. Besides this impulse, which belongs to man's spiritual nature, a whole series of structural forces connected with man's biological nature and with external physical nature go to make up the state. Hereditary qualities, which are biologically determined, characterize a people and the physical and mental make up of its political community. No less extensive is the influence of environment on the political community, that

[12] Cf. Machiavelli, *Il Principe,* 1513.

[13] Machiavelli, *Discorsi sopra la prima deca di Tito Livio,* III, Introduction.

[14] Nietzsche, *Also sprach Zarathustra; Die neuen Götzen; Menschliches, Allzumenschliches,* par. 473; *Morgenröte,* par. 179; *Der Wille zur Macht,* par. 717; *Der Antichrist,* par. 2; the last quotation in the text comes from Zarathustra: "Gespräch mit den Königen."

is, the geographical situation (e.g., whether continental or insular) and the fertility of the state territory. From the organization of its defensive function and of its means of sustenance to the pattern of its day-to-day activities, the whole life of the political community is governed by environment, whether by adaptation to it or by struggling with it. Both natural elements, inherited characteristics and environment, combine to form the *individuality* of every state, the national character of the political community.

All this causes the state to appear to the individual as a kind of *elemental force* inescapably determining his life. He is born into the state without being consulted. Before he becomes conscious of his own self, it has already received a deep imprint from the tradition and culture of his political community. If we consider further the claim of the state to coercion, which will unfailingly subordinate the interests of the individual to those of the whole, as well as the role of physical power as a means of self-preservation and self-defense into whose service the citizen is coerced, we may indeed say that, in the experience of the individual, the state appears as "elemental force." Besides, there is in the state something of *destiny* for the individual. He sees himself, especially in periods of heightened historical dynamic, bound to the state community for weal or woe. The Second World War, with its effect on the destinies of millions, was a new and dreadful witness of this fact. Between the wars, unemployment wore the same fatal aspect for countless millions in the process of the political community; it confronted the individual with an elemental force which mocked the will and the endeavors of the community.

The state is an elemental force. But it is also a *spiritual power* ordained toward the taming of the irrational elements, so that man can become master of his destiny and pursue the goal indicated for him in the existential ends of his nature. These irrational elements in the actual state can as little alter the fact that it is basically rational in nature and subject to the ordering forces of the spirit as can the irrational and less human elements in human nature cause any doubt to fall upon its moral dignity. Even if the irrational elements be raised to a higher power in the state, the power of the spirit is also increased by the multiplication of effort in the political community. Both sides of the reality of the state, the irrational and the rational, must be viewed by ethics in order that, when it apprehends the state as part of the moral order, it may also appreciate the difficulty and complexity of the task of integrating the political order, and that it may avoid the danger of discussing the state as an abstraction. This is the more imperative since, besides the irrational elements just discussed, other elements have to be kept in mind: those involved in the power instinct, in the acquisitive instinct, and in the historical conditions which have molded the state. We have discussed these in part or shall presently begin to discuss them.

The *materialist and biological theories of the state* seek the ultimate origin of the state in irrational elemental forces. One main trend among such theories is dialectical materialism, which attributes the state to class relations engendered by technico-economic production conditions. The other main trend is the racial biological theory which makes the essence of the state the unity of the people brought about by common blood and destiny. This theory was first developed by *L. Gumplowicz,* who deduced the essence of the state from the natural factors of blood and of race as primitive instinctive elements reaching conscious and formative expression in the state.[1] When he expounded his theory at the beginning of the nineteenth century he could hardly have suspected that, through the medium of the racial theory of the state,[2] analogous ideas would soon be developed as the motive force of a political dynamic which would shake the world.

Mention should be made of the *patriarchal and patrimonial* theories, which are naturalistic inasmuch as they see in the state and the power of the state only a natural development from the family system and paternal authority. Although it may be true that the state in many cases developed simply from the wider family community, its nature is as different from that of the family as are its ends and functions. The ordering power of the state community is no mere extension of paternal authority, as the patriarchal theory following *Aristotle's* account of the origin of the state outlined above, assumes; still less is it an extension of the father's "right of possession" over wife, child, and servants, as is supposed by *Ludwig von Haller* in his so-called patrimonial theory.

118. The State: Unity of Consent

By its nature, the state is fellowship; that is to say, the state is a unity of persons, whose distinguishing characteristic is freedom. Their binding themselves to this unity, consequently, is an essential element in the state. By its nature the state is founded on the *consent* of its members. The great exponents of the natural law philosophy of the state have not hesitated to describe this consent as the contractual element in the nature of the state and, although with reserve, to call it a *pactum.*[1] To be sure, they do not by any means desire to base the state upon man's arbitrary will and on a social contract in the individualist sense, and therefore not

[1] Cf. Ludwig Gumplowicz, *Die soziologische Staatsidee,* 1892; and especially, *Staatsphilosophie im Umriß,* 1910.

[2] Only a minute fraction of National Socialist political writing can claim any scientific quality. The following may be mentioned: W. Dräger, *Primat des Volkes? Ein Beitrag zur Grundfrage einer völkischen Staatslehre,* 1935; K. Larenz, *Rechts- und Staatsphilosophie der Gegenwart,* 1935; O. Koelreutter, *Deutsches Verfassungsrecht,* 1936; *Vom Sinn und Wesen der nationalen Revolution,* 1933; we have touched upon such literature in the section on the "Nation."

[1] Cf. St. Augustine, *De civ. Dei,* Bk. IV, Chap. 4; *Conf.* 1, III, 15: "generale pactum." St. Thomas, *in Rom. 13, 1:* "Quasi quoddam pactum inter regem et populum"; St. Thomas quotes (*Summa theol.,* Ia IIae, q. 105, a. 2) Augustine's definition of the state (*De civ. Dei,* Bk. II, Chap. 21), which he took over from Cicero: "Est coetus multitudinis, iuris consensu, et utilitatis communione sociatus."

upon the actual will of the people. But, since they seek its root in the nature of man with his spiritual will, they find a contractual element in it, a sort of *union of wills,* as an essential constituent of the state. Were the state not a union of free selves it would not differ fundamentally from the community of bees; the most highly organized slave state might well be the highest form of human society. The ultimate standards that should govern its order and functions, then, must be drawn from man's own responsibility for his existential ends. His nature itself informs him that the performance by the state of the fundamental functions of society is a necessary condition if he is to integrate his nature in accordance with this responsibility. He finds political unity indicated in his natural social impulse. Consent to the order of society based upon this is, accordingly, a matter of man's will bound up with "right desire" (cf. Chap. 3). Hence, the political community is fellowship in virtue of the reflecting reason and the self-binding will, that is, in virtue of consent.

This consent embraces the following elements: (1) the union of wills, in the sense of consent of the individuals to the order designed in human nature for the fulfillment of the fundamental social functions: the effect is political fellowship; (2) the union of wills as consent to the actualization of this order as dependent on an established authority: the effect is political obedience. Summing up the discussion of the subject, one may, with *Pufendorf,* designate these two aspects of consent as *pactum unionis* and *pactum subjectionis.*[2] *Pufendorf* himself, however, anticipates the fallacy of the later individualist social contract theories which place the origin of the state and also state power in an alleged constitutive act of consent, instead of in the obligatory consent to the order of the political community predesigned in human nature. For the natural law school, the *pactum unionis* is not a constitutive act from which state and state power could be derived, but the union of free persons following their "essential" will. This aspect of consent, therefore, emphasizes the spiritual and moral nature of the unity of order, which is the state. Now, since this union of wills belongs to the moral order, it is a duty for all; therefore, it cannot be unconditional.

The juridical consciousness and the legal customs of a people, stimulated by natural instinct and developed by experience and reflection, determine the basic order of law for its political fellowship and thus also for the exercise of political authority.[3] We know from our discussion of

[2] Cf. Samuel Pufendorf (1632–94), *Jus naturale et gentium,* Bk. VII, Chap. 2; cf. the Latin edition and the English translation published by the Carnegie Endowment for International Peace.

[3] It is this fact that De Maistre (1754–1821) is establishing when, in opposing the theory of the absolute sovereignty of the people, in his aggressively exaggerated, although substantially realistic form, he says that man cannot really make a constitution, but that he discovers it in the nature of the state and can only develop it; constitutions, he observes, are not the results of arbitrary decisions but of a natural growth, and, if they are written, are only declarative records of previously existing law (*Le Principe Générateur des Constitutions Politiques,* 1809, I and XXVIII): for

the establishment of the juridical order that the actualization of its principles depends on their being concretely defined. A definition of this kind comes about through legal custom, in which the at first unconscious consent of the people regarding the basic legal order or constitution of its communal life (basic norm, fundamental law, *lex fundamentalis;* the conception originated in the sixteenth century) [4] achieves expression; this constitution concerns the obedience of the members and the exercise of power by the authority. This part of the consent may be designated *pactum subjectionis.* Our theory of consent shows that the individual does in fact find his own essential will in the fundamental juridical order of the community in which the united will expresses itself.[5] Hence, there is a grain of truth in *Rousseau's* formula that every man obeys himself if he obeys the law of the state, although *Rousseau's* perspective is completely at variance with ours, as will be seen from our later discussion of state sovereignty.

Thus, in all essential points the *natural law theory of consent diverges from the individualist theory.* 1) Sovereign individuals do not unite in consent, binding themselves by virtue of their autonomy; rather, man finds political fellowship predesigned in his nature and morally commanded. 2) The source of the state and state power is not sought in the consent; rather, its character as an ordered unity of moral persons is sought. 3) It is not left to the arbitrary will of the political community to determine the substance of the consent; rather, this is predesigned in its natural constitution.

119. The State: A Welfare Community

The end of the state is not confined to the preservation of law and order; in addition, it consists in making possible the fulfillment of all the existential ends of its citizens. To distinguish this function from the purely ordering function, which the state carries out by maintaining law, we shall describe it as the welfare function. *Aristotle* summarized its content as "the good life," [1] man's self-fulfillment in happiness, physically, mentally, and morally.

This idea of the state, as making possible in all respects the good life, together with a Christian interpretation of the material and cultural values

---

neither in the physical nor in the moral sphere can man create anything new, but can only modify what he finds at hand. He can as little really make a constitution as he can make a tree. "L'homme peut tout modifier dans la sphère de son activité, mais il ne crée rien: telle est sa loi, au physique comme au moral . . . Il ne s'est figuré qu'il avait le pouvoir de faire un arbre. Comment s'est-il imaginé qu'il avait celui de faire une constitution?" (*Considérations sur la France,* 1796, Chap. 6.)

[4] Cf. G. Jellinek, *Allgemeine Staatslehre,* 3rd ed., 1919, p. 508.

[5] Cf. St. Thomas, *Summa theol.,* Ia IIae, q. 90, a. 3: "Et hoc modo unusquisque sibi est lex, inquantum participat ordinem alicuius regulantis."

[1] Cf. Aristotle, *Politics,* I, 2, 8; III, 9, 6–14.

implied, has always been the notion endorsed by the traditional natural law school. It is still found clearly in their great follower, *Hugo Grotius,*[2] and in the great political thinkers who preceded the rise of individualism. We mention especially *Edmund Burke,* who describes the state as "a partnership in all science, a partnership in all art, a partnership in every virtue and in all perfection."[3] We need only refer to our discussion of the common good (Chaps. 23–29), the result of which, applied to the state, should be formulated as follows: The state must create the legal basis for social cooperation as well as the other conditions which enable all citizens to obtain their proportionate share of the fruits of social cooperation, materially and spiritually. Admittedly, "society" shares with the "state" in these tasks of justice. Nevertheless, they belong largely to the political sphere and to the departments of economic and social policy.

Individualist thinking, with its laissez-faire *state,* restricted the competence of the state to the legal order, to the exclusion of welfare functions.[4] These functions determine the idea, today almost universally accepted, of the "*social welfare state.*" This may be defined as the state which accepts the commonweal function in the sense just described. Today, the true idea of the state is challenged from the opposite direction: the new conception is that of the "*provider state.*" The latter regards it as its function to provide directly, by central planning and controlling of social cooperation, for all the material and cultural needs of the citizens and to supply them with everything necessary for every eventuality of life. This is the state born of the socialistic and communistic interpretation of "social security." This idea of the state is what lies at the root of modern movements for state-planned economy and society. It does not allow for the full development of personality, which is dependent on man's self-responsibility in fulfilling the tasks bound up with his existential ends, leaving to the state only subsidiary functions; and it is inconsistent with the common good, whose optimum development depends on the development, by all the members of the community, of their own powers and their own responsibility.

120. The State: Political Pluralism

When we say that the state is of its nature a community for social cooperation to enable its members fully to satisfy their material and cultural needs, we do not mean that the members of the community are altogether agreed among themselves concerning their respective shares in this cooperation or concerning the distribution of its fruits. Here the natural in-

[2] Hugo Grotius says: "Est autem civitas coetus perfectus liberorum hominum, juris fruendi et communis utilitatis causa sociatus" (*De jure belli ac pacis,* I, 1, par. 14), thus making welfare a distinct end.

[3] Edmund Burke, *Reflections on the Revolution in France,* 1790, p. 143.

[4] Cf. A. Müller-Armack, *Das Jahrhundert ohne Gott,* 1948; *Diagnose unserer Gegenwart,* 1949.

stinct of self-interest comes into operation, urging groups to seek out rewards for themselves in their activities and in their income, and to try to exert influence on the social system to this end. Hence, those whose interests in the working of the social system are alike form groups within the state community. This splitting up of the community into groups with opposing interests may be called political pluralism: the state of free democracy is the *state of pluralistic society*. Not only do economic interests and class interests, as is sometimes assumed, seek to gain influence over the organization of the functions of the state and aim at political pluralism, but also military, national, and cultural interests and anything that may be championed by individual groups as a political ideal seek the same thing.

Neither the nature of the state as a community nor the nature of the common good excludes conflicts of interest groups and ideologies. Limits are set to the dynamics of political pluralism only by the fundamental order of law, which is proper to the state as a natural community, with its function of serving the common good; this fundamental order must be respected by the opposing groups in their efforts to secure their own interests. From the foregoing considerations, political ethics must draw the following conclusions.

1. The actual state is characterized by *antagonisms,* in the sense just described, of conflicting interests, even if its unity is essentially and morally based on a condition of amity. This fact may be illustrated by the organizing and mobilizing of group interests in the party state, which, within the limits stated, is consistent with the nature of the state.

2. Since the plurality of opposing forces within the state involves their balancing, *compromise* is an indispensable factor in the formation of the political will of the whole. This balancing may be achieved by democratic forms or it may be brought about by a ruler who, in considering measures, takes these forces under consideration. Every compromise, however, is bound up with the fundamental claims of the common good and, therefore, with justice, which is above group interests.

3. The state, however, is more than the mere resultant of political pluralism and of the dynamics of power in which this tends to result. Precisely because the state is a unity in fellowship of the whole people, it is contrary to its nature if an individual group, by reason of the supremacy of its numerical or organizational forces, tries to gain advantages at the expense of other sections of the community, or if one group identifies itself with the state, forcibly excluding others from its management, as the single-party state does, with its principle that the party is the state. This is the fundamental political principle of all totalitarian states.

The State: Only *Political Pluralism?*

Some recent writers seek to regard the state as an exclusively political pluralism, for which there is already (not uniformly) a new expression, "politology."

In Germany a collapse of the traditional philosophical and theoretical conceptions of the state is spoken of. What is actually in question is the exchange of the earlier one-sided metaphysical conception of the state as derived from *Hegel* for an equally one-sided sociological mechanistic conception. The political order is understood as the resultant of opposing interests of groups, which try to use their power to secure the service of the state in their own interests, and appeal to the "legality" of their procedure in accordance with the principles of formal democracy. (Note that, in the liberalist conception, the state was regarded as the resultant of opposing individual interests, but not without the idea of a juridical order, and thus of "legitimacy.") In the "new" sociological mechanistic political theory the moral conception of the state, with its basic principles of justice and the common good, is abandoned; this means the surrender of the state to the power groups and group interests. The state and state power are regarded more as the outcome of the antagonism of pressure groups, the balancing mechanism of accumulated forces. The political theory based on the self-balancing of a political pluralism misjudges the nature of personality and society characterized by moral responsibility: it is contrary to reality. Should it become the standard for the political life of the West, it would have to be paid for with bitter experience in the evolution of free democracy.

This theory is inconsistent with reality, as *R. M. MacIver* in his well-known book emphasizes with regard to such ideas in America (the more recent German books are to no small extent offshoots of this). The whole logic of democracy, he says, depends on the conception that there is still a national unity and a common welfare. Although the common welfare cannot be organized like business interests, its existence and the need cannot be denied, for democracy guarantees the value of personality as a universal good and implies the enhancement of that value in all men; the values implied in the human person deny to any power group the right to impose its will upon the rest; the theory that a legislative act is always the calculable resultant of a struggle between pressure groups, and never a decision between opposing conceptions of national welfare, is not new; modern developments in all industrialized countries merely give it a new emphasis. He refers to the literature of the period preceding the Second World War.[1]

The so-called "new theory of the state" only elevates the actual situation to a theory, which is, therefore, in reality no philosophical theory at all. Important as empirical sociology, investigating and coordinating the facts of reality, may be for political theory and political philosophy and also for state policy and party politics, the new sociology of the state passes over such a great reality in free democracy as the belief in human personality. This is fully taken into account only in a moral conception of the state. It is true that the fundamental moral and legal order of the political community, as has been said, leaves a wide scope to group interests and pressure groups, but they are subject to the law of justice, which is the law of life of the free democracy and the safeguard of its future. (Of course, merely to establish that democracy is en-

[1] Cf. R. M. MacIver, *The Web of Government*, 1948, pp. 220 f.; literature quoted by him: A. F. Bentley, *The Process of Government, A Study of Social Pressures* (U.S.A.), 1908, 2nd ed., 1949; W. B. Munro, *The Invisible Government*, 1928; H. D. Lasswell, *Politics: Who Gets What, When, How*, 1936; F. R. Kent, *The Great Game of Politics*, 1924.

dangered by the policy of interest groups is of as little effect as merely to give them warning and exhortation; rather, efforts should be made toward a constitutional form of group activity; cf. Chaps. 85, 134.)

The fact that the state is exclusively the outcome of political pluralism is also the root idea of the political theory of *Carl Schmitt:* the state is a resultant of the grouping of society springing from the *"friend-foe relationship"* and of the power relationships which this involves.[2] The consequence of this theory is that the ideal situation is seen in the complete elimination of all "enemy" elements by the friend group, in other words, by the one-party state. The "friend-foe" relationship itself is accepted as the primal fact, that is, as the irrational, instinctive, elementary impulse in group life. The theory is based on a doctrine of man derived from the axiom, *homo homini lupus.* The theory puts the "political" *before* the state and derives the state from the "political," that is, the will of a group for domination over other groups, the state is the means to such domination. Racialist political science was based on such an irrationalistic interpretation of the "political": "The state has no political value of its own. . . . The state is the instrument for the political leadership, but only an instrument"; [3] hence, the "unpolitical conception of the state," which regards the state not as the political unity itself, but merely as a "tool" [4] for "political," ends. This irrationalistic conception of the "political" amounts to precisely the opposite of what has been understood as "politics" since the days of classical Greek philosophy, namely, the administration of the life of the community in accordance with the laws of justice indicated in man's nature.

State without *Political Pluralism?*

Dialectical materialism (*Marx* and *Lenin*) regards any pre-communistic society as one characterized by class relationships and by the domination of a single class, namely, the owners of the means of production. In the transition from the class society to the classless society the dictatorship of the proletariat occurs, which means the denial of political pluralism, and, instead, domination by a single class, the proletariat.[5] The Marxian *"classless society"* is a state entirely without political pluralism. The Marxian assumption of the classless society rests on a Utopian misconstruction of human nature, which fails to take into account the instincts for self-interest, and the nature of social cooperation, with which the emergence of groups possessing different interests is inseparably connected. Indeed, in the light of all available experience, no socialistic or communistic society will escape the development of new classes, which will be constituted by the ruling political party as well as by the different ranks of political, economic, and technical executives with their privileges and social advantages.

The idea of the political monopoly of the proletariat and, with it, a fundamental opposition to pluralism, is also a feature of *syndicalism.* What distinguishes this from Marxism primarily is its different conception of the transition from the capitalistic to the socialistic society. *Marx* thinks of an automatic

[2] Cf. Carl Schmitt, *Hüter der Verfassung,* 1931; *Der Begriff des Politischen,* 1932.
[3] O. Koellreutter, *Deutsches Verfassungsrecht,* 1936, p. 11.
[4] Cf. K. Larenz, *Rechts- und Staatsphilosophie der Gegenwart,* 1935, p. 146.
[5] Cf. Lenin, *State and Revolution,* 1942.

development toward the dictatorship of the proletariat through the process of capitalistic accumulation of capital, on the one hand, and increasing pauperization on the other, resulting in the "expropriation of the expropriators." The syndicalists do not believe in this automatism. Their chief representative, *Georges Sorel,* at first a champion of Marxism, later turned against its determinism. The proletarian revolution, he says, cannot be expected as the result of an automatic development, but only as the result of proletarian action. Like all political, social, moral, and religious revolutions in history, it must proceed from a minority. The proletarian revolution must be set in motion by a proletarian élite, which he found in the syndicates (trades unions). These must educate the mass of the proletariat for the general strike, and hence for the socialistic revolution.[6] Nothing conveys more clearly the antipluralistic attitude of syndicalism than its principle, *La classe, c'est la patrie.* In contrast to Marxism, syndicalism bases the organization of socialistic society, not on the nationalization of the means of production, but on the self-government of industrial groups in the administration of the socialized means of production. The political weakness of syndicalism as a socialistic movement should not delude us with regard to its influence. It is well known that *Mussolini* made clear his debt to *Sorel's* ideas in the establishment of fascist corporatism. On the other hand, Sorel himself has admitted the kinship between his ideas and those of communism by hailing *Lenin* as the liberator of the proletariat. The influence of syndicalism is also recognizable in those trends in modern socialism whose aim is to take the main control of economy away from the state and place it in the hands of self-governing industrial groups, thus assigning a leading role to trade unions as a political power.

That the state is, of its nature, wholly inconsistent with political pluralism and is only the concern of one group is also one of the propositions of *Spann's universalism:* the state is an "estate" among the other estates of society and possesses like any estate its unique function and sovereignty; this "group in charge of the state," within a people, consists of the leaders, the military, and also the civil servants.[7] The parallelism between his "aristocratic" theory of the state and *Plato's* ideas cannot conceal its fallaciousness; for since, owing to the equality of human nature, no individual can in justice wield power over others, in the same way no group can. By its nature as a community the state is the concern of all.

121. The State: An Arbitrary Structure

In respect to the two fundamental social functions, the legal function and the welfare function, the state and its structure pertain at least as much to men's free will and pleasure as does the style in which they build their houses. In the course of history the architecture of states manifests as great a variety in different countries and among different peoples

[6] Cf. G. Sorel, *Réflexion sur la violence,* 1908, 5th ed., 1925; *La décomposition du marxismus,* 3rd ed., 1922; M. Freund, *Der falsche Sieg, aus Worten und Werken von G. Sorel,* 1944.

[7] Cf. O. Spann, *Der Wahre Staat,* 3rd ed., 1931, pp. 184 ff., 237.

as domestic architecture. A glance at the constitutions, the legal systems, the legislative and administrative procedure, of individual states will suffice to show that they vary in form and in content. They differ no less in the means by which they achieve the common utility in the organization and administration of transportation, health, and educational and social services. It could not be otherwise, for the way in which its general utility can best be served depends on the concrete needs and desires of the population. The mode of organization of the legal and welfare functions of the state is open to free choice in the whole sphere lying beyond the borders of the order of law designed in human nature.

The political order laid down by natural law doctrine does not involve a detailed constitution, which would imply even approximately a morally obligatory idea of a permanent, concrete type of state. It leaves *a wide field to political self-determination.* This fact has never been overlooked by natural law doctrine throughout its long tradition. In its view, legislation and government have the sole purpose of serving the concrete common good, and it is through the people (*multitudo*) and their needs that the concrete content of the common good is determined.* The will to self-determination in organizing the functions proper to the state is *limited only by the order of ends and values* implied in natural law. This sharply distinguishes the natural law conception of the state from the liberalist and utilitarian conceptions, which make the subjective evaluations of individuals the sole and ultimate judge of what constitutes the whole substance of the common utility, and which make the state and the order of values upon which it is to be built entirely a matter of the "absolute" will of the people. The partial truth contained in the utilitarian doctrine of the state, however, will appear from our argument. Likewise, the natural law conception of the state, with its ends and values designated in human nature itself, is marked off from the arbitrary socialistic and pragmatist economic and social planning, which is based on ideological programmes.

122. The State: A Functional Institution

The immediate experience through which the individual becomes aware of the state, in normal times, does not convey to him the picture of a communal organism. As a rule, his first impression is only that of an immense functional institution. His direct contacts with the state are limited to such organs of state administration as the tax collector and the police. The ends served by the *apparatus* of the state may become familiar to the great mass of citizens by the teaching of civics in the school, by the treatment of public affairs in the press and radio, and by their discus-

* Cf. St. Thomas, *Summa theol.*, Ia IIae, q. 90. a. 3: "Ordinare autem aliquid in bonum commune est vel totius multitudinis, vel alicuius gerentis vicem totius multitudinis."

sion in the course of parliamentary election and debate. Even then the average citizen hardly becomes aware that the state is intrinsically a community, and therefore more than an apparatus in the service of the interests of all. Only in rare cases, when the nation celebrates its public holidays, and when the people gather round their symbols and sing their national hymns or attend church services to commemorate national occasions, does the state become more clearly apprehended as a community. Especially at times of external danger, the feeling of corporateness and common destiny in the political community attains greatest strength.

We have already mentioned that the receding of a nation's state consciousness is something natural in normal times, in contrast to the overemphasis of this consciousness by all totalitarian systems in their "education for the state." Besides, it is natural that the citizen should form his picture of the state from his immediate experience of how it subserves his efforts toward the "good life." But he must do this chiefly by referring to the functional apparatus of the state and to the handling of this apparatus by the government. And after all, the "*institutional,*" as a means of obtaining the assured, orderly and continuous fulfillment of its ends, is an essential component of any communal system. It is doubly essential for the state, whose purpose is the comprehensive performance of the fundamental functions of society.

To be a functional mechanism, a practical organization, an administrative apparatus, belongs to the nature of the state. But this aspect is not its whole nature, as is assumed by the utilitarian, mechanistic theories of the state, which make the state, in the individualist version, exclusively an organization for serving the interests of the individual, or, in the collectivistic version, an exclusively coordinating apparatus in the service of some collective values. This *purely functional conception of the state* misses the true reality as certainly as does the purely metaphysical conception, which raises the state to an end and a being for itself, independent of its members, of their good, and of their interests. The state is both. It is a community with its own end, independent of the arbitrary will of the individuals. Hence, it has a supraindividual character. On the other hand, it is a means in the service of the individual person and his existential ends, and therefore is of a subsidiary character.* The *coordination of the metaphysical and functional views* of the state by the natural law school, however, still leaves room for the stressing of one aspect or the other if no exclusive justification is claimed for either. It is well known, for example, that the English-speaking nations incline more toward a functional, the German and to some extent the Latin nations more toward a metaphysical, idea of the state—whence the profound differences in their respective writings on political theory.

* Cf. the valuable attempt to coordinate the two conceptions of the state, outside the traditional natural law doctrine, by L. T. Hobhouse in *The Metaphysical Theory of the State,* 1918.

In the modern state three trends of development have been of special influence in causing the mechanistic idea of the state to predominate in the minds of the citizens. First, modern party politics and the character of the party struggle for political power make the state seem to be a means in the service of opposing interest groups; this is all the more true since the citizen is compelled to view the state mainly through the spectacles of party propaganda, and his direct participation in the business of the commonwealth is confined almost entirely to election day. Secondly, the modern territorial state, because of the hypertrophy of its bureaucracy, assumes an anonymous, impersonal character, which is apt to choke the consciousness of a live community. Thirdly, the notion of the provider state, which is becoming in increasing measure the political idea held by the modern masses, works in the same direction. This notion regards the state as a functional mechanism for the purpose of providing economic and social "security"; the state, by direct assistance, is to be "planned" as an apparatus for bringing about this function.

123. The State: Its Historical Character

To what extent are states the product of history? To what extent are they the product of nature? In their actual existence their origins lie in historical development: they are the work of men. Nothing more vividly illustrates this than the fact that, until recent times, history has been regarded almost exclusively as political history, and that the study of cultural, economic, and social history is of recent date. It is no accident that political history has been primarily the history of wars; for war, as an instrument of politics, is one of the most important forces shaping history. In the individual state *nearly everything* is historically determined: [1] the form of the state and the exercise of political authority; the structure of institutions; the social system as the resultant of its class structure; the national character of the political body as marked by inherited physical and mental qualities and by environment. Thus, we reach the conclusion that states are determined in their actual existence by history, just as "the state" is determined by nature in its essential existence.

A political philosophy minimizing the extent of the historical nature of the state will remain doctrinaire and partly blind to the reality of the state and the flexibility of its functions. The followers of the great classics of the traditional natural law school in their textbooks have not always avoided the danger of seeing the state too exclusively from the point of view of its essential order and, in appearance at least, of reducing the complex, changing, concrete reality in history to a handful of rather general concepts. But we must not overlook the fact that the

[1] Cf. St. Thomas, *in I Pol.*, lect. 1: "Civitates sunt institutae humana industria."

thorough examination of the reality of the state from the sociological and historical points of view is of fairly recent date even in the sphere of the social sciences.

The opposite danger is that of introducing historical elements into the idea of the essence of the state, and hence into the notion of supratemporal natural law. Historical forms and manifestations of political life have been identified with the nature of the state by some schools of political theory. The idea of the divine right of princes, which was upheld in the sixteenth and seventeenth centuries, the period of rising absolutism, is one of these errors. It derives the power of the prince directly from God and makes him responsible exclusively to God. Writing on a similar distortion of reality by monarchist political thinkers in the nineteenth century, *Constantin Frantz* makes the following observation: "It became customary to speak of 'Throne and Altar' as the foundations of political life; but only Hearth and Altar should be named in such close association." Political philosophy must carefully guard against the *infiltration of historical elements into its concepts.* Anyone who proceeds to the analysis of the state with the aid of historical concepts will gain from them a colored, distorted picture. As will be seen from our discussion of the concept of sovereignty, modern political philosophy received many of its features of sovereignty from its historical background. The natural law theory will be safer from such deviations the more it keeps in mind that the natural order in the sphere of the state, as in other spheres, is confined to elementary principles of a general character.

The State in Historicist Theory

Modern historicism believes that it can usurp the function of political philosophy to determine the nature of the state and to understand it exclusively both historically and sociologically. Political theory, we are told by *F. Meinecke,* one of the foremost champions of historicism, "still remains largely under the influence of the old method of searching for the best, the ideal, and normal state and making it an absolute. To comprehend the individual institutions of historical mankind, but also their timeless core, that which is general in the laws of their life, that which is universal in the interrelations of these laws, is the essence and function of modern historicism." [2] The natural law school also is of the opinion that, for a complete explanation of the nature of the state, reference must be made to historical reality, because the state is substantially a historical phenomenon, which lives and works only in historical forms; therefore, it can be studied only in the individual modes in which it manifests itself. But, on the other hand, the human mind has always felt itself impelled to examine the fundamental universal human forces operating in the historical forms of the state, and has thereby become convinced that man will not be satisfied to be mere driftwood carried along by historical processes. The inquiry into the ideal and normal state springs from man's conviction that every political order

[2] Friedrich Meinecke, *Die Idee der Staatsräson,* 2nd ed., 1925, p. 23.

must receive its definitive standards from man and his nature. Political ethics, in its analysis of the state, goes back to the metaphysical aspect in the essential reality of man, while historicism relies on the historical reality of the state.

Our second argument against the historicist exaggeration is directed toward its methodological foundations. The researches of *Dilthey, Simmel, Rickert,* and *M. Weber,*[3] which were concerned with the possibilities and limits of historical inquiry, seem to leave no doubt that historicism places its hopes too high. As *Meinecke* correctly points out, history deals with "individualities": historicism proceeds from the "individual forms" of historically existing states. Therefore, it cannot achieve more than a comprehension of constants in the behavior of states. Its methods make possible only generalizing laws which convey pronouncements on constants in the behavior of the individual forms. It cannot infer from the observation of ways of behavior alone whether these constants are the outcome of internal forces or only of external circumstances. The inherent laws of life of the state could not be discovered without ontological analysis, which, in the "nature" of the state, would also allow the apprehension of the nature of man. The limits to such empirically established generalizing laws appeared clearly, in the comprehensive criticism on *Spengler's* work, to come from all angles of historical and philosophical investigation (cf. Chap. 159).

Our third argument is directed against the proposition in which *Meinecke* sees the main finding of historicism: the state is first and foremost power; to be guided by power is its fundamental, universal law. This proposition is not borne out by history. History knows of states that have not actively entered the circle of modern power politics: Holland, Sweden, Norway, Portugal, Switzerland. Also, the champions of historicism themselves are compelled to limit their universal law by the observation that, when it is in evidence as a determining characteristic in political action, in general power is also bound up with ends of an ideal or material nature. If they begin to examine these ends, they will find human nature and its impulses as motive forces. To make the irrational impulse toward power the predominant force is an obvious narrowing of the view regarding the full reality of human nature, in which the rational impulses, with the superiority of the mind, stand opposed to the irrational. It may be said along with *Benedetto Croce* that, "From the point of view of the historian it is absurd to suppose that the moral flame which burns in the heart of humanity has ever been or can ever be extinguished—the flame which gives the historian the very light by which to understand events. . . . [They speak] as if the problem were the historical one of understanding the facts and not, as is actually the case, the ethical problem of changing them, that is, of creating new facts."[4]

Our arguments are not intended to deny the possibility or to underrate the value of historical methods and the significance of historicism for political

[3] William Dilthey, *Der Aufbau der geschichtlichen Welt in den Geisteswissenschaften,* 1910; Heinrich Rickert, *Grenzen der naturwissenschaftlichen Begriffsbildung,* 5th ed., 1929; *Kulturwissenschaft und Naturwissenschaft,* 7th ed., 1926; Max Weber, *Gesammelte Aufsätze zur Wissenschaftslehre,* 1922; Georg Simmel, *Die Probleme der Geschichtsphilosophie,* 3rd ed., 1907; Theodor Litt, *Individuum und Gemeinschaft,* 3rd ed., 1926; *Geschichte und Leben,* 3rd ed., 1920; Ernst Troeltsch, *Der Historismus und seine Probleme,* 1922; *Der Historismus und seine Überwindung,* 1924. Cf. also F. Meinecke, *Die Entstehung des Historismus,* 1936.

[4] Benedetto Croce, *Politics and Morals,* trans. by S. J. Castiglione, 1946, pp. 127 ff.

theory. There are no objections to historicism on grounds of natural law doctrine, if it does not maintain that by its methods alone we can discover the whole nature of the state or claim a scientific monopoly for its conception of the state, which lays chief emphasis on its power character. The natural law theory is also in agreement with historicism in regarding it as indispensable for practical statesmanship, to take account of historical experience in the life of states and statesmen. The theory of *Meinecke* will be further discussed in the section on "Reason of State" (Chap. 149). Advocated unconditionally, the historicist conception of the state would signify a new turn in the power-state principle.[5]

The State in Idealistic Theory

Idealism regards the state as the highest manifestation of the spirit. According to *Hegel* the "spirit of the world" executes its law upon peoples "in world history, as world judgment": all law rests with the people, which represents "the present stage of development of the world spirit." Opposed to it, "the spirits of other peoples are without rights and they, like those whose epoch is past, count no more in world history." [6] It was easy for the power state theory to gain from this some corroboration of the principle of the law of facts, of "political realism." *Hegel's* idea, that history is also judgment, is as old as the historical sense of mankind: [7] Natural law implies that human frustration must follow any radical deviation of states from it, although it also implies that history cannot be the whole of world judgment, since the existence of a personal God implies the personal responsibility of man.

The fact that a wholly unhistorical political philosophy can also be derived from *Hegel* is shown by *Spann* with his universalist political philosophy. *Spann* views society as a "spiritual whole" which divides into spiritual "partial wholes" according to spiritual partial functions in human cultural life: systems of action such as religion, philosophy, science, art, the life of the senses. These systems are in the hands of organized groups of persons, the "estates." Such an estate is the state.[8] A causal mode of viewing society is rejected by the universalist, who recognizes only "validities," "ramifications," and, at most, "reasons," in the sense of an explanation by means of meaningfully correlated action.[9] By confounding reality and idea *Spann* obstructs the view of reality and hence of truth. "According to Spann the true state has no truth because it is a reality neither time-bound nor man-bound; for it is, according to his method, evolved spiritually as an eternally identical form, from an eternally identical basic structure." [10] The result is that *Spann's* state is wholly devoid of historical truth, because the state proceeds from spiritual reality by a purely ideal unvarying process of the development of the spirit. "Thus seen, Spann's doctrine discloses

[5] Cf. the long list of such thinkers in Lord Acton, *The History of Freedom,* 1907, pp. 220 ff.

[6] Hegel, *Grundlinien der Philosophie des Rechts,* 1821, pars. 340, 345 ff.

[7] Cf., e.g., Thucydides' account of the treatment of Melos by the Athenians and of the fate of their expedition to Sicily.

[8] Cf. O. Spann, *Der Wahre Staat,* 3rd ed., 1931, pp. 158 ff., 183 ff.; *Gesellschaftslehre,* 3rd ed., 1931, pp. 249 ff., 386 ff.

[9] Cf. O. Spann, *Gesellschaftslehre,* 1931, pp. 562 ff.; *Kategorienlehre,* 1924, pp. 6 ff., 294 ff.

[10] H. Heller, *Staatslehre* (Leyden), 1934, p. 51.

itself as a genuine emanatism, with all the dangers of emanatist thought, especially the antagonism to history which is peculiar to it. Just as in metaphysical emanatism the real world, so also in sociological emanatism real society, becomes an essentially unhistorical system."[11]

124. The State: Sin

Of all the factors shaping the actual existence of the state, sin is one of the most potent. Christian thought, especially at the time of the decline of the ancient world, painted this fact in such realistic colors that not a few moderns thought themselves justified in suggesting that Christianity attributed the origin of the state mainly to sin or even that the early Christian Fathers had identified the state with sin. The misunderstanding of *Augustine's* description of the *civitas terrena* in contrast with the *civitas Dei* has been largely responsible for this error.[1] In the same way Pope *Gregory VII's* mention of pride, robbery, murder, and every crime in the behavior of rulers has been presented as the Christian notion of the origin of the actual supremacy of the state.[2]

In the light of the latest researches on Augustinian political theory,[3] today we may take it as proved that by *civitas terrena* and *civitas Dei, St. Augustine* did not mean state communities at all, but the "City of God" as a religious, moral community, and the "Earthly City" as the totality of opposing forces. Where antimoral forces are dominant in the historical existence of the state and in its exercise of authority, the state approximates to the *civitas terrena* as *civitas impiorum* or *civitas diaboli.* If justice is wholly abandoned, then states, that is, those in authority with their power organization, are simply large bands of gangsters,[4] a view not to be too lightly dismissed in the light of recent experience.

Indeed, for *St. Augustine* (and the same is true of Pope *Gregory VII*) there is no doubt that the state originates in human nature by virtue of the divine will and that it possesses a moral and cultural value. With this conception of the state, *St. Augustine* has laid the foundation for all later Christian thought. Throughout traditional natural law theory

[11] H. Freyer, *Soziologie als Wirklichkeitswissenschaft, Logische Grundlegung des Systems der Soziologie,* 1930, pp. 75 ff.

[1] Cf. G. Jellinek, *Allgemeine Staatslehre* (*Das Recht des modernen Staates,* Vol. I), 1905, pp. 180 f.

[2] Thus, O. von Gierke, *Johannes Althusius,* 1880, 4th ed., 1929, p. 62, trans. by B. Freyd, *The Development of Political Theory,* 1939, p. 72. Pope Gregory's observations are contained in a private letter of March 15, 1081, to Bishop Hermann of Metz (*Registrum,* VIII, 21). Cf. R. W. and A. J. Carlyle, *A History of Medieval Political Theory in the West,* 1909, II, p. 145.

[3] Cf. J. Mausbach, *Die Ethik des Hl. Augustinus,* 2nd ed., 1929, I, pp. 326 ff.; II, pp. 410 ff.; O. Schilling, *Die Staats- und Soziallehre des heiligen Augustinus,* 1910; E. Troeltsch, *Augustin, Die Christliche Antike und das Mittelalter,* 1915, pp. 38 ff.

[4] Cf. St. Augustine, *De civ. Dei,* Bk. IV, Chap. 4: "Remota itaque justitia quid sunt regna nisi magna latrocinia? Quia et latrocinia quid sunt nisi parva regna?"

it is not the state as such that is regarded as the consequence of sin, but only the physical compulsion which is bound up with state authority, likewise the misuse of political authority and executive power. It was *Luther* who first abandoned the line of thought set out by *St. Augustine* and consigned the state wholly to the realm of sin and fallen nature.

Inevitably Demoniac?

Present-day thought, guided by historical experience since the First World War, is occupied anew with the undeniable perversion of the state by sin. "Why is there not at least a clean theory of political life even if the practice remain dirty?" *Meinecke* asks. He replies: "Repeated attempts have been made to erect a clean theory of this kind that will uncompromisingly subordinate the state to the decrees of morality and law but, as already said, without historical result." The common good, the physical, moral, and mental health of the community, is indeed a "high, moral purpose, but the means (the power) of attaining it is and remains crude and elementary. It is, Christianly speaking, subject to sin and only too easily exposed to abuse." Besides, it is of the nature of the state that it "must pollute itself by violations of morality and law," if only through the seemingly indispensable means of war. "The state, so it seems, must sin. Although the moral sense rises up against this anomaly again and again, yet it is really without historical result. It is the most awful and shattering fact of world history that there is no hope of radically moralizing that human community which comprehends all other communities, protecting and fostering them, which at the same time also embraces the richest and most diverse body of culture and which, therefore, ought to act as a beacon to all other communities by the purity of its being." The state, therefore, says *Meinecke,* cannot escape the "demoniac effect" of power, power being indeed essential to it.[5]

This view of the state within the framework of historicism must undoubtedly be allowed the credit of making transparently clear the concentrated effect, often rising to demoniac effect, of the perversion of human nature in the state. Yet, it seems to leave out of consideration the not less strong moral potentialities of man and mankind. Further, it does not seem to take sufficient account of the efforts made in recent history by these forces to organize the community of nations in order to ban power politics and war. Admittedly, the results obtained so far give grounds for scepticism. But it must not be forgotten that the evolution of moral consciousness among peoples toward the organization of peace, as well as the evolution of international law itself, is still recent in the history of mankind.

Finally, the misuse of power by the state, although it is a characteristic feature of its actual existence, can in itself be as little regarded as the essence of the state as can the essence of man be deduced from his abuse of his faculties. It has already been shown how man is impelled by his moral nature to check the demoniac element in the dynamism of power and to make war impossible as an instrument of policy for the individual state. Internationally organized power itself may then become a means of overcoming power which is contrary to jus-

[5] Cf. Friedrich Meinecke, *Die Idee der Staatsräson,* 1925, pp. 7, 15, 17, 513.

tice (and hence sinful), and thus become a means of subjecting power to law (cf. the following chap.).

125. The State: A Moral Value

Since the state is a community having its foundation in the existential ends of man, it is *part of the moral order* and is a moral value. It is part of the reality of human nature at its full stature; its function for the common good is part of the moral responsibility of the human person. As a community, therefore, the state is invested with moral dignity. And since its functions are fundamental for the performance of all man's tasks in the material and cultural spheres, its value is the most comprehensive in comparison with the individual values in these spheres; hence, it is a distinct moral value of very high rank. *St. Thomas* does not hesitate to describe the state, following *Aristotle,* as the most excellent creation of human reason; accordingly, he gives politics the highest place among the arts.[1]

To place the state in the order of values appears strange to those with a background of *political utilitarianism,* who conceive the state only as an organizational, technical institution serving self-ordained interests. The utilitarian theories are right in emphasizing that the state has the status of a means toward the fulfillment of human life. But they do not see that the state forms a true element in human nature as an end fundamental to the other ends and therefore existential. Individualism and collectivism are agreed in this utilitarian view, which denies the state any moral substance or value of its own. The former sees in the state the mere servant of the individual and his interests. Collectivism makes it a large economic concern in the service of "the mode of production in material life" (*Marx*). In both cases the primacy of the human person is sacrificed, together with the distinct value of the state, precisely because the essential connection of the state with man's moral existence is not recognized.

The status assigned here to the political community within the order of values does not imply that the state is paramount in the life of man. Such a role is suggested by *political mysticism,* which assigns to the state a selfhood completely independent of the individual man and absolutely transcending him. Only, however, by an emanatist identification of the reality of the Spirit with God and the state can *Hegel* say: "The state is divine will, as present spirit unfolding itself to actual form and organization." And only thus can he conclude that the state "has the supreme right against the individual, whose supreme duty it is to be a member of the state." The state is not, as *Hegel*[2] supposes, itself the "moral uni-

[1] Cf. St. Thomas, *in I Pol.,* lect. 1; *in I eth.,* lect. 2.

[2] Cf. Hegel, *Grundlinien der Philosophie des Rechts,* 1821, Einl., p. XXI; cf. also pars. 258, 270.

verse." In the same way all those present-day political theorists err—even though their rationalism takes a different turn—who, proceeding from a superstitious overestimation of "scientific reason," view the state when aided by science as an all-wise planner. Indeed, the end of the state is a universal and a comprehensive one, but only *one* within the sphere of man's existential ends insofar as their fulfillment depends on cooperation. Above this sphere, and hence above the sphere of "what is Caesar's" (Matt. 22:21), there stands the human person with his existential ends.

There is no clearer indication of the moral nature of the state than its function of realizing the minimum of morality in the coexistence of men. It performs this task by the institution of the legal order, as we have shown. This is what gives moral justification to the method of force, which is also at the disposal of the state, and a moral character to its use. The state curbs the "less human elements in human nature" in favor of true humanity. Thus, in the state *the human spirit asserts itself in safeguarding true human existence* in social life. To be sure, the mind succeeds in this effort only partially, but to make progress in it is an unmistakable command of the spirit. Hence, we are able to separate truth from error in the Hegelian idea of the state: the state is not in itself the reality of the spirit and not "the reality of the moral idea"; [3] rather, the state is the agency by which man's spirit can subdue the social dynamic of the irrational forces in his nature; hence, it is the agency for realizing the moral idea, the moral principles which are indispensable to the life of society. For these various reasons a high function falls to the state in regard to the self-education of the community, an educative function which, since the time of *Plato* and *Aristotle,* has never ceased to impress itself upon the human mind, although as this has reached greater self-consciousness the limits of this function have become more clearly apprehended.

The state's function of realizing the moral idea is not confined, however, to the individual political community, but extends over the *political development of mankind as a whole.* The effective power both of rational and irrational elements in human nature is magnified many times by the state. States thereby become mighty forces, in a positive or negative direction, in man's struggle to attain the moral, juridical, political, and social ideals that spring from his existential ends. This struggle is an oscillating process; it is *the meaning of history.* The political ruling power often plays a destructive part, dragging nations down from the level of true human freedom and of respect for human personality and culture which they have reached. But the development of mankind's legal consciousness is an undeniable fact. This is the effect of natural law operating in man. Assuredly it is not immediately through the state that the dynamic of natural law and the progress of moral consciousness becomes effective; rather, it becomes effective through the endeavors of the

[3] *Ibid.,* par. 257.

great ethical and political thinkers and through social and political movements. But if one reflects how great a role such thinkers and social movements assign to the state for the realization of their ideals and programs, and how the actualization of social liberty depends on the political order, one can hardly be in doubt about the significance of the state in the historical dynamic of natural law as a motive force in the moral and cultural development of mankind.

Therefore, we may conclude that the natural law conception of the state is *teleological;* nevertheless, the juristic, the sociological, and the historical conceptions of the state also find their place in natural law doctrine. A teleologically ordained reality in the human sphere is always of a moral character: the essential ends constitute imperatives. The actual reality of the state, however, is a resultant of many forces and impulses of a physical, spiritual, or moral nature; in this sense, it is the result of a process of integration. This integration, like everything human, may be imperfect when measured by the standard of essential humanity; there can be no doubt about the standard for this integration, if the values producing true humanity are established.

An integration without a determinative standard is assumed by the *integration theory* of *Rudolf Smend.*[4] The process of growth of the plant, which is a resultant of many physical, chemical, and biological forces, is not the nature of the plant; the juristic and the sociological conceptions of the state are inadequate, says *Smend,* because the state is the process of integration from the forces comprehended in these two conceptions. These forces, according to *Smend,* may be political ideals, ideas of social justice, or systems of values; the media of integration may be of a personal, a national, or a political character (e.g., symbols, a national myth, political leaders). The integrating forces act in the manner of an entelechy since they are never fully actualized but keep the process of actualization permanently in motion. Hence, the individual states are merely stages in this process of integration; consequently, as such they are subject to valuation. With his idea of integration, *Smend* tries to comprehend the state as a unity of idea and of actuality, excluding any moral imperative idea of the state and rejecting the natural law doctrine of the state.

His critics argue, however, that his theory provides new evidence of how difficult it is for political theory to escape from the natural law ideas. We have ourselves pointed out that the one-sided juridical, sociological, historical conceptions of the state are contrary to reality. We may well speak of an integration of the state, just as we speak of the full realization of human nature in personality. In both cases, however, we must first establish what is the nature of man and the nature of the state before any judgment about their integration or the stages of their integration is logically possible.

[4] R. Smend, *Verfassung und Verfassungsrecht,* 1928; a first sketch of his theory is to be found in *Festschrift der Berliner juristischen Fakultät für W. Kahl,* 1923, under the title, "Die politische Gewalt im Verfassungsstaat und das Problem der Staatsform." Smend is influenced by T. Litt's theory that the mind strives after an optimum of objective sense connections in social wholes. A critique of the theory is presented by H. Kelsen in *Der Staat als Integration,* 1930.

PART TWO

The Sovereignty of the State

126. Political Authority as Sovereignty

A good many modern political theorists are accustomed to describe political authority as sovereignty and in doing so to make it an absolute right. They have tried to read into the nature of the state what they have found the modern state to claim. This concept of sovereignty is a modern one. As long as the states of Western civilization remained incorporated in the unity of the medieval Christian Commonwealth (*Respublica Christiana*) of the Holy Roman Empire, their sovereignty was limited by its Christian constitution and natural law. But already in the conflict of powers which arose in the twelfth century and occasioned the famous Bull, *Unam Sanctam,* of *Boniface VIII* in 1302, the claim to sovereignty of the national state in the modern sense was hinted at. The appearance of sovereign states in history, as *v. d. Heydte* has shown,* falls in the period from 1250 to 1350. The Renaissance, with its emphasis on the freedom of the individual personality in contrast with the previous religious and social bonds in all spheres of life, formed the next stage in the development of the modern idea of sovereignty. Just as in the economic sphere the modern entrepreneur type arose, so also in the political sphere the prince type arose, which gave *Machiavelli* the inspiration for his study in statesmanship. The Protestant attack on the spiritual foundations of the unitary culture of the Middle Ages and the transfer of religious authority to the princes (on the principle, *Cuius regio eius religio*) cleared the way for the later development of the idea of sovereignty. In the sixteenth century the power of the prince was further strengthened when, in a number of European countries, the people leaned upon him in the process of emancipation from the predominance of the nobility, and he obtained their support in his struggle to assert his supremacy over the nobility. Then, in the nineteenth century, nationalism sought in *absolute* sovereignty the political means for securing its ends, thus giving the idea its final modern stamp.

This same development led, however, to the first disillusionment. The absolute sovereignty of the national state and the community of na-

* Cf. Friedrich A. Frh. v. d. Heydte, *Die Geburtstunde des souveränen Staates: Ein Beitrag zur Geschichte des Völkerrechts, der allgemeinen Staatslehre und des politischen Denkens,* 1952.

tions, the organization of which became more and more a vital necessity for all nations as contact between them grew closer, inevitably proved to be two incompatible ideals. Political theory also had its difficulty with the concept of absolute sovereignty: the concept could not be applied to the development of interconnections between individual states in the nineteenth century. On the one hand, sovereign states formed federations which resulted in many limitations of their authority. On the other hand, states yielded up a portion of their authority to another without being deprived of their sovereignty. When *Jellinek,* with the support of facts such as these, undertook his assault on the modern conception of sovereignty, contending that it was only a "historical" category, he had at first only a small following among political theorists. *Kelsen's* attack, however, has already found a strong echo. We have spoken in detail of both these contributions to political theory (cf. Chaps. 54, 101). Today, more and more political theorists are showing themselves ready to divest the concept of sovereignty of its historical elements and to reduce it to its essential content. Indeed, there are some who regard it as mere ballast in political theory and would jettison it altogether. But it is as wrong to reject the concept of sovereignty altogether and to put the political authority of the state on a level with the other authorities in society as it is to make the state absolute. For, as it will appear from our further discussion, sovereignty or supremacy is *a distinguishing characteristic of the state.*

127. The Root of Political Authority

If all men are by nature equal, how can one person or one body be entitled to authority and be supported by physical coercion? Is there any *moral justification for a political authority* with a power to enforce obedience, in view of the dignity of the human person as a free moral being? Answers to this question range between two extremes: the authority of the state in its concrete form issues directly from the will of God; the authority of the state issues from the will of man alone. The first view occurs sporadically in the Middle Ages and is only later taken up with enthusiasm by the advocates of absolute monarchy, who form from it a theory of the divine right of kings, the theory according to which the king receives his mandate directly from God and is responsible solely to God. The second view is at the root of the modern theory of sovereignty.

Our own answer springs from what has been said about the nature of society and the common good and about the origin of law and of social authority. The specific ordering power of the political community is rooted in its function of creating the social conditions necessary for full human existence; in other words, its function of realizing the all-embracing common good. The immediate origin of political authority is thus the nature of the political community as determined by man's existential ends. The legal basis of the state's authority, therefore, lies in the natural constitution of the communal order necessary for the fulfillment of the fundamental functions of society. Just as the communal order is rooted in man's nature, and therefore in the will of the Creator and the moral order, so also is authority itself. Thus, subordination to political authority, functioning as it does on behalf of the common good, is ordained by man's nature, and hence it is part of right reason and rests upon man's own ordered or essential will (cf. Chap. 118 on the state as unity of will; on the conception of essential will cf. note 3 below). We find elements of truth in each of the extreme theories mentioned regarding the origin of political authority. Against the former, however, we have established that political authority only indirectly springs from God's will: God manifests his will in human nature, and man finds the direction of his essential will indicated in his nature.

It is also evident from our argument that the power of *command* and the power of *coercion* spring from different facts of human nature. From this there follows an important distinction that will cause insoluble difficulties for political philosophy if it is neglected. The basis of the power of command lies in human nature and in its orientation toward the common good as a condition of the personal integration of all. The basis of the power of coercion lies in the impairment of human nature and in its perversity, that is, in the irrational elements because of which man's will, in its ends and means, readily sets itself in opposition to the order designed in essential nature. Christian natural law, throughout its whole tradition, has never left in doubt the fact that it seeks the basis of the power of coercion in the sinfulness of human nature. In the language of natural law philosophy, political authority as power of command has its source in primary natural law; as power of coercion it has its source in secondary natural law.

Theories on the Origin of Political Authority

1. The *social-contract theories* find the origin of political authority in the consent of the individuals. Although in their original form they are abandoned today as untenable, their basic idea is still at work in the theories that make the will of the people the sovereign law of the state. Their exponents proceed from various postulates of a "state of nature" (*Hobbes:* in society man overcomes his "natural state" as an unsocial being; *Rousseau:* in society man reaches his "natural state" as a social being) and reach a variety of conclusions about the original location of political authority (*Hobbes:* the government; *Locke* and *Rousseau:* the political community). They arrive at opposite definitions of the respective orbits of the rights of people and government (*Hobbes* attributes absolute sovereignty to the government, *Rousseau* to the people). Their views

on the revoking of the social contract are also contradictory (*Hobbes:* alteration of the social contract by the people is a breach of contract; *Rousseau:* such alteration is the elementary right of the people). *Locke* takes up a midway position with his distinction between a contract of union and one of consent, deriving from the latter the limitation of political authority. He says: "Nobody can transfer to another more power than he has in himself; and nobody has an absolute arbitrary power over himself, or over any other, to destroy his own life, or take away the life or property of another." [1] A simple logical extension of this argument, however, discloses the untenability of the individualist theory of consent and also of any social-contract theory. All social-contract theories overlook the fact that the individuals cannot transfer something which they do not possess, namely, a *public* right such as political authority. It is a right having its basis in the common good as something different from the individual good. Therefore, it cannot be derived from individual rights and the individual will, as we have urged in our study of legal philosophy.

2. The *corporative theories* (cf. Chap. 42) see only the "institutional" unity of the group, whether its basis is sought in the idea of solidarity or in some *fait normatif.* In this they take up an essential element in the origin of political authority which we have called the natural, objective constitution of the political community. These theories, however, seem to be unable to explain satisfactorily the relationship of the individual will to the objective forces molding the community and its authority, namely, to explain the fact that the institutional unity is also to be understood as based in the "essential" will of its members.

3. In this fact is to be sought also the chief objection to Bosanquet's *theory of mind.* He takes over from *Rousseau* the distinction between the general will and the will of all. As *Bosanquet* pertinently shows,[2] *Rousseau* neither thinks out this distinction to its theoretical conclusion nor is he in fact able to avoid enthroning the will of all as a mere resultant of the interests of isolated individuals. But, like the other critics of *Rousseau's* theory of sovereignty, *Bosanquet* does not see the deeper reason which led *Rousseau* to think that, as the resultant of the will of all, the true "general will" finally emerges. This reason lies in the rationalistic dogma of the absolute goodness of human nature, which will best develop through freedom. On the other hand, as *Bosanquet* rightly observes, *Rousseau* tried to explain the general will as something more than the resultant of the absolutely free expression of the individual will, and to link the general will with what we have called the essential will. *Bosanquet* associates himself with this attempt in his account of political authority, the source of which he places in the rational or "real" will of all with its intrinsic tendency toward objective good. Externally, then, he comes close to the natural law view. But his concepts are tinged with Neo-Hegelianism. Consequently, in his theory the common and the "real" will are not correlated with a definite conception of the moral and social nature of the human person. And, clearly following *Hegel,* he identifies the real common will with the "national mind" or "social mind." This, he holds, becomes objective in the customs and institutions of a society, including the exercise of political authority as its organ. In

[1] Locke, *Second Treatise on Civil Government,* XI, 1698.

[2] Cf. Bosanquet, *The Philosophical Theory of the State,* 1899, pp. 111 ff., 236 ff.; 3rd ed., 1920, pp. 103 ff., 218 ff.

this "mind" *Bosanquet* finally sees the sovereign, and hence also the source of political authority.

4. The *command theory* is one which traces political authority ultimately to irrational elements in human nature. Among them we shall first mention absolute scepticism. Truth, justice, and freedom, according to this theory, are not unambiguous concepts, because, as the various philosophical systems show, reason evolves mutually contradictory truths, justices, and freedoms. To achieve social order it is necessary to apply irrational principles, that is, to subject reason to pure power of command. Authority must decide what truth, what freedom, and what justice shall prevail in society, in order that society may exist at all. That this scepticism ends in Machiavellianism is shown by the conclusion to which it is logically worked out by Professor *G. Renzi*. He explains that his aim is to restore to their rights the old, solid, irrational foundations of political theory, namely, despotism, force, war, and revolution.[3]

5. With his *theory of infallibility, De Maistre,* also stressing the irrational elements in human nature, reached the conclusion a hundred years earlier that political authority must possess an essential feature of infallibility. There can be no human society without government, he says in his famous book on the pope, no government without sovereignty, no sovereignty without infallibility; were the decision of the political authority not infallibly binding in spite of its not being in fact infallible, the dissolution of society would appear inevitable.[4] His pessimistic estimate of human nature made him regard as absurd the idea of liberal democracy with its favorable judgment on human nature and reason, and caused him to lay such stress on the authoritarian principle, that he became one of the most resolute and brilliant supporters of monarchy as a political form. He must by no means, however, be classed as an advocate of a theory of unlimited sovereignty, since political authority is for him part of the juridical order, which is designed in human nature by the will of the Creator and fixes the limits of authority (cf. Chap. 118, note 3). With his idea of the infallibility of political authority he touches upon one of its essential features. At the same time, his idea shows up an element of truth in the sceptics' interpretation of political authority which we have just discussed.

In explanation, we can say the following: The political order is sketched only in outline by the principles of natural law; the actualization of the common good in detail is left to man's will, so that only by acts of decision, which concern a variety of possible purposes and expedient means, can matters be settled. One of the principal functions of political authority in such cases is to form decisions that will be final and binding on the whole community. Thus far *De Maistre* is undoubtedly uttering a thought of natural law political philosophy (cf. Chap. 43) concerning the juridically binding character of power of decision for all members of the state. And indeed he came much nearer to the truth than did the schools of democratic political theory, which attribute a kind of infallibility to the will of the people based on the majority principle, without being able to explain why the minority should be bound by it.

[3] Cf. Giuseppe Renzi, *La filosofia dell'autorità,* 1920, pp. 155–77, 216–44.

[4] Cf. De Maistre, *Du Pape,* 1817, Bk. I, Chap. 19: "Il ne peut y avoir de société humaine sans gouvernement, ni de gouvernement sans souveraineté, ni de souveraineté sans infaillibilité; et ce dernier privilège est si absolument nécessaire, qu'on est forcé de supposer l'infaillibilité, même dans les souverainetés temporelles (où elle n'est pas), sous peine de voir l'association se dissoudre."

128. The Character of Political Authority

Political authority is the ruling power which belongs to the state so that it may fully discharge the fundamental functions of society. It consists in a right founded in the end of the political community and embracing all functions necessary for the realization of its specific common good. Political authority, therefore, exists for the sake of the general interest of the political community, not for the sake of the private interest of a ruler, a ruling party, or a ruling class. Its nature and its justification lie in the fact that it is service to the community. To restore sovereignty to its true perspective seems necessary in face of the theories which consider it only from the point of view of political obedience and see its character only in its power to command and in its power to legislate. *Aristotle* already pointed out that such a conception is disproved by the state's function of self-preservation against external attacks. Furthermore, although international treaties and declarations of war are reserved to the lawgiver, the routine of foreign policy and the diplomacy of government play no less an important role. In fact, *government is more than merely the administration of law,* in the sense of an application of the mere letter of the law. It is the utilization by the government of the powers at its disposal, in the light of its best judgment, for the greatest good of the commonwealth in its internal and external needs. Otherwise one could not speak of an art of statesmanship, and government would be nothing more than the technique of administration. In fact, all political theorists, beginning with *Plato* and *Aristotle*, who have considered the state an entity with an existence of its own, its own end, and its own moral value, have taken the view that the field of activity of political authority, although bound by law and rights, comprises nothing less than the farsighted and vigorous advancement of the common good.

Hence, we may offer the following definition. Political authority is the right to govern, founded in the end of the state and specified by the law of the individual state, for the actualization of its common good. For the purpose of clarifying the characteristics of political authority, we may conveniently follow the order of the *characteristics* which we connected with the modern concept of sovereignty. According to this concept, sovereignty is supreme, indivisible, inalienable, and unlimited.

1. Political authority is the *supreme* social authority, so that to it alone belongs the appellation of sovereignty. This is because it guarantees the foundations of social order, upon which depends the realization of all the ends of human existence. All other social structures depend on the state in carrying out their functions. This comprehensive end, which makes the state the "perfect" society, is the reason for the comprehensive nature of the right of political authority; and political authority reaches its highest level in the hierarchy of social authorities,

because all the "lesser" social units depend upon the political society, the "universal" society, in fulfilling their respective ends. This end of political authority explains at the same time why the individual state is legally independent of other states, since, unless it is made secure from external interference, it is not capable of establishing the necessarily uniform legal order without which social coexistence and cooperation are impossible. The authority of the state, therefore, ranks highest in the natural sphere; because it is limited to the natural sphere and to the common good of the individual state, any claim to absolute sovereignty is untenable.

2. From this argument it is evident that political authority is *indivisible,* inasmuch as the complete discharge of the fundamental functions of society admits of only one single sovereign authority. But it is not indivisible in the sense that its exercise cannot be shared among a number of organs.

3. Its authority is inalienable. This pertains to the nature of the political community: ordered society cannot exist without the right to command and the corresponding obligation of civil obedience. For these reasons the state cannot be doomed to "wither away." Political power is not merely historically determined and the product of a political, economic, or social process of development; it is founded in the essential reality of human nature. Only in its concrete form is political authority historically determined.

4. Political authority is "unlimited," exercising its right, without being answerable to any other authority, within the orbit of its functions; thus, it enjoys full autonomy. This autonomy is not absolute in the sense that it is exempt from restriction by justice or from accountability before justice. Any political theory which holds that all law originates in the state, or which even regards sovereignty as identical with the right to legislate, must logically reach the conclusion that the sovereign stands above the law and cannot come into conflict with it. Among the precursors of the modern theory of sovereignty, only *Hobbes* and the followers of *Rousseau* draw this extreme conclusion; *Bodin, Locke,* and *Bentham* maintain that the sovereign is bound by moral law. It would not be enough, however, to understand by moral law and natural justice in this connection only the general moral and jural principles, for political authority is also bound by the elementary legal order of the political community, which finds its expression in the moral and juridical consciousness of a society and in its legal customs. In consequence, as we shall argue later on, for parliamentary majorities, as for the absolute monarch, there exists no absolute legislative sovereignty.

Coercion the Essence of Political Authority?

Among the theories which seek the essence of political authority in effective power of command within a community, we would draw attention to those of

J. Austin and *M. Weber*. *Austin's* definition of political authority is: "If a determinate human superior, not in the habit of obedience to a like superior, receive habitual obedience from the bulk of a given society, that determinate superior is sovereign in that society, and the society (including the superior) is a society that is political and independent." [1]

Against this, *Maine* has raised the conclusive argument that every political power of command is restricted in its exercise by the moral and legal principles governing a society.[2] *Maine* further contends that the definite superior, who is vested with power of command, is often not to be identified, a fact which has been much cited in later political theory in reference to federated states like the United States, where legislation is shared between the Congress of the Union and the legislatures of the states. But the conclusive objection to *Austin's* theory of the nature and origin of sovereignty is that he does not relate sovereignty to the popular will or to moral consciousness, but only to the force which ensures the effectiveness of the will of the superior.

In a very similar way, *M. Weber* regards the "monopoly of legitimate physical force" as the essence of political sovereignty. For *Weber*, sovereignty is "the *chance* of obtaining obedience from specifiable persons for a command of determinate content"; and the state is "an association with institutionalized ruling power," which "successfully claims for itself the monopoly of legitimate physical coercion." *Weber* regards his idea as a purely sociological one and does not attempt to define the nature of sovereignty in terms of political philosophy or of legal science; he himself says: "Coercion is by nature not the normal or the sole expedient of the state—of this there is no question." [3] For sociology, the science of social reality, the question must be on which grounds the political power of command is seen in "physical coercion." The conception of a monopoly of "legitimate" coercion seems, moreover, almost a contradiction in terms, since "legitimacy" indicates grounds of justification for the exercise of coercion, that alone give coercion the character necessary for true ordered human social life. In fact, the monopoly of physical coercion is true of human sovereign power over an animal herd as well as of the slave state. It is a well-established sociological fact in political history (cf. Chap. 116) that physical coercion, if it is to last any length of time, must justify itself before the human mind and before the juridical consciousness. More fruitful than such generalizing theories for providing insight into the power relationships of modern democracy with its parties and pressure groups, are the sociological investigations concerned with these relationships, among which those of *Max Weber* himself provide exemplary beginnings.

Leadership, the Essence of Political Authority?

The charismatic basis of political authority, namely, the founding of authority on the "personal gift" (*charisma*) of the "leader," [4] dealt with by *Max*

[1] Cf. J. Austin, *The Province of Jurisprudence Determined*, 1832.

[2] Cf. Sir H. Maine, *Early History of Institutions*, 1875, pp. 380 ff.; cf. Machiavelli, *Il Principe*, Chap. 116.

[3] M. Weber, *Wirtschaft und Gesellschaft*, 1922, pp. 28 f.; *Gesammelte politische Schriften*, 1921, pp. 397, 402. Cf. also M. Weber, *Staatssoziologie, Anord., Einf., u. Erläut. durch Johannes Winkelmann*, 1956.

[4] Cf. M. Weber, *Wirtschaft und Gesellschaft*, pp. 124 ff.

Weber as one of the three bases of legitimacy, was developed to a unique kind of completion by racialist political theory. In this theory, political authority is not rooted in the natural order of the community, but in the personal character of the leader; it is "bound up with the personality of the one in whom it is invested," who "embodies popular mind and popular will." [5] The racialists themselves see the difference between their view and that of the natural law school in that, through the "idea of a ruling power rooted in itself, the conception of office is at the same time rid of the character of being merely a constituent of order." [6] Political authority, thus founded upon the personality of the leader, is burdened with the "risk of the extraordinary." [7] The criterion of leadership is that "the people instinctively and unerringly distinguishes the true leader, the representative of political values, from the 'pseudo-leader,' the mere holder of a position of power which alone he is bent on maintaining." [8] Fundamentally, neither the personal qualities of a man nor the instinctive feelings of a people give political authority its essential character; rather the objective reality of the essential order of the political community does this.

This distinction made by natural law doctrine between the *leadership principle* and the *authority principle* can, however, be readily harmonized with the conviction that it is an immense boon for a community if those who exercise political authority are personalities possessing real qualities of leadership and capable of rousing the nation to its best ideals in its public life. The distinction makes it clear, however, that genuine leadership exists only when it keeps its tables of values in harmony with the objective laws of political order.

129. The Original Location of Political Authority

Closely connected with the question of the origin and nature of political authority, is the question which asks in whom it is originally invested. Although the former question is concerned with the basis of the right constituting political authority, the latter is concerned with the subject of the right. The solution of the decisive question regarding the principles for the exercise of political power obviously depends, in great measure, upon the answer. Is political authority originally vested in the state, as conceived in *Bodin's* doctrine of state sovereignty; or is it vested in *Hobbes*' absolutist prince; or in the people, as in *Rousseau's* theory of popular sovereignty? Our answer emerges from what has been said about the origin of political power: Political authority resides originally *in the people as a unity actualizing the political order.* The end of a society, as we have urged, is the root of its authority; [1] hence, political

[5] O. Koellreutter, *Deutsches Verfassungsrecht,* 1936, pp. 130 f.

[6] W. Dräger, *Primat des Volkes? Ein Beitrag zur Grundfrage einer völkischen Staatslehre,* 1935, pp. 65 f.

[7] E. Forsthoff, *Der totale Staat,* 1934, p. 12.

[8] O. Koellreutter, *op. cit.,* p. 132.

[1] To determine the original bearer of political authority the principle given by St. Thomas (*Summa theol.,* Ia IIae, q. 90, a. 3) applies: "Quia et in omnibus aliis ordinare in finem est eius, cuius est proprius ille finis."

authority resides in the people who are organized for carrying out the fundamental functions of society, that is, in the *body politic* (*corpus*

By pointing out the characteristics of our theory in comparison with the theories of absolute state sovereignty, the absolute sovereignty of the prince, and the absolute sovereignty of the people, we may try further to elucidate its bases and its significance. Since the common good of the people as a unity forms the foundation of political authority, the state cannot be regarded as originally something above and independent of the people, nor can it even raise itself above a merely subservient function. Thus, absolute state sovereignty, as postulated by *Bodin*[2] or as developed by *Hegel*, or as applied by the modern totalitarian state, has no basis in the true nature of the state. At the same time, political authority cannot originally be vested in the absolute prince or in an absolute body whose right is composed, as *Hobbes* thought, of portions of the rights to absolute freedom of all citizens, which the latter resign, thereby creating something new, namely, political authority, in order to safeguard their remaining freedom.

Political authority does not owe its existence to an act of will of the citizens, but it is coexistent with the unity of the people, who are organized for the fulfillment of the functions of the political order. It resides juridically in the "institution" (cf. Chap. 42) of the body politic in the sense of its natural "constitution" being determined by the fundamental social functions. Since it is not in the will of the people, but in the people as a political body, that political authority originally resides, absolute sovereignty of the people has no foundation in the nature of the state, as *Rousseau* maintains. The current popular will, therefore, is not the original foundation and absolute master of political power. But, insofar as it is constituted of the actual political common good, the will of the people is a determining factor in the exercise of political authority. We shall study this question in the next chapter.

politicum).

Ideological Limitations of Political Theories

In scarcely any other realm of thought is the dependence of philosophical and scientific theories upon the circumstances of the time so clearly indicated as in the attempts of modern political theory to determine the original location of political authority (concerning the conception of ideology cf. Chap. 58). Hence, these attempts offer a most interesting field for the sociology of knowledge, all the more so since one can hardly ever speak of a conscious intent, but only of an influence of contemporary circumstances on thought. Thus, *Bodin* sets out to justify the rising absolute monarchy of France, *Hobbes* the absolute mon-

[2] Cf. Jean Bodin, *De republica*, 1586, I, 8. Bodin recognizes that political authority is bound by divine and natural law, but not that it is bound by human law. It is in this sense only that he can be classed among the upholders of the absolute sovereignty of the state.

archy in England, *Locke* the English revolution of 1688 and the deposition of *James II, Rousseau* the forces working toward the modern idea of sovereignty of the people, *Hegel* the enlightened absolutism of the Kingdom of Prussia. No less do the anti-individualist and antidemocratic theories of the recent past bear the stamp of having been conditioned by events.

Spann, for example, in his "universalism," makes political authority reside originally in the estate, which is responsible for the state as a group within it. *W. Heinrich,* one of his pupils, expressly declares that *Spann's* state is the antithesis of democracy; this signifies equal participation by all in the government of the state and in the formation of the political will. And he further explicitly remarks (in 1934!) that, with such a reorientation of view regarding the location of political authority, social science "is falling in with the historical developments of our days." [3]

No nearer to the truth is the pure corporatism of Professor *Manoilescu,* who denies that there exists either a divine right of the sovereign or a divine right of the people; there are only original rights, which are based on the functions of the corporations as functional units into which the nation is organized for the purpose of social cooperation. The origin and the original location of political authority, therefore, should be sought in the totality of the corporations.[4] Both universalist and pure corporatism fail to see that the political community must be a unity in itself which is determined by its own end if it is to make the idea of member communities in the form of estates or corporations at all possible; the purpose of these, therefore, can be derived only from the end of that unity and cannot form the basis of authority for the whole. *Manoilescu* also forgets that political authority existed long before the "century of corporatism." By confining political authority to a governing estate, the universalist theory may be used in support of trends toward a single-party or single-class system; pure corporatism supports the surrender of the state to the forces of economic interest organized in corporations.

130. Popular Sovereignty

Political authority, as we have seen, originally resides in the people as a political unity. Does it follow that persons in whom it is actually vested can lawfully exercise it only through and with the consent of the people? Since it was often due to historical factors that particular persons or bodies came to exercise political authority (for instance, the gradual transformation of family authority, or military conquest), historical experience does not bear out the assumption that any special act of transfer is a necessity for the vesting of political authority in a particular person or body. On the other hand, there seems to be no doubt that, in the event of the lapsing of all existing rights to the exercise of political authority in a community, as when a ruling dynasty becomes extinct, the community itself is called upon to appoint its actual ruler.

[3] W. Heinrich, *Ständewesen,* 2nd ed., 1934, pp. 6, 41.

[4] Cf. Manoilescu, *Le siècle du corporatisme,* 1934, pp. 164 ff.

It seems also certain prima facie that no ruler can juridically be completely independent of the will of the people in the exercise of political power, if one holds that the state is a community of moral persons existing for their best interest, and not an organization of higher animals existing in the best interest of their master. Indeed, if the common good is the concern of all members of the community, since they are responsible for the fulfillment of their essential tasks which are rooted in the existential ends, the exercise of political authority cannot be altogether independent of the will of the community. The question is, then: *How far must any exercise of political authority be legitimated by the consent of the people?* Consent as a characteristic trait in the nature of the state has already been discussed. Here we are investigating the dependence of the exercise of political authority upon consent. We are concerned, of course, only with the relationship between popular consent and political authority, which applies to every form of government, and not with its concrete form in modern constitutional democracy.

In perhaps no other question is the separation of the moral and the historical issues so difficult as in this. The notion of an original express act of consent in the determination of those who have to exercise political authority seems inescapable if one admits it to be a fact that the community in which political authority originally resides cannot, as a mass, exercise political authority itself, and hence must necessarily delegate it to an individual or to a body. What is certain, however, is that, like all principles of natural law, the juridical principle of political authority is a general principle, the concrete application of which cannot be derived from itself alone. Only the *principle* of authority, and not the concrete form of its determination, belongs to the natural, and hence to the divine, dispensation. With regard to the concrete form of its determination, however, the second principle of natural law, that political power originally resides in the people as a political community, is important; this determination can come only from the will of the community in some form. It comes about through the juridical will of the people evolving through usage and custom; this juridical will, in turn, is determined by both the primary and the developed legal consciousness of the people, and lastly by the moral conscience. It is a concrete form of natural law (cf. Chap. 48).

In addition, of particular significance is the fact that the juridical principle of authority becomes effective through the establishment of the political community, which can be constituted only as a juridical community; thus, in the necessarily concrete legal order of the political community, the concrete form of authority is implied.

Thus, in the natural law sphere (*quaestio iuris*) there is *no historical sequence of events;* that is, the establishment of the political community does not come first, followed by an act of consent to the law governing political authority. The two sides to the moral foundation of political order cannot be disjoined; only if this is kept in view will it be possible to find the approach to the essential relationship between popular will and political authority. In both directions we find historical factors at work, insofar as the concrete determination of the juridical principles in question implies the operation of such factors. But political philosophy and political ethics are concerned with this determination here only in its general nature, and not with actual acts of its historical basis and formation (*quaestio facti*).

It follows that the exercise of political authority is itself part of the legal order by which the *juridical consciousness of the people* gives the principles of political fellowship and political authority their concrete determination and in which the political community is constituted. In this sense, the lawful exercise of political authority depends on popular consent. With this concrete legal order the people, therefore, gives itself a fundamental law for the exercise of political authority in its community: the primordial constitution. This law is *morally and legally binding upon those charged with the exercise of political authority.* In this sense, therefore, *by virtue of natural law, a sovereignty of the people* exists. The juridical consciousness of mankind does not doubt this fact. In questions of sovereignty, the whole history of Western law is, as the *Carlyle* brothers have shown, a defense of the principle that the exercise of political authority is subject to the will of the people as expressed in legal usages and customs, and that the holder of power does not stand above the law. Upon this principle rests the distinction, pointed out by the *Carlyle* brothers, of such importance in the legal consciousness of the Middle Ages, between the lawful prince, himself protected by the law in the exercise of power, and the usurper who places himself outside the law.[1]

The part played by legal usages and customs in the determination of the juridical order for the exercise of political authority has been borne out by modern comparative history of law; indeed, it is among its major discoveries. It is well known that *H. S. Maine,* one of its originators, saw in this fact that a sovereign is in one way or another bound by a higher law than himself a decisive argument against *Austin's* theory of sovereignty.[2] Our conclusion does not, of course, exclude the possibility that the exercise of political authority may be, and has in history

[1] Cf. R. W. and A. J. Carlyle, *A History of Medieval Political Theory in the West,* 1909; cf. also A. J. Carlyle, *Political Liberty, A History of the Conception in the Middle Ages and Modern Times,* 1941. A telling example of the medieval idea of the limitation of legislative sovereignty is shown in the competence of the medieval English parliament, for which, as C. H. McIlwain, *The High Court of Parliament and Its Supremacy,* 2nd ed., 1934, p. 99, emphasizes, the law is primarily a body of custom of which the Parliament's enactments are only declaratory and for which certain great principles of this law were beyond its power to change; although this law was often called the law of nature, its inviolability was due above all to its universality as a custom.

[2] Cf. Sir H. Maine, *Ancient Law,* 10th ed., 1884, pp. 7 ff

been, transferred and regulated by the express consent of the political community, that is, by a constitutional act; or that after revolutionary changes such consent can also take the form of tacit acceptance and recognition of the rule of a usurper.

What are the *practical conclusions from the natural law idea of popular sovereignty?*

1. The exercise of political authority is governed by the legal convictions rooted in the legal conscience of a people: no ruler and no government stands above the law or may create law at will. The fact that they are bound by natural law is a matter of course; but they are also, in accordance with natural law, subject to existing law, insofar as this is the expression of the juridical consciousness and the juridical will of the people in the sense described. This was a standing principle for the whole of medieval thought and that of early modern times.

2. State power is lawfully exercised not in the private interest of the ruler, whether a monarch or a party, but in the general interest of the people. Again, however, what is in question is not only the general principle that the end and juridical basis of political authority are to be found in the common good, but also the common good in its relationship to the concrete popular will and to what it considers to be the "good life," its "welfare," within the framework of the fundamentals of political order. The popular will can be passive, leaving nearly everything to the government; it can also lack conscious and articulate expression. Nevertheless, it is there, and political authority must discover its substance, and, in conformity with it, make the welfare of the people its guiding principle. In this respect every government must assure itself of the consent of the people in what it proposes to do for the common good. No absolute sovereign power of any government can decide for "guns or butter."

3. Connected with this is the further implication of the natural law doctrine of popular sovereignty that, in all forms of government, absolutist or democratic, adequate means should be provided to insure that the will of the people may be taken into account. Consequently, traditional natural law teaching arrived at the conclusion that the democratic principle should not be absent from any form of government (cf. Chap. 133).

A further series of conclusions shows the *radical difference between the natural law doctrine of popular sovereignty and the modern theory of absolute popular sovereignty that is liberalist or totalitarian in character.*

1. No actual government fundamentally exercises political authority as a mandate of the people (even in constitutional democracy), but in virtue of the natural order of the political community, and therefore in the name of God. As soon as political authority has passed into the hands of a lawful government, the moral authority accompanying the

political is vested in the government independently of the constitutional machinery. This means that, ultimately, we obey the orders of the government not because it is elected by the people, but because such obedience is commanded by the natural moral order. If, then, political authority does not reside in the people, in the sense that the government exercises its authority only as the representative (*vicarius*) of the people, and there is no intrinsic dependence of the essential political authority upon its constitutional form, no conclusions can be drawn from the natural law theory of popular sovereignty in support of a higher right for democracy than for other forms of government.

2. The people cannot lawfully seek to change the basic powers of the political authority. In other words, the popular majority will, even under democracy, cannot lawfully give any government a mandate releasing it from the observance of the natural juridical order. Parties and party groups, in a free democracy, which violate natural liberties (education, school, marriage) by appealing to a legality dependent on the parliamentary majority principle, fundamentally act as unlawfully as the totalitarian governments when they appeal to the popular will (by plebiscite) in disregarding human rights.

3. Legal titles to the exercise of political authority cannot be annulled by the people simply by appeal to the original sovereignty of the people. The people cannot, by infringing such titles, lawfully alter its form of government and, for example, depose a legitimate monarch.

In summary, we can say: Contrary to the natural law principles discussed, the *theory of absolute popular sovereignty* bases political authority exclusively on the popular will, asserts its unqualified dependence on the popular will, and holds that it can be withdrawn at the pleasure of the popular will. This theory thus becomes a theory of the *right to revolution* (cf. Chap. 156).

The Controversy over Popular Sovereignty in Traditional Natural Law Theory

In the nineteenth century, *differences of opinion within the traditional natural law school* emerged concerning the implications of popular sovereignty, although previously there had been unanimity throughout the whole development of natural law theory.[3] The reason was that isolated propositions of the great representatives of the natural law tradition in the sixteenth and

[3] Cf. Taparelli, S. J., *Saggio teoretico di Diritto Naturale,* 1839; Balmes, *Portestantismus und Katholizismus,* 1861; T. Meyer, S.J., *Institutiones Iuris Naturalis,* II, 1900; V. Cathrein, *Moralphilosophie,* 6th ed., 1924; P. Tischleder, *Ursprung und Träger der Staatsgewalt nach der Lehre des heiligen Thomas und seiner Schule,* 1923; O. Schilling, *Staats- und Soziallehre des heiligen Thomas von Aquin,* 2nd ed., 1930; F. X. Arnold, *Die Staatslehre des Kardinals Bellarmin,* 1934; J. Brodrick, S.J., *Life and Work of Cardinal Bellarmine,* 1928, I, pp. 216–51, where he discusses in detail the arguments of the opponents of the Bellarminian theory; similarly, H. Rommen, *Die Staatslehre des Franz Suárez,* 1936, pp. 177–215, argues for Suárez.

seventeenth centuries were now considered in the perspective of the theory of absolute popular sovereignty originated by *Rousseau*. Criticism was directed especially toward the theses of *Robert Bellarmine* (d. 1621) and *Francisco Suárez* (d. 1617). They themselves declare, however, that they are speaking only in accordance with the whole tradition of natural law theory, including *St. Thomas Aquinas*.

What the critics consider erroneous are statements such as the following: political authority, by whomsoever exercised, has lawfully been derived only from the people, whether directly or indirectly, and cannot come into the possession of a man in any other way if it is to be just; [4] the community cannot itself exercise political authority, and must therefore transfer it to one or a few persons, so that it depends on the consent of the people whether it will have a king or consuls or other rulers and, if legitimate cause exists, the people can change a monarchy to an aristocracy or a democracy or vice versa, as in fact happened at Rome.[5]

A careful interpretation of such passages, in the light of the whole theory of these thinkers, indicates that they really do not deviate from the tradition of the natural law doctrine. They merely lay more stress on the consent element, but without neglecting the institutional element, namely, the foundation of political authority in the body politic as such. What they are concerned with is more the fact that the actualization of the principle of political authority cannot be thought of apart from the law in which the people come to see the fundamental order of its social life. Consequently, they especially emphasize that this actualization cannot take place "without the intervention of the will and consent of men," [6] but only "through the intermediacy of human judgment and human choice." [7] This we ourselves have urged in our interpretation of the natural law theory of popular sovereignty.

Their main contentions are that the ruling power comes indeed from God, but the power only, not the rulers or the forms of government,[8] and that no sovereign, whether a monarch or the people itself, stands above the law. Hence, their first conclusion is this: consent in some form is necessary so that political

[4] Cf. Suárez, *De legibus,* Bk. III, Chap. 4, n. 2: "Sequitur ex dictis, potestatem civilem, quoties in uno homine vel principe reperitur, legitimo ac ordinario jure, a populo et communitate manasse, vel proxime, vel remote, nec posse aliter haberi, ut justa sit." The passages in St. Thomas to which Suárez refers are: *Summa theol.*, Ia IIae, q. 90, a. 3 (cf. our quotation in Chap. 118) and Ia IIae, q. 97. Suárez, therefore, sums up: "Potestas regia formaliter ut talis est de jure humano."

[5] Cf. Bellarmine, *De laicis,* Chap. 6: "In particulari singulas species regiminis esse de iure gentium, non de iure naturae; nam pendet a consensu multitudinis constituere super se regem vel consules vel alios magistratus, ut patet; et si causa legitima adsit, potest multitudo mutare regimen in aristocratiam aut democratiam et e contrario, ut Romae factum legimus."

[6] Suárez, *op. cit.,* Chap. 3. n. 6: "Haec potestas datur communitati hominum ab auctore naturae, non tamen sine interventu voluntatum et consensuum hominum, ex quibus talis communitas perfecta congregata est"; Chap. 4, n. 1: "Licet haec potestas absoluta sit de iure naturae, determinatio eius ad certum modum potestatis, et regiminis est ex arbitrio humano."

[7] Bellarmine, *op. cit.,* "Nota, ex dictis sequi, hanc potestatem in particulari esse quidem a Deo, sed mediante consilio et electione humana, ut alia omnia, quae ad jus gentium pertinent. Jus enim gentium est quasi conclusio deducta ex jure naturae per humanum discursum."

[8] Cf. St. Thomas, *Epist. ad Rom., XIII.*

authority may lawfully come into effect in a particular person and, in this sense, its transfer by the political community takes place. The popular will in this consent may be unconscious, as in the case of the transition of family authority into the political authority of the elders of the tribe, or it may be articulate, as when the political community exercises its right to appoint a ruler or form of government if there is no one left with a legitimate title to political authority.

Their second conclusion is that the sovereign—and they would certainly say, whether monarch or, in modern democracy, people—is a usurper if he disregards the law that binds him by one or other form of such transfer. They write with their eyes on the rising absolute sovereignty of princes, but they would equally reject the absolute sovereignty of the people, since they emphatically deny that the people possesses any right to alter the form of the state at will by infringing existing rights (e.g., by deposing a legitimate ruler).

The fundamental idea of the medieval doctrine of popular sovereignty—that every government, whether prince or parliament, is subject to law—undoubtedly continues to exert its influence even in the modern social-contract theories in their concern for the rule of law,[9] even though their foundation of political philosophy leaves much to be desired. The fact that this fundamental idea of the medieval doctrine of popular sovereignty is also at work in modern democratic constitutions is beyond doubt. Concerning the Scholastic theory of the state and the previously mentioned controversy, such an acute thinker as Professor *Alfred O'Rahilly* says: "Its significance—especially for our times—consists in the passionate belief that man does not live *for* the State, that he cannot (like a bee or ant) be merged in the whole, that even the state is subservient to higher law and purpose. . . . By an irony of fate, while we Scholastics have largely forgotten the great seventeenth-century exposition of Christian democracy, the influence of Suárez, working through English Whigs and Puritans and culminating in the American Declaration of Independence (July 4, 1776), is once again inspiring men toward freedom." [10] *O'Rahilly* is referring to the proclamation of human rights in the Declaration of Independence.

The Controversy about the Transfer Problem in Traditional Natural Law Doctrine

There is agreement in traditional natural law doctrine that political authority, since it is part of the moral order, has its origin in God. Nevertheless, opinions are divided on the question of how political authority arrives at the person who wields it in the historically existing form of state. The *theory of translation* maintains that there is an actual transference by the citizens of the state, in whom, as a political unity, political sovereignty originally resides. On the other hand, the *theory of designation* maintains that the people can only designate the person who is to exercise political authority, since political authority itself comes directly from God to the person specified to exercise it. It is clear that the

[9] Cf. A. J. Carlyle, *Political Liberty, A History of the Conception in the Middle Ages and Modern Times,* 1941, pp. 27–30, 133–42, 182–87.

[10] A. O'Rahilly, "Suárez and Democracy," in *Studies* (Dublin), March 1918, pp. 3 f., 21; "The Sources of English and American Democracy," in *Studies,* June 1919, pp. 199 ff.

controversy about the question of transfer is closely allied with the controversy previously discussed, for *Suárez* and *Bellarmine* are the most resolute advocates of the theory of translation. We believe (cf. the beginning of this chapter) that, to the reasons advanced by these two, we have added another, namely, that the concrete origin of political authority is not to be thought of at all in terms of a *historical* series of events; rather, the political community can only be constituted in concrete form as a legal community, and the form of exercise of political authority is determined by the consent underlying its concrete legal order, through which, therefore, the transfer of authority comes about.[11]

131. Political Obedience

If political obedience has always been a primary topic in political theory, this is because of its special character. As soon as the individual, in the course of man's development, acquired an increased sense of the fact that he had existence and rights of his own, it became a problem for the human mind *why* and still more *to what extent,* if all men are equal, an individual or a body can claim and compel obedience from the whole of society.

The answer which we have found in the foregoing discussion of political authority is that the *moral right of command* of the political authority is based on man's existential ends and on the fulfillment, demanded by these ends, of the fundamental social functions by the political community. Therefore, the special character of political obedience does not, as is assumed by all individualistic theories of the state, rest on any form of consent in which the individuals bind themselves. Political obedience derives its specific character from the particular nature of the common good, and thus from the political community's institutional or intrinsic order. The political power of command is not only the necessary condition for the unfolding of particular sides of human nature, like that which underlies other forms of authority (e.g., obedience to parents), but the condition for the realization of all men's tasks in the material and cultural spheres. Being rooted in the common good, civil or political obedience is a special kind of legal obligation, an obligation of legal justice, and accordingly, it can be insured by the use of physical force.

Consequently, *legality,* in the sense of the readiness of those subject

[11] A detailed account of the controversial question may be found in H. Rommen, *The State in Catholic Thought,* 1945, pp. 424–76; *Die Staatslehre des Franz Suárez,* 1926, pp. 177–215; it is dealt with exhaustively in P. Tischleder, *Ursprung und Träger der Staatsgewalt,* 1923; a more recent work is Gabriel Bowe, O.P., *The Origin of Political Authority,* 1955. Many think that the theory of translation is untenable on account of the utterances of Leo XIII on the origin of political authority; that this is not so, rather that Leo XIII only wishes to stress the origin of political authority in God in face of the theory of absolute popular sovereignty (cf. above), is conclusively demonstrated by H. Rommen in the first-mentioned work, pp. 469 ff., in the second, pp. 208–15.

to law to obey the civil law of the state, is a *moral virtue* belonging to the virtues of justice. Its immediate foundation lies in the natural law principle of legal justice, whereby obedience to the lawgiver is an obligation; its more remote foundation lies in the general natural law principle, whereby obedience to lawful authority is commanded. The obligation of legality, therefore, is intrinsically related to the authority, rooted in the moral order, of the lawgiver; on the other hand, the obligation of legality is limited to the demand of outward conformity with the law of the lawgiver (cf. Chap. 38).[1] With regard to the lawgiver, in particular cases the question of the legitimization of his authority, with which we shall deal presently, arises. Since the lawgiver himself is bound in principle by moral law and cannot arbitrarily create morally binding law, his disregard of these principles could lead to a divergence between "legality" and "legitimacy" in legislation. Out of this grows the danger of a legal positivism, which places the legality of legislation in a democracy in the will of the majority as the ultimate source of law; this of necessity leads to an outcome in which "legality has become a poisoned weapon" (*C. Schmitt,* cf. Chap. 48, note 11).

From the same reasons that make political obedience a moral duty, the *limitation* of this duty is derived: it does not go beyond the order of justice. The command and the law of political authority, therefore, are not binding if they are *unjust in themselves* or if the authority lacks *legal foundation.*[2] First, we shall deal with the question of the limitation of political obedience because of the injustice of the commands or laws. The question gains added significance at a time when the state, as a result of totalitarian tendencies and the claim to omnicompetence, is

[1] Cf. Thomas Würtenberger, "Die Legalität, Versuch einer Deutung ihres rechtsphilosophischen Sinngehaltes," in *Gegenwartsprobleme des international Rechtes und der Rechtsphilosophie: Festschrift für Rudolf Laun,* D. S. Constantopoulos and Hans Wehberg, editors, 1953, pp. 622 ff., pertinently regards consideration of the claims and sphere of legality as an important question for our generation. Würtenberger's distinction should be noted: "Whoever pays respect toward law as such gives silent assent to the 'moral' task of law, to serve freedom and realize justice in the order of mutual human relations"; however, "the particular status of *legality* in regard to *morality* consists . . . above all in a recognition of the existence of the legal *order* as such. . . . In respect for the ordering of human relations realized in law lies the true core of all legality. In this above all is also to be seen the *degree of its independent value* for social and law-regulated life. . . . Whoever thus regards the norms of law in dealing with legality pays homage above all to the idea of legal order embodied in law. Other elements need not be included in the intention of one acting in accordance with law." By the example of penal law Würtenberger shows that the claims of legality are restricted to a certain standard of outward behavior: hence, the aim of penal action is not the formation of the moral personality of the lawbreaker, but to bring him "to a simple acknowledgment of the binding power of the legal order as a whole," that is, legality. As in traditional natural law doctrine (cf. beginning of following chap.), Würtenberger also stresses that the support of legality does not exclude awareness of the imperfection of all legislative work.

[2] Cf. St. Thomas, *Summa theol.,* IIa IIae, q. 104, a. 6: "Principibus saecularibus intantum homo obedire tenetur, inquantum ordo justitiae requirit. Et ideo si non habent justum principatum, sed usurpatum, vel si injusta praecipiant, non tenentur eis subditi obedire; nisi forte per accidens, propter vitandum scandalum vel periculum."

prone to overstep the bounds of its rights. The following principles emerge from what has been said about the political power of command as a right and about its foundation.

1. Laws and commands are *unjust* if they conflict with existential human ends (*St. Thomas: bonum humanum*): if the ruler (prince or party or parliamentary majority) imposes oppressive laws that are not required by the common good but spring from the avarice or pride of the ruler; if the ruler exceeds the authority granted him by the constitution; if burdens, even when necessary for the common good, are inequitably apportioned. *St. Thomas,* whom we have followed in this enumeration, adds: "All these are infringements of law rather than law; therefore, they do not bind in conscience."[3] Infringements of rights by modern states affect especially the spheres of education, marriage legislation, the relation of Church and state, freedom of property and labor, and taxation (e.g., excessive taxation for the purpose of experiments in planned or socialist economy).

2. The lapsing of the duty of obedience presupposes *certainty* regarding the injustice of the laws in question. By reason of the function of political authority as a power for securing social order, the ordinance of the lawful superior must prevail in case of doubt as long as the contrary is not established.[4]

3. The observance of orders and laws of political authority may be a moral duty, *in spite of their injustice*, on the grounds of the common good, which can impose an obligation to avoid still graver prejudice to order and peace; or it may be morally permissible on the grounds of prudence, that is, it can impose an obligation to take precautions against incurring the severe penalties attached to the refusal of obedience. Thus, under totalitarian dictatorships, fathers of families may be compelled to show an external loyalty in order to keep their jobs and be able to support their families. In the latter case, the observance of laws is divested of the character of political obedience and can only externally appear as such, since its moral basis is essentially different from that of political obedience. Obligations of prudence naturally give way when, in conflict with clear duties of conscience, one must "obey God rather than man."

The extent to which obedience to a *usurping government* is permissible or forbidden is also the question which asks whether the government, on the whole, lacks legal foundation. Have the inhabitants of areas that have been annexed by an aggressor state as a result of an unjust war a moral duty of political obedience to the conqueror, or can such a duty arise? When a government or dynasty which has been forcibly deposed upholds its claim and title to be the legitimate political authority of their country

[3] *Ibid.*, Ia IIae, q. 96, a. 4, where the *bonum humanum* is also mentioned.

[4] Cf. Suárez, *De leg.*, lib. I, c. 9, n. 9: "Necessarium esse, ut de iniustitia legis certo moraliter constet: nam si res sit dubia, praesumendum est pro legislatore."

against the usurping government, to which government is it permissible or obligatory for the citizen to render obedience? Can an unlawfully acquired political authority ever become lawful? The relevant principles of natural law are as follows:

1. The mere fact of the taking over of power in the territory of a state can establish *no right to legitimate authority.* In recent times attempts have been made in one way or another to give a legal color to naked acts of force: by appealing to the "will of the people" as shown by plebiscite after the *fait accompli* in the forcibly annexed territory; or by appealing to the "law of historical facts" (e.g., to a former territorial connection), although long dissolved by legal facts, between the annexed and the annexing countries; or by appealing to the so-called natural right of a race or a nation to political unity (e.g., such movements as Pan-Germanism and Pan-Slavism); or by appealing to the alleged right of revolution made by groups on their seizure of power. In all such cases, modern usurpers have felt urged to have their title to political power later "confirmed" by plebiscite. But plebiscites can never rectify the legal wrong of a usurpation by a foreign power or by a group within the state, quite apart from the fact that plebiscites can be "made" to do so, as the evidence of recent history amply shows. Rights cannot be established by physical facts alone, but only by legal facts, so-called legal titles. In the modern state, the necessary legal title to the exercise of political authority is usually based upon the constitutional transfer of power.

2. Although the law of mere facts establishes no moral authority for the usurper, there is a *limited obligation upon the citizens of obedience* to his orders as soon as he has gained assured control. The legal basis for this lies not in the fact of assured control but in the necessity of insuring public order in the political community, which would otherwise fall a victim to anarchy and chaos. This qualified duty does not exist as long as the usurper is struggling for power, because then obedience is still due to the lawful government, and to render obedience to the usurper would be equivalent to supporting him. Even after this stage the obligation is confined to obedience to such decrees as are required for ordered legal and political administration. Thus, an oath of allegiance given to such a government by a public servant is intrinsically restricted to the special duties of his office; obedience to the instructions of a usurper is not permissible where it would involve recognition (e.g., an invitation to enter a government formed by him or to take part in a "constituent assembly" convoked by him in order to recognize his government). A qualified duty of obedience, as here defined, does not imply any prejudice to the right of the legitimate ruler or the legitimate government to try to regain political power by appropriate means and to call the citizens to active resistance against the usurping government.

3. Although the fact of the usurpation of power cannot of itself create legitimacy, yet subsequently the actual fact of the resulting reconstitution

of the political common good in its essential implications, in the course of time can establish the legitimacy of a government which, because it is assured in the exercise of its authority, has become an integral element of the actual common good. The consequences of this are: (1) the government then acquires the moral power of command of a legitimate political authority, and the moral duty to obey it comes into full force; (2) every legal claim of a former legitimate ruler becomes obsolete. The condition of this is that the existing government is in assured possession of power, and that the common good indubitably depends upon its peaceful continuance. The validity of this legal principle, that *the de facto government becomes legitimate in time,* finds confirmation in the legal consciousness of peoples; this has often been manifested in the course of history after revolutionary changes.

What is the legal foundation of such legitimacy? In our view it is to be sought in the fact that *the actual common good is dependent upon historical factors.* The common good is actualized only as an interdependence of the citizens in their legal and factual relations, by means of social institutions which are essentially connected, directly or indirectly, with the actual political authority. In the course of time, this connection, in its concrete form, becomes an integral constituent of the actual common good. How much would the citizens in the economic field alone leave undone, to the detriment of their own and the general interest, if they could not, with some confidence, rely upon legal certainty, stability, and continuity, apart from the fact that there would be no end to the danger of civil war and anarchy in a commonwealth so situated? Owing to the inextricable involvement of an established government, illegitimate in itself, with the complex historical reality of the actual common good in the course of time, its purely de facto authority passes over to a real de iure authority.

The fact that the former usurper now exercises authority, which imposes legal obligations upon the subjects, is not because the seizure of power creates a right or because public order demands an authority (as pointed out under (2), but because such authority has itself become a constitutive element of the actual common good. It will certainly take a considerable *time* before the necessary historical process is completed. To describe this process as a quasi-prescription, which some natural law theorists would do, does not seem to do justice to the public-law character of political authority; besides, it seems to be inconsistent with the necessary conditions laid down for prescription in the sphere of private law (good faith). In the historical reconstitution of the common good in its actual form, which we have accepted, the *consent* of the people, tacit or expressed, has its place. Of course, it is not to be understood as an act recognizing a right of usurpation as such; but rather as an act recognizing the fact that the common good exists under the concrete conditions obtaining, including the government in power.

In this whole question the traditional natural law doctrine has always been guided by *"historical" thinking,* even though its exponents go different ways in establishing the connection between the two aspects of the political common good, that is, between its moral idea and its historical reality. In thus recognizing the historical nature of the state and the common good, the natural law school has sometimes been reproached for allowing itself to be led into admitting a law of mere facts. In truth, however, it avoids developing the moral principle of the common good *in vacuo,* thus avoiding doctrinairism, just as on the other side it rejects historicism by refusing to base moral principles merely on historical processes. But because the moral and legal principles lead back to the *existential* ends of man, the guiding principle of political ethics must, for the natural law doctrine, be the actual reality of the political common good.

A further question for discussion, in connection with the duty of obedience toward the political power, is the *right and the duty of political resistance* in case of wrongful use or wrongful acquisition of political authority. This question calls for a separate chapter.

132. The Right of Resistance

In the treatment of political resistance natural law theory has always begun by emphasizing the moral duty of obedience, which Christian thinkers read out of the words of the Apostle *Paul,* that obedience is imperative because power is of divine ordination (cf. Rom. 13:1). Similarly, the exhortation of the Apostle *Peter* that servants should be subject not only to good and kind masters, but also to perverse ones (cf. I Pet. 2:18), has been applied also to political authority throughout the whole tradition of natural law political theory. With the sense of reality belonging to this theory, the sometimes unjustified use of authority, which is to a greater or lesser degree bound up with its exercise because of the impairment of human nature, has been expressly characterized as irrelevant with regard to the duty of political obedience.

Natural law theory, however, is not less definite about the fact that the individuals and the lesser communities possess natural rights that are equally original with those of the state itself. But he who possesses inviolable rights also has the right, and often the duty, of protecting them against infringements. The reason is that he possesses these rights for the sake of existential ends, and therefore for the sake of inalienable duties. Where, then, the bidding of the state and the bidding of conscience are in conflict, the principle, "God is to be obeyed rather than man," applies. The first conclusion from this is that, in the ordered commonwealth, the citizen must have opportunity to safeguard his natural rights against political authority. The absence of this possibility distinguishes the totalitarian, dictatorial state. As long as the right of the citizens to the judicial protection of their rights from state interference is respected, there is little possibility of the emergence of state totalitarianism. But when the legal tribunal is replaced by police, concentration camps, deportation, or political proscription, then the citizens are deprived of their rights against the state.

What action are the citizens justified in taking if the legal government abuses its power, oppressing them with unjust laws and decrees? In such a case the citizens have the right, and sometimes the duty, of *passive resistance,* that is, of refusing obedience. The bases of this right and the conditions for its application in particular cases are to be found in the intrinsic limitation of political authority, which has been discussed already. From the nature of political authority it likewise follows that, should the conditions for passive resistance exist, the general duty of loyalty to the legitimate government remains. Furthermore, for good reasons the natural law school has always upheld the principle that, apart from altogether exceptional circumstances, passive resistance is, politically as well as morally, the only proper means of protecting the liberties of the citizens against the abuse of power by the government. Should such an abuse be combined with despotism, violence, or revolution in defense of the citizens' rights, generally result in still graver harm to the common good than is involved in the abuse of power by the government. Civil war usually does greater harm to a commonwealth than even grievous violations of rights by the government. This *principle of non-violence* in political resistance has been further endorsed for the traditional natural law school by religious considerations.

When is *active resistance* against the abuse of political power by the legal government justified? Active resistance is the organized defense of the people against such abuse. This defense may be carried out with or without the use of force. *Nonviolent* defense may take the form of mobilizing public opinion or of appealing to a superior forum of justice, of which in former times traditional natural law doctrine chiefly thought. Both became obsolete in the era of the totalitarian state, but could indeed become the chief methods of nonviolent active resistance as soon as the organized community of nations has secured the recognition of basic human rights by all states. Today the general strike, on the other hand, can be a very effective means of nonviolent active resistance; it could be the only justifiable form of "political strike." *Violent* (armed) resistance is today often called revolution. This is, however, an ambiguous term. Revolution (*seditio*), in the traditional natural law doctrine, is usually applied only to illegitimate action (attack) against a just government. The traditional natural law doctrine regards active resistance as a legitimate right of the people when the highest goods of the community, such as the essential freedoms of the citizens, are directly exposed to the gravest danger, owing to the abuse of political power, and when no constitutional and peaceful possibilities of defense exist. What is meant is defensive action, not attack; not a private undertaking by individuals, but an action in the name of the community whose common good is being defended; hence, an organized defense undertaken by a substantial proportion of the people. The goods in question, as has been said, can be constitutionally guaranteed rights on which the basic political order is founded; or the existence of state and people may be at stake if the government, through its armament policy and its foreign policy, aims at an aggressive war or at provoking one. The object of resistance may be to bring back the government within the bounds of constitutional legality or, if this is not attainable, to remove, to overthrow the government.

The foundation generally accepted by the older natural law tradition for the right of active resistance lies in the *right of self-defense* against an unjust attack, which belongs to the communal person, the body politic, in exactly the same way and under the same conditions as to the individual person. These conditions call for a limitation of the action to the end and means of defense against the aggressor. This does not exclude killing the aggressor, if other methods of exercising the right of resistance are doomed to failure. In fact, it has always been the idea of natural law thinkers that, if the legitimate ruler abuses political power to the grave detriment of the community, he becomes a usurper and the enemy of the community, and the latter is justified in using the right of self-defense. The tyrant himself is the rebel, says *St. Thomas,* rather than the people; such a ruler may be resisted as one may resist robbers.[1] The ruler who abuses his power, *Grotius* says, following the natural law tradition, becomes the enemy of the people and thereby abdicates.[2] The objection that the abuse of a right does not cancel that right, has no force, because the right becomes altogether void through abuse if the abuse frustrates its end. This is precisely the condition for active resistance.

The representatives of the traditional natural law doctrine, like *Bellarmine* and *Suárez,* who justify active resistance not by appeal to the right of self-defense but by appeal to a right of the people as the original repository of political authority, come to the same practical conclusion. In their view, the tyrant (cf. Chap. 131) is acting contrary to the condition of legitimate exercise of power, according to which he is bound by the fundamental juridical order willed by the people, so that he surrenders his title. But the exercise of the right to transfer power to a new ruler, which thus reverts to the people, is justified, they say, only if the common good is in extreme danger and as long as existing rights are not infringed.

The whole traditional natural law doctrine emphasizes the idea that

[1] Cf. St. Thomas, *Summa theol.,* IIa IIae, q. 42, a. 2: "Magis autem tyrannus seditiosus est"; q. 69, a. 4: "Sicut licet resistere latronibus, ita licet resistere in tali casu malis principibus."

[2] Cf. Hugo Grotius, *De jure belli ac pacis,* Bk. I, chap. 4, n. 11: "Consistere enim simul non possunt voluntas imperandi, et voluntas perdendi; quare qui se hostem populi totius profiteretur, in eo ipso abdicat regnum."

the justification of the right of active resistance (apart from the two conditions just mentioned) depends on the *condition* of certainty that there will not arise from it an equal or a greater ill for the common weal than the tyranny which is to be overthrown.[3] They point out that, as the result of political disturbances, small, violent, and radical groups often eventually attain to power, or groups which are less concerned with the common good than with their own interest. For a twofold reason, therefore, traditional natural law doctrine has attached to the right of active resistance the condition that it be sufficiently organized: because it is in the interest of law to lead to a quick decision against an existing tyranny while avoiding a long civil war; to prevent the rise of a new tyranny from radical groups. The dangers in question explain why the natural law school of social ethics urges passive resistance (nonviolence) as the means by which the common good is best served in the great majority of cases, and why in practice it is very sceptical of armed active resistance. This need not conflict with the fact that, in certain circumstances, when the highest goods of a people are gravely threatened, it can be a duty for groups in key positions to organize active resistance, and a duty for individual citizens to take part.[4]

A *revolution* differs from active resistance in that it is against the legitimate political authority lawfully exercising its rights. Revolution, in the proper sense of the word, is violent insurrection to depose a legitimate government or to secure a considerable change in the constitution. It differs from active resistance inasmuch as there is no grave threat to the common good on the side of the government, and the government does not therefore forfeit its rights because of a grave abuse of power: revolution is an aggressive, not a defensive, action. According to natural law theory no reason can justify such a revolution: there is *no right to revolution* as a means of settling internal affairs with a legitimate government.

[3] Cf. the detailed and cautious discussion of the right of active resistance in T. Meyer, S.J., *Institutiones juris naturalis,* 1900, II, 523–36. On the German catastrophe 1933–45, cf. Max Pribilla, S.J., *Deutsche Schicksalsfragen* (2nd ed. of *Deutschland nach dem Zusammenbruch*), 1950, pp. 287–319, "Das Widerstandsrecht des Volkes," with references to old and new literature; *Die Vollmacht des Gewissens, Europäische Publikation E. V.,* 1956, pp. 13–135, "Deutsche Gespräche über das Recht zum Widerstand," especially the opinions of Hermann Weinkauf, Max Pribilla, Walter Künneth; Gerhard Ritter, *Carl Goerdeler und die deutsche Widerstandsbewegung,* 1954.

[4] With good reason Max Pribilla, S.J., *Deutsche Schicksalsfragen,* 1950, p. 310, condemns a one-sided emphasis on the dangers of active resistance, and even the transformation of passive resistance into a patient bearing of injustice, especially if political criminality, which recognizes no law, can only be kept within bounds by force: "At such times situations can arise, where it is not sufficient for Christians to pray and endure, but they also have the serious duty to defend themselves by returning force for force, in order to protect their members from untold injustice and sorrow and the gravest dangers to faith and morality; for we must not allow the power of the wicked to increase in the world through the weakness and faintheartedness of the good."

Any party or group conjuring up such a revolution and civil war is branded with all the wrong of a war of aggression; it is a crime against the community and its foundations.

A last form of resistance is the overthrowing of a tyranny by the *murder of the tyrant*. In the sixteenth and seventeenth centuries this was the subject of debates, both within and without the traditional natural law school, which brought the greatest minds into the field. The question was: Is assassination of a tyrant permissible or not? Some Catholic exponents of natural law doctrine thought they could give an affirmative answer under very special conditions; a number of outstanding Protestants came to the same conclusion. *Melanchthon* did not hesitate to suggest the murder of a tyrant to be a work pleasing to God, and to express the wish that someone might be found to assassinate *Henry VIII* of England.[5] The long and agitated debate fundamentally mirrored the deep, universal conviction of the entire Middle Ages that the political ruler does not stand above the law.

The outcome of the debate about the assassination of tyrants, for natural law theory, is the principle that the *murder* of a ruler by a private individual on his own responsibility or at the instigation of a factious minority can *never be a legitimate method of achieving political ends.* From our discussion of political resistance, it is evident that neither the killing of a legitimate ruler, who has not become a usurper by abuse of power, nor that of a usurper whose power has become legitimate and is not abused, can be justified as the overthrowing of a tyrant: in either case it would be sheer murder. The position is different (cf. above) if the tyrant has become a usurper by a serious abuse of political power. Then a legitimate authority still holding office (perhaps a court of justice) can inflict a death sentence which anyone is empowered to carry out; [6] more probably, however, the conditions for the citizens' right to self-defense, which justify the killing of the usurper as an ultimate means of defense if other means are wanting, can be found in people with a high sense of responsibility, who are sure that the will of the people supports their decision.[7]

[5] Cf. Melanchthon, "Ep. ad Vit. Theod.," 24 Aug., 1540, in *Corp. Reform.*, III, 1075 f.

[6] This seems to be the considered opinion of St. Thomas. In an earlier work he approves of Cicero's verdict (*De officiis*, I, 25) in favor of Caesar's assassins; he is praised and rewarded, says Thomas, who for the liberation of his country kills the tyrant who has usurped power by force, against the will of the citizens or by obtaining their consent through compulsion, and if there is no possibility of appeal to a superior authority (*II Sent.*, d. 44, q. 2, a. 2). In his later work he stresses the point that an evildoer may in no case be killed by a private person for the sake of the common good without a sentence having been passed by a competent authority; cf. *Summa theol.*, IIa IIae, q. 64, a. 3: "facere aliquid ad utilitatem communem . . . si sit cum nocumento alterius, hoc non debet fieri, nisi secundum judicium eius ad quem pertinet aestimare quid sit subtrahendum partibus pro salute totius."

[7] Thus also says Eberhard Welty, *Der Aufbau der Gemeinschaftsordnung*, Vol. II, *Herders Sozialkatechismus*, 1953, p. 268, of an unjust attack of an usurper: "Any one

In setting forth the principles of natural law on the right of resistance, especially active and violent resistance, social ethics can only describe hypothetical situations. In *political reality* the facts and conditions affecting the application of natural law principles as a rule are of great complexity and obscurity. In addition, rapidly changing political situations often require rapid decisions, which, for all these reasons, are a matter for the *individual conscience.* Ethics, however, has to show the gravity of the moral responsibility involved in such decisions and has to develop the principles that must govern them.

133. Forms of Government

When *Aristotle* in his *Politics* works out the classification of political forms, he is obviously not guided by a purely theoretical interest. His object is to examine the forms of government that history sets before him, with regard to their ability to realize justice. Since the deciding factor is the exercise of political power, which is governed by the form of constitution,[1] he proceeds from the fact that political power is always "in the hands of one or of a few or many," and names the three corresponding modes of exercise of political power: monarchy, aristocracy, and polity. Aristotle gives the criterion of justice by which they are to be judged: whether they are fit to exercise political authority in the *general interest.* Where the private interest of the rulers becomes predominant, there arise the deteriorations corresponding to these three forms: tyranny, oligarchy, and "democracy" (by "democracy" *Aristotle* means mob rule). Obviously a considerable change, now universally accepted, has taken place in this classification since *Aristotle's* day: democracy is no longer applied to mob rule but to a "government of the people, by the people, for the people," in the interest of justice.

Numerous other classifications have since been attempted.[2] What is true of nearly all theoretical classifications in the sphere of the social sciences holds true for this: reality is so complex, that any classification can only be a makeshift, enabling it to be more easily comprehended con-

---

of the people may obstruct him and in so doing, if necessary kill the usurper." Similarly, A. Bride in an exhaustive examination of the many opinions collected on the question, in *Dictionnaire de Théologie Catholique,* XV (Paris), 1947, column 2014, although with the well-founded proviso that with the development of modern democratic forms of government the killing of tyrants could only be justified in extremely rare cases. On the other hand, it must be taken into consideration that usurpation means precisely an encroachment in the basic democratic order by application of unlawful power.

[1] Cf. Georg Jellinek, *Allgemeine Staatslehre,* 3rd ed., 1919, p. 664: "It is a most ingenious thought of ancient political science that forms of government are identical with forms of constitution."

[2] Jellinek, *ibid.,* p. 667, indicates the contrast between monarchy and republic as "the most widely diverging fundamental types," but says himself that the dividing line is a purely formal one and reality knows only subspecies and mixed forms.

ceptually. As *Aristotle* himself is evidently aware, all three sound forms of political power, as well as the three perverted forms, can be divided into subspecies which differ widely from one another and admit of many transitional forms. An absolute monarchy, which is bound by moral and customary law, but not by positive law, is essentially different from constitutional monarchy, in which the ruler is bound by constitutionally fixed rules in the exercise of his functions; both share merely the name with titular monarchy, in which the exercise of political authority lies with a parliament; in the last case a polity, like the English, may well feel itself to be a democracy in a distinctive sense. Again, it can hardly be doubted that *Aristotle,* with his conception of the subordination of the individual to the state, would have included at least some of the totalitarian states of recent history, namely, the elective, or, as we should say today, the plebiscitary dictatorships, among the justifiable forms of monarchy, in spite of their suppression of the civil liberties held as fundamental to Western democracy. Indeed, all modern totalitarian states profess to be democracies in a higher sense, finally realizing the principle of "government of the people, by the people, for the people," whereas the formal democracies, it is claimed, have not passed beyond the stage of plutocracies.

Social ethics is concerned only with the principles for judging forms of states, not with appraising these forms individually, which, in view of the many transitional forms, could only lead to a casuistry with scant profit to understanding. These principles may be defined in the following way:

1. The fundamental consideration is the capacity of a political form to function for the realization of the greatest measure of the *common good.* Since historical experience has shown monarchies, aristocracies, and democracies, in their various forms, to be capable of this function, none of them is in itself less good than another as a political form. With obstinate firmness, therefore, natural law political theory has maintained the *moral neutrality of forms of government.* Their ability to serve the common interest is dependent, first, on legal rules binding on the government, whether based on a written constitution or on customary law. Next come the sociological conditions in which it has to work. Among these conditions, as *Aristotle* saw, a special place must be given to the economic and social ones. In a feudal system in which the ownership of land is accompanied by special duties of armed defense, an aristocracy may be the appropriate political form. The disproportionate inequality of ownership and of the distribution of industrial and financial power can, on the other hand, turn a democracy into a plutocracy. In the third place, among the conditions for the functioning of political forms, *moral* attitudes are of great significance. No unprejudiced person will deny that the perversion of historical political systems has nearly always been preceded by the moral perversion of the rulers, whether these have been Caesars or a patriciate or the people.

2. Since the common good itself is the product of a great number of

active forces, all political forms carry their inherent *advantages and disadvantages* according as they more or less make room for the one or other of these forces. These advantages are primarily the capability for quick action in the interest of the political community (political authority), stability of law and order, the security of the citizens' natural rights to freedom, and the possibility of progressive development of its common weal. Without doubt monocracy, in the form of a monarchy as well as in that of a dictatorship, is marked by a heightened capacity for action, since it is able to make swift decisions and take effective measures with relatively little interference from opposing parties, conflicting opinions, and changing moods. Hereditary monarchy has an added advantage since it guarantees, to an increased extent, stability and a continuity of development of the common weal. On the other hand, the safeguarding of the rights of the citizens and of the possibility of a progressive development of the common weal is more readily to be expected from a democracy, although the decline of Athens, after its unique development in the fifth century B.C., brought about by the undignified rivalries of parties, will always remain an example of how the "progress" and the prosperity of a polity are by no means necessarily best assured in a democracy.

3. The moral neutrality of individual forms of government and their relative advantages and disadvantages do not prevent our asking whether there is not a *best form*, namely, one that serves the purpose of insuring the exercise of political power in the best interest of the common good. The answer can be gained only from the experience of how human nature, on the average, reacts to the various forms of government. Supported by this experience, the traditional natural law school concludes with *Aristotle* that the *mixed* form of government is best.

Human nature being as it is, men readily give way to the inclination to misuse political power, held for the sake of the common good, for their own purposes and interests. The exercise of political power, therefore, should be subject to control. And since the moral limits of political authority are found in the rights of all the members of the community, and in the good of the people, which is its goal, and since, moreover, political authority is originally vested in the people as a whole (cf. Chaps. 129–130), there can be no question that the people's collaboration is demanded by the nature of the state to bring about the common good and to preserve the individual rights. Consequently, any good form of government must in practice embody the *democratic principle*. Concerning the form of collaboration, however, natural law principles of themselves say little, except by reference to definite historical, social, and cultural conditions.[3]

[3] Only in this qualified sense can one say with Jacques Maritain, *Man and the State* (London), 1954, p. 117, that whatever the form of the political regime may be, democratic philosophy appears as the only true political philosophy. In fact, however, there does not seem to be a democratic philosophy in the same sense for all peoples in the various conditions of their development; and also there is the radical difference between representative and plebiscitary democracy; in any case, modern democratism should be distinguished from a theory of democracy to be considered within the framework of natural law.

At the same time, a government cannot function in the real interest of the common good unless it is raised above the influences of an irresponsible demagogy and self-centered party politics and possesses a certain stability and sufficient authority for a vigorous initiative. Indeed, just as the people must be protected against the abuse of political authority, so also must political authority itself be protected against the abuse of political liberties to the detriment of the common good. Thus, in every political system which is to work in the interest of its intrinsic end, the *authoritarian principle* must be made sufficiently effective.

A detailed concern with the business of the state, however, is not every man's affair. Not all the citizens, as *St. Thomas* remarks, have the will or the capacity to concern themselves particularly with the polity. This requires a high sense of responsibility and more than average insight into the necessities of the common weal; all this implies a special education. A healthy state, then, needs a class which possesses these advantages. Above all, it must be the guardian of the great traditions and ideals of the nation; but it must also foresee future developments and requirements of the common good, and rouse the people to comply with these ideals and demands. For these reasons a strong admixture of the *aristocratic principle* is indispensable to any constitution. (We shall presently comment on the aristocratic principle in modern democracy in reference to *De Tocqueville*).

Our account of the mixed form of constitution will show that what is meant is not a mixture of political forms but a mixture of principles which is compatible with any political form. In whatever way these principles are combined, the constitution must lay special stress on one of these principles, insofar as the final decisive responsibility for the exercise of political power must be determined.

134. Modern Democracy

I *Its Basis*

Hardly anyone would dispute the proposition that modern democracy is the appropriate political form for culturally advanced peoples. If we begin our discussion of modern democracy with this proposition, we are in line with our earlier remarks on political ethics, except for the reservation that the idea of the absolute sovereignty of the people and two further ideas derived from it and characteristic of the individualist and collectivistic interpretations of democracy, the identification of democracy with the republican system and its identification with the totalitarian system, are to be regarded as in a separate category. In these two cases the principle of the absolute sovereignty of the people is pushed to obviously contradictory extremes: (1) the sovereignty of the people is irreconcilable with the rights of a hereditary monarch; (2) the people can by a plebiscitary surrender of its sovereignty, invest a party which claims totalitarian authority with absolute power.

One further point in our initial thesis requires comment. We said that democracy is the appropriate political form for culturally advanced peoples. In this we are thinking of peoples in whose members the responsibility for the management of the common weal is awake, so that cooperation in this is seen as part of the rights of man. Hence, the right of the citizens to a democratic political system does not have its foundation in the legal fact that political authority is originally vested in the people; rather, it has its foundation in the development of its juridical consciousness. In other words, the modern democratic political form is not drawn from primary natural law, which would make it an ideal to be striven for in all circumstances and by every political community. From the same premises it follows also that it is not an ideal to be forced upon peoples indiscriminately as socially progressive; still less is it an ideal to be foisted in a definite form, that has been developed by one people, upon other peoples. The fact that the democratic system cannot be derived from the abstract rights of the abstract individual, as individualist and collectivistic thinkers try to derive it, is sufficiently proved by the completely contrary systems which have been founded upon this premise. According to legal philosophy and legal ethics, the modern form of democracy can be founded only on the development of the concrete juridical consciousness of a people.

11 *The Characteristic Features of Modern Democracy*

The following features distinguish the modern idea of democracy from earlier forms of democracy. 1) *Sovereignty of the people:* modern democracy, in the well-known words of *Abraham Lincoln,* consists in "government of the people, by the people, for the people." The extent of the powers of government is defined by popular mandate in a constitution. 2) *The mass:* the people of a modern democracy is a mass in the quantitative sense of a large population of the territorial state in comparison with the city-state; it is a mass in the qualitative sense of a principle of formal equality, whereby every vote carries equal weight; and, in the sociological sense, it is a mass since the people constitutes itself politically by grouping itself in accordance with the free choice of the citizens, and not on the basis of military, political, economic, or other social functions, as, for example, in the democracy based on estates or occupational communities in the Middle Ages. By contrast with the latter, the democracy of the present day is mass democracy. 3) *Representation:* the people exerts its will in government not directly but through the representatives it elects. These, however, do not represent their constituency alone but the people as a whole. Hence, in their parliamentary activity, they are not exclusively committed to a special mandate from their constituencies and to the representation of quite definite and limited interests, but are primarily bound by their conscience in what they think to be in the interest of the common good. 4) *Universal franchise:* the representatives of the people are chosen by means of universal, direct, equal, and free franchise. The franchise is universal; it is not confined to classes distinguished by property or privileges, or to the male sex (exception: Switzerland). The election is direct: every vote is given directly for a deputy or a list, and not for an intermediary. It is equal: every citizen has one vote. It is free: the ballot is secret.

5) *Parliament:* the sovereign lawgiver in modern democracy is the parliament; it frequently takes the form of a two-chamber system. Decisions are made by means of a simple majority of the members or, in matters of great import, with a qualified (usually two-thirds) majority. 6) Modern democracy obtains its special character from the *party system:* by means of parties the people forms itself into groups sharing ideological and material interests. In contrast with, for example, the ancient city-state, the parties in the mass democracy are an indispensable agency for the formation of the political will and for the establishment of the mechanism necessary for this. In the party democracy it is the parties and not the electorate that nominate the parliamentary candidates. In order to influence and to win over the electorate, the parties make use of their party apparatus, which consists of party organization, propaganda (press, local offices, meetings), and party funds (made up of donations and members' contributions). Furthermore, the parties direct the voting in parliament with the aid of party discipline. 7) *The rule of law:* the rights of the government and the rights of the citizens are defined in the constitution (fundamental law of the state). The modern free democracy is a "constitutional democracy." No one, and no government, stands above a law thus constituted; all are responsible before the law and all are equal before it.

8) Western democracy is *pluralistic in character* (in contrast to the totalitarian single-party state). Western democracies are divided into those with two-party systems (the U.S.A., the United Kingdom), in which the majority party holds legislative power, and those with a majority-party system, in which legislative power is exercised by majority groupings of parties (coalitions), formed permanently or *ad hoc*, on the basis of compromise. 9) A basic feature of the free democracy is *control over the exercise of political authority:* provision against the abuse of political power by the government is made the most important element in the constitution and in the rights of parliament. 10) *Separation of powers* is regarded as indispensable to this control.[1] Underlying the principle of the separation of powers is the proposition that political liberties are assured only if the legislative and executive functions are performed by different

[1] It is generally admitted today that when Montesquieu developed his theory of the separation of powers in his famous work, *De l' esprit des lois,* 1748, he partly misunderstood the English Constitution, upon which he based his arguments. It is equally

persons or organs acting as a check on one another and keeping one another within their legal bounds. Experience has shown, however, that safeguards against the misuse of power are exercised no less advantageously by means other than the rigid separation of powers.

In *England,* the Cabinet, in which the executive power is vested, is formed from the majority party in Parliament; in practice, Parliament exercises the legislative power; thus, the executive can legalize all its acts so long as it holds the majority in Parliament. In addition, decisions of the courts can be set aside by legislation, but the judiciary cannot reverse acts of Parliament. Control is sought not in the separation of powers, but in ministerial responsibility: the ministers are answerable to Parliament for their conduct of office, and in regard to this they are called to account at "question time" in Parliament. To keep watch to see that Her Majesty's Government does not evade its responsibility to the people is the constitutional function of the opposition in the British Parliament, which is designated Her Majesty's Opposition. Of the separation of powers in the strict sense, therefore, there exists little more than the independence of the judges.

By contrast, as a result of a doctrinaire interpretation of the principles of *Montesquieu, France* in the time of the Third Republic sought to protect the rights of the citizens by means of a special administrative law and court of administration; furthermore, ministerial responsibility was pushed so far that the stability of governments was undermined. A number of democratic constitutions set up after the First World War followed France in these forms of separation of powers, particularly in establishing courts of administration and constitutional courts before which the citizen can seek his rights against the state.

In the *United States* the principle of separation of powers found its most rigid application in the Constitution of 1787. The executive power is vested in the president; he is directly elected by the citizens for a fixed period, and cannot be deposed by a vote of no confidence; the heads of departments of state are responsible solely to the president personally; the legislative power is vested in the Congress, consisting of the Senate and the House of Representatives, but the president can initiate legislation by a message to Congress, and he has a right to veto bills, which, however, can become law by a fresh vote taken by a qualified majority. Through the judicature, called the Federal Supreme Court, acts of the executive and the legislature can be declared contrary to the Constitution; should the legislature in such a case insist upon its will, it can carry through the law in question by the very complicated procedure of an amendment of the Constitution. Thus, the separation of powers is almost complete.

III *Criticism of Modern Democracy*

The criticism of modern democracy follows three main lines. They all refer to vital points in its structure.

certain that he himself was misunderstood when his theory was used as a basis for the American Constitution of 1787, with painstaking regard for strict separation of powers. Montesquieu himself does not think of a rigid separation of powers, but speaks of a distribution "de trois pouvoirs" (*ibid.,* Bk. XI, Chap. 6). The problem itself was not first seen by Montesquieu; it is already anticipated in Aristotle, *Politics,* IV, 14.

1. The principal objection is that democracy has failed in the face of the modern *social question.* In the century of modern democracy social antagonisms in nearly all countries have become extremely acute and have already led, in a considerable number of states, to the abolition or transformation of democracy. Democracy has not succeeded in achieving an economic and social system harmoniously combining freedom and order, or even in developing an idea of such a system. What democracy was able to do was no more than to alleviate, by means of social policy, the socially harmful consequences of unrestricted economic freedom. The welfare development must not blind us to the fact that the real problem, namely the socially just economic and social order, is still unsolved; rather, the conflicts of the organized economic and social interest groups in the pluralistic democracy make obvious the precarious situation of the commonweal, particularly when seen with an eye to the future.

2. A further point in the criticism of modern democracy relates to its actual *political mechanism.* It is far from being a government by the people. To a large extent it is a domination over the people by parties and party machinery. The nomination of electoral candidates depends upon the party organization and not upon the will of the people. In an expression of will in the legislative body the representative of the people is bound by party discipline; he knows that his re-election will not be supported by the party if he comes into conflict too often with party discipline. The direction of party policy itself, to some extent, is laid down by extra-parliamentary forces, above all today by economic interest groups (pressure groups), in no way answerable to the people. The parties themselves, when they are in power, are always prone to shape policy in the party interest; in order to exist in the struggle of party politics they must determine governmental policy with an eye to the next election. Thus, party politics readily comes before the abiding interests of the political common good in the conduct of the state. This is all the easier because the modern government has at its disposal a considerable propaganda apparatus, with which public opinion can be guided, lack of success can be concealed, minor failures can be turned into successes, and obvious blunders can be laid at the door of enemies of the government and of the "people."

On the other hand, opposition parties, by utilizing parliamentary methods, can cripple the whole parliamentary machinery and the work of the government purely as a matter of party tactics. Opposition parties have often prevented the passing of bills by means of filibustering speeches, at the same time making the parliament a forum for party propaganda. Party democracy, with its technique of propaganda, also provides a great opportunity for *demagogy,* especially at times of internal and external difficulties.

3. A still more serious point of criticism of modern democracy concerns the *limited capacity for action* of democratic governments. The reason is

very often the necessity of forming coalition governments and the dependence of these on the interest-based policies of the parties to the coalition. Such weakness in governments prevents a continuity of policy and the planning of far-sighted, necessary measures, particularly economic measures. There is danger of instability, particularly for "young" democracies, as a result of lack of tradition and experience, and this danger may be great in newly formed democracies in what were formerly colonial territories. The relatively great stability of the governments of Europe after the Second World War shows, as was already to be observed in the governments of Great Britain and America, that democracy is more than merely a political mechanism. Its expedient functioning presupposes moral and political qualities in the people which cannot be gained overnight, particularly political judgment and a political sense of responsibility. The limited power of action of democratic governments, in comparison with other political forms, constitutes a disadvantage particularly in international complications, a disadvantage which obviously needs consideration in the era of nuclear energy, with the hitherto undreamed of possibilities of military surprise. Not without reason, therefore, are questions such as these uttered: Will a centralization of powers be the outcome, incompatible alike with political and with social democracy, but imperative for the purpose of enhancing the possibility of quick decision and action? To what extent will the economic utilization of nuclear energy strengthen internal developments leading toward a centralized or socialistic planned economy? Because of these questions the criticism of democracy can but close with a large question mark with regard to the future even if, on the other hand (cf. Chap. 104), the nuclear age would not urgently demand an international organization in order to secure minimum standards of free society and democratic institutions in all countries, which alone can secure the preservation of mankind and civilization. Hence, democratic ideals may materialize in a different form, but the future of mankind seems to be bound up with them more than ever.

4. After the Second World War, developments leaving *popular representation out of account* are the subject of increasingly strong criticism of democracy and of concern for its future. Important decisions are transferred to extra-parliamentary bodies, but the authority of parliament and hence "legality" are procured for them. Dangers come from three directions. First, they come from the pressure groups, the industrial combinations (cf. Chap. 120). Groups seek to attain their will directly through their own organizations. This is done for the most part by influencing the formation of the political will (legislation) by means of "pressure" on the parties, and occasionally by direct pressure on the legislator (e.g., the threat of a political strike for the purpose of satisfying economic and social demands). In connection with this development, representation is turned into mechanical voting on preconceived decisions, that is, on

compromises, which are prepared beforehand by pressure groups outside parliament and are then brought forward by the parties for parliamentary approval. In addition, a considerable number of party members who hold leading positions in parliamentary life make up the secretaries and officials of these groups. In all countries having free democracy today, the literature [2] which is concerned with these facts is on the increase, however widely the development in different countries may vary, and however different the rates of progress.

Secondly, a constant extension of functions occurs at the expense of the legitimate sovereign power of the people and the government appointed by them, through administrative bureaucracy. "In view of the fundamental fact of the irresistible advance of bureaucratization," *Max Weber* as early as 1917 posed this as the vital question of democracy: "How can any warranty be offered, in view of the increasing indispensability of political bureaucracy and the resulting increase in its power position, since forces are available to keep this class, which is steadily gaining importance and predominance, within bounds and really control it? How will democracy be possible at all even only in this restricted sense?" [3]

Thirdly, the status of parliament and popular representation is en-

[2] Cf. Messner, *Der Funktionär, Seine Schlüsselstellung in der heutigen Gesellschaft,* 1961; Georges Burdeau, *Traité de science politique,* Vol. VI, *La démocratie gouvernante, son assise sociale et sa philosophie politique,* 1956. The theory of democracy in its original sense as starting out from the individual, says Burdeau, is not in keeping with the interplay of pluralistic social forces in the mass, with their "constitutional" consequences; he sees the necessity for some way for the state to assert itself in face of the "society" intent on the furtherance of group interests, but does not know what to suggest. In German, special mention may be made of Ernst Forsthoff, *Verfassungsprobleme im Sozialstaat,* 1954. For a sociological analysis of the development underlying the danger to democracy cf. Hans Freyer, *Theorie des gegenwärtigen Zeitalters,* 1955, especially the conception of the "secondary system" ("secondary" in contradistinction to the natural "primary" forms of community), namely, the kind of control exercised by the organized material world over man, the formation of man through economic organization and political apparatus, technique and party ideology. How clearly Max Weber saw the facts in question and understood how to interpret them can be seen from his *Gesammelten politischen Schriften,* 1921, pp. 149 ff., now Max Weber, *Staatssoziologie,* J. Winckelmann, editor, 1956, pp. 45 ff. The constitutional legal aspect of the development in question is stressed by Hans Huber, "Die Umwälzungen im Staatsgefüge durch die Verbände," in *Ordo, Jahrbuch für die Ordnung von Wirtschaft und Gesellschaft,* Vol. VII, 1955, p. 192: "In the Western states, constitutional coordination is lacking with regard to the egoistic group organizations. These have actually, but not legally, become a constitutional factor of the first order. The written constitution keeps quiet about them and their role. Through this the normative constitution with its distribution of powers is in reality left out of consideration. The groups, to be sure, do not wish to change their label of status: it is to their advantage if they only appear to be private legal organizations, which strive for so-called 'solutions in private law' to social and economic questions and of whose power and influence on the state nothing is said. It is not, however, a question of designation, but of actual functions. Already today the unions distinguish themselves by playing an intensive part in political will-formation and power of decision, in various degrees and in various forms."

[3] Max Weber, *op. cit.,* pp. 152 f.

dangered by a kind of self-effacement, that is, by delegating its legislation, particularly in the form of authorizing ministries to execute laws [4] (cf. Chap. 139).

IV *The Reform of Democracy*

The rise of totalitarian states has again confirmed the old lesson of experience that political liberty offers the best opportunities for truth and justice, those two fundamental poles of the whole of human and social life, and that even the possibility of the misuse of this liberty can be no real argument against a democratically founded order of freedom. With this experience the conviction of the natural law school is fully in accord, that truth and justice by themselves, when they are brought sufficiently close to man, appeal to the deepest instincts of his spiritual nature. But if democracy offers such an opportunity for political liberty, what are the *conditions for making democracy itself secure?* What reforms are necessary to meet the dangers threatening modern democracy?

1. Undoubtedly the fundamental reform must be considered to be the development of formal democracy toward *socially integrated democracy*. This means the joint responsibility and partnership of all citizens in the performance of those very ordering functions of economic and social life, upon which depends the attainment of the end of the national economy, the general welfare. Political democracy denies its own ideals and its spiritual foundations if it is not capable of evolving socially integrated democracy. Political franchise alone can lead only to the formation of a government in whose hands lies the responsibility for the guidance of the social economy: socially integrated democracy signifies direct participation of all members of the social and economic community in this responsibility. Socially integrated democracy is in no way synonymous with the right of joint control, profit-sharing, joint ownership. It is not the socialist provider state and not the socialist "economic democracy" or "communal economy" (*gemeinwirtschaft*). The expression, "industrial democracy," used in America denotes in a different way what we mean by our expression. We prefer the expression "socially integrated democracy" first, because it is not only a question of economy, still less of the industrial sector, but of the whole social system; and secondly, because what is in question is an ordering function concerned with the social process, and not the democratic management of business concerns by the workers or state authorities. The aims, organization, functions, and methods of socially integrated democracy, taken from the economic angle, will be dealt with in Book IV.

2. A further crucial question for the development of democracy is that

[4] How much the question also occupies English thinking may be seen from C. K. Allen, *Law and Orders: An Inquiry into the Nature and Scope of Delegated Legislation and Executive Powers in England*, 1945; for examples, cf. J. Messner, *Die soziale Frage*, pp. 623 f.

of *leadership*. The representatives whom the people send to parliament do not receive a limited mandate merely to represent their constituents, but a commission to act conscientiously for the good of the polity. The question is then: Are these representatives capable of the task of governing, are they conscious of their responsibility, and are they also willing to assume responsibility where measures are required which, although at the moment unpopular, are in the true interest of the polity? The answer is that democracy, to fulfill its true functions, requires an aristocracy of mind and character. With every problem in political, economic, and social life becoming more complex, the solution of the leadership problem in modern democracy has become steadily more difficult as well as more urgent. Besides, the overwhelming influence of party organizations and the rule of "party bosses," the high average age of the representatives nominated by the ruling party clique, the financial dependence of a large portion of the representatives upon the party coffer, subjection to party discipline—these factors go a long way to prevent the emergence of an intellectual aristocracy in modern democracy. Evidently the problem is fundamentally an educational one.[5]

This problem of an aristocracy, however, is by no means simply a problem of the education of leaders; it is also a problem of their selection. *De Tocqueville* is certainly right with his remark, in a letter to *J. S. Mill,* that it is a lesser question for democracy to find the means for government by the people than to bring the people to elect the men most fitted for governing.[6] This question, too, has ultimately only one answer: the education of the electorate. Modern democracy can function and continue to exist only if the people's political judgment and sense of political responsibility develop. Not that the amount of knowledge and judgment which must be expected of the professional politician and the statesman could be expected of every citizen. His education should, however, equip him to see through political catchwords and slogans and to appraise ideological illusions for what they are, and not as genuine solutions. In this process of education the principal role belongs to the press, and in particular to the popular press.

[5] In England, the public schools, recently much criticized, from which for a long time the greater part of the members of the British Parliament have been drawn, have notably been able to supply, by means of the intellectual and moral attitude which they foster, an essential requirement for the functioning of British democracy up to now.

[6] Cf. De Tocqueville, *Oeuvres et correspondance, inédites,* 1861, II, p. 56: "Il s'agit bien moins pour les partisans de la démocratie de trouver les moyens de faire gouverner le peuple, que de faire choisir au peuple les plus capables de gouverner, et de lui donner sur ceux-là un empire assez grand pour qu'il puisse diriger l'ensemble de leur conduite, et non le détail des actes, ni les moyens d'exécution. Tel est le problème. Je suis parfaitement convainçu que de la solution dépend le sort des nations modernes." J. S. Mill, the convinced adherent and champion of the liberalist idea of the world and society, shows in his work, *Considerations on Representative Government,* 1861, 1907 ed., pp. 70 ff., 94, the necessity of safeguards against the danger for democracy in the lack of education of the citizens, and even considers the possibility of plural voting.

But here again there is a vicious circle. The *newspapers* read by the broad mass of the pople are party inspired organs. These make abundant use of the greatest power in the hands of the press, which, according to a well-known remark of a newspaper magnate, is the power to suppress information. That is to say, matters are withheld from the public, the knowledge of which is needed for the formation of an objective judgment in questions of public interest. It is not too much to say that, as long as the press itself is not fully conscious of its responsibility, the education of the people to a sense of responsibility and of political judgment is almost impossible, and hence the future of democracy itself is in danger. All this shows unmistakably that *democracy is at bottom a moral problem,* and that it ultimately depends upon moral qualities whether, and how far, the "government of the people, by the people, for the people" can become and remain a reality.

3. A further problem of reform, upon which much depends for the future of democracy, is the strengthening of the government's *authority,* which, although bound by law, is indispensable for the fulfillment of the common weal function of the government. This is of vital importance in the pluralist party state, when the government is formed by the coalition of parties and is subject to the interests of short-sighted party policies and chance majorities in parliament. In the two-party state, on the other hand, as in England (the liberal party is too small to be effective), all authority rests, at least theoretically, in the majority party in power, so that all the liberties characteristic of English democracy "are admittedly at the mercy of a party majority in parliament."[7] The reason for this is the lack of any legally binding authority by written constitution. The majority party is of course subject to a very alert public opinion, constantly activated by the opposition. A valuable suggestion for answering our question may be gained from the Constitution of the United States. There the government is made independent of the whims of parliamentary machinery, since the Constitution confers on the president, who is elected directly by the people, more powers and functions than those exercised by the prime minister in any other democracy; furthermore, he is free from ministerial responsibility to the Congress. In view of the dangers of concentration of power in the mass democracy, and on the other hand of the necessity of strengthening the "authoritarian principle" in the puralist party state, one may well say that among modern deliberately chosen democratic institutions, the American, with the controls provided, has so far steered the safest course between the Scylla of a paralyzing governmental impotence and the Charybdis of a hypertrophic governmental authority. Indeed the powers of the government can be very wide if there are correspondingly strong control institutions to guard against their abuse.

4. A most urgent problem is set before democracy by the inroads made into the political field by the *pressure groups.* Possibilities of reform can

[7] J. W. Gough, *Fundamental Law in English Constitutional History,* 1955, p. 211.

be seen to take chiefly two directions. First, great hope is placed on a progressively better instructed public opinion. In fact, developments in all Western democracies since the Second World War show that, if they go too far in their policy of self-interest, the big pressure groups come up against the opposition of public opinion, which has made it possible for governments somehow to guard the general interest. In the last hundred years the mode of functioning of public opinion has undergone a fundamental change as a result of the great increase in general education as well as the providing of information by press, radio, and television. Another hope of subordinating group interests to the common interest may rest, as *Grabowsky* realistically remarks, on the "existence of large parties," since "within the parties and sections the same happens as with a government conscious of its task: a balancing of group interests, which nearly always strive against each other, and also a considering of the standpoint of the consumer." As an illustration of his view he refers to the United States; there is nevertheless the danger, he concedes, that the two large parties may compete for the support of the great pressure groups and agree to demands which run counter to the common interest; should this be done by one party, however, the other would gain a valuable weapon of propaganda.[8]

The second main direction in which the solution of our problem is to be sought is that of a *constitutional "incorporation" of the pressure groups.* The proposals concerning this are not very precise. Proposals to allow the institution for political will-formation to be constituted by representations of interest groups instead of by political parties are wholly misleading. *H. J. Laski,* speaking of the United States, suggests "an independent political party" of the trade unions; [9] logically, political parties for the other pressure groups should also be considered. A very massive attempt was made in connection with the corporatist movement by *Michael Manoilescu,* at that time Professor in Bucharest, to account for all state law in terms of the will of the people grouped in economic organizations, and even to assign entirely to these the right of political will-formation. According to his proposals, the "corporative parliament" would have to exercise the entire legislative power, which in present-day democracy belongs to the parliament.[10] Few today would be inclined to subscribe to such opinions, which are incompatible with the whole idea of democracy.[11] For, democracy should insure respect for just those values in public

[8] Cf. A. Grabowsky, *Politik im Grundriß,* 1952, pp. 223 f.

[9] Cf. H. J. Laski, *Trade Unions in the New Society* (Sidney Hillman Lectures, 1949; U.S.A.), 1950, p. 102.

[10] Cf. M. Manoilescu, *Le siècle du corporatisme: Doctrine du corporatisme intégral et pur* (Paris), 1934, pp. 164 ff., 325–49; Manoilescu has become internationally known, especially through his book which appeared in French in 1931, and in German, in a revised and enlarged edition in 1937; *Die nationalen Produktivkräfte und der Außenhandel: Theorie des internationalen Warenaustausches.*

[11] The fact should not be overlooked that on the socialistic side, with its idea of "economic democracy," a train of thought is pursued which would give the central

life and in the ordering of public affairs which must be placed above the particular interests of organized social and economic groups and which must determine how the general interest is to be secured.

In fact, the constitutional incorporation of pressure groups could only come about through the separation of political and economic representative bodies and the division of their functions. The balancing of economic interests would be a matter for an economic chamber. On the other hand, political will-formation is exclusively the concern of the body of elected representatives, which has to care for the common interest in accordance with viewpoints and standards of values which are not purely economic. Only this body can look after the common interest, because it represents the whole nation, whereas the representatives of pressure groups always serve their group interests first. Moreover, the economic power of the groups works to the prejudice of those which have a weaker organization or even none at all. Details of the status and function of an economic chamber will be discussed (cf. n. V, 2 of this chapter) when we deal with systems of representation.

v *Crucial Points in the Democratic Machinery*

Modern democracy has developed primarily *four* devices for ascertaining the will of the political community and for insuring its influence on the executive. These are the electoral system, the system of representation, the compromise, and the majority decision. All these devices offer an abundance of questions of expediency for the political theory. It is for ethics to bring into the foreground the ends which these devices must ultimately serve.

1. *The electoral system.* Democracy is meant to be government of the people by the people. The first problem is, then, to find the real will of the people. Since the people does not exercise power directly, but only through representatives, this question becomes that of the method of electing the representatives. Two main systems have been evolved, majority representation and proportional representation. Under the majority system, as used in England, several candidates can contest the single seat in one constituency. The candidate obtaining the most votes is elected, however small his majority. Under the system of proportional representation, which is the rule in most democratic countries today, large constituencies are formed, so that, for example, eight deputies are allotted to about half a million inhabitants. Votes are given for party lists. The number of candidates elected from each list corresponds to the number of votes cast for that list as a multiple of the figure which forms the proportion of the total poll necessary for the election of one candidate. The

---

organs of economic autonomous corporations legislative powers in common with the political parliament; cf. Messner, *Die soziale Frage*, 1956, pp. 597 f.

ineffective votes cast for any list in each constituency are totalled for the whole country and credited to other candidates of the same party.

To what extent do these two electoral systems answer their purpose? The manifest advantage of the *majority system* is the greater contact between the candidate and his constituency, and consequently the strengthening of his sense of responsibility as a deputy; other benefits are a grouping of the community into a smaller number of parties (e.g., the two-party and later three-party system in England) and possibly a more active interest on the part of the electors in the questions at issue in an election. The chief disadvantage of majority representation is that, if three party candidates are nominated, the successful candidate often obtains fewer than half the total of the possible votes for the constituency. The majority of the constituency is then without representation. Possibly the government itself may obtain fewer than half the votes of the electorate, and yet these votes give it the constitutional authority to exercise a deep and lasting influence on the destiny of the nation. In the country which is the classical example of majority representation, Great Britain, critical voices are raised today in favor of proportional representation, although in view of the English respect for tradition they cannot count on success.

What are the pros and cons of the *proportional system*? Since the time of *J. S. Mill*, the chief advantages quoted are that the people's will is ascertained with numerical exactness, political programs of every shade can find adequate expression in the representative body, and minority parties can exert the full influence warranted by their numbers. Among the disadvantages, the first is the danger of a multitude of parties, because the collecting of votes cast for individual parties from the whole country gives even small parties their chance to obtain seats. Recently, attempts have been made to set limits to party splintering, so that parties which do not obtain a minimum percentage of the total votes are denied any mandate; with this there is the danger, however, that the formation of new parties with worthwhile aims will be prevented or made difficult. The result of party splintering is that, as a rule, only coalition governments can be formed that lack stability because they are based upon too many parties. A particular disadvantage is that the parties, under pressure of the organizations closely connected with them, have to nominate officials of such organizations for election who, hardly known to the electors, strengthen the influence of the pressure groups on the formation of the political will of the parliament. As a final disadvantage it may be mentioned that voting for a list encourages decisions in favor of sweeping programs, with catchy slogans thrown out by a financially powerful electoral propaganda machine, thus tending to open the door to electoral demagogy and radicalism.

If we review the advantages and disadvantages of the two electoral systems, one thing will become clear: [12] in the ascertainment of the peo-

[12] Any further purely abstract discussion of the two electoral systems must remain unfruitful. Only an inquiry into the sociological conditions determining the functioning

ple's will it must always be remembered that the body of elected representatives is not an expression of the real will of the people, but an approximation, and thus only a *fiction.* It is all the more a fiction since a very large part of the electorate has no well-considered will on the questions at issue. This would require a sober examination of party programs, party promises, and party tactics, as well as of the internal and external needs of the country, which many voters are not willing or even in a position to undertake. The fictitious character of the popular will is hardly essentially reduced by the direct plebiscite ("direct democracy") in individual questions of importance. For, only in rare cases can the questions be formulated other than in a simplified form. Their importance, therefore, is either not conveyed to the minds of the masses or a battle of catchwords is encouraged.[13]

Two main forms have developed: by popular vote (referendum), in a general plebiscite on a specific question the individual voter replies with a Yes or No; by popular demand (initiative), if a given number of electors demand it, a bill dealing with a certain question must come up for consideration, according to the regular procedure, before the legislative body. In spite of objections seriously raised, the plebiscite, in face of ideologically stiffened parliamentary fronts in individual questions of conscience (e.g., educational rights of parents, constitutional changes involving basic liberties), can be an indispensable method of arousing consciences. For this very reason the direct referendum should be envisaged for only very rare and exceptional cases. Totally different from direct democracy is plebiscitary democracy in the form it takes in the totalitarian states, by which the direct plebiscite serves to "legalize"[14] a government and its program.

Nothing will so much reduce the fictitious character of the popular will as expressed in general elections as a developed *sense of responsibility in the citizens.* This must show itself chiefly in three ways: first, by a conscientious participation in the elections; secondly, by keeping close contact with their representatives and urging their will upon them in all

---

of the one or the other electoral system in the democracy of the individual country can lead to a grasp of concrete purposes of reform. There is, however, a principle, with the help of which the defects connected with the two systems may really be overcome and for which good reasons, based on natural law, can be adduced. Whoever maintains it to be wholly utopian may be startled to find it expressed many years ago (before 1933) by the chairman of the German Reich electoral authority, E. F. Wagemann, *Wagen, Wägen, Wirtschaften,* 1954, p. 16: "Why, I ask, do not minors have the right to participate in elections just as they have property rights and the right of succession? As this right would have to be exercised by their parents, it is attacked from the radical side, purely because they could see it would be augmenting the fathers' and mothers' votes."

[13] Cf. Hans Nawiasky, "Von der unmittelbaren Demokratie; die Bereitschaft der Schweiz—die Zurückhaltung in Deutschland," in *Rechtsstaat und Demokratie,* in *Festg. für Z. Giacometti* (Zürich), 1953, pp. 195 ff.

[14] These words are true of the last-mentioned form of plebiscite: "The plebiscite is a manifestly undemocratic institution, since its source lies in the government, not in the people, and since it uses democratic forms purely as camouflage" (A. Grabowsky, *Politik im Grundriß,* 1952, p. 209).

questions of importance; thirdly, by continuous alertness to the activities and behavior of the parties with regard to the vital issues of the polity. The first of these responsibilities calls for further comment. In times when the legal fundamentals in a polity are assured and it is chiefly matters of expediency that are in question, the individual citizen has no serious moral obligation to trouble himself about his part in the formation of the political will of the community. It is quite otherwise when elections to parliament involve decisions about questions of the fundamental order of the common weal which affect the essential functions of the common good and the natural rights of the citizens. Then, participation in the general election becomes a question of conscience. If an election offers well-grounded expectations of a decisive success for parties which, for example, seek to deny religion its place in public life, eliminate religious education, curtail the parents' rights over the education of their children, or other rights connected with the freedom and the responsibility of the human person, there is no doubt that the Christian has a serious moral duty to vote, and to vote to the best of his judgment in such a way as to frustrate those expectations.

2. *The system of representation.* The combinations of Upper House and Lower House in England, Senate and House of Representatives in the United States, Council of the Republic and National Assembly in France, Federal Council and Federal Diet in the German Federal Republic, National Council and Federal Council in Austria, may be regarded as the main types of systems of representation. Among the most prominent purposes of popular representation in the history of modern democracy is the preservation of the rights and interests of the people from governmental encroachments. Protection against arbitrary and extortionate taxation has been almost everywhere the strongest motive force in the evolution of constitutional democracy. The right of granting power to levy taxes offered a means for increasing parliamentary control over the whole activity of the government. To be the people's champion vis-à-vis the government is the fundamental function of a parliament.

But, it is ever more obvious that the state, as a unity, equally needs a protector of its essential and permanent interests, in view of the progressive encroachment by party and group forces. The state itself needs some safeguard against the people, the political authority against a misuse of political liberties, and the political common good against the vested interests in society.[15] The real function of a second chamber may be said to consist in this. The second chamber performs a genuine function only when it is an advocate for the polity as against the people, when it

[15] C. Frantz, whom we are following in these ideas, remarks in his *Naturlehre des Staates*, pp. 356 ff.: "The people requires only one representative body; a second is more than a luxury, since it would mark the first as defective." Together with "people's representation," he therefore calls for "state representation" to "assert the ideas and interests of the state; this cannot be expected or demanded of the people's representative body; it would be contrary to its origin and even its end."

defends the essential and permanent interests of the common good against the mere group interests of parties and against a sheer opportunist policy of balancing these interests.

Hence, the second chamber must serve to realize the aristocratic principle in the state (cf. Chap. 133). Those appointed to the second chamber, then, should be persons of repute, experience, character, and judgment. In nearly all discussions of the two-chamber system a further, and apt, reason given for the need of the second chamber is that the rights of the people would not be sufficiently guaranteed by a single chamber, since parliamentary controls might fail against a government which could rely on the absolute majority of a single party. To offer a further guarantee against the unconstitutional ambitions of a government is certainly an important function of a second chamber, particularly at a time when political and economic power can be concentrated in the hands of the government, for instance, by an extensive nationalization of big concerns. The second chamber will, it is true, be able only to exercise the controlling function on behalf of state interests as such, if it is constitutionally endowed with the necessary authority. It will not be able to do this insofar as it is merely a repetition of the first chamber, if, for instance, its members are appointed strictly on the federative principle (which certainly calls for some defense in face of the present-day tendency in states toward centralization) in accordance with the position of the parties in the territorial bodies ("federal states"), or if they are appointed wholly by their governments.

Closely connected with the question discussed above of a regulation of the constitutional position of interest groups is the question of an *economic chamber*. Much has been said for and against it. Should it possess legislative power? What laws should it pass? Economic laws? But nearly all economic questions also affect the general interest, whose protection is the task of the parliament itself. Besides, the parties in the existing parliaments are themselves largely grouped according to economic and class interests, so that an economic chamber with a share in legislation would be a repetition rather than something new; therefore, it would duplicate, instead of diminishing, the frictions in the working of the parliamentary machinery. Moreover, if an economic chamber exercised a determining influence on the legislative power the result would be a still further amalgamation of economics and politics, a malady from which democracies of the present day are already suffering severely.

These arguments against legislative economic chambers do not, however, tell against a chamber with advisory functions. Such a chamber could prove itself most suitable in face of the dangers which arise for democracy in the pluralist society organized according to group interests. A prerequisite for such a constitutional central economic chamber would be the development of economic and social infrastructures with self-government on the national, regional, and local levels. Members would be appointed by the self-governing economic bodies of the functional groups (agriculture, industry, crafts, trade, etc.), and not by general vote. Only the local and, at the most, the regional self-governing organs would be elected by all group members. The fundamental questions of national economic policy would have to be discussed by the central economic chamber, which would in particular provide permanent committees for important sectors of the economy, and special committees, as required, for specific questions. These committees would have to furnish the legislative body with expert advice in all questions of economic and social legislation; well-documented majority and minority opinions could be put forward by the various groups concerned (cf. Chaps. 85, 181). A chamber with such functions would link up with a development which has grown out of the parliamentary system itself: the development of permanent and special parliamentary committees with their advisory functions. The chief burden in dealing with economic questions of particular interest for individual groups of society, would be transferred to committees directly concerned with such questions. These would not be parliamentary committees but committees of the economic chamber, formed by self-governing bodies of the social economy. In these committees the interest groups would have to try to balance the conflicting interests (possibly with majority and minority opinions), and to consider carefully the implications of such balancing for the individual groups and the general interest. The legislative body, freed from the immediate pressure of interest groups, would be able to do justice to its task and give first consideration to the general interest. The state would be more free for its task of serving the common interest, the common good, because the balancing of interests would take place prior to reaching parliament, and therefore in the nonpolitical sphere. Only by transferring the balancing of interests to this sector is it possible to conceive a constitutional incorporation of the interest groups in the order of democracy without prejudice to its foundations.

It is often rightly emphasized that the interest groups "relieve the state in many ways, since through their offices, their secretaries, their inquiries, and their records they are active in clarification and preparation; did they not exist, other officials and authorities would be necessary." *Grabowsky* is of the opinion that this would not be wrong, "but on the other side the groups again burden the state with their stormy, never-ending demands; for they demand thorough investigations to clarify the questions raised and to balance interests." The inference, however, seems to be other than that which *Grabowsky* links with the fact "that the groups are no longer to be thought out of existence and that every move against them is tilting against windmills." The provision of material for group discussions is certainly their own affair, but they should themselves be obliged to seek and to argue a compromise which can be vindicated before the general interest. Only thus will the political parliament as a legislative body, that is the state, be able to satisfy the obligation toward the common good, because then the pressure of the groups will be substantially removed. No solution of the crisis of democracy which has grown out of the advance of the interest groups in the political field, is provided by the mere claim: "In this situation the state, as a political factor, has the eminent task of balancing the interests of the groups against one another, and then, where they overlap, of restoring them to their limits," and therefore has "superior, supervisory, and determining functions." [16] This claim is no solution, because the "state" in the pluralistic democracy is the government, which is appointed by parliament under pressure of the groups. That the legislator, the parliament, and the government, and hence the "state," is today so continuously exposed to the pressure of interest groups, and therefore lacks ability to fulfill its "eminent task" (as *Grabowsky* too sees it), this is the situation and the problem: the menace to the foundations of democracy.

3. *Compromise.* Modern democracy is an offspring of the belief in human reason of the Enlightenment period. The idea was that the government to which the maximum amount of reason was applied must yield a maximum of general welfare. In this theory of democracy the maximum application of reason is expected from the all-round discussion of questions of public life and from the participation of all the citizens. Discussion alone, however, is not yet decision. The way to arrive at decision is likewise in the appeal to reason, that is, persuasion. The decision in favor of a cause would then be determined by the superiority of rational arguments. The object would be the consent of the governed as the basis of government, the way to which is prepared by discussion and persuasion. Consent itself does not necessarily consist in the unqualified agreement of all. It often takes the form of compromise, agreement in spite of conflicting opinions. Against this theory of democracy the reality of pluralist society today proves just as much to be the outcome of the groups' confidence in their *power* as the working of *reason.* Consequently added significance is given to the ethics of compromise.

The test of the *genuine* compromise is whether it does justice to the essential positions from different points of view, so that consent is conscientiously possible for all participating groups. On the enactment of a bill based on such a compromise, the opposition, even though it formally voted against it, would in fact accept the law if it found that its point of view was sufficiently respected. According to the whole idea of democracy, true compromise is the positive goal for the machinery for the formation of the will of the democratic community. Essentially different from true compromise is *tactical* compromise, the object of which is only a temporary solution. Parties give their consent to it as the lesser evil, with the immediate intention of by-passing some difficulty in the

[16] A. Grabowsky, *op. cit.,* pp. 223 f.

democratic machinery, and the further intention of resuming the struggle, when opportunity offers, in order to improve the compromise in their favor. Another reason why a party enters into tactical compromises may be that, in matters which lie closer to its more fundamental interests, it finds other parties accommodating and hence is able to reach an acceptable compromise in such matters. A party adhering to natural law principles with regard to private property may be justified in entering into a compromise in questions of socialization, even if it regards a compromise that is inconsistent with the real demands of the common good. But such a party, by compromising, may be able to prevent much more radical measures; it may also hope to exert a moderating influence in the process of socialization; and it may expect by this means to work more easily for a later rehabilitation of the principle of private property. In nearly all matters where moral principles are involved, similar borderline cases may arise in which tactical compromise can be justified in order to avoid a greater evil.

By no means, therefore, need all justification be denied to tactical compromise; situations may arise, even in questions concerning religious and moral principles, in which the common good not only justifies but demands the policy of the lesser evil. It may be remembered that the idea of such compromise was already thoroughly familiar to the great champions of natural law in the Middle Ages, although they did not use the expression (cf. Chap. 49, esp. note 15), which is the more remarkable in view of the outwardly solid acceptance of religious and moral principles in those centuries. Likewise, the wide value of compromise as a constituent part of the legal and political order was seen and discussed by them (cf. Chaps. 40–41) in connection with their realistic interpretation, in line with natural law ethics, of the historical and social factors governing the realization of law. We have endeavored in these chapters to carry their ideas further; in the modern democracy of a pluralist society, with its party and group interests, almost all decisions regarding state, economy, and social policy, as well as foreign policy and international relations, are for the most part matters of compromise.[17]

Compromise is indeed the very *touchstone of democracy*. The further the tactics of compromise remain removed from true compromise, the more a *fiction* determined by party and power interests takes the place of a democratic way of life. The politically irresponsible then refuse to see the essential lasting interest of the community, are intent on party interests, and reject concessions out of sheer party dogmatism. The result is tactical compromises so precarious that, if they are frequently

[17] Cf. W. Adolf Jöhr, *Der Kompromiß als Problem der Gesellschafts-Wirtschafts- und Staatsethik,* 1948; Hans Steubing, *Der Kompromiß als ethisches Problem,* 1955, deals with compromise from the standpoint of Protestant theological ethics, and hence only as a matter for the individual conscience, with the unsatisfactory conclusion: "Thus also here, *faith* is left as the final and only *answer* to all problems of compromise."

employed, they not only render impossible any government in the true interest of the general weal but also gravely discredit democracy. The purely tactical compromise can, on the other hand, also be the instrument of a cheap *opportunism* which, sparing itself the trouble of seeking for real solutions based on principles and serving the common good, follows the path of least resistance and watches for every opportunity of exploiting the situation for party interest. But, according to the whole logic of democracy, such an opportunism must sooner or later end in disaster: either the democratic machinery eliminates unprincipled parties or else it comes to grief through them. We shall not be in error in regarding it as a general rule that as soon as purely tactical compromise begins to prevail, the spiritual and moral foundations of democracy fail and there arises a growing threat from antidemocratic forces ready to replace the majority rule based on objective discussion and the demands of public opinion by minority rule based on physical power.

4. *The majority decision.* The real crux of the democratic machinery for the expression of the will of the community is the majority principle. In itself democracy is that form of state in which the people as a whole is responsible for the conduct of the business of state. In fact, if the will of the people is not united, a decision concerning the conduct of the state can only be made according to the majority principle. From this, theorists of democracy, like *Bryce* in his important work on the theory of democracy, draw the simple conclusion that democracy is a form of political community in which the ruling power belongs to the majority; no other method of determination may be found.[18] By such a proposition, however, an obvious inconsistency in the theory of democracy would be admitted: according to the idea of democracy, it is in the people as a whole that the political authority resides; in fact, however, as *Bryce* says, in democracy the majority rules over the minority. All that can be done, says *Bryce,* is to place a bridle on majority rule and to protect the community against hasty, ill-considered legislative acts of the majority. He arrives, in substance, at the following possibilities: [19] restriction of the field of normal legislation by the constitution, so that legislation in exactly defined spheres will assume the character of an alteration in the constitution, which can take place only by means of a cumbersome procedure; a right of veto to be held by the executive, as in the United States, requiring the initiation of a fresh process of legislation; direct consultation of the people; a two-chamber system, in which the second chamber would be given the function of sharing in decisions or revising them; the division of powers.

What is the deeper connection between these methods of checking majority rule and the idea of democracy, which makes *reason, objective argument,* and *free consent* the basis of government? This connection

[18] Cf. J. Bryce, *Modern Democracy,* 1921, I, p. 23.
[19] Cf. *ibid.,* II, pp. 428 ff.

lies, as Professor *Ernest Barker* shows in his outstanding book on the theory of democracy,[20] in the resumption of public discussion, with the object of prolonging it in time and widening the circle of those taking part in it. The provision for a veto has as its aim a new discussion of a measure already voted upon. The more roundabout procedure of constitutional changes involves a retarding of legislation on momentous questions, which precludes precipitancy and causes an all-round examination of the subject. The two-chamber system, and still more the consultation of the people, extend the circle of the discussion. Consequently, the mental character of democracy does not admit the simplified majority principle, as suggested in *Bryce's* definition. For, since by the idea of democracy a discussion is only formally ended by a majority decision in which opinions have not only been counted but weighed by the value of their arguments, the will of the minority is also always represented, as *Barker* points out, in the votes of the majority. In fact, every government that is put in power by a majority vote knows that it must take into account the minority will. In this, realistic considerations support the democratic sense of responsibility, since the government, if it wishes to remain in office, must exert itself to convince as many as possible of the propriety of its actions and to win public opinion to its cause. In spite of this, there is a gap between the theory and the practice of democracy. In reality, the crude majority mechanism, with its counting, instead of weighing, of votes, remains operative in the democratic machinery to such an extent that it is *the most serious of all the fictions* with which modern democracy is burdened.

We have already said much concerning the deeper reason for this. Through the majority principle the principle of absolute popular sovereignty is effective. Instead of repeating what has already been said about the latter (cf. Chaps. 37, 38, 118, 130, also note 7 in the present chap.), we may refer to the judgment of an outstanding Swiss professor of public law, *Werner Kägi,* who says (italics his): *"Rousseau has transferred Hobbes' notion of absolute sovereignty from the monarch to the people. It is one of the most ominous facts in the history of democracy and of the constitutional state, that the most influential theorist of modern democracy belongs, not to the constitutional tradition, but to the absolutist tradition of Western political thought."* [21]

VI *The Most Urgent Problems*

Only when men perceive the extent to which modern democracy rests on fictions and works with fictions, can those who see in it a chance

[20] Cf. E. Barker, *Reflections on Government,* 1942, pp. 50 ff.

[21] W. Kägi, *Rechtsstaat und Demokratie,* in *Festg. für Z. Giacometti* (cf. note 13 above), pp. 109 f.

for man to rise to real freedom and full human dignity in social life have real hope that it will continue to exist and will increasingly serve these ends. The political philosophy of natural law is realistic enough to be aware that such fictions cannot be fully eliminated from any machinery of political fellowship. This is because of the limitations of human reason in the business of government. If the essence of democracy is to be considered as the maximum use of reason, then one of its fundamental principles of reform must be the endeavor to reduce the fictitious character in its political machinery.

1. The first is the recognition of the *sovereignty of law* before the sovereignty of the people, that is, of the absolute authority of law immune from any human interference, to which the nature of man bears witness. By this means legitimacy would again assume its priority before all mere legality, which relies on the arbitrary law established by man. The legal principles form the inviolable basis of the life of political society and therefore they must be kept apart from the mechanism of the majority principle. We recall the warning words of *Werner Kägi,* mentioned above, and refer to those of *Guglielmo Ferrero* which will be quoted later (Chap. 156).

2. A further condition for reducing the fictitious element in modern democracy is that a knowledge of all facts which are relevant for settling public affairs must be widely propagated: *truthful information.* Only then can discussion fulfill its purpose. If the facts on which public opinion has based its judgment are distorted or incomplete, the political will is bound to be in error. Since the greater part of the press consists of the party press, the supreme aim of which is effective party propaganda, and the commercial press, which sagaciously follows every shade of public opinion, flattering every emotion, we see how hard a task it must be for democracy to purge itself of the fictions besetting its vital nerve. The way to bring the press to fulfill its responsibility toward the public is a vocational organization of the press with autonomous regulation of professional discipline, and standards of professional honor, with the possibility of calling to account journalists who are careless of their duty and of excluding them from exercising their profession, in the same way that doctors in many countries can be struck off the register for unprofessional conduct.

3. But the reduction of the fictions of the democratic machinery depends not only on truthful information; it depends also on *political judgment.* The paramountcy of numbers in the majority decision loses its merely quantitative character and gains in qualitative value the more broadly it is based on real judgment with regard to the pros and cons in public issues. Only thus can democracy pass progressively to a genuine rule of reason in the service of the common good. The development of political judgment in the mass of the citizens is a matter of general, civic,

and moral education, with regard to the sense of responsibility to truth and justice. Thus, we return to the fundamental fact that the future of democracy is a question of education.[22]

135. The Modern Totalitarian State

Like modern liberal democracy, the modern totalitarian state has its forerunners in antiquity, although it differs from the ancient *tyrannis* as much as modern democracy differs from ancient democracy. The differences can be attributed to the two main conditions that make possible the development of the totalitarian state. The totalitarian state is, first, ideologically based on a *collectivistic philosophy,* with views about man and society that claim dogmatic authority throughout the whole life of the community, and in consequence of which, the state demands total subordination of the individual human personality and of social units to collectivistic ends. Secondly, it is based sociologically upon the possibility of a total *organization of the mass society* for the purposes of the ruler. The ancient *tyrannis* also was intended primarily to serve its master and his desire for power and enrichment. But it sought no justification in ideological systems and did not claim a historical mission for a nation or for the world. It is otherwise with the modern totalitarian state, which, on the basis of an elaborate ideology, seeks to arouse the people to a new consciousness of life, to revolutionary social reform, and to a historical mission.

The *preconditions* for the existence of present-day totalitarian states are quite different from those which made the ancient *tyrannis* possible. The ancient city-state could easily be terrorized by a handful of men. Dictatorship as the permanent form of state in the modern territorial state presupposes that the thinking of a great part of the population is ideologically molded and that there is an efficient apparatus for political control. Both conditions have been made possible by the modern state. From the ideological aspect, the levelling influence of technology, the workshop, and the objectivization of human relations created the conditions, the administrative apparatus being the result of the growth of centralization and of bureaucracy in connection with the immensely increasing demands on the state. Thus, the totalitarian state has in its hand the conditions and means for organizing the whole social and political life according to its aims and intentions. We need not concern ourselves here in detail with this ideological and sociological process,

[22] In Western countries, since the end of the Second World War an abundant literature has been published on the criticism and reform of democracy, which is still increasing yearly with important new publications. In addition to those already mentioned, reference may be made to the works, cited in the Bibliography, of Berggrav, Ferrero, Heydte-Sacherl; E. and F. v. Hippel, Hollis, Lippmann, McKean, MacIver, Maritain, Keeton, Key, Künneth, Percy, Talmon, Windolph.

since we have had to deal step by step throughout our study with the reality of present-day society.

As the *deeper causes* of the genesis of the totalitarian state have often been referred to in the course of our inquiry, they need only be briefly summarized here. First, there is the secularization of the idea of man by rationalism and individualism, resulting in the undermining of the moral and religious guaranty of the dignity of the human person; linked with this is the secularization of the state with the idea of its absolute sovereignty; another factor was the secularization of the idea of law, with the principle which asserted itself in the nineteenth century, that all law comes from the state. While individualism had elevated the individual to be the absolute and final end of human existence and granted him absolute autonomy, collectivism, by a dialectical twist, made a collective individual, that is, the egalitarian community (communism) or the state (fascism) or the race-nation (National-Socialism), the absolute end and invested it with absolute autonomy. At the same time, individualism, with its principle of neutrality in regard to values, created a vacuum which was now open to a new interpretation of life based on those collective values. Another factor was the inability of liberalist democracy to solve the social question of capitalism. Lastly, mention must be made of the catastrophic intensification of economic and social problems as a result of the First World War and the consequently increased psychological receptivity for radical schemes, both factors gaining in strength by the fact that the totalitarian states, as is generally admitted, were able to achieve notable successes in these very fields from the outset.

We turn, then, to the *characteristics of the modern totalitarian state.* They may be summarized as follows.

1. The rights of political *authority* are unlimited, and the purposes which it sets up prevail over all other human ends (whence the totalitarian state has its name). All endeavors for individual ends must be coordinated with the purposes of the state; hence, any social function of a group or community, as often as it touches upon a function of the state, will be subordinated to the principle of "one function, one authority."

2. The individuals and the smaller communities possess no rights independent of the state. Hence, for the totalitarian state there is no distinction between society and state; there is *no free society,* but society is regulated by the state according to its aims and will.

3. The totalitarian state, therefore, recognizes *no right against the state.* Here may be seen the distinctive mark of the totalitarian state, that is, that the citizen possesses no guaranteed opportunity of vindicating his rights against the state by legal process. Insofar as constitutional rights of citizens are laid down, they have a different meaning from those guaranteed by the constitutions of "Western" democracy. They are freedoms such as the totalitarian government understands and is

willing to guarantee, not freedoms to be respected absolutely by the government and based on an order of law by which the government itself is bound.

4. The totalitarian state is a *single-party state.* State and monopoly party are identified; the state is the agency for carrying out the will of the party in the political community. The party, therefore, holds all important posts in the machinery of the state, in the direction of industry, and in the occupational organizations.

5. The political will of the community is formed by the political leader of the monopolistic party and his group. This political will is made effective by the party throughout the life of society and is communicated to the people by the propaganda machine. *Responsibility* in the totalitarian government, therefore, is *"from above to below,"* all vital decisions being made at the top. In liberal democracy the direction of responsibility is the reverse, the regulation of the exercise of political authority going back to the popular will.

6. *Parliament* in the totalitarian state is merely an institution for receiving the will of the dictator, whose propaganda instrument it is rather than an instrument for the formation of the will of the community.

The following features further characterize the practice of the totalitarian state in carrying out the principles just mentioned.

7. The totalitarian state is a *police state;* that is, the executive power of the state has untrammeled sway in carrying out the will of the government, especially in preventing or eliminating anything in which the government or the one party sees an immediate or remote danger to its power. The most potent agency of this police rule is the terrorizing of the population, which is kept under psychological pressure by drastic measures against all manifestations of opposition: the concentration camp, deportation, forced labor, the removal of officials from office.

8. The government can no more be called to account by an independent constitutional or administrative judiciary than by an independent parliament. Thus, *no institutional control* is allowed over the exercise of political power.

9. *No free public opinion* exists which could exercise an informal control over the government. The press, publication of books, the organization of meetings, the radio, motion pictures, all are controlled and directed by the state and the single party, if they are not indeed in their direct possession.

10. *No right of free association* exists. Thus, forces opposed to the regime are prevented from combining. All occupational and cultural organizations are monopoly organizations standing under the determining influence of the one party and the control of the state.

11. *Human rights* rooted in the freedom of conscience, such as the practice of religion, the religious and moral education of children by the

parents, are not recognized in principle. Even when they are given constitutional recognition they are rendered inoperative in practice, for, more than in anything else, the totalitarian state is *interested in men's souls,* asserting its primary and absolute right to influence them in accordance with its ideological dogmas. It sees in such a right the very basis of its future existence.

12. Lastly, the totalitarian state asserts even a kind of right of *ownership over its citizens,* since it regards men first and foremost as an instrument in the service of its ends. It refuses them the right of free withdrawal from the state community by leaving the country.

To sum up, we may say that the criterion of the totalitarian character of a state is its ideological and practical *valuation of man* as merely a means to subserve collective ends. This criterion definitely distinguishes the totalitarian state from the constitutional state in the Western sense even when the latter, owing to some grave emergency in its internal or external affairs, such as war or an attempted coup d'état, is compelled for a time partially to suspend constitutional rights. Isolated, merely external resemblances do not justify the classification of an "authoritarian" state as totalitarian as long as this principle is not interpreted in practice according to the totalitarian valuation of man. It is of course equally certain that nontotalitarian, "authoritarian" governments, resulting from a national emergency, are under obligation, as soon as circumstances permit, to return to constitutional rule or, if new foundations must be laid for such a rule, to make due arrangements for the formation of a constituent assembly. We shall deal with the principles applying to such occasions in our discussion of constitutional changes.

PART THREE

The Functions of the State

---

136. The Subsidiary Nature of the State's Function

It is a law of sociology, as we have shown, that power strives to extend itself. The state of its very nature is power; and, being invested with sovereignty, it is also in a true sense invested with a plenitude of power. But, again because of its nature, its power is subject to the order of the existential human ends, which every social unit must ultimately serve. Therefore, we must open the discussion of the functions of the state with some account of the implications of the principle of subsidiary function. This we must do especially because the opposite principle, that of state omnicompetence and omnipotence, is steadily gaining in influence even in the democratic countries. In free democracies this is the outcome of "social security" and "social welfare" in disregard of the limits set by personal responsibility and social freedom. Thus, there is a continuous and expanding process of usurpation of fresh functions by the state in the spheres of education, the care of health, provider functions, social policy, and budget policy.

The principle of subsidiarity is what brings the functions of the state into the perspective of the actual common good. This is characterized by the fact that the political community is an association of individual and social persons with their own existential ends and their corresponding tasks, rights, and powers, who can reach their essential self-fulfillment only by complying with the corresponding responsibilities implied in these ends. The state is the institution for coordinating these powers and activities for the good of all. Therefore, it has functions and acquires rights where the powers and wills of individual persons and smaller communities fail in the service of their existential ends. Its function, accordingly, is limited to facilitating, stimulating, supplementing, and coordinating the activities of the individuals and social groups. In the perspective of social reality, then, we cannot doubt that the social functions are essentially different from one another by reason of their immediate ends in the service of human existence.

The function of child education in the family has a different end in the service of full human existence from that of state education. It is directed to the forming of the human, religious, and moral personality in its foundations. Education by the state, on the other hand, is governed by the needs of the political community. To the state are assigned functions only with regard to tasks whose fulfillment depends wholly on the cooperation of all in the "universal" society—tasks such as the establishment and preservation of law and order, military defense, and the raising of funds for these tasks by taxation. Such specific ends give rise to functions and thus rights of the state. Based as they are in the comprehensive common good, these are certainly rights of very high rank; in fact, they are rights of *sovereignty* but limited in substance in accordance with the principle of *subsidiarity.*

This summary of our earlier analysis of the principle of subsidiary function (cf. Chap. 45) is confirmed by a glance at the actual process by which the general good, the "good life" (*Aristotle*), is realized in society. The full development of the human person is not something given to man from without, something that can be put on like a garment. Rather, as we have shown, it is his self-realization in the fulfillment of his essential tasks in life, and thus it can only come about through personal effort and responsibility. Any social grouping, including the state, therefore, can assume merely an ancillary role. The principle of subsidiary function, therefore, is an expression of the fact that the *full vitality of the human personality* only results from the exercise of his freedom and the discharging of his particular responsibility. Moreover, the principle of subsidiary function signifies the fullest mobilization of all forces for the *full realization of the common good.* For this ultimately rests upon no other forces than those of the individuals, and these forces are set in motion by nothing so effective as individual interest. Give a man stony ground for his own, says an old Chinese proverb, and he will make a flourishing garden of it.

The principle of subsidiary function, therefore, signifies that the best possible development of the intellectual and bodily talents and powers of the members of the community, as brought about by the personal responsibility and the *personal interest of the individual,* is in the interest of the common good—if the coordination of their activities is secured. This applies to the economic and social as well as to the spiritual and cultural common good. Among other objections against the socialist planned economy, one which carries great weight is the following: the general interest, that of consumers, is certainly not best served by transferring all responsibility to a planning authority, which takes the place of many thousands of planners, in the form of larger and smaller entrepreneurs, who, provided that their efforts are coordinated, exert themselves for the consumers. The same applies as much to the cultural as to the material common good. The common good is realized in the multiplicity of cultural ends in which members of society can find the fulfillment of themselves through responsible activity, although helped by social cooperation. Acceptance of the principle of subsidiary function denotes *richness of life in a political community.* In proportion as this principle is made inoperative by the unification, direction, and regimentation of society, society's richness of life, development, and vitality must be choked at the roots.

Since the individual and social persons, with their own ends and their own responsibility, constitute society as distinct from the state, the principle of subsidiary function *stands for the rights of "society"* as against the state. For a positive definition of the character of society, therefore, we can draw from the principle of subsidiary function this conclusion: The principle of subsidiary function demands *the free society and the open society.*

The characteristic of the *free society* consists in the freedom of the citizens, their natural communities, and their associations to pursue their ends and interests untrammeled in the religious, intellectual, political, economic, social, and charitable spheres, within the bounds set by the common good. Two legal principles, therefore, are essential to the existence of the free society: respect for natural rights by the state, wherever they are found, and the possibility of safeguarding these rights, by legal process, from encroachment by the state. These rights comprise the civil, political, economic, and social freedoms: freedom of conscience, freedom of worship, the freedom and inviolability of the person, the right of parents over the education of their children, the freedom of citizens to associate for any purposes compatible with the common weal, the freedom of the citizens to order their public life in accordance with the demands of their conscience, and freedom of public opinion. Assured freedom of public opinion is a touchstone of the free society: this is the society in a state which is not afraid of the free judgment of public opinion.

Secondly, the principle of subsidiary function demands the *open society.* By this is meant the political community whose citizens, individually and in their social groupings, enjoy the right of unhindered intercourse with the outside world, and which grants to foreigners the same full civil (not political) rights as to its own citizens. Of course these liberties, like all others, have no foundation outside the framework of the natural law principles, including those of the political common good. The open society, therefore, does not imply a right of conspiracy with foreign powers for revolutionary groups in a state, or a right of espionage for foreigners. What the principle does demand, however, is free international contact with citizens of other countries in all domains of activity: in the religious sphere for the Churches and their members, and equally in the intellectual and cultural sphere, including the departments of art, literature, and science. It demands free economic interchange as far as is compatible with the national economic interests of a country, and free contact with foreign national groups, such as trade unions or political parties, with like ideals and aims in the social and political fields.

Not less essential is the other aspect of the open society, the fact that it is open to citizens of other states, allowing them such rights as are essential to a free society. The free right of immigration into a state's territory is not in question, but simply free interchange between foreign nationals and the members of a state under the conditions of life in a free society. Not least among the rights of free contact in the domains outlined above is that of obtaining information about conditions, opinions, aims, and developments in a country, if these are of any public world interest, that is, if the good of a part or of the whole of the international community is affected. In other words, the open society is the political society which needs to fear the judgment of world public opinion as little as its own.

A fundamental trait of *the totalitarian state* is that it is a *state without a free society:* it proclaims the identity of state and society and usurps the functions and rights of society. The totalitarian state, in its modern form, is the outcome of a dialectical process. This process began with the uprising of society against the state; the absorption of society by the state is the end of the process. Individualism gave to the free society a significance whereby all rights were centered ultimately in the autonomous individual. All state authority was conferred by the individual's alleged inborn right to freedom, and thus gave the people the right to change the form of state and government at will and made absolute popular sovereignty a feature of the free society; at the same time, however, it surrendered the state to the class warfare of groups seeking political power. When any group succeeded in eliminating political pluralism by the party monopoly, the hour of the totalitarian state had struck: the aims of the monopoly party began to assert a total predominance over all other ends of society. Individualism made the rights of society absolute: now the rights of the state were made absolute; the individualist revolution of society against the state was followed by the identification of society with the state. It is perhaps not so urgent today to warn people against an individualist misinterpretation of the rights of society as to see clearly that the individualist misuse of the privileges of the free society and that the collectivistic, totalitarian elimination of the free society spring from a common root. This root is legal philosophy, which has no place for genuine political pluralism, and which is founded in law itself but is also bridled by it. This pluralism is represented by the principle of subsidiary function and flourishes in the free and open society.

Among the various *factors that have contributed to the accumulation of functions of the modern state,* those which resulted from the difficulties of individualistic capitalism must be mentioned especially. The state was compelled to try to alleviate the harshest effects of competitive capitalism on the working classes by regulating child labor, by factory legislation, and by social policy. The enormous increase in the population, with the problems of housing, public health, and education, to mention only these, imposed further tasks on the state. All these commitments far exceeded the financial capacities of local authorities, and when the state assumed their burdens it appropriated powers over them. In addition, there was the growing force of nationalism, also a child of the individualist development, and, linked with it, the endeavor to give absolute sovereignty and power to the state. The associated desire to give the nation an intellectual pattern resulted in an increasing political influence on educational services, from elementary school to university. In the economic sphere, nationalism involved efforts to achieve the maximum degree of economic strength and prosperity under the economic and political maxims of a new mercantilism. The object of this policy was the greatest possible development of industry and agriculture with a consequent accretion of functions to the state administrative machinery.

Militarism, too, had one of its chief roots in nationalism, with the incessant armaments race between states; as a result of this competition, the life of the community, in considerable measure, came under the dictate of the military exigencies of a possible war. The creation of the industrial and financial prerequisites for building up armaments, the military training of the population, the planning of strategic roads and railways and of production important for war economy, all extended the sphere of competence of the state. We now sum up what we have been saying. Of the factors contributing to the hypertrophy of the functions of the state since the middle of the nineteenth century, the concomitant rapidly spreading collectivization of "society," and the widening of the power of the state and bureaucracy since the end of the First World War, the chief are the great forces of modern society—capitalism, nationalism, and militarism—all of them owing a substantial part of their existence ultimately to individualism.

137. The Primacy of Politics

The common good constitutes the supreme law of the state community. From this unmistakably follows the primacy of politics. This fact may appear strange after all that has been said in the foregoing section concerning the subsidiary nature of the functions of the state. To appreciate the principle of the primacy of politics, however, one need only remember how the primacy of economics became the slogan in country after country in face of the economic difficulties which followed the First World War, and how it is championed in theory by Marxist thinkers for the whole of national and international life. Often it meant simply that it should be left to economic forces organized in the large interest groups ultimately to determine the governance of the state in accordance with "economic necessities" as they understood them. Indeed, industry organized in producers' associations knew to a significant degree how to control the activity of elected parliaments and the governments drawn from them by calling a halt, through hinting at a threatening contraction of production, in view of difficulties arising from forthcoming laws or measures (as in the field of social policy) which were unwelcome to industry. But also, in various countries, organized labor was able to assume a similar role, with various modifications of the idea, "bread before politics." The outcome of all these influences was a far-reaching domination of political life by economic factors; in other words, as we have frequently indicated, the domination of political life by pressure groups; these groups are high finance (working most silently but most effectually), industry, agriculture, and trade unions. All seek in this way to identify their interests with the general interest and to make them a dominating aim of politics.

Without doubt, in this tendency, often the most essential interests of these groups and indeed the real common good of the state are at stake, though equally often the political maneuvers of professional politicians, which in fact spring only from party interest or even only from personal interests. Yet, against all particular interests of groups, whether they are industrial or financial forces or trade unions or parties, the law of the common good prevails, and hence the law of the primacy of politics. "*Politics*" is here understood in its fundamental sense, that is, as relating to the political community as a whole and thus to the all-round establishment and preservation of the common good. "The primacy of politics," therefore, means that it is the fundamental function of the political community to restrain the various groups with their particular interests and claims to power, and by so doing to prevent the exploitation of some groups by others. The fact that this function is not the merely negative one of silencing these interests, but the positive one of incorporating them in the dynamic process of the progressive realization of the common good in the interest of all, is obvious in view of what has been said concerning the common good.

It follows from the essential primacy of politics that the political *authority* must possess ample power to enable it to carry out the function just described; hence, the necessity of an internally strong state and government, capable of protecting and asserting the pre-eminent interests of the common weal despite the efforts of the organized interest groups. *The principle of subsidiary function, then, in no way implies a weak state,* which would of course inevitably be at the mercy of the stronger pressure groups. On the contrary, the principle of subsidiary function has its necessary counterpart in the authority principle, which must be realized to such an extent that the state, as guardian of the common weal, will be strong enough to guarantee the general interest in its nearer or remoter perspective. One of the dangers of democracy, especially on the soil of a utilitarian view of life and of society, is to make the state appear as a mere clearing house for the group interests of society and to make politics seem synonymous with party quarrels. Because the state has the function of securing the interests of all, in opposition to group interests, the common good as the fundamental law of the state implies the primacy of politics and a plenitude of authority in the service of the common good.

138. The Legal Function of the State: A. The Constitution

By "constitution" or constitutional law is understood the positive legal order which determines the rights of the state and the rights of its citizens. Therefore, it regulates first and foremost the exercise of political authority, the legal form of its transfer to the government, the extent of its powers, and the rights of the citizens in relation to it. A constitution is the outcome of *historical factors.* We must first mention those factors that we have seen at work in the forming of the character of a state, such as its need for self-defense in foreign relations and its internal class structure. Historical factors, furthermore, influence the development of the juridical consciousness of peoples, which expresses itself in the legal usages or customs that enter into the constitution. Also of a historical nature are the qualities of individual peoples which urge them to adopt a more liberal or a more authoritarian form of government. To the realm of history belong, finally, those state-founding acts of individuals or groups by which, as often in recent times, constitutions have been established after wars or revolutions. From the nature of these historical factors it is evident that constitutions need not be written or fixed by statute, but may simply take the form of customary law. England provides the often-quoted example of an unwritten constitution. But the necessity of safeguarding civil liberties resulted, in the nineteenth century, in a growing tendency to set them down in written constitutions. How justified this tendency was may be seen from the unexpected growth of a new absolutism of the totalitarian states which was so much more violent than earlier types.

What are *the constitutional principles of natural law?* After our previous discussions on the nature of the state and political authority, they may be defined as follows.

1. There exists an unwritten basic norm for every state in the *law of the common good,* in its two aspects as an order of unity through authority and as an order of freedom grounded in natural rights. Few modern constitutions are willing expressly to recognize God as the ultimate source of all law, a truth which follows logically from the supreme unwritten constitutional principle as implied in natural law. On the other hand, the oft-recurring formula in the preambles of modern constitutions, that all law proceeds from the people, must not be taken in itself as a declaration of the secularistic state. It may be intended to be such, but it may only refer to the democratic appointment of the organs chosen to exercise political authority and to the orbit of the powers invested in them by the will of the people on whom such provisions depend; in the latter case, such a formula is consonant with the natural law idea of popular sovereignty.

2. A further unwritten constitutional law, valid for every state, resides in the *principle of legitimacy,* the principle that political authority has a moral and legal obligation toward the basic principles of the natural conscience and, developed therefrom, toward the juridical consciousness of the people. In this is seen the most essential role of the united will of the citizens as a political unity, the united will which is an essential factor in popular sovereignty and fundamental law, the "consensus" of the political community (cf. Chaps. 118, 130). The natural law constitutional principle of legitimacy excludes any state absolutism or state totalitarianism in the sense that the state is raised above the law; but it equally excludes any popular sovereignty in the sense that a constitution founded on positive law could justify any and every act of the government or of groups in agreement with it. Such a merely formal legality can be in complete contradiction to the legal principle of legitimacy founded in the constitution of the state according to natural law (cf. Chap. 131).

3. To the ample scope which these natural law principles leave for the operation of historical factors, described above in the variety of *constitutional forms,* there is only one further limitation: the respect for acquired legal titles. Natural law finds a place, as we have shown, for all the diverse forms of constitution which history displays, as long as they do not impair fundamental human natural rights.

4. It is the natural right of the people to give itself a constitution when it has to make new departures in its political life, as many peoples have had to do after international catastrophes like the two World Wars. Since such a right to sovereignty is invested in the people only as a political unity, the condition of its exercise is that the people constitutes itself as a unity, thereby showing itself capable of organizing a machinery for expressing its will, especially by setting up a provisional government to conduct general elections for a constituent assembly. Recent history shows that the general juridical consciousness regards this as the way of law for *establishing a constitution* in the circumstances stated. If, under pressure from foreign powers or from groups in possession of power in a community, there is any substantial limitation of freedom in the appointment of a provisional government or in the elections of the constituent assembly, then, as we have also seen in recent times, the resulting government is recognized as legitimate neither in its own country nor by other countries. When, in times of chaotic disruption in a state, individual personalities or groups take it upon themselves to reorganize the political community and, if they succeed, to give the state a new constitution, this can never have more than a provisional character. It requires legitimation by at least the tacit consent of the people. The earlier the express consent of the people is sought in an appropriate form, the more evident it will be that the originators of such a constitution have really acted in accordance with the will of the people. The fact that

the natural juridical consciousness does not condemn such a process of establishing a constitution in the circumstances we have mentioned, is suggested by the title "Father of his country," which has often been conferred upon such an innovator by his people.

5. Since every constitution depends on historical and, therefore, on changing factors, whereas the common good as the supreme law of the political community must be ever newly actualized, there is no natural law foundation for unalterability in a constitution and none can be considered so final as to be unalterable, even though its originator may have intended it so.

This raises the question of the *revision of a constitution.* The methods that have actually been followed, in history, of altering constitutions vary between assassination and revolution, at one extreme, and reform by constitutional means of existing constitutions or the establishment of a new constitution by plebiscite, at the other. What are *the principles of natural law?*

1. The *forcible overthrow* of an existing lawful constitution is always illegal: it is always an attack against the fundamentals of the constitution, which rests on the popular will as the expression of the juridical conscience and juridical consciousness, and thus against the principle of legitimacy inherent in this constitution. In addition, it implies the violation of existing rights. Rebellion against the illegal exercise of political authority is to be distinguished from the overthrow of a constitution; such rebellion has been dealt with in connection with the right of political resistance.

2. Since the actual constitution is an instrument for realizing the political common good, it is a duty to alter it if it ceases to be capable of performing this function. Rulers, parties, or classes who oppose such alteration are acting against natural law.

3. Since stability and continuity of law, and thus the highest good of the community, depend upon the tranquil evolution of the constitution, every constitution which is dependent on the popular will must *provide for ordered change.* Such measures have a double purpose to fulfill since they must afford the possibility of initiating constitutional reforms in harmony with the people's will, and also create assurances that the real will of the people can make itself felt.

The recent history of constitutional changes shows how easily parties may be able to utilize the parliamentary machinery to impose their will on the people. Experience and caution have taught the nations to find various means to give force to the people's considered will in constitutional changes. Above all, constitutional change is placed outside the ordinary process of legislation and submitted to a special procedure. Such procedures depend on political tradition, national individuality, and considerations of expediency; it is not possible to lay down general natural law rules for these. Often collaboration between the two legislative bodies in a two-chamber system, or between these and the head of the state, is laid down. Nearly always, in contrast with normal legislation, a qualified (usually two-thirds) majority is required, and sometimes direct consultation of the people. The purpose of the rather complicated procedure is to make the people aware of the significance of constitutional legislation as well as to secure time and opportunity for calm reflection.

4. If a constitution makes no provision for constitutional procedure in case of constitutional changes, essential changes can lawfully be carried out only by the people as a political unity and consequently only with the *collaboration of government and people.* For although sovereignty is originally invested in the people as a unity, the existing lawful government is a constituent element in this unity; without it the people could not give lawful and ordered expression to its will. Any different kind of procedure could only be described as revolution: one-sided changes in the constitution made by the government or by a group claiming to represent the people are forms of a coup d'état.

5. In times of *national emergency,* when the basic juridical order and the common good are gravely imperiled, the existing constitution, insofar as it proves inadequate to the situation, gives way to the higher juridical principle: *Salus populi suprema lex.* This presupposes that, owing to circumstances, the government is not in a position to provide itself with the necessary powers by constitutional means. The causes of the state of emergency may be a sudden war of aggression or an actual or immediately threatening attempt at a coup d'état. Only the gravest dangers, and then only temporarily, entitle a government to *suspend the constitution,* as the principle mentioned implies. The custom whereby retrospective approval ("indemnity") is given to such governmental measures by the legislative body shows that the legal principle just developed is recognized by the juridical consciousness of peoples.

139. The Legal Function of the State: B. Legislation

The critical discussion which the natural law school has always devoted to the duty of the legislator often astonishes the present-day jurist. Why speak so much about duty in legislation, it is asked, if the principle of popular sovereignty is in force and parliament is jealously guarding its prerogatives? But it is precisely this supposition that is erroneous. Parliament has to a large extent allowed its rights to be substantially pruned away and has evaded its responsibility. Two factors have contributed to this development: the complexity of the matters which have required legislation, and the increasing number of laws which have had to be passed. Representatives have not felt confident enough to cope with the details of matters under discussion; on the other hand, administrative departments have been very ready to undertake the working out of the details. And there are liberalist-socialistic theories of democracy which have made a principle out of this, as out of other mistaken developments, namely, that the legislature should not have to concern itself with the details, but only with matters of principle. When this theory is put into practice, a *government* can, to a considerable extent, shelter itself from the control of the elected representatives, since it is a well known characteristic of skeleton laws, that their use cannot easily be checked. The principle also promotes the centralizing and bureaucratic tendencies of the *executive,* which is thereby enabled to usurp part of the function of the legislature. Thus, the actually responsible legislator in democracy, the parliament, has taken upon itself a restriction to which it is not entitled to submit. It has no such right because, as a rule, the detail of a law is no less important to the actual common good than the principles which it embodies. Hence, the duty of the legislator does not permit a shifting of one-half of his responsibility. The legislator today largely renounces his responsibility by delegated legislation.

By *delegated legislation* is meant legislation by inferior authorities on the basis of an authorization by the legislature. It takes the form of government orders and regulations issued by the government, by ministries, or by bodies, particularly in the form of permission for the execution or application of laws. Formally, delegated legislation is justified under the authorization granted by the competent legislative authority: it is a justification according to the principle of legality in contradiction to the natural law constitutional principle of legitimacy. In that case, when it is a question of more than merely technical matters, parliament has no real right to delegate. For no one can give up a right rooted in a duty unless the attainment of the object of the right is assured; this is not left to his discretion, but he remains responsible for it. Such a responsibility lies upon the legislator, whether monarch or elected body. The consequences of the principle of delegation are being noted today with increasing anxiety: this portion of legislation easily escapes the control of the legislator; responsibility can often be ascertained only with great difficulty; because of the unavoidable elasticity of general rules a wide opening is left for arbitrary government; uncontrolled power is concentrated in the hands of the government and the administrative bureaucracy; centralism increases without warning. These are phenomena doubly grave in view of the tendencies of state capitalism and state socialism.

Does *formal democracy offer any remedy?* Devices for controlling the drafting and carrying through of delegated legislation, such as parliamentary committees in cooperation with representatives of the interested groups of the community, may be useful as emergency measures, but only as such. The abuse of delegated legislation points to a deeper evil, of which we have already spoken. Why is the modern parliament, with regard to the details of laws, unequal to its task? Because it is entrusted with legislation in matters that properly fall within the competence of the self-government of occupational communities. In such a perspective, the maxim that only legislation in matters of principle belongs to the legal function of the state acquires its true validity. The details, which today are covered by delegated legislation, do not fall within the competence of ministerial departments but within that of the occupational self-governing communities. The true solution of the problem, therefore, forms one of the objects of a more radical social reform, as we have already pointed out and shall later discuss in greater detail. A reversal of the tendency toward centralism and bureaucracy and a notable contraction of the grossly hypertrophied apparatus of state administration would be the inevitable effects of the transfer of this portion of legislation to the self-government of the occupational organizations. This would at the same time put an effective brake, probably the only effective one, on the concentration of power in the hands of state capitalism and state socialism.

Brief mention must be made of another source of law binding upon a community, namely, *customary law.* The interest of modern jurisprudence in customary law is mainly of a historical, and not a theoretical, character, since it upholds the absolute legislative sovereignty of the state. The political theorists of the natural law school, however, found high interest in customary law (cf. Chaps. 47–48) from the conviction that the legislator himself is bound by law as it lives in the consciousness and the usages and customs of a people,* because this legal custom is an essential component of the constitution. But if there is a legislative authority positively established, the question arises how far a recently arisen custom can obtain legal force against or alongside the law enacted by the authority. In natural law theory, this validity is logically made conditional upon the legislator's consent, at least upon his tacit consent.

140. The Legal Function of the State: C. The Administration of Justice

The state's function of administering justice consists in the protection of the rights of the community and of its citizens, by judicial process and by the execution of the judgments of the courts. From the general

* St. Thomas Aquinas thus gives the reason for the law-creating power of popular custom: "Sicut autem ratio et voluntas hominis manifestantur verbo in rebus agendis, ita etiam manifestantur facto . . . scilicet per exteriores actus multiplicatos interior voluntatis motus, et rationis conceptus efficacissime declaratur. Cum enim aliquid multoties fit, videtur ex deliberato rationis judicio provenire" (*Summa theol.*, Ia, IIae, q. 97, a. 3).

principles of distributive justice we can deduce the following *natural law principles* for the administration of justice by the state.

1. The judicial process must be based on the *law in force* in the political community, whether statutory or customary. One of the fundamental principles today of legal representation in the constitutional state is that judgment can be passed on an act only by the laws in force at the time of its commission, and not by laws subsequently introduced.

2. The judicial process must be in accordance with a *procedure* that insures the ascertainment of the relevant facts. The corresponding principles of the modern constitutional state are the following: no one can be sentenced by the judiciary for a crime unless the fact of the crime has been established by process before the regular courts; no one may be held in custody without judicial sentence being passed; no one may be sentenced without ample opportunity for defense and for preparing the necessary evidence. Special courts are justified at times of grave emergency in the state (e.g., when martial law is declared), but only if all necessary safeguards are applied to avoid judicial errors, which in martial law procedure can easily lead to judicial murders.[1] (In totalitarian states a subsequent rehabilitation of the victim of such a judicial murder, when there is a change in the course of politics, can only make more obvious the subordination of justice to political ends.)

3. In the application of the law, the principle of *equality before the law* must be observed. Although this stands formally as a principle of the administration of justice in the modern constitutional state, there is no doubt that much remains to be done to realize it fully in practice. No one would dispute the fact that there is some truth in the saying: "One law for the rich and one law for the poor." Fortunes are often acquired by clever circumvention of the law; and even though this is apparent, the legal administration is unable to take any steps. Still more open to objection seems the inequality before the law which is due to the high costs of litigation, whereby the poorer classes are often deprived of the recourse to law. This condition arises from the complexity of the law and legal procedure and the consequent quasi-monopoly enjoyed by the legal profession. A remedy seems to be promised in the attempts being made in some countries to provide legal facilities at moderate fees for people of slender means, through various forms of cooperation between the state, the local authorities, and the lawyers' associations.

4. In addition to these principles, which are essentially recognized as such and accepted, it is especially necessary today to stress the principle of *legality in the political administration.* In all Western countries, developments are seen in which this basic principle of the constitutional

[1] Hans Schima, *Verfeinerung des Rechtsschutzes, Rektoratsrede an der Universität Wien,* 1956, p. 9, says: "As *ultima ratio* for the constitutional principle," must be stressed the obligation of the state to make good when a public organ wrongfully causes damage to anyone; "only by this regulation is the system of legal protection really completed."

state in the administrative sphere is set aside by other considerations. Thus, the attempt is often made to avoid difficulties and delays which the administration experiences owing to the increasing complexity of legislation and legal practice. Among the methods of which administrative authorities make use are contracts with citizens (e.g., between the tax authorities and tax debtors), or agreements with interest groups, which evade the legally prescribed constitutional or administrative channels.[2] When those officially concerned with judicial and legal duties do not observe right and law with complete conscientiousness, from whom can such conscientiousness be expected? The citizens and the groups, in rapidly increasing measure, make use of the possibilities thus offered them; the result must be a serious upheaval in the foundations of the constitutional state. The development indicated is furthered by the surrender of judicial power to the various administrative authorities: administrative decisions take the place of judgments by the regular courts. Arbitrary action can be prevented with certainty only if the natural principles of justice [3] are fully preserved in the administrative proceedings and if, in addition, there is the possibility of appeal to a higher court (administrative or constitutional court of justice); to this must be added the vigilance of parliaments.

As far as *the judge* is concerned, the indispensable condition for the maintenance of justice is that, in giving judgment, he is free to follow his conscience and is protected against influence from political sources. Therefore, it is a principle of the modern constitutional state that the judiciary shall be independent of the executive. A consequence of this is the principle that no judge must be dismissed or transferred by the executive except in the case of legally proven unprofessional conduct. Regarding the independence of the judge, much depends on the method of his appointment. It is best if judges are appointed by the ministry responsible for the administration of justice in consultation with representatives of the judges' professional associations; the election of judges by representative bodies, as is customary in some places, at least for

[2] Hans Huber, "Die Umwälzungen im Staatsgefüge durch die Verbände," in *Ordo, Jahrbuch für die Ordnung von Wirtschaft und Gesellschaft,* Vol. VII, 1955, p. 192, points to "the deflection of typical principles and institutions of free democratic (and federated) states through organized group egoism. A significant phenomenon of this tendency is perhaps the prevalence of agreements between the state and private (individual or legal) persons for the regulation of affairs which, from a constitutional point of view, pertain to the 'domaine de la loi.' These agreements offend against the principle of legality of the administration and finally loosen the constitutional concept of law. They are often concluded for the purpose of by-passing a control, the supervision of administrative jurisdiction, of finance, of parliament, etc."

[3] Richard Warner, *The Principles of Public Administration, A Study in the Mechanics of Social Action,* 1947, p. 85, calls special attention in his distinguished work on the English administration to four principles of *Natural Justice:* No one may be judge in his own cause; no one may be sentenced without being given a hearing; the party to a decision has a claim to know the reason for it; in case of an inquiry the report of the official conducting it should be made known to the parties.

certain categories of judges, is obviously attended with the danger that political considerations may influence the administration of justice.

An important condition today for the proper administration of justice is the *adequate training of the judge* and of administrators. A mere technical training in law is not sufficient, that is, a training which simply makes the future judge familiar with the letter and perhaps with the history of the law. The following may be taken as generally recognized principles for the interpretation of the law: (1) it shall correspond with the letter of the law; (2) it shall follow the precedent of judgments given in similar previous cases; (3) it shall accord with the intention of the lawgiver as expressed in the law. But to ascertain the intention of the lawgiver, the judge in the modern state must go back to sources such as the reports of commissions set up by the government to inquire into the subject matter of new laws. There he will find, in cases of modern industrial legislation, for example, references to complicated institutions of economic life as well as to the present state of legal theory in regard to the questions involved. It follows, then, that merely legal training is not enough; rather, the judge (and the lawyer) also must be familiar with political economy, ethics, and psychology. Accordingly, in most countries of Europe, the courses of legal studies at the universities have more and more been made to embrace these spheres.[4]

One thing the judge cannot learn at school is insight into the actual working of *present-day industrial and cultural life.* This must be gained from experience. For example, consider the complicated process by which a large combine fixes prices for its various products, including the allied processes of shifting costs from one subsidiary company to another and building up concealed reserves. Such manipulation of prices by combines is very prejudicial to weaker individual competitors. These manipulations will never be understood so fully by the judge, from purely theoretical study, that he will be able clearly to see their rights and wrongs. Only the man who is engaged in the economic field can form an adequate view of all the factors involved. All these considerations illustrate the fact that an important area of jurisdiction can be expertly covered only by jurisdiction of the professional self-governing bodies. Such an idea of jurisdiction may cause surprise at first glance. Yet, the idea is not new. In a large number of countries professional organizations of doctors and lawyers and craft guilds, for example, exercise such a jurisdiction in their own province and often have power to impose penalties going so far as the exclusion of members from the exercise of their trade or profession. Similarly, judgment in cases of unfair methods of competition would belong to the jurisdiction of self-governing occupational bodies

[4] Concerning the "instruction of organs administering law," Hans Schima, *op. cit.*, pp. 7 f., says: "To a substantial degree, knowledge is necessary which does not pertain to the juridical faculty but to another. There is no department of life which cannot fall to an administrative authority for judgment."

(cf. Chaps. 85, 181). There must, of course, be a right of appeal, and when it is shown that a case goes beyond the occupational sphere, the possibility of referring it to the regular courts must be insured.

The *theories of criminal law* associated with the rationalistic, naturalistic, humanitarian theories, to which in the nineteenth century considerable significance was attached, call for no detailed examination today. To a doctrine of human nature which denies the freedom of the will, and hence the responsibility of the criminal, attributing his actions rather to a disease of the human organism (*C. Lombroso*) or to influences in the social environment (*F. von Liszt* and others), the state's right to punish must seem meaningless. Humanitarian thought, with its belief in the unimpaired innate goodness of human nature, was bound to demand the substitution of education for punishment. Since then, owing to the disillusionment of the naturalistic humanitarian hopes, mankind has returned to more realistic views and has absorbed the lesson that society cannot subsist without the threat and execution of punishment.

The following is, in fact, the root of the state's right to punish: punishment is indispensable for the maintenance and restoration of the order of society, which is a highly important feature of the common good, particularly since human nature is impaired in its will to conform with this order. The idea of reparation for the wrong done to the order of society is, of course, meaningful only if this order is recognized as part of the moral order. With our theory it should not be difficult to reconcile what there is of truth in the principal modern theories of the right to punish. 1) The state's right to punish is the necessary means of safeguarding law and order. In this the *deterrence theory* is given its place: The root of the right to punish is certainly to be sought in the state's duty toward the common good, but it works also as a deterrent to crime. A theory of the right to punish must, however, justify the actual execution of punishment and not only its deterrent effect.

2) In its execution, punishment serves to restore the violated legal order, whose stability (the rule of law) is one of the highest goods of the community. The so-called *vindication theory* emphasizes this. It comes nearest to the natural law theory of the right to punish, but fails to point out the necessity of punishment rooted in the order of the common good in face of the impairment of the will to order in human nature (original sin); in addition, the vindication theory cannot explain the prerogative of mercy, which would of course impede the restoration of the juridical order.

3) Since in legal philosophy the juridical order and the rule of law, as fundamental goods of the common weal, form the basis of the state's right to punish (cf. the reference to *T. Würtenberger* in Chap. 131, note 1), the *correction theory,* which seeks to base the right to punish exclusively upon the end of the improvement of the criminal, and thus upon the individual good, is also inadequate. The very greatest im-

portance should, however, be attached to efforts to educate criminals to be better men and to lessen criminality by improving environment.

The natural law theory also provides us with clear principles for judging of the justification of the *death penalty*. Since the end of punitive authority is to safeguard and restore legal order, the death penalty is in itself justified as a necessary means to this end, but the exercise of this authority must not go beyond what is necessary in the particular circumstances in which a society finds itself. Hence, for one and the same crime at different periods and in different circumstances different penalties may be necessary and justified, and the death penalty can, in certain circumstances, be indispensable and justifiable, in other circumstances not necessary and therefore unjustifiable. And even if in particular circumstances the death penalty is justified, it is imperative that absolutely adequate measures be taken to insure that judicial error, and hence judicial murder, are precluded. For this reason alone there must be constitutional provision for a right of reprieve, but also for the reason that the circumstances which justified the establishment of the death penalty for certain crimes may have altered so that it may have lost its intrinsic justification.

141. The Welfare Function of the State: A. The Economic Order

There are still to be found advocates of the absolute nonintervention principle which rules out any intervention of the state in economic life apart from quite a few exceptional cases.[1] This principle found its positive expression in the theory of laissez faire and Manchester liberalism. With strong arguments in favor of reliance on the widest possible free play for competition and price mechanism as guaranties of the greatest economy in the employment of goods and labor resources for the general good, neo-liberalism stands for the principle of the minimum of state intervention.[2] Socialism favors a maximum of state interference, associated with the democratic freedoms but not limited by any other principle, in the social economy. Totalitarian socialism (communism) claims for the state the whole organization and direction of the economy.

In general, the danger at present is of accepting state intervention as the natural thing, assigning to the state *a right of intervention* unlimited in principle, and expecting salvation from that alone in every difficulty of economic and social life. In natural law theory there was never any question of the right and duty of the state to intervene in the economic field; for, by the principle of the common good it is the business of the

[1] Cf. L. Mises, *Die Gemeinwirtschaft. Untersuchungen über den Sozialismus,* 1922, 2. Aufl. 1932, trans. by J. Kahane under the title, *Socialism,* 1936.

[2] Cf. the works of W. Eucken, F. A. Hayek, L. C. Robbins, W. Röpke, Adolf Weber.

state to care for the realization of the common good through the economic cooperation of its members.

Neither was there any doubt where the *limits of state intervention* should be fixed, since the principle of subsidiary function gives the state only the function of coordinating, checking, stimulating, and assisting the economic activity and planning of the individuals and their associations. Thus, primary and secondary competencies are clearly demarcated: the duty and right of self-help on the part of the individuals and their associations are primary, all functions of the state are secondary and are limited to securing for them the possibility of attending to their purposes and interests by their own efforts and on their own responsibility within the framework of the common good. Thus, the principle of subsidiary function clearly points in this direction: to establish and promote, as far as is compatible with the common good, the largest possible sphere of economic freedom and self-responsibility for the individual and of freedom and self-government for the vocational groups.[3] The state's functions in the economic sphere will be fully discussed when dealing with the ethics of economic life (cf. Book IV).

142. The Welfare Function of the State: B. Social Policy

Social policy consists in measures and institutions of the state to protect social groups against a disadvantageous position in regard to sharing in the common weal as a result of the social system. The characteristics of this concept and the difference between social policy and social reform we have already discussed when dealing with the defects in the social order (Chaps. 65 ff.). The effect of the individualist capitalistic social system was the economic insecurity of the employee, since his employment depended upon the profit-making prospects of capital and could be swept away by economic crises. Conditions of pay were almost entirely subject to the will of the employer. The life and health of employees were endangered by physically and morally unhealthy conditions of work in factories, a result of the effort to keep down production costs. In

[3] Worthy of note is the pertinent description of this principle by J. S. Mill, who belongs to the classical school of political economy (*Principles of Political Economy*, Bk. V, Chap. 11, par. 16): "In the particular circumstances of a given age or nation, there is scarcely anything really important to the general interest, which it may not be desirable, or even necessary, that the government should take upon itself, not because private individuals cannot effectually perform it, but because they will not. . . . A good government will give all its aid in such a form as to encourage and nurture any rudiments it may find of a spirit of individual exertion. It will be assiduous in removing obstacles and discouragements to voluntary enterprise, and in giving whatever facilities and whatever direction and guidance may be necessary. . . . Government aid, when given merely in default of private enterprise, should be so given as to be, as far as possible, a course of education for the people in the art of accomplishing great objects by individual energy and voluntary cooperation."

general, "labor" was persistently denied an income proportionate to the productivity of the social economy and thus denied its share in the common good. "Property" had the prerogative in the distribution of the product of the national economy and well knew how to utilize it in its own interest. On this account, the state, being responsible for the common good of the citizens, had to intervene on behalf of large groups of the working class which suffered various kinds of disadvantages. In the meantime other groups, too, had disadvantages to complain of. Not least among these groups it was the family, which, lying under a disadvantage in present-day society, had to be helped by the state. The measures taken for these purposes constitute social policy.

Some observations on the *history of social policy* are necessary. To begin with, it is incompatible with the legal nature of modern social policy to consider the state regulations governing pauperism in the sixteenth, seventeenth, and eighteenth centuries as a preliminary stage, a view which is often taken. These were thought of more as protecting society than as protecting the poor, and their application bore, in part at least, a punitive character; the workhouses established under the English Workhouse Act of 1723 are an example of this. Modern state social policy, on the contrary, is founded on the idea of the right of the worker to such a status as will correspond to his human dignity and to his function in the process of economic cooperation. Furthermore, we may recall that, in accordance with the principle of the state's responsibility, the idea of comprehensive and systematic social policy was able to make its way only as a result of hard struggles on two fronts: against economic liberalism and against Marxian socialism. Liberalism fought against it with its principle of laissez faire and nonintervention, fearing an increase in production costs, a loss of ground for the national economy in face of competition on world markets, and an undermining of the worker's sense of responsibility. Marxian socialism at first opposed social policy because it feared interference with the dialectical process of transition from a capitalistic to a socialistic economy; in other words, it feared a slowing up of the supposedly inevitable process of impoverishment of the working class and of the formation of proletarian class consciousness and the fighting spirit of the proletariat in the transition to socialistic dictatorship. The first isolated efforts toward social policy are found long before the era of social policy; they were directed against the gravest excesses in the employment of children. Already in 1802 a law was passed in England to protect children engaged in factory work (*Health and Morals of Apprentices Act*), but since there was no independent inspection of factories it had no real effect. The *First Factory Act* in 1833 created the necessary inspectorate. In Germany (Prussia) also, the first law inspired by social policy, in 1839, dealt with child labor.

From these beginnings to systematic social legislation was a long road; the lead was taken by Germany (Sickness Insurance, 1883; Accident Insurance, 1884; Invalids' and Old Age Pensions, 1889) and by Austria (Accident Insurance, 1887, Sickness Insurance, 1888). With regard to aiming at regulating working conditions, the trade unions became of the greatest significance. Fundamental to their position was freedom of combination (right of free association in order to safeguard and further the economic and social interests of the worker in labor relations), which for the most part was recognized by the constitutions as a basic right. This recognition by the legislator of trade unions as representatives of the workers meant that they had authority to conclude collective agreements, their conditions having binding force for labor relations within the scope of the agreements and hence being inviolable in the individual labor contract; a further result was that trade union representatives were drawn into the functions of institutions set up by state social policy in the service of industrial peace (arbitration, labor courts) and in addition they participated in the directing of self-governing social insurance bodies. The development of social policy has reached different stages of progress in different countries, and in what has been said we have dealt only with the average position.

The *ends and means* of social policy may be reduced to two groups: they concern labor conditions and income security. As regards labor relations, social policy comprises the protection of the worker's person, life, and health by regulations concerning workshop space, power-driven machines, means of transportation, lavatory and cloakroom accommodations. To these are added regulations concerning the labor of women, youths, and children (prohibition or restriction of employment, prohibition of night work, protection of pregnant women and mothers in confinement). An assured effectiveness is given to these regulations by the institution of a state factory inspectorate and by the cooperation of chosen representatives of the workers (shop stewards) in seeing to the maintenance of the regulations. Further, there are rules regarding minimum intervals between shifts and breaks during shifts, hours of work (the first great achievement is the forty-eight hour week), paid holidays, and length of notice.

The other chief aim of social policy, security of livelihood, is served primarily by general and compulsory social insurance with contributions payable by employers, employees and the state: it provides for cases of loss of income through sickness, accident, disability, and unemployment. Security of livelihood is also served by employment exchanges (they should be under the joint control of employers and employees on a basis of parity) providing the particulars of labor supply and labor demand in their region, and bound up with this, advisory and training centers for the purpose of facilitating transfer to branches of industry where there is a demand for labor.

The fundamental task of social policy in securing the worker's livelihood is an employment policy aiming at the maximum of full employment (having regard to the demands of social and economic productivity). To be distinguished from this general full employment policy are the measures to be taken to provide employment for particular situations (economic recessions), such as road building and drainage schemes. Social policy also includes the exercise of influence by the state to bring about a proportionate distribution of income; this will be spoken of in other connections.

The object of social policy mentioned can also be designated the objects of *social security* or of the *welfare state.* It follows from what has been said, and it will be more fully shown later, that the conceptions of social security, welfare state, and social policy may not be confined to the functions of state social insurance; neither, however, are they to be understood in the sense of a responsibility of the state, as though it were the function of the state to make direct provision for all necessities in all vicissitudes in the lives of its citizens, as is posited in the collectivistic and socialistic interpretations of social security and of the welfare state.

I *The Foundation of the State's Obligation of Social Policy*

According to the *common good principle,* social policy is part of the state's function, an obligation of common good justice; seen from the viewpoint of the underprivileged groups, it is an obligation of distributive justice (cf. Chap. 50). Further abstract discussions of its position under categories of justice seem to be superfluous. It would seem to be more important to glance at the deeper practical connections. The chief province of social policy is connected with the labor contract. In this, from the point of view of fundamental connections in the light of natural law, property and labor enter into association with each other. By natural law, social obligations are connected with property (cf. Chap. 171), and some of these gain acceptance especially in the labor relationship (e.g., use of property without harming others, hence protection of health in the workshop; proportionate social benefits to fellow workers in the use of productive property; the duty to confer such benefits in the form of "social insurance" of members of the family and others working in the family business was considered a natural precept).

As soon as a large proportion of owners of productive *property* are unwilling to fulfill these social obligations belonging to private ownership, there arises an obligation for the state to regulate them through legislation and to guarantee their observance; it does this by "labor law" as the chief part of social legislation. Labor law, therefore, stands in an essential relationship to the social obligations of private ownership and is correlated to property law. The deeper real foundation of the state's obligation toward social policy is shown equally on the side of *labor.* The labor contract is a particular kind of contract (cf. Chap. 172). There are natural law conditions bound up with it which are irreducible, since work is associated with the human person and its existential ends. As soon as large groups in society have no guarantee that these conditions will be observed in the labor contract, there falls to the state the obligation in common good justice of guaranteeing their observance by social legislation. Accordingly, legal obligations and legal claims of a natural law kind, the former with regard to property, the latter with regard to labor, have to be given effect in the labor contract: it is an obligation of common good justice for the state to define and guarantee their force. Our analysis of the state's obligation toward social policy is of no mere theoretical interest, as will be shown by our examination of the limits of this obligation, which now becomes necessary.

II *The Limits of the State's Competence for Social Policy*

To give a precise account of these limits is today just as important as to explain the natural law foundation of social policy. What limits does natural law set to social policy? The authority of the state ceases where its obligation ceases, an obligation which has its foundation in the common good. This is the general *principle of subsidiary function,* namely, the principle that responsibilities and competencies only fall to the state to the extent that the members of society, on their own resources and on their own responsibility, are not capable of fulfilling the essential purposes founded in the existential ends.[1] The order of subsidiary function, which holds good for social policy, also provides the natural law limits to social security and social welfare policy. If these limits are overstepped, there is the danger that social policy will result in increasingly collectivistic tendencies in economic and social life, because the social measures then necessary would require economic planning, which would be accompanied by inevitable encroachments on the rights of freedom, rights protected by the order of subsidiary function in accordance with natural law. Labor itself, whose protection is the object of social policy, would be exposed to the danger of encroachments by the overexpansion of social security policy. Labor cannot remain outside the necessary planning if the overall plans and the economic yield expected from them are not to suffer.[2] Before we attempt to describe the limits in question in detail, it should be emphasized that a wide measure of social policy will always be an obligation of natural law for a state with an industrial society, because of the particular relationship of property and labor obtaining in it.

1. The natural law limits of the state's social policy are overstepped if the social function of private property is infringed; this happens as soon as savings (provision for the vicissitudes of life) decline so far that the rise in the rate of consumption in a social economy forces down the

[1] Even social justice places the obligation first on the social groups (cf. Chap. 50). There seems to be too little regard for the limits of the state's social policy when it is laid down as a principle that the primary duty of the modern state is the enforcement of social justice; cf. Jacques Maritain, *Man and the State* (London), 1954, p. 18.

[2] This is the certain finding of the investigations of Joseph Schumpeter, *Kapitalismus, Socialismus und Demokratie,* 1946, pp. 276–94.

rate of capital formation to an extent that the fulfillment of the social end of the economy is jeopardized. Some points to be considered are the present-day standard of living, the population structure (future old-age pensions), international economic development (automation), and the international situation. The social function of private property is likewise involved when, through compulsory insurance, portions of wages are expropriated, with adverse effects on responsibility and the willingness to save, so that large numbers of the insured seek to make unjustified and extravagant insurance claims (sickness and convalescence benefits, premature disability pension, and unemployment assistance).

2. From the viewpoint of labor, the limit of the state's obligation, and hence competence, for social policy is reached if the workers themselves are capable of looking after their economic and social rights. Good reasons exist for assuming that, in present-day industrial society with its pressure groups, especially with the present-day links between trade unions and political parties in the mass democracy, labor and capital are equal in power.

3. Social policy is certainly on the wrong road insofar as it paves the way for new positions of power in society. While it was, and is, one of the essential objects to protect labor against the domination of the owners of the means of production who have social power, the national insurance bodies have become social powers to a very large extent by their centralization of competencies and of administrative bureaucracy. Their power stretches equally over the contributions of compulsorily insured persons and the form and extent of insurance benefits; in sickness, insurance patients, doctors, hospitals, and chemists fall equally under the control of their power. Through their connection with parties and trade unions, the national insurance bodies possess further political power. There is a well-founded demand for decentralizing the national insurance institutions [3] by transferring the burden of organization to vocational bodies, territorially distributed, while the central organization would have to protect the aggregate interests of the insured, to assess risks, and to exercise a controlling function over the self-governing vocational bodies.

4. As a result of the connection of the state's welfare function with the order of subsidiary function, social policy can never be an end in itself; rather, the chief aim of all social policy is the restoration of their own power to the underprivileged groups, to enable them to fulfill, on their

[3] Cf. Gerhard Weisser in the very cautious article, *Soziale Sicherheit, Handwörterbuch der Sozialwissenschaften,* Vol. IX, 1956, p. 411: "According to all experience of governmental and economic organization, it can cause no undue disadvantage if the organ or organs become increasingly decentralized. The cultural interest speaks for decentralization on the basis of freedom. . . . Equally, no overwhelming prejudice need be feared if those to be insured have a share in the decisions of the organ or organs. . . . In each case, democratically constituted committees of management and the like will be appropriate." On the centralist structure and the state socialistic impact of Bismarck's German "classical national insurance" see Georg Kliesch, *Neue Ordnung,* 1956, n. 4, pp. 222–28.

own responsibility, through participation in social cooperation, the tasks imposed by the existential ends. It must be the aim of state social policy, therefore, to render itself, as far as possible, superfluous, by influencing the functioning of the social economy so that it will be able to attain its social end by its own working. Social policy, therefore, must aim at social reform: the immediate aim is direct help for underprivileged groups; the further aim, by natural law, is to cure the evil at the roots.

5. Social policy reaches its limits as soon as its influence goes against the full extent of productivity and output, and thus against the social end of the economy and of the economic common good. All social policy implies the obligation to an economic policy which guarantees the fulfillment of the social end of national economy. Within this framework, first and absolute priority belongs to insurance for cases of sickness, accident, disability, age, and unemployment; but these must be under the control of the self-governing vocational bodies in regard to the question whether a claim to social insurance benefit is justified. Second in order of priority is an employment policy which assures to all members of society the possibility of gaining a livelihood while strictly preserving a stable currency. As third priority there are the tasks concerned with the distribution of income by means of fiscal policy; in carrying out these it is necessary to safeguard the relationship mentioned earlier between the rate of consumption and the rate of capital formation.

A fundamental condition of the order of subsidiary function in social policy is stability of currency: above all, *social security* demands *currency stability*. If the true principle of insurance is maintained, any gradual decrease in the value of currency will cause a depreciation in value of the enormous sums of insurance contributions, so that the insured persons are in danger of receiving only a fraction of what they have a right to expect in insurance payments. The case is different if the currency remains stable, thereby creating for the social economy the most important condition of all social security. For this reason alone the assurance of a stable currency is one of the most important fundamental natural law precepts for the state's economic and social policy; another reason is that only with a stable currency can competition fulfill its social function (cf. Chap. 181), namely, to maintain the movement of prices toward the socially necessary costs. If these conditions are fulfilled, workers, employees, and officials could expect full value in wages and pensions; in addition, when prices fall as a result of a rise in economic productivity, they would receive their due share in the increased output of the political economy. To this they have a right, since certainly in the political economy the work they have done in advance continues to have effect and to contribute to the growth of productivity.

From the point of view of the natural law order of the social economy, two much discussed questions are considered to be, in part at least, *illusory problems*. The first concerns the question of security: whether for old-age pensions under national insurance, capital security or the contribution method is to be preferred; in a political economy with guaranteed currency stability and guaranteed social functioning of competition (of the market), there can be no doubt that the method of capital security corresponds to the nature of the facts. It would mean the full acceptance of the principle of insurance. The other question concerns the gearing of pension rates to the upward trend of wages (dynamic pensions, productivity pensions). Only on the supposition of the existing severe injustice of a rapid or slow inflation, and the further injustice of the impairment of the market economy in its social function, will a higher valuation of pensions in harmony with the inflation and the rate of growth of socio-economic productivity become a real question of justice. Obviously, such a solution of the pension problem results in developments toward the provider state. It is at once clear also that, in such cases, injustices which are not eradicated engender fresh injustices accompanied by the relevant "emergency solutions" (these always deal only with the symptoms, and not the removal of the cause). This applies particularly to the new inflationary pressure arising from dynamic pensions. In addition to that which is always in operation, the increased demand for consumer goods accompanying wage increases in a boom period already portends the danger of inflationary overexpansion; this tendency would be directly strengthened by the increased volume of purchasing power accompanying the demand for consumer goods as bound up with a dynamic pension scheme. Inversely, the fall in wages in an economic depression at a critical point of time would mean an accompanying loss in pensions, which would be harmful to demand and would tend to discourage any fresh turn toward business prosperity and full employment.

6. The principle of subsidiary function permits no nationalization, "socialization," of production and of services in spheres where it is the business of state social policy to make them sufficiently available to lower income groups by social policy methods, which can be provided, however, on the basis of private ownership and private initiative. According to the principle of subsidiary function, there are grounds in some circumstances for the nationalization of railways or the communalization of public supply undertakings, such as gas and electricity. Quite different would be the nationalization of house building or of medical services, even though it were not complete nationalization but only nationalization of the major part of such services. By nationalization of the medical service, elementary rights of the doctor (the free exercise of his profession) and of the patient (free choice of doctor) are adversely affected. Such considerations are all the more serious since the performance and the employment of medical services are closely bound up with questions of conscience and confidence. As a state official the doctor may be expected to follow directives from above which are unacceptable to his own conscience and

to the conscience of his patient.[4] Also incompatible with the principle of subsidiarity is the extensive nationalization and communalization of house property and building, which is advocated by the socialists, and which has already been referred to in connection with the family (cf. Chap. 74). Equally unjustifiable is a socializing of charity (e.g., of hospitals supported by voluntary charitable activity) or of similar welfare work. The socialization of charitable undertakings is nothing less than a violation by the state of human rights, of which the right of free association to practice charity on the grounds of religion and humanity is not the least.

143. The Cultural Function of the State: A. The School

What right has the state with respect to education? We are thinking not of universities, but of elementary and secondary education, that is, of all schools in which the mind and character receive their basic formation. The care of the general good, which unquestionably is the task of the state, undoubtedly empowers it to provide for general instruction sufficient to enable its citizens to be equal to the claims made upon them in their political and economic life by present-day civilization. Modern industrial life itself makes demands on a very large number of workers which cannot be met except by those who have had considerable schooling. The same is true of the administrative tasks in the modern state, including the tasks of local government. Indeed, the very existence and development of modern civilization presuppose certain standards of education in all citizens. Only if a minimum of instruction is obligatory for all children can there be any possibility of a selection of real talent as needed for the more important tasks in culture, administration, and government. All this makes clear the right of the state to insure the necessary measure of instruction for all [1] by compulsory school attendance if parents cannot prove that a child otherwise obtains the instruction which would guarantee the attainment of the educational standard prescribed by the state.

Like all functions of the state, this and the rights based on it are only of a subsidiary character. For clear reasons, which we have discussed

[4] On the socialization of health services in England under the socialist government after the Second World War and on the experience of socialistic policies and the policy of social security, cf. J. Messner, *Das englische Experiment des Sozialismus, dargestellt auf Grund ökonomischer Tatsachen und sozialistischer Selbstzeugnisse,* 1954, Japanese trans., 1961. One may observe the lack of incentive for the state doctor to pursue his education further.

[1] Cf. W. E. Ketteler, *Freiheit, Autorität und Kirche,* 1862, in which the famous German bishop was one of the first on the side of the Church to emphasize the right of the state to introduce compulsory school attendance under modern conditions, provided that the primary educational rights of the parents and the Church are respected.

when dealing with the educational rights of the parents, the primary right over the education of their children belongs to the parents. This means the right, in the first place, to determine the fundamentals of education, chiefly the religious and moral education of their children; in the second place, to make their own provision for their instruction as demanded by the state in accordance with its specific right; in the third place, the right of the parents to codetermine the spirit of the state school according to their religious convictions and according to their view of life. These rights, based on the freedom of conscience, constitute the natural *right to the free school.* Hence, from what has been said, the following applies.

1. There is no jural basis either for a state school monopoly or for compulsion to attend state schools. Parents have a natural right to found private schools if they wish and if their economic situation permits; in that case the state has merely the right to see that its standard of instruction is maintained. The state not only may not prevent the founding of private schools, but is even obliged by distributive justice to allot subsidies to these private schools out of the taxes, subsidies equal to the expenditure it saves through the private schools.

2. In its own schools, the legal status of the state is in the sphere of essential, particularly religious and moral, education, a representative of the parents to whom the parents' inalienable rights are delegated. In the realm of religious and moral education, next to that of the parents ranks the right of the religious community, that is the Church to which the child belongs, because of its mission in the sphere of the religious and moral existential ends. Only the denominational schools correspond with these rights of the parents and the Church. These owe their character to the uniformity between education and instruction: the latter often touches on fundamental questions of human existence and therefore must be guided in this ambit by the determining values that are to form the child's mind. This character of the school calls for separate schools for children of different denominations, staffed by teachers of their own denomination, and with the Church having the opportunity to fulfill her moral and religious educational mission. Certainly, such a solution may not always be possible, when, for example, in small local communities a common school has to suffice. In this case the educational rights of parents and of the Church will be complied with through provision for moral and religious education in cooperation with the Church communities.

3. If their educational rights are threatened by the state, the parents have a grave obligation to do everything in their power to reach a settlement of the schools question in harmony with their duties in the education of their children. Their rights are inalienable in the sense that parents remain responsible for the attainment of the ends of these rights as long as these ends and corresponding duties remain unfulfilled.

J. S. Mill,[2] one of the leading representatives of liberalism, stressed that a state school monopoly would not only be incompatible with the parents' rights and liberty, but is bound to become a great danger to the general good and to the development of civilization. He observes that the state may justifiably require of everyone the possession of certain knowledge; but to prescribe how and from whom this knowledge is to be obtained is not within its rights. The totalitarian states have fully proved how true it was that a government which can make use of a state school monopoly can make of the young whatever it wills. Indeed, the demands for civic and national education, which in liberalist society were largely the pretext for the introduction of general compulsory attendance at state schools, were almost always understood as a basis for the title to make the teaching of a political and of a national creed, which the state has no real right to teach, part of an obligatory education. Precisely this right, with the exclusion of all rights of parents and of the Church, is claimed by the totalitarian state with its system of complete state monopoly of schools, compulsory schooling, and secularized schools.

144. The Cultural Function of the State: B. Cultural Policy

By cultural values is here meant values belonging strictly to the sphere of the mind. Has the state any functions in this sphere, for example, in philosophy, science, art? On this topic, Western political theory begins with *Plato's* opinion that the state must decidedly concern itself with art and literature, even though only in the direction of averting influences detrimental to the commonwealth. He thinks music and literature should be subjected to a thoroughgoing state censorship; they should find a place in the education of his political aristocracy only after rigorous selection. Although he goes too far in the standards which he applies, nevertheless he remains clearly aware that the function of the state can only be protective and not productive. The state, it is implied, is to protect the common weal, and is not to inspire, to direct, or to regulate production in the intellectual sphere.

The modern state went to the extreme in both directions. The individualist-liberalist political theory of the nineteenth century denied the state any right of interference in the sphere of culture. Yet, the twentieth century sees in the totalitarian states a disciplining and regimentation of all spheres of cultural life—of philosophy, science, art, literature, book publishing, and the press—such as has never before been experienced in human history. Not only are whole classes of works of philosophy and literature placed on the state's "Index" of prohibited books in these countries and destroyed when they are found, but under the disciplining in-

[2] Cf. J. S. Mill, *Principles of Political Economy,* 1848, Bk. V, Chap. 11, par. 8.

fluence of the monopolistic professional organizations a tendency inspired by dogmatic collective values is enforced upon every activity of the mind.

With the development of the modern liberalist state and of the modern totalitarian state the problem of *state tolerance* was posed anew. Previously the state, since it had a religious foundation, considered itself justified and bound, at its own wish or at the wish of the authorities of the religious communities, to prevent intellectual activities in which were seen a threat to the fundamental spiritual values of the common good of the existing unitary culture. The situation is different today in several respects.

First, freedom itself is differently assessed as the result of a development in which, on the one hand, autonomous freedom was claimed for man and unrestricted freedom for social life; on the other hand, however, moral and jural consciousness progressed to the recognition of human rights and, with this, to the recognition of what is fundamental to all these, freedom of conscience as man's primal right.

Secondly, the situation is changed in that, at the center of the worldwide ideological warfare determining the cultural future of mankind, is the interpretation of the nature of man and thus, above all, the recognition of his rights of freedom. The society wishing to fight for freedom can count on success only if it gives evidence that the principle of freedom is a reality in its life, to the whole extent demanded by freedom of public opinion as a fundamental value of the free society.

Then, thirdly, in modern society culture of the mind is no longer only the concern of a privileged class united by strong ties of tradition, but also the concern of ever new forces emerging by a constant process of selection; at the same time, the growth of culture itself is understood in the perspective of the free creative forces stirred up by itself, so that, for the consciousness of the free society, the freedom compatible with the demands of the common good forms not only the basic value of social order, but also the prime moving force of cultural development. We stress the change in the situation strongly, because in the situation new demands are made which arise from the existential ends of man, and new applications of natural law principles are called for in the changed world. The preceding considerations have significance not only for the question of the relationship of state and of culture occupying us now, but also for the relationship of state and religion, which will be dealt with in the following chapter.[1]

These considerations lead to this conclusion: In the free society, which provides access for all to cultural values and to a share in creative cultural activity, the general principle of the *maximum degree of freedom* compatible with the actual common good applies uniquely to the sphere of

[1] Cf. concerning the wide range of fundamental and particular problems which cannot be further dealt with here, and also concerning public opinion, J. Messner, *Kulturethik,* esp. Chap. 77.

mental culture. As soon as the historical situation has developed thus far, as previously mentioned, the deeper ontological foundation of our thesis will also be evident: human personality and social culture expand in the creative struggle for values and in mutual fructification, and therefore only in freedom. The state's function as guardian of the common good in the sphere of intellectual culture is limited to the averting of direct and grave threats to the common good, which are conjured up by misuse of freedom. Indeed, its chief function plainly becomes the protection and security of the maximum degree of freedom, since on this depends the future of freedom and of culture. In present-day democracy, on the grounds of the principle of subsidiary function, *primarily "society" is called upon* to generate forces to oppose destructive developments in the intellectual sphere. And, indeed, only in this way can the healthy forces themselves grow vigorous. Thus, natural law theory must, in this matter, also rely upon the self-regulating powers of society and insist that only when these fail and the common good, social order, and peaceful development are directly threatened, does the function of regulative intervention in the interest of the common good devolve upon the state.

To illustrate the application of these principles by a concrete example, we may consider the often discussed question of atheistic or revolutionary teaching at universities, particularly when these are maintained or supported by the state. The chief facts to be taken into consideration are the condition of public opinion and the concrete prospects of success of particular methods. In the circumstances of the present day this seems to lead to the following conclusions. Normally it would hardly serve a useful purpose to ban any given political or philosophical tenets from the universities or to dismiss their exponents from their chairs, as overzealous idealists sometimes imagine. It is a lesson of history that revolutionary doctrines do not lose in potency and may even become more dangerous if their public expression is banned. Besides, undue haste in calling for state interference may often spring from the indolence of groups who are aware of the baneful influences, but are not so quick in the use of the opportunities offered by the free society to counteract such mischief by their own efforts. The methods available include these: positive work of scholarship in the fields in question; effective scientific criticism of destructive philosophical and social doctrines; vigorous support of scholarly exponents of sound doctrines; discussion and criticism in a well-organized press; the providing of opportunities in university towns for discussing pernicious doctrines among students and others; and not least, the awakening of the critical faculty and intellectual powers of resistance in the young. Indeed, in order to have regard for the mentality of modern society, it seems of the highest importance to train the youth of the universities to active resistance to such influences, if they are later to take their places in this society for the general good of all.

In the sphere of tolerance by the state there is a question of special importance on the mental and cultural level which calls for careful consideration: the problem of *public morality.*[2] Basically, the same principles are valid, from a spiritual and cultural point of view, as for the rest of the functions of the state. In contrast to the individualist-liberalist indifferentism toward values, traditional natural law ethics has always upheld the principle that public morality belongs to the highest goods of the common weal and of human culture. From this it has drawn the conclusion that it is a function of the state, as defender of the common weal, to avert destructive forces in this sphere. In the modern state, the discussion centers mostly on radio, television, literature that is a danger to the young, amusements accessible to the young, the motion picture, the theater, "night life," and prostitution. By public morality is to be understood the moral standards which a society sets itself in its conduct outside the purely private sphere. The *criterion of what is meant by "public"* is to be sought in the circumstance that, from particular conduct, there can proceed effects morally harmful to members of the community who do not possess the necessary power to resist such influences. This definition can surely not be regarded as a narrow one; it explicitly presupposes a certain power of resistance derived from education and even admits the necessity of a kind of inurement to an atmosphere in which standards are comparatively low. Indeed, the concept of "public" cannot be considered to be as precise as is often assumed. In any case, the moral standards must be set higher where the public also comprises children and adolescents. In no way is it the business of the state to intervene in the purely private sphere; its function is to act solely as defender of the common good.[3]

It is all the more difficult to arrive at an absolutely unequivocal conception of public morality, because public authority must estimate what methods and what degree of control are expedient in existing circumstances, that is, what methods will really serve the common good. Very strict and rigid measures may do more harm than good at times. Furthermore, the legislator will hardly be able to prevent evasions of the law. It is well known that clubs are set up as "private" which are open to almost anyone on payment of a membership fee. That there is, however, a *public conscience* in these matters, which can be aroused, is shown by the existence of organs of film censorship in all civilized countries, which owe their origin to the initiative of social groups. Or again, we may think

[2] Natural law doctrine has included these questions in the treatment of phenomena which the lawgiver is unable to prevent, in spite of their perverseness, and to which is applied the rule thus expressed by Suárez (*De leg.*, Bk. III, Chap. 12, n. 16), following Aristotle and St. Thomas: "Quando autem vitia non sunt noxia communitati, vel ex rigorosa punitione illorum maiora mala timentur, permittenda potius sunt, quam cohibenda per leges civiles. Quapropter in particulari ad applicandam hanc regulam necessaria est prudentia legislatoris: neque aliquid certum in hoc puncto dici, aut affirmari posse existimo."

[3] Suárez, *ibid.*, Chap. 11, n. 8: "Non spectat ad leges civiles . . . privata honestas singulorum, ut tales sunt, sed solum ea modo rectitudo per has leges constituitur, quae bono civili vel necessaria, vel valde utilis est."

of the abolition of houses of ill fame in France after the Second World War as a result of the mobilization of public opinion by a fearless woman, in spite of the powerful resistance of profit-making interests.

In nearly all modern states, the *civil law* also contains a kind of minimum code of public morality; certain acts are made punishable because of their relation to the moral goods of the community (e.g., disorderly conduct, the supplying of alcohol to intoxicated persons, certain sexual offenses, blasphemy). Such legal regulations may be the heritage of a Christian tradition. Notwithstanding the most vigorous attempts to abolish culpability, as in the last-named two spheres, the natural and Christian conscience has successfully asserted itself in almost all states.

145. State and Religion

Among the natural rights of man, which are rooted in his existential ends and to be respected and guaranteed by the state, are those in the religious sphere. Has the *state itself a religious existence?* Only on doctrinaire grounds can it be denied that it has. If human existence is seen in its full reality, the error of the principle "religion is a private affair" is evident. Of course, the absolutely self-contained and autonomous individual of individualist theory allows no extension of his religious existence into the political community, and, again, the state that follows the collectivistic theory has no place for the religious existence of the community, because it makes its own being and its own collective ends absolutes. But as soon as we look at the whole reality of human existence and the absolute character of its existential ends in the religious sphere, it becomes evident that the state itself has a religious existence, that religion is also a public affair, and that the state community, no less than the individual himself, has obligations to God, the Creator of his nature, which is ordered toward the state. A dogmatic political secularism finds as little basis in social reality as does a dogmatic anarchism.

That we do not deviate far from the prevailing convictions of the Western world with these ideas may be seen from the fact that its statesmen, as in England and in the United States, do not hesitate to call their countries Christian; they know that, while for the greater part of their people Christianity is not a lived reality, yet they have fundamentals in common, namely, those rooted in Western Christian civilization. These statesmen know that, on this account, their state as a community is bound to the *basic values of the Christian cultural tradition.*

A Christian state in the true sense, which, in view of the *common Christian profession* of the great majority of its citizens, considers itself bound by Christian beliefs about truth and value will, if not in its constitution, at least in its conduct, recognize God as the origin of all rights, including those of political authority, and accordingly will recognize the sanctity and inviolability of natural rights in every sphere. In its marriage law it must fully comply with the sacramental character of Christian marriage (e.g., in England, where the Anglican Church is the state Church, the marriage of Catholics is first performed in Church before a Catholic priest, and is followed directly afterwards by a civil ceremony in the sacristy before the same priest representing the authority of the state); in its educational services it will honor the right of the parents to have their children brought up according to their moral and religious convictions; in public institutions and those in which it has a controlling influence (such as broadcasting), it must not only counteract influences detrimental to the substantially Christian character of its people but it must also, in a positive way, try to promote the cultural ideas arising from this Christian character; in its foreign policy it will exert what influence it can in support of the Christian cultural tradition in times when this is threatened, and will render aid to other nations that are struggling for their Christian existence.

The principles mentioned seem theoretically incontestable if one thinks of a state whose citizens are united in the profession of one Christian faith. In the *nation of mixed religion,* especially when the greater part of the population does not profess or actually practice any religion, the state cannot profess and promote the religion of a minority without causing grave conflicts of conscience among the majority of its citizens. The majority in such a case could find themselves compelled to take part, at least indirectly, in acts of public authority which were not acceptable to their consciences. Connected with this is the problem of *state tolerance with regard to religion,* namely, the guaranteeing of freedom of belief and conscience. In detail this means: (1) the right to worship, in the sense of the right to the private and public practice of religion or to the practice of none without suffering any disadvantage in civil life; (2) the right to association on the ground of common religious duties and interests; (3) the right to champion the convictions of one's religious community in accordance with the right of expression and information maintained in the modern free society.[1]

[1] On the principles founded in *Christian* faith concerning the question of tolerance in the state; on the fact that truth is undivided, but that this does not exclude a proportion of truth in non-Christian religions; on the question of tolerance as one of justice and charity; on the basis of the claim of tolerance in the right of the individual conscience; on the claim that Catholic states should not deny those of other beliefs what the Catholic Church claims with justice for its adherents in non-Catholic states, cf. the prudent and well-considered opinion of Albert Hartman, S.J., *Toleranz und christlicher Glaube,* 1955. Concerning the history of tolerance cf. J. Lecler, S.J., *Histoire de la tolérance au siècle de la reforme,* 2 vols. (Paris), 1955. Especially worthy of note is the reference to the fact that, until the middle of the sixteenth century, the principle of uniformity of religion in the state was represented as a demand of the good of the state, and then toleration of a second religion was upheld here and there also by appeal to the benefit of the state; the right of conscience was not thought of at all. Cf. in addition Roger Aubert, Louis Bouyer (*et al.*), *Tolérance et communauté humaine: Chrétiens dans un monde divisé* (Paris), 1952; A. Dordett, *Die Ordnung zwischen Kirche und Staat,* 1958.

For the most part, the state can deal justly with the situation described only by basing its relation to religion on the *principle of the separation of Church and state.* The formula of a free Church in a free state, therefore, can acquire a correct sense, namely, that the Church should, according to circumstances, be in a position to exercise its own specific rights without hindrance from the state. The formula involves a fallacy, however, if the freedom of the state is understood as an expression of formal religious indifferentism (suggesting that one religion is as good as another), or if the freedom of the Church is reduced to the general freedom of association laid down in the constitution; for then the status of the Church is put on a par with that of a merely private association, irrespective of its ends, which cover the religious, existential ends of man embracing the whole of human existence, and in which, therefore, even purely by the law of nature, are to be found the roots of her public mission and of her autonomous rights.[2]

If traditional natural law theory has always maintained a universal *competence of the Church* in matters which belong to the sphere of its inherent ends, and in this sense has claimed a superior competence to that of the state, it has been able to offer logically unassailable grounds for this attitude. When once the order of precedence of the existential ends and of the responsibilities springing from them is settled, as well as the fact that rights are founded upon them, there can be no mistaking the autonomy as well as the paramount position of that community whose function lies in the religious and moral sphere, and hence in absolute existential ends, in relation to the state, whose ends lie outside the sphere of religious salvation.[3] For the same reason, the natural law tradition, at least in its most authoritative representatives, has always regarded it as evident that the Church possesses no competence outside the sphere of the religious and moral existential ends, that is, no sort of competence in the province which is assigned to the state by reason of its purpose of fulfilling the fundamental functions of society. Here the state is autonomous, and the nature of the Church itself precludes *clericalism,* which would consist in an assumption of competence by the Church or its ministers as such in the province of the state.

From the principles mentioned we may derive the following conclusions. The Church cannot, without being false to its nature, place itself at the service of a state or of a nation so that precedence to ends other

[2] To suppose that the rights of the Church are grounded only in its supposed status as one of the lesser communities in the universal society, is the error of J. N. Figgis (*Churches in the Modern State,* 1913), although he must be accounted in modern political philosophy as one of the outstanding pioneers, following Von Gierke and Maitland, of the theory of social and legal pluralism (cf. Chaps. 32, 42). Concerning the relation of Church and state cf. J. Lecler, *L'église et la souveraineté de l'état* (Paris), 1946, Engl. trans., *The Two Sovereignties: A Study of the Relationship between Church and State,* 1952.

[3] Cf. Alec R. Vidler, *The Orb and the Cross,* 1946; Jacques Maritain, *Primauté du spirituel,* 1927, trans. by J. F. Scanlan, *The Things That Are Not Caesar's,* 1930.

than the absolute existential ends is granted; a "National Church" based upon such an intermingling of ends makes itself a constituent element and an instrument of a single political society, whereas the claim of the Church in its own sphere can only be a universal one. Again, the state can never derive from its nature a title to subject the work of the Church, which is prescribed by its mission, to a control founded on state interest; any such Gallicanism, which may even go so far as to claim a right to forbid or to sanction forms of prayer (England), is a manifest overstepping of the competence of the state. A conclusion from the intrinsic relation of the spheres of competence of the two communities, Church and state, is, further, that those matters in which their spheres meet are most expediently settled by agreement. "Most expediently" here means in the manner most conformable to man's existential ends, which both Church and state have to serve in their own spheres, in view of the fact that the individual belongs to both communities and hence is subject to both competencies. The principal domains in which these competences intersect are marriage, the school, and the education of youth after school age. We have dealt with these domains in the relevant parts of this study. These domains form the main object of treaties, known as *concordats,* between the state and the Catholic Church.

The principles that have been developed above also indicate *a competence of the Church in the political sphere,* that is, insofar as the absolute existential ends of man are affected in the life and activity of the state; hence, the question of the Church's missionary sphere arises. The fact that during the Second World War a great number of non-Catholics on the side of the Allies made it a source of bitter complaint against the Catholic Church that it did not use its jurisdiction to exert pressure on the consciences of Catholics serving in the armed forces of the Axis powers, bears evidence that even outside the natural law tradition there is no doubt of the range of ecclesiastical jurisdiction. But these very accusers overlook the fact that this jurisdiction of the Church is solely concerned with the best means of safeguarding the spiritual interests of *all* members of the Church in existing conditions, and not political interests.[4]

Direct intervention in the sphere of conscience, such as was possible (e.g., by dispensation from the oath of allegiance to a prince in an unjust

[4] In the case in question the situation was in the highest degree complicated by the fact that on whichever side such pressure by the Church had been applied it was to be feared that psychological prejudice would treat the matter as one of political partisanship; untold harm might thus have ensued for the religious well-being of a great number of the members of the Church. Had no other ground existed for such anxiety, the struggle which had continued against its authority during two hundred years must have given the Church reason to fear that great numbers of its members might not possess the strength to hold out in the conflict of conscience which such intervention would have occasioned. The reproach, therefore, should be directed against those who have striven with inflexible tenacity through the nineteenth and twentieth centuries to banish the Church from the public life of Western man and Western society.

war), is not, however, the only way the authority of the Church can be exercised in the political sphere when religious or moral principles are concerned. Another method is the arousing of consciences by public declarations about the irreconcilability of political principles and acts of governments with religious and moral rights. A third method, especially fostered by the Catholic Church today, is the systematic training of lay people for the exercise of their obligations in all walks of life as citizens, in order to make moral and religious principles again effective in the secularized society. This is what is called Catholic Action, defined by *Pius XI* as "the Church at work in society."

146. The Defensive Function of the State: Defensive War

Self-defense against external aggression is, for the state, the indispensable condition for the performance of the fundamental social functions which constitute its nature. Self-protection can force the state into war. We have already discussed the nature of war, the laws of war, and the international machinery for avoiding war in connection with international law (cf. Chaps. 104–105). Because it is bound up with fearful evils, war is never justified as a means of policy but only for defense. Accordingly, *the conditions for a just war are:* (1) it must be waged for the defense of vital goods of a state community, such goods being violated or directly and gravely threatened by attack from another state; (2) no superior authority can be called upon to restore the violated right; (3) war must not jeopardize still higher goods than those which are to be defended; (4) the intention of the defender does not go beyond the defense and restoration of the violated right; (5) the means of defense employed must not be unlawful in themselves; (6) the means employed must be proportionate to the purpose of defense, that is, they must not cause more evil than is necessitated by this purpose. If one of these conditions is lacking, a war cannot be just.

Certain representatives of a Christian and humanitarian *pacifism* raise objections to this view with the argument that, although it may once have been justifiable as a means of defense, under no conditions can war be regarded as justified today, that is, in the age of nuclear weapons. Present-day warfare, so runs the argument, with its mass murder, its destruction, its propaganda of hate, its moral evils, and the danger of the annihilation of all human culture, indeed of humanity itself, is so frightful in its effects that no attack on the goods of a commonwealth can make it into a proportionate means of defense, since the evils it causes always outweigh the harm that might otherwise have befallen the polity. There may perhaps have been some truth in this argument when the world knew nothing of the totalitarian states. But since mankind has learned with what consistency such states are capable of eradicating almost every possibility of a revival of freedom and justice in a conquered state, it can hardly be doubted that the possibility of preserving those goods, all the more if they include the religious and moral freedoms, establishes not only a *right* but a *duty* to wage defensive war. Even nuclear weapons cannot provide a valid argument against such a proposition (cf. Chap. 105), precisely since the totalitarian state is, because of this weapon, given a real chance of world domination, and is, according to all recent experience, not likely to be reluctant to use any weapon for such a purpose. Thus, the old principle of the traditional natural law doctrine holds good in theory: War becomes a right and even a duty when the highest goods of the state community or of a community of states are in danger from an aggressor. The conclusion arising from this principle, in face of the present-day situation, is that the utmost efforts must be made to prevent war under any circumstances through international guarantees of peace.

The *difficulties for the citizens* in forming a judgment on the justice of a war should not be underestimated. It is a fact that, in most wars, the majority of the people on each side have been convinced in greater or lesser degree of the justice of their cause. How difficult it is for the great mass of a people to form a real judgment of their own cause may be seen from the fact that, in former times, the mass of the citizens was simply unable to obtain reliable information, and today public opinion is formed under the influence of the propaganda which is at work in the educational services, the press, the literature, the news services, and the radio and television services of a country. Countless citizens, who credit themselves with independent judgment, necessarily become, to a large extent, the victims of this propaganda. Therefore, the average citizen lacks the facilities needed for arriving at a true and adequately based opinion on the justice of his country's cause; he may, consequently, as the traditional natural law theory has always held, as far as his conscience is concerned in the matter, trust his government, provided that he is convinced of its integrity and sense of responsibility and has not good reasons to believe that a war which it undertakes is an unjust aggression.

Often enough the *difficulty* of judging the question of right and wrong exists no less *for the government itself*. In spite of the most thorough examination of the facts and circumstances of a dispute, it is often impossible to form a definite judgment on the justice of the cause of one's own state. For the tension between natural and positive law in the international sphere may easily give rise to an apparent legal title on both sides, especially if the one party can take its stand more on positive international law, the other more on natural law. Take the case in which one state insists upon the positive law of peace treaties while the other can summon to its aid the natural right to have such treaties revised in given circumstances; or the case in which a state with a rapidly increasing population and inadequate territory insists upon its right to a greater share of the natural resources of the earth, while other states consider themselves obliged to defend the positive rights, which they have inherited, to their national territory, raw materials, and markets. It is an indication of the great sense of reality embodied in traditional natural law ethics that, for situations of the kind described, the solution was reached (by *Suárez,** for example) that a war which a government decides to wage is just if the government has sufficient evidence that the greater probability of a just cause lies on its own side. In view of the possibly far-reaching consequences of modern war, however, it is evident that nothing less will do than a high degree of moral certainty about the justice of the cause. The analysis of the difficulties of forming a judgment on the justification of war makes it clear afresh that there is nothing more important than to prevent the disputing parties from being their own judges, as we have urged in our discussion of the preservation of peace through an international machinery.

This is made still clearer by the consideration of circumstances which complicate judgment concerning the defensive character of a war. For, the *distinction between offensive and defensive warfare* itself is partly relative and dependent on the concrete situation. Not only the ordinary man, but also writers on international law often incline to the oversimplified view that defensive war is war for the purpose of resistance to an actual armed aggression and that the guilty party is he who first takes up arms. But a prima facie "preventive war" on this principle may, in fact, be a true defensive war if a state or the community of states is compelled to avert by war a certain and unquestionably threatening deadly aggression which cannot be averted in any other way. Only when it becomes possible in the further development of international law to bind all states, before resorting to arms, to submit to international jurisdiction in cases of dispute concerning facts pointing to plans of aggression, only then will the first-mentioned view of offensive war come into its own as far as the individual state is concerned. There is an absolute difference between a defensive war undertaken in the case of a direct and extreme threat, as in the situation previously described, and a preventive war which

* Cf. Suárez, "De bello," Tract III of *De Fide, Spe, et Charitate,* disp. XIII, s. VI, par. 2: "Ponamus enim titulum belli esse, quod rex hic contendat hanc urbem ad se pertinere, vel jure haereditario sibi obvenire denuo. Jam si facta diligentia illud certo constat, aperta est assertio. Quando vero res est pro utraque parte probabilis, tunc se debet rex gerere, ut justus judex; quare si sententia sibi favens invenitur probabilior, potest etiam juste prosequi jus suum, quia ut verum existimo, in sententiis ferendis, sequenda est semper probabilior pars, quia ille est actus justitiae distributivae: in qua dignior est praeferendus. Est autem dignior, cui probabilius jus favet, de quo latius infra." The greater probability of a state's cause would provide no sufficient reason for waging war in present-day circumstances when international complications threaten, and in the given case not even certainty, because not the possession of a town but only the physical and moral existence of a political community must be at stake to make a defensive war just.

is undertaken to prevent a feared, but not certain and imminent, aggression, or even an aggression which only appears possible or probable in an uncertain future. Such a preventive war is always a war of aggression and is especially unjust and a grave crime in the present day, since it may involve the use of nuclear and bacteriological weapons; besides, if the danger is not imminent, appeal may be made to the organs of the United Nations and world public opinion may be mobilized.

I *Universal Conscription*

Does the defensive function of the state establish a right to introduce universal conscription? In this system, the state enlists young men fit for service in its armed forces for a given period under threat of severe penalties in case of refusal. The purpose is to have a trained army ready for action in case of war. No element in the nature of the state points unmistakably to an unconditionally existing right to conscript on these terms. This right can arise only from circumstances in which the state has to fulfill its function of self-defense. If the international situation is in a continuous state of tension and the security of a state demands such precautions, the necessary conditions may exist for the right to institute universal conscription. Thus, the actual existence of this right is essentially bound up with questions of fact. A further condition necessary is that no alternative means are available which would allow lesser inroads to be made into the freedom of the citizens. Such possibilities are offered by voluntary military service or a militia in which the training would be carried out over a number of short periods, thus sparing the young man a prolonged period of deprivation of freedom just at the time when he is beginning a career and founding a family. There is no need to stress the obligation on the part of all nations to cooperate in abolishing universal conscription in conjunction with general disarmament. Indeed, the existence of standing armies based upon universal conscription has, in recent history, immensely favored militarism and constituted a perpetual danger to peace.

II *The Refusal of Military Service*

May military service be refused altogether or at least armed service on grounds of religious or moral conviction—hence, on grounds of conscience? The distinction between religious and moral conviction is of importance for the reason that some religious sects (Quakers, Mennonites) maintain that war is morally impermissible because it involves killing people, so that the actual conviction of conscience is easily tested. This testing is more difficult in the individual case, although it is not impossible, as is shown by the example of Great Britain, where the conscientious objector is examined before a legal tribunal with regard to his conscientious convictions. The corresponding natural law principles may be described as follows. On the one hand, there is the duty of the political community to defend itself as well as the duty to distribute the resulting burden equally among all in accordance with their capacity. On the other hand, there is the elementary right of the individual person to freedom of belief and of conscience. Men who have serious conscientious objections to the use of lethal weapons or to war as a means of national defense must be exempted by the state from combatant service. Conscientious objectors may justly be required to take part in the many vital tasks bound up with the self-defense of the state, such as serving in ambulance units at the front. In the First and Second World Wars numerous English objectors thought it fair that they should perform service which was vital to defense and not less dangerous than combatant service (e.g., in the latter war, in the medical units of parachute companies). The clergy, because of their office in the service of religion and of the idea of peace founded on religious and moral values, cannot properly be conscripted for combatant service, as every conscience not warped by doctrinaire prejudices is convinced. Only a state that makes the rejection of these values a principle of its policy can act against this conviction.

147. Self-Preservation of the State Community

I *The Quantitative Population Problem*

Since the alarming decline in their birth rates, the population problem has become an alarming one for the nations of the *white race* in Europe (concerning the population movement, world political dynamics, utilization of the world's food-producing resources, cf. Chap. 151). What can be done?

1. Neo-Malthusians and their opponents are agreed that the change in sexual morality since the end of the nineteenth century is the deepest cause of the decline in the population of the white race. History likewise shows that the decay of marriage morality is one of the decisive causes of the decline of nations and of cultures. The future of the nations of the white race depends on the return to the *natural moral law*,[1] which, with

[1] Concerning the unbending attitude of the Catholic Church (cf. Pius XI, encyclical on *Christian Marriage*, on the question of artificial birth control), the firm condemnation of all artificial methods of birth control by the Free Church Council, and the more indefinite attitude of the Church of England (Lambeth Conference, 1930) and the Methodists (Conference, 1930), cf. D. V. Glass, *Population, Policies and Movements in Europe*, 1940, p. 430. Concerning the only methods of birth control permitted by natural law principles, that is, without preventing conception but by using the periods of sterility having regard to the temperature rhythm connected with ovulation, cf. H. Knaus, *Die Physiologie der Zeugung des Menschen*, 4th ed., 1951; *Die fruchtbaren und unfruchtbaren Tage der Frau und deren richtige Berechnung*, 25th ed., 1956; J. Lyle Cameron, *Motherhood and the Safe Time Simplified* (London), 1955; John A. O'Brien, *Natural Birth Control*, 5th ed. U.S.A., German trans. *Natürliche Geburtenregelung*, 1956.

regard to this decisive question, is manifestly the true law of life of the nations.[2]

2. At the same time, everything depends on the reinvigoration of the life-cell of the community, the *family*. A primary and indispensable condition for this is the reawakening and the promoting of respect for the family and for the values associated with it. Although successful population policy can fundamentally only be family policy, this was and is barely mentioned in the nondenominational literature of population theory.[3] The greatness of the errors that can be made by naturalistic "scientific" thinking, is shown by the advocacy of "professional motherhood"; if it were proved that the fall in the birth rate is due to the inability of the family to adapt itself to the conditions of modern society, then, according to this project, the possibility of replacing the family as a biological reproductive unit by a childbearing profession would have to be considered.[4]

3. Of paramount importance for the biological functioning of the cell of society is its *economic basis*. The aim is to safeguard the family income and the family dwelling (concerning family values and family policy, cf. Chaps. 70 ff.).

4. Alongside the family idea the *community idea* can claim merely a

[2] In the widely ranging discussion about *"the pill,"* natural law and "population explosion," natural law is taken too one-sidedly as concerning only the individual sexual act. In fact, however, natural law also concerns conjugal love and the supporting and strengthening of its bonds. Science, as is to be hoped, will be able to develop a pill that makes the safe period safer; then the use of such a pill as will demand sexual abstinence for only a few days will result in an increase in the interpersonal tension of the conjugal partners with an increase in love and affection; in consequence, this method of achieving responsible parenthood in accordance with natural law will turn out to be in the best interest of conjugal love, the unity of matrimony and the well-being of the family community as a whole. (It is not to be forgotten that steroids leave it to the woman when to apply them, indeed with or without the knowledge of the husband). However, there are still wider aspects of natural law involved. It is surprising that the question of birth regulation through steroids has obtained such momentum particularly in the welfare states. Should they not in natural law feel obliged to apply their affluence to first ends first, namely, to the problem of providing accommodation for the oncoming generation instead of allowing to spend such great portions of the national income on goods of secondary importance? Natural law and the order of values implied in it leaves no doubt about the obligations of the affluent society in this direction. And, then, there is the natural law imperative of the use of the resources of the earth for the support of its growing population; indeed it is a crime against the clear imperatives of natural law that up to a third of the resources of the great powers are used for rearmament with the intent of possible destruction instead of being made fruitful for supporting the growing numbers of the world population. If the great nations pooled their resources for research into intensive agriculture and for help to the countries in need, the feeding of the future world population would offer no insurmountable difficulty. The many tasks thereby involved for international cooperation will be discussed in Chap. 151. Concerning this, cf. especially Hermann Muckermann, *Ewiges Gesetz*, 1947; *Die Familie im Lichte der Ehegesetze*, 2nd ed., 1952; *Der Sinn der Ehe, biologisch, ethisch, übernatürlich*, 3rd ed., 1952.

[3] As an exception we may mention F. Lorimer and F. Osborn, *Dynamics of Population*, 1934, p. 339.

[4] Cf. Kingsley Davis, "Reproductive Institutions and the Pressure for Population," *Sociological Review*, July, 1937.

subordinate value. The community idea implied in "social charity" is something completely different; when we dealt with social charity we outlined the duties concerning the population problem which it involves. Experience speaks clearly in this matter. *D. V. Glass* sums it up concisely when he says: "Whatever pronatalist propaganda may say on the subject, parenthood is not generally undertaken for altruistic motives." [5]

5. In democratic states, special attention should be paid to the education of the masses in the knowledge that, in the sphere of population policy, as in other spheres of social life, the individual cannot separate his own interest from that of the community.[6] Such a socially flavored utilitarianism means in fact only an appeal to the enlightened self-interest of the parents; if, as is the opinion of Professor *Myrdal,* "What a democratic society can do—is, therefore, restricted to providing truthful information and education to aid private individuals better to understand their own interests," [7] then the future hope for the white races would be very slight.

11 *The Qualitative Population Problem*

1. *Negative eugenics.* The qualitative aspect of the problem of population, eugenics, is today hardly less the subject of extensive studies and programs than the quantitative aspect. *Francis Galton,* who conceived the modern idea of eugenics in the 1880's and coined the word "eugenics," defines it thus: "Eugenics is the study of agencies under social control which may improve or impair the racial qualities of future generations either physically or mentally." For the same subject the name "racial hygiene" came to be used in Germany soon after the turn of the century. *Eugenics* is applied human biology. In general, *biology* is the science of the form, functions, origin, and variations of living beings, taking into account their nature and environment. *Genetics* is the department of biology concerned with the phenomena and laws of heredity. The science which investigates the nature and causes of biological phenomena determined by social conditions is termed *social biology.*

By negative eugenics we understand measures to improve the racial qualities of future generations by the elimination of undesirable hereditary qualities. What are these harmful qualities? In answering this first question, opinions differ according to the philosophical, political, economic, and social principles on which eugenic programs are based. To begin with, among the laws and draft bills the Sterilization Law of National-Socialism may be mentioned; it specified the following as hereditary qualities: congenital feeble-mindedness, schizophrenia, manic depressive insanity, inherited epilepsy, Huntington's chorea, inherited blindness, in-

[5] D. V. Glass, *op. cit.*, p. 372.
[6] Cf. R. and K. Titmuss, *Parent's Revolt*, 1942, p. 120.
[7] G. Myrdal, *Population, A Problem for Democracy*, 1940, p. 223.

herited deafness, severe inherited physical malformation, and severe alcoholism. An English Voluntary Sterilization Draft Bill concerned mental defectives, all who have ever suffered from mental disturbances or suffer from any grave and probably hereditary physical disability, and finally all who may be considered likely to transmit a mental defect or a grave physical disability. The model law, resting on "scientific" considerations, drafted by *H. H. Laughlin* (in the United States, where at one time half the states were engaged in drafting sterilization laws) includes the following classes: the feeble-minded, the insane (including psychopathic), the criminal (including the delinquent and wayward), the epileptic, the inebriate (including drug addicts), the diseased (including tuberculous, syphilitic, leprous, and others with chronic diseases), the blind (including those with seriously impaired vision), the deaf (including those with seriously impaired hearing), the deformed (including the crippled), the permanently dependent (including orphans, the homeless, tramps, and paupers).[8] A comparison reveals the surprising fact that the English Draft Bill not only admits to sterilization classes of defects which are not comprised in the German law, but it would admit all persons who are likely to transmit a defect even though it has not shown up in themselves. The Laughlin Scheme goes further still in defining eugenic defects that would justify the state in imposing compulsory sterilization; it is a proposal which claims the adherence of a great number of modern biologists and eugenicists.

How far can such proposals claim the support of *serious genetic thought?* Genetics is a very young science, and much of it is still in dispute. Therefore, it seems best to follow an accepted leading authority such as *J. B. S. Haldane.*[9] He (in his fifteenth year as an active communist) can certainly not be suspected of prejudice based on religious dogma; he himself sees no objection to admitting sterilization in certain circumstances.

1. *Haldane* points out that, to prevent the birth of the hereditarily ailing, would involve the loss of a much greater number of hereditarily healthy children. Thus, in order to exclude a few feeble-minded or schizophrenic children we would have to prevent the birth of ten times as many normal children, since only between eight and ten per cent of the children of a parent suffering from one of these hereditary maladies are themselves affected by it. Not even if both parents are feeble-minded is it certain that all the children will also be feeble-minded. In spite of the sacrifice of a large number of hereditarily healthy persons, no appreciable success would be attained by sterilization in combating these hereditary maladies (except in the case of deaf-mutes, who commonly intermarry) in less than thirty to forty generations, since the defect of those carrying

[8] In this survey we follow J. B. S. Haldane, *Heredity and Politics,* 1938, pp. 16, 77, 94.

[9] Cf. *ibid.,* pp. 68–103.

the diseases is very often not detected until they have produced affected children. Other hereditary maladies sometimes skip a generation, with the result that affected parents can have normal children.

2. Compulsory sterilization would eliminate not only many healthy children but also some of very high hereditary abilities. For examples, *Milton* and *Beethoven*, if the above-mentioned *Laughlin* scheme had been in existence, would have been denied to the world; *Dostoievski* would not have been born because of a hereditary predisposition to epilepsy, and *Van Gogh* because of a predisposition to insanity.

3. According to *Haldane*, most biologists maintain the theory that, with regard to mental defectives, who figure at the head of all such programs, it is not possible to predict with certainty from knowledge of the parents that their children will be less adequate members of society than the majority. Only in a very few cases can a physical defect be predicted before the birth of a child, such as that children of two albinos will probably be albinos. But our knowledge of the heredity of psychological traits is too scanty to allow of such predictions. Hence, *Haldane* reaches the conclusion that we do not know enough to accord rights to any individual, or to deprive him or her of any rights, on the basis of ancestry only.

4. He further poses the question whether the feeble-minded are really socially valueless; they can carry out work, such as very simple manipulations, which fully normal people are capable of performing only with great difficulty; thus, in a society in which there was work for all and occupational selection there would perhaps be employment for the greater part of those who are today regarded as feeble-minded (with the proviso that careful control be maintained to prevent the economic exploitation of such people).

5. Sterilization is bound up with a lowering of the dignity of marriage; *Haldane* mentions as an example cases in which feeble-minded girls in California were married after sterilization, the husbands thereby being assured of security from procreation. *Haldane* remarks that any course of action which reduces it (marriage) to that level appears to be at least as antisocial as one which allows an occasional defective to be born. Another objection to sterilization is that, for women, it is a serious operation, and a human life must not be endangered—a fundamental principle of English law—except to avoid a greater danger to the person.

6. *Haldane* affirms that, even if biology should be in a position to make safe pronouncements on heredity, human interference, such as compulsory sterilization, still would be a question outside the scope of biology; it would be a question of the relative value of different goods, health and freedom respectively. But if the principle of compulsory interference were accepted, it would no longer be possible to see where a limit should be set. *Haldane* finds evidence for this in the proposal of Dr. *Blacker*, Secretary of the Eugenics Society, namely, that not only the mentally defective

should be sterilized but all those who are somewhat below the average in intelligence.

Haldane's statements make it clear that the attitude taken by natural law ethics toward sterilization is in harmony with the sciences of biology and of genetics, and that no well-founded scientific objection to it can be raised. Ethics proceeds from the existential ends of man, in which man's moral responsibilities and the rights resting on them are designed, establishing the moral principle of absolute respect for the bodily integrity no less than for the sanctity of human life and for the dignity of the human person in general. No right to impair this integrity exists in itself, either for the individual in respect to himself or for the state in respect to its citizens. A right to admit an impairment of this integrity exists for the individual only in order to avert immediate grave danger to life or health (when an operation is justified), and for the state only as a punitive measure. Therefore, compulsory or voluntary sterilization, that is, temporary or permanent deprivation of the power of procreation as a eugenical measure, cannot be justified. If it is imperative to hinder the propagation of hereditary ailments because of grave and certain danger to the general good, this may be done only by the setting up of impediments to marriage and the segregation of affected persons, if their individual sense of responsibility does not offer enough surety.

Although many eugenicists consider only sterilization and contraception, which are ruled out by natural law ethics, as adequate methods of negative eugenics, *Haldane* himself enumerates the following methods, which are also compatible with natural law if the defined limits are observed: discouraging the marriage of affected persons and carriers; forbidding such marriages; encouraging continence within or outside marriage; segregation. The only argument against segregation, *Haldane* says, is the cost. But this argument, he goes on, would be quickly disposed of by the reflection that, for instance, the cost of segregating the 300,000 genuine mental defectives in England and Wales would be about the same as the cost of maintaining 100,000 unemployed, a small consideration by the standards of recent decades. And it is with a fine sensibility that *Haldane* replies to the view that the care and pity given to the weak mean little for civilization by saying that care and pity are an essential part of civilization and worthwhile for their own sakes; should they tend to harm civilization to some degree by fostering the spread of undesirable genes, he suggests the remedy may be found in practicing still more care and pity by segregating mental defectives under humane conditions.[10]

One of the eugenic measures available in the case of ailments which are transmitted if both parents are carriers, is the prohibition or discouragement of marriages between first cousins. *Haldane* points out that, for instance, in England the Catholic Church is the only body which in principle prevents marriages between cousins. Should the biologist reach definite

[10] Cf. *ibid.*, pp. 102 f., note.

conclusions about the grave harmfulness to the common interest of marriage between persons with certain inherited diseases, there could be no ethical objection to the introduction of new impediments by Church or state. In this, however, not only the degree of danger for the progeny and the racial inheritance of a people must be taken into account, but also those values of marriage which lie beyond biology, that is, the help which the partners derive from marriage morally, psychologically, and in other ways. Eugenic propositions of such a kind must, therefore, at least allow for exceptions, that is, the possibility of dispensation.

Another important measure of negative eugenics would be a legal obligation for all persons intending marriage to undergo a medical examination and to produce their pedigree, on the basis of which a certificate of fitness for marriage, with regard to inherited qualities, would be issued. Although such a certificate (except in the few cases of legal impediment) could not in itself form the basis of a prohibition of marriage, yet when a person's sense of responsibility has been awakened by education, instruction, and propaganda, it might be the means of preventing many eugenically unsound marriages, if those intending to marry can be clearly shown what danger awaits their children, their families, and the community itself.

2. *Positive eugenics.* By positive eugenics we mean measures to improve racial qualities by promoting an increase in the desirable qualities. One might say its aim is to enhance the general vitality of a nation, which means the capacity of its members, or the greater number of them, to fulfill the whole of man's essential functions—moral, social, and cultural. We say vitality, because the Darwinian concepts "fit" and "unfit" cannot be applied in eugenics without qualification, since fitness in the Darwinian sense of natural selection is determined only by the greater or lesser number of the surviving offspring.[11] Our definition of vitality includes the improvement of congenital qualities and also meets the views of the many biologists and eugenicists who regard positive eugenics as primarily a matter of shaping environment. Social biology rightly sees in poverty and the kind of environment that accompanies poverty one of the greatest obstacles to the development of valuable hereditary qualities. Many of its exponents draw from this the simplifying conclusion that the principal means for improving this environment is the restriction of births among the poor population. As an example of the lengths to which such eugenicists are prepared to go, *Haldane* mentions the proposal put forward by Professor *MacBride* in *Nature* (1936) to "punish" with compulsory sterilization parents who have to resort to public assistance in order to support their children.[12] Such a demand, at a time when nearly all coun-

[11] The biologist must, Haldane thinks, be excused if he prefers the word fitness in the same sense as Darwin used it; but if it is so used, says Haldane, in many cases the eugenicists are demanding the sterilization of the fit (cf. *ibid.*, pp. 91 ff.).

[12] Cf. *ibid.*, pp. 119 ff.

tries are providing or planning family allowances for children after the birth of the first, seems astonishingly unrealistic. It is even more astonishing when social reformers, whether economists or politicians, make family limitation the beginning of social reform instead of making it their business to study the economic reforms required for securing the best possible eugenic conditions of environment for family life. Indeed, these reformers seem to regard it as their task to put the cart before the horse.

We shall first turn to the question of improving the *mental qualities* of the population. Positive eugenics concerns itself above all with the examination of the "*differential birth rate*," that is, the relatively higher birth rate of the poorer population groups, and with the question of the effect which this differential birth rate has on the average intelligence of a population. Following *Haldane*, we may here sum up the results of extensive statistical research.[13] The children of larger families are, on the average, less intelligent than those of smaller families, but the results of intelligence testing depend largely upon environment, and, on the whole, the home environment weighs more heavily in the scale than the school environment; in intelligence tests the children of wealthier families surpass poorer children to a barely appreciable degree; but the children of the professional classes (doctors, teachers, clergy, and others) do show a marked superiority. Nevertheless, according to *Haldane*, if the differential fertility of the classes continues, the average intelligence may decline in England by between one and two per cent per generation. *Lorimer* and *Osborn* think they can detect a similar trend in regard to the United States.[14]

Obviously, such opinions hold true only for unchanging conditions of social environment. A number of other facts make such suppositions appear dubious. *Haldane* himself observes that, although well-to-do Mohammedans have practiced polygamy for over a thousand years, and therefore their offspring, on account of their elevated social environment, should show a higher intelligence, they do not in fact surpass the Jews and Christians in intellectual qualities. He further points out, and this is an important fact of experience, that in the wealthier classes can be observed a connection between genes making for high ability and genes making for infertility, so that economic success and biological success are contradictory; and since there is no evidence of any substantial lack of mental qualities among the children of the poorer classes, *Haldane* remarks, compulsory measures in consideration of the differential birth rate would involve a considerable sacrifice of potential ability, unless the fertility of the rich can be greatly increased. Furthermore, the poorer and more prolific classes possess certain desirable qualities not as common among the rich, such as meekness, whereas international aggressiveness largely

[13] Cf. *ibid.*, pp. 113–27. Cf. also Sir C. Burt, *Intelligence and Fertility* (The Eugenics Society), 1946.

[14] Cf. F. Lorimer and F. Osborn, *op. cit.*, 1934, p. 347.

issues from socially elevated classes. We have discussed (cf. Chap. 73) in some detail the reasons why, in large families, the spirit of mutual understanding and mutual helpfulness is more highly developed.

In connection with these eugenic observations, *Haldane* gives a surprising exegetical turn to one of the eight Beatitudes. In his opinion the words, "Blessed are the meek; for they shall possess the land," point to the fact that the conquering classes and peoples are short-lived compared with the ordinary people. One might, he observes, even say that the eugenic movement is partly a passionate protest against the hard fact that the meek do inherit the earth.

The following *methods of positive eugenics* (racial hygiene), therefore, are to be stressed:

1. All that has been stated previously leads up to the main objective always upheld in traditional natural law ethics: *family policy*, which will provide the economic, social, hygienic, and spiritual conditions and thus the environment needed for the development of the family in conformity with the particular existential ends proper to its nature. Natural law ethics thought in terms of social biology long before social biology was spoken of as a science. We have discussed at some length the conditions of a healthy family life; they include an adequate income, suitable dwelling accommodation, a public opinion sympathetic to family values, the training of youth in the appreciation of these values, and the practicability of early marriage. Modern eugenics, as *Lorimer* and *Osborn* assure us, leaves no doubt that the basis of any practical program of positive eugenics must be a combination of early marriage and economic security for young married couples.[15]

2. Next after the family must come the *school*. In *Haldane*'s view, a free, uniform school system would probably be good from a eugenic point of view simply because parents would no longer limit their families in order to give their children a good education. And it would be eugenically desirable also because it would make possible the selection and encouragement of talent; for then opportunities of higher education would be the same for the gifted children of the poor as for the rich.

3. The next point in the program of positive eugenics should be the strong encouragement of the *farming population*. For the past hundred years the decline of the birth rate has gone hand in hand with the growth of the big towns. Provision should be made so that the large family on the land will again be a natural economic advantage instead of merely increasing economic difficulties. And when families outgrow their economic resources, a well-planned scheme for the creation of new farming settlements should strive to hold the sons and daughters of the farming population on the land; or, at least, there should be area planning with the provision of industrial and trading settlements so as to offer the overspill population opportunities for earning a proper income.

[15] Cf. *ibid.*, p. 339.

4. With regard to *intelligence* itself, the transmission of valuable qualities should be greatly aided by the intermarriage of the sons and daughters of the most highly endowed families, namely, those of the professional classes, as mentioned above.

5. Lastly, there is yet one aspect of positive eugenics which receives no attention at all in discussions on mental qualities. Although some eugenists do ask what precisely is meant when one speaks of high abilities, yet they see chiefly those abilities that can be measured by intelligence tests and expressed in intelligence quotients (I.Q.). The other world of mental values, that is, of *personality* and its moral foundation, is, however, undoubtedly at least as important as that of mere intelligence. A glance at the history of the rise, the great achievements, and the decline of nations shows what decisive importance moral values possess in their life. Among the moral values, those in the realm of sexual morality are of outstanding eugenic importance; only those who are blind to the lessons of experience can be deceived concerning the position of sexual morality in the education of the young.

We need not deal at length with the dreams of a section of modern eugenists on the subject of *artificial insemination* (eutelegenesis) and their hopes for breeding a race of "supermen." Since the end of the sexual function is linked to marriage and the family, artificial insemination outside the marriage bond is not possible without violation of the natural law; in marriage itself it is possible only as an aid in reaching the end of the natural process of procreation.[16] Although from his ethical point of view not fundamentally opposed to it, *Haldane* observes that even from a genetical point of view, because of our present very slight knowledge of the genetical basis of the characters found in great men, such projects are premature; furthermore, artificial insemination would lend itself to grave abuses and, as a means of producing more great men, equality of educational opportunity is much more likely to be of immediate value. Thus, again the actual scientific findings of social biology point toward the propositions of natural law ethics. On the other hand, one hard fact sets a definite limit to the hope that with the progress of biology and genetics it will yet be possible to produce a race of supermen, a fact which biologists and eugenicists almost without exception overlook, namely, that there is a hereditary quality which affects the constitution of the whole of mankind. We refer to the consequences of original sin. Its effects extend not only to man's qualities but to his environment. These consequences are not hereditary qualities in the genetic sense. But the fact, which human biology itself must acknowledge, that almost all men must be regarded as bearers of some undesirable hereditary qualities, even if these

[16] From the literature on this subject cf. A. Niedermeyer, *Handbuch der speziellen Pastoralmedizin,* Vol. II, 1950, pp. 185–232; H. Davis, S.J., *Artificial Human Fecundation* (New York), 1951; A. Gemelli, O.F.M., *La fecondazione artificiale* (Milan), 2nd ed., 1949.

are not manifest, is to be ultimately explained by the effects of original sin on man's physical and spiritual qualities.

This does not mean, however, that a great deal cannot be done, by a qualitative population policy, to improve the physical and intellectual qualities of a nation. Since such an improvement would make possible a more perfect fulfillment of the tasks in life founded on the existential ends of the individual and society, ethics must regard the *qualitative population policy* not merely as morally valuable but, within the framework of what is possible, as a *moral duty* for society. On the same grounds, ethics must insist that the aims and methods of the policy remain in harmony with the order of ends. It is not true that biological values are everything, as was held by biological philosophies of one stripe or another, including National-Socialist racialism. The values of the spiritual, moral person rank higher, and in cases of conflict, such as we have discussed above, they take precedence. The Christian philosophy of life further maintains that supernatural values are relatively independent of inherited biological qualities and social biological environment; sickness and poverty do not absolutely prevent man's spiritual growth, they may even encourage it; the sick and the poor can be holy and, therefore, can realize the highest values attainable by man. A certain measure of suffering, so says the testimony of poets and of thinkers on the experience of mankind, can even be of advantage to man in a purely natural sense in the process of attaining and preserving his highest self. But, as we would urge again, excessive difficulties in the shape of illness or environment present to the average man an insurmountable obstacle to a life lived in conformity with the demands of the higher moral values; therefore, positive and negative eugenics provide society with some essential obligations.

148. Fiscal Policy and Budgetary Policy

Natural law affords two *general principles* for the fiscal policy of the state. The first concerns the right of the state to levy taxes, which is rooted in the state's need of financial means in order to fulfill its functions in the interest of the common good. This principle, therefore, belongs to the realm of legal justice. The second general principle concerns the equitable distribution of burdens in accordance with capacity. This principle, therefore, belongs to distributive justice.

From these general principles are to be drawn the *particular principles* which apply to the conditions of development in present-day states. Among these the following call for special attention before we go into details. 1) A criterion of a just fiscal and budgetary policy arising from the principle of the common good is *socio-economic productivity* (cf. Chap. 164). The maintenance and promotion of productivity form the basis of material and cultural life for the citizens in the present and for the future;

they are also the condition for raising sufficient revenue for the growing functions of the state. 2) Closely connected with this is the principle concerning the effect of taxation on the *economic order;* today, fiscal policy is an essential part of economic policy and therefore has an important function in the service of the social end of the economy. One thinks of functions with regard to the market system and the structural order of the national economy, and with regard to monetary policy and antidepression policy. 3) Closely connected with the social end of the economy is the principle of fiscal policy as applied to the *social order:* the principle that it must serve toward a socially just distribution of the national income, insofar as this is not achieved by virtue of the socio-economic process itself; the first consideration is the necessary minimum for the economic and cultural existence of the family. 4) Natural law principles today also assign *cultural functions* to the fiscal and budgetary policy of the state.[1] The extent of these principles, at least in the most important respects, will be discussed later. To obtain further clues we must first of all inquire into the following.

I *The Basis and the Limits of the Right to Levy Taxes*

The *foundation* of the state's right to levy taxes is laid in the principle of the common good, that is in a principle of justice. To speak of principles of justice for taxation and budgeting by the state, today is no longer contrary to the spirit of the prevailing political theory and financial theory to the same extent it was in the period of belief in the value neutrality of the social sciences. Nevertheless, there is no lack of opponents of the

[1] Only insofar as it concerns the social end of the society, the state, the economy, and culture is fiscal and budgetary policy the subject of social ethics. For individual ethics and moral theology no less difficult questions arise with regard to determining the form and extent of the taxpayer's obligation in justice in the case of a state which has become extravagant with public money, makes the burden of taxation excessively high, and in which the apportionment of taxes is somewhat arbitrary, especially when political power relations play a decisive part in determining such matters. In dealing with the question of the justification of taxation it seems that social ethics and individual ethics are often insufficiently distinguished, and that attention is too exclusively devoted to the citizen's obligation to pay taxes; far less attention is paid to the duty of the legislator in fixing taxes, and too little emphasis is given to the fact that the just form of resistance against a defective fiscal morality in the state is not a defective morality of the citizens, rather may they use all democratic means to improve the justice of taxation. Paul Jostock, *Grundzüge der Soziallehre und der Sozialreform,* 1946, p. 68, says that excessive taxation does not justify the individual in gaining relief on his own account by reducing his tax payment, since this would only increase the injustice, especially in the case of the wage and salary earner who could not make use of this method: "Where the burden of taxation is too heavy, reform must be sought by legal methods, and by influencing public opinion and parliament. Most would be gained by a revision of the whole financial policy, perhaps by more strictly confining the state to its proper functions." Cf. the reference in note 7 to Jostock; cf. also Jostock's comprehensive discussion in "Über den Umfang des der Besteuerung entgehenden Einkommens, ein Beitrag zur Volkseinkommenstatistik," in *Weltwirtschaftliches Archiv,* Vol. LVII, 1943, pp. 27–80.

principle of justice today; this may be seen from the position adopted by so important an exponent of economics and of the science of finance as *Alfred Amonn.* The principle of justice, he holds, may be rejected for fiscal theory, because there could be no general formulation of a principle of which the financial could only be a particular application; furthermore, because the principle of justice in the science of finance would lead to absurd and impossible consequences; lastly, because all demands which would be made in its name would be much better based on the principle of economic expediency. In this, *Amonn* sees the basis of taxation as "regular, compulsory revenue"; the only "chief purpose" of taxation is gaining revenue for the commonwealth, a "secondary" socio-political purpose is denied. In discussing the "principles for taxation," he arrives, however, at the "general principle" for the public economy: "The general well-being should be raised as much as possible." In addition, he expressly states as "the general principle of expenditure" that it should most fully promote the general welfare; furthermore, the general principle of revenue raising is that "the payment of taxes should be so arranged that the least damage is caused to the general welfare. This can only come about through influence on production and distribution." [2]

These considerations hardly show that the basis of taxation should not lie in the common good and in the principles of justice which apply to it; and *Amonn*'s "principle of economic expediency" can only rest on principles of value by which expediency is judged. Since these principles of value are principles for shaping a sphere of social order, they can substantially be nothing other than principles of justice. How widely today principles of value, and thus the principle of the common good and that of justice, are considered to apply to national economy, the pattern of revenue and of expenditure, is shown by the social and political aims linked with these functions, such as full employment, the proportionate distribution of income, the business cycle policy for the purpose of maintaining and raising the standard of living, the bringing about of a well-balanced economic structure, and especially the maintaining of a sound economic foundation of agriculture and of the one-man business and family business in crafts and trades. The change of interpretation in this becomes particularly obvious if one recalls that individualist-liberalist thinking looked for the basis of taxation in the services performed by the state for the individual; thus, it was based on the interest and advantage of the individual, including the protection of his person, of his freedom, of his property, and of his freedom to work for his own profit; fundamentally, taxation was considered an evil that must be kept to a minimum.

In the discussion of the *limits* of taxation, financial science has for so long proceeded almost entirely from the negative idea that the state, by excessive taxation, causes its sources of revenue to fail, thus acting to its own disadvantage. With regard to the limits of taxation, too, the natural

[2] A. Amonn, *Grundsätze der Finanzwissenschaft,* Part I, 1947, pp. 7, 177 ff., 190, 192.

law principles of the common good and of subsidiarity show us the way by their criterion of economic productivity, as previously mentioned. Thereby, the formal principle of "economic expediency" advocated by *Amonn* not only obtains the necessary concrete contents, but at the same time, production and distribution, which, according to him, should be influenced by fiscal policy, are brought into their proper relationship. (Concerning the concept of economic productivity, cf. Chap. 164.)

II The Principle of the Common Good in Fiscal and Budgetary Policy

1. *Economic productivity,* in accordance with the principle of the common good and the principle of subsidiary function, is at the same time both the purpose and the limit of state fiscal policy. Everyone knows that a sufficiently exact calculation of the productivity of national economies is not possible (in spite of the socio-economic accountancy theory). There are certain factors which can be used to estimate productivity, definite enough to serve as a basis for economic policy, with which fiscal policy must be consistent. Attention must be drawn to two of these factors in particular. The first is the cost and price structure of a country's economy; the second is the rate of capital formation and of investment. It is easy to see that each of these factors comprises a whole group of interdependent factors. On both sides the connection between productivity development and fiscal policy has not yet been sufficiently examined by students of political economy and finance. With regard to the first mentioned, cost and price structure,[3] the present steadily increasing interaction of national economies, with their export and import relationships in international competition, will set compelling standards of productivity on the individual national economy. Professor *Schmölders* asserts, with regard to the present position, that economic productivity "is today threatened by nothing so much as by taxation." *Schmölders* refers to the fact that the call to a fundamental fiscal reform in all countries is motivated by ideas of maintaining and reviving productivity; the aim of this is especially to be seen "in a reform of such taxes as most gravely prejudice production, the will to commercial enterprise, and exports from the domestic economy"; therefore, in countries with excessive taxation of incomes and of corporations, as in Great Britain and Germany, their reform would take first place; while in other countries, such as France, with a system of purchase taxes causing excessive taxation of undertakings, reform of the purchase taxes would be first in importance.[4]

[3] Cost and price structure is also stressed as one of the principal standards for judging economic productivity in *Productivity Measurement,* Vol. I, *Concepts,* publ. by the European Productivity Agency (Paris), 1955, pp. 78 f. (contribution by G. Fürst, President of the statistical federal office of the German Federal Republic).

[4] Cf. Günter Schmölders, *Finanzpolitik,* 1955, p. 303.

Taxation substantially exceeding the twenty-five per cent limit of national income was considered as retarding productivity by *Keynes*, "whose name was so much taken in vain by the advocates of unlimited taxation." [5] Although before the First World War taxation in European countries claimed on the average barely ten per cent of the national income, the amount rose between the two wars to over twenty per cent, and after the Second World War to thirty and forty per cent (taxation amounted in England in 1938 to twenty-two per cent, in 1949 to forty per cent,[6] whereas in the United States in 1938 to 19.5 per cent, in 1949 to 22.6 per cent). So prominent an advocate of Christian social doctrine and social reform, and at the same time an expert in socio-economic accountancy, as *P. Jostock* thinks of economic productivity and the national prosperity dependent on it when he warns: "Prosperity cannot be successfully built without a powerful restraint of the so severely inflated public finance economy. Taxes swallow much too large a part of the national income—this applies not only to the years since 1933—and this means that considerable portions of the economic output do not find optimal use. On the whole, public departments cost more in administration and deal with money and goods less economically than private concerns." [7]

Among the causes of the *restrictive effect* of excessive taxation on productivity those generally admitted today are: uneconomic increased expenditure of business concerns merely for the purpose of tax evasion by increasing the expenses (travelling expenses, advertisement outlay, office expenses, group conferences, etc.), thereby raising the rate of consumption to the detriment of the rate of capital formation (at a vital point of the economy); inflation pressure through tax shifting by the producer on to the consumer (rising prices); evasion of tax by limiting activities which become unremunerative (for example, English authors who limited their literary work to an income of 10,000 pounds sterling); or through restriction in the consumption of goods which are subject to a special tax. The limits of taxation are determined, therefore, by the principle of economic productivity, according to its effects on industrial enterprise in general, the will to economic venture, and capital formation. For the development of productivity, the continuous formation of capital available for long-term investment is decisive. *Adolf Weber* can hardly meet with opposition when he says: "This capital formation will be impaired by

[5] Colin Clark, *Welfare and Taxation*, 1954, pp. 4 f.; he says that Keynes, in a letter to him in 1944, considered twenty-five per cent of the national income as the limit of economically harmless taxation after the Second World War. Professor Colin Clark who, as the author of the comprehensive work *The Conditions of Economic Progress*, 2nd ed., 1951, is singularly to be relied on for an expert opinion, maintains that it may well be shown from economic facts that the extreme limit of harmless taxation amounts to twenty-five per cent of the social product.

[6] Cf. Ursula Hicks, in *Handbuch der Finanzwissenschaft*, W. Gerloff and F. Neumark, editors, Vol. I, 1952, p. 339.

[7] P. Jostock, *Grundzüge der Soziallehre und der Sozialreform*, 1946, p. 156; cf. also, *Die Berechnung des Volkseinkommens und ihr Erkenntniswert*, 1941.

nothing so much as by existent and expected tax burdens."[8] The principle derived by *Anton Tautscher* from the "law of tax yield" ("that with rising taxation rates the tax yield increases progressively to the optimum"), "From the law of tax yield the limit of taxation follows when the maximum is reached and there is no further progressive increase in yield,"[9] may serve as a rule of thumb for judging when individual taxes reach the limits which are critical for productivity. We shall presently return to individual "maxims for the limits of taxation," of which *Tautscher* lists over five dozen.

Points from which to initiate a fiscal policy *conducive to productivity* are in particular the amount and kind of investment, the depreciation process, and the building up of business reserves. The appropriate particular measures of fiscal policy depend to a great extent on the prevailing circumstances of a national economy and on its position in world economy. Hence, in different states, directly contrary fiscal policies could be in the interest of furthering productivity. In a country greatly lacking in capital, it could be economically right to favor by fiscal policy the building up of reserves (nondistributed profits), depreciation, and ploughing-back; on the other hand, in a country with a market tending to overexpansion, a fiscal policy restraining ploughing-back, especially in the consumer goods industries, could be an indispensable means for transferring the surplus yield of business concerns to the capital market, and thus lead to farsighted economic planning. The following is another consideration concerning the influence of fiscal policy on depreciation: The increased speed of technical development (automation) and the technical rationalization of manufacture can make necessary a much faster depreciation than before, and therefore a fiscal policy to meet this would be needed; on the other hand, a similar depreciation percentage quota for all sizes of undertakings would favor a structurally harmful acceleration of growth in the large undertakings. (The fiscal and budgetary possibilities in business cycle and employment policy will be dealt with fully under the *Ethics of Social Economy*, Book IV.)

2. The fact that fiscal and budgetary policy is of great significance for the *economic order* is undisputed today. The separation of national economy and public finance (with taxation down to a minimum) has given way to a close involvement of the two: The theory of the public economy was "freed from the autonomy of a theory of public bookkeeping, and has again become a real part of political economy," as *Tautscher* expresses

[8] Adolf Weber, *Kurzgefaßte Volkswirtschaftspolitik*, 6th ed., 1951, p. 90. With regard to individual effects of taxation hampering productivity: on savings, on work, on pricing policy, on real capital formation, cf. Fritz Neumark in *Handbuch der Finanzwissenschaft,* W. Gerloff and F. Neumark, editors, 2nd ed., Vol. I, pp. 622–30, and Carsten Welinder, *ibid.*, Vol. II, 1956, pp. 336–56; cf. also Fritz Terhalle, *Die Finanzwirtschaft des Staates und der Gemeinden*, 1948, pp. 200 ff.; A. Amonn, *op. cit.*, pp. 196–206.

[9] A. Tautscher, *Grenzen der Besteuerung*, 1954, pp. 56 f., 90 ff.

it.[10] "Taxes are," says *Amonn,* "purely a portion of the economic order"; [11] he adds: "They are of necessity tied up with the individualist economic order"; by this he means the market economy resting on private ownership in contradistinction to the collectivistic (communistic) economy based on state ownership of the means of production. The distribution of private property, therefore, is of key significance for the economic order; hence, for fiscal policy the question, on the one hand, is one of avoiding harm to small or medium-sized producitve property, and on the other hand, of striving for the greatest number of owners of productive property. For such a fiscal policy the principle that, wherever there are smaller undertakings the majority of which are no less productive than the large undertaking, the former should be encouraged, is decisive. Economic productivity, is, then, at least as well, if not better, served on account of the greater application of private initiative; the accumulation of capital power is precluded; the social function of competition is more certainly realized as a result of the greater equality of the market position of the producers.

Connected with private ownership are certain *principles of structural order* relating to industry and to the market. It seems particularly important to stress these natural law principles for fiscal policy at a time when the social function of private property is underestimated to a large extent, when, moreover, large undertakings and combines are intensifying their power over the economy, and when large portions of the population, with a kind of self-deception, are ready to expect economic and social advantages from the nationalization of branches of production. To this is added the influence of the decrying of private property by Marxian and other socialistic movements; socialistic programs in general see in a fiscal policy which undermines private ownership a way to the form of economic democracy for which they strive, in which the chief emphasis is placed on state and communal economy.

Fiscal policy can affect the *structural order* chiefly in three directions: it can influence the order of magnitudes by differential taxation of medium and small businesses in comparison with large businesses and combines; it can further the desired expansion of branches of the economy or restrain that which is not desired; it can be used for a policy of industry location by means of differential treatment of desirably or less desirably situated undertakings and businesses.[12] What is to be regarded as "desirable" cannot in general be established; it depends on the internal development of the national economy (which is in constant flux), on necessary measures for development areas, and on its adjustment to world economic development. The influence of taxation as a means of market

[10] Cf. A. Tautscher, "Die öffentliche Wirtschaft als Ordnungsfaktor der Volkswirtschaft," in Lagler-Messner, *Wirtschaftliche Entwicklung und soziale Ordnung, Festschrift für Degenfeld-Schonburg,* 1952, p. 329.

[11] A. Amonn, *op. cit.,* p. 191.

[12] Cf. A. Tautscher, *Grenzen der Besteuerung,* pp. 43 ff.

policy can also be very considerable. On the supply side of the market the order of competition can be affected by taxation in favor of medium and smaller businesses; and also especially by the severer taxation of monopolistic and oligopolistic undertakings, and, not least, of cartel gains and other exceptional profits, which depend on competition restrictions and on explicit or implied agreement (cf. Chap. 177, esp. the reference to *R. Liefmann*). It is a demand of fiscal justice, of far-reaching significance for the ordering of the market and for fair competition, to have regard for equal conditions in the competition between consumer and production cooperatives and government concerns on the one hand and private undertakings on the other. There are opportunities of influencing price relations by a higher or lower purchase tax (e.g., on goods in general demand and of luxury mass goods: tobacco, alcohol, cinema tickets). On the supply side, fiscal policy can have effects on the market order, particularly by influencing the distribution of income.

3. With this we arrive at the *social order* as the object of fiscal and budgetary policy; on the one hand, income and property distribution are to be considered, on the other hand, economic growth and full employment. Today, there is hardly any difference of opinion on the social tasks of fiscal and budgetary policy, although perhaps wide differences exist with regard to the ends, the means, and the limits. The end could be described thus, in accordance with previous considerations, in the light of the principle of justice: the proportionate levelling of incomes, while preserving the principle of service and efficiency as the basis of income adjustment (cf. Chap. 172), and hence the principle of economic productivity. The means for such an income policy lie in the sphere of income tax and purchase tax: increasing taxation of higher incomes (progressive income taxation), and the progressively lower taxation of goods in general need (regressive purchase tax) in contradistinction to luxury mass consumption. A social policy of levelling the income and property distribution (apart from the limited possibilities of estate tax and death duties) is served by apportionment of tax-free allowances to individual citizens' incomes, especially of the tax-free allowance for the family (cf. Chap. 72). *Fritz Neumark* draws the conclusion, from experience with progressive income tax, that "in the higher income scale this more or less considerably exceeds what mere compliance with the capacity principle would demand, but that the private enterprise economy may exist with much slighter differences in property and lower profits than was previously regarded as essential," and that "it cannot be gainsaid that taxation policy as such, not to mention the totality of measures comprising fiscal policy, often finds itself in the dilemma, whether and to what extent the '*nivellement*' [income and property levelling, *J.M.*] undertaken from *social* motives can be permanently reconciled with economic necessities, hence also—indirectly—with the possibilities of social policy."[13]

In fact, a decisive question in any income redistribution policy is: Who

[13] F. Neumark, *op. cit.*, pp. 624, 626.

undertakes the *function of capital formation* which is essential for the growth of productivity and the general standard of living? The example in England of the fiscal and budgetary policy of the welfare state, much discussed in scientific financial literature, seems without doubt to be more of a warning than an encouragement, if it is considered that there the investment rate has fallen to eight per cent [14] and has become one of the lowest in Europe. The relation between the national income, the rate of investment, and the rate of consumption is of decisive significance for the economic development of a country but not less of its position in world politics. *Economically*, on this depends the ability of a country to compete in external trade, and hence to procure raw materials through the necessary exports, at the same time developing the standard of living. With regard to world politics, highly industrialized countries must be prepared to raise capital for economic aid to the underdeveloped countries, since the future of the West depends on this.[15] The fundamental problem for fiscal and budgetary policy is, therefore, to what extent, by redistribution of the national income, the necessary capital formation may be expected from the *working class* who benefit by the redistribution; in other words, whether a new distribution of income is accompanied by a new distribution of property by reason of the new opportunities provided for saving, or whether the higher incomes of the masses, in conjunction with social security, will be used only for increased consumption. If one wants to bear in mind common good justice with regard to fiscal and budgetary policy, one cannot overlook the considerations just mentioned. In the fiscal policy of the Western countries attention should be paid to encouraging the masses to save and to invest, not least to invest in equities and securities, by means of which at the same time economic and social ends would be served.

4. The *cultural tasks* of fiscal and budgetary policy spring from a real *emergency of the common good* in the present-day society, with its withdrawal from the spiritual-cultural values and the turning toward other values. Again, both internal and international considerations are to be taken into account. The task of the state in its internal policy is to promote educational efforts on all levels and in all spheres—science and research, art and literature—because the spiritual values in question are in themselves real, indeed fundamental, values of the common good. The loss in spiritual values by a people would mean the withering of its roots of life, for like everything else in man, the biological life force of a people is at bottom dependent on mental attitudes. In internal policy it must also be remembered that the development of the present-day political economy, from a purely technical and economic standpoint, calls for resources

[14] Ursula Hicks, *Steuerpolitik im Wohlfahrtsstaat—Die Erfahrungen Großbritanniens*, 1954, enters more into the financial side than the economic policy of the welfare state. Concerning the effects on the efficiency of the political economy, cf. J. Messner, *Das englische Experiment des Sozialismus*, 1954, pp. 30–39.

[15] Cf. J. Messner, *Die Soziale Frage* (from the point of view of future international developments), 1956, Chaps. 34, 65, 128.

of skilled personnel, which can be insured only by extensive state support for the necessary educational institutions; in most Western countries today there is a shortage of skills appropriate to the tasks of managers, engineers, and technicians. It is known that in Soviet Russia alone there are more engineers and technicians coming from the specialized educational centers than in the whole of the West. In the economic race between East and West a decisive role will be played by the engineer and the technician. Thus, tasks arise for budgetary policy in the cultural sphere which are of immense significance in international policy, of which the West is only slowly beginning to be aware.

In addition to the specific tasks of international cultural policy, especially through the participation of states in the work of the United Nations and UNESCO, there are also those of direct cultural contact between nations, by means of cultural institutes, interchanges of students and professors, exhibitions, etc. And there is a kind of fiscal policy which fosters culture, not perhaps to be mentioned as an obligation of the state, but for which sound common sense provides sufficient reasons. I refer to cases when contributions to charitable purposes, scientific research units, national educational institutions, and the like, could qualify for a tax refund. It goes without saying that this must be limited, for example, to a definite percentage of taxable private income or of the taxable profits of companies (corporation tax); in addition, it must be restricted to definite kinds of institutions, to which donations qualifying for rebate could be made. Thus, in Great Britain, contributions to charitable institutions, within defined lower and higher limits, are recognized as qualifying for a refund of tax, provided that the taxpaying contributor enters into a "covenant."

Lastly, there are important cultural points of view to be considered when deciding policy regarding death duties. The high and sharply progressive rates of duty in some countries must already provoke misgivings, since they affect the institution of property as such. A class of property owners is largely becoming dispossessed owing to the confiscatory character of death duties, without the emergence of a new broad class of property owners which could take over the social and cultural functions of the former. One thinks of the importance for the common good, vital for a settled democracy, of an economically independent class which can afford to sustain its own opinions and attitudes and to withstand the forces working for the development of a state-dependent mass society and collectivization. As the entire history of nations shows, greater possessions carry with them the means for nurturing values surpassing the material values, which are essential for the life and the growth of culture.

III *The Principle of Capacity in Fiscal and Budgetary Policy*

If the functions of fiscal and budgetary policy on behalf of the community are considered from the standpoint of the common good principle which we have discussed, we must next consider the position of the individuals in the distribution of the burdens of taxation. Up to most recent times, in the development of the science of finance, the position of the individual was the first consideration when fiscal justice was spoken of. Among the well-known fiscal maxims enumerated by *Adam Smith* (ability, certainty, convenience, cheapness), justice, that is, taxing according to ability, takes first place; and *Fritz Terhalle*, a high-ranking expert on fiscal policy of the present day, says with good reason, thinking of democracy: "Less than ever before can the fiscal policy of the present day evade the fundamental political objective of fiscal justice." Since the Second World War efforts have been made, both theoretically and politically, to place the emphasis in the question of justice on the distribution of income by fiscal policy (the welfare state), and to treat justice in the apportionment of burdens as a question of second rank. *Terhalle*, of course, sees the difficulties of decision and of carrying out the demands of justice in a democratic commonwealth. He points to the various beliefs about value and justice which influence public opinion; but even were it unequivocally established what kind of taxation is just, the difficulties, he says, would be still very great, because with the demands of justice other purposes of fiscal policy are to be reconciled, such as the raising of the necessary revenue for the maintenance of the military services and of the civil service; he adds the fact of experience that, as the need for revenue grows, it often becomes less possible to conform with the demand of justice, namely, when this is felt to be especially urgent, as with a purchase tax, which must be stretched to a particularly great extent in case of an extraordinary need for revenue. Last but not least, *Terhalle* mentions the distinction, essential for just taxation, between the legal tax debtor and the actual taxpayer, on account of the possible shifting of liabilities as, for instance, when taxation of corporation profits is made up by higher prices. In spite of everything and especially with regard to the forces acting on public opinion, *Terhalle* maintains: "It is admittedly the concern of responsible politicians and statesmen . . . to gather available suggestions but not to allow themselves to be governed by the opinion of the day; rather, they must keep the reins in their own hands." "Fundamentally, there is only one single aim for a fiscal policy seeking a just distribution of burdens: to apportion to each what is his own." [16] This is the demand of justice which the traditional natural law doctrine has always advocated, considering the principle of distributive justice as the chief principle of fiscal justice.

With which taxes is the aim of fiscal justice best attainable? Time and again these questions have been answered with the assertion that a single tax would best correspond with the principles of fiscal justice; this could

[16] F. Terhalle, *Die Finanzwirtschaft des Staates und der Gemeinden,* 1948, pp. 161–66.

be, it is thought, income tax, property tax, expenditure tax,[17] or tax on land values (*Henry George*). Today, it may be regarded as the unanimous conviction of scientific fiscal experts that the apportionment of the tax burden corresponding to the taxable capacity of the individual is most completely attainable by a combination of taxes on income, property, and expenditure. The first two have preference, as *direct taxes,* from the point of view of the principle of justice; for, the actual amount of income from business activity or ownership of property offers a comparatively reliable criterion of taxable capacity; in addition, it involves the state in proportionately cheaper costs in raising taxes. In fact, *Fritz Neumark* can say that the "shifting of the center of gravity in the system of taxation toward direct personal taxes . . . corresponds to the modern conception of the principles of justice and capacity, and has in fact been operative in the course of the last decades in the majority of countries."[18] The principle of capacity undoubtedly demands the increasingly higher taxation of higher incomes (progressive income tax); on the other hand, the principle of the common good (common good justice) sets limits to this progression, namely, insofar as readiness to save, capital formation, the will to invest, and economic productivity are affected.

In consequence of these limits and of the heavy financial needs, the present-day state cannot manage without a considerable degree of *indirect taxation,* which, as distinct from income, falls on the expenditure of the taxpayer; such indirect taxes constitute about half of the tax yield of most industrial countries. Among the indirect taxes are reckoned purchase tax and the customs duties. They are collected from producers or traders and increase the price of goods (on an average from ten to twenty per cent). They are unjust if they hit the small income relatively much harder, and especially unjust if they fall most heavily upon the essential requirements of families with many children. If the purchase tax, as in European countries, is applied at several production stages of an article, to be paid by the producers concerned, then this article is subjected to multiple taxation before it reaches the consumer. Such a tax can be an incentive to industrial concentrations, since in a production process of several stages within one factory the burden of multiple taxation would be avoided; thus, big concerns gain an advantage in price formation. In countries where this multiple taxation applies efforts are made, with good

[17] Nicholas Kaldor in his book, which is highly regarded by experts, *An Expenditure Tax,* 1955, pleads for a tax on expenditure instead of the excessive and progressive surtax on income taxation; he recalls that the proposal to tax expenditure as the basis of a fiscal system may be traced back to Hobbes' *Leviathan,* and he can refer to such important political economists as J. S. Mill, Alfred Marshall, and Irving Fisher as advocates of the conviction that such a system of taxation would not only be more just, but would also be more profitable politically and financially on account of the stimulus to save which it provides; he does not of course close his eyes to the difficulties involved in the making of the necessary statement of expenses by the tax-debtor.

[18] F. Neumark, *op. cit.,* Vol. I, p. 660. The course of development laid down by Neumark does not correspond with that of Soviet Russia, where the chief emphasis in tax raising is placed on purchase tax, while the highest tax on income does not exceed 12.5 per cent (as given in the *Economist* of December 17, 1956, p. 1010).

reason, to have it "assessed in bulk." Because taxing the daily necessities of life affects small incomes, in particular and most severely the family, the chief object for indirect taxation must be luxury goods of all kinds. This should include the luxury expenditure of propertied classes, although regard must be had for the risk of a decline of orders and of employment setting in in the industries concerned, and the luxury expenditure of the masses, that is, alcohol, tobacco, tickets for motion pictures, places of amusement, racing; such taxation, however, must allow for the demand of goods for leisure use by the lower income groups.

IV *Budgeting and Fiscal Policy*

Until the Second World War it was a dogma of scientific finance that budgets should be balanced yearly, because in case of a budget deficit there is the danger of undesirable creation of money by the state, coupled with devaluation or with the taking on of debt burdens in an irresponsible fashion. After the Second World War the view was widely held, following *Keynes'* theory, that an important function of fiscal policy was to serve economic and trade policy; this meant, above all, the expansion or restriction of the flow of money and credit by way of tax surpluses or tax deficit. The often very agitated discussion about the possibilities and limits of such fiscal planning are not yet settled. *Fritz Neumark* aptly sums up the state of the discussion:

> Unanimity exists . . . on this, that fiscal policy, as well as its purely financial task, *can* and *should* fulfill (social and) economic functions by means of which the aim of mitigating economic fluctuations, as completely as possible, and of insuring the maintenance of a state of maximum employment of productive forces would be set in the foreground. It is conceded by most that the realization of this end requires recourse *also* to other than financial means, in particular to methods of credit policy, yet it is believed that its attainment is utterly impossible *without* a sensible policy of expenditure and of reimbursement.[19]

Another expert in scientific finance, *Gerhard Colm,* cautions:

> The dogma of a yearly balancing of the budget would provide at least a norm which could be used in considering expenditure programs and fiscal policy. Do we not surrender all rules and do we not open the doors to interest policies, if we assert that a concrete budgetary policy entirely depends on economic circumstances . . . ? The chief point to be stressed here is that for each country or each period a relatively fixed budget target should exist, estimated on the assumption of a high employment level, whether there be at the time a moderate or substantial surplus, a balanced budget or a moderate deficit.[20]

[19] F. Neumark, "Grundsätze und Arten der Haushaltsführung und Finanzbedarfsdeckung," in *Handbuch der Finanzwissenschaft,* Vol. I, p. 636; cf. the essentially more sceptical attitude taken by Günter Schmölders, *Finanzpolitik,* 1955, pp. 262 ff.; especially worthy of note seems Schmölders' sociological explanation of "fiscal policy-making," *op. cit.,* pp. 48–125.

[20] G. Colm, *Die öffentliche Haushaltswirtschaft,* pp. 534 ff.

The application of such a long-term budget target would provide sufficient breathing space to allow for additional expenditures or reductions of taxes necessitated by an antidepression policy.

The possibilities and the tasks of fiscal policy with regard to the business cycle policy will occupy us further (in Book IV: *Ethics of Social Economy*). Here we must mention the *first among the principles* of common good justice imposing obligations upon the state, which natural law ethics emphasizes in questions of economic policy in general and fiscal policy in particular: *the principle of a stable currency.* It applies as much against measures leading to deflationary, as against those leading to inflationary currency fluctuations. The great danger of an antidepression fiscal policy is effects of an inflationary kind, above all those of a creeping inflation. As we shall see, the inflationary undermining of the stability of currency means a grave injustice against whole large groups of income-earners (people with fixed incomes) and property-owners (owners of savings, debentures, state loans, etc.), and thus against the stability of ordered property conditions, a main foundation of social order. The undermining of currency stability further means a grave injustice on the part of the legislator (parliament), because with currency instability a basic condition for expedient business management is lost. Short-term antidepression successes of fiscal policy, insofar as they impair currency stability, always involve a falling short of the full realization of the social end of the economy, which can be achieved only as a result of long-term planning and occasional sacrifices. In addition, as *Schmölders* points out, one must bear in mind "how much the development of the public exchequer and revenue finding depend on the stability of currency, which, in 'deficitary budget policy,' is in jeopardy. Each devaluation of a currency hastens and increases the effective personal and material expenditure of the exchequer, just as it diminishes and retards state revenue in real terms, as soon as its development nears or possibly exceeds the expected additional amounts in tax, levied because of taxpayers' delays." [21]

[21] G. Schmölders, *op. cit.*, p. 269.

PART FOUR

State Dynamics

149. Reason of State

In the foregoing discussion of the nature of the state we have often noted dynamic forces in the actual reality of the state, which have far-reaching influence on its life, on its development, and on its conduct. Among these *sociological* factors are war, the endeavor to broaden the basis of its economic existence, the will to power, and the growth and decline of the population. In the modern state a large proportion of these forces converge in nationalism, capitalism, militarism, and imperialism; within the life of the state there are also political pluralism, social class antagonisms, and dynamic forces springing from these two causes. We must not forget the moral impulses, with the elementary impulse toward law and justice, and also the moral impulses toward economic, social, and cultural progress. It is the operation of all these rational and irrational driving forces in the life of the state that we would comprehend under the heading of *state dynamics*. An inquiry into state dynamics is faced with the problem of how far the state is subject to necessities originating in these irrational factors, and whether they give the state a status placing it outside the moral order.

The dominance of such necessities in the conduct of the state is termed *reason of state*. This expression (*ragione di stato*) comes from the period after *Machiavelli*. It did not attain general currency until the middle of the seventeenth century, but it was at once understood more or less in the sense of the principle originated by *Machiavelli:* that the law governing the acts of the statesman must be determined solely by expediency, and that "state reason," that is, state interest, may require a mode of conduct contrary to the moral law. Yet, few political theorists have been found to defend pure Machiavellianism, for the simple reason that the natural moral law protests too clearly against it in the conscience of the majority of mankind. The advocates of absolute reason of state have generally sought at least a certain moral veneer, whether, with *Hegel*, they chose to see in the state a moral being of a higher order or, with *Treitschke*, have claimed for it immanent life purposes and cultural purposes which raise it above the general moral order. In fact, political ethics and individual ethics can come to different, even opposite, conclusions in the application of the general principles of natural law. To give an example: The patient acceptance of a serious attack on his honor can be a high virtue in the individual, if he alone is involved; in the statesman, if serious harm should arise for the state, it can be a grave wrong. Clearly, then, there is a core of truth in the idea of "reason of state," which therefore must have an admissible meaning in natural law doctrine. That such a meaning is not alien to it is clear from the fact that, for natural law philosophy, the fundamental principle of morality consists in "right reason" (cf. Chap. 3). We must then ask what "right reason" is for the state, in order to give reason of state its place in natural law doctrine.

The solution of our problem will have to begin from the distinction between the common good and the individual good. On this is founded the precedence which natural law accords to the former in given circumstances. The further conclusion is seen in the peculiar form of the *obligations arising from the common good.* These obligations mean that state interest can command modes of conduct which differ from those the moral order imposes upon the individual. This is an obvious consequence of the position of the idea of end, which, as we have urged, affords the concrete criterion of the good in natural law ethics. It would be remarkable if the great representatives of the natural law tradition had not expressed themselves unmistakably on the propriety of reason of state.

St. Thomas, in fact, leaves no doubt on the matter, and he frequently appeals to the authority of *St. Augustine.* The discussion of the virtues of patience and fortitude and of virtues in war gives him occasion to consider the divergence between the norms of political ethics and those of individual ethics. He is occupied with the question of how far the state itself is bound by the precepts of *Christ* and of the apostles expressed in the Sermon on the Mount and elsewhere, such as: "But I say to you not to resist evil: but if one strike thee on thy right cheek, turn to him also the other" (Matt. 5:39); or: "Revenge not yourselves . . . but give place unto wrath, for it is written: Revenge is mine, I will repay, saith the Lord" (Rom. 12:19). With *Augustine,* he replies: These precepts constitute a universal obligation of spiritual preparedness to accept injustice with patience and not to defend oneself; but they do not demand the same kind of action in every case.

For obvious reasons the position of the teacher requires that any wrongdoing on the part of the pupil against himself be prevented or punished; similarly, the common good can demand that wrong be resisted. Not to resist a threatened injustice or to allow a perpetrated injustice to go unpunished where, for example, the state's duty of self-defense is involved, is, according to *St. Thomas,* morally wrong or may even indeed be a crime.[1] All this follows from the general principles of natural law ethics:

[1] St. Thomas, *Summa theol.,* IIa IIae, q. 40, a. 1, commenting on the passage quoted from St. Matthew, refers to St. Augustine, *De serm. Dom. in monte,* I, 19: "Huiusmodi praecepta semper sunt servanda in praeparatione animi, ut scilicet semper homo sit

The existential ends, insofar as their fullfillment depends on the fundamental social functions, confer a moral priority on the necessities of the political common good. Therefore, the conduct of the state is not thereby raised above the general moral order. There can be no question of a special political morality as opposed to the universal. The general moral principles apply without restriction to the acts of the state, although their application to the particular conditions of these acts and to the "situation" affecting the good of the state may lead to practical consequences which differ from those which would ensue for the individual.

Reason of state, accordingly, is the demand of the objective common good as the concrete political task in a given situation. Questions such as this one made necessary our previous exhaustive inquiry into the process of realization of the common good with regard to its nature, causes, structure, and functions (cf. Chaps. 22 ff.). From this inquiry *three conclusions* clearly emerge:

1. There is *no absolute* reason of state which would entitle the state to take action in violation of law and morality, but there is a moral reason of state which invests the state with the right and the duty to act in accordance with the claims of the objective common good in a given situation.

2. Acts that are immoral in themselves are immoral in politics also. The *moral law* applies without restriction to politics. The principle that the end justifies the means cannot be a principle of true reason of state. A lie, including the propaganda lie in time of war, is never permissible in politics; mere reticence in regard to facts or truth, or concealment (e.g., as a stratagem in war), is a different matter. Similarly, breach of treaty can never be justified as a political means, nor can the conclusion of a treaty for the purpose of deceiving a rival, since this involves the intention to break the treaty; different again is the extinction of a treaty owing to a complete change in the circumstances, foreknowledge of which would have prevented its being concluded. Hence, a state is not bound by a defensive pact if the observance of it would gravely endanger the existence of the state, unless the acceptance of such a risk is expressly included in the treaty.

3. A further conclusion arising from our former discussion of the common good is that the actual common good can never be more than an approximation. Therefore, reason of state can command the more imperfect in order not to make the more perfect impossible, and hence can

---

paratus non resistere, vel se non defendere, si opus fuerit. Sed quandoque est aliter agendum propter commune bonum, vel etiam illorum cum quibus pugnatur." Not to resist wrong in the latter case, says St. Thomas (*ibid.*, q. 188, a. 3), "ad imperfectionem pertinet, vel etiam ad vitium, si aliquis potest convenienter injurianti resistere." Cf. also *ibid.*, q. 108, a. 1; q. 140, a. 2; in q. 136, a. 4, appealing to St. Augustine, *Epist. 138, ad Marcellinum,* St. Thomas urges that patience can lay divergent obligations on the individual and on the state: "Praecepta patientiae non contrariantur bono reipublicae, pro quo conservando contra inimicos pugnatur."

command what is most expedient in the circumstances. Therefore, reason of state enjoins a policy of *"the possible."* The statesman who neglects the realities of political forces, however idealistic his motives, lends himself to measures which bring the state into unnecessary danger; in fact, he acts against the common good. The fact that the true realistic policy as prescribed by reason of state has nothing in common with mere opportunism has already been explained in our discussion of the nature of the common good.

Because moral reason of state prescribes a realistic policy in accordance with the prevailing conditions governing the realization of the common good, it is *a field of most serious and involved conflicts of conscience.* For, in the weighing of the necessities of the political common good, countless factors have to be considered, a great number of which do not admit of an exact valuation of their import. This is particularly true in circumstances in which reason of state gains an immensely increased significance e.g., when a state is simultaneously threatened from within and without. The necessary decisions are made uncommonly difficult at such times if the radical groups within the state can secure the help of foreign powers pursuing parallel ideological and political aims. The demands of reason of state are complicated still further in cases where a Christian statesman of sensitive conscience finds himself faced with situations which, however they turn out, would almost inevitably imperil the moral and religious substance of the political common good. Thus, as an example, unless such a statesman takes resolute action against internal radical groups, he condemns to failure his own policy that is inspired by moral ideals, while those very moral ideals may be blamed for the severities accompanying such resolute action in the eyes of many and may thus provide opponents with powerful propaganda weapons. In the period before and during the Second World War, for instance, there was more than one Christian statesman who, facing the immensely complicated problems of reason of state, put the question to himself whether his Christian conscience was not an obstacle in the way of necessary decisions and whether a statesman with neutral religious convictions would not find it easier, under existing conditions, to act in accordance with the true reason of state.

One of the gravest dilemmas of conscience into which reason of state can plunge a statesman is the *decision for or against war* as a means of national defense. We are, of course, thinking solely of a just defensive war. A country that finds itself drawn into the sphere of influence of another state which has an overwhelming preponderance of power may have to choose whether to try a temporizing policy, preserving its existence temporarily by concessions which will compromise its sovereignty, or embroil itself in a war which offers no hope of success but will secure for the country an incomparably better moral position in the eyes of the world. This was the situation of some states before and during the Second World War. Only exceptional resolution and energy, rooted in moral principles, can take the responsibility for deciding such conflicts of conscience. Even more difficult for the statesman is the decision regarding a *preventive war of defense* (cf. Chap. 146). Take the case when war is undoubtedly inevitable because another power is decidedly arming and preparing for it; a preventive war of defense gives the threatened country a chance of survival, or of survival with far smaller losses. What action is the statesman entitled, or rather obliged, to take on the grounds of moral reason of state? In all such cases conflicts of duties arise, to be resolved on the basis of the universal moral order, not conflicts resulting from an intrinsic antagonism between the nature of the state and the moral order.

Reason of state is misconceived by political theory in two opposite ways: on the one hand, it is not considered to have any justification at all; on the other hand, it is made the sole law of political action. The former attitude is that of absolute pacifism; the latter that of political utilitarianism.

Absolute Pacifism

Absolute pacifism denies any justification even to purely defensive war. We need not repeat (cf. Chap. 146) the arguments by which natural law philosophy, today as ever, holds that under certain conditions defensive war is justified. It is no real objection to these arguments to say that nonviolent, purely passive resistance is a method more likely to succeed in the defense of a nation's highest goods, such as its moral and religious existence. For there is ample evidence in recent history that the modern totalitarian aggressor state may well be able to destroy the spiritual substance of a nation. Furthermore, there can be no doubt that a nation engaged in a war of defense, conscious that it has to fight for its highest spiritual and national values, can summon up moral forces which, even in the event of external defeat, can be of greatest significance for the future spiritual, moral, religious, and even biological existence of a nation.

When absolute pacifism appeals to the Christian conscience in support of its opposition to defensive war, and of a mere trust in Providence, it falls into the further error of presuming to anticipate Providence by determining, notwithstanding circumstances, the manner of trial which a people is to be prepared to accept from the hand of the Ruler of history. The pacifist decides independently for nonviolent, passive resistance. Yet, how can he say whether active, armed resistance by a state, as prescribed by the moral reason of state, may not, even if actually condemned to failure, release moral and spiritual forces destined to have a substantial influence in giving to the course of history a direction corresponding to its Christian significance. It is one of the fundamental errors of absolute pacifism that it is not prepared to look beyond the situation of the moment and to think in the light of history, and a fundamental error of absolute Christian pacifism that its concept of the Christian conscience denies submission to the Lord of history.

It is not, then, for nations to choose the "Way of the Cross" advocated by *F. W. Foerster,* one of the most resolute champions of absolute pacifism, and to rely upon the "Eternal Laws" whereby law and justice must prevail.[2] We have it

[2] Cf. Friedrich Wilhelm Foerster, *Politische Ethik,* 1918, pp. 254 ff.

from no less an authority than *St. Thomas* that this is not the sense in which we are to understand the words of the Apostle that evil is not to be resisted and that vengeance must be left to the Lord. Rather, the moral function of the state is to realize the common good in given circumstances, as far as this lies within human understanding and human power. Beyond this, giving the moral order its fuller reality lies in the hands of the Creator.

Political Utilitarianism

Political utilitarianism upholds the principle that any means demanded by the "necessities" of the state, that is, by considerations of expediency, is justified. This principle hardly ever appears in all its nakedness, but it is generally clothed in an ethical garb. Recent history indeed shows to what an extraordinary degree, as far as their power permitted, states allowed themselves to be guided by reason of state in the utilitarian sense, in order to pursue a policy of interest. Political utilitarianism shows itself to be a Machiavellianism, softened out of regard for world opinion. Reason of state in this version is "the calculation of what is expedient, useful and advantageous, what the state must do in order to attain at a given moment the optimum of its existence." It is "the idea informing its life, its entelechy." It is "state exigency," "the situation of constraint in which the state finds itself with regard to both internal and external threats to its power and which compels it to adopt means of defense and combat of quite specific character," so that in acting in accordance with reason of state, "the state is apparently lifted by a compelling force above law and morality." [3]

This idea of reason of state, propounded by *Meinecke* between the two World Wars, is based on two obviously fallacious presuppositions. The first is that he does not see in power merely an integrating element in the state and its common good, but the essence and criterion of its very existence. *Meinecke* makes this quite clear when he sums up the essence of the state thus: "We may say that power is the most original, indispensable, and enduring factor in the nature of the state," while "law, morality, and religion also contribute integrally to its being, or at least claim to do so, as soon as the state has attained the prime elementary feature of being power." [4] Our analysis (cf. Chap. 116) has shown a different relationship between power and the spiritual factors in the nature of man and of society. *Benedetto Croce,* historian as well as philosopher, does not hesitate to declare: "Whenever we hear someone refer to 'historical necessity' rather than to his conscience to justify an impending decision about some line of action, we can be sure that we are faced with a case of lack of moral sensibility, or with an attempt to defraud the inescapable law of duty." [5]

The second erroneous presupposition in the idea of reason of state set forth by *Meinecke* consists in this, that the conflicts of conscience and the possibility of error which beset the life and activity of the state and which are only an intensified form of the tragedy surrounding all human life and activity, is interpreted as an essentially necessary conflict with the moral order. History itself, on which the historian *Meinecke* thinks to found his idea of reason of state, shows unmistakably that states are likely to be tempted to make reason of state

[3] Friedrich Meinecke, *Die Idee der Staatsräson,* 2nd ed., 1925, pp. 6, 12, 17.
[4] *Ibid.,* pp. 496 f.
[5] Benedetto Croce, *Politics and Morals,* trans. by S. J. Castiglione, 1946, p. 128.

an absolute only when their relative preponderance of power brings an "optimum of their existence" within reach. But it also shows that all states, as soon as they are threatened by a stronger state, bethink themselves of the moral order and call upon justice to defend them.

Even states that act on principles of absolute reason of state and of Machiavellianism, always strive outwardly for some moral justification of their actions, however tenuous it may appear. It follows, then, that the sense of responsibility before the moral order is not lacking, however great may be the temptation to act solely in accordance with political utilitarianism. Besides this, *Meinecke's* book reveals how easily political philosophy can fall into the error of utilitarian state philosophy. Writing of the collapse of Germany at the end of the First World War and her helplessness in face of the victor states, *Meinecke,* struck by the reverse side of reason of state (the outcome of the Second World War gives a much more tragic significance to his words), writes: "The pitiless reason of state of the ancient republics seems to be reviving, with its intolerance of the mere existence of an opponent who has once been dangerous and its relentless pursuit of his complete destruction. Assuredly, it was from this cause that the ancient republic perished at the core. And now for the same reason, extinction threatens the essence of modern European political life, that hitherto self-restoring equilibrium of free, independent states, feeling toward one another as members of one great family. This will mean that Europe has played out her historic role, and that Western civilization is in fact doomed to decay." [6]

Reason of State and Moral Dualism

The advocates of the idea of reason of state who insist on its inherent conflict with the moral order while yet seeking a moral justification for it, ultimately come to accept a double morality: a general morality and a political morality. They try with *Hegel* to give this ethical dualism a foundation by ascribing to the state a special higher moral being or, following *Schleiermacher's* ethics, by claiming a particular kind of individual morality for the state. As "every individual, in order to assert himself, requires a minimum of power," *Meinecke* argues, so does the state, in order to "save and preserve its distinct individuality"; and one can only say that if by the state's action this aim "is achieved at the expense of the general moral imperative, as often happens, it is tragic guilt." [7] Such action, therefore, he maintains, cannot be judged by general moral rules. Yet, the individual needs power in order to fulfill the moral responsibilities issuing from the existential ends: this was the idea of our philosophy of law. Nevertheless, it seems evident that only the power of law, founded upon the general moral order, is able to guarantee for all men and all peoples their equal claim, founded on their equal human nature, to the development of their individuality. The question is how this equal claim of all men and all peoples, concerning which the unbiased conscience is in no doubt, is to be enforced and realized on the basis of an isolated "individual morality."

Indeed, the whole possibility of a social morality and of any political and international order rests on the fact that everything individual is linked with

[6] Meinecke, *op. cit.,* pp. 529 f.
[7] *Ibid.,* pp. 533 ff.

something common and therefore universal. By universal we mean the personality values with the individual and social rights and duties bound up with them. Consequently, a collective body like the state is subject, just as is the individual, to the universal moral law, however much this may appear as individual morality for such a body in particular circumstances, as we have shown by a number of examples of complications of reason of state. The allusion to "*tragic guilt*," as inevitably associated with action in accordance with reason of state, invokes an idea which may have possessed its justification in ancient tragedy but which today less than ever can be regarded by the developed moral and legal consciousness as a real solution of ethical problems. The more the conscience of mankind comes to see that the subordination of the dynamics of power to a generally binding order is indispensable for mankind's continuance and development, the less can the political sphere be regarded as an exception.

150. War

Among the factors in political dynamics which exercise a determining influence on the existence, on the life, on the development, and on the destiny of the state, first place must undoubtedly be given to war. The history of mankind is at least as much a history of its wars as of its civilization. War very often marks the beginning and end of states, elevates them to new heights of development after victory, or makes them the puppets of their conquerors after defeat. If war is such a power in the life of the state, then the first question that must present itself is: What are the *causes of war?* A glance into history will show us that these causes are closely connected with roots from which, as we have shown, the state itself by its nature arises. Among them the following must be noted: the natural growth of peoples and the resulting pressure toward living space; the acquisitive instinct in its primitive and modern forms; the power instinct in the ruling classes of almost every society; the instinct to expand resources with the drive for colonies and export markets in modern times, particularly intensified by the motive forces of capitalism; nationalism with its principle of absolute sovereignty; militarism with its focusing of the whole life of the nation and of its expanding vitality on the increasing of its actual war potential; religious conviction, whose significance as a cause of war is shown by the history of religious wars; lastly, those philosophies of life and history which see in war a momentous expression of the life of peoples and an indispensable means of education toward the development of their vitality. The causes of war just mentioned will be dealt with more thoroughly in the following chapters.

Here we need only point out that, in spite of all the complexity and urgency of the *forces directly responsible* for releasing war in the modern, and especially in the present-day, world, nothing justifies the fatalistic assertion that they are outside human responsibility and control. The exhaustive analysis, aided by many thousands of documents, of so complicated a drama as that which preceded the First World War, leads *L. Albertini* to the conclusion that even here uncontrollable forces ultimately did not tie the knot and decide the fate of nations, but the men who held the threads in their hands.[1] And concerning the outbreak of the Second World War, it may be seen from Professor *Freund's* collection of documents that opportunities existed for those concerned to show a sense of, and a willingness for, responsibility. *Freund* himself, in the Preface, pointing to the outcome of his argument, speaks of the wish that "he could communicate a little to the reader that profound convulsion, how shamefully everything happened—with what shamefully criminal intention, with what shameful incompetence and excellent routine—as a world began to decline." [2]

Certainly voices are continually making themselves heard whose question regarding the causes of war seems much less meaningful than this: Is not *war the motive force of cultural progress?* The spiritual forbears of *Treitschke,* who thought that to exclude war is to mutilate human nature, can be traced back to *Heraclitus,* who sharply opposed *Homer* and his condemnation of war, in conformity with his general axiom that "war is the father of all things." *Nietzsche* seeks to go more deeply into the connections of war and culture:

> War is indispensable. It is nothing but fanaticism and beautiful-soulism to expect very much (or even, much only) from humanity when it has forgotten how to wage war. For the present we know of no other means whereby the rough energy of the camp, the deep impersonal hatred, the cold-bloodedness of murder with a good conscience, the general organized ardor in destroying the enemy, the proud indifference to great losses, to one's own existence and to that of one's friends, the elemental earthquakelike convulsion of the soul, can be as forcibly and certainly communicated to enervated nations as is done by every great war: owing to the brooks and streams that here break forth, although they sweep boulders and rubbish of all sorts along with them and destroy the meadows of delicate cultures, the mechanism in the workshops of the mind is afterwards, in circumstances again favorable, rotated by new power. Culture can by no means dispense with passions, vices, and malignities.[3]

Even he who assigns to suffering an irreplaceable function in the maturing of individual personality and of the cultures of nations, will include the prevention of war by an international legal body for safeguarding peace among the highest cultural aims of mankind. And if mankind is viewed as a whole, there is such an excess of suffering that a sociologically based ethics believes it must see precisely in the lessening of suffering a chief criterion of true moral activity; [4] today one thinks not least of the

[1] Cf. Luigi Albertini, *Le Origine della guerra del 1914,* L. Magrini, editor, Vols. I–III (Milan), 1945, especially Vol. II.

[2] Michael Freund, *Weltgeschichte der Gengenwart in Dokumenten: Geschichte des zweiten Weltkrieges in Dokumenten,* Vol. III, *Der Ausbruch des Krieges* (1939), 1956, VI.

[3] F. Nietzsche, *Menschliches, Allzumenschliches,* 1879, par. 477.

[4] Cf. Leopold v. Wiese, *Ethik in der Schauweise der Wissenschaften vom Menschen und von der Gesellschaft,* 1947.

position of the countless millions of people of the underdeveloped countries.

In the discussion of state dynamics we are concerned primarily with the *consequences of war.* All history provides evidence that after a war the principle which is almost invariably acted upon is this: The victor knows no law; he creates law. He treats the conquered in the manner best suited to his own present and presumed future interests. For absolute reason of state, *vae victis* is as much an affair of cold-blooded calculation as any other means of policy. What, then, are the *principles of justice* that should govern the peace settlement after a war? First of all, war of itself never creates new genuine law. This is fully evident in the case of a state unjustly attacked, which is compelled to bow before the victor and to accept a peace treaty. The same applies however even to the victor in a just war, since its reason consists only in the vindication of the violated right. Only to the extent that actual rights are violated, does justice entitle the victor in a war of defense to exact from the defeated enemy compensation ("reparations"), punishment, and guaranties of peace. Their extent can be determined only if the immediate and remoter responsibilities for the war are conscientiously ascertained. Even the right to punish the unawful aggressor is measured, and therefore limited, by the guilt which has been incurred by the nation, or the government, or both together. But even when guilt is established, we must not forget that punishment is not an end in itself; rather, it must minister to the restoration of justice and peace. If it becomes an end in itself, then it is an exhibition of revenge.

Furthermore, it is a principle of internal criminal law with all civilized peoples, and thus of modern *ius gentium,* that punishment presupposes the *establishment of guilt* by disinterested and impartial judges. No other method of assessing the fact and the extent of war guilt would comply with justice than that which is employed for the trial of a lawbreaker by a criminal court in a constitutional state: the proceedings must be in accordance with existing law, the judges must be independent (applied to international criminal law: they must, above all, not belong to a party to the conflict), and there must be adequate opportunities for defense. The war guilt clause in the *Versailles Treaty* may well serve as an instance of how questionable the decreeing of war guilt by the victors appears, since there were jurists of all nations, apart from the Germans, who found this clause untenable. Typical are the conclusions arrived at by three American jurists who examined the question closely: only one, Professor *Schmitt,* attributes the responsibility to Germany; Professor *Barnes* assigns it to France, Russia, and Serbia; Professor *Fay* assigns to the other powers as much guilt as to Germany.[5]

On the other hand, the fact that even under modern conditions a whole nation may share the *collective guilt* of a war of aggression has been main-

[5] Cf. Professor Magrini in his Preface to Albertini's work, mentioned above, note 1.

tained, but has never been proved. The fact that during the Second World War the leading powers among the Allies made it their business in their propaganda to single out a party among the German and Italian nations as responsible for the war, is evidence enough for the existence of a clear consciousness that, especially in totalitarian states, whole nations cannot be made responsible when the all-powerful group provokes a war. The dependence of any government on public opinion does not answer the question, since the opportunities of misleading public opinion which are available with modern methods of propaganda to the modern state, and especially the totalitarian state, are too extensive.

The territorial changes following almost every war on the grounds of more or less justified claims to compensation or guaranties of peace in recent times have been associated with extensive *deportations of population*. The intention was the elimination of minority problems, which have proved to be among the primary causes of wars since the rise of nationalism. The first time a peace treaty provided for a large-scale compulsory exchange of populations was the Turco-Greek agreement of 1923. Such agreements on the basis of reciprocity may be justified if they are made freely by both sides and proper arrangements are made for the resettlement of the populations. On the grounds of justice no objection can be made to expulsion from old or new state territory of those members of a minority who are convicted by judicial procedure of having cooperated with the aggressor in a war. But no justification exists for indiscriminate deportation of a minority population if its disloyalty is not established. Even in cases of guilt the punishment must be in accordance with the degree of guilt: confiscation of all possessions in addition to deportation may be justified in cases of graver guilt; but to those who have not taken part in political actions, a fair chance to remove the bulk of personal property must be given. Deportation of minorities for any other reason is incompatible with the cultural standards of the European nations, let alone the demands of natural justice and, even more, of Christian charity.

A grave injustice also exists, according to natural law principles, when the victor state retains *prisoners of war* for too long. As soon as it is certain that there is no fear of the defeated aggressor state disturbing international peace, and that it can be expected to pay the reparations imposed on it, the obligation of justice to release prisoners of war subsists. The retention of large numbers of prisoners up to ten years or more by one of the victorious powers after the Second World War, and the indifference of the public opinion of the world recalls the time when the enslavement of portions of the defeated nation was regarded as the victor's right. The injustice is proved by the consideration that the splitting up of families in such an event would be felt by many as sorely as death itself. It is only because the family has lost so much in estimation as a human, social, and ethical value that the possibility of such a relapse into barbarism can be explained.

Among the guaranties of peace which may justly be demanded from a defeated aggressor, may be counted his *military and economic disarmament,* that is, the restriction of his military forces and armament industry insofar as they constitute a threat, all circumstances considered, to the security of the state unjustly attacked or to international peace. There is no doubt, however, that it would conflict with natural law principles of justice to deprive a nation of all the means of defense as long as there is no working international organization, especially if such a nation were directly threatened by a well-armed state, apart from the fact that prolonged unilateral disarmament is such a severe humiliation for a nation that it can hardly be expected to serve the purposes of peace, and is thus simply bad policy. Compulsory limiting of armaments to the extent required by internal peace and order would, however, assume an altogether different aspect if carried out as part of a general disarmament of all nations under international control. Again, with regard to economic disarmament, to impose on a nation conditions which leave it no prospect of material and cultural rehabilitation, apart from the injustice involved in such an enforced debasement of the standard of living (the "reagrarianization" of Germany, as planned by some American circles during the Second World War), is not a policy likely to serve the interests of peace.

In all these questions *justice and readiness for reconciliation* are the best realistic policy. The longer a war lasts the more violently it arouses the passions of the nations, so that at the moment of its conclusion hatred and the spirit of revenge carry them away, and reason scarcely obtains a hearing. There is perhaps only one method of bringing about a spirit of understanding and reconciliation: to postpone the final peace settlement until passions have cooled and it becomes possible to view as a whole the catastrophe in which modern war, as evidenced by most recent history, inevitably plunges all the belligerent nations. Then mature judgment may acknowledge that the future of all depends on their good will for cooperation and on the conditions which the victors provide to enable such a will to emerge.

151. Movements of Population in State Dynamics

I *Increase of Population*

Overpopulation in a state has always claimed the attention of political science as a factor operating with the strength of an elemental force. We find it already discussed in *Plato* and with stronger emphasis in *Aristotle.* This is not surprising in view of the small "living space" of the city-state, which was rapidly threatened by the natural growth of population.[1] To-

[1] The like conditions in regard to the medieval town urged the same problem upon the natural law ethics of that time. St. Thomas had in view two main solutions, following suggestions made by Aristotle: first, the limiting by law of the size of the family; secondly, the founding of colonies or, as we should say today, emigration. As for

day, the world's living space seems to be growing too small for the expected world population. It is calculated [2] that the population of the earth will increase from 2.45 to 3.6 billions between the years 1950 and 1980, that is to say, in only one generation. By the turn of the century it would reach the six billion limit. This means that population pressure is becoming a factor of incalculable importance for present-day state dynamics. The general questions of population policy connected with this have already been dealt with (cf. Chap. 147 and the literature cited there).

Taking into consideration the figures mentioned, there arises the world problem of the relationship between population increase and *foodstuffs potential*. Many can see a solution only in a return to the population theory of *Malthus*, after this seemed to be abandoned owing to actual development as inconsistent with the facts. His theory is: The population multiplies in geometrical progression, but the means of subsistence only in arithmetical progression; thus, the population is necessarily limited by the means of subsistence. The population invariably increases where the means of subsistence increase, unless prevented by some powerful checks; these checks may all be reduced to moral restraint, vice, and misery.[3] The progress of industry and of agriculture and the unforeseen increase of population pronounce against the *economic* presuppositions of *Malthus'* theory. Whereas in the eighteenth century, toward the end of which he was writing, the population of England rose from about 5,000,000 to 9,000,000, it increased in the nineteenth century from 9,000,000 to 33,000,000. The respective figures for Germany are 15,000,000 to 20,000,000 and 22,000,000 to 66,000,000.[4] But the *biological* presuppositions of

---

the prospects of success of both methods, that of limitation of the size of the family is subject to restrictions imposed upon its application by the natural law itself. It is, therefore, not without surprise that one finds St. Thomas (*in II Pol.*, lects. 8, 17) suggesting the restriction of procreation after a certain number of children without discussing the ethical problems arising from such a measure; he confines himself (*ibid.*, lect. 15) to rejecting the chief means which the ancient state applied for controlling the birth rate, namely, the toleration of homosexuality. But he defines the problem with his usual responsiveness to realities when he says (*ibid.*, lect. 6, 8, 13) that one cannot aim at a proportionate equality in the distribution of property which is vital for a political community, and at the same time allow an infinite growth of the population.

[2] According to the calculations communicated to the Congress for Population Questions held in Rome in 1954.

[3] Cf. Malthus, *Essay on the Principle of Population as It Affects the Future Improvement of Society*, 1798.

[4] The optimum theory of population policy may be regarded as a derivative of the Malthusian theory of limitation of population by natural causes. It was first expounded in England by E. Cannan and is today widely held in the United States. According to this theory, it is more or less an arithmetical problem what the optimum population is for a country when once one has investigated its economic potential. Professor Myrdal, *Population, A Problem for Democracy*, 1940, pp. 26 f., is right when he says that this theory is one of the most sterile that political economy has produced. Indeed, it is merely an evasion of the economic problem presented by the movement of population; this problem is that of finding an economic policy whereby the basis of existence for a growing population may be provided

Malthus' theory are also doubtful. His theory of "geometrical progression" of population growth is based on the assumption that biologically there is an established and unchangeable figure of fertility for human propagation. Of this, however, there is no proof. Rather, the biologists who believe that there are natural, that is, biological, forces counteracting excessive growth of population (not to be confused with unnatural methods of birth control) may be right. We may recall the observation of *Haldane* (cf. Chap. 147), namely, that in the wealthier classes a connection between genes is to be found, one group causing the betterment of hereditary qualities, the other, however, causing a diminution of fertility; he explicitly observes that in this way economic success and biological success are incompatible; elevated economic conditions result in a diminished biological fertility. The founder of eugenics, *Francis Galton,* mentioned in the same chapter, made the observation (to which *C. B. Goodhart* alludes, cf. below, *op. cit.*), that daughters of well-to-do families with fewer than average children inherit and retransmit a below average fertility. The fact established by *Lujo Brentano* is well known, that in the last 150 years the fall in the birth rate has moved parallel with the rise in prosperity; [5] still, his assessment of the causes may prove insufficient in the light of the present-day social sciences, especially social biology. Whereas he tends to concentrate excessively on moral degeneration as a cause of infertility, present-day biology is inclined to assume also natural biological barriers to growth of population. Thus, *C. B. Goodhart* points out a physiological and psychological decrease in fertility, which appears in individuals, classes, and nations whose attitude is conditioned by ideas of success; in such cases qualities of high selective value, such as intelligence, health, and strong power of sexual attraction, can be linked with decreased fertility; physiologically it causes less frequent births, and psychologically it results in the inclination to seek fulfillment in life in values other than those of marriage and the family. *Goodhart* emphasizes that this form of natural limitation of increase of population can take effect only if the mortality figures in overpopulated countries suffer a drastic decline; a merely slight improvement in subsistence or a raising of the standard of living, which would affect the mortality figures, not only would not retard but would probably promote an increase in population. His conclusion is: What we are obliged in any case to do, if done at once, may save our descendants from facing an inevitable ruin; [6] he thinks of the duty of advanced nations to promote ways and

[5] Cf. L. Brentano, *Konkrete Grundbedingungen der Volkswirtschaft, Ges. Aufs.,* Vol. II, 1924, pp. 196–338; in addition, cf. the sixty-two pages of statistics in the Appendix.

[6] As an example of diminishing fertility founded on psychology, Goodhart mentions the fact, emphasized in the literature of social biology and of population policy, of the diminished readiness to marry in Catholic Southern Ireland. Among the population of Southern Ireland artificial birth control would not be in use, rather is it the case that women who marry young have many children, but that proportionately few marry young and many do not marry at all; no less large a number of men remain

means of quickly assimilating the standard of living of underdeveloped countries to their own. *Goodhart* is not thinking of a socio-biological law. In fact, if we question history about the decay of nations, Professor *Ilse Schwidetzky* will be right with the answer which she gives after a scientific examination of the biological population development of twelve nations: "The historical biology of population only teaches how things may turn out, not how they must of necessity." [7] It may be taken as established, however, that economic progress and well-being is neither a chief cause of over-population, as *Malthus* supposed, nor can we see in it, as *Brentano* supposes, the chief cause of degeneration of nations (sexual diseases, mental illnesses, decline in morals). There are, rather, reasons for the supposition that the prosperity of a people can produce biological effects on population, which may be claimed to be a natural regulation of population increase, and hence a factor in solving the fateful problem of the adaptation of the population increase to the resources available.

With regard to the political dynamics arising from increase of world population, *natural law principles* of the greatest importance are in question.

1. Common good justice obliges the advanced peoples to offer help to peoples of underdeveloped countries toward a real and speedy raising of their standard of living. Two world problems are closely involved in this: repulsing communism, which sees its great opportunity in the low living standard of underdeveloped countries; providing the necessities of life for the greatly increased world population, which is to be expected in one or two generations, according to present fertility figures.

2. Common good justice demands that every nation devote its strength to exploiting to the utmost the still available sources of foodstuffs and to maintaining and extending the existing granaries. Tasks discussed in an extensive literature at the present time are chiefly set by soil erosion, plant diseases, and food parasites. With regard to new sources of foodstuffs we may recall the work of the biologist, seeking to raise plants of greater yield for food and fodder, studying possibilities of gaining vegetable foodstuffs from the sea (it is seriously estimated that thirty billion tons could be gained annually out of the sea; that is about as much as is obtained annually from the land). In addition there are the extensive possibilities of cultivating as yet unused surface soil in Asia, Australia, Africa, and the Pacific Islands [8] (in India with its inadequately nourished popula-

---

unmarried. Reasons of an economic nature certainly account for this in both sexes, yet the economic position before the famine in the middle of the last century, when the Irish were actually famous for the high number of marriages and births, was without doubt on a very low level.

[7] I. Schwidetzky, *Das Problem des Völkertodes,* 1954, p. 159 (many references to the literature are contained here).

[8] From the wealth of literature these concise expositions may be mentioned: Jacob Oser, *Must Man Starve?* 1956 (contains a wealth of examples); Alfred Sauvy, *Théorie générale de la population,* Vol. I, *Economie et population,* 1952; Vol. II, *Biologie*

tion only two-thirds of the cultivable land is made use of, and only by inadequate methods; the same holds good of the greater part of the South American continent).

3. Common good justice demands, lastly, close international cooperation. Without it none of the problems mentioned can be overcome. It is necessary in order to produce the enormous financial resources required. These resources could be found without going further if the greater part of what is now spent on armaments were devoted to providing the necessary conditions for the increasing world population. International cooperation is further required in order to create an international administrative authority to facilitate and to regulate emigration from countries with a population whose food requirements exceed foreseeable supplies (cf. Chap. 108). It is rightly pointed out in this respect by politicians, regarding the overpopulated countries of the Far East, that the Asiatics have the same right of emigration to underpopulated countries of the West as had the Europeans who "emigrated" to underdeveloped countries dominated by them.

Emigration and acquisition of territory are not the only means of balancing the pressure of population. If overpopulated countries have access to raw material markets and commodity markets, they can create the economic living space which they require in their own country by means of work and trade. The fact that the conscience of mankind is quite clear about this demand of natural law, is shown by the *Atlantic Charter* (1941). More than this, however, we cannot infer from it, since in practice its principles have largely been abandoned in the postwar world. The highly developed countries often obstruct imports from underdeveloped countries; yet these can only attain a higher standard of living by exports which will enable them to acquire the necessary raw materials and machinery. A glance at the history of colonialism and the accompanying exploitation of at present underdeveloped countries, shows that there are good reasons for the assertion that the European countries, which up to quite recent times shared in this exploitation, have duties, not only of social and international justice, but of commutative justice, of strict justice, which can only be discharged if there is considerable readiness to make sacrifices in face of the development problems of the formerly exploited, underdeveloped peoples.

Neo-Malthusianism

The remedy proposed by the neo-Malthusians for population pressure is artificial birth control. Its methods are contraception and abortion. In Germany,

---

social, 1954; *L'Europe et sa population,* 1953; L. D. Stamp, *Our Undeveloped World,* 1953; Le Gros and N. W. Pirie, editors, *Four Thousand Million Mouths,* 1951; S. Chardrasekhar, *Hungry People and Empty Lands,* Preface by William Vogt, 1954; M. K. Bennett, *The World's Food, A Study in the Interrelation of World Population, National Diets and Food Potentials* (New York), 1954; Fritz Baade, *Welternährungswirtschaft,* 1956.

according to the estimate of serious authors, the number of abortions between the two World Wars amounted to about a million a year; in France and Belgium on an average half of all pregnancies were artificially terminated.[9] Nowadays, contraception is a highly popularized method. It is well to note that just as "Darwinism" was not the teaching of *Darwin* himself, "Malthusianism" was not that of *Malthus*. *Malthus* rejects birth limitation in marriage. As a means of regulating the growth of population, he suggests "moral restraint." Today, neo-Malthusianism has become the keystone in the program of many who are concerned with population policy, in view of the nutrition difficulties of the world in the next generations, which may not be overcome by other means. In the Second World War voices were heard advocating a form of pressure toward birth limitation for the purpose of making Germany and Japan "innocuous" as dynamic forces in world policy, namely, by imposing on them living conditions which would impel them toward birth limitation and thus to national suicide. Recent developments in world political realities have speedily made these short-sighted politicians better informed, now that both states form bridgeheads in the fight against world communism. Political realities in the world today speak no less surely against the propaganda of neo-Malthusianism as a remedy for the present and future difficulties of world and population policy. For, the communistic world powers consider the increase in the numbers of their population, and in those of nations they hope to have under their influence, as their strongest forces in the struggle for world domination. Their various tactics brought them considerable progress but they rely chiefly on the one law of history, already mentioned, which is confirmed by facts: history moves with the nations which show decisively higher birthrates. At first, while still in the naïve intoxication of its materialist ideological faith, Soviet Russia believed it possible to permit abortion and to make divorce merely a matter of form. With the Second World War there was a complete change of attitude. The Soviet dictators learned that also, especially in the age of nuclear weapons (which most probably will never be brought into use), the Russian mother offers the greatest hope for her imperialistic aims; hence it is that Russia today stands in the first rank of countries with a far-sighted population policy. The propaganda of neo-Malthusianism as a means of world policy and of population policy is not only unrealistic because a definite success cannot be expected from it, but also because it provides communism with a highly effective weapon of propaganda, namely, that the capitalistic West is completely failing in so fundamental a question concerning the entire existence of men and of peoples, while the communistic economy and society are creating the conditions for the natural development of life of the peoples. Although in the last few years Russia and China have changed their population policy and their birthrate is now falling considerably, the above mentioned law of history is still on their side.

11 *The Declining Birth Rate*

At first glance only population increase seems to act as a factor in state dynamics. Close examination of the effects of the present decline in population in a large area of the world testifies to the contrary. In Pro-

[9] Cf. D. V. Glass, *Population, Policies, and Movements in Europe*, 1940, pp. 162 ff.

fessor *Myrdal's* view,[10] no other factor, not even war, is of such critical significance for the long-term destinies of democracies as the population movement. Democracy, with all its content of civic ideals and human life, must solve this problem or perish. In this proposition Professor *Myrdal* is joined by a number of prominent students of population theory.

The statistics of population movements show [11] a birth rate (i.e., live births per thousand of population) of about thirty from 1881–85 in all countries of the white race. From 1933–36 in all countries of western Europe except Holland, Hungary, Italy, Spain, and Portugal, the figures dropped well below twenty, whereas those of eastern Europe were still above twenty-five, the highest being that of Russia. In 1958, according to the *Demographic Yearbook, 1959,* published by the Statistical Office of the United Nations, Department of Economic and Social Affairs, there is not much change apart from the fall of the birth rate below twenty in Hungary (16.1) and Italy (17.9); the relative figures for 1958 in the U.S.A. and U.S.S.R. were 24.3 and 25.3. Birth rates in themselves of course do not accurately enough reveal the reproductive capacity of a nation, since they convey nothing with regard to the age, sex, or mortality of the population. To overcome this weakness of statistics, *R. R. Kuczynski* introduced the so-called "net reproduction rate," which is not indeed unobjectionable but allows quick comparison of tendencies in population movements. This figure gives the ratio of daughters of child-bearing age to mothers in a population. The basic ratio is one to one. This signifies that each mother is being replaced by one potential mother, so that the population will be just able to maintain itself numerically; a higher or lower figure will show the degree of increase or decline.

Kuczynski calculates the following ratios for the years immediately preceding the Second World War: the basic ratio was no longer reached by any countries of western, northern, or central Europe, or by Australia or New Zealand; this ratio was exceeded in southern Europe (Portugal, Spain, Italy, and the Balkan States), and still more in eastern Europe (Poland, Rumania, Bulgaria) and, of course, Russia and China. The figures quoted refer to the period before the Second World War. Since then the birth rate has increased in many of these countries, as a result of large-scale family policies, but on the whole the number of children for a normal family has not been reached. The decline in the birth rate need not have a proportionate effect on the absolute population figures if mortality rates likewise fall because of improved medical and health services. The result will show itself in the age pyramid of the population: the proportion of older people will increase. Thus, most countries with steeply falling birth rates have so far kept their population figures stable or even

[10] Cf. G. Myrdal, *Population: A Problem for Democracy,* 1940, p. 33.

[11] Cf. R. R. Kuczynski, *The Measurement of Population Growth: Methods and Results,* 1935; "World Population," in T. H. Marshall, editor, *The Population Problem,* 1938; D. V. Glass, *op. cit.;* Carr-Saunders, *World Population: Past Growth and Present Trends,* 1936; R. and K. Titmuss, *Parents' Revolt,* 1942.

increased them. Another stabilizing factor is immigration. For a long time past, France has been able to maintain a stable population by this means, in spite of a declining birth rate.

The causes of the decline in the birth rate

1. In most inquiries into the causes of the decline in population, *economic* factors are given the first place. Certainly, in the period between the two wars the parallelism between the curves of this decline and of economic depression is so marked that there can be no doubt of the importance of economic factors. The connection between bad harvests and a fall in the birth rate among the agricultural population had long been observed, even though on the whole the influence of economic fluctuations was of no considerable extent. That we must be careful, however, not to overrate the significance of economic causes, is shown by the fact already mentioned and strongly stressed by *Lujo Brentano,* that in modern Europe the principal cause of the fall in the birth rate was increasing prosperity. For a long period this was confined to the wealthier classes.

2. An important "social" cause is the desire to uphold or to secure certain social standards of living. The middle classes particularly, especially the salaried classes, sought to secure for themselves by limitation of births a higher social standard with more expensive houses, cars, better holidays, and better education for fewer children. The causes mentioned also, and especially, favor the increase of late marriages, or rather the decrease in early marriages, one of the chief causes of diminished fertility among all peoples.[12]

3. Public and secret *propaganda* for family limitation ("family planning," birth control) played its part also, inspired partly by "humanitarian" reasons, and partly by profit motives on the part of the producers of contraceptives. Simpler and safer methods of birth control, "scientifically" devised, have so popularized the practice that many neo-Malthusians themselves began to fear the consequences of further "progress" in this direction.

4. Closely connected with this are causes of a *moral* character: the utilitarian view of life, which is able to regard the hardships and sacrifices of pregnancy and motherhood merely as a diminution of pleasure values and enjoyment of life.

5. A further group of causes of the decline in the birth rate follows from the attitude of the state and of public opinion toward the *family.* In the individualist capitalistic era the state did nothing to protect the normal and large family economically; it tolerated the crowded, unhealthy slum dwellings which have throttled the family life of the working population in the large towns, and for a long time it took no account of the family in its social policy, or did so only when it was too late. To this was added the influence of public opinion, which ridiculed parents with

[12] Cf. J. B. S. Haldane, *Heredity and Politics,* 1943, p. 109.

more than one or two children as simpletons unaware of their own interests, or as hidebound by moral and religious prejudices.

6. Lastly, we must mention the group of diverse *physiological* causes, among which we include here all those which result in a reduction in procreative power. The idea that an industrial environment, as some biologists suggested, diminishes fertility, is now generally rejected. Influence on the biological decline of a race, however, is exercised, as was shown at the International Congress for Population Research in 1933, by the excessive use of alcohol, tobacco, morphia, by work with heavy metals, and undernourishment. "It is the sexual ailments which are of really general danger to the individual as well as for the existence of the race. . . . Gonorrhoea is the greatest foe of marital fecundity. Probably a quarter of all childless marriages are due to a gonorrhoeal malady contracted by husband or wife. . . . Whereas gonorrhoea reduces the number of offspring without impairing the quality of the race, syphilis has disastrous consequences for quality as well as for numbers"; [13] its effects are seen in miscarriages and in mental defectiveness in children. On the whole, however, in the opinion of experienced students of population movements, involuntary sterility due to physiological causes is much rarer than is generally supposed.[14]

The consequences of the decline in the birth rate and of the change in population structure

In the first place we must remember that the effects of the present population shrinkage of the white race will not be fully felt for one or two generations. At the time of heavy unemployment between the two World Wars the opinion was widely held that the decline in the birth rate provided an escape from unemployment; the International Federation of Trade Unions, at its Congress in 1936, recommended birth control for workers' families as one of the most reliable methods for relieving the labor market. Nevertheless, professional political economists assert the opposite, saying that declining birth rates would aggravate economic difficulties and unemployment.[15] The reasons for this, which are only in part and temporarily invalidated by the present-day understanding of methods of antidepression policy, can be stated briefly.

1. The fall in the numbers of children and young people will result in a lessening of the *demand* for the very goods that depend on mass production (e.g., all kinds of food, houses, clothing, shoes, sweets, motion

[13] Cf. *Bericht des Internationalen Kongresses für Bevölkerungswissenschaft,* 1935, Professor Harmsen, editor (Munich), 1936, pp. 875 ff.

[14] Cf. R. R. Kuczynski, "Childless Marriages," in *Sociological Review,* October 1938.

[15] Cf. H. D. Henderson in *The Population Problem: A Symposium,* T. H. Marshall, editor, 1938, pp. 84–106; Lord Keynes, "Some Economic Consequences of a Declining Population," in *The Eugenics Review,* April 1937; R. R. Kuczynski, *Population Movements,* 1936, pp. 61–79; D. V. Glass, *Population Policies and Movements in Europe,* 1940, pp. 363 ff.

picture tickets, radio and television sets), and in consequence, a process of contraction will set in over considerable sections of industry. The result would be a considerable destruction of capital accompanied by "structural" unemployment, which would result from a change in demand.

2. In the thoughts of these political economists this is bound up with the fear that the change in the *age structure* of the population will absorb a great deal of the possible economic advantages of birth control. The reason for this is that a greatly increasing number of older people will have to be supported by the work of a decreasing number of younger people, irrespective of whether they live on the earnings of relatives or on old-age pensions.

3. The aging of the population would have another economic result, perhaps no less dangerous. In a senile population the spirit of courageous economic enterprise gives way, as a natural *psychological* tendency, to the desire for economic security. On the part of capital this means the wish to safeguard profits, and hence monopolization and the formation of combines; on the part of labor it means the desire to insure an income for the vicissitudes of life, leading to inordinate commitments with a throttling effect on initiative.

4. Hand in hand with this goes the aging of the *politicians* responsible for the direction of the affairs of the state. Today, in the democratic states, this is already an often deplored weakness; in the future it will curb their ability to solve the problems of internal and external policy which will be raised by the aging of the population.

5. The tasks involved in adapting economy to the new conditions resulting from the changing population structure would be so difficult that it would not be possible to deal with them without far-reaching *state intervention.* A continually growing productive capacity will have to be harmonized with a continually declining demand. Thus, the cry for state-planned economy will become steadily louder, while the state, owing to the fall in the birth rate, will see itself faced with increasing claims for old-age pensions and an increasing national debt; the economy, on the other hand, will see itself faced with an increasing need of capital (for automation).

6. The effects of extended economic regulation on the *life of the individual* must not be overlooked. A peculiar brand of socialism will develop under a continued decline of population, as Professor *Myrdal* thinks, and will take on an administrative, bureaucratic, senile character: the bureaucratic administration of the liquidation of a people.[16]

The question is, however, whether the *liquidation of a people* can be carried out in such a well-regulated manner, for the falling birth rate must affect external as well as internal policy. Most advocates of neo-Malthusianism almost entirely ignore this side of the population problem, although

[16] Cf. G. Myrdal, *op. cit.*, pp. 22 ff., 165.

the effects on world politics may be of dire proportions within a generation or two and may determine the fate of our children and grandchildren.

Among the consequences of a continuous decline in population still another group must be considered: the accompanying decline in *moral and cultural creative powers.* Concerning the deeper cause we have already spoken in dealing with the family as an educational community: the loss of the educative influence of the child. *Wordsworth* summed up one of the laws of the life of peoples in his well-known words: "The child is father of the man."

152. Nationalism in State Dynamics

When *Arnold Toynbee* wrote in the year 1915 that the ideal of nationality was a threat to our civilization,[1] he touched upon one of the mightiest forces in modern state dynamics. Since the principle of nationality was made the basis of European peace in 1919, history has provided tragic evidence of the destructive effects of these forces. The *development of nationalism* in the second half of the nineteenth century is distinguished by the individualist-collectivistic perversion of the idea of nation and nationalism. 1) Following the decline of the Christian pattern of values as a formative power in the life of nations, secularized spirituality sought new absolute values; among these was the collective value of the nation. In particular the middle classes found in it a new purpose in life, a substitute for the values and ideals denied to them by the economic preoccupations of day-to-day existence, something promising future greatness. 2) The idea of the state called for a fresh vision. Utilitarian liberalism had emptied it of its fundamental meaning, making the state the servant of the individual as well as of his economic interests, and thus its machinery an object of party strife. Nationalism partly filled the resulting vacuum and gave the state, in national values, a new meaning capable of rallying all classes. 3) Nationalism was further nourished by capitalism, which after a period of free trade suggested to each nation as an aim the industrial development of its own country, the protection of its national capital, the internal market, the development of its supply of raw materials through the acquisition of colonies, and the attempt to achieve national self-sufficiency (*autarky*), aims which taken together constitute the advanced form of economic nationalism.

These spiritual, political, and economic energies found their outlet in making the collective value of the nation absolute. Thus, the nationalistic movements became the most powerful motive powers in history. Hardly any other social and historical phenomenon reveals so much the inner relationship and connection between individualism and collectivism as does individualist nationalism with its collectivistic self-deification of

[1] Cf. A. Toynbee, "The New Europe," in *The Nation,* 1915, Vol. XVII, p. 248.

the nation. As a collectivistic version of individualist mentality, nationalism makes the nation the symbol of man's sovereignty over himself and of the realization of this sovereignty through power; thus, *R. Niebuhr* pertinently characterizes nationalism as the expression of the pride of modern man.[2]

If the question is asked whether present-day nationalism is essentially more liberal or conservative, more democratic or totalitarian, the answer, from what has been said, can only be that it is all these together, and that it depends upon historical forces and circumstances what characteristic form it takes in any one country. The history of the twentieth century shows that any political system, totalitarian or democratic, can embark on a *nationalistic policy*. Such a policy reveals itself, first, in the claim to the absolute predominance in the state of one nationality over others. It is a well-known fact that the states of Central Europe, whose separate existence after 1918 was founded on the principle of the right to national self-determination, denied the same right of self-determination to their own national minorities. Secondly, the policy is also revealed in efforts to incorporate in the state ethnically related elements living in neighboring states. The consequence of these attempts is a policy of expansion on ethnological grounds, such as Pan-Germanic and Pan-Slav movements. A third evidence of this policy appears in endeavors by great nations to secure political hegemony on racial, historical, or ideological grounds. The forms of this policy vary. The policy of annexation or influence, sufficiently exemplified in the recent past, is one form; another has been the opposition on the part of colonial empires to the efforts of the colonial peoples toward self-government and independence.

Is nationalism, then, *altogether suspect?* In our discussion of the phenomenon of the modern nation we have found that, among the elements binding it together are strong, natural, socially formative forces, such as common ancestry, homeland, customs, usages, tradition, culture, and destiny, and that all these elements are charged with an ethical character. The idea of the nation itself is an ethical idea. Just as every man with his special endowments is a distinct idea of God, so also the individual nations with their powers and their historical tasks in regard to the great common purposes of humanity reveal special ideas of the Creator. Nationalism is the endeavor to realize and to assert the values in which a nation finds "its soul" (*Toynbee*) as a community. Nationalism is, then, not only justified, provided that these values do not claim greater importance than is their due in the order of values, but it can be a virtue, a kind of patriotism.

Serious *obligations for the individual, as for the nation,* may arise from these values. For the individual, duties arise especially in times of national crisis caused by external threats or internal decline. Here we may

[2] Cf. R. Niebuhr, *The Nature and Destiny of Man,* 1941, Vol. II, pp. 201 f.; Niebuhr, the American Protestant theologian, traces the roots of modern nationalism back to Lutheran ethics, which dissevered the social sphere from the moral, placed it entirely under the domination of sin, and made state authority the executor of God's will. Lutheranism thus made its contribution toward justifying the omnipotence of the national state on religious and moral grounds.

mention the duty to place national unity above party differences and sectional interests, to cooperate in sustaining and reinforcing national ideals and values, the duty of remaining single in the case of persons with hereditary ailments, and for married couples who are physically and financially capable the duty of increased willingness to have children, particularly in periods of a dangerously declining birth rate. The nation as a whole likewise has the duty to preserve and to nourish the values and forces that weld it into a live community. Thus, homeland, tradition, and national history will always form an essential part of the pattern of values for the education of the young and of the mature. Of no less importance is the duty to coordinate the nation with the others in the fellowship of nations, in spirit as well as in organizational form. To bring up the young to respect this fellowship is not the least important of the nation's tasks, for only if this is done can the dynamic force of the national idea be guided into fruitful channels. But from all these considerations we also see that an internationalism which denies the intrinsic justification of the national idea, or an ethical system which indiscriminately rejects all nationalism, is in conflict with the facts that form the basis of the social and moral values invested in the nation.

Marxian *dialectical materialism* judges national movements in each individual country by the hopes they afford for the international proletarian cause. Their evaluation, consequently, is a matter of interpreting historical "necessities." If they conflict with the world movement of the proletariat, they are "reactionary." Thus, *Marx* sympathized with the national movement in Poland and its struggles to gain independence from Czarist Russia. In 1914, on the other hand, as is well known, the Marxist parties in all countries except Serbia and Russia declared in favor of war, and thus thought and acted "nationalistically." Until the year 1923, Soviet Russia was guided by *Marx's* idea that the world revolution would occur simultaneously in the majority of industrial countries, and saw in the Comintern (the Communist International), which extended throughout the world, the beginning of the world revolution. After *Lenin's* death, the principle of "socialism in the individual state" was adopted, and in 1943 the Comintern was nominally dissolved.

153. Capitalism in State Dynamics

In the course of history the genesis of the modern state goes hand in hand with the development of modern capitalism. They furthered each other's development. On the part of the princes, they had learned to think capitalistically under the pressure of state financial exigencies, with the result that they furthered capitalistic development in the interest of the state. Indeed, one must ask: How was it possible for modern capitalism to arise in face of the opposition of public opinion, with its firm rejection of interest as usury, and in face of the usury laws of Church and state?

The answer is, as Professor *J. Strieder* has shown, that political factors were at work. Military campaigns, state administration, the royal household, and the desire of princes for luxury made increasing demands on the financial resources of state and of city from the sixteenth century onwards. To obtain loans from the owners of wealth in industry and commerce, they found themselves compelled to agree to the cartel licences demanded by these capitalistic entrepreneurs and thus to the foundation of monopolies. In Germany, under the influence of the Kaiser, the prohibitions on monopolies in the crucial sphere of the ore trade were removed (by laws, 1525). *Strieder* numbers these laws, with good reason, among the most important documents in the history of modern capitalism. Just as in Germany, so also in other countries, political developments finally wrested the victory from the medieval usury legislation and made the decisive contribution to the genesis of modern capitalism.[1]

But the later stage also in the development of capitalism is not thinkable without the modern state. As *Max Weber* has shown, the process of production and capital investment in modern economy depends on the "rational" state, that is, on one with a legal and administrative apparatus whose functioning can be reliably calculated in advance. Only thus can the risks of extensive capital investment in long-term producers' goods, with a view to recovering the capital with profit, be estimated.[2] Thus, modern capitalism is possible only in the modern state.

Yet, it is no less true to say that the modern state is impossible without modern capitalism. The expenditure of the modern state alone makes the state dependent on an economic system fully exploiting all factors of production: expenditure for national defense, education, health, economic and social welfare, especially for public services such as communications (post, telephone, telegraph) and transportation (roads, railways); in addition, for the administrative departments of the modern state with its bureaucracy (agriculture, commerce, and labor ministries). In mentioning social welfare we have touched upon one of the strongest forces of development in the dynamics of industrial society. It is from the class antagonisms of this society that a good part of those forces of development emanated. The working class, through its trade unions and parties, was able to gain increasing influence on the functioning of the state, resulting in the transition from the laissez-faire state of the nineteenth century to the present-day welfare state. Class antagonism in the capitalistic society has proved to be one of the most potent driving forces in the *internal* dynamics of the modern state, so much so that it is impossible to consider present-day capitalism and that of a hundred years ago as the same thing. In another direction, capitalism has given a fresh character

[1] Cf. Jakob Strieder, *Zur Genesis des modernen Kapitalismus,* 1904; *Studien zur Geschichte kapitalistischer Organisationsformen,* 2nd ed., 1925; *Jakob Fugger der Reiche,* 1926.

[2] Cf. Max Weber, *Wirtschaft und Gesellschaft,* 1922, p. 94; *Wirtschaftsgeschichte,* 1923, trans. by F. H. Knight, *General Economic History,* 1927.

to democracy. For generations, the capitalistic class was able to manage the democratic machinery of the state in its interest. The monopolistic control of the state by this class in most democracies has been terminated by the rise of the working class organizations. The capitalistic class became one of the political pressure groups, the organized working class another. The dynamics of capitalism characterizes the present-day state, along with the antagonisms of the economic interest groups, which all seek to gain advantage by influencing the working of the democratic machinery. The ideal of the common good of the state thus is largely degraded to a mere balancing of group interests and is given over to internal political strife; indeed, it becomes the reflection of the constellation of interest blocs (e.g., industry, finance, agriculture, trade unions, parties) in the development of the capitalistic system.

The fact that capitalism constitutes one of the most powerful forces in the *external* dynamics of the state is shown by the power which the modern state derives from capitalism, be it Western welfare state capitalism or Eastern communist state capitalism, in the war potential which it can achieve with the aid of the industrial exploitation and organization of its economic resources, in the influence of "armament capitalism" [3] on international disputes, and, above all, in the development characterized by the "hot" and "cold" war in the struggle for world markets and sources of raw materials to which the state is driven by the capitalistic impetus toward expansion (concerning imperialism cf. the following chap.).

If one will take into account all relevant facts, however, in judging capitalism, one must also consider its favorable effects in the direction of peace. Take an example from recent history: It was primarily capitalistic calculation, that, after the First World War, decided the revision of the reparations demands upon Germany. The determining interest was that of the economic systems of the creditor nations, on account of the complete involvement of all, including Germany, in world economy. The motive for this revision was clearly enunciated in the governing principle of the *Dawes Plan:* "Business, not politics." The operation of the rational factor in capitalism is a fact, even though the estimation of its effects may give rise to such conflicting opinions as those of Lord *Keynes* and *Étienne Mantoux.*[4] That the *Marshall Plan* (E.R.F.), apart from political motives, was also largely inspired by economic motives, is well known.

The laws of development of the capitalistic state, according to *dialectical materialism* after *Marx,* are inconsistent with two features which actually characterize this development. According to *Marx,* the state is merely the instrument

[3] That the interest of economic groups in armament production and in armed conflicts between states is not confined to the capitalistic system, is shown by the distinction drawn by Aristophanes between industries which profit from war and others; cf. Max Weber, *Wirtschaft und Gesellschaft,* p. 624.

[4] Cf. Lord Keynes, The Economic Consequences of the Peace, 1920; Étienne Mantoux, *The Carthaginian Peace, or the Economic Consequences of Mr. Keynes,* 1946.

in the hand of the exploiting class to hold down the exploited. The development of the capitalistic system, with its continuing process of accumulation of capital on the one side and the process of pauperization on the other, according to this theory, must result in violent revolution and the dictatorship of the proletariat.[5] In fact, however, the working class did not believe in this deterministic dialectic scheme of pauperization and dictatorship, but through its trade unions and political parties brought about social reforms in its interest. The second fact is the degree of balance of interests reached by the economic pressure groups in the democracies. Although these facts are, as we have pointed out, far from indicating that capitalism is developing toward a substantially just economic system, they certainly show that this development does not follow the Marxist laws, as long as only economic factors are in operation and not force inspired by noneconomic motives.

154. Imperialism

Imperialism is the tendency of great states, rooted in power politics, to seek territorial expansion and the increase of their influence in world politics. Only such a general conception covers all the manifestations of imperialism which we find in history. The concept "great state" is relative; the determining factor is the power potential of a state in relation to the international environment. The radius of imperialistic efforts may extend to individual countries or even to the whole world. The latter form of development is already indicated in the Roman Empire, the beginning of imperialism in the Western world. If the object was then the whole known world, a "world empire" covering the entire globe has become the aim of imperialism in its most recent development, although for political realism continents subjugated by power politics will remain the steppingstones in the struggle for world domination.

Our general definition of imperialism must, of course, meet with opposition from a doctrinaire theory such as that of dialectical materialism. In this theory, imperialism is, as *Lenin* expresses it, the manifestation of "capitalism in transition." "The economic quintessence of imperialism is monopoly capitalism"; monopoly itself is "the transition from the capitalistic system to a higher socioeconomic order." [1] According to his theory, five features are essential to imperialism: the formation of monopolies as a result of the concentration of capital; the monopolistic sway of finance capital arising from the merging of bank capital and industrial capital; the export of capital as distinct from the export of commodities; the parceling out of the world among the international capitalistic cartel monopolies; the territorial parceling out of the world among the biggest capitalistic powers.[2]

Marx himself did not reach the point of discussing imperialism as a stage in

[5] Cf. Marx and Engels, *The Communist Manifesto*, 1848; for the interpretation of the Marxian theory, cf. Lenin, *State and Revolution*, 1917.

[1] Cf. Lenin, *Imperialism: The Highest Stage of Capitalism*, 1916. Laurence & Wishart, 1942, p. 107.

[2] Cf. *ibid.*, p. 77.

the dialectical development of capitalism. The first attempt to extend *Marx's* theory in this direction was undertaken by *R. Luxemburg* and *R. Hilferding. Hilferding* sets out from the necessity of concentration and monopoly formation in industry for the sake of stabilizing the profit rate, which results in the dependence of industry on the banks. Capital at the disposal of the banks and employed by industry he terms finance capital. In the setting up of cartels and trusts, finance capital, he holds, reaches its highest stage of power. The cartel means extra profits, and therefore the accumulation of capital; but it implies also the narrowing of possibilities of investment owing to the monopolistic restriction of production. This conflict leads to the export of capital, and hence to the struggle for countries with possibilities of capital investment, and to an imperialist policy.[3] *Rosa Luxemburg* starts from the Marxian under-consumption theory and the discrepancy between production capacity and consumption capacity in capitalistic society, which arises from the accumulation of capital and drives capital to a continuous search for new markets and new labor to be exploited. The methods pursued, she says, are colonial policy, the international loan system, the policy of spheres of interest, and wars—in short, the imperialistic military system.[4] Without any doctrinaire fusion with the Marxist theory of capitalism, the theory of underconsumption (i.e., maldistribution), as a leading cause of "parasitic" imperialism in the train of modern capitalism, was already developed at the turn of the century by *J. A. Hobson*,[5] who is much quoted by *Lenin.*

The facts of history do not bear out the theory of imperialism originating with *Marx.* With Professor *W. Sombart* one may first of all point out that the capitalism of Czarist Russia and that of Japan, by means of which Japan in 1905 entered the circle of the Great Powers, were a far cry from the systems of highly capitalistic countries, and that the capitalism of England in its early stages was by no means of the character of finance capitalism. Furthermore, there is a paramount force such as population pressure giving rise to expansionist needs; its causes do not lie in capitalism, and are only secondarily economic.

Another non-economic main cause of imperialism is the purely political need for security on the part of great states, by virtue of which, through the partitioning of large areas into "spheres of influence," they pursue chiefly political and strategic aims. The role played by geographical factors also may be gathered from the emergence of geopolitics as a new branch of political science. Geopolitics deals with the geographical bases of world politics and with the economic and political conditions resulting therefrom. It was first expounded by Sir *Halford Mackinder*[6] and then developed by *Karl Haushofer.* The "oil imperialism," which is chiefly concentrated in the Near East, cannot be reckoned as an example of imperialism governed by the laws of development of capitalism, but simply by the need for sources of raw materials. It is due to the pressure to make sure of

[3] Cf. Rudolf Hilferding, *Das Finanzkapital,* 1910.
[4] Cf. Rosa Luxemburg, *Die Akkumulation des Kapitals,* 1913.
[5] Cf. J. A. Hobson, *Imperialism,* 1902; 3rd ed., 1938.
[6] Cf. H. J. Mackinder, *Democratic Ideals and Reality,* 1919.

sources of oil and to acquire new ones for mechanized industries and for mechanized warfare. Another variety which claims attention is ideological imperialism, with its consciousness of a political and cultural mission, such as was to be found in the imperialism of later Victorian England and of which the name *Rudyard Kipling* (*Recessional*) is a symbol; or such as may be seen in the forceful ideas of dialectical materialism, expressing the hopes of international communism and with the names of *Marx* and *Lenin* on its banners.

Besides, we must not forget the national, non-economic aims of an imperialism, in which the aspirations of nations toward historical greatness and influence in world politics converged at the end of the nineteenth century. Finally, there is the power of the great personality in the dynamics of expansionism. Who would maintain that the driving forces behind the enterprises of an *Alexander*, a *Peter the Great*, or a *Napoleon* were economic?

From the facts enumerated we can draw some *important conclusions:* 1) Imperialism is not a phenomenon connected exclusively with the present stage of development of modern capitalism. Imperialism gained from capitalism only fresh stimuli and special features. Even these cannot be attributed solely to monopoly capitalism, but to commence with the struggle for export markets and for sources of raw materials. Capitalistic imperialism is merely one form of imperialism, although admittedly one of immense influence on the political dynamics of the modern world. 2) The view, spread by Marxist theory, of an absolute primacy of economics in international life is groundless. Lord *Keynes* is probably right when he says that the power of vested interests is vastly exaggerated compared with the gradual encroachment of ideas, and that, sooner or later, ideas, not vested interests, are the danger for good or evil.[7] 3) Political imperialism can operate in the socialistic state, with its great concentration of power, at least to the same degree as in any other economic system. The imperialism of the communistic big state in recent history clearly proves this. But economic interests of a socialistic state can also lead to imperialistic exploitation of weaker states; this is due, observes *Max Weber*, to a situation which "would hardly undergo any fundamental change if we imagined for a moment, as an intellectual experiment, that the individual political communities were somehow state-socialist, in other words, bodies satisfying a maximum of economic needs through socialistic planned economy. Every political body with such a social economy would seek to obtain in the 'international' market those indispensable commodities which are not produced in its own territory (e.g., in Germany, cotton) as cheaply as possible from those states which possess a natural monopoly of it and which would endeavor to exploit this. There seems to be no likelihood that, where force would most easily lead to

[7] Cf. J. M. Keynes, *The General Theory of Employment, Interest, and Money,* 1936, pp. 383 ff.

favorable conditions of exchange, it would not be used. Thus, there would arise, if not a formal, yet an actual duty on the part of the weaker to render tribute; furthermore, it is not possible to see why the strongest state-socialistic communities should disdain to exact from weaker states, where they could, quite specific tribute for their partners, exactly as was the universal custom in early history." [8]

155. Militarism

Militarism may be defined as the constant actual readiness for war on the part of a state, with military authority exercising a determining influence simultaneously on the management of the state machinery. Militarism is not the outcome of a direct external threat and the consequent preparation for an imminent defensive war. It springs rather from the principle that peace cannot be preserved except through readiness for war: *Si vis pacem para bellum.* The necessary presupposition for militarism is a political philosophy which regards conflict in international life as the normal condition, and peace as an exceptional phenomenon. The outcome of militarism is a powerful impulse to competition in armaments. For, if only one or two great states are given up to militarism, other states within their sphere of operation will be compelled, for security's sake, to compete proportionately in the armaments race. Thus, a dynamic force of tremendous power will come into play in the internal and external life of the states. The history of Europe since the Seven Years' War and the catastrophes of two World Wars offer convincing evidence of this dynamic force. We cannot go into the question of how far this is a modern phenomenon and how far, for example, Sparta and Rome were military states, or how far geopolitics comes into play; in reference to these states it is often affirmed that the tendency to militarism may be found chiefly in continental powers.

In modern militarism we can discover the following *characteristic traits:* a standing army; universal conscription; a socially privileged officer class; traditional military science; influence of the generals on the government; the permeation of the whole educational sphere with a military spirit; glorification of war; systematic strategical planning of traffic routes and the location of industrial plants; relatively high budgetary expenditure for military purposes; the fostering of arms industries; the striving for a self-supporting economy. Most of these features exercise influence in varying degrees on the dynamics of internal and external political life.

One side of the working of these factors must be briefly touched upon. Militarism is not preparation for a definite war, but an element in the institutional side of a society. The institutional, we discovered, is marked

[8] Max Weber, "Wirtschaft und Gesellschaft," in *Grundriß der Sozialökonomie,* 1922, p. 625.

by a tendency to make its end an end in itself: militarism makes the soldier, readiness for war, and education for war ends in themselves. The high rank due to the soldierly virtues in a true perspective of ends is perverted when these ends are made absolute. And since the institutional is further characterized by a tendency toward hypertrophy, under militarism the military system assumes an ever-increasing importance in the life of the state, if only for the reason that it secures power for the military caste in and through the state, which the military caste in turn seeks to enlarge. Finally, since in the institutional there is a tendency toward independent activity apart from the purely ancillary function which is proper to it, the military machine, which is inspired by militarism, gravitates toward activity, that is, toward war.

156. Revolutionism

Revolution as an element in political dynamics accompanies mankind throughout its history. It remained for modern political theory, however, to elevate *revolution into a principle.* To the modern individualist, collectivistic political theory, this principle seems such a self-evident conclusion from its other principles that it remains unconscious of the fact that it is governed by a principle of this kind. The word "revolution," in the sense of a principle, therefore has not been found for a very long time in the indexes of present-day textbooks of political theory or even in those great encyclopedias which purport to supply information on everything of interest to the modern man. Yet, all modern history is incomprehensible without reference to the revolutionary principle springing from modern secularistic thought. Only if one is aware of this principle is it possible to grasp the dynamics of national and international political life since the French Revolution, with the development of plebiscitarian democracy and the rise of the totalitarian states after the First World War and the complete reorganization of international power relations after the Second World War. This was accompanied by the emergence of a vast number of new states and forms of government whose sole justification was the principle of revolution.

This principle is founded on the theory of *absolute popular sovereignty,* a theory consisting of the three following principles. 1) Political authority is based solely on the will of the people. 2) It is wholly dependent on the will of the people. 3) Accordingly, it can be reconstituted at any time by the people. Thus, in principle, the actual will of the people stands above the existing, legitimate order of the state, only recognizing the legality created by itself, and the right of revolution above that of legitimacy. As *Guglielmo Ferrero,* that great representative of the finest European thought, who died in exile in Paris during the Second World War, pointed out: revolutionary popular sovereignty breaks with the principle of legitimacy, which alone can justify the exercise of political power, and it is the negation of those fundamental principles founded in the natural order of society which "are the unseen spirits of the commonwealth and the foundations of universal order." *

The effect of the principle of revolutionary popular sovereignty on the dynamics of the state is magnified by the fact that the popular will needs a mechanism to be able to form and to express itself. The prevailing mechanism for this purpose is that of representative democracy. Those groups in the political community which control this mechanism and the propaganda accompanying it, whether by employing superior financial resources or by appealing to stronger emotions, or by monopolizing propaganda, or by manipulating election results, are always able to present their own will partly or wholly as the actual will of the people. Itself a principle of perpetual change, the revolutionary principle thus becomes an instrument in the hands of changing political groups struggling for power in the state. It releases the tumult of passions into political life, as the companions of *Odysseus,* in their folly, released the storm winds from *Aeolus'* bag.

157. Ideological Forces in Political Dynamics

Under the heading of ideological forces we have classed views about nature and the end of man and society as far as these exert any influence on the form and development of society (cf. Chap. 58). Religious faith, sociologically seen as such a force, is the source of some of the most powerful dynamic influences in the life and development of states. To visualize the extent of the religious forces we need only think of the great religions of mankind, the theocracy of Israel, Buddhism, Mohammedanism, and especially Christianity, not to mention such a close amalgam of religion and state as was represented by Japanese Shintoism. At first sight one may be tempted to ascribe to religions mainly a stabilizing and restraining influence. But it is enough to remember the punitive expeditions undertaken by the Israelites at the command of their divine Lord, proselytizing wars such as those of Charlemagne, the Holy War of the Mohammedans at the beginning of the modern era, wars of religion like the Thirty Years' War, the Crusades, the influence of conflicts between state and Church in the development of the Western state, to see that the dynamic factors springing from religion in the life of the state are no less considerable than the stabilizing factors. It is not our purpose here

* Guglielmo Ferrero, *Pouvoir: Les Génies invisibles de la Cité,* 1942. Concerning the historical roots of the principle of revolution, cf. Wilhelm Hohoff, *Die Revolution,* 1877, which is still very instructive.

to do more than note the fact of this influence of religion. Its detailed analysis as a universal phenomenon is a matter for the sociology of religion and falls outside the province of ethics.*

Along with the secularization of thought, since the beginning of modern times *antireligious ideological forces* have emerged in the dynamics of the state alongside and in opposition to the religious forces, without falling behind them in effective power. Again a brief citation of facts must suffice, since throughout this study we have dealt often in general and in particular with the individualist-liberalistic and collectivistic-socialistic ideologies as factors of social and political life. Claiming as they do to mold social life, these secularistic forces are bound to come into conflict with religious forces, which make the same claim. Such conflicts mark the discussions on the relative competences of Church and state in the liberalist state of the nineteenth century, especially in questions of education and marriage. A further point for consideration is the ideological foundations of party organizations in the free democracy. The dynamic effects on political life are incomparably greater when an ideological force succeeds in securing a monopolistic totalitarian influence on a society. Its aim then is to transform the whole social order in virtue of its principles concerning the nature and status of human personality in society and the entire significance of civilization. The facts of recent history which illustrate the power of the political dynamics originating in such ideologies are well known.

In the liberal democracies a new dynamic is becoming evident in the form of a debate between differing humanisms, or fundamental notions of man and society. There has arisen the conception of the *ideologically pluralistic society* as distinct from the ideological monopoly of the totalitarian state. There are two main ideological beliefs in opposition, the Christian and the "humanist." The latter presents itself in the mantle of science and stands for a naturalistic view of man with nuances in which are mingled elements of the naturalistic humanist theories which were discussed in Chapter 1. These philosophies or ideologies use the word "humanist" to emphasize their opposition to the Christian conception of man, and they seek to gain ground from Christianity by influencing the forms of society and culture. Their humanism claims to rest on scientific foundations and to be free of otherworldliness, by contrast with Christian humanism with its ground in revelation and its idea of transcendence. In fact, the humanist idea of the dignity of man is derived from two ideas of Christianity: first, the idea of man's likeness to God, found in Genesis and made part of Christian teaching; secondly, worship of God, offered to all men through Christ, the mediator.

* Concerning the sociology of religion, cf. especially the studies of Max Weber, *Wirtschaft und Gesellschaft,* 1922, pp. 227–356; *Gesammelte Aufsätze zur Religionssoziologie,* 1921; A. Mueller-Armack, *Religion und Wirtschaft,* 1959.

158. Moral Forces in Political Dynamics

Of all the forces contributing to the dynamics of the state, the moral forces reveal themselves as the strongest. This assertion may surprise many. Were it not true, mankind could not continue to exist. Except for the primacy of these forces mankind would long ago have fallen prey to the irrational forces operating in political dynamics and could never have reached the heights of civilization which it has attained in spite of everything. To the moral impulses of man can be traced the establishment of legal order *within the state,* and thus, that minimum of social morality which is indispensable for men's coexistence and cultural life. With regard to moral impulses, the state is the means of restraining in society the rank growth of the "less human elements" in man's nature, to the advantage of his true nature. The moral impulses, in fact, avert the war of all against all; thus far we can find a core of truth in *Hobbes'* theory of the state.

This is far from exhausting the dynamics of the moral tendencies of human nature in the state. Not only is the state negatively an institution for averting mankind's self-destruction in the war of all against all, but, positively, it is even more an *institution for achieving fully human existence,* the "good life" (*Aristotle*), or, as we should say today, the general good, the good of all. Through the aid of the state the human mind succeeds in fundamentally coordinating the impulses, ends, and energies of the individuals to the good of all. In our inquiry into the foundations of the state from the point of view of social psychology, we found a great number of such impulses, ends, and forces; they are effective, for instance, in the system of power and of ownership, in technical, economic, national, and cultural endeavors. In the state, man's mind creates the institution which is to bring about the coordination of these impulses and forces in the interest of the common good. At the same time, the will of the groups and classes of society for an increasing participation in an ever more amply fulfilled common good finds its instrument in the state: the state becomes the field of operation for the dynamics of social justice, juridical consciousness, and legal will. Certainly, the human mind never wins more than partial success in this, but the dynamic aiming at such progress is the natural law of mankind operative in man's discernment of, and striving for, the realization of the truly human values (cf. Chap. 47).

With this we can make a clear distinction between truth and error in *Hegel's* idea of the state: the state is not in itself the reality of the spirit, and is not the "reality of the moral idea." * It is, however, the instrument of the spirit for conquering the social dynamic of the irrational forces in human nature, and hence is the means of realizing the "moral idea," the moral principles indispensable for the life of society. For these reasons, a high function belongs to the state in the self-education of the community

* Hegel, *Philosophie des Rechts,* par. 257.

in accordance with the individual and cultural ends designated in human nature, an educational function which the human spirit has become growingly aware of since *Plato* and *Aristotle,* although the limits, too, of this function have become more precisely known.

This realization of the moral idea by the state is not confined to the individual political community but takes place also progressively in the historical development of *mankind as a whole,* and hence internationally. Obviously the motive power of the rational and irrational elements in human nature is greatly magnified in states: these become colossal forces, positively and negatively, in the conflict between good and evil, between justice and injustice, in the international sphere. Obviously also, however, the ideals and values shown to man in his existential ends assert themselves in this dynamic, pre-eminently through the joint efforts of the morally developed societies. These efforts form a fluctuating process. They are the *meaning of history.* This is the conclusion from what has been said concerning the dynamic impulsion of natural law (cf. Chaps. 3, 46–48). The explanation of these efforts is one of the crucial *tests of every political philosophy:* it reveals the doctrine of man and the philosophy of history implied in a political philosophy.

In fact, history testifies to a gradual rise in the moral and legal demands which mankind makes of the order of municipal and international life. The state is called upon in the realization of these demands. Even if the course of development from the society whose keyote is slavery, to that which we describe today as the free society is by no means an unbroken one and is not even secure against renewed setbacks, the decisive values and ideals are today not only much more clearly visible than ever before, but also the will to advance on the hard road toward them was never so strong as today, and the amount of political power committed to the efforts to attain them was never so great.

To be sure, the state often plays a negative part by dragging nations down from the height they have reached in the realization of freedom and progress as demanded by the existential human ends. But the evolution of the jural consciousness of mankind in the direction of these values and ideals of international life cannot reasonably be denied. Indeed, it is not through the state alone that the dynamics of natural law and the progress of the moral consciousness in the national and international community operate. They are in operation no less in the work of the great ethical and political thinkers as well as in social and political movements, which themselves, however, assign a principal role to the state in the realization of their ideas and programs. In addition, the history of international law is basically the history of the efforts, inspired by belief in the dignity of human personality and hence in moral values and ideals, to subject the relations between states to an order corresponding to the moral nature of man. And it was chiefly through states that the dynamics of the natural moral law, which tend toward such ideals, became effective.

159. The Rise and Decline of Nations

The discussion of the dynamics of the state cannot be concluded without a glance at the rise and decline of nations. Analyzing the moving forces of history we must keep in view that they are by no means only political, but also cultural and economic. It has been held that the developing life of peoples may be described in terms similar to that of individual human life—childhood, growth, maturity, and decline. "This growth and decay follows higher, inscrutable laws," says *Jakob Burckhardt.*[1] *Oswald Spengler* thought he had discovered these laws. His basic idea is that cultures are organisms whose development obeys universal laws; these laws can be ascertained by means of a "scientific morphology of history." Historical development, therefore, can be predicted. "In this book," *Spengler* begins, "is attempted for the first time the venture of predetermining history." He foresees in a few centuries the final downfall of Western culture, which today spans the globe. Fresh "young" peoples with new cultures and political forces may in the meantime grow to maturity and determine future development.[2] *A. J. Toynbee* rejects the idea of societies as organisms and contends that the breakdowns of civilizations are not brought about by forces outside human control, nor are they repetitions of laws of nature.[3] The recent history of the frictions between East and West, however, gives him occasion for a pessimistic view of the future of Europe,[4] which is not far removed from the notion of *Spengler.*

Does there exist such a *historical determinism* in the development of nations, as *Spengler* maintains? Surveying the extraordinarily numerous discussions about *Spengler's* work, which have been conducted by experts in the many branches of knowledge touched upon by *Spengler,* one is led to assume that not only is the morphological view of history a fruitful method, but also the fact that a certain parallelism in the development of cultures and nations is established.[5] On the other side, there is general agreement among his critics that his historical determinism is a conclusion which the evidence does not substantiate.[6] The main argument against his approach to historical morphology is that he regards the development of

[1] Jakob Burckhardt, *Reflections on History,* trans. by M. D. H., 1943, p. 56.

[2] Cf. Oswald Spengler, *The Decline of the West,* trans. by C. F. Atkinson, 1926.

[3] Cf. A. J. Toynbee, *A Study of History,* IV, pp. 39, 119. Cf. Somerwell's abridgment, 1946, pp. 255, 275.

[4] Cf. A. J. Toynbee, *The World and the West,* 1952; facts and possibilities are well weighed in a realistic criticism of Toynbee's work by the Dutch historian, Pieter Geyl, *Debates with Historians,* 1955.

[5] Cf. Manfred Schroeter, *Der Streit um Spengler,* 1922; G. Briefs, *Der Untergang des Abendlandes,* 2nd ed., 1921.

[6] We may again refer to the investigation carried out by I. Schwidetzky with outstanding scientific method, *Das Problem des Völkertodes,* 1954, with her evidence that there are no laws discernible which could justify historical determinism.

other cultures from the point of view of a son of the Western culture and interprets them in terms of its cultural phases. Indeed, *Spengler* himself admits that his own philosophy can only express the Western soul as distinct from the classical, the Indian, etc.[7]

Not less cogent is the argument that, if certain parallels do exist in the historical development of cultures, it is impossible to prove that this parallelism is the result of the same causes; for, the number of cultural units which can be compared is too small, the material is vast and indeterminate, and the historical periods are of enormous length. Again, it is urged that we cannot dispute the possibility that entirely new causes may arise, fitting into no scheme of development and giving a completely new direction to the progress of events. Reference is made to the unique advances of science and technology in the nineteenth and twentieth centuries, to which there is no parallel in history. It may finally be asked, with justification from the point of view of the "sociology of knowledge," to what extent *Spengler's* pessimism is an expression of the period following the First World War, which was marked by the beginning of scepticism in the nineteenth-century belief in progress. Even had his work, however, no other significance than this, it would remain an outstanding contribution to the criticism of modern civilization and would provide the Western nations, in its analysis of modern culture, politics, science, art, and the like, with grounds for a serious examination of conscience.

From the point of view of a *Christian philosophy of history*, the objection has been raised that *Spengler* underestimates the one factor in history which can of its nature supply a constant impulse to the regeneration of peoples, namely, Christianity. At the same time, many of his critics, who profess a Christian philosophy of history, overlook the fact that Christian eschatology does not suggest a final victory of the faith and forces of Christianity in the natural realm of culture. From various remarks of Christ it may be gathered also that his real followers will always be in a minority. Even after the redemption, original sin remains a powerful operative force in history, which can be effectively opposed by the power of the redemption only to the extent to which men surrender themselves to it. It is, however, no less true that Christianity is indeed a never silent call to men and nations to bethink themselves of the inherent laws of their life, and an inexhaustible source of regeneration of their innermost life from the forces of the supernatural.

Supported by such reasoning, the Christian philosophy of history rejects the deterministic "decline" pessimism as well as the deterministic nineteenth-century "progress" optimism. The supernatural forces are, in fact, the decisive contribution of Christianity to the life of peoples and cultures. For, since these forces alone can again and again renew the moral roots of people, it is through them that they are able to retain or

[7] Cf. Spengler, *op. cit.*, p. 46.

to restore their youth.[8] It was the error of the so-called cultural Christianity of the liberalist tendency of all Christian churches in the nineteenth century to believe that Christianity must justify itself in an apologetic, showing that it holds its own among the cultural forces of the world. Yet, although its mission is not directly concerned with the temporal life of nations, indirectly it is of hardly less significance than if it had been destined for that purpose (cf. *Augustine,* Chap. 57). For, its aims are always and not least the clarification, renewal, and increase of the operative power of the natural law, which is the law of life for the nations and for their cultures.[9]

A discussion of political philosophy and political ethics cannot end otherwise than with a glance at the philosophy of history. For, any political philosophy, just as it contains its particular philosophy of human existence, so also it contains, openly or covertly, its philosophy of history. The systematic study of the philosophy of history is a relatively young province of human scientific endeavor. The founder of the modern philosophy of history, *Giovanni Battisti*

[8] We find evidence for our argument in three such outstanding historians of our age as Toynbee, Croce, and Grousset. Toynbee (*op. cit.,* IV, p. 583; in Somerwell's abridgment, p. 359), after his comprehensive analytical study of history, sees for Western civilization no other source of regeneration "at this hour of decision at which we now live" than the spirit and the forces of a reborn *Respublica Christiana.* Benedetto Croce, *Politics and Morals,* pp. 125 ff., points out: "Leopold Ranke used to say that history is always the history of the relations and struggle between Church and state," i.e., that the Church opposes the state when the latter makes itself the end, and man the mere means; the doctrine advocated by the Church is "unanswerable," it signifies fundamentally the defense of the moral conscience; modern history itself shows the superiority of the "ecclesiastical" or ethical, since it has its origin in the *historia ecclesiastica* founded by Christianity. Lord Acton, *History of Freedom,* 1907, mentions the deeper reason: "The Christian notion of conscience imperatively demands a corresponding measure of personal liberty. The feeling of duty and responsibility to God is the only arbiter of a Christian's actions. With this no human authority can be permitted to interfere. We are bound to extend to the utmost, and to guard from every encroachment, the sphere in which we can act in obedience to the sole voice of conscience, regardless of any other consideration. The Church cannot tolerate any species of government in which this right is not recognized." René Grousset, the noted expert on the history of the East, says in one of his last works, in which he undertakes to strike a "balance of history" (*Bilan de l'histoire,* 1946), that the question of the meaning of history can only be answered by the Christian solution and that in the shipwreck of all hopes, healing lies in the mission of Christianity: "Nous savons et nous venons de voir qu'en dehors de la solution chrétienne, en dehors de la solution spiritualiste, il n'y en a désormais plus d'autre, j'entends de solution acceptable pour la raison et pour le coeur. Si le monde n'est que ce qu'il parait être, au point où l'ont mené,—avec une probité dont il faut leur savoir gré,—la science et la philosophie scientifique de ce temps, il est absurde pour la raison, révoltant pour le coeur. Le christianisme représente aujourd'hui contre un si monstrueux néant, cette révolte de la raison et du coeur, cette défense de l'esprit. Est la mission dans le naufrage —s'il n'était là,—de toute espérance, est plus que jamais salvatrice" (*ibid.,* p. 306). Concerning the whole question cf. especially Christopher Dawson, *Religion and the Rise of Western Culture,* 1950; *Dynamics of World History,* 1957, and other works of his cited in the bibliography.

[9] On questions of philosophy and ethics relating to culture inseparably bound up with the philosophy of history, cf. J. Messner, *Kulturethik,* 1954, Chaps. 73–76, 79–80.

Vico (1668–1744), who is so keenly appreciated today, was neglected in the nineteenth century since he did not allow enough room for the belief in unlimited progress which was then in the ascendancy. His chief work, *Principii di una scienza nuova d'intorno alla natura commune delle nazione,* 1725, is mostly cited in shortened form as *Scienza nuova.* The reason why *Vico* wished his philosophy of history to be understood as natural theology is that history moves in accordance with the laws implanted in men by divine Providence. His ideas may be summarized as follows. Just as the physicist ascertains the laws of external nature by the study of phenomena, so also the philosopher should discover the laws of historical evolution by investigating the history of the human mind, as shown in the historical development of law, language, mythology, and religion; after the emergence of humanity from its original condition, historical development proceeds in three periods, the divine, the heroic, and the human, each with its own forms of political, legal and cultural life. The human is characterized by democracy and the "empires" which succeed it; at the end of the third period there occurs the transition to barbarism, and the process begins all over again. In this "law of cycles," *Vico* has anticipated essential ideas of the modern morphology of culture. How far *Spengler* was inspired by *Vico* cannot be established, since he tells us nothing of the influences that assisted him in molding his basic ideas. The influence of *Vico* on the historical school of jurisprudence of *Savigny* is established.

The modern philosophy of history has largely identified itself with the positivist *sociology of history.* Its epistemological foundations are questionable in more than one respect. Because of its narrowed view of freedom and hence of the spiritual world in general, it cannot dispute the great conceptions of the Christian philosophy of history which, beginning with *St. Augustine's City of God,* crystallized in the Middle Ages in the theory of the Sacrum Imperium,[10] and once again came to a mighty synthesis in *Bossuet's Histoire universelle.*

The various naturalistic schools of the philosophy of history are also far from agreeing on a fundamental pattern of laws of history; this is shown by their diverse and contradictory schemes of periods, cycles, and morphologies. In fact, man's freedom determines the basic substance of history, finding in it opportunity for expression of ever new creative impulses. Hence, history is not accessible to the methods of the natural sciences. Besides, the arrival of the God-man in history was, indeed, a direct intervention which, while it did not substantially modify the sphere of natural forces accessible to purely empirical methods, nevertheless set in motion spiritual forces in the realm of freedom, of freedom which admits no other than an eschatological meaning of history. Freedom must be understood as responsibility before the Lord of history, as man is informed by his moral reason and, in addition, with unmistakable clarity, by the faith bound up with the historical personality of Christ.

From its beginnings, therefore, Christianity had its philosophy of history. It leaves room enough for the evolutionary theories and morphologies of an empirical philosophy of history. Such a philosophy, however, if it does not mean to overstep the bounds of scientific methods into the realm of phantasy (and of this procedure *Comte's* positivism is an astonishing example), must itself admit that, with the means at its disposal, it cannot dispute the validity of a transcen-

[10] Cf. Alois Dempf, *Sacrum Imperium, Geschichts- und Staatsphilosophie des Mittelalters und der politischen Renaissance,* 1929.

dental interpretation of history. The mistake of identifying the philosophy of history with the sociology of history, which, in the sense mentioned, prevailed for a long time, may be regarded as overcome by the present-day standard of the epistemology of science and by its methods.[11]

Fundamental to the nineteenth-century philosophy of history, in its idealistic as well as its materialist trends, is the *idea of progress,* the elements of which originated in the eighteenth century Enlightenment. It dominates such fine thinkers as *J. G. Herder* (1744–1803), although he still remains inspired by the Christian interpretation of history. In his famous work on this subject [12] he tries to explain history as a continuous evolution toward "humanity," man being the crowning result of the development of nature, and Christianity the fulfillment of the religious development of mankind. The great idealist attempt at a philosophical interpretation of history is that of *Hegel.* World history is "the exposition and actualization of the Universal Spirit." [13] In this process, "the principles of the successive phases of spirit that animate the nations in a necessitated gradation, are themselves only steps in the development of the one universal Spirit, which, through them, elevates and completes itself to a self-comprehending totality." "Nothing in the past is lost for it, for the Idea is ever present; Spirit is immortal, with it there is no past, no future, but an essential now." [14] The character of his philosophy is that of a philosophy of immanence denying the duality of the universal Spirit and the historical world.

The idea of progress took a new direction with the *materialist philosophy of history* of *Marx* and of modern socialism influenced by him. In the system of dialectical materialism ("historical materialism," cf. Chap. 16), the movement of the human spirit in history becomes the mere "superstructure" of "the mode of production in material life" and its evolution. It is Marx's scientific service to the philosophy of history to have turned attention to the economic forces and the political forces connected with them. On the other hand, there emanated from him powerful incentives to replace the philosophy of history by the sociology of history. He himself, as we have shown (cf. Chap. 41), was not able to manage without ideals independent of economic factors. Moreover, *Marx,* in spite of himself and his "scientific socialism," remains attached to that deepest characteristic of all socialism, which, as *Max Weber* put it, is ultimately a kind of "faith"; indeed, *Weber* also points out, because of this element of "faith" in any kind of socialism, it cannot be disposed of ultimately by rational and scientific argumentation. "I think," says *Weber,* "there is no means of doing away with the socialistic conviction and the socialistic hopes. Every working class will always, in one sense or another, be socialistic." [15] This may prove true, however, only so long as man has not reached the goal of a "*social humanism*" as understood by a philosophy of history and an ethics of culture, which, proceeding

[11] It may be observed how severely such a leading sociologist and social scientist as P. A. Sorokin, *Fads and Foibles in Modern Sociology and Related Sciences* (U.S.A.), 1956, criticizes the pseudoscientific methods, borrowed from the natural sciences, in social and cultural sciences, and with this the unsparing self-criticism with which he condemns some of the scientific attitudes in his earlier works.

[12] Cf. J. G. Herder, *Ideen zur Philosophie der Geschichte der Menschheit,* 1784–91.

[13] Hegel, *Grundlinien des Philosophie des Rechts,* 1821, par. 342.

[14] Hegel, *Vorlesungen über die Philosophie des Geschichte,* 1837, trans. by J. Sibree, *Lectures on the Philosophy of History,* 1857, pp. 40, 81 f.

[15] Max Weber, *Der Sozialismus,* now in *Gesammelte Aufsätze zur Soziologie und Sozialpolitik,* 1924, p. 517.

from the development of the moral and juridical consciousness and socio-economic relations, is aware of its scientific duty to interpret the tasks of the historical moment (cf. Chap. 181).

BIBLIOGRAPHY

Abel, W., *Die Alterssicherung der bäuerlichen Bevölkerung,* 1956.

Achinger, H., *Wirtschaftskraft und Soziallast,* 1948.

——— *Soziale Sicherheit,* 1953.

Acton (Lord), *History of Freedom,* 1907.

Albertini, L., *Le origine della guerra del 1914,* L. Magrini, editor, 3 vols. (Mailand), 1945.

Albertini, R. v., *Freiheit und Demokratie in Frankreich: Die Diskussion von der Restauration bis zur Résistance,* 1957.

Albrecht, G., *Sozialpolitik* (*Grundriß der Sozialwissenschaft,* Vol. XVI), 1955.

Allen, Carleton Kemp, *Law and Orders: An Inquiry into the Nature and Scope of Delegated Legislation and Executive Powers in England,* 1945.

Allport, G. W. and Portman, L., *The Psychology of Rumor,* 1947.

Amonn, A., *Grundsätze der Finanzwissenschaft,* 2 vols., I, 1947, II, 1953.

d'Arcy, M., S.J., *Communism and Christianity* (Penguin Books), 1956.

Arnold, F. X., *Die Staatslehre des Kardinals Bellarmin,* 1934.

Aron, R., *The Century of Total War,* 1955.

——— *L'opium des intellectuels,* 1955.

Aubert, R., Bouyer, L., *et al.*, *Tolérance et communauté humaine: Chrétiens dans un monde divisé* (Paris), 1952.

Baade, Fritz, *Welternahrungswirtschaft,* 1956.

——— *Brot für ganz Europa: Grundlagen und Entwicklungsmöglichkeiten der europäischen Landwirtschaft,* 1952.

Barker, E., *Reflections on Government,* 1942.

——— (Editor), *From Alexander to Constantine: Passages and Documents Illustrating the History of Social and Political Ideas,* 336 B.C.–A.D. 337, 1956.

Baumeister, W. and Lochner, H., editors, *Der unbewältigte Wohlstand,* 1957.

Beales, A. C. F., *The Catholic Church and International Order,* 1941.

Beck, Robert N., *The Meaning of Americanism: An Essay on the Religious and Philosophic Basis of the American Mind* (New York), 1956.

Belloc, H., *The Servile State,* 1912, reprinted 1949.

Bennett, M. K., *The World's Food: A Study in the Interrelation of World Population, National Diets and Food Potentials* (New York), 1954.

Bentley, A. F., *The Process of Government: A Study of Social Pressures* (U.S.A.), 1908, reprinted 1949.

Berggrav, E., *Der Staat und der Mensch,* 1946.

Bochenski, J. M. and Niemeyer, G., *Handbuch des Weltkommunismus,* 1958.

Boettcher, E., editor, *Sozialpolitik und Sozialreform* (Veröff. d. Akad. f. Gemeinwirtschaft Hamburg), 1957.

Böhm, Franz, *Der Rechtsstaat und der soziale Wohlfahrtsstaat,* 1953.

Borch, H. v., *Obrigkeit und Widerstand: Zur politischen Soziologie des Beamtentums,* 1954.

Bosanquet, *The Philosophical Theory of the State,* 1899, 3rd ed., 1920.

Boyd Orr, J., *The White Man's Dilemma,* 1953.

Bowe, G., O.P., *The Origin of Political Authority: An Essay in Catholic Political Philosophy,* 1955.
Brauer, T., *Sozialpolitik und Sozialreform,* 1931.
Brentano, L., *Konkrete Grundbedingungen der Volkswirtschaft, Ges. Aufs.,* Vol. II, 1924.
Briefs, G., *Der Untergang des Abendlandes,* 2nd ed., 1921.
Brodrick, J., S.J., *Life and Work of Cardinal Bellarmine,* 1928.
Brogan, D. W., *An Introduction to American Politics,* 1954.
Bryce, J., *Modern Democracy,* 1921.
Buchheim, K., *Geschichte der christlichen Parteien in Deutschland,* 1953.
Burckhardt, J., *Weltgeschichtliche Betrachtungen,* 1905.
Burdeau, G., *Traité de science politique;* Vol. VI, *La démocratie gouvernante, son assise social at sa philosophie politique,* 1956.
Burgdörfer, F., *Geburtenschwund, Die Kulturkrankheit Europas,* 1942.
——— *Bevölkerungsdynamik und Bevölkerungsbilanz,* 1951.
Burnham, J., *The Machiavellists,* 1943.
——— *The Managerial Revolution,* 1941.
Burt, C., *Intelligence and Fertility,* 1946.
Butterfield, H., *Christianity, Diplomacy, and War,* 1953.
Carlyle, A. J., *Political Liberty: A History of the Conception in the Middle Ages and Modern Times,* 1941.
Carlyle, R. W. and A. J., *A History of Medieval Political Theory in the West,* 6 vols., 1903–36.
Carr-Saunders, A. M., *World Population: Past Growth and Present Trends,* 1936.
Castro, J. de, *The Geography of World Hunger,* 1952.
Catlin, G. E. G., *A Study of the Principles of Politics,* 1930.
——— *The Science and Method of Politics,* 1927.
——— *What Does the West Want?* 1957.
Chambers, R. W., *Thomas More,* 1945; cf. Donner, H. W., *Introduction to Utopia,* 1945.
Chandrasekhar, S., *Hungry People and Empty Lands,* 1954.
——— *Population and Planned Parenthood in India,* 1955.
Chase, S., *Democracy under Pressure* (New York), 1945.
Clark, Colin, *Welfare and Taxation,* 1954.
——— *The Conditions of Economic Progress,* 2nd ed., 1951.
Colm, G., "Die öffentliche Haushaltswirtschaft," in *Handbuch der Finanzwissenschaft,* Vol. I, 1952.
Conrad, H., *Dantes Staatslehre im Spiegel der scholastischen Philosophie seiner Zeit,* 1946.
Conrad-Martius, H., *Utopien der Menschenzüchtung: Der Sozialdarwinismus und seine Folgen,* 1955.
Croce, B., *Politica e Morale,* 1947, Engl. trans. by S. J. Castiglione, *Politics and Morals,* 1946.
David, Jakob, S.J., *Soziale Grundströmungen: Soziale Sicherheit, soziale Mündigkeit und ihr Verhältnis zum Staat,* 1948.
Davis, H., S.J., *Artificial Human Fecundation* (New York), 1951.
Dawson, C., *The Judgment of Nations,* 1943.
——— *Religion and the Modern State,* 1935.
——— *Progress and Religion,* 1929.

—— *Beyond Politics,* 1939.
—— *Religion and Culture,* 1948.
—— *Dynamics of World History,* 1957.
—— *Religion and the Rise of Western Culture,* 1950.
—— *Understanding Europe,* 1952.
—— *The Making of Europe: An Introduction to the History of European Unity,* 1932, 8th ed., 1948.
Dechamps, B., *Macht und Arbeit der Ausschüsse: Der Wandel der parlamentarischen Willensbildung,* 1954.
Dempf, A., *Sacrum Imperium: Geschichts- und Staatsphilosophie des Mittelalters und der politischen Renaissance,* 1929.
—— *Christliche Staatsphilosophie in Spanien,* 1937.
—— *Kritik der historischen Vernunft,* 1957.
Djilas, M., *The New Class* (New York), 1957.
Dombois, H. A., *Strukturelle Staatslehre,* 1952.
Dordett, A., *Die Ordnung zwischen Kirche und Staat,* 1958.
Dulles, John Foster, *War and Peace,* 1950.
Dürrenmatt, P., *Der Kleinstaat und das Problem der Macht,* 1955.
Duverger, Maurice, *Les partis politiques,* 1954.
Eder, K., *Der Liberalismus in Altösterreich,* 1955.
Eggleston, F. W., *Reflections of an Australian Liberal,* 1953.
Ehler, S. Z. and Morrall, J. B., *Church and State through the Centuries: A Collection of Illustrative Documents,* 1954.
Einaudi, M. and Goguel, F., *Christian Democracy in Italy and France,* 1952.
Engels, F., *The Origin of the Family, Private Property, and the State,* trans. London, 1940.
d'Entrèves, A. P., *Dante as a Political Thinker,* 1952.
Ernst, Alfred, *Die Schranken der Pressefreiheit (nach schweizerischem Recht),* 1945.
Eschenburg, T., *Staat und Gesellschaft in Deutschland,* 1956.
—— *Herschaft der Verbände?* 1955.
Europäische Publikation E.V. (ed.), *Die Vollmacht des Gewissens,* 1956. Gutachten v. Hermann Weinkauf, Max Pribilla, Walter Künneth zum Widerstandsrecht.
Faller, F., *Die rechtsphilosophische Begründung der gesellschaftlichen und staatlichen Autorität bei Thomas v. Aquin,* 1954.
Fechner, E., *Recht und Politik in Adalbert Stifters Witiko: Stifters Beitrag zur Wesensbetrachtung des Rechts und zur Charakterologie und Ethik des politischen Menschen,* 1952.
Federici, F., *Der deutsche Liberalismus: Entwicklung einer politischen Idee von I. Kant bis T. Mann,* 1946.
Ferrero, G., *Pouvoir: Les génies invisibles de la cité,* 1942.
Field, G. C., *Political Theory,* 1956.
Figgis, J. N., *Churches in the Modern State,* 1913.
Fischer, M., *Die öffentliche Verantwortung des Christen heute,* 2nd ed., 1953.
Foerster, F. W., *Politische Ethik,* 4th ed., 1957.
Fogarty, M. P., *Christian Democracy in Western Europe 1820–1953,* 1957.
Forsthoff, E., *Der totale Staat,* 1934.
—— *Verfassungsprobleme im Sozialstaat,* 1954.

Freund, M., *Weltgeschichte der Gegenwart in Dokumenten: Geschichte des zweiten Weltkrieges in Dokumenten;* Vol. III, *Der Ausbruch des Krieges* (1939), 1956.
Freyer, H., *Theorie des gegenwärtigen Zeitalters,* 1955.
——— *Soziologie als Wirklichkeitswissenschaft: Logische Grundlegung des Systems der Soziologie,* 1930.
Gardiner, G., *Capital Punishment as a Deterrent and the Alternative,* 1956.
Geck, L. H. Ad., *Sozialpolitische Aufgaben,* 1950.
Gemelli, A., O.F.M., *La fecondazione artificiale,* 2nd ed. (Milan), 1949.
Gerloff, W., *Die öffentliche Finanzwirtschaft,* 2nd ed., 2 vols., Vol. I, 1948, Vol. II, 1950.
Geyl, Pieter, *Debates with Historians,* 1955.
Gilson, E., *Dante et la philosophie,* 1939; Engl. trans. by D. Moore, *Dante, the Philosopher,* 1948.
——— *Les Métamorphoses de la Cité de Dieu,* 1952.
Gladden, E. N., *Civil Service or Bureaucracy?* 1956.
Glass, D. V., *Population Policies and Movements in Europe,* 1940.
Gordon Walker, P., *Restatement of Liberty,* 1951.
Gough, J. W., *Fundamental Law in English Constitutional History,* 1955.
——— *John Locke's Political Philosophy,* 1950.
Grabowsky, A., *Politik im Grundriß,* 1952.
Gregoire, R., *La fonction publique* (Paris), 1954.
Grousset, R., *Bilan de l'histoire,* 1946.
Guardini, R., *Die Macht: Versuch einer Wegweisung,* 1951.
Gumplowicz, L., *Die soziologische Staatsidee,* 1892.
——— *Staatsphilosophie im Umriß,* 1910.
Haldane, J. B. S., *Heredity and Politics,* 1943.
Hartmann, Albert, S.J., *Toleranz und christlicher Glaube,* 1955.
Heckel, J., *Naturrecht und christliche Verantwortung im öffentlichen Leben nach der Lehre M. Luthers,* 1952.
Heer, F., *Der Aufgang Europas,* 1949.
——— *Die Tragödie des Heiligen Reiches,* 1952.
——— *Europäische Geistesgeschichte,* 1954.
Hegel, *Grundlinien der Philosophie des Rechts,* 1821.
——— *Vorlesungen über die Philosophie der Geschichte,* 1837, 2nd ed., 1840.
Heinrich, W., *Ständewesen,* 2nd ed., 1934.
Heller, H., *Staatslehre,* 1934.
Hellpach, W., *Einführung in die Völkerpsychologie,* 3rd ed., 1954.
——— *Kulturpsychologie,* 1953.
Herder, J. G., *Ideen zur Philosophie der Geschichte der Menschheit,* 1784–91.
Hermens, F. A., *Democracy or Anarchy: A Study of Proportional Representation,* 1941.
——— *Mehrheitswahlrecht oder Verhältniswahlrecht?* 1949
Heyde, L., *Abriß der Sozialpolitik,* 10th ed., 1953.
Heydte, Fr. A. v. d., *Die Geburtsstunde des souveränen Staates,* 1952.
——— (with K. Sacherl), *Soziologie der deutschen Parteien,* 1955.
Hicks, Ursula, *Steuerpolitik im Wohlfahrtsstaat: Die Erfahrungen Großbritanniens,* 1954.

—— in, *Handbuch der Finanzwissenschaft*, W. Gerloff and F. Neumark, editors, Vol. I, 1952.
Hilferding, R., *Finanzkapital*, 1910.
Hippel, Ernst v., *Geschichte der Staatsphilosophie*, Vol. I, 1955.
—— *Vom Wesen der Demokratie*, 1947.
—— *Gewaltenteilung im modernen Staat*, 1948.
—— *Die Krise des Staatsgedankens und die Grenzen der Staatsgewalt*, 1950.
—— *Staatsdenker der Antike*, 1957.
Hippel, Fritz v., *Die Perversion von Rechtsordnungen*, 1955.
Hobhouse, L. T., *The Metaphysical Theory of the State*, 1918.
Hobson, J. A., *Imperialism*, 1902, 3rd ed., 1938.
Höffner, J., *Soziale Sicherheit und Eigenverantwortung*, 2nd ed., 1956.
Hofstätter, P., *Die Psychologie der öffentlichen Meinung*, 1949.
—— *Sozialpsychologie*, 1956.
—— *Gruppendynamik*, 1957.
Hohoff, W., *Die Revolution*, 1877.
Hollis, C., *Can Parliament Survive?* 1949.
Huber, Hans, "Niedergang des Rechts und Krise des Rechtsstaates," in *Demokratie und Rechtsstaat, Festg. f. Z. Giacometti*, 1953.
—— "Die Umwälzungen im Staatsgefüge durch die Verbände," in *Parteien und Verbände*, N. Z. Zeitung, editor, with contributions by E. Küng, E. Geyer, H. Häberlin, H. Huber, C. Mötteli, 1955.
—— "Die Umwälzungen im Staatsgefüge durch die Verbände," in *Ordo, Jb. f. d. Ordnung v. Wirtschaft u. Gesellschaft*, Vol. VII, 1955.
Hugelmann, K. G., *Stämme, Nation und Nationalstaat im deutschen Mittelalter*, 1955.
Humboldt, W., *Ideen zu einem Versuch, die Grenzen der Wirksamkeit des Staates abzugrenzen*, 1851, written 1792.
Hyman, S., *The American President* (New York), 1954.
Internationales Arbeitsamt (Ed.), *Systems of Social Security* (Genf.), 1957.
Jellinek, G., *Allgemeine Staatslehre*, 3rd ed., 1919.
Joad, C. E. M., *Decadence: A Philosophical Inquiry*, 1948.
Jöhr, W., *Der Kompromiß als Problem der Gesellschafts-, Wirtschafts- und Staatsethik*, 1957.
Jostock, P., *Krisis der Sozialpolitik*, 1952.
—— *Grundzüge der Soziallehre und der Sozialreform*, 1946.
—— *Die Berechnung des Volkseinkommens und ihr Erkenntniswert*, 1941.
—— "Aufbringung und Verteilung der öffentlichen Sozialleistungen," in *Jahrb. f. Caritaswissenschaft u. Caritasarbeit* (Freiburg i. Br.), 1957.
Jouvenel, B. de, *Du Pouvoir: Histoire naturelle de sa croissance*, 1945.
—— *De la souveraineté: A la recherche du bien politique*, 1955; Engl. trans. 1957.
Kägi, W., "Rechtsstaat und Demokratie," in *Festg. f. Z. Giacometti*, 1953.
Kahl, J., *Macht und Markt: Vom Ausbau unserer Wirtschaftsordnung*, 1956.
Kaiser, J., *Die Repräsentation organisierter Interessen*, 1956.
Kaldor, N., *An Expenditure Tax*, 1955.
Keeton, G. W., *The Passing Parliament*, 1953.
Kelley, S., Jr., *Professional Public Relations and Political Power*, 1957.

Kelsen, H., *Hauptprobleme der Staatslehre*, 2nd ed., 1923.
——— *Allgemeine Staatslehre*, 1925.
——— *Der soziologische und der juristische Staatsbegriff*, 2nd ed., 1928.
——— *Der Staat als Integration*, 1930.
Kenny, T., *The Political Thought of John Henry Newman*, 1957.
Kent, F. R., *The Great Game of Politics*, 1924.
Ketteler, W. E. (Bishop), *Freiheit, Autorität und Kirche*, 1862.
Key, V., *Politics, Parties, and Pressure Groups* (New York), 1942.
Kirk, R., *The Conservative Mind: From Burke to Santayana*, 1953.
Kluth, H., *Sozialprestige und sozialer Status*, 1957.
Knaus, H., *Die Physiologie der Zeugung des Menschen*, 4th ed., 1951.
——— *Die Fruchtbaren und unfruchtbaren Tage der Frau und deren richtige Berechnung*, 25th ed., 1956.
Koellreutter, O., *Deutsches Verfassungsrecht*, 1936.
Kroll, G., *Was ist der Staat?* 1950.
Kuczynski, R. R., *The Measurement of Population Growth: Methods and Results*, 1935.
——— in, T. H. Marshall, editor, *The Population Problem*, 1938.
Kuehnelt-Leddhin, E. R. v., *Freiheit oder Gleichheit? Die Schicksalsfrage des Abendlandes*, 1953.
Künneth, W., *Politik zwischen Dämon und Gott: Eine christliche Ethik des Politischen*, 1954.
Lakeman, E. and Lambert, J. D., *Voting in Democracies*, 1955.
Larenz, K., *Rechts- und Staatsphilosophie der Gegenwart*, 1935.
Laski, H. J., *Trade Unions in the New Society* (Sidney Hillman Lectures, 1949), 1950 (U.S.A.).
——— *Grammar of Politics*, 1925, many reprints.
Lasswell, H. D., *Politics: Who Gets What, When, How*, 1936.
——— *The Analysis of Political Behaviour: An Empirical Approach*, 1947.
Lecler, J., S.J., *Histoire de la tolérance au siècle de la reforme*, 2 vols. (Paris), 1955.
——— *L'église et la souveraineté de l'état* (Paris), 1944; Engl. trans., *The Two Sovereignties: A Study of the Relationship between Church and State*, 1952.
Leder, G., *Kriegsdienstverweigerung aus Gewissensgründen: Zur Problematik des Artikels 4, Absatz 3, des Grundgesetzes*, 1957.
Lees-Smith, H. B., *Second Chambers in Theory and Practice*, 1923.
Le Gros and Pirie, N. W., editors, *Four Thousand Million Mouths*, 1951.
Leibholz, G., *Der Strukturwandel der modernen Demokratie*, 1952.
Leiserson, A., *Organised Labor as a Pressure Group*, 1951.
Lenin, *Staat und Revolution*, 1917.
Lentner, L., *Der Christ und der Staat: Grundsätzliche Feststellungen in den Rundschreiben Leos XIII und ihre Gültigkeit für die Gegenwart*, 1952.
De Lestapis, S., S.J., *Family Planning and Modern Problems*, 1961.
Lindsay, A. D., *The Modern Democratic State*, 1943.
Lippmann, W., *The Public Philosophy*, 1955.
——— *The Good Society*, 1937.
Litt, T., *Individuum und Gemeinschaft*, 3rd ed., 1926.
——— *Geschichte und Leben*, 3rd ed., 1920.

—— *Die Frage nach dem Sinn der Geschichte,* 1950.
Lorimer, F. and Osborn, F., *Dynamics of Population,* 1934.
Lorson, P., S.J., *Un chrétien peut-il être objecteur de conscience?* (Paris), 1950.
Machiavelli, *Discorsi sopra la prima deca di Tito Livio.*
—— *Il principe,* 1913.
McIlwain, C., *The High Court of Parliament and Its Supremacy,* 2nd ed., 1934.
MacIver, R. M., *The Web of Government,* 1947.
—— *Academic Freedom in Our Time,* 1956.
McKean, D. D., *Party and Pressure Politics,* 1949.
Mackenroth, G., *Bevölkerungslehre, Theorie, Soziologie und Statistik der Bevölkerung,* 1953.
McKenzie, R. T., *British Political Parties,* 1955.
Mackinder, H. J., *Democratic Ideals and Reality,* 1919.
Maine, H. S., *Early History of Institutions,* 1875.
—— *Ancient Law,* 10th ed., 1884.
de Maistre, *Le principe générateur des constitutions politiques,* 1809.
—— *Considérations sur la France,* 1796.
—— *Du Pape,* 1817.
Malthus, *Essay on the Principle of Population as It Affects the Future Improvement of Society,* 1798.
Manoilescu, *Le siècle du corporatisme,* 1934.
Mantoux, E., *The Carthaginian Peace, or the Economic Consequences of Mr. Keynes,* 1946.
Marcic, René, *Vom Gesetzesstaat zum Richterstaat: Recht als Maß der Macht, Gedanken über den demokratischen Rechts- und Sozialstaat,* 1957.
Maritain, J., *Man and the State,* 1954.
—— *The Things That Are Not Caesar's,* 1930.
—— *Christianity and Democracy,* 1945.
—— *The Rights of Man and Natural Law,* 1944.
—— *Scholasticism and Politics,* 1940.
—— (with others), *Le Pouvoir* (Paris), 1957.
Martin, Alfred v., *Ordnung und Freiheit, Materialien und Reflexionen zu Grundfragen des Soziallebens,* 1956.
Martini, W., *Das Ende aller Sicherheit,* 1954.
Marx, *The Communist Manifesto,* 1848.
Mausbach, J., *Die Ethik des hl. Augustinus,* 2 vols., 2nd ed., 1929.
Mayer, J. P., *Prophet of the Mass Age: A Study of Alexis de Tocqueville,* 1939.
Meinecke, F., *Die Entstehung des Historismus,* 2 vols., 1936.
—— *Die Idee der Staatsräson,* 2nd ed., 1925.
Mesnard, P., *L'essor de la philosophie politique au XVIe siècle* (Paris), 1952.
Micklem, N., *The Theology of Politics,* 1941.
—— *The Theology of Law,* 1949.
Mill, J. S., *Principles of Political Economy,* 1848.
Milne, R. S. and Mackenzie, H. C., *Straight Fight,* 1954.
Mises, L., *Die Gemeinschaft,* 1922; Engl., *Socialism,* 1936.
Möbus, G., *Politik des Heiligen: Geist und Gesetz der Utopie des Thomas Morus,* 1953.

Montesquieu, *De l'esprit de lois,* 1748.

Moody, J. N. (Ed.), *Church and Society: Catholic Social and Political Thought and Movements 1789–1950* (New York), 1953.

Morrison, Herbert, *Government and Parliament: A Survey from the Inside,* 1954.

Mosca, G., *Elementi di scienza politica,* Preface by B. Croce.

Müller-Armack, A., *Das Jahrhundert ohne Gott,* 1948.

——— *Zur Diagnose unserer Gegenwart,* 1949.

——— *Religion und Wirtschaft,* 1959.

Myrdal, G., *Population: A Problem for Democracy,* 1940.

Namier, L., *Personalities and Powers,* 1955.

Nawiasky, H., "Von der unmittelbaren Demokratie; die Bereitschaft der Schweiz, die Zurückhaltung in Deutschland," in *Demokratie und Rechtsstaat, Festg. f. Z. Giacometti,* 1953.

——— *Allgemeine Staatslehre;* Part I, *Grundlegung,* 1945; Part II, *Staatsgesellschaftslehre,* 1952; Part III, *Staatsrechtslehre,* 1956.

——— *Staatstypen der Gegenwart,* 1934.

——— "Das Eigenrecht der kleineren Gemeinschaften," in *Politeia,* 1951.

Nell-Breuning, O. v., S.J., *An der Grenzscheide von Sozialpolitik und sozialer Strukturpolitik,* 1955.

Nell-Breuning, O. v., S.J. and Sacher, H., *Zur christlichen Staatslehre* (Beitr. zu einem Wörterb. d. Politik, Heft II), 2nd ed., 1957.

Neundörfer, L., *Die Sozialreform,* 1957.

Neuordnung der sozialen Leistungen, Denkschrift auf Anregung des Herrn Bundeskanzlers, erstattet von den Professoren H. Achinger, J. Höffner, H. Muthesius, L. Neundörfer, 1955.

Niedermeyer, A., *Grundriß der Sozialhygiene,* 1957.

Nietzsche, *Der Wille zur Macht.*

——— *Also sprach Zarathustra.*

——— *Die neuen Götzen.*

——— *Menschliches, Allzumenschliches.*

——— *Morgenröte.*

——— *Der Antichrist.*

Nikisch, A., *Arbeitsrecht,* 2 vols, 2nd enlarged ed., 1955.

Noack, Ulrich, *Politik als Sicherung der Freiheit: Nach den Schriften von John Dalberg-Acton, dem Historiker der Freiheit 1834–1902,* 1947.

O'Brien, John, *Natürliche Geburtenregelung,* 1956.

Oppenheimer, J. Robert, *Atomkraft und menschliche Freiheit,* 1957.

O'Rahilly, A., "The Sources of English and American Democracy," in: *Studies* (Dublin), June 1919.

Ornstein, Hans, *Macht, Moral und Recht,* 1946.

Ortega y Gasset, J., *Der Aufstand der Massen,* 1931.

Oser, J., *Must Men Starve? The Malthusian Controversy,* 1956.

Oswald, W., *Ideologie und Wirklichkeit in der demokratischen Staatstheorie,* 1943.

——— *Die christlichen Grundlagen unseres Staates,* 1944.

Parkin, C., *The Moral Basis of Burke's Political Thought,* 1956.

Percy of Newcastle (Lord), *The Heresy of Democracy,* 1954.

Pfister, B. (Ed.), *Das Widerstandsrecht und Grenzen der Staatsgewalt: Bericht*

über die Tagung der Hochschule für politische Wissenschaften München und der Evang. Akademie Tutzung, 1956.
Pieper, A., *Der Staatsgedanke der deutschen Nation,* 1929.
Pribilla, Max, S.J., *Deutsche Schicksalsfragen,* 2nd ed., 1950.
——— *Mut und Zivilcourage des Christen,* 1957.
Pütz, T., *Politische Weisheit,* 1955.
——— *Neue Wege und Ziele der Sozialpolitik,* 1954.
——— *"Witiko" als Urbild des politischen Menschen,* 1950.
Rahner, Karl, *Die Chancen des Christentums heute,* 1952.
Readings in Fiscal Policy, selected by a Committee of the American Economic Association, 1955.
Reding, M., *Der politische Atheismus,* 1957.
Reinhart, M., *Handbuch der Sowjetverfassung,* 1955.
Reiwald, P., *Vom Geist der Massen. Handbuch der Massenpsychologie,* 1948.
Renzi, G., *La filosofia dell'autorità,* 1920.
Reynolds, E. E., *St. Thomas More,* 1953.
Riesmann, David, *The Lonely Crowd* (U.S.A.), 1950.
Ritter, G., *Carl Goerdeler und die deutsche Widerstandsbewegung,* 1954.
——— *Vom sittlichen Problem der Macht,* 1948.
Roegele, O. B., *Kirche und Politik,* 1956.
Rolin, Jean, *Police Drugs,* trans. with Foreword by L. J. Bendit; with an appendix on narcoanalysis by E. V. Saher, 1955.
Rommen, H., *Die Staatslehre des Franz Suárez,* 1926.
——— *Der Staat in der katholischen Gedankenwelt,* 1935; Engl. trans., *The State in Catholic Thought* (U.S.A.), 1945.
Röpke, W., *Die Krise des Kollektivismus,* 1948.
——— *Die Gesellschaftskrise der Gegenwart,* 1942.
——— *Das Kulturideal des Liberalismus,* 1947.
Rothacker, E., *Probleme der Kulturanthropologie,* 1948.
Rüfner, V., *G. B. Vico: Autobiographie: Mit einer Einleitung in Vicos philosophische Bedeutung,* 1948.
Rüstow, A., *Ortsbestimmung der Gegenwart: Eine universalgeschichtliche Kulturkritik;* Vol. I, *Ursprung der Herrschaft,* 1950; Vol. II, *Weg der Freiheit,* 1952; Vol. III, *Herrschaft oder Freiheit?* 1954.
Saitschick, R., *Der Staat und was mehr ist: Ein Buch über die Grundlagen der künftigen Gesellschaft,* 3rd ed., 1946.
——— *Josef Görres und die abendländische Kultur,* 1952.
Salin, E., *Geschichte der Volkswirtschaftslehre,* 4th ed., 1951; Engl. (U.S.A.), 1953.
Santayana, G., *Dominations and Powers: Reflections on Liberty, Society and Government,* 1951.
Sauvy, Alfred, *Théorie Générale de la population;* Vol. I, *Economie et population,* 1952; Vol. II, *Biologie sociale,* 1954.
——— *L'Europe et sa population,* 1953.
Schilling, O., *Die Staats- und Soziallehre des heiligen Augustinus,* 1910.
——— *Die Staats- und Soziallehre des heiligen Thomas von Aquin,* 2nd ed., 1930.
——— *Naturrecht und Staat nach der Lehre der alten Kirche,* 1914.

Schima, Hans, *Verfeinerung des Rechtsschutzes, Rektoratsrede an der Universität Wien,* 1956.
Schmaus, M., *Beharrung und Fortschritt im Christentum,* 1952.
Schmitt, Carl, *Politische Theologie,* 1922.
——— *Hüter der Verfassung,* 1931.
——— *Der Begriff des Politischen,* 1932.
——— *Donoso Cortés in gesamteuropäischer Interpretation,* 1950.
——— *Gespräch über die Macht und den Zugang zum Machthaber,* 1954.
——— *Die geistesgeschitliche Lage des ht. Parlamentarismus,* 2nd ed., 1926.
——— *Legalität und Legitimität,* 1932.
Schmitz, Hans, *Die Zukunft der Altersversorgung,* 3rd ed., 1954.
——— *Die Angestelltenversicherung,* Tl. I, 1948; Tl. II, 1951; Tl. III, 1955.
Schmölders, G., *Finanzpolitik,* 1955.
Schnabel, F., *Deutsche Geschichte im 19. Jh.,* 4 vols., new ed. 1948.
Schneider, Reinhold, *Friede der Welt,* 1956.
Schnürer, G., *Kirche und Kultur im Mittelalter,* 3 vols., 1924–29.
——— *Die Anfänge der abendländischen Völkergemeinschaft,* 1932.
Schöllgen, W., *Ohne mich! Ohne uns? Recht und Grenzen des Pazifismus,* 1951.
Schreiber, Georg, *Zwischen Demokratie und Diktatur,* 1949.
Schreiber, Wilfried, *Existenzsicherung in der industriellen Gesellschaft: Vorschläge zur "Sozialreform,"* 1955.
Schroeter, M., *Der Streit um Spengler,* 1922.
Schütz, A., *Gott in der Geschichte,* 1936.
Schwartz, B., *American Constitutional Law,* Foreword by A. L. Goodhart, 1955.
Schwidetzky, I., *Das Problem des Völkertodes,* 1954.
Seidlmayer, M., *Dantes Reichs- und Staatslehre,* 1952.
Sell, F., *Die Tragödie des dt. Liberalismus,* 1953.
Sellmair, J., *Der Mensch in der Tragik,* 3rd ed. 1948.
——— *Humanitas Christiana: Geschichte des christlichen Humanismus,* 1949.
——— *Bildung in der Zeitwende,* 1952.
Simmel, G., *Die Probleme der Geschichtsphilosophie,* 3rd ed., 1907.
Simon, Yves R., *Philosophy of Democratic Government* (U.S.A.), 1951.
Smend, R., *Verfassung und Verfassungsrecht,* 1928.
Somary, F., *Krise und Zukunft der Demokratie,* 1952.
Sorel, Georges, *Réflexion sur la violence,* 1908, 5th ed., 1925.
——— *La décomposition du marxisme,* 1908, 3rd ed., 1922.
Sorokin, P. A., *Fads and Foibles in Modern Sociology and Related Sciences* (U.S.A.), 1956.
Spann, O., *Der wahre Staat,* 3rd ed., 1931.
——— *Gesellschaftslehre,* 3rd ed., 1931.
——— *Kategorienlehre,* 1924.
——— *Geschichtsphilosophie,* 1932.
——— *Religionsphilosophie,* 1947.
——— *Spanns philosophisches Gesamtwerk, im Auszug hrsg. v. H. Riehl,* 1950.
Spengler, *The Decline of the West,* trans. by C. F. Atkinson, 1926.
Stamp, L. D., *Our Undeveloped World,* 1953.
Stanka, R., *Geschichte der politischen Philosophie,* Vol. I, *Die pol. Phil. d. Altertums,* 1951; Vol. II, *Die pol. Phil. d. Mittelalters,* 1958.
Steffes, J., *Religion und Politik,* 1929.

—— *Die Staatsauffassung der Moderne,* 1921.
Steinbüchel, T., *Zerfall des christlichen Ethos im XIX Jh.* 1951.
Steubing, Hans, *Der Kompromiß als ethisches Problem,* 1955.
Stewart, J. D., *British Pressure Groups,* 1958.
Syrup, F., *Hundert Jahre staatliche Sozialpolitik,* 1839–1939, hrsg. v. J. Scheuble, bearb. v. O. Neuloh, 1957.
Talmon, J. L., *The Origins of Totalitarian Democracy,* 1952.
Tautscher, A., *Die Grenzen der Besteuerung,* 1954.
—— *Die öffentliche Wirtschaft,* 1953.
Tawney, R. H., *Equality,* 1931.
Terhalle, F., *Die Finanzwirtschaft des Staates und der Gemeinden,* 1948.
Thielicke, H., *Die evangelische Kirche und die Politik,* 1953.
—— *Der Nihilismus, Entstehung, Wesen, Überwindung,* 1950.
Thistlethwaite, F., *The Great Experiment: An Introduction to the History of the American People,* 1955.
Thompson, D., *Equality,* 1949.
Tillich, P., *Love, Power, and Justice,* 1954.
Tischleder, P., *Ursprung und Träger der Staatsgewalt nach der Lehre des heiligen Thomas und seiner Schule,* 1923.
—— *Staatslehre Leos XIII,* 1925.
Titmuss, R. and K., *Parents' Revolt,* 1942.
Tocqueville, A. de, *Oeuvres et correspondances, inédites,* 1861.
—— *Oeuvres, papiers et correspondances;* edition définitive publiée sous la direction de J.-P. Mayer, 10 vols. Vol. I, *De la démocratie en Amérique,* Intro. by H. J. Laski, 1951; Vol. II, *L'ancien régime et la Révolution,* Intro. by G. Lefebvre, 1952; Vol. VI, *Correspondance anglaise,* 1954; Vol. V, *Mélanges: Voyages en Sicile et aux États-Unis,* 1957.
Toynbee, A. J., "The New Europe," in *The Nation,* Vol. XVII, 1915.
—— *A Study of History,* 10 vols., 1936–54.
—— *The World and the West,* 1953.
Treitschke, H. v., *Politik,* Vol. I, 1897, Vol. II, 1898.
Troeltsch, E., *Der Historismus und seine Probleme,* 1922.
—— *Der Historismus und seine Überwindung,* 1924.
—— *Augustin, die christliche Antike und das Mittelalter,* 1915.
—— *Die Bedeutung des Protestantismus für die Entstehung der modernen Welt,* 5th ed., 1928.
Ullmann, Walter, *The Growth of Papal Government in the Middle Ages: A Study in the Ideological Relation of Clerical to Lay Power,* 1955.
Unkelbach, H., *Grundlagen der Wahlsystematik: Stabilitätsbedingungen der parlamentarischen Demokratie,* 1956.
Venzmer, G., *Krankheit macht Weltgeschichte,* 1956.
Verdroß, A., *Völkerrecht,* 3rd ed., 1955.
—— *Grundlinien der antiken Rechts- und Staatsphilosophie,* 2nd ed., 1948.
Vidler, A. R., *The Orb and the Cross,* 1946.
Vierkandt, A., *Gesellschaftslehre,* 1923.
—— *Familie, Volk und Staat,* 2nd ed., 1948.
—— (Editor), *Handwörterbuch der Soziologie,* 1931.
Voegelin, E., *Politik als Wissenschaft,* 1957.
—— *The New Science of Politics* (U.S.A.), 1952.

Wagemann, Ernst, *Wagen, Wägen, Wirtschaften: Erprobte Faustregeln-Neue Wege*, 1954.
Ward, Barbara, *The Interplay of East and West*, 1957.
——— *Faith and Freedom: A Study in Western Society*, 1954.
Warner, R., *Principles of Public Administration*, 1947.
Weber, Adolf, *Der Kampf zwischen Kapital und Arbeit*, 6th ed., 1954.
Weber, Alfred, *Abschied von der bisherigen Geschichte*, 1946.
Weber, Max, *Gesammelte Aufsätze zur Soziologie und Sozialpolitik*, 1924.
——— *Wirtschaft und Gesellschaft*, 1922.
——— *Gesammelte Aufsätze zur Wissenschaftslehre*, 1922.
——— "Politik als Beruf," in *Gesammelte politische Schriften*, 1921.
——— *Staatssoziologie*, 1956.
Weddigen, W., *Grundzüge der Sozialpolitik und Wohlfahrtspflege*, 1957.
Weiss, R., *Volkskunde der Schweiz* (besonders Kapital über Staat, Recht und Volkscharakter), 1946.
Welty, E., *Der Aufbau der Gemeinschaftsordnung;* Vol. II, *Herders Sozialkatechismus*, 1953.
Westphalen, F., *Die theoretischen Grundlagen der Sozialpolitik*, 1931.
Wheare, K. C., *Government by Committee: An Essay on the British Constitution*, 1955.
——— *Modern Constitutions*, 1951.
Wick, Karl, *Der konservative Staatsgedanke und seine soziale Verpflichtung*, 1948.
Wirsing, G., *Die Menschenlawine: Der Bevölkerungszuwachs als weltpolitisches Problem*, 1956.
Woytinski, W. S. and E. S., *World Population and Production: Trends and Outlook* (New York), 1953.
Wünsch, G., *Evangelische Ethik des Politischen*, 1936.

BOOK IV

THE ETHICS OF SOCIAL ECONOMY

PART ONE

The Economic Process

160. Social Economy

Social economy means the economic cooperation of the members of the political community in the process of supplying, on their own responsibility, their material and cultural wants. This conception of social economy equally draws attention to the two poles in its nature: man and society. Man and society always have been the poles in traditional natural law ethics when social economy has been under review.

The classical economists, doubtless following the mercantilists and physiocrats, saw their study as an *Inquiry into the Nature and Causes of the Wealth of Nations,* to quote the title of *Adam Smith's* famous work (1776). They described wealth as "all useful and agreeable things that possess exchangeable value," which is the definition given by *J. S. Mill* in the preliminary remarks to his equally celebrated book, *Principles of Political Economy* (1848). The classical economists examine the economic process as bound up with the genesis of wealth; it forms the basis of their position in the history of social economy, which is that they sought to comprehend the laws of this process in their interaction. But there is one serious omission in their study of wealth and the laws of its genesis: *man.* "The living garment of divinity" becomes in their hands a sackcloth which is thrown over goods, as Professor *Gottl-Lilienfeld,* alluding to the description of man in *Goethe's Faust,* expressed it. Everyone knows that in today's economic theory, man has come to occupy the foreground.

With the latest development of economic theory the second pole in the economic process, the social one, which has always been put forward by natural law ethics as essential, comes into prominence: social economy is viewed from the point of view of the social end of the *community.* This does not follow solely from the dominant position occupied by the theories of full employment and of the distribution of income; rather, it looks to the world and to the future from the theory of economic expansion and the world-wide economic tasks in regard to the underdeveloped countries. The concept of "social welfare," which has always been current in natural law ethics, is thus the most important topic in economic theory. Even the heirs of classical economics speak today of welfare economics and "social market economy"; a theory of economic growth and a social theory of world economy are in full development.

Our definition of social economy is intended to do justice equally to both elements, the human and the social: the particular individual responsibility and the social fellowship of the members of the nation. The national economy is a part of men's social cooperation in the tasks given them along with their existential ends. Therefore, it is subordinated to the social end, the common good. Therefore, all that we have said about the nature of society (cf. Chaps. 14–33) as well as about existential ends (cf. Chap 3), and about conformity of ends with right reason, fully applies to the social economy. All that need be said here about this is that the principles already developed are to be applied to the special field of present-day national economy.[1]

A few *fundamental facts and concepts* need to be defined. The fundamental fact governing the process of the satisfaction of human needs is that *means are scarce* in relation to needs. In this lies reason's ("right reasons") task: to achieve, with the means available, the optimum fulfillment of the demands imposed by man's personal and social existential ends. The expression "rationality principle," which is commonly used in economics, thus acquires an ethical significance for economic ethics; indeed, when truly human action is under discussion, it cannot have any other meaning. We may then define economy as the utilization of scarce means in the service of tasks set by the existential ends in accordance with right reason.[2] Thus, it may at once be inferred that the financial success of an undertaking is not by itself sufficient proof of economically sound

[1] It has been thought that I should also have offered a metaphysics of economy. It is not possible to see, however, that any ontology and metaphysics could be at issue other than social ontology and social metaphysics, which we have undertaken to offer in the course of our general discussion of the nature of society and of the common good. For, social economy is part of the social cooperation of men in the performance of the tasks given them by the existential ends; the social end of economy is central to our economic ethics, an essential constituent of the ends of the common good. If the desire for a metaphysics of economy implied that it was to be sought in a metaphysic of values, then I think that in this respect too the essentials have been discussed in our treatment of the existential ends, the relationship of values to them, and the metaphysical and ontological coordination of both with the nature of man (cf. Chaps. 3 ff.).

[2] The attempt is constantly being made to assign economy to the realm of *means* exclusively. This is an error in two ways; Max Weber, *Wirtschaft und Gesellschaft,* 1921, p. 32, points to the first: "How absurd it is to declare that economy (as currently defined) is in concept only a 'means'—in contradistinction, for example, to the state—is revealed by the fact that the state can be defined only in terms of the means (force) of which it today wields a monopoly. Practically considered, economy means, if anything, careful choice between ends, *but* orientated on the scarcity of means which appear to be available or obtainable for these several ends." Even more serious is the second error involved in assigning economy to the category of means; for economic life is part of culture in the full sense of the word: men cannot otherwise conform with the material and cultural demands imposed by the existential ends than by cooperation in society. That "economy is an aggregate of means for ends" is the teaching of O. Spann, *Fundament der Volkswirtschaftslehre,* 4th ed., 1929, p. 25, and his school; on this cf. J. Messner, *Die Teleologie in O. Spann's "Fundament der Volkswirtschaftslehre," Tijdschrift voor Philosophie,* 9th year, May 1947, p. 25; on economy and culture cf. also J. Messner, *Kulturethik,* pp. 336 ff.

action, for financial success does not necessarily mean that economic activity is planned in accordance with the rationality principle, that is, in accordance with the due respect for the human and social side of all economic action. Serving as it does the existential ends of man, economy is linked with the order of ends as designed in man's nature (cf. Chap. 3).

Thus, a satisfactory way of disentangling a problem that has always been troublesome for economic theory—the *problem of value*—seems to offer itself. Economic theory has distinguished particular aspects of economic value and accordingly has established certain categories of value, which we shall shortly mention, but a real synthesis has remained beyond its reach. Presumably, for this reason a large proportion of present-day economists simply proceed, after a brief mention of the concept of value and its subspecies, to declare that, in economic theory, value and price are identical. Indeed, to economic theorists, with the exception of the Marxians and the marginal utility school, the conception of value is an erratic element which has no real logical connection with the rest of their systems and concerning which one cannot understand why the question is introduced at all.

Like every other phenomenon of value, economic value has its subjective and its objective aspects. The subjective aspect is the determining element in the concept of "*utility value*" or "value in use": the capability of goods and services to satisfy human wants. In the concept of "*cost value*," the determining element is objective: the expenditure of labor and material required for the production of goods and services to satisfy human wants. In social economy, both aspects of value are linked by *their social nature*. The utility value, or use value of goods and services, rests on "general valuation," as the medieval natural law school perceived, and it is the outcome of the homogeneity of wants in a society. Therefore, for this reason alone, it is determined by social factors, and also because the calculation of the use value of goods and services depends upon their inherent scarcity, whence all members of the economic community are compelled to make a choice (related to their income) in regard to the satisfaction of their wants. On the other hand, those offering goods of utility value must aim at the lowest possible production costs in order to compete for choice. In the social economy, therefore, use value has an intrinsic relation to cost value. Conversely, cost value has also an inherent relation to use value. The reason is that the material goods and labor forces available in a community for the satisfaction of existing and increasing needs are always scarce. The "scarcity value" which they possess depends essentially on social factors, because the members of society must be able to afford the cost of the goods and services they desire, which tends to reduce the cost. Thus, in both respects, that of cost and that of use, value proves to be of a social nature. The synthesis of the two aspects of economic value, which has caused so much difficulty to economic theory, is therefore to be sought in its social nature.

In *exchange value,* which means the quantity of goods (including services) which can be obtained in exchange for a good, the subjective and objective components of economic life interact. Insofar as such interaction takes place, the exchange value of a good forms its *"natural value."* It is characteristic of it that all factors contributing to the social nature of value are codeterminant so that they are related to the existential ends; hence the economic value possesses ethical value quality. Thus, the principle of economic value becomes a most general ethical principle of order in social economy: in the rightly ordered social economy, the significance of a good is actualized in the exchange value as the outcome of satisfying needs in accordance with the existential ends through social cooperation. This principle of order derived from economic value is necessarily a very general one; it indicates clearly enough that its essence is that of social justice.

I *The Theory of Labor Value*

There was no need for the explicit statement of *J. S. Mill* to make it clear that the individualist theory of economics was unable to see a moral quality in economic value.[3] On the other hand, all socialistic thought proceeds from the tacit assumption of an ethical quality in economic value. Only because of this could the idea of the right to the full product of labor have so strongly influenced its thought. The theory of labor value has been developed principally by *Marx.* The sole constitutive element of economic value, says *Marx,* consists in the labor "crystallized" in it. Together with his "theory of history," *Marx's* theory of value, in *Engels'* opinion, makes his socialism "scientific." The exchange value of goods, says *Marx,* although governed by their utility value, contains "not an atom of utility value," for some common element must make goods interchangeable. Their utility value, however, rests on their diversity, on the various geometrical, physical, chemical and other qualities of goods; utility value, therefore, must be left out of account in the investigation of exchange value. This leaves goods with one characteristic only, namely, they are products of human labor; hence, the value of goods consists in their being "crystallized," "abstract" labor. The measure of the value of particular goods is the "working time socially necessary" for their production at a given stage in production technique. How *Marx* proceeds from his doctrine of value to his doctrine of surplus value will be dealt with later (cf. Chap. 170); here we must examine only his doctrine of value.

One feature in the nature of economic value which *Marx* emphasizes, by contrast with the English economists, is its social character. But, with the first steps in his reasoning in support of his doctrine of value, *Marx* commits an error of logic that has never been pointed out in Marxian criti-

[3] Cf. J. S. Mill, *Principles of Political Economy,* Bk. III, Chap. 2.

cism. He compares concrete qualities with abstract qualities, the utility derived from concrete qualities with the abstract "quality of being products of human labor." Yet, if we compare goods according to the concrete labor which has gone into them, we shall find that they vary as much in this as in their use value; and if we conceive of use value as the property of satisfying human wants, then evidently goods are comparable in their use value in exactly the same way as in their abstract labor value devised by *Marx.* A second fallacy occurs where *Marx,* with his concept of "socially necessary working time," unconsciously reintroduces the utility value which he thought to have eliminated from the notion of value. For, "socially necessary" means that not all, but only a certain, working time is recognized by society as "useful." A third inconsistency between the Marxian theory of value and the facts, which is generally pointed out by critics, lies in the fact that there is a considerable number of goods the value of which is obviously governed, not by the labor crystallized in them, but almost entirely by their rarity. Such goods are works of art, antiques, wines of certain districts or vintages and, especially, agricultural land. In view of this, *Marx* himself excludes from his theory of value, goods that cannot be reproduced at will, expressly mentioning agricultural land. But he does not state how he can then sustain his claim to explain by his theory of value the laws of the economic process in society. Fourthly, there is another conflict with facts in that even goods produced by process of labor do not obey his law in the values they acquire. Indeed, his assertion that "complicated labor" is only a multiple of "simple labor" is made without any clear specification of the multiplying factor. The truth is that goods produced by more highly skilled labor are not exchanged in accordance with a scale of labor, but in accordance with the higher "utility value" which is expected of them and the scarcity of the labor which goes into them. "Scientifically," therefore, the Marxian theory of labor is untenable, and is indeed upheld only by doctrinaire Marxists, particularly in the communist world. To what extent, however, *Marx's* theory, by pointing out the relationship between social value and "socially necessary" costs, draws attention to something essential, will be shown later (cf. Chap. 164, esp. note 1).

11 *The Method of the Ethics of Social Economy*

The method of ethics applied to economic life is that of ethics in general as developed in Book I. Natural law, we said, is nature and therefore must be ascertained from the nature of man and his relation to reality. We found consistency with nature to be the criterion of morality as demanded by natural law. Morality in the economic field, accordingly, is what is demanded by the nature of social economy, in other words, what is socio-economically right. Only by an analysis of social economy, its functions, and its institutions, can social ethics arrive at a valuation of it.

In this inquiry it must make use of the findings of empirical economic theory. Here we have *a body of generally accepted doctrine* which suffices for the ethical discussion of economy. Theories lying outside this realm of generally accepted doctrine must be left out of account in our inquiry into economic ethics, except when dubious ethical or political conclusions are drawn from such theories; such economico-political conclusions are, indeed almost without exception, also of an ethical nature. Tempting as it may often be to embark on a discussion of rival economic theories, social ethics must submit to a twofold restriction: 1) It must exclude questions which are purely questions of economic theory. 2) It must also exclude questions raised solely by the technical-organizational aspect of the socio-economic process. For, ethics is concerned only with the principles and their application as governed by circumstances. (Social ethics must submit to a further restriction in the use of the technical expressions of economics: it will avoid these as far as possible, and, being in a particular way a science of life, it must serve life and seek as far as possible to use the language of life.)

161. The End of Social Economy

By means of economic cooperation, as we indicated in our definition, the members of the body politic provide for their material and cultural wants. Only through social cooperation can men obtain satisfaction of their material needs in a manner substantially superior to that of the beasts. In the primitive history of mankind this cooperation takes place within the family community. But if every family were to supply all its own needs and do the work of farmer, baker, blacksmith, cobbler, tailor, and mason for itself, men would never emerge from the first primitive level. A higher standard of life is achieved only when the members of a larger group share the work of satisfying their aggregate needs, that is, cooperate. This type of social economy is essentially *cooperation based on division of labor:* the needs of all will be better and more abundantly satisfied as individuals take up specialized trades. What is true of the material sphere is even truer of the spiritual. Without economic cooperation men could never rise to levels of higher spiritual culture; they would lack leisure and, still more, the necessary resources; one need only consider what society today spends on higher and lower education. Thus, the end of social economy is the generally ampler and better satisfaction of human needs.

This, however, illustrates but one side of the truly human satisfaction of human needs. Like the animals, man could, as it were, be led to the feeding trough for the satisfaction of all his needs, and could be required to keep it filled by his labor. Obviously, however, such a procedure is quite alien to his nature, for by virtue of the spiritual element in his nature he is a creative being. Man wishes to shape his life and the manner of his fulfillment himself; therefore, he wishes to take an active part in the shaping and satisfaction of his needs. Furthermore, the existential ends designed for him in his nature, because they mean responsibility for man, cannot be realized except in personal decision. And again, the development and ripening of the human personality are linked with the individual's responsible fulfillment of the tasks implied in the existential ends, including economic tasks (cf. Chaps. 24 ff.). For all these reasons, in our introductory definition of social economy (cf. Chap. 160) we have emphasized the *personal responsibility of the individual* within the scope of economic cooperation.

Two principles of order, therefore, can be inferred from the end of social economy, for the personal choice and self responsible activity in question proceed in two ways. First, the individual may choose which needs he prefers to satisfy, and with what kind of goods he will satisfy them. This means the *right and freedom of consumer's choice.* One man prefers to live in town, another in the country; one spends more on food, another on clothes; one likes to indulge in a drink, another prefers to buy a book or go to a concert. Secondly, and even more important, is man's personal choice and activity in connection with his instinct to improve the satisfaction of his wants qualitatively and quantitatively. Man seeks to expand creatively his opportunities for self-fulfillment; he desires scope to obtain by his work possibilities of development for himself and for his family; he wishes to enrich the economic process in order to gain a greater share in its output. This means *the right and freedom to economic enterprise,* that is, to acquire and extend one's livelihood by work and private initiative. These two rights are limited only by the rights of others and of society as a whole; since freedom of consumer's choice is impossible without freedom to economic initiative, the main stress can be laid on this as a principle of economic order in the free society.

The end of economic cooperation is, we have said, wholly and entirely part of the end of man's social cooperation in general, ordained by his nature for the realization of the existential ends. To the economic sector of social cooperation, therefore, apply all the principles which we developed for the constitution and function of society in the portions of this work dealing with social and legal philosophy, and which we summed up as the *principle of the common good and the principle of subsidiary function* (cf. Chaps. 44–45). The implications of the former in regard to social economy is that its end is attained only if all who participate in economic cooperation receive a proportionate share in the aggregate output; in other words, the end of social economy is the material and cultural common good; hence, its regulative principle is *social justice.* The principle of subsidiary function has the same significance for economic society as it has for society in general, namely, as we have shown, that there should be *as much freedom as possible, as much regulation as neces-*

sary, that is, as much as the interest of the common good requires; or, in other words, the end of social economy demands the highest degree of freedom of consumer's choice and freedom of enterprise consistent with the common good. It must be borne in mind that the establishment and preservation of natural rights and freedoms belongs to the basic substance of the common good, and, furthermore, a maximum of free initiative for the members of society is a prerequisite of a maximum of the common good (cf. Chaps. 24–25). We may express this law as follows: As much scope as possible for the free creative activity of the individual both on the part of "labor" as well as of "capital"; as much restriction as is demanded by the common interest.

Therefore, we may make the following definition: *The social end of economy consists* in the full measure of the all-round common good, to be attained by a maximum of freedom of economic enterprise consistent with it in using the natural goods and labor forces available to social economy.[1]

The application of these principles to the socio-economic process, to the market mechanism, to price, wage and interest formation, to the forms of economic organization, and to the integration of social economy must engage our attention in what follows. One thing is clear already: These principles contain the *outline of an economic order predesigned by natural law:* that of *ordered freedom.*[2]

162. The Market as Organ of the Socio-Economic Process

Since social economy is economic cooperation by means of the division of labor, the exchange of goods by the members of society belongs to the natural structure of the social economy. The economic community, therefore, is a community based on exchange relations. The exchange process within the whole economic process constitutes the market; this, therefore, is an essential organ of social economy. Because in natural conditions goods throughout the whole range of social economy move toward the place which offers the best opportunities of exchange, the market is a unity even though it is organized territorially (local markets, provincial and metropolitan exchanges) and by branches (cotton market, copper

[1] Many an economist fundamentally gives the same definition. Adolf Weber, *Allgemeine Volkswirtschaftslehre,* 6th ed., 1953, p. 7, and *Der Kampf zwischen Kapital und Arbeit,* 6th ed., 1954, VI, says: "The goal of economy must be the unflagging maintenance and betterment of the real income from work while preserving the freedom and dignity of the working man."

[2] It has been pointed out that, in our account of economic ethics, there is less mention of existential ends; in fact, they have been made the whole criterion of the "natural" order of social economy, even though preponderantly under the guiding notion of the "social end of economy"; this notion emphasizes social justice as the determining principle of order, but, as it appears from the text above, it comprises the individual and the social existential ends, the personal values and the community values.

market, etc.). All the sectional markets are, however, linked together and interdependent.

The market performs *a threefold social function:*

1. It is one of the most powerful *society-forming* forces. This statement may seem surprising to many, and probably no less so the fact that this was also the opinion of that realistic thinker, *St. Thomas Aquinas* (cf. Chap. 171). It is one of the remarkable features of the present-day literature of sociology, of social philosophy and of social ethics that they have next to nothing to say about the primal factor of social unity except in the sense of *Toennies'* one-sided notion of society (cf. Chap. 16), in which there is no room for the exchange community of the national economy. The mutual dependence of individual men in the fulfillment of the material and cultural tasks laid down by their existential ends is the essential basis of society. Because they are bound up with individual interests, these forces acquire a special effectiveness in the social economy. This involves the danger of a "commercialization" of society; yet, to see in economy, in exchange cooperation, and in the market nothing but commercialization would be as mistaken as to see in man, because he requires nourishment, nothing but a biological entity.

2. The market performs the further social function of *directing the economy* toward its end. In the form of demand, it conveys the orders of the consumer to the producer and it shows the producer what goods he can dispose of at economic prices in the light of production costs. A deeper reason for the social function of the market lies in the process of value-formation which is bound up with it, whether goods or services are in question. The market is the medium through which the two factors determining value operate: the general valuation of goods by the economic community ("utility value") and the socially necessary expenses involved in their production ("cost value"). Thus, the market which functions in accordance with the law of value (cf. Chap. 160) realizes the *law of gravitation of social economy:* the movement of the exchange value of goods toward least costs, that is, toward the *"natural value."* It operates so that, with the available goods and labor forces, the best possible provision is made for the material and cultural needs of the economic society.

3. Closely connected with this is the social function of the market in the service of *economic progress,* of economic development, or, in the language of today, of economic growth. It mobilizes all possible forces in the economic society in order to secure ampler and better provision for material and cultural needs (in other words, a progressive standard of living). Those who offer goods and services can hold their own in the exchange process if the prices obtained for their goods and services replace their cost in material and labor. They secure a surplus, or a profit, if they are able to produce goods in equal quality at lesser cost or of better quality at equal cost to average exchange value. Hence, we may conclude, and we shall go into this more fully later, that competition is an essential

part in the order of social economy. Cooperation takes place through competition.

Just as all other social institutions fall short in the accomplishment of their end and function, so also the market fulfills its social end and social function only more or less imperfectly. Natural law ethics must, however, think first and foremost in terms of the natural order so as to be able to judge in accordance with the principle of objective right reason, to identify abuses, and to define claims.

I *The "Anarchy" of Competition*

Hardly anyone denies today that, in the age of individualist laissez-faire capitalism, the fulfillment of the social function of the market was seriously hampered. The consequence was periodical economic crises with their accompanying unemployment and capital destruction. On these facts the socialists built their "general theory" that market economy and competition must simply mean anarchy. This is notably *Marx's* theory, which he endeavored to strengthen with his laws of movement of capitalistic economy. The capitalist, says *Marx*, must make profit in the struggle of capitalistic competition if he is to survive in competition. Profit comes, however, only from the "variable capital" employed in wages and not from "fixed capital," which is capital invested in machinery. In order to survive competition, the capitalists must be constantly seeking to introduce new production techniques, and hence to increase the amount of fixed capital. Since profit arises only from the use of variable capital, there ensues a constant sinking of the rate of profit ("law of the declining profit rate"), and hence constant pressure toward mechanization on the part of the capitalists. The "coercive law" of competition thus causes the increase of fixed capital and the expansion of production, but at the same time the diminution of "variable capital," namely, wages, and hence of purchasing power. The consequences of this are said to be, inevitably, recurrent constantly-worsening crises.

Experience has not borne out *Marx's* analysis of the market mechanism. In particular, he overlooks the fact that the augmentation of fixed capital does not come about of itself; rather, labor forces are necessary for it. The process of capital employment, too, by no means reveals in actuality a one-sided change from variable to fixed capital. On the contrary, the development of production technique is accompanied by a growing need of qualified workers; indeed, the continuing augmentation of fixed capital through technical process involves a progressive increase in wage incomes or variable capital. A further argument against *Marx's* theory is the fact that entrepreneurs have shown as little inclination as the workers to submit to the capitalistic market mechanism; just as the workers formed trade unions for self-protection, so also the employers banded together in cartels in order to prevent ruinous competition. Besides this, millions of small entrepreneurs in industry have confuted the Marxian prognosis by remaining in business. All this shows that *Marx's* "inescapable law" of competition accords as little with reality as does the deterministic formula of the "anarchy" of competition. The deep-seated frictions in the market are, of course, another matter; this leads to the question of giving order to the market, a question which will be dealt with later (cf. Chap. 181).

11 *The "Laws" in Economic Theory*

The market as the organ of social cooperation forms the subject of economic theory. With few exceptions its laws are market laws: laws concerning the interrelation of supply and demand and the associated movement of prices, wages, interest, rents. Economic theory, if it is to be possible at all, must proceed, like any other theory concerned with human and social conduct, from presuppositions corresponding to the "pure type" of a social phenomenon—from "ideal types," as *Max Weber* describes such notions in his well-known methodological inquiries.[1] The "model" notion which is greatly in vogue today is based, however, on the more or less arbitrary assumption of certain conditions governing the process of certain economic ("macroeconomic") interrelations for the purpose of analysis (akin to "model thinking" is the method of "economic analysis" in the American economic science); if model and reality are far too frequently identified, this is because no epistemological or methodological clarification of the presuppositions and validity of model-thinking remotely approaching *Weber's* work has yet been attempted. Since theory must start from ideal-type presuppositions, its generalizations about the interrelations of factors in social economy ("laws"), in which generalizations it comprehends the economic process, possess only the value of an approximation: the process will never follow exactly the course marked out for it in these laws.[2] Nevertheless, insofar as the "ideal type" presuppositions are in accord with essential human nature, they are natural laws of social economy. True, a society can construct an economic order which wholly or in part discards them, but it will do so only at the cost of some sacrifice of general economic well-being.

Economics itself has partly misunderstood its basic ideal-type presuppositions and has, in consequence, been led into false conclusions, which have in turn been the source of erroneous views concerning the principles of economic order through several generations. One such ideal type is

[1] Cf. Max Weber, *Wirtschaft und Gesellschaft,* 1922, pp. 1–31; *Methodische Grundlagen.*

[2] Cf. J. Messner, *Sozialökonomik und Sozialethik,* 2nd ed., 1929; "Wirtschaftsgesetz und Naturrechtsgesetz," in *Wirtschaftstheorie und Wirtschaftspolitik, Festschrift für Adolf Weber,* A. Kruse, editor, 1952; "Law in Economics and Ethics," in *Review of Social Economy* (Milwaukee), Sept., 1955; "Wirtschaftstheorie, und Wohlfahrtstheorie," in *Wirtschaftliche Entwicklung und Soziale Ordnung, Festschrift für Degenfeld-Schonburg,* Lagler-Messner, editors, 1952.

homo oeconomicus: the man who acts in conformity with economic reason. This ideal type is indispensable to economic theory. Manchester liberalism has confused economic reason with economic interest and interpreted *homo oeconomicus* as the purely economic man, who acts solely according to his own economic interest, who ought to act thus, and who has a right to act thus. The practical consequence of this was the laissez-faire principle of economic policy, which makes freedom the sole ordering principle of social economy (linked with the idea of "harmony of interests"; cf. Chap. 22). The results of these were the concomitant features of the individualist-liberalist economic and social system: crises, unemployment, class warfare. *Homo oeconomicus* must be understood in terms of his whole rational nature [3] and not merely as an economic calculating machine. And the economic system itself must insure that the limitations implied in the common good concerning individual freedom of initiative are maintained by social institutions; only then can the market perform its social function in the fullest measure.

111 *The Value-Free Theory*

The sector of political economy which is concerned exclusively with interrelations in the course of the economic process is known as economic theory, social economics, or as the "*pure theory*" of economics. This pure theory excludes from its competence any consideration of ends and, therefore, also of human, social, cultural, and moral values. It seeks to examine only the causal connections or, better, since interrelations are under discussion, the functional connections in the economic process; judgment about ends, which are to be sought in this process, it leaves to ethics, since value-judgments are involved, and it declares in favor of leaving the actual choice of ends for the fashioning of a social economy to politics.

There is no real reason why such a pure theory cannot be justified on ethical grounds, if it remains aware of the limits of its method. No one will deny that medical science is justified, in order to form a basis for the art of healing, in confining itself to the investigation and elucidation of the functional connections of the human body, that is, to the biological

[3] A. Marshall, the distinguished economist, who carried on the tradition of the classical school in England, clearly sees how wrong is this narrowness of view, *Principles of Economics,* 5th ed., 1907; Preface to first edition, 1890: "But ethical forces are among those of which the economist has to take account. Attempts have indeed been made to construct an abstract science with regard to the actions of an 'economic man,' who is under no ethical influences and who pursues pecuniary gain warily and energetically, but mechanically and selfishly. But they have not been successful, nor even thoroughly carried out; for they have never really treated the economic man as perfectly selfish. No one could be relied on better than the economic man to endure toil and sacrifice with the unselfish desire to make provision for his family; and his normal motives have always been tacitly assumed to include the family affections. But if these motives are included, why not also all other altruistic motives, the action of which is so far uniform in any class at any time and place, that it can be reduced to a general rule? There seems to be no good reason against including them."

side of human nature, without regard to man as a person. It is likewise justifiable to investigate the economic functional connections in the social body, and to elucidate them, independently of its nature as community. The end of the community, the common good, can be properly attained only if the causal connections in the economic process are understood. This pure theory has an instrumental character; it is indispensable for anyone who sets value-goals before the national economy, whether as economist, ethicist, or politician. In the preceding chapter we have made it clear that national economy is altogether more than a mere complex of economic interrelations. Its essence is the social cooperation of men in the fulfillment of the tasks imposed by their existential ends; its essential end is the economic, social, and cultural common good. Unlike the "pure theory," a "general" economic theory will have to be orientated to this end. Then, possibly, economist and ethicist may meet, if in searching for this end and accordingly for the fundamental end of the national economy they keep strictly to the "nature of the facts," namely, the nature of social economy as the cooperation of members of a state community in the endeavor to provide for their material and cultural needs (cf. Chap. 161, note 1).

The scientific justification, and also the limits, of a "pure" theory can be summed up by reasoning out *Max Weber's* famous propositions regarding the value problem in economic theory, which have aroused so much discussion up to the present day. The theory offers, he says, an instrument for objective consideration of, and inquiry into, the means serving economic and social purposes; and it is able to state what economic effects, and especially unwanted side effects, will be involved in the use of means applied for definite ends (e.g., in measures of state economic policy). On the other hand, the "pure" theory, as its principal exponents themselves emphasize, has no inherent right to make any pronouncement on ends in the name of science. When exponents of this kind of theory make such pronouncements, they are speaking as politicians or social reformers guided by value-assumptions.[4] Such a restriction of economics to pure science, if consistently applied, is a great advance for that liberalist economics which, as already indicated, converted its methodological pre-

[4] Cf. Max Weber, "Die Objektivität der sozialwissenschaftlichen und sozialpolitischen Erkenntnis," in *Gesammelte Aufsätze zur Wissenschaftslehre,* 1922. For the logical analysis of the intellectual presuppositions and value-beliefs of thinkers and researchers in the sphere of the social sciences, a useful instrument has been forged in the analytical philosophy (logical positivism) which holds sway in Anglo-Saxon countries; how fruitful its use can be in the discussion of the value-beliefs prevailing in present-day welfare theory may be seen from I. M. D. Little, *A Critique of Welfare Economics,* 1950. As an example of the criticism of the postulates of classical economics Keynes, *The General Theory of Employment, Interest, and Money,* 1946, pp. 4–34, may be mentioned. For the analysis of the wider presuppositions of classical economics cf. G. Briefs, *Untersuchungen über die klassische Nationalökonomie,* 1915; on the general postulates of Adam Smith's economics cf. T. Pütz, *Wirtschaftslehre und Weltanschauung bei A. Smith,* 1932; that the sociology of Max Weber itself offers a rewarding field for such analyses was shown by Leo Strauss (cf. Chap. 40, note 8).

suppositions into ethical and political postulates. This methodological attitude could even help to overcome the belief, nurtured by individualism and collectivism (Marxism), in the inescapable deterministic domination of economic factors over the whole of social, cultural, and political life, since this belief sprang from the economic theory which mistook its philosophical presuppositions.

If no unanimity has been attained in the far-reaching discussion on freedom from value in economic theory, this is due to the impreciseness of the concepts employed, and especially the concept of economic theory. Agreement is not attainable if, on the one hand, like *Francesco Vito,* one simply equates economics with "political economy," without distinction between "pure" and "general" theory, and, on the other hand, like *W. Weber* and *E. Topitsch,* altogether denies the possibility of a scientific understanding of value. Both *Vito* and *Weber-Topitsch* dispute my arguments on the question of the value-judgment in economic theory, the former because he numbers me among the exponents of freedom from value, the latter because they include me among the advocates of the value idea; such directly contradictory judgments seem to me a not inconsiderable testimony to the rightness of my position, which is founded on the *distinguo* without which, in so complex a human reality as social economy, one easily arrives at theories divorced from actual truth.[5]

In the logical sphere, the discussion continues; in economic theory, since the end of the Second World War there has occurred an often uncritical transition from the value-free to the value-directed economic theory. This is particularly true in "welfare theory," which today holds such wide sway, and which is often guided in establishing goals of economic policy, less by the "nature of the facts" than by preconceived political and ideological ideas. It is a fundamental task of the "general" theory of economics, as we have seen, to discover from the "nature of the facts" the social end of economy. In his cautious, critical inquiry into the social end and the value-judgment in economic theory, *Theodor Pütz* also reaches a *distinguo:* "If one understands by ideological (*weltanschaulichen*) valuations, opinions governed by subjective factors which consciously or unconsciously are put forward with a claim to scientific objectivity, then freedom from value undoubtedly must be regarded as an essential condition of scientific economic understanding"; "scientific economic analysis, however, can very well reveal an intrinsic end of national economy as a whole, which is to be, and, in view of it, also assess the correctness of the functioning of economic life." [6]

[5] Cf. F. Vito, *Introduzione alla economia politica,* 2nd ed., 1952; Weber-Topitsch, "Das Wertfreiheitsproblem seit M. Weber," in *Zeitschrift für Nationalökonomie,* 1952. For a critique of the treatment of the question of value by F. Vito cf. the discussion of his book *L'Economia al servizio dell'uomo: I nuovi orientamenti della politica economia e sociale,* 4th ed., 1954, by Josef Solterer, in *Review of Social Economy* (Milwaukee), 1955, pp. 160 ff.

[6] T. Pütz, *Theorie der allgemeinen Wirtschaftspolitik und Wirtschaftslenkung,* 1948, pp. 34, 46 ff., 78–84. After a critical examination of some dozen definitions of the essen-

163. Demand

As a factor in the process of social economy, demand is to be taken as meaning demand backed by purchasing power. Social economy means social cooperation, whereby the members of the economic society receive goods and services from others in exchange for their own. Demand, therefore, is not the sum of the wants of an economic society, the satisfaction of which is desired; rather, it comprises only those wants which can be satisfied by the supply of goods and services of equal exchange value. Thus, in the socio-economic process *effective* demand constitutes only a portion of the aggregate needs. This is a hard fact. It is an unavoidable result of even the most ideal form of economy that elementary needs cannot be satisfied from income resources whereas luxury wants are satisfied. The artisan father of a numerous family may not be able from his earnings alone to provide the necessities of life for his children, yet a much sought-after professional man can afford a collection of valuable paintings. Such effects of economic cooperation, as our example shows, can take place without any injustice being done and without being due to any fundamental disorder in the economic structure and the social system. They spring from the difference in value of the services in question, upon which purchasing power is based in the particular cases. In such cases there may then arise tasks of social policy or of social charity. If, however, whole classes of the economic community are permanently unable to provide the necessities of life out of the earnings of their labor, or if their standard of living remains disproportionately lower than that of other classes, then evidently inherent defects exist in the economic system and the social end of the economic cooperation is not being attained.

In the perspective of the end of social economy, however, a still wider aspect of effective demand in the economic process comes to view: namely, all members of the community should find work and income in economic cooperation. In other words, it means *full employment.* Social economy is a process of exchanging goods, which is destined to offer opportunities of income for as many members of the community as possible. One of the reasons for seeing in this a principal end of the national economy is man's right, in accordance with natural law principles, to earn a livelihood through work. Besides, it is only in case of full employment that one can expect a sufficient measure of effective demand to absorb the products of the fully employed productive forces of the national economy, namely, *full economic productivity.* Effective demand proves to be the basic mo-

---

tial aim of political economy in specialized literature, Pütz himself gives all-round social welfare as this aim, which means for economic policy, "Well established provision of the means of physical existence and the promotion of cultural development as required by the process of forming coexistence into community."

tive force of the economic process. In view of what has already been said, this seems so self-evident that one is surprised to find that it had to be rediscovered between the two World Wars.[1]

Natural law principles, accordingly, call for an economic policy which will bring about effective purchasing power whereby the extension of demand and increase of productivity must be seen in interdependence and interaction. Among the means toward this end, we need to mention a *distribution of income* aimed at a level of general expenditure on goods of immediate consumption, such as will be compatible with the growing productivity of the economic process. The expenditure connected with the demand for such consumer goods is marked by relative stability. This demand depends primarily on the proportion of the national income which is allocated to wages. A corresponding distribution of incomes, therefore, has a substantially stabilizing influence on effective purchasing power, and hence on the economic process and the level of employment. Thus, the principle, always upheld by natural law economic theory, of a proportionate distribution of income in accordance with the standards of justice and the common good, receives confirmation from the new tendencies in the development of economic theory.

Closely connected with the goal of income distribution is the goal of a better *distribution of property;* it is a goal which economic theory has in view today also, and one which has always been advocated unremittingly by natural law economic theory as a postulate of justice and the common good. The guiding idea was that the economic existence of the individual, especially of the breadwinner, should be guaranteed by private property. Far beyond the school of natural law economic ethics, political economists today ascribe essential significance for the course of the economic process to the formation of property by the workers in the shape of savings and co-ownership in industrial capital.[2] (We have dis-

[1] The classical theory, narrowly orientated as it was toward cost value, understood the socio-economic process principally in terms of the producer. Thus, it arrived at the view that supply creates demand and that "all sellers are inevitably and by the meaning of the word, buyers," as J. S. Mill, *Principles of Political Economy,* III, 14, par. 2, expresses it; but this at once leaves the question open, whether they are always willing to sell—in a time of progressive devaluation of money, for example. In the way mentioned, Say, and with him a good number of the later economists, came to the opinion that it was only a matter of obstruction of the channels of trade if supply did not create for itself the necessary demand. They would have been much nearer to the truth if they had said obstruction of the arteries of circulation, including money. The consequence for practical economic policy of this error of theory was that, for a long time, the belief was held that economic progress must be kept in motion from the production side, neglecting the demand side, by insuring opportunities of profit for capital.

[2] *The Report on Economic Depressions: Economic Stability in the Post-War World* (League of Nations, Geneva), Part II, 1945, which was drawn up by leading international economists, including Professors Carter Goodrich (IAA), F. L. McDougall, Oskar Morgenstern, Gottfried Haberler says (par. 294): "There would be a still greater assurance of stability of demand were the distribution not only of income but of capital more evenly spread than is characteristic of most modern industrial econ-

cussed here one principal group of means of stabilizing effective demand; the second principal group, stabilization by the aid of money and credit policy, will be discussed in connection with money and credit policy and full employment.)

Consumer's Ethics

If effective demand is of such importance, it is the *consumer* whom we must regard as the lord of the economy. Consequently, the question of the right economic system is also essentially a question of the right exercise of the function of demand. In other words, the question of economic ethics is basically also one of *consumption ethics.* If the majority of the consumers are clear and articulate about their wishes, the producers must conform or suffer loss. Instead, however, the consumers allow themselves to be largely dictated to by the producers or to be guided by their advertisements; or they merely follow habit instead of taking an active part in the economic process by choosing the most suitable and economical goods. They nourish the capitalism which they at the same time decry. Indeed, for the construction of an economic order corresponding with the social end of economy, it is as necessary that there should be a new type of consumer as that there should be a new type of entrepreneur, although the latter is a favorite theme today.

The ethics of consumption and the attitude of the consumers acquire an enhanced importance in a time of full employment and increasing standard of living, particularly when the individual is, to a large extent, protected against the vicissitudes of life by means of social insurance. Thrift has hitherto been appreciated chiefly as a basic individual virtue of consumption ethics, but in the circumstances described it is also a social virtue of great significance. In social ethics, the latter particularly concerns us. Every luxury consumption which is not economically justifiable constitutes an offense against the thrift which is enjoined by social ethics, that is, against consumption ethics. The social economy cannot justify luxury consumption which takes place on the excuse of economically necessary capital formation, upon which depend the foundation of the economy and the fulfillment of its social end in the future. Expenditure of this kind is equally unjustifiable in the case both of large and of small incomes. With generally increasing incomes, the *order and value pattern of consumption* become principal questions of social pedagogy, that is, questions of education toward a consumer's morality, with the consequence of new obligations in both personal ethics and social ethics. Only if the consumer himself firmly cooperates will a fundamental task of social reform also succeed, namely, the task of restoring the consumer to

omies today." The following argument is adduced in support of this (par. 132): "For in such circumstances the demand of the great mass of the population will be kept up to some extent by drawing on its reserve of savings."

his paramount role in social economy. The extent to which the producers dominate the economy today and are able to maintain their control by powerful organizations makes it quite evident how difficult this task will be.

Systems of *dirigist planned economy* further the process of depriving the consumer of his rights. Certainly, they plan for the consumer, but a consumer such as they visualize and hope for, and such as they hope to bring about with the aid of their powerful instruments of propaganda. His deprivation of rights is complete in the communistic state. The control of the market belongs to the consumer in his exercise of the function of demand. The reason for this is his right of ownership of his income and his right to freedom of consumer's choice: he has the right to say what he wants and how he wishes to be served. He will possess this right only when he knows how to use it energetically.

To be aware of this right and of the duties linked with it is an essential part of consumer's ethics. Consumer's morality, the fundamental significance of which we have just mentioned, means the orientation of consumers' choice and demand toward the material and cultural tasks indicated by the existential ends and to the related hierarchy of needs and values. Such orientation calls for consumers who are aware of this hierarchy and of its obligatory force and also who possess the necessary insight into the quality of goods and who have the will to assert the corresponding claims in purchasing, that is, in demand. The task of educating the consumers in the right exercise of the function of demand falls upon the family, the school, the press, the consumers' associations and consumers' advisory bodies, and the many secular and ecclesiastical institutions for adult education.

An important factor in this respect is the position of the *housewife* in social economy. Economic science, indeed, likes to describe the consumer as the sovereign of the economy, but generally hastens to declare in the same breath that its interest excludes housekeeping. This is one of its inconsistencies. How much depends on the right fulfillment of the function of demand by housewives may be gathered from the fact that, in present-day economies, more than half the national income passes through their hands.[3] In fact, when we speak of *homo oeconomicus* we should think not only of production and investment; the function of demand and disbursement is, as we have shown, of no small importance for the development of a well-founded and permanent state of national welfare. Family housekeeping and family income have already been spoken of (cf. Chap. 72) from other points of view. The principles and postulates discussed there receive further confirmation from the question of the order of social

[3] Cf. P. Jostock, *Die Berechnung des Volkseinkommens und ihr Erkenntniswert*, 1941, pp. 125 f.: "If rent is included (without the rent-value of owners' dwellings), then fully two-thirds of the national income might be at the disposal of the housewife, and without rent about three-fifths."

economy discussed here. For three things seem to be beyond dispute: first, the demand function is, on the whole, exercised by the mother of the family, in accordance, at least in the great majority of cases, with the implications of the order of precedence of needs; secondly, a demand that is consistent with values, provided that there is a sufficiency of normal families of three or four children to insure the continuance of a nation, guarantees an expanding demand, which must have a consolidating influence on the foundations of the economy and tend to keep it in a state of permanent development; thirdly, thc social virtue of thrift is nowhere so reliably learned as in the well-ordered family home. Just as everywhere else in social life, we find the family to be the life center of the economy.[4]

164. Supply

Supply means the provision of goods (for use and production) and services (banking, transport, insurance, trade, cultural services). The fulfillment of the end of social economy obviously depends wholly on supply. If, as wc showcd, according to natural law principles the maximum material and cultural common good attainable, with the available natural resources and labor, forms the end of the social economy, then everything depends on the proportion in which these means are expended for the end in question. This proportion we term *socio-economic productivity*: the third fundamental concept of natural law ethics, along with "socio-economic cooperation" and "socio-economic value-principle." In order to avoid misconceptions, it may be well to state that our concept in no way eliminates man, but rather, being linked with the common good, places man in the center of social economy, which is social cooperation, made possible by the process of exchange, in the accomplishment of the material and cultural tasks indicated in the existential ends.

[4] Thus, the family income involves essentially a problem for economic theory; one may compare also (cf. Chap. 151) what economists and population students of the standing of H. D. Henderson, G. Myrdal, R. R. Kuczynski, and D. V. Glass have to say about the economic significance of decreasing populations, basing their ideas on the demand function arising out of the income of the normal family; attention is due also to the conclusions which Erich Egner, *Der Haushalt*, 1952, suggests for the position of housekeeping in the economy along with market exchange. All this speaks against a generalization like that of Bernhard Stein, *Der Familienlohn*, 1956, p. 144, concerning the income which should be the object of family policy: "What is ultimately involved is not a question of economic theory." Without doubt, however, Stein is right with his rejection of an "economic theory" basing income demands of family policy on economic services rendered by the family, namely, the investment made by the parents in the form of expenses incurred on behalf of the growing generation and for the provision of labor forces necessary to the national economy; in this sense, with Stein one must sharply distinguish between reasons of economic theory and reasons of social policy in the question of family income. Erich Egner, "Ökonomische Probleme der Familienpolitik," in *Schmollers Jahrbuch*, 75th year, 1955, p. 89, rightly warns us against such arguments from economic theory for the just family income, pointing to the danger of degrading man to a factor in economic calculation.

Because economic cooperation is completed in the exchange process with free consumer's choice and free initiative (private ownership of the means of production), this process, if its functioning is not restricted, causes the exchange value of goods to gravitate toward the lowest costs of production. The exchange value moves toward the natural value (cf. Chap. 162). In other words, if the quality is the same the cheapest goods will find most purchasers, and similarly, if the prices are the same, the best quality goods will sell best. This movement of exchange value is a movement toward *"socially necessary" costs:* a higher expenditure on costs would leave the producer without an income, for the expenditure would not be made good in the exchange process. The exchange process of the market economy enables the consumer, through the medium of demand, to determine what goods shall be produced with the available factors of production and what amount of these is to be expended as costs for particular kinds of goods.[1] With the notion of "socially necessary" costs, the idea of *"socially necessary" income* is linked inseparably. By the latter is understood the income which is necessary in a social economy to guarantee the full utilization of its productive forces. The basis in economic theory of the idea of socially necessary income can no longer be questioned in view of the importance assigned by economic theorists to effective demand for the full expansion of productivity (cf. preceding chap.).

In the concept of socially necessary income, as a constituent of the concept of socio-economic productivity, three aspects are to be noted. It means the aggregate income (the volume of purchasing power), which guarantees the absorption of what is produced, and excludes gaps in the production process which impede productivity; it also means a distribution of income which issues in a demand for goods and services resulting in productive exploitation of all available labor forces (full employment); thirdly, it means the raising of the necessary means (capital formation) for the economic progress, the economic expansion, which is indispensable for the fulfillment of the tasks accruing to society as a result of the growth of population, increasing material demands, and increasing cultural commitments.

The idea of economic productivity is, as has been mentioned, one of the fundamental ideas of social ethics for answering the question concerning the natural order of social economy.[2] The implications of our concep-

[1] It is hardly necessary to mention that, in our concept of the "socially necessary costs," the element of truth in Marx's theory of labor value is taken into account. Marx sees the working time which is "socially necessary" at a given stage of production technique as the sole factor regulating value; he is thinking of a productivity governed by technique. In our concept of socio-economic productivity we have avoided narrowing down cost value to labor value, and to cost value altogether, since utility value also, the "general valuation," is included by reason of the demand function (free consumers' choice) of the members of society with their income obtained in the socio-economic process.

[2] Our concept of socio-economic productivity clearly indicates a divergence from purely *"technical"* productivity, viz., from the quantity of goods which can be pro-

tion and principle of economic productivity for this order in general and in particular will come up for discussion again and again in what follows.

I *The Concept of "Economic Productivity"*

This concept has been the subject of widespread debate among political economists. In natural law ethics, it has a definite meaning determined by the social end of economy (cf. Chap. 160). Only if one has in view a concept of economy or productivity which does not relate this end wholly to man are the following criticisms possible: such a concept of socio-economic productivity would demand that every usable material e.g., every tree in town, every bit of earth and every available capacity of man is used to produce goods. Man, however, lives not by bread alone, still less by industrial goods; nor is he a mere robot in the service of the production of goods. In other words, the social end of economy does not consist exclusively or even principally in the production of ponderable and measurable goods and services. Man is a cultured being with an abundance of needs of a nonquantitative nature: a town needs parks and open spaces in order to preserve the biological prerequisites of life in it, and also to satisfy spiritual needs; they therefore form part of man's indispensable natural and cultural environment, the creation of which is implied in the social end of economy. And because human and cultural values are bound up fundamentally with the soil and the ownership of the soil, it is a precious good which must be preserved from ruinous exploitation (technical considerations of profit) and waste (the claims of motor traffic). The same is true of woodland, the vital substructure of national economies, for only its preservation prevents the soil from becoming barren and water from becoming a scarce commodity. To amplify these brief observations by mentioning the position of man in the economy seems not inappropriate today in the age of automation with its possibilities of overstress in the rhythm of work. Such a rhythm of work chiefly ministers to the production of the goods of a material standard of life and comes about through the subordination of man to the requirements of technique, both of which take place at the cost of his responsibility in regard to his tasks in the realm of the values proper to man as a cultural being.

Man in his entirety, with all the existential ends designed for him in his human and social nature, is essential for the idea of the social end of economy and socio-economic productivity: all the *ends in the order of rank and in the range* which, for the individual, link material to per-

duced with a technical production apparatus; such quantities can mean overproduction, so that, if they cannot be disposed of, the market reveals the production apparatus to be economically an unsound investment either wholly or in part. Our concept also reveals its divergence from productivity wholly "accounted" for in the books of the individual business concern, i.e., the financial return of an undertaking which, either wholly or partly, does not derive from the performance of a service in accordance with the social end of economy.

sonal values, and for society link social economy to common good values. Because they link it with the common good values, the conceptions of the social end of economy and of socio-economic productivity are also to be viewed in the light of the *future of society* and not merely from the point of view of a short-term calculation of profit, nor again from the point of view (perhaps based on socio-economic accountancy) of output accruing and available for distribution. The probable opportunities of meeting the future capital and cultural needs of a society form part of the fundamentals of socio-economic productivity—two aspects of the social end of economy which call for insistent emphasis, in view of today's trends toward consumption.

11 *The Entrepreneurial Function*

The function of supply, which we are considering, is guided in the market economy by the desire to make gain by business activity: those engaged in the exchange process, wish to acquire, by the provision of goods and of services, an income. This they achieve insofar as the goods and services they provide satisfy effective demand, thus contributing to the fulfillment of the social end of the economy. Providing such supply is the essence of the function of the entrepreneur. Its fundamental law, accordingly, is the law of economic productivity, but, also, *a maximum of private enterprise* is a constituent of the order of social economy, because it is necessary for the attainment of its end. Detailed *reasons* can be given for this from natural law principles: 1) From the point of view of the *individual:* the individual obeys a natural impulse when he seeks to obtain an income or an increase of income by supplying goods and services in the process of economic exchange. 2) From the point of view of the principle of *subsidiary function*: the general law of the greatest measure of individual activity and responsibility, consonant with the interest of society, is true also for the supplying of material and cultural wants (this means as much private enterprise as possible). 3) From the point of view of the *common good principle*: the more that planning minds are at work in economic cooperation, the more abundant will be the economic productivity; this is the case when there exists a maximum of private enterprise. If, for example, in a population of forty million there are two million large, medium, and small entrepreneurs in agriculture, industry, trade, and commerce striving to provide for needs under the pressure of competition, there will be a better assurance of attaining economic productivity and a rising standard of living than if twenty or two hundred officials, the case under socialistic economic planning, possess an economic planning monopoly. 4) From the point of view of *social order*: the maximum of private enterprise means the widest distribution of economic power, which is the most efficacious means of preventing the socially and politically dangerous concentration of economic power, whether in the hands of financial or industrial magnates or in the hands of the state and the government.

The entrepreneurial function can be *exercised in two ways*: by the utilization of familiar and tried methods for satisfying the demands of customers; or by striving for a better and ampler satisfaction of needs. The latter is the entrepreneurial function distinctive of modern dynamic, against medieval static, social economy; in other words, it is the decisive factor in economic development, progress, and expansion. It extends into the field of production and into the field of the market. This *entrepreneurial function consists,* in particular: (1) in the increase of productivity by *fresh combinations of production factors.* All factors of production can ultimately be reduced to labor and natural resources. Through their combination, consumer goods or producer goods can be produced. All enterprise, including that of the craftsman, signifies the combination of these factors of production. The entrepreneurial function which belongs to the modern economic process rests, however, on much longer-range planning: because of the necessity of more or less extensive technical production methods, it must adopt "roundabout production ways," calling for long-term capital investment and only after a considerable time making possible the supply of consumption goods. A man who manufactures and uses a machine for producing needles must calculate in advance the combination of factors of production employed and also the prospective market for the surplus production. The effect of this new combination of production factors is that, in the well-known illustration of *Adam Smith,* many thousands of needles can be produced in a single day, whereas the individual workers unaided "certainly could not each of them have made twenty, perhaps not one a day." (2) The other side of the specific function of the entrepreneur lies in the *expansion of the market* and, with this, the opening up of new trading outlets. This comes about through the discovery of latent wants and through the awakening of new wants by the production of goods or new qualities of goods. The expansion of the market also includes essentially the opening up of new sources of raw materials, whether by the exploitation of new domestic materials or by importation from the world markets. Summing up, we may say that the specific function of the entrepreneur in modern social economy consists in the opening up of new possibilities of economic progress and expansion, resulting in the raising of the general standard of living; in the words of *W. Sombart*: "The perfect entrepreneur is inventor, discoverer, conqueror, and organizer." His motives, besides that of making a living, include the impulse toward creative development, the spirit of adventure, and the desire for power. The function is exercised both by the independent entrepreneur and by the managers of joint stock enterprises.

The supply function is guided by the *profit motive,* particularly in the market economy, and very specially in the exercise of the entrepreneurial function in the modern social economy. What is the *moral character* of the entrepreneur's profit? First, the entrepreneur's profit is economically quite different from capital profit. One of *Marx's* most surprising errors was the confusion of capital profit and entrepreneur's profit. The entrepreneur's profit is the price for his services, as already indicated; capital profit is the price for the use of capital. *Marx's* error is all the more astonishing in that the economic theory of the natural law school in the fourteenth century distinguished between entrepreneur's profit and interest on capital. The basis of it lay in the ideas of *Duns Scotus* [3] (d. 1308), who was followed by his pupil and fellow Franciscan, *Bernardine of Siena,* these two being followed later by theologians like *Antoninus of Florence, Dominic Soto, Gregory of Valencia,* and *Ludovico Molina* (d. 1600). Their fundamental idea is that the entrepreneur performs a useful service to the community, and to that extent is entitled to profit.[4] This is in fact the guiding principle for the ethical valuation of the entrepreneur's profit: it is justified to the extent to which it is matched by productive service in the social economy. Profit not based on such service is morally unsound and generally synonymous with usury in one form or another, a topic that will call for discussion from time to time in the further course of this study.

Economic historians like *Max Weber, Werner Sombart, Jakob Strieder,* and others state that the modern entrepreneur type has only begun substantially to determine the pattern of European social economies since the Renaissance. At the same time they do not forget to emphasize that isolated examples of bold economic enterprise are to be found long before that. Ancient colonization would not be comprehensible without the courageous entrepreneur. But the aforesaid historians assign the emergence of the typical entrepreneur of modern social economy to the Renaissance. With the development of the vigorous individual personality and the concomitant loosening of the social bonds of the Middle Ages, the Renaissance produced in the economic sphere, as well as in the spheres of art, literature, science, and politics, a new type of creative man. The customary narrowing of the idea of the Renaissance to the artistic and literary fields does not do justice to the facts. The medieval master had been guided and restricted in his enterprise by the principle of "adequate livelihood," which governed the static character of the municipal economy. The newly emerging type of entrepreneur thought of profit, economic advance, social success, political influence, and the promotion of material and spiritual culture. It was not without a stubborn struggle that the old economic spirit abandoned the field; until far into the sixteenth century the profit of the entrepreneur was disputed in vigorous public discussions and debates. Yet, as early as the fourteenth century leading theologians were

[3] Cf. Duns Scotus, *IV Sent.,* disp. 15, q. 2.

[4] On the status of these medieval theologians cf. particularly the study by Franz Keller, *Unternehmung und Mehrwert,* 1912.

arguing the justification of the new entrepreneur type and his profits, provided they are based on a genuine economic service to the community.

III *Producer's Ethics*

The basic principle is the principle of socio-economic productivity, as already mentioned. A number of conclusions are to be derived from it.

1. The *profitableness* of an undertaking as the goal of business activity is morally justified according to the economic productivity which is realized in it. If it is inconsistent with the latter then it is morally questionable. This does not signify a fundamental scepticism toward the principle of profitableness; on the contrary, profitableness is a prerequisite of productivity. It becomes, therefore, an obligation in social ethics, because unprofitable undertakings are a liability to the economy and they cause loss of employment. But it is also an obligation in individual ethics, because an undertaking can only exist on the principle of profitability and by producing a surplus, and hence an income. The principle of profitability, however, always remains bound up with the principle of economic productivity.

2. Our principle also concerns the *kind of goods* which forms the object of production and of supply. Production of goods of inferior quality ("trash"), whose value for satisfying needs is more apparent than real, conflicts with the professional ethics of the producer; similarly, the expenditure of capital and labor on the production of goods of antivalue character, especially the kind which will cause harm to some (e.g., obscene literature); the first category comprises goods with morally indifferent ends, the second comprises goods with morally reprehensible ends. The boundary is not always easy to draw; in particularly critical cases the paramount consideration is the conscience of the purchasers. This is true of the often-raised question of the manufacture of means of artificial birth control; in countries such as England, where the Church of England holds contraception to be morally permissible in certain cases (cf. Chap. 147), it may appear to the subjective conscience of many as a justified and possibly imperative mode of conduct. It can be morally permissible to meet a demand supported in this way by conscience; but a different matter, and certainly impermissible, is the supplying of contraceptives through public dispensing machines or the advertising of them (in England the Church of England stepped in at once to oppose the public sale of such goods by dispensing machines).

3. One part of producer's ethics, which is supremely important today, is the *producers' associations,* which fix and enforce prices. Cartels and trusts are but one example, for similar arrangements are made in craft trades, in agriculture and by trade unions. Such agreements serve the group interest. The group as such thereby becomes responsible. The

individual association member is wrong to consider itself free from any moral responsibility if he enjoys the advantages which leaders and the officials of the association secure in the interest of the group. In fact, purely arbitrary action cannot be taken, because action against the principle of economic productivity must eventually prejudice the interest of the group itself; on the other hand, the pressure of interest groups based on economic and social power may even result in the increase of socio-economic productivity.[5] The prices and wages policies of producers' associations, however, are preponderantly dominated by the profitability principle, without sufficient regard to socio-economic productivity. In the light of experience, there is little hope that any substantial change in the outlook of the associations is to be expected from the individual consciences of their members or officials. It can be expected only from an order of social economy, which compels the associations to subject their decisions to the principle of socio-economic productivity. It will be one of the main objects of our economic ethics to indicate such an order (cf. Chap. 181) with competitions as its basis.

4. An essential part of producer's ethics concerns the social problems of the *factory shop*, which we shall deal with when discussing the organization of social economy (cf. Chap. 173).

5. Finally, the responsibilities in advertising call for consideration.

IV *Ethics of Advertising*

All the principles just set down are true for advertising ethics. The first precept in advertising is truth. This concerns the nature of the goods (the eulogizing of inferior or worthless goods; misleading statements about component parts, properties, or advantages of goods; deception through misappropriation of trademarks used by competitors) and quantities (concealment of true quantity by packing or stating false weight; pretense of especially favorable bargains, as at "sales"); the general principles of morality and justice are contravened by advertising procedures directly involving economic harm to other producers (disparagement of their goods) or any other harm to groups (e.g., to young people by the display of pictorial advertisements which tend to arouse lower instincts).

Also objectionable from a socio-economic, and therefore from a socio-ethical, standpoint is the immense and unproductive expenditure of capital which advertising represents in all advanced economies; unproductive, because very often a considerable proportion of the costs which are passed on as prices are advertising costs; such advertisements are especially objectionable when, as a result of heavily financed advertising campaigns, goods are sold at many times their true cost price (this is true of some "brand name" goods).

[5] John Kenneth Galbraith has succeeded unintentionally in making this evident to a large extent in *American Capitalism, the Concept of Countervailing Power,* 1952.

All this does not mean that advertising does not perform an important function according to the principle of economic productivity; indeed, it represents an essential part of the entrepreneur function which, as emerges from our definition above, is indispensable for economic progress and economic growth.[6]

165. Money

Although money passes daily through everyone's hands, hardly any other phenomenon presents so many riddles to economic theory. The uncertainties and differences of opinion on monetary theory give proof of this. Yet, there is almost complete unanimity on the four functions of money. Money is, first, a medium of *exchange*. It is almost impossible in general to acquire a typewriter in exchange for toothbrushes, simply because the typewriter dealer has no use for a large quantity of toothbrushes. There arose spontaneously the practice of using generally accepted exchange goods, especially pieces of metal, whose quality and weight would first be tested before each transaction but were then standardized by the stamp of a guaranteeing authority. The second function of money is to serve as a *measure* of value. How many toothbrushes are equivalent to a typewriter? This is determined by the universal exchange commodity. Since this can be exchanged for any other goods and services, yet forms its exchange value in exchange for all things, it becomes the standard of value for all goods. Thirdly, money is a means of *saving*. If someone wishes to buy a typewriter he must as a rule save a portion of his current income for some time in order to afford it. Money is a means of storing value. Fourthly, in the socio-economic process, money is the indispensable means of *calculation*. The producer has to disburse costs and has to count on replacing them by the prices he charges for the goods produced. The means for calculation is offered by the valuation of the cost factors in money units, and hence by comparison with the price expected. The factors of production are paid for in money value, which is later replaced from the money value of the goods sold. Because modern social economy, owing to the advanced stage reached by the division of labor and capital investment, must be based on money calculation, it is essentially a money calculation economy, to use an expression of *Max Weber*.[1]

During most of its history, money has exercised its functions by virtue of its *material value*, especially in the form of metal pieces. Today it exercises them independently of its material value. The banknote was formerly a claim on a definite institution to pay a quantity of the currency

[6] Evidence for this is shown in the critical inquiries of Burckhardt Röper, *Die Konkurrenz und ihre Fehlentwicklungen: Untersuchungen über Störungen der Marktwirtschaft,* 1952, pp. 157 ff., 163 ff.

[1] Cf. Max Weber, *Wirtschaft und Gesellschaft,* 1922, pp. 45 ff., 58 f.

commodity, such as silver or gold. Today it represents a claim to any goods of specified value out of the yield of socio-economic cooperation. Such money is simply "purchasing power," a claim by the holder on the economic community. Today, it possesses a predominantly *functional* character.[2] Two conclusions of great significance can be drawn by natural law ethics from the fact of the change in the character of money. First, since money no longer possesses any (material) value of its own, but rather its main significance consists in (functional) service in the socio-economic process, there emerges *a new form of its social function* which assigns to society the whole responsibility for insuring that it performs its function as well as possible in accordance with the social end of economy. Secondly, since money now represents only a claim on society, it indicates *a new form of private property.* Society, therefore, bears all the responsibility for seeing that the right of ownership acquired along with money is fully guaranteed; in other words, society is responsible for the stability of the value of money.

Since money today takes the form we have been considering, the *value of money* is determined in accordance with the relationship of the demand, which issues from the available money, to socio-economic productivity (which sets the standard for supply). We deliberately resort to the concepts of demand and productivity, which indicate no fixed quantities. This brings out clearly the status of money as a means, its functional character in social economy, and at the same time the evolutionary character of social economy. Thus, the dynamic as well as the static aspect in the concept of money is emphasized, namely, its position in the service of economic and social progress. Its *static* character, its stability of value, is fundamental to all its functions, not least to its function as a standard of measurement for goods and services entering into the economic process. If the standard of measurement changes its magnitude, then obviously there will be a diminution in the standard of conformity with it, and hence in fulfillment of the social end of economy. In order to appreciate the significance of the question we may recall the economic and political effects of changes in the value of money. Without the devaluation of the ruble in Russia after the First World War, the Bolsheviks could hardly have seized power; in Germany, without the inflation of the twenties and

[2] The natural law doctrine of the early Middle Ages strongly emphasized the functional character of money and is in this respect surprisingly modern; it was thus able to prove the lack of justification for interest charged purely on money. The determining purpose of money, says St. Thomas, is to serve as a medium of exchange; whereas its intrinsic value is mainly of importance in foreign dealings (cf. St. Thomas, *Summa theol.*, IIa IIae, q. 78, a. 1; *in Pol. I,* 5–6; *in Eth.* V, 5; *Quaest. disp. de malo,* q. 13, a. 4 c.). In face of the continual debasements of coinage at the end of the Middle Ages, natural law thinkers came to find themselves engaged in a much higher degree, as Thomas did, with the problem of the intrinsic value as a condition of the fulfillment of its function in exchange and calculation. The result of the most recent development is that the metallic theory of money (based on the intrinsic value of the currency commodity) and the juristic (based on the claim to a quantity of the currency commodity) have moved further and further from reality.

its disastrous consequences for the middle classes (destruction of savings) National Socialism could never have secured totalitarian authority.[3]

Accordingly, nothing seems more important in the question of money than to be clear about the *function of money in regard to socio-economic order.* This ordering function is wholly and entirely bound up with the stability of money. Since the unit of money represents a claim to shares of the output of socio-economic cooperation, the value of the money is obviously determined by socio-economic productivity and, depending on that, by the volume of money.[4] A development which alters the relationship between the volume of goods and the volume of money and the resultant value of money must result in the rising or falling of prices, accompanied by a relative *reduction or increase in the value of money*—inflation and deflation. *Inflation* is caused by an expansion of purchasing power which, not being accompanied by an expansion of economic productivity, brings about an increased demand for consumption as well as for investment goods. *Deflation,* on the other hand, accompanies a falling off in purchasing power, which brings about a reduction in demand and in socio-economic productivity.

What are the *consequences of changes in the value of money,* whether inflationary or deflationary? The effects can be considered from two points of view, from that of the individual or from that of the community or, which is the same thing, from that of commutative justice or from that of social justice. Inflation for the *individual,* as summarized by *Irving Fisher,* hit the creditor class and creditor-like class, including savings

[3] Professor Irving Fisher, *Stable Money* (English edition under the title, *Stabilized Money*), 1935, pp. xix f., hopes that some day a professional historian will write a history of the role of unstable money in history itself; he would find that other historians, subject to the money illusion, or entirely innocent of monetary economics, have repeatedly missed the point of outstanding events in history. The waning of Hoover and the waxing of Roosevelt were the political reaction to an enlargement of the dollar. Only a few historians realize that deflation "made" Bryan politically and that subsequent inflation "unmade" him; and only a few economic historians are aware that inflation during wars causes a calamity boom after war, ending in a crisis, as after the Napoleonic Wars in 1818, after the Crimean War in 1857, after the Civil War in 1866, after the Franco-Prussian War in 1873, after the World War in 1920; the falling ruble led to Bolshevism in Russia.

[4] It is the error of the champions of the "*quantity theory of money*" to regard the volume of money as alone significant; this theory maintains that the value of money is dependent upon its volume in comparison with the available quantity of goods, and most of its exponents also trusted in "self-regulation" in the money question. The consequence was a rigidity in money policy that was liable to produce deflationary effects. The second objection to the "quantity theory" arises from the fact that it does not allow sufficient scope to the psychological factors in the functioning of the money system, viz., the greater or lesser willingness to spend (e.g., liquidity preference or the flight from paper money with its associated deflationary and inflationary effects). Two other well-known objections to the "quantity theory" are, thirdly, that it does not take into account the speed of circulation of money (a banknote can be used for one purchase or ten in the same space of time), and fourthly, it does not take into account the additional means of circulation (checks, which are based upon the legal currency). With these qualifications the quantity theory is still useful as a rule of thumb.

bank depositors; deflation strikes at the debtor and debtor-like classes, including farmers, businessmen, and stockholders. The wage is harmed during inflation through the high cost of living, and during deflation through unemployment. Finally, both inflation and deflation affect all classes badly by throwing the whole economic mechanism out of adjustment.[5]

The consequences for the *community* as a whole are the *misdirections of social economy,* its disequilibrium. Inflation is accompanied by a rise in demand, followed by claims for higher wages from organized labor and at the same time increased investment by enterprises, because of the readiness of banks to grant credit, which in turn is due to the prospects of increased profits, all this being accompanied in turn by a renewed expansion in demand, a new rise in prices, new wage claims—the familiar "spiral." The situation becomes especially grave if confidence in the currency wanes abroad and then, soon afterwards, at home. If the process of inflation must come to an end, for example, owing to the inability of an economy dependent on external markets to compete, the economic process will show breaks at various points: firms must close down, unemployment will spread. The capital and labor which have been misdirected into the now stagnant industrial undertakings are lost. They have been misdirected because money has failed, owing to the change in its value as a measure of value and as a means of calculation, and because, therefore, opportunities for the productive employment of capital and labor, which have been held out, have proved illusory. Under deflation, with the contraction of the volume of money and purchasing power, goods produced remain unsalable; the stagnation of demand results in falling prices, production cuts, and hence unemployment. The changed value of money is the cause, for the calculations and plans of producers based on the assumption of a definite demand prove to be fallacious.

Among the foremost *causes* of the instability of the value of money *Fisher* pointed to the creation of money by the banks, which forms part of the process of granting credit. It is true, the banks are not at liberty to create money in the form of credit by opening banking accounts, because they are bound by law to maintain a reserve of cash. But, in the granting of short-term loans, the banks can be more liberal or more cau-

[5] Cf. I. Fisher, *op. cit.,* XIX. A similar description is given by Richard Gaettens, *Inflationen, das Drama der Geldentwertungen vom Altertum bis zur Gegenwart,* 1955, pp. 300 f., of the effects, which have remained the same "from the third century A.D. until today." "Fantastic increases in prices, the disappearance of gold and silver and of all essential goods, currency regulations and economic regulations under threat of the severest penalties, the undermining of all conceptions of morality in that state and private persons discharge their debts with worthless money, the flight from money toward so-called real values, wild speculation and the upsurge of the most ancient and primitive form of economy, barter: such is the picture presented to us." Even though one may differ from Gaettens in the interpretation of historical details, his conclusion is incontestable: "Inflations are the greatest crime against one of man's basic rights, against private property."

tious, so that more or less money will flow into the economic system. The profit motive induces them to be as generous as possible in their credit policy as soon as economic development permits an optimistic view. On the other hand, when economic development suggests a pessimistic view, they see themselves under the necessity of exercising restraint in the granting of credit and in the prolonging of short-term loans. Thus, the policy of the banks contributes substantially to the instability of money and fosters inflationary or deflationary tendencies. *J. M. Keynes* sought the principal cause of the change in the value of money in another direction: the fulfillment of the function of money depends not only on the volume of money but also on its circulation; hence, the withholding of money from circulation by the public must have deflationary effects and bring about restraints on the economic process. With his psychological law of the diminishing readiness to spend while incomes are rising (cf. the section on *Keynes*' general theory, in Chaps. 166–167), he thought that he had found a fundamental human attitude with deflationary effects. What experience teaches is that, in times of economic or political uncertainty, cash is hoarded, especially gold and securities, with adverse effects upon circulation and investment and the further consequences of economic depression and unemployment.

Today, the main causes of the continuing creeping or open inflation in the West, the "New Inflation"[6] (cf. Chap. 182), is constant overconsumption, measured by the standard of socio-economic productivity, resulting from exceptionally high money incomes and state expenditure. The excessive raising of money incomes is due to the race for a greater share of the social product, with the exercise of power influence by pressure groups on the side of both employers and employees; the increased money incomes attained in this way result in higher production costs, higher prices, and again, higher money incomes. Next comes excessive expenditure by the state, which is due in the first place to the maintenance of a swollen bureaucracy, secondly to the desire of economic groups for subventions, and thirdly to the gigantic cost of armaments.

It should now be evident that, in money ethics, the *maintenance of the stability of the value of money* is *the fundamental obligation of justice,* and indeed of all species of justice—legal, distributive, social, commutative, and international (the export of inflation harms other states). The obligations involve the interest groups with their demands, which govern the movement of prices; the state with its money, expenditure, economic, and social policies; and the finance and credit institutions. These obligations will be discussed in detail when we deal with the organizations and institutions in question.

[6] The new inflation is regarded as "inflation of costs" (especially excessive wage costs) as distinct from earlier forms which are defined as "inflation of demand"; both forms, however, are ultimately traceable to an excessive circulation of money because not backed by increased productivity.

The first conclusion to be drawn from the supreme natural law principle of all *monetary policy,* the stability of the value of money, is that the management of monetary policy must be the task of one special independent public organ. One single organ, because money policy must be unified; public, because it is not the business of banks which are largely guided by private interests; and, it must be independent of the government. Such an organ has evolved in most countries in the form of the *central issuing bank.* Its principal instrument of monetary policy consisted and consists, as is today increasingly recognized in view of postwar experience, in discount policy, the raising or lowering of the *discount rate* (bank rate). This means the rate of interest at which the central issuing bank grants short-term loans against sound securities. It cannot be fixed arbitrarily, but only with regard to the actual conditions of supply and demand in the money and capital markets. Nevertheless, as a basic price for money it exercises a supporting or a restrictive influence on supply and demand in these markets: when it is lowered it increases the fluidity of money; when it is raised it tends to make money scarce. The argument that the discount policy has proved to be an ineffective means of money, of credit, and of market policy may correspond to theoretical conceptions associated with the "new economics," but it conflicts with actual experience; generalizations about ineffectiveness in very special circumstances, such as the economic crisis after the First World War and the boom after the Second World War, are, just because they concern exceptional cases, scientifically inadmissible. Certainly, however, as we shall see, further measures to bring about an economically useful circulation of money must be added to discount policy.

The effectiveness of the discount policy of the central bank depends, however, on how far the central bank is supported or thwarted by the *commercial banks* and their credit policy. In most countries, partly under the leadership of the United States, methods of influencing the money and credit policy of the banks have developed. In particular, it has been made possible to carry out necessary changes, as required, in the size of the *cash reserves* which the banks are legally obliged to maintain; by this means, the possibility of creating money and credit on the part of the banks can be either narrowed or broadened. A further instrument of monetary policy which has emerged is the *open market policy* of the central bank: the purchase and sale of securities to the banks. The purchase of securities by the central bank brings to the selling banks claims on the central bank which function as cash reserves, and hence result in an expansion of credit and money circulation (approximately tenfold, if the banks are under obligation to maintain a ten per cent cash reserve); the sale of securities by the central bank has the opposite effect. Furthermore, the central issuing banks can influence the *selection of credit* by exercising greater strictness in granting credit to banks for rediscounting (U.S.A.: "selective controls") with regard to the quality of their credits. Finally, and not least, there is the exercise of *direct influence* on the banks (U.S.A.: "moral suasion") by the central bank in regard to a more restrained or more liberal credit policy which it considers to be necessary [7] (on this whole question also cf. Chap. 178, on banks).

Keynes' "General Theory"

In the last chapter of his *General Theory, Keynes* emphasizes the fact that, when full employment is reached by means of the central money and investment policy, from this point on the classical economic theory comes into its own again.[8] Had more attention been paid to this caution, the argument about the New Economics would hardly have flamed up so vigorously, and the New Economics itself, which somewhat unjustly claims his authority, would have had much less need to revise its theories than it has found to be necessary in the last few years. In fact, years before this debate began, we drew attention in the first edition of this book to a number of findings in *Keynes'* theory which are important to natural law economic ethics; but criticism was also necessary of many points in which his theory, in its approach or in its conclusions, is incompatible with the "nature of the facts," or by which spokesmen of the "new economics" in particular have been led on to a false trail theoretically and have arrived at dubious postulates in economic policy. Our criticism thus followed its own path, so that *The Times Literary Supplement* (London) of April 27, 1951, observed that the part of the book on economic theory and practice contains "some interesting views critical of Lord *Keynes*." That was at a time when the neo-Keynesian theory was in full vogue.

It is not our task here to go further into the controversies in question.[9] The primary object of our criticism was the generalization of the temporary situation after the First World War into a basic economic situation on which *Keynes* hoped to build a "general theory" of economics. This situation was marked by inadequate capital investment and a tendency to hoard cash, which was induced by the prevailing political and social uncertainty; perhaps a later period will see in *Keynes'* thought a parallel to the thought of *Marx*, another great theorist of the capitalistic economy. *Marx*, too, thought to found a "general theory" of capitalistic economy on the then existing situation of laissez-faire capitalism. In the light of the experience of the English experiment in socialism from 1945–1951, which was guided by the "new economics," we also pointed out the error of two psychological assumptions made by *Keynes: Keynes*, as every economist

[7] A very apt, clear introduction to the questions under discussion, and to economic thinking generally, is offered by M. A. Robinson, H. C. Morton, and J. D. Calderwood, *An Introduction to Economic Reasoning* (Brookings Institute, Washington), 1956, pp. 195–206; another introduction, though in part written for the expert, is provided by a work which has recently achieved recognition, A. C. Day, *Outline of Monetary Economics* (Oxford), 1957.

[8] Cf. J. M. Keynes, *The General Theory of Employment, Interest, and Money*, 1936; 1946 edition, p. 378.

[9] A useful, if compressed, survey with exhaustive bibliography can be found in Wilhelm Weber, *Theorie und Politik der Beschäftigung. Der Stand der Debatte um die "Vollbeschäftigung,"* 1954; also: *Wirtschaftswissenschaft von heute: Ein Überblick über moderne ökonomische Forschungen*, 1953.

knows, lays claim to the discovery of a supposed fundamental law of the use of income, namely, that men are disposed, as a rule and on the average, to increase their consumption as their income increases, but not by as much as the increase in their income. The English experiment has shown that there is not really any such psychological law. Experience also revealed a second fundamental psychological error of *Keynes:* he believes that it is possible in a society with liberal democracy and free trade unions to put a stop to wage movements as soon as full employment is reached. *Roy Jenkins,* one of the followers of *Keynes* who greatly influenced the socialistic financial policy of England during the socialistic experiment, was impelled to state that the pursuit of wage increases by organized labor could, except in a highly advanced community, be attempted only with the weapons of totalitarian propaganda. Not to have seen this is an error in psychology on the part of *Keynes,* who says that, with full employment, the old classical economics comes wholly into its own again, with its principle that all depends on "stable" wages and flexible prices.[10] In this criticism of two of *Keynes'* psychological assumptions we are not, of course, denying all significance in the shaping of demand to psychological factors involved in the function of money in social economy; nor do we criticize the forms of market and employment policy promoted by his doctrines, as long as the limits set by the social end of economy are observed. In succeeding chapters we shall have occasion to return to various details of *Keynes'* theory.

166. Capital

The essential feature characterizing the modern socio-economic process is the extensive use of manufactured producer goods. With the available labor and the available natural resources, means of production are manufactured for use in the socio-economic process in order to make possible a more abundant production, and hence later, a more abundant consumption. Goods are withheld from immediate consumption and used for initiating "roundabout ways of production," as *Böhm-Bawerk* expresses it. We have already noted *Adam Smith's* example of the needle manufacturing machine as an illustration of increased productivity of labor. Capital is, accordingly, "stored labor" (*Adolf Weber*), making current labor more productive. Since capital can be created, increased, and renewed only by

[10] Cf. J. Messner, *Das englische Experiment des Sozialismus, auf Grund ökonomischer Tatsachen und sozialistischer Selbstzeugnisse dargestellt,* 1954, pp. 42, 44 f.; Keynes, *General Theory,* p. 96; Roy Jenkins, *Pursuit of Progress,* 1953, p. 172. The doubtful psychological assumptions of the Keynesian theory are discussed in detail by R. Schröder, *J. M. Keynes als "Psychologe,"* in the book of that name by G. Schmölders, R. Schröder, H. St. Seidenfus, 1956. Cf. especially the thorough criticism of Keynes' assumptions by Schröder, pp. 89–95; regarding Keynes' basic law of the use of income cf. also the previously mentioned (Chap. 163, note 12) *Report of the Delegation on Economic Depressions:* Part II, *Economic Stability in the Post-War World* (League of Nations, Geneva), 1945, p. 306, which plainly states that its authors (Professors Carter Goodrich of the I.L.O., Oskar Morgenstern, Gottfried Haberler and others) are not convinced that a chronic tendency for savings to exceed investment expenditure has ever been found or that it is likely to be found in any reasonable time.

the withholding from immediate consumption of a portion of the current resources of goods and labor, a kind of "abstinence" (*Senior*) or "saving" is necessary. This postponement of immediate consumption, at the same time means "waiting" (*Cassel*) for the more abundant consumer goods which are produced with the aid of the factories and machines created by the investment of capital. Capital formation can be the result of voluntary saving by individuals, as in the free society, or of compulsory saving by the holding down of money incomes, as in the totalitarian socialistic economy.

It would be wrong to assume, however, that factories and machines are in themselves capital. The goods produced may be unsalable and then the production plants are worthless. Or the production plants may be obsolete, and their products are going to be priced out of the market, so that again the plants are on the point of becoming worthless. Production plants must not only be renewed, but also constantly must be improved because of competition and because of the growing demands on the national economy by the desire for increasing incomes. The result is the constantly increasing demand for capital. Hence, in addition to the two essential features of the idea of capital which have been mentioned, saving and waiting, there is also a third, from a socio-economic point of view, namely, the growth factor. It is not only the "reproduction" of which *Marx* speaks, and thus not only the power to replace the production plant out of the yield of production, to make good wear and tear and to overhaul it. *The social function of capital* essentially involves a growth factor. Capital is, then, used in accordance with the principle of socio-economic productivity, when its use is accompanied by the formation of more capital, which can satisfy the constantly expanding tasks of the social economy, the tasks of the future, of economic, and of social progress, of economic growth.[1]

Upon what does the realization of this social function of capital and of capital formation depend? In the preceding chapter we said that in earlier and simpler social economies simple money calculation sufficed. The master in the medieval town could see by this means whether the market was absorbing his goods at the prevailing market prices. In the present-day social economy, with its complex ramifications of production, such money calculation does not suffice. Economic calculation now must judge whether the goods and labor forces withdrawn for production from present consumption are actually employed for the improvement of future consumption and for the further growth of capital formation; that is, whether the available scarce capital is really used to increase socio-economic productivity. Because capital is scarce, a price must be paid

[1] Our concern is to determine the social function of capital, not to engage in the wide-ranging technical debate on the concept of capital. On this and on the literature cf. Adolf Weber, *Allgemeine Volkswirtschaftslehre*, 6th ed., 1953, pp. 190–211; cf. also the essay by Adolf Weber, *Kapitalbildung als Voraussetzung für den volkswirtschaftlichen und sozialen Fortschritt*, 1957.

for it as for any other scarce good. This price makes possible economic calculation in the social economy that works with elaborate methods of production. This price for the use of capital must be recovered with capital from the yield of production, that is, from the prices charged for the goods produced and the produced means of production. Thus, economic calculation passes from pure money calculation to *"capital calculation."* We have adopted this expression, which epitomizes one of the essential features of modern social economy, from *Max Weber*.[2] Capital calculation is money calculation based on the money price for use of capital. Therefore, it becomes evident why capital is to be understood both as *real capital* (capital goods) and as *money capital* (the purchasing power necessary to acquire the capital goods). Neither is capital by itself alone. We have shown that real capital, a production installation, taken by itself, is not capital. We shall now consider the question why money by itself alone is not capital.

The fact that the notion of capital has a goods aspect and a money aspect has aroused the special interest of natural law ethics. The reason is that the interest problem became linked with it. Since purchasing power may be money capital as well as simply money, the question arises: *When will money be capital and when will it simply be money?* The money yield obtained for an entrepreneur's services or for the sale of raw materials or products of the soil in economic cooperation, represents quantities of purchasing power and hence claims to a portion of the yield in goods from socio-economic cooperation. All goods which are demanded in one way or the other with this purchasing power can only be withdrawn from the supply of goods already available in the social economy. For the purpose of improving and expanding production and future consumption, portions of the aggregate yield of socio-economic cooperation are withheld from immediate consumption and are used to produce means of production. Available purchasing power then appears on the capital market. If the total demand exceeds the total output of goods, the result must be inflationary effects. There is agreement today, however, also with regard to the fact that the nonappearance of purchasing power balanced by the supply of goods in the social economy produces disturbances in the opposite direction; capital demand is then lacking, labor remains unemployed, the productivity of the economy is impaired; deflationary effects follow. *Keynes* has shown that this aspect was neglected by the classical economists, on the assumption that the equilibrium of supply and demand on the market for money capital always automatically establishes itself, so that saving is always balanced by investment. Where this is not the case, available goods and available labor remain inactive. Therefore, not only may the money remain unfruitful, as the natural law theorists of the Middle Ages saw it, but also available goods may be rendered unfruitful by causes that proceed from money and prevent the attainment of the

[2] Cf. Max Weber, *Wirtschaft und Gesellschaft*, 1922, pp. 48 ff., 58 f., 89.

maximum of socio-economic productivity. Accordingly, money is capital when and insofar as it represents purchasing power matched by supplies of goods (at least as basis of credit; cf. following chap.), and it is used in order to put these supplies to work for the maintenance and expansion of economic productivity.

The foregoing considerations make it evident that, from the monetary point of view, there is no question of the exercise of any arbitrary influence on the capital market and the scale of investment. Capital formation is possible only by way of the withdrawal of goods from the existing supply. No mere creation of money (e.g., as "social credit") can, in disregard of this fact, lead to a more abundant yield from socio-economic production; in this respect, it is altogether certain that *money in itself is unfruitful.* Money is not in itself capital, and the creation of money and the expansion of purchasing power do not create capital. Only available supplies of goods can be made productive by money. *Money, then, becomes capital* when socio-economic productivity is increased by the use, facilitated by money, of supplies provided in the process of social economy. Then, it is possible, out of the augmented yield of production, to pay the price (interest) for the use of that supply of goods.

A society which is content with what it can wrest from nature by the work of its hands will think less about tools and machines than a society which has already reached a comparatively high standard of living and is striving for a still higher standard. More perfect implements must then be interposed between nature and work, in order to increase the productivity of labor.[3] The capital formation thus necessitated for the growth of the economy and the rising standard of living in the future always involves conflict with the desire for a higher standard of consumption in the present. From the point of view of the desire for economic and social progress, *capital is the scarcest factor of production.* "Like every scarce good which gives rise to costs, this production element also obtains a price in the market, the price called 'interest,' which is calculated to stimulate increased supply but also, and especially, indicates the best possible investment. The higher the interest, the higher the yields which must be expected from branches of industry to which this element of production is directed; and the less capital is available for investment at any given time, the greater is the preference for investments which will reproduce as rapidly as possible the capital invested"; with this explanation *Adolf Weber* calls the *free capital market "the heart of the market economy,"* namely, "the free capital market, under state control, where the interest due to socio-economic conditions is arrived at." *Weber* sees the principal causes of the adulteration of the capital market in the assumption that capital can be replaced by money and by the creation of money, and

[3] In the highly industrialized countries, the United States and Germany, the capital expenditure per worker ten years ago was reckoned more than 10,000 dollars and 15,000 marks respectively; 1964 it is certainly much more.

in the fact that, for reasons of social policy, the level of interest is artificially forced down by legislative or fiscal measures. This does not mean, however, he declares, that existing interest burdens should not be lightened by suitable measures for reasons of social policy; but, especially, "we do not need unrestricted private profits." [4] In fact, if natural law social ethics has always rejected, as unjust, gains not justified on the principle of socio-economic productivity, that is, in the form of monopoly profiteering and interest usury, then, just as the ordered market has the decisive role in realizing the just price, so also the capital market has the decisive role in realizing the just interest. This will be treated more fully when we deal with interest (cf. Chap. 170).

Keynes' "Socialization of Investments"

With regard to the possibility and the effects of the existence of money which does not become capital, and hence is excluded from investment purposes, so that producer goods lie fallow and unemployment ensues, there is hardly any theoretical difference of opinion among economists. Not so with the diagnosis of the causes of shortcoming in investment activity and the means of averting this. *Keynes,* starting from the unemployment between the two World Wars, sees the cause in oversaving, judged by his fundamental law of economic psychology that increased income is not bound up with a similarly increased willingness to spend. Other schools of economics see the causes of inadequate investment and of unemployment between the two World Wars in the too rigid production and price policies of monopolies, the equally inelastic wage policies of trade unions, the deflationary credit policies of the banks, the interventionist policy of the state vis-à-vis the national economy, the disintegration of world economy as a result of protectionism, political uncertainty, and the accompanying increased risks for long-term investments.

With regard to methods to counteract the falling off in investment, *Keynes* comes to the conclusion that a more or less comprehensive socialization of investment is the only means, together with central controls for the adjustment of the propensity to consume and the inducement to invest, resulting in a far-reaching extension of traditional functions of government.[5] His fundamental idea is the *socialization* of investments. By this he means principally a policy of state disbursements for investment purposes while mopping up by fiscal means the money which would otherwise lie fallow, and going beyond this level by means of "deficit spending." Contrariwise, the schools of economics, which place the responsibility for the economic depression and mass unemployment of the twenties on the functional and structural causes mentioned, demand *"liberalization,"* or the removal of the obstacles to economic recovery and development which arise from these causes. It can hardly be disputed today that countries like Germany, which pursue an economic policy of liberalization, are in advance in their economic development in comparison with those which

[4] Adolf Weber, "Der freie Kapitalmarkt, das Herzstück der Marktwirtschaft," in *Wirtschaftsfragen der freien Welt, Festschrift für Ludwig Erhard,* E. v. Beckerath, Fritz W. Meyer, A. Müller-Armack, editors, 1957, pp. 417–19.

[5] Cf. J. M. Keynes, *The General Theory of Employment, Interest, and Money,* pp. 378 f.

have followed the principle of socialization of investment in their economic reconstruction after the Second World War.

In this entire discussion we are concerned with the fundamentals of economic policy, which are at the same time *fundamentals of economic order.* "Socialization" and "controls," which *Keynes* advocates, greatly reinforce the tendency of the modern state toward the accumulation of power. At an earlier stage in his thought (cf. Chaps. 85, 181) *Keynes* himself saw a prime danger of evolution in the ousting of the free system of economy by a collectivistic system; he regarded it as a main task of economics to meet this danger by working out a new order of social economy on the principles of a democratic corporativism. This is the sort of economic order which traditional natural law theory has always advocated.[6] *Keynes* never attempted to clear up this obvious inconsistency in his two theories of economic order.

167. Credit

Credit is the lending of money for the purpose of mobilizing capital in the socio-economic process. Such a loan may consist, in the first place, of stored up purchasing power to which there is a corresponding stock of goods in the economy; secondly, it may consist of purchasing power newly created on the assumption that a yield of goods to correspond with it will be created in the process of capital utilization by the increase of productivity. The two processes are inextricably linked, since the mobilization of capital by means of credit is effected under a twofold control, social and private.

The social control consists in this: a price must be paid for credit, that is, a price for the use of capital which is made possible by credit. This price must be recovered together with the amount of the credit itself when the goods acquired with it are used. Only one who has a prospect of repaying not only the credit but also the price for it can seek to obtain economically justifiable credit. Whether he can or cannot repay in this way depends upon the sale of his goods: thus, the market exercises a control over the volume and the application of credit.

Moreover, the giver of credit himself does not let it depend on the opinion of the receiver of credit whether he is able to repay capital and interest, whether he is worthy of "credit." The giver endeavors to secure himself. Therefore, he asks for "securities," which may be in the form of house property, land, stocks of goods, claims outstanding, bonds, furniture, life insurances, and jewelry. Should the recipient of credit be unable to repay the credit and interest, the creditor can recoup himself by realizing such securities. Thus, there is a private control over the receipt of credit: the recipient is required to exercise foresight.[1]

[6] Cf. J. M. Keynes, *The End of Laissez Faire,* 1926 (cf. the passages cited in Chaps. 85, 181, n. V).

[1] These controls and their effect are too often overlooked. A surprising example of unawareness was met by the author when a well-known philosopher and writer ex-

At the same time the *limit* to which the social end of economy can be promoted by the provision of credit (creation of credit) becomes evident. Credit creates purchasing power, and hence demand. If the latter exceeds the supply of goods currently created, the result must be an increase of the price level and inflation with devaluation of money: this would be contrary to a fundamental precept of social justice implied in the social end of economy, the precept concerning the stability of the value of money. It is to be observed that inflation must set in at once if an increase in production is not accompanied by capital formation which can give the increase in socio-economic productivity engendered by credit a sound footing and lay the foundation for its further growth.

From the function of credit in the socio-economic process, certain conclusions are to be drawn relating to the structure of credit, the form of instruments of credit, credit organization, and credit policy. The time factor obviously acquires special significance for the *structure of credit.* In the highly capitalized economy, long-term credit is necessary for plant machinery and for the mining of raw materials; repayment will become possible only when the capital invested begins to yield returns exceeding the current outgoings. Besides this, short-term credit (from a few days to several months) is necessary for the running expenses of an undertaking, to cover wages, raw materials, fuel; such credits are repaid out of the current sales of the business. Between the two forms of credit and the two markets there are transitional stages governed by the variety of production methods and the speed of turnover of capital in individual branches of industry: the turnover is relatively quick in commercial undertakings; firms which produce complicated machinery have a rather slow turnover; in agriculture, the production process is largely governed by natural factors. The credit structure must correspond to these conditions and modifications of the demand for credit if credit is to fulfill its function in the service of socio-economic productivity. In today's social economy, the credit structure is radically biased in favor of short-term credit. The banks see greater opportunities of profit in short-term loans because the aggregate interest yield of these exceeds the simple annual interest rate; the banks also see in short-term credit a greater assurance of their liquidity, because it can be recalled at short notice. Natural law economic theory has always been sceptical with regard to the preponderance of short-term credits, because of the greater possibilities of usurious interest charges and the risks to the socio-economic equilibrium. Today, more and more economists regard it as an essential cause of the fluctua-

---

plained to him how he used credit to illustrate to his students the corruptness of capitalism. Capitalism, he would say, makes it possible for me to raise credit on my large and very valuable library; I can then build a factory, manufacture goods, and make profits while continuing in the possession and enjoyment of my library. On his attention being drawn to the possibility of losing his library if the undertaking should prove a failure, he grew more thoughtful.

tions in markets that short-term credit is so prevalent[2] (e.g., today the danger of a boom with the accompanying fear of recession).

The question of the structure of credit is at the same time a question of the *instruments of credit.* The first thing to be considered, along with the time factor, is the basis of security in credit. The universal complaint today is that large-scale credit is at an advantage, whereas it is only with difficulty and under oppressive conditions that the small businessman can obtain credit. The reason for this is that the large and safe undertaking offers better and more easily accessible securities and also makes possible big credit transactions, which are far more advantageous to the banks than many dealings with small traders. Indeed, for medium-sized and small industrial and farming businesses credit is characterized by the personal link between the entrepreneur and his business and the relative lack of adequate security. Consequently, credit for these businesses must be based at least as much on the personal reliability and business soundness of those concerned as on the securities which they have to offer. Since, therefore, credit business demands accurate knowledge of the personal and business status of the borrower, it is necessary to have recourse to vocational credit organizations on a cooperative basis. Security can then be provided chiefly by guarantees on the part of business friends of the borrower in collaboration with the organizations mentioned.

These considerations also suggest conclusions with regard to the *organization of credit.* It must satisfy credit requirements in accordance with the variation in the time factor, risk, and productive capacity. The nature of the facts itself has led to a division of work in banking to accord with the particular conditions of credit demand in agriculture, industry, trade, commerce, export business, and so on. For credit which is dependent on personal factors, particularly in the case of farmers and small businessmen, cooperative organizations have evolved. There is still substantial progress to be made in this direction; the credit cooperatives could greatly increase their financial strength by links between them and by their linking up with the big banks.

Credit policy is a principal means for guiding the social economy. The object is to mobilize capital to such an extent and in such forms that, if all the available factors of production are utilized to the best of their capacity, the maximum of economic productivity will be reached, with opportunities of work for all who are willing to work and a corresponding income for all. The instruments of credit policy consist in the measures previously mentioned for achieving an expansion or contraction of the granting of credit by the commercial banks, in accordance with the requirements of the social end of economy. Of these, two are of decisive importance for credit policy: the first is the requirement of economic stability, meaning the stability of the value of money and a price-level which is stable, on the whole, though mobile in regard to particular prices,

[2] Cf. Irving Fisher, *100% Money,* 1936, pp. 147 ff.

failing which the wage-price spiral will be set in motion; the second requirement based on the social end of economy is that of economic growth as a prerequisite of the fulfillment of the continuously increasing economic, social, and cultural tasks. The possibility of real economic dynamics depends upon economic stability, that is, upon freedom from depression and unemployment and from artificial booms and inflation. The two requirements, economic stability and growth, provide an important scope for credit policy, but also set clear limits to it. The limits to the expansion of the economic process by means of credit policy are fixed by the actually attainable increase in productivity. A credit policy which attempts to overleap these limits may bring about an appearance of prosperity for some years; but it will cause an influx of money, and hence of purchasing power, into the national economy and thus bring about an expansion of demand not matched by a similar expansion in the supply of goods: the result of this will be price inflation followed by wage claims and then further price inflation. Because of the opportunities and also the dangers which it involves, credit policy as a means of steering the process of social economy is a matter of grave responsibility, according to the natural law principles of justice rooted in the social end of economy and in the common good in general.

Is Keynes' Theory Dynamic?

In the chapter on capital we pointed out, in harmony with the natural law theory of money, that money in itself is not capital but can become capital only under certain conditions. Credit money, or money which flows into the national economy by reason of credit, is not in itself capital. Credit money can become capital only under the same conditions as money in general: if it becomes a means of making available supplies of goods which serve to raise economic productivity. *Keynes* taught that the volume of saving should not exceed that of investment; he did not state that the volume of saving must be less than that of investment; he was even further from saying that credit is in itself capital and can be a means of economic growth and of policy of economic expansion independently of the formation of capital by saving. One of the most serious misunderstandings made by exponents of the "new economics" was to conceive *Keynes'* theory as a dynamic theory of constant economic expansion and economic growth and to see in credit and money the means toward this.

A competent witness like *Harrod* declares that the formulation and handling of its subject matter shows *Keynes' General Theory* to be essentially static. *Keynes'* notions of liquidity preference, with its significance for unemployment and the overcoming of unemployment, belong, *Harrod* says, to the conceptual framework of static equilibrium; only a single concept in *Keynes'* general theory is of an essentially dynamic nature, that of "positive saving." *Harrod* illustrates this: The year-by-year continuing allocation of one-tenth of one's income to house rent is not a dynamic process; it is consistent with a stable equilibrium of yearly prices and rates of socio-economic output; a steady allocation of one-tenth of one's income to saving, however, is essentially dynamic, because it involves a continuing growth in one of the fundamental determinants of the socio-economic process, namely, the quantity of capital available.[3]

It would be a complete misinterpretation of *Keynes'* ideas to equate capital with money, to exclude the notion of capital altogether from economic thought, and to try to work only with such ideas as creation of money, investment, saving. *Erich Preiser* seeks to do this on the ground that, although new real income probably appears only when the expansion of production has taken place, "production cannot be expanded at all unless the quantity of money is first increased and, with that, new nominal income is created."[4] Such theories obviously rest on the assumption that higher labor costs (nominal wages) lead to higher mechanization and that this in turn brings about a higher productivity of labor. Professor *Joan Robinson*, a socialist in the front rank of present-day British economists, makes conclusions which are critical of all such theories in her much acclaimed book on capital; it is, she says, a widely held error that the connection between rising wages and increasing mechanization is a causal one. Her argument shows that the accumulation of capital tends to raise wages; this she holds to be true of both capitalistic and socialistic economies.[5]

Theories which attempt to equate credit money and investment capital are following out *Keynes'* theory in a wrong direction. *Keynes'* thought, according to *Harrod*, was static, not dynamic, with full employment as its principal object; to produce a dynamic theory, as *Harrod* clearly indicates at the end of his book, although himself a follower of *Keynes'* theory, a reappraisal of *Keynes'* theory is necessary, indeed its development in a direction opposite to that of the money creation theories.[6]

168. Price

The exchange value of goods expressed in money is their price. It is the outcome of the interaction of the factors of supply and demand, and the essence of the market is that it is the process of interaction of these factors. Price, however, is not only the outcome of the relationships involved, but also an efficient cause in them. Every price stands in a mutual relationship to other prices: for the seller of a commodity the price is the replacement of the labor and raw material costs, as well as income; for the person who buys raw materials, plant, and labor, with a view to production, their prices are component elements in his costs. The market, as we have said (cf. Chap. 162), is the organ in the socio-economic process serving to bring about the maximum of economic productivity; and the means by which this is achieved is the movement of prices toward the "*natural price*" level, which takes place when supply and demand develop in the proper way. Supply and demand develop properly when neither side makes use of the ignorance or weakness of the other. Dis-

[3] Cf. R. F. Harrod, *Towards a Dynamic Economics*, 1948, pp. 10 f.
[4] E. Preiser, *Bildung und Verteilung des Volkseinkommens*, 1957, pp. 67 ff.
[5] Cf. J. Robinson, *The Accumulation of Capital*, 1956, p. 151.
[6] Cf. R. F. Harrod, *op. cit.*, pp. 145 f.

tortions are caused by the withholding of supplies for the purpose of speculation: by underselling; by monopolistic price-fixing in association with production restrictions; by official fixing of maximum prices resulting in the exclusion of goods from the market; and quite generally by fluctuations in the value of money. If the market guarantees the orderly interaction of supply and demand, the result is a distribution of the social product through prices which allow the members of the social economy to receive back their raw material and labor costs in the prices of their products, in accordance with the productivity of the production factors they have used; with this, they also receive recompense for any entrepreneur service contributing toward increases in productivity, as well as for the "differential gains" made by firms as a result of advantages in the market.

From what has been said about the social end of economy and the social function of the market (cf. Chaps. 161–162), we can derive a *fundamental principle of natural law price ethics* (developing the traditional natural law of the Middle Ages): [1] justice, in general, is satisfied only by the movement of prices to the natural price which goes with the proper interaction of suppy and demand. On the demand side, the decisive factors are the subjective ones, which are expressed in utility value or use value: on the one hand, the significance of a good for the satisfaction of need according to common valuation (*communis aestimatio*), and on the other hand, its significance for the individuals according to the portion of income which they are prepared to use on particular goods in the course of making their necessary choice in the satisfaction of needs ("marginal utility" in the language of the economist). Note that common valuation is also in question insofar as the general income level determines the aforesaid choice: the kinds of goods selected belong to a higher range of exchange value when the general level of income rises

[1] For a picture of the natural law price ethics of medieval scholasticism the following are of value: Edmund Schreiber, *Die volkswirtschaftlichen Anschauungen der Scholastik seit Thomas v. Aquin,* 1913; Joseph Höffner, "Der Wettbewerb in der Scholastik," in *Ordo,* 1953, pp. 181–202; Höffner declares, contrary to the opinion of Jakob Strieder, *Studien zur Geschichte der kapitalistischen Organisationsformen,* 2nd ed., 1925, p. 58, that the scholastic doctrine of price was not built upon a rigid principle of adequate sustenance. That this principle, however, played a vital role in the price policy of the guilds in the medieval town can hardly be disputed; the medieval scholastic price ethics remains attached to the wholly static thinking of the scholastic ethics of the time, according to which the ordered acquisitiveness of man is confined to *exteriores divitias, prout sunt necessariae ad vitam eius secundum suam conditionem* (Thomas Aquinas, *Summa theol.,* IIa IIae, q. 118, a. 1); only when capitalism began to evolve (cf. Chap. 164) does more dynamic thinking emerge in scholastic ethics also. The dynamic consequence of lowering of costs, which is integral to competition, remained unknown to it even then. The initial assumption was, as Höffner himself says, that "prices, on the supposition of human needs, would be determined by costs and by the play of supply and demand. Hence, the price-raising and price-lowering effect of competition was recognized, whereas its cost-lowering function was not clearly perceived, although suspected; this undoubtedly is connected with the fact that the scholastics critically examined first and foremost the price-formation in commerce, but paid little attention to the sphere of production."

(and progressively: at a first general increase in income the choice is made between, e.g., expenditure on clothing, on housing, or on holidays; at another rise the choice will be perhaps between a motorcycle, a television set, a camera). On the supply side, the objective factors are decisive; these are expressed in cost value, which is governed by the "socially necessary costs" ("marginal costs," in economists' language). These are the costs which the producers endeavor to reduce by using better production methods in order to increase sales; the buyers, on the other hand, press for their reduction by means of their choice in the satisfaction of their needs and their endeavors to achieve with their income the highest possible satisfaction of needs (i.e., to buy the best quality as cheaply as possible). Therefore, not every replacement of costs is demanded by justice in accordance with natural law principles, but only "socially necessary costs." This is price formation on the principle of socio-economic productivity, as implied in the social end of economy. That is to say, the social end of economy also involves the end of economic progress and economic growth, which are indispensable for the fulfillment of the material, cultural, and social tasks bound up with man's existential ends, including especially those posed by the natural increase in population.[2]

Connected with the principle discussed are three *further general principles* of the natural law price order which were already initially recognized by traditional natural law theory and today again are receiving attention among economists who are aware of the social end of economy. The first is the principle of *price elasticity*: the movement of prices to the natural level must not be prevented. Even in the static economy of the Middle Ages it was evident to the exponents of the natural law doctrine that new factors are perpetually arising on the side of supply and demand, for which the price mechanism must make room if the principle of the common good is to be realized. The just price, therefore, is not regarded as an exactly determined and fixed sum, but is thought of rather as

[2] Professor A. E. Napp-Zinn, "Gerechtigkeit in der Volkswirtschaft, eine sozialethische Betrachtung," in *Festschrift für Albert Stehr* (Jahrbuch für das Bistum Mainz), 1950, pp. 265 ff., opposes the views set down here, as already developed in *Sozialökonomik und Sozialethik* (1927); he upholds the view that the expenses of the producer must determine the amount of value he receives in his prices and that this is a postulate of justice. As a universal principle this would mean the end of any economic progress, without which there would not exist the means of subsistence for a growing population nor the necessary conditions for the fulfillment of growing social and cultural tasks. The fact that in cases such as Napp-Zinn discusses it may be necessary to take into account the cost situation in conjunction with other circumstances in determining the justice of *individual* prices is clear from what follows, as will be seen; but the general principle arrived at in the text above is obviously needed in order to evaluate the individual case. On the oversimplifying cost-principle in price theory, O. v. Zwiedineck-Südenhorst, "Einige Parerga zur Lehre vom Preis," in *Wirtschaftstheorie und Wirtschaftspolitik, Festschrift für Adolf Weber*, Alfred Kruse, editor, 1951, p. 351, says: "The once generally formulated assertion, 'Costs determine price,' has long been recognized as wholly inadequate and impracticable in face of the evident fact that the commodity which reaches the market and is offered for sale on a particular day has been produced at a great variety of costs."

pretium summum, medium, and *infimum*; and it can range, therefore, between the limits known today as the price margins, provided that the causes of differences in price lie in actual differences in the local and temporal, quantitative and qualitative, price-determining factors. Apart from exceptional cases, price agreements (by monopolies) which impede the movement toward the natural price are contrary to the price formation demanded by socio-economic productivity in the movement toward the natural prices of individual goods.

Another principle of natural law price order is that of *price stability*: the price level in general is to be assured, whereas only particular prices move in accordance with the principle of elasticity just mentioned. Natural law ethics is here guided by the idea that the market cannot fulfill its function in the service of socio-economic productivity if the uncertainty of prices makes reliable long-term calculation and planning impossible for the producers; it is also guided by the thought that, with the uncertainty of prices, many producers will be priced out of the market, with unemployment as the result. The principle of price stability, therefore, is contravened by price uncertainties due to speculation which distorts the actual relationship of supply and demand (e.g. forms of exchange speculation, land speculation), but especially by the general price uncertainty, which goes with concealed or open deflation or inflation. Price movements, which necessarily accompany economic progress and growth in the train of unceasing technical discoveries, must be subordinated to the social end of economy: such movement of prices must be gradual and not sudden (a notable example of the consequences of sudden technical progress was the distress among handweavers after the invention of the mechanical loom). The price stability discussed here is, as may be readily seen, something different from absolute price stability, which was made the supreme principle of price policy between the two World Wars and was pursued along with cartel and protective tariff policies with the result of lasting depression and mass unemployment.

What distinguishes the price doctrine of traditional natural law theory is that it comprehends the principles of price elasticity and price stability in their inner relationship, namely, as based on the third general principle of price justice—the social function of *ordered competition.* The regulation of competition was made possible in the static social economy of the Middle Ages, centered on the town, by the guild system. At the end of the era, the guild system, already in a state of torpor, was out-stripped by the dynamic economy animated by the progressive forces of modern enterprise and modern technology. A new realization of the principle of ordered competition in conformity with modern social economy is, as we shall see in our discussion of the ordering of the socio-economic process (cf. Chap. 181), the most urgent task in the endeavors to bring about a competition fully in harmony with the social end of economy or, what is the same thing, the market order postulated by this end. For if, as we have shown, the just price is the price appropriate to socio-economic productivity, then the surest means for bringing about price justice is free but ordered competition.

The following *particular principles* emerge: Because price formation is bound up with the social end of economy, *social justice* is the fundamental principle of price justice in the economy. The determining factor here is the twofold function of price in the ordered market economy; price distributes the social product, hence income, and, if issuing from competition, brings about the highest possible income level (living standard) by means of socio-economic productivity. Hence, the following principle arises: Normally the first task of price justice is not the calculation of price quantities and the fixing of prices, but the establishment of the order of competition and the market, so that the factors of supply and demand become generally effective. The fact that this should be aimed at is of special significance, because the justice of the individual price can be realized only in its relationship to all other prices, and hence to the price structure in general. When buying a pair of shoes one can compare the price asked with prices in other shops. Even so, shoe prices in general may be unjust; they may be too high if controlled by a monopoly, or too low if dumping from abroad causes undercutting. Again, the dependence of shoe prices on other prices extends into every branch of the economy. Leather prices (different grades) depend on cattle prices, cattle prices on land prices, land prices on grain prices (because of the varied possibilities of use of land), grain prices depend on costs of production of grain abroad, and so on; this is but one line of interconnected prices affecting a commodity. Similar lines lead from the prices of machines and tools used in footwear manufacture into every part of the socio-economic process. And from the wages and living costs of the producers (accommodation, food, clothing) a whole group of such lines radiates. Then there come the price margins according to place, time, quality, style. Only the market and competition can bring into play all these factors and their relevance in suppy and demand; statistical methods, however good, cannot ascertain these in any case, particularly because they are constantly in motion and therefore variable. Even if they were comprehended by the most perfect electronic brain they would in the very next moment no longer correspond with the facts; therefore, prices fixed by the authorities on the basis of these factors would be inconsistent with the requirements of social justice in the ordering of prices.[3]

[3] Medieval scholastic price ethics also had other very realistic reasons for rejecting price-fixing by authority and for relying on a monopoly-free competition; thus J. Höffner, *op. cit.*, pp. 199 ff.: 1) "Official price-regulation threatens to distort the *price-structure*," because any interference with the price-structure leads to interference at other points, whereas it is the duty of the state to eliminate monopolistic price usury. 2) "The system of price-regulation and other official encroachments threatens to lead to *administrative corruption*." 3) "Price-regulation leads to numerous illegalities and thus undermines respect for law"; the modern terms for these evils are black market, profiteering, and hoarding.

When it is a question of the price in the individual buying and selling transaction, the obligation of price justice is one of *commutative justice.* This is the "strict" justice which imposes an obligation of equivalence between service and recompense, and, in case of departure from such equivalence, prescribes restitution. Equivalence, accordingly, is the deciding factor. The following are the individual principles of commutative justice for commerce in goods and for the just price: 1) Prices in the open market may be taken by buyer and seller as the just prices at which they can buy and sell with a good conscience as long as they do not have reasons for presuming the contrary. It has always been a principle, firmly held by the traditional natural law school, that the presumption is in favor of the prevailing prices being just. This shows that they regarded price justice as completely bound up with the actual supply and demand conditions operating in the properly working market. 2) Reduced production costs justify selling at a lower price in order to increase turnover and profits. 3) Increasing the value of goods by improving the quality justifies an increase in price; this needs stating because today most competition takes the form of improvements in quality rather than reductions in price (although fundamentally there is an indirect reduction in price, viz., the same price for higher quality). 4) The exploitation of the momentary market situation in order to buy or sell more advantageously is justified as long as no speculative influence on the market is applied. A man who takes his vegetables to a neighboring town in order to profit by the higher prices consequent upon a temporary scarcity, does not offend against commutative justice; nor does anyone who draws moderate profit from the sale of worthless glass beads in Central Africa. In the former case there are special circumstances surrounding the actual relationship of supply and demand because of the momentary local shortage, in the latter because of the "general valuation" of the articles of adornment.[4]

We must now discuss *legal and distributive justice,* the functions of the state in the establishment of price justice. 1) From what has been said it may be gathered that the principal task of the state is its concern for ordered freedom of competition, and hence for the movement of prices toward the natural level implied in the social end of economy. 2) Even in case of necessary encroachments into price-formation processes when prices are forced up by monopolies, its most important task is not

[4] In view of the constantly recurring misunderstandings which result from an untenable "metaphysics of economy," we would point out that the great exponents of traditional natural law theory have always realistically seen that "economic value" is not identical with the "essential value" of a good, but that it is governed by its relationship to human need. Hence, says St. Augustine, *De civ. Dei,* Bk. XI, Chap. 16, a horse will fetch a higher price than a male slave, a precious stone will fetch a higher price than a female slave. Similarly, St. Thomas, *in Eth.* V, Lib. 9, says that every living thing has a higher intrinsic value than an inanimate thing; in economic dealings, however, the decisive factor is the utility value: "(Commutabilia) non enim appretiantur secundum dignitatem naturae ipsorum . . . sed rebus pretia imponuntur secundum quod homines indigent eis ad suum usum."

fixing prices but bringing about a state of competition (e.g., by reducing customs tariffs), which will make excessive prices impossible. 3) For reasons of economic policy, that is, to safeguard or augment the aggregate economic productivity in the present or the future, the state may be obliged to support prices. Industries may need their prices supported in the face of foreign competition, so that they may be able to meet the competition later on by improving productivity; the state can help in such cases by means of customs duties or subsidies. Such price support, however, is always at the expense of the community, which in these cases either pays higher prices for the goods protected by tariffs or contributes from revenue to the subsidies which keep prices down. It is, therefore, a question of price justice how far the state may go with such measures. If the same objectives can be attained by other means, such as credits or credit facilitation, direct price support measures cease to be just.

4) For reasons of social policy, the state may be obliged, as an exceptional measure, to exercise a lasting influence on portions of the price structure. Thus, the lowering of the cost of living by means of subsidies may be necessary for a time in order to create a just wage level. Even in this case, however, the purpose must be to take suitable steps to enable the economy itself to raise productivity, thus achieving a just wage level. 5) Direct price regulation by the state authorities can only be applied as an emergency measure when a just price formation is, for the time being, unattainable by other means. The authorities must always understand that fixed prices exert influence on supply and demand, and this means a serious lowering of price morality. Experience in and after the two World Wars clearly confirms this sociological law: supply is driven out of the open market and consequently the black market opens, which is always a real hotbed of usury.

6) It emerges clearly from our argument that the task of the state, by means of its economic policy, is to intervene against the distortion of the supply-demand relationship by speculators with their special profits which are not based on services to productivity. 7) On the other hand, special profits made by firms and based on productivity are the results of the natural movement of price and market. Therefore, it is not the business of the state to prevent them, but rather to carry out economic and fiscal policies favoring competition, thus tending to make them result in a more general price development on the cost principle, a development in which the firms in question are ahead.

Usury

The violation of price justice is one of the forms that usury assumes. Usury in general is the overreaching of others in economic exchange, that is, the appropriation of economic value without corresponding value being rendered in return. Thus, it is an infringement of equivalence in the exchange of goods, in wage conditions, and in credit business. Its most important manifestations, therefore, are price usury, wage usury, and interest usury. Because it is linked with the socio-economic process and market economy, usury is different from theft and normal fraud: usury is the appropriation of surplus value in the socio-economic process, whereas theft and fraud are not intrinsically connected with this process. An appropriation of surplus value by usury can be made by whole branches of the economy or by whole classes, because of power positions, at the expense of the rest of the economic community or other classes; in this case it is *social usury*. It can be carried out by individual persons or undertakings at the expense of one or more individual persons or undertakings, and it is then called *individual* usury.

Modern legislation, if it uses the expression usury at all, recognizes only individual usury and defines it usually as exploitation of the need or ignorance of others; it restricts this definition mainly to moneylending, and hence to excessive interest charges. Only one form of social usury has claimed the particular attention of the modern legislator, without, however, being called usury; this is price usury, insofar as it forms the object of monopoly legislation. Already in his encyclical *Rerum novarum* (1891), *Leo XIII* spoke about usury "in modern form," although sociology and social ethics did not come to grips with the problem in detail. Our distinction between social and individual usury is intended to do justice to the facts in question.

Social usury is an offence against social justice through the exploitation of a part of society by economically more powerful groups. It is the form of usury characteristic of the social economy which is distinguished by class power or the economic power of particular groups. The instrument of social usury is principally monopolistic power in its various forms, whether that of "capital" in wage bargaining by employers, price-fixing by cartels, the fixing of interest rates by financial institutions, or the monopolistic power of "labor" in the enforcement of wage claims disproportionate to the development of productivity. The vast extent of social usury in modern economy linked with powerful group interests does not, however, in any way diminish the significance of individual usury. In business between individuals, profit is too readily considered as justified merely because it involves no conflict with the criminal law; and in individual exchange or labor contracts which are not subject to regulated prices (repairs, "servicing" etc.), the criterion is all too often the maximum of profit with too little regard for honest dealing. It is another mark of the easy conscience in business dealings that the sense of a duty of restitution of what has unjustly been gained by such profiteering is almost entirely lost.

169. Wages

The wage is the contractual remuneration for labor service. The wage problem relates to dependent work which is carried out on the orders of an employer in accordance with a work contract. It includes not only manual labor, skilled, semiskilled (involving knowledge of few manipulations), or unskilled, the remuneration of which is called "wages" in the narrower sense, but also most categories of work that are performed for a salary. Two features characterize the nature of the labor relationship: dependent work (1) is participation in socio-economic cooperation; (2) it is performed in accordance with a labor contract between an employer and an employee. The consequences of this twofold character of employed labor are that its remuneration represents an income for the worker, but at the same time an element in costs for the employer. The two sides are inseparably linked: as an element in costs, labor is a factor of production for the employer, the value of which he must take into account on the basis of its productivity. But it is, on the other hand, upon this productivity that the size of the wage share in the output of the combined factors of production, the *suum* of labor, rests. We said that the employer must assess the value of the factor of production, labor, according to its productivity, for he must recover his labor costs from the prices realized by the sale of his goods. Ultimately, then, it is not the employer who judges of the productivity of the labor he employs, but the consumer who, by paying the prices demanded, gives a judgment on the productivity of the factors expended. Thus, wages are the price of labor as a factor of production; as long as they correspond to the productivity of the labor employed in a social economy which fulfills its purpose, it is the economically correct wage. It was necessary to begin by following up these socio-economic relationships because the working out of natural law principles of justice must always be guided by the nature of the facts.

The following emerges as the *supreme principle of wage justice:* The share in the output of socio-economic cooperation received in wages is just if it corresponds to the relative amount of work which goes into the attainment of the economic productivity appropriate to the social end of economy. This general principle indicates the intrinsic connection between the two principles of justice to which, in accordance with natural law, the just wage must conform. These are the principle of social justice and the principle of commutative justice (its demand: equivalence between service and remuneration). In both respects, the productivity of labor determines the ethically just wage: the productivity of labor in the economic process as a whole as a contribution to the general well-being, and the productivity of labor as part of the productivity of the single undertaking; the latter, like the former, is economically evaluated through the prices of the goods produced.

In reference to the individual aspects of the supreme principle set down above, these *general principles* emerge:

First, the full realization of wage justice presupposes *full employment*,[1]

[1] Full employment can never mean one hundred per cent employment or a complete absence of unemployment (certainly not the absence of unemployed registered at employment offices, since the figures of unemployed at the latter include those who are quite unwilling to work). Economic progress and expansion derive from ever-new combinations of the production factors—labor, natural resources, and capital; this involves, for a portion of the working population, a change of occupation and tem-

namely, that the productivity of labor with the means technically available in an economy is fully utilized. The end of social economy is obviously not fulfilled if a large part of the community does not participate in socio-economic cooperation; and the wage level of the employed must be reduced because of the diminished aggregate economic output. Hence, the employment of all who are willing to work in a social economy is a necessary condition for a wage system which is just in the full sense. Not to have seen this is one of the most serious errors of the classical economists. In fact, classical theory is obviously at odds with itself since, although regarding labor as the most valuable factor of production, it makes wages dependent on the process of capital investment in the social economy. The productivity of labor is dependent on the capital equipment of a social economy, but this itself depends on the productivity of labor, and hence also on the full employment of labor. The classical theory of wages and employment proceeds too much upon a conception of available capital as a given or static quantity, whereas economically the real problem is how to expand the capital foundation of the socio-economic process while making full use of labor as a factor of production. Therefore, classical theory has seen only one way of overcoming unemployment: the reduction of wages, which should set the capital factor in motion by cheapening the labor factor, that is, assuring capital of profits and thus offering an incentive to investment. The truth is that circumstances may demand (cf. Chap. 167) immobilized capital to be set in motion by the agency of credit in the economic process and full economic productivity to be aimed at.[2]

The second principle concerning the realization of wage justice, which is derived from our supreme principle, is that it is bound up with the *full productivity* of social economy. If this does not obtain, the actual average wage is too low.[3] Even then, of course, the question remains

porary unemployment. If boom conditions and full employment mean that such labor forces are not available for a long period, then the process of sound general economic advance is bound to be hindered.

[2] J. M. Keynes was the first to take the classical economists to task for the error we have mentioned above. But his own theory does not do justice to the essential end of social economy: he is more concerned with full employment than with a just wage based on productivity; he concerns himself, therefore, only with one side of the problem, giving also too much weight to the nominal wage (cf. note 12 below). Indeed, his theory of full employment has no real criterion for judging when a rise in wages, with its possible inflationary effects, is consistent with a real increase in productivity; just as the classical theory has no criterion for judging when wage reductions, with their possible deflationary effects, prejudice the social end of the economy.

[3] This is borne out by two facts mentioned by K. W. Rothschild, *The Theory of Wages,* 1954, pp. 162–70: (1) in the past the relative share of wages in the growing national income seems remarkably constant in view of the increasing power of the trade unions; (2) the wage share in the national income proves in the past to have been dependent on the degree of monopolization in economy. Rothschild observes that obviously there is no reason for supposing that this stability of the relative wage share in the past constitutes a "law" of capitalistic economy and must continue also in the future. In fact, the future development of the wage share depends upon the full de-

whether and how far better income distribution will result in an increase of wage incomes. Hardly anyone familiar with the elements of economic theory, however, today could maintain that justice is served by a mere measure of distribution with a lower economic productivity. On the whole, the sole means of achieving a higher wage income is the increasing of productivity. If the shortcoming in productivity is the fault of the owners of means of production (land and capital) as in countries inadequately developed industrially, measures of economic and fiscal policy can be used to influence the development of productivity; in case of resistance, it may be justifiable for the state temporarily to undertake administration of economic concerns. For highly industrialized economies our supreme principle yields this conclusion: just as full productivity cannot take place without full employment, full employment does not necessarily mean the full productivity of the social economy.[4] The productivity of labor itself depends on the relative degree of capital equipment, and hence on progressive capital formation; but it also depends on the will and capacity to work of the employed workpeople. If a wage policy inspired by supposed findings of the "new economics" leads to excessive wage increases which go beyond the limit set by socio-economic productivity, it conflicts with wage justice as much as does the policy of wage cuts based on "classical economics."

The reason is that the realization of wage justice is not just a question of the distribution of the current aggregate economic output, but also a question of making provision for future economic growth; *present and future* must be seen as inseparably linked. In no sphere is the common good implied in the existential ends merely a matter of the immediate present; it is at least equally a question of the conditions of future developments, especially those tasks arising from the growth of the population (the increasing need for consumer goods, schools, hospitals), from social policy (particularly provision for the aged in aging societies), and from the preservation of peace (armaments). Capital formation and capital investment for this very reason are a basic obligation of social justice, particularly when the expansion of productivity, owing to the prospective scarcity of labor forces because of the aging of the population, depends to a greater extent on the capital equipment of the national economy (automation). Along with the question of wage justice there is the problem of the *proportion between consumption rate and investment rate* in

velopment of socio-economic productivity, which in its turn depends on the full development of ordered competition and on the repression of monopolistic restrictions on competition, except for cases justified by the principle of productivity itself: thus, it is necessary to break the shackles of monopoly (on monopolies cf. Chap. 177).

[4] The following examples show that full employment does not mean full productivity: In the communistic economy of Soviet Russia there has been full employment for thirty years without socio-economic full productivity being achieved, as is shown by the relatively low wages; similarly, the English experiment in socialism has shown that such a connection does not exist (cf. J. Messner, *Das englische Experiment des Sozialismus,* pp. 31 ff.).

the employment of the aggregate economic output. How much can and should be devoted to capital investment and how much to immediate consumption certainly depends in part on the arbitrary will of society. A nation can, if the political and economic future is predictable, allow itself a considerable present consumption at the expense of capital formation, if it clearly understands that it is thereby forestalling a greater increase in future consumption, and hence a future rise in the standard of living. When wage incomes are low, their rise is desired, and political and economic conditions are stable, a relatively high rate of consumption may be just, although it results in a retarded rate of growth of socio-economic productivity. Conversely, the maintenance of a relatively low rate of consumption may be even a demand of justice, as in an underdeveloped country in which for weighty reasons a very rapid expansion of economic capacity must be attained. Then, only *a comprehensive national wage policy* aligned equally with present and future tasks conforms with the common good: the common good (and hence social justice) lays upon the economic groups the obligation to help to establish guiding maxims for such a national wage policy and to do their best in their own spheres to comply with them in their wage policy. Such guiding maxims of national wage policy must be established with the *cooperation of the economic groups,* the self-governing vocational bodies as well as the interest groups, since questions of balancing interests are to be solved particularly in the matter of price movement and price policy. *Ideas such as the following are gaining ground today*:

In a considerable number of countries today, there is discussion, in the realm of theory as well as of politics, of the idea of a comprehensive *national wage policy* with the cooperation of a joint economic organ. The pressing occasion for this is afforded by the constantly rising wage-price spiral and the consequent inflation. This idea has a twofold aspect: first, the movement of wages, prices, and all the factors which contribute to inflation (investment expenditure, wage and dividend policies) must be seen in terms of their mutual economic relationship; secondly, an organ consisting of members of the groups responsible for the movement of the factors in this reciprocal relationship is necessary for agreement on the guiding principles of such a comprehensive wage policy and on the corresponding attitude of the groups.

Considering the position of interest groups in liberal democracy one sees little prospect in a comprehensive wage policy. *Erich Arndt* remarks: "This collaboration may today seem Utopian; nevertheless, it is necessary. . . . A wage policy of the groups which ignores this fact must sooner or later provoke the intervention of the state." [5] *Arndt* points out that *Lloyd G. Reynolds* predicts that, in the United States, with a view to carrying out a national wage policy, the state will intervene in the collective agreement negotiations between employers and employees in the determination of a general wage-level.[6] Nevertheless, the hope should not be given up that finally the understanding

[5] E. Arndt, *Theoretische Grundlagen der Lohnpolitik,* 1957, p. 287.
[6] Cf. L. G. Reynolds, *Labor Economics and Labor Relations,* 1949, pp. 454 f.

of the necessity of agreement by democratic methods instead of the power struggle will prevail among the economic groups, and not least as a result of apprehension of the dangers which can arise for democracy through the penetration of the state into the sphere of collective agreement.

For, the intervention of the state at so vital a point in the economic system associated with liberal democracy would inevitably result in a progressive conversion to a system of dirigist planned economy. Obviously, if the state makes itself responsible for wages it must necessarily take measures in regard to all the factors which influence the purchasing power of wages, namely, the pattern of prices, interest rates, dividends, and the commodity, money, and capital markets. *Arndt* sees the necessary condition for a general wage policy in the formation of joint committees, in which cooperation would take on an institutional character and the representatives of bodies concerned with the labor market and agents of the state social and economic policies would be united in an atmosphere of mutual trust; there is no valid reason to suppose, he declares, that decisions on wage policy, which are so important to the national economy, cannot be taken in an atmosphere in which such committees let themselves be guided by the relevant facts, so that labor conflicts would be more and more avoided. The fact that the idea, in spite of all, is not Utopian is shown by the example of the long-term "peace settlements" in Switzerland.[7] It should be remembered that these ideas point to one of the fundamentals of traditional natural law thought: social justice in wage policy is a matter of weighing considerations which take into account all the relevant factors, and only committees consisting of representatives of all groups are competent to do this (cf. Chap. 181).

In the question of wage justice many points must be borne in mind concerning the relationship between consumption rate and investment rate, which we have discussed. First and foremost is the *stability of the value of the currency.* No wage policy based on justice could tamper with the stability of money, since this, being vital to the whole process of realizing the social end of economy, is the first precept of justice. Some other points call for special emphasis. In a country dependent on foreign markets, the working of competition must be taken into account, for the development of its wage incomes and its economic growth depend not least on its competitive capacity. Special attention is due to the condition of the technical apparatus of the economy; if it is obsolete owing to neglected investment or war destruction, then considerable renewal may be necessary. Other needs will be those concerning capital formation and investment, which arise from the growth of population. Those who regard "family policy" as a function of the state and society must not forget that for a growing population, if family incomes are to be in accord with the principles of family allowances for balancing family burdens, a corresponding growth of the economy is required, and this can take place only through a corresponding capital formation. But those who think that family planning (or "rationalizing") by means of birth restriction is the

[7] Cf. E. Arndt, *op. cit.,* pp. 289 f.

way to a higher standard of living are in error if they hope for a substantially higher present consumption with a reduction in capital formation; the resulting shortage of labor in the foreseeable future must, if the standard of living is to be maintained or raised, be balanced by machinery and automation, that is, by capital formation and investment. The world political situation is another factor not to be forgotten: the industrial nations of today have a grave responsibility, for reasons which need not be enlarged upon here, concerning the political, social, and economic fate of the peoples of underdeveloped countries. Rendering them the aid which they need presupposes the availability of enormous capital sums, which means a capital formation at the expense of increases in consumption. Therefore, obligations both of social and of international justice are involved, along with an obligation of self-preservation on the part of the nations of the West in the face of the opportunities and hopes which the communists see for themselves in the social and economic conditions of underdeveloped countries.

The principles hitherto discussed also determine the relationship between *needs and incomes,* which is appropriate for wage justice. The wage is income for the worker and an element in costs for the producer. The latter's expenditure in costs is decided by the market price of the goods produced. But the market prices decide also how far the recipient of income can meet his needs with his wage income. What are these needs? If they are described as material and cultural needs or, which is the same thing, as the economic and cultural minimum of existence, this is to use an intrinsically relative concept. Obviously, the average needs of the citizen of the United States are not the same as those of an average citizen of Japan. Hardly anyone would maintain that the needs to be satisfied in both countries are the same. Material needs depend on food customs, and cultural needs depend on cultural tradition, which can comprise much higher values than those which prevail in the cinema and in television. But, most important, average need is a relative quantity because the economic productivity of a country permits of nothing else; for, income cannot permanently exceed economic output. Consequently, the principle of need is not to be separated from the principle of efficiency; the latter like the former is a relative concept. In the first place the capacity and the will for efficiency are variable. If both are present to a high degree, however, the level of the efficiency remains dependent on capital equipment and on the productivity of labor, which is governed by this, and hence also the average wage income. With regard to the individual wage income, the productivity principle gives rise to a clear requirement of justice: higher efficiency is entitled to a wage remuneration, as its *suum,* as far as higher productivity is implied. From the point of view of "individual" ethics, this seems to be a logically inevitable principle, although today it is by no means regarded so, for under the influence of the equality principle and the majority principle, especially in European countries, the movement of wages for a long time has been biased in favor of the general workers. From a "social" ethics point of view, such a wage movement is no less objectionable, because the growth of productivity in the national economy depends quite fundamentally on the performance of work of higher value, and only if the pattern of incomes is adjusted to the services rendered can it secure the more valuable labor forces which are indispensable for an economy and its growth with regard both to productivity and incomes. Higher pay for higher services, therefore, is demanded equally by commutative and by social justice. A wage policy which goes against these requirements of justice and is guided too much by the equality principle, therefore, is prejudicial at a vital point to the growth of welfare in the national economy, which is dependent on the growth of productivity.

Summing up the principles discussed, we can use the expression *social wage* to describe the wage demanded by wage justice. This social wage is related to the social end of economy and to socio-economic productivity; it can also be called the family wage if it is the wage of a fully capable and willing workman. Another conclusion from the principles discussed is that the social wage, the maintenance of its purchasing power and growth, are primarily a matter of economic policy and not of a mere distribution policy. Again, the social wage, since it is essentially related to the growth of productivity, is not a fixed quantity. Nor is it a quantity exactly ascertainable by formula. Neither mathematical economic theory (econometrics, whose chief value is in the elucidation of complex relationships, although it has not succeeded in gaining any substantially new knowledge) nor socio-economic accountancy can offer any clues for the ascertainment of such a quantity.[8] In discussing price ethics we found also that the just price is not an exactly calculable quantity. The reasons stated there are applicable equally to the just wage: the essential factors consist entirely of variable quantities which not only are constantly changing but must be constantly changing in accordance with the dynamic nature of the social end of economy, both on the side of productivity and on the side of income, because of the indivisible interrelationships between them. Hence, automatically operating wage regulations are inconsistent with the principles of wage justice; thus the sliding wage scale [9] (index wage)

[8] Paul Jostock, *Die Berechnung des Volkseinkommens und ihr Erkenntniswert,* 1941, pp. 96 ff., comes to the conclusion, in regard to one of the factors indispensable for such a calculation—the annual percentage growth of the national income—that "here there is still much uncertainty, and pronouncements of universal application are still impossible." A particularly dubious aspect of income statistics, as applicable to the general accounting of the national economy, is revealed by the Swedish Professor Erik Lundberg, *Business Cycles and Economic Policy,* 1957: the various forms of price control (administrative prices) cause a disarrangement of the pattern of values in the economy with the result that only a relative validity is due to the statistical data in detail and in general.

[9] The experiment of the *sliding wage scale* in Australia has been instructive. According to the *Labour Report,* 1954, n. 43, and the *Year Book of the Commonwealth*

and the principle of the guaranteed annual wage, if by such is meant fixed wage sums irrespective of the trading position of the individual undertaking and the market situation in general.[10] (In Europe, ideas have even sprung up here and there according to which the "contractual" labor relationship would be replaced by a kind of civil servant relationship, with security of tenure, fixed income, and pension rights.)

A further general observation: The measure of economic productivity governing the social wage is only partly a question of the wealth of a country in natural resources. Of much greater importance is the willingness and skill of a people, provided that it has access to *world markets* and thus can offset its lack of natural resources (today, it is one of the most tragic questions of social and international justice that nations, especially economically underdeveloped ones, are cut off from such trading

---

of Australia, 1956, n. 42, edited by the Commonwealth Bureau of Census and Statistics, Canberra, the basic wage principle was already discussed in 1890. In 1907, for the first time an industrial court gave a decision on a minimum wage. In the same year the Commonwealth Court of Conciliation and Arbitration in its famous "Harvester Judgment" established the minimum wage for an unskilled workman with a family of five at £2.2.0 per week. In 1921, the system of automatic wage adjustments was introduced with a quarterly automatic adjustment to the price index, which was based on the movement of prices for food, clothing, rent of five rooms, light, fuel, travel costs, and tobacco. From 1911 to 1955 the price index figure rose from a basic 1,000 to 3.970, the nominal wages from 1,000 to 5,773 (in 1953 the minimum wage was £11.16.0), real wages from 1,000 to 1,454. This means an increase of almost fifty per cent in real wages in this period; in addition, in 1931 the working week was reduced to 44 hours, and in 1949 to 40 hours; unemployment on the average reached 3%–4%. In this period (1907–53) the Australian £ was devalued to almost a third of its former value. In face of the accelerating inflation, the Court of Conciliation and Arbitration suspended the system of automatic wage adjustment for the reason that it was undoubtedly a factor in hastening the rapid increase of prices in Australia, especially in the years 1951 and 1952. In 1951, the price index had risen from 2,589 to 3,124, in 1952 from 3,124 to 3,645. Therefore, one can justifiably speak of an acceleration of inflation as bound up with the system. If one compares the increase in real wages with that of other countries it becomes clear that the development of wages in Australia was by no means more favorable to the workers (in the industrial countries it amounted to fifty per cent or more on the average), but was purchased at the price of a severe inflation as a result of the index wage system. Discussion in Australia on the system, and particularly social-ethical discussion, is to a remarkable extent dominated by an exaggerated emphasis on the needs principle (on the part of the workers) and the capacity-to-pay principle (on the part of the employers). The wage index system has also been in force in New Zealand for some decades, and experience has been similar there; France also has had a wage index system for several years, whereby a rise in the price index by a certain number of points meant an automatic raising of minimum wages. An additional objection to such systems is that, although the workers are somewhat protected against an inflationary depreciation of income, other large groups, especially the middle classes, are seriously harmed, which is in obvious conflict with social justice.

[10] In discussions of the *annual wage system* introduced here and there in the United States, it is very often overlooked that, in this, the wage structure is not the main question at issue but the employment throughout the year of a large proportion of the workers in seasonal industries such as the automobile industry, which was, accordingly, compelled to alter its production plans so that the greater part of the overtime in the seasonal period vanished. Thus, more is heard today of guaranteed employment than of guaranteed annual wage.

opportunities and are thus denied the social wage which they should be capable of achieving).

To strive for the *greatest possible expansion of productivity* proves to be the first task if wages in a country are substantially lower than those of other countries. Social policy, then, is presented with important tasks, but the principal one, that which is connected with the growth of productivity, is a task of economic policy.

The *particular principles of justice* still remain to be discussed.

I *Social Justice*

From the foregoing there emerges as a general principle of social justice that the just share (the *suum*) of labor in the product of socio-economic cooperation, in the form of wages, is proportionate to the stage of development and the growth requirements of economic productivity. The twofold aspect of the principle of socio-economic productivity which this indicates points to a twofold aspect of social justice: the claim to a growing wage income and, at the same time, the limitation of this claim in accordance with the present and future tasks bound up with the growth of productivity and the social end of economy. The chief obligation of social justice in the question of wages lies with the parties to the collective agreement.[11] Everything that has been said previously on full employment and full productivity, on the stability of the value of money, on the conditions necessary for the growth of productivity and of the economy as demanded by the social end of economy, on the relationship of

[11] Regarding the widespread opinion that wage obligations resulting from collective agreements must eliminate all competition in the sphere of work and wages, Bernard Pfister, "Die Gefährdung der Marktwirtschaft in der Vollbeschäftigung," in *Die Aussprache* (Bonn), October, 1956, pp. 182 ff., draws attention to the following facts: "Trade union rates are minimum wage rates, and labor agreements can be variously adjusted, either upwards or downwards. The fact that trade union rates are minimum wage rates has brought it about that in the structure of fixed wage rates efficiency wage rates have been developed. And hence, because of these, the competitive element operates alongside these agreements: the efficiency wage, which to a quite large extent contains genuine elements of competition; it sets in motion with increased strength personal capacities, personal effort, and personal achievements." Pfister gives evidence to show that, with a uniform fixed wage the difference between individuals in productivity reaches thirty per cent: "These differences make the desire of the workers for differential rates based equitably on efficiency understandable and clear. Competitive wages and factory social services have now induced a certain feeling of weakness in the trade unions, and their answer to this feeling was and is the demand for the forty-hour week." The introduction of the forty-hour week means, says Pfister, that overtime pay begins from the forty-first hour, and "it is understandable today that workers ask for overtime, since they have become very consumption-conscious and wish to make use of extra earnings to rise to a higher level of consumption. This is one of the *decisive revolutions* of the present time. The possessor of a motor-scooter or a small car, new or second-hand, is in the long run outside the reach of class war infection! He has now something to lose! The political effects of this are among the crucial facts in the *social revolution* in the midst of which we now find ourselves."

consumption rate and investment rate, on the quantitative relationship between needs and efficiency, is comprised in this general principle of social justice. Four aspects of social justice in the wage question are to be emphasized:

1. The question of social justice is concerned chiefly with the *wage structure* of the economy as a whole, since wages in their entirety distribute the share of the social product accruing to the labor factor of production. Excessive wages in particular branches of industry may have the effect of too low a wage level in dependent branches of industry, which may have to reckon with excessive prices for their instruments of production or raw materials. Excessive wages may occur in sectors of the economy as a result of comparatively strong trade union organizations, which can secure special advantages, or as a result of excessive monopolistic prices, in which the employers give the workers a vested interest by means of higher wages. In their wage policy, then, the individual groups of workers should take account of the claims of other groups affected.

2. As elements in production costs, wages influence the price level and the price structure of the whole social economy; hence, the level of purchasing power of incomes in general, including the *real wages* of the workers (the purchasing power of wages), is influenced. Individual groups of workers who obtain a lead in wage increases may gain temporary advantages at the expense of consumers in general, including therefore the other groups of workers. But when the general level of prices rises, the wage and price curves approximate each other and increases in money wages then signify only a transitory increase in real wages. If such a wage policy oversteps the limits set by the growth of productivity it is bound to produce inflationary effects and then offends against social justice in two directions: on the one hand because monetary stability is a basic requirement of social justice; and on the other hand because in this way special advantages are being secured for particular groups to the disadvantage of organizationally weaker groups of workers and of sections of the population dependent on fixed incomes. The real wage, related to the development of productivity and monetary stability, must, therefore, from both the economic and the ethical points of view, serve as the standard for wage policy. This is obviously in the interest of the workers themselves.[12]

3. Socio-economic productivity and the associated full employment are essentially a matter of economic cooperation in general; hence, the social end of economy and social justice are satisfied only if all have a proportionate share in increased output, not only those who are at present employed but also those who have contributed in the past to the creation of conditions for the current economic productivity (and now living on old-

[12] Neither his theory nor the consequences of the wage policy influenced by it have provided proof that, as Keynes says, *The General Theory of Employment, Interest, and Money,* 1946, pp. 14 f., the workers themselves are so much "more reasonable economists than the classical school," for the reason that they are so much more concerned with money wages than with real wages.

age pensions). This *general participation* in the growth of socio-economic productivity is possible only if the increase of productivity in individual branches of the economy leads to reduction of prices and thus to the raising of the purchasing power of incomes. It constitutes the only sure way to a general raising of real wages and of the aggregate living standard of society. This does not mean that increased productivity in a branch of the economy, particularly when it is the result of greater efforts by the workers, cannot benefit them in the form of increased shares in the output. In the event of higher yields from undertakings in certain branches of the economy, due not to services performed but to market conditions (e.g., reductions in raw material prices, a temporary seller's market for finished goods abroad), there is not necessarily a claim in justice to higher wages, because such profits are part of the risk element of enterprise, and trade fluctuations may bring about an opposite trend.

4. Since the factors determining the wage which conforms with social justice are so complex, their individual ramifications so difficult to assess, and since they are nevertheless always linked in general with the social end of economy, wage policy cannot be the concern of the individual branch of economy of an employers' association or a trade union. Every wage movement in the individual branch of the economy concerns the economy as a whole, its price structure and wage structure, the movement of money value and the capital market situation, and, along with all this, the present and the future. The *national wage policy in general,* aiming at a wage structure as postulated by social justice but also taking into account the other (political, cultural, economic) common weal requirements, falls within the competence, as we have seen, of committees for working out principles of a national wage policy, as an organ comprising all groups of the national economy in association with a supreme economic council and giving an equal say to employers and employees.

11 *Commutative Justice*

The principle of commutative justice, of the equivalence between service and reward, chiefly concerns the agreed wage and the agreed work. The following aspects of commutative or contractual justice in regard to wages are of special importance:

1. The labor contract is a two-sided contract whereby wage level and nature of work are today agreed mainly through the collective agreement, whereas it is the individual labor contract which gives effect to the obligation to work and the entitlement to wages applicable to a particular rate group of the collective agreement. The *contract commits both parties,* the employer to pay the agreed wage and the worker to perform the agreed work. Thus, the principle of equivalence can be violated by either partner, by the employer in not paying the agreed rates or in demanding services not provided for in the agreements, by the worker

through bad work or restrictive practices; the latter may be the result of working to rule sometimes maintained by the trade unions or may be intended to make the work last longer (as in road making, building, or other trades where work is hard to oversee). Since the labor contract falls within the sphere of "strict justice," it involves the duty of restitution of services withheld.

2. Even though work and wage conditions are decided by collective agreement, it still remains possible to take account of the favorable or unfavorable trading situation of the particular undertaking in fixing the pattern of wages. Consideration of the *situation of the individual undertaking* may call for concessions on the part of the employer in regard to wages, and not only the employer but also the employee. Assessment of the conditions and extent of such obligations, where obligations of commutative justice exist, is generally very difficult. In the event of unfavorable trading due to external circumstances, wage claims in accordance with contract remain in force, but the continuance of the undertaking may call for temporary sacrifices, and here the consent of the personnel is indispensable (in every country, when a company goes bankrupt, wage claims have first call on the assets). If special efforts by the workers result in a specially favorable position for a business, they should, in most cases in accordance with special agreements, receive a share in the distributed profits [13] as a matter of "strict" justice.

3. Since the possibility of fluctuations in business constitutes the main part of the *risk* involved in the entrepreneurial function, the entrepreneurs have a right to compensation for risk for an extended period. The workers, for their part, have a corresponding right that firms shall not seek to offset loss of earnings by dismissals of workers or by reduction of working hours, as long as this is not unavoidable owing to the economic situation of the business. As distinct from participation in the risks of business it is in the interest of social economy and of the working people that there should be long-term stability of wages with a raising of the purchasing power of wages by price reductions or by improvements in the quality of goods, accompanied by security of employment.

4. Since the labor contract is a contract of services, although not to be separated from the bond of solidarity in the employer-employee relationship, obligations can arise which have not been the subject of explicit contractual agreements. By the nature of this bond its sphere is the in-

[13] The trade unions insist partly, in both directions, on a rigid policy of fixed wage rates, which is hard to reconcile with commutative justice. They are more willing to accept the dismissal of some of the workers than wage reductions, which a great number of employees would be ready to accept in order to insure continuance of employment for all. Certainly there are employers who would be willing to exploit the possibility of departing from the union wage. But in all such questions there are individual cases which must be examined as such in order that justice may then be satisfied. There are also well-known cases in which the trade union, at the instigation of a section of employees, prevents a productive effort going beyond the "norm," and hence prevents the corresponding higher wage claim.

dividual factory or the individual undertaking, and not the branch of industry or an overall organization. Such obligations may include within their sphere benefits of a business concern as, for instance, profit sharing, which correspond rather to requirements of equity than to those of justice in the true sense. Justice is violated, however, when organizations such as employers' associations or trade unions harm the factory personnel by opposing such participation; this can also occur when the demand is made for it to be governed by collective agreement, for profit sharing, which goes beyond the agreed wage, is dependent upon the profit situation of the particular undertaking and the risk compensation already mentioned; hence the decision about these matters belongs essentially to the entrepreneurial function. The forms of industrial social policy and of voluntary social benefits are those which in the majority of cases comply best with the aforesaid actual duty of solidarity (the employees, therefore, if possible, having their say with regard to the use of that which the individual undertaking can spare out of its extra profits; cf. Chap. 173).

III *Legal and Distributive Justice*

The state is only exceptionally obliged by principles of legal and distributive justice to intervene *directly* in wage settlement in order to bring about wage justice. In liberal democratic countries the government has no such opportunity; it would mean an encroachment on the freedom of action of the parties to the collective agreement, which they would not be willing to tolerate. Nevertheless, tasks of great moment fall upon the state in which it can exercise *indirect* influence. These are chiefly three: the economic task of creating the conditions for wage justice, that is, an economic policy of full employment and full productivity; the social task of labor legislation and of exercising influence on the distribution of income and property (with special regard for the lower income groups of workers), chiefly through fiscal measures; finally, the task of bringing about the organizational conditions for a national wage policy, to be worked out by an organ of a supreme economic council, with authority to act as adviser on wage policy in the individual branches of the economy.

IV *The Relationship of the Various Principles of Wage Justice to One Another*

When wage justice is lacking, one or the other or several species of justice may be infringed. This may be shown by a few examples. If collective agreements or extra contract exist, commutative justice is violated when employers or employees do not keep to the agreed terms. In collective negotiations the one party or the other offends against social justice if it puts forward or, alternatively, rejects wage claims inconsistently with the requirements of the social end of economy and the productivity principle; in either case, might is being put before right. Just as commutative or social justice is violated, wage usury (cf. Chap. 168) can be individual or social usury. If the state has established minimum wages (basic wage in Australia generally; in other countries for out work), any failure to honor these on the part of the employer is a violation not only of legal justice but also of commutative justice, involving a duty of restitution.

Wage-movement and Trade Union Power

In the discussion of wage justice, as we have seen, social ethics is involved with a considerable number of principles. From the point of view of the social end of economy, which is an essential part of the common good, the end of society, *socio-economic productivity* becomes the principle and criterion of the social justice of the wage share in the aggregate yield of socio-economic cooperation ("economic output," "national income"). Regarding the relevant aspects of the "nature of the facts," social ethicists must consult political economy and economic theory. With the strengthening of the trade union movement in the early twentieth century, a vigorous debate broke out among economists on the question concerning what the organized workers with their unquestionable power can achieve in the wage movement. A decisive contribution was made to this discussion by *Adolf Weber* with his book, which has long been recognized as *the* work on this question.[14] Few other economists can claim so unique a victory in such a long-drawn-out debate. In the latest evolution of wage theory, the productivity principle occupies the central position which *Weber* had always been demanding for it. Two of the most important recent works on wage theory may be mentioned, a German and an English one. In his theoretical principles of wage policy, *Erich Arndt* declares that "all efforts toward an increase of the real wage are not to be aimed at the problem from the angle of the nominal wage; rather, the problem has to be approached from the angle of the determinants of the net marginal product of labor, among which the clear pre-eminence in this connection belongs to productivity. It is not by gazing spellbound at the nominal wage and pushing it upwards that the living standard of the working people can be raised, but only by common effort to increase the productivity of the whole economy." [15] To social ethics, the productivity principle means not only the limit of successful wage policy but also a permanent task; for this reason we said that the wholly just wage presupposes full productivity of the social economy. Economic theory says the same thing in its own way: like *A. Weber* before him, *Arndt* states that "every wage policy must be fitted into the great aims of the state economic and social policies"; it is universally agreed among economists that these aims are comprehended in national welfare. The productivity principle also occupies a central place in the important book by *K. W. Rothschild* previously mentioned: the

[14] Cf. Adolf Weber, *Der Kampf zwischen Kapital und Arbeit,* 1st ed., 1910, 6th ed., 1954.

[15] E. Arndt, *Theoretische Grundlagen der Lohnpolitik,* 1957, pp. 286, 290.

whole question of labor's bargaining power, he holds, is reduced to the question of how far it can make inroads into capitalistic consumption without endangering the capital formation on which labor's own productivity and income depend; as species of capital income he mentions rent, interest and profits. Only if cuts on the consumer side succeed in the direction mentioned can trade union policy prosper, according to *Rothschild,* and the higher wage levels reached remain permanent, but not if they are accompanied by cuts on the investment side. With today's technical progress and the associated growth of national income he sees opportunities for an increase in wages at the expense of consumption, which is based on capital income; he again emphasizes, however, that the struggle for higher wages can succeed by slowing down the increase of consumption only from capital income when the growth of investment and, in consequence, labor's productivity is not seriously affected.[16]

The Right to the Full Product of Labor

The "right to the full product of labor" is the natural correlate of a rejection of "unearned income," that is, of income which is a return on privately owned capital. This alleged right forms the fundamental juristic-economic idea of the whole of modern socialism; it is to be realized by the socialization of the means of production, which precludes income from private property put to use in the economy. The right to the full product of labor was first advocated in England before the end of the eighteenth century by *William Godwin,* and in the 1820's by *William Thompson.* Of the latter *Menger* says, in his account of the development of the idea of this right,[17] that all later exponents of the idea, the *Saint-Simonists, Proudhon,* and *Marx* himself, came directly or indirectly under his influence. In his work the theory of labor value, which attributes the exchange value of goods exclusively to labor, is found already. All modern socialistic thinking, particularly that of *Marx,* uses the theory of labor value as support for the right to the full product of labor and the demand to socialize the means of production in order to abolish income from capital. Such a claim to the full product of labor has no justification as soon as it is admitted that capital goods contribute toward the productivity of the socio-economic process and that the private ownership principle is a principle of social and economic order. For then it is clear that the owner of capital goods has a right to a corresponding share in the output of production, especially by reason of the right of property, which implies the right to the enjoyment of its fruits. From what has been said about the just wage, however, it is equally certain that a right to the full product of labor does exist to the extent to which the output of production is the output of labor and is not the result of other factors of production (entrepreneur's services, capital, land).

Profit Sharing

Profit sharing can be thought of as surplus-sharing, if a higher yield is brought about through special efforts of the workers. These may take the form of in-

[16] Cf. K. W. Rothschild, *The Theory of Wages,* 1954, pp. 110–15.

[17] Cf. A. Menger, *Das Recht auf den vollen Arbeitsertrag,* 1886; Engl. trans. by E. Tanner, *The Right to the Whole Produce of Labour,* 1899.

creased output or economy in material and labor costs. The greatest possible extension of profit sharing systems on these principles is equally implied in the social end of economy and in the lasting interest of the workers, because they are guided by the productivity principle and represent an ideal way of increasing labor income. From these two reasons it follows as a *general principle* that *profit sharing so related to effort and efficiency* forms a fundamental object of social reform. According to "the nature of the facts," profit sharing schemes of this kind must vary in accordance with the relevant existing conditions in the *individual undertaking*.

Attempts to prove in addition that, *without such qualifications,* a universal principle of profit sharing by the workers is a principle of justice are faced with the fact that not all undertakings are capable of earning profits which permit of payments to the workers over and above wages. If they all were in such a position, social justice would demand a corresponding general increase in wages. As it is, however, social justice demands in the first place that higher yields resulting from socio-economic factors (and not from special efforts within the undertakings concerned) should benefit all members of society and groups of workers in the form of price reductions and resultant increases in incomes and wages. In terms of economics, groups of workers who benefit from profit sharing in more prosperous undertakings would, in comparison with other groups, become recipients of rent-income by reason of the fact that they have better positions; a large proportion of workers, however, are compelled to work in undertakings whose output does no more than keep them going; another portion are perhaps thrown upon unemployment relief.

We must not overlook the effect of a general principle of profit sharing on the *structure of society:* since big concerns are generally in a position to attain relatively much higher profits, the effect would be a ready influx of labor to the bigger firms, and hence opportunities for their expansion, which is undesirable on many grounds (cf. Chap. 185). The duty of solidarity among the various groups of workers, which is in this case also an obligation of social justice, supports the idea that increased productivity and increased output should benefit the workers by way of price reductions. Indeed, it is an essential part of the social function of the market to bring about by competition a reduction of production costs to marginal costs, and hence a reduction of prices and a general raising of incomes. Only a higher productivity based on special efforts and efficiency confers a title to special income, whereas in social justice all members of the social economy are entitled to their share in the output of an increase in productivity resulting from socio-economic factors.

These reservations about an inappropriate extension of the profit sharing principle are wholly different in kind from those put forward on the part of the trade unions. Trade union objections derive from apprehensions that profit sharing may have the effect of making the workers dependent on the factory and weakening the trade union movement. (On co-ownership cf. Chap. 171.)

170. Interest

Capital interest is the price for the use of capital. Attempts to explain interest by saying that it is simply a recompense for "saving" ("abstinence" from consumption), or for "waiting," provide only half an explanation. No fruitful result is produced by abstinence and waiting in themselves, but only by the investment of the resources saved in the socio-economic process. For the sake of the expected higher output, *a price,* interest, is paid for the scarce factor of production, capital. But a distinction is necessary even with the productivity theory of interest. Not every major yield resulting from the use of capital signifies in itself socio-economic productivity; it can simply mean higher technical productivity (cf. Chap. 164). Whether economic productivity exists is decided by the sale of the goods manufactured with the capital. Thus, the production costs incurred as capital must be recovered from the selling prices of the goods. If they are not recovered, the capital invested in technical equipment goes to waste. Thus, it is the application of capital demanded by socio-economic productivity that justifies interest as price. Because the entrepreneur is compelled by the selling price of goods to apply capital in accordance with the principle of "socio-economically necessary costs," interest as price directs capital to the appropriate point in the economic process.[1] Interest, therefore, is the indispensable instrument of economic calculation (cf. Chap. 166) in the service of socio-economic productivity for the industrial society dependent on the use of capital.

The analysis of the interest problem, as of any phenomenon of the socio-economic process, can begin only with a simplification of the complex relationships. Such simplifications are justified provided that they do not disregard fundamental facts or proceed from false assumptions. The operation of the function of interest may be subject to serious disturbances. But this does not affect the establishment of its essential function. It is one of the fundamental tasks of economics, social ethics, and social reform to study the normal functioning of the socio-economic organism. Only such a procedure makes it possible to see how this organism can be brought to perform its functions adequately. Thus, we have had to concern ourselves with discovering the grounds on which "pure" interest is to be explained as the equivalent of the productivity dependent on capital, and hence with finding the starting point for a *natural law appraisal of interest.* From the point of view of social ethics, it is the nature of the facts, objective reality (cf. Chap. 3), that decides whether social or economic institutions conform with the pattern implicit in natural law principles. We have seen from the nature of the facts that there is a twofold socio-economic function of interest: it promotes capital formation and it guides the use of capital. Hence, it is justified in social ethics. This, however, implies nothing concerning the *raison d'être* of private income from interest. The answer to this second question depends upon the social function and ethical justification of private ownership of the means of production, with which we shall deal later (cf. Chap. 171).

[1] It is perhaps one of the most serious objections to Keynes' theory that it misses the function of directing capital in the socio-economic process, which is exercised by interest as the price for the use of capital.

When the ethical justification of interest is granted, the crucial question in the ethics of interest is: What *rate of interest* is just? Since interest is the price for the use of capital, the general principles of price justice apply: interest is just when it corresponds to the undistorted relationship between capital supply and capital demand, namely, the actual scarcity relationships. The need for capital, which is expressed in *demand,* depends upon circumstances such as population movement (with the ensuing need for new housing, schools, hospitals, etc.); upon the strength of the general desire for a higher standard of living; upon the need for extending public services (transport, roads, sources of power); upon the need for technical equipment in the various branches of industry; upon the progress of technology (automation); upon confidence in future development (from political as well as other points of view); upon the need for reconstruction after war or natural catastrophes; upon the changing pattern of wants; upon fashion; upon the population's willingness to spend and the consequent volume of effective demand; upon the extent of new investment opportunities associated with a more or less buoyant or retarding condition of the business cycle. The *supply* of capital is governed by savings activity; by state fiscal policy (the restrictive effect of excessive taxes on income, output and profits); by the desire for securities (the hoarding of gold, cash, etc.); by the extent of new capital formation out of the available capital; by the self-financing policies of firms and, linked with this, their dividend and depreciation policies; by the building up of funds by the social insurance institutions out of compulsory contributions; by the movement of purchasing power in consequence of monetary and credit policy; by the structure of incomes and the saving and spending habits associated with particular classes; and especially by the willingness to take risks in putting down capital (risk capital is of crucial importance for economic progress).

Since, in the price formation process, all the factors of supply and demand in the whole social economy achieve uniform operation, interest is fundamentally a uniform phenomenon. Just as with other prices, this does not rule out the setting up of sectional markets by reason of special conditions of capital demand and supply, and therefore variations in the level of interest for agricultural credit, industrial credit, commercial credit, financial credit, government credit. The uniformity of capital interest also does not exclude the conjunction of the price for the use of capital with other price elements, for instance, with the price for risk-taking in capital investment or with the price for an entrepreneur's services. Capital profit and the entrepreneur's profit, therefore, are to be distinguished from "pure" interest.

In fact, "pure" interest is always linked with *other price-formation factors.* Thus, the rates of interest at which banks issue credits contain a number of elements of the bank's costs. These include: (1) the bank's prime costs (buildings, furniture and equipment, salaries); (2) liquidity costs (holding cash in readiness for repayments on demand); (3) capital costs (the payment of interest on their own capital, profits to shareholders; (4) risk costs (the building up of reserves to counterbalance irrecoverable credits). Pure interest, therefore, does not present itself as such in the capital market. The nearest approach to it is the *interest rate of the central bank,* which is based on exact observation of all market factors and is fixed as discount rate for credits extended to banks and for first-class bills of exchange. But even this discount rate is charged with cost elements.

If the just interest is thus the price for the use of capital, determined by the factors of supply and demand on the capital market, interest justice is a question of *ordering the capital market.* On the factors of capital supply and capital demand depends the movement of the price for the use of capital to the level corresponding to the social end of economy, and therefore interest justice. If the medieval natural law theory of interest considered the ethics of the question from the point of view of the essence and function of money in accordance with the position of money in the economy of that time, the conditions have changed owing to the present-day potential capital quality of money; yet, economists are again aware even today how much depends on the money quality of capital.[2] Money obviously possesses an intermediate status in the capital market: both on the supply and on the demand side of the capital market the volume of money entering the economic process exercises an expansive or a restrictive effect.[3] The intermediary role of money in the capital market further makes it possible that the investment risk can be separated from money capital. Money capital can be used to purchase safe securities

[2] Keynes, *The General Theory,* pp. 182 f., is certainly touching on an essential lack in the classical theory when he points out that it disregards the inner connection between the theory of value and the theory of money and that, in the question of the interest rate, it accordingly attaches insufficient importance to the factors operating on the money side. Keynes himself, however, sees the problem of interest only in the money perspective: to him interest is only the price which equilibrates the desire to hold wealth in the form of cash with the available quantity of cash (*ibid.,* p. 167); hence, essentially it is a compensation for parting with the liquidity which belongs to money as distinct from other goods. In fact, the means of supplying needs are always scarce in comparison with the needs; the same is true (with a stable currency) of money for the acquisition of the scarce capital goods which are necessary for the better supplying of needs, with the result that a price, namely interest, is formed for money capital.

[3] Keynes' general theory rests on the role played in this by, among other factors, the liquidity preference, lack of willingness to invest, lack of disposition toward consumer spending (cf. *ibid.,* pp. 166 ff., 183 f.). In his critique of the "classical theory" he points out that it proceeds from the erroneous assumption that saving automatically means investment on the ground that money always strives for fructification. His own economic psychology, however, is based exclusively on the consumption aspect, whereas the real motive forces of modern social economy are to be found, under normal conditions, in the desire for enterprise and profit; this is a side of economic psychology which has received no thorough treatment except in the work of F. v. Degenfeld-Schonburg, *Die Motive des volkswirtschaftlichen Handelns und der deutsche Marxismus,* 1920.

bearing assured yields (debentures, etc.) instead of being invested with participation in risk (industrial shares or private business). In the former case, debts arise on the part of the productive economy which are bound up with a rigid debt-service regardless of the actual yield of economic enterprise and which, therefore, can exercise a disadvantageous effect on the development of productivity. This fact induced *Adam Smith* to advocate a suitable application of usury laws.[4]

Far-reaching disturbances of the order of the capital market can also originate from *monopolistic tendencies* on the two sides of the capital market. On the supply side, finance capital, because of its monopolistic position, is able to strengthen by means of credit policy the influences which the money side exerts on the capital market. On the demand side of the capital market, the monopoly tendencies in industry (cartels) and in trade (price-fixing) have strongly inhibiting effects. They restrict competition, opportunities of capital investment in branches of production, and indeed, owing to their long-range effects, throughout the whole of social economy. These effects can reach so far that even an abnormally low rate of interest cannot stimulate capital demand; such was the experience between the two World Wars. Here lay a principal cause of the alleged excessive saving;[5] it consisted of hindrances to capital investment, and hence to capital demand, brought about by contractions of the market in the train of monopolistic restrictions on competition in industry and trade.

The *state* has vital functions to perform if the capital market and the fixing of interest rates are to be patterned on the social end of economy. First, it must not counteract the development of a capital market capable of functioning in this sense. It does this when it makes use of the capital market for its own investment purposes at uneconomic interest rates by means of big loans which are favored by taxation and in other ways. The same is true of a similarly constituted loan policy on the part of regional and municipal communities. On the supply side, the state works against the development of an efficient capital market by over-taxation of the principal sources of capital formation, namely, capital yields (double taxation: on business profits and on dividends). A well-ordered pattern of the capital market and of interest rates is furthermore impaired when business profits are not, to a relatively large extent, passed on to the shareholders, but are ploughed back into the business for self-financing purposes (cf. Chap. 182). If the state promotes self-financing by means of tax concessions, the capital market is deprived of substantial sums and the development of a rate of interest indispensable for its functioning and corresponding to the actual market situation is gravely hampered. The

[4] Cf. A. Smith, *Wealth of Nations,* Bk. II, Chap. 4; J. M. Keynes, *op. cit.,* p. 352.

[5] Were Keynes' theory of excessive saving not open to question on other grounds it would be for the reason that he neglects the organizational factors in the powerful monopolistic restriction of investment opportunities mentioned above and ascribes exclusively to psychological causes the lack of willingness to invest.

effect of overtaxation is quite generally detrimental if the state thereby accumulates surpluses which tax justice would forbid it to take from enterprise (cf. Chap. 148). This is true for two reasons: first, because it should receive from taxation only what is necessary for the fulfillment of its functions (and hence should accumulate no surpluses); secondly, because it goes against its supreme principle, the common good, if it weakens instead of strengthening an organ so important for the social end of economy as the capital market. From this criticism of state action, it may be seen what are its proper tasks with regard to the order of the capital market and with regard to the formation of the interest rate. In addition, precautionary measures will be necessary in order to render harmless economically inexpedient speculation on the capital market, a matter which must be treated in connection with the Exchange (cf. Chap. 179).

In an economy aiming at the expansion of economy and welfare, special attention must be devoted to promoting the investment of *risk capital:* the goal should be to discourage the pure *rentier* type, who is solely concerned with securing his capital and profits, in favor of capital investments which share in the risk of the socio-economic process. This can be brought about only if risk capital is offered the attraction of an appropriate profit, which is necessary for the sake of its function in the interest of economic growth and prosperity. The capital market, which is efficient according to the criterion of the social end, must, in the evolution of interest, on the whole express the scarcity conditions in the capital market, and especially if the economically correct and ethically justified interest is relatively high. But risk capital must be able to have confidence that its yields, even comparatively high ones, will not be annihilated by inordinate taxation; for a national economy aiming at economic growth and prosperity this would be all the more reprehensible since these very profits would mostly flow back into capital formation and the capital market. The fact that in medieval scholastic thinking the function of risk capital and the justification of its appropriate interest yields was a central point in its interest theory will be seen from the two sections which immediately follow.

The Church and Usury

Profit resulting from a loan agreement, the object of which is a "fungible" thing (*res fungibilis*), is usury, and therefore is unjust: this is what the traditional natural law theory has said consistently from the time of the Fathers until today in the Code of Canon Law (cf. Can. 1534). A fungible good is one which is measurable in quantity and quality, is consumed in use and cannot, therefore, be used fruitfully; hence if it is borrowed, it is to be restored only in quantity and kind; for instance, a loaf of bread. Appealing to this traditional teaching on usury, writers, since the beginnings of modern capitalist economy, have repeatedly insisted that interest on capital is, according to the doctrine of the Church, necessarily and always usury and that, therefore, capitalistic economy is essentially a usurious economy. The reasoning is that capital is money, and this is a "fungible" thing, serving only as a medium of exchange; hence, it is intrinsically unfruitful. A decision on the question seems intended in the encyclical *Quadragesimo Anno* (1931). In the German-speaking countries, after the appearance of the encyclical *Rerum novarum* (1891), the opponents of the moral justification of interest maintained that in the sentence, *non res sine operâ nec sine re potest opera consistere,* the word *res* was not to be translated "capital," thus insisting on the "unfruitfulness" of money as a claim to capital. In the Latin text of *Quadragesimo Anno,* however, the word *capitale* is appended in brackets to the word *res* in the heading of the section on "capital and labor," obviously implying money capital with its claim to a share in the product of the cooperation of capital and labor.

In fact, the traditional natural law teaching has always recognized the justification of genuine interest rooted in the productivity of capital in its doctrine of "titles to interest," that is, grounds on which compensation is justifiable in case of a money loan. One of these was *damnum emergens* (loss actually incurred). Its significance can be shown by an illustration. If a man has a store of grain lying unused in a granary and gives some of it as a loan, later receiving back the same quantity and quality, he is, according to the traditional usury teaching, entitled to no compensation; if, however, he lends a quantity which he would otherwise have used for sowing, the right to compensation is allowed him. Besides, *lucrum cessans* (profit lost on forgoing investment of money in one's own undertaking or that of others, e.g., in an overseas trading company) was also a chief title to interest. The two titles to interest which we have mentioned indicate a direct connection with the productivity of capital; only an indirect connection appears in the other two current titles to interest: *periculum sortis* (special risk of nonrecovery of the money lent) and *poena conventionalis* (specially agreed penalty in case of delayed repayment).[6]

Reappraisal of the Medieval Scholastic Theory of Interest

Whereas the interest theory of the medieval natural law school was the object of vigorous criticism in the nineteenth century on the part of liberalist economic theory, the social sciences later produced an altogether different judgment. *W. Sombart* writes: "The very simple formula in which ecclesiastical authority expressed its attitude to the question of profit making is this: Interest on a pure money loan, in any form, is forbidden; profit on capital, in any form,

[6] One of the best expositions of the traditional teaching on interest and usury in ancient and medieval Christendom is to be found in G. Ratzinger, *Die Volkswirtschaft in ihren sittlichen Grundlagen,* 1891, 2nd ed., 1895; Ratzinger reaches this conclusion: "Interest as compensation for the use of capital finds its moral and juristic justification in the rights of property; its economic justification and necessity lie in the scarcity of natural resources and capital goods." Concerning the interest question in early Christian times cf. Ignaz Seipel, *Die wirtschaftlichen Lehren der Kirchenväter,* 1907; on the Middle Ages and scholasticism cf. the works of W. Endemann (a liberalist in outlook): *Die nationalökonomischen Grundsätze der kanonistischen Lehre,* 1863; *Studien in der romanisch-kanonistischen Wirtschafts- und Rechtslehre,* 2 vols., 1874–83. For a critical account of his work cf. F. X. Funk, *Geschichte des kirchlichen Zinsverbotes,* 1876; for a short historical account cf. A. M. Knoll, *Der Zins in der Scholastik,* 1933; cf. in the text above the appreciative judgments on the medieval doctrine and attitude by Sombart and Keynes.

is permitted, whether it flows from commercial business or from an industrial undertaking . . . or from insurance against transport risks; or from shareholding in an enterprise . . . or however else." *Sombart* comments: "Basically, this is by no means so astonishing when we consider more closely the men whom we generally know as scholastics. We have been accustomed to do them a great injustice in regarding them as unpractical, abstruse-minded bookworms, treating of unreal topics with endless repetitions and intolerable prolixity. . . . If one attentively peruses the writings of the scholastics, especially the wonderful work of the very great Thomas Aquinas, the monumental quality of which was equalled only by the creations of Dante and Michelangelo, one gains the impression that the work of education which they had at heart was something different from our education in middle-class respectability: that it was the education of their contemporaries to be upright, courageous, alert, and energetic men." [7]

In a passage of striking similarity, *J. M. Keynes* writes: "I was brought up to believe that the attitude of the medieval Church to the rate of interest was inherently absurd, and that the subtle discussions aimed at distinguishing the return on money loans from the return to active investment were merely Jesuitical attempts to find a practical escape from a foolish theory. But I now read these discussions as an honest intellectual effort to keep separate what the classical theory has inextricably confused together, namely, the rate of interest and the marginal efficiency of capital. For it now seems clear that the disquisitions of the schoolmen were directed toward the elucidation of a formula which should allow the schedule of the marginal efficiency of capital to be high, while using rule and the moral law to keep down the rate of interest." [8]

Marx's Theory of Surplus Value

Marx makes no distinction between interest and profit on capital. For him profit on capital is the surplus value which accrues to the capitalist from the employment of labor. Value itself (cf. Chap. 160) consists in "crystallized labor," that is, in the working time socially necessary for the production of a commodity. Work is a commodity like any other, and, as for any other, the purchaser pays in the exchange value for the amount of labor which went into production in order to receive thereby the use value. With the use value of labor, however, the capitalist produces a multiple of the exchange value which he has paid for it. This surplus value falls to the capitalist as owner of the means of production. Capital is accumulated solely from the surplus value arising from labor. The capitalist mode of production, therefore, is essentially a system of exploitation. Thus runs the Marxian argument.

This surplus value theory rests logically on a fallacy. It seeks to examine the question: What is labor's due share in the yield of the capitalist production process? It answers the question by stating that labor is a commodity like any other and that, therefore, the theory of economic value is as true for labor as for any commodity. But it should have been his task to show that labor follows the

[7] Werner Sombart, *Der Bourgeois: Zur Geistesgeschichte des modernen Wirtschaftsmenschen,* 1920, p. 314.

[8] J. M. Keynes, *The General Theory of Employment, Interest, and Money,* 1946, pp. 351 f.

same principle in value-formation. *Marx* thus assumes what he should have proved, as *H. Dietzel* first showed. Secondly, the facts too refute the Marxian theory. According to the theory, wages in the capitalistic economy could never rise above production costs, that is, above the bare minimum standard of existence. Yet, in fact, they have doubled in the course of a century in the capitalistic countries. His law of the diminishing profit rate [9] also rests on a fallacy. The profit rate, says *Marx,* is the relationship of the total surplus valuc accumulating in social production to the total capital expenditure; forced by the pressure of competition the capitalist must, as far as possible, replace variable capital (labor) by constant capital (machinery). Hence, since surplus value can be won only through variable capital, the rate of profit must sink. In this process the replacement of labor by machinery goes ahead, and impoverishment and proletarianization advance with the growing accumulation and concentration of capital, which takes place by means of impersonal legal titles (in the form of the shareholders' company). Hence, "with the inevitability of a natural process" class antagonisms develop and the transition from capitalistic to collective ownership of the means of production takes place ("The expropriators are expropriated" says the *Communist Manifesto*). The facts of evolution contradict this theory of *Marx:* there is neither a constant lowering of the profit rate (especially in the form of dividends) nor a constant increase of impoverishment. The error is obvious: *Marx* does not see that interest (as an element in profit) is a price for the use of capital and that this price is governed by the scarcity of capital in relation to constantly widening needs in the course of the progressive development of society.

[9] The inherent weakness of Marx's theory of value is clearly seen in the well-known contradictory accounts of the rate of profit in the first and third books of *Das Kapital.* According to the theory expounded in the first book, the rate of profit should vary in accordance with the relationship of variable (expended on labor) and fixed (machinery) capital, since profit can arise only from variable capital. In the third volume, however, Marx takes for granted the existence of an average profit rate (independently of the composition of the capital), as it takes shape in consequence of the price-formation process, whereas it should have been his task to explain this profit rate by means of his value theory.

PART TWO

The Organization of Social Economy

171. Private Ownership

Private ownership is fundamental to the natural law order of social economy. From the principle of private ownership, a pattern of the social economy follows which rests on the free exchange of goods and services: the market economy. Thus it is the means of production that primarily constitute the problem of the natural law order of economic life, not private ownership of consumer goods, the use of which, if rightfully acquired, falls to the responsibility of the consumer. In private ownership, the essential nature of a right is most perfectly realized, for it means the exclusive and unrestricted right of control over things. A right, we have seen, is always power of control. When this power relates to things, it is not limited by the object of the right, whereas the right to the labor of another is inherently restricted by the status of the human person. According to traditional natural law doctrine, therefore, the right of ownerships involves the owner's exclusive power of disposal [1] over the property (use, consumption, sale, donation, bequest); the right to the fruits of property; the right to make the property a source of gain [2] within the framework of the socio-economic process; the right to restitution in the event of unlawful deprivation.

The right of private ownership, like all other rights, finds its justification in the end proper to it. The *social end* must have first place: the goods of the earth are destined for the use of all men in the fulfillment of their existential ends, so that in this respect everything is common to all.[3] The conclusion which natural law theory draws from this in the sphere of individual ethics is that every man has the right, in case of extreme need, to appropriate what is necessary to life, without regard to existing property law. The conclusion in social ethics is that any system

[1] Cf. St. Thomas, *Quaestiones quodlibet.*, VI, 12: "Quantum pertinet ad conditionem ipsius rei potest re sua uti ut vult"; *Summa theol.*, IIa IIae, q. 118, a. 2: ". . . possessiones . . . quarum sumus totaliter domini."

[2] Cf. St. Thomas, *Summa theol.*, IIa IIae, q. 66, a. 1: "Habet homo naturale dominium exteriorum rerum, quia per rationem et voluntatem potest uti rebus exterioribus ad suam utilitatem." This is further defined (*ibid.*, a. 2) as "potestas procurandi et dispensandi," i.e., the right to use the thing owned for economic enterprise in order to earn an income in the process of economic exchange.

[3] Cf. St. Thomas, *ibid.*, a. 2: "*secundum ius naturale omnia sunt communia.*"

of social economy is in conflict with natural law to the extent that it precludes a proportionate distribution of the goods, which social cooperation produces, by exploiting the resources available in a community. Thus, it is not the nature of the goods themselves that points to the necessity of private property, for it makes no pronouncement about which piece of land should belong to this man and which to that man, nor does the fulfillment of any of the existential ends of man directly require his ownership of this or that particular thing. The "communism" of smaller communities (e.g., religious orders), therefore, conforms pre-eminently with natural law, but presupposes especially ennobled "nature."

The order of society must, however, proceed from the behavior of human nature in general; and reason and experience led men to the conviction that the realization of their existential ends is best served and the purpose of the goods of the earth in the interest of all is best fulfilled by private property. All peoples, guided by the requirements of common utility, thus have arrived at a system of private property, even though this system has appeared under a variety of forms in their positive law. Hence, the *natural law principle of private ownership* does not form part of primary natural law, but of secondary, or supplementary natural law [4] and of the *ius gentium.* In our treatment of *ius gentium* we have shown how natural law and positive law play complementary parts in it, without however any diminution of the natural law character of *ius gentium.*

The grounds, connected with the existential ends, for the *natural law character of private ownership* may be analyzed under two main headings: the first is centered on man as an individual person; the second on man's being part of society as a condition of the fulfillment of his ends.

1. The *nature of the individual person* demands the institution of private ownership for the following reasons: 1) Man has a *natural desire* for property; *St. Thomas,* following *Aristotle,* points to the satisfaction which the possession of property confers; this desire thus belongs to ordered self-love, that is, to self-love governed by the order of ends.[5] 2) Man has a disposition to *help friends* or strangers; he is capable of helping them effectively only if he is in possession of goods. In thus basing private ownership on the essentially altruistic side of human nature, man's impulse toward love of neighbor, *St. Thomas* likewise follows *Aristotle.*[6] 3) Only on his *own responsibility* can man be what he is destined by his nature to be, and in this respect he is bound up with the world of material goods; this personal responsibility, therefore, presupposes the power of disposal over such goods. 4) An essential element in human nature is the impulse toward *creative development,* which we have already more than once pointed out; this impulse seeks satisfaction also in the economic

[4] Cf. St. Thomas, *ibid.,* Ia IIae, q. 94, a. 5: "Distinctio possessionum et servitus non sunt inductae a natura, sed per hominum rationem ad utilitatem humanae vitae et sic etiam in hoc lex naturae non est mutata nisi per additionem."

[5] Cf. St. Thomas, *in Lib. IX Eth.,* lect. 4 a; *De regimine principum,* lib. VII: "Inest animis hominum, ut proprium bonum quaerant."

[6] Cf. St. Thomas, *in II Pol.,* lect. 4 d.

sphere, apart from the fact that its fulfillment in this sphere is an essential condition of development in the other spheres of life. 5) There is an impulse in human nature to provide for the *future* in order to make man independent of chance and the power of others; such provision can be based only on private property (this principle of natural law, and also the following one, was first emphasized by *Leo XIII* in his encyclical *Rerum Novarum*). 6) The *family* as a domestic, economic, and educational community presupposes private ownership; it is one of the most durable instincts of the parents to insure the future well-being of their children; this instinct is best served by private property; the family is not merely a group of consumers, for its development depends rather upon economic enterprise, and hence implies private ownership of the means of production.

All these reasons which demonstrate the derivation of private ownership from the nature of man as an individual person may be summed up in this way: Private ownership is the extension of the human person into the material world for the purpose of fulfilling his existential ends.

2. The *nature of society and its end* demand the institution of private ownership for the following reasons: 1) The basic social function of private ownership is the clear demarcation of *mine* and *thine;* private ownership serves to maintain *peace in society* and obviates disputes. This is true of property for consumption, but also and especially of property for production, because with common property there inevitably arises the question concerning who is entitled to control it, a question which will almost unfailingly become the object of political strife; furthermore, changes of government may have adverse effects on the conduct of public industrial concerns, as may be seen in the modern democratic state with its alternative parties ready to take over government.[7] 2) Private ownership brings about *a better utilization* of the goods available in the interest of all, since the individuals have a personal interest in their utilization; the individual has less interest in what is common to all, he treats it with less care and is reluctant to devote work, effort, and self-sacrifice to it: this is a universal experience.[8] 3) *St. Thomas* stresses the importance of private ownership for the *socially cementing force* of the exchange of goods; only if the individuals possess their own right of disposal can real commerce on the basis of division of labor take place, and thus perform its function of promoting men's social cooperation; [9] public ownership, on the other hand, can lead only to the supplying of goods

[7] St. Thomas, *ibid.*, lect. 5 c, is very decided about these dangers of common ownership, for it must lead to "accusationes et disceptationes et omnia alia mala."

[8] Cf. St. Thomas, *ibid.*, *lect.* 2 a: "commune multorum valde parum curatur, quia omnes maxime curant de propriis."

[9] Cf. St. Thomas, *Summa theol.*, Ia IIae, q. 105, a. 2: "Est autem duplex communicatio hominum ad invicem; una quidem quae fit auctoritate principium [the state]; alia autem quae fit propria voluntate privatarum personarum [society]"; in both cases, power of control is in question, in the former case over persons, in the latter case over things: "Potestati vero privatarum personarum subduntur res possessae; et

from communal warehouses. 4) As *Aristotle* and *St. Thomas* mention,[10] private ownership also entails the *natural order* of the social body. Under private ownership, the members of society and groups in society work for one another in independence, not for the state as distributor of the economic output; under exclusively public ownership there are only dependent labor and dependent existences. 5) Private ownership servcs to insure the *social freedom* of the human person. This natural law idea first became quite clear with the development of the modern totalitarian state. As long as private property continues to be protected by the legal system of a state, the citizens have far better opportunities for passive resistance to encroachments by political authority into the sphere of natural rights. Only when the citizens and their families are in complete material dependence upon the state does there remain no further institutional obstacle to the totalitarian claim of political authority. 6) The recent development of modern society was needed to reveal another social function of private ownership: private property tends toward a *distribution of power* in society, whereas common ownership entails a gigantic concentration of power in the hands of the state with all the dangers of the misuse of such power, especially in the modern social economy with its huge production apparatus. The two last-named social functions of private ownership are still performed when the existing system of private ownership is very imperfect: there is still the possibility of resistance to state domination even in case of great concentration of private property and also there is the possibility of an endeavor to bring about a right distribution of property. The story is entirely different, however, when public ownership concentrates all economic and political power in the hands of the ruling group.

The social functions of private ownership, therefore, can be summed up in this way: Private property promotes and protects the natural order of society and state. For this order, because it ministers to the human person, is essentially an order of freedom.

To sum these functions up, we speak of the *social function of private ownership*. This includes the function of private ownership in the service of the common good order, but equally the function in the service of the order of freedom, which, of course, is itself a fundamental part of the order of the common good. Because of this, private ownership belongs essentially to natural law, although its concrete *forms are governed by historical circumstances.* Just as the common utility, which is the purpose of law, must give rise to varying applications and manifestations of natural law principles in varying circumstances, so also the principle of private property. This is the reason why the traditional natural law school assigned the institution of private property entirely to *ius gentium* (cf.

---

ideo propria auctoritate in his possunt sibi invicem communicare, puta emendo, vendendo, donando, et aliis huiusmodi modis"; later, he specifically mentions "mutuum" (loan) as part of the process of exchange.

[10] Cf. St. Thomas, *in Lib. II Pol.*, lect. 5 a.

Chap. 48), which is applied natural law, not primary natural law. To give the institution of private property the form most suited to the fulfillment of its essential functions on behalf of the common utility, is a matter for society and the social authority. Thus, the system of private property in every society is, to a large extent, dependent on social and historical factors: social, including the agreement of wills in society; [11] and historical, namely, those connected with the evolution of society and culture.

Therefore, the idea of private ownership, throughout its history, has always involved *two basic questions:* first, a question concerning the natural law character and therefore the permanence of private ownership; secondly, a question concerning the socially conditioned and the variable character of private ownership. The first is basically the question about private ownership as an essential ordering principle in society; the second concerns the right order of property in view of the sociohistorical conditions governing the realization of this ordering principle. The second question has always involved the further question of property reform, which is one of the most fundamental questions of social reform and hence of the social system.

Only as a normative principle can the principle of private ownership become a *principle of reform*: that is, according to whether in existing circumstances the social function of private property is fulfilled in both respects, the individual and the social. If, however, private ownership is not itself conceived as a principle inherent in the natural order of society, as in all collectivistic-socialistic ideologies, then private ownership is made exclusively a functional principle in the service of a preconceived social system. Private ownership then becomes completely *relativized* and its natural law character is denied, with the result that no bounds to the principle of state intervention remain; the concept of property itself is sociologized, that is, it is regarded entirely as an expression of socioeconomic development.[12] Equally opposed to the natural law principle of private ownership is the making of forms of ownership an absolute, which was implicit in the individualist-liberalist principle of the "sanctity of private property," according to which the existing forms of property were considered inviolable and unalterable. Natural law doctrine demands the institution of private property with its essential functions for social order, but it likewise demands the reform of this institution in harmony with these functions.

Change in Forms of Ownership

Social history reveals an immense diversity in forms of ownership among different peoples and at different epochs. We find mixed prop-

[11] Cf. St. Thomas, *Summa theol.*, IIa IIae, q. 66, a. 2: "Distinctio possessionum . . . (est) secundum humanum condictum, quod pertinet ad ius positivum."

[12] Richard Schlatter, *Private Property: The History of an Idea*, 1951, is informative in many respects, but tends to sociologize.

erty systems with common property for general use (common land) and private property (arable land and cattle); feudal property systems with overlordship (*dominium altum*) of the king and ownership for use (*dominium utile*) on the part of the vassal, subject to the latter's obligation to render military service and service at court; manorial systems with political and judicial functions delegated to the landlord, who is entitled to the economic contributions (tithes) of his tenant farmers. With the rise of commerce at the end of the Middle Ages, the *modern forms of property* evolve, especially in regard to money and loans: forms of property arise that make possible a wide separation between ownership and use, as in the forms of capital loan; instruments arise for the transfer of property over great distances without movement of goods, thereby avoiding the risk of loss or theft (already in the fifteenth century remittances of money were effected from Germany to the Roman Curia through the agency of the business houses of the *Fuggers*); soon, instruments of exchange are developed as means of transferring value securely over intervals of time; joint ownership is developed, first in the form of shares in mines, then in the form of shares in commercial and industrial undertakings because of the large capital required for trading over great distances and because of the progressive technical development of industry. Another signal development is joint ownership by trusts and combines in industrial undertakings for the purposes of organization, profit-sharing, control, and management, resulting in the massive concentrations of capital which we see today. Further recent developments are proprietary rights in inventions, patents, and trademarks. A significant development is the form of ownership constituted by present-day use of paper money as a claim to a portion of the goods resulting from socio-economic cooperation. The evolutionary progress is not at an end, as we can see from the system of ownership of dwellings, which gives ownership of flats, with the accompanying part-ownership of staircases, ground, garden, laundries, and cellars.

From the natural law principle of private property there follow further principles concerning the obligations of ownership, the rights of ownership, and the distribution of property.

1 *The Obligations of Ownership*

These are obligations either of justice or of charity.

1) The obligations of *justice* bound up with private property belong to social justice, in accordance with the end of socio-economic cooperation. In present-day social economy they are the following. a) The purpose for which the goods of the earth are destined imposes a general duty to employ property in the socio-economic process, especially large possessions, in order to create opportunities of work and remuneration. By this means the propertyless will be able to acquire income, and thus property, themselves. Restrictions on production by monopolies, in order to safeguard parasitic

profits, which have the effect of hindering the growth of income for labor, are a violation of social justice. b) Another group of obligations relates to the distribution of the output of social cooperation between property income and labor income; this involves the questions of just price, wage, and interest, which have already been discussed. c) Any monopolistic status ("quasi-monopoly") of private property is irreconcilable with the social obligation bound up with private property. Land property and capital property assume a monopolistic character when they tend toward class formation and when the propertied classes are able so to dominate the social system that a real redistribution of property on a just pattern is prevented. Land monopoly has the effect of preventing the acquisition of land for settlement; capital monopoly prevents the working people from acquiring property.

2. The second group of obligations bound up with private property comprises duties of *charity* and concerns the rendering of aid to needy individuals or groups in society by owners of property, out of their superabundant possessions, as enjoined by the natural moral law. What constitutes such possessions has been defined in traditional natural law doctrine in terms of the means adequate to the owner's station and the relative poverty of the needy. The form and manner in which these duties are to be complied with are a matter for the conscience of the owner of property.[13] Duties of both individual charity (helping one's "neighbor") and of social charity (especially in connection with the social end of economy) are involved here. The latter include the following particular features: a) The obligations of social charity pertaining to property can, in certain circumstances, have an extraordinary significance for social economy. More liberal spending at a time of depression can be a social virtue tending to stimulate investment and the volume of employment; at other times, however, what is required in the interest of the propertyless classes may rather be moderation in the use of income from property for the purpose of increased capital investment and the creation of opportunities of work. b) Charity may require the productive use of property; thus, large-scale property may entail, besides obligations in social justice to create opportunities of work, obligations of social charity, as when the creation of such opportunities would involve a relatively heavy capital risk, which justice itself could not impose. c) An obligation of social

[13] Cf. St. Thomas, *Summa theol.,* IIa IIae, q. 66, a. 7: "res, quas aliqui superabundanter habent, ex naturali iure debentur pauperum sustentationi . . . sed . . . committitur arbitrio uniuscuiusque dispensatio propriarum rerum, ut ex eis subveniat necessitatem patientibus." In considering the words "debentur pauperum sustentationi" one should observe that St. Thomas speaks of this in discussing the question of the appropriation of consumer goods in case of extreme need, so that he is thinking of the superfluity of such goods; this appears especially clearly in the passage from Ambrose mentioned by him, as well as from the conclusion which Thomas himself reaches in discussing the question, that "if there is an obvious and urgent necessity, so that help must indubitably be given in immediate need (e.g., when someone is in danger and there is no other possibility of assistance), then one may permit oneself to obtain assistance in one's need from the property of others, either openly or secretly; this is in no sense theft or robbery"; the repeated qualifications should be noted.

charity also exists in the sense that property imposes an obligation, when it is in a stronger position vis-à-vis employed labor, to deal in an accommodating and benevolent spirit in collective bargaining between capital and labor.

In regard to obligations of justice *rights and duties of the state* must also be considered. These can arise if private property is used in a way inconsistent with its purpose to serve all, for example, when land or mineral resources are wastefully used to the substantial impairment of the general interest, or when property is used to harm others (through neglect or malice) or the community (e.g., for purposes of revolution). Most modern constitutions guarantee the rights of rightfully acquired property. It must be remembered that, as we have already seen in discussing the nature of law, the misuse of private property does *not in itself* cancel its rights. Regarding the rights and duties of the state, the general principle holds that, in state law, the social duties bound up with private property must be defined to the necessary extent and their performance must be assured. In natural law itself we find only the principles governing the use of private property; it is by positive law that their implications for the special conditions of a society must be worked out. In fact, Roman law and most modern legal codes contain provisions against the misuse of property to the detriment of individuals. Furthermore, most modern states have procedures for the confiscation of property in case of its employment in direct opposition to the interests of the community (e.g. in case of treasonable activity). It is not, however, these cases that principally interest us here, but the nonfulfillment of the obligations *bound up with the ownership of the means of production.* Three main groups of legal institutions have been developed by the modern state to insure the fulfillment of the social obligations attached to it and to guard against a distribution of income inconsistent with natural law. 1) Legislation for the protection of workers: factory owners are required by law to take minimum measures for the protection of the health and life of workmen. 2) Social insurance: owners of productive property are obliged to contribute toward insuring their employees against unemployment, sickness, accident, and age. 3) Taxation to bring about a better distribution of property and income. 4) In exceptional cases even the nationalization of private property may be justifiable; the conditions for this will be considered later (cf. Chap. 186). All these measures, however, have not solved the "property question" of modern society, the question of a just distribution. In order to be in a position to clarify this problem, we must first turn to the much discussed problem of income from property.

II *Property Rights*

The right to an income from property, or capital income, is the crucial one among the claims rooted in property with regard to the organization of social economy. Its justification is evident as soon as the productivity of the property, the capital, is established. This last point has already been dealt with (cf. Chap. 170). The legal principle that the fruit of property accrues to the owner (*fructus cadet domino*) is a principle of natural law because it is grounded in the functions of private property to be subservient to the needs of the human person and social order. It makes no difference whether the productivity of the thing owned depends on its natural forces (like that of an apple tree) or on the work of the owner (like the productivity of land) or on the cooperation of others (as when labor and capital become jointly productive through agreed cooperation); the cooperation of others does not in itself involve any claim to a share in the product, but only to the agreed remuneration (which may amount to more or less than the yield thereby attained from the thing owned).

The fundamental thesis of *modern socialism* states that there is no justification for income from capital, namely, the creation of new property as the fruit of property employed in the economic process. Economic value, in this theory, springs only from work; hence, capital property in itself confers no claim to a share in the social product. *Proudhon* gave a famous turn to this argument in his essay: *Qu'est-ce que la propriété?* (1840). To the question, "What is property?" he replied: Property is theft, because it facilitates "income without work," whereas the total product of social economy springs from work, and the worker, therefore, possesses the "right to the full product of labor" (cf. Chap. 169). *Marx* himself brings us nearer to a solution. He diagnoses the malfunctioning of private capital ownership correctly when he says that in individualist-capitalistic society this ownership constitutes "social power," which enables "capital" to exploit labor in the free and untrammelled labor contract. We have already pointed out to what extent in individual capitalism capital was a repository of social power. *Marx*, however, falls prey to the fallacy of conceiving private ownership of the means of production always and in all circumstances as social power. In fact, it is precisely from the position of capital property as social power that it can be clearly seen what is the real goal of social reform: not the elimination of private property, but the elimination of its social power. The means to achieve this is a social system in which labor is raised to an ordering principle alongside property, on a footing of parity in directing the socio-economic process (cf. Chaps. 169, 181). With this is linked intimately the further end of social reform: the bringing about of a distribution of property which will enable the greatest possible proportion of the members of society to enjoy an income from property.

A right of property, today widely forgotten in its full significance, is *protection by the state*. The notion is widespread today that anything which is done against private property is "social," and anything that is done by the state in this direction proclaims it specially as a social state or welfare state. In fact, the state is obliged to protect private property because its fundamental task is to establish and to maintain the order of freedom in accordance with natural law; and the right of private ownership, as we have said, is the strongest bulwark of this order of freedom. It is a duty of the lawgiver and of the administration to resist the undermining of the social function of private ownership by a welfare, social, fiscal, nationalization, or socialization policy guided by collectivistic-socialistic aims. It is mainly socialism that today recognizes no bounds set by the natural law private ownership principle to such governmental measures. An obligation which falls upon the state of respecting and of preserving private property concerns very particularly the stability of the value of money, because money is a form of private property for the greatest number of citizens (cf. Chap. 165).

111 *Distribution of Property*

The principles for the distribution of property are derived from the general natural law principles regarding private ownership and its functions in the service of social order. 1) The greatest possible number of members of society should possess, or be enabled by the social system to acquire by means of income from work, the necessary property to secure the fulfillment of the tasks set for them by the individual and social existential ends. 2) The greatest possible proportion of society should possess an income from property; this would most effectively exclude any social or political predominance of private and collective property. 3) The medium-sized property should be so common that large-scale property and poverty would be exceptions; this is one of the best, if not *the* best safeguard of social peace and of the ordered development of society and state.

These principles call for a brief commentary. They partly overlap, although each emphasizes a particular aspect of the influence of income distribution on social order. At the outset it must be observed that these principles do not obviate every possibility of the existence of large-scale property or of poverty in a society. Distribution of property depends upon factors which are connected with the inequality of human nature, namely, the diversity of ability (entrepreneur qualities) and industry among individuals; both large-scale property and widespread poverty become serious defects only when they are occasioned by the social system or when they determine a social system. Our first principle of property distribution is an application of the natural law principle of private ownership: The *economic existence* of all members of society is best assured by means of the widest possible distribution of ownership; in addition, their social and political independence is best safeguarded in this way. The second principle concerns the *class structure*. A class structure with conflicting economic and social interests is unavoidably bound up with the development of society and is an important factor of true social progress; we have seen this in our discussion of the class as a sociological phenomenon (cf. Chap. 86). But class formation threatens the foundations of social order if the bond of community between the classes is severed. Improper property distribution and the conflicts of interest associated with it in the socio-economic process are among the most important class-forming factors, and community of interest in the existing property system is one of the strongest bonds of unity in a society; this is especially evident today when the free world is under the threat of communism. Since the strength of the social order in a community grows in proportion to the spread of middle-sized possessions, traditional natural law theory has, since *Aristotle's* time, seen in a strong middle class the surest symbol of a healthy social body; where it exists one can expect to find the social functions of private ownership and the mutual support of social order and individual freedom most completely fulfilled. A middle class based on ownership does not mean merely craftsmen working with their own tools, but includes also the owners of dwellings, of industrial shares, of loan deeds, and of savings deposits.

Two further guiding principles for the *reform of the system of ownership* must also be mentioned: First, not the abolition of private property but the creation of private property for the greatest possible number of members of society is the object of social reform.[14] Secondly, not a mere redistribution of property is the aim of social reform, but a socially just distribution of income out of the yield of socio-economic cooperation in order to make possible the acquisition of private property by the propertyless.

Co-ownership

By workers' co-ownership is to be understood part-proprietorship in company undertakings. Three basic forms are being discussed: co-ownership *within the firm,* which means the owning by the worker of part of the capital of the undertaking in which he is engaged; it is conceived either as voluntary capital sharing from profits by the undertaking, and hence as a bringing together of capital and labor which will give the worker a sense of working in his own firm with all the ensuing psychological, social and economic consequences for the firm as well as for the individual, or, as a statutory system providing that firms with a certain number of employees must give the workers a share in the profits in the form of proprietary shares over and above the agreed wages; such participation in profits is called "investment wage." The protection of the interests of such co-owners, it is suggested, must be carried out by an organ appointed by them for the purpose (the trade unions, insofar as they accept the idea at all, regard this as a function of the relevant trade union; in some countries unions advocate a contractual regulation of profit sharing).

[14] The communism of the primitive Christian community was not conceived as a form of organization of economic cooperation, but as an ideal form of a charitable community on a religious basis; therefore, it has nothing to do with our problem.

The second basic form which is being discussed and progressively realized is ordinary *share proprietorship*. It also has two versions: either co-ownership by acquisition of shares in the usual form or co-ownership by the acquisition of quasi-shares, "certificates," of investment trusts which invest their capital in the shares of a considerable number of undertakings with probably assured yields and out of these pay an average dividend. In both cases the worker acquires co-ownership of firms to which he does not himself belong, but the property and property income may be both substantially more secure than those of his own firm. The way to such co-ownership is laid by "investment saving," that is, the saving of portions of earnings for the purpose of investment in the manner mentioned.

A third form of co-ownership is that of the *production cooperatives,* which is contained in a "company contract" as distinct from the "labor contract." This form also is propagated in two ways: either the workers are owners in their totality (the individuals possibly with variously high capital participation and corresponding voting rights) or the proprietor of the stock and the employees with (or without) capital participation combine in a form of limited liability company and agree about the division of the profits.

In the years following the Second World War great hopes were variously placed in the producer's cooperative solution (cf. Chap. 172); in Germany today the idea of "investment wage" is the focus of attention. In this, two ideas are associated: profit sharing and property formation on the part of the workers. The first idea depends on the increase in economic productivity accompanying a constantly brisk market and full employment. In regard to capital formation out of distributed profits, the economically essential point [15] is that a disbursement of profits in the form of cash would mostly be put to consumption purposes instead of to capital formation and capital investment, which are demanded by the more immediate and the more remote economic and social tasks. However a number of *principles of justice* make a generalizing postulate with regard to investment wages, particularly for the establishment of a statutory obligation to pay investment wages, appear of doubtful justification. Social justice requires the fullest possible *participation by all the workers* of the social economy in increases of productivity, and therefore price reductions, and not the favoring of individual groups, namely, those engaged in undertakings with bigger yields (a particular example is the disadvantageous position of agricultural laborers). Social justice also requires that the comprehensive development of socio-economic productivity be assured to the greatest possible extent, since on it urgently depends the future social welfare of the workers in general. Therefore, it demands the promotion of an efficient *capital market*. The investment wage, however, leads to a further measure of self-financing with its adverse effects on the development of the capital market and structural development of the national economy (cf. Chap. 182), all connected with questions of social justice. Further criticism is suggested by the principle of commutative justice; for if higher wage shares in the yield of a firm are claimed on grounds of justice, they must then pass over into the *workers' property right* and right of disposal; to add this to investment is an encroachment on these rights, a form of compulsory saving which differs only in degree

[15] Cf. O. v. Nell-Breuning, S.J., *Wirtschaft und Gesellschaft,* Vol. I, 1956, pp. 436 ff., 443 ff.

from the compulsory saving by means of which the Eastern communistic economies apportion the national income to consumption and investment ("for the good of the working classes").

With regard to legal justice: Would *the state* be justified, in view of the economic and social effects we have mentioned, in making investment wages obligatory by statute? Other reservations occur also. What would be the result if firms had to reduce the number of their employees owing to a bad run of business? Would not the dismissed workers claim the right to cash in their investment shares and hence bring the firms into even greater difficulties? And would there not be divisions among the workers with regard to the question of how the investment wages were to be calculated as shares of profits: whether simply in accordance with the standard wage rates or according to years of service, or even taking into account the voluntary social services of the particular firm? Besides, in the competition for labor that goes with a lively market there would be a stream of labor pouring into the big firms and those with higher investment wages, which would have an adverse effect, from the point of view of structural policy, on the relative scale of undertakings in the national economy. Discrepancies would also occur in the assessment of the workers' annual claim to income from their invested property, since the individual items in the profit and loss account of firms are linked, to a large extent, with questions of evaluation. From this point of view alone, therefore, it is by no means sure that social peace is served by a legally obligatory investment wage.

The picture is quite different when share co-ownership is thought of, based on saving out of wage income and investment in equities of any, or the worker's "own," undertaking. This idea is inspired by a strong *social realism,* namely, an outlook which springs from the actual conditions and seeks to find the road to the goal in view which best corresponds with these conditions. If, however, the investment wage is made the panacea or the principal remedy for the social question, the boundary is then crossed into *social romanticism,* especially as such demand for the investment wage is governed not least by a momentary favorable economic situation, which can in no wise be regarded as assured. With this is linked the further question of social justice, namely, how far the workers should be exposed to the risk of loss of property or income in a time of recession.

In any case, the question arises concerning what form of share property is expedient for the working population. It seems to be certain that forms of equity shares must be found which do not deprive the worker of his freedom of movement, do not expose him to too great a risk of loss, do not burden him excessively with the risk of enterprise, and give him investment property without immobilizing his means. The reverse side of this picture, the undertakings themselves, must not be overlooked. To carry the special status of workers' shares too far, for instance, by conferring prior rights on them in case of the liquidation of an undertaking, or by an obligation in certain cases to purchase the worker's share, or by guaranteeing fixed dividends, might have adverse effects on the flexibility of management, on the readiness to invest on the part of the capital market, and on the security of the capital basis of the undertaking. The institution of the "preferential share" is a very old one and may offer several suggestions for the pattern of the worker's share holdings in the respects we have mentioned. These considerations also indicate that much the more useful field to explore is the field of ordinary share property, and that co-ownership in the worker's "own" firm can only be considered on a voluntary basis. Indeed, the workers themselves may often prefer to seek more secure and profitable investment opportunities than those provided by their own firm, if they are willing to incur the risks of investment in shares or in other industrial part-proprietorship; besides, investing by means of the capital market safeguards full freedom of disposal over one's property and the income therefrom, which would not only be desirable for the working people intent on owning industrial property but is also in accord with the nature of private ownership.

Therefore, many weighty reasons exist for ordinary share co-ownership in the form of investment through the acquisition of equities on the capital market directly, or indirectly by means of an *investment trust,* which, itself a capital company, establishes a connection between workers' savings capital and the capital market in a manner which safeguards the worker's property and income. Two prerequisites for the attainment of such a system of ownership call for special mention. The first is a sufficient willingness to save on the part of the working population, which today, with its greatly increased earnings, thinks to a large extent in terms of increased consumption; and in conjunction with the first, is a spirit of co-enterprise on the part of the workers (cf. Chaps. 172–73). The second prerequisite concerns the capital market: small and very small shares (and also portions of shares) must be able to be acquired and sold without formalities on the capital market (English proposals would say: over the bank counter); the result would be shareholding by the mass of workers and, in the end, a "property-owning democracy." In principle, the share with voting rights is to be preferred in conjunction with a special representation of the holders of such small shares at the general meeting of the company, and even on the board of directors when such shares account for a larger proportion of the whole capital. (Concerning this whole question cf. also what is said on profit sharing in Chap. 169.)

172. Labor

Labor is a principle of socio-economic order and, as we shall see, one of *higher rank* than property, whose ordering function in society we have just discussed. The fact that individualistic capitalism has succeeded in completely excluding the ordering function of labor and in securing to capital property and its profit interest the exclusive control of the process of social economy is perhaps the most compelling evidence of the perverseness of the principles informing individualistic capitalism. In fact, *the whole essence of the modern social question* can be summed up thus: How can labor be made the determining principle of order in social economy, and how can the usurped predominance of private property be broken? This has also been ultimately the motivating question in all varieties of socialism. The socialistic answer runs: by abolishing private ownership. In fact, as we shall see, the ordering function of private property in society is the prerequisite for establishing the full right of labor to be a principle of order in social economy. What we are concerned with primarily here is dependent labor. To a very great extent labor in modern social economy is dependent: first, because the majority of labor is executive, being organized and directed by management; no kind of socialism could alter that in any way. Secondly, labor is dependent because it is engaged by the owners of the means of production under the labor contract; here, too, socialism would change nothing, but rather the dependent character of labor would become much more of a problem owing to the heightened power status of the managers.

Does not the *labor contract* make labor a chattel, a mere accessory of the means of production in a manner inconsistent with the dignity of the human person? The moral justification of the labor contract and of capitalistic economy, of which the labor contract is an integral element, has often been impugned on this account. Under individualistic liberalism labor has been made an instrument of capital property and of its profit interest and the labor contract has been treated as a hiring contract. The work performed has been regarded as a commodity in exactly the same way as any other commodity which the entrepreneur requires for his production process. The labor contract, however, differs fundamentally in natural law from the contract of hire or sale, since the work performed is inseparably linked with the human person, thus investing the labor contract with two qualifications that cannot be set aside. First, since it is the human person who performs work, the services stipulated must not be such as to interfere with the accomplishment of the tasks set by man's existential ends; this would happen in the case of a twelve-hour day which engrossed all the workman's energies and time to the detriment of other responsibilities based on existential ends, such as those of family life or of religious life. Secondly, the workman is, like all members of society, the end of socio-economic cooperation and must not be made a mere instrument or merely "calculated" as a factor of production in the service of capital profit.

In traditional natural law doctrine, therefore, the labor contract is a contract *sui generis,* that is to say, a contract in whose substance there are predetermined *natural law conditions* which, even if they are not specifically stipulated, are automatically added to the agreed terms by virtue of the natural law as often as man's work for remuneration is the object of a contract. With this proviso, however, the labor contract is to be regarded, according to the whole natural law tradition, as morally unobjectionable since it is not in itself inconsistent with the responsibilities founded in the existential ends.

In the modern democratic society the *labor contract* usually contains *three groups of conditions:* The first group consists of *natural law conditions.*

Besides this first class there is a second class, the *collective agreement conditions. Marx* was right in holding that the individual worker under laissez-faire capitalism is only formally free, being compelled to sell day by day the only "commodity" at his disposal, his labor. But he failed to see that the workers could organize and thus make their freedom a reality in their negotiations with the employers. The organization of labor supply by the trade unions made possible the collective labor contract which provides that individual labor contracts can be concluded only in accordance with the conditions laid down in the former, regarding hours, wages, and paid holidays.

A third class of conditions which form part of the individual labor contract is *state labor law conditions.* If the labor contract *eo ipso* contains terms derived from its essence in natural law, then the state evidently has an obligation to take such measures as will insure that these conditions are observed, insofar as they are not already guaranteed by social morality or by social institutions. To a limited extent this is always necessary because it is a question of the legal definition of duties which, like all other natural law principles, require definition in the particular circumstances of the existing social system. The obligations directed toward the protection of the rights of labor are fulfilled by the state by the creation of labor law, which lays down minimum conditions for health protection at work, maximum weekly hours of work, and social insurance benefits. In discussing labor law (cf. Chap. 142) we pointed out that the social obligations of private property giving employment to labor receive their legal definition through labor law; labor law, therefore, is the correlate of property law.

In dealing with trade unionism (cf. Chap. 88) and social policy (cf. Chap. 142) we showed that the regulation of labor conditions by means of collective agreement and state labor law has by no means attained the goal mentioned at the outset, namely, making labor itself a regulative principle in social economy, as demanded by the personal dignity of work and the social end of economy which is linked with it. Labor and private property are both fundamental ordering principles of social economy. Placed on an equal plane with private property, labor must be a principle of order in social economy. This can occur only if *labor, on an equal footing with property, obtains its due place assured at the levers of the socio-economic process.* The course and development of the socio-economic process depend, as we have seen (cf. Chap. 168), on the price mechanism corresponding to the social end of economy. In order to become a regulative principle with equal rights as the ordering factor in social economy, labor must have such influence on price developments that the fulfillment of the social function of competition and the market will be realized. The result would be a slow and cautious, but general and lasting movement of prices to the "natural prices," that is, to the "socially necessary" costs. This would bring about the maximum of socio-economic productivity. Thus, on the economic side the essential prerequisite for the maximum wage income would be assured, and on the social side this would be realized by the collective agreement. The predominance of property would thus be broken both on the social and on the economic side: the worker would not only be at the levers of the socio-economic process, but also at the switchboard of the distribution process. The agencies to direct the economic process and to distribute its yield would be joint committees with parity of rights of "capital" and "labor," whose members would be appointed by the employees' and employers' organizations. Concerning the constitution and procedures of such a socially integrated democracy we shall have more to say later (cf. Chap. 181).

Our solution of the question of how labor can be made the decisive principle of order in social economy is distinguished from all other modern attempted solutions by two factors. First, it is guided by the two fundamental principles of the personal dignity of work and the common good purpose of economy (social justice); secondly, it not only preserves inviolate but renders fully effective the two other fundamental principles of the order of social economy: the principle of private ownership and the principle of subsidiary function. Private ownership as a principle of order becomes fully effective in our solution because it is compelled to fulfill its social function. The institution of private ownership, therefore, remains fully preserved, but capital is placed in an auxiliary role. The principle of subsidiary function is made fully effective because it is not through the state but through the agency of "social" organs that labor is constituted the ordering principle of social economy; these organs are the joint committees mentioned, formed on the principle of equal rights of "capital" and "labor." In contradistinction to our solution, modern proposals for constituting labor the decisive principle of organization in social economy follow two main trends, state socialism and cooperative socialism; both are connected with the development of socialism since the first half of the nineteenth century. Both of them need some further discussion.

I *The State Socialistic Solution of the Problem of Labor*

The solution of the labor problem which today dominates half the world is the Marxist one. The Marxists like to call it a democratic solution. Actually, in this socialistic solution "economic democracy" and the importance of labor as an ordering principle of social economy are mere fictions; for the direction of social economy is exclusively in the hands of central economic authorities with dictatorial powers. Not only can labor exercise no decisive influence directly on the course and development of the economic process, its dependence upon capital, even though this is now public property, is more likely to be increased than diminished. For, labor remains a mere production factor in the plans of the central authorities, who are also compelled to secure far-reaching powers of control over this production factor if their plans for the various branches of the economy and the overall plan are to be realized. The result is that, in this socialistic economy, the socialization of the means of production must be accompanied with the force of an inner logic by a form of *socialization of labor.* Public ownership of the means of production must lead to encroachments upon the freedom of labor, which at best differ only in kind from those which characterize individualist capitalism. Freedom of labor in the socialistic economy is guaranteed to no greater extent than is freedom of labor, in *Marx's* judgment, under capitalism. Socialism, therefore, is not the solution to the problem of labor and of the establishment of labor as the regulative principle of social economy.

11 *The Cooperative Socialistic Solution of the Labor Problem*

The early socialism of the first half of the nineteenth century, which *Marx* dubbed "Utopian," discovered a great number of constructive ideas on social reform, some of which have more future in them than the "scientific" socialism of Marx. The "organization of labor," which *Charles Fourier, Robert Owen,* and *Louis Blanc* had in mind, aimed at solutions which make the worker himself the owner in an organization of cooperative production. *Fourier* would achieve this by the organization of large economic units (*phalanges*) producing almost their entire requirements themselves; they would only secondarily carry on exchange with other such economic units; their families would run common domestic establishments (*phalanstères,* organized like big hotels); these economic units are to be settled on their own land (he is one of the first with the call "back to the land!") and organized as limited companies, the shares in which are to be held by the individual members of the economic units. *Robert Owen,* himself an employer, who was far ahead of his time with the model social institutions which he introduced into his business, would eliminate capital profit and money; money would be replaced by work vouchers recording the hours of work which the producer had given to the product. *Owen* took a practical step in this direction by setting up a labor exchange bank in London where the members delivered their products, receiving in exchange vouchers to the value of the hours of work which they had expended (according to their own statement); these vouchers could be exchanged for goods. *Owen's* organization was soon forced to go into liquidation because a majority of the members brought in only products which were unsalable on the market. His errors were overcome by two of his followers who achieved world-wide fame with the twenty-eight poor weavers as the "Pioneers of Rochdale" and founders of the *consumers' cooperatives.* When the poverty of the weavers in England reached its climax in the middle of the 1840's, these men formed an association, founded a store by means of contributions of money, with the object of sharing the profit after expenses had been covered, in proportion to the money value of the goods purchased by each from their shop. Thus, the problem of eliminating capital profit was basically solved in one sector of social economy, but it was also shown that the elimination of money is not the way.

Proudhon's idea also was to abolish profit by means of a moneyless exchange system: through the institution of "free credit" he would give the worker access to the means of production. In his Exchange Bank the producers were to deliver their products against vouchers recording their value calculated on the basis of working time and material expenditure. With these vouchers they could purchase commodities, raw materials, and instruments of production for future use. *Proudhon* calls this system of natural exchange that of "mutual aid," or mutualism. Attempts to realize this were destined to fail for similar reasons to *Owen's* system. *Louis Blanc* again aimed at an "organization of labor" (this is the title of his pamphlet) by means of "social workshops," in which the workers were to be associated under their own administration for cooperative production. All profits would go to the workers and would be devoted to increasing wages, to "social insurance" (to sum up his idea in the modern phrase) and to renewing and expanding the cooperative capital; the initial capital of the cooperatives was to be provided by the state. These "social workshops," in *Blanc's* opinion, would, in competition with "individualist workshops," because of their more efficient organization, not only hold their own but would eliminate private concerns. In fact, however, the clumsiness of the democratic management which he envisages must put his producers' cooperatives at a disadvantage compared with private concerns. Besides, the whole risk arising from competition falls upon the worker alone. The experiments that were made with cooperative production in Paris in 1848 under the influence of his ideas did not succeed, partly owing to lack of labor discipline. But with the idea of *producers' cooperatives* an idea had been initiated in social reform which has never since been abandoned. *Lassalle* took up the idea again and essayed a comprehensive organization of social economy built upon labor. The idea has been revived from time to time since then and attempts have been made to realize it (cf. Chap. 174 on the labor cooperative enterprise).

The Right to Work

The right to work forms an integral part of early socialistic thought. *Proudhon* speaks of it as a necessary correlate of the right to property; it forms the foundation of *Fourier's* thought and it is upheld by the most ardent champion of Fourierism, *Victor Considérant;* the "right to work" forms an integral element especially in *Blanc's Organization of Labor*. Being one of the dominating ideas of the revolution of 1848, the right to work gained recognition by the establishment of "national workshops." These are to be distinguished from *Louis Blanc's* projected "social workshops," mentioned above; their purpose was not one of industrial organization, but only the creation of work by means of public works, such as road improvements in and around Paris. In 1848, the guarantee by the state of a general right to work could not succeed. The government was unable to find the money necessary to satisfy all claims to work; the maintenance of labor discipline was another difficulty, and the attempt to maintain it by organizing the people into companies and brigades came to grief; in June, further measures to secure the necessary labor discipline were met by a revolt on the part of the workers which cost them hundreds of lives.

Obviously there exists the natural human *right to work* in the sense that man is entitled to work in order to earn a livelihood. From this right must be distinguished the *right to employment,* which is what is meant by the right to work in socialistic thought and in other less articulate thought. The state could guarantee a right to employment only if it were in control, not only of all means of production, but of labor as well, that is, if it could determine how and where workers were to be employed. The natural law regulative principle of private property and likewise the natural law principle of freedom of labor rule out a right to employment. But the right to work, in the sense just defined, does exist. For, we have seen (1) that the most important social obligation of property is the creation of opportunities of work by its application in the socio-economic process; social justice, therefore, gives the propertyless a claim against private property for the fulfillment of this obligation; and we have also seen (2) that the state has the duty to see to the fulfillment of this obligation of private property; in this respect, therefore, there does exist a claim by the propertyless on the state. Natural law theorists in the last few decades have not always given sufficient emphasis to these obligations of private property and the state when, on grounds which we have set down above, they have recognized only a natural human right to (do) work in order to earn a livelihood. A mere right to work without an obligation on the part of the state to guarantee the carrying out of the social obligations of private property is of little value to the propertyless worker; it leaves him to the benevolence of the propertied classes. Rightly, therefore, a policy of "full employment" is regarded today as an obligation of the state. This obligation of the state is one of legal and distributive justice; it does not confer upon individuals titles to employment by a state-organized economy. (The fact, on the other hand, that the natural human right to work can be seriously violated by monopolizing employment through the establishment of the closed shop has been discussed in Chap. 88.)

173. The Plant

The plant is the organization of labor for the continuing production of certain goods in conjunction with the organization of raw materials and tools. The plant is organized by the management, which obtains the necessary labor by means of the labor contract. Because of its key position in socio-economic cooperation, thinkers inspired by moral principles found themselves increasingly compelled, with the intensification of the social question in the nineteenth century, to take the plant as the starting point for their solution of the labor question. The principles of laissez-faire capitalism had made the entrepreneur absolute "master in his house," that is, in the factory, a situation irreconcilable with the moral character of the labor contract (cf. preceding chap.). This claim of the employer, based on a mistaken idea of the position of the right of private property, was countered by labor law. This not only included general regulations on labor conditions, but also gave the workers a voice in matters not concerning the running of the factory. Since the First World War, works committees, in Europe at least, have increasingly become an organizational element in the social system, although their status and functions have not been settled in the same way in all countries. There is considerable diversity in their forms, in their machinery, and in their results. Employers' organizations and some trade unions also have impeded their development: the former saw in them a danger to freedom of management; the latter a danger to the unity and strength of the labor movement, to which a direct understanding between employers and workers was regarded as prejudicial. Not until the Second World War was there a far-reaching change in these attitudes, together with the growth of a new science of *"human relations in industry."*

In the sphere of human relations, the *works committee* or works council has important functions. Its purpose is the agreed settlement of all matters of common interest to management and workers. These include especially: (1) assisting in the organization of work in the factory, including such matters as hours of work, shifts, breaks, and holidays; (2) applying the collective agreement in force to the special circumstances of the factory, such as the classification of workers into the agreed wage categories, the regulation of piecework, piecework rates, and bonus payments; (3) the disposal of day-to-day problems and difficulties, such as differences between management and workers, culpable absenteeism, unpunctuality, and carelessness in the handling of machinery and materials; (4) consultation on general questions of management, particularly the technical improvement of work organization and institutions in the factory; (5) sharing in the organization and direction of social welfare institutions in the factory, such as canteens, sports clubs, and institutions to care for the families of workers; (6) playing a part in the building up of a community spirit in the plant, on which more will be said presently. All these functions of the works committees are of an internal nature; their performance presupposes that the representatives of the workers are freely chosen by the latter, particularly the shop stewards appointed to represent the workers vis-à-vis the management. If, however, the trade unions have the deciding voice in their election, the factory committee becomes more an agency of these outside organizations, which may be injurious to the development of industrial democracy. As we have already shown (cf. Chap. 88), the social ordering functions of the trade union concern the whole branch of industry, not the individual factory as such (except in countries where, in big concerns, trade unions are formed exclusively by their employees).

The supreme goal in the realm of social relations in the factory is *fellowship in efficiency and interest* between management and labor. Social psychologists know today how much in error is the purely psychotechnical science, with its stop-watches and the purely commercially calculating social plant policy based on the idea of what "pays" in the end. They know that the worker wishes to find in his world of work acceptance as a complete personality and a full member of a community, because his human nature demands this. Both on the individual and on the social side, fulfillment of personality depends on social relations in the factory. The first, the vital prerequisite for such fulfillment of personality is mutual *confidence* between labor and management, confidence in mind and attitude. Everyone knows how much inner distrust and outward reserve have to be overcome in order to bring this about. A further prerequisite is a common *understanding* of the connections between the vocational-technical and the personal-human sides of the world of work; the workman cannot apply himself to his work with full interest unless he can understand that his contribution is a part of the technical and industrial whole, but he must also be assured of the interest of the management in his vocational and personal endeavor and success. In the latter respect, employers have something vital to learn regarding human relations in industry: industry has not merely an economic and technical aspect, but a psychological aspect as well. Another prerequisite of a social order governed by the idea of fellowship between labor and management in the plant is that the worker should have the maximum *co-responsibility,* and hence co-determination, which is compatible with the particular economic responsibility of the management, or rather which is necessary for the best fulfillment of both the social and the economic purposes of the plant.

These purposes will be best served if both sides are united in the will to achieve the highest possible *productivity* and if the share of the workers in the result is fully commensurate with their contribution to that end. This contribution may consist of better training for the job, of greater efforts (abandonment of "go slow" and "ca' canny") and also of saving costs (greater care with machinery and raw materials). The sharing in the result will mean forms of profit sharing (cf. Chap. 169), especially voluntary social services provided by firms. Social policy in the factory has hitherto undertaken the following tasks: a more agreeable layout of work shops, the provision of entertainment in the longer breaks, the development of the bonus system, the creation of opportunties of economic and social advancement for the workers, further education facilities, maternity homes, sports clubs and sports facilities, and, not least in importance, the guaranteeing of jobs for considerable numbers of employees (important for the factory not only from the economic-technical point of view, because trained and experienced workers can be counted upon, but especially for the development of solid social relations in the factory and in the factory community itself); especially worthy of mention is the provision of housing, preferably for private ownership by the occupiers, if only in order to avoid disputes in questions of maintenance.

In connection with the social order of the factory, *the question* has been posed to me whether the plant is *an elementary social unit of a natural law character* and consequently an autonomous structure with intrinsic principles of order, rights, and duties. The question has also been put in this way: Is the plant the cell of the economic community in the sense in which the family is the cell of society? There are a number of reasons which argue against an affirmative reply: 1) The plant is a *functional organization* in the service of an undertaking, and hence an organization working for purposes which, in their special character, are not determined by nature. Nature says only in a general way that men have to perform in social fellowship the tasks appointed by their existential ends; but it does not say how the individual factory is to be organized, socially and technically, in the division of labor in society. With regard to the family, the village, and the state, however, it is entirely different; their ends are specifically determined by nature and thus form the basis of elementary communities with, in consequence, natural rights of their own. The pattern of social cooperation is outlined in the natural units by their own inherent ends; in the factory this is not so. 2) Certainly, as we have seen, the community idea should govern the plant; but it is the idea of association and the duty of *solidarity* resting on the voluntary and freely dissoluble bond of employees and employers linked together in the plant. This bond of solidarity is rooted in the personal nature of men as coworkers in a factory, whether in a managerial, an administrative, or an executive capacity. The duty of solidarity demands not only the avoidance of measures and attitudes which must be an obstacle to the integration of personality, in one's occupation as indicated in the existential ends, but also mutual advancement in this objective, insofar as it depends upon vocational factors. But these are obligations derived from freely chosen cooperation and not from a particular pattern of cooperation prescribed by man's social nature and by the ends proper to it. 3) The social relationship in question is fundamentally not different from that which links the farmer working with his family on his own farmstead and the worker employed by him, who is also intent on providing a livelihood for his family. This example shows that earning a livelihood jointly in the same plant does indeed establish social relationships but not in itself any social structure of a natural law character. Since, in the economy based on a division of labor, which by natural law principles can only be a market economy, factory and firm rest on private ownership and the labor contract, there arises a community of interest and responsibility, a bond of *loyalty* as a particular form of the duty of solidarity. Expressed in terms familiar from the legal and social history of industrial society: the basic pattern of plant fellowship between labor and management is not "institutional" (as understood by institutional theory, cf. Chap. 42), but "constitutional" in character (hence not, as was once thought, of a "patriarchal" nature, nor a "leader and followers" relationship in accordance with an authoritarian or aristocratic theory of society). 4) The plant is not the cell of the economic society, in the sense that the family is the cell of society, for this reason alone, that the justification in terms of ends of its structure and function does not lie within itself; it is ultimately derived from its place in the *socio-economic process* and from its efficiency therein, as ascertained from the judgment of the market. So true is this that, even with a workers' production cooperative, so predominant is the control exercised by the market and the mutual control of the members of the cooperative that the community sense becomes paramount only in rare and ideal instances. For, at the beginning of the economic process stands interest, in all its forms, even though it be in the form of ordered self-love. 5) The bond of solidarity gives a basis for the right of the employees to a voice in deciding about the common concerns of the plant; these may include all aspects of social relations, although the running of the business itself is excluded. The extent of this codirection is a question requiring further discussion.

Codetermination

From what has been said about fellowship between labor and management it follows assuredly that a principal aim of social reform must be the greatest possible degree of all-round coresponsibility and codetermination by the employees in the plant. A sharp distinction, however, must be made between codetermination in the social sphere and codetermination in the economic sphere, namely, in the running of the business. Hitherto, we have been discussing the former. Hardly any management will be opposed to a codetermination which results in increasing productivity and thus presupposes a kind of joint entrepreneurship on the part of the employees, since the increasing yield benefits both owners and management. Rather different is the question whether on natural law principles the labor relationship as such gives a basis for the right of codetermination for the employees in the conduct of the business. No such basis exists. Still less is there any justification for such a right on the part of interest groups outside the plant, such as trade unions. If such a right is enforced, it means infringing the owners' right of disposal, which is protected by the natural law principles of ownership.

The lawgiver, however, may be compelled to institute forms of codetermination. This can happen, first, in accordance with the natural law principle of permitting violations of principles of justice in order to avoid graver wrong, as, for instance, if otherwise the socialization of large-scale firms would be unavoidable owing to party power politics. Secondly, the institution of a form of codetermination can be required by the natural law principle of the clear command of the common good, which empowers the state to interfere in property rights, as when big business conjures up the danger of far-reaching unemployment and grave harm to the national economy, whether in order to exert pressure on the working population in the social struggle or in order to sabotage the economic policy of a government; in such a case, a right of codetermination would be participation in a trusteeship falling to the state. Both cases, then, would be wholly exceptional in character.

Two forms of codetermination are in harmony with natural law principles. The first is that based on free agreement of the owners of undertakings, or the management representing them, with the workers; this form, being altogether in accord with the concrete points mentioned, has proved to be the most successful. The second form is that based on capital investment and thus on participation by the workers in the ownership of an undertaking, especially in the co-ownership of their "own" firm. These two forms of the right of codetermination are especially distinguished by coentrepreneurship and coresponsibility; they form, therefore, not only a task for the employers, but also for the employees, since they concern their readiness for such coentrepreneurship.[1] (On co-ownership cf. Chap. 171.)

Automation

Automatic production presents hardly any special natural law problems. For, if one refuses to be misled by the often sensational literature of automation, regarding the conditions for a realistic judgment, it can hardly seem doubtful that the proclaimed new industrial "revolution" is basically only another phase of the technical industrial evolution which has been in progress for over a century. This evolution may be advancing rather rapidly; nevertheless, the industrial society has acquired wide experience in the course of technological development up to now which will stand it in good stead in the present and future phases of this process. For this reason alone the economic and social crisis phenomena, which are variously predicted, will not occur. Besides, all the groups interested in automation and its effects possess influential positions of power, which they can bring to bear in order to control and regulate the evolution in question in order to obviate far-reaching economic and social abuses prejudicial to their group interest and to the general interest. The fear of "technical" unemployment is exaggerated for the reason that the increasing production of automation machines will itself call for labor forces. Just as in the rest of technical industrial development, there will be an increasing need for more highly qualified labor, which will entail longer training; a number of countries have already experienced the need of extended school education. This results in a lightening of the pressure on the labor market; in addition there will be the accelerated rhythm of work which goes with automation, together with the raising of the productivity of labor, and will reduce working hours (the present demands for a five-day week are based on this).

[1] From the literature on codetermination: H. D. Ortlieb and H. Schelsky, editors, *Wege zum sozialen Frieden: 14 Beiträge zur Mitbestimmung und sozialen Partnerschaft in der Wirtschaft* (Akademie für Gemeinwirtschaft, Hamburg), 1954: "A collection of personal opinions which, although at times in disagreement or cutting across one another, are nevertheless linked by the common purpose of smoothing the approaches to objective consideration and decision in an important question of our social destiny" (from the Preface); contains a very comprehensive bibliography. For a fundamentally different basic position cf. Franz Böhm, "Das wirtschaftliche Mitbestimmungsrecht der Arbeiter im Betrieb," in *Ordo, Jahrbuch für die Ordnung von Wirtschaft und Gesellschaft,* Vol. IV, 1951.

On the whole, only a relatively very small sector of production is technically suited to automation, and even for this sector there is the question of economic possibilities. This means that only a fraction of the workers would be moved from their places of work by reason of automation. The economic aspect chiefly involves the question of raising capital and paying interest on it. If the capital market is sluggish and interest rates are high, possibilities of automation are reduced. Along with this, automation will involve a higher demand for energy, whereas energy requirements are already causing concern throughout the world. The provision of this requirement again makes heavy demands on capital, not least in view of the possibilities of nuclear energy which are opening up. If one does not shut one's eyes to all the factors which come into play with automation, then one need hardly fear economic and social developments which cannot, with today's experience and knowledge of technical-economic interrelationships, be steered into orderly paths, as indicated by the general principles linked with the social end of economy.[2]

The decisive factor will be the demand of justice that the increase in production made possible by automation should benefit not merely the individual industry or firm, but society in general. The conditions necessary for automation and for the increase of productivity attainable from it are created on the mental, scientific, technical, and economic sides substantially by social cooperation as a whole; hence, the increasing yields, where they are not clearly due to special services, should be apportioned among all the members of society. This is obviously a question of price formation and hence of the market system, with which we shall be concerned later (cf. Chap. 181).

174. The Enterprise Organization

In our study of the supplying of the market with goods and services within the framework of the socio-economic process, we have found that the essential features of this today are the services and the concomitant profits of the entrepreneur. The undertaking, or firm, is the organization of production factors (natural resources, labor, technique) for the purpose of producing goods or services for the market, and motivated by the desire for profit. Its object is to secure a return in excess of the costs expended. Its method is the calculation of these costs in money, in accordance with the existing and expected prices for the employed goods and services compared with the existing and expected prices for the goods to be produced and to be sold. Money calculation and capital calculation, which is associated with it, form therefore, as we have seen (cf. Chaps. 165–66), the basis for judging the success of economic enterprise; therefore, profit is its directly determining motive. To appreciate the significance of enterprise as an organizational form in modern social economy,

[2] For a realistic judgment on automation cf. Adolf Weber, *Drei Phasen der industriellen Revolution, Sitzungsbericht d. bayrischen Akad. d. Wiss.*, 1957, n. 10; Friedrich Pollock, *Automation*, 1956; John Diebold, *Automation: The Advent of the Automatic Factory*, 1954; R. H. Macmillan, *Automation, Friend or Foe?* 1956.

we must have before our eyes the consequences involved when money calculation or capital calculation becomes institutional. 1) It rationalizes business management: for the medieval masters, and still today for small traders, their business is, as it were, a part of their household, and sustenance for their families and employees must be provided out of the regular returns of the business. The modern firm is an entity in itself. 2) Rationalized business management is carried out by means of bookkeeping, which enables an accurate check to be kept on costs and returns so that the surplus and the profit over and above costs, which are booked as capital expenditure, can be ascertained. 3) Profit on capital becomes the immediate purpose of production; the satisfaction of needs the means to that purpose.[1]

The ethical valuation of the undertaking as an organizational form, in the sense described, will have to take account of the unprecedented increase in the productivity of the economic process and the unparalleled expansion of the basis of economic existence in the capitalistic countries in the nineteenth century, with their rising living standard accompanying rapidly increasing population figures. These developments are to be attributed substantially to the rationalization of industry, which is associated with private enterprise, and to the largely automatic operation of the profit motive in private enterprise. With this a number of doubts come into mind: together with competition and the technical production process, the profit motive, operating through the organizational form of enterprise, results in a kind of independence, whereby enterprise becomes an essential vehicle of the *autonomy* of the capitalistic dynamic. The consequent danger is the depersonalization of industry, affecting employer and employee alike: man is in danger of becoming the *accessory of the organization* which he has created. There can hardly be another form of organization in which the tendency of the institutional (cf. Chap. 59) to become independent and autonomous is so strongly realized as in private enterprise under the organizational form of capitalism. The profit motive becomes the immediately governing force in industry.

This brings us to the crucial question in the *ethical valuation of modern capitalism:* Is the profit interest, as a direct motive factor of the economic process, compatible with the real end of this process? The answer to this question depends upon whether the dynamic of the profit interest can be so directed that it will tend to promote, and not hinder, the social end of economy. The answer must be sought in a socio-economic process ordered by institutions to guarantee the realization of the social end of economy. And since the market is the basic organ of social economy (cf. Chap. 162), the fundamental question is that of ordering the market: there must be *institutions* to insure that the dynamic of the profit motive,

[1] This sociological description of the modern enterprise organization follows Max Weber, *Wirtschaft und Gesellschaft,* 1921, pp. 31–53: "Soziologische Grundkategorien des Wirtschaftens."

which is bound up with private enterprise, will work equally in the general interest (the social end of economy) as in the individual interest. As already pointed out (cf. Chaps. 85, 172), this seems to us the fundamental question also of ordering the economic system based on private ownership of the means of production. We hope to show how such an economic order can be conceived (cf. Chap. 181) in which nothing is taken away from the driving force of the profit motive in the process of economic and social progress, but this motive would function wholly in the service of the economic and social common good.

Producers' Cooperative of Workers

Early socialism, as we have seen (cf. Chap. 172), to which state-socialistic thinking was alien, looked for a solution of the labor problem in the cooperative principle: the workers were to be their own entrepreneurs and were thus to receive the entire returns of the undertaking. Understood as a member of the market economy, the producers' cooperative can be an ideal form of replacement of the labor agreement by a company agreement and of the reunion of labor and ownership of the means of production. The workers would have exclusive control (not only a share in control) in all questions of policy concerning factory and firm, including questions of distribution of profits and capital investment.

But the prerequisites for the success of such undertakings have precluded their durable existence being anything more than exceptional up to now. These prerequisites concern the workers, who must be animated by a like mentality and attitude regarding fellowship and work, for otherwise the inevitable mutual check on their respective willingness to contribute would lead to conflicts. These prerequisites concern also the nature of the undertaking, since there must be a certain similarity in services performed in order to preclude discrepancies in the allocation of work and in the distribution of the profit, which must depend on work and efficiency. Not the least important prerequisite is the assent of the members to the necessity of capital formation and capital investment, which must be provided out of the yield of the business and are indispensable for its competitive capacity.

Nevertheless, this form of enterprise is to be aimed at and promoted by all means consistent with the principle of socio-economic productivity. But the workers' cooperative must be brought into being by the workers themselves, relying on enterprise and initiative, the application of capital, and the willingness to risk. It would be a gratifying thought if attempts at workers' cooperative productive enterprises were to succeed to a greater extent, and particularly in greater style, and hence in large-scale undertakings. Even a representative of economic liberalism like *J. S. Mill* saw in the workers' cooperative undertaking promising possibilities of social reform; indeed, he maintained that a system founded on this came nearest to the demands of social justice and the general interest. *Mill* thought of the replacement of the labor relationship by a shareholder relationship, the directorate being appointed by the workers; from such an organization of social economy he expected a great increase in productivity resulting from the shrinkage of the commercial apparatus merely serving the purpose of distribution and from the stimulus to enthusiasm on the part of the workers; he expected also that the spirit of democracy would become effective in the economic community.[2]

175. The Joint Stock Enterprise

Among the various forms of undertaking, social ethics is chiefly interested in that particular organization which, by its prevalence and its method of capital utilization, is most typical of modern capitalism. This is the business company, and particularly the *joint stock company,* or shareholders' company. The industrial production of all economically advanced countries is organized to the extent of about forty per cent in joint stock companies; the joint stock company is also the principal instrument for the organization of the large combinations which characterize the development of capitalism since the turn of this century. The joint stock company arouses the interest of social ethics also, especially because of the institutional objectivization of the profit motive occurring in it, through which the capital utilization process assumes a largely impersonal and "anonymous" character (in France the corporation is called outright *société anonyme*). This anonymity is evident in the impersonal designations of firms which tell the outsider nothing with regard to who are the owners of the business and often nothing with regard to who is really responsible for its management. Another aspect of it is seen in the fact that, generally, the shareholders have no other interest in a business than safe and ample dividends and have no particular personal connection with it. Shares, as a rule, are marketable, their value being assessed in terms of capital risk and prospects of profit. The management itself is subject, if not to the pressure of "immanent coercive laws" (*Marx*) of the movement of the profit rate, in any case to the pressure of the abstract profit interest of the shareholders coupled with the dynamic force of competition. Thus, in the organization of these undertakings, experience shows, the human and social aspects are readily thrust into the background.

On the other hand, the function of a joint stock enterprise in social economy is beyond dispute: the liability of the owners in the undertaking is limited to the amount of the shares they have acquired, with the result that large sections of the community can participate in big undertakings without excessive risk. By thus splitting up enterprise capital, the joint stock company makes possible the gathering together of greater and

[2] Cf. J. S. Mill, *Principles of Political Economy,* Vol. IV, Chap. 7, pars. 4, 6.

smaller amounts of ready capital in the interest of their economically productive application. Finally, it enables the entrepreneur function, which would otherwise be lost to the social economy, to be exercised independently of personal capital. And the joint stock enterprise makes possible mass production, which is necessary for a progressive living standard in modern society.

The peculiar character of the joint stock company has given rise to considerable abuses. The experiences of the period of development of the joint stock enterprise (in most countries the 1870's) impelled the industrial countries one after another to take legal precautions by special company *legislation* for the protection of the general economic interest, of the public willing to invest, and of shareholders. Such legislation created controls in three main directions: (1) in regard to the promotion of the corporation (in many countries, compulsory registration, including the giving of particulars about the responsible promoters, the proposed amount of share capital, the board of directors, and the powers proposed for the directors); (2) in regard to business management (general and particular responsibility of directors; in various countries: obligatory audit of books by accountants, internal organs of supervision like the *aufsichtsrat* [board of supervisors] in Germany and Austria, submission of an extract of the annual report to the authorities, obligatory publication of names of all directors, as in England); (3) in regard to rights of shareholders (the obligatory calling of an annual general meeting of shareholders by the directors and the presentation of an audited balance sheet).

These provisions of company law, however, have remained rather loose in all countries, since they have been made to fit the pattern of the economic morality of laissez-faire capitalism. The following defects have appeared in them: 1) The investing public has been misled by inaccuracies or omissions in prospectuses; promoters have secured advantages for themselves by the speculative purchasing of land or plant and reselling to the corporation at higher prices, thus influencing prices before the issue of shares, with the result that prices subsequently fall, to the detriment of the investing public. 2) The exercise of control over business management through the auditing of accounts has often become a mere formality, especially since the various methods of window dressing made it impossible even for the experienced auditor to gain an insight into the real state of a company's affairs. The purpose of window dressing may be to conceal unsuccessful speculations, special emoluments of officers of the company, unsound dividend policy, unjustified accumulation of reserves, and transactions by the directors on the corporation's account for their own benefit and the like. The institution of the *aufsichtsrat* (board of supervisors) in Germany and Austria has frequently been reduced in value because the accumulation of lucrative appointments to such boards of a number of firms in a single person made it impossible for the individual to carry out the supervisory task undertaken, or their excessive number was a burden to firms (the German company law reform of 1931 limited the number of members of the *aufsichtsrat* in a firm to thirty, the number of appointments to be held by an individual to twenty). 3) The legal protection of shareholders has often proved ineffective because of methods which have given to the directors or a group of shareholders far-reaching or complete control of the undertaking; these methods included in certain countries expedients such as shares carrying more than one vote, management shares, namely, shares at the disposal of the management to use in the best possible way, reserve shares, beneficiary ownership of packets of shares for the purpose of exercising control over the undertaking (as when anonymous firms such as banks are registered as the nominal, i.e., legal holders of shares, while the rights of control and of drawing dividends are exercised by the "beneficial," i.e., the real proprietor). By such means the remainder of the shareholders have often been almost entirely deprived of influence over the firm and general meetings have become a mere formality.

From this may be inferred the main lines for *reform of company law.* The governing principle must be the greatest possible *publicity.*[1] The first object is truth in prospectuses. The law should require that sufficient information be given to the investing public with regard to prospectuses in order to preclude the manipulations which occur in connection with the floating of a company and new issues of shares. In particular, it would be well to establish the liability of all signatories of the prospectus: promoters, directors, accountants, and valuers. The duty of publicity should next extend to the annual balance sheet and the associated profit and loss account. The objects here are truth (the truthful presentation of individual items without transfers), clarity (the specification of individual items without mixing them), and continuity of form (accounts to be presented in identical form, as far as possible, from year to year, to facilitate comparison). A measure of fundamental importance for the attainment of this object would be the laying down by law of a form of presentation of accounts.[2] The auditor, whose qualifications should be legally defined, should be under an obligation to draw attention in his

[1] The *Cohen Report on Company Law Amendment,* 1945, expressly declares that it takes this principle as basis: "Much of our report is based on the principle of the validity of which we are convinced, that the fullest information practicable about the affairs of companies should be available to the shareholders and the public." The *Report* contains a number of valuable concrete suggestions; they are often parallel with measures provided in the German Supplementary Company Law of 1931.

[2] Under the German and English reform schemes, measures such as the following are provided or proposed. On the assets side, there should be specified: fixed assets (land, buildings, machinery, tools, vehicles, patents) and current assets (raw materials, finished goods and goods in process of production, securities, own shares, claims on subsidiary companies, bills, checks, cash balances); on the liabilities side should be specified: long-term debts, including debentures and mortgages, and short-term debts, including in particular acceptances. Other rules concern the valuation of the several classes of assets and depreciation; disclosure of the amount of paid-up share capital and of reserves created for the securing of creditors is made obligatory; also the disclosure of directors' fees and of other emoluments and "expenses," of the purchase or sale of shares or debentures as well as of all capital transactions between the directors and the company.

report to deficiencies in the balance sheet or in the profit and loss account in the light of official regulations or to any reluctance on the part of the board of directors to furnish information. The annual report to the shareholders' meeting should afford a real view of the actual condition of the undertaking, especially in the perspective of the general trend of economic development, and should deal particularly with reserves and dividend policy; it should reveal also the relation of the company to cartels or trusts.

Closely linked with the aims mentioned is that of a stricter delimitation of the *powers of the directors* in the determination of the general policy of the corporation, which always involves far-reaching decisions on the handling of the corporation's funds, that is, the property of the shareholders. This delimitation of the powers of the management may take the form of reserving such decisions to the general meeting, or establishing a right of veto for a qualified minority of shareholders in the statute of the corporation. Such measures, however, can hardly intend more than the exclusion of business manipulations by the directors for their personal benefit. It should not be forgotten that the position of the managing directors is essentially different from that of trustees or employees; for, the exercise of the entrepreneur function, which falls upon the directors, calls for a considerable degree of freedom of decision.

A much discussed question is that of *secret reserves*. These are created principally by not passing on profits to the shareholders, but also by undervaluing capital assets in the accounts. One purpose of secret reserves is to conceal the extent of profits in years of good business and to use them to maintain the level of dividends in bad years. Another purpose is to furnish the management with the means of avoiding the contracting of loans or the issue of new shares so that the business can be self-financing. Sometimes the purpose pursued is that of enabling the directors to engage in financial manipulations going beyond their powers. The shareholders are then placed at a disadvantage, since they do not receive the dividends to which they are entitled in the current business year, and perhaps in later years they cannot receive higher declared profits because of the sale of their shares; besides, higher dividends in later years might cause a rise in the price of shares, a benefit which is lost to one who wishes to sell beforehand; finally, the creation of secret reserves might prevent an otherwise possible reduction in the prices of the products of the corporation or an increase in the wages of its employees. The socio-economic aspect of the creation of excessive secret reserves, insofar as they contribute to the self-financing of undertakings, must not be overlooked: undertakings create capital out of profits without having recourse to the capital market; considerable funds, which would have flowed into the capital market if all available profits had been distributed, are withheld and applied to investment without being subjected to the economic control of the interest rate of the capital market, which goes along with socio-economic productivity; self-financing also has a detrimental effect on the structural order of the national economy, since it is chiefly possible for the big undertakings and therefore causes their expansion, to the disadvantage of independent and small-scale enterprise. Besides, self-financing often facilitates the formation and expansion of combines through the taking over of smaller enterprises, and thus it can be used for the purpose of exercising power. In the individual case, the problem of secret reserves can be decided only in the light of the prevailing circumstances. The majority of shareholders would doubtless be in agreement with a limited reserve policy which, especially in times of economic uncertainty and a sickly capital market, guaranteed a steady development of the business and a relatively stable dividend. Ethically, the creation of reserves becomes particularly open to objection when the big shareholders, setting aside the dividend claims of the small shareholders, hold back profits in order to increase the substantive value of the shares, with the object of securing economic influence, etc. The above-mentioned schemes of reform contain provisions for preventing abusive manipulations, such as the establishment of an obligation to disclose reserves in detail, their sources and their application, and especially the laying down of bases for the valuation of individual assets. The state will have to take care that it does not favor the withholding of profits to the detriment of the social economy and the interests of the shareholders, through excessive taxation of distributed profits, too great freedom in the valuation of production installations, and too great opportunity to set down self-financing expenditure as allowances against tax.

There is a further question, the sense of *responsibility of the shareholders* and the way it can be strengthened. Proposals to admit only inscribed shares, to make the transfer of shares difficult, and thus to create more personal sense of responsibility on the part of the shareholders, can command only very limited support. Such measures may be useful when it is a matter of safeguarding undertakings of national importance against coming too much under the influence of foreign capital or of preventing undertakings that have a special responsibility toward the general good, such as organs of the press, from becoming the tool of anonymous forces. On the whole, the inscribed share with less easy transferability means a substantial reduction in the socio-economic function of the joint stock company, which, as already shown, depends upon ready transferability of shares. The experience of those countries where shareholders are required to be registered in the books of the company has not shown that anonymous share proprietorship can really be abolished in this way. The British Cohen Committee recommends statutory measures to secure the disclosure of so-called beneficial ownership in the company's books and of transfers of such ownership as soon as a single person is directly or indirectly a beneficial owner to the extent of one per cent of the capital of the company.

Production Unit Size

Marx's attempt to establish a law that the capitalistic undertaking necessarily tends toward a maximum size has not been borne out by the facts. Instead, there is a law covering the optimum size of concerns, with regard to the process of production and marketing possibilities for the individual classes of goods. The superiority of big business over small business is a fact where the law of mass production holds undisputed sway, so that, when greater quantities of the same kind of goods are manufactured, production costs diminish per unit of production. But the big concern is not economically possible for all classes of goods (e.g., in the production of bread, which must be consumed before it becomes too stale); even in the big town the mass production of bread is possible only within limits, and the wholesale bakery has by no means been able to supersede the small business. Another barrier to mass production is individual wants and tastes (e.g., the demand for shoes and clothing), which will certainly not be satisfied by mass production as long as there is free individual consumer's choice. The expansion of large-scale production may also be restricted in the free society, with its fluctuating demand by the movement of costs, if the fixed costs (which recur unchanged notwithstanding incomplete utilization of productive capacity) impose too great a burden of risk upon expansion. Finally, capital costs also have a restrictive effect on size: the small producer to some extent can withstand the competition of large-scale business because he can forgo interest on the capital which he has invested in his own business, whereas the joint stock company is largely dependent upon outside capital, which must be given a share in the profit in the form of interest or dividends. These economic limits to the superiority of the large-scale undertaking had the result that the extinction of medium-sized and small concerns, especially crafts, is out of the question. Indeed, in the course of capitalistic evolution there have even arisen new branches of small industry, sometimes in direct connection with the development of the large industry (e.g., for repairs and installations).

176. The Combination

The combination is the grouping of undertakings into one organization under unified direction (whereas the cartel is a temporary association of firms for the purpose of regulating the market while the individual firms retain their full independence). Combination structures can assume various forms according to the way in which the management of the combined undertakings is unified. We speak of "horizontal" combination when firms at similar stages of production and distribution combine, or "vertical" combination when firms at different but mutually complementary stages of production and distribution are associated. In either case,[1] a firm may,

[1] Three forms of association, from loose to close, may be mentioned: 1) The grouping based on interest, or syndicate, an association of firms founded upon exchange

by acquiring the equities of other firms, be enabled to control them (holding company, combine, *konzern* in Germany), or a number of firms may be grouped together to form one (trust, corporation, or, in the United States, big business simply).

Among the *advantages* causing the growth of combinations are, first of all, economies of various kinds. Hence, in the purchase of raw materials, the combination may enjoy a substantially more favorable position as a large-scale or even monopolistic purchaser. In the consumption of raw materials, too, economies are often achieved by the more efficient utilization of raw materials, in particular through better opportunities for using waste materials and energy. Production costs can be reduced by increased rationalization, reduction of labor costs, amalgamation of plants and the concentration of production in specialized plants. In marketing also, economies in costs can be made, especially in freight costs, by the allocation of particular markets to the best-situated factories; there can also be savings on advertising and travelling representatives. Again, the combination makes it possible to employ the most capable and experienced personnel in key positions. The financial power of the combination enables it to be to a high degree independent of the banks and their monopolistic power; they often have their own banks. Furthermore, and not least, the combination provides opportunity for long-term planning of capital investment, which, in view of the vast amounts involved in some branches of industry (e.g., iron and steel and nuclear energy), may be a matter of great importance for the economic community. For all these reasons, the combination can be in the interest of economic productivity, all the more since, as *Oswald Lehnich*, one of the best authorities on the prerequisites and workings of combinations, maintains, "the object of combination is primarily the strengthening of efficiency and not the curtailment of competition." [2]

But these advantages are counterbalanced by grave *perils* to social economy and to the general interest. Chief among these is the purpose of controlling the market, although "the prerequisite for restriction of competition first exists when the combination has assumed a definite magnitude," and this prerequisite is generally confined to the horizontal combination (uniformity in supply of goods); [3] as an example, the oligopolies in the motor industry may be cited. In the endeavor to expand and to control

of shares with regulations with regard to the accounting and distribution of business profits; the firms retain their independence, but they are subject to a unitary control either by links between the boards of directors or by the paramount influence of one firm. 2) A tighter form is the holding company, based on the acquisition by a firm of the shares of another; after the First World War certain large banks in Central Europe obtained control in this way over considerable sectors of industry in the course of reconstruction or of investment policy. 3) The strictest form of association is the amalgamation or fusing of firms, which continue to exist nominally as separate firms but in fact become parts of another undertaking; provincial banks have in this way been annexed to large banks, and smaller industrial undertakings have been acquired by large companies.

[2] O. Lehnich, *Die Wettbewerbsbeschränkung: Eine Grundlegung*, 1956, p. 47.

[3] Cf. *ibid.*, p. 49.

the market, the combination often has at its disposal financial means, which it is able to acquire out of profits. This involves another danger: the profits which the combination obtains from the above-mentioned advantages and economies are only exceptionally passed on to the public in the form of reduced prices, especially since, as *Lehnich* points out, the combinations like to manufacture standardized goods in order to influence prices. Moreover, the foundation of such combinations is often associated with stock exchange maneuvers and questionable share dealings on a grand scale, so that Professor *Liefmann* remarks that most American trust millionaires have owed their immense fortunes not to the earnings of businesses which they control, but to speculation. Still more undesirable is the economic and financial power which combinations secure through the acquisition of the majority of the shares in other firms; in the words of *Liefmann,* this power "enables capitalists to control two hundred times as much capital as they themselves possess." *Walter Rathenau* declared that the world is ruled by an upper three hundred in the realm of finance; there is, therefor, as *Liefmann* says, "the danger that states within the state are being built up, organizations which, with the aid of their capital strength, can gain an immoderate influence over the state and exploit and control it against the interests of the public." People do not form, he says (and what he says of Germany is true of all capitalistic countries), an accurate picture "of the influence wielded by the great capitalistic magnates on the money market, the press, public opinion, the government, even science." Some disquiet must be caused, too, by the underlying cause of all this: equity capitalism, the fact that, to quote *Liefmann* again, "an increasing proportion of the nation's capital is embodied in equities and is therefore mobilized." [4]

The task of subordinating the combination to the social end of economy, and with that especially the elimination of market control by the combination, when it is inconsistent with this end, will vary to some extent according as the combination is horizontal or vertical. The measures implied in the end in question will be aimed principally in two directions. The first is indicated by economic reasons in the interest of the combinations themselves and of the social economy as a whole. Chief of these measures is the decentralization of the powers and functions of the managements of the different establishments within the framework of the general policy set out by the overall management. Decentralization would mean chiefly allowing considerable independence to individual managements in their decisions, so that they would themselves be primarily responsible for the disposal of their goods on the open, competitive market. Enterprise would thus be fully effective, and competition would insure the productivity of

[4] R. Liefmann, "Trusts," in *Handwörterbuch der Staatswissenschaften,* Vol. VIII, 1928, pp. 311 ff., 318 f.; on the economic and political power of the trusts in the United States cf. A. A. Berle, Jr., *The Twentieth Century Capitalist Revolution* (U.S.A.), 1954.

individual units.[5] With a decentralized organization of the combination, the cost principle and the principle of socio-economic productivity would remain effective for all production units, and thus for the interest of the public. Limits also would be set to the drive for power.

Owing to the possibilities of market-control and the exercise of power, serious tasks fall upon the *state*. It will have to provide, by law, for a measure of publicity regarding the business policy of combinations, which will make it possible to guard the general interest through effective controls. This involves particularly a duty of publicity in regard to balance sheets and profit and loss accounts,[6] the disclosure of the extent to which subsidiary companies are subject to the control of the holding company or to the control of other subsidiary companies. Like American law, the English Cohen Report makes the status of a holding company dependent upon the exercise of *de facto* control by an undertaking over a subsidiary, whether by possession of a majority of vote-carrying shares or by the right of appointing a majority of the directors. There must be a publication of balance sheets and profit and loss accounts of all subsidiary companies individually, together with those of the holding company itself, drawn up in accordance with the regulations governing the presentation of accounts of joint stock companies (the relevant principles were discussed in the preceding chapter). The interests of the holding company and its subsidiaries in other joint stock companies must be disclosed where these are not controlled by the holding company in its capacity of holding company. Auditors will have an increased responsibility to ascertain whether the balance sheets and profit and loss accounts of the holding company and its subsidiaries are in accordance with the legal requirements of publicity binding such companies. The competent government department must also have the right to demand any further particulars necessary in the general interest of social economy. These measures will, first, give the public an insight into the interrelationships of firms within the combination and their respective capital holdings, and the concentration of power in the hands of the controlling firm and its directors. They will also hinder the camouflaging of the profit and reserves items in the accounts of the individual companies, an object which is often achieved as the result of complicated schemes of part-ownership and indebtednesses, whereby companies become subsidiaries and sub-subsidiaries, and the

[5] The same conclusion is reached by P. F. Drucker, *Big Business*, 1947, in his examination of the organization and managerial methods of General Motors. He calls this undertaking an essay in federalism, which attempts to combine the greatest corporate unity with the greatest divisional autonomy and responsibility. Drucker sums up the essence and advantages of such decentralization under the following heads: Speed and certainty in decisions; absence of conflict; scope for personal initiative; internal mobility; absence of social antagonisms; opportunities for promotion and a supply of qualified candidates; the stimulus of mutual rivalry; democratic policy-making.

[6] Cf. especially the *Cohen Report on Company Law Amendment*, 1945, pars. 115–22: "Relations between Holding and Subsidiary Companies."

camouflaging of the respective incomes of their directors. Means are also provided for revealing price-manipulations by individual firms in a combine, whereby the combine secures for itself opportunities of unfair competition vis-à-vis other similar but independent firms. An expert like *Liefmann,* who was one of the first to call for the greatest practicable degree of publicity concerning the affairs of combinations and, with this object, to propose regulations concerning the details to be shown in their balance sheets and profit and loss accounts, warns us against undue irresolution in this respect: "One need not hesitate even to demand disclosure of the wealth and incomes of big capitalists. From a social point of view, it is much better if there is no concealment of what the wealthiest people in commerce, industry, and agriculture possess in capital, what incomes they enjoy and what taxes they have to pay." [7] The principles which will be discussed in the following chapter for the public control of monopolies also apply to combinations, insofar as they attempt to secure monopolistic control of the market.

Proposals for *control of combinations* in the United States, which in part run parallel to those following from the Cohen Report in England, are discussed by *Fritz Machlup.* He maintains that the most far-reaching privilege granted to companies, and one which greatly fosters the growth of combinations, is the unrestricted right of acquiring share property in other undertakings, a right which, as *Walter Lippmann* (*The Good Society,* 1937) points out, would have been inconceivable fifty years ago; the proprietors of many joint stock companies have been deprived of their voting rights and, besides, of substantial portions of their profits, which have been "ploughed back" and used for expansion of the business, so that a large amount of the country's investment capital is withdrawn from the competition of the capital market; and, on the whole, no limit whatever is set to the expansion of the joint stock company. Further objects of reform discussed by *Machlup* are an obligation on every combination to declare all holdings and the names of all share proprietors (citing the important book by *C. D. Edwards, Maintaining Competition: Requisites of a Government Policy,* 1919); a limit would be set to combination-forming if directors were obliged to hold an interest, up to a definite percentage, in the stock of the company; he also discusses the limitation of companies in respect to capital, volume of sales, and numbers of employees, except when it is proved that reasons of productivity demand larger entities. With regard to taxation policy, *Machlup* has two observations to offer: the tax system is not neutral toward large and small undertakings; rather, the former has an advantage over the latter and the tax system must be organized with a prejudice against the large undertaking and the combination, which has not yet happened. *Machlup,* of course, has certain reservations to make, in detail, especially by reason of the criterion that the

[7] Cf. R. Liefmann, *op. cit.,* p. 320.

volume which is expedient according to the productivity principle varies in particular industries.[8]

Our principles of socio-economic productivity and social policy lead to the following conclusion: The medium and smaller independent firms and companies should be encouraged in their competition with combinations and corporations, not only when they reach a relatively higher degree of productivity but also when they reach an equal degree, and this encouragement should take place in every possible form of economic policy, credit policy, and fiscal policy.

177. The Cartel

Firms may try to secure increased profits by gaining the advantage in competition, or they may try to obtain high and assured profits by agreements to regulate or to restrict competition. Because the forms and the extent of restriction of competition differ, the definition of this kind of association, the cartel, must be a general one, such as put forward by Professor *Oswald Lehnich,* one of the best authorities on the history and forms of the cartel, in his *Grundlegung:* "It is a question of agreements between undertakings of the same kind which, while remaining independent, are intent on bringing about, with the help of a control and restriction of competition, a market situation inconsistent with free competition." [1] The market controls may cover production, conditions of sale, or prices.[2]

The *advantages* of such combinations for private enterprise and social economy rest on the restriction or elimination of ruinous competition. For the individual firm, these advantages mean an increased and secure rate of profit brought about by price fixing (undercutting is eliminated), economies in marketing (restriction of advertising), reduction of production

[8] Cf. F. Machlup, *The Political Economy of Monopoly,* 1952, pp. 240–65.

[1] O. Lehnich, *Die Wettbewerbsbeschränkung: Eine Grundlegung,* 1956, p. 15. Cf. Fritz Machlup, *The Political Economy of Monopoly* (U.S.A.), 1952, p. 85: cartels are business agreements with the purpose or effect of restricting or regulating competition.

[2] Among the various forms of cartels the following may be mentioned in particular: (1) those which lay down general conditions of sale, such as credit purchasing, charging for packing materials, rates of discount for payment in cash, the calculation of interest on deferred payments; (2) combinations whose members pledge themselves to certain standard or minimum prices, and perhaps also to schemes of calculation; such combinations are often called price rings; (3) by some combinations certain areas are assigned to individual firms or groups for exclusive selling; (4) others allocate all orders received in an industry to the member firms, generally through a bureau, called a syndicate; (5) other combinations lay down the aggregate output of an industry and allocate quotas to the individual firms in order to restrict supply and thereby stabilize prices; if quotas are exceeded the firms concerned must make corresponding payments to the combination; (6) profit-sharing combinations, whose members pledge themselves to pay their profits into a common fund administered by a syndicate, whence they are paid out to the individual members according to agreed quotas.

costs (rationalization by means of standardization), and economies in the purchasing of raw materials (elimination of the middleman through the creation of purchasing agencies). Cartels can also bring substantial benefits to social economy, in particular by eliminating economically harmful effects of competition, the ensuing destruction of capital, and hence unemployment. This can be of special importance in time of depression if the purifying process is already completed and if unregulated competition, by cutting out sound businesses, would lead to further economically disastrous destruction of capital. Again, the greater stability of prices makes possible longer-range economic planning, especially with regard to the vast capital investments on which highly technical industries depend. Moreover, by means of rationalization, cartels can make possible an expansion of production together with a lowering of costs and prices for the benefit of the consumer. Furthermore, the higher prices resulting from combination in certain branches of industry may result in the payment of higher wages. Not the least of the advantages of the cartel lies in its power of winning and of retaining foreign markets; at times there may even be justification for a temporary reduction of export prices, especially when it is a question of finished goods for which export markets are yet to be found and the export of which would foster home industry. Lastly, the usefulness of the cartel in the field of raw material production (coal, oil, minerals) is generally admitted, because it can help to prevent exploitation and wasting of natural resources.

Such combinations, however, may also involve grave *dangers* to social economy and at the same time to individual enterprise. First, there is the curtailment of competition, which is the natural outcome of cartel combination. Such curtailment may, of course, be in the interest of social economy, although cartel policy is usually engendered for private interests. The means by which it is operated is the maintenance of a fixed level of prices by keeping down supply. Supply is kept down by methods such as restriction of output (the allocation of production quotas to particular firms), the closing down of firms on the payment of premiums for cessation of production, the purchase of patents and inventions in order to prevent their exploitation in the process of production. The cartel marketing policy often involves methods of unfair competition, in order to bring to heel outside firms or to drive them from the market. Outsiders, namely, firms in a branch of industry which are not members of the cartel (or "ring"), are forced out of the market by temporary undercutting, by refusal to buy raw materials from firms supplying outsiders, and so on. Extensive combination can bring the social economy to a condition of rigidity and inelasticity and thus can give rise to a chronic state of crisis and unemployment (e.g., the period between the two World Wars). There is also the danger of technical overexpansion because the quota of total output allocated to individual cartel members is determined by the capacity of each firm. Hence, firms tend toward overinvestment in order to obtain a higher quota. The incidental result is the struggle for quotas and the purchase of quotas within the combination. This overexpansion may contribute substantially to the intensification of a subsequent economic depression. Cartel formation again increases the power of capital in relation to the consumer with the standardization of goods at which the cartel producers often aim. But, above all, cartels seek power as interest groups (cf. Chap. 134) for the purpose of imposing their special interests on legislation, economic policy, and government. They can also use their financial power to influence public opinion in various ways (e.g., by withholding advertisements from organs of the press that are not responsive to their wishes). The dumping of half-finished goods or raw materials on foreign markets can be very detrimental to the national economy, since it favors the foreign producer and hampers the competitive strength of the home industry with its finished goods. Even with finished goods, dumping is sometimes carried so far that home produced goods purchased abroad and reimported are cheaper, in spite of customs duty, than the same goods purchased direct from the works at home. This kind of dumping can amount to a squandering of the national wealth.

Monopoly and Oligopoly

Cartel combinations use "monopolistic" methods in order to control and to restrict competition. In *economic theory*, along with the powerful growth of combinations in modern economy, there developed a specific monopoly theory and, in the one-sided process of thought that is familiar on such occasions, competition and monopoly came to be spoken of as two forms of the socio-economic process. This overlooked the fact that monopoly is a relative concept, the meaning of which depends on the idea of competition. Meanwhile, a change has come about: the monopoly problem is approached again principally in terms of *perfect and imperfect competition*. In the course of this change it became clear that the actual reality of markets and prices is far too complex to be grasped by theories of perfect competition and perfect monopoly, especially since in the more recent development of social economy there is an increasing number of cases in which a few large suppliers try to regulate competition without any one of them having the power or will to dominate the market. Oligopoly is also discussed.[3] *Machlup* points out that, in the con-

[3] The notion of oligopoly is by no means uniform in economic theory. It is perhaps best to follow the realistic suggestion of Burkhardt Röper, *Die Konkurrenz und ihre Fehlwirkungen,* 1952, p. 203, and think of it as a collective notion for all possible market phenomena which are not covered by the concepts of monopoly or competition. Alexander Mahr, "Zur Systematik der Marktformen," in *Festschrift für Degenfeld-Schonburg,* Lagler-Messner, editor, 1952, pp. 279–87, who was probably the first to use the term oligopoly, declares that with oligopoly there are very varied possibilities of price-formation, and that the appraisal of the existing form of market is an extremely important, but by no means the only, condition for accurate analysis of price-formation, since it depends upon the often very significant differences in the *attitude*

cept of monopoly so often used by monopoly theorists, any price policy, no matter of what kind, is by definition a monopolistic policy, presupposing other than purely economic factors in price formation, and that in this sense even the smallest general store can be considered a kind of monopoly because of advantages of situation or service.

If monopoly is a relative concept for theory, it is no less so for *economic policy.* With regard to economic policy, it is related to a social end of economy conceived in a definite way. Indeed, *Fritz Machlup,* one of the foremost experts on monopoly theory, declares that discussions of "monopoly" are only practicable insofar as the general effects of "monopoly" on the aggregate output and in particular on the use of the auxiliary sources of production, are concerned.[4] This means that there cannot be any discussion on the question of "monopoly as such," but that there are always particular questions concerning whether and how far definite monopolies and monopolistic methods are economically undesirable and therefore to be eliminated. With these two points of view, which bring out the relativity of the monopoly concept, we have insured that we are looking at reality, the "nature of the facts," which is the prerequisite for the ethical appraisal of monopoly. The economic theory of competition and monopoly need not detain us further here, especially since a serious theorist like *Machlup* comes to the conclusion that no clear methods exist for ascertaining the extent to which access to individual industries or branches of industry or competition in their sphere is restricted; but when and the extent to which such restrictions of competition are found out, they can be removed, even if their effects are not exactly measurable.[5]

In judging the economic consequences of monopoly, it is necessary first to observe that inherent factors exist which set *limits* to its development and power, since the incentive of economic life is the desire for gain; where this meets with obstacles it seeks possibilities of by-passing them. Thus, there is no really complete monopoly on the basis of mere agreement, which is the prerequisite of cartel combination, but only a more or less complete curtailment of competition. In the market sphere of the combination an open as well as a covert competition always exists. Open competi-

of the parties toward the market. There is an abundance of kinds of attitudes on the supply side and on the demand side to be considered; one of these is referred to by Röper, *op. cit.,* p. 204, in criticizing the thinking in "enterprise models": "Here an essential phenomenon seems to have fallen short, namely the *compromise,* which plays an important role in economy as in daily life. Reality shows that for the market form of oligopoly also the compromise is rather the normal phenomenon, and conflict situations are exceptional." Similarly Machlup draws our attention to a too little considered kind of attitude, *op. cit.,* p. 104, in discussing the idea of *domination* of businesses by others, a situation which is always thought of as one of conflict between controllers and controlled, whereas frequently the controlled firms feel themselves "protected" rather than abused, and are prepared to stand for the controlling firms when these are exposed to political attacks. Cf. Röper, *op. cit.,* p. 226.

[4] Cf. Machlup, *op. cit.,* p. 20 (also pp. 39 and 83 on the function of competitive prices, or, as we express it, the social function of competition).

[5] Cf. *ibid.,* p. 528.

tion arises through the supply of goods of equal value by outsiders (producers not belonging to the combination) or through the supply of substitute products which, although not of equal value, are cheaper than those supplied by the cartel. Covert competition may be carried on within the combination itself through the struggle for quotas, the purchase of quotas, and the exchange of quotas, in the course of which firms of higher capacity reduce their production costs, thus securing higher profits; as a result, there is a ceaseless incentive to improvement of production methods. Covert competition is forced upon the members of the cartel by the ever-present possibility that the combination may break up and free competition must be resumed: the separate interests of the individual firms, therefore, provide a constant spur to increased productivity. Besides this, there are also limits to the price policies of monopolies. Since the demand for a commodity is always somewhat elastic, a monopoly would be restricting its profits if it reduced sales too much owing to excessive prices; on the production side, fixed costs work in the same direction, costs, that is to say, which remain constant without regard to the volume of output and therefore increase per unit of production as output diminishes, thus reducing profits.

But even when the inherent limitations of monopoly and its possible good effects are taken into account, grave *dangers* remain for the national and individual economy. In the national economy, restrictions on competition prevent the movement of prices in accordance with the cost principle ("natural prices"), and hence prevent the attainment of the optimum socio-economic productivity. Such restrictions of competition, private monopolies, therefore, on natural law principles can be justified only on the ground of special circumstances; [6] even the public monopoly is justified only to a very limited extent, as in the case of public services and the isolated case of a monopoly for fiscal purposes. When monopoly is criticized on natural law grounds, both the common good principle and the freedom principle are applicable; the order of freedom is to be seen as an essential part of the order of the common good itself; this was also true

[6] J. Höffner, "Der Wettbewerb in der Scholastik," in *Ordo,* 1953, p. 197, summarizes the natural law doctrine of the Middle Ages as follows: "Monopolies are to be rejected as attacks on the freedom of the market and hence against just price-formation." The modern economist judges with equal severity: "Every industrial monopoly represents an extremely harmful foreign body, socially and economically, within a system of free competition" (Adolf Weber, *Kurzgefaßte Volkswirtschaftslehre,* 7th ed., 1957, p. 262). O. Lehnich, *Die Wettbewerbsbeschränkung,* 1956, sums up his extensive researches based on experience in Germany thus: "As well as economic dislocations, restriction of competition within the framework of the general problem of organization causes a number of profound changes in the legal order: the formation of new centers of power with jurisdiction and coercive power equal to the state's, if not superior; a new sense of organization, even perhaps a special organization morality; then a not essentially new but gradually intensified pressure on personal freedom of will; and finally the partial elimination of one of the foundations of modern economy, equality among entrepreneurs as a condition of freedom of contract."

in earlier and later medieval scholasticism.[7] Encroachments on the sphere of freedom are as manifold and diversified as the forms of effective restriction of competition. If a monopoly is able to block access to a branch of industry, the primal freedom of economic activity in this branch of industry is cancelled; this freedom is the fundamental "right to work" (in this case with the application of economic enterprise and of means of production on the principle of free use of private property). The consumers also are not to be forgotten, since they may have to pay excessive prices for the supply of basic requirements; an example could be a severe housing shortage at a time when building costs are high, materials (cement, bricks, metal piping, glass) and labor (in trade unions) being controlled by combinations. In fact, combinations, with their monopolistic methods of market control and price fixing resulting in excessive prices, become an instrument of widespread social usury.

If, as has been suggested already, monopoly and restrictions of competition are a question of the common good, then the *state* acquires the duty of establishing and of maintaining the fundamental order of social economy and the market. It is, however, exceedingly difficult to find the right methods and approaches, as may be seen from the experience of American and German legislation.[8] The reason is that, in the free society, there exist not only incalculable opportunities for evading legal regulations governing profit-making, but the lawgiver himself is subject to the pressure of

[7] Monopolies are condemned because they impair the freedom of economic enterprise: such methods of controlling the market, it is objected, take away from the market its freedom and constitute an attack on the general freedom; the harm to the consumer, who is forced to pay a higher price, is also emphasized; in addition it is pointed out that monopolies harm the common good, the state, more "than bad harvests and grasshoppers." Cf. Höffner, *op. cit.;* and on the monopoly question, also J. Höffner, *Wirtschaftsethik und Monopol im 15. und 16. Jh.*, 1941.

[8] It is not fortuitous that the most lasting efforts by the state to combat unfair competition occur in the *United States,* with its decided notions of freedom. The Sherman Antitrust Law goes back as far as 1890; it was concerned chiefly with restrictions on trade between the states of the Union and foreign states. In 1914, under the Federal Trade Commission Act, a Commission was set up with the power to inquire into companies (banks excepted) or individuals in case of any supposed unfair or dishonest methods in competition or business, which should be then eliminated by administrative procedure. The Clayton Act of 1914 was directed against restrictions of competition by price-fixing, differential prices for particular purchasers, exclusive sale agreements, and the buying up of the stock of a rival corporation. In 1923, *Germany* created a Cartel Inspectorate and set up a Cartel Court; all agreements for the regulation by cartels, syndicates, and similar combinations of output, the market, and prices had to be deposited in writing before they could become legal; such agreements could be declared invalid by the Cartel Court on grounds of public interest or could be cancelled by one of the parties on the ground of unfair restraint of economic freedom or other reasons; exclusive sale, boycotting, and embargoes on delivery were prohibited. The *experience* of both countries points unmistakably to the fact that, in practice, only secondary importance can be assigned to state control of combinations and that the primary and deciding factor is business morality in industry, which can be made effective only by the vocational groups in industry themselves. Real progress was made, therefore, in both countries only when the industrial groups themselves began to brand unfair methods of competition and of restricting competition.

interest groups in drafting and carrying out the law. *Machlup* declares that, in the United States, the legislation against cartel agreements has actually furthered the growth of monopolies; firms have evaded the law by creating corporate combines or mergers (cf. preceding chapter). Secondly, the failure of antitrust legislation is, to no small extent, caused by the interest groups, as *Fredrik Neumeyer* points out, and by those who manipulate public opinion in their service; furthermore, it is caused by the many exceptions (trade unions, cooperative societies, banks, shipping companies, railways, export corporations). *Machlup* and *Neumeyer* also point to the omission of the duty of publicity in regard to subsidiaries in combinations which control the market, and, especially, the failings of patent law, although, for the reasons stated, no legal reforms are to be expected in either direction.[9] The slight success which antitrust legislation has had in combatting monopoly is commonly admitted. In Germany, experience has been similar with the prohibition of cartels by the occupation authorities after the Second World War; *Lehnich* goes so far as to state: "It is to be clearly seen that the lawgiver is powerless in face of the economic tendency to restrict competition. In spite of prohibition, cartels have revived themselves in invisible form. They have merely undertaken skillful adaptations and have replaced the legal pressure, which is forbidden them by law, with a moral pressure." A favorite method of evasion is the corporate combine with an extensive system of vertical price agreements.[10] The law of 1957 represents only a partial success in the struggle against restrictions of competition; cartels are prohibited, yet numerous exceptions are envisaged in the law, so that "there must be doubt about the effect," [11] as that leading German economist, *Adolf Weber,* puts it, in the light of long acquaintance with trust legislation, especially since, as *Lehnich* also mentions in the passage quoted, with the complexity of tacit understandings (as distinct from true cartel contracts) it is no longer possible as a rule to perceive whether an individual price within the discipline of such combinations derives from monopolistic conditions or not.

If we inquire into the role of the *state* in the struggle against monopolistic tendencies, we shall first have to remember that it was the state itself that supported these tendencies, even though unwittingly, in almost all the greater industrial countries; *Adolf Weber* adds a gloss to this: state economic policy "was influenced by the erroneous notion that the private losses of weak entrepreneurs were fundamentally bad from the viewpoint of social economy, although they often mean only a beneficial adaptation of entrepreneurs working at fixed costs to the economic progress which tends to leave them behind." *Weber* mentions the help given

[9] Cf. Machlup, *op. cit.*, pp. 232, 207 ff., 285 f.; F. Neumeyer, *Monopolkontrolle in USA*, 1953, pp. 216–33.

[10] Cf. Lehnich, *op. cit.*, pp. 477 ff.

[11] Adolf Weber, *op. cit.*, pp. 261 f.; for an account of the preparatory work on the law cf. Lehnich, *op. cit.*, pp. 479–609.

to such undertakings by protective tariffs which ward off foreign competition; fiscal practice, which has favored the manufacture of long-term production goods, and has discouraged the distribution of profits and promoted ploughing back, with the consequence of raising fixed costs. Another impetus was given to monopolistic tendencies, according to *Weber,* by the credit policy of the banks, which preferred large-scale credit for long-lived production firms (cf. Chap. 167), and also the false thinking about techniques, which caused large production plants to be considered as more efficient, whereas often because of the high fixed costs they increased the difficulties of adaptation and hence the need for protection. "Thus, the big firms secured the upper hand in more and more individual spheres of the economy, and the power groups—the cartels, combines and trusts—arose in their manifold varieties. They were used in the attempt to make the interests of the organized suppliers predominant at the expense of the interests of *all* parties to the market." [12]

The pressure of vested interests on the state and its economic policy is much greater at a time of depression than at a time of prosperity, especially since, during a depression, the entrepreneurs emphasize the necessity of dismissing workers if the protection which they have desired is refused. *Lehnich* regards a "constitutional economic law" as a most important measure to combat monopolistic methods, a law which could be altered only by a qualified majority necessary for changes in the constitution and not at any mere change of government; besides, legal protection for restrictions of competition must in principle be granted only exceptionally and only for brief transitional periods. State legal protection was a main support of the cartels because they were recognized as agreements binding in law, and prosecution could follow their violation by members. When *Lehnich* finally proposes "an office for economic order with supreme authority" [13] as a measure to combat restrictions of competition, he invites serious objections. One recalls how little, in *Lehnich's* own opinion, is to be expected from the state; besides, it is not possible to see how, in a liberal democracy, such a "supreme authority" can enjoy a status and function alongside the government, particularly since American experience shows that the firms subjected to examination under the antitrust laws are carefully chosen, with an eye on the power of combinations.

In the pluralistic society with its group interests and pressure groups, which under democracy seek to attain their ends by exercising direct influence on the state and on the executive power, certainly very serious responsibilities will fall upon the state; yet, the crucial function is a settlement which primarily concerns not political, but economic, forces. Our fundamental idea (cf. Chap. 181) is that, on the one hand, the state has

[12] Adolf Weber, *Allgemeine Volkswirtschaftslehre,* 6th ed., 1953, pp. 533 f.
[13] Lehnich, *op. cit.,* pp. 499 ff., 612 f.

to establish and guarantee a basic economic order, but above all it must be possible for entrepreneurs willing to compete effectively to insure their freedom and to make a stand against existing restrictions on competition. In that basic order the state would have to create the necessary *conditions* for an effective control springing from the forces of competition itself. About such necessary conditions *Liefmann* has submitted suggestions which have not yet been made obsolete by the new literature on trusts and monopolies.[14] They are: a duty of publicity for all trusts, on the fulfillment of which must depend the legal validity of the agreements underlying them; the duty of trusts to convey to the competent authorities all information required; the duty of publishing detailed periodical reports on the state of the associated firms and of their branch of industry in order to make possible the exercise of control by the wider public; the obligation to publish classified production and consumption statistics as necessary data for appraising the price and production policy of cartels.[15] With the Monopolies Act of 1956, the United Kingdom undertook the following measures: an obligation to declare any restrictions on competition to the Registrar of Restrictive Trading Agreements, so that information is available at all times about any such agreements and their conditions and about those participating in them (the Register can be inspected in the principal towns of England and Wales, Scotland and Northern Ireland); a Restrictive Practices Court decides whether such practices are in the public interest, failing which they come under prohibition (there is no provision for the middle course, whereby, as in the United States, the authorities agree to a modification of the regulation of competition and have the power to terminate the legal procedure); the burden of proof of the fact that a restriction of competition is in the public interest lies with the partners to business agreements on prices and conditions of sale.[16]

[14] Cf. K. Liefmann, "Kartelle," in *Handwörterbuch der Staatswissenschaften,* Vol. V, 1923, pp. 625 f.

[15] The question whether legislation to combat restrictions of competition should follow the prohibition principle, permitting exceptions, or the abuse principle, which is directed against competition restrictions contrary to the public interest, seems to be of mere theoretical significance, since with the former the rules for exceptions must in practice be elastic, and with the latter the same result can be achieved if the law is strictly applied.

[16] As direct effects of the British law the following are noteworthy: On the last day before the expiry of the time for registration over 1,000 notifications were received; in the preceding weeks a large number of agreements to regulate competition were altered in form with the assistance of lawyers in order to evade the provisions of the law, and since new agreements had to be notified within three months a new large batch of notifications followed; numerous agreements were simply abandoned because there was fear of a far-reaching duty to give information before the court, including the submission of documents, correspondence, and details, with lawyers' and experts' costs, so that even in case of clearance by the court the advantages of business agreements would not balance the expenditure and so were foregone at the outset (*Manchester Guardian,* March 2, 1957).

The Law of Concentration

Marx correctly observed that, in individualist capitalism, there is a law of concentration at work, but he misjudged its causes, its extent, and its effects. He explains it by his law of the diminishing profit rate. The diminution of profits, he argues, compels the capitalist to replace labor by machinery; parallel with this, competition leads to the elimination of the weaker undertakings with the result that many capitalists are "killed" by the continually decreasing number of the really big ones. Hand in hand with this process goes "the transformation of the individual and dispersed means of production of many into the massed property of the few, so that the great popular masses are dispossessed of their land, of their means of livelihood, and of the instruments of their labor." Typical of this process of accumulation is, in *Marx's* view, the continual increase and expansion of the stock corporation.

In fact, however, statistics show that share ownership has extended, parallel with the growth of the joint stock corporation, into the middle class, so that it has been possible to speak of a "democratization" of ownership in big business through the stock corporations. Again, the development of industry with its cartel agreements has largely run counter to the tendency which Marx predicted for it: that of eliminating competition, which should have led to the progressive demise of firms. Concentration in the form of the combine reached massive proportions, but even that has proved limited owing to the competitive strength of smaller undertakings, with the result that these are not only continuing to exist but increasing in number. Although concentration in the form of cartel and trust marks a structural change in capitalism from competitive to monopoly capitalism, with detrimental effects on the social end of economy, yet, prognoses of an inevitable fundamental change in the economic system along the lines of Marxian determinism, however fashionable they may be, are not really borne out by the facts. At the session of the Verein für Sozialpolitik in Zürich in 1928, Professor *H. Diehl* rejected Professor *W. Sombart's* forecast of a fundamentally new economic system, with the paradoxical observation that monopolistic cartels do not represent a new form of economic organization; on the contrary, they represent the culmination of a free competition, since they are essentially the outcome of an economic system resting on the competitive principle. The economic development of the United States, with its firm adherence to the competitive principle in spite of all combinations, at any rate shows that these need not of themselves lead to an altogether new economic system and that the hypothesis of a deterministic evolution is scientifically untenable. Of course, monopolies in the hands of the state, organized in the form of cartels and trusts, can become typical forms of socialistic economic organization or of state-planned economy. Thus, the separate branches of industry in Soviet economy are organized as trusts.

One of the main goals of reform in Western society indicated by the social end of economy is the greatest possible "democratization" of ownership in companies, particularly through the coproprietorship of the workers in industrial capital by means of shareholdings (cf. Chap. 171).

178. Banking

The bank is the undertaking which serves as an intermediary in money transactions and in credit transactions. As such it not only provides, like other branches of the economy, a particular commodity, but keeps the whole modern economic process in operation. Besides the two main groups of functions mentioned, the banks perform other functions of a more secondary nature: the safe deposit of valuables [1] (coin, bullion, securities, etc.) and the purchasing and selling of foreign exchange. To facilitate the making of payments the banks perform first and foremost their deposit service, holding money at the disposal of customers in deposit or in current accounts, which they can withdraw by check or in cash.[2] To facilitate credit business the banks advance loans in the various forms already mentioned (cf. Chap. 167), part of their service being the conversion of savings deposits into investment capital. Such deposits are entrusted to the banks in expectation of a definite rate of interest, and the banks, in order to meet this expectation, must apply the deposits to investment; the credit services of banks also include issue business (the underwriting or placing of loans on behalf of public bodies, of bonds, namely, fixed-interest bearing debentures of undertakings, of shares of corporations in the process of flotation or of increasing their capital) and commission business (the purchase and sale of securities on behalf of customers). Banks of the kind described are also known as commercial banks to distinguish them from the central issuing bank, whose function it is to supply the national economy with cash in virtue of its sole right to issue banknotes (legal means of payment).

The nature of the commercial bank's function in the service of money and credit supply, demands that it undertake no obligations which it cannot currently carry out in accordance with sound business principles. This maxim is essentially the same as that which is true for every undertaking: sufficient cash must be held in readiness to meet current obligations. As the *principle of liquidity,* it gains all the greater importance from a natural law point of view because the essential function of the bank is the entering upon current payment obligations, so that the danger of insolvency is incomparably greater than with other undertakings. Bank insolvency causes losses to the customers as well as having far-reaching effects on the socio-economic process as a whole. The economic history of the last hundred years throws abundant light on all this. The principle of liquid-

[1] The true *depositum* of older natural law theory. This confers on the banker no proprietorship over the object, which must be restored on demand.

[2] These deposits are essentially different from the *depositum,* since they concern a fungible object and represent a debt on the part of the bank to the customer (a *mutuum*).

ity means that a bank's liabilities (money received in deposits) must be so covered by its assets (cash, credit with other finance institutions, claims arising from loans granted), so that the bank can discharge liabilities arising at any time by means of realizable assets. The extent of the liquidity to be maintained is governed by the cash requirements of customers, and these again by business custom (e.g., seasonal demands) and psychological factors (a buoyant economy, confidence in the solvency of the bank). At any given time, then, the bank has to discharge only a fraction of its total liabilities; therefore, it need keep only a percentage of its deposits in cash (in normal times about ten per cent) in order to meet demands as they arise. Offenses against the liquidity principle, which mark the history of bank failures, include the following: the granting of credit on too large a scale (in the process of competing for big customers); loans against inadequate securities (especially the granting of loans on the strength of fluctuating shares); blank credits; the acceptance of accommodation bills, which are based on no transaction in real value; unwontedly risky participation in stock exchange transactions; carrying too far the practice of issuing securities on the banker's own account; the advancing of funds not sufficiently secured, for purposes of speculation on the stock market; in the more recent history of finance, the use of short-term credits from abroad for the granting of long-term industrial loans: this was one of the main causes of the bank crisis of 1931, which originated in Central Europe and had such far-reaching effects on world economy.

The position which the banks occupy in the economy confers important tasks upon the *state.* Since the modern commercial banks are mostly joint stock corporations, the same principles apply to the tasks of the lawgiver in regard to banks as we have developed for the control of the joint stock corporation in general. The lawgiver must make provision for the soundness of the business management of the banks and thus of their solvency. The prime condition for this is an increased duty of publicity in balance sheets and in obligatory periodical reports. In the balance sheets of hardly any other form of undertaking is there so much camouflage to mystify the public as in those of banks. A detailing of the individual items, therefore, has unceasingly been demanded as the prerequisite to any real check on a bank's affairs by the public. Under assets, to mention only some examples, should be disclosed the average holding of cash since the publication of the last balance sheet or periodical report, and not merely the holding on the day when the accounts are made up, a figure which could be reached by various manipulations; balances with other banks should be shown separately under the central bank, clearing banks, and other banks; securities should be classified according to character as Treasury Bills, government loans, fixed interest securities, shares, and so on; advances should be classified according to term. On the liabilities side a distinction should be made between demand deposits (current account), time deposits, and savings deposits proper; losses and the writing off of bad debts should be clearly visible. Legislation should also provide for publicity regarding the combination of companies in the banking sphere and the range of influence exerted by the banks on industry. In almost all countries the banks are exempted from the antitrust and cartel legislation; yet, publicity regarding combination of any kind is undoubtedly in the public interest. Concentration in the banking world leads to a high degree of monopoly on the part of finance capital. In all countries, the big banks have absorbed a large number of smaller houses and with their nationwide networks of branches they enjoy a virtual monopoly in the granting of credit. Theoretically, of course, it can be objected that banks can, "in the long run," make profits only if productive industry brings in returns, and therefore that banks must have regard for the needs of industry; and certainly the few big banks in each country are in competition with one another for customers (oligopoly), especially for the bigger ones. And yet, there exists among them, as in no other branch of economy, a tacit understanding about business policy. In no other branch is the profit interest so homogeneous as in finance capital. The big financial institutions exert power by making easy or difficult new industrial and commercial projects, by their dominating position in the provision of credit for medium-sized and smaller industry, and by their influence on economic and commercial policy and on politics in general (cf. Chaps. 153–54).

The mighty influence which finance capital exercises on economics and politics makes it easy to understand why the call for nationalization of the banks is continually heard. But this would obviously transfer into the hands of the state, of the government, and of the party or parties behind it the power possessed by the financial houses. Such a gigantic concentration of economic and political power can provide no solution. What the social end of economy requires, rather, is the following: Decentralization of management in the realm of the big banks, and thus a transfer of responsibility to the provincial and branch banks, an organization of the banking system to correspond with credit requirements, a professional organization inspired with the sense of responsibility and socio-economic thinking of all its members; and, in addition to the legal measures already proposed, the institution of an agency formed from a supreme economic council and consisting of representatives of the main spheres of economic activity, for the purpose of watching over the credit policy from the point of view of the general economic interests of the nation. We shall presently be discussing this in detail.

Today more than ever before it is the general belief that the functions of the commercial banks in *money and credit business* exercise a most far-reaching influence on the whole course and development of the socio-economic process. All this business is carried on through the medium of money. A widening or narrowing of the stream of money inconsistently with the requirements of socio-economic productivity means inflation or deflation. If the supreme principle of natural law for the whole management of the banks is liquidity, the *supreme natural law principle* for all money and credit business is stability of value. Banks create money (cf. Chap. 165) by opening current account credits for customers, which the latter can dispose of by check. Thus, the volume of money in circulation in the social economy is to a considerable extent dependent upon the loan business of the banks. It is upon this that the profits of the banks mainly depend, and consequently they endeavor, in favorable market conditions, to extend their credits as widely as possible. Thus, the flow of money is increased, and with it demand. If this is not accompanied by a like increase in socio-economic productivity based on savings capital, inflation is the inevitable result. On the other hand, if unmistakable signs of recession appear, the banks, in order to maintain liquidity, call in short-term loans, thereby hastening the recession and bringing about the collapse of undertakings whose situation might have been serious but not desperate. Thus, in accordance with the nature of the facts, namely the function of money and credit in the service of the social end of economy, natural law ethics will have two further principles to state in accord with the economist: "(1) that the capital investments for which the bank is directly or indirectly responsible should bear the proper relationship to the level of savings in the national economy, and (2) that, what is required in the interest of an increased liquidity, especially the calling in of credits, should not entail the collapse of inherently sound creditors." [3]

Two more principles remain to be mentioned which are of great importance in nearly all countries. No one could maintain that the chief blame for inflation falls on the banks and on their credit policy; rather, the organized interest groups with their excessive income demands and the state with its excessive expenditure are responsible for the progressive expansion of the volume of money and thus of demand, for the increase in production costs and the price level, and hence for the progressive devaluation of money. Indeed, bank directorates in nearly all countries have shown a significant sense of responsibility for what the national economy requires, particularly in collaboration with government and central banks, when they have appealed to the banks to cooperate in fighting inflation through a cautious and selective lending policy. Nevertheless, a further principle to be mentioned is a heightened sense of *responsibility* to the national economy on the part of the boards of directors of banks, not only because the commodity in which they deal is the vital element of the national economy, but also because their special position gives them a far better vantage point for surveying the whole national economy than is given to other branches of the economy with their conflicting interests; therefore, they have an obligation toward the whole of the national economy and its present and future development.

The last principle to be stated is securing the *independence* of financial

[3] Adolf Weber, *Geld, Banken, Börsen,* 5th ed., 1955, p. 221.

and credit policy from political party and interest groups; under democracy this means, above all, the independence of the central bank from such influences, and hence also its independence from the government of the day. In the democratic system, governments are dependent on the wishes and demands of parties and pressure groups. They have to make economic policy more or less with one eye on the next election and on the wishes and demands of people seeking a greater share of the economic output and the national income. To meet these wishes and demands would mean an expansion of the stream of money and of credit, which would have inflationary effects. A central bank with the necessary degree of autonomy can be a bulwark against an inflationary economic policy. Since governments fear that it may make their economic policies more difficult, they dislike too much independence of this kind; therefore, it should be anchored in constitutional law to the extent necessary for insuring the stability of the currency.

A matter of great significance for the fulfillment of the socio-economic functions of the banks is the *structural organization of banking,* vertically and horizontally. Vertically, the object is a decentralization of banking to the extent necessitated by the nature of regional economic requirements. Certainly the great banking institutions cannot be dispensed with in the centers of trade and of industry, but the branches should enjoy the necessary managerial independence in satisfying regional and local credit needs. Even more important is horizontal division, in the sense of a division of labor among the banks corresponding with the particular credit requirements of the different branches of social economy (cf. Chap. 170). What is needed is a development of important beginnings, which already exist in most countries, with the differences between joint stock banks and private banks, between commercial banks and cooperative institutions (e.g., for agriculture and small-trade credit), between banks for industrial and commercial credit, between savings banks and mortgage banks. Another necessary objective is the separation of deposit business from investment business in banking organization, in such a way that the security of moneys entrusted to the bank is not endangered by the latter. This becomes even more important because the banks are making ever more strenuous efforts to attract savings, while on the other hand their credit business is rapidly expanding. The separation need not go so far as the setting up of separate bank institutions, but certainly legislation must "make it difficult for short-term moneys to be used for long-term purposes, and for long-term moneys (savings) to be used for purposes of day-to-day payments." [4]

In addition to the principles of legal regulation, structural organization, and business policy, which have already been discussed, there re-

[4] Adolf Weber, *Depositen- und Spekulationsbanken, Ein Vergleich deutschen und englischen Bankwesens,* 1st ed., 1902; 4th ed., 1938; separate departments are suggested also by Irving Fisher, *100% Money,* 2nd ed., 1936.

mains to be mentioned the role of the banks in the *general economic policy and planning policy.* This is fundamentally the affair of the state, although this does not mean that, in a democracy, the state must be equated with the government in power at the moment. The common good is altogether more than a matter of opinion for governments to decide. Governments are constituted by parties whose will represents only that of a fraction of the population, whereas the good of the whole population should form the rule of their action, a rule which is of the greatest importance in the question we are discussing because it confers obligations not only toward the present but toward future generations. Credit economy is of its nature *economy for the future.* Therefore, it follows that credit policy must not be left wholly to the arbitrary will of the commercial banks; rather the nation must have a voice in all essentials. In this respect the nation is indubitably represented by the state, but equally it must be represented by the central organizations of its vocational groups. From a long-term point of view, the leading principles of credit policy will have to be worked out by an agency composed of representatives of the central organizations of the vocational groups (including representatives of the central bank and the relevant ministries). These principles would be directives for state economic policy, for the interest policies of the different groups, and indeed for the central bank (its fundamental task as set down above must remain inviolate). In the working out of these principles, the following points are to be taken into account: the necessity of integrating the structure of social economy (e.g., by guiding credit into agriculture, if national and international circumstances demand increased production); the foreign trade situation (circumstances may necessitate that certain export industries in a country should be favored); the technical development and the consequent emergence of new industries or the necessary reorganization of existing ones (here may be an opportunity of influencing the tempo of mechanization, rationalization, and automation); the social stratification of a country (the encouragement of the economic middle class can be especially desirable); current or expected difficulties in particular vital branches of the economy; the aid to be given to underdeveloped countries by the national economy. A development in the direction of an organ of the kind discussed here is to be seen in a number of countries in the form of advisory national committees to assist the government in questions of credit policy.

179. The Over-all Markets

Over-all markets affect the entire social process and its immediate future development. Therefore, they call for separate treatment in a discussion of the organization of social economy. They deal principally in foreign bills, securities (the capital market), and primary products of world-wide importance, such as grain, cotton, and copper (the commodity market). As the principal centers of exchange for capital and commodities, at the same time establishing contact with world markets, the over-all markets are distinguished by an extreme sensitiveness to any influence bearing on the socio-economic process and by the considerable influences which they themselves exert upon it. Hence, more information can be gained as a rule about the developments and tendencies in international politics from the exchange reports in the daily press than from the editorials. The stock exchange indexes are often a more reliable barometer of actual economic development and its undercurrents than statistics of production, consumption, and exports.

The functions of the over-all markets may be grouped under four heads. First, they serve as trading institutions of the highest *efficiency*. This is because the goods they deal in are specified only as to quantity and quality, so that substitution is possible, times of delivery and payment are precisely regulated, and consequently, supply and demand are brought into contact over the widest extent of space and time. The result is that any commodity is available at any time and in any place. Under a free social economy, a producer in a remote town can reckon on receiving the quantity of cotton which he requires through the agency of a merchant who deals on the cotton exchange; similarly, anyone can obtain through his bank any particular shares in which he wishes to invest his savings. Secondly, these markets perform the function of *levelling prices* by ascertaining supply and demand over wide areas and long periods. In this they provide industry and commerce with essential data for calculation and planning. Thirdly, they have the function of affording *insurance* against price risks by means of forward dealings, or "futures." A cotton spinner who purchases raw cotton must envisage the possibility that, on the day of selling his finished products, cotton prices may be lower and he may thus lose a corresponding portion of his invested capital; he can, however, sell the same quantity of cotton on the exchange at the expected date of sale of his finished products: if cotton prices fall, he is covered by the price in forward dealing; if they rise, he is covered by the higher price of the finished article. A similar kind of safeguard comes into play against foreign exchange risks in the purchase of raw materials for manufacturing for export. Fourthly, these markets provide the opportunity for a *speculation* useful to the social economy. Speculation in general means business activity involving risks caused by the fluctuations of the socio-economic process. By speculation on the over-all markets, risks in markets of the highest economic importance are made the object of trade, and this from the motive of private profit, which is always the motive when risks are undertaken in economic life. By the fact that these risks are undertaken by the dealers in these specialized markets, the industrial or commercial undertakings concerned are relieved of part of their otherwise much greater risks and at the same time they are enabled to form a more exact estimate of the remaining risks and a sounder calculation.

The *dangers* which the investment markets hold for the economic process are rooted chiefly in their character as a forum of speculation. No other institution of modern social economy has been so much condemned on this account as these markets. Often enough they are regarded as simply a field for commercial bandits who extort gigantic profits from productive industry by criminal methods. To reply by idealizing them, as theorists often do, and to explain away the depredations of "speculation," that is of economically unsound speculation, as merely harmless occurrences in the socio-economic process, is to be equally far removed from reality. Anyone who seriously attempts to deal with this question must find himself continually wondering what constitutes economically useful speculation. Since the growth of the modern exchange there has been almost ceaseless debate on the subject in every country, and it has become particularly lively when stock exchange scandals have come to light. We must now try to define more closely the kind of speculation that is beneficial to social economy. Concerning the principle itself there can be no doubt: speculation is ethically justifiable when it fulfills a useful function in the socio-economic process; it is ethically reprehensible when it is harmful in this respect. (We are concerned here only with the socio-economic aspect. How far the individual is obliged on moral grounds to abstain from gambling on the stock exchange is a question for individual ethics and moral theology; such an inquiry must take into account the danger of a passion for gambling and of the inadequate fulfillment of duties to family, to creditors, and to the needy, as a result of the squandering of means in speculative investments.)

The kind of *speculation* which performs a *necessary function* in the modern economic process includes the following features: knowledge of the existing state of the market; study of the influences bearing on the possible development of supply and demand in the markets concerned; an endeavor to foresee probable tendencies; the contracting of business liabilities in spite of the remaining factor of uncertainty. This factor constitutes the risk which is always bound up with true speculative enterprise,[1] whether in the form of capital investment in equities or in the form of the entrepreneur's proper function. There is a double risk involved in investment in securities: first, the profit risk, since a share can bring in greater or less dividends, and secondly, the valuation risk bound up

[1] J. M. Keynes, *The General Theory of Employment, Interest, and Money,* 1946, p. 158, wants to appropriate the term *speculation* for the activity of forecasting the psychology of the market, and the term *enterprise* for the activity of forecasting the prospective yield of assets over their whole life. This does not seem to be quite in accord with the author's own very acute definition of the stock exchange as an institution whose purpose is to direct new investment into the most profitable channels in terms of future yield (p. 159); for, such a function cannot be performed without genuine enterprise in the acceptance of the risks involved in speculation on the future course of the capital market and investment chances.

with fluctuations in price for risk capital in accordance with supply and demand. An investor who purchases a security on the exchange, consequently, will have to consider not only the prospective yield on his investment but also the likely tendencies of the capital market. From what has been said, we see that speculation becomes *harmful to socio-economic efficiency* when price gains are made the sole purpose and a share is made the object of speculation independently of any expert appraisal of the yield prospects and of the undertaking in question. Such speculation is indeed a kind of gamble and must cause harmful disturbance to the social economy: harmful to the development of the equity market, harmful to the public's judgment on the relevant undertakings, and harmful to capital investment, because productive economy is deprived of moneys which are held in reserve for exchange speculations. This last statement is not invalidated by the argument that capital is not lost to the economy as a whole through such speculation, but that capital sums merely change hands.

Such, then, is our verdict on *speculation by the public* on the stock exchange. The general public lacks the expert knowledge for socially useful speculation. In fact, it is the speculating public that is primarily responsible for many of the abuses on the exchange, and not the exchange as an institution. How can speculation by the public be curtailed? 1) The members of the *stock exchange* itself can make a substantial contribution by insuring that all who deal on it conform to the necessary standard of business morality; this naturally means forgoing some profits, since profits rise with increased turnover. This object will be best achieved when the exchange is organized on a professional basis in the way in which we shall presently describe. 2) The *banks* can have a restraining effect by discriminating in their loan business for speculation on the stock exchange, and also by advising the public. This, too, involves loss of profits, since a considerable part of the profits of the banks is made up of the proceeds of commission on the purchase and sale of securities. The rate of interest on loans in continuation business (*contango*) is of great importance: an increase acts as a brake on speculation, a reduction as a stimulus.[2] 3) The

[2] Thus, when bull or bear operators, owing to an unfavorable movement of prices, are unwilling to settle a time bargain by payment or by delivery of the security, the banks, either directly or indirectly through brokers, provide accommodation to make it possible to carry over the transaction and so await a more favorable tendency, the shares in question serving as security (the method varies in different countries). How unfair stock exchange speculations can be carried on by irresponsible banks in this kind of loan business is well demonstrated by Adolf Weber, *Depositen- und Spekulationsbanken, ein Vergleich deutschen und englischen Bankwesens*, 4th ed., 1938, p. 207: By granting loans readily they can stimulate the desire to purchase and bring about a rise in exchange prices; "but it is also possible for the banks to depress prices in that they 'block' capital which they perhaps have held available up to then in excess for *contango* purposes. The superfluity of money seems to have given way to a scarcity; the uninitiated is disturbed, he thinks that he must act in accordance with the market situation, and he sells; because of this sale prices are further depressed and further sales are occasioned. The banks may also perhaps participate ostentatiously in

state can influence speculation by the public chiefly through the central bank with its power over the money market. Direct legislation to prohibit speculation in the form of stock exchange gambling does not seem expedient for reasons stated in our discussion of the tasks of the legislator in cases when he finds himself faced with emotions which preventive legislation would simply divert into other channels (such as the black market) more detrimental to the common interest. 4) Lastly, we must not overlook the role of the *press* in keeping unsound speculation in check. If all those who are responsible work together, then speculation by the public may well be reduced to harmless proportions. For indeed, as *Keynes* says, speculation may do no harm "as bubbles on a steady stream of enterprise," but it is harmful "when enterprise becomes the bubble on a whirlpool of speculation"; with the eye on capital development, he says, this cannot be a by-product of the activities of a casino, if things should not go very wrong.[3]

The principles which we have derived from the socio-economic function of speculation apply also to those *professional dealers* on the exchange. Indeed, they apply with even greater force because a special professional responsibility rests upon the latter and because their conduct exercises a far-reaching influence on speculation by the general public. The ethical criterion is, in this case, also the socio-economic effect of speculation and of its methods, especially their effect on the possibility of appraising the factors of supply and demand. Any methods to secure profits from speculation are morally reprehensible if they tend to mislead the market. Such *stock exchange maneuvers* can make use of two principal methods: the spreading of false reports about factors which directly or indirectly influence supply and demand, or the falsifying of the market situation by influencing actual supply and demand. As a rule, both methods are used in conjunction. Their aim is to influence the mood of the investment mar-

selling activity; at the same time they unobtrusively increase their purchases to a large extent, and—the business is done. It is worth mentioning too that the *contango* position provides opportunity for acquiring legal proprietorship of great quantities of securities. This temporary proprietorship can be used for voting at general meetings of shareholders, with the possibility that the temporary shareholder may pursue quite different interests from the true shareholder." Weber further points out how the vagueness of the distinction between dealing on one's own account and commission dealing on the stock exchange has had the effect of making it possible for the banker "with one hand to induce the financially weak client to speculate, and with the other hand, when market conditions become unfavorable, to ruin him" by burdening him with securities which otherwise he, the banker, would have purchased for himself (*ibid.*, p. 214). Thus, in the third edition of the work quoted (1922, p. 222) Weber states: "It is perhaps possible to say that in share transactions rather 'too much' division of labor is better than 'too little.' The close connection between dealing on one's own account and commission dealings, which is the rule in Germany, undoubtedly entails greater disadvantages than the perhaps too elaborate division of labor in England." Weber was here referring to the division of labor between banks, brokers, and jobbers: the brokers receiving loans from the banks and the jobbers being engaged mainly in the pricing process, and therefore mostly specializing in markets for certain industrials.

[3] Cf. Keynes, *op. cit.*, p. 159.

ket, whose extreme expressions are stock exchange fever and panic, or to influence the prices of the particular securities in which the speculator is interested. The mood of the stock exchange is affected by exaggerated or false reports of an optimistic or pessimistic nature regarding possible tendencies in trade, or in politics at home or abroad, by reports concerning changes in the bank rate, by projected measures of taxation, by measures to promote or restrict imports or exports, by governmental loan policy, and by difficulties or favorable prospects in leading industrial undertakings. Equally far-reaching are the effects of methods adopted to influence the actual factors of supply and demand and thereby to influence prices for the purpose of obtaining purely speculative profits. Firms or groups of speculators with a strong backing of capital, banks or stockbrokers can rig the market by means varying with the constitution of the stock exchange in different countries, in order to be able to sell better or to buy more cheaply. A long catalogue of such maneuvers could be compiled from the history of stock exchanges. They vary from year to year; for this reason alone there would be no purpose in going into detail. Only one principal method, that of forward dealings (futures), calls for special consideration.

Forward dealings (as distinct from cash business) are based on the exploitation of expected price movements in the hope of profiting from the difference between buying and selling prices. In simple forward dealings, securities or goods are bought or sold for acceptance or delivery at a later date, at a fixed price, in the expectation that in the meantime prices will rise (bull transaction) or fall (bear transaction), thus resulting in a profit. (In time, bargains, or option business, one party reserves the right to withdraw from the contract on payment of a premium; this method has greatly receded in importance in most countries or has become obsolete.) The argument against these transactions, that the turnover in securities or goods exceeds by several times the actual quantities in existence or that a seller sells goods which he does not possess, does not in itself rule them out morally, for they are features inseparable from trade and are indeed common practice in commerce: merchants sell goods which they do not yet possess but can presumably obtain and deliver. It is true that a large proportion of forward dealings are not aimed at the actual purchase of securities or goods, but at the making of a differential profit. Yet, there is no doubt that they possess the character of genuine commercial dealings, because in exchange dealings obligations are always entered into by both buyers and sellers actually to take up or to deliver the securities or goods, even though they endeavor to rid themselves of these obligations where possible by appropriate transactions.[4] Whether

[4] On the proposition that transactions based on mere payment of price differences in forward dealings do not really occur on the stock exchange and are often confused with the option, cf. O. von Nell-Breuning, *Grundzüge der Börsenmoral,* 1928, pp. 168 ff. On the other hand, there is point in the observation of W. Prion, "Börsenwesen," in *Handwörterbuch der Staatswissenschaften,* 4th ed., 1924, Vol. II, p. 1063, that the

the speculation which is involved in these dealings is for the good of social economy depends, however, chiefly upon how far it is compelled to remain in contact with the concrete price-determining factors which govern the socio-economic process, and with the actual state of the undertakings whose shares are priced on the stock exchange. Hence, we come to the question of creating the conditions for fulfilling the socio-economic function of the over-all market.

The subordination of activity in this market to the general interest can, as experience shows, be achieved only by a combination of *regulative forces* on the part of the professional organizations and on the part of the state. Relatively little can be done by the state alone. Such is the sure lesson of the German exchange reform of 1896, which placed legal restrictions on forward dealing. It was not merely that its purpose, the protection of the inexperienced public, was not attained, since speculation by the public hardly diminished, but the price system itself became uncertain and unbalanced because of the predominance of cash business, quite apart from the fact that a portion of the business of the stock exchanges was simply transferred to the joint stock banks because of the high capital expenditure possible for them.[5] On the other hand, features that proved their value, and thus were incorporated in the German law of 1908, were the regulations regarding classes of persons [6] permitted to engage in forward dealings and classes of securities and commodities [7] in which forward dealings would be permitted. Only in certain continental countries, including Germany, Austria, and to some extent France, are the over-all markets subject to state regulations or state supervision. In the United Kingdom and the United States there is no state sanction or supervision, and the exchanges are completely autonomous organizations. Experience bears out that the lion's share in the task of insuring a proper functioning of the over-all markets in the interest of the social economy falls, as implied in the natural law principles, mainly upon the *self-government of the vocational body* representing those professionally engaged in the business of the exchange markets.[8] The most important conditions for this are

existing procedure in forward dealings, whereby accounts are finally settled by the payment of resulting balances, "can easily lead to the view that forward dealing consists only in the payment of price differences. This view must gain even greater force if another speciality of the stock exchange, the continuation, is taken into account."

[5] Cf. Prion, *op. cit.*, p. 1063.

[6] On the stock exchange: such transactions to have legal effect only when concluded by legally qualified traders, registered companies, persons now or formerly engaged in banking, or persons specially admitted to these dealings; on the corn exchange: futures completely ruled out except when concluded between producers, manufacturers, or merchants.

[7] Securities: admitted only under special conditions for certain categories, such as mining shares, a certain minimum amount of authorized capital required; commodities: forward dealing permitted only after consultation with the industrial groups directly interested.

[8] The "berufsgenossenschaftliche Organization" was already advocated before the turn of the century by so realistic a thinker as G. Ratzinger, *Die Volkswirtschaft in ihren sittlichen Grundlagen*, 2nd ed., 1899.

an educated sense of professional responsibility, a professional code of business morality, and professional tribunals with adequate powers to administer penalties for breaches of the code. No other form of control can really take the place of control through vocational self-government or even achieve its own purpose without it. The professional body must lay down the conditions for the admission of members to the exchange markets, first emphasis being placed on character, commercial training, and experience, with financial means being placed second. Next, there must be standards governing the classes of securities in which dealings, and especially forward dealings, will be permitted. Another important field is the development of standards governing the procedure to be accepted for the various transactions, and here very much will depend on a sense of responsibility in all members of the organization, safeguarded by vigilant and strict tribunals. Past experience shows that a professional organization of the kind we have indicated is not Utopian: in nearly all the stock exchanges of the world, standards of business methods and forms of tribunals have been evolved. At least they are beginnings which suggest the possibility of future development along the lines indicated. It can hardly be doubted that, in addition, indispensable functions would fall to an organ whose members are elected by the organized bodies of the branches of industry which directly depend on the functions of the exchange markets. For the stock exchange this will mean the principal organizations of industry and commerce and the banks; for the corn exchange, agriculture, the milling concerns, the import trade. On all such committees the consumers must be adequately represented. For the stock exchange, the tasks of these committees will include the elimination of economically harmful methods of speculation, the exclusion of unsuitable securities from exchange dealings, and the settling of approved methods of quotation; for the corn exchange, these tasks will include the grading of qualities in accordance with the needs of the country, the arranging of rates of compensation in case of deliveries above or below the stipulated grade of quality, and the prevention of fictitious bargains and speculation maneuvers ("gambling with the bread of the people"). Indeed, almost all the functions mentioned above in connection with the German legislation fall within the competence of a professional organization or the superior organ referred to.

If the importance of the over-all markets has somewhat diminished in European countries since the First World War, this does not make the discussion of the relevant natural law principles less topical. The exchanges are essential organs for fulfilling the social function of the highly developed market economy. Where they fail in this task, the restoration of its full functioning capacity will be a requirement of a just market system. This is even more true in that the over-all markets are of decisive importance for the building up of a capital market which can guarantee economic and social progress, economic growth in the countries of the

West and, depending on this, economic help for underdeveloped countries. *Adolf Weber* rightly warns us against the bypassing of the exchanges by the big banks when they do not pass on to the exchanges most of the business which comes their way in the buying and selling of equities, but balance their business between branches and head offices or with the aid of friendly banks, "allowing only the few remaining items to reach the exchange." This development is, to some extent, part of the process of concentrating capital and power in the few big banks; "but insofar as this is the case, the exchange has ceased to be the organ of a *free* market economy. It is becoming the organ of monopolistic or large-scale capitalistic power factors." [9]

[9] Adolf Weber, *Geld, Banken, Börsen,* 5th ed., 1955, pp. 313 f.

PART THREE

The Integration of Social Economy

---

180. The Economic System

When the expression "economic system" was coming into general use, Professor *Adolf Wagner,* one of the so-called "socialists in a professor's chair" in the Germany of the 1870's, first urged that "every economic system actualizes a mixture of principles, not merely one principle." In the economic theory of the natural law school there has never been any doubt that a plurality of principles is essential for an ordered economic system. In all spheres, the social order is determined by the common good principle and the principle of subsidiary function. The principle of subsidiary function expresses itself in two special principles: the self-responsibility of the individual in the fulfillment of the tasks laid upon him by the existential ends, and the self-ordering of society in the fulfillment of the tasks implied in the existential ends. We speak of "society" as distinct from the state. This right of self-ordering empowers the smaller community to safeguard its common interest against the individual interests of its members and against the authority of the state. The organizational function of the state, namely, that of coordinating, overseeing, stimulating, and assisting, is rooted in the common good principle. Thus, *three principles* exist which must underlie any ordered economic system, that is, one which is capable of fulfilling its end: self-responsibility for the individual (freedom), self-ordering (self-governing) for society, and a community order for the state. Hence, the natural law principles for the order of social economy point to a *"mixed economic system,"* on the analogy of the mixed form of state in the political order.

Natural law principles, however, offer only a very general outline of an order of social economy, and not a concrete detailed economic system, just as natural law implies no legal systems and has no preference between democracy, monarchy, and aristocracy. This must not be taken to mean, however, that, applied to social and economic reality in time and place, natural law principles do not yield some definite demands. For, as our whole inquiry has shown, although natural law principles are general principles, nevertheless they are not empty conceptual shells, but principles with the purpose and the power to give order to the spheres of social life. The fact that natural law principles contain an *outline of economic order* is (1) evident from the fact that they exclude both the individualist and the collectivistic economic systems, and hence both forms of monism, that of total individual freedom and that of the total authority of the state; (2) again, natural law principles rule out systems which represent only a mixture of these two systems, a mere *compositum mixtum* of two contrary principles. The economic order based on natural law principles rests rather on a coordination of three principles, none of which may be omitted. That is why natural law thinking has always had to reject liberalist and socialistic systems which adhere to an exclusive, absolute priority of one principle: liberalism places the essential ordering function in the free play of forces (although with correctives); socialism places it in state organization of economy (although recognizing a sphere of individual freedom to be secured by democracy).

No other sphere of human life is so characteristically a sphere of *relative natural law* as that of social economy. Since man's existential ends are based on natural law principles, the fulfillment of the tasks bound up with them is dependent on circumstances, and hence on time and place. The economic and social common good, therefore, imposes in one country tasks different from those in another, in every country today tasks different from tomorrow's, and therefore it calls for an appropriate choice and application of methods: permanent or temporary socialization of branches of industry, or denationalization and return to private hands; central controls or restoration of private initiative; monopoly organizations or extension of competition. Natural law principles demand a harmonizing of economic order and economic policy in accordance with the long-term and short-term ends of the common good, but at the same time they lay down the principle of subsidiary function as a general rule, constantly to be preserved, for all interference in social economy: "As much freedom as possible, as much control as necessary."

Thus, the natural law principles clearly indicate the direction in which the fundamental order of social economy is always and in all circumstances to be sought. The three principles cause a system of coordinates for an order of social economy in conformity with the existential ends, that is to say, an order with man as its central point. One of the most important, and yet most difficult, tasks of a modern natural law is undoubtedly to sketch the form of this order of economy which accords with present-day intricate conditions (thus also *Keynes;* cf. Chaps. 85, 181, n. V). The fulfillment of the tasks in question presupposes an understanding of the organization and functioning of present-day social economy, together with knowledge of the failings of this organization and of their immediate and remoter causes. Another prerequisite is an estimation of the short-term and long-term effects of measures and reforms in the existing economic system, which natural law principles appear to dictate; for they may produce effects which may prove the existing failings in the economic system the lesser evil in the circumstances. Idealistic demands, appealing to natural law principles, can then be misguided, since it is one of the fundamental principles of natural law that the immediate goal is the best possible arrangement in the prevailing circumstances, and not the absolute best (cf. Chap. 49); in this respect natural law ethics is, as otherwise, realistic. Today, natural law economic ethics is therefore faced with a very wide range of complex questions of fact, of justice, and of expediency.

The *nomenclature* of an order of economy based on natural law principles should be governed mainly by two considerations: it should bring into relief the essential interconnections of this order, but should equally be characterized by an awareness of the ideological currents which it is to encounter. The expression "solidarism" brings out the coordination of individual and of society which is demanded by natural law principles. The idea behind the expression "vocational order" is the notion of the "social" ordering forces of economy, and in particular the autonomy of the vocational communities; it has the disadvantage that it does not emphasize at the same time the other two principles of order, and therefore that it does not obviously confront the liberalist and socialistic systems of social thought; on the other hand, the idea is gaining ground that, in the pluralistic society, as characterized today especially by the pressure groups with their interests, only by balancing the group interests themselves on the principle of justice can the perils which threaten democracy be overcome. Again, the expression "social market economy" can be used to designate a social economy organized in accordance with the three principles mentioned, if "social" is not merely related externally to "market economy," but the market economy is understood as part of social cooperation, for the arranging of which each of the three principles is equally relevant. Another possible expression (but cf. Chap. 184) is "socially integrated democracy," which has connotations of individual freedom, the state's ordering function, and the autonomy of vocational communities; in addition, it seems sufficiently apt for the extension of democracy from the political into the social field, which is in such general demand today. The expression "economic democracy" seems unsuitable because it is misleading and was misinterpreted from the beginning by the socialists; on the other hand, the designation "industrial democracy," which is commonly used in the United States, is not colored by socialistic ideology, and its reference is mainly to "social" ordering forces in the sense of self-governing vocational communities.

181. The Order of Social Economy

Although liberalist classical economic theory has for some time been vigorously criticized, its fundamental error regarding the order of social economy has not yet, as far as we can see, been assessed with sufficient exactness. This error did not consist in the fact that the classical theory assigned a function to competition in the economic order, since competition, as we have seen, actually contributes to the attainment of the optimum economic productivity. On the other hand, the socialistic hope, that the ordering function of competition can be simply replaced by centralized planning, direction, and control, has proved illusory. Both in theory and in practice the socialists are today concerned with insuring that the function of competition is exercised in their economic system. No, it is not the fundamental error of classical theory that it expects the ordering of social economy to come from competition; rather, its fundamental error is that it holds that competition need only be completely free, "perfect," in order to perform this function. The classical economists think that competition bears its own regulative principle within itself and will automatically and necessarily bring about the highest level of general well-being by virtue of the free play of forces which it entails.

Admittedly, the exponents of liberalist economics have hastened to say that free competition can never completely become a reality. Nevertheless, their theory was governed by the presuppositions mentioned, and these were false. They were so false that modern socialism, since its beginnings, has been able to focus its criticism of laissez-faire capitalism on the "anarchy" of competition. But in doing so, socialism was led to its own fundamental error of seeing the ordering principle of social economy only in centralized planning, direction, and control, with its theory of collective ownership as the philosophical substratum. Thus, the radical error of the socialistic economic theory is the counterpart of the radical error of the classical theory.

We must deal, therefore, with both errors at the same time by forming a precise idea of the ordering function of competition in social economy and simultaneously of the ordering principle that should govern competition itself. What kind of principle will it be, then, which should regulate competition?

I *Competition as an Ordering Principle in Social Economy*

We have said (cf. Chap. 162) that competition has a social function of crucial importance, namely, in bringing about the best possible fulfillment of the social end of economy. Therefore, it is itself an ordering principle of social economy. This is an evident conclusion from a number of natural law principles and ideas implied in the "nature of the facts":

1. It is an obvious conclusion from the principle of subsidiary function, the principle of man's personal and primary responsibility in the performance of the tasks assigned him by his existential ends, and hence from the basic principle of freedom: "As much freedom as is compatible with the common good." A root principle in the social sphere, it applies also without restriction to the economic sphere. In this sphere also the principle

is based on man's existential ends. These involve the task of providing for the economic existence of oneself and one's family for the present and the future. We refer deliberately to tasks laid upon man by the family; indeed, man's being ordained for family life is one of the most evident and incontrovertible existential ends. The clear witness of this end is corroborated by the fact that family responsibility provides one of the strongest motive forces in the process of safeguarding and extending the economic basis of life. This is accompanied generally by the acquisitive instinct characteristic of man's nature, although this expresses itself with great variety in individual cases. The acquisitive instinct means the exploitation of one's own abilities or resources in order to obtain better economic conditions of life. In both respects mentioned, the desire for gain is one of the basic impulses of human nature. Thus, it seems evident that only an economic system based on *private enterprise* corresponds to the demands of man's nature; such a system will necessarily be competitive. Competition is, accordingly, an essential feature of an economy organized on the principle of subsidiary function.

2. The same conclusion is reached from the principle of *private ownership,* which, as we have seen, is a fundamental natural law principle of social order. In the society which has private ownership of the means of production, economic cooperation must mean the free exchange of the goods produced by its individual members and the concurrent endeavors of the various producers to make the conditions of exchange more advantageous for themselves by offering better or cheaper products. This is competition. In the society regulated by natural law principles, then, economic "cooperation" can only take the form of "competition."

3. Competition is indispensable for the fulfillment of the *social end of economy.* This is a logical conclusion from our analysis of economic productivity and its realization by the movement of prices to the natural level. In the social economy, with its complex division of labor, economic calculation is economically not possible (cf. Chap. 165) without competition, and such calculation is the necessary condition for the best possible use of the available labor and natural resources as required by the social end of economy. Besides, psychologically, only competition can mobilize all the forces of economic cooperation, and it is thus rooted in the social end of economy as a sector of the common good, with its demands for economic, social, and cultural progress.

4. The next argument is closely related to the last: Competition is the indispensable means for realizing the *just price.* The just price (cf. Chap. 168) is the economically correct price, and this means the price which truly expresses the relationship between demand and supply. Demand and supply can be fully effective only in a system of competition resting on private ownership and private enterprise.

Thus, we may sum up the results of our four arguments, of which the first two are based on the *freedom* of the individual, the last two on the *common end* of economy: Competition is the natural constitution of economy in the sense of the social cooperation of men in the fulfillment of the material and cultural tasks laid upon them by their existential ends.

11 *The Principle for the Ordering of Competition*

Competition has the function of a fundamental principle of order in social economy. But it itself requires a regulative principle to guarantee that it will function in the service of the end of social economy. Hence, the aim is *ordered competition.* Only a complete misunderstanding of human nature could have led the classical economists to assume that unrestricted free self-interest in competition must lead to a harmony of interests. Natural law theory, it is true, also holds that the idea of order is inherent in that of freedom; but it is equally aware that human nature, in its use of its freedom, is prone to overstep the bounds set by this order: a large proportion of the members of society will always seek to assert their own self-interest at the expense of the rights of others. In the laissez-faire system, the result is unfair, ruinous, or too expensive competition, with the consequences of business collapses, economic crises, and unemployment. Economic order, therefore, is not something resulting automatically from the interplay of individual economic interests; rather, it is an aim depending on man's ordered will and is to be guaranteed by the ordering will of society. Competition, therefore, if it is to perform its social function, itself has need of a regulative principle.[1] This principle is that of the common good or the social good, namely, the principle of social justice with all that is implied in the social end of economy.

Competition thus involves two equally important tasks: first, the ordering of competition in accordance with the claims of the social end of economy; secondly, the maintenance of competition for the sake of its own ordering function in social economy. In brief: the establishment of order and the preservation of freedom in competition are equally the object of the ordering function under discussion. On natural law principles, then, competition cannot be "perfect," but only "imperfect," in the sense that the free play of forces must be kept within the framework of the order of the common good. But to *make competition as "perfect" as pos-*

[1] Neo-liberalism, on the other hand, is distinguished by the idea that freedom of competition is fundamentally the sole principle of order in market economy. Admittedly, state interference in the organization of the market is considered necessary and self-help measures by groups justifiable, yet only on the principle of "market conformity." But this again makes freedom of competition the ultimate principle and criterion of the order of the market, and hence of the system of competition. All deviations from this market conformity are regarded only as exceptions to the general rule of the one principle of freedom. In the neo-liberalist view, the social element in the "social market economy" is only a secondary principle with a restrictive force as regards the primary principle of freedom; whereas, according to natural law ethics the common good principle is rooted in human nature exactly as is the principle of freedom, and the social end of economy is valid for the ordering of freedom exactly as is the freedom to business activity which underlies competition.

sible within this framework, since upon this depends the degree of attainment of the social end of economy, is itself required by the order of common weal justice.

Because liberalist competition contained no real principle of order, it led from the original laissez-faire capitalism to monopoly capitalism. The very great curtailment of competition under monopoly capitalism has exposed the error of older liberalist theory in supposing that competition carries its own regulative law within itself and that this operates automatically. In fact, the social end as the regulative principle of economy requires that the social function of competition shall be fulfilled to the fullest possible extent—on the one hand through protection of the freedom of competition against attempts at curtailment by exercise of social or economic power, and on the other hand through control of this freedom in order to prevent its abuse to the detriment of the general interest of the economic community. The fact that freedom of competition does not come about spontaneously is today generally admitted; the result is the legislation against restrictions of competition, which today is regarded as necessary in all states. Yet, with state regulation an order of competition insuring its social function has not been achieved. Concerning the reason for this there can be no doubt.

State regulation can work only through general laws with generally prescribed exceptions. In the liberal democracy, laws are passed in accordance with party strengths, with the result that they always reflect power relationships and are subject to change when these change; furthermore, such laws, because they depend on power relationships, are substantially determined by the disposition of the special interests of the groups and not by the overriding social end of economy. The radical weakness of such legislation is that the decisive ordering function is shifted outside the realm of social economy and that the state is assigned a function which it cannot fulfill. If infringements of the order of competition are made by individuals or monopolies, the state can take legal or administrative steps in accordance with such regulations. In combating unfair methods of competition in this way, however, the state must always be in the wake of actual developments because methods of restricting competition are too numerous, and hence there are always opportunities of circumventing legal regulations. To combat new methods, the state must once again set the machinery of legislation in motion; the result will again be the same.[2] This can be seen by recent developments in countries which

[2] Our remarks above are confirmed by so eminent an authority as J. F. Schaer, *Handelsbetriebslehre*, 1921, p. 285: "Like the whole of industrial life, commerce is in a perpetual flux of development. Every day brings new ways, new methods, new combinations, and in the field of competition especially inventiveness is unlimited. New inventions of burglar-proof safes are followed closely by new devices for bursting them open. So also, unfair competition, which knows how to slip into a thousand hidden recesses of economic life, can discover all the loopholes and weaknesses in the law and can continue its job without coming to grief before the courts. Conse-

have legislation against restrictions in competition: the laws are bypassed by forming big corporations, a development which calls for fresh legislation.

Experience has shown the ineffectiveness of much legislation in different countries to combat restrictions of competition. Such experience has further taught that state legislation cannot achieve an order of competition serving its social function unless the organized vocational communities of the individual branches of the economy themselves provide rules of fair competition and insure that these are observed in business. Furthermore, the state must always, when adopting measures to regulate competition, and again when putting such measures into effect, consult the vocational organizations. If these facts of experience are taken together, the only possible conclusion is that the ordering of competition is primarily a matter for the organized industrial bodies, that is, for *"social" organs,* and not for the "state." The task of the state is, in this respect, only a subsidiary one: it has only to do what the vocational bodies cannot accomplish themselves. Its main function is to create the legal conditions for the activity of vocational organizations and in carrying out the measures which these bodies consider necessary against existing restrictions in competition. These functions of the state are implicit in its essential sphere of functions, but also are adequate to forestall arbitrary action by industrial bodies and by powerful concerns.

We come then to the conclusion that the maintenance and ordering of competition are tasks for the economy itself, namely, for "society" and not for the state: they are a matter for the self-government of the organized vocational bodies, separately and in cooperation.

111 *The Key to Free and Ordered Competition*

The nature of the socio-economic process leaves no doubt concerning the point from which it can be kept in order so as to fufill its social function to the greatest possible extent. This point is the *price.* Price is the resultant of supply and demand and of the factors of competition operating in them. By means of price-formation, competitors try to make special profits for themselves, whereas, the function of market price-formation is to keep prices moving toward the natural price level. Since the natural price for particular goods consists in the "socially necessary costs" (cf. Chaps. 162, 168) of their production, including the "socially necessary income" as a factor in costs, this price results in the optimum socio-economic productivity in relation to the social end of economy. The ordering of competition, therefore, means that, through the

---

quently, the machinery of legislation must be kept in motion almost uninterruptedly if it is to keep pace with new practices in the field of unfair competition; hardly has a new law appeared, however, when it seems already too loosely woven to catch the crafty and unscrupulous businessman."

price-mechanism, the law of economic value, which is operative in the *movement of prices toward the natural price,* is made unfailingly effective in every case. This means that no one who is capable of satisfying demand with cheaper or better goods should be prevented by any form of restriction of competition: his freedom of enterprise and his readiness to give better service in the general economic interest must be protected from all endeavors to eliminate such competition by monopolistic methods based always on unauthorized use of power (on these methods see Chap. 177); in addition, the consumers themselves must be enabled to take steps in their own defense against excessive prices.

In fact, all recent attempts to establish an optimum measure of fair competition have shown that, ultimately, prices are the focus of measures to promote the social function of competition. This is evident in the case of legislation against unfair competition. The unfairness consists in traders' selling at below average prices by not paying their creditors, not meeting their taxes or social welfare dues. Often they relieve themselves of their liabilities by means of a composition with their creditors and the inland revenue in order to start up again in a fresh business. Price is equally the focus of efforts to combat unfair checks on competition by monopolistic power. Their aim is the securing of extra profits by high prices, and these are maintained, generally under the leadership of dominant firms in the branch of industry, by agreements or understandings. The idea that prices are the key to control of competition is confirmed also by the fact that the central point of the whole traditional natural law economic theory has been the question of the just price as the social purpose of competition.

But if the price is the key to fair competition, is not the fixing of prices by authorities the simplest means? No, because the economically correct price is the resultant of a complex of variable flexible factors, and the individual price itself influences a number of factors in price-formation; and no authority could survey all these effects and countereffects, much less assess their significance for the use and cost value of goods. Again, the price fixed by authority can be circumvented and, from all experience, price-fixing demoralizes competition, for which reason alone it cannot contribute to the establishment of sound competition. For one result of price-fixing is the growth of a black market for the goods affected. In fact, no one today thinks in terms of price-fixing by authority as a general measure. Neither does price-fixing play any part in the procedure which we have in mind for achieving all-round fair competition. What is needed is not price-fixing, but *keeping prices moving* toward the level of "economically necessary costs" (cf. Chap. 168).

There is more significance in the argument that today price competition plays only a relatively minor role and that it is indeed largely rejected by industry and commerce; and that the stability of existing prices is seen as a principal aim of all economic policy. This may be so, although to different degrees in different countries. But such a fact is as little a valid argument against the importance of price in an order of competition in conformity with its end as is the fact of an unjust exercise of power by interest groups a valid argument against the democratic order postulated by justice. In any case, when questions of social order are under discussion, one should never be satisfied with an answer which simply establishes the existing defects and leaves the matter there. "Sociologically," it is perfectly clear from the start that all social systems, not least the economic market, and competition systems, are always defective; just for this reason there always exists the moral responsibility, seen from the point of view of the intrinsic ends to be realized by those systems. Besides, it is only *direct* price-competition that can truly be said to be largely eliminated; *indirect* price-competition dominates social economy. Direct competition takes the form of price reductions, indirect competition takes the form of improvements in quality of goods or services at a stable price. Since the cost element must be incorporated in the price, the latter form of competition is also price-competition, although indirect. The methods are well known. The following is an example of *quality competition:* The price of a particular electric razor may be kept stable, but its quality may be improved and this information conveyed to purchasers through advertising; thus, the various manufacturers must constantly seek to improve their quality in order to remain in business. Indeed, quality competition has always played a vital role (it was the chief form of competition in the Middle Ages). Another kind of indirect competition takes forms such as discounts, allowing credit for goods sold, lengthened hire-purchase periods; these methods are applied to wholesale trade as well as retail. And we must not forget the indirect price-competition in the service of the customer, in the form of better equipped premises and more efficient staff; both involve costs, and hence both come under indirect price-competition. But the question, price-competition or not, is by no means left to the free choice of industry and commerce. For no national economy, especially in the Western area, can shut itself off from other economies; they are entangled in competition and will be so to an increasing degree; this means an extending market, and more competition will result in an ever increasing *direct price-competition* (which is at the same time quality competition). Furthermore, competition in world markets, particularly with the development of industry in under-developed countries and the substantially lower labor costs in those countries, will inevitably result in a rapidly intensifying direct price-competition. To dispute this is to underestimate the economic and political realities facing the Western economies in the foreseeable future. Thus, the *question of price-competition and the gravitation of prices toward marginal costs will become increasingly urgent.*

A further argument must be mentioned: it has been thought that, when the issue is price-competition, the simplest procedure is that the state should prevent restrictions on competition and regulate its foreign trade policy in order to admit a flow of goods from abroad which will compel price-competition. This would be correct if we lived in times when a ruler, wholly and exclusively devoted to the welfare of the whole people, were in a position to exercise the necessary authority unhindered. Where then is the state to whom one can entrust such a task? In the modern democracy, the government is subject to party influence, and the parties in turn to the influence of economic groups. If the "state" seeks to bring about intensified competition in some sphere the interests affected will simply turn at the next elections to those likely to carry out the counter-measures which they hope for. We live in the age of the pluralistic society, in which pressure groups impose their will as far as possible on the democratic "state." However good a law a state may bring in against unfair competition practices, pressure groups and vested interests will be able to tamper with the application of it; this is one of the reasons why such laws have had so little success. The same is true of foreign trade policy: these groups will obstruct the lowering of tariff barriers, which will mean the undercutting of their prices. One should not be deluded into thinking that the liberalizing of international trade in European countries came about through the "state" acting on its own initiative; it was, in fact, enforced by developments beyond the control of the individual states.

Thus, we may conclude: Price is the key to free and ordered competition, that is, to preventing restrictions on competition inconsistent with the social end of economy; but the social economy itself, and not the state, must provide the organ qualified to maintain the movement of prices demanded by this social end.

IV *The Machinery for Establishing Free and Fair Competition*

What, then, must be the nature of this *institution* for the ordering of competition by means of the movement of prices? It can only be done through an organ representing all interests concerned in the level and movement of a price, so that the movement of the price toward the lowest production costs, the "socially necessary costs," is assured. This organ, therefore, is not to be thought of as a supreme national price tribunal, but should be constituted for each individual case of competition defects as a committee of representatives of all groups directly interested in the particular price. Indirectly, the whole economic community is always interested in any price, because every price has influence on all other prices; each such control organ, therefore, must include representatives of the consumers. Those directly interested in a particular price are not only the employers concerned but also the workers, since their wages depend on it: those who finish products affected by the price in question or who deliver raw materials to the branch of industry whose price is under discussion. All this points to organs in the form of *functional bodies,* that is, of joint committees, each composed of one representative from the employers' and one from the workers' organizations in the industry to which the producer belongs whose price is being disputed; also with a representative each from the corresponding organizations in the branches of industry directly interested in the price; and with at least two consumers' representatives. The formation of such committees from case to case, and the procedure to be followed by them, are, as we shall presently see, so simple that everything speaks in their favor against national tribunals.

Let us take an example. If the price fixed by a sugar cartel is contested, the committee in question should contain representatives of the employers' and workers' associations in the sugar industry and in the sweetmeat (candy) and confectionery industries using sugar, representatives of the corresponding trades and of the sugar importers and exporters, of the sugar-cane or beet producers who supply the raw material, and two consumers' representatives. The composition of such a committee will insure that all special interests in the individual branches of industry can assert their claims where they are directly interested in a price, while the final judgment of the committee regarding competition always tends in the direction of the general interest of the economic society. Indeed, the only members of the control committee interested in a high price are the employers' and workers' representatives from the branch of production whose incomes from profits and wages are in question, and, at most, those of the raw materials producers and the import trade; the other members all represent consumers and therefore are interested in the lowest possible price, whether the price they are interested in is for producer goods or goods for direct consumption. This control of competition, accordingly, would insure the *gravitation of prices* to the lowest cost level, and thus serve the social function of competition.

The fact that our system of competition control rests on *sound economic principles* and is in harmony with practical experience may be seen from the fact that so outstanding an economist and expert on the monopoly policies employed by cartels as Professor *Liefmann* reaches the following conclusion: "If state interference in price-fixing by a cartel should appear necessary, only price commissions for each industry would be adequate, to be made up not only of government officials but of all groups of those concerned: entrepreneurs, workers, merchants, manufacturers, raw material suppliers, and others." [3] It is also *Liefmann's* expressed view that not only price agreements in cartels, but also tacit agreements formed between businessmen in the smaller towns and villages should be subjected to such control. Our scheme for price control is thus the logical development of an idea toward which theorists concerned with the problems of restrictions of competition were already moving.[4]

[3] R. Liefmann, "Kartelle," in *Handwörterbuch der Staatswissenschaften,* Vol. V, 1923, p. 625.

[4] That some practical experiments have been made in this direction is clear from Liefmann, who points out that in Germany, the country where cartels were most

The *application* to start the procedure of price control can be made by competitors or consumers who wish to contest a price demanded by a producer or merchant, and his competition methods, also by the organizations of producers, workers, consumers, and by state authorities. The committee will have to examine the footing on which the price that is challenged rests. In case of undercutting, the facts (such as lowering of quality, irresponsible incurring of debts, tax payments in arrears) may be so obvious, or, in case of overcharging, standards of comparison may be so readily available (e.g., comparison of cartel prices with world market prices) that a judgment will be easy to arrive at. Otherwise, the committee will have to check the data upon which such prices are based, and the same opportunity must be open to the party arraigned. The object of these inquiries will be to ascertain whether the costing on which the price is based is reasonable, that is, whether the viability of the undertaking is assured in case its prices are challenged by competitors as too low; or whether excessive profits are secured when the prices of a cartel are challenged as too high. Such checking of cost calculations almost always necessitates an inspection of accounts. Naturally the producers and firms concerned cannot be expected to expose their books to the committee itself and surrender their trade secrets, for this would obviously lead to abuse. The inspection of accounts should be carried out by auditors under oath, only the findings being communicated to the committee. The auditors must be under the same responsibility, but also enjoy the same protection, as the judiciary: abuse of official position must be punishable with the severest penalties; the taking up of any industrial or commercial activity on retirement from office must be prohibited, in order that the auditor may not exploit, in the service of competing firms, information gained in the course of his official duties. Mischievous lodging of complaints (e.g., by competitors) can be prevented by sufficiently high penalties.

The *verdict* of the committee can be to the effect that unfair competition by undercutting has been proved, or that the lower price is justified and is therefore in the interest of the social economy. In the complaint of overpricing by a monopoly, the verdict may be that a price is justified in view of the special situation of the industry (e.g., owing to temporary need for protection against competition from abroad), or that the higher price is harmful to the interest of the social economy. The producer or merchant whose prices are challenged as being too high or too low must be given the opportunity to *appeal* to a higher judicial body. This can be formed from the same committee with the addition of a chairman with a casting vote who could be taken from the governing body of a central organization of industry, agriculture, trade unions, etc., according to the particular question to be dealt with, or could be a professional judge familiar with economic problems; or again, the appeal committee could

---

fully developed before the Second World War, such price commissions were provided by law along with compulsory cartels.

be formed at a higher level of the employers' and workers' organizations. The machinery must further allow for minority reports in cases in which a qualified number of the members of a committee disagree with the verdict of the majority. The findings and such reports would be sent to the state authorities responsible for free and fair competition, whether in the form of criminal or civil proceedings or through economic policy (e.g., lowering of tariffs). Such state intervention would be made easier through procedures of this kind, because of the effects of these verdicts on public opinion; and public opinion would be made much more sensitive to excessive prices due to defective competition; furthermore, the flexibility of such procedure and its influence on public opinion would tend to inspire caution and restraint in producers with regard to a price policy restrictive of competition. In all this the state, in its measures of economic policy, would be able to count on the force of public opinion, without which, in the view of experts in general, free competition on a large scale cannot be achieved. For the details of the technical side of procedure, naturally only experience can be the teacher.

How will the *committees be constituted?* As has been made clear already, they would not be permanent committees but will be constituted *ad hoc,* for each particular case as it arises. The members should be selected from lists to be submitted periodically by employers', workers', and consumers' organizations; jurors' lists in normal legal procedure could offer a model in this respect. Anyone summoned to be a member of a committee would be obliged to attend unless serious reasons for exemption were produced. Service would be honorary, although expenses should be allowed. In a society with an advanced degree of regional economic autonomy, the authorities empowered to summon the control committees would be the provincial or regional bodies of the vocational groups; otherwise, governmental officials in collaboration with the organizations of employers, workers, and consumers would be so empowered.

This machinery of competition control involves three great advantages: it is elastic, swift, and cheap; elastic, because a special committee is set up for each case, so that the function of control cannot be limited by bureaucracy or congestion of business; swift, because the members will be persons engaged in their own occupations, who will have no interest in protracting their inquiries; cheap, because of the saving of costs, since membership of the committees will be honorary.

v *Competition Proper through Industrial Democracy*

The critical aspect of the problem of economic self-government is how to determine its *sphere of functioning* so that the various groups in the economy are able to look after their own special interests, but are thereby obliged at the same time to promote the general interest. To determine the functions of economic self-government in this manner is, in the words of Lord *Keynes,* perhaps the *chief task of economists at this hour.* This bold thinker and great expert on modern social economy acutely described this task as follows:

> We have to discriminate between what Bentham, in his forgotten but useful nomenclature, used to term Agenda and Non-Agenda, and to do this without Bentham's prior assumption that interference is, at the same time, "generally needless" and "generally pernicious." Perhaps the chief task of economists at this hour is to distinguish afresh the Agenda of government from the Non-Agenda; and the companion task of politics is to devise forms of government within a democracy which shall be capable of accomplishing the Agenda.[5]

Keynes then goes on to say that, "in many cases the ideal size for the unit of control and organization lies somewhere between the individual and the modern state. I suggest, therefore, that progress lies in the growth and the recognition of semi-autonomous bodies within the state-bodies" (the passage is quoted at length in Chap. 85, note 4). The criterion of action of these semi-autonomous bodies would be solely the public good as they understand it; in this they would be autonomous, although subject to the sovereignty of democracy, as expressed in parliament.

Keynes has not attempted to offer a solution of this problem which he so sharply delineates and which he describes as perhaps the most important for present-day economists. We believe that the solution is to be sought in the direction indicated in the foregoing section (n. IV). Our system allows the industrial groups to pursue their interest unhindered, but under such conditions that they will at the same time be pursuing the general interest. And the autonomous bodies in our machinery of competition control do in fact occupy that intermediate position between the individual and the state, which *Keynes* was thinking of, for they consist of the industrial groups and the functional committees set up by them. These groups can be entrusted with a very wide field of self-government, since the procedure of competition control operates to the advantage of socio-economic productivity; therefore, what takes place in the sphere of economic self-government remains closely connected with the demands of the general interest. The decisive point in our solution is, then, that this fundamental function of self-government is identical with the fundamental function of economic order implied in the social end of economy: the freeing and ordering of competition. Since the general interest is secured by the efforts of self-governing bodies to insure their group interests, there is no need for any further limitation of the sphere of self-government of the individual branches of the economy.[6]

[5] J. M. Keynes, *The End of Laissez Faire,* 1926, p. 40.

[6] Our solution does not fall into the error of theories of industrial self-government, such as are found in guild socialism and universalism, which call for a completely autonomous self-government of the individual branches of the economy, but are unable to say how with such autonomy the general interest is to be preserved. What these theories lack is an institution within the economy for harmonizing the special interests of the vocational groups, so that this function inevitably falls to the competence of

Cooperation in the planning and direction of the whole socio-economic process in accordance with the requirements of the general interest thus becomes the principal function of economic self-governing, namely, semi-autonomous bodies; and bound up with the fulfillment of this is the second main function, the best possible protection and furtherance of the special interests of the group.

Thus, our solution realizes the *root principle of all social order:* that individuals and groups have a right to the full measure of freedom in the conduct of their own affairs that is consistent with the common good; and it realizes the further principle that this relationship of freedom and order must be safeguarded by suitable institutions against infringements from both sides. In our solution, a self-governing branch of industry has at its disposal all possibilities from complete freedom of competition to the elimination of competition by a monopolistic cartel. But producers who, with progressive methods, are capable of producing better and cheaper, and thereby better serve the community, will always be able to make their way, whereas producers who see themselves threatened by unfair competition can protect themselves. Another advantage of our solution is that it functions against state monopolies and nationalized undertakings as well as against private monopolies. The crucial advantage of our method is that, as *Keynes* envisaged, the road becomes clear toward an economic and social order beyond the conflict of individualist-liberalist and collectivistic-socialistic principles, which has split our society for a century. It would be a system of justice, insuring all groups in society, including the workers, equally their place in the direction of the social economy and in the distribution of its product. This system, therefore, would mean social reform,[7] such as would be capable of radically solving the social problem of today; it would mean *"industrial democracy"*

---

the state. But this brings into question the autonomy of economic self-government itself, since the state can achieve such a condition of harmony only with the aid of far-reaching centralistic controls. Besides, with such a harmonizing of interests there is the danger that, under democracy, those economic groups which at the moment control the state may assert their own interests, and the further danger that the economy may become organized into pressure groups, each embracing one branch of industry, the strongest of which will be able to promote their own interest by means of compromise at the expense of the rest. Some of these theories go so far as to see the principal task of self-government in restriction of competition (including combination as a method) and to accord to the autonomous branches of industry even their own monetary and credit policies with fixing of their own interest rates. On such ideas in Spann's universalism cf. O. Spann, *Der wahre Staat,* 3rd ed., 1931, and Heinrich, *Das Ständewesen mit besonderer Berücksichtigung der Selbstverwaltung der Wirtschaft,* 2nd ed., 1934. Concerning this and on more literature about universalism cf. the comprehensive critical study by Adolf Weber, *Über die berufsständische Idee in Deutschland, Jahrbücher für Nationalökonomie und Statistik,* 1936.

[7] Measures of *social policy* are being variously described as *social reform,* notably in the English-speaking countries and in Germany, in connection with the reform of the National Insurance pension schemes. While it is the purpose of social policy to remove particular faults in the existing economic and social system, the purpose of social reform is to solve the social question radically (cf. Chaps. 62–66).

with the widest possible range: the working of the process of social economy as a whole.

VI *Industrial Democracy and Social Reform*

Fully actualized justice must secure to all groups in socio-economic cooperation direct participation with equal rights and responsibility in the planning and working of the social economy. We speak first of the *economic* aspect of the modern social problem, which is characterized by the predominance of property as against labor in the direction of the social economy. The self-government just described would secure the *collaboration of property and labor* through the institution of committees to be composed of members of all industrial groups concerned with the matter to be settled and, in particular, of employers and workers *on the principle of complete parity*. In the hands of these functional bodies, and hence within the domain of economic self-government, lies the "*planning*" of the social economy; the method for achieving this would be a price structure governed by the principle of "economically necessary" costs, thereby resulting in the highest standard of economic productivity and the highest standard of living for the community. As we have seen, this end is automatically attained through freedom and order in competition. Harmful consequences to individual groups from sudden price movements can be excluded; and again, the groups can protect themselves against sudden changes in production technique (automation), if it involves "structural" unemployment and a gradual transition is in the general interest of society. The "directing" of the socio-economic process is exercised by such industrial self-government, since, by means of the competition control committees, the industrial groups are able to intervene and to influence the movement of prices in the interest of the social economy, and in their own interest, at every moment and in every individual case. With these functions, workers and employers exercise *joint control* over the whole process of social economy, collaborating in the committees with equal rights, so that the economic process may best fulfill its purpose in the general interest. Thus, *the worker would at last have his hand directly on the lever for planning, directing, and controlling the process of social economy.*

On the other hand, the worker in the *socialistic planned economy* enjoys no direct voice in the planning, direction, and control of social economy as a whole. First, socialism gives the worker only an indirect opportunity of exercising control over economy, through parliament; his power of control is restricted to the vote at elections. Secondly, it is a well-known fact that the industrial society is increasingly characterized by the predominance of the "managers," so that economic-technical considerations are paramount in the organization of the economy; socialism is certainly no remedy against further development in this direction, but is more inclined to promote it. Thirdly, the average parliamentarian, owing to lack of economic experience, is not in a position to judge whether the socialized undertakings are really conducted in the interest of the social economy, especially as these concerns can exploit every possibility of camouflaging accounts in order to conceal failures. In the socialistic planned economy, there is only one real means for estimating the efficiency of social economy, that is the rise or fall of the standard of living when its products and prices are no longer competitive in the free markets. By the time public opinion is aware of such a fall, an enormous misdirection of capital has already taken place, and in the complex structure of present-day economy the damage done to socio-economic productivity cannot easily, and at any rate not quickly, be undone. All this shows that socialistic economy gives the worker no direct control of the economy, but only the power to appoint those who carry out the planning, direction, and control.

We have spoken of the economic aspect of the social reform implied in our scheme of free and fair competition; there remains to be discussed the *social* aspect: the wage and labor conditions. All the machinery for their settlement already exists, created and tested by some three generations of social progress. These elements exist in the *functional committees for collective bargaining.* They would form an integral component in economic self-government; in fact, only under a social economy adjusted in this way could the collective agreement fully perform its function in the interest of the workers. Conscious of their share, on equal terms, in the control of the socio-economic process, they would be primarily intent on the general interest of the economy, knowing that thereby they were best promoting their own interest. In collective bargaining, special attention would be paid to possibilities of *increasing productivity,* since the workers would expect increases in real income from price reductions while nominal wages themselves remained relatively stable. This relative stability of nominal wages would not prevent the workers from putting forward wage claims in particular instances. The interest of the workers in productivity would then give such institutions as joint industrial production councils in factories a basis on which to exist and to function entirely different from that which they can possess today. For the reasons given, an atmosphere of real understanding between workers and management would be attained at the same time, since the common purposes of both parties in the control of the economic process and in the raising of economic productivity would prevail.

Thus, the essential conditions for the *existing antagonism between capital and labor would be removed:* the workers would no longer see themselves as the exploited class, because they would be assured of an equal share in the control of the social economy and in the distribution of the social product. As an equal partner in economic cooperation, they would possess a consciousness of the status of a fully responsible member of society and of the vocational dignity of labor. The conditions would exist for lasting *social peace* and for the long-sought solution of the labor question.

VII *Possible Criticisms and Reservations*

Such a system of industrial democracy naturally gives rise to a number of questions, particularly questions concerning the effects of the system on the worker, the entrepreneur, and the trade cycle. With regard to the *worker,* it may be objected that our solution fails in its purpose of insuring parity of responsibility and control to him in the guidance of the economy, when he becomes unemployed owing to mechanization. In fact, however, much as our proposed machinery works in favor of a maximum of economic productivity, in the functional committees the workers would be in a position to exercise decisive influence on the tempo of mechanization. If mechanization involved extensive and prolonged unemployment, the inevitable reduction of purchasing power would jeopardize the economic productivity of capital equipment. Mechanization itself would not be prevented, but its tempo and extent would be controlled with the object of the general interest of the whole economic society. In fact, our solution would create the basic conditions for permanent *full employment with increasing productivity and increasing income.* For, free and fair competition keeps the price level tending toward marginal production costs, and hence results in a continuous extension of the division of labor, of the home market, and of the use of all available production factors, including labor. Hence, a competitive system orientated toward the social end of economy means the best possible conditions for natural economic growth, with the consequence of full employment. The machine will no longer be man's master, but his servant, since technical productivity will be subordinated to socio-economic productivity.

A second possible criticism of our solution relates to the position of the *entrepreneur.* Will not his freedom of decision in the conduct of his business be impaired? The reverse is true, for the responsibility and control which the workers share concern not the running of the individual undertaking but the social function of the whole economy. Not only would the rights of business management not suffer, but free and fair competition would result in fully securing those rights, rooted in private ownership. Our solution would permit no profit from an undertaking without corresponding real service to the social economy; competition, compelling the movement of prices toward marginal costs, would see to that. But the performance of the social function of private property would be assured by institutions; there would be no more interest in restricting the rights of property by social or fiscal measures and, as is so common today, in curtailing through them the freedom of decision to the detriment of productivity. Furthermore, nothing would open up a wider field for vigorous enterprise than a system which would remove all unjustified checks on competition. Such a system would, by linking entrepreneur income and capital profit closely with economic productivity, certainly make life harder for entrepreneurs and managers; on the other hand, it would make things easier for the entrepreneur by insuring his freedom of decision and of opportunities for profit through efficiency. No doubt such an economy of ordered freedom would presuppose, for full efficiency, a regeneration of the spirit of enterprise, but it would also contribute decisively toward it. This would be the kind of entrepreneur who could appreciate the fresh wind of a competition as free as possible, subject to the demands of the economic common good, rather than seek to insure profits by restricting competition and pursuing a policy of group interest to the detriment of the general interest.

A third criticism of a system of competition which keeps prices gravitating toward marginal costs relates to its effects on the *business cycle.* Would it not have deflationary consequences? The movement of prices on the cost principle would mean a gradual increase in the purchasing power of money. However, deflationary effects would not follow because, first, deflation springs from a contraction of the volume of money and purchasing power, so that part of the industrial output cannot be absorbed. But the effect of our scheme of free and fair competition would be exactly the opposite, namely, an increase in the purchasing power of the existing volume of money as a result of a very slow but continuous fall in prices. Such a natural increase in the purchasing power of the national income would provide a steady stimulus in the form of increasing effective demand. Secondly, the notorious effect of deflationary economic depressions, namely, that debt burdens become heavier owing to the increase in the value of money, would not occur, since our method of competition control would never bring about a general fall in the price level, as happens in deflation, but only an adaptation of particular prices to the cost level, so that the movement of the whole price system would be very gradual. Thirdly, and most important, it would be a decisive advantage of our solution that the stability of the currency would remain untouched and would not be subject to experiments; instead, the individual prices would be kept in motion toward a minimum cost level, while the fixed yardstick indispensable to sound costing would be preserved. Fourthly, *common sense* tells us that in a well-ordered economy it is the most natural thing that *goods should become more plentiful and cheaper with the development of skill and technique.*[8]

[8] Siegfried L. Gabriel, "Lohn- und Arbeitsproduktivität," in Bombach-Gabriel, editors, *Löhne und Preise,* 1957, pp. 64 ff., may be right: the statement that price reductions, which follow increases in productivity, always signify deflationary effects, he says, rests on a confusion of two things: "A deflation which has its cause in the monetary sphere and derives from an underprovision of the economy with means of payment must be distinguished from falling prices resulting from a number of productivity increases in individual undertakings and not conflicting with their earning

VIII *The Organization of Industrial Democracy*

An advantage of the greatest importance in our solution of the problem of free and fair competition is that self-government in industry can be carried out with a *minimum of organization.* Its main function is that of bringing about and maintaining the normal working of the economic process, and therefore it interferes only occasionally where this process is impeded, and accordingly requires only the institution of *ad hoc* committees. Thus, this self-government needs no special organizational apparatus for executing its chief function, but uses the existing organizations of workers and employers. Further development of this foundation of organization is required only insofar as it needs to be extended to every branch of economic activity to enable all concerned to have their interests represented, and thus to cooperate in economic self-government. Adequate beginnings have already been made in this direction, for in all socially advanced countries there exist organs to negotiate some form of collective settlement of labor questions.

Even the formation of superior organs of economic self-government would mean no more than a development of already existing organizations; in various countries already, national advisory councils on the principle of parity of labor and capital have been set up to advise governments on economic questions of national importance, to work out suggestions, to lend the government moral support when necessary but unpopular measures have to be adopted, and to assist in the technical execution of such measures by influencing the bodies which they represent. Such national organs of economic self-government should be constituted by the central organizations of the different industries on a basis of parity. The supreme organ of economic self-government would be an economic council, a representational body alongside the lower house, or chamber of deputies, of the parliament (cf. Chaps. 85, 134). It would exercise advisory functions, not powers of decision, after preparation by committees

---

capacity. When the economy is underprovided with means of payment, the entrepreneur, owing to the relative rigidity of costs, runs automatically into difficulties. It is different with price reductions which are the outcome of improvements in productivity, since here the reduction is the result of cheapened production. Whereas with deflation caused by monetary factors there are bound to be crises of earning capacity, which unfavorably influence the management relative to employment, investments, etc., there is in the second case no necessary conflict with earning capacity. . . . Probably this fear of a slowly crumbling price-level comes from a time in which prices, because of a general underprovision of means of payment, were under pressure —a situation which is to be distinguished sharply from the gradual process of cheapening of thousands of commodities which can now be manufactured with lesser costs." Gabriel points out that Spurgeon Bell, *Productivity, Wages, and National Income,* 1940, declared that, in the American industry from 1923 to 1937, eighty per cent of productivity profits were passed on to the consumer in the form of price reductions; Bell's work, he informs us, is the only work which has studied the distribution of the gains of productivity, and therefore merits special attention.

for the individual questions of general economic interest, and hence for an economic policy on the principles of free and fair competition, for a national wage policy, for fiscal policy, but equally for monetary and credit policy including the direction of capital and credit, social policy, full employment policy, and foreign trade policy. On the same principle of parity, industrial councils or industrial chambers would have to be formed on a regional basis for matters which concern only the district. Thus, at district, regional, and national levels the whole organization of economic self-government would be built up on a vocational basis. Their basic function would be to look after the social end of economy and the demands of economic productivity, while having full competence to look after the special interests of the vocational groups.

Inevitably, all the economic issues mentioned in the foregoing discussion fall ultimately to the competence of the government, and hence of the parliament. But the obligation to collaborate with a supreme organ of industrial self-government would obviously provide a healthy corrective to the usual attitude of parliamentary majorities, which is so much the outcome of ideological dependence and vested interests, in favor of the general economic and social interest. Here would be found the solution of a problem of *momentous importance for liberal democracy.* The most objectionable effects of the pressure of interested groups on parliament and government would be prevented, *the balancing of interests would be removed from the political to the economic sphere,* and, with the basic principle of free and fair competition, the deciding factor in all disputes and policy problems would be the social end of economy, and hence social justice.

IX *Maximum of Competition, Minimum of Regulations*

A social economy such as we have described, with the greatest possible freedom of competition, does not exclude regulations for competition when they are necessary in the general interest. They may even be necessary for insuring the best conditions for the growth of freedom of competition. Thus, competition may proceed in a particular branch of industry under conditions which involve a wastage of capital, so that restrictions on competition may be required in the national interest; or regulation of competition may be necessary because there is such an inequality of conditions that smaller undertakings, in spite of an equal ability to serve productivity, would be forced out of the market. Both possibilities are well illustrated by transportation in many countries today; in the first place, there is the competition between road and rail transport; in the second place the competition between big, heavily capitalized undertakings and smaller ones; in addition, there is the competition between manufacturing and commercial firms which run their own transport. In such cases, regulations may be necessary in order to create equal conditions for different sizes of firms, to prevent squandering of capital in new investment, and to make monopoly power unworkable. The object is to bring about competition in which prices will correspond with socio-economic productivity. Examples such as these given will show that the small firm is not less efficient in its own sphere than the large one; consequently, as soon as the necessary steps have been taken, it can be adequately protected by simple competition control against unfair pricing by large and powerful rivals.

From what has been said on the function of fair competition the following *principles for regulations,* in accordance with the social end of economy, may be derived.

1. The *fundamental aim* is always the creation of the necessary conditions for fair competition, and hence not merely the restriction or abolition of competition. Insofar as restrictions are required, they can have a merely temporary character: the "imperfect" competition, which is the result of regulations, must as far as possible prepare the way for "perfect" competition. This goal can be achieved if such regulations are linked with measures to strengthen the weaker competitors, so that they can then hold their own in competition. First in importance among these measures is self-help carried out by means of cooperative organizations, for the purpose of joint purchase of raw materials, machinery, tools and fuel, the maintenance of joint machinery and repair depots, and the provision of cheap credit in suitable form (in exceptional cases even with the assistance of loans from public funds on favorable terms).

2. The *immediate aim* of the regulation of competition must be the establishment and maintenance of equitable conditions. This equitableness is chiefly threatened by the preponderance in capital power of large corporations which are able to drive weaker competitors out of the market by direct or indirect (giving "extras") price-cutting, in order first to achieve a monopoly or oligopoly position and then to secure increased profits. It is probably one of the principal advantages of our committees for competition control that they can reach to the foundations of pricing in the individual case and find out how to approach the establishing of equitable conditions of competition. In connection with them, and not otherwise, it will be possible for a general law to prevent unfair competition methods from succeeding and taxation measures taken against undertakings which use a preponderance of capital power to stultify competition, can achieve their purpose.

3. The *long-term goal* of all regulation of competition must be to bring about a sound structural proportion among the firms of different sizes in a branch of industry. It remains a long-range objective because, after a century of unfettered competition and monopoly capitalism, with their resultant ill-effects on the economic structure, it can be attained only by a process of gradual development. As we have seen, there is no practical or scientific evidence for the belief that the large production unit has

higher efficiency in all spheres of industry. For a realistic economic theory like that based on natural law, which applies the criterion of efficiency in conjunction with that of proportional distribution of property, there is this principle for the regulation of competition: *As great a number of medium-sized and smaller undertakings as is consistent with socio-economic productivity*, and *as much protection for them as is necessary, in face of the superior competitive power of big firms, which is derived from capital power rather than economic productivity.* Our whole inquiry into the function and order of competition should make it clear that the economically and socially right proportionate pattern of large, medium, and small undertakings cannot, as is sometimes thought, be brought about by inhibiting new industry and trade or by limiting the size of capital; this is unrealistic because the size of capital cannot be appropriately enough determined, and because legal means can be found of circumventing such regulations. In each individual case, the expedient methods to be used must be decided by the criterion of productivity, and only an institution like competition control by our functional committees is capable of providing the necessary data.

x *Self-governing Industrial Democracy and the State*

It is for the state to carry out the executive measures and decisions arrived at by the functional competition committees. There are principally two classes of procedure which need to be considered.

Legislation should empower the state administration to intervene as a result of verdicts by the committees. This is a domain in which the *delegation of executive power* is justified. The decisions of the competition control committees (and appeal committees) would concern cases which detailed legislation on competition in various countries had hitherto failed to cover successfully. Such cases include dishonest advertising, abuses of the seasonal "sale" (regulations are made with regard to the timing and frequency of such sales), misrepresentation of weight and quantity, bribery, tendentious statements about the business situation of other firms (protection of credit is then necessary), misuse of trademarks and colophons, betrayal of trade secrets, industrial and factory espionage; besides these there are the following methods of ensnaring customers: making untrue statements about price or quality or quantity of available stocks; unsound competitive methods, such as certain forms of credit, of instalment systems, and of discount on cash payments; and, of course, all the methods of unfair competition which we have enumerated, such as undercutting by firms which do not pay their debts to supplier firms or to tax authorities, or which make occasional use of their greater capital strength to sell under cost in order to break weaker competitors; again, price agreements by monopolistic combines or quasi-monopolies which are able to exert a decisive influence on a market without fully controlling it; similarly, price-fixing methods practiced by combines which arrange for a subsidiary company to be supplied by another subsidiary at manipulated prices lower than the market prices in order to create a more favorable market for the products of the former. All such offenses against just competition, hitherto the concern of state legislation, would come under the purview of economic self-government. The advantage of our machinery is that skeleton legislation suffices, which assigns to the competition committees the discovery of cases of unfair competition, and to the state authorities the execution of their decisions.

The second group of measures for carrying out the decisions of the committees for competition control come within the scope of *economic policy.* Such measures are particularly expedient in order to insure the movement of prices in accordance with the cost principle to counteract monopolistic price agreements. They include the removal of restraints, intended to protect established undertakings, on new business enterprise, the withdrawal of tax concessions, and the cancellation of subsidies; to these can be added measures of trade policy, such as the reduction of tariffs and the lifting of import quotas (cf. n. IV above on the altered conditions of such governmental measures). In the internal market and in external trade, "*liberalization*" would be the trend of policy. As temporary measures to bring about free and fair competition in conformity with the social end of economy (e.g., in order to break a monopoly), it may even be necessary to resort to the setting up of state undertakings, state trusteeship of firms, or the nationalization of monopolistic concerns.

XI *Some Effects of the Economy of Ordered Freedom*

1. The movement of prices toward the natural level governed by socially necessary costs means a progressive *general increase in income,* namely, a gradual growth in the purchasing power of money incomes, and hence a growth in real income.

2. This is accompanied by a natural progressive expansion of *effective demand,* the fundamental motive force in economic and social progress, particularly when the value of money is stable.

3. By freeing competition to the furthest extent consistent with, and at the same time required by, the common good, our system would lead to the greatest possible expansion of the internal market and hence to a *balanced growth* of the economy.

4. At the same time such a system, with its constant movement of prices on the cost principle, would uniquely enhance the competitive capacity of the national economy in world markets and create the best opportunities for *export trade.* The great significance of this advantage need hardly be stressed.

5. Such ordered competition works automatically toward *full employment* because it brings about a continuous expansion of the internal

market and facilitates access to world markets. The principal factor in this is the tendency toward optimum socio-economic productivity resulting from the full operation of the principle of costs in conjunction with stable money. Contrasting with such a solution of the problem of full employment are the solutions based on an expansion of the volume of money and a policy of public debt, since they admittedly have to accept a rising price level, and hence inflationary consequences, so that the fruits that appear to be within reach always evade the grasp of the economic Tantalus. Creeping inflation makes increase in money incomes necessarily partly illusory and brings in its wake fresh income demands and fresh inflation.

6. The economy of the ordered freedom of competition is the realization of *industrial democracy,* with the worker sharing on equal terms in the planning, direction, and control of the economy. In contrast to this, all collectivistic-socialistic and centralist-planning systems refuse the worker a direct influence in the running of the economy; therefore, they cannot claim to solve the social problem which is rending society and the world.

7. The system of ordered competition means the realization of *social justice,* for it is a social system in which labor and property are equally principles of order in socio-economic cooperation. In such a system, private property, or capital, no longer possesses any social predominance, since labor shares equally in controlling the socio-economic process. Furthermore, not only are the workers enabled by the collective agreement to secure their share in the national income, but they are also enabled to insure the attainment of the optimum productivity, and hence the highest wage-level and standard of living. Labor would be installed in its full rights. This would be the way to social peace. At the same time our system of ordered economic freedom affords the widest scope for private enterprise and private interest by the freeing of competition in conformity with the prevailing requirements of the social economy.

8. In the social economy of ordered freedom, then, *individual interest and general interest are inextricably interdependent:* the individual can benefit himself only by serving the common interest, and the community insures its economic and social progress only by providing the maximum of incentive to serve the general interest by means of freedom for individuals and groups. In such a correlation lies the *essence of social order.*

182. The Functional Integration of Social Economy

By the functional integration of social economy we mean that the process of social economy is made to follow a course which best fulfills the present and future requirements of the social end of the economy.

I *Business Fluctuations*

Economic depressions are more or less serious functional disturbances in the realization of the social end of economy. Their characteristic is that capital goods already produced are unusable owing to a lack of effective demand, and hence there is unemployment. Four kinds of depression can be distinguished by their causes: 1) *External* causes of depressions are exemplified by natural catastrophes (e.g., the prolonged blizzard conditions in Great Britain in February 1947, which brought about a change from virtually full employment to an unemployment figure of two million), especially poor harvests, and worst of all, war. 2) *Cyclic* depressions arise from inherent defects in the functioning of the process of social economy. 3) *Structural* defects resulting in depressions are caused by defects in the equilibrium of the socio-economic process, such as those brought about by changes in demand for capital goods or consumption commodities (decline of the population, fashion). 4) *Technical* unemployment as a phenomenon of depression arises when new machines temporarily displace workers in abnormal numbers from the production process; this technical unemployment can be particularly acute when at a time of high wages employers seek to "rationalize" their establishment by replacing men with machines.

Economic depressions may affect one or more branches of industry (partial depressions) or an entire social economy or a large sector of world economy (general depressions). Business fluctuations with their *periodic character* formed one of the most critical problems of individualist-liberalist social economy: regularly recurring depressions or crises with resultant mass unemployment and destruction of capital (since production plants become useless). The explanations attempted by economic theorists fall into two main groups: the *underconsumption theories* and the *overproduction theories.* The series of underconsumption theories was begun by *Robert Owen,* who thought that profit raises the prices of goods, with the result that a portion of the social product cannot be purchased with wages. In fact, *Malthus* and a number of his contemporaries thought that the increased productivity of capitalistic economy could be balanced only by an unproductive consumption, that is, by an extensive luxury consumption. Among the underconsumption theories, that of Lord *Keynes* must be counted; he explained depressions in terms of psychological causes, lack of willingness for investment and consumption; he suggested as the principal remedy a public investment policy. Among the *overproduction theories* that of *Simone de Sismondi* (1793–1843) comes first. He thought that the extensive use of machines results in such an expansion of production that the aggregate income of one year does not suffice to buy the following year's production. Overproduction, according to *Marx,* arises in the capitalistic economy from the necessity, which competition imposes on the capitalists, to counteract the inevitable diminution of the profit rate by increasing the capital invested in mechanization; the result is a contraction of the amount of capital expended in wages, so that more and more unsalable commodities are thrown upon the market and increasingly acute disturbances of equilibrium and crises must ensue.

In fact, the intensity of cyclic economic crises in the period before the First World War steadily diminished, so that cyclic unemployment at the beginning of the century no longer exceeded a proportion of from two to five per cent of the working population. The underconsumption and the overproduction theories are, radically, concerned with the same manifestation of the misfunctioning of social economy. Economic science, in its close investigation of the deeper causes of cyclic business fluctuations, has increasingly endeavored to locate the *actual point in the interconnections* of the economic process where "the chain is broken" and the equilibrium between actual supply and effective demand is finally upset. The value of such investigations for antidepression policy is beyond question. Many such attempts, however, seem to rest primarily upon the assumption that the process of social economy is a mechanism which will continue to function correctly if only its weak point can be found and the fault rectified. Social economy is not, however, a mechanism but a highly complex network of human interests, purposes, activities, and endeavors. The cause of fluctuations, therefore, basically is psychological. It is to be found especially in the tendencies to overestimate the possibilities of profit, resulting in overinvestment, and to take a pessimistic view of the (e.g. politically unsafe) conditions of economic development, resulting in restraint in capital investment and spending in general. With this is linked the uncertainty of human foresight in calculating the evolution of the economic process, which, because of the extensive use of technical means of production, of roundabout means of production, makes long-term planning necessary. In the complex and far-ranging modern economy, the data necessary for such planning are subject to incalculable fluctuations: prices, wages, interest rates and, linked with all these, the value of the supplies of goods available in an economy.

Our analysis seems to suggest the *means for overcoming economic fluctuations*. They can be divided into two groups: 1) To eradicate the evil, the forces of order must be brought into operation, which will guarantee the natural development of the economic process in accordance with its intrinsic end. This is to be achieved through the institution described for insuring the gradual but constant movement of prices toward "socially necessary costs." Thus, the general upward movement of prices, which is economically unjustified and which is a prime cause of the overestimation of prospects of profit and accordingly of overinvestment, will disappear. This will also insure the stability of the value of money, so that planning by the entrepreneur can be on a much more secure foundation.

Along with this, the belief in the automatic self-regulation of the socio-economic process would be superseded by the idea that it is the responsibility of society to establish order in economy and to insure the fulfillment of its social end. 2) The other group of means for overcoming economic fluctuations is directed toward attacking the symptoms rather than the causes of the trouble. Chief among them are the methods of monetary and credit policy to guide the economy, as already mentioned (cf. Chaps. 165, 167). By ranging these among the methods of treatment of symptoms, we are again stressing the limitation of their fruitful application. It is a frequent mistake today that economic fluctuations are spoken of as an affair of the past simply because a recession can be counteracted by monetary and credit measures. It is difficult to reconcile this optimism with the annually recurring anxious question of those who have their finger on the pulse of economic life: whether there will be a recession or not. And everyone knows that the principal reason for concern is that for some years such measures have been tried to the uttermost and hence the persisting business cycle is beset with inflationary forces. These forces are today a great danger to the functional integration of social economy. This now calls for closer discussion.

II *The "New Inflation"*

Inflationary effects also accompanied the economic fluctuations in the nineteenth century. After the Second World War, inflation became, in many countries, an essential element in the continuous boom conditions. Linked with this process are novel factors which seem to justify the widely used expression "new inflation," which is chiefly thought of as a cost inflation. Rising production costs are said to be the cause of the rising price level and the concomitant fall in the purchasing power of money, which means inflation. The question is, then: Which are the increased costs of production? Rising wage costs are to be considered but, I think, to look only at wage costs is to simplify the problem.

In fact, high prices are also due to the structure of costs on the *capital side,* taken in conjunction with too high a measure of ploughing back, or self-financing, that is, the practice, common among big firms, especially joint stock firms, of retaining a considerable proportion of profits for the purposes of investment, of renewing and extending production plants. For the small firm, ploughing back savings and profits is the natural thing. Not so, however, for the big firm. An excess of ploughing back holds up the natural movement of prices toward marginal costs: prices remain static, instead of the increase in productivity indicated by profits leading to a reduction in prices. On the contrary, excessive ploughing back results in an upward movement of prices, since it is accompanied by an increased demand for capital goods. This demand is excessive because it is largely freed from the control by an interest rate corresponding to the scarcity conditions on the capital market and too closely related to immediate possibilities of return. It is quite different when financing is done through the medium of the capital market, so that arbitrary manipulations of interest accounts and writing off of sums invested are not so easy; the financing of undertakings is then more dependent on the requirements of socio-economic expediency and less on considerations of mere profit-making by the individual firm. It must be emphasized that, in many branches of industry, the big firms determine prices, and just those firms which have wider opportunities for self-financing. It is also too little observed that these are more independent of investment credit, so that they can render partly ineffective monetary policy (raising the interest rate in order to bring about price reductions) as a means of stemming inflation. Ploughing back is encouraged by overtaxation of company profits: these seek to set an increased expenditure account against their profit account.

Ploughing back is important not least because it results in wage claims on the part of the *workers,* which is psychologically comprehensible, on the very ground of high profits.[1] The workers are conscious of their right to a share in the increasing productivity; if they do not obtain it through falling prices and a consequent rise in real income they demand higher nominal wages. Thus, the upward trend of prices continues. This is because, after the wage increases, price increases regularly follow on the often wrongful ground of increased production costs. "Often wrongful" because entrepreneurs are too ready to increase prices when higher wage costs may be met at least partly out of profits and could be recovered in part by rationalization. Prospects of profit in boom conditions also lead to rivalry among firms for labor, with offers of better overtime rates and other rewards; higher overtime rates form a significant proportion of wage incomes. But this particular kind of wage-formation is associated, not with increased, but rather with reduced, productivity. For, again understandably enough, the worker often yields to the temptation to stretch out the work of the normal day in order to create overtime and earn the higher rates. Undoubtedly, one of the principal causes of the new inflation is the general rise in wage incomes, often unduly emphasized. They are a novel factor because they are due to the new position of the trade unions as interest groups, possessing unique power resources, and in the full employment economy, possessing a unique position as partners in negotiation. In the course of these proceedings not only increasing productivity but also increasing prices and cost of living are given as support for wage claims. It is too little considered that rising prices and costs of

[1] In Great Britain an important factor in the inflationary wage claims, accompanied by repeated strikes and threats of strikes, has been the particularly high level of ploughing back (after 1950 about sixty per cent of investments!). On the continent of Europe, in most economies today ploughing back averages about forty per cent; one would not be far wrong if one estimated the average before the First World War as less than half. On German conditions cf. Paul Jostock, "Kritische Stimmen zum Thema Selbstfinanzierung," in *Die neue Ordnung,* 1957, pp. 219–25.

living with creeping inflation occur also because, owing to the falling value of money, higher prices have to be paid for imported foodstuffs and other commodities. These raise the cost of living index and thereby become again in their turn a cause of new wage claims. Thus, the wage-price spiral extends not only to production costs but also to the higher costs for imported goods caused by persistent inflation.

Another main cause of the new inflation is a too easygoing monetary and credit policy. The new inflation would not be possible at all without assistance from an inflationary *monetary and credit policy.* In the circles of the "new economics," inflation was simply seen as a permanent device for maintaining economic and social progress; this is another reason why it is right to speak of "new inflation." [2] Today, among experts the opposite view is gaining ground, although there are still some stragglers who hold that a gentle, "controlled" inflation is indispensable for a continuous and growing prosperity. Undoubtedly, wage inflation, and price inflation too, could be avoided if the credits were not granted by which it is enabled to continue. The reason is that, for wage payments, to a great extent short-term credits are taken, but at the same time credit advances accompany ploughing back investments, because the retained profits of firms are very often only "on the books" and can be applied to investment only by means of credits obtained on such "securities." Obviously, new inflation, just insofar as it is cost inflation, would soon come to a halt if the credits sought were not available, or were available only at high interest rates. What would be the result? Curtailment of production consequent upon restricted and dearer credit would cause temporary unemployment. What government is in a position to assume responsibility for a higher degree of unemployment and yet remain in office? To this question we must presently return.

One of the causes of the new inflation is *excessive government expenditure.* It is among the causes of the new inflation because it has developed on an unprecedented scale only since the First World War and especially since the Second. Excessive government spending is inflationary in two respects: (1) from the point of view of expenditures: the expenditure occasioned by an enormously expanded administrative apparatus and civil service means an increased demand for consumer goods for immediate use or of a durable character (radio and television sets, cameras, auto-

[2] From the inflationary economic policy of individual countries may result inflationary effects on national economies which adhere to the principle of stable currency: they can be hit by "imported inflation." (This is the counterpart to the "exported unemployment" between the two World Wars; this meant that countries put up tariff barriers to imports in order to maintain employment, thus causing unemployment in other countries.) A country with a stable currency, which also holds to the principle of a stable exchange, is liable to receive increased exports from inflationary countries with payments in the currency of the importing country kept as accounts at its banks, which increase their deposits; in addition, there is an influx of foreign currency to the banks; both these resources can be used to provide credit, with inflationary results.

mobiles), whereas the services of the bureaucracy cannot be deemed equally productive; (2) from the point of view of revenues: enlargement of the administrative apparatus necessitates increased taxation, which places a burden on industry, and of which a considerable proportion goes as costs toward raising the price level. Increased governmental expenditure includes also the gigantic sums which modern states spend in subsidies, for instance, to promote industrial exports, to maintain agricultural prices, to make up the deficits in social insurance funds, and to carry out foreign aid programs.

Linked with the causes mentioned are those of a *political* nature. The ending of the new inflation would call for the limitation of consumption to the volume justified by economic productivity, and hence a limitation of money incomes and of private spending. The recipients of excessive incomes are those large organized interest groups in the social economy which can make use of their power to obtain a disproportionate share of the national income, so that, on the whole, more income is acquired than is really earned. As production costs these incomes force prices upward and cause inflation, either creeping or open. To call a halt to inflation would mean the pruning of an illusory prosperity, insofar as inflation is responsible for it; on the other hand, inflation itself causes the constant renewal of wage claims, since rising prices partly make money incomes turn out to be illusory in value. But to prune specious prosperity would require a conversion in the minds of the masses, which in a democracy makes the task of carrying the necessary measures very difficult for a government, since in most countries there are parties, waiting for the opportunity to take over government, who are ready to grant further concessions to overconsumption and inflationary forces.

Thus, it will appear that there are, sociologically speaking, new kinds of causes of inflation in its present form; it is, however, *basically demand inflation* deriving from a demand for consumption and investment goods above the level of productivity attained. This demand is based upon incomes which enter into prices as costs, cause the upward movement of prices, and make the concomitant decline in the value of money appear as cost inflation.

This discussion of the causes of the new inflation should make it plain that we are dealing here with *questions of justice of the greatest significance* for the more immediate and remoter future of social economies and for nations themselves. The basic cause of inflation is excessive consumption in comparison with what is justified by the level of economic productivity. The prevention of inflation would require the cutting back of incomes and of consumption to what is actually produced in the economy. This would depend on the following conditions: (1) that one should think in terms of real incomes, not money incomes; (2) that the natural way of bringing about a general increase in real incomes with growing economic productivity should be pursued, namely, that of a gradual lowering of prices; (3) that state and government should be kept out of the battlefield of conflicting economic interests and should be able to direct their economic and social policies, as far as possible, in accordance with justice and the general interest. Certainly the groups and sectional interests will always seek and find ways to advance their particular advantage; they have the right to do so. What matters is that in so doing they have an obligation to the common good. Mere exhortations in this respect are quite useless. Institutions are required with a twofold purpose: first, the balancing of interests among the groups must be located in the social economy itself, so that it cannot give rise to a political dynamic threatening the foundations of democracy; secondly, this balancing of interests must be linked with the principle of socio-economic productivity and the movement of prices to marginal costs. A general, but steady, rise in real incomes would be the result. The institutions in question are those serving free and fair competition, as described in the preceding chapter. An aspect which appears in this is of decisive importance: the state, standing above the conflict of interests, would recover its sovereign rights, and then in its economic policy, especially in its monetary, credit and taxation policies, it would be able to correspond with the demands of the social end of economy, namely, soundly based and increasing national prosperity, including that fundamental postulate of justice, stable money.

In consequence, it is quite obvious that the new inflation has imposed on statesmanship new tasks of *internal and international policy* which involve the gravest responsibility. At present a boom, which in many countries is based on a scarcely controlled inflation, can give way to a depression involving unemployment. It is then that the communists could gain victories, not sufficiently anticipated by the West with its concentration on a policy of armed defense and controlled disarmament.[3] Everyone recoils from the horror of a nuclear war; in consequence, it is very much the question how far the future of the West will be decided more by economic and social development than by anything else. If the phrase "economy decides destiny" was ever true, it is applicable to the future of the West. The decisive question will be whether a social order of economy is attained which will subdue new inflation.

111 *Economic Growth*

We have already devoted some attention to the question of economic growth because economic progress, the expansion of the productivity of

[3] For a fuller account cf. J. Messner, *Die soziale Frage im Blickfeld der Irrwege von gestern, der Sozialkämpfe von heute, der Weltentscheidungen von morgen*, 7th ed., 1964, Chap. 65: "Der Kommunismus." It is surprising to see no mention, in the thoughtful book by Jean Fourastié, *Le grand espoir du XXe siècle*, 3rd ed., 1952, of the economic question mark of communism, which hangs over the hope discussed by him; there is also no mention of the other great question mark for the Western world: inflation.

the social economy, is the essential condition for the fulfillment of the social end of the economy: that is to say, for the fulfillment of the tasks arising from the natural growth of population and from the universal natural desire for better conditions of living. Because the tasks in question are implicit in the social end of economy and hence in the nature of things, fundamental questions concerning the ordering of social economy in accordance with natural law are at issue.

The question of economic growth has *two sides,* which have too long been regarded as separable, but which, in the present state of the world, show themselves to be *inseparable,* however gradually this may be perceived: these are *the national and the international.* The state of the underdeveloped countries and the danger of the spread of communism are unmistakable warning signs that the two must be seen in their interrelation. To the Western countries this is not only a question of justice, since the countries with colonial possessions could not have attained their economic growth without their colonial sources of materials, but it is also a question of the economic and political future, if only because of the opportunities otherwise presented to world communism. The case of India exemplifies glaringly the interconnection between the national and international sides of economic growth. India's yearly national income amounts to £20 sterling per head of population (*Manchester Guardian,* August 15, 1957), and even the greatest efforts cannot improve on this figure because of the increase in population. To think only of the national economy is the one great error in the matter of economic growth in the Western countries.

The best introduction to the question of economic growth is provided by *economic history,* and particularly that of Europe, since it is in Europe that economic growth and development have been most pronounced in modern times. Other continents have been marked by stagnation or hardly perceptible development. What were the causes of the development of European economies? It goes back to the beginning of the modern era; in the fifteenth century it is already in full swing, reaches a climax toward the end of the nineteenth century, and has mounted to a new climax since the middle of the twentieth century. At the commencement of this process is *man's mind* and the extension of his gaze to new horizons. *Marx's* theory of dialectical materialism, with its emphasis on "the mode of production of material life," failed to see that only the human mind was able to give such impetus to the forward development of the mode of production. It was the German triumvirate of *Werner Sombart, Max Weber,* and *Jakob Strieder* that showed mental factors to be the decisive ones in economic history itself, contrary to *Marx's* theoretical argument. They demonstrated that these mental forces are to be sought in the fields of religion and ethics as well as in the fields of natural science and politics. An abundance of interrelationships between these forces has thereby been revealed. Details need not be considered here, although something has already been said on the subject (cf. Chaps. 16, 153, 164, 170).

These intellectual factors governing modern economic development received their most important expression in the modern *entrepreneur spirit,* which already emerges sporadically in the fourteenth century and becomes in the fifteenth century the essential motive force of capitalistic economic development. It breaks through the traditional links by means of economic forms and economic thinking, and seeks to find in long-distance trading and financial business new approaches for new enterprise. The scholars mentioned brought further into light the connection between these causes and the vital significance of *capital formation;* in this they again collaborated by complementing and correcting one another. *Striodor* finally showed that the trading profits of big businessmen were the source of capital formation ("capital accumulation") and that the employment of capital directed thus toward its own growth (cf. Chap. 166) became a substantial cause of economic growth.

Other relationships which were seized upon by the scholars named, with their eyes on the causes of the economic development of early and later European capitalism, and which are today of fundamental importance for the question of economic growth in the underdeveloped countries, concern the bearing of the *natural sciences and technology* on economy. The development of the natural sciences received powerful stimuli from the possibilities of technical application, yet these applications in turn are governed by economic conditions and mental attitudes. The theory which perceives in technical inventions and innovations the principal incentive to economic growth is not borne out by the facts. History points to other principal incentives, as the economic historian *W. W. Rostow* (U.S.A.) indicates, namely, the pressure issuing from growing needs in relation to the available resources for satisfying them, and the resultant capital investment which aims at higher productivity.[4] In this,

[4] Cf. W. W. Rostow, *The Process of Economic Growth,* 1953, pp. 94 f. Rostow (pp. 83 f., 141 f.) opposes the theory of Schumpeter, *Theorie der wirtschaftlichen Entwicklung,* 5th ed., 1952, who, he holds, gives too much importance to technical discoveries as an impetus to development, whereas technical discoveries and their economic application are the outcome of the necessity to seek after means of satisfying growing needs. Nevertheless, growing needs alone are not sufficient; there must also be the spirit of enterprise, the service of the entrepreneur, "a use of national productive forces different from what has gone before," whereby "these forces are withdrawn from their previous uses and made to serve new combinations" as Schumpeter defines in "Unternehmer," in *Handwörterbuch der Staatswissenschaften,* 4th ed., Vol. VIII, 1928, p. 483. He was the one who pointed once again to the importance of the entrepreneur function for economic development, and also (*ibid.,* p. 476) to the fact that, in the economic theory of the eighteenth century and in the works of the classical economists, the entrepreneur function is hardly dealt with (lately Schumpeter has referred to this in his *History of Economic Analysis,* 1954, pp. 554 ff.). Gerald M. Meier and Robert E. Baldwin, *Economic Development,* London and New York, 1957 (with an extensive bibliography) merits attention as a book which treats of economic growth both historically and theoretically.

population growth is undoubtedly an important factor; nineteenth century capitalism would have been impossible without the unique increase in population of those times; on the other hand, the population increase during that period would have been impossible without the growth of economic productivity in the course of capitalistic development. It was only because the great majority of the growing population worked long hours for many decades at very low wages and because this was accompanied by massive capital formation that in the twenty years before 1914 there occurred so widespread and pronounced a rise in the standard of living and that now, in the middle of the present century, another unprecedented increase is possible. A period of considerable restriction of consumption is an indispensable condition for the economic growth of any social economy. Linked with this is the hard historical fact that, whereas the curtailment of consumption chiefly affected the broad laboring classes, on the other hand the necessary large capital formation must be brought about other than by the broad consumer classes. This is true equally of the history of capitalism in Europe and of communism in Russia [5] and will be true with regard to the future of the underdeveloped countries.

In the *relationship between economic development and political democracy* there is also a reciprocal connection: private ownership as a legal and economic institution is one of the strongest supports, if not *the* strongest, of political democracy; this is again a cause of a mobility of consumption and private initiative extremely important to economic development. History warns us, however, in this regard also, against biased judgments; we need only remember the position of mercantilist dirigism in the development of European economies, or the gigantic efforts and indeed successes of the communistic economy of Russia, which are made possible only by a totalitarian system, and are obviously unthinkable under democratic conditions with mass parties in the ascendant; this implies no value-judgment of the economic and political order in Russia, but is simply a statement of fact. Biased theoretical thinking can easily lead to fallacious judgments regarding the causal connections of reality and to false conclusions regarding the political and economic forms on which economic

[5] How one's view of the facts can be impeded by thinking in terms of "theoretic models" is shown by the statement of Joan Robinson, *The Accumulation of Capital,* 1956, p. 4, that an essential feature of capitalistic economy is that of a small number who hire the labor of a large number at agreed wage rates directly or through managers. A glance at H. Parkinson, *The Ownership of Industry,* 1951, pp. 3 f., 53 ff., 68, would have informed her that in Great Britain, before nationalization (from 1945 onwards), small-scale proprietorship was greatly in the ascendant in the industries concerned, large-scale proprietorship had no majority position, and certainly a few active shareholders were by no means able to exercise a decisive influence on business management. In the communistic economy of Russia, capital property is at the disposal of a far smaller number of persons than in any capitalistic economy, and, besides, these authorities have imposed upon the masses restrictions of consumption with compulsory saving which exceeds anything under capitalistic economy.

growth depends.[6] An inference of great importance is to be derived from the history of the working class under capitalism in the nineteenth century: that it is necessary to strive for a *steady course* of economic growth with the exclusion of economic friction and social malaise inconsistent with the social end of economy. Indeed, economic growth and a high living standard are not the highest of values; rather there are values of substantially higher rank and of determinant significance for the social end of economy itself. To learn from historical experience will be an obligation in regard to the tasks awaiting in the underdeveloped countries, and also for the West itself regarding the new period of economic growth to be expected from automation and nuclear energy (cf. Chap. 164).

It should by now be evident that the essential immediate conditions for economic growth are the spirit of enterprise and capital formation. These are interdependent: enterprise cannot avail without capital formation; capital formation for the purpose of economic growth becomes possible only if entrepreneurs employ initial capital in an endeavor to make effective the predisposition of risk capital to grow by being put to its purpose (cf. Chap. 166). These two factors are more important than science and technology, for the most advanced technology remains fallow if there is no spirit of enterprise, and cannot be used if the necessary capital is not forthcoming. Only the spirit of enterprise can create the conditions necessary for work with technical means of production, especially in regard to the training of the skilled workmen necessary for the production of machinery and for its use.[7] Capital formation is again required to insure the continuation of the growth process when wages are increas-

[6] P. T. Bauer and B. S. Yamey, *The Economics of Underdeveloped Countries* (Cambridge Economic Handbooks), 1957, pp. 161–257 *passim,* try to show, in long discussions inspired by neo-liberalist thinking, that, by the path of collectivism, there is nothing to be achieved for economic growth; but if one looks back over the century of capitalistic progress in Europe up to 1900, one may agree with the best Western experts on Russian economy that it is highly possible that the Soviet regime may in the foreseeable future overtake this economic growth. In this particular case it is vitally necessary to see the hard reality of facts, since otherwise the West will arrive at quite false judgments regarding the underdeveloped countries and the possibilities of Russian help for them. Cf. A. Bergson, editor, *Soviet Economic Growth, Conditions, and Perspectives* (U.S.A.), 1954; D. Shimkin, *Minerals, a Key to Soviet Power* (U.S.A.), 1953; H. S. Ellis, *The Economics of Freedom,* with Preface by Dwight D. Eisenhower (U.S.A.), 1950; Mende Thibor, *South-East Asia between Two Worlds,* 1955; R. Nurkse, *Problems of Capital Formation in Underdeveloped Countries,* 1953; A. Weber, *Marktwirtschaft und Sowjetwirtschaft,* 2nd ed., 1951; *Sowjetwirtschaft und Weltwirtschaft,* 1959.

[7] W. A. Lewis, *The Theory of Economic Growth,* 1953, p. 164, identifies as the immediate causes of economic growth economic endeavor, the accumulation of knowledge, and the accumulation of capital. But these are *conditions,* whereas the *causes,* as Rostow indicates (see above), are to be sought elsewhere. The factors mentioned by Lewis become causative, as European history shows, only in association with the service of the entrepreneur, which Lewis in this connection does not mention at all. The necessity of private initiative is strongly emphasized by Bauer and Yamey, *op. cit.,* pp. 102 ff.; also that, although knowledge is vital, the essentials must be learned through practice.

ing: expensive labor is replaced by machinery which is then made productive at higher levels than attained before by more highly skilled workers.[8] In connection with this progressive mechanization and rationalization, the question of capital formation and the raising of capital constantly arises.[9] Capital formation is the result of saving; by credit it can only be brought about insofar as the expansion of productivity, which it facilitates, leads to the formation of new savings capital; if this is not the case, the process of growth rests on more or less unsure foundations.[10]

It is unnecessary to repeat here what was said in the preceding section and in previous chapters about whether and how far economic and social

[8] The definition of economic growth will have to be based on productivity per head of the labor force; surprisingly, a definition is only rarely attempted in the literature. Rostow, *op. cit.,* p. 81, bases his definition on the rising of per capita output related to increase in capital and labor force in connection with the increase in population (because of the increase in needs to be satisfied).

[9] Seymour Melman, *Dynamic Factors in Industrial Productivity,* 1956, pp. 179 ff., shows that the main feature of economic growth consists in the increase of the productivity of labor, and the cause of this increase is the better equipment of labor with machinery and tools. But it seems impossible to accept his assumption that the principal cause of the better technical equipment of labor is higher labor costs, viz., increasing wages, which drive the entrepreneur to keep continually expanding technical methods. He tries to show this by contrasting the growth of productivity of labor in Great Britain and in the U.S.A., starting with the fact that in the first half of the twentieth century the productivity of labor in Great Britain only doubled, whereas in the United States it increased fourfold. He passes over the question of how the capital formation took place, which was necessary for this process of the replacement of dear labor by machines, and the further question, to what extent a spirit of enterprise is required to keep this process in motion. Here we should think of the genuine *entrepreneur function,* and also of the spirit of enterprise in the working population, which in the United States accepts the unemployment that belongs to this process (very high in comparison with other countries), knowing that, through installing of new and better means of production, new jobs are constantly being created. This spirit of enterprise shows itself in the United States also in the participation of the workers in capital formation by the purchase of shares. The decisive factor in the United States is capital formation out of capital profits in the form of dividends which are invested by way of the capital market, supplemented by a considerable volume of ploughing back. Both the spirit of enterprise and capital formation receive powerful impulses from *competition,* which has always been freer in the United States in comparison with other countries, especially with Great Britain. That Melman's thesis is untenable in the simplified form he gives it, is shown by developments in Australia, where rising wages did not at all result in the increased productivity of labor which his thesis requires (cf. the data in Chap. 169).

[10] W. A. Lewis, *op. cit.,* pp. 222 ff., considers that the capital formation necessary for economic growth is possible by way of creating money and inflation; he seems to be guided by the belief that, in every case, inflation aimed at useful capital formation is self-destructive because the increased stream of consumer goods deriving from the new capital formation would end the upward movement of prices or even cause price reductions. This belief in the automatic painless ending of inflation is as yet not borne out by the facts. Exponents of the "new economics" still uphold the view that inflation and rising price level are inseparable from economic and social progress; the opponents of such theories argue that the end of an inflationary economic policy, according to all evidence, will be accompanied by the danger of economically, socially and politically dangerous reverses. In any case, the questions touched upon make it clear that the *"theory of economic growth"* cannot dispense with the *"theory of economic equilibrium,"* and indeed would sacrifice any realistic foundation.

progress can be promoted by means of *credit*. But it may be pointed out that economists whose attention is focused on recent economic history, rather than on the "new economics," conclude that capital formation in the sense here described is the decisive factor of sound and lasting economic growth. Researches made in countries with a rising economic development show that what is required is, first, capital formation through saving, and, secondly, a kind of investment that will lead as far as possible to the formation of new capital; [11] furthermore, it is vitally important for lasting economic growth to know what relationship exists between capital investment in producer goods industries, on the one hand, and in consumer goods industries on the other hand, and again, in the former case, the relationship between capital investment for the manufacture of production of producer goods (e.g., steel works, power stations) and capital investment for the manufacture of means of production for consumer goods (e.g., machinery for textile and footwear manufacture).[12]

In these researches and studies two things stand out: (1) they approach their subject matter from a *social end of economy,* which is suggested by the nature of social economy; (2) they arrive at an *order of priority* in the immediate and long-term satisfaction of needs, in accordance with the order which we have mentioned for the manufacture of producer goods and consumer goods, on which economic growth depends. Stress is laid on the necessity of adaptability of production and investment development in the production spheres mentioned, and equally on the dangers to steady economic growth arising from the overstraining of the requirements of adaptability by allowing too keen competition (e.g. the period

[11] Much light is thrown on this by Simon Kuznets, "International Differences in Capital Formation and Financing," in *Capital Formation and Economic Growth: A Conference of the Universities-National Bureau Committee for Economic Research* (Princeton), 1955, pp. 19–110; the whole volume offers an abundance of empirical material on the question of economic growth. Cf. also Kuznets, "Problems in Comparison of Economic Trends," in S. Kuznets, W. E. Moore, J. J. Spengler, *Economic Growth: Brazil, India, Japan* (Duke University Press), 1955, pp. 3–28; Kuznets, editor, *Income and Wealth of the United States,* Series II of *Income and Wealth,* 1952. On the whole field an indispensable source is Colin Clark, *The Conditions of Economic Progress,* 2nd ed., 1952.

[12] Cf. Adolph Lowe, "Structural Analysis of Real Capital Formation," in *Capital Formation and Economic Growth* (cf. preceding note), pp. 586 ff.; Lowe may rightly insist that for the theory of economic growth as distinct from the "*linear*" theory originated by Böhm-Bawerk, which attributes all end products technically to labor and natural resources alone, everything depends on the "*structural*" organization of the sectors of production in a national economy as explained above. Starting from this, Lowe (*ibid.*, p. 587) demands a "*dynamic equilibrium theory*" along with the "*static equilibrium theory.*" Lowe (*ibid.*, pp. 581 f.) also stresses the priority of "*macroeconomics,*" the socio-economic point of view, over "*microeconomics,*" on which too much weight is laid by those whose theory of economic growth begins one-sidedly with the individual firm and its progressive enterprise and progressive technique. On the two attitudes cf. also the observations of Irving H. Siegel in reply to W. R. Maclaurin to the effect that the conception of economic growth as the mere accumulation of economic innovations cannot be the foundation of any adequate macroeconomic theory; cf. Siegel in the work mentioned in the preceding note, *Capital Formation, etc.*, pp. 573 f.; Maclaurin, *op. cit.*, pp. 551 ff.

of laissez-faire capitalism, with its enormous economic growth, together with enormous disadvantages on the human side owing to pauperism and proletarianism). Since the question of economic growth is thus intimately linked with the social end of economy, with the order of priority in the satisfaction of needs in face of the available resources of labor and materials both on the production and on the consumption sides, and with the rhythm of development, which is subject to man's control and therefore confers an obligation upon him: for these reasons it *is a question of natural law ethics* and of the order of justice. That is why this question, today so much in the foreground, has been treated here more thoroughly from the point of view of the principles elaborated earlier. There are two reasons why economic inquiry is today focused on this question: first, because in the highly developed lands of the West an unprecedented economic growth is taking place, and linked with it the anxious questions which persist year by year: Whether it is permanent, whether it rests on sound foundations, whether a reverse is imminent—questions prompted by consciences made uneasy by the continuing inflation in almost all these countries; secondly, because the question of economic growth in the underdeveloped countries of Africa, Asia and Latin America will be the crucial question on which will depend the issue of the conflict between liberal West and communist East to decide the future of the world.[13]

So much for economic growth in general. To consider in detail the prerequisites and the methods of economic growth in underdeveloped countries does not fall within the scope of our present discussion of natural law ethics. The application of the principles discussed depends too much on *circumstances* which are only rarely referable to general categories. With regard to such circumstances, from a psychological point of view, *traditional habits* of thought and of attitudes toward a high birth rate, toward business activities, and toward saving, are very diverse, so that a policy of economic growth cannot be carried out according to strict formulae, but must operate in different countries with different means. If one considers only the right to a national way of life, one can see that organized economic growth is possible in certain cases only as the result of a long and patient education, which must go hand in hand with the relevant measures of economic policy. This concerns especially countries where particular ties of family, extended family, and tribe are observed; to incorporate such social organizations into an expanding national econ-

[13] If the *literature of economic growth* in the United States and to a lesser extent also in England is incomparably richer than in Europe, this is because in European countries after the Second World War the main problem was to overcome the effects of the war on the national economies; besides, because of its leading position in the Western world, the foreign policy of the United States encompasses wider political horizons; Great Britain is somewhat similarly situated because of her responsibility toward the economic and social progress of the different members of the Commonwealth. The fact discussed here is made especially clear in the work which today provides probably the best survey of the relevant ideas and literature, G. M. Meier and R. E. Baldwin, *Economic Development* (New York and London), 1957.

omy and to utilize them for economic development will be just as much in the interest of assured economic growth as at later stages gradual reshaping of such organizations may become unavoidable. However, essential community values may be at stake which cannot be counterbalanced by the material values of a growing standard of living. New and difficult problems of social structure, in conjunction with new tasks of economic policy, will arise.[14] For these reasons, categories derived from the experience of highly developed economies cannot be applied without a differentiation in every stage of economic growth in underdeveloped regions—ideas like aggregate output, supply of labor, saving, and capital formation.[15]

Special difficulties will be provided by questions associated with the necessary *capital formation*. Here, particular attention will have to be paid to natural law considerations of far-reaching importance. The underdeveloped countries will have to build up, from their own resources, the capital foundation of economic growth, although with help from the economies of the West. The smallest portion of this help will consist of the export of money capital from these economies, for the reason that there is too little guarantee that, under the pressure of social and political conditions, such capital may not be applied to the increase of immediate consumption. The capital aid of the West will have to be provided mainly in the form of means of production for the establishment of basic industries, including agriculture, transport, and power installations. An important instrument for this purpose will be international finance institutions, which we shall discuss in connection with the natural law order of world economy. The capital formation to be undertaken by the underdeveloped countries themselves is not to be expected from voluntary saving with a low standard of living, so that *compulsory saving* will be unavoidable. *Lewis* illustrates this by the example of India: The country invests four to five per cent of the national income (this estimate is probably too low today, seven or eight per cent may well have been reached); its population likewise increases by four to five per cent annually; if India wishes to raise its standard of living by one per cent annually (we mentioned earlier that the yearly income per head of the population is about

[14] Lewis, *op. cit.*, p. 426, speaks of such tasks: The individual in such societies is a member of a group or of a whole series of groups, and the life and development of such societies depend upon the recognition of these small communities with their organization and authority. Bauer and Yamey, *op. cit.*, pp. 64 ff., on the other hand, take a one-sided individualist and economic view, and see in the extended family principally a hindrance to economic development, as if economic values were everything.

[15] Kuznets, *Problems in Comparisons of Economic Trends, op. cit.*, pp. 27 f., points out, along with other leading exponents of the growth theory, that this theory suffers from a deficiency of critical analysis of the notions employed, and especially that, on the whole, the questions of growth in the underdeveloped countries are discussed with notions founded in experience in one or two highly industrialized countries with which the author is familiar. For an appreciation of the wholly different prerequisites of economic growth cf. Rostow, *op. cit.*, pp. 10–79.

£20), it must double its current investments.[16] Any other possibility than compulsory saving to attain a higher investment rate will not be discoverable in many cases; [17] compulsory saving, to the extent necessary, in such countries for this purpose means, however, since inevitably a large measure of state investment will be linked with it, enhanced opportunities for a dirigist economic policy. To maintain a strict limit to socialistic state planning and to encourage private initiative and private capital formation, but especially foreign private capital investment, will then be the hallmark of statesmanship seeking the highest things for the nation.

Thus, vitally important fundamental principles of natural law in the fields of political, economic, social and international order are involved in the question of economic growth in underdeveloped countries. All of them concern obligations of international social justice, of which a summary will be given in Chapter 197.

183. The Integration of Social Economy through Full Employment

By the integration of social economy through full employment we mean a policy which makes it possible for all members of the community, who are able and willing to work, to play their part in economic cooperation in society, while preserving the freedom of labor and the optimum economic productivity. The qualifications introduced into this definition are derived from the essential nature and end of social economy. It is easy, even under the most difficult conditions, to attain full employment in a society if wages are kept at a relatively low level, and easier still if basic rights of the worker, such as the right to choose or change his occupation, particularly the right of free collective bargaining, are curtailed. The complete absence of unemployment in communistic states is explained by such a wage policy and such restrictions of freedom. The fact that the workers even in countries of western Europe (Germany, Italy) before the Second World War accepted inroads into liberties as a condition of full employment shows how grave an evil they had found chronic unemployment to be. One is reminded of the Grand Inquisitor's words in

[16] Cf. Lewis, *op. cit.*, pp. 207 f.

[17] W. W. Rostow, *op. cit.*, 1953, pp. 259 ff., in dealing with this question points out that the Keynesian hope of achieving the most by means of effective demand is falsified by the facts; what is needed, rather, is an economic policy aimed at bringing about the necessary measures of capital formation and investment. With regard to the Western democracies, he points to the serious issues arising from a policy of full employment and the accompanying chronic inflation, and, at the same time, from a policy aiming at the appropriate pattern and scale of investment. The solution of these tasks, he holds, demands a change on the part of the economic sciences, politicians, officialdom, and especially the peoples of the democratic world. Economic science must seek solutions which curtail the direct interference of the state to a minimum, notwithstanding its increasing functions. This aim was the underlying motive of our concern with the idea of a social economy of ordered freedom (cf. Chap. 181).

Dostoevsky's The Brothers Karamazov: "In the end they will lay their freedom at our feet, and say to us, 'Make us your slaves, but feed us.' And then they will understand that freedom and food in plenty for all are incompatible." We have tried to show (cf. Chap. 181) that a system of social economy, which tends permanently toward full employment, is possible, thus making freedom of labor and freedom of private enterprise the fundamental principles of order, and at the same time guaranteeing the full measure of productivity and the standard of living attainable with a given supply of natural goods and labor.

The favorite *instruments of employment policy* today are monetary and credit policies together with deficit and expenditure budgeting. The possibilities and limits of market policy by these means have been discussed already (cf. Chaps. 165, 167, 182). The results of this discussion must be summed up at this point and expanded with an eye to full employment. The field of *monetary and credit policy* includes, above all, the interest rate policy of the central bank; there is also the method of reducing the cash-holding obligations of the banks, especially in conjunction with an open market policy on the part of the central bank. The effect of such measures is to provide the economy with cheap loans (a cheap money policy) and hence provide a stimulus to investment by private persons and also by public bodies, that is, in health services, education services, housing, and road construction. Not a few economists see in credit policy the principal method, while viewing interest rate policy with scepticism. It is certainly true that in the persistent depression between the two World Wars, the very great reduction of interest rates proved to be ineffective. Yet, it by no means follows that the interest rate policy in normal conditions is not generally the most expedient means because of its flexibility, so that with its use future developments are not endangered; to this point we shall presently return.

The second main group of measures consists chiefly in *government spending* to create work, based on budget deficits and loans: in a time of depression the community borrows money from itself to be paid back in better times from revenue. Such credit is used for financing or supporting public works projects, such as road building and drainage works; for industrial subsidies, aid to exports, price guarantees to individual industries for the purpose of maintaining, extending, or improving production equipment, as in mining or agriculture; and also for carrying out long-range aims in town planning, housing, school building and office building. Among the various possibilities of public investment, those are the most useful which exercise the most widespread effects on the whole social economy,[1] above all by stimulating private investment activity in the dif-

[1] These remote effects are what Keynes, following R. F. Kahn, terms the "*multiplier*," and G. Haberler the "multiplication process"; cf. Keynes, *The General Theory of Employment, Interest, and Money*, 1946, pp. 113 ff.; G. Haberler, *Prosperity and Depression*, 3rd ed. (League of Nations, Geneva), 1941, pp. 455 ff. According to the *accelerator* principle, the stimulation of demand for end products increasingly

ferent economic fields whose raw materials, machines, or other products are used for carrying out public works and for making them profitable. A good example is the far-reaching effects of housing policy, which stimulates various branches of industry and trades, such as building, brick making, cement production, plumbing, carpentry, and glazing, which themselves in turn exert a stimulating indirect influence, if only a slight one, on other branches of industry, and hence on the level of employment of the whole economy. In road building, however, the indirect effects are much more narrowly circumscribed.

The *limits* of market and employment policy, with the means stated, are ultimately determined by the increase in socio-economic productivity attainable therewith.[2] These limits are overreached by a full employment policy when linked with a policy of economic growth with the aid of expanded credit. Then, inflationary effects are to be expected. This is generally the case when a rising movement of wages continues after the attainment of full employment. It is a fact that the workers are especially inclined to make wage demands under full employment, and that equally the employers in particular branches of industry, in order to obtain labor, are often ready to make wage concessions in the form of overtime or bonus payments. With the wage movement is linked the price movement: the increase of prices associated with the expansion of demand and higher wage costs results in a diminution in the purchasing power of money, or inflation. This is the already discussed "new inflation." If prices rise with full employment, then this indicates a demand in excess of socio-economic productivity, and overconsumption at the cost of future economic and social development. State expenditure for public works may also tend to restrict productivity if it is not managed with the strictest regard for its limits. For it can be carried out only by means of a higher taxation revenue, which partly curtails private capital formation. This merits special thought because public works always mean that a substantial amount of capital is tied down for a considerable time to come, since, once begun,

---

results in an expansion of production and investment in the preceding stages of pro duction; cf. G. Haberler, *op. cit.*, pp. 85–105; also the book already mentioned, *Economic Stability in the Postwar World* (League of Nations), 1945, pp. 50 ff., 177 ff. The two principles can receive only limited acceptance, because an antidepression and full employment policy founded on them, although it could achieve rapid successes, could bring about detrimental results by tying down capital and labor resources to sectors of production of secondary importance in the true process of economic recovery; this will be further referred to in the text.

[2] "Unproductive" investments may be an extreme emergency measure; some are inclined grossly to overestimate the extent of its justification, as for instance Keynes in his judgment on the building of the pyramids and of the medieval cathedrals. Here he seems to be overlooking the following facts: at the periods when the pyramids and the cathedrals were built there was no opportunity at all for large-scale private investment; and the great period of cathedral construction took place during the static medieval economy with its *chronic labor shortage* (cf. Chap. 60, note 4). The economic history of the period of cathedral building can therefore hardly be adduced in favor of an antidepression and employment theory of the Keynesian kind.

they cannot easily be broken off. But, this tying down of capital affects not only the capital immediately necessary for the execution of public works; it also affects investments made in various sectors of industry in connection with public works (reverse operation of the multiplier and accelerator principle; cf. note 1). This is particularly so since, as *G. N. Halm* points out, investments in the public sector can for the most part only be made according to scales of priority instead of interest and yield calculation; in consequence in one sector too much, in another too little, is invested, so that the necessary balance is not even established in the public economy.[3]

Mechanization and Unemployment

The special character of *"technical" unemployment* received remarkable attention and was the subject of extensive discussion at the time of the chronic mass unemployment between the two World Wars. It all began with the realization that mechanization and rationalization temporarily caused steep rises in unemployment. Both processes were in part motivated by the idea (on the part of the employer) of cutting down labor in order to avoid not only high wage bills but also substantial social burdens. They sought, in accordance with the law of substitution of the factors of production, to diminish their production costs. To counteract such technical unemployment, a variety of automatic controls were proposed. One proposal was that social insurance contributions should be payable, not on the basis of the number of workers employed and the amount of wages paid in a business, but in accordance with the amount of capital invested; thus, social insurance would act at the same time as a brake on the overhasty introduction of technical methods and as a protection of the workers against dismissal. According to another proposal, any fresh introduction of technical methods should be charged during a period of unemployment with a contribution to social insurance funds corresponding to the earnings lost by the discharged workers until they have obtained work again. Even forms of machinery tax have been put forward as a check on "antisocial" mechanization. Such proposals and attitudes are understandable in view of the tragic experience of mass unemployment between the two World Wars. As late as the middle of the present century workers in England tried strike action to enforce the abandonment of technical development plans (e.g., in open-cast coal mining), not to speak of the riots among weavers a hundred years ago. In this sphere, wholesale solutions and wholesale measures are never justified. For the productivity of labor in a sector of industry and in the social economy as a whole, and hence the standard of living also, depend on the standard of equipment with tools, and hence on the state of the means of production. One may wonder what the standard of living of Great Britain would be today with its doubled population if the machine breakers of a century ago had had their way. The experience of Great Britain with its coal industry after the Second World War may serve as a warning; economic reconstruction, exports, and even the standard of living in Great Britain were endangered because the productivity of

[3] G. N. Halm, *Wirtschaftssysteme,* 1960, 303 (not in English edition of 1951).

the coal industry lagged behind owing to technical backwardness. A reason for this backwardness is to be found in the fact that for decades, because of the chronic unemployment, there was an unlimited supply of labor available to the coal industry at relatively low wages; this state of affairs had a retarding effect on mechanization, exactly the effect which the proposed controls for the avoidance of technical unemployment were to achieve. All automatic controls on technical development prove to be a two-edged sword. But there is undeniably a problem of overhasty and too widespread technical development and rationalization which have not only caused unemployment unnecessarily, especially when, contrary to the principle of socio-economic productivity, it consists only in "technical productivity" (cf. Chap. 164). This can be checked by controls such as those outlined in Chapter 181, which will make it possible to have due regard to socio-economic productivity and to weigh current difficulties and future needs against one another.

184. The Social Integration of Economy

From the social viewpoint, by the integration of economy is meant the bringing about of a status of complete social equality of labor compared with the other groups in society ("deproletarianization"). Modern democracy brought legal and political equality for all, but not social equality. Under the individualist-capitalistic social system the social status of the worker was marked by three characteristics: (1) economic insecurity; (2) social dependence; (3) lack of partnership in the control of the socio-economic process as a whole. The economic insecurity of the worker consisted in the uncertainty of his income: the capitalistic labor market mechanism threw him out of the economic process if capital saw no possibilities of profit for itself. His lot, therefore, was the perennial threat of unemployment. Unemployment benefit was able to alleviate the material consequences for the worker but did not alter the mechanical operation of the labor market. The social dependence of the worker was the result of the social power of capital. The individualist-capitalistic social system gave capital the upper hand in settling the conditions of labor. For a long time there were no safeguards to guarantee the observance of the conditions of the labor contract demanded by the human dignity of the worker in accordance with the principles of natural law. Besides, the worker was denied any share in the direction and control of the economic process: in the individualist (and also the collectivistic) economic system, the worker is merely a planned, and not a planning, factor in the economic process.

In comparison with his status under individualist capitalism in the middle of the nineteenth century, *the status of the worker today is fundamentally altered:* 1) The policy of full employment has made the economic existence of the working population incomparably more secure. 2) With the growth of the trade union movement, the social status of labor has so changed that today it is on a par with capital in power. 3) In the direction of the total economic process also, the position of the workers has changed so much that, by means of their own political parties, they have obtained a significant influence over economic legislation and policy. 4) In addition, the modern state carries out an extensive social and welfare policy, with the strong cooperation of the workers through their trade union and political organizations. 5) Finally, the consumers' cooperative movement not only offers the workers, as consumers, economic advantages, but also represents considerable economic power.

The fact that, in spite of all this, the worker still does not see himself as a full partner in the economic community is shown by the social tensions and disagreements which continue almost unabated and by the fact that the *social question in its modern form remains unsolved* in its root element, the relationship between labor and capital. A radical solution must (1) base the economic security of labor on an order of economy which of itself comprehensively fulfills the social end of economy, and hence, of itself, leads to full employment without constantly endangering the increasing incomes of labor by inflation. (2) The social dependence of the worker must be eliminated by institutions and organs which, appointed on the principle of parity, guarantee that, for the regulation of all social concerns, justice is the determining factor, so that there will not be, as today, a confrontation of social power (capital) by social power (labor) and the conflict between them will not be a permanent institution. (3) Labor must become a regulative principle of social economy on equal terms with property, so that the workers can be equal partners in the planning, direction, and control of social economy as a whole. We have tried in the preceding chapters to sketch what would be the chief features of an order of social economy which should secure to labor, in these three directions, the status due to it in accordance with natural law principles.*

Such an order of social economy would also provide the necessary conditions for the other decisive change in the status of the workman, the change resulting from the *acquisition of property* out of income. Only when the majority of workers are able to accumulate property will the social order of economy be fully integrated and the social end of economy realized, as far as this is humanly possible. The principles of economic order which we have developed guarantee rising productivity, rising real wages, and hence increasing possibilities of forming property; and they insure the stability of the value of money, that basic requirement of a secure

* In the first edition of this book the social order built on such foundations was termed "socially integrated democracy," the idea being that this suggested the hitherto incompleted political democracy on the social side, by means of the equal participation of the workers in the direction of the social economy, in order best to fulfill its social end. This expression (German *soziale Demokratie*) is only occasionally used in this edition to avoid confusion with a corresponding socialistic expression, as used by E. Heimann, *Vernunftglaube und Religion in der modernen Gesellschaft: Liberalismus, Marxismus und Demokratie,* 1955, p. 305.

status of the worker in a just social order. It is a remarkable inconsistency today that, whereas from many directions the call is heard for property in the hands of the workers as a principal means of social reform, and consequently wages are demanded which will make this possible by saving, nevertheless it is taken for granted that the economic growth necessary for such wages will inevitably lead to inflationary effects. Saving out of wage incomes will always be a long-term process, if it is to have any significance for the reshaping of the social and economic order. The forms which we have already discussed are principally three: savings bank deposits, investment in securities (especially in equities and in investment trust certificates), and, above all, the acquisition of a family home; the last should be envisaged preferably in association with a piece of land, which would be cultivated by the family, could provide a not-to-be-despised supplementary income, and in turn could be combined with the wage income of members of the family to accumulate further property, particularly for sons and daughters. The advantages of the last-mentioned form of property acquisition are manifold and are hardly to be disputed on any concrete grounds. These advantages are: socially, a more even distribution of wealth; economically, better utilization of labor and more intensive utilization of the soil; politically, closer bonds between the worker on his own land and the rest of the community; for population policy, better conditions for the natural increase of population if the family can find a substantial part of the sustenance for its growing children on its own land, along with wage incomes; for health policy, better conditions for a natural mode of life. The fact that these advantages cannot be reconciled with some preconceived theories says nothing against their significance: A widely spread family income of this kind would be one of the strongest bulwarks against the advance of communism, and of socialism too. But it is also clear that, without a change in the psychological and economic outlook of large sectors of the industrial workers, it is not to be expected that there will be considerable saving in the foreseeable future, with a rapid development of such family property and the necessary enthusiasm in managing it. Such a change in attitude would have to be accompanied by a change in attitude toward the fundamental values of life, and in particular by a widespread rejection of the illusory values of present-day civilization.

185. The Structural Integration of the Socio-Economic Process

By the structural integration of social economy is meant the coordination of the different branches of the economy so that the labor and natural resources available to a community may be most usefully employed in the service of the social end of economy.

I *The Principle of the Relative External Independence of Social Economy*

As long as there is no international authority to guarantee peace and close cooperation among the nations, the individual nation will have to strive to attain the end of social economy out of its own resources, to such an extent that it retains the power to plan and direct the economic process; and hence is less subject to the fluctuations of world economy. If this relative independence is lacking, a social economy will be more sensitive to price and market fluctuations in other countries and more responsive to setbacks in their own economic evolution, with all the consequences flowing from economic depressions and uncertainty.

The principle of relative independence cannot be reconciled with communistic large-scale economic planning any more than with the laissez-faire economy, which would leave the individual social economy at the mercy of the free play of forces in international competition. Whereas the former increasingly places its economy at the service of its international political aims, individualist theory is blind to the goods and values of the political community as such. The order of ends gives a clear indication of the principles of economic policy in this regard. A political community, which would be able to achieve stability in its social order, balanced progress in its economy, and assured power of action in face of the dynamic of international affairs only by making sacrifices of economic well-being, is bound to strive, in its economic structure, for the all-round development demanded by the social end of economy. Economic and social welfare are high values in the common good of a nation, but not the highest. The relative independence of the national economy, of which we have spoken, does not mean, however, that the economy is to be cut off from world economy, but it means sufficient autonomy in regard to the development of the national economy that it can be adapted to the rhythm of international economic trends without grave setbacks. The social end of economy also involves the provision of the requirements of military defense, which will mean developing resources in order to be able to meet contingencies in the international political field.

II *The Principle of the Relative Internal Equilibrium of the Economic Structure*

The principle now to be discussed relates to the fullest possible development of the social economy in all its branches. Here again socio-economic productivity is to be invoked, this time as a criterion of what is possible, and also necessary. Only a harmonious development of all branches of economy will bring about the fullest socio-economic cooperation through the process of exchange, or of the "home market." A social economy with a sound structure and an established internal market possesses a more adequate power of resistance to depressions because the external markets are restricted to a more complementary role, and also because the economic process can be more easily guided by methods of economic policy; besides, the burdens which are imposed upon the individual economic groups by the necessity of adapting to fluctuations in world economy can be more easily distributed over the whole.

This aspect of structural integration, too, is concerned only with a relative equilibration, of such a kind that the benefits thereby gained for the community are in proportion to the price paid. Accordingly, the principle of the equilibration of the economic structure is by no means a principle of economic self-sufficiency (*autarky*). Such a goal could be pursued only by countries that possessed an inexhaustible supply of all economic resources and might cut themselves off from international economic cooperation without any economic and political disadvantages to themselves or the family of nations. Any other country would have to pay heavily in terms of its standard of living or its capacity for political action, and would thus expose itself to the danger of social, political, and international difficulties. On the other hand, it is clear that the separate social economies are the more valuable members of a well-constructed international economic system, the more they themselves are enabled by their own structural integration to reach their highest efficiency. International economy would correspondingly be a cooperative system of social economies rather than a struggle for world markets.

III *The Principle of Gradation of Size in Accordance with Productivity*

This principle relates to the sizes of concerns in the various branches of economy, especially industry and agriculture, but also commerce and credit business. How desirable, from the point of view of the social end of economy, is the large, the medium or the small industrial undertaking, the small or medium factory, the large-scale, medium, or small farming unit? Our principles yield a conclusion of great importance for the structural order of economy: *The medium and smaller economic unit is altogether to be preferred to the large unit where the productivity of the former equals or exceeds that of the latter.* The reason is that the common weal order of society demands the greatest possible number of undertakings in which property and labor are directly associated. Property which yields profit in conjunction with the work of the owner is the surest guarantee of a sound social order; it is certainly the strongest, if not the only, safeguard of liberal democracy. Freedom in democracy obtains from private property its firmest support: personal interest; all other safeguards are subject to the vagaries of the majority will; and economic security based on the widest distribution of private ownership of medium and smaller businesses exerts an incomparable stabilizing influence in face of the communistic dynamic which today threatens democracy. This is one of the *social functions of private property* if it is correctly distributed. The danger of rigidity in a social order thus secured by private property is prevented by the linking of business property to the principle of economic productivity, that is, as we have shown, by incorporating the social function of competition. The social function of private property and the social function of competition are thus brought into an intrinsic, essential relationship, which is rooted in the social end of economy, this being itself part of the common good purpose of society.

The position of *agriculture* in the whole structure of national economy requires special mention in this context. In the industrial countries of Europe at the turn of the century liberalist economic theory and practice were content with the idea that agriculture in these countries, with the development of the international division of labor, could play only a very subordinate role; some, like Professor *Lujo Brentano,* openly declared that it had best disappear altogether since food can be obtained more cheaply from the world market in exchange for industrial products. The lasting economic and social difficulties, which in those days fell upon the farming communities, are well known: the disparity between agricultural and industrial incomes, between agricultural and industrial prices; the decay of valuable agricultural land; the flight from the land; and the movement to the towns, with such consequences, for example, as the decline of the population. All this meant severe shortcomings in the realization of the end of social economy and of the common good of the political community. The structural principles which we have developed demand that the political community shall develop its agriculture to the highest degree compatible with the principle of socio-economic productivity. Fundamental values of the political community and of social order must weigh heavily by comparison with a relatively slight increase in material welfare. A degree of tariff protection and state subvention for agriculture, therefore, is indispensable. I say a degree, because the measures in question must always be aimed at bringing about an increase in the efficiency of farming which will render such measures superfluous or at least keep them within bounds in order not to burden the community with disproportionate costs.* Factors which must contribute toward

* Two facts characterize the development of incomes in agriculture: first, with a growing aggregate income of an economy, a relatively small proportion is expended on agricultural produce, in addition to which agricultural production increases as a result of the use of technical methods of production. "From this relationship there arises the necessity for the aggregate social product to increase much more steeply each year than agricultural production, so that this can be absorbed by the consumer without pressure of prices" (H. Niehaus, *Leitbilder der Wirtschafts- und Agrarpolitik in der modernen Gesellschaft,* 1957, p. 262). The second fact: as far as there has been a big increase in agricultural wages in the advanced economies it has been due to the replacement of human labor by machines; "The one who pays for the deficiency in technical progress in production methods is not the consumer of agricultural

this end are a sound proportion in the size of units (cf. following section), mechanization, and rationalization (within the limits set by the conditions of agricultural management and the protection of rural cultural values), an adequate supply of credit, well-developed self-help organizations (producers' and credit cooperatives), the best possible general and vocational training of the farming community, dwellings for farm workers, full social insurance benefits for the farming population, and the opportunity for farm workers to rise to independence.

It is generally recognized today that the small independent farm can be much more productive than the large estate. Among the advantages of the small farm are the greater working capacity per head of the farmer's family, owing to their love for their own homestead and soil; better utilization of the manifold productive resources, owing to the greater ease in combining the various necessary operations; and greater resistance to economic fluctuations in a unit which is largely self-supporting and can more easily adapt its production to the market. There are also strong reasons connected with the common good in general for small farms: the socially stabilizing effect of a strong farming community and its significance for the biological self-preservation of the nation, especially at a time of suicidal decline in the birth rate. All this is not, however, a denial of any justification for large estates: the large estate may be more productive economically because of the opportunities it provides for the use of technical equipment, for rotation of crops, and for the conservation of the soil.

With regard to the gradation of sizes in *industry*, it is an undoubted fact that the large-scale business is by no means always and universally more productive; it should be remembered that economic and technical productivity are to be distinguished and that for large-scale business there are inherent limits to productivity (cf. Chap. 175). Where the predominance of big business in an economy depends only on greater capital strength, the state has definite tasks in bringing about a structural pattern of economy on the principles described. The means to this end are chiefly the following: a competitive system which will preclude advantages based on capital power; a fiscal policy which will impede the automatic growth of the big concern through nondistribution and the ploughing back of profits. It would, of course, be a mistake to place too much hope in the state alone in this matter. The regulative forces of economy itself, which work for a free and fair competition (cf. Chap. 181), must also be brought into play. A very great deal can and must be done by the smaller and medium-sized businesses themselves. The chief agency will be cooperative self-help organizations: purchasing cooperatives to obtain raw

---

products, but the producer in all those concerns where too many heads and hands are engaged in production" (Niehaus, *ibid.*, p. 263); similar ideas are to be found in Fritz Baade, *Brot für ganz Europa: Grundlagen und Entwicklungsmöglichkeiten der europäischen Landwirtschaft*, 1952, esp. pp. 119–26: "Acht Grunderkenntnisse."

materials on favorable terms; cooperative workshops for joint use of machinery (e.g., repair depots); marketing cooperatives for the sale and storage of products; and credit cooperatives for the provision of credit in suitable forms. General and professional training are also indispensable factors, for it is largely by the quality of their work that small-scale industry and crafts must assure their economic existence. Not least in importance, vocational training must be concerned with the organizational and technical business equipment, since upon this depends to a considerable extent their efficiency and competitive strength in face of the greater capital resources of the large concern.

Along with agriculture and industry, we must give particular consideration to *commerce and trade,* the distributing apparatus of social economy. The productivity of commerce rests upon its service to the consumer and to the producer, to whom it transmits the aggregate orders of the consumers. In relation to its economic productivity, it readily overexpands, since it involves smaller risks, easier opportunities of profit, and less demanding work in comparison with other economic activities. In almost all industrial countries, one can observe an overexpansion of commerce in general, particularly in the intermediate trade between producer (especially agricultural) and small retailer. The existence of the latter is today threatened on many sides. Producers with strong capital backing, particularly combines, have turned to the creation of their own selling organizations. On the other hand, large groups of consumers have emancipated themselves from privately owned retail shops by means of consumers' cooperative societies. The independent tradesman also suffers because of the department store and the one-price store. But whereas the department store can perform a function economically useful since, as a large-scale buyer, it can more easily resist the price dictates of the producers' cartels and hence sell more cheaply to the purchaser, besides saving him trouble in shopping, there is hardly anything convincing to be said in favor of the one-price store; its prosperity often rests on the fact that it surrenders quality to the illusion of cheapness and offers inferior goods (in some countries the one-price store is prohibited by law). If the smaller independent tradesman is to be able to compete he must contribute most himself. He must be prepared to modernize his shop and his business methods, particularly with regard to bookkeeping and stocktaking, and to display his goods attractively, with care for the external appearance of his establishment and for tidiness within; other requisites are civility toward customers and flexibility in his individual treatment of them; in short, the tradesman must engage his whole personality in his business. These methods of strengthening competitive capacity would have to go together with a selective process, with the result that trading will be reduced to an amount which will not place too heavy a burden on socio-economic productivity, so that the present undeniable overexpansion will be curbed.

We have dealt only by way of illustration with the aims and methods of a structural system, in accordance with the end of social economy, from the point of view of relative sizes of economic units; what we have been illustrating is the principle of the greatest possible number of small undertakings consistent with the demands of socio-economic productivity and the purpose of state and society, the common good.

186. The Function of the State in the Integration of Social Economy

In the course of our discussion of the process of social cooperation, its ordering and integration, we constantly found that the state has tasks of great importance. At this point we shall survey briefly the status and functions of the state in the realm of economy.

1. *Economic order.* The functions of the state are authorized but also restricted by natural law, that is, by the common good principle and the subsidiary function principle. According to the latter, economy falls primarily within the sphere of the personal responsibility and activity of the individual, that is, private initiative, a principle of order which, especially in conjunction with the principle of private ownership, produces market economy or competition. It belongs to the state, on the basis of the principle of the common good, to coordinate the particular activities and responsibilities of the members of society, to promote and regulate them as the social end of economy requires. Here the fundamental principle of every activity of state authority comes into play: that it best complies with its common good function when it can so influence the free activity of the members of society (individuals and groups) that these, by pursuing their own interest, serve the general interest (cf. Chap. 25), so that the motive power of individual interest, private initiative, becomes fully effective for the general welfare.

2. *Economic legislation.* The skeleton of a system conforming with the principles mentioned must be created by economic legislation. The guiding principle must be that the legal order is basically an order of freedom, namely, the defining and guaranteeing of liberties in accordance with the common good. Economic legislation concerns mainly the rights and duties bound up with private property, economic exchange of goods and services (commercial law), economic institutions and forms of organization (such as legislation concerning restrictive trading agreements, joint stock companies, combines, and banks).

3. *Economic policy.* Economic policy is also known today as economic planning. It comprises measures taken by the state to promote general economic well-being. The general principles, when applied to state economic policy, yield the two principles of consistency and continuity. Con-

sistency requires [1] that all measures are to be viewed in the light of their interrelationship and of their overall influence on the attainment of the social end of economy. Continuity demands the avoidance of spasmodic changes in important measures, because the resulting uncertainty will have a crippling effect on private initiative and the entrepreneur function. Continuity can be jeopardized, especially under democracy, by changes of government with programs varying between a greater measure of free enterprise and state socialism. This is well-exemplified by the situation in Great Britain after the Second World War; the Labor Government of 1945–51, with its program of nationalization, was succeeded by a government which carried out denationalization measures to the constant accompaniment of hopes and warnings of subsequent renationalization from the other side, should they succeed to power. We have dealt with the methods of state economic policy in detail when discussing the process and organization of social economy and also in our immediately preceding observations on its functional, social, and structural integration; these methods include policies in regard to full employment and trade fluctuations, money, credit, currency, investment, prices, wages, interest, property, income, agriculture and industry, foreign trade, foreign exchange rate and tariffs; further tasks will be discussed when we treat of international economy.

4. *Social policy.* Social policy aims at the attainment of the social end of economy by legislation in favor of the economically weaker groups by social insurance schemes (concerning the principles cf. Chap. 142), family allowance schemes.

5. *Fiscal policy.* By means of fiscal policy the state can first influence the expansion or contraction of different kinds of consumption, since it can

[1] Adolf Weber, *Kurzgefaßte Volkswirtschaftspolitik,* Preface to 1st ed., 1935 (7th ed., 1957), vividly explained that everything depends on the *consistency* of economic policy if it is to succeed in promoting the general welfare: "The national economy is not a box of toys of which portions can be assembled at will; in the national economy all the parts are interdependent, and everyone who overlooks this connection and does not grasp its special nature will try in vain to replace bad by better, and will almost certainly be led into experiments which will only magnify the chaos." Walter Eucken, *Die Grundlagen der Nationalökonomie,* 6th ed., 1950, p. 240, says the same thing: "Individual economic questions—whether questions of agricultural policy, trade policy, credit policy, monopoly policy, taxation policy, company law, or bankruptcy law—are elements of the question, how the economic system as a whole, nationally and internationally, with the special rules of the game, is to be shaped. For many decades it has been customary to single out, casuistically, individual questions of economic policy. But the whole interrelationship of all economic phenomena demands that they be seen in this interrelationship and treated accordingly." What is meant here is the economic laws in their interaction, but understood in the perspective of man as the central point of social economy. Hence, Bernard Pfister, "Wirtschaftspolitische Entscheidung und wirtschaftspolitische Verantwortung," in *Festschrift für Ludwig Erhard,* 1957, pp. 38 f., can say that "much can be achieved by governmental laws and administrative regulations, but only if these laws have had incorporated into them an understanding of man's nature and the actual problems of every economy."

influence prices by means of purchase taxes; and it can influence the volume of purchasing power itself by means of income tax; secondly, it can also influence the formation and investment of capital; thirdly, it can influence the distribution of incomes (concerning the principles cf. Chap. 148).

6. *State economic activity.* On principle it is, as pointed out (under n. 1), not the business of the state to run economic enterprises except in cases when special reasons make it necessary according to the common weal principle. Economic activity may have the form of state enterprises for the purpose of supplying the public with certain necessary services or of producing necessary revenue for the state; state participation in large private concerns for the purpose of exercising necessary supervision; if necessary, the nationalization of particular branches of industry. The qualification *necessary* sets narrow limits to state activity in all these directions. As long as the services of private enterprise are available to the public and the state there can only exceptionally be any real ground for specific activity by the state in the role of entrepreneur. And since its expenditure can be met by taxation, the state will only in rare and exceptional cases have any justification for setting up revenue-earning enterprises, such as the state tobacco and salt monopolies in Austria, which are of historical origin. Participation by the state in large private concerns may be imperative for control purposes, as in the case of the peaceful uses of atomic energy. But nationalization proper can be necessary; this calls for special discussion.

I *The Nationalization of Branches of Industry and Large Concerns: General Principles*

1. The right of *private ownership* as a social institution has its foundation in the natural law itself and is, therefore, independent of the arbitrary will of the state.

2. Only the interest of the general well-being can provide justification for interference by the state in the sphere of private ownership, so that, in every single case in which nationalization is under consideration, it must be shown that it is in the interest of the general good.

3. Expropriation for the purpose of nationalization can, in justice, be carried out only on payment of full compensation to the owners.

II *Possibilities and Limits of Nationalization*

Nationalization may be defined as the transfer of the greater or a greater part of the means of production to state ownership. The aim is mostly to secure a monopoly of business in order to make economic planning possible in the industry concerned and in the economy as a whole. Nationalization of individual concerns can only exceptionally lead to monopoly, but the nationalized undertaking can acquire a predominant position in an oligopoly. Applying the second of the general principles let us now consider some possibilities of justified nationalization in certain branches of industry.

1. Undoubtedly there is always justification for nationalizing the production of materials for the military or economic use of *nuclear energy.*

2. Nationalization may be necessary for so-called *key industries,* namely, industries producing goods upon which a large proportion of a country's industries depends if their functions are indispensable in the social economy and cannot otherwise be guaranteed. Furthermore, state enterprise may be justified in the production of goods upon which the community is dependent if the necessary private capital and the necessary private enterprise are lacking. Similarly, the nationalization of a branch of industry may be justified if it holds a determining position in the external political-military situation. It must be noted, however, that neither the monopolistic organization of an industry nor the exercise of political influence in itself justifies nationalization as long as other means exist of averting dangers to the political, economic, or social common good. Such means may include the breaking of a monopoly or the breaking up of political influence by parliamentary control (e.g., the cooperation of all parties in a parliamentary committee).

3. With regard to the consumer goods industries, there might be grounds for nationalizing those supplying *basic needs* of the community, the satisfaction of which cannot be left to the caprice of private enterprise. Such industries may include water, gas, electricity, and public transport services. Today, services of this kind are under state or municipal ownership in a number of free democratic countries.

4. In the advanced society there cannot be any sufficient grounds for nationalization of *agricultural land* for the purpose of cultivation by the state itself. Political, social, and economic reasons make it a rather vital task of the state to promote such a distribution of property in land, so that as many families as possible can obtain economic and social security by their own work on their own soil.

5. *Minerals,* like coal and ores, may justifiably become an object for nationalization when it is necessary in the interest of the national economy, either because a better utilization of deposits is required, involving costly improvements of technical equipment which the owners are unable or unwilling to carry out, or because it is necessary to prevent exploitation, which would be harmful to the future development of the national economy, as in the case of ores necessary for the production of nuclear energy.

6. No adequate grounds exist for the nationalization of the *banks.* Credit possesses a fundamental importance for the whole of social economy, which is surpassed only by that of the soil. He who controls credit controls the economy. If the state controls it, the whole of the economy is in the grip of the state. State ownership of a bank or the nationalization

of the central issuing bank is a different matter, however (on this cf. the provisos in Chap. 178).

7. For obvious reasons, enterprises with *cultural aims* must be completely exempt from nationalization. Such enterprises are the press and book publishing. This does not preclude the state's maintaining, for example, its own printing press or publishing house or newspaper, provided that these do not make use of unfair methods of competition.

Clearly, then, the nationalization of sectors of industry or nationalization of big business firms can be applied only in exceptional cases. There are other reasons too why nationalization can be justified only as a matter of unavoidable necessity. First, all experience shows that the state and state officials possess no special aptitude for managing economic undertakings; indeed, *Otto Bauer*, onetime head of the Austrian Social Democratic Party, did not hesitate to say: "No one manages industrial concerns worse than the state"; the reason is that the entrepreneur function and the administrative function are quite different things. There is also, as *Bauer* points out, danger for democracy: "If the government controlled all possible concerns it would become all-powerful in comparison with the people and the parliament"; that is the danger envisaged by leading English socialists toward the end of the socialistic experiment in Great Britain, the danger of a "new despotism," namely, the despotism of the manager.[2]

III *Compensation*

The compensation of expropriated owners in the course of nationalization is a question of commutative justice: this means that it must essentially be carried out on the principle of equivalence. Now the ascertainment of the value of undertakings often meets with the greatest difficulties (owing to wear and tear, fluctuations in the markets for their products, psychological influence on the equity market arising from the nationalization policy of a government). Therefore, it is a matter of justice and equity that the state, in settling the amount of compensation, should come to an honorable understanding with the owners. The amount of a just compensation is especially hard to arrive at when money is steadily decreasing in value. In compensation, real values are exchanged for money values, and these lose in value, especially when government stock is used to pay the shareholders of large undertakings.[3] For all these reasons, it should

[2] Cf. Otto Bauer, *Der Weg zum Sozialismus,* 1919, p. 19, republished 1947; J. Messner, *Das englische Experiment des Sozialismus, dargestellt auf Grund ökonomischer Tatsachen und sozialistischer Selbstzeugnisse,* 1954, pp. 101 f.

[3] In Great Britain the shareholders in railways, the coal industry, etc., were compensated by means of government stock (Coal Industry Nationalization Act, 1946, par. 21; Electricity Act, 1947, par. 20; Gas Act, 1948, par. 25); the shareholders had to accept certain losses in market values, besides reductions in purchasing power of the money value of government stock, owing to the constant decline in the value of money.

be settled by agreement between state and owners how much is to be paid in cash, how much in gilt-edged securities, how much at a later date (with compensation for any diminution in the value of money), what new investment opportunities are to be offered to make up for the loss of real value, and so on. Fundamentally, all these questions are questions of strict justice, and therefore demand most careful arrangement if a state is not to be guilty of grave injustice, which would also burden it with a long-term duty of restitution.

IV *Socialism in Search of New Ways*

Here we shall speak only of socialism in a free democracy, or liberal socialism, not communism. In the Western democracies, the conception of socialism prevalent before the Second World War received a profound shock. This conception rested on the principle of the nationalization of the means of production as a necessary preliminary to the defeat of the "social power" (*Karl Marx*) of capital and to a form of economy raised to the highest pitch of efficiency by means of general planning, guidance, and control by central authorities. Two causes were mainly responsible for the change in socialistic outlook. The first is the experience of actual socialism of the old type in Russia; communism there and the totalitarian form of state bound up with it have effected such disillusionment in the Western world that the older idea of socialism seems completely discredited; the outcome of this is a new and very radical "revisionism" (the first began in the 1880's) of Marxism. Besides, the free industrial society has proved so efficient and has achieved such an increase in the standard of living that the full socialization advocated by the old school of socialists seemed too risky.[4]

The questionable character of the idea of socialism based on the nationalization of the means of production has been a subject of study from early days. The older school of socialists held that socialistic economy would achieve a much higher productivity because it eliminated the "anarchy of competition"; but they never ask themselves *how a socialistic system could function.* This was the question which had to be answered. A critical point was that prices in the socialistic economy meant something different from what they meant in the free economy. In the former they are fixed by decree, admittedly in the light of demand and production figures calculated statistically, but without supply and demand being able to exercise their reciprocal influence; this means that use value and cost value of goods cannot become effective in order to make prices move toward the natural level. In the socialistic economy, this is not possible, since there is neither a market for capital goods (these being of course nationalized) nor a free consumers' choice (since only "planned" goods are on sale).

[4] There is a full treatment of socialism in J. Messner, *Die soziale Frage,* 7th ed., 1964, Chap. 54–91.

Therefore, no price-formation exists which would guarantee the best possible use of the available factors of production. Hence, an increased efficiency in socialistic economy is out of the question; indeed the attainment of the maximum economic productivity is impossible. For, without the price mechanism of the free market, the basic conditions of *economic calculation* are lacking. These are indispensable for the attainment of the economically most productive employment of natural resources, capital and labor (on economic calculation cf. Chaps. 165–66).

The problem of the *economic efficiency of the socialist economic system* was first taken up by *Max Weber* and *Ludwig Mises,* and somewhat later by *Georg Halm.*[5] Then the socialistic theorists themselves began to face up to the problem. The Germans *Heimann* and *Landauer,* both now in America, *H. D. Dickinson* in England, and *A. P. Lerner* in the United States may be mentioned.[6] They came to the conclusion that the socialistic economy, if it is to achieve the maximum productivity and standard of living, needs a price-formation based on the interaction of supply and demand and that therefore a market with real competition is indispensable.[7] Now they tried to show that even with common ownership of the means of production a market for capital goods, and hence a genuine *interest rate* and price-formation guided by it, was possible if the individual concerns had to "buy" their raw materials and means of production from one another and also to pay capital interest from their balance of returns over outlay. They could then obtain credits only if they were in a position to pay interest on them. The rate of interest would be fixed by the planning authorities in accordance with the desired capital investment rate. Competition and incentive would be created by bonus systems, differential wages, preferential entitlements to consumer goods. Would these methods achieve the purpose? The rate of interest as a cost element to be reckoned by factory managements would no doubt present the central planning authorities with a means to control the relative productivity of individual production units. But in no way would such statistical figures

[5] Cf. Max Weber, *Wirtschaft und Gesellschaft,* 1921, pp. 55 f.; L. Mises, *Die Wirtschaftsrechnung, Archiv für Sozialwissenschaft,* Vol. XLVII, 1920; Vol. LI, 1924; Vol. LX, 1928; Mises, *Die Gemeinwirtschaft,* 2nd ed., 1932; G. Halm, *Ist Sozialismus wirtschaftlich möglich?* 1926; cf. also the contributions by Mises and Halm, in F. A. Hayek, editor, *Collectivist Economic Planning,* 1935.

[6] Cf. E. Heimann, *Sozialistische Wirtschafts- und Sozialordnung,* 1932; "Planning and the Market System," in *Social Research,* Vol. I, 1934; C. Landauer, *Planwirtschaft und Verkehrswirtschaft,* 1931; H. D. Dickinson, *Economics of Socialism,* 1939; A. P. Lerner, *The Economics of Control,* 1944.

[7] It is one of the most disappointing features of J. A. Schumpeter's book, *Capitalism, Socialism, and Democracy,* 1942, that he does not discuss more fully the question of the possibility of economic calculation under socialism. Schumpeter says that the central authorities should fix a price for every kind and quality of producer goods at a level such that the available quantity of goods will be fully absorbed and the market therefore cleansed. Nothing is easier than to fix prices that will cleanse the market, but the question is not the emptying of the market of produced goods, but the supplying of the market while satisfying the demand in the best possible way with the natural resources and labor forces available to an economy.

perform the social function of the freely-developed interest rate, since the fixing of the interest rate itself would not be the result of a real price-formation process in the capital market, and therefore would remain more or less arbitrary.

As the proposed bonus systems, it too would mean no competition as a prerequisite of price-formation, new socialistic theories, such as *Lerner's*, seek to base *price-formation* directly on the free market in consumer goods and in factors of production. The managers of the individual factories would have to increase or decrease production according as the production factors achieved a productivity above or below their market price, and also to produce as cheaply as possible in each case. The principal task of the central planning authorities would be confined to making use of monetary credit and investment policy to insure that market price formation fulfilled its function in the service of economic productivity.[8] Even such a socialistic economy would be founded upon a "socializing of capital investment" and hence would make a free capital market impossible, so that an essential condition for an efficiently functioning price system would be lacking. Besides, as *Lerner* assumes, the possibility of receiving some sort of consumer goods is not yet a "free" market. Essentially, the free market means that goods are available to the consumer in such quality and quantity as he desires. The example quoted by *Lerner* of four gasoline stations belonging to different firms close together at a street corner [9] offers an excellent illustration of this: The squandering of entrepreneur capital and labor time of the employees through waiting for customers may indicate, as *Lerner* suggests, a flaw in the free market economy; but in a socialistic economy, it would be the customers, according to all experience, who would have to wait, to queue up and thus waste time, and would indeed often be left to the mercy of the distribution apparatus and of those who serve it. Examples of this today are plentifully provided by industries run by the state or municipalities. There is also the *restriction of free choice of consumption:* in the socialistic economy, only those goods can be bought whose production is planned and provided for by the authorities; under "socialization of investment," no goods can be manufactured unless their production is envisaged by the authorities who plan investments.

A good survey concerning the problems just discussed, that is, of price-formation and economic calculation in socialistic economy, is offered by *T. I. B. Hoff*, who concludes that socialistic economy can no doubt attain an increased "technical" productivity in various branches of industry, but only at the cost of "socio-economic" productivity (cf. Chap. 164): the planning authorities can authorize capital investment on a large scale in individual branches of industry, so that goods of a particular kind are manufactured in quantities, but only by curtailing the manufacture of

[8] Cf. A. P. Lerner, *The Economics of Control*, 1944, pp. 58–67, 123–32, 264.
[9] Cf. *ibid.*, p. 183.

goods of other kinds, and hence at the cost of satisfying needs which would be asserted under free choice of consumption.[10]

V *The Mixed Economic System in Socialistic Thought and in Natural Law*

In the free democracies of the West, socialism is thought of today only as a "*mixed economic system.*" As a matter of fact, the social economy organized according to natural law principles is, as we saw (cf. Chap. 180), a "mixed economic system." Yet, this is something entirely different from the socialistic mixed economic system. The natural law system rests on the equal importance of three principles of social order, the socialistic on the predominance of one principle and the subordination of the other principles. The natural law principles are, first, the principle of freedom as rooted in the suprasocial being and value of man as a person; in conjunction with this, the principles of man's primary responsibility in the fulfillment of his economic functions and his primary right in the use of the appropriate means; from this follows the principle of the priority of private initiative in economic enterprise; this follows likewise from the idea of private ownership as a principle of social order implied in the principle of freedom as derived from natural law; its bearing on the basic structure of social economy, therefore, may not be arbitrarily confined, that is, in accordance with ideologically patterned party programs. Secondly, the principle of decentralization in society, with their own responsibility and competence for the smaller social units, which for the economic order means vocational intermediate bodies between state and individual, possessing autonomy and regulative functions. Thirdly, the principle of the general good, with the duties and rights of the state for the purpose of coordinating, regulating and encouraging in the economic sphere, although with a limitation of its competence to measures which are necessary for the attainment of the social end essential to economy. None of the principles, as often pointed out, is of absolute validity; all are coordinated. The two first-named groups of principles make up the principle of subsidiary function in social economy, the principle that generally limits the application of the third, the competency of the state (cf. Chap. 45). Consequently, the *principle of subsidiary function is central to the mixed economic system* in accordance with natural law. It is precisely the principle of subsidiary function that is denied its authority by every school of socialism; instead, they assign the paramount place to a common good principle, in conformity with the socialistic idea of equality, and accordingly, they assume for the state the right of centralized direction of the economy with powers unlimited in themselves, so that all the other principles named—private ownership, private initiative, and also the value of the human person and his freedom—become of relative validity.

[10] Cf. T. I. B. Hoff, *Economic Calculation in the Socialist Society,* 1949, p. 190.

Socialism today, therefore, is understood as an economic system marked by the *nationalization and socialization* of a considerable sector of the economy and central control of the remaining sphere of market economy. But within the framework thus outlined, socialism and planned economy are given a great variety of meanings today; any discussion of socialism, therefore, must begin with definitions. The *three following tendencies* may be mentioned as more sharply defined.

1. There is a school which is still strongly under the influence of the idea of as far-reaching a *nationalization* of the means of production as possible.[11] It earmarks for nationalization all branches of economy, whose complete control by the planning authority is a necessary condition for the effective control of the rest of the economy. These include transportation, credit, and the key industries (especially coal mining, the iron and steel industries, electric power production, according to the character of the social economy of a country). Among the central controls are those relating to currency, exchange, foreign trade, the control of investment (the prohibition, restriction, or the encouragement and facilitation of investments in various sectors of industry in accordance with periodical "plans"), control of the labor market (direction of labor), and control of purchasing power and supply (influencing private expenditure by mopping up purchasing power through state loans, taxation, and rationing of goods). There is no uniform opinion concerning the road to this form of socialistic economy; some think in terms of immediate nationalization, others of a gradual transition. The latter, who seem to be gaining in influence, see the way in a progressive extension of state ownership in the sphere of large undertakings and of governmental participation in business management through the purchase of shares in corporations, monopolistic undertakings, and other big business, by means of large funds made available in the annual budget and fed from the dividends of governmental packets of shares.[12] This first system would be socialistic planned economy, today also called centralized administrative economy.

2. A second school looks toward an economic system in which there are coexisting sectors of market economy and common ownership economy. The social economy in general would be directed by governmental measures of economic planning. Here, "indirect" measures would get preference over "direct" measures; measures of monetary, credit, and in-

[11] Very logically presented by Schumpeter, *op. cit.*, with all the antidemocratic implications; particularly to be noted is his summing up in the section "Democracy in the Socialist Order," which reaches the conclusion (p. 301) that effective management of the socialist economy means dictatorship not *of* but *over* the proletariat in the factory; people would be sovereign at the elections, but because of the necessity to enforce labor discipline, socialistic democracy may prove to be more of a sham than capitalistic democracy ever was.

[12] Formerly advocated by Carl Landauer, *Planwirtschaft und Verkehrswirtschaft*, 1931; *Theory of Economic Planning*, 1944; similar ideas are now to be found in the British Labor Party policy statement, *Labour's Policy in Future Public Ownership*, 1957.

vestment policy would be preferred to direct intervention by means of price regulation, prohibition of investment, and import restrictions. Common ownership would not mean merely nationalization; this would be the exception; but there would be a broad sector with the socialization of the means of production in various forms of ownership by cooperatives of different kinds and organization, largely independent public corporations owned by local authorities, that is, public utility services, or municipalities, state (e.g., the British Broadcasting Corporation), limited liability companies and stock corporations in the proprietorship of trade unions or the "foundations" (e.g., big firms appropriated to the employees by the original owner). Another possibility considered, although with more reserve, is labor-codetermination at factory or suprafactory level.[13] A thorough inquiry into the economic efficiency of such a form of socialistic economy has not yet been offered.

3. A third trend in socialistic theory envisages a "state directed market economy," with the calculated transition from "a merely subsidiary economic policy to central economic direction." The chief means would be a combination of methods as a "general instrument of economic policy": credit policy, financial policy, fiscal policy, especially in the service of investment policy, the principal aims being the stabilization of the economic cycle and the maintenance of full employment.[14] Nationalization is not excluded. Concerning details, there are different views in this group too. There is even a kind of recognition of the subsidiary position of the state, as when the principle is stated: "Competition as far as possible, planning as far as necessary," which implies that, when a restriction of freedom is considered to be necessary, the burden of proof lies with the planner; with the principle, "as much competition as possible," it is also maintained that "liberal socialism" partly goes along with neo-liberal theory, but only partly, not as far as "perfect" competition. The representatives of this brand

[13] Cf. among others, H. Ritschl, *Die Grundlagen der Wirtschaftsordnung,* 1954, pp. 98–104; H.-D. Ortlieb, editor, *Wirtschaftsordnung und Wirtschaftspolitik ohne Dogma,* 1955. A catalogue of contemplated forms of socialization which was set out in the *Hamburger Sozializierungsgutachten* in 1947 is reproduced by K. Schiller in *Aufgaben und Versuche zur Neuordnung von Gesellschaft und Wirtschaft,* 1953, pp. 155 f.; most of the ideas mentioned are anticipated by O. Bauer, *Der Weg zum Sozialismus,* 1919, republished 1947; with regard to similar ideas, recently expressed by British socialists, cf. Socialist Union, *Socialism: A New Statement of Principles,* 1952.

[14] Cf. Erich Preiser, "Wesen und Methoden der Wirtschaftslenkung," in *Gesammelte Aufsätze "Bildung und Verteilung des Volkseinkommens,"* 1957, pp. 241, 268; *Die Zukunft unserer Wirtschaftsordnung,* 2nd ed., 1955, pp. 70 f., 73, 87 f. Preiser takes over the Keynesian fundamental psychological law (cf. above Chap. 167) with the even more generalizing statement that, "with the growing wealth of a nation an ever greater percentage of the national income is saved," so that it is the rule for investment to lag behind savings. Facts do not corroborate this opinion: the growth of national income in the economies of the West since the Second World War has by no means led to the situation that an ever greater percentage of national income is saved; indeed, the opposite has proved true, namely, there is an increasing desire to spend and consume far beyond the actual national income (therefore, inflationary effects follow).

of socialist economy, however, think that the expression "directed market economy" is objectionable because the market economy as the aim of economic policy stands too much in the foreground.[15]

A remarkably indefinite notion is the *notion of freedom,* by which socialism is guided in its new paths toward its envisaged system of economy and society. *Preiser* says that this is a system "in which the freedom of each individual can develop within the limits set by the freedom of all others." [16] Here, one is reminded that *Marx* also regards the future socialistic economic and social system as one "in which the free development of each is the prerequisite for the free development of all" (*Communist Manifesto*). This is the formal principle of freedom which, as we have pointed out (cf. Chap. 34), can satisfy the individualist and the collectivistic ideas of law; communism, as is well known, claims to realize this principle of freedom most perfectly.

The groups mentioned propose their systems almost exclusively, as *Marx* did, without a thorough economic analysis of the conditions of their expected efficiency in the service of optimum socio-economic productivity and satisfaction of needs with the resources and labor available to an economy, the main types being the possibilities of economic calculation, with interest- and price-formation as its prerequisites, as discussed above. The particular problems posed by the socialistic theories in the fields of ethics, social philosophy, jurisprudence, social policy, government, economics, ideology, and sociology, have already been dealt with in the appropriate contexts (cf. Index).

[15] Karl Schiller, *Sozialismus und Wettbewerb,* 1955, pp. 29 ff., 41; *Aufgaben und Versuche zur neuen Ordnung von Gesellschaft und Wirtschaft,* 1953, p. 149, mentions a number of modes of expression used by different authors for the distinction between market economy and socialistic planned economy: "regulated market economy" (Zorn, Dahrendorf); "socialist market economy" (Eduard Heimann, Alfred Weber); also "planned market economy" or "liberal planned economy"; but the latter expression, he says, offers in "popular debate" a constant cause for confusion with "centralized administrative economy."

[16] Preiser, *Die Zukunft unserer Wirtschaftsordnung,* p. 93.

PART FOUR

The Cooperation of the Social Economies: International Economy

---

187. International Economy

When discussing the foundations of international law, we saw that the organized community of nations, like the political community, has two fundamental functions to perform: first, establishing and maintaining peace and order; secondly, promoting the general well-being. We need not recapitulate the reasons that make international economic cooperation an obligation of international justice. These reasons have their origin in man's existential ends. The progressive attainment of these ends depends on this cooperation, since the diverse abilities and resources of nations make it necessary for them to complement one another. We have also shown that cooperation between nations does not destroy their status as individual common selves, but rather presupposes it. Just as cooperation in the political community does not destroy the existence or self-responsibility of the individuals, legally or economically, similarly, international cooperation must leave room for individuality and the relative economic independence of nations.

Two groups of phenomena in the development of world economy since the First World War have led to a substantial strengthening of the feeling, which is in agreement with natural law principles: international economic cooperation is indispensable for the economic prosperity of all nations; it is the function of the organized community of nations, by means of suitable organs, to bring order into this cooperation in the interest of all.

To the first group belong those phenomena which induced in nations the conviction that none of the more highly developed social economies can isolate itself from the general current of international economic development. It is the general conviction today that the extent of the economic progress attained by even the richest nations essentially depends on their participation in international economic cooperation and especially on how far nations of backward development are enabled to share in the economic and social progress of the others. The encouragement of the backward economies will provide new markets for the highly industrialized countries; in addition, those foci of danger to world peace, which countries depressed by a state of economic and cultural backwardness represent, will be eliminated.

The second group of factors, which today press for international economic cooperation, is marked especially by the dependence of all industrial countries, whether already highly industrialized or still in the process, on sources of raw materials. Since the economic and social progress of all nations depends on their economic cooperation, access to these sources by way of trade must be made available to them. For this purpose, measures must be taken by the organized society of nations. Similarly, since the individual national economies are continually inclined to master their difficulties by an economic policy of import and export control, currency control and currency manipulation, and control of the movement of capital, it is recognized in theory that coordinating measures by an international organ with the necessary authority are indispensable. Only by this means can the greatest possible expansion and intensification of international economic cooperation, and thereby of economic progress, be attained by all nations.

In all questions of the organization of international economic cooperation, with which we shall be concerned in the following sections, ethics must confine itself to a statement of the relevant principles and abstain from speculation on purely organizational and technical matters. Our discussion of international economic cooperation can thus be comparatively brief, the more so since in the light of experience there is still a long way to go before the organized community of nations is able to cope with its tasks and to give its agencies the necessary authority to perform their functions. The principle of absolute sovereignty still holds the field in the economic and political spheres; accordingly, a great proportion of the many organizational plans for closer international economic cooperation, which form the topic of much literature since the Second World War represent "heroic suggestions" * rather than any rapidly developing reality, with one great exception, EEC (European Economic Community–EWG Europäische Wirtschaftsgemeinschaft), which is well under way and seems destined to become a model for the formation of similar communities in other continents.

188. The Order of International Economic Cooperation

The instrument of international economic cooperation is trade, with the principle of costs as its driving force. In this sense, no difference exists between domestic and international economic cooperation. The purpose of both is best achieved when the demand for goods and services is universally satisfied at minimum production costs. From this the principle necessarily follows: as much *free trade* as possible, that is, as much as is

* J. B. Condliffe, *The Reconstruction of World Trade,* 1941, p. 390.

compatible with the social ends of the national economies and with the ends of international economy. For the ordering of international economic cooperation, we thus reach a fundamental principle which we found to be a fundamental law of the functioning of every social order. Limits are set to the free trade principle, first, as we emphasized in discussing the structural integration of national economy, to the extent that the ends of the common good of the political communities demand the utilization of their own resources. In a system of free trade the means of preserving the special interests of the individual social economy is customs tariffs, which protect particular industries in a country against a too keen foreign competition in prices. These may have the twofold purpose of insuring the efficiency of industries which are politically or economically indispensable (at the cost of permanent sacrifices) or of making it possible for such industries, and particularly infant industries, to develop their full efficiency in face of competition. Secondly, limits are set to free trade by the common end of international economic cooperation, inasmuch as it forbids the exploitation of the economically weaker and politically dependent nations. Their protection belongs to the sphere of functions of the organized community of nations, which was dealt with at some length in our discussion of international law.

International trade, on the cost principle, involves an *international division of labor.* This is, accordingly, the form of economic cooperation in the international sphere exactly as in the national economy. And the international division of labor, similarly, has two inherent purposes: it affords the opportunity of optimum satisfaction of wants, and the opportunity of optimum employment. The former cannot admit of doubt; the latter became a vast problem in the disintegration of world economy after the First World War. In their economic embarrassments, with unemployment as the outcome, almost all countries saw in the restriction of imports the most direct means for maintaining the level of employment in their own industries and thus protecting their labor markets. This represented an "export of unemployment." For the result was a decline of exports from other countries, an increase of unemployment in these countries with protective restrictions on imports on their side. Hence, international economy was caught in a vicious circle. In this lies one of the principal economic causes of the chronic unemployment throughout the world between the two wars. The guiding principle of the world trade system thus developing, put into practice by most states, was to export as much as possible and to import as little as possible. This could lead only to a *reductio ad absurdum,* for the outcome must be a continuous contraction of world trade. The principle is the exact reverse of the fundamental principle inherent in the end of international economic cooperation and thus in *natural law.*

The national economies may, in such a system of international trade, secure a certain protection for their labor markets through import restrictions, but they will soon find themselves faced with a hardening of the unemployment position and also with a lowering of the standard of living. This is because production in the more heavily protected industries will be carried on at higher cost than in other countries: that is to say, they will supply goods to the home and world market only at relatively higher prices. The consequence is that incomes decline and unemployment is stabilized. Actually, the lesson of the period between the two World Wars has been drawn with the *principle of the liberalization* of international trade relations, effected by international agreement, whereby the participating states bound themselves to minimum rates in the liberalization of their imports. This development has been substantially supported by the soaring market and full employment. However, the lesson is not yet learned completely; as soon as economic difficulties arose, one or other state again hoped to remedy the situation by trade or currency exchange restrictions.

In the sections which follow, we shall examine the detailed conclusions to be drawn from the principle laid down for the ordering of international economic cooperation.

189. International Trade

Undoubtedly, it will be conceded that the economic and social progress of the family of nations as a whole depends upon the progressive expansion of international trade. If, nevertheless, the short-sighted economic interest of the individual nations prevails, it is because they very often act under the political and social pressure exerted by the different interest groups within the state. Obviously, only a supranational counterpoise in the form of the authority of the organized community of nations can remedy such tendencies and preserve the good of all nations. In fact, a considerable amount of international economic literature is moving in the direction of these ideas.

Since the development of the economic well-being of all nations depends on the development of international trade, it is, on natural law grounds, evidently the task of the organized community of nations, first, to lay down the principles of a system of international trade which guarantees the minimum of free trade demanded for the progressive economic development of all and, secondly, to see that these principles are observed and to give assistance to those national economies which, under such a system, may temporarily be faced with difficulties. The first task may be fulfilled by a world-trade charter set up by the organized community of nations. The second task points to an international agency charged with supervising the compliance of the individual nations with the provisions of the world-trade charter, and accordingly with supervising all arbitrary import restrictions by individual states. All trade treaties would thus need the sanction of this agency.

As long as an organized community of nations is unable to discharge the appropriate functions itself, much could be achieved in organizing international trade by the cooperation of the leading industrial nations. In accordance with these principles, the aim would be a *multilateral system of trade* which would establish equality of conditions in the trade relations between the greatest possible number of countries. An approach to multilateralism in international trade was made in the most-favored nation clause in trade agreements in times when the chief means of protection was the tariff system. On the same principle is based an agreement concluded in 1947 by eighteen nations for the removal of import restrictions, called the GATT (General Agreement on Tariffs and Trade). Its effectiveness is fundamentally lessened by modifications which are made possible by exceptions of various kinds, including regional tariff unions. To be fully effective, a multilateral system of trade would presuppose a multilateral system of payments, by which nations in their trade and exchange policies would collaborate "in the elimination of foreign exchange restrictions which hamper the growth of world trade," as the Bretton Woods Plan (1944) formulates one of its purposes. There is, however, a long way to go before multilateralism will be the general principle in international trade. For, at times of temporary difficulties the state with absolute sovereignty all too easily dismisses the postulates of a policy that would bear tangible fruits only at some future time.*

The reverse of such a trade policy is the *bilateral system,* with differential tariff agreements on the basis of reciprocity. Its various forms are based on methods of protectionism, of safeguarding the individual national economy by measures to restrict imports. The means employed to restrict imports are prohibitive tariffs, foreign exchange control, and systems of multiple currencies. As was shown in the period between the wars, the bilateral system necessarily results in a return to a kind of primitive barter: quantities of goods are exchanged for quantities of goods; this entails a minimum of international economic cooperation, and nations have paid dearly for it by severe economic losses and chronic mass unemployment.

A restricted form of the multilateral trade system which is employed

* Alexander Mahr, "International Economic Integration and Prosperity," in *Economia Internazionale,* Vol. VIII, 1955, pp. 9 f., shows the shortsightedness of those who fear harm for the individual nation in the removal of trade barriers in a multilateral trade system. Undoubtedly an extension of imports could cause difficulties for industries making goods for home consumption, but the greater opportunities for exports would have the effect of new investments in the engineering industry and in the building trade; these would radiate through numberless branches of the economy, resulting in more new opportunities for profit than would be lost. Indeed, the replacing of existing opportunities for production and profit by new and more extensive opportunities based on wider markets and competition is the characteristic feature of all increase in economic welfare.

is the *customs union:* several countries abolish all trade barriers between themselves, while maintaining a common tariff in trade with countries outside their circle. Thus, a large economic unit is formed with a common market, tending toward lower production costs and a higher standard of living. The principle of customs union is the basis of the "Common Market" of the European Economic Community (Treaty of Rome, 1957), including the Benelux countries (Belgium, Holland and Luxemburg), and Germany, France and Italy, which also formed the European Coal and Steel Community in 1953. Provision is made for a period of transition in order to solve the many difficult questions which arise before the Common Market can be fully operative. The difficulties concern: the inclusion and adaptation of branches of economy which hitherto have had guaranteed prices, particularly agriculture, the danger of large-scale concentrations of capital and industry; the equalization of social burdens on account of their importance for price formation; the coordination of economic and business cycle policies by the nations concerned; the arrangement of the mutual relationship of currencies insuring their stability and convertibility. In addition, there is the possibility of restrictions of trade by such large economic units with countries outside their Community. Such a union may counterbalance large unions already in existence such as the Soviet bloc and the United States with their economic hegemony, and in particular the latter's protectionism; yet, it will again be seen how essential the already mentioned international authority would be in order to restrain an economic policy of these units detrimental to international trade relations. Already efforts are being made in South America to link together the national economies of the continent into a large unit. What will be the position of those countries which, for geographical reasons, are denied union with such large units? What will be the position of the underdeveloped countries for whose economic growth trade with the industrial countries of the West is of vital importance, and of critical importance for world politics?

190. The International Monetary System

The international division of labor cannot achieve its purpose any more than can the division of labor within the nation if there is no firm basis of calculation. A basic condition of a successful international economic cooperation is the *stability of foreign exchange rates.* It is the general conviction today that the lessons of the effects of the instability of the international monetary system on economic development between the two wars cannot be taken seriously enough; in a world trade recession they could be of the utmost importance. For countries in economic difficulties, the temptation to devalue their currencies was great, because in this they not only found the easiest method of temporarily avoiding unpopular deflationary measures (result, a reduction of incomes or unemployment), but they also temporarily secured an increase in exports and a decrease in imports (this, however, only as long as foreign trade was not controlled by import and export quotas). Moreover, on paper at least, currency devaluation brought in considerable gains to the treasury (devaluation of debts, nominal increase in value of gold and foreign currency holdings at the central bank). The consequences were correspondingly unfavorable to countries having trade relations with the devaluing country. The former often tended to balance these consequences by a similar devaluation or to secure advantages by a greater devaluation.

But such a policy met one big obstacle, namely, the impairment of the credit of the country which devalued too much or too often, resulting in an extensive flight of capital. Monetary instability came to a head when such financially powerful states as Great Britain in 1931 and the United States in 1933 themselves proceeded to devalue. The result was a serious aggravation of the chaotic state of currency relations, characterized by discriminatory currency agreements between states and multiple currency practices on the part of states for the purpose of neutralizing balances held by other countries and of securing advantages for themselves from foreign trade relations. A further result was the flight to gold and a flight of gold to the safest countries. To keep their currencies under control, these countries were compelled to "sterilize" quantities of the gold in their hands, that is, to restrict its monetary function.

Today, there is unanimity regarding the goal of an international exchange policy. This goal is virtual stability in the currency exchange rates, together with the greatest measure of free currency movement in payments for current transactions. The goal is seen today in the *convertibility of currency*. The condition for the attainment of this goal is a maximum of free trade in goods among states, so that prices can move in accordance with the demands of the actual state of the market, and, in consequence, the purchasing power of money, that is, the price of currency itself. In an international payments system, the value of currency cannot be rigidly fixed (hence, "virtual" stability), but depends on its purchasing power in relation to the purchasing power of other currencies. This purchasing power depends on the amount of goods and services a national economy can provide, commensurate with its production resources, to meet the demand exercised by the purchasing power in foreign currency. Therefore, it is not only "balance of trade" (goods traffic) that is decisive, but the whole "balance of payments" (including the inflow of currency through tourist traffic and other sources). Two deductions follow from this: first, international exchange relations, by the nature of things, depend on the development of the balance of payments of the individual economies; secondly, the extent to which the relative stability of exchange rates will be attained depends on the economic and monetary policy of the states. Because on this depends the fulfillment of the social end of international economic cooperation, it raises grave obligations of international justice as well as social justice for the states.

The very largely accepted standard for the value of currency today is the American dollar. Before 1914 it was gold. In view of the lamentable state into which international exchange relations have fallen, one may well recall the fact that world economy once had a universal and stable medium of currency in gold. Regarding the advantages and the deficiencies of *gold as an international currency basis,* little division of opinion exists today. Its advantages are its stability and its mechanical operation, which compels a country, by sending gold abroad (if the transportation of gold is cheaper than discount credit at the official rate), to limit the volume of money and to reduce the level of incomes and thus production costs, with the result of an increase in exports and a favorable balance of payments. The disadvantages are that the quantity of gold available as a basis for currencies, and hence the available volume of money, depends upon the production of gold, and the price of gold upon production costs: gold entails a certain inflexibility in the supply of money to an expanding world economy, and hence can lead to deflationary effects. These disadvantages could, however, be counterbalanced by an elastic international money policy.

This seems to be one of the underlying ideas of the multilateral international payment system envisaged by the Bretton Woods Plan in the form of the International Monetary Fund. Under this system, a practicable relationship of the value of currencies to gold is intended as a means of achieving exchange stability. The establishment of a multilateral system of payments is aimed at in the Fund Agreement by clauses that require the avoidance of restrictions on current payments and discriminatory currency practices, and by the principle of convertibility of foreign held balances. Under this principle, each member of the Fund has to buy balances of its currency held by any other member against payment in the latter's currency or in gold, insofar as such balances originate in current transactions and their conversion is necessary for the making of payments for current transactions. But the Fund will also give assistance out of its resources to its members so that they can "correct maladjustments in their balance of payments without resorting to measures destructive of national or international prosperity." These resources are built up by subscriptions from all the members according to quotas; part of the subscriptions must be paid in gold and United States dollars.

The object of these endeavors was attained only in part, since, as pointed out, the stability of the exchange rate depends mostly on the economic and monetary policy of individual countries. A great measure of success has been achieved by the European Payments Union (EPU) formed in 1950 within the framework of the OEEC (Organization of European Economic Cooperation), in which the countries of Europe, including England, were united for the purpose of balancing the demands and obligations in foreign exchange of the member states. Since the end of international cooperation in the economic sphere is unattainable without exchange stability, with a wide measure of free convertibility in the course of current transactions, it would be a task for the organized community of nations to provide for an international monetary authority with the necessary powers and means. The powers of such an authority would have to correspond with its threefold task of insuring exchange stability, of establishing a multilateral system of international payments, and of assisting countries with endangered currencies.

The function of such an authority would be a kind of supervision and coordination of the monetary policies of the different countries in the interest of the greatest prosperity of all. The individual countries would have to be left a certain scope for their own monetary policies. (Today, there is fair agreement among students of the theory of international economic cooperation that this scope may be restricted to approximately two per cent of the exchange rate of the individual country within definite and not too short periods.) As long as the authority of the organized community of nations is not strong enough, the question of exchange rates will depend on the enlightened self-interest of the nations and on the measures connected with this. Countries with inflationary or weakened currencies will have to be prepared for crises of confidence. As a useful expedient to support the exchange rates of such currencies, reserve stocks of gold and foreign currencies (exchange equalization funds) are held by the central banks. If the means at disposal are insufficient, the country affected can turn to the International Monetary Fund. If there is no prospect that the endangered currency will recover, the result must be devaluation, always most harmful to the country concerned and to international development as a whole.

191. The International Movement of Capital

The severe international economic crisis of the 1930's will always stand as an illustration of the devastating effects on international economy that can spring from movements of capital. A rich stream of short-term loans had flowed from America and Britain into the economic systems of Europe, especially of central Europe, and had contributed substantially to the prosperity which commenced in the later twenties. At the first signs of a turn in the business cycle, these short-term credits were recalled. The result was an enormous acceleration and also intensification of the international depression. But this was only one aspect of the ruinous effects of the movement of capital. The exchange fluctuations that accompanied the onset of the depression and the fear of impending devaluations caused a large-scale flight of capital. The result was a further shrinkage of the volume of capital in the many national economies at a time when they had a special need of capital; an outflow of gold, which further rocked the foundations of currencies; and finally the utter lack of proportion in the distribution of the world's gold. A persistent deflation set in, and the international economic crisis assumed a chronic character. Obviously, where the mechanism of the capitalistic desire for profit, liquidity, and security is in operation, the uncontrolled movement of capital acts as a disintegrating force on international economy.

The purpose of international economic cooperation leaves no doubt with regard to the proper kind of international movement of capital. First, capital movement has an indispensable function as a means of international antidepression policy. Capital loans from wealthy capitalistic countries should be made available, by suitable institutions, to countries whose capital foundations are weakened or inadequate. Secondly, the international movement of capital has a decisive function in the encouragement of underdeveloped economies. These require the help of foreign capital in order to build up their capital equipment without excessive delays in the rise in their standard of living. Wider markets will be opened for the capital exporting countries, since the borrowing countries will purchase capital goods, and with the growth of their own production will also have means available for the purchase of consumer goods. It is a well-known fact that, in normal circumstances, the export of capital to a country intent on economic growth is followed by the export of goods, chiefly in the form of capital goods.

Indispensable as the function of the international movement of capital is, its fulfillment depends on conditions that cannot be secured except through the operation of an international authority. Natural law principles, therefore, impose certain tasks on the organized community of nations. The fact that the necessity of an international institution charged with such tasks is generally accepted today, is evidenced by the principles worked out at Bretton Woods for the establishment of the International Bank for Reconstruction and Development. Of the functions that should be given to such an international financial institution, there is, in international theory, wide agreement on the following.* The institution would have to make loans available for the purposes we have stated above. In the performance of such a function it may facilitate the raising of loans in the capital markets, or act as guarantor for such loans, or may itself assume the task of granting loans from its own funds. It must further try to insure that foreign capital does not flow into the borrowing country in the form of bank loans, but is productively employed for investment in industries of the borrower country.

Another function of the international financial institution would consist in the supervision of the application of loans granted to a country. The purpose of such loans is obviously frustrated if they are used, not for

* Cf. also *Economic Stability in the Postwar World:* Report of the Delegation on Economic Depressions, Part II (League of Nations, Geneva, 1945), Chap. 20.

expanding the productivity of the social economy by means of new or renovated capital equipment, but for the purchase of consumer goods or luxury goods, and thus to bring about a merely temporary rise in the standard of living. Only the raising of the productivity of the social economy, with the help of borrowed capital, can help it to join profitably in the international economy and also to give a guarantee that the creditors will receive their capital back together with normal interest.

A further function of the international financial institution would be to insure that no restrictive conditions are laid down regarding purchases to be made from loan funds, since the object of such loans will be fulfilled as well as possible only if the borrowing country can buy in the most favorable markets the investment goods and raw materials it needs for expanding its productivity; such conditions might be that definite quotas of capital goods should be bought in the countries taking part in making loans. The appropriate functions of such an international financial organ can thus be summed up as control and the direction of the international movement of capital, the effect of which is, first, that capital is directed to the danger points in order to prevent or mitigate depressions in the international economic process, and, secondly, that capital is directed to underdeveloped social economies in order to bring about an expansion of world trade and the integration of world economy. For tasks of the kind mentioned, the International Finance Corporation (IFC) was formed, which, working in conjunction with the International Bank, arranges loans for undertakings of underdeveloped countries and to these countries themselves; a foundation of the UN itself is the Special United Nations Fund for Economic Development (SUNFED). We have frequently pointed out the fateful responsibility which today is laid on the Western countries for the raising of the economic and social conditions in the underdeveloped countries in view of the international political situation and the hopes of communism. All too slowly are consciences awakened!

192. The International Foodstuffs Market

Among the international markets, those concerned with primary production are the most important, that is to say, the markets for agricultural products and for raw materials. Both are focal points of international market fluctuations. We shall deal first with the markets for agricultural products. An example of the many difficulties is given by the destruction of corn or coffee in producing countries while in other parts of the world millions of people are starving or could not afford the high price of even so modest a luxury as coffee.

The underlying problem is, however, that of prices for the producers, who see a threat to their economic existence and to that of their workers in the collapse of prices consequent upon outstandingly big harvests. A particular aspect of this is the problem of the balance of payments of the countries concerned: big falls in prices disturb the equilibrium, and their harmful effects not only threaten these countries themselves with depression but also exert far-reaching and deleterious influences on wide sectors of international economy, because the countries weakened by such falls in prices have to reduce their demands and their imports. On the other hand, international economic depressions are felt with exceptional severity by such countries, because the falling off of purchasing power in the industrial countries causes the demand for agricultural products and raw materials to decline, with the result that prices fall.

States with an extensive agricultural production, however, have not only been faced with the problem of the dependence of their business cycle on the movement of prices of agricultural products, but also with the problem of maintaining the productive capacity of their agriculture and the structure of their economy in general. They have undertaken a variety of methods to counteract the disturbances of economic equilibrium proceeding from the agricultural markets. Among the cruder methods, we may mention direct price guarantees; among the more refined, the organizing of credit supplies. They are intended to help in stabilizing the prices and in maintaining the income of the producers, and at the same time in keeping up productive capacity. The guaranteeing of prices by way of subsidies from public funds means that the community is making a contribution to the income of a particular branch of industry. This may place an unduly heavy burden on the community and on the national income, and, moreover, may result in an expansion of production which will serve to intensify the disturbances of equilibrium in national and international economy. Guaranteed home prices in connection with lowered export prices can also result in a boosting of exports to the disadvantage of other exporting countries. The outcome of this will be that the latter countries will take countermeasures, and thus channels of trade will become blocked.

Nevertheless, direct subsidies, as was indicated in our discussion of the structural integration of national economy, may be justified in a limited degree. But it will always be a question of finding a form that will attain the object of such subsidies to the fullest possible extent without burdening the community excessively or prejudicing international economic cooperation. A number of countries have made successful attempts in this direction through *credits* for agriculture, the servicing of the debts being largely adjusted to the fluctuations of prices for agricultural products. Thus, Denmark has organized credits with a sliding scale of interest corresponding to the movement of a price index for selected agricultural products. Another instrument, made use of by the U.S.A., is the control of supply by the setting up of buffer stocks and fixing minimum prices for agricultural products; they sell when prices are rising and buy up stocks when prices are falling. In one case, however, such a policy of price stabilization is not essentially different from price support by means of subsidies, which we have just criticized, namely, when a government, during a prolonged downward trend of prices in the world markets, finds itself compelled to buy up surplus harvests with the effect of accumulating stocks of more than a year's total output or to sell at heavy losses when stocks must finally be discharged. A stabilization policy aided by purely national buffer stocks, therefore, must be confined to comparatively narrow limits.

The successes attained by such national buffer stocks, however, have had their effects on plans for a stabilization policy for agricultural prices based on *international buffer stocks.* Such an institution, it is considered, could more easily avoid the difficulties of the national buffer stocks, because it would not only operate within a vastly wider range of risks, which could to some extent be balanced, but would at the same time be able to carry on a farsighted policy of expanding consumption. Since it is a question of men's fundamental needs and since the subsistence situation of countless millions still leaves very much to be desired, so that "freedom from want" forms one of the primary aims of international cooperation, the principles of natural law lay down definite tasks for the organized community of nations. To accomplish these tasks it requires an organ whose competence would embrace functions such as those which were drawn up by the United Nations Conference on Food and Agriculture at Hot Springs (1943).[1] These functions would be assigned to the United Nations Food and Agricultural Organization and its subagencies.

In addition, an *international financial institution* for agricultural credit would have to come to the aid of the corresponding national institutions with loans in times of exceptional difficulty.[2] Such an organ for the control of the international agricultural market would, of course, have to work in close collaboration with the other organs for the control and encouragement of international trade and for the coordination of international antidepression policy. The prime determining factor in all questions of economic and antidepression policy is the sovereign will of the individual state; even when states make international agreements regarding concerted economic policies, they seek by means of clauses to safeguard their freedom of action in the immediate national interest under the changing conditions of international trade, very often to the detriment of in-

[1] The Final Act of the United Nations Conference on Food and Agriculture (Hot Springs, Virginia, 1943) contains in two dozen pages an invaluable synopsis of criticism on national and international agricultural policies before the Second World War, as well as a detailed synopsis of ideas on policies aimed at achieving freedom from want in the future.

[2] Cf. the discussion of such proposals, especially the emphasis on the necessity and the functions of international buffer stocks in *Economic Stability in the Postwar World:* Report of the Delegation on Economic Depressions, Part II (League of Nations, Geneva, 1945), Chap. 19; cf. also Chap. 18, on the possibilities and limits of a purely national antidepression policy in the agricultural sphere.

ternational economic cooperation and, in consequence, in the end, of themselves.

Not a few advocates of an international planned economy take pleasure in evolving detailed schemes of quantitative controls, aiming in particular at restrictions on production in order to stabilize prices. The possibility of realizing such plans is very slight because of the interest of the individual states in the maintenance of their productive capacities and their economic and social structures. An obstacle will be found, too, in the farmer, whose struggle for existence rests on his love for his soil and homestead and who will continue to exist in spite of restrictions on production. Again, agriculture depends like no other branch of industry on the weather. In one part of the world it may cause harvests above the average, and in another below the average, so that the task is not so much to plan production quantities as to balance them through international trade. In particular, planning by means of restrictions seems absurd as long as people still go hungry in any part of the world. A positive task for international planning, the difficult details of which are hardly touched upon by such theorists of planning, would be the provision of the necessary means of *transportation* to convey surpluses of agricultural products to scarcity areas. This task may well be described as one of the most urgent for international collaboration in the field we have been discussing. In general terms, this problem was envisaged in a recommendation of the United Nations Conference on Food and Agriculture at Hot Springs, which speaks of a necessary reduction of distribution costs in international trade and particularly of abolishing discriminatory policies in international transportation.

193. The International Raw Materials Market

Like fluctuations in foodstuff prices, fluctuations in raw materials prices signify disturbances of the nerve centers of international economic cooperation. Fluctuations in prices of raw materials affect all industrially developed national economies; fluctuations of these economies in turn have far-reaching effects on prices of raw materials. Their boom period brings about higher demands, recessive trade movements bring about a falling off of demand, which depreciates the stocks of raw materials and can strike hard at the balance of payments of countries exporting raw materials particularly of the development countries.

How enormous can be the fluctuations of prices of raw materials may be seen from the following facts:

Between the World Wars the price of wheat and of jute has been halved three times within about twelve months, the price of cotton three times in periods under eighteen months. The price of copper and of lead was halved four times within periods of two years, and doubled three times even more rapidly. The price of zinc was halved twice in eighteen months, of tin twice in twenty-four months; zinc and lead doubled in price three times in two years or less; copper three times in eighteen months. On one occasion the price of coffee was halved in eight months, on another the price of sugar trebled in four months. Between 1920 and 1933, the price of crude rubber fluctuated between four cents a pound and twenty-five times that amount and was, on several occasions, doubled or halved in the space of a few months.[1]

The wide disparity of these prices was, for a long time, caused in particular by ruthless competition of producers of raw material. In consequence, they sought to organize the markets for the purpose of safeguarding prices. Thus, a network of *international cartels* spread itself over almost the whole raw material production of the world.[2] Hence, before the Second World War nearly all the most important raw materials were the object of international economic agreements: copper, zinc, tin, nickel, aluminium, mercury, sulphur, petroleum, cotton, cement, and dye-stuffs. The total number of international cartels before the Second World War far exceeded a hundred. With the rise of the former colonial peoples to independent national states they try to stabilize the prices for their raw materials, which is understandable since the capital aid they receive from industrialized countries is at times swallowed up altogether by the falling of prices of raw materials, on the export of which they depend. Yet their endeavor for a regulation of these prices at the Geneva Conference of the United Nations in 1964 would mean a planned world economy and the end of free trade, in which consists the main hope for an all-round prosperity of world economy. However, undoubtedly there are important tasks of international economic policy for a United Nations agency aiming at stabilizing prices and production (cf. Chap. 196).

The *methods* employed by international cartels vary like those employed by national cartels for regulating markets and production. They fix prices or allocate export markets or control supplies or fix production quotas or restrict imports to countries to the advantage of producers belonging to the cartel; often such methods are combined. International cartels are analogous to national combinations in their effects. They were able to prevent a complete chaos in price movements and thus, to some extent,

[1] *The Transition from War to Peace Economy:* Report of the Delegation on Economic Depressions, Part I (League of Nations, Geneva, 1943), pp. 23 f.

[2] The majority of the literature dealing with the problem of international cartels still holds as tightly to the erroneous assumption that the international cartel is a product of the nineteenth century as it does to the equally false assumption that international trade is an altogether modern phenomenon. Price protection and the safeguarding of profits are, however, already clearly in evidence as driving forces at the foundation of the first international cartels in the fifteenth and sixteenth centuries. Cf. J. Strieder, *Zur Genesis des modernen Kapitalismus,* 1904; *Studien zur Geschichte kapitalistischer Organisationsformen,* 2nd ed., 1925; F. Roerig, *Mittelalterliche Weltwirtschaft, Blüte und Ende einer Weltwirtschaftsperiode,* 1933; H. Pirenne, *Economic and Social History of Medieval Europe,* 1937.

exercise a steadying influence on the fluctuations of international trade and to contribute to a more sparing use of sources of raw materials. Their price and production policies, however, were primarily directed toward their profit and the protection of invested capital. Since they often try to anticipate market movements in their policies, by taking advantage of their monopoly power, they tend to sharpen the transitions between the different phases of the trade cycle, in spite of a certain leveling of prices on the whole. Through the excessive prices, they exercise a restraining influence on the growth of national economies. Certainly, there are also natural limits to market control by cartels. For, on the one hand, production costs in the individual countries are so varied that the producers of raw materials are not easily led to limit production sufficiently to safeguard the higher cartel prices demanded by producers with high production costs. On the other hand, demand is not really very elastic, since it is conditioned by the pattern of needs of the individual national economies.

The fact that an organized community of nations must exercise influence on the distribution of raw materials, on which the majority of national economies and international economic cooperation itself depend in the present conditions of economic development, seems to be an unassailable conclusion from the supreme principle of natural law concerning the distribution of the goods of the earth, namely, that these goods must be at the service of all men in the fulfillment of their cultural tasks as prescribed for them in the existential ends. This does not mean that all states should have direct access to the sources of raw materials by the possession of colonies. It does mean, however, that the raw materials should be made equally available to all nations through trade. The fact that that principle of natural law is perceived by the moral consciousness of humanity today is shown by its recognition in the Atlantic Charter, although this document has lost all significance as a political instrument.

The conclusion to be drawn from this principle is that a task for the organized community of nations is to make it possible for all nations to acquire the necessary raw materials by trade. This makes imperative the supervision of cartel policies in regard to prices, the market, and production, by an agency of the organized community of nations. Today, there is considerable agreement on this among writers who are not tied by doctrinaire prejudices. The way toward such a control, however, still seems a long one in view of the principles operative at present in the international sphere.

The very first prerequisite for the carrying out of such control seems to be faced with insuperable obstacles. This prerequisite consists in an obligation to register all international agreements, private or governmental, dealing with production and markets in the field of raw materials. Secret clauses in the sphere of international economic treaties are as possible as in the political sphere. Apart from the possibility of such clauses, the control of sources of raw materials and also the maintenance of their productive capacity form, for both capitalistic and noncapitalistic states, a very important element in their economic and military potential. In fact, this element is so important that the great international cartel organizations themselves are principal movers in the international political dynamic (e.g., "oil imperialism"). They are equally forces of economic and political imperialism and a means of defense against it. Besides, the large profits of cartels provide the state with a highly appreciated source of revenue. In this respect there has been no change since the first emergence of international cartels in the fifteenth and sixteenth centuries: as we have pointed out elsewhere, the state then had already a direct financial interest in them.

Notwithstanding these difficulties, which must be fully appreciated for a realistic view, the aims indicated by the principles of natural law hold true: first, the provision for access by all nations on equitable conditions to the raw materials they need through commerce; secondly, the control of private and governmental agreements on market and production restrictions; thirdly, a measure of stabilization of prices through an international economic policy. The attainment of the first objective depends largely on the keeping open of the channels of international trade by the organized community of nations, through methods we have already discussed. A condition for the attainment of the second objective is that the organized community of nations should be able to maintain peace by means of international organs, for this would in part deprive countries of a motive for seeing in international cartels an instrument of economic or political imperialism or of national defense. Then, the cooperation of states with an international organ for cartel control could more easily be secured. Only when the first two tasks are approached successfully, will the necessary stabilization of prices of raw material, in conjunction with an international economic policy, really come into sight. As a method of stabilization, market operations based on the use of international buffer stocks for the various raw materials, set up by international organs and linked with a farsighted price policy, would have to be considered. Such controls promise even better success than controls in the foodstuffs market, because the conditions of production can more easily be manipulated.[3]

194. The International Debt Problem

The problem of international debts, for a very long time has been considered by economists predominantly from the point of view of the movements of capital involved in the contracting and servicing of debts. The difficulties arising from the German reparations obligations after the First World War made it evident that, for the present-day social economy, it

[3] Cf. *Economic Stability in the Postwar World:* Report of the Delegation on Economic Depressions, Part II (League of Nations, Geneva, 1945), Chaps. 18–19.

is a problem how to accept the transfer of large payments from other social economies. The means for such payments must be gained by sales on the world market. The ensuing competition tended to throw the home markets of the creditor countries out of equilibrium, to bring their production partly to a standstill, and to cause unemployment. For the sake of their domestic markets, these countries resorted to protectionism, which did not allow the needed international economic cooperation to thrive. Yet, payment by the debtor country without access to the world markets must upset its balance of payments, undermine its currency, and thus result in disturbances of international economy. This was practically recognized in the Dawes Plan, which limited the German debt service to an amount consistent with the stability of the German exchange rates.

The conclusions with regard to the international debt problem in general, to which these experiences lead, are mainly two, and both point to functions of the organized community of nations, since the natural law principles founded on the end of international cooperation seen in terms of the common good are in question. First, measures must be taken to insure that the creditor countries are prepared to accept a proportionate quantity of goods. The reason is that payments from one social economy to another can take place only on the basis that the values used for payment, including particularly gold and foreign currency, are acquired by export sales on the world markets. A policy of protection in creditor countries, therefore, must be guarded against. Secondly, there must be safeguards to prevent the debt service of a country having a detrimental effect on the stability of its rate of exchange. This can be achieved if the continuous debt service (amount of repayment and interest) is automatically restricted to the amount permitted by the stability of the exchange rate of a country. Or, provision should be made that debt service payments may be transmitted in the currency of the debtor country by an international financial agency. Such a method would take one step further a principle which is fundamentally recognized in the institution of the International Bank for Reconstruction and Development. This bank in empowered to enter into agreements whereby the debt service for loans granted by it can be carried out in the currency of the debtor up to a period of three years; at the same time, provision is made for agreements on conditions governing the employment of repaid quantities of currency of the debtor country, on the repurchase by it of quantities of its currency, and on the maintenance of its rate of exchange. The no less important function of assisting countries which are in difficulties with their debt service by further credits on favorable terms would, as circumstances demand, also fall to a financial institution of the organized community of nations.

Unforeseen developments in world economy and in the economy of the debtor country may make it an obligation of fair play to write off debts in whole or in part. In the liquidation of such debts, considerable importance should be given to an extended application of the principles underlying the lend-lease procedure during the Second World War. This principle is particularly applicable to loans granted by countries with advanced economies for economic development in backward countries.

195. International Antidepression Policy

One lesson to be learned from the great depression of the period between the World Wars is that any purely national antidepression policy must fail. National policies in that period were inspired by the shortsighted idea of attacking unemployment with an eye only to one's own country. The principal way to set about this was to encourage exports and to keep out imports by the means we have discussed. This policy has been aptly described as a policy of "exporting unemployment." Its result was the chronic world unemployment, which marked this depression and gave it an acuteness unprecedented in world history. It was basically a deflation crisis. Today, the international economy is endangered in the opposite direction, by the unsound antidepression policy of a large number of countries, inspired by sectional interests and carried out by means of the "new inflation" and, in some cases, to the detriment of countries with a stable currency by way of "imported inflation." We have (cf. Chap. 182) spoken of this in detail and also of the increasing international political dangers due to constantly threatening recessions. These considerations provide undoubted evidence that the collaboration of all nations in an international antidepression policy is a matter of international justice, and the organizing of this collaboration is a task for the community of nations. A special institution would have to be created for the tasks in question.

The first fundamental task of the community of nations would be to uphold the principle of cooperation itself against the internationally harmful isolationist trade policies of individual countries, policies that look to immediate but transient advantages rather than to the more distant but abiding advantages of well-developed cooperation.

Among the particular functions that would fall to such an institution and are today widely discussed, the following may be especially noted: the influencing of the credit and money policies of individual countries in order to counteract deflationary tendencies or to halt inflationary tendencies upsetting international cooperation; the exercise of influence with a view to coordinating the full employment policies of individual countries; the granting or arranging of credits to countries whose balances of payments and currencies are imperiled; control of the movement of capital, in particular the reduction of the undue prevalence of short loans, a factor that creates and intensifies depressions, and of purely speculative credit often associated with them. Hand in hand with all this goes a further task which would have to be completed by the organized community of nations: the integration of international economy. And at this point we must discuss this integration.

196. The Integration of International Economy

By the integration of international economy is to be understood an ordering of international economic cooperation which best conforms with its end, the achievement of the economic, social, and cultural progress of all members of the family of nations. This, therefore, will relate to the cultural as well as to the material values, to the level of employment in the national economies as well as to the volume of their output. From what has been said in earlier sections it will be evident that such integration imposes tasks of both negative and positive character on an international authority. Negatively, the authority would have to counteract trade policies hampering international cooperation on the part of individual states and to work for the utmost reduction of trade barriers in general. Any policy of discrimination in trade is, especially in times of economic difficulties, necessarily followed by measures of a like character taken by other states and finally by a system of protection which will prevent the integration of international economy. Positive objectives: an international authority would have to aim generally at the maximum productivity of international cooperation as a whole by securing a concerted economic policy among the individual states, and thus also to have regard to an optimum measure of structural coordination of the social economies. By this, we think primarily of the balancing of agricultural and industrial production, the balanced development of basic industries and the manufacture of consumer goods, the progressive and balanced expansion of world trade, development aid for economically backward countries, and the coordination of efforts in the highly developed industrial countries by the fulfillment of the tasks imposed by this development.

The fact that the moral consciousness of mankind admits of no doubt regarding the principles of international economic integration, which we have derived from the general principles of natural law, can be inferred from the United Nations Charter (1945). In Chapter IX, "International Economic and Social Cooperation," the Charter sets out these ends: a higher standard of living, full employment, the economic and social progress of all nations, and also the promotion of spiritual values, of human rights and fundamental freedoms for all without distinction of race, sex, language, or religion. For the attainment of these purposes the Charter envisages a coordination of various specialized agencies established by intergovernmental agreements in the sphere of international economic cooperation, and the initiation of negotiations among the states for the creation of new agencies when necessary.

Owing to the continuing dominance of the principle of absolute sovereignty, it is not possible for the organization of the United Nations to set up organs equipped with sufficient powers to discharge, on its own authority, the functions discussed. The activity of the agencies mentioned in Chapter IX of the Charter is thus essentially limited to that of influencing the member states, by advice and suggestion, to the effect that they adapt their economic policies along the general lines laid down; these agencies would also come to the aid of weaker countries, or to those that find themselves in temporary difficulties, with international funds, thereby preventing disintegrating repercussions on international economy.

197. World Justice (International Social Justice)

It need surprise no one to find a chapter on international social justice at the end of a study on natural law in the modern world. The first edition of this work did not contain a chapter specially devoted to this subject, since it was chiefly written with an eye on the social, political, economic, and international problems as they presented themselves under the conditions in and immediately following the Second World War. In many respects, these conditions have rapidly developed further. For this reason, the present work is much larger than the previous edition. One of the new problems, overshadowing all others, is that of international social justice. There is no doubt that it raises questions on which the future of the world depends. The author may perhaps mention that he has, since the middle 1950's, been among the first to discuss the position of the underdeveloped countries as the present-day international social question and indeed a question of worldwide social justice (cf. among other writings *Die Soziale Frage,* 1956).

Like any other species of justice, international social justice imposes an obligation to render to another, as *suum,* what is due to him. For every form of social justice this *suum* consists in a proportionate sharing by major groups in a society in the common weal, which is to be actualized through social cooperation. Because it aims at the actualization of a common good, social justice has the task of ordering a community. What this community, these large groups and their *suum* are in the conception of *international* social justice does not admit of any doubt. We can, therefore, give a definition: International social justice consists in the principles of an order of the community of nations, which will make it possible for every nation, by virtue of its own effort and responsibility, helped by other nations, to secure the proportionate share in the common good of all nations attainable by their cultural, political, economic, and technical cooperation. "Nations" and "countries" are from the point of view of international social justice primarily states, and, in particular, communities which have only recently achieved their complete or almost complete political independence. But the rights and duties rooted in international social justice also include those which concern claims to sovereignty and the duties of colonial powers to grant it.

Thus, in the concept of international social justice there are *two inseparable determinants:* first, the *suum* (what is one's due), to which each nation has a title; and secondly, social cooperation as an essential factor in the actualization of this *suum.* The problem is often too simply seen as merely one of distribution, whereas far more is it one of cooperation. (Concerning the entire question of economic growth cf. Chap. 182, n. III).

It seems imperative, therefore, to speak first of the problems involved in *cooperation.* We must, as always, begin with the "nature of the facts" when we come to deal with the whole question of international justice. We have earlier (cf. Chap. 171) laid it down that social justice does not demand the redistribution of property but the *creation of income* for those lacking it so that they can acquire property. No more does international social justice call for a mere redistribution of the existing wealth achieved by the highly industrialized countries. A clear and concrete conclusion regarding cooperation follows: transfers of financial funds, which could only promote a temporary increase of consumption, are neither necessary nor expedient. What is needed is capital, and capital aid must be given in such a way as to promote sources of new and higher income for the development countries.

Closely connected with this is another essential feature of social justice, of great significance for its international aspect, regarding the cooperation of nations in the community of nations. In discussing the nature of the common good, we were at pains to show that the main groups in the state are not only entitled to a share in the current store of goods in society but ought also to be given the opportunity to work for an expansion of this store of goods, by applying their energies and effort, and at the same time to strive for an increase of their own share. This means that the main groups, in our present context the underdeveloped countries, have a claim in the name of justice to play a full part in international economic cooperation. It follows, first, that they are not to be regarded as recipients of gifts or alms, as they are represented in some discussions of the problem of development aid. A second and most important consequence, again quite clear and concrete, is that they must enjoy *access to world markets.* International economic cooperation is carried out by means of trading on world markets. We shall return presently to this difficult aspect of development aid. To doubt that this is a fundamental question of international social justice would be to deny the equal rights of nations in the family of nations on the ground of the theory, prevalent in the nineteenth century and well into the twentieth, of a distinction rooted in the nature of man himself between "higher" and "lower," namely, ruling and ruled, races.

Full membership of underdeveloped countries in international economic cooperation has the practical result that the highly developed economies are obliged to create scope for such cooperation. This involves not only the opening of their markets to the growing industries of the underdeveloped countries, but also the necessary *adjustment of their own national economies* to facilitate such cooperation. Progress, of course, must be gradual. The international division of labor bound up with international cooperation will involve structural changes in the economy of the Western industrial countries. These changes will be unavoidable. They are, unquestionably, imperatives of justice in international cooperation, even though they may sometimes entail difficulties and sacrifices. For the industrial countries of the West, it is an advantage that the necessary adaptations are to be made at a time of prosperity. But they call for a farsighted economic policy, a necessary condition of which is increased capital formation accompanied by the necessary restriction of consumption. The unmistakable and concrete conclusion is that, in international social justice, the more *highly developed counrties should be satisfied with the standard of living* which they have attained and should make available to the underdeveloped countries the resulting economic means. Naturally, this does not preclude the highly developed countries from carrying out the requirements of social justice toward underdeveloped areas in their own spheres.

There is yet another side to the idea of cooperation in the order of international social justice. Cooperation, as we have said, does not mean that the prosperity of the industrial countries can simply be shared with the underdeveloped countries. This would be only momentary aid such as one might offer to a hungry person: charitable aid. Such aid, of course, is also indispensable. But the cooperation we are speaking of involves obligations of justice with regard to jural claims of economically underdeveloped large groups of human society, with the object of enabling these to attain, by means of social cooperation, to the full all-round development to which their equal human nature entitles them. *Man is a social being, in the international as well as in the national sphere.* It is strange that this fact has to be emphasized. It was possible to regard man chiefly as a "political" being in a narrow national sense as long as, in classical antiquity, the polity was able to satisfy its needs on its own soil and by its own work. Indeed, under the then prevailing circumstances, this society found it necessary to meet all possible material needs from their own resources. From this was derived the principle of *autarky,* which dominated political science and ethics in ancient times. States endeavored to extend their own productive areas by founding colonies, which in the ancient world primarily meant the settlement of citizens abroad. *Colonia dicta est a colendo:* the name colony connotes the cultivation of the land; the *colonus* was a farmer. It is, however, a familiar story how the exploitation of subject peoples marked ancient Greek colonization, later Roman colonization in the provinces, and lastly modern colonial history. The conscience of civilized peoples is answerable for grave deficiencies in the fulfillment of fundamental duties of international social justice. Up to most recent times, no one has awakened men's consciences with regard to this grave injustice. It may be said in excuse that the "internal proletariat" in their own countries was bound to appear as the immediate task to the advanced peoples, so that their consciences could not be stirred by the injustice with regard to the "external proletariat" (*Toynbee*), namely, the proletariat of peoples in the colonies. But just as in the nineteenth century, the internal proletariat became increasingly able to vindicate the rights due to it under internal social justice; thus, in the twentieth century, the time has come for the external proletariat, under international social justice.

These reflections have the purpose of bringing out the *fundamental significance of the idea of cooperation* in the principle of international social justice. Owing to the equality of their nature and the inequality of their individual capabilities, as we have seen, individual men are social beings. It is because of this twofold aspect of human nature that men can achieve the integration of their nature by social cooperation and are also obliged to take part in it. Exactly the same can be said of peoples as parts and members of humanity as a whole. As soon as *the world becomes a unity*, so that events at one point affect the common good of the whole community of nations, all nations become interdependent in their further material and cultural development. All individual nations can progress in the material and cultural expansion of their common good only through cooperation, and the general good of the community of nations as a whole can expand only by means of growing cooperation. *Coresponsibility* for the international common good becomes a duty for all nations. This means *partnership* in the full sense of the word, and nothing less than full partnership in cooperation between highly developed and underdeveloped countries can satisfy the imperatives of international social justice. *Codetermination* becomes the right of all.

If partnership is spoken of, when rights and duties are spoken of, we must not think exclusively of duties of the highly developed countries and rights of the underdeveloped. Rights and duties exist on both sides, although of a different substance. On neither side are there exclusively receivers or givers. The basic duties and basic rights of all relate to cooperation as such, under the principle of the common good of the community of nations, in its political, cultural, and economic spheres. Again there emerge quite concrete conclusions regarding the cooperation of nations which is based on international social justice.

Among the forces which brought about the unification of the world, with its nations and countries, so that the good of all depends on their close cooperation, first mention must be made of technology and the concomitant development of communications. Technology alone, however, would have accomplished little had it not at the same time also opened up an intellectual current through which the peoples of the underdeveloped countries reached awareness of their own worth and rights, or, in other words, national consciousness. With this self-awareness is linked *a new legal sense:* the underdeveloped countries' knowledge of their *rights* based on social justice. This means first and foremost claims on the rest of the world by virtue of justice. Hand in hand with their national feelings goes an awareness of their position and power in the world today as politically divided between East and West. It is quite understandable that the underdeveloped countries exploit this position in order to advance more rapidly to the economic and cultural prosperity that have been withheld from them for so long. They accept development aid from either of the antagonistic world camps and seek to obtain material gain from their struggle for influence. Thus, *self-interest,* quite rightly, plays a large part in connection with the claims of the underdeveloped countries on the basis of international social justice. They should not forget, however, that social justice establishes not only rights, but *also duties.* These are duties of common good justice. They confer the responsibility for the preservation and safeguarding of the common good of the community of nations. In the concrete case this is the international political common good. It would be quite wrong if, in international social justice, these obligations of political justice were not also seen. Those responsible for government in the underdeveloped countries are obliged by international social justice to take account of the effect of their actions on the wider world political situation and on the development of the common good of the nations. Since vital issues depend on their political attitude in this matter, they have obligations of international social justice as serious as the obligations of the more highly developed countries to render development aid.

We spoke of two determinants by which we may understand international social justice from a natural law point of view: the principle of social cooperation and the principle of *suum cuique.* The former principle is a principle of social philosophy and social anthropology, issuing as we have seen in a number of very concrete imperatives of justice; the latter is a principle of social ethics and law proper, which we now have to discuss.

Regarding the principle *suum cuique,* it is necessary to recall first the very hard fact of a long standing blindness of conscience: the peoples of the underdeveloped countries have to a great extent been robbed of that which nature itself has given them as *suum,* namely, their labor force and their natural resources. With industrialization, the colonial countries reached out to where they could find raw materials and labor forces in the "enlightened" belief that the economically advanced countries might appropriate what the natives could not make use of. The ruling classes of the advanced countries knew how to form an "easy conscience," as they had done over the exploitation of their own working people, with theories of social Darwinism and an individualistically conceived "natural order."

On the other hand, the serious significance of the economic side in the moral-legal principle of *suum cuique,* again must not lead to viewing this principle as merely one concerning the distribution of material goods and prosperity. What is due in justice to the peoples of the underdeveloped countries, their *suum,* relates primarily to the *status and function of these peoples* in the community of nations, precisely what we have hitherto called their full membership in international cooperation. Certainly, most of these nations today enjoy membership in the United Nations. But one need only recollect the "internal proletariat" of European countries in the nineteenth century. The working population finally possessed all its rights, but remained, at least until the Second World War, at a serious economic and social disadvantage (cf. Chap. 184). Not until after the Second World War was there real substantial progress toward equal rights of the workers in status and function as a major group in the industrial society. It was the social, ethical, and legal principle of the *suum* that gave the workers, in virtue of justice, the claim to this position. And it is the same principle in the international sphere that today gives the peoples of the underdeveloped countries the same claim on the international level: equal rights regarding status and function in the community of nations.

The material claims of the peoples of the underdeveloped countries involved in the international side of the principle *suum cuique* relate to their right to the necessary *economic basis for their material and cultural advancement.* The reasons for this are self-evident if three principles are established: (1) the equality of the human nature of members of all nations with their similar purposes and tasks in life (the "existential ends") outlined in their nature; (2) the goods and forces which can be won from the earth are destined for the members of all nations, to enable them to fulfill their equal ends and tasks in life; (3) the right of access to the necessary means to comply with these ends and tasks, through the exchange of labor and goods, through international cooperation by way of the international division of labor. It would be possible to deny one of these principles if the equality of natural human rights could also be denied. Traditional natural law doctrine has also regarded the obligation in question as rooted in the social function, which by natural law is bound up with all property: in the fact that the goods of the earth are destined for all men (cf. Chap. 171, and also Chaps. 26–27). Hence, international justice obliges economically advanced nations to provide underdeveloped countries with the opportunity of acquiring income and property with the object of approximating to their own standard of living.

In addition to the (already discussed) grounds of the obligation to render development aid there is a further very special one if one considers the concrete historical development of the industrial countries. It is a fact of economic history that the present prosperity of the industrial countries of Europe has been due in great part to the fact that raw materials in almost unlimited supply were available from the present underdeveloped countries. When, therefore, the obligations of international social justice toward the underdeveloped countries are discussed, such obligations arise for the more highly developed countries on account of their acquisition of the raw materials necessary for their industrial development under conditions which represented substantial advantages for themselves. These obligations, of course, fall more upon *colonial powers* which have obtained immediate and greater advantages. But for other highly industrialized countries it would not have been possible to advance to present-day prosperity without the advantages conferred by trade links with colonial powers. From this point of view, therefore, there are *obligations for all* individuals toward the underdeveloped countries.

Up to now, we have spoken simply of the more highly developed countries or of the advanced countries. It would be wrong to think of these countries as a unity or concretely of the *states* concerned. This would impose a major obligation on their *governments*. But this is correct only in a limited sense; for governments are, since we are thinking almost exclusively of democracies, dependent on parliaments. As recent years have repeatedly shown, *parliaments* are in this very matter greatly reluctant to follow the lead of government. What a government proposes can be carried out only by means of revenue. But the parties forming the government in a democracy are primarily intent on satisfying their electorate by guaranteeing and increasing prosperity. Thus, it is quite clear that the obligations of international justice are also, and not least, *obligations of each individual citizen* of the more highly developed countries. Concretely, this obligation means that the citizens are satisfied with the level of prosperity attained, and although they aim at a just distribution of wealth in their country, they are prepared to renounce further increased consumption in order to make funds available for development aid. A special obligation falls upon those citizens, or upon their powerful companies, who are capable of giving substantial help to underdeveloped countries through the founding of *business enterprises of a private character*, under normal business conditions but without the excess profits which private companies have hitherto sought in underdeveloped countries. Among the obligations of social justice must be included also the creation of *international financial institutions* which can organize capital aid to the underdeveloped countries and can, partly at least, undertake guarantees for the private capital invested (cf. Chap. 191). Thus, the risks would be distributed and a bigger stream of private capital could flow into the development countries.

Finally, we must mention a special kind of obligation, the *arousing of public opinion* to a consciousness of the grave and portentous obligations of the more highly developed countries toward the underdeveloped. Although the subject is now much canvassed in the press and on radio and television, much of the comment is too general and it is not pointed out that the obligations in question fall upon each individual person, and indeed concern him fundamentally. The *officials of the organized interest groups* speak too little or hardly at all of these obligations, or, if a word is dropped, it is hinted at to others instead of the members of their particular group being told what justice and, indeed, their own future demand.

Again, it would be unrealistic not to see that, where there is a *suum* at stake, *self-interest* is in operation. It has been mentioned above that, on the part of the underdeveloped countries, such self-interest is a natural phenomenon and it is not surprising if it induces them today to exploit to their advantage the position in which they find themselves between East and West. Likewise, from a realistic point of view, it is necessary to recognize and to appreciate the fact that the more highly developed countries, in their readiness to help underdeveloped countries, are motivated primarily by self-interest rather than moral reasons. The precarious situation of the common good order in the community of nations threatens their own physical existence. Ultimately, it is their fundamental *suum*, their right to survival, and to a future, that they seek to secure through their contribution to a worldwide order of social justice. There is a further motive of enlightened self-interest, which is at the present time little regarded, but which, if once operative, would achieve precisely what the moral conscience enjoins as a duty of international justice. For the highly developed countries, there arises today the difficult problem of continuous growth: the production of goods can be enormously increased, but the absorptive capacity of their markets has limits which prove to set limits to growth itself. The reasons are complex, and need not be discussed here in detail. Two ways of escape from such growth crises present themselves: first, instead of working for a dubious increase in consumption, such national economies can turn to more vigorous capital formation, producing the goods needed by underdeveloped countries; secondly, such national economies can turn at the same time to importation from underdeveloped countries, which presupposes changes in their economic structure, accompanied by production of new goods made possible by capital formation. These capital-formation and conversion processes would result in the attainment and maintenance of a high level of employment, in strengthening the foundations of growth, but also in a substantial extension of development aid. It would be a process in the very self-interest of the more highly developed countries.

But is it not inconsistent to speak of social justice as enjoining a readiness to give aid, and at the same time of self-interest as the actual motivating force? It is no more inconsistent than it is to speak of the community of nations when one sees the nations split asunder so deeply that mankind's self-destruction has become an imminent peril. Everyone knows that self-interest, the desire for self-preservation, prevents the forces of destruction from being released. When we speak of the community of nations we are, of course, thinking of an ethical idea and a postulate of justice. But we are also thinking of much more. It is an idea and a postulate with a very real and concrete basis. Everyone knows that the society of men and of nations cannot exist on the principle of *homo homini lupus* or, which is the same thing, on the principle of the war of all against all. Everyone knows also that, if man is to be true to his destiny as a cultural being, peace in society and in international life is the first and indispensable prerequisite, that is, human nature demands secured peace and therewith a minimum of international order. Everyone also knows that men and nations find themselves irresistibly impelled, even compelled, by their desire for a life worth living and capable of being enriched in value, to strive for an order of coexistence. The fact that this instinct and this endeavor move on the brink of catastrophe cannot call in question the fact of their existence. On the contrary, according to the whole disposition of human nature, the way to the goals and ideals mentioned is that of the conflict of opposites in human nature, which assume immense proportions in international life. In the internal life of the state, according to the experience of history, all progress toward juster social systems is marked by the struggle of opposing groups. In international life it cannot be otherwise, and indeed with the worldwide extension of the opposing fronts the dangers must become proportionately greater.

Hopes for forces arising from purely moral motives are probably illusory. This, however, does not make the discussion of questions of justice less useful or necessary. It should be clear to anyone that ultimately a real hope of a world peace which will guarantee the future of mankind cannot be attained by a settlement of the differences on the principle of might, but only on the principle of justice. In the nineteenth century, individual states were threatened at their foundations by social conflicts before social justice began to assert itself. It will be the same in the twentieth century in international life: the way to the realization of the all-embracing community of nations on the principle of justice as opposed to the power principle will be marked by bitter, even the bitterest, experiences and fears, but it will follow the direction of justice, which, just because of these experiences and fears, will prevail in the legal consciousness of world public opinion. If, therefore, the self-interest of the highly developed countries, namely, their *interest in self-preservation,* is able to determine their readiness to help the underdeveloped countries, it will be working in the service of international social justice. In the dynamic of international politics, forces and counterforces are at work which prevent a policy of pure self-interest and in the end will assert the authority of the authentic claims of human nature. The endeavor to attain the best possible assured realization of the special interest of the nations will have to be seen as linked with the special interests of all others within the general ambit of the "nature of the facts." *The logic of the nature of the facts* in international connections is relentless: it compels progressive recognition of the claims of social justice in their international dimension and also progressive realization of these claims even in spite of temporary overstressing of sectional interests. This is *ethical realism.*

Those forms of self-interest, on the other hand, are wholly questionable in which blindness to the claims of social justice toward the underdeveloped countries is outdone by the shortsightedness of self-interest concerned only with immediate advantage. This happens on the part of groups in industrial countries which look on development aid only as a means of promoting national exports with the help of taxation funds, with the sole idea of further market expansion and further increase of prosperity. If nothing else opens their eyes, the terrible dynamic of the world political situation of today should. In a situation where the national income of some nations comprises only a small fraction of the national income of the industrial countries, *there can be no isolated growth of prosperity* in one of the latter; there can be no "neutral" prosperity policy in the sole interest of one country. If a balance is not reached through the sense of responsibility of the prosperous countries, it will certainly come in other ways which will leave little remaining of the precious prosperity. The fact that time is pressing today must be obvious to all. Tomorrow it will press more urgently and the requirements of development aid will rapidly increase. What is today left undone through shortsightedness may perhaps, if undertaken tomorrow, be too late. A reason for this will be the speedy development of the national self-consciousness of nations, who will then endeavor to speed up the expansion of their national economies. Another cause of the rapidly increasing need for development aid is the competition of international communism for influence on the future of the underdeveloped nations by material and ideological methods. It is no doubt regrettable that thereby questions of development aid are thrust on to a different level from that of justice. But the groups mentioned, which still think exclusively of the promotion of their own welfare, seem to be quite deaf to the argument of justice. Thus, on this side there remains only the hope of the *argument from hard facts.* For the demands of international social justice, if understanding were otherwise to be lacking, this at least must be expected on the part of the workers in the more highly developed countries, who themselves had to fight for a hundred years for what was due to them in social justice and who now have a share in the growing prosperity but also share the responsibility for decisions in questions relating to prosperity policy.

Finally, it seems necessary to emphasize that cooperation and the *suum,* in which we found the two basic determinants of international social justice, are by no means limited to the economic aspect, but also apply to the *mental and cultural aspects* of the new future of mankind. Concerning intellectual cooperation in this regard, the West must rapidly disabuse itself of its idea of intellectual-cultural superiority. To begin with, this sense of superiority is wholly unfounded because of the catastrophic intellectual disorientation of the nations of the West. It is catastrophic because it is a principal cause of the weakness of the West in face of the threat of international communism. The intellectual disorientation of the West concerns all the fundamental questions of life: What is the nature of man; what is the meaning of his existence; what is the freedom, in short, what is the humanism that the West would consider as its distinguishing feature? What the Western countries have to offer to the underdeveloped countries intellectually is scientific knowledge and technical skill. With regard to the rest, what the people of the underdeveloped countries see in the life of the West is a disorientation in questions of essential values, with an attachment to values of material prosperity, which provides one of the greatest surprises for members of the underdeveloped nations who come into contact with Western countries. On the other hand, among the peoples of the economically underdeveloped countries, there are still established spiritual outlooks and unused creative cultural resources. Again, in the moral and religious spheres, these peoples may possess reserves of strength where the more highly developed countries have used theirs up. Cooperation, therefore, implies the recognition of equal rights of status and of function in the intellectual-cultural field. One would like to see a regeneration of the soil of Western culture, enriched by new forces of intellectual growth, resulting in a great movement of world public opinion, inspired by the moral conscience, gradually but irresistibly championing the cause of fundamental human values, assigned to man by his dignity and his freedom enshrined therein, against the forces of evil, that is, of power politics.

In the cooperation which social justice demands between underdeveloped and industrialized countries, the latter must regard themselves as receivers as well as givers. In several respects, the West will have to recognize that *social and cultural questions of the widest significance* are bound up with material aid. It will be one of the most difficult intellectual-cultural tasks of real development aid to warn the underdeveloped countries against the social and cultural consequences involved in overhasty industrialization. The social history of the period of industrialization in Europe tells a fearful tale. The capital aid pouring into the underdeveloped countries, if spent too exclusively on industrialization, can have a powerful disintegrating and destructive effect on social structures with strong family and tribal bonds and, in a short time, will produce a mass humanity with all the consequences of a radicalism to which it would be especially responsive. Already, urbanization is advancing to a disturbing extent in a large number of these countries, as the best experts declare, namely, the missionaries who live in the original homelands of the indigenous populations. Besides, in not a few underdeveloped countries it is thought that speediest results can be obtained with forms of state planning and nationalization of wide spheres of industry, and inflationary extension of credit and manipulation of currencies by means of artificial exchange rates. Perhaps the most difficult of all development aid measures is to convince those in authority in the countries concerned that such a policy must hold up sound economic progress and thus represent a violation of social justice, in whose name the world's conscience is summoned to render development aid.

Not only on the side of cooperation but also on the side of the *suum,* simple considerations show that claims and obligations of international social justice exist in the intellectual-culture sphere as well as in the material. What the underdeveloped countries need besides capital aid is the help of advice in economic and technical matters. This will be best rendered by an *intellectual elite in the underdeveloped countries.* If these countries today are glad to be advised by foreign specialists, growing national consciousness will very quickly insist on the performance by native personnel of the essential functions in government, economy, technology, health service, and higher education. And only an indigenous elite can be really familiar with the special conditions affecting all branches of political, economic, and cultural life. We have seen (cf. Chap. 182) how unfortunate it is in the economic sphere if, with regard to the development countries, categories and concepts are used which originate in the special kind of experience in the industrial countries of the West. In the underdeveloped countries, problems of social policy are posed which call for accurate knowledge of the existing social structures and the possibility of usefully incorporating them in the desired development policies. To help the underdeveloped countries in building up this intellectual elite is an undeniable obligation of international social justice. A full range of training in science, economics, technology, and medicine, in the universities of the advanced countries, should be available to as large a number of students as possible from the underdeveloped countries. The financial burden involved would be part of the material sacrifices due from the countries of the West.

Once again, in connection with the intellectual-cultural sphere in the cooperation of the underdeveloped and highly developed countries, it is necessary to mention duties of international social justice which fall upon *each single citizen* in the Western countries. In this sphere also, the idea is prevalent that everything depends on state and institutions. It must also be remembered that many members of today's intellectual classes in the underdeveloped countries have studied at Western universities and returned home with a nihilistic attitude toward truth and values. Hence, arises the danger that what the West communicates intellectually may go against it in the underdeveloped countries. Of course, the task would be misunderstood if it were assumed in the West that development aid should prominently include the imparting of religious beliefs and values. Rather, in today's crisis of humanity, Western man should demonstrate in his own life what are the values which bind him by virtue of his Christian cultural tradition, instead of letting his life appear to be an affirmation of materialism. This is an obligation of international social justice and it concerns *every single person.*

Again, in this respect too, there will probably prove to be a fateful connection between justice and self-interest: there will be little readiness on the part of the Western countries to provide the funds required by the underdeveloped countries, unless the necessary changes come about in the sphere of the mind; but, on the other hand, the continuing and intensifying world crisis and the advance of the underdeveloped countries into key positions in the struggle between East and West may promote the mental changes tending to lead to such readiness. Then, the consciousness of obligations of social justice on the part of the highly developed nations may develop to a breadth and depth which could give a new shape to public opinion and public life: the conscience of the majority of the citizens of the West would admit to the obligations toward the rest of the world, on the intellectual and cultural planes, in their thought and in their life. Only when the new forces of such thinking and living become effective can one envisage any ultimate hope that mankind will find the way out of its present crisis to a world order of justice.

198. World Economy and World Peace

The state of international economy and the development of international security are closely interrelated: they promote or obstruct each other. In the first place, an assured peace creates the most essential psychological prerequisite for a development of economic activity. This prerequisite is confidence in the stability of the international political situation. Today, there is general agreement among those who are not tied to ideological and doctrinaire theories that the great economic depression of the period between the wars was, in its deepest roots, a crisis of confidence due to the political instability which prevailed over great parts of the world. Without assured confidence in future political stability, there can be no long-range planning of private enterprise and capital investment or of state economic policy and trade policy.

From yet a second viewpoint, the structural integration of international economy depends on a secure peace. In our analysis of the structural integration of the national economy, we came to the conclusion that such integration involves a relative independence, since it is subject to the claims of national defense as long as there exists no effective international means of preserving peace. If peace is assured, however, the national economies can adapt themselves much more fully to a system of international division of labor, with the result that its structure would be determined by the aim of a fuller actualization of the principle of costs and hence of the economic productivity of all. The outcome would be a steady increase in well-being for all nations and, at the same time, the attainment and consolidation of full employment for all.

Conversely, an advanced integration of international economy would itself be a highly effective means for insuring peace. For, in the first place, if the individual countries are, in their economic structure, organized to a considerable degree for international cooperation, they are largely dependent upon the import of foodstuffs, raw materials, and manufactured goods, and they will therefore be slower to decide for aggressive wars. The integration of international economy would thus be a better safeguard against the greatest danger for world peace—surprise attack—than any merely politically conceived system.

Secondly, the integration of international economy would have to take *international social justice* as its guiding principle, thus warding off the next greatest danger for world peace: the danger facing the Western world from the "outer proletariat" (*Arnold Toynbee*), that is, from the populations of the economically backward and undeveloped countries, which, in the era of world communism, threaten to become the strongest determining factors in international politics (Cf. the foregoing chapter).

BIBLIOGRAPHY

Abel, W., *Die Alterssicherung der bäuerlichen Bevölkerung,* 1956.

D'Arcy, M., S.J., *Communism and Christianity* (Penguin Books), 1956.

Arndt, E., *Theoretische Grundlagen der Lohnpolitik,* 1957.

Arnold, F. X., *Zur christl. Lösung der sozialen Frage,* 2nd ed., 1949.

Baade, F., *Brot für ganz Europe: Grundlagen und Entwicklungsmöglichkeiten der europäischen Landwirtschaft,* 1952.

Bauer, O., *Der Weg zum Sozialismus,* 1919, wiederaufgelegt 1947.

Bauer, P. T. and Yamey, B. S., *The Economics of Underdeveloped Countries,* 1957.

Baumeister, W. and Lochner, H., editors, *Der unbewältigte Wohlstand,* 1957.

Bednarik, K., *An der Konsumfront: Zwischenbilanz des modernen Lebens,* 1957.

——— *Der junge Arbeiter von heute, ein neuer Typ,* 1954.

Belloc, H., *An Essay on the Restitution of Property* (Distributist League, London), 1936.

Below, G. v., *Probleme der Wirtschaftsgeschichte,* 1920.

Bentele, Max, *Das Recht auf Arbeit in rechtsdogmatischer und ideengeschichtlicher Betrachtung,* 1949.

Berge, Wendell, *Cartels: Challenge to a Free World* (American Council of Public Affairs, Washington), 1944.

Berle, A. A., Jr., *The Twentieth Century Capitalistic Revolution,* 1954.

——— (with G. C. Means), *The Modern Corporation and Private Property,* 1932, 17th ed., 1954.

Bienert, W., *Die Arbeit nach der Lehre der Bibel: Eine Grundlegung evangelischer Sozialethik,* 1954.

Binder, Paul, *Die Stabilisierung der Wirtschaftskonjunktur,* 1956.

—— *Kaufkraft, Produktivität: freie Kapitalbildung,* 1956.

Bishop, F. P., *The Ethics of Advertising,* 1949.

Boarman, P., *Der Christ und die soziale Marktwirtschaft,* contributions by W. Schreiber, B. Kunze, A. Rüstow, A. Müller-Armack, O. v. Nell-Breuning, 1955.

Böhler, Eugen, *Nationalökonomie,* 3rd ed., 1957.

Böhm, Franz, *Wirtschaftsordnung und Staatsverfassung,* 1950.

—— *Die Grundordnung der Wirtschaft als geschichtliche Aufgabe und rechtsschöpferische Leistung,* 1937.

—— *Die Aufgaben der freien Marktwirtschaft,* 1951.

Bombach, G. and Gabriel, S. L., editors, *Löhne und Preise,* 1957.

Brauer, T., *Der moderne deutsche Sozialismus,* 1929.

—— "Mittelstandspolitik," in *Grundriß der Sozialökonomik,* 1927.

—— *Produktionsfaktor Arbeit, Erwägungen zur modernen Arbeitslehre,* 1925.

—— *Konsumgenossenschaften und Entproletarisierung der breiten Schichten,* 1928.

Briefs, G., "Sozialform und Sozialgeist der Gegenwart," in *Handwörterbuch der Soziologie,* A. Vierkandt, editor, 1931, pp. 160 ff.

—— *Untersuchungen über die klassische Nationalökonomie,* 1915.

—— *Die Verantwortung des christlichen Unternehmers heute,* 1955.

Brown, J. A. C., *The Social Psychology of Industry: Human Relations in the Factory,* 1954.

Buchanan, N. S. and Ellis, H. S., *Approaches to Economic Development* (New York, Twentieth Century Fund), 1955.

Bückers, H., C.SS.R., *Die biblische Lehre vom Eigentum,* 1947.

Bühler, O., *Steuerrecht der Gesellschaften und Konzerne,* 2nd ed., 1953.

Bunting, J. Whitney, editor, *Ethics for Modern Business Practice* (New York), 1953.

Burghardt, A., *Eigentumsethik und Eigentumsrevisionismus: Vom Abfindungslohn zum Miteigentum,* 1955.

Bürgi, F. W., Gutersohn, A., Röpke, W., Siegfried, A., *"Beiträge,"* in *Handwerk und Kleinhandel in der modernen Volkswirtschaft: Entwicklungsmäglichten und Rechtsgrundlagen* (St. Gallen), 1947.

Burns, Arthur F., *Prosperity without Inflation* (U.S.A.), 1948.

Buttinger, J., *Am Beispiel Österreichs: Ein geschichtlicher Beitrag zur Krise der sozialistischen Bewegung,* 1953.

Capital Formation and Economic Growth, A Conference of the Universities National Bureau Committee for Economic Research (Princeton), 1955.

Chamberlin, E. H., *The Theory of Monopolistic Competition,* 1938. 6th ed., 1949.

Cirillo, R., editor, *Catholic Social Thought: An International Symposium,* 1956.

Clark, Colin, *The Conditions of Economic Progress,* 2nd ed., 1952.

—— *The Economics of 1960,* 1942.

Clark, Evans, editor, *Partners in Production: A Basis for Labor-Management Understanding,* A Report by the Labor Committee of the Twentieth Century Fund (New York), 1949.

Clark, M. Gardner, *The Economics of Soviet Steel,* 1957.
Condliffe, J. B., *The Reconstruction of World Trade,* 1941.
Coser, L., *The Functions of Social Conflict,* 1956.
Cronin, J. F., *Catholic Social Action* (Milwaukee), 1948.
——— *Catholic Social Problems in Economic Life* (U.S.A.), 1950.
——— *Social Principles and Economic Order,* 1956.
Crossman, R. H. S., Crosland, C. A. R., Jenkins, Roy, et al., *New Fabian Essays,* 1952.
David, J., S.J., *Der Arbeitnehmer nach kath. Soziallehre,* 1950.
Day, A. C., *Outline of Monetary Economics* (Oxford), 1957.
Degenfeld-Schonburg, F. v., *Geist und Wirtschaft,* 1927.
——— *Die Motive des volkswirtschaftlichen Handelns und der deutsche Marxismus,* 1920.
Demant, V. A., *Religion and the Decline of Capitalism,* 1952.
Demelius, H. and Lagler, E., editors, *Wiener Studien des Forschungsinstitutes für Genossenschaftswesen,* Vol. I, 1954, with contributions by E. Lagler, J. Rois, A. Vukovich, A. Tautscher; Vol. 4, 1956, with contributions by F. Klein, R. Pohle, H. J. Seraphim, H. Westermann.
Dempsey, B. W., S.J., *The Functional Economy,* 1958.
Deploige, S., *Le conflit de la moral et de la sociologie* (Paris), 3rd ed., 1923.
Dessauer, F., *Streit um die Technik,* 1956.
Dickinson, H. D., *Economics of Socialism,* 1939.
Diebold, J., *Automation, the Advent of the Automatic Factory,* 1953.
Dobretsberger, J., *Das Geld im Wandel der Wirtschaft* (Bern), 1946.
Drucker, P., *The New Society: The Anatomy of Industrial Order,* 1950.
——— *Big Business,* 1947.
——— *The Practice of Management,* 1955.
Dupriez, L. H., *Economic Progress: Papers and Proceedings of a Round Table Held by the International Economic Association* (Louvain), 1955.
Economic Growth, Brazil, India, Japan, S. Kuznets, W. E. Moore, J. J. Spengler, editors (London), 1955.
Economic Stability in the Post-War World, Report of the Delegation on Economic Depressions, League of Nations, Geneva, 1945.
Edwards, C. D., *Maintaining Competition: Requisites of a Government Policy,* 1919.
Egner, Erich, *Der Haushalt,* 1952.
——— "Ökonomische Probleme der Familienpolitik," in *Schmollers Jahrbuch für Gesetzgebung, Verwaltung und Volkswirtschaft,* 1955.
Eickhoff, A., *Christliches Ordnungsbild und soziale Wirklichkeit,* 1949.
Ellis, H. S., *The Economics of Freedom,* with Preface by Dwight D. Eisenhower, 1950.
Endemann, W., *Die nationalökonomischen Grundsätze der canonistischen Lehre,* 1863.
——— *Studien in der romanisch-canonistischen Wirtschafts- und Rechtslehre,* 2 vols., 1874–83.
Engel, J., *Das Unternehmen zwischen sittlicher Verantwortung und wirtschaftlicher Notwendigkeit,* 1956.
Erhard, L., *Wohlstand für alle,* 1957; Engl. trans., *Prosperity for All,* 1957.
Eucken, W., *Grundsätze der Wirtschaftspolitik,* 2nd ed., 1955.

——— *Die Grundlagen der Nationalökonomie,* 6th ed., 1950.
Fernandez, J. M., S.J., *Justitia social. Ni comunismo ni propriedad absoluta, comunidad de bienes creados* (Bogotá), 1955.
Fischer, Guido, *Neuzeitliche Betriebsgestaltung durch Ordnung der menschlichen Arbeitsverhältnisse,* 1955.
——— *Allgemeine Betriebswirtschaftslehre,* 6th ed., 1952.
Fischer, H., *Industrielle Sonntagsarbeit,* 1957.
Fisher, Irving, *Stabilized Money,* 1935.
——— *100% Money,* 1936.
Fleck, R., *Weltwirtschaftlicher Solidarismus* (Berlin), 1952.
Fogarty, M. P., *Personality and Group Relations in Industry,* 1956.
——— *The Just Wage,* 1961.
Forstmann, A., *Neue Wirtschaftslehren, Theorien und Hypothesen,* 1954.
Fourastié, Jean, *Le grand espoir du XXe siècle,* 3rd ed., 1952.
Funk, F. X., *Geschichte des kirchlichen Zinsverbotes,* 1876.
Gaettens, R., *Inflation, das Drama der Geldentwertungen vom Altertum bis zur Gegenwart,* 1955.
Galbraith, J. K., *American Capitalism, the Concept of Countervailing Power,* 1952.
Geck, Ad., *Soziale Betriebsführung, zugleich Einführung in die betriebliche Sozialpolitik,* 1953.
Gehlen, A., *Sozialpsychologische Probleme in der industriellen Gesellschaft,* 1949.
Gemelli, A., O.F.M., *L'operaio nell'industria moderna,* 2nd ed., 1946.
Gerloff, W., *Geld und Gesellschaft: Versuch einer gesellschaftlichen Theorie des Geldes,* 1952.
Gottl, F., *Die Herrschaft des Wortes: Untersuchungen zur Kritik des nationalökonomischen Denkens,* 1901.
Grégoire, F., *Aux sources de la pensée de Marx:* I. *Période Hegelienne (1836–41),* II. *Période Feuerbachienne (1841–44)* (Louvain), 1947.
Gundlach, G., S.J., *Die Ordnung der menschlichen Gesellschaft,* ed. by Katholische Sozialwissenschaftliche Zentralstelle Mönchengladbach, 2 vols., 1964, with introduct. note by Bishop Joseph Höffner and foreword by Anton Rauscher, S.J.; contains all publications by Gundlach with name and subject index.
Guth, W., *Der Kapitalexport in unterentwickelte Länder,* 1957.
Haavelmo, T., *A Study in the Theory of Economic Evolution* (Amsterdam), 1954.
Haberler, G., *Prosperität und Depression, eine theoretische Untersuchung der Konjunkturbewegungen,* 1948, 2nd ed., 1955.
Halm, G., *International Monetary Cooperation,* 1945.
——— *Ist Sozialismus wirtschaftlich möglich?* 1926.
——— *Geld, Kredit, Banken,* 1935.
——— *Geld, Außenhandel und Beschäftigung,* 3rd ed., 1957.
——— Economic Systems, A Comparative Analysis (New York), 1960.
Handwörterbuch der Staatswissenschaften, 4th ed., L. Elster, Adolf Weber, F. Wieser, editors, 1923–29.
Handwörterbuch der Volkswirtschaft, 4th ed., L. Elster, editor, 1931–33.
Harrod, R. F., *Towards a Dynamic Economics,* 1948.

Hayek, F. A. (ed.), *Collectivist Economic Planning*, 1935.
—— *The Road to Serfdom*, 1944.
Heimann, E., *Wirtschaftssysteme und Gesellschaftssysteme*, 1954.
—— *Vernunftglaube und Religion in der modernen Gesellschaft: Liberalismus, Marxismus und Demokratie*, 1955.
—— *Freedom and Order* (New York), 1947.
Heinrich, W., *Die soziale Frage*, 1934.
—— *Wirtschaft und Persönlichkeit: Die Führungsaufgaben des Unternehmers und seiner Mitarbeiter in der freien Welt*, 1957.
—— *Wirtschaftspolitik*, 1. Hdb., 1952, 2. Hdb., 1954.
Hicks, J. R., *The Social Framework: An Introduction to Economics*, 2nd ed., 1947.
—— *A Contribution to the Theory of the Trade Cycle*, 2nd ed., 1951.
Hoff, T. J. B., *Economic Calculation in the Socialist Society*, 1949.
Hofmann, W., *Die volkswirtschaftliche Gesamtrechnung*, 1954.
Höffner, J., *Christentum und Menschenwürde, das Anliegen der spanischen Kolonialethik im goldenen Zeitalter*, 1947.
—— *Wirtschaftsethik und Monopol im fünfzehnten und sechzehnten Jahrhundert*, 1941.
—— *Das Ethos des Unternehmers*, 1956.
—— "Der Wettbewerb in der Scholastik," in *Ordo*, 1953.
—— *Statik und Dynamik in der scholastischen Wirtschaftsethik*, 1955.
Horn, Adam, *Wert und Zeit als Kategorien der wirtschaftlichen Wirklichkeit* (Nachr. d. Gieß. Hochschulg.), 1957.
Hünermann, J., Müller, E., Röpke, W., *Wirtschaftsethik heute: Drei Reden an jeden, der produziert, kauft und verkauft*, 1956.
Huppert, W., *Erfolgsbeteiligung der Arbeitnehmer*, 1953.
—— *Betriebliches Miteigentum der Arbeitnehmer*, 1954.
Industry and Society: *Labour's Policy on Future Public Ownership*, edited by the English Labour Party, 1957.
Jenkins, Roy, *Pursuit of Progress*, 1953.
Jöhr, W. A., *Theoretische Grundlagen der Wirtschaftspolitik*, Vol. I, 1943.
—— *Die Konjunkturschwankungen*, 1952.
—— *Ist ein freiheitlicher Sozialismus möglich?* 1948.
—— *Die Beurteilung konkreter wirtschaftspolitischer Probleme*, 1947.
Jostock, P., *Die Berechnung des Volkseinkommens und ihr Erkenntniswert*, 1941.
—— *Die sozialen Rundschreiben*, 1948.
—— *Das Sozialprodukt und seine Verteilung*, 1955.
—— "Wie weit sind Volkseinkommen international vergleichbar?" in *Weltwirtschaftl. Archiv*, Vol. XLIX, 1939.
—— "Aufbringung und Verteilung der öffentl. Sozialleistungen," in *Jhrb. d. Caritaswissenschaft u. Caritasarbeit*, 1957.
Kahl, J., *Macht und Markt*, 1956.
Kalveram, W., *Der christliche Gedanke in der Wirtschaft*, 1949.
Karrenberg, F., *Mitbestimmung in der Wirtschaft*, 1953.
—— *Versuchung und Verantwortung in der Wirtschaft*, 1954.
—— (with Joachim Beckmann), editor, *Verantwortung für den Menschen, Festg. f. H. Held*, 1957.

Keller, Franz, *Unternehmung und Mehrwert,* 1912.
Keynes, J. M., *The Economic Consequences of the Peace,* 1920.
——— *The General Theory of Employment, Interest and Money,* 1936.
——— *The End of Laissez Faire,* 1926.
Klein, F., *Christ und Kirche in der sozialen Welt: Zur Stellung der Caritas im Spannungsfeld von Liebe und Recht,* 1956.
Kliesch, G., *Das neue Dorf: Ein Ordnungsbild aus christlichem sozialem Geiste,* edited by Führungsstelle der Kath. Jugendbewegung Düsseldorf, 1957.
——— *Landvolk in berufsständischer Ordnung,* 2nd ed., 1950.
Kluth, H., *Sozialprestige und sozialer Status,* 1957.
Knoll, A. M., *Der Zins in der Scholastik,* 1933.
——— *Der soziale Gedanke im modernen Katholizismus,* 1932.
Koch, W. editor, *Grundsatzfragen der Wirtschaftsordnung,* with contributions by F. Böhm, H. Meinhold, O. v. Nell-Breuning, G. Weisser, 1954.
Kraus, O., *Der Kapitalzins im Kreuzfeuer,* 1951.
——— *Kreislauf und Entwicklung der Volkswirtschaft,* 1953.
Kruse, A., *Wo steht die Nationalökonomie heute,* 1951.
——— editor, *Wirtschaftstheorie und Wirtschaftspolitik, Festschr. für Adolf Weber,* 1952.
Küng, Emil, *Allgemeine Kosten- und Preissenkung? Eine Untersuchung über ihre Zweckmäßigkeit als Mittel der Außenwirtschafts- und Konjunkturpolitik* (St. Gallen), 1946.
Kuznets, S., *Economic Change,* 1954.
——— "International Differences in Capital Formation and Financing," in *Capital Formation and Economic Growth: A Conference of the Universities National Bureau Committee for Economic Research* (Princeton), 1955.
——— "Problems in Comparison of Economic Trends," in *Economic Growth, Brazil, India, Japan;* cf. above.
——— *Income and Wealth of the United States,* Series II of *Income and Wealth,* 1952.
Lagler, E., with A. Mahr and W. Weber, editors, *Ordnungsprobleme der Wirtschaft,* with contributions by J. M. Back, H. Drimmel, L. Erhard, A. Gutersohn, O. Howald, A. Mahr, A. Müller-Armack, K. Schiller, H.-J. Seraphim, 1957.
——— editor, *Wiener Studien zur Agrarpolitik und Agrarsoziologie:* Heft I, *Das Dorf in der industriellen Entwicklung der Gegenwart,* 1957, contributions by W. Abel, E. Lagler, A. Steden, G. Weipert, F. Westphalen; Heft II, *Das Agrarproblem in Industrieländern,* 1957, W. Kahler.
Lagler-Messner, editors, *Wirtschaftliche Entwicklung und soziale Ordnung, Festschr. für Degenfeld-Schonburg,* 1952.
Landauer, C., *Planwirtschaft und Verkehrswirtschaft,* 1931.
Latouche, R., *Les origines de l'économie occidentale* (Paris), 1956.
Lerner, A. P., *The Economics of Control,* 1944.
Lester, R. A., *Economics of Labor* (New York), 1948.
Lewis, W. A., *The Theory of Economic Growth* (London), 1955.
Liefmann, R., *Kartelle, Konzerne und Trusts,* 8th ed., 1930; Engl. trans., *Cartels, Concerns, and Trusts,* 1932.
——— "Kartelle," in *Handwörterbuch der Staatswissenschaften,* Vol. V, 1923.
Lippmann, W., *The Good Society,* 1937.

Little, I. M. D., *A Critique of Welfare Economics,* 1950.

Lowe, Adolph, "Structural Analysis of Real Capital Formation," in *Capital Formation and Economic Growth;* cf. above.

Lundberg, E., *Studies in the Theory of Economic Expansion* (Oxford), 1955.

Lutz, F. A. and Hague, D. C., editors, *The Theory of Capital,* 1961.

Machlup, F., *The Political Economy of Monopoly,* 1952.

Maclaurin, W. R., "Innovation and Capital Formation in Some American Industries," in *Capital Formation and Economic Growth;* cf. above.

Mahr, A., *Volkswirtschaftslehre: Einführung in das Verständnis der volkswirtschaftlichen Zusammenhänge,* 1948, new ed. shortly.

Mann, Adolf, *Arbeit und Muse: Möglichkeiten der Persönlichkeitsentfaltung für den Menschen in der heutigen Industrie,* 1957.

——— *Sozialprodukt, Lohnpolitik, Produktivitätssteigerung,* 1957.

——— *Aus der Praxis einer Ertragsbeteiligung,* 1954.

Marshall, A., *Principles of Economics,* 1st ed., 1890, 5th ed., 1907.

Maurach, R., *Handbuch der Sowjetverfassung,* 1955.

Mayo, E., *The Social Problems of an Industrial Civilisation,* 1945.

Meinhold, W., *Grundzüge der allg. Volkswirtschaftslehre,* 1954.

——— *Volkswirtschaftspolitik,* 1955.

Melman, Seymour, *Dynamic Factors in Industrial Productivity,* 1956.

Mendès-France, P. and Ardant, G., *La science économique et l'action,* 1954.

Menegazzi, G., *Method and Foundations of Social Science* (Italy), 1957.

Menger, A., *Das Recht auf den vollen Arbeitsertrag,* 1886; Engl. trans. by E. Tanner, *The Right to the Whole Produce of Labour,* 1899.

Meier, G. M. and Baldwin, R. E., *Economic Development,* 1957.

Meier, Viktor, *Das neue jugoslawische Wirtschaftssystem* (Switzerland), 1956.

Messner, J., *Sozialökonomik und Sozialethik,* 2nd ed., 1929.

——— *Die Theologie in O. Spanns "Fundament der Volkswirtschaftslehre," Tijdschrift voor Philosophie,* 9. Jg. May, 1947.

——— *Das englische Experiment des Sozialismus, auf Grund ökonomischer Tatsachen und sozialistischer Selbstzeugnisse dargestellt,* 1954.

Michel, Ernst, *Sozialgeschichte der industriellen Arbeitswelt,* 3rd ed., 1953.

Mill, J. S., *Principles of Political Economy,* 1848.

Mulcahy, R. E., S.J., *The Economics of Heinrich Pesch* (New York), 1952.

Müller, Franz H., *Economic Aspects of Industrial Decentralisation,* 1947.

——— *Soziale Theorie des Betriebes,* 1952.

Müller-Armack, A., *Wirtschaftslenkung und Marktwirtschaft,* 2nd ed., 1948.

——— *Entwicklungsgesetze des Kapitalismus,* 1932.

——— *Zur Diagnose der wirtschaftlichen Lage,* 1947.

Myrdal, G., *An International Economy: Problems and Prospects,* 1957.

Nell-Breuning, O. v., S.J., *Wirtschaft und Gesellschaft,* 2 vols., 1957.

——— *Mitbestimmung,* 1950.

——— *Die Funktion des Grundeigentums in der Rechts- und Sozialordnung unserer Zeit,* 2nd ed., 1952.

Nell-Breuning, O. v., S.J. and Sacher, H., unter Mitarb. v. L. Wirtz, "Zur Wirtschaftsordnung," Heft IV in *Wörterbuch der Politik,* 1949.

Neumeyer, F., *Monopolkontrolle in USA,* 1953.

Niehaus, H., *Leitbilder der Wirtschafts- und Agrarpolitik in der modernen Gesellschaft,* 1957.

—— with Priebe, H., editor, *Agrarpolitik i. d. soz. Marktwirtschaft,* 1956.
Nurkse, R., *Problems of Capital Formation in Underdeveloped Countries,* 1953.
Ortlieb, H.-D., editor, *Wirtschaftsordnung und Wirtschaftspolitik ohne Dogma,* 1955.
Parkinson, H., *The Ownership of Industry,* 1951.
Pesch, H., S.J., *Liberalismus, Sozialismus und christliche Gesellschaftsordnung,* 3 vols., 2nd ed., 1901.
—— *Lehrbuch der Nationalökonomie,* Vols. I–V, 2nd–5th ed., 1924/26.
Pfister, B., Mertens, P., Mann, A., Winschuh, J., *Probleme des Eigentums und Miteigentums,* 1954.
Pigou, A. C., *Keynes's General Theory: A Retrospective View,* 1952.
—— *Socialism versus Capitalism,* 1949.
Pirenne, H., *Economic and Social History of Medieval Europe,* 1937.
Pölnitz, G. Fr. v., *Jakob Fugger, Kaiser, Kirche und Kapital in der oberdeutschen Renaissance,* 1949.
—— *Jakob Fugger: Quellen und Erläuterungen,* 1951.
Preiser, E., *Bildung und Verteilung des Volkseinkommens,* 1957.
—— *Die Zukunft unserer Wirtschaftsordnung,* 2nd ed., 1955.
—— *Die soziale Problematik der Marktwirtschaft,* 1951.
Priebe, H., *Wer wird die Scheunen füllen? Sozialprobleme der deutschen Landwirtschaft,* 1954, 2nd ed., 1955.
Productivity Measurement: Vol. I, *Concepts;* Vol. II, *Plant Level Measurements, Methods and Results,* 1956 (pub. by the European Productivity Agency, Paris), 1955.
Pütz, T., *Theorie der allgemeinen Wirtschaftspolitik und Wirtschaftslenkung,* 1948.
—— *Das Bild des Unternehmers in der Nationalökonomie: Versuch einer aufbauenden Kritik,* 1936.
—— *Wirtschaftslehre und Weltanschauung bei Adam Smith,* 1932.
Ratzinger, G., *Die Volkswirtschaft in ihren sittlichen Grundlagen,* 1891, 2nd ed., 1895.
Report on Economic Depressions, *Economic Stability in the Postwar World* (League of Nations, Geneva), 1945.
Reynolds, L. G., *Labor Economics and Labor Relations,* 1949.
Riener, W., *Soziales Handbuch. Katholische Soziallehre und soziale Gegenwart,* 1956.
Ritschl, H., *Grundlagen der Wirtschaftsordnung: Gesammelte Aufsätze zur Lehre von der Wirtschaftsordnung,* 1954.
Robinson, E. A. G., *Monopoly,* 1941.
Robinson, Joan, *Accumulation of Capital,* 1956.
Robinson, M. A., Morton, H. C., Calderwood, J. D., *An Introduction to Economic Reasoning* (pub. by the Brookings Institute, Washington), 1956.
Roerig, F., *Mittelalterliche Weltwirtschaft, Blüte und Ende einer Weltwirtschaftsperiode,* 1933.
Rollet, H., *L'action sociale des catholiques de France, 1871–1901* (Paris), 1948.
Röper, Burckhardt, *Die Konkurrenz und ihre Fehlentwicklungen: Untersuchungen über Störungen der Marktwirtschaft,* 1952.
Röpke, W., *Internationale Ordnung,* 2nd ed., 1956.

——— *Civitas Humana,* 3rd ed., 1949.
——— *Das Kulturideal des Liberalismus,* 1947.
——— *Die Ordnung der Wirtschaft,* 1948.
——— *Die Gesellschaftskrise der Gegenwart,* 5th ed., 1950.
Rostow, W. W., *The Process of Economic Growth* (Oxford), 1953.
Rothschild, K. W., *The Theory of Wages,* 1954.
Rüstow, A., *Das Versagen des Wirtschaftsliberalismus,* 2nd ed., 1951; on this cf. B. Pfister, *Ordo,* Bd. IV, 1951, 440–43.
Salin, Edgar, *Geschichte der Volkswirtschaftslehre,* 4th ed., 1952.
Samuelson, P. A., *Economics,* 3rd ed., 1955.
Schaer, J. F., *Handelsbetriebslehre,* 1921.
Schäfer, W., *Industriebetrieb und Öffentlichkeit vor den sozialen Aufgaben der Gegenwart,* 1956.
Schelsky, H., editor, *Arbeiterjugend, gestern und heute,* 1954.
——— *Die skeptische Generation: Eine Soziologie der deutschen Jugend,* 1957.
Schelsky, H. and Ortlieb, H.-D., *Wege zum sozialen Frieden,* 1954.
Schiller, Karl, *Sozialismus und Wettbewerb,* 195[illegible]
——— *Aufgaben und Versuche zur neuen Ordnung von Gesellschaft und Wirtschaft,* 1953.
Schilling, O., *Die soziale Frage und ihre Teilgebiete,* 1931.
——— *Christliche Wirtschaftsethik,* 1954.
Schlier, Otto, *Wegweiser zur Statistik,* 1954.
Schmalenbach, E., *Kostenrechnung und Preispolitik,* 7th ed., 1956.
——— *Die Aktiengesellschaft,* 7th ed., 1950.
Schmid, H., *Neoliberalismus und kath. Soziallehre,* mit Einf. v. O. v. Nell-Breuning, S.J., 1955.
Schmitz, Wolfgang, *Die wirtschaftliche Integration Europas: Stand und Möglichkeiten nach dem Wiener Kongreß der International Handelskammer,* 1953.
Schmölders, G., *Konjunkturen und Krisen,* 1955.
Schmölders, G., Schröder, R., Seidenfuß, H. S., *John Maynard Keynes als Psychologe,* 1956.
Schreiber, Edmund, *Die volkswirtschaftlichen Anschauungen der Scholastik seit Thomas v. Aq.,* 1913.
Schumpeter, J., *History of Economic Analysis,* 1954.
——— "Die Entwicklung der Sozialökonomik zur Wissenschaft," in *Grundriß der Sozialökonomik,* 1924.
——— *Aufsätze zur Soziologie,* Erich Schneider and Arthur Spiethoff, editors, 1953.
——— *Dogmenhistorische und biographische Aufsätze,* Schneider and Spiethoff, editors, 1954.
——— *Theorie der wirtschaftlichen Entwicklung,* 5th ed., 1953.
——— *Kapitalismus, Sozialismus und Demokratie,* 1946, Engl. 1942.
Schwendimann, J., *Der Bauernstand im Wandel der Jahrtausende,* 1946.
Scott, W. H., *Industrial Leadership and Joint Consultation,* 1952.
Seipel, I., *Die wirtschaftlichen Lehren der Kirchenväter,* 1907.
Seraphim, H.-J., *Theorie der allgemeinen Wirtschaftspolitik,* 1955.
——— *Die genossenschaftliche Gesinnung und das moderne Genossenschaftswesen,* 1956.

—— "Europäisches Bauerntum und europäische Agrarunion," in *Probleme einer europäischen Agrarintegration,* with contributions by W. Abel, O. Howald, E. Lagler, H.-J. Seraphim, 1953.
Socialist Union, *Socialism, A New Statement of Principles,* 1952.
Sombart, W., *Der moderne Kapitalismus,* 2 vols., 6th ed., 1924.
—— *Der Bourgeois: Zur Geistesgeschichte des modernen Wirtschaftsmenschen,* 1920.
Spann, O., *Fundament der Volkswirtschaftslehre,* 4th ed., 1929.
—— *Der wahre Staat,* 3rd ed., 1931.
Spiegelhalter, F., *Gewinnbeteiligung, Illusionen und Möglichkeiten: Mit einer Zusammenfassung praktischer Erfahrungen aus 300 Großbetrieben,* 1951.
—— *Die Lohn-Preis-Spirale und ihre Überwindung,* 1957.
Spiethoff, B. K., *Gesicherte Löhne—freie Preise,* 1950.
Staley, E., *The Future of Underdeveloped Countries,* for the Council of Foreign Relations, 1954.
Stein, Bernhard, *Der Familienlohn,* 1956.
Steinbüchel, T., *Der Sozialismus als sittliche Idee,* 1923.
—— *Sozialismus* (*Gesammelte Aufsätze zur Geistesgeschichte I*), 1950.
Strieder, J., *Zur Genesis des modernen Kapitalismus,* 1904, 2nd ed., 1935.
—— *Studien zur Geschichte kapitalistischer Organisationsformen: Monopole, Kartelle u. Aktiengesellschaften im Mittelalter und zu Beginn der Neuzeit,* 2nd ed., 1925.
—— *Levantinische Handelsfahrten deutscher Kaufleute des 16. Jh.,* 1919.
—— *Jakob Fugger der Reiche,* 1926; Engl. trans., *Jacob Fugger the Rich,* 1931.
—— "Entstehen und Vergehen großer Vermögen im älteren Europa," in *Hist. Jhrb. d. Görres-Ges.,* Bd. 55, 1935.
—— "Finanznot des Staates u. Entstehung des neuzeitlichen kapitalistischen Wirtschaftslebens," in *Neue Jahrbücher,* Jg., 1932.
—— *Die dt. Montan- und Metallindustrie im Zeitalter der Fugger,* 1931.
—— "Negerkunst von Benin und deutsches Metallexportgewerbe im 15. u. 16. Jh.," in *Zeitschrift für Ethnologie,* 64. Jg., 1932.
Taucher, W., *Gedanken zur Planwirtschaft,* 1949.
—— *Beschäftigungspolitik,* 1954.
Tautscher, A., *Geschichte der Volkswirtschaftslehre,* 1949.
—— *Wirtschaftsethik,* 1957.
—— *Grenzen der Besteuerung,* 1954.
—— *Einkommenspolitik und Genossenschaftswesen,* 1955.
Tawney, R., *Religion and the Rise of Capitalism,* 1927.
Thielicke-Pentzlin, *Mensch und Arbeit im technischen Zeitalter: Zum Problem der Rationalisierung,* 1954.
Veil, Klaus, *Das Wesen von Unternehmung und Unternehmer,* 1956.
Veit, O., *Volkswirtschaftliche Theorie der Liquidität,* 1948.
—— *Die veränderte Währungspolitik und ihre Folgen: Währungspolitik auf richtigem Kurs,* 1957.
Vito, F., *Introduzione alla economia politica,* 11th ed., 1956.
—— *L'economia a servizio dell'uomo: I nuovi orientamenti della politica economia e sociale,* 4th ed., 1954.
Vocke, W., *Gesundes Geld,* 1956.

Warriner, Doreen, *Land and Poverty in the Middle East,* 1948.
—— *Land Reform and Economic Development* (Cairo), 1955.
Weber, Adolf, *Allgemeine Volkswirtschaftslehre,* 6th ed., 1953.
—— *Kurzgefaßte Volkswirtschaftslehre,* 7th ed., 1956.
—— *Kurzgefaßte Volkswirtschaftspolitik,* 7th ed., 1957.
—— *Agrarpolitik, neubearb. v. W. Meinhold,* 1951.
—— *Weltwirtschaft,* 4th ed., 1950.
—— *Der Kampf zwischen Kapital und Arbeit,* 6th ed., 1954.
—— *Marktwirtschaft und Sowjetwirtschaft,* 2nd ed., 1951.
—— *Hauptfragen der Wirtschaftspolitik: Abhandlungen, Erinnerungen, Erfahrungen,* 1950.
—— *Depositenbanken und Spekulationsbanken, ein Vergleich deutschen und englischen Bankwesens,* 4th ed., 1938.
—— *Hochkonjunktur und Produktivität in weltwirtschaftlicher Sicht,* 1956.
—— *Stand und Aufgaben der Volkswirtschaftslehre in der Gegenwart,* 1956.
—— *Kapitalbildung und Lohnkämpfe,* 1955.
—— *Kapitalbildung als Voraussetzung für den volkswirtschaftlichen und sozialen Fortschritt,* 1957.
Weber, H. and Tischleder, P., *Wirtschaftsethik,* 1931.
Weber, Max, *Wirtschaft und Gesellschaft,* 1922.
—— *Gesammelte Aufsätze zur Religionssoziologie,* 1920.
—— *Gesammelte Aufsätze zur Sozial- und Wirtschaftsgeschichte,* 1924.
—— *Gesammelte Aufsätze zur Wissenschaftslehre,* 1922.
Weber, Wilhelm, *Wirtschaftswissenschaft und Wirtschaftspolitik in Österreich,* 1949.
—— *Theorie und Politik der Beschäftigung: Der Stand der Debatte um die "Vollbeschäftigung,"* 1954.
—— *Wirtschaftswissenschaft von heute: Ein Überblick über moderne ökonomische Forschung,* 1953.
—— *Österreichs Wirtschaftsverfassung und Wirtschaftsordnung im Lichte moderner Wirtschaftstheorie und Wirtschaftspolitik,* 1957.
Weddigen, W., *Wirtschaftsethik: System humanitärer Wirtschaftsmoral,* 1951.
Welty, E., O.P., *Vom Sinn und Wert der menschlichen Arbeit: Aus der Gedankenwelt des hl. Thomas v. Aquin,* 1946.
—— *Recht und Ordnung im Eigentum,* 1947.
—— *Verantwortung und Mitverantwortung in der Wirtschaft,* 1949.
—— *Die Ordnung des Wirtschaftslebens: Arbeit und Eigentum.* Bd. III, v, *Herders Sozialkatechismus,* 1958.
Westphalen, F., *Die Lohnfrage: vom ehernen Lohngesetz zum gerechten Lohn,* 1934.
Wiener, N., *The Human Use of Human Beings,* 2nd ed., 1955.
Winschuh, J., *Das neue Unternehmerbild,* 2nd ed., 1955.
Wootton, Barbara, *The Social Foundation of Wage Policy,* 1955.
Wünsch, G., *Evangelische Wirtschaftsethik,* 1927.
Zimmermann, L. Z., *Geschichte der theoretischen Volkswirtschaftslehre,* 1954.
Zinkin, M., *Development of Free Asia* (London), 1957.
Zwiedineck-Südenhorst, O. v., *Von der älteren zur neuren Theorie der politischen Ökonomie,* 1952.
—— *Allgemeine Volkswirtschaftslehre,* 2nd ed., 1948.

——— *Weltanschauung und Wirtschaft,* 1942.
——— "Einige Parerga zur Lehre vom Preis," in *Wirtschaftstheorie und Wirtschaftspolitik, Festschr. f. Adolf Weber,* A. Kruse, editor, 1951.
——— *Lohntheorie und Lohnpolitik, in Hwbd. Staatsw. VI,* 4th ed., 1925.
——— *Lohnpolitik und Lohntheorie,* 1900.
——— "Die Lohnpreisbildung," in *Grs. der Sozialök. IV,* 1925.

INDEX OF PROPER NAMES

Prepared by Miss N. L. Munton, Birmingham, England

GENERAL INDEX

Prepared by Frau Dr. R.-M. Steinbauer, Vienna